The Theory of Knowledge

Classical and Contemporary Readings

Third Edition

Louis P. Pojman

United States Military Academy

 WADSWORTH
CENGAGE Learning

Australia • Brazil • Japan • Korea • Mexico • Singapore • Spain • United Kingdom • United States

WADSWORTH
CENGAGE Learning

The Theory of Knowledge: Classical and Contemporary Readings, Third Edition
Louis P. Pojman

Publisher: Holly J. Allen

Philosophy Editor: Steve Wainwright

Assistant Editor: Lee McCracken

Editorial Assistant: Anna Lustig

Technology Project Manager: Susan DeVanna

Marketing Manager: Worth Hawes

Advertising Project Manager: Bryan Vann

Print/Media Buyer: Robert King

Permissions Editor: Bob Kauser

Production Service: Ruth Cottrell

Copy Editor: Ruth Cottrell

Cover Designer: Bill Stanton

Cover Image: Relativity. © M. C. Escher/Cordon Art, Baarn, Holland

Compositor: Ruth Cottrell Books

© 2003 Wadsworth, Cengage Learning

For product information and technology assistance, contact us at
Cengage Learning Customer & Sales Support, 1-800-354-9706

For permission to use material from this text or product, submit all requests online at **www.cengage.com/permissions**
Further permissions questions can be emailed to
permissionrequest@cengage.com

Library of Congress Control Number: 2002106308

ISBN-13: 978-0-534-55822-2

ISBN-10: 0-534-55822-4

Wadsworth
20 Davis Drive
Belmont, CA 94002
USA

Cengage Learning is a leading provider of customized learning solutions with office locations around the globe, including Singapore, the United Kingdom, Australia, Mexico, Brazil, and Japan. Locate your local office at **www.cengage.com/global**

Cengage Learning products are represented in Canada by Nelson Education, Ltd.

To learn more about Wadsworth, visit **www.cengage.com/wadsworth**

Purchase any of our products at your local college store or at our preferred online store **www.CengageBrain.com**

Printed in the United States of America
6 7 8 9 10   17 16 15 14 13

To
Robert Audi
and
Jim Landesman,
Two Men Worthy of the Name *Philosopher*
Whom I Am Privileged to Have as Friends,
This Book Is Dedicated

Contents

Preface

I am grateful for the enormously positive response to the first two editions of this anthology and have taken the suggestions of the users and reviewers of this book into serious consideration in compiling the third edition. It is gratifying to see epistemology receiving so much attention, especially since I believe that it, along with metaphysics, constitutes the very heart of philosophy. This anthology has been strengthened in many places, especially in the parts on foundationalism/coherentism and internalism/externalism. A new section on philosophy of science and epistemology, dealing with the nature of scientific method and the demarcation problem (the criterion differentiating science from nonscience), fills an important niche in contemporary epistemology. The book now contains eleven parts. I have increased its size to sixty-four articles, having deleted five but added eighteen articles.

Here are some of the additions: Rene Descartes, "Meditations 3 and 4"; Roderick Chisholm, "Foundationalism"; Thomas Reid, "Direct Realism"; John Greco, "Virtue Epistemology"; A. J. Ayer "Verificationism" and "The Elimination of Metaphysics" ;Carl Hempel, "The Scientific Method of Hypothesis Testing"; Karl Popper, "Conjectures and Refutations"; Imre Lakatos, "Science and Pseudoscience"; Paul Feyerabend, "Science as Myth"; and Karl Popper, "Knowledge without a Knowing Subject." I have also updated the introductions and bibliographies.

I have chosen the best articles I could find on the eleven subjects treated, aiming at philosophical cogency and accessibility. Although philosophy takes concentration and perseverance, philosophical articles do not have to be convoluted and tortuous reading. Students should find these selections exciting and worthy of serious study.

Although many philosophers have written or spoken to me about suggestions for improvement, I would especially like to thank Tim McGrew, Western Michigan University; Juli Eflin, Ball State University; Jim Landesman, City University of New York Graduate Center; Carol Caraway, Indiana University of Pennsylvania; Steven Hales, Bloomsburg University; Paul Tang, California State University at Long Beach; Jeffrey Tiel, Ashland University; and Robert Welshorn, University of Colorado at Colorado Springs. In addition I would like to thank Daniel H. Cohen, Colby College; David DeGrazia, George Washington University; Sally Ferguson, University of West Florida; and Jack C. Lyons, University of Arkansas. Their advice has been invaluable. The result is a much better book. I want to thank Kara Kindstrom, associate editor at Wadsworth, for encouraging me throughout this revision. Ruth Cottrell did an excellent job bringing this book into production. As always my wife, Trudy, was a constant source of critical examination and loving support.

Over the years two philosophers have greatly influenced my epistemic views. Robert Audi and Jim Landesman have taught me more than I can say. Both of these men have helped me throughout this project. I am rich in having them as friends. To them this book is dedicated.

I would be happy to receive any feedback from users and reviewers of this work.

Louis P. Pojman
United States Military Academy
April 18, 2002

Part I

General Introduction: The Theory of Knowledge

What can we really know? How can we be certain that we have the truth? How can we be certain that we know anything at all? What is knowledge, and how is it different from belief? If we know something, must we know that we know it?

The theory of knowledge—or *epistemology* (from the Greek, "the science of knowing")—inquires into the nature of knowledge and justification of belief. Many philosophers believe it is the central area of philosophy, for if philosophy is the quest for truth and wisdom, then we need to know how we are to obtain the truth and justify our beliefs. We need to know how to distinguish the true from the false and justified beliefs from unwarranted beliefs.

If we consult the *Oxford English Dictionary*, we find the following definition of the verb *to know:* "to recognize, to identify, to distinguish, to be acquainted with, to apprehend or comprehend as a fact or truth." This sort of definition gives us a ballpark understanding of the term, but it is still too broad for philosophical purposes. So let us note some typical uses of the verb *to know:*

1. "I know my friend John very well."
2. "I know how to speak English."
3. "I know that Washington, DC, is the capital of the United States."

The three sentences illustrate three different types of knowledge: knowledge by acquaintance, competence knowledge, and descriptive or propositional knowledge. We may characterize each of them this way:

1. *Knowledge by acquaintance.* A person S knows something or someone X (where X is the direct object of the verb). We are familiar in this way with the objects in the world and with our thoughts and sensations. We have acquaintance knowledge of our pains, our beliefs, our friends, the town in which we grew up, and so forth.

2. *Competence knowledge (sometimes called skill knowledge).* Person S knows how to D

(where *D* stands for a verb infinitive). This is *know how*. You know how to speak English and get around campus (or at least your room, when it isn't too cluttered). You may know how to ride a bicycle or play the piano or swim.

3. *Propositional knowledge (or descriptive knowledge)*. Person S knows that *p* (where *p* is some statement or proposition). Propositions have truth value; that is, they are true or false. They are the objects of propositional knowledge. When we claim to know that *p* is the case, we are claiming that *p* is true. Here are three examples of propositional knowledge: "I know that the sun will rise tomorrow," "I know that I have a mind," and "I know that Columbus discovered America in 1492."

Epistemology is primarily interested in this third kind of knowledge, propositional knowledge, and it is the kind of knowledge we shall be examining in this work. But this statement of purpose only scratches the surface of what we are concerned with in the theory of knowledge.

The field of epistemology seeks to throw light on the following kinds of questions:

1. What is knowledge? That is, what are the essential characteristics of this concept?

2. Can we know anything at all? Or are we doomed to ignorance about the most important subjects in life?

3. How do we obtain knowledge? Through the use of our senses, or our intellect, or both? Let us examine each of these questions.

What is knowledge? As mentioned, propositional knowledge is knowledge of true propositions. To claim to know something is to claim to possess a truth. If you claim to know that $10 \times 10 = 100$, you implicitly claim that the statement $10 \times 10 = 100$ is true. It would be a misuse of language to make a statement such as "I know that $10 \times 10 = 13$, but it is false," for knowledge claims are claims about grasping the truth. Of course, we may be wrong about our knowledge claims. The drunk claims to know

that there are pink elephants in the room, the child claims to know that Santa Claus exists, and two witnesses may make contradictory knowledge claims in reporting an accident. We often believe falsely that we know. Sometimes the evidence on which our knowledge claim is based is inadequate or misleading, or we misremember or misperceive. Sometimes our knowledge claims are contradicted by those of others, as when two people of different religious faiths each claims that his or hers is the only true religion or when one person claims with certainty that abortion is morally wrong and the other person claims with equal certainty that it is morally permissible.

Knowledge involves possessing the truth but includes more than having a true belief. Imagine that I am holding up four cards so that I can see their faces but you can only see their backs. I ask you to guess what types of cards I am holding. You feel a hunch (have a weak belief) that I am holding up four aces and correctly announce, "You are holding four aces in your hands." Although we both possess the truth, I have something you don't—an adequate justification for my belief that there are four aces in my hand. So knowledge differs from mere true belief in that the knower has an adequate justification for claiming truth.

Now the question shifts to the nature of justification. What exactly does it mean to be justified in believing some proposition? Are we justified when the evidence is undeniable, such as when we believe that $2 + 2 = 4$ or when we feel pain and cannot help believing that we are in pain? Can we have sufficient evidence to justify belief in physical objects? Our belief in other minds? Beliefs about metaphysical propositions such as the existence of God or freedom of the will? How much evidence must one have before one can claim to know a belief is true? Questions of justification will occupy us in most of this work, especially Parts V, VI, VIII, IX, and X.

Let us turn to the second question: Can we know anything at all? Or are we doomed to ignorance about the most important subjects in life? What do we really know? Could it be that we really know nothing at all? *Skepticism* is the theory that we do not have any knowledge. We cannot be completely certain that any of our beliefs are true. Radical skepticism goes even further and claims that *we cannot even be certain of the belief that we cannot be completely certain that any of our beliefs are true.* We cannot even know that we cannot have knowledge. Skepticism can also differ with regard to the skeptical thesis; for example, some skeptics claim that we cannot have empirical knowledge but allow mathematical knowledge.

Skepticism does not deny that we should not act from the best evidence available, but it insists that we can never be sure that we are correct in our truth claims. For all we know, the universe and everything in it could have been created ten minutes ago, and all our apparent memories created with it. Or the universe and everything in it may have doubled in size last night while we were sleeping. How could we check on this? It wouldn't help to use a ruler to measure our height to see if we doubled in size, would it?

Can you defeat the skeptic? Arguments for and against skepticism are examined in Parts I and II.

Let's turn to the third question: How do we obtain knowledge? through our senses, or our intellect, or both? There are two classic theories on the acquisition of knowledge. They are called *rationalism* and *empiricism*. "Rationalism" may be a misleading name for the first theory, because both theories use reason in acquiring knowledge. It is simply that rationalists believe that reason is sufficient to discover truth, whereas empiricists hold that all knowledge originates through sense perception (through seeing, hearing, touching, tasting, and smelling).

René Descartes (1596–1650) in Reading II.1 holds that the mind alone, even apart from empirical experience, can discover its truth.

Similarly, Immanuel Kant (1724–1804) in Reading VII.1, A. C. Ewing (VII.3), and Roderick Chisholm (VII.6) argue for the reality of a priori knowledge. The whole of Part VII considers that issue.

Empiricism is the doctrine that all knowledge originates in the senses. In Part III, we examine two classical empiricist philosophers, John Locke and Bishop George Berkeley. John Locke (1632–1704) systematically attacked the notions of innate ideas and a priori knowledge, arguing that if our claims to knowledge are to make sense they must be derived from the world of sense experience:

> Let us then suppose the mind to be, as we say, white paper, void of all characters, without any ideas; how comes it by that vast store, which the busy and boundless fancy of man has painted on it with an almost endless variety? Whence has it all the materials of reason and knowledge? To this I answer, in one word, from experience: in that all our knowledge is founded.

Locke goes on to set forth a representational theory of knowledge, which claims that the core of what we know is caused by the world itself, although some qualities are the products of the way our perceptual mechanisms are affected by the world. The former qualities—called *primary qualities*, such as motion, size, shape, and number—are the true building blocks of knowledge because these qualities are accurate representatives of the objective features of the world. The *secondary qualities* are modes of apprehending the primary qualities; examples are taste, color, odor, and sound. Because the color or taste of the same object can appear differently to different people or to the same person at different times, secondary qualities are subjective, even though they are caused by the objective primary qualities.

The difference between rationalism and empiricism may be illustrated by the following schema with regard to two important questions:

Question 1. How do we acquire ideas?

Answer A. Rationalism: Some *nonanalytic propositions** are innate or known a priori (independent of experience).

Answer B. Empiricism: All propositions are acquired from experience. No nonanalytic propositions are known a priori.

Question 2. How is knowledge organized in the mind?

Answer A. Rationalism: The mind brings to experience principles of order from the mind's own nature.

Answer B. Empiricism: The mind arranges and stores materials that are given in experience.

The selection from Descartes's *Meditations*, illustrate rationalism. Selections from the work of Locke (III.1), Berkeley (III.2), and Hume (II.2) illustrate classical empiricism. This book considers nine perennial epistemological topics:

Part II, "Skepticism": Can we have any knowledge at all?

Part III, "Perception": Can we have knowledge of the external world?

Part IV, "The Analysis of Knowledge": Is knowledge true justified belief?

Part V, "Theories of Justification (I)": Is the structure of justification foundational or coherentist or neither?

Part VI, "Theories of Justification (II)": Is the correct account of the justification process one of externalism or of internalism?

Part VII, "A Priori Knowledge": Is there synthetic a priori truth? Is the analytic–synthetic distinction itself valid?

Part VIII, "Induction": Which is the correct solution to the problem of inductive knowledge?

Part IX, "Science: Science, Justification, and the Demarcation Problem": This section, deals with the nature of scientific method and the demarcation problem (the criterion differentiating science from nonscience).

Part X, "The Ethics of Belief": Are there epistemic obligations? Are there moral obligations to seek the truth or to have the best set of justified beliefs?

Part XI, "Challenges and Alternatives to Contemporary Epistemology": Is knowledge essentially social or individualistic? Is the Cartesian ("egocentric") paradigm the correct model of knowing? Are truth and reality relative to agents or communities? Is all justification intrinsically perspectival or contextual, or can we transcend social contexts and understand the world impartially? Is the sex of the knower relative to the process of acquiring knowledge or is it irrelevant? Is knowledge political?

These topics and the questions that surround them form the heart of the philosophical enterprise. Nearly everything in philosophy refers to them. Although, first of all, they are purely theoretical, an understanding of their significance promises to make one a more enlightened human being, more aware of the structures of the cognitive dimension of existence.

We begin this part with an introductory essay on the question of what we know by Bertrand Russell and then an important essay by Roderick Chisholm on the problem of the criterion for a theory of knowledge.

---

* An *analytic proposition* is one in which the predicate term is contained in the subject—for example, "All mothers are women"—whereas a *nonanalytic* or *synthetic* proposition is one where the predicate adds something to the subject—for example, "Mary Smith has just become a mother." The nonanalytic propositions referred to by the rationalists typically are metaphysical propositions such as "God exists," "I have a free will," and "All things have sufficient reasons to explain them." See Part VII for more on this subject.

I.1 What Can We Know? Appearance and Reality

BERTRAND RUSSELL

Bertrand Russell (1872–1970) is one of the most important philosophers of the twentieth century. A Cambridge University philosopher, his works cover virtually every area of philosophy from logic and philosophy of mathematics (*Principia Mathematica*, 1910) to philosophy of religion ("Mysticism") and ethics. Russell's concern to live out his philosophy in his life led him to found a special school on his philosophy of education, go to prison for opposing his government's involvement in World War I, become a leader in Britain's "Ban the Bomb" (the atom bomb) movement, and speak out on moral and political issues, sometimes at personal risk.

In the following passage from *The Problems of Philosophy,* Russell asks whether there is any knowledge we can be certain about. He then examines a range of things in daily life about which we seem to be certain. Then he shows that there is reason to doubt each of these. His probing questions serve as a good starting point for both contemporary skepticism and the quest for knowledge itself.

Is there any knowledge in the world which is so certain that no reasonable man could doubt it? This question, which at first sight might not seem difficult, is really one of the most difficult that can be asked. When we have realized the obstacles in the way of a straightforward and confident answer, we shall be well launched on the study of philosophy—for philosophy is merely the attempt to answer such ultimate questions, not carelessly and dogmatically, as we do in ordinary life and even in the sciences, but critically after exploring all that makes such questions puzzling, and after realizing all the vagueness and confusion that underlie our ordinary ideas.

In daily life, we assume as certain many things which, on a closer scrutiny, are found to be so full of apparent contradictions that only a great amount of thought enables us to know what it is that we really may believe. In the search for certainty, it is natural to begin with our present experiences, and in some sense, no doubt, knowledge is to be derived from them. But any statement as to what it is that our immediate experiences make us know is very likely to be wrong. It seems to me that I am now sitting in a chair, at a table of a cer-

Reprinted from *The Problems of Philosophy* (Oxford University Press, 1912).

tain shape, on which I see sheets of paper with writing or print. By turning my head I see out of the window buildings and clouds and the sun. I believe that the sun is about ninety-three million miles from the earth; that it is a hot globe many times bigger than the earth; that, owing to the earth's rotation, it rises every morning, and will continue to do so for an indefinite time in the future. I believe that, if any other normal person comes into my room, he will see the same chairs and tables and books and papers as I see, and that the table which I see is the same as the table which I feel pressing against my arm. All this seems to be so evident as to be hardly worth stating, except in answer to a man who doubts whether I know anything. Yet all this may be reasonably doubted, and all of it requires much careful discussion before we can be sure that we have stated it in a form that is wholly true.

To make our difficulties plain, let us concentrate attention on the table. To the eye it is oblong, brown and shiny; to the touch it is smooth and cool and hard; when I tap it, it gives out a wooden sound. Anyone else who sees and feels and hears the table will agree with this description, so that it might seem as if no difficulty would arise; but as soon as we try to be more precise our troubles begin. Although I believe that the table is "really" of the same color all over, the parts that reflect the light look much brighter than the other parts, and some parts look white because of reflected light. I know that, if I move, the parts that reflect the light will be different, so that the apparent distribution of colors on the table will change. It follows that if several people are looking at the table at the same moment, no two of them will see exactly the same distribution of colors, because no two can see it from exactly the same point of view, and any change in the point of view makes some change in the way the light is reflected.

For most practical purposes these differences are unimportant, but to the painter they are all-important: the painter has to unlearn the habit of thinking that things seem to have the color which common sense says they "really" have, and to learn the habit of seeing things as they appear. Here we have already the beginning of one of the distinctions that cause most trouble in philosophy—the distinction between "appearance" and "reality," between what things seem to be and what they are. The painter wants to know what things seem to be, the practical man and the philosopher want to know what they are; but the philosopher's wish to know this is stronger than the practical man's, and is more troubled by knowledge as to the difficulties of answering the question.

To return to the table. It is evident from what we have found, that there is no color which pre-eminently appears to be the color of the table, or even of any one particular part of the table—it appears to be of different colors from different points of view, and there is no reason for regarding some of these as more really its color than others. And we know that even from a given point of view the color will seem different by artificial light, or to a color-blind man, or to a man wearing blue spectacles, while in the dark there will be no color at all, though to touch and hearing the table will be unchanged. This color is not something which is inherent in the table, but something depending upon the table and the spectator and the way the light falls on the table. When, in ordinary life, we speak of the color of the table, we only mean the sort of color which it will seem to have to a normal spectator from an ordinary point of view under usual conditions of light. But the other colors which appear under other conditions have just as good a right to be considered real; and there-

fore, to avoid favoritism, we are compelled to deny that, in itself, the table has any one particular color.

The same thing applies to the texture. With the naked eye one can see the grain, but otherwise the table looks smooth and even. If we looked at it through a microscope, we should see rough-nesses and hills and valleys, and all sorts of differences that are imperceptible to the naked eye. Which of these is the "real" table? We are naturally tempted to say that what we see through the microscope is more real, but that in turn would be changed by a still more powerful microscope. If then, we cannot trust what we see with the naked eye, why should we trust what we see through a microscope? Thus, again, the confidence in our senses with which we began deserts us.

The shape of the table is no better. We are all in the habit of judging as to the "real" shapes of things, and we do this so unreflectingly that we come to think we actually see the real shapes. But, in fact, as we all have to learn if we try to draw, a given thing looks different in shape from every different point of view. If our table is "really" rectangular, it will look from almost all points of view, as if it had two acute angles and two obtuse angles. If opposite sides are parallel, they will look as if they converged to a point away from the spectator, if they are of equal length, they will look as if the nearer side were longer. All these things are not commonly noticed in looking at a table, because experience has taught us to construct the "real" shape from the apparent shape, and the "real" shape is what interests us as practical men. But the "real" shape is not what we see; it is something inferred from what we see. And what we see is constantly changing in shape as we move about the room; so that here again the senses seem not to give us the truth about the table itself, but only about the appearance of the table.

Similar difficulties arise when we consider the sense of touch. It is true that the table always gives us a sensation of hardness, and we feel that it resists pressure. But the sensation we obtain depends upon how hard we press the table and also upon what part of the body we press with; thus the various sensations due to various pressures or various parts of the body cannot be supposed to reveal directly any definite property of the table, but at most to be signs of some property which perhaps causes all the sensations, but is not actually apparent in any of them. And the same applies still more obviously to the sounds which can be elicited by rapping the table.

Thus it becomes evident that the real table, if there is one, is not the same as what we immediately experience by sight or touch or hearing. The real table, if there is one, is not immediately known to us at all, but must be an inference from what is immediately known. Hence, two very difficult questions at once arise; namely, (1) Is there a real table at all? (2) If so, what sort of object can it be?

It will help us in considering these questions to have a few simple terms of which the meaning is definite and clear. Let us give the name of "sense-data" to the things that are immediately known in sensation: such things as colors, sounds, smells, hardnesses, roughnesses, and so on. We shall give the name "sensation" to the experience of being immediately aware of these things. Thus, whenever we see a color, we have a sensation of the color, but the color itself is a sense-datum, not a sensation. The color is that of which we are immediately aware, and the awareness itself is the sensation. It is plain that if we are to know anything about the table, it must be by means of the sense-data—brown color, oblong shape, smoothness, etc.—which we associate with the table; but, for the reasons which have been given, we cannot say that the table is the sense-data, or even that the sense-data are directly properties of the table. Thus a problem arises as to the relation of the sense-data to the real table, supposing there is such a thing.

The real table, if it exists, we will call a "physical object." Thus we have to consider the relation of sense-data to physical objects. The collection of all physical objects is called "matter." Thus our two questions may be re-stated as follows: (1) Is there any such thing as matter? (2) If so, what is its nature?

The philosopher who first brought prominently forward the reasons for regarding the immediate objects of our senses as not existing independently of us was Bishop Berkeley (1685–1753). His *Three Dialogues Between Hylas and Philonous, in Opposition to Sceptics and Atheists*, undertake to prove that there is no such thing as matter at all, and that the world consists of nothing but minds and their ideas. Hylas has hitherto believed in matter, but he is no match for Philonous, who mercilessly drives him into contra-

dictions and paradoxes, and makes his own denial of matter seem, in the end, as if it were almost common sense. The arguments employed are of very different value: some are important and sound, others are confused or quibbling. But Berkeley retains the merit of having shown that the existence of matter is capable of being denied without absurdity, and that if there are any things that exist independently of us they cannot be the immediate objects of our sensations.

There are two different questions involved when we ask whether matter exists, and it is important to keep them clear. We commonly mean by "matter" something which is opposed to "mind," something which we think of as occupying space and as radically incapable of any sort of thought or consciousness. It is chiefly in this sense that Berkeley denies matter; that is to say, he does not deny that the sense-data which we commonly take as signs of the existence of the table are really signs of the existence of something independent of us, but he does deny that this something is non-mental, that it is neither mind nor ideas entertained by some mind. He admits that there must be something which continues to exist when we go out of the room or shut our eyes, and that what we call seeing the table does really give us reason for believing in something which persists even when we are not seeing it. But he thinks that this something cannot be radically different in nature from what we see, and cannot be independent of seeing altogether, though it must be independent of our seeing. He is thus led to regard the "real" table as an idea in the mind of God. Such an idea has the required permanence and independence of ourselves, without being—as matter would otherwise be—something quite unknowable, in the sense that we can only infer it, and can never be directly and immediately aware of it.

Other philosophers since Berkeley have also held that, although the table does not depend for its existence upon being seen by me, it does depend upon being seen (or otherwise apprehended in sensation) by some mind—not necessarily the mind of God, but more often the whole collective mind of the universe. This they hold, as Berkeley does, chiefly because they think there can be nothing real—or at any rate nothing known to be real except minds and their thoughts and feelings. We might state the argument by which they support their view in some such way as this:

"Whatever can be thought of is an idea in the mind of the person thinking of it; therefore nothing can be thought of except ideas in minds; therefore anything else is inconceivable, and what is inconceivable cannot exist."

Such an argument, in my opinion, is fallacious; and of course those who advance it do not put it so shortly or so crudely. But whether valid or not, the argument has been very widely advanced in one form or another, and very many philosophers, perhaps a majority, have held that there is nothing real except minds and their ideas. Such philosophers are called "idealists." When they come to explaining matter, they either say, like Berkeley, that matter is really nothing but a collection of ideas, or they say, like Leibniz (1646–1716), that what appears as matter is really a collection of more or less rudimentary minds.

But these philosophers, though they deny matter as opposed to mind, nevertheless, in another sense, admit matter. It will be remembered that we asked two questions; namely, (1) Is there a real table at all? (2) If so, what sort of object can it be? Now both Berkeley and Leibniz admit that there is a real table, but Berkeley says it is certain ideas in the mind of God, and Leibniz says it is a colony of souls. Thus both of them answer our first question in the affirmative, and only diverge from the views of ordinary mortals in their answer to our second question. In fact, almost all philosophers seem to be agreed that there is a real table. They almost all agree that, however much our sense-data—color, shape, smoothness, etc.—may depend upon us, yet their occurrence is a sign of something existing independently of us, something differing, perhaps, completely from our sense-data whenever we are in a suitable relation to the real table.

Now obviously this point in which the philosophers are agreed—the view that there is a real table, whatever its nature may be is vitally important, and it will be worthwhile to consider what reasons there are for accepting this view before we go on to the further question as to the nature of the real table.

Before we go farther it will be well to consider for a moment what it is that we have discovered so far. It has appeared that, if we take any common object of the sort that is supposed to be known by the senses, what the senses immediately tell us is not the truth about the object as it is apart from us, but only the truth about certain sense-data which, so far as we can see, depend upon the relations between us and the object. Thus what we directly see and feel is merely "appearance," which we believe to be a sign of some "reality" behind. But if the reality is not what appears, have we any means of knowing whether there is any reality at all? And if so, have we any means of finding out what it is like?

Such questions are bewildering, and it is difficult to know that even the strangest hypotheses may not be true. Thus our familiar table, which has roused but the slightest thoughts in us hitherto, has become a problem full of surprising possibilities. The one thing we know about it is that it is not what it seems. Beyond this modest result, so far, we have the most complete liberty of conjecture. Leibniz tells us it is a community of souls; Berkeley tells us it is an idea in the mind of God; sober science, scarcely less wonderful, tells us it is a vast collection of electric charges in violent motion.

Among these surprising possibilities, doubt suggests that perhaps there is no table at all. Philosophy, if it cannot answer so many questions as we could wish, has at least the power of asking questions which increase the interest of the world, and show the strangeness and wonder lying just below the surface even in the commonest things of daily life.

I.2 The Problem of the Criterion

RODERICK M. CHISHOLM

Roderick Chisholm (1916–1999) was professor of philosophy at Brown University and the most influential epistemologist in the United States. He also made significant contributions in the fields of metaphysics and ethics. Among his works are *Perceiving* (1957), *The Theory of Knowledge* (1977 and 1989), and *The Foundations of Knowing* (1982) from which the present selection is taken.

Chisholm begins by raising the problem of the *criterion:* To know anything—that is, to distinguish the "good" kind of beliefs from the "bad" kind—we need a *method* or *criterion*, a process that guarantees that what we claim to know is truly knowledge. On the other hand, before we can know whether our method or criterion is reliable, we must be able to recognize particular instances of knowledge. So which comes first, our method or particular instances? Chisholm labels those who begin with *method* "methodists" and those who begin with *particulars* "particularists." He then goes on to provide his solution to the puzzle.

1

"The problem of the criterion" seems to me to be one of the most important and one of the most difficult of all the problems of philosophy. I am tempted to say that one has not begun to philosophize until one has faced this problem and has recognized how unappealing, in the end, each of the possible solutions is . . .

2

What is the problem, then? It is the ancient problem of "the dialectus"—the problem of "the wheel" or "the vicious circle." It was put very neatly by Montaigne in his *Essays*. So let us begin by para-paraphrasing his formulation of the puzzle. To know whether things really are as they seem to be, we must have a *procedure* for distinguishing appearances that are true from appearances that are false. But to know whether our procedure is a good procedure, we have to know whether it really *succeeds* in distinguishing appearances that are true from appearances that are false.

And we cannot know whether it does really succeed unless we already know which appearances are *true* and which ones are *false*. And so we are caught in a circle.

Let us try to see how one gets into a situation of this sort.

The puzzles begin to form when you ask yourself, "What can I really know about the world?" We all are acquainted with people who think they know a lot more than in fact they do know. I'm thinking of fanatics, bigots, mystics, various types of dogmatists. And we have all heard of people who claim at least to know a lot less than what in fact they do know. I'm thinking of those people who call themselves "skeptics" and who like to say that people cannot know what the world is really like. People tend to become skeptics, temporarily, after reading books on popular science: the authors tell us we cannot know what things are like really (but they make use of a vast amount of knowledge, or a vast amount of what is claimed to be knowledge, to support this skeptical conclusion). And as we know, people tend to become dogmatists, temporarily, as a result of the effects of alcohol, or drugs, or religious and emotional experiences. Then they claim to have an inside view of the world and they think they have a deep kind of knowledge giving them a key to the entire workings of the universe.

Reprinted from *The Foundations of Knowing* (University of Minnesota Press, 1982) by permission. Notes deleted.

If you have a healthy common sense, you will feel that something is wrong with both of these extremes and that the truth is somewhere in the middle: we can know far more than the skeptic says we can know and far less than the dogmatist or the mystic says that he can know. But how are we to decide these things?

3

How do we decide, in any particular case, whether we have a genuine item of knowledge? Most of us are ready to confess that our beliefs far transcend what we really know. There are things we believe that we don't in fact know. And we can say of many of these things that we know that we don't know them. I believe that Mrs. Jones is honest, say, but I don't know it, and I know that I don't know it. There are other things that we don't know, but they are such that we don't know that we don't know them. Last week, say, I thought I knew that Mr. Smith was honest, but he turned out to be a thief. I didn't know that he was a thief, and, moreover, I didn't know that I didn't know that he was a thief; I thought I knew that he was honest. And so the problem is: How are we to distinguish the real cases of knowledge from what only seem to be cases of knowledge? Or, as I put it before, how are we to decide in any particular case whether we have genuine items of knowledge?

What would be a satisfactory solution to our problem? Let me quote in detail what Cardinal Mercier says:

> If there is any knowledge which bears the mark of truth, if the intellect does have a way of distinguishing the true and the false, in short, if there is a criterion of truth, then this criterion should satisfy three conditions: it should be *internal, objective,* and *immediate*.
>
> It should be *internal*. No reason or rule of truth that is provided by an *external authority* can serve as an ultimate criterion. For the reflective doubts that are essential to criteriology can and should be applied to this authority itself. The mind cannot attain to certainty until it has found *within itself* a sufficient reason for adhering to the testimony of such an authority.

The criterion should be *objective*. The ultimate reason for believing cannot be a merely *subjective* state of the thinking subject. A man is aware that he can reflect upon his psychological states in order to control them. Knowing that he has this ability, he does not, so long as he has not made use of it, have the right to be sure. The ultimate ground of certitude cannot consist in a subjective feeling. It can be found only in that which, objectively, produces this feeling and is adequate to reason.

Finally, the criterion must be *immediate*. To be sure, a certain conviction may rest upon many different reasons some of which are subordinate to others. But if we are to avoid an infinite regress, then we must find a ground of assent that presupposes no other. We must find an *immediate* criterion of certitude.

Is there a criterion of truth that satisfies these three conditions? If so, what is it?

4

To see how perplexing our problem is, let us consider a figure that Descartes had suggested. . . . Descartes' figure comes to this.

Let us suppose that you have a pile of apples and you want to sort out the good ones from the bad ones. You want to put the good ones in a pile by themselves and throw the bad ones away. This is a useful thing to do, obviously, because the bad apples tend to infect the good ones and then the good ones become bad, too. Descartes thought our beliefs were like this. The bad ones tend to infect the good ones, so we should look them over very carefully, throw out the bad ones if we can, and then—or so Descartes hoped—we would be left with just a stock of good beliefs on which we could rely completely. But how are we to do the sorting? If we are to sort out the good ones from the bad ones, then, of course, we must have a way of recognizing the good ones. Or at least we must have a way of recognizing the bad ones. And—again, of course—you and I do have a way of recognizing good apples and also of recognizing bad ones. The good ones have their own special feel, look, and taste, and so do the bad ones.

But when we turn from apples to beliefs, the matter is quite different. In the case of the apples, we have a method—a criterion—for distinguishing the good ones from the bad ones. But in the case of the beliefs, we do not have a method or a criterion for distinguishing the good ones from the bad ones. Or, at least, we don't have one yet. The question we started with was: How *are* we to tell the good ones from the bad ones? In other words, we were asking: What is the proper method for deciding which are the good beliefs and which are the bad ones—which beliefs are genuine cases of knowledge and which beliefs are not?

And now, you see, we are on the wheel. First, we want to find out which are the good beliefs and which are the bad ones. To find this out we have to have some way—some method—of deciding which are the good ones and which are the bad ones. But there are good and bad methods—good and bad ways—of sorting out the good beliefs from the bad ones. And so we now have a new problem: How are we to decide which are the good methods and which are the bad ones?

If we could fix on a good method for distinguishing between good and bad methods, we might be all set. But this, of course, just moves the problem to a different level. How are we to distinguish between good methods for choosing a good method? If we continue in this way, of course, we are led to an infinite regress and we will never have the answer to our original question.

What do we do in fact? We do know that there are fairly reliable ways of sorting out good beliefs from bad ones. Most people will tell you, for example, that if you follow the procedures of science and of common sense—if you tend carefully to your observations and if you make use of the canons of logic, induction, and the theory of probability—you will be following the best possible procedure for making sure that you will have more good beliefs than bad ones. This is doubtless true. But how do we know that it is? How do we know that the procedures of science, reason, and common sense are the best methods that we have?

If we do know this, it is because we know that these procedures work. It is because we know that these procedures do in fact enable us to distinguish the good beliefs from the bad ones. We say

"See—these methods turn out good beliefs." But *how* do we know that they do? It can only be that we already know how to tell the difference between the good beliefs and the bad ones.

And now you can see where the skeptic comes in. He'll say this: "You said you wanted to sort out the good beliefs from the bad ones. Then to do this, you apply the canons of science, common sense, and reason. And now, in answer to the question, 'How do you know that that's the right way to do it?', you say 'Why, I can see that the ones it picks out are the good ones and the ones it leaves behind are the bad ones.' But if you can *see* which ones are the good ones and which ones are the bad ones, why do you think you need a general method for sorting them out?"

5

We can formulate some of the philosophical issues that are involved here by distinguishing two pairs of questions. These are:

> A.   "*What* do we know? What is the *extent* of our knowledge?"
>
> B.   "How are we to decide *whether* we know? What are the *criteria* of knowledge?"

If you happen to know the answers to the first of these pairs of questions, you may have some hope of being able to answer the second. Thus, if you happen to know which are the good apples and which are the bad ones, then maybe you could explain to some other person how he could go about deciding whether or not he has a good apple or a bad one. But if you don't know the answer to the first of these pairs of questions—if you don't know what things you know or how far your knowledge extends—it is difficult to see how you could possibly figure out an answer to the second.

On the other hand, *if*, somehow, you already know the answers to the second of these pairs of questions, then you may have some hope of being able to answer the first. Thus, if you happen to have a good set of directions for telling whether apples are good or bad, then maybe you can go about finding a good one—assuming, of course, that there are some good apples to be found. But if you don't know the answer to the second of these pairs of questions—if you don't know how to go about deciding whether or not you know, if you don't know what the criteria of knowing are—it is difficult to see how you could possibly figure out an answer to the first.

And so we can formulate the position of *the skeptic* on these matters. He will say: "You cannot answer question A until you have answered question B. And you cannot answer question B until you have answered question A. Therefore you cannot answer either question. You cannot know what, if anything, you know, and there is no possible way for you to decide in any particular case." Is there any reply to this?

6

Broadly speaking, there are at least two other possible views. So we may choose among three possibilities.

There are people—philosophers—who think that they do have an answer to B and that, given their answer to B, they can then figure out their answer to A. And there are other people—other philosophers—who have it the other way around: they think that they have an answer to A and that, given their answer to A, they can then figure out the answer to B.

There don't seem to be any generally accepted names for these two different philosophical positions. (Perhaps this is just as well. There are more than enough names, as it is, for possible philosophical views.) I suggest, for the moment, we use the expressions "methodists" and "particularists." By "methodists," I mean, not the followers of John Wesley's version of Christianity, but those who think they have an answer to B, and who then, in terms of it, work out their answer to A. By "particularists" I mean those who have it the other way around.

7

Thus John Locke was a methodist—in our present, rather special sense of the term. He was able

to arrive—somehow—at an answer to B. He said, in effect: "The way you decide whether or not a belief is a good belief—that is to say, the way you decide whether a belief is likely to be a genuine case of knowledge—is to see whether it is derived from sense experience, to see, for example, whether it bears certain relations to your sensations." Just what these relations to our sensations might be is a matter we may leave open, for present purposes. The point is: Locke felt that if a belief is to be credible, it must bear certain relations to the believer's sensations—but he never told us *how* he happened to arrive at this conclusion. This, of course, is the view that has come to be known as "empiricism." David Hume followed Locke in this empiricism and said that empiricism gives us an effective criterion for distinguishing the good apples from the bad ones. You can take this criterion to the library, he said. Suppose you find a book in which the author makes assertions that do not conform to the empirical criterion. Hume said: "Commit it to the flames: for it can contain nothing but sophistry and illusion."

8

Empiricism, then, was a form of what I have called "methodism." The empiricist—like other types of methodist—begins with a criterion and then he uses it to throw out the bad apples. There are two objections, I would say, to empiricism. The first—which applies to every form of methodism (in our present sense of the word)—is that the criterion is very broad and far-reaching and at the same time completely arbitrary. How can one *begin* with a broad generalization? It seems especially odd that the empiricist—who wants to proceed cautiously, step by step, from experience—begins with such a generalization. He leaves us completely in the dark so far as concerns what *reasons* he may have for adopting this particular criterion rather than some other. The second objection applies to empiricism in particular. When we apply the empirical criterion—at least, as it was developed by Hume, as well as by many of those in the nineteenth and twentieth centuries who have called themselves "empiricists"—we seem to throw out, not only the bad apples but the good ones as well, and we are left, in effect, with just a few parings or skins with no meat behind them. Thus Hume virtually conceded that, if you are going to be empiricist, the only matters of fact that you can really know about pertain to the existence of sensations. "'Tis vain," he said, "to ask whether there be body." He meant you cannot know whether any physical things exist—whether there are trees, or houses, or bodies, much less whether there are atoms or other such microscopic particles. All you can know is that there are and have been certain sensations. You cannot know whether there is any you who experiences those sensations— much less whether any other people exist who experience sensations. And I think, if he had been consistent in his empiricism, he would also have said you cannot really be sure whether there have been any sensations in the past; you can know only that certain sensations exist here and now.

9

The great Scottish philosopher, Thomas Reid, reflected on all this in the eighteenth century. He was serious about philosophy and man's place in the world. He finds Hume saying things implying that we can know only of the existence of certain sensations here and now. One can imagine him saying: "Good Lord! What kind of nonsense is this?" What he did say, among other things, was this: "A traveller of good judgment may mistake his way, and be unawares led into a wrong track; and while the road is fair before him, he may go on without suspicion and be followed by others but, when it ends in a coal pit, it requires no great judgment to know that he hath gone wrong, nor perhaps to find out what misled him."

Thus Reid, as I interpret him, was not an empiricist; nor was he, more generally, what I have called a "methodist." He was a "particularist." That is to say, he thought that he had an answer to question A, and in terms of the answer to question A, he then worked out kind of an answer to question B. An even better example of a "particularist" is the great twentieth century English philosopher, G. E. Moore.

Suppose, for a moment, you were tempted to go along with Hume and say "The only thing about the world I can really know is that there are

now sensations of a certain sort. There's a sensation of a man, there's the sound of a voice, and there's a feeling of bewilderment or boredom. But that's all I can really know about." What would Reid say? I can imagine him saying something like this: "Well, you can talk that way if you want to. But you know very well that it isn't true. You know that you are there, that you have a body of such and such a sort and that other people are here, too. And you know about this building and where you were this morning and all kinds of other things as well." G. E. Moore would raise his hand at this point and say: "I know very well this is a hand, and so do you. If you come across some philosophical theory that implies that you and I cannot know that this is a hand, then so much the worse for the theory." I think that Reid and Moore are right, myself, and I'm inclined to think that the "methodists" are wrong.

Going back to our questions A and B, we may summarize the three possible views as follows: there is skepticism (you cannot answer either question without presupposing an answer to the other, and therefore the questions cannot be answered at all); there is "methodism" (you begin with an answer to B); and there is "particularism" (you begin with an answer to A). I suggest that the third possibility is the most reasonable.

10

I would say—and many reputable philosophers would disagree with me—that, to find out whether you know such a thing as that this is a hand, you don't have to apply any test or criterion. Spinoza has it right. "In order to know," he said, "there is no need to know that we know, much less to know that we know that we know."

This is part of the answer, it seems to me, to the puzzle about the diallelus. There are many things that quite obviously, we do know to be true. If I report to you the things I now see and hear and feel—or, if you prefer, the things I now think I see and hear and feel—the chances are that my report will be correct; I will be telling you something I know. And so, too, if you report the things that you think you now see and hear and feel. To be sure, there are hallucinations and illusions. People often think they see or hear or feel things that in fact they do not see or hear or feel. But from this fact—that our senses do sometimes deceive us—it hardly follows that your senses and mine are deceiving you and me right now. One may say similar things about what we remember.

Having these good apples before us, we can look them over and formulate certain criteria of goodness. Consider the senses, for example. One important criterion—one epistemological principle—was formulated by St. Augustine. It is more reasonable, he said, to trust the senses than to distrust them. Even though there have been illusions and hallucinations, the wise thing, when everything seems all right, is to accept the testimony of the senses. I say "when everything seems all right." If on a particular occasion something about *that* particular occasion makes you suspect that particular report of the senses, if, say, you seem to remember having been drugged or hypnotized, or brainwashed, then perhaps you should have some doubts about what you think you see, or hear, or feel, or smell. But if nothing about this particular occasion leads you to suspect what the senses report on this particular occasion, then the wise thing is to take such a report at its face value. In short the senses should be regarded as innocent until there is some positive reason, on some particular occasion, for thinking that they are guilty on that particular occasion.

One might say the same thing of memory. If, on any occasion, you think you remember that such-and-such an event occurred, then the wise thing is to assume that that particular event did occur—unless something special about this particular occasion leads you to suspect your memory.

We have then a kind of answer to the puzzle about the diallelus. We start with particular cases of knowledge and then from those we generalize and formulate criteria of goodness—criteria telling us what it is for a belief to be epistemologically respectable. Let us now try to sketch somewhat more precisely this approach to the problem of the criterion.

11

The theory of evidence, like ethics and the theory of value, presupposes an objective right and wrong.

To explicate the requisite senses of "right" and "wrong," we need the concept of *right preference*—or, more exactly, the concept of one state of mind being *preferable*, epistemically, to another. One state of mind may be *better*, epistemically, than another. This concept of epistemic preferability is what Cardinal Mercier called an *objective* concept. It is one thing to say, objectively, that one state of mind is *to be preferred* to another. It is quite another thing to say, subjectively, that one state of mind is in fact preferred to another—that someone or other happens to prefer the one state of mind to the other. If a state of mind A is to be preferred to a state of mind B, if it is, as I would like to say, intrinsically preferable to B, then anyone who prefers B to A is *mistaken* in his preference.

Given this concept of epistemic preferability, we can readily explicate the basic concepts of the theory of evidence. We could say, for example, that a proposition p is *beyond reasonable doubt t* provided only that believing p is then epistemically preferable for S to withholding p—where by "withholding p" we mean the state of neither accepting p nor its negation. It is evident to me, for example, that many people are here. This means it is epistemically preferable for me to believe that many people are here than for me neither to believe nor to disbelieve that many are people here.

A proposition is *evident* for a person if it is beyond reasonable doubt for that person and is such that his including it among the propositions upon which he bases his decisions is preferable to his not so including it. A proposition is *acceptable* if withholding it is *not* preferable to believing it. And a proposition is *unacceptable* if withholding it is preferable to believing it.

Again, some propositions are not beyond reasonable doubt but they may be said to have *some presumption in their favor*. I suppose that the proposition that each of us will be alive an hour from now is one that has some presumption in its favor. We could say that a proposition is of this sort provided only that believing the proposition is epistemically preferable to believing its negation.

Moving in the other direction in the epistemic hierarchy, we could say that a proposition is *certain*, absolutely certain, for a given subject at a given time, if that proposition is then evident to that subject and if there is no other proposition that is such that believing that other proposition is then epistemically preferable for him to believing the given proposition. It is certain for me, I would say, that there seem to be many people here and that 7 and 5 are 12. If this is so, then each of the two propositions is evident to me and there are no other propositions that are such that it would be even better, epistemically, if I were to believe those other propositions.

This concept of epistemic preferability can be axiomatized and made the basis of a system of epistemic logic exhibiting the relations among these and other concepts of the theory of evidence. For present purposes, let us simply note how they may be applied in our approach to the problem of the criterion.

12

Let us begin with the most difficult of the concepts to which we have just referred—that of a proposition being *certain* for a man at a given time. Can we formulate *criteria* of such certainty? I think we can.

Leibniz had said that there are two kinds of immediately evident proposition—the "first truths of fact" and the "first truths of reason." Let us consider each of these in turn.

Among the "first truths of fact," for any man at any given time, I would say, are various propositions about his own state of mind at that time— his thinking certain thoughts, his entertaining certain beliefs, his being in a certain sensory or emotional state. These propositions all pertain to certain states of the man that may be said to manifest or present themselves to him at that time. We could use Meinong's term and say that certain states are "self-presenting," where this concept might be marked off in the following way.

A man's being in a certain state is *self-presenting* to him at a given time provided only that (i) he is in that state at that time and (ii) it is necessarily true that if he is in that state at that time then it is evident to him that he is in that state at that time.

The states of mind just referred to are of this character. Wishing, say, that one were on the moon is a state that is such that a man cannot be in that state without it being evident to him that he is in that state. And so, too, for thinking certain thoughts and having certain sensory or emotional experiences. These states present themselves and are, so to speak, marks of their own evidence. They cannot occur unless it is evident that they occur. I think they are properly called the "first truths of fact." Thus St. Thomas could say that "the intellect knows that it possesses the truth by reflecting on itself."

Perceiving external things and remembering are not states that present themselves. But thinking that one perceives (or seeming to perceive) and thinking that one remembers (or seeming to remember) *are* states of mind that present themselves. And in presenting themselves they may, at least under certain favorable conditions, present something else as well.

Coffey quotes Hobbes as saying that "the inn of evidence has no sign-board." I would prefer saying that these self-presenting states are sign-boards—of the inn of indirect evidence. But these sign-boards need no further sign-boards in order to be presented, for they present themselves.

13

What of the first truths of reason? These are the propositions that some philosophers have called "a priori" and that Leibniz, following Locke, referred to as "maxims" or "axioms." These propositions are all necessary and have a further characteristic that Leibniz described in this way: "You will find in a hundred places that the Scholastics have said that these propositions are evident, *ex terminis,* as soon as the terms are understood, so that they were persuaded that the force of conviction was grounded in the nature of the terms, i.e., in connection of their ideas." Thus St. Thomas referred to propositions that are "manifest through themselves."

An axiom, one might say, is a necessary proposition such that one cannot understand it without thereby knowing that it is true. Since one cannot know a proposition unless it is evident and one believes it, and since one cannot believe a proposition unless one understands it, we might characterize these first truths of reason in the following way:

A proposition is *axiomatic* for a given subject at a given time provided only that (i) the proposition is one that is necessarily true and (ii) it is also necessarily true that if the person then believes that proposition, the proposition is then evident to him.

We might now characterize the *a priori* somewhat more broadly by saying that a proposition is a priori for a given subject at a given time provided that one or the other of these two things is true: either (i) the proposition is one that is axiomatic for that subject at that time, or else (ii) the proposition is one such that it is evident to the man at that time that the proposition is entailed by a set of propositions that are axiomatic for him at that time.

In characterizing the "first truths of fact" and the "first truths of reason," I have used the expression "evident." But I think it is clear that such truths are not only evident but also certain. And they may be said to be *directly,* or *immediately,* evident.

What, then, of the indirectly evident?

14

I have suggested in rather general terms above what we might say about memory and the senses. These ostensible sources of knowledge are to be treated as innocent until there is positive ground for thinking them guilty. I will not attempt to develop a theory of the indirectly evident at this point. But I will note at least the *kind* of principle to which we might appeal in developing such a theory.

We could *begin* by considering the following two principles, M and P; M referring to memory, and P referring to perception or the senses.

M. For any subject S, if it is evident to S that she seems to remember that *a* was F, then it is beyond reasonable doubt for S that *a* was F.

P.   For any subject S, if it is evident to S that she thinks she perceives that *a* is F, then it is evident to S that *a* is F.

"She seems to remember" and "she thinks she perceives" here refer to certain self-presenting states that, in the figure I used above, could be said to serve as sign-boards for the inn of indirect evidence.

But principles M and P, as they stand, are much too latitudinarian. We will find that it is necessary to make qualifications and add more and more conditions. Some of these will refer to the subject's sensory state; some will refer to certain of her other beliefs; and some will refer to the relations of confirmation and mutual support. To set them forth in adequate detail would require a complete epistemology.

So far as our problem of the criterion is concerned, the essential thing to note is this. In formulating such principles we will simply proceed as Aristotle did when he formulated his rules for the syllogism. As "particularists" in our approach to the problem of the criterion, we will fit our rules to the cases—to the apples we know to be good and to the apples we know to be bad. Knowing what we do about ourselves and the world, we have at our disposal certain instances that our rules or principles should countenance, and certain other instances that our rules or principles should rule out or forbid. And, as rational beings, we assume that by investigating these instances we can formulate criteria that any instance must satisfy if it is to be countenanced and we can formulate other criteria that any instance must satisfy if it is to be ruled out or forbidden.

If we proceed in this way we will have satisfied Cardinal Mercier's criteria for a theory of evidence or, as he called it, a theory of certitude. He said that any criterion, or any adequate set of criteria, should be internal, objective, and immediate. The type of criteria I have referred to are certainly *internal,* in his sense of the term. We have not appealed to any external authority as constituting the ultimate test of evidence. (Thus we haven't appealed to "science" or to "the scientists of our culture circle" as constituting the touchstone of what we know.) I would say that our criteria are *objective.* We have formulated them in terms of the concept of epistemic preferability—where the location "*p* is epistemically preferable to *q* for S" is taken to refer to an objective relation that obtains independently of the actual preferences of any particular subject. The criteria that we formulate, if they are adequate, will be principles that are necessarily true. And they are also *immediate.* Each of them is such that, if it is applicable at any particular time, then the fact that it is then applicable is capable of being directly evident to that particular subject at that particular time.

15

But in all of this I have presupposed the approach I have called "particularism." The "methodist" and the "skeptic" will tell us that we have started in the wrong place. If now we try to reason with them, then, I am afraid, we will be back on the wheel.

What few philosophers have had the courage to recognize is this: we can deal with the problem only by begging the question. It seems to me that, if we do recognize this fact, as we should, then it is unseemly for us to try to pretend that it isn't so.

One may object: "Doesn't this mean, then, that the skeptic is right after all?" I would answer: "Not at all. His view is only one of the three possibilities and in itself has no more to recommend it than the others do. And in favor of our approach there is the fact that we *do* know many things, after all."

Bibliography

Audi, Robert. *Belief, Justification, and Knowledge.* Belmont, CA: Wadsworth, 1988.

Ayer, A. J. *The Problem of Knowledge.* London: Penguin, 1956.

Baergen, Ralph. *Contemporary Epistemology.* Fort Worth, TX: Harcourt Brace, 1995.

Capaldi, Nicholas. *Human Knowledge.* New York: Pegasus, 1969.

Chisholm, Roderick M. *The Foundations of Knowing.* Minneapolis: University of Minnesota Press, 1982.

Chisholm, Roderick M. *Theory of Knowledge.* 3d ed. Englewood Cliffs, NJ: Prentice Hall, 1988.

Dancy, John. *Introduction to Contemporary Epistemology.* London: Blackwell, 1985.

Dancy, Jonathan, and Ernest Sosa, eds. *A Companion to Epistemology.* Oxford: Blackwell, 1992.

Everitt, Nicholas, and Alec Fisher. *Modern Epistemology.* New York: McGraw-Hill, 1995.

French, Peter, Theodore E. Vehling, Jr., and Howard Wettstein, eds. *Midwest Studies in Philosophy.* Vol. 5: *Studies in Epistemology.* Minneapolis: University of Minnesota Press, 1980.

Goodman, Michael, and Robert Snyder, eds. *Contemporary Readings in Epistemology.* Upper Saddle River, NJ: Prentice Hall, 1993.

Lehrer, Keith. *Theory of Knowledge.* Boulder, CO: Westview, 1990.

Locke, John. *An Essay Concerning Human Understanding.* Oxford: Oxford University Press, 1975.

Harman, Gilbert. *Thought.* Princeton, NJ: Princeton University Press, 1975.

Landesman, Charles, ed. *The Foundations of Knowledge.* Englewood Cliffs, NJ: Prentice Hall, 1970.

Malcolm, Norman. *Knowledge and Certainty.* Ithaca, NY: Cornell University Press, 1963.

Moser, Paul, and Arnold Vander Nat, eds. *Human Knowledge.* Oxford: Oxford University Press, 1987.

Nagel, Ernest, and Richard Brandt, eds. *Meaning and Knowledge.* New York: Harcourt, Brace & World, 1965.

O'Connor, D. J., and Brian Carr. *Introduction to the Theory of Knowledge.* Minneapolis: University of Minnesota Press, 1982.

Plato. *Phaedo, Meno, Theaetetus,* and the *Republic.*

Pojman, Louis P. *What Can We Know? An Introduction to the Theory of Knowledge.* Belmont, CA: Wadsworth, 2001.

Pollock, John L. *Contemporary Theories of Knowledge.* Totawa, NJ: Rowman & Littlefield, 1986.

Popkin, Richard. *A History of Skepticism from Erasmus to Spinoza.* Berkeley: University of California Press, 1979.

Russell, Bertrand. *Human Knowledge: Its Scope and Limits.* New York: Simon & Schuster, 1948.

Russell, Bertrand. *The Problems of Philosophy.* Oxford: Oxford University Press, 1912.

Steup, Matthias. *An Introduction to Contemporary Epistemology.* Upper Saddle River, NJ: Prentice Hall, 1996.

Part II

Skepticism

What can we really know? How can we be certain that we have the truth? How can we be certain that we know anything at all? If we know something, must we know that we know it? Is the skeptic right in claiming that we know almost nothing at all?

Can we know anything at all? Or are we doomed to ignorance about the most important subjects in life? What do we really know? Could it be that we really know nothing at all? Could it be that either none of our beliefs are completely true or that none of our true beliefs are sufficiently justified to constitute knowledge? How can we show that we really do know anything at all?

Skepticism is the theory that we do not have any knowledge. We cannot be completely certain that any of our beliefs are true. There are two classic types of skepticism, both originating in ancient Greek philosophy: Academic skepticism and Pyrrhonian skepticism. Academic skepticism was first formulated by Arcesilaus (about 315 to about 240 BCE), a philosopher in Plato's Academy, and builds on Socrates' confession in the *Apology,* "All that I know is that I

know nothing." It argues that the only thing we can know is that we know nothing. The Academics argued that there is no criterion by which we can distinguish veridical perceptions from illusions and that at best we have only probable true belief.

Pyrrhonian skepticism, named after Pyrrho of Elis (about 360 to 270 BCE), flourished in Alexandria in the first century B.C. The Pyrrhonians rejected Academic skepticism and dogmatism, the view that we could have knowledge, and set forth "tropes," skeptical arguments leading to *equipollence,* the balancing of reasons on both sides of an issue that led to *epoche,* the suspension of judgement. Whereas the Academics claimed to know one thing (that they didn't have any other knowledge), the Pyrrhonians denied that we could know even that. The Greek Pyrrhonist, Sextus Empiricus (second century A.D.), said that Pyrrhonism was like a purge that eliminates everything, including itself.

One other distinction regarding skepticism needs to be made: that between global and local skepticism. Global skeptics maintain universal doubt. They deny that we know that there is an external world, that there are other minds, that we can have knowledge of metaphysical truths, such as whether we have free will, whether God exists, whether we have souls, and so forth. Some superglobal skeptics even deny that we can know simple mathematical truths or that the laws of logic are valid (an evil genius could be deceiving us). In the following readings, René Descartes (1596–1650) and Keith Lehrer both represent global skepticism. The other type of skepticism is local skepticism, which admits that we can have mathematical and empirical knowledge but denies that we can have metaphysical knowledge (God's existence, the nature of matter, whether all events have antecedent causes, whether there are other minds, and so forth). David Hume (1711–1776) entertains the possibility of both forms of skepticism. As Richard Popkin accurately puts it,

> Hume sometimes held a most extreme skeptical position . . . questioning even the knowledge claims of science, mathematics, and logical reasoning, and sometimes held a limited mitigated skepticism allowing for probabilistic standards for evaluating beliefs about what is beyond immediate experience. When Hume examined the general nature of all beliefs, he tended toward complete skepticism. When he examined metaphysics and theology, in contrast with science, he tended toward a positivistic, limited skepticism. And when he developed his own views about human nature and conduct, his doubts tended to recede and his positive views became more pronounced.[1]

Skepticism does not deny that we should act from the best evidence available, but it insists that we can never be sure that we are correct in our truth claims. For all we know, the universe and everything in it could have been created ten minutes ago, and all our apparent memories created with it. Or the universe and everything in it may have doubled in size last night while we were sleeping. How could we check on this? It wouldn't help to use a ruler to measure our height to see if we have doubled in size, would it?

How do you know that you are not the only person who exists and that everyone else is a robot who is programmed to speak and smile and write exams? Can you prove that other people have consciousness? Have you ever felt their consciousness, their pain, or their sense of the color green? In fact, come to think of it, how do you know that you are not just dreaming right now? All you are experiencing is part of a dream. Soon you will awake and be surprised to discover that what you thought were dreams were really minidreams within your maxidream. How can you prove that you are not dreaming? Or perhaps you are simply a brain suspended in a tub full of a chemical solution in a scientist's laboratory and wired to a computer that is causing you to have the simulated experiences of what you now seem to be experiencing? If you are under the control of an ingenious scientist, you would never discover it, for he has arranged that you will only be able to compare your beliefs to experiences that he simulates. Your tub is your destiny!

In the first reading, from the *Meditations,* Descartes begins by rejecting all sensory perception, arguing that the senses are not reliable witnesses because they sometimes deceive. Essentially, we do not have a criterion by which to distinguish illusory experience from veridical perception. His argument may be formulated thus:

1.   To have knowledge we need to be able to tell the difference between a hallucination (deception) and a perception. (Where there is no relevant difference, no epistemological distinction can be made.)

2. It is impossible to distinguish between an hallucination (or deception) and a normal perception.

3. Therefore, we do not know whether any of our perceptual beliefs are true.

But Descartes goes on to doubt even our mathematical judgements. He imagines that an ingenious demon is deceiving him about everything, even about the most secure mathematical sums, so that it is possible that he is mistaken about adding 2 plus 3. In Meditations 2 through 4 Descartes offers his solution to skepticism.

In the second selection, David Hume admits that we can know mathematical truths but claims that we cannot have empirical knowledge. He supposes that all our beliefs (or ideas) are caused by impressions (both internal and external, the passions and the perceptions). But we cannot get behind the impressions to check whether the world is really like what we are experiencing, so we can never know to what extent our impressions and ideas resemble the world. Hume goes on to argue that since all our beliefs are founded on these insecure impressions, we can have no metaphysical knowledge. We cannot even trace our belief in cause and effect, the self, the existence of God, or free will to impressions; hence, they are entirely without justification. In the fourth reading, Keith Lehrer argues that knowledge entails complete justification of belief, but that if it is possible that the skeptical hypothesis is true, no one is completely justified in any belief. Hence, no one knows anything at all.

Can you defeat the skeptic? Two attempts are offered in this part of the book. In the third reading, G. E. Moore claims we *can* know there is an external world, for we can know we have bodies. There are many empirical beliefs that we can be absolutely certain of, so that skepticism may justly be refuted. In the fifth reading, Norman Malcolm distinguishes two types of knowledge, weak and strong. When I use the weak sense of knowledge, I am prepared to let an investigation determine whether my knowledge claim is true or false, whereas when I use the strong sense I will not concede that anything whatsoever could prove me mistaken.

Note

[1] Richard Popkin, "Skepticism," *Encyclopedia of Philosophy*, Vol. 7 (New York: Macmillan, 1967), p. 455.

II.1 Global Skepticism and the Quest for Certainty (Meditations 1 through 4)

René Descartes

René Descartes (1596–1650) was born in France and educated by the Jesuits at the College of La Fleche. In this classic work, *Meditations on First Philosophy* (1641), Descartes declares that because his education and experience in general have resulted in a shaky house of knowledge, he must use the method of universal doubt to raze the entire edifice, foundations and all, and erect new and solid foundations on which to build a permanent dwelling, an indestructible system of knowledge. This selection contains the first four of six meditations on the subject of knowledge.

[handwritten: DESCARTES WAS NOT A SKEPTIC, DESPITE THIS ARGUMENT.]

First Meditation

Of the Things Which May Be Brought Within the Sphere of the Doubtful

[handwritten: REALIZED HE HAD NO KNOWLEDGE]

It is now some years since I detected how many were the false beliefs that I had from my earliest youth admitted as true, and how doubtful was everything I had since constructed on this basis; and from that time I was convinced that I must once for all seriously undertake to rid myself of all the opinions which I had formerly accepted, and commence to build anew from the foundation, if I wanted to establish any firm and permanent structure in the sciences. But as this enterprise appeared to be a very great one, I waited until I had attained an age so mature that I could not hope that at any later date I should be better fitted to execute my design. This reason caused me to delay so long that I should feel that I was doing wrong were I to occupy in deliberation the time that yet remains to me for action. Today, then, since very opportunely for the plan I have in view I have delivered my mind from every care [and am happily agitated by no passions] and since I have procured for myself an assured leisure in a peaceable retirement, I shall at last seriously and freely address myself to the general upheaval of all my former opinions.

Now for this object it is not necessary that I should show that all of these are false—I shall perhaps never arrive at this end. But inasmuch as reason already persuades me that I ought no less carefully to withhold my assent from matters which are not entirely certain and indubitable than from those which appear to me manifestly to be false, if I am able to find in each one some reason to doubt, this will suffice to justify my rejecting the whole. And for that end it will not be requisite that I should examine each in particular, which would be an endless undertaking; for owing to the fact that the destruction of the foundations of necessity brings with it the downfall of the rest of the edifice, I shall only in the first place attack those principles upon which all my former opinions rested.

All that up to the present time I have accepted as most true and certain I have learned either from the senses or through the senses; but it is sometimes proved to me that these senses are deceptive, and it is wiser not to trust entirely to any thing by which we have once been deceived.

But it may be that although the senses sometimes deceive us concerning things which are hardly perceptible, or very far away, there are yet many others to be met with as to which we cannot reasonably have any doubt, although we recognise them by their means. *[handwritten: FIRE PLACE EX.]* For example, there is the fact that I am here, seated by the fire, attired in a dressing gown, having this paper in my hands and other similar matters. And how could I deny that these hands and this body are mine, were it not perhaps that I compare myself to certain persons, devoid of sense, whose cerebella are so troubled and clouded

Reprinted from the *Philosophical Works of Descartes,* trans. Elizabeth Haldane and G. Ross, vol. I (Cambridge University Press, 1931), by permission of the publisher.

by the violent vapors of black bile, that they constantly assure us that they think they are kings when they are really quite poor, or that they are clothed in purple when they are really without covering, or who imagine that they have an earthenware head or are nothing but pumpkins or are made of glass. But they are mad, and I should not be any the less insane were I to follow examples so extravagant.

At the same time I must remember that I am a man, and that consequently I am in the habit of sleeping, and in my dreams representing to myself the same things or, sometimes even less probable things, than do those who are insane in their waking moments. How often has it happened to me that in the night I dreamt that I found myself in this particular place, that I was dressed and seated near the fire, whilst in reality I was lying undressed in bed! At this moment it does indeed seem to me that it is with eyes awake that I am looking at this paper; that this head which I move is not asleep, that it is deliberately and of set purpose that I extend my hand and perceive it; what happens in sleep does not appear so clear nor so distinct as does all this. But in thinking over this I remind myself that on many occasions I have in sleep been deceived by similar illusions, and in dwelling carefully on this reflection I see so manifestly that there are no certain indications by which we may clearly distinguish wakefulness from sleep that I am lost in astonishment. And my astonishment is such that it is almost capable of persuading me that I now dream.

Now let us assume that we are asleep and that all these particulars, e.g. that we open our eyes, shake our head, extend our hands, and so on, are but false delusions; and let us reflect that possibly neither our hands nor our whole body are such as they appear to us to be. At the same time we must at least confess that the things which are represented to us in sleep are like painted representations which can only have been formed as the counterparts of something real and true, and that in this way those general things at least, i.e. eyes, a head, hands, and a whole body, are not imaginary things, but things really existent. For, as a matter of fact, painters, even when they study with the greatest skill to represent sirens and satyrs by forms the most strange and extraordinary, cannot give them natures which are entirely new, but merely make a certain medley of the members of different animals; or if their imagination is extravagant

[margin note: COULD BE DREAMING AT ANY MOMENT]

enough to invent something so novel that nothing similar has ever before been seen, and that then their work represents a thing purely fictitious and absolutely false, it is certain all the same that the colors of which this is composed are necessarily real. And for the same reason, although these general things, to wit, [a body], eyes, a head, hands, and such like, may be imaginary, we are bound at the same time to confess that there are at least some other objects yet more simple and more universal, which are real and true; and of these just in the same way as with certain real colors, all these images of things which dwell in our thoughts, whether true and real or false and fantastic, are formed.

To such a class of things pertains corporeal nature in general, and its extension, the figure of extended things, their quantity or magnitude and number, as also the place in which they are, the time which measures their duration, and so on.

[margin note: SIZE LOCATION QUANTITY ETC.?]

That is possibly why our reasoning is not unjust when we conclude from this that Physics, Astronomy, Medicine and all other sciences which have as their end the consideration of composite things, are very dubious and uncertain; but that Arithmetic, Geometry and other sciences of that kind which only treat of things that are very simple and very general, without taking great trouble to ascertain whether they are actually existent or not, contain some measure of certainty and an element of the indubitable. For whether I am awake or asleep, two and three together always form five, and the square can never have more than four sides, and it does not seem possible that truths so clear and apparent can be suspected of any falsity [or uncertainty].

[margin note: EXT WORLD NOT KNOWN LETSGAME INTELLIGIBLE WORLD]

Nevertheless I have long had fixed in my mind the belief that an all-powerful God existed by whom I have been created such as I am. But how do I know that He has not brought it to pass that there is no earth, no heaven, no extended body, no magnitude, no place, and that nevertheless [I possess the perceptions of all these things and that] they seem to me to exist just exactly as I now see them? And, besides, as I sometimes imagine that others deceive themselves in the things which they think they know best, how do I know that I am not deceived every time that I add two and three, or count the sides of a square, or judge of things yet simpler, if anything simpler can be imagined? But possibly God has not desired that I should be thus deceived, for He is said to be supremely good. If, however, it is contrary to His goodness to have made me such that I constantly deceive myself, it would also appear to be contrary to His goodness to permit me to be sometimes deceived, and nevertheless I cannot doubt that He does permit this.

There may indeed be those who would prefer to deny the existence of a God so powerful, rather than believe that all other things are uncertain. But let us not oppose them for the present, and grant that all that is here said of a God is a fable; nevertheless in whatever way they suppose that I have arrived at the state of being that I have reached—whether they attribute it to fate or to accident, or make out that it is by a continual succession of antecedents, or by some other method—since to err and deceive oneself is a defect, it is clear that the greater will be the probability of my being so imperfect as to deceive myself ever, as is the Author to whom they assign my origin the less powerful. To these reasons I have certainly nothing to reply, but at the end I feel constrained to confess that there is nothing in all that I formerly believed to be true, of which I cannot in some measure doubt, and that not merely through want of thought or through levity, but for reasons which are very powerful and maturely considered; so that henceforth I ought not the less carefully to refrain from giving credence to these opinions than to that which is manifestly false, if I desire to arrive at any certainty [in the sciences].

But it is not sufficient to have made these remarks; we must also be careful to keep them in mind. For these ancient and commonly held opinions still revert frequently to my mind, long and familiar custom having given them the right to occupy my mind against my inclination and rendered them almost masters of my belief; nor will I ever lose the habit of deferring to them or of placing my confidence in them, so long as I consider them as they really are, i.e. opinions in some measure doubtful, as I have just shown, and at the same time highly probable, so that there is much more reason to believe in than to deny them. That is why I consider that I shall not be acting amiss, if, taking of set purpose a contrary belief, I allow myself to be deceived, and for a certain time pretend that all these opinions are entirely false and imaginary, until at last, having thus balanced my former prejudices with my latter [so that they can-

not divert my opinions more to one side than to the other], my judgement will no longer be dominated by bad usage or turned away from the right knowledge of the truth. For I am assured that there can be neither peril nor error in this course, and that I cannot at present yield too much to distrust, since I am not considering the question of action, but only of knowledge.

I shall then suppose, not that God who is supremely good and the fountain of truth, but some evil genius not less powerful than deceitful, has employed his whole energies in deceiving me; I shall consider that the heavens, the earth, colors, figures, sound, and all other external things are nought but the illusions and dreams of which this genius has availed himself in order to lay traps for my credulity; I shall consider myself as having no hands, no eyes, no flesh, no blood, nor any senses, yet falsely believing myself to possess all these things; I shall remain obstinately attached to this idea, and if by this means it is not in my power to arrive at the knowledge of any truth, I may at least do what is in my power [i.e. suspend my judgement], and with firm purpose avoid giving credence to any false thing, or being imposed upon by this arch deceiver, however powerful and deceptive he may be. But this task is a laborious one, and insensibly a certain lassitude leads me into the course of my ordinary life. And just as a captive who in sleep enjoys an imaginary liberty, when he begins to suspect that his liberty is but a dream, fears to awaken, and conspires with these agreeable illusions that the deception may be prolonged, so insensibly of my own accord I fall back into my former opinions, and I dread awakening from this slumber, lest the laborious wakefulness which would follow the tranquility of this repose should have to be spent not in daylight, but in the excessive darkness of the difficulties which have just been discussed.

Second Meditation

The Nature of the Human Mind, and How It Is Better Known Than the Body

So serious are the doubts into which I have been thrown as a result of yesterday's meditation that I can neither put them out of my mind nor see any way of resolving them. It feels as if I have fallen unexpectedly into a deep whirlpool which tumbles me around so that I can neither stand on the bottom nor swim up to the top. Nevertheless I will make an effort and once more attempt the same path which I started on yesterday. Anything which admits of the slightest doubt I will set aside just as if I had found it to be wholly false; and I will proceed in this way until I recognize something certain, or, if nothing else, until I at least recognize for certain that there is no certainty. Archimedes used to demand just one firm and immovable point in order to shift the entire earth; so I too can hope for great things if I manage to find just one thing, however slight, that is certain and unshakeable.

I will suppose then, that everything I see is spurious. I will believe that my memory tells me lies, and that none of the things that it reports ever happened. I have no senses. Body, shape, extension, movement and place are chimeras. So what remains true? Perhaps just the one fact that nothing is certain.

Yet apart from everything I have just listed, how do I know that there is not something else which does not allow even the slightest occasion for doubt? Is there not a God, or whatever I may call him, who puts into me the thoughts I am now having? But why do I think this, since I myself may perhaps be the author of these thoughts? In that case am not I, at least, something? But I have just said that I have no senses and no body. This is the sticking point: what follows from this? Am I not so bound up with a body and with senses that I cannot exist without them? But I have convinced myself that there is absolutely nothing in the world, no sky, no earth, no minds, no bodies. Does it now follow that I too do not exist? No: if I convinced myself of something then I certainly existed. But there is a deceiver of supreme power and cunning who is deliberately and constantly deceiving me. In that case I too undoubtedly exist, if he is deceiving me; and let him deceive me as much as he can, he will never bring it about that I am nothing so long as I think that I am something. So after considering everything very thoroughly, I must finally conclude that this proposition, I am, I exist, is necessarily true whenever it is put forward by me or conceived in my mind.

But I do not yet have a sufficient understanding of what this 'I' is, that now necessarily exists.

So I must be on my guard against carelessly taking something else to be this 'I', and so making a mistake in the very item of knowledge that I maintain is the most certain and evident of all. I will therefore go back and meditate on what I originally believed myself to be, before I embarked on this present train of thought. I will then subtract anything capable of being weakened, even minimally, by the arguments now introduced, so that what is left at the end may be exactly and only what is certain and unshakeable.

What then did I formerly think I was? A man. But what is a man? Shall I say 'a rational animal'? No; for then I should have to inquire what an animal is, what rationality is, and in this way one question would lead me down the slope to other harder ones, and I do not now have the time to waste on subtleties of this kind. Instead I propose to concentrate on what came into my thoughts spontaneously and quite naturally whenever I used to consider what I was. Well, the first thought to come to mind was that I had a face, hands, arms and the whole mechanical structure of limbs which can be seen in a corpse, and which I called the body. The next thought was that I was nourished, that I moved about, and that I engaged in sense perception and thinking; and these actions I attributed to the soul. But as to the nature of this soul, either I did not think about this or else I imagined it to be something tenuous, like a wind or fire or ether, which permeated my more solid parts. As to the body, however, I had no doubts about it, but thought I knew its nature distinctly. If I had tried to describe the mental conception I had of it, I would have expressed it as follows: by a body I understand whatever has a determinable shape and a definable location and can occupy a space in such a way as to exclude any other body; it can be perceived by touch, sight, hearing, taste or smell, and can be moved in various ways, not by itself but by whatever else comes into contact with it. For, according to my judgement, the power of self-movement, like the power of sensation or of thought, was quite foreign to the nature of a body; indeed, it was a source of wonder to me that certain bodies were found to contain faculties of this kind.

But what shall I now say that I am, when I am supposing that there is some supremely powerful and, if it is permissible to say so, malicious deceiver, who is deliberately trying to trick me in every way he can? Can I now assert that I possess even the most insignificant of all the attributes which I have just said belong to the nature of a body? I scrutinize them, think about them, go over them again, but nothing suggests itself; it is tiresome and pointless to go through the list once more. But what about the attributes I assigned to the soul? Nutrition or movement? Since now I do not have a body, these are mere fabrications. Sense-perception? This surely does not occur without a body, and besides, when asleep I have appeared to perceive through the senses many things which I afterwards realized I did not perceive through the senses at all. Thinking? At last I have discovered it—thought; this alone is inseparable from me. I am, I exist—that is certain. But for how long? For as long as I am thinking. For it could be that were I totally to cease from thinking, I should totally cease to exist. At present I am not admitting anything except what is necessarily true. I am, then, in the strict sense only a thing that thinks; that is, I am a mind, or intelligence, or intellect, or reason—words whose meaning I have been ignorant of until now. But for all that I am a thing which is real and which truly exists. But what kind of a thing? As I have just said—a thinking thing.

What else am I? I will use my imagination. I am not that structure of limbs which is called a human body. I am not even some thin vapor which permeates the limbs—a wind, fire, air, breath, or whatever I depict in my imagination; for these are things which I have supposed to be nothing. Let this supposition stand; for all that I am still something. And yet may it not perhaps be the case that these very things which I am supposing to be nothing, because they are unknown to me, are in reality identical with the 'I' of which I am aware? I do not know, and for the moment I shall not argue the point, since I can make judgements only about things which are known to me. I know that I exist; the question is, what is this 'I' that I know? If the 'I' is understood strictly as we have been taking it, then it is quite certain that knowledge of it does not depend on things of whose existence I am as yet unaware; so it cannot depend on any of the things which I invent in my imagination. And this very word 'invent' shows me my mistake. It would indeed be a case of fictitious invention if I used my imagination to establish that I was something or other; for imagining is simply contemplating the shape or image of a corporeal thing. Yet now I know for certain both that I exist and at the same time that all such images and, in general, everything relating to the nature of body, could be mere dreams <and chimeras>. Once this point has been grasped, to say 'I will use my imagination to get to know more distinctly what I am' would seem to be as silly as saying 'I am now awake, and see some truth; but since my vision is not yet clear enough, I will deliberately fall asleep so that my dreams may provide a truer and clearer representation.' I thus realize that none of the things that the imagination enables me to grasp is at all relevant to this knowledge of myself which I possess, and that the mind must therefore be most carefully diverted from such things if it is to perceive its own nature as distinctly as possible.

But what then am I? A thing that thinks. What is that? A thing that doubts, understands, affirms, denies, is willing, is unwilling, and also imagines and has sensory perceptions.

This is a considerable list, if everything on it belongs to me. But does it? Is it not one and the same 'I' who is now doubting almost everything, who nonetheless understands some things, who affirms that this one thing is true, denies everything else, desires to know more, is unwilling to be deceived, imagines many things even involuntarily, and is aware of many things which apparently come from the senses? Are not all these things just as true as the fact that I exist, even if I am asleep all the time, and even if he who created me is doing all he can to deceive me? Which of all these activities is distinct from my thinking? Which of them can be said to be separate from myself? The fact that it is I who am doubting and understanding and willing is so evident that I see no way of making it any clearer. But it is also the case that the 'I' who imagines is the same 'I'. For even if, as I have supposed, none of the objects of imagination are real, the power of imagination is something which really exists and is part of my thinking. Lastly, it is also the same 'I' who has sensory perceptions, or is aware of bodily things as it were through the senses. For example, I am now seeing light, hearing a noise, feeling heat. But I am asleep, so all this is false. Yet I certainly seem to see, to hear, and to be warmed. This cannot be false; what is called 'having a sensory perception' is strictly just this, and in this restricted sense of the term it is simply thinking.

From all this I am beginning to have a rather better understanding of what I am. But it still appears—and I cannot stop thinking this—that the corporeal things of which images are formed in my thought, and which the senses investigate, are known with much more distinctness than this puzzling 'I' which cannot be pictured in the imagination. And yet it is surely surprising that I should have a more distinct grasp of things which I realize are doubtful, unknown and foreign to me, than I have of that which is true and known—my own self. But I see what it is: my mind enjoys wandering off and will not yet submit to being restrained within the bounds of truth. Very well then; just this once let us give it a completely free rein, so that after a while, when it is time to tighten the reins, it may more readily submit to being curbed.

Let us consider the things which people commonly think they understand most distinctly of all; that is, the bodies which we touch and see. I do not mean bodies in general—for general perceptions are apt to be somewhat more confused—but one particular body. Let us take, for example, this piece of wax. It has just been taken from the honeycomb; it has not yet quite lost the taste of the honey; it retains some of the scent of the flowers from which it was gathered; its color, shape and size are plain to see; it is hard, cold and can be handled without difficulty; if you rap it with your knuckle it makes a sound. In short, it has everything which appears necessary to enable a body to be known as distinctly as possible. But even as I speak, I put the wax by the fire, and look: the residual taste is eliminated, the smell goes away, the color changes, the shape is lost, the size increases; it becomes liquid and hot; you can hardly touch it, and if you strike it, it no longer makes a sound. But does the same wax remain? It must be admitted that it does; no one denies it, no one thinks otherwise. So what was it in the wax that I understood with such distinctness? Evidently none of the features which I arrived at by means of the senses; for whatever came under taste, smell, sight, touch or hearing has now altered—yet the wax remains.

Perhaps the answer lies in the thought which now comes to my mind; namely, the wax was not after all the sweetness of the honey, or the fragrance of the flowers, or the whiteness, or the shape, or the sound, but was rather a body which presented itself to me in these various forms a lit-

tle while ago, but which now exhibits different ones. But what exactly is it that I am now imagining? Let us concentrate, take away everything which does not belong to the wax, and see what is left: merely something extended, flexible and changeable. But what is meant here by 'flexible' and 'changeable'? Is it what I picture in my imagination: that this piece of wax is capable of changing from a round shape to a square shape, or from a square shape to a triangular shape? Not at all; for I can grasp that the wax is capable of countless changes of this kind, yet I am unable to run through this immeasurable number of changes in my imagination, from which it follows that it is not the faculty of imagination that gives me my grasp of the wax as flexible and changeable. And what is meant by 'extended'? Is the extension of the wax also unknown? For it increases if the wax melts, increases again if it boils, and is greater still if the heat is increased. I would not be making a correct judgement about the nature of wax unless I believed it capable of being extended in many more different ways than I will ever encompass in my imagination. I must therefore admit that the nature of this piece of wax is in no way revealed by my imagination, but is perceived by the mind alone. (I am speaking of this particular piece of wax; the point is even clearer with regard to wax in general.) But what is this wax which is perceived by the mind alone? It is of course the same wax which I see, which I touch, which I picture in my imagination, in short the same wax which I thought it to be from the start. And yet, and here is the point, the perception I have of it is a case not of vision or touch or imagination—nor has it ever been, despite previous appearances—but of purely mental scrutiny; and this can be imperfect and confused, as it was before, or clear and distinct as it is now, depending on how carefully I concentrate on what the wax consists in.

But as I reach this conclusion I am amazed at how weak and prone to error my mind is. For although I am thinking about these matters within myself, silently and without speaking, nonetheless the actual words bring me up short, and I am almost tricked by ordinary ways of talking. We say that we see the wax itself, if it is there before us, not that we judge it to be there from its color or shape; and this might lead me to conclude without more ado that knowledge of the wax comes from what the eye sees, and not from the scrutiny of the mind alone. But then if I look out of the window and see men crossing the square, as I just happen to have done, I normally say that I see the men themselves, just as I say that I see the wax. Yet do I see any more than hats and coats which could conceal automatons? I judge that they are men. And so something which I thought I was seeing with my eyes is in fact grasped solely by the faculty of judgement which is in my mind.

However, one who wants to achieve knowledge above the ordinary level should feel ashamed at having taken ordinary ways of talking as a basis for doubt. So let us proceed, and consider on which occasion my perception of the nature of the wax was more perfect and evident. Was it when I first looked at it, and believed I knew it by my external senses, or at least by what they call the 'common' sense—that is, the power of imagination? Or is my knowledge more perfect now, after a more careful investigation of the nature of the wax and of the means by which it is known? Any doubt on this issue would clearly be foolish; for what distinctness was there in my earlier perception? Was there anything in it which an animal could not possess? But when I distinguish the wax from its outward forms—take the clothes off, as it were, and consider it naked—then although my judgement may still contain errors, at least my perception now requires a human mind.

But what am I to say about this mind, or about myself? (So far, remember, I am not admitting that there is anything else in me except a mind.) What, I ask, is this 'I' which seems to perceive the wax so distinctly? Surely my awareness of my own self is not merely much truer and more certain than my awareness of the wax, but also much more distinct and evident. For if I judge that the wax exists from the fact that I see it, clearly this same fact entails much more evidently that I myself also exist. It is possible that what I see is not really the wax; it is possible that I do not even have eyes with which to see anything. But when I see, or think I see (I am not here distinguishing the two), it is simply not possible that I who am now thinking am not something. By the same token, if I judge that the wax exists from the fact that I touch it, the same result follows, namely that I exist. If I judge that it exists from the fact that I imagine it, or for any other reason, exactly the same thing follows. And the result that I have grasped in the case of the wax may be applied to

everything else located outside me. Moreover, if my perception of the wax seemed more distinct after it was established not just by sight or touch but by many other considerations, it must be admitted that I now know myself even more distinctly. This is because every consideration whatsoever which contributes to my perception of the wax, or of any other body, cannot but establish even more effectively the nature of my own mind. But besides this, there is so much else in the mind itself which can serve to make my knowledge of it more distinct, that it scarcely seems worth going through the contributions made by considering bodily things.

I see that without any effort I have now finally got back to where I wanted. I now know that even bodies are not strictly perceived by the senses or the faculty of imagination but by the intellect alone, and that this perception derives not from their being touched or seen but from their being understood; and in view of this I know plainly that I can achieve an easier and more evident perception of my own mind than of anything else. But since the habit of holding on to old opinions cannot be set aside so quickly, I should like to stop here and meditate for some time on this new knowledge I have gained, so as to fix it more deeply in my memory.

Third Meditation

The Existence of God

I will now shut my eyes, stop my ears, and withdraw all my senses. I will eliminate from my thoughts all images of bodily things, or rather, since this is hardly possible, I will regard all such images as vacuous, false and worthless. I will converse with myself and scrutinize myself more deeply; and in this way I will attempt to achieve, little by little, a more intimate knowledge of myself. I am a thing that thinks: that is, a thing that doubts, affirms, denies, understands a few things, is ignorant of many things, is willing, is unwilling, and also which imagines and has sensory perceptions; for as I have noted before, even though the objects of my sensory experience and imagination may have no existence outside me, nonetheless the modes of thinking which I refer to as cases of sensory perception and imagination, in so far as they are simply modes of thinking, do exist within me—of that I am certain.

In this brief list I have gone through everything I truly know, or at least everything I have so far discovered that I know. Now I will cast around more carefully to see whether there may be other things within me which I have not yet noticed. I am certain that I am a thinking thing. Do I not therefore also know what is required for my being certain about anything? In this first item of knowledge there is simply a clear and distinct perception of what I am asserting; this would not be enough to make me certain of the truth of the matter if it could ever turn out that something which I perceived with such clarity and distinctness was false. So I now seem to be able to lay it down as a general rule that whatever I perceive very clearly and distinctly is true.

Yet I previously accepted as wholly certain and evident many things which I afterwards realized were doubtful. What were these? The earth, sky, stars, and everything else that I apprehended with the senses. But what was it about them that I perceived clearly? Just that the ideas, or thoughts, of such things appeared before my mind. Yet even now I am not denying that these ideas occur within me. But there was something else which I used to assert, and which through habitual belief I thought I perceived clearly, although I did not in fact do so. This was that there were things outside me which were the sources of my ideas and which resembled them in all respects. Here was my mistake; or at any rate, if my judgement was true, it was not thanks to the strength of my perception.

But what about when I was considering something very simple and straightforward in arithmetic or geometry, for example that two and three added together make five, and so on? Did I not see at least these things clearly enough to affirm their truth? Indeed, the only reason for my later judgement that they were open to doubt was that it occurred to me that perhaps some God could have given me a nature such that I was deceived even in matters which seemed most evident. And whenever my preconceived belief in the supreme power of God comes to mind, I cannot but admit that it would be easy for him, if he so desired, to bring it about that I go wrong even in those matters which I think I see utterly clearly with my mind's eye. Yet when I turn to the things themselves which I think

I perceive very clearly, I am so convinced by them that I spontaneously declare: let whoever can do so deceive me, he will never bring it about that I am nothing, so long as I continue to think I am something; or make it true at some future time that I have never existed, since it is now true that I exist; or bring it about that two and three added together are more or less than five, or anything of this kind in which I see a manifest contradiction. And since I have no cause to think that there is a deceiving God, and I do not yet even know for sure whether there is a God at all, any reason for doubt which depends simply on this supposition is a very slight and, so to speak, metaphysical one. But in order to remove even this slight reason for doubt, as soon as the opportunity arises I must examine whether there is a God, and, if there is, whether he can be a deceiver. For if I do not know this, it seems that I can never be quite certain about anything else.

First, however, considerations of order appear to dictate that I now classify my thoughts into definite kinds, and ask which of them can properly be said to be the bearers of truth and falsity. Some of my thoughts are as it were the images of things, and it is only in these cases that the term 'idea' is strictly appropriate—for example, when I think of a man, or a chimera, or the sky, or an angel, or God. Other thoughts have various additional forms: thus when I will, or am afraid, or affirm, or deny, there is always a particular thing which I take as the object of my thought, but my thought includes something more than the likeness of that thing. Some thoughts in this category are called volitions or emotions, while others are called judgements.

Now as far as ideas are concerned, provided they are considered solely in themselves and I do not refer them to anything else, they cannot strictly speaking be false; for whether it is a goat or a chimera that I am imagining, it is just as true that I imagine the former as the latter. As for the will and the emotions, here too one need not worry about falsity; for even if the things which I may desire are wicked or even nonexistent, that does not make it any less true that I desire them. Thus the only remaining thoughts where I must be on my guard against making a mistake are judgements. And the chief and most common mistake which is to be found here consists in my judging that the ideas which are in me resemble, or conform to, things located outside me. Of course, if I considered just the ideas themselves simply as modes of my thought, without referring them to anything else, they could scarcely give me any material for error.

Among my ideas, some appear to be innate, some to be adventitious, and others to have been invented by me. My understanding of what a thing is, what truth is, and what thought is, seems to derive simply from my own nature. But my hearing a noise, as I do now, or seeing the sun, or feeling the fire, comes from things which are located outside me, or so I have hitherto judged. Lastly, sirens, hippogriffs and the like are my own invention. But perhaps all my ideas may be thought of as adventitious, or they may all be innate, or all made up; for as yet I have not clearly perceived their true origin.

But the chief question at this point concerns the ideas which I take to be derived from things existing outside me: what is my reason for thinking that they resemble these things? Nature has apparently taught me to think this. But in addition I know by experience that these ideas do not depend on my will, and hence that they do not depend simply on me. Frequently I notice them even when I do not want to: now, for example, I feel the heat whether I want to or not, and this is why I think that this sensation or idea of heat comes to me from something other than myself, namely the heat of the fire by which I am sitting. And the most obvious judgement for me to make is that the thing in question transmits to me its own likeness rather than something else.

I will now see if these arguments are strong enough. When I say 'Nature taught me to think this', all I mean is that a spontaneous impulse leads me to believe it, not that its truth has been revealed to me by some natural light. There is a big difference here. Whatever is revealed to me by the natural light—for example that from the fact that I am doubting it follows that I exist, and so on—cannot in any way be open to doubt. This is because there cannot be another faculty both as trustworthy as the natural light and also capable of showing me that such things are not true. But as for my natural impulses, I have often judged in the past that they were pushing me in the wrong direction when it was a question of choosing the good, and I do not see why I should place any greater confidence in them in other matters.

Then again, although these ideas do not depend on my will, it does not follow that they must come from things located outside me. Just as the impulses which I was speaking of a moment ago seem opposed to my will even though they are within me, so there may be some other faculty not yet fully known to me, which produces these ideas without any assistance from external things; this is, after all, just how I have always thought ideas are produced in me when I am dreaming.

And finally, even if these ideas did come from things other than myself, it would not follow that they must resemble those things. Indeed, I think I have often discovered a great disparity <between an object and its idea> in many cases. For example, there are two different ideas of the sun which I find within me. One of them, which is acquired as it were from the senses and which is a prime example of an idea which I reckon to come from an external source, makes the sun appear very small. The other idea is based on astronomical reasoning, that is, it is derived from certain notions which are innate in me (or else it is constructed by me in some other way), and this idea shows the sun to be several times larger than the earth. Obviously both these ideas cannot resemble the sun which exists outside me; and reason persuades me that the idea which seems to have emanated most directly from the sun itself has in fact no resemblance to it at all.

All these considerations are enough to establish that it is not reliable judgement but merely some blind impulse that has made me believe up till now that there exist things distinct from myself which transmit to me ideas or images of themselves through the sense organs or in some other way.

But it now occurs to me that there is another way of investigating whether some of the things of which I possess ideas exist outside me. In so far as the ideas are considered simply as modes of thought, there is no recognizable inequality among them: they all appear to come from within me in the same fashion. But in so far as different ideas are considered as images which represent different things, it is clear that they differ widely. Undoubtedly, the ideas which represent substances to me amount to something more and, so to speak, contain within themselves more objective reality than the ideas which merely represent modes or accidents. Again, the idea that gives me my understanding of a supreme God, eternal, infinite, immutable, omniscient, omnipotent and the creator of all things that exist apart from him, certainly has in it more objective reality than the ideas that represent finite substances.

Now it is manifest by the natural light that there must be at least as much reality in the efficient and total cause as in the effect of that cause. For where, I ask, could the effect get its reality from, if not from the cause? And how could the cause give it to the effect unless it possessed it? It follows from this both that something cannot arise from nothing, and also that what is more perfect—that is, contains in itself more reality—cannot arise from what is less perfect. And this is transparently true not only in the case of effects which possess what the philosophers call actual or formal reality, but also in the case of ideas, where one is considering only what they call objective reality. A stone, for example, which previously did not exist, cannot begin to exist unless it is produced by something which contains, either formally or eminently everything to be found in the stone; similarly, heat cannot be produced in an object which was not previously hot, except by something of at least the same order degree or kind of perfection as heat, and so on. But it is also true that the idea of heat, or of a stone, cannot exist in me unless it is put there by some cause which contains at least as much reality as I conceive to be in the heat or in the stone. For although this cause does not transfer any of its actual or formal reality to my idea, it should not on that account be supposed that it must be less real. The nature of an idea is such that of itself it requires no formal reality except what it derives from my thought, of which it is a mode. But in order for a given idea to contain such and such objective reality, it must surely derive it from some cause which contains at least as much formal reality as there is objective reality in the idea. For if we suppose that an idea contains something which was not in its cause, it must have got this from nothing; yet the mode of being by which a thing exists objectively or representatively in the intellect by way of an idea, imperfect though it may be, is certainly not nothing, and so it cannot come from nothing.

And although the reality which I am considering in my ideas is merely objective reality, I must not on that account suppose that the same reality need not exist formally in the causes of my ideas, but that it is enough for it to be present in them

objectively. For just as the objective mode of being belongs to ideas by their very nature, so the formal mode of being belongs to the causes of ideas—or at least the first and most important ones—by their very nature. And although one idea may perhaps originate from another, there cannot be an infinite regress here; eventually one must reach a primary idea, the cause of which will be like an archetype which contains formally and in fact all the reality or perfection which is present only objectively or representatively in the idea. So it is clear to me, by the natural light, that the ideas in me are like pictures, or images which can easily fall short of the perfection of the things from which they are taken, but which cannot contain anything greater or more perfect.

The longer and more carefully I examine all these points, the more clearly and distinctly I recognize their truth. But what is my conclusion to be? If the objective reality of any of my ideas turns out to be so great that I am sure the same reality does not reside in me, either formally or eminently, and hence that I myself cannot be its cause, it will necessarily follow that I am not alone in the world, but that some other thing which is the cause of this idea also exists. But if no such idea is to be found in me, I shall have no argument to convince me of the existence of anything apart from myself. For despite a most careful and comprehensive survey, this is the only argument I have so far been able to find.

Among my ideas, apart from the idea which gives me a representation of myself, which cannot present any difficulty in this context, there are ideas which variously represent God, corporeal and inanimate things, angels, animals and finally other men like myself.

As far as concerns the ideas which represent other men, or animals, or angels, I have no difficulty in understanding that they could be put together from the ideas I have of myself, of corporeal things and of God, even if the world contained no men besides me, no animals and no angels.

As to my ideas of corporeal things, I can see nothing in them which is so great or excellent as to make it seem impossible that it originated in myself. For if I scrutinize them thoroughly and examine them one by one, in the way in which I examined the idea of the wax yesterday, I notice that the things which I perceive clearly and distinctly in them are very few in number. The list comprises size, or extension in length, breadth and depth; shape, which is a function of the boundaries of this extension; position, which is a relation between various items possessing shape; and motion, or change in position; to these may be added substance, duration and number. But as for all the rest, including light and colors, sounds, smells, tastes, heat and cold and the other tactile qualities, I think of these only in a very confused and obscure way, to the extent that I do not even know whether they are true or false, that is, whether the ideas I have of them are ideas of real things or of non-things. For although, as I have noted before, falsity in the strict sense, or formal falsity, can occur only in judgements, there is another kind of falsity, material falsity, which occurs in ideas, when they represent non-things as things. For example, the ideas which I have of heat and cold contain so little clarity and distinctness that they do not enable me to tell whether cold is merely the absence of heat or vice versa, or whether both of them are real qualities, or neither is. And since there can be no ideas which are not as it were of things, if it is true that cold is nothing but the absence of heat, the idea which represents it to me as something real and positive deserves to be called false; and the same goes for other ideas of this kind.

Such ideas obviously do not require me to posit a source distinct from myself. For on the one hand, if they are false, that is, represent non-things, I know by the natural light that they arise from nothing—that is, they are in me only because of a deficiency and lack of perfection in my nature. If on the other hand they are true, then since the reality which they represent is so extremely slight that I cannot even distinguish it from a non-thing, I do not see why they cannot originate from myself.

With regard to the clear and distinct elements in my ideas of corporeal things, it appears that I could have borrowed some of these from my idea of myself, namely substance, duration, number and anything else of this kind. For example, I think that a stone is a substance, or is a thing capable of existing independently, and I also think that I am a substance. Admittedly I conceive of myself as a thing that thinks and is not extended, whereas I conceive of the stone as a thing that is extended and does not think, so that the two conceptions differ enormously; but they seem to agree with respect to the classification 'substance'. Again, I perceive that I now exist, and remember that I have existed for some time; moreover, I have various thoughts which I can count; it is in these ways that I acquire the ideas of duration and number which I can then transfer to other things. As for all the other elements which make up the ideas of corporeal things, namely extension, shape, position and movement, these are not formally contained in me, since I am nothing but a thinking thing; but since they are merely modes of a substance, and I am a substance, it seems possible that they are contained in me eminently.

So there remains only the idea of God; and I must consider whether there is anything in the idea which could not have originated in myself. By the word 'God' I understand a substance that is infinite, eternal, immutable, independent, supremely intelligent, supremely powerful, and which created both myself and everything else (if anything else there be) that exists. All these attributes are such that, the more carefully I concentrate on them, the less possible it seems that they could have originated from me alone. So from what has been said it must be concluded that God necessarily exists.

It is true that I have the idea of substance in me in virtue of the fact that I am a substance; but this would not account for my having the idea of an infinite substance, when I am finite, unless this idea proceeded from some substance which really was infinite.

And I must not think that, just as my conceptions of rest and darkness are arrived at by negating movement and light, so my perception of the infinite is arrived at not by means of a true idea but merely by negating the finite. On the contrary, I clearly understand that there is more reality in an infinite substance than in a finite one, and hence that my perception of the infinite, that is God, is in some way prior to my perception of the finite, that is myself. For how could I understand that I doubted or desired—that is, lacked something—and that I was not wholly perfect, unless there were in me some idea of a more perfect being which enabled me to recognize my own defects by comparison?

Nor can it be said that this idea of God is perhaps materially false and so could have come from nothing, which is what I observed just a moment ago in the case of the ideas of heat and cold, and so on. On the contrary, it is utterly clear and distinct, and contains in itself more objective reality than any other idea; hence there is no idea which is in itself truer or less liable to be suspected of falsehood. This idea of a supremely perfect and infinite being is, I say, true in the highest degree; for although perhaps one may imagine that such a being does not exist, it cannot be supposed that the idea of such a being represents something unreal, as I said with regard to the idea of cold. The idea is, moreover, utterly clear and distinct; for whatever I clearly and distinctly perceive as being real and true, and implying any perfection, is wholly contained in it. It does not matter that I do not grasp the infinite, or that there are countless additional attributes of God which I cannot in any way grasp, and perhaps cannot even reach in my thought; for it is in the nature of the infinite not to be grasped by a finite being like myself. It is enough that I understand the infinite, and that I judge that all the attributes which I clearly perceive and know to imply some perfection —and perhaps countless others of which I am ignorant—are present in God either formally or eminently. This is enough to make the idea that I have of God the truest and most clear and distinct of all my ideas.

But perhaps I am something greater than I myself understand, and all the perfections which I attribute to God are somehow in me potentially, though not yet emerging or actualized. For I am now experiencing a gradual increase in my knowledge, and I see nothing to prevent its increasing more and more to infinity. Further, I see no reason why I should not be able to use this increased knowledge to acquire all the other perfections of God. And finally, if the potentiality for these perfections is already within me, why should not this be enough to generate the idea of such perfections?

But all this is impossible. First, though it is true that there is a gradual increase in my knowledge, and that I have many potentialities which are not yet actual, this is all quite irrelevant to the idea of God, which contains absolutely nothing that is potential; indeed, this gradual increase in knowledge is itself the surest sign of imperfection. What is more, even if my knowledge always increases more and more, I recognize that it will never actually be infinite, since it will never reach the point where it is not capable of a further increase; God,

on the other hand, I take to be actually infinite, so that nothing can be added to his perfection. And finally, I perceive that the objective being of an idea cannot be produced merely by potential being, which strictly speaking is nothing, but only by actual or formal being.

If one concentrates carefully, all this is quite evident by the natural light. But when I relax my concentration, and my mental vision is blinded by the images of things perceived by the senses, it is not so easy for me to remember why the idea of a being more perfect than myself must necessarily proceed from some being which is in reality more perfect. I should therefore like to go further and inquire whether I myself, who have this idea, could exist if no such being existed.

From whom, in that case, would I derive my existence? From myself presumably, or from my parents, or from some other beings less perfect than God; for nothing more perfect than God, or even as perfect, can be thought of or imagined.

Yet if I derived my existence from myself, then I should neither doubt nor want, nor lack anything at all; for I should have given myself all the perfections of which I have any idea, and thus I should myself be God. I must not suppose that the items I lack would be more difficult to acquire than those I now have. On the contrary, it is clear that, since I am a thinking thing or substance, it would have been far more difficult for me to emerge out of nothing than merely to acquire knowledge of the many things of which I am ignorant—such knowledge being merely an accident of that substance. And if I had derived my existence from myself, which is a greater achievement, I should certainly not have denied myself the knowledge in question, which is something much easier to acquire, or indeed any of the attributes which I perceive to be contained in the idea of God; for none of them seem any harder to achieve. And if any of them were harder to achieve, they would certainly appear so to me, if I had indeed got all my other attributes from myself, since I should experience a limitation of my power in this respect.

I do not escape the force of these arguments by supposing that I have always existed as I do now, as if it followed from this that there was no need to look for any author of my existence. For a lifespan can be divided into countless parts, each completely independent of the others, so that it does not follow from the fact that I existed a little while ago that I must exist now, unless there is some cause which as it were creates me afresh at this moment—that is, which preserves me. For it is quite clear to anyone who attentively considers the nature of time that the same power and action are needed to preserve anything at each individual moment of its duration as would be required to create that thing anew if it were not yet in existence. Hence the distinction between preservation and creation is only a conceptual one, and this is one of the things that are evident by the natural light.

I must therefore now ask myself whether I possess some power enabling me to bring it about that I who now exist will still exist a little while from now. For since I am nothing but a thinking thing—or at least since I am now concerned only and precisely with that part of me which is a thinking thing—if there were such a power in me, I should undoubtedly be aware of it. But I experience no such power, and this very fact makes me recognize most clearly that I depend on some being distinct from myself.

But perhaps this being is not God, and perhaps I was produced either by my parents or by other causes less perfect than God. No; for as I have said before, it is quite clear that there must be at least as much in the cause as in the effect. And therefore whatever kind of cause is eventually proposed, since I am a thinking thing and have within me some idea of God, it must be admitted that what caused me is itself a thinking thing and possesses the idea of all the perfections which I attribute to God. In respect of this cause one may again inquire whether it derives its existence from itself or from another cause. If from itself, then it is clear from what has been said that it is itself God, since if it has the power of existing through its own might, then undoubtedly it also has the power of actually possessing all the perfections of which it has an idea—that is, all the perfections which I conceive to be in God. If, on the other hand, it derives its existence from another cause, then the same question may be repeated concerning this further cause, namely whether it derives its existence from itself or from another cause, until eventually the ultimate cause is reached, and this will be God.

It is clear enough that an infinite regress is impossible here, especially since I am dealing not just with the cause that produced me in the past, but also and most importantly with the cause that preserves me at the present moment.

Nor can it be supposed that several partial causes contributed to my creation, or that I received the idea of one of the perfections which I attribute to God from one cause and the idea of another from another—the supposition here being that all the perfections are to be found somewhere in the universe but not joined together in a single being, God. On the contrary, the unity, the simplicity, or the inseparability of all the attributes of God is one of the most important of the perfections which I understand him to have. And surely the idea of the unity of all his perfections could not have been placed in me by any cause which did not also provide me with the ideas of the other perfections; for no cause could have made me understand the interconnection and inseparability of the perfections without at the same time making me recognize what they were.

Lastly, as regards my parents, even if everything I have ever believed about them is true, it is certainly not they who preserve me; and in so far as I am a thinking thing, they did not even make me; they merely placed certain dispositions in the matter which I have always regarded as containing me, or rather my mind, for that is all I now take myself to be. So there can be no difficulty regarding my parents in this context. Altogether then, it must be concluded that the mere fact that I exist and have within me an idea of a most perfect being, that is, God, provides a very clear proof that God indeed exists.

It only remains for me to examine how I received this idea from God. For I did not acquire it from the senses; it has never come to me unexpectedly, as usually happens with the ideas of things that are perceivable by the senses, when these things present themselves to the external sense organs—or seem to do so. And it was not invented by me either; for I am plainly unable either to take away anything from it or to add anything to it. The only remaining alternative is that it is innate in me, just as the idea of myself is innate in me.

And indeed it is no surprise that God, in creating me, should have placed this idea in me to be, as it were, the mark of the craftsman stamped on his work—not that the mark need be anything distinct from the work itself. But the mere fact that God created me is a very strong basis for believing that I am somehow made in his image and likeness, and that I perceive that likeness, which includes the idea of God, by the same faculty which enables me to perceive myself. That is, when I turn my mind's eye upon myself, I understand that I am a thing which is incomplete and dependent on another and which aspires without limit to ever greater and better things; but I also understand at the same time that he on whom I depend has within him all those greater things, not just indefinitely and potentially but actually and infinitely, and hence that he is God. The whole force of the argument lies in this: I recognize that it would be impossible for me to exist with the kind of nature I have—that is, having within me the idea of God—were it not the case that God really existed. By 'God' I mean the very being the idea of whom is within me, that is, the possessor of all the perfections which I cannot grasp, but can somehow reach in my thought, who is subject to no defects whatsoever. It is clear enough from this that he cannot be a deceiver, since it is manifest by the natural light that all fraud and deception depend on some defect.

But before examining this point more carefully and investigating other truths which may be derived from it, I should like to pause here and spend some time in the contemplation of God; to reflect on his attributes, and to gaze with wonder and adoration on the beauty of this immense light, so far as the eye of my darkened intellect can bear it. For just as we believe through faith that the supreme happiness of the next life consists solely in the contemplation of the divine majesty, so experience tells us that this same contemplation, albeit much less perfect, enables us to know the greatest joy of which we are capable in this life.

Fourth Meditation

Truth and Falsity

During these past few days I have accustomed myself to leading my mind away from the senses; and I have taken careful note of the fact that there is very little about corporeal things that is truly perceived, whereas much more is known about the human mind, and still more about God. The result is that I now have no difficulty in turning my mind away from imaginable things and towards things which are objects of the intellect alone and are totally separate from matter. And indeed the idea I have of the human mind, in so far as it is a thinking thing, which is not extended in length, breadth or height and has no other bodily characteristics, is much more distinct than the idea of any corporeal thing. And when I consider the fact that I have doubts, or that I am a thing that is incomplete and dependent, then there arises in me a clear and distinct idea of a being who is independent and complete, that is, an idea of God. And from the mere fact that there is such an idea within me, or that I who possess this idea exist, I clearly infer that God also exists, and that every single moment of my entire existence depends on him. So clear is this conclusion that I am confident that the human intellect cannot know anything that is more evident or more certain. And now, from this contemplation of the true God, in whom all the treasures of wisdom and the sciences lie hidden, I think I can see a way forward to the knowledge of other things.

To begin with, I recognize that it is impossible that God should ever deceive me. For in every case of trickery or deception some imperfection is to be found; and although the ability to deceive appears to be an indication of cleverness or power, the will to deceive is undoubtedly evidence of malice or weakness, and so cannot apply to God.

Next, I know by experience that there is in me a faculty of judgement which, like everything else which is in me, I certainly received from God. And since God does not wish to deceive me, he surely did not give me the kind of faculty which would ever enable me to go wrong while using it correctly.

There would be no further doubt on this issue were it not that what I have just said appears to imply that I am incapable of ever going wrong. For if everything that is in me comes from God, and he did not endow me with a faculty for making mistakes, it appears that I can never go wrong. And certainly, so long as I think only of God, and turn my whole attention to him, I can find no cause of error or falsity. But when I turn back to myself, I know by experience that I am prone to countless errors. On looking for the cause of these errors, I find that I possess not only a real and positive idea of God, or a being who is supremely perfect, but also what may be described as a negative idea of nothingness, or of that which is farthest removed from all perfection. I realize that I am, as it were, something intermediate between God and nothingness, or between supreme being and non-being: my nature is such that in so far as I was created by the supreme being, there is nothing in me to enable me to go wrong or lead me astray; but in so far as I participate in nothingness or non-being, that is, in so far as I am not myself the supreme being and am lacking in countless respects, it is no wonder that I make mistakes. I understand, then, that error as such is not something real which depends on God, but merely a defect. Hence my going wrong does not require me to have a faculty specially bestowed on me by God; it simply happens as a result of the fact that the faculty of true judgement which I have from God is in my case not infinite.

But this is still not entirely satisfactory. For error is not a pure negation, but rather a privation or lack of some knowledge which somehow should be in me. And when I concentrate on the nature of God, it seems impossible that he should have placed in me a faculty which is not perfect of its kind, or which lacks some perfection which it ought to have. The more skilled the craftsman the more perfect the work produced by him; if this is so, how can anything produced by the supreme creator of all things not be complete and perfect in all respects? There is, moreover, no doubt that God could have given me a nature such that I was never mistaken; again, there is no doubt that he always wills what is best. Is it then better that I should make mistakes than that I should not do so?

As I reflect on these matters more attentively, it occurs to me first of all that it is no cause for surprise if I do not understand the reasons for some of God's actions; and there is no call to doubt his existence if I happen to find that there are other instances where I do not grasp why or how certain things were made by him. For since I now know that my own nature is very weak and limited, whereas the nature of God is immense, incomprehensible and infinite, I also know without more ado that he is capable of countless things whose causes are beyond my knowledge. And for this reason alone I consider the customary search for final causes to be totally useless in physics; there is considerable rashness in thinking myself capable of investigating the impenetrable purposes of God.

It also occurs to me that whenever we are inquiring whether the works of God are perfect, we ought to look at the whole universe, not just at one created thing on its own. For what would perhaps rightly appear very imperfect if it existed on its own is quite perfect when its function as a part of the universe is considered. It is true that, since my decision to doubt everything, it is so far only myself and God whose existence I have been able to know with certainty; but after considering the immense power of God, I cannot deny that many other things have been made by him, or at least could have been made, and hence that I may have a place in the universal scheme of things.

Next, when I look more closely at myself and inquire into the nature of my errors (for these are the only evidence of some imperfection in me), I notice that they depend on two concurrent causes, namely on the faculty of knowledge which is in me, and on the faculty of choice or freedom of the will; that is, they depend on both the intellect and the will simultaneously. Now all that the intellect does is to enable me to perceive the ideas which are subjects for possible judgements; and when regarded strictly in this light, it turns out to contain no error in the proper sense of that term. For although countless things may exist without there being any corresponding ideas in me, it should not, strictly speaking, be said that I am deprived of these ideas, but merely that I lack them, in a negative sense. This is because I cannot produce any reason to prove that God ought to have given me a greater faculty of knowledge than he did; and no matter how skilled I understand a craftsman to be, this does not make me think he ought to have put into every one of his works all the perfections which he is able to put into some of them. Besides, I cannot complain that the will or freedom of choice which I received from God is not sufficiently extensive or perfect, since I know by experience that it is not restricted in any way. Indeed, I think it is very noteworthy that there is nothing else in me which is so perfect and so great that the possibility of a further increase in its perfection or greatness is beyond my understanding. If, for example, I consider the faculty of understanding, I immediately recognize that in my case it is extremely slight and very finite, and I at once form the idea of an understanding which is much greater—indeed supremely great and infinite; and from the very fact that I can form an idea of it, I perceive that it belongs to the nature of God. Similarly, if I examine the faculties of memory or imagination, or any others, I discover that in my case each one of these faculties is weak and limited, while in the case of God it is immeasurable. It is only the will, or freedom of choice, which I experience within me to be so great that the idea of any greater faculty is beyond my grasp; so much so that it is above all in virtue of the will that I understand myself to bear in some way the image and likeness of God. For although God's will is incomparably greater than mine, both in virtue of the knowledge and power that accompany it and make it more firm and efficacious, and also in virtue of its object, in that it ranges over a greater number of items, nevertheless it does not seem any greater than mine when considered as will in the essential and strict sense. This is because the will simply consists in our ability to do or not do something (that is, to affirm or deny, to pursue or avoid); or rather, it consists simply in the fact that when the intellect puts something forward for affirmation or denial or for pursuit or avoidance, our inclinations are such that we do not feel we are determined by any external force. In order to be free, there is no need for me to be inclined both ways; on the contrary, the more I incline in one direction—either because I clearly understand that reasons of truth and goodness point that way, or because of a divinely produced disposition of my inmost thoughts—the freer is my choice. Neither divine grace nor natural knowledge ever diminishes freedom; on the contrary, they increase and strengthen it. But the indifference I feel when there is no reason pushing me in one direction rather than another is the lowest grade of freedom; it is evidence not of any perfection of freedom, but rather of a defect in knowledge or a kind of negation. For if I always saw clearly what was true and good, I should never have to deliberate about the right judgement or choice; in that case, although I should be wholly free, it would be impossible for me ever to be in a state of indifference.

From these considerations I perceive that the power of willing which I received from God is not, when considered in itself, the cause of my mistakes; for it is both extremely ample and also perfect of its kind. Nor is my power of understanding to blame; for since my understanding comes from God, everything that I understand I undoubtedly understand correctly, and any error here is impos-

sible. So what then is the source of my mistakes? It must be simply this: the scope of the will is wider than that of the intellect; but instead of restricting it within the same limits, I extend its use to matters which I do not understand. Since the will is indifferent in such cases, it easily turns aside from what is true and good, and this is the source of my error and sin.

For example, during these past few days I have been asking whether anything in the world exists, and I have realized that from the very fact of my raising this question it follows quite evidently that I exist. I could not but judge that something which I understood so clearly was true; but this was not because I was compelled so to judge by any external force, but because a great light in the intellect was followed by a great inclination in the will, and thus the spontaneity and freedom of my belief was all the greater in proportion to my lack of indifference. But now, besides the knowledge that I exist, in so far as I am a thinking thing, an idea of corporeal nature comes into my mind; and I happen to be in doubt as to whether the thinking nature which is in me, or rather which I am, is distinct from this corporeal nature or identical with it. I am making the further supposition that my intellect has not yet come upon any persuasive reason in favour of one alternative rather than the other. This obviously implies that I am indifferent as to whether I should assert or deny either alternative, or indeed refrain from making any judgement on the matter.

What is more, this indifference does not merely apply to cases where the intellect is wholly ignorant, but extends in general to every case where the intellect does not have sufficiently clear knowledge at the time when the will deliberates. For although probable conjectures may pull me in one direction, the mere knowledge that they are simply conjectures, and not certain and indubitable reasons, is itself quite enough to push my assent the other way. My experience in the last few days confirms this: the mere fact that I found that all my previous beliefs were in some sense open to doubt was enough to turn my absolutely confident belief in their truth into the supposition that they were wholly false.

If, however, I simply refrain from making a judgement in cases where I do not perceive the truth with sufficient clarity and distinctness, then it is clear that I am behaving correctly and avoiding error. But if in such cases I either affirm or deny, then I am not using my free will correctly. If I go for the alternative which is false, then obviously I shall be in error; if I take the other side, then it is by pure chance that I arrive at the truth, and I shall still be at fault since it is clear by the natural light that the perception of the intellect should always precede the determination of the will. In this incorrect use of free will may be found the privation which constitutes the essence of error. The privation, I say, lies in the operation of the will in so far as it proceeds from me, but not in the faculty of will which I received from God, nor even in its operation, in so far as it depends on him.

And I have no cause for complaint on the grounds that the power of understanding or the natural light which God gave me is no greater than it is; for it is in the nature of a finite intellect to lack understanding of many things, and it is in the nature of a created intellect to be finite. Indeed, I have reason to give thanks to him who has never owed me anything for the great bounty that he has shown me, rather than thinking myself deprived or robbed of any gifts he did not bestow.

Nor do I have any cause for complaint on the grounds that God gave me a will which extends more widely than my intellect. For since the will consists simply of one thing which is, as it were, indivisible, it seems that its nature rules out the possibility of anything being taken away from it. And surely, the more widely my will extends, then the greater thanks I owe to him who gave it to me.

Finally, I must not complain that the forming of those acts of will or judgements in which I go wrong happens with God's concurrence. For in so far as these acts depend on God, they are wholly true and good; and my ability to perform them means that there is in a sense more perfection in me than would be the case if I lacked this ability. As for the privation involved—which is all that the essential definition of falsity and wrong consists in—his does not in any way require the concurrence of God, since it is not a thing; indeed, when it is referred to God as its cause, it should be called not a privation but simply a negation. For it is surely no imperfection in God that he has given me the freedom to assent or not to assent in those cases where he did not endow my intellect with a clear and distinct perception; but it is undoubtedly an imperfection in me to misuse that freedom and make judgements about matters which I do not

fully understand. I can see, however, that God could easily have brought it about that without losing my freedom, and despite the limitations in my knowledge, I should nonetheless never make a mistake. He could, for example, have endowed my intellect with a clear and distinct perception of everything about which I was ever likely to deliberate; or he could simply have impressed it unforgettably on my memory that I should never make a judgement about anything which I did not clearly and distinctly understand. Had God made me this way, then I can easily understand that, considered as a totality, I would have been more perfect than I am now. But I cannot therefore deny that there may in some way be more perfection in the universe as a whole because some of its parts are not immune from error, while others are immune, than there would be if all the parts were exactly alike. And I have no right to complain that the role God wished me to undertake in the world is not the principal one or the most perfect of all.

What is more, even if I have no power to avoid error in the first way just mentioned, which requires a clear perception of everything I have to deliberate on, I can avoid error in the second way, which depends merely on my remembering to withhold judgement on any occasion when the truth of the matter is not clear. Admittedly, I am aware of a certain weakness in me, in that I am unable to keep my attention fixed on one and the same item of knowledge at all times; but by attentive and repeated meditation I am nevertheless able to make myself remember it as often as the need arises, and thus get into the habit of avoiding error.

It is here that man's greatest and most important perfection is to be found, and I therefore think that today's meditation, involving an investigation into the cause of error and falsity, has been very profitable. The cause of error must surely be the one I have explained; for if, whenever I have to make a judgement, I restrain my will so that it extends to what the intellect clearly and distinctly reveals, and no further, then it is quite impossible for me to go wrong. This is because every clear and distinct perception is undoubtedly something, and hence cannot come from nothing, but must necessarily have God for its author. Its author, I say, is God, who is supremely perfect, and who cannot be a deceiver on pain of contradiction; hence the perception is undoubtedly true. So today I have learned not only what precautions to take to avoid ever going wrong, but also what to do to arrive at the truth. For I shall unquestionably reach the truth, if only I give sufficient attention to all the things which I perfectly understand, and separate these from all the other cases where my apprehension is more confused and obscure. And this is just what I shall take good care to do from now on.

II.2 Skepticism Regarding the Senses

DAVID HUME

The Scottish empiricist David Hume (1711–1776) accepts that there are truths of reason, mathematical, and logical truths but doubts whether we can have empirical and metaphysical knowledge. According to Hume all learning is based on sensory impressions, and our ideas are mere representations of these impressions. We use these ideas to construct complex ideas, but we have no way of knowing whether the complex ideas represent reality. An example of such a complex idea is the notion of God, the thought of which is a composite made up of our ideas of power, knowledge, and goodness, each of which are joined to the notion of unlimited quantity, to make up the notions of all-powerful, all-knowing, and moral perfection. But there is no way of proving that these ideas are exemplified in reality.

In the present selection from Hume's youthful *Treatise of Human Nature* (1739), Hume asks why we believe in the individual and continued existence of physical objects ("the existence of body"). He admits that we cannot help believing in an external world, but he wants to know whether we are justified in so believing. He offers three hypotheses to answer this question. Our knowledge of the external world is based either on (1) our senses, (2) our reason, or (3) our imagination. He rejects the first hypothesis, because our perceptions change when there is no reason to believe that the external object changes. The senses do not preserve the continued existence of objects, yet we cannot help believing that objects do continue to exist even when we do not perceive them. He rejects the second hypothesis (that reason is the cause of our belief) because reason lacks sufficient premises to establish the existence of physical objects but rather, in order to think about the external world, takes their continued and distinct existence for granted. That leaves the third hypothesis, imagination, as the only plausible cause of our belief in the external world. Constancy and coherence of impressions are the forces that lead us to posit such a belief. But this is no proof of an external world, let alone of the veridicality of our perceptions.

We may well ask, *What causes induce us to believe in the existence of body* [external objects—Ed.]? but 'tis in vain to ask, *Whether there be body or not?* That is a point, which we must take for granted in all our reasonings.

The subject, then, of our present enquiry is concerning the *causes* which induce us to believe in the existence of body; And my reasonings on this shall begin with a distinction, which at first sight may seem superfluous, but which will contribute very much to the perfect understanding of what follows. We ought to examine apart those two questions, which are commonly confounded together, *viz.* Why we attribute a CONTINUED existence to objects, even when they are not present to the senses; and why we suppose them to have an existence DISTINCT from the mind and perception. Under this last head I comprehend their situation as well as relations, their *external* position as well as the *independence* of their existence and operation. These two questions concerning the continu'd and distinct existence of body are intimately connected together. For if the objects of our senses continue to exist, even when they are not perceiv'd, their existence is of course independent of and distinct from the perception; and *vice versa*, if their existence be independent of the perception and distinct from it, they must continue to exist, even tho' they be not perceiv'd. But tho' the decision of the one question decides the other; yet that we may the more easily discover the principles of human nature, from whence the decision arises, we shall carry along with us this distinction, and shall consider, whether it be the *senses, reason,* or the *imagination,* that produces the opinion of a *continu'd* or of a *distinct* existence. These are the only questions, that are intelligible on the present subject. For as to the notion of external existence, when taken for something specifically different from our perceptions, we have already shewn its absurdity.

To begin with the SENSES, 'tis evident these faculties are incapable of giving rise to do the notion of the *continu'd* existence of their objects, after they no longer appear to the senses. For that is a contradiction in terms, and supposes that the senses continue to operate, even after they have ceas'd all manner of operation. These faculties, therefore, if they have any influence in the present

case, must produce the opinion of a distinct, not of a continu'd existence; and in order to do that, must present their impressions either as images and representations, or as these very distinct and external existences.

That our senses offer not their impressions as the images of something *distinct,* or *independent,* and *external,* is evident; because they convey to us nothing but a single perception, and never give us the least intimation of any thing beyond. A single perception can never produce the idea of a double existence, but by some inference either of the reason or imagination. When the mind looks farther than what immediately appears to it, its conclusions can never be put to the account of the senses; and it certainly looks farther, when from a single perception it infers a double existence, and supposes the relations of resemblance and causation betwixt them.

If our senses, therefore, suggest any idea of distinct existences, they must convey the impressions as those very existences, by a kind of fallacy and illusion. Upon this head we may observe, that all sensations are felt by the mind, such as they really are, and that when we doubt, whether they present themselves as distinct objects, or as mere impressions, the difficulty is not concerning their nature, but concerning their relations and situation. Now if the senses presented our impressions as external to, and independent of ourselves, both the objects and ourselves must be obvious to our senses, otherwise cou'd not be compar'd by these faculties. The difficulty, then, is how far we are *ourselves* the objects of our senses.

'Tis certain there is no question in philosophy more abstruse than that concerning identity, and the nature of the uniting principle, which constitutes a person. So far from being able by our senses merely to determine this question, we must have recourse to the most profound metaphysics to give a satisfactory answer to it; and in common life 'tis evident these ideas of self and person are never very fix'd nor determinate. 'Tis absurd, therefore, to imagine the senses can ever distinguish betwixt ourselves and external objects.

Add to this, that every impression, external and internal, passions, affections, sensations, pains and pleasures, are originally on the same footing; and that whatever other differences we may observe among them, they appear all of them, in their true colors, as impressions or perceptions.

Reprinted from *Treatise of Human Nature* (1739).

And indeed, if we consider the matter aright, 'tis scarce possible it shou'd be otherwise, nor is it conceivable that our senses shou'd be more capable of deceiving us in the situation and relations, than in the nature of our impressions. For since all actions and sensations of the mind are known to us by consciousness, they must necessarily appear in every particular what they are, and be what they appear. Every thing that enters the mind, being in *reality* as the perception, 'tis impossible any thing shou'd to *feeling* appear different. This were to suppose, that even where we are most intimately conscious, we might be mistaken.

But not to lose time in examining, whether 'tis possible for our senses to deceive us, and represent our perceptions as distinct from ourselves, that is as *external* to and *independent* of us; let us consider whether they really do so, and whether this error proceeds from an immediate sensation, or from some other causes.

To begin with the question concerning *external* existence, it may perhaps be said, that setting aside the metaphysical question of the identity of a thinking substance, our own body evidently belongs to us; and as several impressions appear exterior to the body, we suppose them also exterior to ourselves. The paper, on which I write at present, is beyond my hand. The table is beyond the paper. The walls of the chamber beyond the table. And in casting my eye towards the window, I perceive a great extent of fields and buildings beyond my chamber. From all this it may be infer'd, that no other faculty is requir'd, beside the senses, to convince us of the external existence of body. But to prevent this inference, we need only weigh the three following considerations. *First*, That, properly speaking, 'tis not our body we perceive, when we regard our limbs and members, but certain impressions, which enter by the senses; so that the ascribing a real and corporeal existence to these impressions, or to their objects, is an act of the mind as difficult to explain, as that which we examine at present. *Secondly*, Sounds, and tastes, and smells, tho' commonly regarded by the mind as continu'd independent qualities, appear not to have any existence in extension, and consequently cannot appear to the senses as situated externally to the body. The reason, why we ascribe a place to them, shall be consider'd afterwards. *Thirdly*, Even our sight informs us not of distance or outness (so to speak) immediately and without a certain rea-

soning and experience, as is acknowledg'd by the most rational philosophers.

As to the *independency* of our perceptions on ourselves, this can never be an object of the senses; but any opinion we form concerning it, must be deriv'd from experience and observation: And we shall see afterwards, that our conclusions from experience are far from being favourable to the doctrine of the independency of our perceptions. Meanwhile we may observe that when we talk of real distinct existences, we have commonly more in our eye their independency than external situation in place, and think an object has a sufficient reality, when its Being is uninterrupted, and independent of the incessant revolutions, which we are conscious of in ourselves.

Thus to resume what I have said concerning the senses; they give us no notion of continu'd existence, because they cannot operate beyond the extent, in which they really operate. They as little produce the opinion of a distinct existence, because they neither can offer it to the mind as represented, nor as original. To offer it as represented, they must present both an object and an image. To make it appear as original, they must convey a falshood; and this falshood must lie in the relations and situation: In order to which they must be able to compare the object with ourselves; and even in that case they do not, nor is it possible they shou'd, deceive us. We may, therefore, conclude with certainty, that the opinion of a continu'd and of a distinct existence never arises from the senses.

To confirm this we may observe, that there are three different kinds of impressions convey'd by the senses. The first are those of the figure, bulk, motion and solidity of bodies. The second those of colors, tastes, smells, sounds, heat and cold. The third are the pains and pleasures, that arise from the application of objects to our bodies, as by the cutting of our flesh with steel, and such like. Both philosophers and the vulgar suppose the first of these to have a distinct continu'd existence. The vulgar only regard the second as on the same footing. Both philosophers and the vulgar, again, esteem the third to be merely perceptions; and consequently interrupted and dependent beings.

Now 'tis evident, that, whatever may be our philosophical opinion, colors, sounds, heat and cold, as far as appears to the senses, exist after the same manner with motion and solidity, and that the difference we make betwixt them in this respect, arises not from the mere perception. So strong is the prejudice for the distinct continu'd existence of the former qualities, that when the contrary opinion is advanc'd by modern philosophers, people imagine they can almost refute it from their feeling and experience, and that their very senses contradict this philosophy. 'Tis also evident, that colors, sounds, &c. are originally on the same footing with the pain that arises from steel, and pleasure that proceeds from a fire; and that the difference betwixt them is founded neither on perception nor reason, but on the imagination. For as they are confest to be, both of them, nothing but perceptions arising from the particular configurations and motions of the parts of body, wherein possibly can their difference consist? Upon the whole, then, we may conclude, that as far as the senses are judges, all perceptions are the same in the manner of their existence.

We may also observe in this instance of sounds and colors, that we can attribute a distinct continu'd existence to objects without ever consulting REASON, or weighing our opinions by any philosophical principles. And indeed, whatever convincing arguments philosophers may fancy they can produce to establish the belief of objects independent of the mind, 'tis obvious these arguments are known but to very few, and that 'tis not by them, that children, peasants, and the greatest part of mankind are induc'd to attribute objects to some impressions, and deny them to others. Accordingly we find, that all the conclusions, which the vulgar form on this head, are directly contrary to those, which are confirm'd by philosophy. For philosophy informs us, that every thing, which appears to the mind, is nothing but a perception, and is interrupted, and dependent on the mind; whereas the vulgar confound perceptions and objects, and attribute a distinct continu'd existence to the very things they feel or see. This sentiment, then, as it is entirely unreasonable, must proceed from some other faculty than the understanding. To which we may add, that as long as we take our perceptions and objects to be the same, we can never infer the existence of the one from that of the other, nor form any argument from the relation of cause and effect; which is the only one that can assure us of matter of fact. Even after we distinguish our perceptions from our objects, 'twill appear presently, that we are still incapable of reasoning from the existence of one to that of the other: So that upon the whole our reason neither does, nor is it possible it ever shou'd, upon any supposition, give us an assurance of the continu'd and distinct existence of body. That opinion must be entirely owing to the IMAGINATION: which must now be the subject of our enquiry.

Since all impressions are internal and perishing existences, and appear as such, the notion of their distinct and continu'd existence must arise from a concurrence of some of their qualities with the qualities of the imagination; and since this notion does not extend to all of them, it must arise from certain qualities peculiar to some impressions. 'Twill therefore be easy for us to discover these qualities by a comparison of the impressions, to which we attribute a distinct and continu'd existence, with those, which we regard as internal and perishing.

We may observe, then, that 'tis neither upon account of the involuntariness of certain impressions, as is commonly suppos'd, nor of their superior force and violence, that we attribute to them a reality, and continu'd existence, which we refuse to others, that are voluntary or feeble. For 'tis evident our pains and pleasures, our passions and affections, which we never suppose to have any existence beyond our perception, operate with greater violence, and are equally involuntary, as the impressions of figure and extension, color and sound, which we suppose to be permanent beings. The heat of a fire, when moderate, is suppos'd to exist in the fire; but the pain, which it causes upon a near approach, is not taken to have any being except in the perception.

These vulgar opinions, then, being rejected, we must search for some other hypothesis, by which we may discover those peculiar qualities in our impressions, which makes us attribute to them a distinct and continu'd existence.

After a little examination, we shall find, that all those objects, to which we attribute a continu'd existence, have a peculiar *constancy*, which distinguishes them from the impressions, whose existence depends upon our perception. Those mountains, and houses, and trees, which lie at present under my eye, have always appear'd to me in the same order; and when I lose sight of them by shutting my eyes or turning my head, I soon after find them return upon me without the least alteration. My bed and table, my books and papers, present themselves in the same uniform manner, and change not upon account of any interruption in my seeing or perceiving them. This is the case with all the impressions, whose objects are suppos'd to have an external existence; and is the case with no other impressions, whether gentle or violent, voluntary or involuntary.

This constancy, however, is not so perfect as not to admit of very considerable exceptions. Bodies often change their position and qualities, and after a little absence or interruption may become hardly knowable. But here 'tis observable, that even in these changes they preserve a *coherence,* and have a regular dependence on each other; which is the foundation of a kind of reasoning from causation, and produces the opinion of their continu'd existence. When I return to my chamber after an hour's absence, I find not my fire in the same situation, in which I left it: But then I am accustom'd in other instances to see a like alteration produc'd in a like time, whether I am present or absent, near or remote. This coherence, therefore, in their changes is one of the characteristics of external objects, as well as their constancy.

Having found that the opinion of the continu'd existence of body depends on the COHERENCE and CONSTANCY of certain impressions, I now proceed to examine after what manner these qualities give rise to so extraordinary an opinion. To begin with the coherence; we may observe, that tho' those internal impressions, which we regard as fleeting and perishing, have also a certain coherence or regularity in their appearances, yet 'tis of somewhat a different nature, from that which we discover in bodies. Our passions are found by experience to have a mutual connexion with and dependence on each other; but on no occasion is it necessary to suppose, that they have existed and operated, when they were not perceiv'd, in order to preserve the same dependence and connexion, of which we have had experience. The case is not the same with relation to external objects. Those require a continu'd existence, or otherwise lose, in a great measure, the regularity of their operation. I am here seated in my chamber with my face to the fire; and all the objects, that strike my senses, are contain'd in a few yards around me. My memory, indeed, informs me of the existence of many objects; but then this information extends not beyond their past existence, nor do either my senses or memory give any testimony to the continuance of their being. When

therefore I am thus seated, and revolve over these thoughts, I hear on a sudden a noise as of a door turning upon its hinges; and a little after see a porter, who advances towards me. This gives occasion to many new reflexions and reasonings. First, I never have observ'd, that this noise cou'd proceed from anything but the motion of a door; and therefore conclude, that the present phaenomenon is a contradiction to all past experience, unless the door, which I remember on t'other side the chamber, be still in being. Again, I have always found, that a human body was possest of a quality, which I call gravity, and which hinders it from mounting in the air, as this porter must have done to arrive at my chamber, unless the stairs I remember be not annihilated by my absence. But this is not all. I receive a letter, which upon opening it I perceive by the hand-writing and subscription to have come from a friend, who says he is two hundred leagues distant. 'Tis evident I can never account for this phaenomenon, conformable to my experience in other instances, without spreading out in my mind the whole sea and continent between us, and supposing the effects and continu'd existence of posts and ferries, according to my memory and observation. To consider these phaenomena of the porter and letter in a certain light, they are contradictions to common experience, and may be regarded as objections to those maxims, which we form concerning the connexions of causes and effects. I am accustom'd to hear such a sound, and see such an object in motion at the same time. I have not receiv'd in this particular instance both these perceptions. These observations are contrary, unless I suppose that the door still remains, and that it was open'd without my perceiving it: And this supposition, which was at first entirely arbitrary and hypothetical, acquires a force and evidence by its being the only one, upon which I can reconcile these contradictions. There is scarce a moment of my life, wherein there is not a similar instance presented to me, and I have not occasion to suppose the continu'd existence of objects, in order to connect their past and present appearances, and give them such an union with each other, as I have found by experience to be suitable to their particular natures and circumstances. Here then I am naturally led to regard the world, as something real and durable, and as preserving its existence, even when it is no longer present to my perception.

But tho' this conclusion from the coherence of appearances may seem to be of the same nature with our reasonings concerning causes and effects; as being deriv'd from custom, and regulated by past experience; we shall find upon examination, that they are at the bottom considerably different from each other, and that this inference arises from the understanding, and from custom in an indirect and oblique manner. For 'twill readily be allow'd, that since nothing is ever really present to the mind, besides its own perceptions, 'tis not only impossible, that any habit shou'd ever be acquir'd otherwise than by the regular succession of these perceptions, but also that any habit shou'd ever exceed that degree of regularity. Any degree, therefore, of regularity in our perceptions, can never be a foundation for us to infer a greater degree of regularity in some objects, which are not perceiv'd; since this supposes a contradiction, *viz.* a habit acquir'd by what was never present to the mind. But 'tis evident, that whenever we infer the continu'd existence of the objects of sense from their coherence, and the frequency of their unions, 'tis in order to bestow on the objects a greater regularity than what is observ'd in our mere perceptions. We remark a connexion betwixt two kinds of objects in their past appearance to the senses, but are not able to observe this connexion to be perfectly constant, since the turning about of our head, or the shutting of our eyes is able to break it. What then do we suppose in this case, but that these objects still continue their usual connexion, notwithstanding their apparent interruption, and that the irregular appearances are join'd by something, of which we are insensible? But as all reasoning concerning matters of fact arises only from custom, and custom can only be the effect of repeated perceptions, the extending of custom and reasoning beyond the perceptions can never be the direct and natural effect of the constant repetition and connexion, but must arise from the cooperation of some other principles.

I have already observ'd, in examining the foundation of mathematics, that the imagination, when set into any train of thinking, is apt to continue, even when its object fails it, and like a galley put in motion by the oars, carries on its course without any new impulse. This I have assign'd for the reason, why, after considering several loose standards of equality, and correcting them by each other, we proceed to imagine so correct and exact a standard of that relation, as is not liable to the least error or variation. The same principle makes us easily entertain this opinion of the continu'd existence of body. Objects have a certain coherence even as they appear to our senses; but this coherence is much greater and more uniform, if we suppose the objects to have a continu'd existence; and as the mind is once in the train of observing a uniformity among objects, it naturally continues, till it renders the uniformity as compleat as possible. The simple supposition of their continu'd existence suffices for this purpose, and gives us a notion of a much greater regularity among objects, than what they have when we look no farther than our senses.

But whatever force we may ascribe to this principle, I am afraid 'tis too weak to support alone so vast an edifice, as is that of the continu'd existence of all external bodies; and that we must join the *constancy* of their appearance to the *coherence,* in order to give a satisfactory account of that opinion. As the explication of this will lead me into a considerable compass of very profound reasoning; I think it proper, in order to avoid confusion, to give a short sketch or abridgment of my system, and afterwards draw out all its parts in their full compass. This inference from the constancy of our perceptions, like the precedent from their coherence, gives rise to the opinion of the *continu'd* existence of body, which is prior to that of its *distinct* existence, and produces that latter principle.

When we have been accustom'd to observe a constancy in certain impressions, and have found, that the perception of the sun or ocean, for instance, returns upon us after an absence or annihilation with like parts and in a like order, as at its first appearance, we are not apt to regard these interrupted perceptions as different, (which they really are) but on the contrary consider them as individually the same, upon account of their resemblance. But as this interruption of their existence is contrary to their perfect identity, and makes us regard the first impression as annihilated, and the second as newly created, we find ourselves somewhat at a loss, and are involv'd in a kind of contradiction. In order to free ourselves from this difficulty, we disguise, as much as possible, the interruption, or rather remove it entirely, by supposing that these interrupted perceptions are connected by a real existence, of which we are insensible. This supposition, or idea of continu'd existence, acquires a force and vivacity from the memory of these broken impressions, and from that propensity, which they give us, to suppose them the same; and according to the precedent reasoning, the very essence of belief consists in the force and vivacity of the conception. . . .

But tho' we are led after this manner, by the natural propensity of the imagination, to ascribe a continu'd existence to those sensible objects or perceptions, which we find to resemble each other in their interrupted appearance; yet a very little reflection and philosophy is sufficient to make us perceive the fallacy of that opinion. I have already observ'd, that there is an intimate connexion betwixt those two principles, of a *continu'd* and of a *distinct* or *independent* existence, and that we no sooner establish the one than the other follows, as a necessary consequence. 'Tis the opinion of a continu'd existence, which first takes place, and without much study or reflection draws the other along with it, wherever the mind follows its first and most natural tendency. But when we compare experiments, and reason a little upon them, we quickly perceive, that the doctrine of the independent existence of our sensible perceptions is contrary to the plainest experience. This leads us backward upon our footsteps to perceive our error in attributing a continu'd existence to our perceptions, and is the origin of many very curious opinions, which we shall here endeavour to account for.

'Twill first be proper to observe a few of those experiments, which convince us, that our perceptions are not possest of any independent existence. When we press one eye with a finger, we immediately perceive all the objects to become double, and one half of them to be remov'd from their common and natural position. But as we do not attribute a continu'd existence to both these perceptions, and as they are both of the same nature, we clearly perceive, that all our perceptions are dependent on our organs, and the disposition of our nerves and animal spirits. This opinion is confirm'd by the seeming encrease and diminution of objects, according to their distance; by the apparent alterations in their figure; by the changes in their color and other qualities from our sickness and distempers; and by an infinite number of other experiments of the same kind; from all which we learn, that our sensible perceptions are not possest of any distinct or independent existence.

The natural consequence of this reasoning shou'd be, that our perceptions have no more a continu'd than an independent existence; and indeed philosophers have so far run into this opinion, that they change their system, and distinguish, (as we shall do for the future) betwixt perceptions and objects, of which the former are suppos'd to be interrupted, and perishing, and different at every different return; the latter to be uninterrupted, and to preserve a continu'd existence and identity. But however philosophical this new system may be esteem'd, I assert that 'tis only a palliative remedy, and that it contains all the difficulties of the vulgar system, with some others, that are peculiar to itself. There are no principles either of the understanding or fancy, which lead us directly to embrace this opinion of the double existence of perceptions and objects, nor can we arrive at it but by passing thro' the common hypothesis of the identity and continuance of our interrupted perceptions. Were we not first persuaded, that our perceptions are our only objects, and continue to exist even when they no longer make their appearance to the senses, we shou'd never be led to think, that our perceptions and objects are different, and that our objects alone preserve a continu'd existence. "The latter hypothesis has no primary recommendation either to reason or the imagination, but acquires all its influence on the imagination from the former." This proposition contains two parts, which we shall endeavour to prove as distinctly and clearly, as such abstruse subjects will permit.

As to the first part of the proposition, *that this philosophical hypothesis has no primary recommendation, either to reason or the imagination,* we may soon satisfy ourselves with regard to *reason* by the following reflections. The only existences, of which we are certain, are perceptions, which being immediately present to us by consciousness, command our strongest assent, and are the first foundation of all our conclusions. The only conclusion we can draw from the existence of one thing to that of another, is by means of the relation of cause and effect, which shews, that there is a connexion betwixt them, and that the existence of one is dependent on that of the other. The idea of this relation is deriv'd from past experience, by which we find, that two beings are constantly conjoin'd together, and are always present at once to the mind. But as no beings are ever present to the mind but perceptions; it follows that we may observe a conjunction or a relation of cause and effect between different perceptions, but can never observe it between perceptions and objects. 'Tis impossible, therefore, that from the existence or any of the qualities of the former, we can ever form any conclusion concerning the existence of the latter, or ever satisfy our reason in this particular.

'Tis no less certain, that this philosophical system has no primary recommendation to the *imagination*, and that that faculty wou'd never, of itself, and by its original tendency, have fallen upon such a principle. I confess it will be somewhat difficult to prove this to the full satisfaction of the reader; because it implies a negative, which in many cases will not admit of any positive proof. If any one wou'd take the pains to examine this question, and wou'd invent a system, to account for the direct origin of this opinion from the imagination, we shou'd be able, by the examination of that system, to pronounce a certain judgement in the present subject. Let it be taken for granted, that our perceptions are broken, and interrupted, and however like, are still different from each other; and let any one upon this supposition shew why the fancy, directly and immediately, proceeds to the belief of another existence, resembling these perceptions in their nature, but yet continu'd, and uninterrupted, and identical; and after he has done this to my satisfaction, I promise to renounce my present opinion. Meanwhile I cannot forbear concluding, from the very abstractedness and difficulty of the first supposition, that 'tis an improper subject for the fancy to work upon. Whoever wou'd explain the origin of the *common* opinion concerning the continu'd and distinct existence of body, must take the mind in its *common* situation, and must proceed upon the supposition, that our perceptions are our only objects, and continue to exist even when they are not perceiv'd. Tho' this opinion be false, 'tis the most natural of any, and has alone any primary recommendation to the fancy.

As to the second part of the proposition, *that the philosophical system acquires all its influence on the imagination from the vulgar one;* we may observe, that this is a natural and unavoidable consequence of the foregoing conclusion, *that it has no primary recommendation to reason or the imagination.* For as the philosophical system is found by experience to take hold of many minds, and in particular of all those, who reflect ever so little on

this subject, it must derive all its authority from the vulgar system; since it has no original authority of its own. The manner, in which these two systems, tho' directly contrary, are connected together, may be explain'd, as follows.

The imagination naturally runs on in this train of thinking. Our perceptions are our only objects: Resembling perceptions are the same, however broken or uninterrupted in their appearance: This appearing interruption is contrary to the identity: The interruption consequently extends not beyond the appearance, and the perception or object really continues to exist, even when absent from us: Our sensible perceptions have, therefore, a continu'd and uninterrupted existence. But as a little reflection destroys this conclusion, that our perceptions have a continu'd existence, by shewing that they have a dependent one, 'twou'd naturally be expected, that we must altogether reject the opinion, that there is such a thing in nature as a continu'd existence, which is preserv'd even when it no longer appears to the senses. The case, however, is otherwise. Philosophers are so far from rejecting the opinion of a continu'd existence upon rejecting that of the independence and continuance of our sensible perceptions, that tho' all sects agree in the latter sentiment, the former, which is, in a manner, its necessary consequence, has been peculiar to a few extravagant sceptics; who after all maintain'd that opinion in words only, and were never able to bring themselves sincerely to believe it.

There is a great difference betwixt such opinions as we form after a calm and profound reflection, and such as we embrace by a kind of instinct or natural impulse, on account of their suitableness and conformity to the mind. If these opinions become contrary, 'tis not difficult to foresee which of them will have the advantage. As long as our attention is bent upon the subject, the philosophical and study'd principle may prevail; but the moment we relax our thoughts, nature will display herself, and draw us back to our former opinion. Nay she has sometimes such an influence, that she can stop our progress, even in the midst of our most profound reflections, and keep us from running on with all the consequences of any philosophical opinion. Thus tho' we clearly perceive the dependence and interruption of our perceptions, we stop short in our career, and never upon that account reject the notion of an independent and continu'd existence. That opinion has taken such deep root in the imagination, that 'tis impossible ever to eradicate it, nor will any strain'd metaphysical conviction of the dependence of our perceptions be sufficient for that purpose.

But tho' our natural and obvious principles here prevail above our study'd reflections, 'tis certain there must be some struggle and opposition in the case; at least so long as these reflections retain any force or vivacity. In order to set ourselves at ease in this particular, we contrive a new hypothesis, which seems to comprehend both these principles of reason and imagination. This hypothesis is the philosophical one of the double existence of perceptions and objects; which pleases our reason, in allowing, that our dependent perceptions are interrupted and different; and at the same time is agreeable to the imagination, in attributing a continu'd existence to something else, which we call *objects*. This philosophical system, therefore, is the monstrous offspring of two principles, which are contrary to each other, which are both at once embrac'd by the mind, and which are unable mutually to destroy each other. The imagination tells us, that our resembling perceptions have a continu'd and uninterrupted existence, and are not annihilated by their absence. Reflection tells us, that even our resembling perceptions are interrupted in their existence, and different from each other. The contradiction betwixt these opinions we elude by a new fiction, which is conformable to the hypotheses both of reflection and fancy, by ascribing these contrary qualities to different existences; the *interruption* to perceptions, and the *continuance* to objects. Nature is obstinate, and will not quit the field, however strongly attack'd by reason; and at the same time reason is so clear in the point, that there is no possibility of disguising her. Not being able to reconcile these two enemies, we endeavour to set ourselves at ease as much as possible, by successively granting to each whatever it demands, and by feigning a double existence, where each may find something, that has all the conditions it desires. Were we fully convinc'd, that our resembling perceptions are continu'd, and identical, and independent, we shou'd never run into this opinion of a double existence; since we shou'd find satisfaction in our first supposition, and wou'd not look beyond. Again, were we fully convinc'd, that our perceptions are dependent, and interrupted, and different, we shou'd be as little inclin'd to embrace the opinion of a double existence; since in that case we shou'd clearly perceive the error of our first supposition of a continu'd existence, and wou'd never regard it any farther. 'Tis therefore from the intermediate situation of the mind, that this opinion arises, and from such an adherence to these two contrary principles, as makes us seek some pretext to justify our receiving both; which happily at last is found in the system of a double existence.

Another advantage of this philosophical system is its similarity to the vulgar one; by which means we can humour our reason for a moment, when it becomes troublesome and solicitous; and yet upon its least negligence or inattention, can easily return to our vulgar and natural notions. Accordingly we find, that philosophers neglect not this advantage; but immediately upon leaving their closets, mingle with the rest of mankind in those exploded opinions, that our perceptions are our only objects, and continue identically and uninterruptedly the same in all their interrupted appearances.

There are other particulars of this system, wherein we may remark its dependence on the fancy, in a very conspicuous manner. Of these, I shall observe the two following. *First,* We suppose external objects to resemble internal perceptions. I have already shewn, that the relation of cause and effect can never afford us any just conclusion from the existence or qualities of our perceptions to the existence of external continu'd objects: And I shall farther add, that even tho' they cou'd afford such a conclusion, we shou'd never have any reason to infer, that our objects resemble our perceptions. That opinion, therefore, is deriv'd from nothing but the quality of the fancy above-explain'd, *that it borrows all its ideas from some precedent perception*. We never can conceive any thing but perceptions, and therefore must make every thing resemble them.

Secondly, As we suppose our objects in general to resemble our perceptions, so we take it for granted, that every particular object resembles that perception, which it causes. The relation of cause and effect determines us to join the other of resemblance; and the ideas of these existences being already united together in the fancy by the former relation, we naturally add the latter to compleat the union. We have a strong propensity to compleat every union by joining new relations to those which we have before observ'd betwixt any ideas, as we shall have occasion to observe presently.

Having thus given an account of all the systems both popular and philosophical, with regard to external existences, I cannot forbear giving vent to a certain sentiment, which arises upon reviewing those systems. I begun this subject with premising, that we ought to have an implicit faith in our senses, and that this wou'd be the conclusion, I shou'd draw from the whole of my reasoning. But to be ingenuous, I feel myself *at present* of a quite contrary sentiment, and am more inclin'd to repose no faith at all in my senses, or rather imagination, than to place in it such an implicit confidence. I cannot conceive how such trivial qualities of the fancy, conducted by such false suppositions, can ever lead to any solid and rational system. They are the coherence and constancy of our perceptions, which produce the opinion of their continu'd existence; tho' these qualities of perceptions have no perceivable connexion with such an existence. The constancy of our perceptions has the most considerable effect, and yet is attended with the greatest difficulties. 'Tis a gross illusion to suppose, that our resembling perceptions are numerically the same; and 'tis this illusion, which leads us into the opinion, that these perceptions are uninterrupted, and are still existent, even when they are not present to the senses. This is the case with our popular system. And as to our philosophical one, 'tis liable to the same difficulties; and is over-and-above loaded with this absurdity, that it at once denies and establishes the vulgar supposition. Philosophers deny our resembling perceptions to be identically

the same, and uninterrupted; and yet have so great a propensity to believe them such, that they arbitrarily invent a new set of perceptions, to which they attribute these qualities. I say, a new set of perceptions: For we may well suppose in general, but 'tis impossible for us distinctly to conceive, objects to be in their nature any thing but exactly the same with perceptions. What then can we look for from this confusion of groundless and extraordinary opinions but error and falsehood? And how can we justify to ourselves any belief we repose in them?

This sceptical doubt, both with respect to reason and the senses, is a malady, which can never be radically cur'd, but must return upon us every moment, however we may chace it away, and sometimes may seem entirely free from it. 'Tis impossible upon any system to defend either our understanding or senses; and we but expose them farther when we endeavour to justify them in that manner. As the sceptical doubt arises naturally from a profound and intense reflection on those subjects, it always encreases, the farther we carry our reflections, whether in opposition or conformity to it. *Carelessness and in-attention alone can afford us any remedy.* For this reason I rely entirely upon them; and take it for granted, whatever may be the reader's opinion at this present moment, that an hour hence he will be persuaded there is both an external and internal world; and going upon that supposition, I intend to examine some general systems both ancient and modern, which have been propos'd of both, before I proceed to a more particular enquiry concerning our impressions. This will not, perhaps, in the end be found foreign to our present purpose.

II.3 A Defense of Common Sense

G. E. MOORE

G. E. Moore (1873–1958) was professor of philosophy at Cambridge University and one of the leading philosophers of the first half of the twentieth century. In this essay—which is a combination of two of his articles, "A Defence of Common Sense" and "Proof of the External World"—Moore argues that skepticism is decisively refuted by common sense. The essence of the argument is as follows:

1. If skepticism is true, we do not have knowledge of the external world.
2. But we do have knowledge of the external world (Moore gives many examples).
3. Therefore, Skepticism is false.

In what follows I have merely tried to state, one by one, some of the most important points in which my philosophical position differs from positions which have been taken up by *some* other philosophers. It may be that the points which I have had room to mention are not really the most important, and possibly some of them may be points as to which no philosopher has ever really differed from me. But, to the best of my belief, each is a point as to which many have really differed; although (in most cases, at all events) each is also a point as to which many have agreed with me.

I

The first point is a point which embraces a great many other points. And it is one which I cannot state as clearly as I wish to state it, except at some length. The method I am going to use for stating it is this. I am going to begin by enunciating, under the heading (1), a whole long list of propositions, which may seem, at first sight, such obvious truisms as not to be worth stating: they are, in fact, a set of propositions, every one of which (in my own opinion) I *know*, with certainty, to be true. I shall, next, under the heading (2), state a single proposition which makes an assertion about

a whole set of *classes* of propositions—each class being defined, as the class consisting of all propositions which resemble *one* of the propositions in (1) in a certain respect. (2), therefore, is a proposition which could not be stated, until the list of propositions in (1), or some similar list, had already been given. (2) is itself a proposition which may seem such an obvious truism as not to be worth stating: and it is also a proposition which (in my own opinion) I know, with certainty, to be true. But, nevertheless, it is, to the best of my belief, a proposition with regard to which many philosophers have, for different reasons, differed from me; even if they have not directly denied (2) itself, they have held views incompatible with it. My first point, then, may be said to be that (2), together with all its implications, some of which I shall expressly mention, is true.

(1) I begin, then, with my list of truisms, every one of which (in my own opinion) I *know,* with certainty, to be true. The propositions to be included in this list are the following:

There exists at present a living human body, which is *my* body. This body was born at a certain time in the past, and has existed continuously ever since, though not without undergoing changes; it was, for instance, much smaller when it was born, and for some time afterwards, than it is now. Ever since it was born, it has been either in contact with or not far from the surface of the earth; and, at every moment since it was born, there have also existed many other things, having shape and size in three dimensions (in the same familiar sense in

Reprinted from G. E. Moore, *Philosophical Papers* (London: George Allen & Unwin, 1959) by permission of Timothy Moore.

which it has), from which it has been *at various distances* (in the familiar sense in which it is now at a distance both from that mantelpiece and from that bookcase, and at a greater distance from the bookcase than it is from the mantelpiece); also there have (very often, at all events) existed some other things of this kind with which it was *in contact* (in the familiar sense in which it is now in contact with the pen I am holding in my right hand and with some of the clothes I am wearing). Among the things which have, in this sense, formed part of its environment (i.e. have been either in contact with it, or at *some* distance from it, however *great*) there have, at every moment since its birth, been large numbers of other living human bodies, each of which has, like it, *(a)* at some time been born, *(b)* continued to exist from some time after birth, *(c)* been, at every moment of its life after birth, either in contact with or not far from the surface of the earth; and many of these bodies have already died and ceased to exist. But the earth had existed also for many years before my body was born; and for many of these years, also, large numbers of human bodies had, at every moment, been alive upon it; and many of these bodies had died and ceased to exist before it was born. Finally (to come to a different class of propositions), I am a human being, and I have, at different times since my body was born, had many different experiences, of each of many different kinds: e.g. I have often perceived both my own body and other things which formed part of its environment, including other human bodies; I have not only perceived things of this kind, but have also observed facts about them, such as, for instance, the fact which I am now observing, that that mantel-piece is at present nearer to my body than that bookcase; I have been aware of other facts, which I was not at the time observing, such as, for instance, the fact, of which I am now aware, that my body existed yesterday and was then also for some time nearer to that mantelpiece than to that bookcase; I have had expectations with regard to the future, and many beliefs of other kinds, both true and false; I have thought of imaginary things and persons and incidents, in the reality of which I did not believe; I have had dreams; and I have had feelings of many different kinds. And, just as my body has been the body of a human being, namely myself, who has, during his lifetime, had many experiences of each of these (and other)

different kinds; so, in the case of very many of the other human bodies which have lived upon the earth, each has been the body of a different human being, who has, during the lifetime of that body, had many different experiences of each of these (and other) different kinds.

(2) I now come to the single truism which, as will be seen, could not be stated except by reference to the whole list of truisms, just given in (1). This truism also (in my own opinion) *I know*, with certainty, to be true; and it is as follows:

In the case of *very many* (I do not say *all*) of the human beings belonging to the class (which includes myself) defined in the following way, i.e. as human beings who have had human bodies, that were born and lived for some time upon the earth, and who have, during the lifetime of those bodies, had many different experiences of each of the kinds mentioned in (1), it is true that each has frequently, during the life of his body, known, with regard to *himself* or *his* body, and with regard to some time earlier than any of the times at which I wrote down the propositions in (1), a proposition *corresponding* to each of the propositions in (1), in the sense that it asserts with regard to *himself* or *his* body and the earlier time in question (namely, in each case, the time at which he knew it), just what the corresponding proposition in (1) asserts with regard to *me* or *my* body and the time at which I wrote that proposition down.

In other words what (2) asserts is only (what seems an obvious enough truism) that each of *us* (meaning by "us," very many human beings of the class defined) has frequently *known,* with regard to *himself* or *his* body and the time at which he knew it, everything which, in writing down my list of propositions in (1), I was claiming to know about *my*self or *my* body and the time at which I wrote that proposition down, i.e. just as *I* knew (when I wrote it down) "There exists at present a living human body which is my body," so each of us has frequently known with regard to himself and some other time the different but corresponding proposition, which *he* could *then* have properly expressed by, "There exists *at present* a human body which is *my* body"; just as *I* know "Many human bodies other than mine have before now lived on the earth," so each of us has frequently known the different but corresponding proposition "Many human bodies other than *mine* have before *now* lived on the earth"; just as *I* know "Many human beings other than myself have before now perceived, and dreamed, and felt," so each of *us* has frequently known the different but corresponding proposition "Many human beings other than *myself* have before *now* perceived, and dreamed, and felt"; and so on, in the case of *each* of the propositions enumerated in (1). . . .

Proof of an External World

In the preface to the second edition of Kant's *Critique of Pure Reason* some words occur, which, in Professor Kemp Smith's translation, are rendered as follows:

> It still remains a scandal to philosophy . . . that the existence of things outside of us . . . must be accepted merely on *faith,* and that, if anyone thinks good to doubt their existence, we are unable to counter his doubts by any satisfactory proof.

It seems clear from these words that Kant thought it a matter of some importance to give a proof of "the existence of things outside of us" or perhaps rather (for it seems to me possible that the force of the German words is better rendered in this way) of "the existence of *the* things outside of us"; for had he not thought it important that a proof should be given, he would scarcely have called it a "scandal" that no proof had been given. And it seems clear also that he thought that the giving of such a proof was a task which fell properly within the province of philosophy; for, if it did not, the fact that no proof had been given could not possibly be a scandal to *philosophy.*

Now, even if Kant was mistaken in both of these two opinions, there seems to me to be no doubt whatever that it is a matter of some importance and also a matter which falls properly within the province of philosophy, to discuss the question what sort of proof, if any, can be given of "the existence of things outside of us." And to discuss this question was my object when I began to write the present lecture. But I may say at once that, as you will find, I have only, at most, succeeded in saying a very small part of what ought to be said about it.

The words "it . . . remains a scandal to philosophy . . . that we are unable . . ." would, taken strictly, imply that, at the moment at which he wrote them, Kant himself was unable to produce a satisfactory proof of the point in question. But I think it is unquestionable that Kant himself did not think that he personally was at the time unable to produce such a proof. On the contrary, in the immediately preceding sentence, he has declared that he has, in the second edition of his *Critique,* to which he is now writing the Preface, given a "rigorous proof" of this very thing; and has added that he believes this proof of his to be "the only possible proof." It is true that in this preceding sentence he does not describe the proof which he has given as a proof of "the existence of things outside of us" or of "the existence of the things outside of us," but describes it instead as a proof of "the objective reality of outer intuition." But the context leaves no doubt that he is using these two phrases, "the objective reality of outer intuition" and "the existence of things (or 'the things') outside of us," in such a way that whatever is a proof of the first is also necessarily a proof of the second. We must, therefore, suppose that when he speaks as if *we* are unable to give a satisfactory proof, he does not mean to say that he himself, as well as others, is *at the moment* unable; but rather that, until he discovered the proof which he has given, both he himself and everybody else *were* unable. Of course, if he is right in thinking that he has given a satisfactory proof, the state of things which he describes came to an end as soon as his proof was published. As soon as that happened, anyone who read it was able to give a satisfactory proof by simply repeating that which Kant had given, and the "scandal" to philosophy had been removed once for all.

If, therefore, it were certain that the proof of the point in question given by Kant in the second edition is a satisfactory proof, it would be certain that at least one satisfactory proof can be given; and all that would remain of the question which I said I proposed to discuss would be, firstly, the question as to what *sort* of a proof this of Kant's is, and secondly the question whether (contrary to Kant's own opinion) there may not perhaps be other proofs, of the same or of a different sort, which are also satisfactory. But I think it is by no means certain that Kant's proof is satisfactory. I think it is by no means certain that he did succeed in removing once for all the state of affairs which he considered to be a scandal to philosophy. And

I think, therefore, that the question whether it is possible to give *any* satisfactory proof of the point in question still deserves discussion.

But what is the point in question? I think it must be owned that the expression "things outside of us" is rather an odd expression, and an expression the meaning of which is certainly not perfectly clear. It would have sounded less odd if, instead of "things outside of us" I had said "external things," and perhaps also the meaning of this expression would have seemed to be clearer; and I think we make the meaning of "external things" clearer still if we explain that this phrase has been regularly used by philosophers as short for "things external to *our minds*." The fact is that there has been a long philosophical tradition, in accordance with which the three expressions "external things," "things external to *us*," and "things external to *our minds*" have been used as equivalent to one another, and have, each of them, been used as if they needed no explanation. The origin of this usage I do not know. It occurs already in Descartes; and since he uses the expressions as if they needed no explanation, they had presumably been used with the same meaning before. Of the three, it seems to me that the expression "external to *our minds*" is the clearest, since it at least makes clear that what is meant is not "external to *our bodies*"; whereas both the other expressions might be taken to mean this: and indeed there has been a good deal of confusion, even among philosophers, as to the relation of the two conceptions "external things" and "things external to *our bodies*." But even the expression "things external to our minds" seems to me to be far from perfectly clear; and if I am to make really clear what I mean by "proof of the existence of things outside of us," I cannot do it by merely saying that by "outside of us" I mean "external to our minds."

. . .

But now, if to say of anything, e.g. my body, that it is external to *my* mind, means merely that from a proposition to the effect that it existed at a specified time, there in no case follows the further proposition that *I* was having an experience at the time in question, then to say of anything that it is external to *our* minds, will mean similarly that from a proposition to the effect that it existed at a specified time, it in no case follows that any of *us* were having experiences at the time in question. And if by *our* minds be meant, as is, I think, usu-

ally meant, the minds of human beings living on the earth, then it will follow that any pains which animals may feel, any after-images they may see, any experiences they may have, though not external to *their* minds, yet are external to *ours*. And this at once makes plain how different is the conception "external to our minds" from the conception "to be met with in space"; for, of course, pains which animals feel or after-images which they see are no more to be met with in space than are pains which *we* feel or after-images which *we* see. From the proposition that there are external objects— objects that are not in any of *our* minds, it does *not* follow that there are things to be met with in space; and hence "external to our minds" is not a mere synonym for "to be met with in space": that is to say, "external to our minds" and "to be met with in space" are two different conceptions. And the true relation between these conceptions seems to me to be this. We have already seen that there are ever so many kinds of "things," such that, in the case of each of these kinds, from the proposition that there is at least one thing of that kind there *follows* the proposition that there is at least one thing to be met with in space: e.g. this follows from "There is at least one star," from "There is at least one human body," from "There is at least one shadow," etc. And I think we can say that of every kind of thing of which this is true, it is also true that from the proposition that there is at least one "thing" of that kind there *follows* the proposition that there is at least one thing external to our minds: e.g. from "There is at least one star" there follows not only "There is at least one thing to be met with in space" but also "There is at least one external thing," and similarly in all other cases. My reason for saying this is as follows. Consider any kind of thing, such that anything of that kind, if there is anything of it, must be "to be met with in space": e.g. consider the kind "soap-bubble." If I say of anything which I am perceiving, "That is a soap-bubble," I am, it seems to me, certainly implying that there would be no contradiction in asserting that it existed before I perceived it and that it will continue to exist, even if I cease to perceive it. This seems to me to be part of what is meant by saying that it is a real soap-bubble, as distinguished, for instance, from an hallucination of a soap-bubble. Of course, it by no means follows, that if it really is a soap-bubble, it did in fact exist before I perceived it or will continue to exist after

I cease to perceive it: soap-bubbles are an example of a kind of "physical object" and "thing to be met with in space," in the case of which it is notorious that particular specimens of the kind often do exist only so long as they are perceived by a particular person. But a thing which I perceive would not be a soap-bubble unless its existence at any given time were *logically independent* of my perception of it at that time; unless that is to say, from the proposition, with regard to a particular time, that it existed at that time, it *never* follows that I perceived it at that time. But, if it is true that it would not be a soap-bubble, unless it *could* have existed at any given time without being perceived by me at that time, it is certainly also true that it would not be a soap-bubble, unless it *could* have existed at any given time, without its being true that I was having any experience of any kind at the time in question: it would not be a soap-bubble, unless, whatever time you take, from the proposition that it existed at that time it does *not* follow that I was having any experience at that time. That is to say, from the proposition with regard to anything which I am perceiving that it is a soap-bubble, there *follows* the proposition that it is external to *my* mind. But if, when I say that anything which I perceive is a soap-bubble, I am implying that it is external to *my* mind, I am, I think, certainly also implying that it is also external to all other minds: I am implying that it is not a thing of a sort such that things of that sort *can* only exist at a time when somebody is having an experience. I think, therefore, that from any proposition of the form "There's a soap-bubble!" there does really *follow* the proposition "There's an external object!" "There's an object external to *all* our minds!" And, if this is true of the kind "soap-bubble," it is certainly also true of any other kind (including the kind "unicorn") which is such that, if there are any things of that kind, it follows that there are *some* things to be met with in space.

I think, therefore, that in the case of all kinds of "things," which are such that if there is a pair of things, both of which are of one of these kinds, or a pair of things one of which is of one of them and one of them of another, then it will follow at once that there are some things to be met with in space, it is true also that if I can prove that there are a pair of things, one of which is of one of these kinds and another of another, or a pair both of which are of one of them, then I shall have proved *ipso facto*

that there are at least two "things outside of us." That is to say, if I can prove that there exist now both a sheet of paper and a human hand, I shall have proved that there are now "things outside of us"; if I can prove that there exist now both a shoe and sock, I shall have proved that there are now "things outside of us"; etc.; and similarly I shall have proved it, if I can prove that there exist now two sheets of paper, or two human hands, or two shoes, or two socks, etc. Obviously, then, there are thousands of different things such that, if, at any time, I can prove any one of them, I shall have proved the existence of things outside of us. Cannot I prove any of these things?

It seems to me that, so far from its being true, as Kant declares to be his opinion, that there is only one possible proof of the existence of things outside of us, namely the one which he has given, I can now give a large number of different proofs, each of which is a perfectly rigorous proof; and that at many other times I have been in a position to give many others. I can prove now, for instance, that two human hands exist. How? By holding up my two hands, and saying, as I make a certain gesture with the right hand, "Here is one hand," and adding, as I make a certain gesture with the left, "and here is another." And if, by doing this, I have proved *ipso facto* the existence of external things, you will all see that I can also do it now in numbers of other ways: there is no need to multiply examples.

But did I prove just now that two human hands were then in existence? I do want to insist that I did; that the proof which I gave was a perfectly rigorous one; and that it is perhaps impossible to give a better or more rigorous proof of anything whatever. Of course, it would not have been a proof unless three conditions were satisfied; namely (1) unless the premiss which I adduced as proof of the conclusion was different from the conclusion I adduced it to prove; (2) unless the premiss which I adduced was something which I *knew* to be the case, and not merely something which I believed but which was by no means certain, or something which, though in fact true, I did not know to be so; and (3) unless the conclusion did really follow from the premiss. But all these three conditions were in fact satisfied by my proof. (1) The premiss which I adduced in proof was quite certainly different from the conclusion, for the conclusion was merely "Two human hands exist at this moment"; but the premiss was something far more specific than this—something which I expressed by showing you my hands, making certain gestures, and saying the words "Here is one hand, and here is another." It is quite obvious that the two were different, because it is quite obvious that the conclusion might have been true, even if the premiss had been false. In asserting the premiss I was asserting much more than I was asserting in asserting the conclusion. (2) I certainly did at the moment *know* that which I expressed by the combination of certain gestures with saying the words "There is one hand and here is another." I *knew* that there was one hand in the place indicated by combining a certain gesture with my first utterance of "here" and that there was another in the different place indicated by combining a certain gesture with my second utterance of "here." How absurd it would be to suggest that I did not know it, but only believed it, and that perhaps it was not the case! You might as well suggest that I do not know that I am now standing up and talking—that perhaps after all I'm not, and that it's not quite certain that I am! And finally (3) it is quite certain that the conclusion did follow from the premiss. This is as certain as it is that if there is one hand here and another here *now*, then it follows that there are two hands in existence *now*.

My proof, then, of the existence of things outside of us did satisfy three of the conditions necessary for a rigorous proof. Are there any other conditions necessary for a rigorous proof, such that perhaps it did not satisfy one of them? Perhaps there may be; I do not know; but I do want to emphasize that, so far as I can see, we all of us do constantly take proofs of this sort as absolutely conclusive proofs of certain conclusions—as finally settling certain questions, as to which we were previously in doubt. Suppose, for instance, it were a question whether there were as many as three misprints on a certain page in a certain book. A says there are, B is inclined to doubt it. How could A prove that he is right? Surely he *could* prove it by taking the book, turning to the page, and pointing to three separate places on it, saying "There's one misprint here, another here, and another here": surely that is a method by which it *might* be proved! Of course, A would not have proved, by doing this, that there were at least three misprints on the page in question, unless it was certain that there was a misprint in each of the places to which

he pointed. But to say that he *might* prove it in this way, is to say that it *might* be certain that there was. And if such a thing as that could ever be certain, then assuredly it was certain just now that there was one hand in one of the two places I indicated and another in the other.

I did, then, just now, give a proof that there were *then* external objects; and obviously, if I did, I could *then* have given many other proofs of the same sort that there were external objects *then*, and could now give many proofs of the same sort that there are external objects *now*.

But, if what I am asked to do is to prove that external objects have existed *in the past*, then I can give many different proofs of this also, but proofs which are in important respects of a different *sort* from those just given. And I want to emphasize that, when Kant says it is a scandal not to be able to give a proof of the existence of external objects, a proof of their existence in the past would certainly *help* to remove the scandal of which he is speaking. He says that, if it occurs to anyone to question their existence, we ought to be able to confront him with a satisfactory proof. But by a person who questions their existence, he certainly means not merely a person who questions whether any exist at the moment of speaking, but a person who questions whether any have *ever* existed; and a proof that some have existed in the past would certainly therefore be relevant to *part* of what such a person is questioning. How then can I prove that there have been external objects in the past? Here is one proof. I can say: "I held up two hands above this desk not very long ago; therefore two hands existed not very long ago; therefore at least two external objects have existed at some time in the past, Q.E.D." This is a perfectly good proof, provided I *know* what is asserted in the premiss. But I *do* know that I held up two hands above this desk not very long ago. As a matter of fact, in this case you all know it too. There's no doubt whatever that I did. Therefore I have given a perfectly conclusive proof that external objects have existed in the past; and you will all see at once that, if this is a conclusive proof, I could have given many others of the same sort, and could now give many others. But it is also quite obvious that this sort of proof differs in important respects from the sort of proof I gave just now that there were two hands existing *then*.

I have, then, given two conclusive proofs of the existence of external objects. The first was a proof that two human hands existed at the time when I gave the proof; the second was a proof that two human hands had existed at a time previous to that at which I gave the proof. These proofs were of a different sort in important respects. And I pointed out that I could have given, then, many other conclusive proofs of both sorts. It is also obvious that I could give many others of both sorts now. So that, if these are the sort of proof that is wanted, nothing is easier than to prove the existence of external objects.

But now I am perfectly well aware that, in spite of all that I have said, many philosophers will still feel that I have not given any satisfactory proof of the point in question. And I want briefly, in conclusion, to say something as to why this dissatisfaction with my proofs should be felt.

One reason why, is, I think, this. Some people understand "proof of an external world" as including a proof of things which I haven't attempted to prove and haven't proved. It is not quite easy to say *what* it is that they want proved—*what* it is that is such that unless they got a proof of it, they would not say that they had a proof of the existence of external things; but I can make an approach to explaining what they want by saying that if I had proved the propositions which I used as *premisses* in my two proofs, then they would perhaps admit that I had proved the existence of external things, but, in the absence of such a proof (which, of course, I have neither given nor attempted to give), they will say that I have not given what they mean by a proof of the existence of external things. In other words, they want a proof of what I assert *now* when I hold up my hands and say "Here's one hand and here's another"; and, in the other case, they want a proof of what I assert *now* when I say "I did hold up two hands above this desk just now." Of course, what they really want is not merely a proof of these two propositions, but something like a general statement as to how *any* propositions of this sort may be proved. This, of course, I haven't given; and I do not believe it can be given: if this is what is meant by proof of the existence of external things, I do not believe that any proof of the existence of external things is possible. Of course, in some cases what might be called a proof of propositions which seem like these can be got. If one of you suspected that one of my hands was artificial he might be said to get a proof of my

proposition "Here's one hand, and here's another," by coming up and examining the suspected hand close up, perhaps touching and pressing it, and so establishing that it really was a human hand. But I do not believe that any proof is possible in nearly all cases. How am I to prove now that "Here's one hand, and here's another"? I do not believe I can do it. In order to do it, I should need to prove for one thing, as Descartes pointed out, that I am not now dreaming. But how can I prove that I am not? I have, no doubt, conclusive reasons for asserting that I am not now dreaming; I have conclusive evidence that I am awake: but that is a very different thing from being able to prove it. I could not tell you what all my evidence is; and I should require to do this at least, in order to give you a proof.

But another reason why some people would feel dissatisfied with my proofs is, I think, not merely that they want a proof of something which I haven't proved, but that they think that, if I cannot give such extra proofs, then the proofs that I have given are not conclusive proofs at all. And this, I think, is a definite mistake. They would say: "If you cannot prove your premiss that here is one hand and here is another, then you do not know it. But you yourself have admitted that, if you did not know it, then your proof was not conclusive. Therefore your proof was not, as you say it was, a conclusive proof." This view that, if I cannot prove such things as these, I do not know them, is, I think, the view that Kant was expressing in the sentence which I quoted at the beginning of this lecture, when he implies that so long as we have no proof of the existence of external things, their existence must be accepted merely on *faith*. He means to say, I think, that if I cannot prove that there is a hand here, I must accept it merely as a matter of faith—I cannot know it. Such a view, though it has been very common among philosophers, can, I think, be shown to be wrong—though shown only by the use of premisses which are not known to be true, unless we do know of the existence of external things. I can know things, which I cannot prove; and among things which I certainly did know, even if (as I think) I could not prove them, were the premisses of my two proofs. I should say, therefore, that those, if any, who are dissatisfied with these proofs merely on the ground that I did not know their premisses, have no good reason for their dissatisfaction.

II.4 Why Not Skepticism?

Keith Lehrer

Keith Lehrer is professor of philosophy at the University of Arizona. In this
essay Lehrer contends that refutations such as Moore's fail to answer the
fundamental problem with knowledge claims, namely, that they need to
show that they satisfy the justification requirement. To know that *p*, one
must be completely justified in believing that *p*. Lehrer argues that we are
never completely justified in our beliefs, so we do not have knowledge.

The sceptic has been mistreated. Sophisticated epistemologies have been developed in defense of dogmatic knowledge claims. Recently, theories of
ignorance have been so rare that the name for such
theories, *agnoiology,* sounds like the antique it is.
Actually, James F. Ferrier[1] introduced both the
terms *epistemology* and *agnoiology* into the philosophical lexicon, but the latter has fallen into disuse
through lack of denotation. Scepticism suffers from
many defects, or so say the dogmatists. Some have
contended that scepticism is contradictory, others
that it is meaningless, and still others that it amounts
to nothing more than an ingenious restatement of
what we already believe. One problem with refutations of scepticism is that they are overly plentiful
and mutually inconsistent. This should create some
suspicion in the minds of the philosophically wary
that some theory of ignorance, an agnoiology, might
sustain the contentions of scepticism. I shall develop
an agnoiology for the defense of scepticism against
dogmatic knowledge claims. By so doing I hope to
convince you of the tenability and importance of
theories of rational belief and action based on probability without knowledge.

   The form of scepticism I wish to avow is more
radical than traditional sceptics have been wont to
defend. Some philosophers have maintained that
we do not know about anything beyond some
necessary truths and some truths about our own
subjective states. But they have not denied that we
do know about those matters. I wish to seriously
consider a stronger form of scepticism, to wit, that
we do not know anything.

Reprinted from *The Philosophical Forum,* 2.3 (1971),
283–298, by kind permission of the author and editor.
[Notes have been edited—Ed.]

I

Some qualification is necessary to avoid misunderstanding and to escape the burden of replying to
overeasy refutations. The form of scepticism that
concerns me does not embody the thesis that we
know that we do not know anything. That thesis is
obviously self-refuting. Rather, the contention is
that no one knows anything, not even that no one
knows anything. You might feel a surge of confidence in the face of such contention simply because
the sceptic has admitted that he does not know that
he is correct, and hence, that he does not know
that you are incorrect when you affirm that you do
know something. But this confidence is misplaced
because scepticism entails that, just as the sceptic
does not know that we do not know anything, so
we do not know that we do know anything, and,
moreover, that we do not know anything.

   In setting out to develop an agnoiology, the
sceptic looks as though he must inevitably fall into
embarrassment. For, in saying why he says what he
does, must he not fall back on the claim that he
knows various things to be true which support his
conclusion? Again the answer is negative. The
sceptic is not prevented by his agnoiology from
believing most of the same things that we believe;
indeed, all his position debars him from is believing in such things as would entail that we have
knowledge. About devils, dust, and delight, he
may believe what he wishes. He may even consider
some beliefs to be more prudent than others or
more useful, and he surely may distinguish
between what is true and what is false.

   He affirms that we know nothing, but he
believes most of what most men believe. He

affirms much else besides, only here he must be careful not to mislead with his sceptical speech. For often when a man speaks we take him to be claiming to know, though he does not say he knows. Indeed, it is perhaps more common than not to attach such implications to the acts of speech we confront. However, there is nothing inevitable or irreversible in this practice. When a man wishes to tell us what he thinks has transpired but does not wish to be understood as making any pretense to knowledge in the matter whereof he speaks, we may understand him without any confusion or perplexity. The agnoiologist who is about to defend scepticism must be understood as speaking in a similar manner. The premises of his agnoiology must not be understood as claims to knowledge but only formulations of what he believes and hopes we shall concede. Not even the claim that conclusion follows from premise would be taken as a claim to knowledge. His words are addressed to us in the full conviction that they are the truth but without any pretense to knowledge.

II

Before attempting to offer any argument for so general a thesis as one affirming universal ignorance, it is essential to include in our agnoiology an account of what knowledge entails. And here we immediately confront the problem that whatever one philosopher has said knowledge is another philosopher has rejected. Hence it is impossible to avoid controversy. Having written elsewhere on this subject, I shall have to rely on those results. I shall consequently assume that if a man knows *that p*, then it is true *that p*. It has seemed evident to most epistemologists that no one can know anything to be true which is not true. Second, I shall assume that if a man knows *that p,* then he believes *that p.* This has been controverted, but I shall not undertake any defense of the assumption here. Next, I shall assume that if a man knows *that p,* then he is completely justified in believing *that p.* A word of explanation. As I am using the locution, "completely justified," it is logically possible that a man should be completely justified in believing something even though he has no justificatory argument to support his belief. However, as an agnoiologist I shall deny the exis-

tence of such beliefs. Though completely justified true belief is a necessary condition of knowledge, it is not sufficient for reasons that might further aid the cause of scepticism.

III

We may best serve the purposes of scepticism by developing our agnoiology in an area where the dogmatist considers himself to be the most invulnerable, namely with respect to those claims to knowledge that he considers to be most certain and beyond doubt. Two classes of such claims are those concerning some logical and mathematical truths as well as those concerning some of our present conscious states. Let us consider necessary truths.

One argument against the sceptic in these matters is that such beliefs are ones where all possibility of error is excluded by logical necessity. This argument is worth a moment of consideration, because by so doing the first agnoiological strong-hold of scepticism may be secured. It is logically impossible to be mistaken in believing any necessary truth. If I believe that the axiom of choice is independent of the continuum hypothesis, and if it is a necessary truth that the axiom of choice is independent of the continuum hypothesis, then it is impossible that I should believe that the axiom of choice is independent of the continuum hypothesis and also be in error. Of course, this is also true of more mundane beliefs like my belief that there is a natural number greater than two and less than five which is prime.

However, the above-mentioned fact, if it constituted any defense of dogmatism, would constitute equally good grounds for the wildest forms of speculation concerning the necessary and the impossible. For, it is logically impossible to be mistaken when one believes any statement which is a necessary truth no matter how speculative or groundless such a belief may be. If it is necessarily true *that p*, then the statement that I am mistaken in believing *that p* would be equivalent to the conjunctive statement that I believe *that p* and it is false *that p.* If it is necessarily true *that p,* then the statement that it is false *that p* cannot possibly be true. Moreover, no conjunctive statement entailing that it is false *that p* could possibly be true either. Therefore, if it is necessarily true *that p,* then it cannot possibly be true that I am mistaken in believing *that p.* No one can possibly be mistaken in believing any necessary truth.

What the preceding proves is that if the dogmatist argues that a person knows that a statement is true whenever it is logically impossible for him to be mistaken in believing it, then he will be committed to the implausible conclusion that a person knows a mathematical statement to be true whenever he correctly believes it to be so no matter how foolish or groundless his belief. However, this violates our assumption that a belief must be completely justified as well as true or else we lack knowledge. Before any proof was forthcoming, someone might have believed that the axiom of choice was independent of the continuum hypothesis, but he did not know it. There is a distinction of justification between being right in mathematics and knowing that one is right. Of course, our agnoiology does not imply that anyone ever does know anything but it does imply that *if* anyone knows anything, then that person must not only have true belief, but complete justification as well.

Thus the preceding argument shows that we cannot assume a man knows whereof he believes simply because it is logically impossible that he should be mistaken in what he believes. For, he may have no proof or justification for believing what he does. Indeed, we might wish to say of the man that he could have been mistaken even though it was logically impossible that he should have been mistaken. What is the force of the *could* which defies logical possibility? In what sense could he have been mistaken? The answer is—he could have been mistaken in the sense that, for all he knows, what he believes is false. This, in turn, means that what he knows does not establish that what he believes is true. And, so, if he knows nothing, then he could have been mistaken even though it is logically impossible that he should be mistaken.

The logical impossibility of error in beliefs concerning the impossible and necessary, that is, statements which if true are necessary and if false are impossible, is no bulwark against scepticism. The logical impossibility of error in such matters is perfectly consistent with complete ignorance. Thus our agnoiology shows that there is no refutation of scepticism to be built on such logical impossibility of false belief.

IV

Let us, however, leave the realm of the necessary and the impossible for that of the contingent. Suppose a man believes some contingent statement to be true, a statement which is neither logically necessary nor logically impossible. What if, in such a case, it is logically impossible for the man to believe falsely? Must not we concede that the man knows?

Before answering this question let us note how few beliefs have the character in question. Some philosophers have thought that beliefs about one's current psychological states were ones that excluded the logical possibility of error. But this is, I am convinced, mostly mistaken. Let me explain why.

First, there are almost no beliefs about one's own present states of consciousness that it is logically inconsistent to suppose should be false. The best candidates for such incorrigible beliefs are ones concerning one's present sensations or thoughts. But it is logically possible for such beliefs to be mistaken. Consider sensations first. Suppose it is affirmed that if a person believes that he is having sensation S, a pain for example, then it is logically impossible that such a belief should be mistaken. This is not so. One might believe one is having a sensation S, a pain for example, because one is having a different sensation, S*, an itch for example, and one has mistaken S* for S, that is, one has mistaken an itch for a pain. How could this happen? It might happen either because of some general belief, to wit, that itches are pains, which one has been led to believe by some authority, or one may simply be misled on this occasion because one has been told by some authority that one will experience a pain. In short, one might have some false belief which together with the sensation of an itch produces the belief that one is in pain. Beliefs about sensations can be inferential, and one can infer that one is in a conscious state that one is not in by inferring from some false belief that this is so. One might believe that sensation S* is S, just as with respect to thoughts, one might believe that some thought T* is T, and thus arrive at the mistaken conclusion that one is in state S or state T because one is in state S* or T*.

The preceding argument might be bolstered by examples to please the fancy, but the argument is so simple as to render them superfluous. For all that I have assumed is that it is logically possible for a person, under the influence of authority, to mistake one conscious state for another and thus to believe that he is in a conscious state when in fact he is not in that state. The argument applies to almost all conscious states with a notable exception. If I believe that I believe something, then the first belief does seem to be one such that it is logically impossible that I should be mistaken. For, it is logically inconsistent to suppose both that I believe that I believe something and that I do not believe anything. It would be tempting to rid oneself of such troublesome cases by saying that it does not make sense to speak of believing that one believes, but I do not believe that such a contention is correct. So, I concede that the set of incorrigible beliefs about one's own conscious states is not null.

V

The preceding argument shows how little contingent knowledge we would need to concede to the dogmatist even if we conceded that we know those beliefs to be true which are such as to exclude the logical possibility of error. But the sceptic need not concede that we know even that. It is not the logical impossibility of error that could yield knowledge but rather our *knowledge* of the logical impossibility of error. Consider the mathematical case again. If I know that something is logically impossible, for example, if I know that it is contradictory to suppose that the axiom of choice and the continuum hypothesis are not independent, then I know that the axiom of choice is independent of the continuum hypothesis. It is not the logical impossibility of error by itself that guarantees knowledge but only *knowledge* of the logical impossibility. *If* we know that it is logically impossible that certain of our beliefs are mistaken, then, no doubt, we know that those beliefs are true. But this *if* is the noose that strangles dogmatism. For, even if we agree it is logically impossible for certain contingent beliefs to be mistaken, still it does not follow that we *know* that it is logically impossible for those beliefs to be mistaken, and, hence it does not follow that we know that the beliefs are true. A sceptic may contend that we do not *know* that

anything is logically impossible however strongly convinced we may be. And he may conclude that we do not know that those beliefs are true even where the logical possibility of error is excluded, because we do not know that the logical possibility of error is excluded.

. . . I have argued that scepticism is logically consistent. . . . He denies what we assert and there is nothing inconsistent or semantically unacceptable in so doing. Language allows for such radical disagreement as that between the sceptic and his detractors. It is this resource of language that provides for possibility of speculation and innovation. Thus, the question to which we must now turn is this—if the position of scepticism is neither meaningless nor contradictory, then why not scepticism?

VIII

The most common answer stems from Thomas Reid. It is based on the assumption that some beliefs are completely justified, because they are beliefs of a special kind which are justified without any supporting justificatory argument.[2] Beliefs of this kind are *basic* beliefs. Thus, if a man believes *that p*, where this is a basic belief of kind K, then he is completely justified in believing *that p* without argument unless there is some good reason for believing *p* to be false. The kind K of basic beliefs may be specified differently by philosophers of different epistemic biases, which already offers succor to the sceptic, but dogmatists have generally agreed that at least some kinds of perceptual beliefs, memory beliefs, and beliefs concerning our conscious states are among them.

Now it is not at all difficult to conceive of some hypothesis that would yield the conclusion that beliefs of the kind in question are not justified, indeed, which if true would justify us in concluding that the beliefs in question were more often false than true. The sceptical hypothesis might run as follows. There are a group of creatures in another galaxy, call them Googols, whose intellectual capacity is 10^{100} that of men, and who amuse themselves by sending out a peculiar kind of wave that affects our brain in such a way that our beliefs about the world are mostly incorrect. This form of error infects beliefs of every kind, but most of our beliefs, though erroneous, are nevertheless very nearly correct. This allows us to survive and manipulate our environment. However, whether any belief of any man is correct or even nearly correct depends entirely on the whimsy of some Googol rather than on the capacities and faculties of the man. If you are inclined to wonder why the Googols do not know anything, it is because there is another group of men, call them Googolplexes, whose intellectual capacity is 10^{100} that of the Googols, and who amuse themselves by sending out a peculiar wave that affects the brains of Googols in such a way that . . . I think you can see how the story goes from here. I shall refer to this hypothesis as the *sceptical hypothesis*. On such a hypothesis our beliefs about our conscious states, what we perceive by our senses, or recall from memory, are more often erroneous than correct. Such a sceptical hypothesis as this would, the sceptic argues, entail that the beliefs in question are not completely justified.

The reply of the dogmatist to such imaginings might be that we are not only justified in those basic beliefs, we are also justified in rejecting any hypothesis, such as the sceptical one, which conflicts with those beliefs. But the sceptic may surely intercede long enough to protest that he has been ruled out by fiat. The beliefs of common sense are said to be basic and thus completely justified without any justificatory arguments. But why, the sceptic may query, should the dogmatists' beliefs be considered completely justified without argument and his hypothesis be rejected without argument? Dogmatists affirm that the beliefs of common sense are innocent until proven guilty, but why, the sceptic might inquire, should his hypothesis not receive comparable treatment before the bar of evidence? Why not regard the sceptical hypothesis as innocent until proven guilty? Indeed, the sceptic might continue, why not regard all belief as innocent until proven guilty? And, he might add, where all is innocence, nothing is justified or unjustified, which is precisely the agnoiology of scepticism.

Some opponents of scepticism have been willing to concede that unless we hold some beliefs to be justified without argument, then we must surely accept the conclusion of scepticism. But, when replying to the sceptic, it will not do to say that we must regard the beliefs of common sense as justified or else we shall wind up on the road to scepticism. For that is precisely the route the sceptic would have us travel.

Let me clarify the preceding argument. In one passage, Bishop Berkeley replies to a dogmatist by appeal to the agnoiological precept that the burden of proof always lies with the affirmative. The precept could be doubted, and generally arguments about where the burden of proof lies are unproductive. It is more reasonable to suppose that such questions are best left to courts of law where they have suitable application. In philosophy a different principle of agnoiology is appropriate, to wit, that no hypothesis should be rejected as unjustified without argument against it. Consequently, if the sceptic puts forth a hypothesis inconsistent with the hypotheses of common sense, then there is not burden of proof on either side, but neither may one side to the dispute be judged unjustified in believing his hypothesis unless an argument is produced to show that this is so. If contradictory hypotheses are put forth without reason being given to show that one side is correct and the other in error, then neither party may be fairly stigmatized as unjustified. However, if a belief is completely justified, then those with which it conflicts are unjustified. Therefore, if neither of the conflicting hypotheses is shown to be unjustified, then we must refrain from concluding that belief in one of the hypotheses is completely justified.

We have here an argument that does not prejudicially presuppose that the burden of proof rests on one side or the other but instead takes an impartial view of the matter and refuses to side with either party until some argument has been given. Thomas Reid was wont to argue that the beliefs of common sense had a right of ancient possession and were justified until shown to be unjustified. But such epistemology favors the sentiments of conservative defenders of the status quo in both philosophy and politics. And the principle that, what is, is justified, is not a better principle of epistemology than of politics or morals. It should be supplanted by the agnoiological principle of impartiality. Thus, before scepticism may be rejected as unjustified, some argument must be given to show that the infamous hypotheses employed by sceptics are incorrect and the beliefs of common sense have the truth on their side. If this is not done, then the beliefs of common sense are not completely justified, because conflicting sceptical hypotheses have not been shown to be unjustified. From this premiss it follows in a single step that we do not know those beliefs to be true because they are not completely justified. And then the sceptic wins the day.

IX

The preceding agnoiological argument can be extended to defeat a whole range of alleged refutations of scepticism. For example, some philosophers have rejected scepticism on the grounds that the sceptic is denying our standards of evidence or our criteria of justification or something of the sort. Now, of course, this may be trivially true; obviously the sceptic is denying that we are completely justified in certain beliefs which we consider to be completely justified, and if that constitutes rejecting our ordinary standards or criteria of evidence, then the sceptic is indeed denying them. But that is no argument against the sceptic; it is a restatement of his position. Unless we can show that the sceptical hypothesis is false, we cannot justly conclude that it is unjustified. In that case our beliefs, which contradict the sceptical hypotheses, are not completely justified. So much the worse for our standards or criteria of evidence.

Next, there are arguments claiming that the sceptic is making proposals which undermine our conceptual framework and change the very concepts we use to formulate our beliefs. The reply is twofold. Sometimes talking about changing concepts is a disguised way of talking about changing meaning of words. I have already argued that scepticism does not have that consequence. So I discount that contention. Other than that, the change of concepts implied by scepticism seems to me, to amount to no more than a change of belief, perhaps of very fundamental beliefs. The reply to this objection is that first, the agnoiology of the sceptic allows him to embrace most of the same beliefs we do. He need not *believe* the sceptical hypothesis to argue that if the sceptical hypothesis is true, then our more familiar beliefs are more often false than true. By thus employing the hypothesis, he has placed us in a position of either showing the hypothesis to be false, or else conceding that our beliefs are not completely justified. Thus the sceptic need not advocate ceasing to

believe those fundamental hypotheses which constitute the assumptions, presuppositions, or what not of our conceptual framework. He only denies that we know those beliefs to be true.

Thus appeals to ancient rights, standards of evidence, and conceptual frameworks are all equally ineffective against the basic challenge of scepticism, to wit—either show that the sceptical hypothesis is false and unjustified or concede that beliefs inconsistent with that hypothesis are not completely justified!

X

We must now turn to a rather different sort of maneuver against the sceptic. It might be conceded that we cannot show that our beliefs are true and the sceptical hypothesis false, but contended that we can show that our beliefs are completely justified, not perhaps for the purpose of arriving at the truth, but for other epistemic ends. Thus it has been proposed that we believe whatever will facilitate explanation and increase our information. If a person is seeking to have beliefs which facilitate explanation and increase information, then he is completely justified in adopting beliefs contributing to those objectives. This argument against scepticism is, I believe, the very strongest that can be offered. For, even if we can offer no argument to show that our beliefs are true and the sceptical hypothesis false, still we may be completely justified in our beliefs in terms of objectives other than truth.

Finally, the move has an intuitive appeal. For, the sceptical hypothesis according to which most of our beliefs arise because of the deception of Googols yields results that would make it difficult to explain in a satisfactory manner what we believe to be the case and, it would make it even more difficult for us to increase our information about the world. Many generalizations about the world, and theories as well, would turn out to be incorrect on that hypothesis, thus making explanation difficult and complicated. Moreover, we would, by hypothesis, have no way of telling when our beliefs give us information about the world and when we are simply being misled by the Googols. All in all the sceptical hypothesis is quite unsatisfactory from the standpoint of explaining things and increasing our information; so unsatisfactory that anyone seeking to explain as much as possible and to increase his information as much as possible would be completely justified in rejecting it.

Is there any reply to this line of argument? The sceptic might reply that he is under no obligation to accept the ends of facilitating explanation and increasing information. But this will not refute the claim that we who do accept such ends are completely justified in believing what we do for the sake of obtaining those objectives. There is a better line of reply available to the sceptic, namely, that our disregard for truth will, in the final accounting, destroy our assets. For agnoiology shows that such pragmatic justification of belief ultimately depends on the assumption that the beliefs are true. Suppose we adopt those beliefs that are most full of explanatory power and informative content, and those admirable beliefs turn out to be false. In that case, by adopting those beliefs we shall have correctly explained nothing and increased our genuine information not at all. For any belief to correctly explain or genuinely inform it must first be true. Only what correctly explains or genuinely informs can constitute knowledge. Therefore, we must be completely justified in believing what we do simply because by so doing we shall obtain true beliefs, or else our beliefs are not completely justified in the manner requisite for knowledge.

XI

The preceding line of argument leads to an inevitable conclusion. To meet the agnoiological challenge of scepticism, we must provide some argument to show that the sceptical hypothesis is false and that the beliefs of common sense are correct. And this leads to a second equally inescapable conclusion. The challenge cannot be met. Many reasons may be given for not *believing* the sceptical hypothesis. Indeed, a sceptic himself need not believe the sceptical hypothesis, and he might agree that there are practical disadvantages in believing such a hypothesis. But he might justifiably insist that we are not completely justified in concluding that the hypothesis is *false*. The hypothesis might seem silly, it might interfere with the attempt to explain things, and it might make it

very difficult to arrive at any sensible set of beliefs for conducting practical affairs and scientific investigations. There are perfectly cogent practical considerations, the sceptic might concede, for not believing the hypothesis. However, agnoiology rejects the premiss contending that inconvenient hypotheses are false. To suppose that would be to trip back into the clutches of a simplistic pragmatism from which we have been rescued all too recently.

The principal argument offered to show that sceptical hypotheses are false is simply that they conflict with our dogmatic beliefs. Since it is precisely the justification of the latter that is in question, this conflict cannot be taken to adjudicate against the sceptical hypothesis. We are not completely justified in rejecting the sceptical hypothesis, and thus we are not completely justified in believing the others. We do not know that the sceptical hypothesis is false, and thus we do not know that anything else is true. That is the agnoiology that sustains scepticism.

XII

In conclusion, let me remark that we need not mourn the passing of knowledge as a great loss. The assumption of dogmatists that some beliefs are completely justified and that they are true, is not a great asset in scientific inquiry where all contentions should be subject to question and must be defended on demand. Moreover, the sceptic is not deprived of those practical beliefs necessary to carrying on the business of practical affairs. Indeed, economists and philosophers have suggested that an analysis of rational choice requires only subjective probability, which is a coherent measure of belief, and the utilities we attach to various outcomes.

It might seem that to introduce an appeal to probabilities is to concede the day to scepticism because the probabilities must be based on observational evidence and the latter must be something we know to be true. But this objection is unsound. First, as Richard Jeffrey has shown, we may employ a concept of subjective probability in which no observation statement is assigned a probability of unity.[3] Moreover, we may reassign probabilities on the basis of sense experience without assigning the probability of unity to any such statement. Finally, even if we do assign a probability of unity to a statement, for example, to a tautology, we need not interpret this assignment as meaning that we know the statement to be true. To be sure, the statement must have a kind of subjective certainty, but this may be analyzed in terms of the betting preferences of the subject rather than as knowledge. If there is any statement of which a person feels so certain that he would prefer to bet the statement is true rather than false no matter what the odds, then the subjective probability of that statement for that man is unity. It does not follow that he knows the statement to be true.

Finally, I would contend that just as we can give an analysis of rational decision in terms of probabilities and practical values, so we can give an analysis of rational belief on the basis of probabilities and epistemic values. In the first case we maximize practical utilities and in the second case we maximize epistemic ones. Neither analysis requires the assumption that we know anything. We can instead regard practical action and scientific inquiry as aiming at the satisfaction of objectives appropriate to each sphere. We change our beliefs to better satisfy those objectives. Thus, we may, while remaining sceptics, contend that our beliefs and actions are rational even though we agree that such beliefs are not so completely justified as to constitute knowledge. As such, all beliefs, even those we consider rational, are subject to critical review. None can be exempted from evaluation on the grounds that it is known to be true without need of supporting argument. Such are the fruits of agnoiology.

Notes

[1] James F. Ferrier, *Institutes of Metaphysics* (Edinburgh and London: William Blackwood & Sons, 1854).

[2] Thomas Reid, *The Works of Thomas Reid, D.D.* (Edinburgh: Maclaugh and Steward, 1863), p. 234.

[3] Richard Jeffrey, *The Logic of Decision* (New York: McGraw-Hill, 1965).

II.5 Two Types of Knowledge

NORMAN MALCOLM

Norman Malcolm (1911–1990) was for many years professor of philosophy at Cornell University. Malcolm begins this essay with a quotation from the British philosopher H. A. Prichard to the effect that we can discover in ourselves whether we *know* some proposition or whether we merely *believe* it. Does knowledge light up a mental state different from that lighted up by belief? Malcolm rejects this thesis on one level of discourse, but he argues that Prichard's distinction does convey insight. Some beliefs or knowledge claims seem so self-evident that we cannot conceive of anything undermining them. Malcolm distinguishes two types of knowledge: weak and strong. Regarding our weak knowledge claims, we are willing to let further investigation determine whether we really have knowledge or not, but regarding strong knowledge we feel absolute certainty, so that no evidence could count against it.

"We must recognize that when we know some-thing we either do, or by reflecting, can know that our condition is one of knowing that thing, while when we believe something, we either do or can know that our condition is one of believing and not of knowing: so that we cannot mistake belief for knowledge or vice versa."[1]

This remark is worthy of investigation. Can I discover *in myself* whether I know something or merely believe it?

Let us begin by studying the ordinary usage of "know" and "believe." Suppose, for example, that several of us intend to go for a walk and that you propose that we walk in Cascadilla Gorge. I protest that I should like to walk beside a flowing stream and that at this season the gorge is proba-bly dry. Consider the following cases:

(1) You say "I believe that it won't be dry although I have no particular reason for thinking so." If we went to the gorge and found a flowing stream we should not say that you *knew* that there would be water but that you thought so and were right.

(2) You say "I believe that it won't be dry because it rained only three days ago and usually water flows in the gorge for at least that long after a rain." If we found water we should be inclined to say that you knew that there would be water. It would be quite natural for you to say "I knew that it wouldn't be dry"; and we should tolerate your remark. This case differs from the previous one in that here you had a *reason*.

(3) You say "I know that it won't be dry" and give the same reason as in (2). If we found water we should have very little hesitation in saying that you knew. Not only had you a reason, but you *said* "I know" instead of "I believe." It may seem to us that the latter should not make a difference— but it does.

(4) You say "I know that it won't be dry" and give a stronger reason, e.g., "I saw a lot of water flowing in the gorge when I passed it this morn-ing." If we went and found water, there would be no hesitation at all in saying that you knew. If, for example, we later met someone who said "Weren't you surprised to see water in the gorge this after-

noon?" you would reply "No, I *knew* that there would be water; I had been there earlier in the day." We should have no objection to this statement.

(5) Everything happens as in (4), except that upon going to the gorge we find it to be dry. We should not say that you knew, but that you *believed* that there would be water. And this is true even though you declared that you knew, and even though your evidence was the same as it was in case (4) in which you did know.

I wish to make some comments on the usage of "know," "knew," "believe," and "believed," as illustrated in the preceding cases:

(a) Whether we should say that you knew, depends in part on whether you had grounds for your assertion and on the strength of those grounds. There would certainly be less hesitation to say that you knew in case (4) than in case (3), and this can be due only to the difference in the strength of the grounds.

(b) Whether we should say that you knew, depends in part on how *confident* you were. In case (2), if you had said "It rained only three days ago and usually water flows in the gorge for at least that long after a rain; but, of course, I don't feel absolutely sure that there will be water," then we should *not* have said that you knew that there would be water. If you lack confidence that *p* is true then others do not say that you know that *p* is true, even though *they* know that *p* is true. Being confident is a necessary condition for knowing.

(c) Prichard says that if we reflect we cannot mistake belief for knowledge. In case (4) you knew that there would be water, and in case (5) you merely believed it. Was there any way that you could have discovered by reflection, in case (5), that you did not know? It would have been useless to have reconsidered your grounds for saying that there would be water, because in case (4), where you *did* know, your grounds were identical. They could be at fault in (5) only if they were at fault in (4), and they were not at fault in (4). Cases (4) and (5) differ in only one respect—namely, that in one case you did subsequently find water and in the other you did not. Prichard says that we can determine by reflection whether we know some-thing or merely believe it. But where, in these cases, is the material that reflection would strike upon? There is none.

There is only one way that Prichard could defend his position. He would have to say that in

Originally published in *Mind* 51 (1952), 178–189. Reprinted in its revised form from *Knowledge and Certainty: Essays and Lectures by Norman Malcolm* (Englewood Cliffs, N.J.: Prentice Hall, 1963).

case (4) you did *not* know that there would be water. And it is obvious that he would have said this. But this is false. It is an enormously common usage of language to say, in commenting upon just such an incident as (4), "He knew that the gorge would be not dry because he had seen water flowing there that morning." It is a usage that all of us are familiar with. We so employ "know" and "knew" every day of our lives. We do not think of our usage as being loose or incorrect—and it is not. As philosophers we may be surprised to observe that it *can* be that the knowledge that *p* is true should differ from the belief that *p* is true *only* in the respect that in one case *p* is true and in the other false. But that is the fact.

There is an argument that one is inclined to use as a proof that you did not know that there would be water. The argument is the following: It could have turned out that you found no water; if it had so turned out you would have been mistaken in saying that you would find water; therefore you could have been mistaken; but if you could have been mistaken then you did not know.

Now it certainly *could* have turned out that the gorge was quite dry when you went there, even though you saw lots of water flowing through it only a few hours before. This does not show, however, that you did not know that there would be water. What it shows is that *although you knew you could have been mistaken*.[2] This would seem to be a contradictory result; but it is not. It seems so because our minds are fixed upon another usage of "know" and "knew"; one in which "It could have turned out that I was mistaken," implies "I did not know."

When is "know" used in this sense? I believe that Prichard uses it in this sense when he says that when we go through the proof of the proposition that the angles of a triangle are equal to two right angles we *know* that the proposition is true (p. 89). He says that if we put to ourselves the question: Is our condition one of knowing this, or is it only one of being convinced of it? then "We can only answer 'Whatever may be our state on other occasions, here we are knowing this.' And this statement is an expression of our *knowing* that we are knowing; for we do not *believe* that we are knowing this, we know that we are" (p. 89). He goes on to say that if someone were to object that we might be making a mistake "because for all we know we can later on discover some fact which is

incompatible with a triangle's having angles that are equal to two right angles, we can answer that we *know* that there can be no such fact, for in knowing that a triangle must have such angles we also know that nothing can exist which is incompatible with this fact" (p. 90).

It is easy to imagine a non-philosophical context in which it would have been natural for Prichard to have said "I know that the angles of a triangle are equal to two right angles." Suppose that a young man just beginning the study of geometry was in doubt as to whether that proposition is true, and had even constructed an ingenious argument that appeared to prove it false. Suppose that Prichard was unable to find any error in the argument. He might have said to the young man: "There must be an error in it. I know that the angles of a triangle are equal to two right angles."

When Prichard says that "nothing can exist which is incompatible with" the truth of that proposition, is he prophesying that no one will ever have the ingenuity to construct a flawless-looking argument against it? I believe not. When Prichard says that "we" *know* (and implies that *he* knows) that the proposition is true and *know* that nothing can exist that is incompatible with its being true, he is not making any *prediction* as to what the future will bring in the way of arguments or measurements. On the contrary, he is asserting that *nothing* that the future might bring could ever count as evidence against the proposition. He is implying that he would not *call* anything "evidence" against it. He is using "know" in what I shall call its "strong" sense. "Know" is used in this sense when a person's statement "I know that *p* is true" implies that the person who makes the statement would look upon nothing whatever as evidence that *p* is false.

It must not be assumed that whenever "know" is used in connexion with mathematical propositions it is used in the strong sense. A great many people have *heard* of various theorems of geometry, e.g., the Pythagorean. These theorems are a part of "common knowledge." If a school-boy doing his geometry assignment felt a doubt about the Pythagorean theorem, and said to an adult "Are you *sure* that it is true?" the latter might reply "Yes, I know that it is." He might make this reply even though he could not give proof of it and even though he had never gone through a proof of it. If subsequently he was presented with a "demonstration" that the theorem is false, or if various persons reputed to have a knowledge of geometry soberly assured him that it is false, he might be filled with doubt or even be convinced that he was mistaken. When he said "Yes, I know that it is true," he did not pledge himself to hold to the theorem through thick and thin. He did not absolutely exclude the possibility that something could prove it to be false. I shall say that he used "know" in the "weak" sense.

Consider another example from mathematics of the difference between the strong and weak senses of "know." I have just now rapidly calculated that 92 times 16 is 1472. If I had done this in the commerce of daily life where a practical problem was at stake, and if someone had asked "Are you sure that 92 × 16 = 1472?" I might have answered "I *know* that it is; I have just now calculated it." But also I might have answered "I know that it is; but I will calculate it again to *make sure.*" And here my language points to a distinction. I say that I *know* that 92 × 16 = 1472. Yet I am willing to *confirm* it—that is, there is something that I should *call* "making sure;" and, likewise, there is something that I should *call* "finding out that it is false." If I were to do this calculation again and obtain the result that 92 × 16 = 1372, and if I were to carefully check this later calculation without finding any error, I should be disposed to say that I was previously mistaken when I declared that 92 × 16 = 1472. Thus when I say that I know that 92 × 16 = 1472, I allow for the possibility of a *refutation*, and so I am using "know" in its weak sense.

Now consider propositions like 2 + 2 = 4 and 7 + 5 = 12. It is hard to think of circumstances in which it would be natural for me to say that I know that 2 + 2 = 4, because no one ever questions it. Let us try to suppose, however, that someone whose intelligence I respect argues that certain developments in arithmetic have shown that 2 + 2 does not equal 4. He writes out a proof of this in which I can find no flaw. Suppose that his demeanor showed me that he was in earnest. Suppose that several persons of normal intelligence became persuaded that his proof was correct and that 2 + 2 does not equal 4. What would be my reaction? I should say "I can't see what is wrong with your proof; but it *is* wrong, because I *know* that 2 + 2 = 4." Here I should be using "know" in its strong sense. I should not admit that

any argument or any future development in mathematics could show that it is false that 2 + 2 = 4.

The propositions 2 + 2 = 4 and 92 × 16 = 1472 do not have the same status. There *can* be a demonstration that 2 + 2 = 4. But a demonstration would be for me (and for any average person) only a curious exercise, a sort of *game*. We have no serious interest in proving that proposition. It does not *need* a proof. It stands without one, and would not fall if a proof went against it. The case is different with the proposition that 92 × 16 = 1472. We take an interest in the demonstration (calculation) because that proposition *depends* upon its demonstration. A calculation may lead me to reject it as false. But 2 + 2 = 4 does not depend on its demonstration. It does not depend on anything! And in the calculation that proves that 92 × 16 = 1472, there are steps that do not depend on any calculation (e.g., 2 × 6 = 12; 5 + 2 = 7; 5 + 9 = 14).

There is a correspondence between this dualism in the logical status of mathematical propositions and the two senses of "know." When I use "know" in the weak sense I am prepared to let an investigation (demonstration, calculation) determine whether the something that I claim to know is true or false. When I use "know" in the strong sense I am not prepared to look upon anything as an *investigation;* I do not concede that anything whatsoever could prove me mistaken; I do not regard the matter as open to any *question;* I do not admit that my proposition could turn out to be false, that any future investigation *could* refute it or cast doubt on it.

We have been considering the strong sense of "know" in its application to mathematical propositions. Does it have application anywhere in the realm of *empirical* propositions—for example, to propositions that assert or imply that certain physical things exist? Descartes said that we have a "moral assurance" of the truth of some of the latter propositions but that we lack a "metaphysical certainty." Locke said that the perception of the existence of physical things is not "so certain as our intuitive knowledge, or the deductions of our reason" although "it is an assurance that deserves the name of knowledge." Some philosophers have held that when we make judgements of perception such as that there are peonies in the garden, cows in the field, or dishes in the cupboard, we are "taking for granted" that the peonies, cows, and dishes exist, but not knowing it in the "strict" sense.

Others have held that all empirical propositions, including judgements of perception, are merely hypotheses. The thought behind this exaggerated mode of expression is that any empirical proposition whatever *could* be refuted by future experience—that is, it *could* turn out to be false. Are these philosophers right?

Consider the following propositions:

i. The sun is about ninety million miles from the earth.
ii. There is a heart in my body.
iii. Here is an ink-bottle.

In various circumstances I should be willing to assert of each of these propositions that I know it to be true. Yet they differ strikingly. This I see when, with each, I try to imagine the possibility that it is false.

(i) If in ordinary conversation someone said to me "The sun is about twenty million miles from the earth, isn't it?" I should reply "No, it is about ninety million miles from us." If he said "I think that you are confusing the sun with Polaris," I should reply, "I *know* that ninety million miles is roughly the sun's distance from the earth." I might invite him to verify the figure in an encyclopedia. A third person who overheard our conversation could quite correctly report that I knew the distance to the sun, whereas the other man did not. But this knowledge of mine is little better than hearsay. I have seen that figure mentioned in a few books. I know nothing about the observations and calculations that led astronomers to accept it. If tomorrow a group of eminent astronomers announced that a great error had been made and that the correct figure is twenty million miles, I should not insist that they were wrong. It would surprise me that such an enormous mistake could have been made. But I should no longer be willing to say that I *know* that ninety million is the correct figure. Although I should *now* claim that I know the distance to be about ninety million miles, it is easy for me to envisage the possibility that some future investigation will prove this to be false.

(ii) Suppose that after a routine medical examination the excited doctor reports to me that the X-ray photographs show that I have no heart. I should tell him to get a new machine. I should be inclined to say that the fact that I

have a heart is one of the few things that I can count on as absolutely certain. I can feel it beat. I know it's there. Furthermore, how could my blood circulate if I didn't have one? Suppose that later on I suffer a chest injury and undergo a surgical operation. Afterwards the astonished surgeons solemnly declare that they searched my chest cavity and found no heart, and that they made incisions and looked about in other likely places but found it not. They are convinced that I am without a heart. They are unable to understand how circulation can occur or what accounts for the thumping in my chest. But they are in agreement and obviously sincere, and they have clear photographs of my interior spaces. What would be my attitude? Would it be to insist that they were all mistaken? I think not. I believe that I should eventually accept their testimony and the evidence of the photographs. I should consider to be false what I now regard as an absolute certainty.

(iii) Suppose that as I write this paper someone in the next room were to call out to me "I can't find an ink-bottle; is there one in the house?" I should reply "Here is an ink-bottle." If he said in a doubtful tone "Are you sure? I looked there before," I should reply "Yes, I know there is; come and get it."

Now could it turn out to be false that there is an ink-bottle directly in front of me on this desk? Many philosophers have thought so. They would say that many things could happen of such a nature that if they did happen it would be proved that I am deceived. I agree that many extraordinary things could happen, in the sense that there is no logical absurdity in the supposition. It could happen that when I next reach for this ink-bottle my hand should seem to pass *through* it and I should not feel the contact of any object. It could happen that in the next moment the ink-bottle will suddenly vanish from sight; or that I should find myself under a tree in the garden with no ink-bottle about; or that one or more persons should enter this room and declare with apparent sincerity that they see no ink-bottle on this desk; or that a photograph taken now of the top of the desk should clearly show all of the objects on it except the ink-bottle. Having admitted that these things *could happen*, am I compelled to admit that if they did happen then it would be proved that there is no ink-bottle here *now*? Not at all! I could say that when my hand seemed to pass through the ink-bottle I should *then* be suffering from hallucination; that if the ink-bottle suddenly vanished it would have miraculously ceased to exist; that the other persons were conspiring to drive me mad, or were themselves victims of remarkable concurrent hallucinations; that the camera possessed some strange flaw or that there was trickery in developing the negative. I admit that in the next moment I could find myself under a tree or in the bathtub. But this is not to admit that it could be revealed in the next moment that I am now dreaming. For what I admit is that I might be instantaneously transported to the garden, but not that in the next moment I might *wake up* in the garden. There is nothing that could happen to me in the next moment that I should call "waking up"; and therefore nothing that could happen to me in the next moment would be accepted by me now as proof that I now dream.

Not only do I not *have* to admit that those extraordinary occurrences would be evidence that there is no ink-bottle here; the fact is that I *do not* admit it. There is nothing whatever that could happen in the next moment or the next year that would by me be called *evidence* that there is not an ink-bottle here now. No future experience or investigation could prove to me that I am mistaken. Therefore, if I were to say "I know that there is an ink-bottle here," I should be using "know" in the strong sense.

It will appear to some that I have adopted an *unreasonable* attitude towards that statement. There is, however, nothing unreasonable about it. It seems so because one thinks that the statement that there is an ink-bottle *must* have the same status as the statements that the sun is ninety million miles away and that I have a heart and that there will be water in the gorge this afternoon. But this is a *prejudice*.

In saying that I should regard nothing as evidence that there is no ink-bottle here now, I am not *predicting* what I should do if various astonishing things happened. If other members of my family entered this room and, while looking at the top of this desk, declared with apparent sincerity that they see no ink-bottle, I might fall into a swoon or become mad. I *might* even come to believe that there is not and has not been an ink-bottle here. I cannot foretell with certainty how I should react. But if it is *not* a prediction, what is the meaning of

my assertion that I should regard nothing as evidence that there is no ink-bottle here?

That assertion describes my *present* attitude towards the statement that here is an ink-bottle. It does not prophesy what my attitude *would* be if various things happened. My present attitude towards that statement is radically different from my present attitude towards those other statements (e.g., that I have a heart). I do *now* admit that certain future occurrences would disprove the latter. Whereas no imaginable future occurrence would be considered by me *now* as proving that there is not an ink-bottle here.

These remarks are not meant to be autobiographical. They are meant to throw light on the common concepts of evidence, proof, and disproof. Every one of us upon innumerable occasions of daily life takes this same attitude towards various statements about physical things, e.g., that here is a torn page, that this dish is broken, that the thermometer reads 70, that no rug is on the floor. Furthermore, the concepts of proof, disproof, doubt, and conjecture *require* us to take this attitude. In order for it to be possible that any statements about physical things should *turn out to be false* it is necessary that some statements about physical things *cannot* turn out to be false.

This will be made clear if we ask ourselves the question, When do we *say* that something turned out to be false? When do we use those words? Someone asks you for a dollar. You say "There is one in this drawer." You open the drawer and look, but it is perfectly empty. Your statement turned out to be false. This can be said because you *discovered* an empty drawer. It could not be said if it were only probable that the drawer is empty or were still open to question. Would it make sense to say "I had better make sure that it is empty; perhaps there is a dollar in it after all?" Sometimes; but not always. Not if the drawer lies open before your eyes. That remark is the prelude to a search. What search can there be when the emptiness of the drawer confronts you? In certain circumstances there is nothing that you would call "making sure" that the drawer is empty; and likewise nothing that you would call "its turning out to be false" that the drawer is empty. You *made* sure that the drawer is empty. One statement about physical things *turned out to be false* only because you *made sure* of another statement about physical things. The two concepts cannot exist apart. Therefore it is impossible that *every* statement about physical things *could* turn out to be false.

In a certain important respect some a priori statements and some empirical statements possess the same logical character. The statements that 5 × 5 = 25 and that here is an ink-bottle, both lie beyond the reach of doubt. On both, my judgement and reasoning *rests*. If you could somehow undermine my confidence in either, you would not teach me *caution*. You would fill my mind with chaos! I could not even make *conjectures* if you took away those fixed points of certainty; just as a man cannot *try* to climb whose body has no support. A conjecture implies an understanding of what certainty would be. If it is not a certainty that 5 × 5 = 25 and that here is an ink-bottle, then I do not understand what it is. You cannot make me doubt either of these statements or treat them as hypotheses. You cannot persuade me that future experience could refute them. With both of them it is perfectly unintelligible to me to speak of a "possibility" that they are false. This is to say that I know both of them to be true, in the strong sense of "know." And I am inclined to think that the strong sense of "know" is what various philosophers have had in mind when they have spoken of "perfect," "metaphysical," or "strict certainty."

It will be thought that I have confused a statement about my "sensations," or my "sense-data," or about the way something *looks* or *appears* to me, with a statement about physical things. It will be thought that the things that I have said about the statement "Here is an ink-bottle" could be true only if that statement is interpreted to mean something like "There appears to me to be an ink-bottle here," i.e., interpreted so as not to assert or imply that any physical thing exists. I wish to make it clear that my statement "Here is an ink-bottle" is *not* to be interpreted in that way. It would be utterly fantastic for me in my present circumstances to say "There appears to me to be an ink-bottle here."

If someone were to call me on the telephone and say that he urgently needed an ink-bottle I should invite him to come here and get this one. If he said that it was extremely urgent that he should obtain one immediately and that he could not afford to waste time going to a place where there might not be one, I should tell him that it is an absolute certainty that there is one here, that nothing could be more certain, that it is some-

thing I absolutely guarantee. But if my statement "There is an ink-bottle here" were a statement about my "sensations" or "sense-data," or if it meant that there *appears* to me to be an ink-bottle here or that something here *looks* to me like an ink-bottle, and if that is all that I meant by it—then I should react quite differently to his urgent request. I should say that there is probably an ink-bottle here but that I could not *guarantee* it, and that if he needs one very desperately and at once then he had better look elsewhere. In short, I wish to make it clear that my statement "Here is an ink-bottle" is strictly about physical things and not about "sensations," "sense-data," or "appearances."

Let us go back to Prichard's remark that we can determine by reflection whether we know something or merely believe it. Prichard would think that "knowledge in the weak sense" is mere belief and not knowledge. This is wrong. But if we let ourselves speak this way, we can then see some justification for Prichard's remark. For then he would be asserting, among other things, that we can determine by reflection whether we know something in the strong sense or in the weak sense. This is not literally true; however, there is this truth in it—that reflection can make us realize that we are *using* "I know it" in the strong (or weak) sense in a particular case. Prichard says that reflection can show us that "our condition is one of knowing" a certain thing, or instead that "our condition is one of believing and not of knowing" that thing. I do not understand what could be meant here by "our condition." The way I should put it is that reflection on *what we should think* if certain things were to happen may make us realize that we should (or should not) call those things "proof" or "evidence" that what we claim to know is not so. I have tried to show that the distinction between strong and weak knowledge does not run parallel to the distinction between a priori and empirical knowledge but cuts across it, i.e., these two kinds of knowledge may be distinguished *within* a priori knowledge and *within* empirical knowledge.

Reflection can make me realize that I am using "know" in the strong sense; but can reflection show me that I *know* something in the strong sense (or in the weak)? It is not easy to state the logical facts here. On the one hand, if I make an assertion of the form "I know that *p*" it does not follow that *p*, whether or not I am using "know" in the strong sense. If I have said to someone outside my room "Of course, I know that Freddie is in here," and I am speaking in the strong sense, it does not *follow* that Freddie is where I claim he is. This logical fact would not be altered even if I *realized* that I was using "know" in the strong sense. My reflection on what I should say if . . . , cannot show me that I *know* something. From the fact that I should not call anything "evidence" that Freddie is not here, it does not follow that he is here; therefore, it does not follow that I *know* he is here.

On the other hand, in an actual case of my using "know" in the strong sense, I cannot envisage a possibility that what I say to be true should turn out to be not true. If I were speaking of *another person's* assertion about something, I *could* think both that he is using "know" in the strong sense and that nonetheless what he claims he knows to be so might turn out to be not so. But *in my own case* I cannot have this conjunction of thoughts, and this is a logical and not a psychological fact. When *I* say that I know something to be so, using "know" in the strong sense, it is unintelligible *to me* (although perhaps not to others) to suppose that anything could prove that it is not so and, therefore, that I do not know it.

Notes

[1] H. A. Prichard, *Knowledge and Perception* (Oxford: Clarendon Press, 1950), p. 88.

[2] Some readers seem to have thought that I was denying here that "I knew that *p*" entails "that *p*." That was not my intention, and my words do not have that implication. If I has said "*although you knew you were mistaken,*" I should have denied the above entailment and, also, I should have misused "knew." The difference between the strong and the weak senses of "know" (and "knew") is not that this entailment holds for the strong but not for the weak sense. It holds for both. If it is false that *p*, then one does not (and did not) know that *p*.

Bibliography

Burnyeat, Myles, ed. *The Skeptical Tradition.* Berkeley: University of California Press, 1983.

Clay, Marjorie, and Keith Lehrer, eds. *Knowledge and Skepticism.* Boulder, CO: Westview Press, 1989.

Hookway, Christopher. *Skepticism.* London: Routledge & Kegan Paul, 1990.

Johnson, Oliver. *Skepticism and Cognition.* Berkeley: University of California Press, 1978.

Klein, Peter. *Certainty: A Refutation of Scepticism.* Minneapolis: University of Minnesota Press, 1981.

Landesman, J. Charles. *Skepticism.* Blackwell's, 2002.

Pojman, Louis P. *What Can We Know? An Introduction to the Theory of Knowledge.* Belmont CA: Wadsworth, 2001. Chaps. 2 and 3.

Rescher, Nicholas. *Skepticism: A Critical Reappraisal.* Totowa, NJ: Rowman & Littlefield, 1980.

Sextus Empiricus. *Selections from the Major Writings on Scepticism.* Trans. Sanford Ethridge; ed. Philip Hallie. Indianapolis: Hackett, 1985.

Stroud, Barry. *The Significance of Philosophical Skepticism.* Oxford: Oxford University Press, 1984.

Unger, Peter. *Ignorance: A Case for Skepticism.* Oxford: Clarendon Press, 1975.

Unger, Peter. "A Defense of Skepticism." *Philosophical Review 80* (1971).

Williams, Michael. *Unnatural Doubts.* Oxford: Blackwell, 1991.

Part III

Perception: Our Knowledge of the External World

In daily life, we assume as certain many things which, on a closer scrutiny, are found to be so full of apparent contradictions that only a great amount of thought enables us to know what it is that we really may believe. In the search for certainty, it is natural to begin with our present experiences, and in some sense, no doubt, knowledge is to be derived from them. But any statement as to what it is that our immediate experience makes us know is very likely to be wrong. It seems to me that I am now sitting in a chair, at a table of a certain shape, on which I see sheets of paper with writing or print. . . . I believe that, if any other normal person comes into my room, he will see the same chairs and tables and books as I see, and that the table which I see is the same as the table which I feel pressing against my arm. All this seems to be so evident as to be hardly worth stating, except in answer to a man who doubts whether I know anything. Yet all this may be reasonably doubted, and all of it requires much careful discussion before we can be sure that we have stated it in a form that is wholly true.

Bertrand Russell
Problems of Philosophy

What do we really know? Assuming that skepticism is false and that we do know something of the external world, what exactly do we know and how do we know it? Do we ever really see the book that appears in front of us, the table that it rests on, the floor on which we stand, the walls that surround us? What is the direct object of awareness when we perceive? Three answers have traditionally been given to that question: (1) direct realism (sometimes called "naive realism" or "commonsense realism"), (2) representationalism, and (3) phenomenalism. Direct realism claims that the immediate object of perception is a physical thing that exists independently of our awareness of it. Representationalism and phenomenalism answer that the immediate object of perception is a sense datum or sense impression—which cannot exist apart from our awareness of it. But representationalism and phenomenalism divide over the relationship of sense data to the physical world. For the representationalist, the physical world exists independently of and is the cause of our perceptions. Physical objects give rise to sense data that we perceive, so we only have mediate knowledge of the external world. For phenomenalism, physical objects are simply constructions of sense data. They do not exist independently of sense impressions.

Common sense tells us that we—through our five senses: sight, hearing, touch, taste, and smell—do directly perceive the real world. It tells us that the physical world exists independently of our awareness of it and that the things we perceive are pretty much the way we perceive them. They exist here and now. Common sense supports naive or direct realism.

Science casts doubt on common sense. As Bertrand Russell succinctly says, "Naive realism leads to physics, and physics, if true, shows that naive realism is false. Therefore, naive realism, if true, is false; therefore it is false."[1] Science tells us that the physical objects we perceive are not what they seem to be, nor do we ever see things in the present. Colors are not in the objects but are the way objects appear as they reflect light. Since light takes time to reach our eyes, all that we see really existed in the past. It takes eight minutes for the light from the sun to reach us and hundreds of years for the light from distant stars to reach us, so when we look (through the proper filtered lenses) at the sun or at distant stars we are not seeing them as they exist in the present but as they existed eight minutes or hundreds of years ago. In fact, there is nothing we see as it presently exists but only as it existed in the past (near or far).

Likewise, science tells us that the sounds we hear, the flavors we taste, the sensations of touch, and the odors we smell are not what they seem to be. They are mediated through our ways of perceiving so we seldom or never experience them as they really are in themselves.

So representationalism seems to succeed in giving an explanation of perception that is more faithful to science than is direct realism. Representationalism holds that the real world

causes our appearances or perceptions by representing the physical world through sense data, mental entities that are private to individual perceivers.

In the following readings, John Locke (1632–1704) sets forth the classic expression of this view. Attacking the notion that we have innate knowledge of metaphysical truths, Locke argues that all our knowledge derives ultimately from sense experience:

> Let us then suppose the mind to be, as we say, white paper, void of all characters, without any ideas; how comes it to be furnished? Whence comes it by that vast store which the busy and boundless fancy of man has painted on it with an almost endless variety? Whence has it all the materials of reason and knowledge? To this I answer, in one word, from experience; in all that our knowledge is founded, and from that it ultimately derives itself.

Locke held a causal theory of perception in which processes in the external world impinge on the perceiver's sense organs, which in turn send messages to the brain, where they are transformed into mental events. We may diagram Locke's causal theory of perception this way:

Objects and Events in the Real World

(Energy coming to sense organs: insensible particles reflected from the object onto the sense organ or coming into contact with the sense organ)

Sense Organs

(Signals to brain)

Brain Event

(Transformation from physical to mental event)

Perceptual Experience

The mechanical input yields the nonmechanical idea in the mind. Although the process is physical and mechanistic, it yields a nonphysical result, a mental event, the perceptual experience, that subsequent philosophers describe as a *percept* or *sense datum* or *sense impression.*

Locke divides the qualities of physical objects into two basic classes: *primary qualities* and *secondary qualities.* Primary qualities are inseparable from their objects and so truly represent them. Such qualities are solidity (or bulk), extension, figure, movement (and rest), and number. These are the true building blocks of knowledge because they accurately represent features in the world. Secondary qualities are not in the things themselves but are caused by the primary qualities. These qualities include colors, sounds, smells, tastes, touch, and sensations. These secondary qualities are types of powers or potentialities or dispositions that reside in a physical object. Fire has the power to change liquids into gases, sugar is soluble in warm water, and glass is fragile. Solubility, flammability, and fragility are dispositional qualities in bodies. Dispositional qualities cause changes in the external world.

Secondary qualities are powers that produce sensations (that is, perceptions) in the perceiver. The primary qualities (motion or whatever) cause the secondary qualities that we perceive. When, under normal circumstances, we look at an object it looks a certain color—say, red. The redness we are acquainted with is not in the object itself but in the way the light reflects off the object into our eye and is communicated to our brain. Secondary qualities are the ways things have of appearing to us.

Underneath all the qualities is substance, the foundation of matter itself. Locke assumes that there must be an ultimate source of reality that underlies the ideas presented in experience. He describes it as "something I know not what."

There are problems with representationalism. If direct realism, via physics, leads to representationalism, representationalism, on philosophical reflection, seems to lead to phenomenalism.

In the second reading in this part of the book, George Berkeley (1685–1753) holds to a type of phenomenalism that has been called "immaterialism." Berkeley criticized Locke's representationalism on several counts. First, he argued that the primary–secondary qualities distinction was unsound. The primary qualities are no more "in" the objects of perception than are the secondary ones. Second, he argued that there were logical problems in the theory that our perceptions resembled physical objects ("an idea can be like nothing but an idea"). Third, he undermined the whole notion of substance that Locke needed to maintain his theory. What is the difference, Berkeley rhetorically asked, between a "something I know not what" (Locke's notion of substance) and nothing at all? Ultimately, Locke's representationalism leads back to skepticism.

Berkeley held that ideas exist in the mind alone. All perceived qualities are mental or subjective: their reality consists in being perceived ("To be is to be perceived"). There is no material world. Physical objects are simply mental events. "The table I write on, I say, exists, that is, I see and feel it; and if I were out of my study I should say it existed, meaning thereby that if I was in my study I might perceive it, or that some other spirit actually does perceive it." All physical objects are mental phenomena that would cease to exist if they were not perceived. Why do physical objects continue to exist when no one is perceiving them? Well, someone *is* always perceiving them: God's eye keeps the world from dissolving.[2]

Contemporary phenomenalism differs with Berkeley only in this last respect. It doesn't posit God as necessary to hold the physical world in existence. Instead, it views the physical world as a construct of ideas. In Mill's words, objects are "permanent possibilities of sensation," meaning that if one were to get into the appropriate condition, one would experience the sense data. In the third reading for this part, W. T. Stace (1886–1967) argues that the realist's view of the world as containing material objects behind the perceived world is an unjustified faith. The world of scientific discourse (for example, such terms as "atoms," "gravity," and "conservation of energy") is not to be taken literally, but instrumentally, as providing useful fictions that help us to predict experiences.

The fourth reading, by C. H. Whiteley (1911–   ), provides a thorough critical assessment of the phenomenalist position, analyzing its strengths and weaknesses.

Two puzzles for sense data theories, whether representational or phenomenal, which Whiteley doesn't discuss, should be noted. The first is the paradox of the nontransitivity of perception. Take three pieces of red colored paper. Suppose we cannot distinguish between samples A and B. They seem exactly the same color. Likewise, samples B and C are indistinguishable. But say we *can* distinguish between A and C! On the sense data account, this is puzzling, since we should be able to distinguish our sense data from one another.

The second puzzle is that of indeterminateness. Suppose we see a speckled hen. How many speckles does our sense datum hold? If we say that the number is indeterminate, we seem to have a paradox between the indeterminate sense datum and the determinate objects that are supposed to be represented.

The fifth reading contains a contemporary defense of direct realism. Thomas Reid argues against representationalists for a form of direct realism based on common sense. The sixth reading, by Bertrand Russell, (1872–1970) is a defense of representational realism, developing Locke's causal theory of perception in the light of contemporary science. According to Russell, our knowledge of physical objects is inferred from percepts in our brain. One may ask why Russell does not simply accept phenomenalism, since he makes percepts primary to our knowledge. Russell concedes that phenomenalism is not impossible, but views it as implausible for reasons similar to Whiteley's.

Notes

[1] Bertrand Russell, *Inquiry into Meaning and Truth* (London: Allen & Unwin, 1940), 15.

[2] According to Berkeley, there is no sound independent of our hearing it and no reality but a mind's experiencing it. Does this mean that when we leave our rooms, they disappear? There is an old Oxford limerick on this point:

> There was a young man who said, "God
> Must think it exceedingly odd
> If he finds that this tree
> Continues to be,
> When there's no one about in the quad."

> Dear Sir, your astonishment's odd
> I'm always about in the quad,
> And that's why the tree
> Continues to be,
> Since observed by,
>
> Yours faithfully,
> God

III.1 A Representational Theory of Perception

JOHN LOCKE

The English philosopher John Locke (1632–1704) was educated at Oxford University, where he became a tutor in Greek rhetoric and philosophy. Later he was a practicing physician and assistant to the Earl of Shaftesbury. This selection is taken from Locke's *Essay Concerning Human Understanding* (1689).

Locke's work in the theory of knowledge is the first systematic assault on Cartesian rationalism, the view that reason alone guarantees knowledge. Locke argues that if our claims to knowledge make any sense, they must be derived from the world. He rejects the rationalist notion that we have *innate ideas* (actual knowledge of metaphysical truths, such as mathematical truths, universals, and the laws of nature) because (1) there is not good deductive argument establishing the existence of such entities, (2) children and idiots do not seem to possess them, and (3) an empirical way of knowing, which seems far more reasonable, has no place for such entities.

According to Locke, the mind at birth is a *tabula rasa*, a blank slate. It is like white paper, devoid of characteristics until it receives sense perceptions. All knowledge begins with sensory experience on which the powers of the mind operate, developing complex ideas, abstractions, and the like. In place of the absolute certainty that the rationalists sought to find, Locke says that apart from the knowledge of the self, most of what we know we know in degrees of certainty derived from inductive generalizations. For example, we see the sun rise every morning and infer that it is highly probable that it will rise tomorrow—but we cannot be absolutely certain.

Locke holds a representational theory of perception in which objects in the world cause our sense organs to start processes that result in perceptual experience. We are never aware of the thing in itself, the object that is perceived and that causes the idea to arise in our mind, but only of the idea or *representation* of the object. We are directly aware of the idea but inasmuch as the object is the cause of the idea, we may be said to be *indirectly* aware of the object itself.

Locke divides our ideas into two types: primary qualities and secondary qualities. Primary qualities are inseparable from their objects and thus truly represent them. Examples of primary qualities are solidity, extension, figure, movement, and number. These are the building blocks of knowledge. Secondary qualities are not in the things themselves but are caused by primary qualities. They include colors, sounds, tastes, and touch. They are powers that objects have to do certain things. Fire has the power to change liquids into gases, sugar is soluble in warm water, and glass is fragile. Solubility, flammability, and fragility are dispositional qualities in bodies, and as such cause changes in the world.

Reprinted from *An Essay Concerning Human Understanding* (1689).

Book II.

Chapter I. Of Ideas in General, and Their Original.

1. Every man being conscious to himself that he thinks, and that which his mind is applied about, whilst thinking, being the ideas that are there, it is past doubt that men have in their minds several ideas, such as are those expressed by the words, Whiteness, Hardness, Sweetness, Thinking, Motion, Man, Elephant, Army, Drunkenness, and others. It is in the first place then to be enquired, how he comes by them. I know it is a received doctrine, that men have native ideas, and original characters, stamped upon their minds, in their very first being. This opinion I have, at large, examined already; and, I suppose, what I have said, in the foregoing book, will be much more easily admitted, when I have shewn, whence the understanding may get all the ideas it has, and by what ways and degrees they may come into the mind for which I shall appeal to every one's own observation and experience.

2. Let us then suppose the mind to be, as we say, white paper, void of all characters, without any ideas; how comes it to be furnished? Whence comes it by that vast store which the busy and boundless fancy of man has painted on it with an almost endless variety? Whence has it all the materials of reason and knowledge? To this I answer, in one word, from experience; in all that our knowledge is founded, and from that it ultimately derives itself. Our observation employed either about external sensible objects, or about the internal operations of our minds, perceived and reflected on by ourselves, is that which supplies our understandings with all the materials of thinking. These two are the fountains of knowledge, from whence all the ideas we have, or can naturally have, do spring.

3. First, Our senses, conversant about particular sensible objects, do convey into the mind several distinct perceptions of things, according to those various ways wherein those objects do affect them: And thus we come by those ideas we have of Yellow, White, Heat, Cold, Soft, Hard, Bitter, Sweet, and all those which we call sensible qualities; which when I say the senses convey into the mind, I mean, they from external objects convey into the mind what produces there those perceptions. This great source of most of the ideas we have, depending wholly upon our senses, and derived by them to the understanding, I call SENSATION.

4. Secondly, The other fountain from which experience furnisheth the understanding with ideas, is the perception of the operations of our own mind within us, as it is employed about the ideas it has got; which operations, when the soul comes to reflect on and consider, do furnish the understanding with another set of ideas, which could not be had from things without. And such are Perception, Thinking, Doubting, Believing, Reasoning, Knowing, Willing, and all the different actings of our own minds; which we being conscious of and observing in ourselves, do from these receive into our understandings as distinct ideas, as we do from bodies affecting our senses. This source of ideas every man has wholly in himself; and though it be not sense, as having nothing to do with external objects, yet it is very like it, and might properly enough be called internal sense. But as I call the other sensation, so I call this REFLECTION, the ideas it affords being such only as the mind gets by reflecting on its own operations within itself. By reflection then, in the following part of this discourse, I would be understood to mean that notice which the mind takes of its own operations, and the manner of them; by reason whereof there come to be ideas of these operations in the understanding. These two, I say, viz. external material things, as the objects of sensation; and the operations of our own minds within, as the objects of reflection; are to me the only originals from whence all our ideas take their beginnings. The term operations here I use in a large sense, as comprehending not barely the actions of the mind about its ideas, but some sort of passions arising sometimes from them, such as is the satisfaction or uneasiness arising from any thought.

5. The understanding seems to me not to have the least glimmering of any ideas, which it doth not receive from one of these two. External objects furnish the mind with the ideas of sensible qualities, which are all those different perceptions they produce in us: And the mind furnishes the understanding with ideas of its own operations.

These, when we have taken a full survey of them, and their several modes, combinations, and relations, we shall find to contain all our whole stock of ideas; and that we have nothing in our minds which did not come in one of these two ways. Let any one examine his own thoughts, and thoroughly search into his understanding; and then let him tell me, whether all the original ideas he has there, are any other than of the objects of his senses, or of the operations of his mind, considered as objects of his reflection; and how great a mass of knowledge soever he imagines to be lodged there, he will, upon taking a strict view, see that he has not any idea in his mind, but what one of these two have imprinted; though perhaps, within infinite variety compounded and enlarged by the understanding, as we shall see hereafter.

6. He that attentively considers the state of a child, at his first coming into the world, will have little reason to think him stored with plenty of ideas, that are to be the matter of his future knowledge: It is by degrees he comes to be furnished with them. And though the ideas of obvious and familiar qualities imprint themselves before the memory begins to keep a register of time or order, yet it is often so late before some unusual qualities come in the way, that there are few men that cannot recollect the beginning of their acquaintance with them: And if it were worth while, no doubt a child might be so ordered as to have but a very few even of the ordinary ideas, till he were grown up to a man. But all that are born into the world being surrounded with bodies that perpetually and diversely affect them; variety of ideas, whether care be taken of it or not, are imprinted on the minds of children. Light and colors are busy at hand everywhere, when the eye is but open; sounds and some tangible qualities fail not to solicit their proper senses, and force an entrance to the mind; but yet, I think, it will be granted easily, that if a child were kept in a place where he never saw any other but black and white till he were a man, he would have no more ideas of scarlet or green, than he that from his childhood never tasted an oyster, or a pineapple, has of those particular relishes.

Chapter VIII. Some Farther Considerations Concerning Our Simple Ideas.

1. Concerning the simple ideas of sensation it is to be considered that whatsoever is so constituted in nature as to be able, by affecting our senses, to cause any perception in the mind, doth thereby produce in the understanding a simple idea; which, whatever be the external cause of it, when it comes to be taken notice of by our discerning faculty, it is by the mind looked on and considered there to be a real positive idea in the understanding, as much as any other whatsoever; though perhaps the cause of it be but a privation of the subject.

2. Thus the ideas of heat and cold, light and darkness, white and black, motion and rest, are equally clear and positive ideas in the mind; though perhaps some of the causes which produce them are barely privations in subjects, from whence our senses derive those ideas. These the understanding, in its view of them, considers all as distinct positive ideas, without taking notice of the causes that produce them: Which is an enquiry not belonging to the idea, as it is in the understanding, but to the nature of the things existing without us. These are two very different things, and carefully to be distinguished; it being one thing to perceive and know the idea of white or black, and quite another to examine what kind of particles they must be, and how ranged in the superficies, to make any object appear white or black.

3. A painter or dyer, who never enquired into their causes, hath the ideas of white and black, and other colors, as clearly, perfectly, and distinctly in his understanding, and perhaps more distinctly, than the philosopher, who hath busied himself in considering their natures, and thinks he knows how far either of them is in its cause positive or privative; and the idea of black is no less positive in his mind, than that of white, however the cause of that color in the external object may be only a privation.

4. If it were the design of my present undertaking to enquire into the natural causes and manner of perception, I should offer this as a reason why a privative cause might, in some cases at least, produce a positive idea, viz. that all sensation being produced in us only by different degrees and modes of motion in our animal spirits, variously agitated by external objects, the abatement of any former motion must as necessarily produce a new sensation, as the variation or increase of it; and so introduce a new idea, which depends only on a different motion of the animal spirits in that organ.

5. But whether this be so or no, I will not here determine, but appeal to every one's own experience, whether the shadow of a man, though it consists of nothing but the absence of light (and the more the absence of light is, the more discernible is the shadow) does not, when a man

looks on it, cause as clear and positive idea in his mind, as a man himself, though covered over with clear sunshine? and the picture of a shadow is a positive thing. Indeed we have negative names, which stand not directly for positive ideas, but for their absence, such as insipid, silence, nihil, &c. which words denote positive ideas, e.g. taste, sound, being, with a signification of their absence.

6. And thus one may truly be said to see darkness. For supposing a hole perfectly dark, from whence no light is reflected, it is certain one may see the figure of it, or it may be painted: Or whether the ink I write with makes any other idea, is a question. The privative causes I have here assigned of positive ideas are according to the common opinion; but in truth it will be hard to determine, whether there be really any ideas from a privative cause, till it be determined, whether rest be any more a privation than motion.

7. To discover the nature of our ideas the better, and to discourse of them intelligibly, it will be convenient to distinguish them as they are ideas or perceptions in our minds, and as they are modifications of matter in the bodies that cause such perceptions in us: That so we may not think (as perhaps usually is done) that they are exactly the images and resemblances of some thing inherent in the subject; most of those of sensation being in the mind no more the likeness of some thing existing without us, than the names that stand for them are the likeness of our ideas, which yet upon hearing they are apt to excite in us.

8. Whatsoever the mind perceives in itself, or is the immediate object of perception, thought, or understanding, that I call idea; and the power to produce any idea in our mind I call a quality of the subject wherein that power is. Thus a snow-ball having the power to produce in us the ideas of white, cold, and round, the power to produce those ideas in us, as they are in the snow-ball, I call qualities; and as they are sensations or perceptions in our understandings, I call them ideas; which ideas, if I speak of sometimes, as in the things themselves, I would be understood to mean those qualities in the objects which produce them in us.

9. Qualities thus considered in bodies are, first, such as are utterly inseparable from the body, in what state soever it be; such as in all the alterations and changes it suffers, all the force can be used upon it, it constantly keeps; and such as sense constantly finds in every particle of matter which

has bulk enough to be perceived, and the mind finds inseparable from every particle of matter, though less than to make itself singly be perceived by our senses, v.g. Take a grain of wheat, divide it into two parts, each part has still solidity, extension, figure, and mobility; divide it again, and it retains still the same qualities; and so divide it on till the parts become insensible, they must retain still each of them all those qualities. For division (which is all that a mill, or pestle, or any other body does upon another, in reducing it to insensible parts) can never take away either solidity, extension, figure, or mobility from any body, but only makes two or more distinct separate masses of matter, of that which was but one before: All which distinct masses, reckoned as so many distinct bodies, after division make a certain number. These I call original or primary qualities of body, which I think we may observe to produce simple ideas in us, viz. solidity, extension, figure, motion or rest, and number.

10. Secondly, such qualities which in truth are nothing in the objects themselves, but powers to produce various sensations in us by their primary qualities, i.e. by the bulk, figure, texture, and motion of their insensible parts, as colors, sounds, tastes, &c. these I call secondary qualities. To these might be added a third sort, which are allowed to be barely powers, though they are as much real qualities in the subject, as those which I, to comply with the common way of speaking, call qualities, but for distinction, secondary qualities. For the power in fire to produce a new color, or consistency, in wax or clay, by its primary qualities, is as much a quality in fire, as the power it has to produce in me a new idea or sensation of warmth or burning, which I felt not before by the same primary qualities, viz. the bulk, texture, and motion of its insensible parts.

11. The next thing to be considered is, how bodies produce ideas in us; and that is manifestly by impulse, the only way which we can conceive bodies to operate in.

12. If then external objects be not united to our minds, when they produce ideas therein, and yet we perceive these original qualities in such of them as singly fall under our senses, it is evident that some motion must be thence continued by our nerves, or animal spirits, by some parts of our bodies, to the brains or the seat of sensation, there to produce on our minds the particular ideas we

have of them. And since the extension, figure, number, and motion of bodies, of an observable bigness, may be perceived at a distance by the sight, it is evident some singly imperceptible bodies must come from them to the eyes, and thereby convey to the brain some motion, which produces these ideas which we have of them in us.

13. After the same manner that the ideas of these original qualities are produced in us, we may conceive that the ideas of secondary qualities are also produced, viz. by the operation of insensible particles on our senses. For it being manifest that there are bodies and good store of bodies, each whereof are so small, that we cannot, by any of our senses, discover either their bulk, figure, or motion as is evident in the particles of the air and water, and others extremely smaller than those, perhaps as much smaller than the particles of air and water, as the particles of air and water are smaller than peas or hail-stones: Let us suppose at present, that the different motions and figures, bulk and number of such particles, affecting the several organs of our senses, produce in us those different sensations, which we have from the colors and smells of bodies; e.g. that a violet, by the impulse of such insensible particles of matter of peculiar figures and bulks, and in different degrees and modifications of their motions, causes the ideas of the blue color and sweet scent of that flower, to be produced in our minds; it being no more impossible to conceive that God should annex such ideas to such motions, with which they have no similitude, than that he should annex the idea of pain to the motion of a piece of steel dividing our flesh, with which that idea hath no resemblance.

14. What I have said concerning colors and smells may be understood also of tastes and sounds, and other the like sensible qualities; which, whatever reality we by mistake attribute to them, are in truth nothing in the objects themselves, but powers to produce various sensations in us, and depend on those primary qualities, viz. bulk, figure, texture, and motion of parts; as I have said.

15. From whence I think it easy to draw this observation, that the ideas of primary qualities of bodies are resemblances of them, and their patterns do really exist in the bodies themselves; but the ideas, produced in us by these secondary qualities, have no resemblance of them at all. There is nothing like our ideas existing in the bodies themselves. They are in the bodies, we denominate from them, only a power to produce those sensations in us: And what is sweet, blue, or warm in idea, is but the certain bulk, figure, and motion of the insensible parts in the bodies themselves, which we call so.

16. Flame is denominated hot and light; snow, white and cold; and manna, white and sweet, from the ideas they produce in us: Which qualities are commonly thought to be the same in those bodies that those ideas are in us, the one the perfect resemblance of the other, as they are in a mirror; and it would by most men be judged very extravagant, if one should say otherwise. And yet he that will consider that the same fire, that at one distance produces in us the sensation of warmth, does at a nearer approach produce in us the far different sensation of pain, ought to bethink himself what reason he has to say, that his idea of warmth, which was produced in him by the fire, is actually in the fire; and his idea of pain, which the same fire produced in him the same way, is not in the fire. Why are whiteness and coldness in snow, and pain not, when it produces the one and the other idea in us; and can do neither, but by the bulk, figure, number, and motion of its solid parts?

17. The particular bulk, number, figure, and motion of the parts of fire or snow are really in them, whether any one's senses perceive them or no: And therefore they may be called real qualities, because they really exist in those bodies: But light, heat, whiteness or coldness, are no more really in them, than sickness or pain is in manna. Take away the sensation of them; let not the eyes see light, or colors, nor the ears hear sounds; let the palate not taste, nor the nose smell; and all colors, tastes, odours, and sounds, as they are such particular ideas, vanish and cease, and are reduced to their causes, i.e. bulk, figure, and motion of parts.

18. A piece of manna of a sensible bulk is able to produce in us the idea of a round or square figure, and, by being removed from one place to another, the idea of motion. This idea of motion represents it as it really is in the manna moving: A circle or square are the same, whether in idea or existence, in the mind, or in the manna; and this both motion and figure are really in the manna, whether we take notice of them or no: This every body is ready to agree to. Besides, manna, by the bulk, figure, texture, and motion of its parts, has a power to produce the sensations of sickness, and

sometimes of acute pains or gripings in us. That these ideas of sickness and pain are not in the manna, but effects of its operations on us, and are nowhere when we feel them not; this also every one readily agrees to. And yet men are hardly to be brought to think, that sweetness and whiteness are not really in manna; which are but the effects of the operations of manna by the motion, size, and figure of its particles on the eyes and palate; as the pain and sickness caused by manna are confessedly nothing but the effects of its operations on the stomach and guts, by the size, motion, and figure of its insensible parts (for by nothing else can a body operate, as has been proved): As if it could not operate on the eyes and palate, and thereby produce in the mind particular distinct ideas, which in itself it has not, as well as we allow it can operate on the guts and stomach, and thereby produce distinct ideas, which in itself it has not. These ideas, being all effects of the operations of manna, on several parts of our bodies, by the size, figure, number, and motion of its parts: Why those produced by the eyes and palate should rather be thought to be really in the manna, than those produced by the stomach and guts; or why the pain and sickness, ideas that are the effect of manna, should be thought to be nowhere when they are not felt; and yet the sweetness and whiteness, effects of the same manna on other parts of the body, by ways equally as unknown, should be thought to exist in the manna, when they are not seen or tasted, would need some reason to explain.

19. Let us consider the red and white colors in porphyry: Hinder light from striking on it, and its colors vanish, it no longer produces any such ideas in us; upon the return of light, it produces these appearances on us again. Can any one think any real alterations are made in the porphyry, by the presence or absence of light; and that those ideas of whiteness and redness are really in porphyry in the light, when it is plain it has no color in the dark? it has, indeed, such a configuration of particles, both night and day, as are apt, by the rays of light rebounding from some parts of that hard stone, to produce in us the idea of redness, and from others the idea of whiteness; but whiteness or redness are not in it at any time, but such a texture, that hath the power to produce such a sensation in us.

20. Pound an almond, and the clear white color will be altered into a dirty one, and the sweet taste into an oily one. What real alteration can the beating of the pestle make in any body, but an alteration of the texture of it?

21. Ideas being thus distinguished and understood, we may be able to give an account how the same water, at the same time, may produce the idea of cold by one hand and of heat by the other; whereas it is impossible that the same water, if those ideas were really in it, should at the same time be both hot and cold: For if we imagine warmth, as it is in our hands, to be nothing but a certain sort and degree of motion in the minute particles of our nerves, or animal spirits, we may understand how it is possible that the same water may, at the same time, produce the sensations of heat in one hand, and cold in the other; which yet figure never does, that never producing the idea of a square by one hand, which has produced the idea of a globe by another. But if the sensation of heat and cold be nothing but the increase or diminution of the motion of the minute parts of our bodies, caused by the corpuscles of any other body, it is easy to be understood, that if that motion be greater in one hand than in the other; if a body be applied to the two hands, which has in its minute particles a greater motion, than in those of one of the hands, and a less than in those of the other, it will increase the motion of the one hand, and lessen it in the other, and so cause the different sensations of heat and cold that depend thereon.

22. I have in what just goes before been engaged in physical enquiries a little farther than perhaps I intended. But it being necessary to make the nature of sensation a little understood, and to make the difference between the qualities in bodies, and the ideas produced by them in the mind, to be distinctly conceived, without which it were impossible to discourse intelligibly of them; I hope I shall be pardoned this little excursion into natural philosophy, it being necessary in our present enquiry to distinguish the primary and real qualities of bodies, which are always in them (viz. solidity, extension, figure, number, and motion, or rest, and are sometimes perceived by us, viz. when the bodies they are in are big enough singly to be discerned) from those secondary and imputed qualities, which are but the powers of several combinations of those primary ones, when they operate, without being distinctly discerned; whereby we may also come to know what ideas are, and

what are not, resemblances of some thing really existing in the bodies we denominate from them.

23. The qualities then that are in bodies rightly considered, are of three sorts.

First, the bulk, figure, number, situation, and motion, or rest of their solid parts; those are in them, whether we perceive them or no; and when they are of that size, that we can discover them, we have by these an idea of the thing as it is in itself, as is plain in artificial things. These I call primary qualities.

Secondly, The power that is in any body, by reason of its insensible primary qualities, to operate after a peculiar manner on any of our senses, and thereby produce in us the different ideas of several colors, sounds, smells, tastes, &c. These are usually called sensible qualities.

Thirdly, the power that is in any body, by reason of the particular constitution of its primary qualities, to make such a change in the bulk, figure, texture, and motion of another body, as to make it operate on our senses differently from what it did before. Thus the sun has a power to make wax white, and fire to make lead fluid. These are usually called powers.

The first of these, as has been said, I think, may be properly called real, original, or primary qualities, because they are in the things themselves, whether they are perceived or no: And upon their different modifications it is, that the secondary qualities depend.

The other two are only powers to act differently upon other things, which powers result from the different modifications of those primary qualities.

24. But though the two latter sorts of qualities are powers barely, and nothing but powers, relating to several other bodies, and resulting from the different modifications of the original qualities; yet they are generally otherwise thought of. For the second sort, viz. the powers to produce several ideas in us by our senses, are looked upon as real qualities, in the things thus affecting us: But the third sort are called and esteemed barely powers, e.g. the idea of heat, or light, which we receive by our eyes or touch from the sun, are commonly thought real qualities, existing in the sun, and some thing more than mere powers in it. But when we consider the sun, in reference to wax, which it melts or blanches, we look on the whiteness and softness produced in the wax, not as qualities in the

sun, but effects produced by powers in it: Whereas, if rightly considered, these qualities of light and warmth, which are perceptions in me when I am warmed, or enlightened by the sun, are no otherwise in the sun, than the changes made in the wax, when it is blanched or melted, are in the sun. They are all of them equally powers in the sun, depending on its primary qualities; whereby it is able, in the one case, so to alter the bulk, figure, texture, or motion of some of the insensible parts of my eyes or hands, as thereby to produce in me the idea of light or heat; and in the other it is able so to alter the bulk, figure, texture, or motion of the insensible parts of the wax, as to make them fit to produce in me the distinct ideas of white and fluid.

25. The reason why the one are ordinarily taken for real qualities, and the other only for bare powers, seems to be, because the ideas we have of distinct colors, sounds, &c. containing nothing at all in them of bulk, figure, or motion, we are not apt to think them the effects of these primary qualities, which appear not, to our senses, to operate in their production; and with which they have not any apparent congruity, or conceivable connexion. Hence it is that we are so forward to imagine, that those ideas are the resemblances of some thing really existing in the objects themselves: Since sensation discovers nothing of bulk, figure, or motion of parts in their production; nor can reason shew how bodies, by their bulk, figure, and motion, should produce in the mind the ideas of blue or yellow, &c. But in the other case, in the operations of bodies changing the qualities one of another, we plainly discover, that the quality produced hath commonly no resemblance with any thing in the thing producing it; wherefore we look on it as a bare effect of power. For though receiving the idea of heat, or light, from the sun, we are apt to think it is a perception and resemblance of such a quality in the sun; yet when we see wax, or a fair face, receive change of color from the sun, we cannot imagine that to be the reception or resemblance of any thing in the sun, because we find not those different colors in the sun itself. For our senses being able to observe a likeness or unlikeness of sensible qualities in two different external objects, we forwardly enough conclude the production of any sensible quality, in any subject to be an effect of bare power, and not the communication of any quality, which was really in the efficient, when we find no such sensible quality in the thing that pro-

duced it. But our senses not being able to discover any unlikeness between the idea produced in us, and the quality of the object producing it; we are apt to imagine, that our ideas are resemblances of something, in the objects, and not the effects of certain powers placed in the modification of their primary qualities, with which primary qualities the ideas produced in us have no resemblance.

26. To conclude, beside those before mentioned primary qualities in bodies, viz. bulk, figure, extension, number, and motion of their solid parts; all the rest whereby we take notice of bodies, and distinguish them one from another, are nothing else but several powers in them depending on those primary qualities; whereby they are fitted, either by immediately operating on our bodies, to produce several different ideas in us; or else by operating on other bodies, so to change their primary qualities, as to render them capable of producing ideas in us, different from what before they did. The former of these, I think, may be called secondary qualities, immediately perceivable: The latter, secondary qualities, mediately perceivable.

Chapter IX. Of Perception.

1. Perception, as it is the first faculty of the mind exercised about our ideas; so it is the first and simplest idea we have from reflection, and is by some called thinking in general. Though thinking, in the propriety of the English tongue, signifies that sort of operation in the mind about its ideas, wherein the mind is active; where it, with some degree of voluntary attention, considers any thing. For in bare naked perception, the mind is, for the most part, only passive: And what it perceives, it cannot avoid perceiving.

2. What perception is, every one will know better by reflecting on what he does himself, when he sees, hears, feels, &c. or thinks, than by any discourse of mine. Whoever reflects on what passes in his own mind, cannot miss it: And if he does not reflect, all the words in the world cannot make him have any notion of it.

3. This is certain, that whatever alterations are made in the body, if they reach not the mind; whatever impressions are made on the outward parts, if they are not taken notice of within; there is no perception. Fire may burn our bodies, with no other effect, than it does a billet, unless the motion be continued to the brain, and there the sense of heat, or idea of pain, be produced in the mind, wherein consists actual perception.

4. How often may a man observe in himself, that whilst his mind is intently employed in the contemplation of some objects, and curiously surveying some ideas that are there, it takes no notice of impressions of sounding bodies made upon the organ of hearing, with the same alteration that uses to be for the producing the idea of sound? A sufficient impulse there may be on the organ; but it not reaching the observation of the mind, there follows no perception: And though the motion that uses to produce the idea of sound be made in the ear, yet no sound is heard. Want of sensation, in this case, is not through any defect in the organ, or that the man's ears are less affected than at other times when he does hear; but that which uses to produce the idea, though conveyed in by the usual organ, not being taken notice of in the understanding, and so imprinting no idea in the mind, there follows no sensation. So that wherever there is sense, or perception, there some idea is actually produced, and present in the understanding. . . .

8. We are further to consider concerning perception, that the ideas we receive by sensation are often in grown people altered by the judgment, without our taking notice of it. When we set before our eyes a round globe, of any uniform color, v.g. gold, alabaster, or jet; it is certain that the idea thereby imprinted in our mind, is of a flat circle variously shadowed, with several degrees of light and brightness coming to our eyes. But we having by use been accustomed to perceive what kind of appearance convex bodies are wont to make in us, what alterations are made in the reflections of light by the difference of the sensible figures of bodies; the judgment presently, by an habitual custom, alters the appearances into their causes; so that from that which is truly variety of shadow or color, collecting the figure, it makes it pass for a mark of figure, and frames to itself the perception of a convex figure and an uniform color; when the idea we receive from thence is only a plane variously colored, as is evident in painting. To which purpose I shall here insert a problem of that very ingenious and studious promoter of real knowledge, the learned and worthy Mr. Molineaux, which he was pleased to send me in a letter some months since; and it is this: Suppose a man born blind, and now adult, and

taught by his touch to distinguish between a cube and a sphere of the same metal, and nighly of the same bigness, so as to tell, when he felt one and the other, which is the cube, which the sphere. Suppose then the cube and sphere placed on a table, and the blind man be made to see: Quaere, "whether by his sight, before he touched them, he could now distinguish and tell, which is the globe, which the cube?" to which the acute and judicious proposer answers: Not. For though he has obtained the experience of how a globe, how a cube affects his touch; yet he has not yet obtained the experience, that what affects his touch so or so, must affect his sight so or so: Or that a protuberant angle in the cube, that pressed his hand unequally, shall appear to his eye as it does in the cube. I agree with this thinking gentleman, whom I am proud to call my friend, in his answer to this problem; and am of opinion, that the blind man at first sight, would not be able with certainty to say which was the globe, which the cube, whilst he only saw them: Though he could unerringly name them by his touch, and certainly distinguish them by the difference of their figures felt. This I have set down, and leave with my reader, as an occasion for him to consider how much he may be beholden to experience, improvement, and acquired notions, where he thinks he had not the least use of, or help from them: And the rather, because this observing gentleman further adds, that having, upon the occasion of my book, proposed this to divers very ingenious men, he hardly ever met with one, that at first gave the answer to it which he thinks true, till by hearing his reasons they were convinced.

9. But this is not, I think, usual in any of our ideas, but those received by sight: Because sight, the most comprehensive of all our senses, conveying to our minds the ideas of light and colors, which are peculiar only to that sense; and also the far different ideas of space, figure, and motion, the several varieties whereof change the appearances of its proper object, viz. light and colors; we bring ourselves by use to judge of the one by the other. This, in many cases, by a settled habit, in things whereof we have frequent experience, is performed so constantly and so quick, that we take that for the perception of our sensation, which is an idea formed by our judgment; so that one, viz. that of sensation, serves only to excite the other, and is scarce taken notice of itself: As a man who reads or hears with attention and understanding, takes little notice of the characters, or sounds, but of the ideas that are excited in him by them.

10. Nor need we wonder that this is done with so little notice, if we consider how quick the actions of the mind are performed: For as itself is thought to take up no space, to have no extension; so its actions seem to require no time, but many of them seem to be crowded into an instant. I speak this in comparison to the actions of the body. Any one may easily observe this in his own thoughts, who will take the pains to reflect on them. How, as it were in an instant, do our minds with one glance see all the parts of a demonstration, which may very well be called a long one, if we consider the time it will require to put it into words, and step by step shew it another? Secondly, we shall not be so much surprized, that this is done in us with so little notice, if we consider how the facility which we get of doing things, by a custom of doing, makes them often pass in us without our notice. Habits, especially such as are begun very early, come at last to produce actions in us, which often escape our observation. How frequently do we, in a day, cover our eyes with our eye-lids, without perceiving that we are at all in the dark? Men that by custom have got the use of a by-word, do almost in every sentence pronounce sounds which, though taken notice of by others, they themselves neither hear nor observe. And therefore it is not so strange, that our mind should often change the idea of its sensation into that of its judgment, and make one serve only to excite the other without our taking notice of it. . . .

15. Perception then being the first step and degree towards knowledge, and the inlet of all the materials of it; the fewer senses any man, as well as any other creature, hath, and the fewer and duller the impressions are that are made by them, and the duller the faculties are that are employed about them; the more remote are they from that knowledge, which is to be found in some men. But this being in great variety of degrees (as may be perceived amongst men) cannot certainly be discovered in the several species of animals, much less in their particular individuals. It suffices me only to have remarked here, that perception is the first operation of all our intellectual faculties, and the inlet of all knowledge in our minds. And I am apt too to imagine, that it is perception in the lowest degree of it, which puts the boundaries between

animals and the inferior ranks of creatures. But this I mention only as my conjecture by the by; it being indifferent to the matter in hand, which way the learned shall determine of it.

Chapter XXIII. Of Our Complex Ideas of Substances.

1. The mind being, as I have declared, furnished with a great number of the simple ideas, conveyed in by the senses, as they are found in exterior things, or by reflection on its own operations, takes notice also, that a certain number of these simple ideas go constantly together; which being presumed to belong to one thing, and words being suited to common apprehensions, and made use of for quick dispatch, are called, so united in one subject, by one name: Which, by inadvertency, we are apt afterward to talk of, and consider as one simple idea, which indeed is a complication of many ideas together; because, as I have said, not imagining how these simple ideas can subsist by themselves, we accustom ourselves to suppose some substratum wherein they do subsist, and from which they do result, which therefore we call substance.

2. So that if any one will examine himself concerning his notion of pure substance in general, he will find he has no other idea of it at all, but only a supposition of he knows not what support of such qualities, which are capable of producing simple ideas in us; which qualities are commonly called accidents. If any one should be asked, what is the subject wherein color or weight inheres, he would have nothing to say, but the solid extended parts: And if he were demanded, what is it that solidity and extension adhere in, he would not be in a much better case than the Indian . . . who, saying that the world was supported by a great elephant, was asked what the elephant rested on; to which his answer was, a great tortoise. But being again pressed to know what gave support to the broad-backed tortoise, replied, something he knew not what. And thus here, as in all other cases where we use words without having clear and distinct ideas, we talk like children; who being questioned what such a thing is, which they know not, readily give this satisfactory answer, that it is some thing: Which in truth signifies no more, when so used either by

children or men, but that they know not what; and that the thing they pretend to know and talk of, is what they have no distinct idea of at all, and so are perfectly ignorant of it, and in the dark. The idea then we have, to which we give the general name substance, being nothing but the supposed, but unknown support of those qualities we find existing, which we imagine cannot subsist, "sine re substante," without some thing to support them, we call that support substantia; which, according to the true import of the word, is in plain English, standing under or upholding.

3. An obscure and relative idea of substance in general being thus made we come to have the ideas of particular sorts of substances, by collecting such combinations of simple ideas, as are by experience and observation of men's senses taken notice of to exist together, and are therefore supposed to flow from the particular internal constitution, or unknown essence of that substance. Thus we come to have the ideas of a man, horse, gold, water &c. of which substances, whether any one has any other clear idea, farther than of certain simple ideas coexistent together, I appeal to every one's own experience. It is the ordinary qualities observable in iron, or a diamond, put together, that make the true complex idea of those substances, which a smith or a jeweller commonly knows better than a philosopher; who, whatever substantial forms he may talk of, has no other idea of those substances, than what is framed by a collection of those simple ideas which are to be found in them; only we must take notice, that our complex ideas of substances, besides all those simple ideas they are made up of, have always the confused idea of some thing to which they belong, and in which they subsist. And therefore, when we speak of any sort of substance, we say it is a thing having such or such qualities: A body is a thing that is extended, figured, and capable of motion; spirit, a thing capable of thinking; and so hardness, friability, and power to draw iron, we say, are qualities to be found in a loadstone. These, and the like fashions of speaking, intimate, that the substance is supposed always some thing besides the extension, figure, solidity, motion, thinking, or other observable ideas, though we know not what it is. . . .

15. Besides the complex ideas we have of material sensible substances, of which I have last spoken, by the simple ideas we have taken from those operations of our own minds, which we

experiment daily in ourselves, as thinking, under-standing, willing, knowing, and power of begin-ning motion, &c. co-existing in some substance: We are able to frame the complex idea of an imma-terial spirit. And thus by putting together the ideas of thinking, perceiving, liberty, and power of mov-ing themselves, and other things, we have as clear a perception and notion of immaterial substances, as we have of material. For putting together the ideas of thinking and willing, or the power of moving or quieting corporeal motion, joined to substance of which we have no distinct idea, we have the idea of an immaterial spirit; and by putting together the ideas of coherent solid parts, and a power of being moved, joined with substance, of which likewise we have no positive idea, we have the idea of matter. The one is as clear and distinct an idea as the other: The idea of thinking, and moving a body, being as clear and distinct ideas, as the ideas of extension, solidity, and being moved. For our idea of sub-stance is equally obscure, or none at all in both: It is but a supposed I know not what, to support those ideas we call accidents. It is for want of reflec-tion that we are apt to think, that our senses shew us nothing but material things. Every act of sensa-tion, when duly considered, gives us an equal view of both parts of nature, the corporeal and spiritual. For whilst I know, by seeing or hearing, &c. that there is some corporeal being without me, the object of that sensation; I do more certainly know, that there is some spiritual being within me, that sees and hears. This, I must be convinced, cannot be the action of bare insensible matter; nor ever could be, without an immaterial thinking being.

Book IV

Chapter I. Of Knowledge in General.

1. Since the mind, in all its thoughts and reason-ings, hath no other immediate object but its own ideas, which it alone does or can contemplate; it is evident, that our knowledge is only conversant about them.

    2. Knowledge then seems to me to be noth-ing but the perception of the connexion and agreement, or disagreement and repugnancy, of any of our ideas. In this alone it consists. Where this perception is, there is knowledge; and where it

is not, there, though we may fancy, guess, or believe, yet we always come short of knowledge. For when we know that white is not black, what do we else but perceive that these two ideas do not agree? When we possess ourselves with the utmost security of the demonstration, that the three angles of a triangle are equal to two right ones, what do we more but perceive, that equality to two right ones does necessarily agree to, and is inseparable from the three angles of a triangle?

Chapter XI. Of Our Knowledge of the Existence of Other Things.

1. The knowledge of our own being we have by intuition. The existence of a God reason clearly makes known to us, as has been shown.

    The knowledge of the existence of any other thing, we can have only by sensation: For there being no necessary connexion of real existence with any idea a man hath in his memory, nor of any other existence but that of God, with the exis-tence of any particular man; no particular man can know the existence of any other being, but only when by actual operating upon him, it makes itself perceived by him. For the having the idea of any thing in our mind, no more proves the existence of that thing, than the picture of a man evidences his being in the world, or the visions of a dream make thereby a true history.

    2. It is therefore the actual receiving of ideas from without, that gives us notice of the existence of other things, and makes us know that some-thing doth exist at that time without us, which causes that idea in us, though perhaps we neither know nor consider how it does it: For it takes not from the certainty of our senses, and the ideas we receive by them, that we know not the manner wherein they are produced: v.g. whilst I write this, I have, by the paper affecting my eyes, that idea produced in my mind, which whatever object causes, I call white; by which I know that that quality or accident (i.e. whose appearance before my eyes always causes that idea) doth really exist, and hath a being without me. And of this, the greatest assurance I can possibly have, and to which my faculties can attain, is the testimony of my eyes, which are the proper and sole judges of this thing, whose testimony I have reason to rely on as so certain, that I can no more doubt, whilst

I write this, that I see white and black, and that something really exists, that causes that sensation in me, than that I write or move my hand; which is a certainty as great as human nature is capable of, concerning the existence of any thing, but a man's self alone, and of God.

3. The notice we have by our senses, of the existing of things without us, though it be not altogether so certain as our intuitive knowledge, or the deductions of our reason employed about the clear abstract ideas of our own minds; yet it is an assurance that deserves the name of knowledge. If we persuade ourselves, that our faculties act and inform us right, concerning the existence of those objects that affect them, it cannot pass for an ill-grounded confidence: For I think nobody can, in earnest, be so sceptical, as to be uncertain of the existence of those things which he sees and feels. At least, he that can doubt so far (whatever he may have with his own thoughts) will never have any controversy with me; since he can never be sure I say any thing contrary to his own opinion. As to myself, I think God has given me assurance enough of the existence of things without me; since by their different application I can produce in myself both pleasure and pain, which is one great concernment of my present state. This is certain; the confidence that our faculties do not herein deceive us is the greatest assurance we are capable of, concerning the existence of material beings. For we cannot act any thing but by our faculties; nor talk of knowledge itself, but by the help of those faculties, which are fitted to apprehend even what knowledge is. But besides the assurance we have from our senses themselves, that they do not err in the information they give us, of the existence of things without us, when they are affected by them, we are farther confirmed in this assurance by other concurrent reasons.

4. First, it is plain those perceptions are produced in us by exterior causes affecting our senses; because those that want the organs of any sense, never can have the ideas belonging to that sense produced in their minds. This is too evident to be doubted: And therefore we cannot but be assured, that they come in by the organs of that sense, and no other way. The organs themselves, it is plain, do not produce them, for then the eyes of a man in the dark would produce colors, and his nose smell roses in the winter: But we see nobody gets

the relish of a pineapple, till he goes to the Indies, where it is, and tastes it.

5. Secondly, because sometimes I find, that I cannot avoid the having those ideas produced in my mind. For though when my eyes are shut, or windows fast, I can at pleasure recall to my mind the ideas of light, or the sun, which former sensations had lodged in my memory; so I can at pleasure lay by that idea, and take into my view that of the smell of a rose, or taste of sugar. But, if I turn my eyes at noon towards the sun, I cannot avoid the ideas, which the light, or sun, then produces in me. So that there is a manifest difference between the ideas laid up in my memory, (over which, if they were there only, I should have constantly the same power to dispose of them, and lay them by at pleasure) and those which force themselves upon me, and I cannot avoid having. And therefore it must needs be some exterior cause, and the brisk acting of some objects without me, whose efficacy I cannot resist, that produces those ideas in my mind, whether I will or no. Besides, there is nobody who doth not perceive the difference in himself between contemplating the sun, as he hath the idea of it in his memory, and actually looking upon it: Of which two, his perception is so distinct, that few of his ideas are more distinguishable one from another. And therefore he hath certain knowledge that they are not both memory, or the actions of his mind, and fancies only within him; but that actual seeing hath a cause without.

6. Thirdly, add to this, that many of those ideas are produced in us with pain, which afterwards we remember without the least offence. Thus the pain of heat or cold, when the idea of it is revived in our minds, gives us no disturbance; which, when felt, was very troublesome, and is again, when actually repeated; which is occasioned by the disorder the external object causes in our bodies when applied to it. And we remember the pains of hunger, thirst, or the headache, without any pain at all; which would either never disturb us, or else constantly do it, as often as we thought of it, were there nothing more but ideas floating in our minds, and appearances entertaining our fancies, without the real existence of things affecting us from abroad. The same may be said of pleasure, accompanying several actual sensations: And though mathematical demonstration depends not upon sense, yet the examining them by diagrams gives great credit to the evidence of our sight, and

seems to give it a certainty approaching to that of demonstration itself. For it would be very strange, that a man should allow it for an undeniable truth, that two angles of a figure, which he measures by lines and angles of a diagram, should be bigger one than the other; and yet doubt of the existence of those lines and angles, which by looking on he makes use of to measure that by.

7. Fourthly, our senses in many cases bear witness to the truth of each other's report, concerning the existence of sensible things without us. He that sees a fire, may, if he doubt whether it be any thing more than a bare fancy, feel it too; and be convinced by putting his hand in it. Which certainly could never be put into such exquisite pain, by a bare idea or phantom, unless that the pain be a fancy too: Which yet he cannot, when the burn is well, by raising the idea of it, bring upon himself again.

Thus I see, whilst I write this, I can change the appearance of the paper: And by designing the letters tell beforehand what new idea it shall exhibit the very next moment, by barely drawing my pen over it: Which will neither appear (let me fancy as much as I will) if my hands stand still; or though I move my pen, if my eyes be shut: Nor when those characters are once made on the paper, can I choose afterwards but see them as they are; that is, have the ideas of such letters as I have made. Whence it is manifest, that they are not barely the sport and play of my own imagination, when I find that the characters, that were made at the pleasure of my own thoughts, do not obey them; nor yet cease to be, whenever I shall fancy it; but continue to affect my senses constantly and regularly, according to the figures I made them. To which if we will add, that the sight of those shall, from another man, draw such sounds, as I beforehand design they shall stand for; there will be little reason left to doubt, that those words I write do really exist without me, when they cause a long series of regular sounds to affect my ears, which could not be the effect of my imagination, nor could my memory retain them in that order.

8. But yet, if after all this any one will be so sceptical, as to distrust his senses, and to affirm that all we see and hear, feel and taste, think and do, during our whole being, is but the series and deluding appearances of a long dream, whereof there is no reality; and therefore will question the existence of all things, or our knowledge of any thing; I must desire him to consider, that if all be a dream, then he doth but dream, that he makes the question; and so it is not much matter, that a waking man should answer him. But yet, if he pleases, he may dream that I make him this answer, that the certainty of things existing in rerum natura, when we have the testimony of our senses for it, is not only as great as our frame can attain to, but as our condition needs. For our faculties being suited not to the full extent of being, nor to a perfect, clear, comprehensive knowledge of things free from all doubt and scruple; but to the preservation of us, in whom they are; and accommodated to the use of life; they serve to our purpose well enough, if they will but give us certain notice of those things, which are convenient or inconvenient to us. For he that sees a candle burning, and hath experimented the force of its flame, by putting his finger in it, will little doubt that this is something existing without him, which does him harm, and puts him to great pain: Which is assurance enough, when no man requires greater certainty to govern his actions by, than what is as certain as his actions themselves. And if our dreamer pleases to try, whether the glowing heat of a glass furnace be barely a wandering imagination in a drowsy man's fancy; by putting his hand into it, he may perhaps be wakened into a certainty greater than he could wish, that it is something more than bare imagination. So that this evidence is as great as we can desire, being as certain to us as our pleasure or pain, i.e. happiness or misery; beyond which we have no concernment, either of knowing or being. Such an assurance of the existence of things without us is sufficient to direct us in the attaining the good, and avoiding the evil, which is caused by them; which is the important concernment we have of being made acquainted with them.

9. In fine then, when our senses do actually convey into our understandings any idea, we cannot but be satisfied that there doth something at that time really exist without us, which doth affect our senses, and by them give notice of itself to our apprehensive faculties, and actually produce that idea which we then perceive: And we cannot so far distrust their testimony, as to doubt, that such collections of simple ideas, as we have observed by our senses to be united together, do really exist together. But this knowledge extends as far as the present testimony of our senses, employed about particular objects that do then affect them, and no

farther. For if I saw such a collection of simple ideas, as is wont to be called man, existing together one minute since, and am now alone, I cannot be certain that the same man exists now, since there is no necessary connexion of his existence a minute since, with his existence now: By a thousand ways he may cease to be, since I had the testimony of my senses for his existence. And if I cannot be certain, that the man I saw last today is now in being, I can less be certain that he is so, who hath been longer removed from my senses, and I have not seen since yesterday, or since the last year; and much less can I be certain of the existence of men that I never saw. And therefore though it be highly probable, that millions of men do now exist, yet, whilst I am alone writing this, I have not that certainty of it which we strictly call knowledge; though the great likelihood of it puts me past doubt, and it be reasonable for me to do several things upon the confidence that there are men (and men also of my acquaintance, with whom I have to do) now in the world: But this is but probability, not knowledge.

10. Whereby yet we may observe, how foolish and vain a thing it is, for a man of a narrow knowledge, who having reason given him to judge of the different evidence and probability of things, and to be swayed accordingly; how vain, I say, it is to expect demonstration and certainty in things not capable of it; and refuse assent to very rational propositions, and act contrary to very plain and clear truths, because they cannot be made out so evident, as to surmount even the least (I will not say reason, but) pretence of doubting. He that in the ordinary affairs of life would admit of nothing but direct plain demonstration, would be sure of nothing in this world, but of perishing quickly. The wholesomeness of his meat or drink would not give him reason to venture on it: And I would fain know, what it is he could do upon such grounds, as are capable of no doubt, no objection.

III.2 An Idealist Theory of Knowledge

GEORGE BERKELEY

George Berkeley (1685–1753), an Irish philosopher and Anglican bishop, was educated at Trinity College, Dublin, where he subsequently taught. A deeply committed Christian, he sought to reconcile science with his faith, proving that although matter does not exist, the laws of physics, being God's laws, govern a universe made up of ideas. Only two types of things exist: minds and ideas. To exist is to be perceived (*"Esse est percipi"*), and God is that being who, perceiving all things, causes them to exist as ideas in his mind. This position is called philosophical idealism, though "idea-ism" would be a more accurate title.

Note that Berkeley's idealism differs from traditional idealism (such as Plato's) in that it is not rationalistic. It does not adhere to independently existing ideas, but rather it assumes an empirical foundation. It agrees with Locke that all ideas originate in sense experience, and proceeds to show that all we ever experience are ideas, our sensations, or sense perceptions. The only reality there is to be known is perceivers and perceptions.

Reprinted from *A Treatise Concerning the Principles of Human Knowledge* (1710).

Of the Principles of Human Knowledge.

Part I.

I. It is evident to any one who takes a survey of the objects of human knowledge, that they are either ideas actually imprinted on the senses, or else such as are perceived by attending to the passions and operations of the mind, or lastly, ideas formed by help of memory and imagination, either compounding, dividing, or barely representing those originally perceived in the aforesaid ways. By sight I have the ideas of light and colors with their several degrees and variations. By touch I perceive, for example, hard and soft, heat and cold, motion and resistance, and of all these more and less either as to quantity or degree. Smelling furnishes me with odours; the palate with tastes; and hearing conveys sounds to the mind in all their variety of tone and composition. And as several of these are observed to accompany each other, they come to be marked by one name, and so to be reputed as one thing. Thus, for example, a certain color, taste, smell, figure, and consistence having been observed to go together, are accounted one distinct thing, signified by the name apple. Other collections of ideas constitute a stone, a tree, a book, and the like sensible things; which, as they are pleasing or disagreeable, excite the passions of love, hatred, joy, grief, and so forth.

II. But besides all that endless variety of ideas or objects of knowledge, there is likewise something which knows or perceives them, and exercises divers operations, as willing, imagining, remembering about them. This perceiving, active being is what I call mind, spirit, soul, or myself. By which words I do not denote any one of my ideas, but a thing entirely distinct from them, wherein they exist, or, which is the same thing, whereby they are perceived; for the existence of an idea consists in being perceived.

III. That neither our thoughts, nor passions, nor ideas formed by the imagination, exist without the mind, is what every body will allow. And (to me) it seems no less evident that the various sensations or ideas imprinted on the sense, however blended or combined together (that is, whatever objects they compose), cannot exist otherwise than in a mind perceiving them. I think an intuitive knowledge may be obtained of this, by any one that shall attend to what is meant by the term exist, when applied to sensible things. The table I write on, I say, exists, that is, I see and feel it; and if I were out of my study I should say it existed, meaning thereby that if I was in my study I might perceive it, or that some other spirit actually does perceive it. There was an odour, that is, it was smelled; there was a sound, that is to say, it was heard; a color or figure, and it was perceived by sight or touch. This is all that I can understand by these and the like expressions. For as to what is said of the absolute existence of unthinking things without any relation to their being perceived, that seems perfectly unintelligible. Their esse is percipi, nor is it possible they should have any existence, out of the minds or thinking things which perceive them.

IV. It is indeed an opinion strangely prevailing amongst men, that houses, mountains, rivers, and in a word sensible objects have an existence natural or real, distinct from their being perceived by the understanding. But with how great an assurance and acquiescence soever this principle may be entertained in the world; yet whoever shall find in his heart to call it in question, may, if I mistake not, perceive it to involve a manifest contradiction. For what are the forementioned objects but the things we perceive by sense, and what do we perceive besides our own ideas or sensations; and is it not plainly repugnant that any one of these or any combination of them should exist unperceived?

V. If we thoroughly examine this tenet, it will, perhaps, be found at bottom to depend on the doctrine of abstract ideas. For can there be a nicer strain of abstraction than to distinguish the existence of sensible objects from their being perceived, so as to conceive them existing unperceived? Light and colors, heat and cold, extension and figures, in a word the things we see and feel, what are they but so many sensations, notions, ideas, or impressions on the sense; and is it possible to separate, even in thought, any of these from perception? For my part I might as easily divide a thing from itself. I may indeed divide in my thoughts or conceive apart from each other those things which, perhaps, I never perceived by sense so divided. Thus I imagine the trunk of a human body without the limbs, or conceive the smell of a rose without thinking on the rose itself. So far I will not deny I can abstract, if that may properly be called abstraction, which extends only to the conceiving separately such objects as it is possible may really exist or be actually perceived asunder. But my conceiving or imagining power does not extend beyond the possibility of real existence or perception. Hence as it is impossible for me to see or feel any thing without an actual sensation of that thing, so is it impossible for me to conceive in my thoughts any sensible thing or object distinct from the sensation or perception of it.

VI. Some truths there are so near and obvious to the mind, that a man need only open his eyes to see them. Such I take this important one to be, to wit, that all the choir of heaven and furniture of the earth, in a word all those bodies which compose the mighty frame of the world, have not any subsistence without a mind, that their being (esse) is to be perceived or known; that consequently so long as they are not actually perceived by me, or do not exist in my mind or that of any other created spirit, they must either have no existence at all, or else subsist in the mind of some eternal spirit: it being perfectly unintelligible and involving all the absurdity of abstraction, to attribute to any single part of them an existence independent of a spirit. To be convinced of which, the reader need only reflect and try to separate in his own thoughts the being of a sensible thing from its being perceived.

VII. From what has been said, it follows, there is not any other substance than spirit, or that which perceives. But for the fuller proof of this point, let it be considered, the sensible qualities are color, figure, motion, smell, taste, and such like, that is, the ideas perceived by sense. Now for an idea to exist in an unperceiving thing, is a manifest contradiction; for to have an idea is all one as to perceive: that therefore wherein color, figure, and the like qualities exist, must perceive them; hence it is clear there can be no unthinking substance or substratum of those ideas.

VIII. But say you, though the ideas themselves do not exist without the mind, yet there may be things like them whereof they are copies or resemblances, which things exist without the mind, in an unthinking substance. I answer, an idea can be like nothing but an idea; a color or figure can be like nothing but another color or figure. If we look but ever so little into our thoughts, we shall find it impossible for us to conceive a likeness except only between our ideas. Again, I ask whether those supposed originals or external things, of which our ideas are the pictures or representations, be themselves perceivable or no? if

they are, then they are ideas, and we have gained our point; but if you say they are not, I appeal to any one whether it be sense, to assert a color is like something which is invisible; hard or soft, like something which is intangible; and so of the rest.

IX. Some there are who make a distinction betwixt primary and secondary qualities: by the former, they mean extension, figure, motion, rest, solidity or impenetrability, and number: by the latter they denote all other sensible qualities, as colors, sounds, tastes, and so forth. The ideas we have of these they acknowledge not to be the resemblances of any thing existing without the mind or unperceived; but they will have our ideas of the primary qualities to be patterns or images of things which exist without the mind, in an unthinking substance which they call matter. By matter therefore we are to understand an inert, senseless substance, in which extension, figure and motion, do actually subsist. But it is evident from what we have already shown, that extension, figure, and motion, are only ideas existing in the mind, and that an idea can be like nothing but another idea, and that consequently neither they nor their archetypes can exist in an unperceiving substance. Hence it is plain, that the very notion of what is called matter, or corporeal substance, involves a contradiction in it.

X. They who assert that figure, motion, and the rest of the primary or original qualities, do exist without the mind, in unthinking substances, do at the same time acknowledge that colors, sounds, heat, cold, and such like secondary qualities, do not, which they tell us are sensations existing in the mind alone, that depend on and are occasioned by the different size, texture, and motion of the minute particles of matter. This they take for an undoubted truth, which they can demonstrate beyond all exception. Now if it be certain, that those original qualities are inseparably united with the other sensible qualities, and not, even in thought, capable of being abstracted from them, it plainly follows that they exist only in the mind. But I desire any one to reflect and try, whether he can, by any abstraction of thought, conceive the extension and motion of a body, without all other sensible qualities. For my own part, I see evidently that it is not in my power to frame an idea of a body extended and moved, but I must withal give it some color or other sensible quality which is acknowledged to exist only in the mind. In short, extension, figure, and motion, abstracted from all other qualities, are inconceivable. Where therefore the other sensible qualities are, there must these be also, to wit, in the mind and nowhere else.

XI. Again, great and small, swift and slow, are allowed to exist no where without the mind, being entirely relative, and changing as the frame or position of the organs of sense varies. The extension therefore which exists without the mind, is neither great nor small, the motion neither swift nor slow, that is, they are nothing at all. But, say you, they are extension in general, and motion in general: thus we see how much the tenet of extended, moveable substances existing without the mind, depends on that strange doctrine of abstract ideas. And here I cannot but remark, how nearly the vague and indeterminate description of matter or corporeal substance, which the modern philosophers are run into by their own principles, resembles that antiquated and so much ridiculed notion of materia prima, to be met with in Aristotle and his followers. Without extension solidity cannot be conceived; since therefore it has been shown that extension exists not in an unthinking substance, the same must also be true of solidity.

XII. That number is entirely the creature of the mind, even though the other qualities be allowed to exist without, will be evident to whoever considers, that the same thing bears a different denomination of number, as the mind views it with different respects. Thus, the same extension is one, or three, or thirty-six, according as the mind considers it with reference to a yard, a foot, or an inch. Number is so visibly relative, and dependent on men's understanding, that it is strange to think how any one should give it an absolute existence without the mind. We say, one book, one page, one line; all these are equally units, though some contain several of the others. And in each instance it is plain, the unit relates to some particular combination of ideas arbitrarily put together by the mind.

XIII. Unity, I know, some will have to be a simple or uncompounded idea, accompanying all other ideas into the mind. That I have any such idea, answering the word unity, I do not find; and if I had, methinks I could not miss finding it; on the contrary, it should be the most familiar to my understanding, since it is said to accompany all other ideas, and to be perceived by all the ways of sensation and reflection. To say no more, it is an abstract idea.

XIV. I shall further add, that after the same manner as modern philosophers prove certain sensible qualities to have no existence in matter, or without the mind, the same thing may be likewise proved of all other sensible qualities whatsoever. Thus, for instance, it is said that heat and cold are affections only of the mind, and not at all patterns of real beings, existing in the corporeal substances which excite them, for that the same body which appears cold to one hand, seems warm to another. Now why may we not as well argue that figure and extension are not patterns or resemblances of qualities existing in matter, because to the same eye at different stations, or eyes of a different texture at the same station, they appear various, and cannot therefore be the images of any thing settled and determinate without the mind? Again, it is proved that sweetness is not really in the said thing, because, the thing remaining unaltered, the sweetness is changed into bitter, as in case of a fever or otherwise vitiated palate. Is it not as reasonable to say, that motion is not without the mind, since if the succession of ideas in the mind become swifter, the motion, it is acknowledged, shall appear slower without any alteration in any external object.

XV. In short, let any one consider those arguments which are thought manifestly to prove that colors and tastes exist only in the mind, and he shall find they may with equal force be brought to prove the same thing of extension, figure, and motion. Though it must be confessed, this method of arguing doth not so much prove that there is no extension or color in an outward object, as that we do not know by sense which is the true extension or color of the object. But the arguments foregoing plainly show it to be impossible that any color or extension at all, or other sensible quality whatsoever, should exist in an unthinking subject without the mind, or in truth, that there should be any such thing as an outward object.

XVI. But let us examine a little the received opinion. It is said extension is a mode or accident of matter, and that matter is the substratum that supports it. Now I desire that you would explain what is meant by matter's supporting extension: say you, I have no idea of matter, and therefore cannot explain it. I answer, though you have no positive, yet if you have any meaning at all, you must at least have a relative idea of matter; though you know not what it is, yet you must be supposed to know what relation it bears to accidents, and what is meant by its supporting them. It is evident support cannot here be taken in its usual or literal sense, as when we say that pillars support a building: in what sense therefore must it be taken?

XVII. If we inquire into what the most accurate philosophers declare themselves to mean by material substance, we shall find them acknowledge, they have no other meaning annexed to those sounds, but the idea of being in general, together with the relative notion of its supporting accidents. The general idea of being appeareth to me the most abstract and incomprehensible of all other; and as for its supporting accidents, this, as we have just now observed, cannot be understood in the common sense of those words; it must therefore be taken in some other sense, but what that is they do not explain. So that when I consider the two parts or branches which make the signification of the words material substance, I am convinced there is no distinct meaning annexed to them. But why should we trouble ourselves any further, in discussing this material substratum or support of figure and motion, and other sensible qualities? does it not suppose they have an existence without the mind? and is not this a direct repugnancy, and altogether inconceivable?

XVIII. But though it were possible that solid, figured, moveable substances may exist without the mind, corresponding to the ideas we have of bodies, yet how is it possible for us to know this? either we must know it by sense, or by reason. As for our senses, by them we have the knowledge only of our sensations, ideas, or those things that are immediately perceived by sense, call them what you will: but they do not inform us that things exist without the mind, or unperceived, like to those which are perceived. This the materialists themselves acknowledge. It remains therefore that if we have any knowledge at all of external things, it must be by reason, inferring their existence from what is immediately perceived by sense. But (I do not see) what reason can induce us to believe the existence of bodies without the mind, from what we perceive, since the very patrons of matter themselves do not pretend, there is any necessary connexion betwixt them and our ideas. I say, it is granted on all hands (and what happens in dreams, frenzies, and the like, puts it beyond dispute) that it is possible we might be affected with all the ideas

we have now, though no bodies existed without, resembling them. Hence it is evident the supposition of external bodies is not necessary for the producing our ideas: since it is granted they are produced sometimes, and might possibly be produced always, in the same order we see them in at present, without their concurrence.

XIX. But though we might possibly have all our sensations without them, yet perhaps it may be thought easier to conceive and explain the manner of their production, by supposing external bodies in their likeness rather than otherwise; and so it might be at least probable there are such things as bodies that excite their ideas in our minds. But neither can this be said; for though we give the materialists their external bodies, they, by their own confession, are never the nearer knowing how our ideas are produced: since they own themselves unable to comprehend in what manner body can act upon spirit, or how it is possible it should imprint any idea in the mind. Hence it is evident, the production of ideas or sensations in our minds, can be no reason why we should suppose matter or corporeal substances, since that is acknowledged to remain equally inexplicable with or without this supposition. If therefore it were possible for bodies to exist without the mind, yet to hold they do so must needs be a very precarious opinion; since it is to suppose, without any reason at all, that God has created innumerable beings that are entirely useless, and serve to no manner of purpose.

XX. In short, if there were external bodies, it is impossible we should ever come to know it; and if there were not, we might have the very same reasons to think there were that we have now. Suppose, what no one can deny possible, an intelligence, without the help of external bodies, to be affected with the same train of sensations or ideas that you are, imprinted in the same order and with like vividness in his mind. I ask, whether that intelligence hath not all the reason to believe the existence of corporeal substances, represented by his ideas, and exciting them in his mind, that you can possibly have for believing the same thing? Of this there can be no question; which one consideration is enough to make any reasonable person suspect the strength of whatever arguments he may think himself to have for the existence of bodies without the mind.

XXI. Were it necessary to add any further proof against the existence of matter, after what has been said, I could instance several of those errors and difficulties (not to mention impieties) which have sprung from that tenet. It has occasioned numberless controversies and disputes in philosophy, and not a few of greater moment in religion. But I shall not enter into the detail of them in this place, as well because I think arguments a posteriori are unnecessary for confirming what has been, if I mistake not, sufficiently demonstrated a priori, as because I shall hereafter find occasion to say somewhat of them.

XXII. I am afraid I have given cause to think me needlessly prolix in handling this subject. For to what purpose is it to dilate on that which may be demonstrated with the utmost evidence in a line or two, to any one that is capable of the least reflection? it is but looking into your own thoughts, and so trying whether you can conceive it possible for a sound, or figure, or motion, or color, to exist without the mind, or unperceived. This easy trial may make you see, that what you contend for is a downright contradiction. Insomuch that I am content to put the whole upon this issue; if you can but conceive it possible for one extended moveable substance, or in general, for any one idea, or any thing like an idea, to exist otherwise than in a mind perceiving it, I shall readily give up the cause: and as for all that compacts of external bodies which you contend for, I shall grant you its existence, though you cannot either give me any reason why you believe it exists, or assign any use to it when it is supposed to exist. I say, the bare possibility of your opinion's being true, shall pass for an argument that it is so.

XXIII. But say you, surely there is nothing easier than to imagine trees, for instance, in a park, or books existing in a closet, and nobody by to perceive them. I answer, you may so, there is no difficulty in it: but what is all this, I beseech you, more than framing in your mind certain ideas which you call books and trees, and at the same time omitting to frame the idea of any one that may perceive them? but do not you yourself perceive or think of them all the while? this therefore is nothing to the purpose; it only shows you have the power of imagining or forming ideas in your mind; but it doth not show that you can conceive it possible the objects of your thought may exist without the mind: to make out this, it is necessary that you conceive them existing unconceived or unthought-of, which is a manifest repugnancy.

When we do our utmost to conceive the existence of external bodies, we are all the while only contemplating our own ideas. But the mind, taking no notice of itself, is deluded to think it can and doth conceive bodies existing unthought-of or without the mind; though at the same time they are apprehended by or exist in itself. A little attention will discover to any one the truth and evidence of what is here said, and make it unnecessary to insist on any other proofs against the existence of material substance.

XXIV. It is very obvious, upon the least inquiry into our own thoughts, to know whether it be possible for us to understand what is meant by the absolute existence of sensible objects in themselves or without the mind. To me it is evident those words mark out either a direct contradiction, or else nothing at all. And to convince others of this, I know no readier or fairer way, than to entreat they would calmly attend to their own thoughts: and if by this attention the emptiness or repugnancy of those expressions does appear, surely nothing more is requisite for their conviction. It is on this therefore that I insist, to wit, that the absolute existence of unthinking things are words without a meaning, or which include a contradiction. This is what I repeat and inculcate, and earnestly recommend to the attentive thoughts of the reader.

XXV. All our ideas, sensations, or the things which we perceive, by whatsoever names they may be distinguished, are visibly inactive; there is nothing of power or agency included in them. So that one idea or object of thought cannot produce, or make any alteration in another. To be satisfied of the truth of this, there is nothing else requisite but a bare observation of our ideas. For since they and every part of them exist only in the mind, it follows that there is nothing in them but what is perceived. But whoever shall attend to his ideas, whether of sense or reflection, will not perceive in them any power or activity; there is therefore no such thing contained in them. A little attention will discover to us that the very being of an idea implies passiveness and inertness in it, insomuch that it is impossible for an idea to do any thing, or, strictly speaking, to be the cause of any thing: neither can it be the resemblance or pattern of any active being, as is evident from Sect. viii. Whence it plainly follows that extension, figure, and motion, cannot be the cause of our sensations. To say, therefore, that these are the effects of powers resulting from the configuration, number, motion, and size of corpuscles, must certainly be false.

XXVI. We perceive a continual succession of ideas, some are anew excited, others are changed or totally disappear. There is therefore some cause of these ideas whereon they depend, and which produces and changes them. That this cause cannot be any quality or idea or combination of ideas, is clear from the preceding section. It must therefore be a substance; but it has been shown that there is no corporeal or material substance: it remains therefore that the cause of ideas is an incorporeal active substance or spirit.

XXVII. A spirit is one simple, undivided, active being: as it perceives ideas, it is called the understanding, and as it produces or otherwise operates about them, it is called the will. Hence there can be no idea formed of a soul or spirit: for all ideas whatever, being passive and inert (vide Sect. xxv.), they cannot represent unto us, by way of image or likeness, that which acts. A little attention will make it plain to any one, that to have an idea which shall be like that active principle of motion and change of ideas, is absolutely impossible. Such is the nature of spirit, or that which acts, that it cannot be of itself perceived but only by the effects which it produceth. If any man shall doubt of the truth of what is here delivered, let him but reflect and try if he can frame the idea of any power or active being; and whether he hath ideas of two principal powers, marked by the names *will* and *understanding,* distinct from each other as well as from a third idea of substance or being in general, with a relative notion of its supporting or being the subject of the aforesaid powers, which is signified by the name soul or spirit. This is what some hold; but so far as I can see, the words will, soul, spirit, do not stand for different ideas, or in truth, for any idea at all, but for something which is very different from ideas, and which being an agent cannot be like unto, or represented by, any idea whatsoever. Though it must be owned at the same time, that we have some notion of soul, spirit, and the operations of the mind, such as willing, loving, hating, inasmuch as we know or understand the meaning of those words.

XXVIII. I find I can excite ideas in my mind at pleasure, and vary and shift the scene as oft as I think fit. It is no more than willing, and straightway this or that idea arises in my fancy: and by the same power it is obliterated, and makes way for another. This making and unmaking of ideas doth very properly denominate the mind active. Thus much is certain, and grounded on experience: but when we talk of unthinking agents, or of exciting ideas exclusive of volition, we only amuse ourselves with words.

XXIX. But whatever power I may have over my own thoughts, I find the ideas actually perceived by sense have not a like dependence on my will. When in broad daylight I open my eyes, it is not in my power to choose whether I shall see or no, or to determine what particular objects shall present themselves to my view; and so likewise as to the hearing and other senses, the ideas imprinted on them are not creatures of my will. There is therefore some other will or spirit that produces them.

XXX. The ideas of sense are more strong, lively, and distinct than those of the imagination; they have likewise a steadiness, order, and coherence, and are not excited at random, as those which are the effects of human wills often are, but in a regular train or series, the admirable connexion whereof sufficiently testifies the wisdom and benevolence of its author. Now the set rules or established methods, wherein the mind we depend on excites in us the ideas of sense, are called the laws of nature: and these we learn by experience, which teaches us that such and such ideas are attended with such and such other ideas, in the ordinary course of things.

XXXI. This gives us a sort of foresight, which enables us to regulate our actions for the benefit of life. And without this we should be eternally at a loss: we could not know how to act any thing that might procure us the least pleasure, or remove the least pain of sense. That food nourishes, sleep refreshes, and fire warms us; that to sow in the seed-time is the way to reap in the harvest, and, in general, that to obtain such or such ends, such or such means are conducive, all this we know, not by discovering any necessary connexion between our ideas, but only by the observation of the settled laws of nature, without which we should be all in uncertainty and confusion, and a grown man no more know how to manage himself in the affairs of life than an infant just born.

XXXII. And yet this consistent, uniform working, which so evidently displays the goodness and wisdom of that governing Spirit whose will constitutes the laws of nature, is so far from leading our thoughts to him, that it rather sends them a wandering after second causes. For when we perceive certain ideas of sense constantly followed by other ideas, and we know this is not of our own doing, we forthwith attribute power and agency to the ideas themselves, and make one the cause of another, than which nothing can be more absurd and unintelligible. Thus, for example, having observed that when we perceive by sight a certain round luminous figure, we at the same time perceive by touch the idea or sensation called heat, we do from thence conclude the sun to be the cause of heat. And in like manner perceiving the motion and collision of bodies to be attended with sound, we are inclined to think the latter an effect of the former.

XXXIII. The ideas imprinted on the senses by the author of nature are called real things: and those excited in the imagination, being less regular, vivid, and constant, are more properly termed ideas, or images of things, which they copy and represent. But then our sensations, be they never so vivid and distinct, are nevertheless ideas, that is, they exist in the mind, or are perceived by it, as truly as the ideas of its own framing. The ideas of sense are allowed to have more reality in them, that is, to be more strong, orderly, and coherent than the creatures of the mind: but this is no argument that they exist without the mind. They are also less dependent on the spirit, or thinking substance which perceives them, in that they are excited by the will of another and more powerful spirit: yet still they are ideas, and certainly no idea, whether faint or strong, can exist otherwise than in a mind perceiving it.

XXXIV. Before we proceed any further, it is necessary to spend some time in answering objections which may probably be made against the principles hitherto laid down. In doing of which, if I seem too prolix to those of quick apprehensions, I hope it may be pardoned, since all men do not equally apprehend things of this nature; and I am willing to be understood by every one. First then it will be objected that by the foregoing principles, all that is real and substantial in nature is banished out of the world: and instead thereof a chimerical scheme of ideas takes place. All things that exist, exist only in the mind, that is, they are purely notional. What therefore becomes of the sun, moon, and stars? What must we think of houses, rivers, mountains, trees, stones; nay, even of our own bodies? Are all these but so many chimeras and illusions on the fancy? To all which, and whatever else of the same sort may be objected, I answer, that by the principles premised, we are not deprived of any one thing in nature. Whatever we see, feel, hear, or any wise conceive or understand, remains as secure as ever, and is as real as ever. There is a rerum natura, and the distinction between realities and chimeras retains its full force. This is evident from Sect. xxix., xxx., and xxxiii., where we have shown what is meant by real things in opposition to chimeras, or ideas of our own framing; but then they both equally exist in the mind, and in that sense are like ideas.

XXXV. I do not argue against the existence of any one thing that we can apprehend, either by sense or reflection. That the things I see with mine eyes and touch with my hands do exist, really exist, I make not the least question. The only thing whose existence we deny, is that which philosophers call matter or corporeal substance. And in doing of this, there is no damage done to the rest of mankind, who, I dare say, will never miss it. The atheist indeed will want the color of an empty name to support his impiety; and the philosophers may possibly find, they have lost a great handle for trifling and disputation. . . .

CXLV. From what hath been said, it is plain that we cannot know the existence of other spirits otherwise than by their operations, or the ideas of them excited in us. I perceive several motions, changes, and combinations of ideas, that inform me there are certain particular agents like myself, which accompany them, and concur in their production. Hence the knowledge I have of other spirits is not immediate, as is the knowledge of my ideas; but depending on the intervention of ideas, by me referred to agents or spirits distinct from myself, as effects or concomitant signs.

CXLVI. But though there be some things which convince us human agents are concerned in producing them; yet it is evident to every one, that those things which are called the works of nature, that is, the far greater part of the ideas or sensations perceived by us, are not produced by, or dependent on, the wills of men. There is therefore some other spirit that causes them, since it is repugnant that they should subsist by themselves. See Sect. xxix. But if we attentively consider the constant regularity, order, and concatenation of natural things, the surprising magnificence, beauty, and perfection of the larger, and the exquisite contrivance of the smaller parts of the creation, together with the exact harmony and correspondence of the whole, but, above all, the never enough admired laws of pain and pleasure, and the instincts or natural inclinations, appetites, and passions of animals; I say if we consider all these things, and at the same time attend to the meaning and import of the attributes, one, eternal, infinitely wise, good, and perfect, we shall clearly perceive that they belong to the aforesaid spirit, who works all in all, and by whom all things consist.

CXLVII. Hence it is evident, that God is known as certainly and immediately as any other mind or spirit whatsoever, distinct from ourselves. We may even assert, that the existence of God is far more evidently perceived than the existence of men; because the effects of nature are infinitely more numerous and considerable than those ascribed to human agents. There is not any one mark that denotes a man, or effect produced by him, which doth not more strongly evince the being of that Spirit who is the Author of nature. For it is evident that in affecting other persons, the will of man hath no other object than barely the motion of the limbs of his body; but that such a motion should be attended by, or excite any idea in the mind of another, depends wholly on the will of the Creator. He alone it is who, "upholding all things by the word of his power," maintains that intercourse between spirits, whereby they are able to perceive the existence of each other. And yet this pure and clear light, which enlightens every one, is itself invisible.

III.3 Science and the Physical World: A Defense of Phenomenalism

W. T. STACE

W. T. Stace (1886–1967) was born in Britain and served in the British Civil Service in Ceylon. In 1932 he came to the United States to teach philosophy at Princeton University. In this essay Stace defends a phenomenalist view of perception. Drawing on Hume's remarks on causality (see Reading VIII.1), Stace argues that the realist, one who believes in a separate material world apart from sensations, has no good arguments for his or her position. All that the principle of causality tells us is that there are regularities of experiences in the world. Modern science goes beyond its proper domain when it hypostatizes functional concepts such as "atoms," "gravity," "forces," and "the conservation of energy" and treats them as though they were things. For a phenomenalist like Stace, only sensations and the minds that perceive them exist. The rest is mental construction, useful fiction, which help us organize our experience and predict sensations.

This selection is a slight abbreviation of Stace's article "Science and the Physical World," which was published in 1967 in his *Man Against Darkness and Other Essays.* It is reprinted with the permission of the University of Pittsburgh Press. © 1967 University of Pittsburgh Press.

Stars, Atoms and Sensations

So far as I know scientists still talk about electrons, protons, neutrons, and so on. We never directly perceive these, hence if we ask how we know of their existence the only possible answer seems to be that they are an inference from what we do directly perceive. What sort of an inference? Apparently a causal inference. The atomic entities in some way impinge upon the sense of the animal organism and cause that organism to perceive the familiar world of tables, chairs, and the rest.

But is it not clear that such a concept of causation, however interpreted, is invalid? The only reason we have for believing in the law of causation is that we *observe* certain regularities or sequences. We observe that, in certain conditions, A is always followed by B. We call A the cause, B the effect. And the sequence A–B becomes a causal law. It follows that all *observed* causal sequences are between sensed objects in the familiar world of perception, and that all known causal laws apply solely to the world of sense and not to anything beyond or behind it. And this in turn means that we have not got, and never could have, one jot of evidence for believing that the law of causation can be applied *outside* the realm of perception, or that that realm can have any causes (such as the supposed physical objects) which are not themselves perceived.

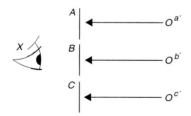

Put the same thing in another way. Suppose there is an observed sequence A—B—C, represented by the vertical lines in the diagram below. The observer X sees, and can see, nothing except things in the familiar world of perception. What *right* has he, and what *reason* has he, to assert cause of A, B, and C, such as a', b', c', which he can never observe, behind the perceived world? He has no *right*, because the law of causation on which he is relying has never been observed to operate outside the series of perceptions, and he can have,

therefore, no evidence that it does so. And he has no *reason* because the phenomenon C is *sufficiently* accounted for by the cause B, B by A, and so on. It is unnecessary and superfluous to introduce a *second* cause b', for B, c' for C, and so forth. To give two causes for each phenomenon, one in one world and one in another, is unnecessary, and perhaps even self-contradictory.

Is it denied, then, it will be asked, that the star causes light waves, that the waves cause retinal changes, that these cause changes in the optic nerve, which in turn causes movements in the brain cells, and so on? No, it is not denied. But the observed causes and effects are all in the world of perception. And no sequences of sense-data can possibly justify going outside that world. If you admit that we never observe anything except sensed objects and their relations, regularities, and sequences, then it is obvious that we are completely shut in by our sensations and can never get outside them. Not only causal relations, but all other observed relations, upon which *any* kind of inferences might be founded, will lead only to further sensible objects and their relations. No inference, therefore, can pass from what is sensible to what is not sensible.

The fact is that atoms are *not* inferences from sensations. No one denies, of course, that a vast amount of perfectly valid inferential reasoning takes place in the physical theory of the atom. But it will not be found to be in any strict logical sense inference *from sense-data to atoms*. An *hypothesis* is set up, and the inferential processes are concerned with the application of the hypothesis, that is, with the prediction by its aid of further possible sensations and with its own internal consistency.

That atoms are not inferences from sensations means, of course, that from the existence of sensations we cannot validly infer the existence of atoms. And this means that we cannot have any reason at all to believe that they exist. And that is why I propose to argue that they do not exist—or at any rate that no one could know it if they did, and that we have absolutely no evidence of their existence.

What status have they, then? Is it meant that they are false and worthless, merely untrue? Certainly not. No one supposes that the entries in the Nautical Almanac "exist" anywhere except on the pages of that book and in the brains of its compilers and readers. Yet they are "true," inasmuch as they enable us to predict certain sensations, namely, the positions and times of certain perceived objects which we call the stars. And so the formulae of the atomic theory are true in the same sense, and perform a similar function.

I suggest that they are nothing but shorthand formulae, ingeniously worked out by the human mind, to enable it to predict its experience, i.e. to predict what sensations will be given to it. By "predict" here I do not mean to refer solely to the future. To calculate that there was an eclipse of the sun visible in Asia Minor in the year 585 B.C. is, in the sense in which I am using the term, to predict.

In order to see more clearly what is meant, let us apply the same idea to another case, that of gravitation. Newton formulated a law of gravitation in terms of "forces." It was supposed that this law—which was nothing but a mathematical formula—governed the operation of these existent forces. Nowadays it is no longer believed that these forces exist at all. And yet the law can be applied just as well without them to the prediction of astronomical phenomena. It is a matter of no importance to the scientific man whether the forces exist or not. That may be said to be a purely philosophical question. And I think the philosopher should pronounce them fictions. But that would not make the law useless or untrue. If it could still be used to predict phenomena, it would be just as true as it was.

It is true that fault is now found with Newton's law, and that another law, that of Einstein, has been substituted for it. And it is sometimes supposed that the reason for this is that forces are no longer believed in. But this is not the case. Whether forces exist or not simply does not matter. What matters is the discovery that Newton's law does *not* enable us accurately to predict certain astronomical facts such as the exact position of the planet Mercury. Therefore another formula, that of Einstein, has been substituted for it which permits correct predictions. This new law, as it happens, is a formula in terms of geometry. It is pure mathematics and nothing else. It does not contain anything about forces. In its pure form it does not even contain, so I am informed, anything about "humps and hills in space-time." And it does not matter whether any such humps and hills exist. It is truer than Newton's law, not because it substitutes humps and hills for forces, but solely because it is a more accurate formula of prediction.

Not only may it be said that forces do not exist. It may with equal truth be said that "gravitation" does not exist. Gravitation is not a "thing," but a mathematical formula, which exists only in the heads of mathematicians. And as a mathematical formula cannot cause a body to fall, so gravitation cannot cause a body to fall. Ordinary language misleads us here. We speak of the law "of" gravitation, and suppose that this law "applies to" the heavenly bodies. We are thereby misled into supposing that there are *two* things, namely, the gravitation and the heavenly bodies, and that one of these things, the gravitation, causes changes in the other. In reality nothing exists except the moving bodies. And neither Newton's law nor Einstein's law is, strictly speaking, a law of gravitation. They are both laws of moving bodies, that is to say, formulae which tell us how these bodies will move.

Now, just as in the past "forces" were foisted into Newton's law (by himself, be it said), so now certain popularizers of relativity foisted "humps and hills in space-time" into Einstein's law. We hear that the reason why the planets move in curved courses is that they cannot go through these humps and hills, but have to go round them! The planets just get "shoved about," not by forces, but by the humps and hills! But these humps and hills are pure metaphors. And anyone who takes them for "existences" gets asked awkward questions as to what "curved space" is curved "in."

It is not irrelevant to our topic to consider *why* human beings invent these metaphysical monsters of forces and bumps in space-time. The reason is that they have never emancipated themselves from the absurd idea that science "explains" things. They were not content to have laws which merely told them *that* the planets will, as a matter of fact, move in such and such ways. They wanted to know "why" the planets move in those ways. So Newton replied, "Forces." "Oh," said humanity, "that explains it. We understand forces. We feel them every time someone pushes or pulls us." Thus the movements were supposed to be "explained" by entities familiar because analogous to the muscular sensations which human beings feel. The humps and hills were introduced for exactly the same reason. They seem so familiar. If there is a bump in the billiard table, the rolling billiard ball is diverted from a straight to a curved course. Just the same with the planets. "Oh, I see!" says humanity, "that's quite simple. That *explains* everything."

But scientific laws, properly formulated, never "explain" anything. They simply state, in an abbreviated and generalized form, *what happens*. No scientist, and in my opinion no philosopher, knows *why* anything happens, or can "explain" anything. Scientific laws do nothing except state the brute fact that "when *A* happens, *B* always happens too." And laws of this kind obviously enable us to predict. If certain scientists substituted humps and hills for forces, then they have just substituted one superstition for another. For my part I do not believe that *science* has done this, though some *scientists* may have. For scientists, after all, are human beings with the same craving for "explanations" as other people.

I think that atoms are in exactly the same position as forces and the bumps and hills of space-time. In reality the mathematical formulae which are the scientific ways of stating the atomic theory are simply formulae for calculating what sensations will appear in given conditions. But just as the weakness of the human mind demanded that there should correspond to the formula of gravitation a real "thing" which could be called "gravitation itself" or "force," so the same weakness demands that there should be a real thing corresponding to the atomic formulae, and this real thing is called the atom. In reality the atoms no more cause sensations than gravitation causes apples to fall. The only causes of sensations are other sensations. And the relation of atoms to sensations to be felt is not the relation of cause to effect, but the relation of a mathematical formula to the facts and happenings which it enables the mathematician to calculate. . . .

It will not be out of place to give one more example to show how common fictitious existences are in science, and how little it matters whether they really exist or not. This example has no strange and annoying talk of "bent spaces" about it. One of the foundations of physics is, or used to be, the law of the conservation of energy. I do not know how far, if at all, this has been affected by the theory that matter sometimes turns into energy. But that does not affect the lesson it has for us. The law states, or used to state, that the amount of energy in the universe is always constant, that energy is never either created or destroyed. This was highly convenient, but it seemed to have obvious exceptions. If you throw a stone up into the air, you are told that it exerts in its fall the same amount of energy which it

took to throw it up. But suppose it does not fall. Suppose it lodges on the roof of your house and stays there. What has happened to the energy which you can nowhere perceive as being exerted? It seems to have disappeared out of the universe. No, says the scientist, it still exists as *potential* energy. Now what does this blessed word "potential"—which is thus brought in to save the situation—mean as applied to energy? It means, of course, that the energy does not exist in any of its regular "forms," heat, light, electricity, etc. But this is merely negative. What positive meaning has the term? Strictly speaking, none whatever. Either the energy exists or it does not exist. There is no realm of the "potential" half-way between existence and non-existence. And this existence of energy can only consist in its being exerted. If the energy is not being exerted, then it is not energy and does not exist. Energy can no more exist without energizing than heat can exist without being hot. The "potential" existence of the energy is, then, a fiction. The actual empirically verifiable facts are that if a certain quantity of energy *e* exists in the universe and then disappears out of the universe (as happens when the stone lodges on the roof), the same amount of energy *e* will always reappear, begin to exist again, in certain known conditions. That is the fact which the law of the conservation of energy actually expresses. And the fiction of potential energy is introduced simply because it is convenient and makes the equations easier to work. They could be worked quite well without it, but would be slightly more complicated. In either case the function of the law is the same. Its object is to apprise us that if in certain conditions we have certain perceptions (throwing up the stone), then in certain other conditions we shall get certain other perceptions (heat, light, stone hitting skull, or other such). But there will always be a temptation to hypostatize the potential energy as an "existence," and to believe that it is a "cause" which "explains" the phenomena.

If the views which I have been expressing are followed out, they will lead to the conclusion that, strictly speaking, *nothing exists except sensations* (and the minds which perceive them). The rest is mental construction or fiction. But this does not mean that the conception of a star or the conception of an electron are worthless or untrue. Their truth and value consist in their capacity for helping us to organize our experience and predict our sensations.

III.4 Phenomenalism: Its Grounds and Difficulties

C. H. WHITELEY

C. H. Whiteley (1911–   ) was until his retirement professor of philosophy at the University of Birmingham in England. In this essay, Whitely analyzes Berkeley's successor, contemporary phenomenalism, identifying its strengths and weaknesses. Its strengths are that it is simpler than its competitors, it lends itself readily to verification, and it refutes skepticism. Its weaknesses are that it tends to blur the distinction between "appearance" and "reality," it cannot account for the seeming permanence of things, it has problems accounting for causation, and it leads to solipsism, the view that "the only experience in the world is my experience, and the only person existing in the universe is myself."

48. The Non-Existence of Matter

From such arguments as these, Berkeley draws the conclusion that Matter does not exist, or at least there is no good reason for believing that it does. This seems a most alarming conclusion. But he assures us that there is no cause for alarm, if we are careful to understand exactly what he is saying. He is denying that there is any such thing as material substance as the materialist philosophers define it; that is, a substance apart from and independent of all awareness, permanent, public, the cause of our sensations, having shape, size, position, motion. He is not denying that there are such things as tables and chairs and clouds and apples and cats, or that we know quite a lot about them and often make true statements concerning them. It is true that there is a table in this room, that it is 3 feet long, etc. It is true that grass is green and snow is white. It is true that water is a compound of oxygen and hydrogen, and malaria is caused by the bite of a mosquito. These statements are false if they are interpreted as referring to some unobservable "material" thing which is outside all experience. But there is another way of interpreting them in which they may well be true. That is to take them as descriptions, not of a mysterious unexperienceable Matter, but of sense-experiences which people have or might have.

From C. H. Whiteley, *An Introduction to Metaphysics,* Methuen & Co. Ltd., London, 1950. Reprinted by permission.

49. The Meaning of Words

And this seems a reasonable way of interpreting our statements when we consider how it is that we come to understand and make use of language. When I am teaching a child the meaning of the word "table," I point to the table, so that he sees it; I put his hand to it, so that he feels it; that is, I cause him to sense certain sense-data. Surely it is with these sense-data that he thereupon associates the sound "table"; when he sees and feels similar sense-data, he repeats "table." It is by the differences in what they look like and feel like that he distinguishes tables from chairs and apples and half-crowns. It is natural to conclude that when he uses the word "table" or "apple," he is using it to describe what he sees, feels, tastes, etc., rather than to propound some theory about an invisible and intangible material substance.

The word "table" *means* a certain visible squareness and brownness, a certain tangible hardness; i.e., it means a certain type of sense-experience. When I say "There is a table in this room" I am describing the sense-data which I am now sensing, and if I do not sense such sense-data, then, being a truthful person, I do not say that there is a table in the room. If someone else says that there is, I test his statement by looking and feeling, i.e., by finding out whether the appropriate sense-data are available; if they are not, I dismiss his statement as false. If I say "Socrates drank his companions under the table," I am not describing any sense-experiences which I have now, but I am describing sense-experiences which I suppose Socrates and his companions to have had at another time and place.

We cannot, of course, identify "the table" with any one single sense-datum; an experience which was entirely unique and did not recur would not be worth naming. The function of words is not to name everything we see or hear, but to pick out the recurrent patterns in our experience. They identify our present sense-data as being of the same group or type as others which we have sensed before. A word, then, describes, not a single experience, but a group or type of experiences; the word "table" describes all the various sense-data which we normally refer to as appearances or sensations "of" the table. So a material thing is not indeed identical with any sense-datum; but neither is it something different in kind from sense-data. It is a group, or class, or system of sense-data; and nothing but sense-data goes to constitute it. So this doctrine may be expressed by saying that every statement we make about a material thing is equivalent to another statement about sense-data.

50. Phenomenalism

This analysis of the notion of a material thing is called Phenomenalism, since it makes of a material thing a group of phenomena, appearances, instead of a transcendent reality distinct from appearances. It is a widespread view, and has been accepted by many philosophers who do not call themselves Idealists and are far from accepting Berkeley's view that the fundamental reality is Mind. The term "idealism" itself, however, though it has shifted in meaning since, does properly denote just this part of Berkeley's theory, that the material world—"the whole choir of heaven and furniture of the earth" says Berkeley—consists of what he calls "ideas" and I have been calling "sense-data." The word in this sense has nothing to do with ideals, and the theory would have been called "ideaism" but for considerations of pronunciation.

Phenomenalism, then, is the doctrine that all statements about material objects can be completely analysed into statements about sense-data. The analysis of any such statement must be very complex; and the value of the "material-object language" is that it enables us to refer in one word, such as "table," to a vast number of sense-data differing very much among themselves. The group of sense-data constituting the table includes all the different views I can obtain at different distances, from different angles, in different lights, no two of them exactly alike, but all of them variations on one central pattern; it includes sense-data of touch, and those of sound (though these last seem somewhat more loosely connected with the main visuo-tactual group); and with other kinds of material things, such as apples, sense-data of taste and smell form important constituents of the thing.

51. Its Advantages

This type of theory has certain clear advantages. On the representative theory, the very existence of a material world or of any given material object must always be in principle doubtful. I am directly aware of my sense-data, and so can be certain of their existence and character: but "material objects" are quite different—their existence and character can be known only by an inference, which cannot give the complete certainty which comes from observation. Descartes, for example, accepts this consequence of the theory, and will not allow himself to believe that there is a material world at all, until he has convinced himself that there exists an omnipotent and benevolent God who would never have led him to believe in the material world if it had not been real. But if Descartes really succeeded in keeping up this attitude of doubt for more than a moment, few men have been able to imitate him. We *cannot* believe that the existence of the table is in any way subject to doubt.

The phenomenalist theory, by making the existence of the table *the same thing* as the occurrence of certain sense-data, removes that doubt; for the system of sense-data constituting the table has beyond doubt come under my observation.

The theory not only removes the doubt, but makes it clear why we cannot seriously entertain it. The Plain Man was right after all: material things are seen and touched, are objects of direct awareness, and it is by seeing and touching that we know that they exist, though no material thing is straightforwardly identical with what I am seeing and touching *at this particular moment*.

So, by accepting the phenomenalist analysis, we escape being involved in any reference to an unobservable Matter. We can preserve our empiricism inviolate, and talk about the things we see and hear and smell and touch, and not about other hypothetical things beyond the reach of our observation. Science, the knowledge of nature, on this view becomes the recording, ordering and forecasting of human experiences. Therein lies its interest for us. If the physical world lay outside our experience, why should we be concerned with it?

52. Criticisms of Phenomenalism

But these advantages of phenomenalism are purchased at a cost. Along several different lines the phenomenalist interpretation of our statements about material things seem to conflict with our usual beliefs, and produces paradoxes not very easy to accept.

"Appearance and Reality"

(1) In ordinary speech we are accustomed to draw a distinction between "appearance" and "reality," and to allow that a thing may appear to be what it is not, as Descartes' stick half under water may appear bent although it is really straight. Hence we reckon some of our perceptions as "real" or "true" or "genuine," and others as "illusions." The representative theory of perception is in accordance with this way of thinking; for on that theory our sense-data are in some respects copies of material things; some are accurate copies, and so are genuine and true, others are inaccurate copies, and so false and illusory. The representative theory differs from common sense mainly in holding that the discrepancies between the sense-datum and the material object which it represents are greater than we realise.

But what is the phenomenalist to make of this distinction? He can admit no essential difference between appearance and reality; for on his view the appearances *are* the reality. Material things consist of appearances—sense-data—and of nothing else. And these sense-data all actually occur and so are equally real. Moreover, they are what they appear to be; their reality consists in appearing, and the

suggestion that they might "really" have qualities which they do not appear to have is without meaning. Thus the phenomenalist has no justification for classifying them into "real" and "unreal," or "genuine" and "counterfeit." The various sense-data which go to constitute a material object, such as my table, are of many different shapes and colors. All of them are equally real, and none of them can be *the* "real shape" or "real color" of the table. Evidently tables are more versatile objects than we thought, and may have as many different shapes and colors as there are occasions of observing them. Why then should we come by the idea that there is only one "real shape," and the rest are mere appearances?

The phenomenalist solution of this difficulty is to allow that in a strict philosophical sense of the word "real," the distinction between reality and appearance cannot be drawn. But the purpose of the common-sense distinction between appearance and reality is not to pry into the ultimacies of metaphysics, but to enable us to deal with the experiences we encounter. What causes us to condemn an experience as an "illusion" is that it leads us astray. A mirage is an illusion because it causes us to make a mistake. But what kind of mistake? Surely, not the mistake of thinking that we now see trees and water, but the mistake of expecting that we shall soon be able to have a drink and sit in the shade. The mistake consists in the false expectation of certain other sense-data. Thus the illusoriness is not in the sense-datum itself, but in the expectation which we form when we sense it.

Error of this sort is possible because sense-data are not chaotic, but in the main are arranged in orderly series. Normally, when the visual sense-data belonging to water are obtainable, so are the gustatory sense-data of drinking water and relieving one's thirst. The mirage deceives us because, abnormally, we get the visual sense-data without the gustatory ones. Mirror-images may deceive us because the things seen in a mirror cannot be observed from the back and cannot be touched. Thus a "real" table consists of a complete set of sense-data of different senses related to one another in certain systematic ways (e.g., visual sense-data become continuously smaller and auditory ones continuously fainter as we move away from a certain region of space). When, as in the case of a table seen in a mirror, you have some members of the set but not others, you say that what is seen in the mirror is not a "real" table, or is not "really" there.

Again, the stick in water may lead us into error because sticks that "look bent" usually "feel bent" as well; and so we are surprised to find that it "feels straight," and say that though it "looks bent" it is not "really bent."

The precise interpretation of the word "real" is different in different contexts. But in general, say phenomenalists, it will be found that what we call the "real world" is not a world different from that of appearances; it is a selection from the world of appearances, a collection of appearances which are normal, systematic, and so reliable. The "unreal" consists of eccentric appearances which in one way or another fail to fit in with the normal type of sets of sense-data, and therefore causes us to form false expectations.

53. The Permanence of Material Things

(2) Sensations come and go. Few of them last for very long, and none of them lasts for ever. If we add up all the occasions in my life on which I have been looking at this table, we get a very short period indeed. And, like the rest of my species, I frequently go to sleep, and cease to perceive any material object whatsoever. That is to say, if a material thing consists of sense-data, its existence must be intermittent. Sense-data belonging to the thing exist only now and again, and most of the time they do not exist at all. But material objects such as tables are normally supposed to be permanent things, which endure uninterruptedly for very long periods. How can a permanent object be made out of momentary sense-data?

If I am alone in the room and close my eyes, there are then no sense-data belonging to the table; are we to suppose that I can annihilate so substantial a material object simply by shutting my eyes? It seems as though the phenomenalist must deny that any such statement as "There is a table in the room" can be true unless there is someone there seeing or touching it; and he must also deny that any such statement as "The table has been here for twenty years" can be true, unless (what seems most improbable) gangs of watchers have been observing it in relays for the whole of that time.

54. Phenomenalist Analysis of Permanence

The phenomenalist answer to these difficulties involves a radical reinterpretation of the whole notion of a permanent material thing. That the existence of the table should be permanent in the way in which my waking experience is uninterrupted, that the table should last for twenty years in the way that my hearing a performance of a symphony can last for three-quarters of an hour, is of course impossible on a phenomenalist view. Whatever kind of permanence is attributed to the table must be understood in another sense.

Clearly, when I say that there is a table in the now uninhabited attic, I am not describing the sense-data of anyone. But, though the statement cannot be a description of *actual* sense-data, it can be a description of *possible* sense-data; and this is what it is according to phenomenalists. To say that there is a table there now is to say that *if* there were anyone in the room he *would be* having the kind of experience which we call seeing a table. "There is a table" means "Go and look and you will see a table." And to say that it has been there twenty years means that if at any time during those years anyone had been in the room, he could have seen or touched a table.

So we must modify our original account of the nature of a material thing. It consists not merely of actual sense-data, but also of possible sense-data; or more precisely, of the fact that under certain conditions sense-data are obtainable. What is permanent is then not any sense-datum or group of sense-data, but the possibility of obtaining sense-data of a certain kind. Hence J. S. Mill defined matter as "the permanent possibility of sensation."

I think this much at least must be admitted: if it is true that there is a table in the attic, it is also true that if anyone with the use of normal eyes in a good light were to be in the attic now, he would have the experience of seeing the table; if it is true that the table has been there for twenty years, it is also true that if anyone has been there under those conditions at any time during those twenty years, he would have had the experience of seeing the table. That is to say, the statement about sense-data is involved in or implied by the statement about the table. According to the phenomenalist, such statements about possible sense-data constitute the whole of what the statement about the table means. All statements about material objects are equivalent to statements about what people have experienced, or would have experienced if circumstances had been different.

He points out that if we try to imagine the presence of the table in the attic, what we do is to imagine what it would look like and feel like. If we want to test the statement that it is there, we go and look. Statements which are not, in the final analysis, about actual or possible experiences, cannot be tested at all, and are therefore without meaning for us.

55. Berkeley's Account of Permanence

Berkeley himself gives another explanation of the permanence of material things. According to his theory, God is eternally perceiving everything, and therefore, at times when neither I nor any other human being or animal is perceiving the table, God is still perceiving it. But whether or not this is really the case, it is obviously not a correct interpretation of what we mean when we attribute continuous existence in time to the table. For if it were, we should not believe in permanent material things at all unless we believed, not only in God, but in an omnisentient God such as Berkeley believed in.

56. Causal Activity

(3) According to our ordinary notions of them, material objects are causally active: they do things. The table supports the tablecloth, the fire warms the room. Material objects exercise force, have influences on one another and incidentally on ourselves, causing, among other things, our sensations of them. This continually active causal interplay makes up the system of nature, which it is the business of science to study and reduce to laws. Does not science explain what happens by referring events to their causes, which in the material realm at least are material things, exercising physical force? Surely, the room cannot be warmed by my visual sense-datum of a fire! Still less can it be warmed by the possibility of a visual sense-datum

of a fire during my absence, when I am not looking at the fire but the room gets warmed all the same. When we all sit round the table and sense sense-data very similar in shape, size and color, what is the explanation of this fact, if not that there is an independent table which is the common cause of all our similar sense-data? Berkeley himself admits, or rather insists, that an "idea" is "inert," and can *do* nothing.

57. Phenomenalist Analysis of Causation

To deal with this problem, we need a fresh analysis and re-interpretation of the notion of cause, parallel to the phenomenalist re-interpretation of the notion of "substance" or "thing." Such an analysis was given in David Hume's *Treatise of Human Nature* (1739), and modern phenomenalists in the main follow his line of thought. Hume's aim is to interpret statements about cause and effect in such a way that the relation between a cause and its effect shall be an observable fact, and shall contain nothing mysterious or occult. For unless the words "cause and effect" described something we could observe, they would not, according to Hume, be intelligible to us.

What, then, do I observe in cases in which I should naturally use causal language? I am watching a game of billiards. I observe the event which I might naturally describe by saying that one ball A moved across the table and made or caused another ball B to roll into a pocket. What do I actually *see:* I see a certain sequence of events: first the movement of A, then the touching of A and B, then the movement of B. This temporal sequence of movements, the one which I call the effect following on the one I call the cause, seems to be all the visible relation there is between them.

But obviously, mere temporal sequence is not the same thing as causation; *post hoc* is not the same as *propter hoc;* plenty of other things preceded the movement of my billiard ball in time which were not causes of it. Yet nothing seems to be observable but temporal sequence—first one event, then the other. Whence do I get this notion of the ball being made or caused or forced to move?

If I were pushing the ball myself, I should be aware of myself making a certain muscular effort, *trying* to make it move; and, when I observe the collision of the two balls and the ensuing movement of B, I may perhaps have a vague image of a similar kind of pushing going on between the balls. But if I do, it is clear that this feeling of muscular effort is not observed in the situation presented to my senses, but is a "projection" of my own past feelings in similar situations. For billiard balls do not have muscles, or make efforts, and even if they did, I could not observe what efforts they were making, I could only observe their movements.

Certainly when I see the collision, I expect that the second ball will move—there is a "felt tendency of the mind" to pass from the "cause" to the "effect"; but this is a psychological fact about me, not a physical fact about the balls. There seems nothing in the observed situation corresponding to the words "cause," "power," "force," which I am inclined to apply to it; only the observed sequence of one event on the other. But how, then, do I distinguish between those temporal antecedents of an event which are its causes, and those which are not? How do I establish the difference between *post hoc* and *propter hoc*?

The answer is plain enough; I repeat the experiment, and if the same sequence of events recurs, I conclude that it was a causal and not an accidental sequence. The reason I believe that the movement of the ball was caused by the impact of the other ball, and not by somebody lighting a cigarette at the same time, is that I know by long experience that balls always move when they are struck by other balls moving fairly quickly, whereas they do not usually move when men light cigarettes in their neighbourhood. When medical men inquire into the cause of cancer, what they are looking for is something which always happens to a man before he becomes ill with cancer, just as, when they say that malaria is caused by the bite of a mosquito, they mean that a man has always been bitten by a mosquito before developing malaria. The observable fact which leads us to say that C is the cause of E is the fact that events of the kind C are followed by events of the kind E, not once or sometimes, but whenever they occur.

Causality, as a fact about the world, is then, according to Hume, a relation of invariable sequence. What is required to convert *post hoc* into *propter hoc* is regular repetition. To say that every event has a cause is to say that for any event E there is another event (or complex of "conditions") C

such that whenever an event of the kind C occurs, an event of the kind E follows. It is to say that the sequence of phenomena is patterned, systematic; that there are in nature discoverable regularities.

But these regularities are discoverable among the observed phenomena themselves, and not between phenomena and something transcending phenomena. Causation, thus interpreted, is a relation between sense-data. The causes, that is to say, the invariable antecedents, of sense-experience, are other sense-experiences.

Of course, not all causes are actually observed phenomena. In the analysis of cause, as in the analysis of substance, we must sometimes refer to possible sense-data which are not actual. But to say, for example, that a burst pipe was caused by the formation of a lump of ice which I have not seen, is not to desert the realm of sense-data; it is only to refer to sense-data which were not actually observed, but which might, in principle, have been observed; if I had been in a position to look at the interior of the pipe, I should have seen a lump of ice there.

Thus Hume and his followers do not deny that the relation of cause and effect is a real feature of the world; but they interpret it as a relation between sense-data, actual or possible. So the principle of causality does not carry us beyond the sphere of the observed and the observable, or compel us to admit the existence of "material substance" over and above systems of sense-data.

Thus, on this theory, the material world consists of sets of sense-experiences, together with the fact that an indefinitely large number of other similar sense-experiences might be had under certain specified conditions. Its "substances" are orderly groups of sense-data; and its causal relations are relations of regular sequence between sense-data of specified kinds. The main business of science is to discover causal laws, i.e., to reveal the patterns in that complex of experiences we call Nature. Science tells us what experiences to expect as the sequel to the experiences we are now having, and so renders our knowledge of the world systematic.

60. Phenomenalism Examined

We thus have, arising out of this discussion, two questions to answer. (1) Is phenomenalism true, that is, can we take the series of sense-data as complete in itself and self-explanatory, or must we postulate some other kind of reality to be its source? (2) Is idealism true, that is, if we assume some other kind of reality to exist, ought we to assume that it is mental?

61. The Relation Between Sense-Data and Material Things

As to the first question, there is one point on which the argument seems to me quite conclusive. Our sense-data are not identical with physical objects, whether these are defined as the plain man, or as the physicist, or even as the phenomenalist define them. They are not identical with the physical objects of the plain man or of the physicist, for both these persons require a physical object to remain unchanged in circumstances in which the sense-data certainly change. Both hold that the table does not change its shape when I change the position from which I look at it, whereas the sense-datum *is* changed. Unless these comparatively stable physical objects are assumed, the scientific explanation of sensation itself falls to pieces. As for the phenomenalist, even on his view no sense-datum is identical with a physical object, for the physical object is a system of possibilities, only a few of which can ever be actualised in any one experience. "This is a table" is never a mere record of what I am now observing, but involves the assertion that I and other people will be able to make further observations of a specific kind; and this possibility of further observations, which is part of what I mean when I say "This is a table," is not a matter of direct observation. So in any case our acquaintance with physical objects is not direct but mediate (to call it "inferential" would suggest a much more deliberate, self-consciously logical process than usually takes place). The properties of the sense-datum are not those of the material thing.

Yet—here is a paradox to be resolved—if I set out to describe a material thing, it seems that I invariably find myself describing sense-data. The table is square, brown, hard . . . all these, and all the other things I can say about the table, are expressed in terms of what is observed through the senses. Three alternatives are open to use here. (*a*) We can say that there is after all a real table which has some

of the properties of our sense-data, though not all of them (Locke's theory). (*b*) We can say that the table consists of a set of actual and possible sense-data, which between them possess the properties which we commonly assign to "the table" (phenomenalism). (*c*) We can say that a statement like "The table is brown" is more complex than it looks. It must be understood to mean, not that anything in the world is both a table (a material object) and brown, but that there is some material object in existence such that, when it comes into a certain causal relation with a normal percipient under certain conditions, there will be a brown sense-datum in that percipient's experience.

Now for alternative (*a*) I cannot see any good reason. Once it is granted that we do not know the properties of the table directly, I cannot see any convincing reason for holding that it has any of the properties of the sense-datum. It cannot have them all; any arguments which can be brought against its having one of them are equally valid against the others; and we cannot produce any evidence of its having any of them except the observation of the sense-data themselves. We cannot, then, permit ourselves to assign to the material object any property of a sense-datum just because it belongs to that sense-datum. We are not entitled, from the square look of the sense-datum of the table, to infer that the material object is square. We are left with the other two alternatives.

62. The Paradoxes of Phenomenalism

If we take the phenomenalist alternative, let us not do so without being clearly and fully aware of what it involves. (1) It involves the denial that physical objects are permanent, or exist unperceived. It must be granted to the phenomenalists that when I say "There is a table upstairs," I am at least implying that if you were to go upstairs and look (given normal eyesight, normal lighting, etc.) you would have certain visual sense-data. But it seems quite clear to me that this is not the whole nor the essential part of what I am asserting. For when I say that the table is there, I am stating something about what exists or happens *in fact, now;* my statement is about the actual present, and not, as the phenomenalists make it, about the possible future. And if the phenomenalist account is to be accepted, we must say that this statement is a mistake. There is nothing at all in the attic now; there is no attic now at all; for there is nobody perceiving it.

(2) We must very seriously revise our opinions about the nature of causality. As a rule, we are in the habit of believing that a cause is something which actually exists or occurs, and that something which does not actually exist or occur can have no effects. This opinion must be given up if we accept the phenomenalist view. For on that view, to say that the bursting of pipes is caused by the formation of ice in them is to say that whenever one observes or could observe sense-data of the set constituting a burst pipe, one either has or could have previously observed sense-data of the set constituting a lump of ice inside that pipe. But quite clearly, in practically every instance of this rule, nobody does actually observe the ice; the sense-data of the ice are possible, not actual. That is to say, causality in such a case is a relation between something and nothing, between an actually observed burst, and a hypothetical proposition to the effect that if something had happened which did not happen and in practice could not have happened, then something else would have happened which also did not happen. This interpretation flouts our usual assumption that what might have happened but did not happen can have no effects. The actual material agents of physics and common sense must be replaced by a set of hypothetical facts relating to unfulfilled conditions. If this is so, it is difficult to see why we should suppose that these hypothetical propositions are true. If I leave a fire in my room, I expect it to be warm on my return; but is this not because I believe that the fire is still now burning, a real present fire exercising an influence on a real present atmosphere? I cannot see what reason can be given for expecting the room to be warmed, independently of my reasons for supposing that the fire *is* burning *now* (and not that, *if* I went and looked, I should see flame). I can see reason for believing in regularities in nature holding between one event and another; but no reason at all for believing in regularities holding between one event which happened and another which might have happened but did not.

(3) A similar paradox arises with regard to other persons. According to the phenomenalist theory, all the statements I make about the consciousness of other people must be interpreted in terms of actual or possible observations of my own. A statement like "Jones is bored but he is not giving any sign of it" is a contradiction in terms, for on this theory the boredom *is* the sign. The only experiences I can intelligibly talk about or think about are my own, and whatever is not expressible in terms of actual or possible observations of mine is not intelligible to me. That is, there is no good argument for phenomenalism which is not an equally good argument for solipsism—the doctrine that the only experience in the world is my experience, and the only person existing in the universe is myself.

These paradoxical conclusions have been accepted by able philosophers, and one cannot therefore say that they are beyond belief. But they are markedly at variance with the ordinary assumptions, not only of common sense, but also of scientific investigation (for, whatever some scientists may manage to persuade themselves, they are not concerned only with the cataloguing and ordering of phenomena, but believe themselves to be dealing with permanent and independent objects). Hence we must demand very strong reasons indeed for accepting them.

III.5   A Commonsense Defense of Direct Realism

THOMAS REID

Thomas Reid (1710–1790), Scottish minister and professor at King's College, Aberdeen, is one of the foremost defenders of commonsense realism. In this selection he examines Hume's indirect realism, the doctrine that we only perceive ideas based on sensory experience and never see or perceive objects themselves. Reid rejects Locke's primary/secondary qualities distinction, holding to the commonsense, direct realist position that we perceive the world directly.

Essays on the Intellectual Powers of Man (in part)

Chapter 14: Reflections on the Common Theory of Ideas

After so long a detail of the sentiments of philosophers, ancient and modern, concerning ideas, it may seem presumptuous to call in question their existence. But no philosophical opinion, however ancient, however generally received, ought to rest upon authority. There is no presumption in requiring evidence for it, or in regulating our belief by the evidence we can find.

To prevent mistakes, the reader must again be reminded that if by ideas are meant only the acts or operations of our minds in perceiving, remembering, or imagining objects, I am far from calling in question the existence of those acts; we are conscious of them every day and every hour of life; and I believe no man of a sound mind ever doubted of the real existence of the operations of mind, of which he is conscious. Nor is it to be doubted that, by the faculties which God has given us, we can conceive things that are absent as well as perceive those that are within the reach of our senses; and that such conceptions may be more or less distinct, and more or less lively and strong. We have reason to ascribe to the all-knowing and all-perfect Being distinct conceptions of all things existent and possible, and of all their relations; and if these conceptions are called his eternal ideas, there ought to be no dispute among philosophers

Reprinted from Thomas Reid's *Essays on the Intellectual Powers of Man* (1785).

about a word. The ideas, of whose existence I require the proof, are not the operations of any mind, but supposed objects of those operations. They are not perception, remembrance, or conception, but things that are said to be perceived, or remembered, or imagined.

Nor do I dispute the existence of what the vulgar call the objects of perception. These, by all who acknowledge their existence, are called real things, not ideas. But philosophers maintain that, besides these, there are immediate objects of perception in the mind itself: that, for instance, we do not see the sun immediately, but an idea; or, as Mr. Hume calls it, an impression in our own minds. This idea is said to be the image, the resemblance, the representative of the sun, if there be a sun. It is from the existence of the idea that we must infer the existence of the sun. But the idea, being immediately perceived, there can be no doubt, as philosophers think, of its existence.

In like manner, when I remember, or when I imagine anything, all men acknowledge that there must be something that is remembered or that is imagined; that is, some object of those operations. The object remembered must be something that did exist in time past: the object imagined may be something that never existed. But, say the philosophers, besides these objects which all men acknowledge, there is a more immediate object which really exists in the mind at the same time we remember or imagine. This object is an idea or image of the thing remembered or imagined.

The *first* reflection I would make on this philosophical opinion is, that it is directly contrary to the universal sense of men who have not been instructed in philosophy. When we see the sun or moon, we have no doubt that the very objects which we immediately see are very far distant from us, and from one another. We have not the least doubt that this is the sun and moon which God created some thousands of years ago, and which have continued to perform their revolutions in the heavens ever since. But how are we astonished when the philosopher informs us that we are mistaken in all this; that the sun and moon which we see are not, as we imagine, many miles distant from us, and from each other, but they are in our own mind; that they had no existence before we saw them, and will have none when we cease to perceive and to think of them; because the objects we perceive are only ideas in our own mind, which can have no existence a moment longer than we think of them!

If a plain man, uninstructed in philosophy, has faith to receive these mysteries, how great must be his astonishment! He is brought into a new world where everything he sees, tastes, or touches, is an idea—a fleeting kind of being which he can conjure into existence, or can annihilate in the twinkling of an eye.

After his mind is somewhat composed, it will be natural for him to ask his philosophical instructor, Pray, sir, are there then no substantial and permanent beings called the sun and moon, which continue to exist whether we think of them or not?

Here the philosophers differ. Mr. Locke, and those that were before him, will answer to this question that it is very true there are substantial and permanent beings called the sun and moon; but they never appear to us in their own person, but by their representatives, the ideas in our own minds, and we know nothing of them but what we can gather from those ideas.

Bishop Berkeley and Mr. Hume would give a different answer to the question proposed. They would assure the querist that it is a vulgar error, a mere prejudice of the ignorant and unlearned, to think that there are any permanent and substantial beings called the sun and moon; that the heavenly bodies, our own bodies, and all bodies whatsoever, are nothing but ideas in our minds; and that there can be nothing like the ideas of one mind, but the ideas of another mind. There is nothing in nature but minds and ideas, says the Bishop;—nay, says Mr. Hume, there is nothing in nature but ideas only; for what we call a mind is nothing but a train of ideas connected by certain relations between themselves.

In this representation of the theory of ideas there is nothing exaggerated or misrepresented, as far as I am able to judge; and surely nothing further is necessary to show that, to the uninstructed in philosophy, it must appear extravagant and visionary, and most contrary to the dictates of common understanding.

There is the less need of any further proof of this, that it is very amply acknowledged by Mr. Hume in his *Essay on the Academical or Sceptical Philosophy*.[1]

It is therefore acknowledged by this philosopher to be a natural instinct or prepossession, a universal and primary opinion of all men, a primary instinct of nature, that the objects which we immediately perceive by our senses are not images in our minds, but external objects, and that their existence is independent of us and our perception.

In this acknowledgment Mr. Hume indeed seems to me more generous, and even more ingenuous, than Bishop Berkeley, who would persuade us that his opinion does not oppose the vulgar opinion, but only that of the philosophers; and that the external existence of a material world is a philosophical hypothesis, and not the natural dictate of our perceptive powers.

A *second* reflection upon this subject is—that the authors who have treated of ideas have generally taken their existence for granted, as a thing that could not be called in question; and such arguments as they have mentioned incidentally, in order to prove it, seem too weak to support the conclusion.

Mr. Locke, in the Introduction to his Essay, tells us that he uses the word idea to signify whatever is the immediate object of thought; and then adds, "I presume it will be easily granted me that there are such *ideas* in men's minds; everyone is conscious of them in himself; and men's words and actions will satisfy him that they are in others.[2] I am indeed conscious of perceiving, remembering, imagining; but that the objects of these operations are images in my mind, I am not conscious. I am satisfied, by men's words and actions, that they often perceive the same objects which I perceive, which could not be if those objects were ideas in their own minds.

Mr. Norris is the only author I have met with who professedly puts the question whether material things can be perceived by us immediately. He has offered four arguments to show that they cannot. *First*, "Material objects are without the mind, and therefore there can be no union between the object and the percipient." Answer, This argument is lame, until it is shown to be necessary that in perception there should be a union between the object and the percipient. *Second*, "Material objects are disproportioned to the mind, and removed from it by the whole diameter of Being." This argument I cannot answer, because I do not understand it. *Third*, "Because, if material objects were immediate objects of perception, there could be no physical science—things necessary and immutable being the only object of science." Answer, Although things necessary and immutable be not the immediate objects of perception, they may be immediate objects of other powers of the mind. *Fourth*, "If material things were perceived by themselves, they would be a true light to our minds, as being the intelligible form of our understandings, and consequently perfective of them, and indeed superior to them.[3] If I comprehend anything of this mysterious argument, it follows from it that the Deity perceives nothing at all, because nothing can be superior to his understanding or perfective of it.

There is an argument which is hinted at by Malebranche, and by several other authors, which deserves to be more seriously considered. As I find it most clearly expressed and most fully urged by Dr. Samuel Clarke, I shall give it in his words, in his second reply to Leibniz, §4: "The soul, without being present to the images of the things perceived, could not possibly perceive them. A living substance can only there perceive, where it is present, either to the things themselves (as the omnipresent God is to the whole universe) or to the images of things, as the soul is in its proper *sensorium*."

Sir Isaac Newton expresses the same sentiment, but with his usual reserve, in a query only.[4]

The ingenious Dr. Porterfield, in his *Essay Concerning the Motions of our Eyes,* adopts this opinion with more confidence. His words are: "How body acts upon mind, or mind upon body, I know not; but this I am very certain of, that nothing can act, or be acted upon, where it is not; and therefore our mind can never perceive anything but its own proper modifications, and the various states of the sensorium, to which it is present: so that it is not the external sun and moon which are in the heavens, which our mind per-

ceives, but only their image or representation impressed upon the sensorium. How the soul of a seeing man sees these images, or how it receives those ideas, from such agitations in the sensorium, I know not; but I am sure it can never perceive the external bodies themselves, to which it is not present."[5]

These, indeed, are great authorities: but in matters of philosophy we must not be guided by authority, but by reason. Dr. Clarke, in the place cited, mentions slightly, as the reason of his opinion, that "nothing can any more act, or be acted upon when it is not present, that it can be where it is not." And again, in his third reply to Leibniz, §11: "We are sure the soul cannot perceive what it is not present to, because nothing can act, or be acted upon, where it is not." The same reason we see is urged by Dr. Porterfield.

That nothing can act immediately where it is not, I think must be admitted: for I agree with Sir Isaac Newton, that power without substance is inconceivable.[6] It is a consequence of this, that nothing can be acted upon immediately where the agent is not present: let this, therefore, be granted. To make the reasoning conclusive, it is further necessary that, when we perceive objects, either they act upon us or we act upon them. This does not appear self-evident, nor have I ever met with any proof of it. I shall briefly offer the reasons why I think it ought not to be admitted.

When we say that one being acts upon another, we mean that some power or force is exerted by the agent which produces, or has a tendency to produce, a change in the thing acted upon. If this be the meaning of the phrase, as I conceive it is, there appears no reason for asserting that, in perception, either the object acts upon the mind or the mind upon the object.

An object, in being perceived, does not act at all. I perceive the walls of the room where I sit; but they are perfectly inactive, and therefore act not upon the mind. To be perceived is what logicians call an external denomination which implies neither action nor quality in the object perceived. Nor could men ever have gone into this notion that perception is owing to some action of the object upon the mind, were it not that we are so prone to form our notions of the mind from some similitude we conceive between it and body. Thought in the mind is conceived to have some analogy to motion in a body: and as a body is put in motion by being acted upon by some other body, so we are apt to think the mind is made to perceive by some impulse it receives from the object. But reasonings drawn from such analogies ought never to be trusted. They are, indeed, the cause of most of our errors with regard to the mind. And we might as well conclude that minds may be measured by feet and inches, or weighed by ounces and drams; because bodies have those properties.

I see as little reason, in the second place, to believe that in perception the mind acts upon the object. To perceive an object is one thing, to act upon it is another; nor is the last at all included in the first. To say that I act upon the wall by looking at it is an abuse of language, and has no meaning. Logicians distinguish two kinds of operations of mind: the first kind produces no effect without the mind; the last does. The first they call *immanent acts*, the second *transitive*. All intellectual operations belong to the first class; they produce no effect upon any external object. But, without having recourse to logical distinctions, every man of common sense knows that to think of an object, and to act upon it, are very different things.

As we have, therefore, no evidence that in perception the mind acts upon the object, or the object upon the mind, but strong reasons to the contrary, Dr. Clarke's argument against our perceiving external objects immediately falls to the ground.

This notion that, in perception, the object must be contiguous to the percipient seems, with many other prejudices, to be borrowed from analogy. In all the external senses there must, as has been before observed, be some impression made upon the organ of sense by the object, or by something coming from the object. An impression supposes contiguity. Hence we are led by analogy to conceive something similar in the operations of the mind.

When we lay aside those analogies and reflect attentively upon our perception of the object of sense, we must acknowledge that, though we are conscious of perceiving objects, we are altogether ignorant how it is brought about, and know as little how we perceive objects as how we were made. And, if we should admit an image in the mind, or contiguous to it, we know as little how perception may be produced by this image as by the most distant object. Why, therefore, should we be led, by

a theory which is neither grounded on evidence nor, if admitted, can explain any one phenomenon of perception, to reject the natural and immediate dictates of those perceptive powers to which, in the conduct of life, we find a necessity of yielding implicit submission?

There remains only one other argument that I have been able to find urged against our perceiving external objects immediately. It is proposed by Mr. Hume, who, in the essay already quoted, after acknowledging that it is a universal and primary opinion of all men that we perceive external objects immediately, subjoins what follows:

> But this universal and primary opinion of all men is soon destroyed by the slightest philosophy, which teaches us that nothing can ever be present to the mind but an image or perception; and that the senses are only the inlets through which these images are received, without being ever able to produce any immediate intercourse between the mind and the object. The table, which we see, seems to diminish as we remove further from it: but the real table, which exists independent of us, suffers no alteration. It was, therefore, nothing but its image which was present to the mind. These are the obvious dictates of reason; and no man who reflects ever doubted that the existences which we consider, when we say *this house* and *that tree,* are nothing but perceptions in the mind, and fleeting copies and representations of other existences, which remain uniform and independent. So far, then, we are necessitated, by reasoning, to depart from the primary instincts of nature, and to embrace a new system with regard to the evidence of our senses.[7]

We have here a remarkable conflict between two contradictory opinions, wherein all mankind are engaged. On the one side stand all the vulgar, who are unpractised in philosophical researches, and guided by the uncorrupted primary instincts of nature. On the other side stand all the philosophers, ancient and modern; every man, without exception, who reflects. In this division, to my great humiliation, I find myself classed with the vulgar.

The passage now quoted is all I have found in Mr. Hume's writings upon this point: and, indeed, there is more reasoning in it than I have found in any other author. I shall, therefore, examine it minutely.

First, He tells us that "this universal and primary opinion of all men is soon destroyed by the slightest philosophy, which teaches us that nothing can ever be present to the mind but an image or perception."

The phrase of being present to the mind has some obscurity, but I conceive he means being an immediate object of thought; an immediate object, for instance, of perception, of memory, or of imagination. If this be the meaning (and it is the only pertinent one I can think of), there is no more in this passage but an assertion of the proposition to be proved, and an assertion that philosophy teaches it. If this be so, I beg leave to dissent from philosophy till she gives me reason for what she teaches. For, though common sense and my external senses demand my assent to their dictates upon their own authority, yet philosophy is not entitled to this privilege. But, that I may not dissent from so grave a personage without giving a reason, I give this as the reason of my dissent: I see the sun when he shines; I remember the battle of Culloden; and neither of these objects is an image or perception.

He tells us, in the next place, "That the senses are only the inlets, through which these images are received."

I know that Aristotle and the schoolmen taught that images or species flow from objects, and are let in by the senses, and strike upon the mind; but this has been so effectually refuted by Descartes, by Malebranche, and many others, that nobody now pretends to defend it. Reasonable men consider it as one of the most unintelligible and unmeaning parts of the ancient system. To what cause is it owing that modern philosophers are so prone to fall back into this hypothesis, as if they really believed it? For of this proneness I could give many instances besides this of Mr. Hume; and I take the cause to be that images in the mind, and images let in by the senses, are so nearly allied, and so strictly connected, that they must stand or fall together. The old system consistently maintained both: but the new system has rejected the doctrine of images let in by the senses, holding, nevertheless, that there are images in the mind; and, having made this unnatural divorce of two doctrines which

ought not to be put asunder, that which they have retained often leads them back involuntarily to that which they have rejected.

Mr. Hume surely did not seriously believe that an image of sound is let in by the ear, an image of smell by the nose, an image of hardness and softness, of solidity and resistance, by the touch. For besides the absurdity of the thing, which has often been shown, Mr. Hume and all modern philosophers maintain that the images which are the immediate objects of perception have no existence when they are not perceived; whereas if they were let in by the senses, they must be, before they are perceived, and have a separate existence.

He tells us, further, that philosophy teaches that the senses are unable to produce any immediate intercourse between the mind and the object. Here I still require the reasons that philosophy gives for this; for, to my apprehension, I immediately perceive external objects, and this I conceive is the immediate intercourse here meant.

Hitherto I see nothing that can be called an argument. Perhaps it was intended only for illustration. The argument, the only argument, follows:

The table which we see, seems to diminish as we remove farther from it; but the real table, which exists independent of us, suffers no alteration. It was, therefore, nothing but its image which was presented to the mind. These are the obvious dictates of reason.

Let us suppose, for a moment, that it is the real table we see: Must not this real table seem to diminish as we remove farther from it? It is demonstrable that it must. How then can this apparent diminution be an argument that it is not the real table? When that which must happen to the real table, as we remove farther from it, does actually happen to the table we see, it is absurd to conclude from this, that it is not the real table we see. It is evident, therefore, that this ingenious author has imposed upon himself by confounding real magnitude with apparent magnitude, and that his argument is a mere sophism.

I observed that Mr. Hume's argument not only has no strength to support his conclusion, but that it leads to the contrary conclusion—to wit, that it is the real table we see; for this plain reason, that the table we see has precisely that apparent magnitude which it is demonstrable the real table must have when placed at that distance.

This argument is made much stronger by considering that the real table may be placed successively at a thousand different distances, and, in every distance, in a thousand different positions; and it can be determined demonstratively, by the rules of geometry and perspective, what must be its apparent magnitude and apparent figure in each of those distances and positions. Let the table be placed successively in as many of those different distances and different positions as you will, or in them all; open your eyes and you shall see a table precisely of that apparent magnitude, and that apparent figure, which the real table must have in that distance and in that position. Is not this a strong argument that it is the real table you see?

In a word, the appearance of a visible object is infinitely diversified according to its distance and position. The visible appearances are innumerable when we confine ourselves to one object, and they are multiplied according to the variety of objects. Those appearances have been matter of speculation to ingenious men at least since the time of Euclid. They have accounted for all this variety, on the supposition that the objects we see are external and not in the mind itself. The rules they have demonstrated about the various projections of the sphere, about the appearances of the planets in their progressions, stations, and retrogradations, and all the rules of perspective, are built on the supposition that the objects of sight are external. They can each of them be tried in thousands of instances. In many arts and professions innumerable trials are daily made; nor were they ever found to fail in a single instance. Shall we say that a false supposition, invented by the rude vulgar, has been so lucky in solving an infinite number of phenomena of nature? This, surely, would be a greater prodigy than philosophy ever exhibited: add to this, that, upon the contrary hypothesis—to wit that the objects of sight are internal—no account can be given of any one of those appearances, nor any physical cause assigned why a visible object should, in any one case, have one apparent figure and magnitude rather than another.

Thus, I have considered every argument I have found advanced to prove the existence of ideas, or images of external things, in the mind; and, if no better arguments can be found, I cannot help thinking that the whole history of philosophy has never furnished an instance of an opinion so

unanimously entertained by philosophers upon so slight grounds.

A *third* reflection I would make upon this subject is, that philosophers, notwithstanding their unanimity as to the existence of ideas, hardly agree in any one thing else concerning them. If ideas be not a mere fiction, they must be, of all objects of human knowledge, the things we have best access to know, and to be acquainted with; yet there is nothing about which men differ so much.

Some have held them to be self-existent, others to be in the Divine mind, others in our own minds, and others in the brain or *sensorium*. I considered the hypothesis of images in the brain, in the fourth chapter of this essay. As to images in the mind, if anything more is meant by the image of an object in the mind than the thought of that object, I know not what it means. The distinct conception of an object may, in a metaphorical or analogical sense, be called an *image* of it in the mind. But this image is only the conception of the object, and not the object conceived. It is an act of the mind, and not the object of that act.

Some philosophers will have our ideas, or a part of them, to be innate; others will have them all to be adventitious: some derive them from the senses alone; others from sensation and reflection: some think they are fabricated by the mind itself, others that they are produced by external objects; others that they are the immediate operation of the Deity; others say that impressions are the causes of ideas, and that the causes of impressions are unknown: some think that we have ideas only of material objects, but none of minds, of their operations, or of the relations of things; others will have the immediate object of every thought to be an idea: some think we have abstract ideas, and that by this chiefly we are distinguished from the brutes; others maintain an abstract idea to be an absurdity, and that there can be no such thing: with some they are the immediate objects of thought, with others the only objects.

A *fourth* reflection is, that ideas do not make any of the operations of the mind to be better understood, although it was probably with that view that they have been first invented, and afterwards so generally received.

We are at a loss to know how we perceive distant objects; how we remember things past; how we imagine things that have no existence. Ideas in the mind seem to account for all these operations:

they are all by the means of ideas reduced to one operation—to a kind of feeling, or immediate perception of things present and in contact with the percipient; and feeling is an operation so familiar that we think it needs no explication, but may serve to explain other operations.

But this feeling, or immediate perception, is as difficult to be comprehended as the things which we pretend to explain by it. Two things may be in contact without any feeling or perception; there must therefore be in the percipient a power to feel or to perceive. How this power is produced, and how it operates, is quite beyond the reach of our knowledge. As little can we know whether this power must be limited to things present, and in contact with us. Nor can any man pretend to prove that the Being who gave us the power to perceive things present may not give us the power to perceive things that are distant, to remember things past, and to conceive things that never existed.

Some philosophers have endeavoured to make all our senses to be only different modifications of touch; a theory which serves only to confound things that are different, and to perplex and darken things that are clear. The theory of ideas resembles this, by reducing all the operations of the human understanding to the perception of ideas in our own minds. This power of perceiving ideas is as inexplicable as any of the powers explained by it; and the contiguity of the object contributes nothing at all to make it better understood; because there appears no connection between contiguity and perception, but what is grounded on prejudices drawn from some imagined similitude between mind and body, and from the supposition that, in perception, the object acts upon the mind, or the mind upon the object. We have seen how this theory has led philosophers to confound those operations of mind which experience teaches all men to be different, and teaches them to distinguish in common language; and that it has led them to invent a language inconsistent with the principles upon which all language is grounded.

Notes

1 *Enquiry Concerning Human Understanding*, 12, I.

2 *An Essay Concerning Human Understanding*, I, 1, 8.

3 *Essay Towards the Theory of the Ideal or Intelligible World*, Pt. II, Ch. 6.

4 *Optics*, Qu. 28.

5 CF. his *Treatise on the Eye*, III, 2, 7.

6 *Principia*, Bk. 3.

7 *Ibid.*, 12; I.

III.6 A Defense of Representationalism

BERTRAND RUSSELL

A biographical sketch of Bertrand Russell precedes selection I.1. Russell defends representational realism as the theory that is adequate to the three central factors of the perceptual process: physics, physiology, and psychology or privileged access. He elaborates on all three factors in the perceptual process, setting forth a causal theory of perception in which mental events are caused by processes in the outside world impinging on the perceiver's body and starting a chain reaction, ending with the percept in the brain. Percepts are the most indubitable things in the world, and from them we infer the reality of the external world.

When we consider perception—visual or auditory—of an external event, there are three different matters to be examined. There is first the process in the outside world, from the event to the percipient's body; there is next the process in his body, in so far as this can be known by an outside observer; lastly, there is the question, which must be faced sooner or later, whether the percipient can perceive something of the process in his body which no other observer could perceive. We will take these points in order.

If it is to be possible to "perceive" an event not in the percipient's body, there must be a physical process in the outer world such that, when a certain event occurs, it produces a stimulus of a certain kind at the surface of the percipient's body. Suppose, for example, that pictures of different animals are exhibited on a magic lantern to a class of children, and all the children are asked to say the name of each animal in turn. We may assume that the children are sufficiently familiar with animals to say "cat," "dog," "giraffe," "hippopotamus," etc., at the right moments. We must then suppose—taking the physical world for granted—that some process travels from each picture to the eyes of the various children, retaining throughout these journeys such peculiarities that, when the process reaches their eyes, it can in one case stimulate the word "cat" and in another the word "dog." All this the physical theory of light provides for. But there is one interesting point about language that should

be noticed in this connection. If the usual physical theory of light is correct, the various children will receive stimuli which differ greatly according to their distance and direction from the picture, and according to the way the light falls. There are also differences in their reactions, for, though they all utter the word "cat," some say it loud, others soft, some in a soprano voice, some in a contralto. But the differences in their reactions are much less than the differences in the stimuli. . . .

The fact that it is possible for a number of people to perceive the same noise or the same colored pattern obviously depends upon the fact that a physical process can travel outward from a center and retain certain of its characteristics unchanged, or very little changed. The most notable of such characteristics is frequency in a wave-motion. That, no doubt, affords a biological reason for the fact that our most delicate senses, sight and hearing, are sensitive to frequencies, which determine color in what we see and pitch in what we hear. If there were not, in the physical world, processes spreading out from centers and retaining certain characters practically unchanged, it would be impossible for different percipients to perceive the same object from different points of view, and we should not have been able to discover that we all live in a common world.

We come now to the process in the percipient's body, in so far as this can be perceived by an outside observer. This raises no new philosophical problems, because we are still concerned, as before, with the perception of events outside the observer's body. The observer, now, is supposed to be a physiologist, observing, say, what goes on

This selection consists of parts of Chapters XII and XIII of The Outline of Philosophy _published by George Allen Unwin in 1927._

in the eye when light falls upon it. His means of knowing are, in principle, exactly the same as in the observation of dead matter. An event in an eye upon which light is falling causes light-waves to travel in a certain manner until they reach the eye of the physiologist. They there cause a process in the physiologist's eye and optic nerve and brain, which ends in what he calls "seeing what happens in the eye he is observing." But this event, which happens in the physiologist, is not what happened in the eye he was observing; it is only connected with this by a complicated causal chain. Thus our knowledge of physiology is no more direct or intimate than our knowledge of processes in dead matter; we do not know any more about our eyes than about the trees and fields and clouds that we see by means of them. The event which happens when a physiologist observes an eye is an event in him, not on the eye that he is observing.

. . . It may be said that we do not in fact proceed to *infer* the physical world from our perceptions, but that we begin at once with a rough-and-ready knowledge of the physical world, and only at a late stage of sophistication compel ourselves to regard our knowledge of the physical world as an inference. What is valid in this statement is the fact that our knowledge of the physical world is not at first inferential, but that is only because we take our percepts to *be* the physical world. Sophistication and philosophy come in at the stage at which we realize that the physical world cannot be identified with our percepts. When my boy was three years old, I showed him Jupiter, and told him that Jupiter was larger than earth. He insisted that I must be speaking of some other Jupiter, because, as he patiently explained, the one he was seeing was obviously quite small. After some efforts, I had to give it up and leave him unconvinced. In the case of the heavenly bodies, adults have got used to the idea that what is really there can only be *inferred* from what they see; but where rats in mazes are concerned, they still tend to think that they are seeing what is happening in the physical world. The difference, however, is only one of degree, and naive realism is as untenable in the one case as in the other. There are differences in the perceptions of two persons observing the same process; there are sometimes no discoverable differences between two perceptions of the same persons observing different processes, e.g., pure water and water full of bacilli.

The subjectivity of our perceptions is thus of practical as well as theoretical importance.

. . . A lamp at the top of a tall building might produce the same visual stimulus as Jupiter, or at any rate one practically indistinguishable from that produced by Jupiter. A blow on the nose might make us "see stars." Theoretically, it should be possible to apply a stimulus direct to the optic nerve, which should give us a visual sensation. Thus when we think we see Jupiter, we may be mistaken. We are less likely to be mistaken if we say that the surface of the eye is being stimulated in a certain way, and still less likely to be mistaken if we say that the optic nerve is being stimulated in a certain way. We do not eliminate the risk of error completely unless we confine ourselves to saying that an event of a certain sort is happening in the brain; this statement may still be true if we see Jupiter in a dream.

But, I shall be asked, what do you know about what is happening in the brain? Surely nothing. Not so, I reply. I know what is happening in the brain exactly what naive realism thinks it knows about what is happening in the outside world. But this needs explaining, and there are other matters that must be explained first.

When the light from a fixed star reaches me, I see the star if it is night and I am looking in the right direction. The light started years ago, probably many years ago, but my reaction is primarily something that is happening *now*. When my eyes are open, I see the star; when they are shut, I do not. Children discover at a fairly early age that they see nothing when their eyes are shut. They are aware of the difference between seeing and not seeing, and also of the difference between eyes open and eyes shut; gradually they discover that these two differences are correlated—I mean that they have expectations of which this is the intellectualist transcription. Again, children learn to name the colors, and to state correctly whether a thing is blue or red or yellow or whatnot. They ought not to be sure that light of the appropriate wave-length started from the object. The sun looks red in a London fog, grass looks blue through blue spectacles, everything looks yellow to a person suffering from jaundice. But suppose you ask: What color are you seeing? The person who answers, in these cases, red for the sun, blue for the grass, and yellow for the sickroom of the jaundiced patient, is answering quite truly. And in each of these cases he is stating something that he *knows*. What he knows in such cases is what I call a "percept." I shall contend later that, from the standpoint of physics, a percept is in the brain; for the present, I am only concerned to say that a percept is what is most indubitable in our knowledge of the world.

I do not in fact entertain any doubts that physics is true in its main lines. The interpretation of physical formulae is a matter as to which a considerable degree of uncertainty is possible; but we cannot well doubt that there is an interpretation which is true roughly and in the main. I shall come to the question of interpretation later; for the present, I shall assume that we may accept physics in its broad outlines, without troubling to consider how it is to be interpreted. On this basis, the above remarks on perception seem undeniable. We are often misled as to what is happening, either by peculiarities of the medium between the object and our bodies, or by unusual states of our bodies, or by a temporary or permanent abnormality in the brain. But in all these cases *something* is really happening, as to which, if we turn our attention to it, we can obtain knowledge that is not misleading. At one time when, owing to illness, I had been taking a great deal of quinine, I became hypersensitive to noise, so that when the nurse rustled the newspaper I thought she was spilling a scuttle of coals on the floor. The interpretation was mistaken, but it was quite true that I heard a loud noise. It is commonplace that a man whose leg has been amputated can still feel pains in it; here again, he does really feel the pains, and is only mistaken in his belief that they come from his leg. A percept is an observable event, but its interpretation as knowledge of this or that event in the physical world is liable to be mistaken, for reasons which physics and physiology can make fairly clear.

Perhaps there is nothing so difficult for the imagination as to teach it to feel about space as modern science compels us to think. This is the task which must now be attempted. . . . The gist of the matter is that percepts . . . are in our heads; that percepts are what we can know with most certainty; and that percepts contain what naive realism thinks it knows about the world.

But when I say that my percepts are in my head, I am saying something which is ambiguous until the different kinds of space have been explained, for the statement is only true in con-

nection with *physical* space. There is also a space in our percepts, and of this space the statement would not be true. When I say that there is space in our percepts, I mean nothing at all difficult to understand. I mean—to take the sense of sight, which is the most important in this connection—that in what we see at one time there is up and down, right and left, inside and outside. If we see, say, a circle on a blackboard, all these relations exist within what we see. The circle has a top half and a bottom half, a right-hand half and a left-hand half, an inside and an outside. Those relations alone are enough to make up a space of sorts. But the space of every-day life is filled out with what we derive from touch and movement—how a thing feels when we touch it, and what movements are necessary in order to grasp it. Other elements also come into the genesis of the space in which everybody believes who has not been troubled by philosophy; but it is unnecessary for our purposes to go into this question any more deeply. The point that concerns us is that a man's percepts are private to himself: what I see, no one else sees; what I hear, no one else hears; what I touch, no one else touches; and so on. True, others hear and see something very like what I hear and see, if they are suitably placed; but there are always differences. Sounds are less loud at a distance; objects change their visual appearance according to the laws of perspective. Therefore it is impossible for two persons at the same time to have exactly identical percepts. It follows that the space of percepts, like the percepts, must be private; there are as many perceptual spaces as there are percipients. My percept of a table is outside my percept of my head, in my perceptual space; but it does not follow that it is outside my head as a physical object in physical space. Physical space is neutral and public: in this space, all my percepts are in my head, even the most distant star *as I see it*. Physical and perceptual space have relations, but they are not identical, and failure to grasp the difference between them is a potent source of confusion.

To say that you see a star when you see the light that has come from it is no more correct than to say that you see New Zealand when you see a New Zealander in London. Your perception when (as we say) you see a star is causally connected, in the first instance, with what happens in the brain, the optic nerve, and the eye, then with a light-wave which, according to physics, can be traced back to the star as its source. Your sensations will be closely similar if the light comes from a lamp at the top of a mast. The physical space in which you believe the "real" star to be is an elaborate inference; what is given is the private space in which the speck of light you see is situated. It is still an open question whether the space of sight has depth, or is merely a surface, as Berkeley contended. This does not matter for our purposes. Even if we admit that sight alone shows a difference between an object a few inches from the eyes and an object several feet distant, yet you certainly cannot, by sight alone, see that a cloud is less distant than a fixed star, though you may *infer* that it is, because it can hide the star. The world of astronomy, from the point of view of sight, is a surface. If you were put in a dark room with little holes cut in the ceiling in the pattern of the stars letting light come through, there would be nothing in your immediate visual data to show that you were not "seeing the stars." This illustrates what I mean by saying that what you see is *not* "out there" in the sense of physics.

We learn in infancy that we can sometimes touch objects we see, and sometimes not. When we cannot touch them at once, we can sometimes do so by walking to them. That is to say, we learn to correlate sensations of sight with sensations of touch, and sometimes with sensations of movement followed by sensations of touch. In this way we locate our sensations in a three-dimensional world. Those which involve sight alone we think of as "external," but there is no justification for this view. What you see when you see a star is just as internal as what you feel when you feel a headache. That is to say, it is internal from the standpoint of *physical* space. It is distant in your private space, because it is not associated with sensations of touch, and cannot be associated with them by means of any journey you can perform.

To make the matter definite, let us suppose that a physiologist is observing a living brain—no longer an impossible supposition, as it would have been formerly. It is natural to suppose that what the physiologist sees is in the brain he is observing. But if we are speaking of physical space, what the physiologist sees is in his own brain. It is in no sense in the brain that he is observing, though it is in the percept of that brain, which occupies part of the physiologist's perceptual space. Causal continuity makes the matter perfectly evident: light-

waves travel from the brain that is being observed to the eye of the physiologist, at which they only arrive after an interval of time, which is finite though short. The physiologist sees what he is observing only after the light-waves have reached his eye; therefore the event which constitutes his seeing comes at the end of a series of events which travel from the observed brain into the brain of the physiologist. We cannot, without a preposterous kind of discontinuity, suppose that the physiologist's percept, which comes at the end of this series, is anywhere else but in the physiologist's head.

It is extraordinarily difficult to divest ourselves of the belief that the physical world is the world we perceive by sight and touch; even if, in our philosophic moments, we are aware that this is an error, we nevertheless fall into it again as soon as we are off our guard. The notion that what we see is "out there" in physical space is one which cannot survive while we are grasping the difference between what physics supposes to be really happening, and what our senses show us as happening; but it is sure to return and plague us when we begin to forget the argument. Only long reflection can make a radically new point of view familiar and easy.

Our illustrations hitherto have been taken from the sense of sight; let us now take one from the sense of touch. Suppose that, with your eyes shut, you let your finger-tip press against a hard table. What is really happening? The physicist says that your finger-tip and the table consist, roughly speaking, of vast numbers of electrons and protons; more correctly, each electron and proton is to be thought of as a collection of processes of radiation, but we can ignore this for our present purposes. Although you think you are touching the table, no electron or proton in your finger ever really touches an electron or proton in the table, because this would develop an infinite force. When you press, repulsions are set up between parts of your finger and parts of the table. If you try to press upon a liquid or a gas, there is room in it for the parts that are repelled to get away. But if you press a hard solid, the electrons and protons that try to get away, because electrical forces from your finger repel them, are unable to do so, because they are crowded close to others which elbow them back to more or less their original position, like people in a dense crowd. Therefore the more you press the more they repel your finger. The repulsion consists of electrical forces, which set up in the nerves a current whose nature is not very definitely known. This current runs into the brain, and there has effects which, so far as the physiologist is concerned, are almost wholly conjectural. But there is one effect which is not conjectural, and that is the sensation of touch. This effect, owing to physiological inference or perhaps to a reflex, is associated by us with the finger-tip. But the sensation is the same if, by artificial means, the parts of the nerve nearer the brain are suitably stimulated—e.g., if your hand has been amputated and the right nerves are skilfully manipulated. Thus our confidence that touch affords evidence of the existence of bodies at the place which we think is being touched is quite misplaced. As a rule we are right, but we can be wrong; there is nothing of the nature of an infallible revelation about the matter. And even in the most favorable case, the perception of touch is something very different from the mad dance of electrons and protons trying to jazz out of each other's way, which is what physics maintains is really taking place at your finger-tip.

Bibliography

Alston, William. *The Reliability of Sense Perception*. Ithaca, NY: Cornell University Press, 1993.

Armstrong, D. M. *Perception and the Physical World*. London: Routledge & Kegan Paul, 1961.

Austin, J. L. *Sense and Sensibilia*. Oxford: Clarendon Press, 1962.

Berkeley, George. *Three Dialogues Between Hylas and Philonous*. Oxford: Oxford University Press, 1713.

Chisholm, Roderick. *Perceiving*. Ithaca, NY: Cornell University Press, 1957.

Clay, Marjorie, and Keith Lehrer, eds. *Knowledge and Skepticism*. Boulder, CO: Westview, 1989.

Cornman, James. *Perception, Common Sense, and Science*. New Haven, CT: Yale University Press, 1975.

Dancy, John, ed. *Perception*. Oxford: Oxford University Press, 1987.

Dretske, Fred. *Seeing and Knowing*. London: Routledge & Kegan Paul, 1969.

Fumerton, Richard. *Metaphysical and Epistemological Problems of Perception*. Lincoln: University of Nebraska, 1985.

Gibson, James J. *Perception of the Visual World*. New York: 1950.

Ginet, Carl. *Knowledge, Perception and Memory*. Dordrecht, Netherlands: Reidel, 1975.

Hardin, C. L. *Color for Philosophers: Unweaving the Rainbow*. Indianapolis: Hackett, 1988.

Heil, John. *Perception and Cognition*. Berkeley: University of California Press, 1983.

Kelley, David. *The Evidence of the Senses*. Baton Rouge: Louisiana State University Press, 1986.

Landesman, Charles. *Color and Consciousness*. Philadelphia: Temple University Press, 1989.

———. *An Introduction to Epistemology*. Cambridge, MA: Blackwell, 1996.

MacLachlan, D. L. C. *Philosophy of Perception*. Englewood Cliffs, NJ: Prentice Hall, 1989.

Price, H. H. *Perception*. London: Methuen, 1932.

Sellars, W. F. *Science, Perception and Reality*. London: Routledge & Kegan Paul, 1963.

Part IV

The Analysis of Knowledge

What are the criteria of knowledge? Can we give an adequate definition of *knowledge*? That is, can we state exactly what the necessary and sufficient conditions of knowledge are? Does knowing entail absolute certainty? In order to know, must we be aware of the evidence on which our knowledge is based?

Jack sees Jill get on Flight 101 for Miami and believes correctly that Jill is now in Miami, but unknown to Jack Flight 101 has been hijacked and diverted to Havana. However, Jill has fortunately taken a boat back to Miami and, two days after her original flight, has just arrived in Miami. Under these circumstances, does Jack *know* that Jill is in Miami? Many would argue that he merely has a true justified belief of this fact. His belief that Jill is in Miami is justified because normally a flight bound to Miami will land in Miami. However, while Jack's belief that Jill is in Miami is true and justified, the reason on which his belief is based is false.

Jane truly believes that the United States dropped an atomic bomb on Hiroshima in August 1945. However, she received this information from her brother John who guessed it on a multiple-choice test and, without believing one way or another, told Jane what his answer was. Jane—falsely believing that John knows what he is talking about (John is usually a reliable witness about such matters)—truly believes John's testimony, but does she *know* that the United States dropped a bomb on Hiroshima in 1945?

Joe has read in two separate newspapers that the Boston Celtics beat the Los Angeles Lakers last night by a score of 100 to 99, so Joe believes that the Celtics won their game last night. The Celtics did win the game last night, only they beat the Detroit Pistons, not the Lakers. A drunken sports reporter made a mistake and wrote down the losing team as the Lakers rather than the Pistons and the score was 109 to 90. A second newspaper simply copied his official report. Does Joe *know* that the Celtics won last night?

On the basis of these reports, Joe also believes that the Lakers didn't win last night. He is right about that, for the Lakers were idle, but does Joe *know* that the Lakers didn't win last night, or does he merely have a justified true belief?

When I was about nine or ten, a day or two before Christmas, I told my brother Vincent that I had snuck into our father's workroom (something forbidden) and had discovered his Christmas present, a railroad and train set. I actually had not gone into my father's room but had made up the story to mislead my brother. But I had guessed correctly, for Vincent was indeed to be given a train set that Christmas.

Vincent told my father that he knew what he was getting for Christmas, and my father, who regarded knowledge of Christmas presents as tantamount to knowledge uttered by the Oracle of Delphi and his workroom as Delphi itself, angrily spanked me for my sacrilege. While I was being spanked, I pleaded that I had not gone into my father's room and had not seen the Christmas presents. "How did you know Vincent was getting a train set?" he asked. "I didn't know it," I responded, "I just made up the story." The question is, did Vincent, on believing my lie two days before Christmas, *know* he was going to get a train set?

Before 1963, the concept of knowledge was either left unanalyzed or defined more or less as true justified belief. In his *Theatetus* Plato offered a tripartite analysis of knowledge, defining it as true belief with a rational explanation or justification (Greek *logos*). Passages asserting the tripartite analysis can be found in C. I. Lewis, Roderick Chisholm, and A. J. Ayer, with similar definitions. Roughly, Person S knows that p if and only if

   a.   S believes that p.
   b.   Belief p is true.
   c.   S's belief that p is justified.

These three conditions constitute the necessary and sufficient conditions of knowledge. If one of them was missing, S did not know that p. If all of them were present, S could not fail to know that p. Let us call this the "tripartite analysis" of knowledge.

Alvin Plantinga reports the following anecdote. In 1962 he was drinking a cup of coffee in the cafeteria of Wayne State University with his colleague Edmund Gettier, when Gettier mentioned that he was concerned that he would be coming up for tenure next year without a lot of publications. He did have an idea of setting forth a few minor counterexamples to the traditional definition of knowledge, but he considered that a minor matter. The next year Gettier's two-and-a-half-page article on the def-

inition of knowledge was published in *Analysis*, and epistemology has never been the same.

Gettier's analysis was based on two counterexamples to the tripartite analysis. The first is as follows. Smith and Jones have applied for a certain job, and Smith has strong evidence for conjunctive proposition (d): "Jones is the man who will get the job, and Jones has ten coins in his pocket."

Proposition (d) entails (e): "The man who will get the job has ten coins in his pocket." We may suppose that Smith sees the entailment and believes (e).

But unknown to Smith, he himself will get the job and happens to have ten coins in his pocket. So, while (d) is false, (e) is true and Smith truly and justifiably believes (e), but we would not say that Smith *knows* that the man who will get the job has ten coins in his pocket.

So the tripartite analysis fails, for he knows neither that he will get the job nor that he has ten coins in his pocket.

Keith Lehrer offers the following variation of Gettier's second counterexample.

A pupil in S's office, Mr. Nogot, has given S evidence e that justifies S in believing "Mr. Nogot, who is in the office, owns a Ford," from which S deduces p: "Someone in the office owns a Ford." But unsuspected by S, Mr. Nogot has been shamming and p is only true because another person in the office, Mr. Havit, owns a Ford.[1] Again the tripartite analysis seems to fail, since the true, justified belief is based on a false proposition.

Gettier's counterexamples have the following form:

   1.   S believes that p.
   2.   Belief p is true.
   3.   S's belief that p is justified.
   4.   Belief p is based on or entailed by some proposition q.
   5.   S is justified in believing q.
   6.   Belief q is false.
   7.   Therefore, S doesn't know that p.

Several proposals have been offered to meet the Gettier-type counterexamples. Four prominent attempts are included in this part of this book. Of course, you could conclude that the traditional concept of knowledge is hopelessly confused and in need of total revision. You may finally choose that alternative, but before you do, you should consider the other four strategies, which consist in supplementing the tripartite analysis with a fourth condition. The four strategies are (1) the no-false-belief condition, (2) the conclusive reasons analysis, (3) the causal condition, and (4) the defeasibility condition.

1. The No-False-Belief Condition

Early on it was thought that the Gettier counterexamples could be defeated by simply stipulating that the belief that p must not be caused or based on a false belief. In the preceding examples, the belief that p is based on a false belief q. However, this attempt at a solution was soon found to be both too weak and too strong. It was too strong because we can think of instances of knowing where a false belief is present. For example, I believe that Joan will be elected president of the student body because I justifiably believe (1) all the fraternity members, constituting 30 percent of the student body, are committed to Joan; and (2) all the sorority members, constituting 30 percent of the student body, are committed to Joan; and (3) all the on-campus independents, constituting 30 percent of the student body, are committed to Joan. Only the off-campus independent students, constituting only 10 percent of the student body, are against Joan. But I may be wrong about item 3. A last-minute change causes the independents to switch their vote. Nevertheless, I may still know Joan will win the election based on my justified true belief. If my belief in h is based on evidence a, b, c, and d, where my combination of two will justify h, I may hold two false beliefs and still be said to know that h.

The no-false-belief condition was also shown to be too weak, and examples were soon forthcoming in which no false belief was present. One of the most famous was set forth by Carl Ginet (it appears in Alvin Goldman's essay in this section, Reading IV.5). Henry is driving in the country and correctly identifies a red barn in the distance. Unknown to Henry, someone has set forth a series of red barn façades in this vicinity so that Henry could not distinguish the real barn from the façades. Hence, Henry cannot be said to know that he is seeing a red barn even though he has a justified true belief. But Henry's failure to know is not attributed to any false proposition on which his belief is based. So the no-false-belief condition does not succeed in saving the tripartite analysis. Our final reading by Richard Feldman also deals with this issue.

2. The Conclusive Reasons Condition

Fred Dretske set forth an ingenious solution to the Gettier puzzle in offering an account that basically argued that S knows that p if S has a reason (R) for p, such that if p were not the case S would not have R.[2] Smith's believing that the man who will get the job has ten coins in his pocket is not based on a conclusive reason, for the man who gets the job would get it even if he were not known to have ten coins in his pocket.

But there are problems with the conclusive reasons condition. George Pappas and Marshall Swain argue that it is too strong. Suppose S were looking at a table on which there was a cup.[3] S truly and justifiably believes that a cup is before him on the table, but unknown to him he is seeing not the cup itself but a hologram caused by rays given off by the cup. So the conclusive reasons account fails, for S would not have the reason he does for believing p if p were not the case, but we would not want to say that S *knows* that a cup is on the table.

3. The Causal Condition

Goldman in "A Causal Theory of Knowledge" (Reading IV.3) sets forth a causal theory that based justification on the way it was caused. If S knows that p, then S's belief that p must be caused by the state of affairs corresponding to p. Returning to the Gettier example, Smith does not know that the person who will get the job has ten coins in his pocket because that belief is not caused in the right way. In knowledge, there must be proper causal connections between the evidence and the belief. This seems promising, and perhaps it can ultimately be refined to do the work Goldman intended, but others quickly pointed out that the notion of causality is very vague here and that explaining via causality is an explanation *obscurum per obscurum* (explaining the obscure by the obscure), for it is not clear how the numbers 2 and 3 cause us to believe that they make 5 or how the future fact that I will die causes me to know this fact or that the universal proposition that all humans are mortal causes me to know the truth.

In Reading IV.5, "Discrimination and Perceptual Knowledge," Goldman sets forth a descendent of his causal theory, which seeks to meet some of the criticisms of his main theory. In Goldman's revised theory, knowledge consists in the ability to discriminate between relevant alternatives. For example, in the case of Henry picking out a red barn in an area where there are barn façades, Henry, on Goldman's account, fails to know that he sees a barn, since he could not distinguish it from the façades.

4. The Defeasibility Condition

The defeasibility requirement, set forth in our readings by Lehrer and Paxson in Reading IV.4, states that if there is no other truth (q) such that S's believing it would have destroyed his justification for believing that p, then this condition,

along with the tripartite conditions, entails that S knows that p. Lehrer and Paxson set forth the following illustration of defeasibility. S sees a man named Tom Grabit steal a book. However, unknown to S, Tom's deranged mothers lies and testifies that Tom is a thousand miles away, so it must have been his twin brother Buck who stole the book. If S had known that Mrs. Grabit had testified the way she did, he would not have been justified in believing that Tom stole the book. The statement "Mrs. Grabit testified that Tom was a thousand miles away at the time in question" would have defeated knowledge. However, one can imagine a defeater to the defeater here. If S knew that Mrs. Grabit was a deranged liar, he would have warrant to dismiss her testimony and continue to hold to his original belief about Tom.

As you may suspect, the defeasibility criterion seems vague and open-ended. For a large number of knowledge claims, we can imagine some true proposition that, if we believed it, would defeat our claim to knowledge, but then we can think of some further true belief that would defeat the defeater, and some other true belief that would defeat the antidefeater, and so on. One may suspect that this condition is really appealing to omniscience. Nonetheless, many epistemologists, like Lehrer and Paxson, believe we can distinguish between defeating and non-defeating conditions. Others, like Gilbert Harman, hold that the best we can do is set forth as a requirement that if a person is justified in inferring that there is no defeating counterevidence to a true, justified belief, then that person *knows* the proposition in question.

These essays represent the tip of the iceberg with regard to the literature generated by Gettier's two-and-a-half-page article. All the positions described have received important criticisms that you may want to look into. A bibliography, including these critical essays, appears at the end of this part of the book. Parts V and VI also contain discussion of some of the ideas discussed in this section.

Let us turn to our readings.

Notes

[1]Keith Lehrer, "Knowledge, Truth and Evidence," *Analysis* 25.5 (1965), 169.

[2]Fred Dretske, "Conclusive Reasons," *Australasian Journal of Philosophy 49* (1971), reprinted in George

Pappas and Marshall Swain, eds., *Essays on Knowledge and Justification* (Ithaca, NY: Cornell University Press, 1978).

[3]George Pappas and Marshall Swain, "Some Conclusive Reasons Against 'Conclusive Reasons,'" in Pappas and Swain, 1978.

IV.1 Is Justified True Belief Knowledge?

Edmund L. Gettier

Edmund L. Gettier (1927–   ) is professor of philosophy at the University of Massachusetts at Amherst.

In this celebrated short essay, Gettier identifies the third condition in Plato and other accounts of knowledge as *justification* and then shows by clear counterexamples that this tripartite analysis of knowledge as true, justified belief is insufficient for knowledge. Something more than mere justification is required before a true belief can qualify as knowledge.

Various attempts have been made in recent years to state necessary and sufficient conditions for someone's knowing a given proposition. The attempts have often been such that they can be stated in a form similar to the following:[1]

> (a) S knows that P   *IFF*
>> (i) P is true,
>> (ii) S believes that P, and
>> (iii) S is justified in believing that P.

For example, Chisholm has held that the following gives the necessary and sufficient conditions for knowledge:[2]

> (b) S knows that P   *IFF*
>> (i) S accepts P,
>> (ii) S has adequate evidence for P, and
>> (iii) P is true.

Ayer has stated the necessary and sufficient conditions for knowledge as follows:[3]

> (c) S knows that P   *IFF*
>> (i) P is true,
>> (ii) S is sure that P is true, and
>> (iii) S has the right to be sure that P is true.

I shall argue that (a) is false in that the conditions stated therein do not constitute a *sufficient* condition for the truth of the proposition that S knows that P. The same argument will show that (b) and (c) fail if "has adequate evidence for" or "has the right to be sure that" is substituted for "is justified in believing that" throughout.

I shall begin by noting two points. First, in that sense of "justified" in which S's being justified in believing P is a necessary condition of S's knowing that P, it is possible for a person to be justified

From *Analysis*, Vol. 23 (Blackwell, 1963), pp. 121–123. Reprinted by permission of the author.

in believing a proposition that is in fact false. Secondly, for any proposition P, if S is justified in believing P, and P entails Q, and S deduces Q from P and accepts Q as a result of this deduction, then S is justified in believing Q. Keeping these two points in mind, I shall now present two cases in which the conditions stated in (a) are true for some proposition, though it is at the same time false that the person in question knows that proposition.

Case I:

Suppose that Smith and Jones have applied for a certain job. And suppose that Smith has strong evidence for the following conjunctive proposition:

> (d) Jones is the man who will get the job, and Jones has ten coins in his pocket.

Smith's evidence for (d) might be that the president of the company assured him that Jones would in the end be selected, and that he, Smith, had counted the coins in Jones's pocket ten minutes ago. Proposition (d) entails:

> (e) The man who will get the job has ten coins in his pocket.

Let us suppose that Smith sees the entailment from (d) to (e), and accepts (e) on the grounds of (d), for which he has strong evidence. In this case, Smith is clearly justified in believing that (e) is true.

But imagine, further, that unknown to Smith, he himself, not Jones, will get the job. And, also, unknown to Smith, he himself has ten coins in his pocket. Proposition (e) is then true, though proposition (d), from which Smith inferred (e), is false. In our example, then, all of the following are true: (*i*) (e) is true, (*ii*) Smith believes that (e) is true, and (*iii*) Smith is justified in believing that (e) is true. But it is equally clear that Smith does not *know* that (e) is true; for (e) is true in virtue of the number of coins in Smith's pocket, while Smith does not know how many coins are in Smith's pocket, and bases his belief in (e) on a count of the coins in Jones's pocket, whom he falsely believes to be the man who will get the job.

Case II:

Let us suppose that Smith has strong evidence for the following proposition:

> (f) Jones owns a Ford.

Smith's evidence might be that Jones has at all times in the past within Smith's memory owned a car, and always a Ford, and that Jones has just offered Smith a ride while driving a Ford. Let us imagine, now, that Smith has another friend, Brown, of whose whereabouts he is totally ignorant. Smith selects three place-names quite at random, and constructs the following three propositions:

> (g) Either Jones owns a Ford, or Brown is in Boston;
> (h) Either Jones owns a Ford, or Brown is in Barcelona;
> (i) Either Jones owns a Ford, or Brown is in Brest-Litovsk.

Each of these propositions is entailed by (f). Imagine that Smith realizes the entailment of each of these propositions he has constructed by (f), and proceeds to accept (g), (h), and (i) on the basis of (f). Smith has correctly inferred (g), (h), and (i) from a proposition for which he has strong evidence. Smith is therefore completely justified in believing each of these three propositions. Smith, of course, has no idea where Brown is.

But imagine now that two further conditions hold. First, Jones does *not* own a Ford, but is at present driving a rented car. And secondly, by the sheerest coincidence, and entirely unknown to Smith, the place mentioned in proposition (h) happens really to be the place where Brown is. If these two conditions hold then Smith does *not* know that (h) is true, even though (*i*) (h) is true, (*ii*) Smith does believe that (h) is true, and (*iii*) Smith is justified in believing that (h) is true.

These two examples show that definition (a) does not state a *sufficient* condition for someone's knowing a given proposition. The same cases, with appropriate changes, will suffice to show that neither definition (b) nor definition (c) do so either.

Notes

[1]Plato seems to be considering some such definition at *Theatetus* 201, and perhaps accepting one at *Meno* 98.

[2]Roderick M. Chisholm, *Perceiving: A Philosophical Study*, Cornell University Press (Ithaca, New York, 1957), p. 16.

[3]A. J. Ayer, *The Problem of Knowledge*, Macmillan (London, 1956), p. 34.

IV.2 An Alleged Defect in Gettier Counter-Examples

RICHARD FELDMAN

Richard Feldman is professor of philosophy at the University of Rochester. He is the author of numerous articles in epistemology, including "Evidentialism"(with Earl Conee) (*Philosophical Studies* 48, 1985), "Fallibilism and Knowing That One Knows" (*The Philosophical Review* 90, 1981), and "Good Arguments" (*Knowledge and the Social,* edited by Fred Schmitt, Rowman and Littlefield, 1994). He also has written *Reason and Argument* (Prentice Hall, 1993). An essay on the generality problem by Earl Conee and Feldman appears in Reading VI.4. In this essay Feldman examines the criticism of Gettier counter-examples that alleges they fail because the justification is based on propositions that are false. Feldman claims to have provided a case in which, although the proposition in question is true, the person who believes it doesn't have knowledge.

A number of philosophers have contended that Gettier counter-examples to the justified true belief analysis of knowledge all rely on a certain false principle. For example, in their recent paper, "Knowledge Without Paradox," Roben G. Meyers and Kenneth Stern argue that "counter-examples of the Gettier sort all turn on the principle that someone can be justified in accepting a certain proposition *h* on evidence *p* even though *p* is false."[1] They contend that this principle is false, and hence that the counter-examples fail. Their view is that one proposition, *p*, can justify another, *h*, only if *p* is true. With this in mind, they accept the justified true belief analysis. D. M. Armstrong defends a similar view in *Belief, Truth and Knowledge*. He writes:

Reprinted from the *Australasian Journal of Philosophy* 50, no.1 (1974) by permission.

This simple consideration seems to make redundant the ingenious argument of . . . Gettier's . . . article. Gettier produces counter-examples to the thesis that justified true belief is knowledge by producing true beliefs based on justifiably believed grounds, . . . but where these grounds are in fact *false*. But because possession of such grounds could not constitute possession of *knowledge,* I should thought it obvious that they are too weak to serve as suitable grounds.[2]

Thus he concludes that Gettier's examples are defective because they rely on the false principle that false propositions can justify one's belief in other propositions. Armstrong's view seems to be that one proposition, *p*, can justify another, *h*, only if *p* is known to be true (unlike Meyers and Stern who demand only that *p* in fact be true).

I think, though, that there are examples very much like Gettier's that do not rely on this allegedly false principle. To see this, let us first consider one example in the form in which Meyers and Stern discuss it, and then consider a slight modification of it.

> Suppose Mr. Nogot tells Smith that he owns a Ford and even shows him a certificate to that effect. Suppose, further, that up till now Nogot has always been reliable and honest in his dealings with Smith. Let us call the conjunction of all this evidence *m*. Smith is thus justified in believing that Mr. Nogot who is in his office owns a Ford (*r*) and, consequently, is justified in believing that someone in his office owns a Ford (*h*).

As it turns out, though, *m* and *h* are true but *r* is false. So, the Gettier example runs, Smith has a justified true belief in *h*, but he clearly does not know *h*.

What is supposed to justify *h* in this example is *r*. But since *r* is false, the example runs afoul of the disputed principle. Since *r* is false, it justified nothing. Hence, if the principle is false, the counterexample fails.

We can alter the example slightly, however, so that what justifies *h* for Smith is true and he knows that it is. Suppose he deduces from *m* its existential generalization:

> (*n*) There is someone in the office who told Smith that he owns a Ford and even showed him a certificate to that effect, and who up till now has always been reli-

able and honest in his dealings with Smith.

(*n*), we should note, is true and Smith knows that it is, since he has correctly deduced it from *m*, which he knows to be true. On the basis of *n* Smith believes *h*—someone in the office owns a Ford. Just as the Nogot evidence, *m*, justified *r*—Nogot owns a Ford—in the original example, *n* justifies *h* in this example. Thus Smith has a justified true belief in *h*, knows his evidence to be true, but still does not know *h*.

I conclude that even if a proposition can be justified for a person only if his evidence is true, or only if he knows it to be true, there are still counter-examples to the justified true belief analysis of knowledge of the Gettier sort. In the above example, Smith reasoned from the proposition *m* which he knew to be true, to the proposition *n*, which he also knew, to the truth *h*; yet he still did not know *h*. So some examples, similar to Gettier's, do not "turn on the principle that someone can be justified in accepting a certain proposition . . . even though (his evidence) . . . is false."[3]

Notes

[1] Robert G. Meyers and Kenneth Stern, "Knowledge Without Paradox," *The Journal of Philosophy* 70, no. 6 (March 22, 1973): 147–160.

[2] D. M. Armstrong, *Belief, Truth and Knowledge* (Cambridge, Eng., 1973), p. 152.

[3] Meyers and Stern, *op. cit.*, p. 147.

IV.3 A Causal Theory of Knowing

ALVIN I. GOLDMAN

Alvin I. Goldman is professor of philosophy at the University of Arizona. Goldman accepts Gettier's contention that the traditional account of empirical knowledge is deficient and seeks to repair the weakness with a causal account of knowledge. Examining Gettier's second counterexample, which involves proposition p, either Jones owns a Ford or Brown is in Barcelona, Goldman argues that p fails to qualify as knowledge, not because it is based on a false proposition but because there is no *causal* connection between the facts that Brown is in Barcelona and that Smith believes p. Goldman shows how perceptual and memory knowledge are such in virtue of the proper causal chains: Pattern 1 and Pattern 2 chains. In Pattern 1 chains, the state of affairs p is involved in the chain that causes a Person S's true belief p. In Pattern 2 chains, a common source causes both state of affairs p and S's belief that p. Goldman's analysis represents a radical departure from traditional epistemology, which views epistemological matters as questions of logic or justification, for rather than focusing on the reasons one has for one's belief, he views knowledge as primarily a causal issue. We will see how Goldman's views further develop in Readings IV.5 and VI.1.

Since Edmund L. Gettier reminded us recently of a certain important inadequacy of the traditional analysis of "S knows that p," several attempts have been made to correct that analysis.[1] In this paper I shall offer still another analysis (or a sketch of an analysis) of "S knows that p," one which will avert Gettier's problem. My concern will be with knowledge of empirical propositions only, since I think that the traditional analysis is adequate for knowledge of nonempirical truths.

Consider an abbreviated version of Gettier's second counterexample to the traditional analysis. Smith believes

(q) Jones owns a Ford

and has very strong evidence for it. Smith's evidence might be that Jones has owned a Ford for many years and that Jones has just offered Smith a ride while driving a Ford. Smith has another friend, Brown, of whose whereabouts he is totally ignorant. Choosing a town quite at random, however, Smith constructs the proposition

(p) Either Jones owns a Ford or Brown is in Barcelona.

Seeing that q entails p, Smith infers that p is true. Since he has adequate evidence for q, he also has adequate evidence for p. But now suppose that Jones does *not* own a Ford (he was driving a rented car when he offered Smith a ride), but, quite by coincidence, Brown happens to be in Barcelona. This means that p is true, that Smith believes p, and that Smith has adequate evidence for p. But Smith does not know p.

A variety of hypotheses might be made to account for Smith's not knowing p. Michael Clark, for example, points to the fact that q is false, and suggests this as the reason why Smith cannot be said to know p. Generalizing from this case, Clark argues that, for S to know a proposition, each of S's grounds for it must be *true*, as well as his grounds for his grounds, etc.[2] I shall make another hypothesis to account for the fact that Smith cannot be said to know p, and I shall generalize this into a new analysis of "S knows that p."

Notice that what *makes* p true is the fact that Brown is in Barcelona, but that this fact has noth-

Reprinted from *The Journal of Philosophy*, 64, 12 (1967), 355–372, by kind permission of the author and editor.

I wish to thank members of the University of Michigan Philosophy Department, several of whom made helpful comments on earlier versions of this paper.

ing to do with Smith's believing p. That is, there is no *causal* connection between the fact that Brown is in Barcelona and Smith's believing p. If Smith had come to believe p by reading a letter from Brown postmarked in Barcelona, then we might say that Smith knew p. Alternatively, if Jones did own a Ford, and his owning the Ford was manifested by his offer of a ride to Smith, and this in turn resulted in Smith's believing p, then we would say that Smith knew p. Thus, one thing that seems to be missing in this example is a causal connection between the fact that makes p true [or simply: the fact that p] and Smith's belief of p. The requirement of such a *causal connection* is what I wish to add to the traditional analysis.

To see that this requirement is satisfied in all cases of (empirical) knowledge, we must examine a variety of such causal connections. Clearly, only a sketch of the important kinds of cases is possible here.

Perhaps the simplest case of a causal chain connecting some fact p with someone's belief of p is that of *perception*. I wish to espouse a version of the causal theory of perception, in essence that defended by H. P. Grice.[3] Suppose that S sees that there is a vase in front of him. How is this to be analyzed? I shall not attempt a complete analysis of this, but a necessary condition of S's seeing that there is a vase in front of him is that there be a certain kind of causal connection between the presence of the vase and S's believing that a vase is present. I shall not attempt to describe this causal process in detail. Indeed, to a large extent, a description of this process must be regarded as a problem for the special sciences, not for philosophy. But a certain causal process—viz. that which standardly takes place when we say that so-and-so *sees* such-and-such—must occur. That our ordinary concept of sight (i.e., knowledge acquired by sight) includes a causal requirement is shown by the fact that if the relevant causal process is absent we would withhold the assertion that so-and-so *saw* such-and-such. Suppose that, although a vase is directly in front of S, a laser photograph[4] is interposed between it and S, thereby blocking it from S's view. The photograph, however, is one of a vase (a different vase), and when it is illuminated by light waves from a laser, it looks to S exactly like a real vase. When the photograph is illuminated, S forms the belief that there is a vase in front of him. Here we would deny that S *sees* that there is a vase

in front of him, for his view of the real vase is completely blocked, so that it has no causal role in the formation of his belief. Of course, S might *know* that there was a vase in front of him even if the photograph is blocking his view. Someone else, in a position to see the vase, might tell S that there is a vase in front of him. Here the presence of the vase might be a causal ancestor of S's belief, but the causal process would not be a (purely) *perceptual* one. S *could not be said to see* that there is a vase in front of him. For this to be true, there must be a causal process, but one of a very special sort, connecting the presence of the vase with S's belief.

I shall here assume that perceptual knowledge of facts is noninferential. This is merely a simplifying procedure, and not essential to my account. Certainly a percipient does not *infer* facts about physical objects from the state of his brain or from the stimulation of his sense organs. He need not know about these goings-on at all. But some epistemologists maintain that we directly perceive only sense data and that we infer physical-object facts from them. This view could be accommodated within my analysis. I could say that physical-object facts cause sense data, that people directly perceive sense data, and that they infer the physical object facts from the sense data. This kind of process would be fully accredited by my analysis, which will allow for knowledge based on inference. But for purposes of exposition it will be convenient to regard perceptual knowledge of external facts as independent of any inference.

Here the question arises about the *scope* of perceptual knowledge. By perception I can know noninferentially that there is a vase in front of me. But can I know noninferentially that the painting I am viewing is a Picasso? It is unnecessary to settle such issues here. Whether the knowledge of such facts is to be classed as inferential or noninferential, my analysis can account for it. So the scope of noninferential knowledge may be left indeterminate.

I turn next to memory, i.e., knowledge that is based, in part, on memory. Remembering, like perceiving, must be regarded as a causal process. S remembers p at time t only if S's believing p at an earlier time is a cause of his believing p at t. Of course, not every causal connection between an earlier belief and a later one is a case of remembering. As in the case of perception, however, I shall not try to describe this process in detail. This is a job mainly for the scientist. Instead, the kind of causal process in question is to be identified simply by example, by "pointing" to paradigm cases of remembering. Whenever causal processes are of that kind—whatever that kind is, precisely— they are cases of remembering.[5]

A causal connection between earlier belief (or knowledge) of p and later belief (knowledge) of p is certainly a necessary ingredient in memory.[6] To remember a fact is not simply to believe it at t_0 and also to believe it at t_1. Nor does someone's knowing a fact at t_0 and his knowing it at t_1 entail that he remembers it at t_1. He may have perceived the fact at t_0, forgotten it, and then relearned it at t_1 by someone's telling it to him. Nor does the inclusion of a memory "impression"—a feeling of remembering—ensure that one really remembers. Suppose S perceives p at t_0, but forgets it at t_1. At t_2 he begins to believe p again because someone tells him p, but at t_2 he has no memory impression of p. At t_3 we artificially stimulate in S a memory impression of p. It does not follow that S remembers p at t_3. The description of the case suggests that his believing p at t_0 has no causal effect whatever on his believing p at t_3; and if we accepted this fact, we would deny that he remembers p at t_3.

Knowledge can be acquired by a combination of perception and memory. At t_0, the fact p causes S to believe p, by perception. S's believing p at t_0 results, via memory, in S's believing p at t_1. Thus, the fact p is a cause of S's believing p at t_1, and S can be said to know p at t_1. But not all knowledge results from perception and memory alone. In particular, much knowledge is based on *inference*.

As I shall use the term "inference," to say that S knows p by "inference" does not entail that S went through an explicit, conscious process of reasoning. It is not necessary that he have "talked to himself," saying something like "Since such-and-such is true, p must also be true." My belief that there is a fire in the neighborhood is based on, or inferred from, my belief that I hear a fire engine. But I have not gone through a process of explicit reasoning, saying "There's a fire engine; therefore there must be a fire." Perhaps the word "inference" is ordinarily used only where explicit reasoning occurs; if so, my use of the term will be somewhat broader than its ordinary use.

Suppose S perceives that there is solidified lava in various parts of the countryside. On the basis of this belief, plus various "background" beliefs about the production of lava, S concludes that a nearby mountain erupted many centuries ago. Let us assume that this is a highly warranted inductive inference, one which gives S adequate evidence for believing that the mountain did erupt many centuries ago. Assuming this proposition is true, does S know it? This depends on the nature of the causal process that induced his belief. If there is a continuous causal chain of the sort he envisages connecting the fact that the mountain erupted with his belief of this fact, then S knows it. If there is no such causal chain, however, S does not know that proposition.

Suppose that the mountain erupts, leaving lava around the countryside. The lava remains there until S perceives it and infers that the mountain erupted. Then S does know that the mountain erupted. But now suppose that, after the mountain has erupted, a man somehow removes all the lava. A century later, a different man (not knowing of the real volcano) decides to make it look as if there had been a volcano, and therefore puts lava in appropriate places. Still later, S comes across this lava and concludes that the mountain erupted centuries ago. In this case, S cannot be said to know the proposition. This is because the fact that the mountain did erupt is not a cause of S's believing that it erupted. A necessary condition of S's knowing p is that his believing p be connected with p by a causal chain.

In the first case, where S knows p, the causal connection may be diagrammed as in Figure 1. (p) is the fact that the mountain erupted at such-and-such a time. (q) is the fact that lava is (now) present around the countryside. "B" stands for a belief, the expression in parentheses indicating the proposition believed, and the subscript designating the believer. (r) is a "background" proposition, describing the ways in which lava is produced and how it solidifies. Solid arrows in the diagram represent causal connections; dotted arrows represent inferences. Notice that, in Figure 1, there is

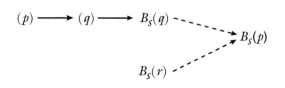

not only an arrow connecting (q) with S's belief of (q), but also an arrow connecting (p) with (q). In the suggested variant of the lava case, the latter arrow would be missing, showing that there is no continuous causal chain connecting (p) with S's belief of (p). Therefore, in that variant case, S could not be said to know (p).

I have said that p is causally connected to S's belief of p, in the case diagrammed in Figure 1. This raises the question, however, of whether the inferential part of the chain is itself a causal chain. In other words, is S's belief of q a cause of his believing p? This is a question to which I shall not try to give a definitive answer here. I am inclined to say that inference *is* a causal process, that is, that when someone *bases* his belief of one proposition on his belief of a set of other propositions, then his belief of the latter propositions can be considered a cause of his belief of the former proposition. But I do not wish to rest my thesis on this claim. All I do claim is that, if a chain of inferences is "added" to a causal chain, then the entire chain is causal. In terms of our diagram, a chain consisting of solid arrows plus dotted arrows is to be considered a causal chain, though I shall not take a position on the question of whether the dotted arrows represent causal connections. Thus, in Figure 1, p is a cause of S's belief of p, whether or not we regard S's belief of q a cause of his belief of p.[7]

Consider next a case of knowledge based on "testimony." This too can be analyzed causally. p causes a person T to believe p, by perception. T's belief of p gives rise to (causes) his asserting p. T's asserting p causes S, by auditory perception, to believe that T is asserting p. S infers that T believes p, and from this, in turn, he infers that p is a fact. There is a continuous causal chain from p to S's believing p, and thus, assuming that each of S's inferences is warranted, S can be said to know p.

This causal chain is represented in Figure 2. "A" refers to an act of asserting a proposition, the expression in parentheses indicating the proposi-

tion asserted and the subscript designating the agent. (q), (r), (u), and (v) are background propositions. (q) and (r), for example, pertain to T's sincerity; they help S conclude, from the fact that T asserted p, that T really believes p.

In this case, as in the lava case, S knows p because he has correctly reconstructed the causal chain leading from p to the evidence for p that S perceives, in this case, T's asserting (p). This correct reconstruction is shown in the diagram by S's inference "mirroring" the rest of the causal chain. Such a correct reconstruction is a necessary condition of knowledge based on inference. To see this, consider the following example. A newspaper reporter observes p and reports it to his newspaper. When printed, however, the story contains a typographical error so that it asserts not-p. When reading the paper, however, S fails to see the word "not," and takes the paper to have asserted p. Trusting the newspaper, he infers that p is true. Here we have a continuous causal chain leading from p to S's believing p; yet S does not know p. S thinks that p resulted in a report to the newspaper about p and that this report resulted in its printing the statement p. Thus, his reconstruction of the causal chain is mistaken. But, if he is to know p, his reconstruction must contain no mistakes. Though he need not reconstruct *every* detail of the causal chain, he must reconstruct all the important links.[8] An additional requirement for knowledge based on inference is that the knower's inferences be warranted. That is, the propositions on which he bases his belief of p must genuinely confirm p very highly, whether deductively or inductively. Reconstructing a causal chain merely by lucky guesses does not yield knowledge.

With the help of our diagrams, we can contrast the traditional analysis of knowing with Clark's analysis (*op. cit.*) and contrast each of these with my own analysis. The traditional analysis makes reference to just three features of the diagrams. First, it requires that p be true; i.e., that (p) appear in the diagram. Secondly, it requires that S believe p; i.e., that S's belief of p appear in the diagram. Thirdly, it requires that S's inferences, if any, be warranted; i.e., that the sets of beliefs that are at the tail of a dotted arrow must jointly highly confirm the belief at the head of these arrows. Clark proposes a further requirement for knowledge. He requires that *each* of the beliefs in S's chain of inference be *true*. In other words, whereas

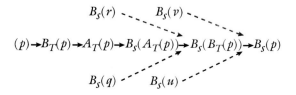

Figure 2

the traditional analysis requires a fact to correspond to S's belief of p, Clark requires that a fact correspond to *each* of S's beliefs on which he based his belief of p. Thus, corresponding to each belief on the right side of the diagram there must be a fact on the left side. (My diagrams omit facts corresponding to the "background" beliefs.)

As Clark's analysis stands, it seems to omit an element of the diagrams that my analysis requires, viz., the arrows indicating causal connections. Now Clark might reformulate his analysis so as to make implicit reference to these causal connections. If he required that the knower's beliefs include *causal beliefs* (of the relevant sort), then his requirement that these beliefs be true would amount to the requirement that there *be* causal chains of the sort I require. This interpretation of Clark's analysis would make it almost equivalent to mine, and would enable him to avoid some objections that have been raised against him. But he has not explicitly formulated his analysis that way, and it therefore remains deficient in this respect.

Before turning to the problems facing Clark's analysis, more must be said about my own analysis. So far, my examples may have suggested that, if S knows p, the fact that p is a cause of his belief of p. This would clearly be wrong, however. Let us grant that I can know facts about the future. Then, if we required that the known fact cause the knower's belief, we would have to countenance "backward" causation. My analysis, however, does not face this dilemma. The analysis requires that there be a causal *connection* between p and S's belief, not necessarily that p be a *cause* of S's belief. p and S's belief of p can also be causally connected in a way that yields knowledge if both p and S's belief of p have a *common* cause. This can be illustrated as follows.

T intends to go downtown on Monday. On Sunday, T tells S of his intention. Hearing T say he will go downtown, S infers that T really does intend to go downtown. And from this S concludes that T *will* go downtown on Monday. Now suppose that T fulfills his intention by going downtown on Monday. Can S be said to know that he would go downtown? If we ever can be said to have knowledge of the future, this is a reasonable candidate for it. So let us say S did know that proposition. How can my analysis account for S's knowledge? T's going downtown on Monday clearly cannot be a cause of S's believing, on

Sunday, that he would go downtown. But there is a fact that is the *common* cause of T's going downtown and of S's belief that he would go downtown, viz., T's intending (on Sunday) to go downtown. This intention resulted in his going downtown and also resulted in S's believing that he would go downtown. This causal connection between S's belief and the fact believed allows us to say that S *knew* that T would go downtown.

The example is diagrammed in Figure 3. (p) = T's going downtown on Monday. (q) = T's intending (on Sunday) to go downtown on Monday. (r) = T's telling S (on Sunday) that he will go downtown on Monday. (u) and (v) are relevant background propositions pertaining to T's honesty, resoluteness, etc. The diagram reveals that q is a cause both of p and of S's belief of p. Cases of this kind I shall call *Pattern 2* cases of knowledge. Figures 1 and 2 exemplify *Pattern 1* cases of knowledge.

Notice that the causal connection between q and p is an essential part of S's knowing p. Suppose, for example, that T's intending (on Sunday) to go downtown does not result in, or cause, T's going downtown on Monday. Suppose that T, after telling S that he would go downtown, changes his mind. Nevertheless, on Monday he is kidnapped and forced, at the point of a gun, to go downtown. Here both q and p actually occur, but they are not causally related. The diagram in Figure 3 would have to be amended by deleting the arrow connecting (q) with (p). But if the rest of the facts of the original case remain the same, S could not be said to know p. It would be false to say that S knew, on Sunday, that T would go downtown on Monday.

Pattern 2 cases of knowledge are not restricted to knowledge of the future. I know that smoke was coming out of my chimney last night. I know this because I remember perceiving a fire

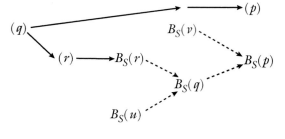

Figure 3

in my fireplace last night, and I infer that the fire caused smoke to rise out of the chimney. This case exemplifies Pattern 2. The smoke's rising out of the chimney is not a causal factor of my belief. But the fact that there was a fire in the fireplace was a cause both of my belief that smoke was coming out of the chimney and of the fact that smoke was coming out of the chimney. If we supplement this case slightly, we can make my knowledge exemplify *both* Pattern 1 and Pattern 2. Suppose that a friend tells me today that he perceived smoke coming out of my chimney last night and I base my continued belief of this fact on his testimony. Then the fact was a cause of my current belief of it, as well as an *effect* of another fact that caused my belief. In general, numerous and diverse kinds of causal connections can obtain between a given fact and a given person's belief of that fact.

Let us now examine some objections to Clark's analysis and see how the analysis presented here fares against them. John Turk Saunders and Narayan Champawat have raised the following counterexample to Clark's analysis:[9]

> Suppose that Smith believes
>
> (*p*) Jones owns a Ford
>
> because his friend Brown whom he knows to be generally reliable and honest yesterday told Smith that Jones had always owned a Ford. Brown's information was correct, but today Jones sells his Ford and replaces it with a Volkswagen. An hour later Jones is pleased to find that he is the proud owner of two cars: he has been lucky enough to win a Ford in a raffle. Smith's belief in *p* is not only justified and true, but is fully grounded, e.g., we suppose that each link in the . . . chain of Smith's grounds is true (8).

Clearly Smith does not know *p*; yet he seems to satisfy Clark's analysis of knowing.

Smith's lack of knowledge can be accounted for in terms of my analysis. Smith does not know *p* because his believing *p* is not causally related to *p*, Jones's owning a Ford *now*. This can be seen by examining Figure 4. In the diagram, (*p*) = Jones's owning a Ford *now*; (*q*) = Jones's having owned a Ford (until yesterday); (*r*) = Jones's winning a Ford in a raffle today. (*t*), (*u*), and (*v*) are background propositions. (*v*), for example, deals with the likelihood of someone's continuing to own the same car today that he owned yesterday. The sub-

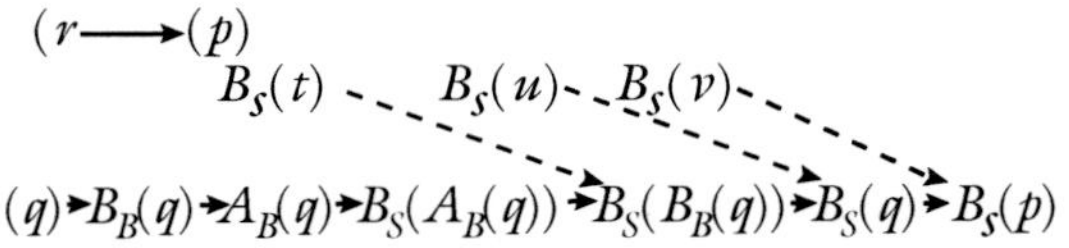

$$(r \longrightarrow (p)$$
$$B_S(t) \dashrightarrow B_S(u) \dashrightarrow B_S(v) \dashrightarrow$$
$$(q) \blacktriangleright B_B(q) \blacktriangleright A_B(q) \blacktriangleright B_S(A_B(q)) \blacktriangleright B_S(B_B(q)) \blacktriangleright B_S(q) \blacktriangleright B_S(p)$$

Figure 4

script "*B*" designates Brown, and the subscript "*S*" designates Smith. Notice the absence of an arrow connecting (*p*) with (*q*). The absence of this arrow represents the absence of a causal relation between (*q*) and (*p*). Jones's owning a Ford in the past (until yesterday) is not a cause of his owning one now. Had he continued owning the same Ford today that he owned yesterday, there would be a causal connection between *q* and *p* and, therefore, a causal connection between *p* and Smith's believing *p*. This causal connection would exemplify Pattern 2. But, as it happened, it is purely a coincidence that Jones owns a Ford today as well as yesterday. Thus, Smith's belief of *p* is not connected with *p* by Pattern 2, nor is there any Pattern 1 connection between them. Hence, Smith does not know *p*.

If we supplement Clark's analysis as suggested above, it can be saved from this counterexample. Though Saunders and Champawat fail to mention this explicitly, presumably it is one of Smith's beliefs that Jones's owning a Ford yesterday would *result* in Jones's owning a Ford now. This was undoubtedly one of his grounds for believing that Jones owns a Ford now. (A complete diagram of *S*'s beliefs relevant to *p* would include this belief.) Since this belief is false, however, Clark's analysis would yield the correct consequence that Smith does not know *p*. Unfortunately, Clark himself seems not to have noticed this point, since Saunders and Champawat's putative counterexample has been allowed to stand.

Another sort of counterexample to Clark's analysis has been given by Saunders and Champawat and also by Keith Lehrer. This is a counterexample from which his analysis cannot escape. I shall give Lehrer's example (*op. cit.*) of this sort of difficulty. Suppose Smith bases his belief of

(*p*) Someone in his office owns a Ford

on his belief of four propositions

(*q*) Jones owns a Ford
(*r*) Jones works in his office

(s) Brown owns a Ford
(t) Brown works in his office

In fact, Smith knows *q*, *r*, and *t*, but he does not know *s* because *s* is false. Since *s* is false, not *all* of Smith's grounds for *p* are true, and, therefore, on Clark's analysis, Smith does not know *p*. Yet clearly Smith does know *p*. Thus, Clark's analysis is *too strong*.

Having seen the importance of a causal chain for knowing, it is fairly obvious how to amend Clark's requirements without making them too weak. We need not require, as Clark does, that *all* of S's grounds be true. What is required is that enough of them be true to ensure the existence of at least *one* causal connection between *p* and S's belief of *p*. In Lehrer's example, Smith thinks that there are two ways in which he knows *p*: via his knowledge of the conjunction of *q* and *r*, and via his knowledge of the conjunction of *s* and *t*. He does not know *p* via the conjunction of *s* and *t*, since *s* is false. But there is a causal connection via *q* and *r*, between *p* and Smith's belief of *p*. And this connection is enough.

Another sort of case in which one of S's grounds for *p* may be false without preventing him from knowing *p* is where the false proposition is a dispensable background assumption. Suppose S bases his belief of *p* on 17 background assumptions, but only 16 of these are true. If these 16 are strong enough to confirm *p*, then the 17th is dispensable. S can be said to know *p* though one of his grounds is false.

Our discussion of Lehrer's example calls attention to the necessity of a further clarification of the notion of a "causal chain." I said earlier that causal chains with admixtures of inferences are causal chains. Now I wish to add that causal chains with admixtures of logical connections are causal chains. Unless we allow this interpretation, it is hard to see how facts like "Someone in the office owns a Ford" or "All men are mortal" could be *causally* connected with beliefs thereof.

The following principle will be useful: *If x is logically related to y and if y is a cause of z, then x is a cause of z.* Thus, suppose that *q* causes S's belief of *q* and that *r* causes S's belief of *r*. Next suppose that *S* infers *q & r from his belief of q* and of *r*. Then the facts *q* and *r* are causes of S's believing *q & r*. But the fact *q & r* is logically related to the fact *q* and to the fact *r*. Therefore, using the principle

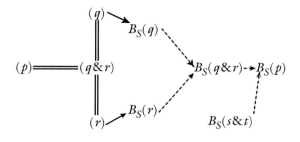

Figure 5

enunciated above, the fact *q & r* is a cause of S's believing *q & r*.

In Lehrer's case another logical connection is involved: a connection between an existential fact and an instance thereof. Lehrer's case is diagrammed in Figure 5. In addition to the usual conventions, logical relationships are represented by double solid lines. As the diagram shows, the fact *p*—someone in Smith's office owning a Ford—is logically related to the fact *q & r*—Jones's owning a Ford and Jones's working in Smith's office. The fact *q & r* is, in turn, logically related to the fact *q* and to the fact *r*. *q* causes S's belief of *q* and, by inference, his belief of *q & r* and of *p*. Similarly, *r* is a cause of S's belief of *p*. Since Smith's inferences are warranted, even setting aside his belief of *s & t*, he knows *p*.

In a similar way, universal facts may be causes of beliefs thereof. The fact that all men are mortal is logically related to its instances: John's being mortal, George's being mortal, Oscar's being mortal, etc. Now suppose that S perceives George, John, Oscar, etc. to be mortal (by seeing them die). He infers from these facts that all men are mortal, an inference which, I assume, is warranted. Since each of the facts, John is mortal, George is mortal, Oscar is mortal, etc., is a cause of S's believing that fact, each is also a cause of S's believing that all men are mortal. Moreover, since the universal fact that all men are mortal is logically related to each of these particular facts, this universal fact is a cause of S's belief of it. Hence, S can be said to know that all men are mortal. In analogous fashions, S can know various other logically compound propositions.

We can now formulate the analysis of knowing as follows:

S knows that p if and only if
the fact p is causally connected in an
"appropriate" way with S's believing p.

"Appropriate," knowledge-producing causal processes include the following:

(1) perception
(2) memory
(3) a causal chain, exemplifying either Pattern 1 or 2, which is correctly reconstructed by inferences, each of which is warranted (background propositions help warrant an inference only if they are true)[10]
(4) combinations of (1), (2), and (3)

We have seen that this analysis is *stronger* than the traditional analysis in certain respects: the causal requirement and the correct-reconstruction requirement are absent from the older analysis. These additional requirements enable my analysis to circumvent Gettier's counterexamples to the traditional one. But my analysis is *weaker* than the traditional analysis in another respect. In at least one popular interpretation of the traditional analysis, a knower must be able to justify or give evidence for any proposition he knows. For S to know p at t, S must be able, at t, to *state* his justification for believing p, or his grounds for p. My analysis makes no such requirement, and the absence of this requirement enables me to account for cases of knowledge that would wrongly be excluded by the traditional analysis.

I know now, for example, that Abraham Lincoln was born in 1809.[11] I originally came to know this fact, let us suppose, by reading an encyclopedia article. I believed that this encyclopedia was trustworthy and that its saying Lincoln was born in 1809 must have resulted from the fact that Lincoln was indeed born in 1809. Thus, my original knowledge of this fact was founded on a warranted inference. But now I no longer remember this inference. I remember that Lincoln was born in 1809, but not that this is stated in a certain encyclopedia. I no longer have any pertinent beliefs that highly confirm the proposition that Lincoln was born in 1809. Nevertheless, I know this proposition now. My original knowledge of it was preserved until now by the causal process of memory.

Defenders of the traditional analysis would doubtlessly deny that I really do know Lincoln's birth year. This denial, however, stems from a desire to protect their analysis. It seems clear that many things we know were originally learned in a way that we no longer remember. The range of our knowledge would be drastically reduced if these items were denied the status of knowledge.

Other species of knowledge without explicit evidence could also be admitted by my analysis. Notice that I have not closed the list of "appropriate" causal processes. Leaving the list open is desirable, because there may be some presently controversial causal processes that we may later deem "appropriate" and, therefore, knowledge-producing. Many people now doubt the legitimacy of claims to extrasensory perception. But if conclusive evidence were to establish the existence of causal processes connecting physical facts with certain persons' beliefs without the help of standard perceptual processes, we might decide to call such beliefs items of knowledge. This would be another species of knowledge in which the knower might be unable to justify or defend his belief. My analysis allows for the possibility of such knowledge, though it doesn't commit one to it.

Special comments are in order about knowledge of our own mental states. This is a very difficult and controversial topic, so I hesitate to discuss it, but something must be said about it. Probably there are some mental states that are clearly distinct from the subject's belief that he is in such a state. If so, then there is presumably a casual process connecting the existence of such states with the subject's belief thereof. We may add this kind of process to the list of "appropriate" causal processes. The more difficult cases are those in which the state is hardly distinguishable from the subject's believing that he is in that state. My being in pain and my believing that I am in pain are hardly distinct states of affairs. If there is no distinction here between the believing and the believed, how can there be a causal connection between them? For the purposes of the present analysis, we may regard identity as a "limiting" or "degenerate" case of a causal connection, just as zero may be regarded as a "limiting" or "degenerate" case of a number. It is not surprising that knowledge of one's own mental state should turn out to be a limiting or degenerate case of knowledge. Philosophers have long recognized its peculiar status. While some philosophers have regarded it as a paradigm case of knowledge, others have claimed that we have no "knowledge" of our mental states at all. A theory of knowledge that makes knowledge of one's own mental states rather different from garden-variety species of knowledge is, in so far forth, acceptable and even welcome.

In conclusion, let me answer some possible objections to my analysis. It might be doubted whether a causal analysis adequately provides the meaning of the word "knows" or of the sentence (schema) "S knows p." But I am not interested in giving the *meaning* of "S knows p"; only its *truth conditions*. I claim to have given one correct set of truth conditions for "S knows p." Truth conditions of a sentence do not always provide its meaning. Consider, for example, the following truth-conditions statement: "The sentence 'Team T wins the baseball game' is true if and only if team T has more runs at the end of the game than the opposing team." This statement fails to provide the meaning of the sentence "Team T wins the baseball game"; for it fails to indicate an essential part of the meaning of that sentence, viz., that to win a game is to achieve the presumed goal of playing it. Someone might fully understand the truth conditions given above and yet fail to understand the meaning of the sentence because he has no understanding of the notion of "winning" in general.

Truth conditions should not be confused with verification conditions. My analysis of "S knows p" does not purport to give procedures for *finding out* whether a person (including oneself) knows a given proposition. No doubt, we sometimes do know that people know certain propositions, for we sometimes know that their beliefs are causally connected (in appropriate ways) with the facts believed. On the other hand, it may often be difficult or even impossible to find out whether this condition holds for a given proposition and a given person. For example, it may be difficult for me to find out whether I really do remember a certain fact that I seem to remember. The difficulties that exist for *finding out* whether someone knows a given proposition do not constitute difficulties for my analysis, however.

In the same vein it should be noted that I have made no attempt to answer skeptical problems. My analysis gives no answer to the skeptic who asks that I start from the content of my own experience and then prove that I know there is a material world, a past, etc. I do not take this to be one of the jobs of giving truth conditions for "S knows that p."

The analysis presented here flies in the face of a well-established tradition in epistemology, the view that epistemological questions are questions of logic or justification, not causal or genetic questions. This traditional view, however, must not go unquestioned. Indeed, I think my analysis shows that the question of whether someone knows a certain proposition is, in part, a causal question, although, of course, the question of what the correct analysis is of "S knows that p" is not a causal question.

Notes

[1]"Is Justified True Belief Knowledge?" *Analysis*, 23.6 (1963), 121–123. I say "reminded" because essentially the same point was made by Russell in 1912. Cf. *The Problems of Philosophy* (Oxford, 1912), ch. 13, pp. 132 ff. New analyses have been proposed by Michael Clark, "Knowledge and Grounds: A Comment on Mr. Gettier's Paper," *Analysis* 24.2 (1963), 46–48; Ernest Sosa, "The Analysis of 'Knowledge that P'," *ibid.*, 25.1 (1964): 1–8; and Keith Lehrer, "Knowledge, Truth and Evidence," *ibid.*, 25.5 (1965), 168–175.

[2]*Op. cit.* Criticisms of Clark's analysis will be discussed below.

[3]"The Causal Theory of Perception," *Proceedings of the Aristotelian Society,* supp. vol. 35 (1961).

[4]If a laser photograph (hologram) is illuminated by light waves, especially waves from a laser, the effect of the hologram on the viewer is exactly as if the object were being seen. It preserves three-dimensionality completely, and even gives appropriate parallax effects as the viewer moves relative to it. Cf. E. N. Leith and J. Upatnieks, "Photography by Laser," *Scientific American* (June 1965), p. 24.

[5]For further defense of this kind of procedure, with attention to perception, cf. Grice, *op. cit.*

[6]Causal connections can hold between states of affairs, such as believings, as well as between events. If a given event or state, in conjunction with other events or states, "leads to" or "results in" another event or state (or the same state obtaining at a later time), it will be called a "cause" of the latter. I shall also speak of "facts" being causes.

[7]A fact can be a cause of a belief even if it does not *initiate* the belief. Suppose I believe that there is a lake in a certain locale, this belief having started in a manner quite unconnected with the existence of the lake. Continuing to have the belief, I go to the locale and perceive the lake. At this juncture, the existence of the lake becomes a cause of my believing that there is a lake there. This is analogous to a table top that is supported by four legs. When a fifth leg is inserted flush beneath the table top, it too becomes a cause of the table top's not falling. It has a causal role in the support of the table top even though, before it was inserted, the table top was adequately supported.

[8]Clearly we cannot require someone to reconstruct every detail, since this would involve knowledge of minute physical phenomena, for example, of which ordinary people are unaware. On the other hand, it is difficult to give criteria to identify which details, in general, are "important." This will vary substantially from case to case.

[9]"Mr. Clark's Definition of 'Knowledge,'" *Analysis*, 25.1 (1964), 8–9.

[10]Perhaps background propositions that help warrant S's inference must be known by S, as well as true. This requirement could be added without making our analysis of "S knows that p" circular. For these propositions would not include p. In other words, the analysis of knowledge could be regarded as recursive.

[11]This kind of case is drawn from an unpublished manuscript of Gilbert Harman.

IV.4 Knowledge: Undefeated Justified True Belief

Keith Lehrer and Thomas D. Paxson, Jr.

Keith Lehrer is professor of philosophy at the University of Arizona, and Thomas Paxson is professor of philosophy at Southern Illinois University, Edwardsville. Confining themselves to nonbasic beliefs—those statements that are based on other statements—Lehrer and Paxson characterize nonbasic knowledge as undefeated justified true belief. That is, "Person S has nonbasic knowledge that h if and only if (i) h is true; (ii) S believes that h, and (iii) there is some statement p that completely justified S in believing that h and no other statement defeats this justification." This third condition is further explicated and qualified.

If a man knows that a statement is true even though there is no other statement that justifies his belief, then his knowledge is basic. Basic knowledge is completely justified true belief. On the other hand, if a man knows that a statement is true because there is some other statement that justifies his belief, then his knowledge is nonbasic. Nonbasic knowledge requires something in addition to completely justified true belief; for, though a statement completely justifies a man in his belief, there may be some true statement that *defeats* his justification. So, we must add the condition that his justification is not defeated. Nonbasic knowledge is undefeated justified true belief. These analyses will be elaborated below and subsequently defended against various alternative analyses.[1]

I

We propose the following analysis of basic knowledge: S has basic knowledge that h if and only if (i) h is true, (ii) S believes that h, (iii) S is completely justified in believing that h, and (iv) the satisfaction of condition (iii) does not depend on any evidence p justifying S in believing that h. The third condition is used in such a way that it entails neither the second condition nor the first. A person can be completely justified in believing that h, even though, irrationally, he does not; and a person can

Reprinted from *The Journal of Philosophy,* 66.8 (1969), 225–237, by kind permission of the authors and editor.

be completely justified in believing that *h,* even though, unfortunately, he is mistaken.[2] Furthermore, the third condition does not entail that there is any statement or belief that justifies *S* in believing that *h.* The analysis, then, is in keeping with the characterization of basic knowledge given above. In basic knowledge, *S* is completely justified in believing that *h* even if it is not the case that there is any statement or belief that justifies his believing that *h.*

There are cases in which a person has some, perhaps mysterious, way of being right about matters of a certain sort with such consistency that philosophers and others have said that the person knows whereof he speaks. Consider, for example, the crystal-ball-gazing gypsy who is almost always right in his predictions of specific events. Peter Unger suggests a special case of this.[3] His gypsy is always right, but has no evidence to this effect and, in fact, believes that he is usually wrong. With respect to each specific prediction, however, the gypsy impulsively believes it to be true (as indeed it is). Whether or not the predictive beliefs of the ordinary gypsy and Unger's gypsy are cases of knowledge depends, we contend, on whether they are cases of basic knowledge. This in turn depends on whether the gypsies are completely justified in their beliefs. It is plausible to suggest that these are cases of knowledge, but this is only because it is also plausible to think that the gypsies in question have some way of being right that completely justifies their prognostications. We neither affirm nor deny that these are cases of knowledge, but maintain that, if they are cases of knowledge, then they are cases of *basic* knowledge.

It is consistent with our analysis of knowledge to admit that a man knows something even though no statement constitutes evidence that completely justifies his believing it. Philosophers have suggested that certain memory and perceptual beliefs are completely justified in the absence of such evidential statements. We choose to remain agnostic with respect to any claim of this sort, but such proposals are not excluded by our analysis.

II

Not all knowledge that *p* is basic knowledge that *p,* because sometimes justifying evidence is essen-

tial. Consider the following analysis of nonbasic knowledge: (i) *h* is true, (ii) *S* believes that *h,* and (iii*) *p* completely justifies *S* in believing that *h.* In this analysis, *p* is that (statement) which makes *S* completely justified in believing that *h.* Note that (iii*), like (iii), does not entail (ii) or (i).

This analysis of nonbasic knowledge is, of course, defective. As Edmund Gettier has shown, there are examples in which some false statement *p* entails and hence completely justifies *S* in believing that *h,* and such that, though *S* correctly believes that *h,* his being correct is mostly a matter of luck.[4] Consequently, *S* lacks knowledge, contrary to the above analysis. Other examples illustrate that the false statement which creates the difficulty need not *entail h.* Consider, for example, the case of the pyromaniac described by Skyrms.[5] The pyromaniac has found that Sure-Fire matches have always ignited when struck. On the basis of this evidence, the pyromaniac is completely justified in believing that the match he now holds will ignite upon his striking it. However, unbeknownst to the pyromaniac, this match happens to contain impurities that raise its combustion temperature above that which can be produced by the friction. Imagine that a burst of Q-radiation ignites the match just as he strikes it. His belief that the match will ignite upon his striking it is true and completely justified by the evidence. But this is not a case of knowledge, because it is not the striking that will cause the match to ignite.

Roderick Chisholm has pointed out that justifications are defeasible.[6] In the examples referred to above, there is some true statement that would defeat any justification of *S* for believing that *h.*[7] In the case of the pyromaniac, his justification is defeated by the true statement that striking the match will not cause it to ignite. This defeats his justification for believing that the match will ignite upon his striking it.

Thus we propose the following analysis of nonbasic knowledge: *S* has nonbasic knowledge that *h* if and only if (i) *h* is true. (ii) *S* believes that *h,* and (iii) there is some statement *p* that completely justifies *S* in believing that *h* and no other statement defeats this justification. The question we must now answer is—what does it mean to say that a statement defeats a justification? Adopting a suggestion of Chisholm's, we might try the following: when *p* completely justifies *S* in believing that *h,* this justification is defeated by *q* if and only if (i) q is true, and (ii) the conjunction of p and q does not completely justify S in believing that h.[7] This definition is strong enough to rule out the example of the pyromaniac as a case of knowledge. The statement that the striking of a match will *not* cause it to ignite, which is true, is such that when it is conjoined to any statement that completely justifies the pyromaniac in believing that the match will ignite, the resultant conjunction will fail to so justify him in that belief. Given this definition of defeasibility, the analysis of nonbasic knowledge would require that a man who has nonbasic knowledge that h must have some justification for his belief that is not defeated by any true statement.

However, this requirement is somewhat unrealistic. To see that the definition of defeasibility under consideration makes the analysis of nonbasic knowledge excessively restrictive, we need only notice that there can be true statements that are misleading. Suppose I see a man walk into the library and remove a book from the library by concealing it beneath his coat. Since I am sure the man is Tom Grabit, whom I have often seen before when he attended my classes, I report that I know that Tom Grabit has removed the book. However, suppose further that Mrs. Grabit, the mother of Tom, has averred that on the day in question Tom was not in the library, indeed, was thousands of miles away, and that Tom's identical twin brother, John Grabit, was in the library. Imagine, moreover, that I am entirely ignorant of the fact that Mrs. Grabit has said these things. The statement that she has said these things would defeat any justification I have for believing that Tom Grabit removed the book, according to our present definition of defeasibility. Thus, I could not be said to have nonbasic knowledge that Tom Grabit removed the book.

The preceding might seem acceptable until we finish the story by adding that Mrs. Grabit is a compulsive and pathological liar, that John Grabit is a fiction of her demented mind, and that Tom Grabit took the book as I believed. Once this is added, it should be apparent that I did know that Tom Grabit removed the book, and, since the knowledge must be nonbasic, I must have nonbasic knowledge of that fact. Consequently, the definition of defeasibility must be amended. The fact that Mrs. Grabit said what she did should not be allowed to defeat any justification I have for believing that Tom Grabit removed the book, because I neither entertained any beliefs concerning Mrs. Grabit nor would I have been justified in doing so. More specifically, my justification does not depend on my being completely justified in believing that Mrs. Grabit did *not* say the things in question.

To understand how the definition of defeasibility must be amended to deal with the preceding example, let us consider an example from the literature in which a justification deserves to be defeated. Suppose that I have excellent evidence that completely justifies my believing that a student in my class, Mr. Nogot, owns a Ford, the evidence consisting in my having seen him driving it, hearing him say he owns it, and so forth. Since Mr. Nogot is a student in my class who owns a Ford, someone in my class owns a Ford, and, consequently, I am completely justified in believing that someone in my class owns a Ford. Imagine that, contrary to the evidence, Mr. Nogot does not own a Ford, that I have been deceived, but that unknown to me Mr. Havit, who is also in my class, does own a Ford. Though I have a completely justified true belief, I do not know that someone in my class owns a Ford. The reason is that my sole justification for believing that someone in my class does own a Ford is and should be defeated by the true statement that Mr. Nogot does not own a Ford.

In the case of Tom Grabit, the true statement that Mrs. Grabit said Tom was not in the library and so forth, should not be allowed to defeat my justification for believing that Tom removed the book, whereas in the case of Mr. Nogot, the true statement that Mr. Nogot does not own a Ford, should defeat my justification for believing that someone in my class owns a Ford. Why should one true statement but not the other be allowed to defeat my justification? The answer is that in one case my justification depends on my being completely justified in believing the true statement to be false while in the other it does not. My justification for believing that Tom removed the book does not depend on my being completely justified in believing it to be false that Mrs. Grabit said Tom was not in the library and so forth. But my justification for believing that someone in my class owns a Ford does depend on my being completely justified in believing it to be false that Mr. Nogot does not own a Ford. Thus, a defeating statement must be one which, though true, is such that the subject is completely justified in believing it to be false.[8]

The following definition of defeasibility incorporates this proposal: when p completely justifies S in believing that h, this justification is defeated by q if and only if (i) q is true, (ii) S is completely justified in believing q to be false, and (iii) the conjunction of p and q does not completely justify S in believing that h.

This definition of defeasibility, though basically correct, requires one last modification to meet a technical problem. Suppose that there is some statement h of which S has nonbasic knowledge. Let us again consider the example in which I know that Tom Grabit removed the book. Now imagine that there is some true statement which is completely irrelevant to this knowledge and which I happen to be completely justified in believing to be false, for example, the statement that I was born in St. Paul. Since I am completely justified in believing it to be false that I was born in St. Paul, I am also completely justified in believing to be false the conjunctive statement that I was born in St. Paul and that q, whatever q is, because I am completely justified in believing any conjunction to be false if I am completely justified in believing a conjunct of it to be false. Therefore, I am completely justified in believing to be false the conjunctive statement that I was born in St. Paul and Mrs. Grabit said that Tom Grabit was not in the library and so forth. Moreover, this conjunctive statement is true, and is such that, when it is conjoined in turn to any evidential statement that justifies me in believing that Tom Grabit removed the book, the resultant extended conjunction will not completely justify me in believing that Tom Grabit removed the book. Hence, any such justification will be defeated.[9] Once again, it turns out that I do not have nonbasic knowledge of the fact that Tom is the culprit.

In a logical nut, the problem is that the current definition of defeasibility reduces to the preceding one. Suppose there is a true statement q such that, for any p that completely justifies S in believing h, the conjunction of p and q does not completely justify me in believing that h. Moreover, suppose that I am not completely justified in believing q to be false, so that, given our current definition of defeasibility, q does not count as defeating. Nevertheless, if there is any true

statement r, irrelevant to both p and q, which I am completely justified in believing to be false, then we can indirectly use q to defeat my justification for believing h. For I shall be completely justified in believing the conjunction of r and q to be false, though in fact it is true, because I am completely justified in believing r to be false. If the conjunction of q and p does not completely justify me in believing that h, then, given the irrelevance of r, neither would the conjunction of r, q and p justify me in believing that h. Hence, my justifications for believing h would be defeated by the conjunction r and q on the current definition of defeasibility as surely as they were by q alone on the preceding definition.

The defect is not difficult to repair. Though S is completely justified in believing the conjunction of r and q to be false, one consequence of the conjunction, q, undermines my justification but is not something I am completely justified in believing to be false, while another consequence, r, is one that I am completely justified in believing to be false but is irrelevant to my justification. To return to our example, I am completely justified in believing to be false the conjunctive statement that I was born in St. Paul and that Mrs. Grabit said that Tom was not in the library and so forth. One consequence of this conjunction, that Mrs. Grabit said that Tom was not in the library and so forth, undermines my justification but is not something I am completely justified in believing to be false, while the other consequence, that I was born in St. Paul, is something I am completely justified in believing to be false but is irrelevant to my justification. The needed restriction is that those consequences of a defeating statement which undermine a justification must themselves be statements that the subject is completely justified in believing to be false.

We propose the following definition of defeasibility: if p completely justifies S in believing that h, then this justification is defeated by q if and only if (i) q is true, (ii) the conjunction of p and q does not completely justify S in believing that h, (iii) S is completely justified in believing q to be false, and (iv) if c is a logical consequence of q such that the conjunction of c and p does not completely justify S in believing that h, then S is completely justified in believing c to be false.

With this definition of defeasibility, we complete our analysis of nonbasic knowledge. We have defined nonbasic knowledge as true belief for which some statement provides a complete and undefeated justification. We previously defined basic knowledge as true belief for which there was complete justification that did not depend on any justifying statement. We define as knowledge anything that is either basic or nonbasic knowledge. Thus, *S* knows that *h* if and only if *S* has either basic or nonbasic knowledge that *h*.

Notes

[1] This analysis of knowledge is a modification of an earlier analysis proposed by Keith Lehrer, "Knowledge, Truth and Evidence," *Analysis,* 25.5 (1965), 168–175. It is intended to cope with objections to that article raised by Gilbert H. Harman in "Lehrer on Knowledge," *Journal of Philosophy,* 63.9 (1966), 241–247, and Alvin Goldman, Brian Skyrms, and others. Criticisms of various alternative analyses of knowledge are given in Lehrer's earlier article, and the reader is referred to that article; such discussion will not be repeated here. The distinction between basic and nonbasic knowledge that is elaborated here was suggested by Arthur Danto in "Freedom and Forebearance," in *Freedom and Determinism* (New York: Random House, 1965), pp. 45–63.

[2] Harman's criticism of Lehrer's earlier article rested on his interpreting Lehrer as saying that a person can be com-pletely justified in believing something only if he does believe it. This interpretation leads to problems and is repudiated here.

[3] "Experience and Factual Knowledge," *Journal of Philosophy,* 64.5 (1967), 152–173, esp. pp. 165–167; see also his "An Analysis of Factual Knowledge," ibid., 65.6 (1968), 157–170, esp. pp. 163–164.

[4] "Is Justified True Belief Knowledge?" *Analysis,* 23.6 (1963), 121–123.

[5] "The Explication of '*X* knows that *p*,'" *Journal of Philosophy,* 64.12 (1967), 373–389.

[6] *Theory of Knowledge* (Englewood Cliffs, N.J.: Prentice-Hall, 1966), p. 48.

[7] Chisholm, "The Ethics of Requirement," *American Philosophical Quarterly,* 1.2 (1964), 147–153. This definition of defeasibility would make our analysis of nonbasic knowledge very similar to one Harman derives from Lehrer's analysis and also one proposed by Marshall Swain in "The Analysis of Non-Basic Knowledge" (unpublished).

[8] In Skyrms' example of the pyromaniac cited earlier, the defeating statement is not one which the pyromaniac need believe; Skyrms suggests that the pyromaniac neither believes nor disbelieves that striking the match will cause it to ignite. Nevertheless, the pyromaniac would be completely justified in believing that striking the Sure-Fire match will cause it to ignite. Hence the statement that striking the match will *not* cause it to light is defeating.

[9] A similar objection to Lehrer's earlier analysis is raised by Harman, p. 243.

IV.5 Discrimination and Perceptual Knowledge

ALVIN I. GOLDMAN

In this essay Goldman modifies his earlier causal account of knowledge, dropping the idea that the knower's belief that *p* must be connected with the fact that *p*. Instead knowledge is defined as beliefs formed by reliable mechanisms, specifically the ability to distinguish the truth of *p* from relevant alternatives. In sections II and III, Goldman works out the details of his discrimination view of perceptual knowledge, and in section IV he shows the significance of his reliabilist theory over against the "Cartesian" justificationist model of perceptual knowledge.

This paper presents a partial analysis of perceptual knowledge, an analysis that will, I hope, lay a foundation for a general theory of knowing. Like an earlier theory I proposed,[1] the envisaged theory would seek to explicate the concept of knowledge by reference to the causal processes that produce (or sustain) belief. Unlike the earlier theory, however, it would abandon the requirement that a knower's belief that p be causally connected with the fact, or state of affairs, that p.

What kinds of causal processes or mechanisms must be responsible for a belief if that belief is to count as knowledge? They must be mechanisms that are, in an appropriate sense, "reliable." Roughly, a cognitive mechanism or process is reliable if it not only produces true beliefs in actual situations, but would produce true beliefs, or at least inhibit false beliefs, in relevant counterfactual situations. The theory of knowledge I envisage, then, would contain an important counterfactual component.

To be reliable, a cognitive mechanism must enable a person to *discriminate* or *differentiate* between incompatible states of affairs. It must operate in such a way that incompatible states of the world would generate different cognitive responses. Perceptual mechanisms illustrate this clearly. A perceptual mechanism is reliable to the extent that contrary features of the environment (e.g., an object's being red, versus its being yellow) would produce contrary perceptual states of the organism, which would, in turn, produce suitably different beliefs about the environment. Another belief-governing mechanism is a reasoning mechanism, which, given a set of antecedent beliefs, generates or inhibits various new beliefs. A reasoning mechanism is reliable to the extent that its functional procedures would generate new true beliefs from antecedent true beliefs.

My emphasis on discrimination accords with a sense of the verb "know" that has been neglected by philosophers. The O.E.D. lists one (early) sense of "know" as "*to distinguish* (one thing) *from* (another)," as in "I know a hawk from a handsaw" (*Hamlet*) and "We'll teach him to know Turtles from Jayes" (*Merry Wives of Windsor*). Although it no longer has great currency, this sense still survives in such expressions as "I don't know him from Adam," "He doesn't know right from left,"

and other phrases that readily come to mind. I suspect that this construction is historically important and can be used to shed light on constructions in which "know" takes propositional objects. I suggest that a person is said to know that p just in case he *distinguishes* or *discriminates* the truth of p from relevant alternatives.

A knowledge attribution imputes to someone the discrimination of a given state of affairs from possible alternatives, but not necessarily all logically possible alternatives. In forming beliefs about the world, we do not normally consider all logical possibilities. And in deciding whether someone knows that p (its truth being assumed), we do not ordinarily require him to discriminate p from all logically possible alternatives. Which alternatives are, or ought to be considered, is a question I shall not fully resolve in this paper, but some new perspectives will be examined. I take up this topic in section.

I

Consider the following example. Henry is driving in the countryside with his son. For the boy's edification Henry identifies various objects on the landscape as they come into view. "That's a cow," says Henry, "That's a tractor," "That's a silo," "That's a barn," etc. Henry has no doubt about the identity of these objects; in particular, he has no doubt that the last-mentioned object is a barn, which indeed it is. Each of the identified objects has features characteristic of its type. Moreover, each object is fully in view, Henry has excellent eyesight, and he has enough time to look at them reasonably carefully, since there is little traffic to distract him.

Given this information, would we say that Henry *knows* that the object is a barn? Most of us would have little hesitation in saying this, so long as we were not in a certain philosophical frame of mind. Contrast our inclination here with the inclination we would have if we were given some additional information. Suppose we are told that, unknown to Henry, the district he has just entered is full of papier-mâché facsimiles of barns. These facsimiles look from the road exactly like barns, but are really just façades, without back walls or interiors, quite incapable of being used as barns. They are so cleverly constructed that travelers invariably mistake them for barns. Having just

Reprinted from The *Journal of Philosophy*, 73.20 (1976), 771–791, by kind permission of the author and publisher.

entered the district, Henry has not encountered any facsimiles; the object he sees is a genuine barn. But if the object on that site were a facsimile, Henry would mistake it for a barn. Given this new information, we would be strongly inclined to withdraw the claim that Henry *knows* the object is a barn. How is this change in our assessment to be explained?[1a]

Note first that the traditional justified-true-belief account of knowledge is of no help in explaining this change. In both cases Henry truly believes (indeed, is certain) that the object is a barn. Moreover, Henry's "justification" or "evidence" for the proposition that the object is a barn is the same in both cases. Thus, Henry should either know in both cases or not know in both cases. The presence of facsimiles in the district should make no difference to whether or not he knows.

My old causal analysis cannot handle the problem either. Henry's belief that the object is a barn is caused by the presence of the barn; indeed, the causal process is a perceptual one. Nonetheless, we are not prepared to say, in the second version, that Henry knows.

One analysis of propositional knowledge that might handle the problem is Peter Unger's non-accidentality analysis.[2] According to this theory, S knows that p if and only if it is not at all accidental that S is right about its being the case that p. In the initial description of the example, this requirement appears to be satisfied; so we say that Henry knows. When informed about the facsimiles, however, we see that it is accidental that Henry is right about its being a barn. So we withdraw our knowledge attribution. The "non-accidentality" analysis is not very satisfying, however, for the notion of "non-accidentality" itself needs explication. Pending explication, it isn't clear whether it correctly handles all cases.

Another approach to knowledge that might handle our problem is the "indefeasibility" approach.[3] On this view, S knows that p only if S's true belief is justified *and* this justification is not defeated. In an unrestricted form, an indefeasibility theory would say that S's justification j for believing that p is defeated if and only if there is some true proposition q such that the conjunction of q and j does not justify S in believing that p. In slightly different terms, S's justification j is defeated just in case p would no longer be evident

for S if q were evident for S. This would handle the barn example, presumably, because the true proposition that there are barn facsimiles in the district is such that, if it were evident for Henry, then it would no longer be evident for him that the object he sees is a barn.

The trouble with the indefeasibility approach is that it is too strong, at least in its unrestricted form. On the foregoing account of "defeat," as Gilbert Harman shows,[4] it will (almost) always be possible to find a true proposition that defeats S's justification. Hence, S will never (or seldom) know. What is needed is an appropriate restriction on the notion of "defeat," but I am not aware of an appropriate restriction that has been formulated thus far.

The approach to the problem I shall recommend is slightly different. Admittedly, this approach will raise problems analogous to those of the indefeasibility theory, problems which will not be fully resolved here. Nevertheless, I believe this approach is fundamentally on the right track.

What, then, is my proposed treatment of the barn example? A person knows that p, I suggest, only if the actual state of affairs in which p is true is *distinguishable* or *discriminable* by him from a relevant possible state of affairs in which p is false. If there is a relevant possible state of affairs in which p is false and which is indistinguishable by him from the actual state of affairs, then he fails to know that p. In the original description of the barn case there is no hint of any relevant possible state of affairs in which the object in question is not a barn but is indistinguishable (by Henry) from the actual state of affairs. Hence, we are initially inclined to say that Henry knows. The information about the facsimiles, however, introduces such a relevant state of affairs. Given that the district Henry has entered is full of barn facsimiles, there is a relevant alternative hypothesis about the object, viz., that it is a facsimile. Since, by assumption, a state of affairs in which such a hypothesis holds is indistinguishable by Henry from the actual state of affairs (from his vantage point on the road), this hypothesis is not "ruled out" or "precluded" by the factors that prompt Henry's belief. So, once apprised of the facsimiles in the district, we are inclined to deny that Henry knows.

Let us be clear about the bearing of the facsimiles on the case. The presence of the facsimiles does not "create" the possibility that the object

Henry sees is a facsimile. Even if there were no facsimiles in the district, it would be possible that the object on that site is a facsimile. What the presence of the facsimiles does is make this possibility *relevant;* or it makes us *consider* it relevant.

The qualifier "relevant" plays an important role in my view. If knowledge required the elimination of all logically possible alternatives, there would be no knowledge (at least of contingent truths). If only *relevant* alternatives need to be precluded, however, the scope of knowledge could be substantial. This depends, of course, on which alternatives are relevant.

The issue at hand is directly pertinent to the dispute—at least one dispute—between skeptics and their opponents. In challenging a claim to knowledge (or certainty), a typical move of the skeptic is to adduce an unusual alternative hypothesis that the putative knower is unable to preclude: an alternative compatible with his "data." In the skeptical stage of his argument, Descartes says that he is unable to preclude the hypothesis that, instead of being seated by the fire, he is asleep in his bed and dreaming, or the hypothesis that an evil and powerful demon is making it appear to him as if he is seated by the fire. Similarly, Bertrand Russell points out that, given any claim about the past, we can adduce the "skeptical hypothesis" that the world sprang into being five minutes ago, exactly as it then was, with a population that "remembered" a wholly unreal past.[5]

One reply open to the skeptic's opponent is that these skeptical hypotheses are just "idle" hypotheses, and that a person can know a proposition even if there are "idle" alternatives he cannot preclude. The problem, of course, is to specify when an alternative is "idle" and when it is "serious" ("relevant"). Consider Henry once again. Should we say that the possibility of a facsimile before him is a serious or relevant possibility if there are no facsimiles in Henry's district, but only in Sweden? Or if a single such facsimile once existed in Sweden, but none exist now?

There are two views one might take on this general problem. The first view is that there is a "correct" answer, in any given situation, as to which alternatives are relevant. Given a complete specification of Henry's situation, a unique set of relevant alternatives is determined: either a set to which the facsimile alternative belongs or one to which it doesn't belong. According to this view,

the semantic content of "know" contains (implicit) rules that map any putative knower's circumstances into a set of relevant alternatives. An analysis of "know" is incomplete unless it specifies these rules. The correct specification will favor either the skeptic or the skeptic's opponent.

The second view denies that a putative knower's circumstances uniquely determine a set of relevant alternatives. At any rate, it denies that the semantic content of "know" contains rules that map a set of circumstances into a single set of relevant alternatives. According to this second view, the verb "know" is simply not so semantically determinate.

The second view need not deny that there are *regularities* governing the alternative hypotheses a speaker (i.e., an attributer or denier of knowledge) thinks of, and deems relevant. But these regularities are not part of the semantic content of "know." The putative knower's circumstances do not *mandate* a unique selection of alternatives; but psychological regularities govern which set of alternatives are in fact selected. In terms of these regularities (together with the semantic content of "know"), we can explain the observed use of the term.

It is clear that some of these regularities pertain to the (description of the) putative knower's circumstances. One regularity might be that the more *likely* it is, given the circumstances, that a particular alternative would obtain (rather than the actual state of affairs), the more probable it is that a speaker will regard this alternative as relevant. Or, the more *similar* the situation in which the alternative obtains to the actual situation, the more probable it is that a speaker will regard this alternative as relevant. It is not only the circumstances of the putative knower's situation, however, that influence the choice of alternatives. The speaker's own linguistic and psychological context are also important. If the speaker is in a class where Descartes's evil demon has just been discussed, or Russell's five-minute-old-world hypothesis, he may think of alternatives he would not otherwise think of and will perhaps treat them seriously. This sort of regularity is entirely ignored by the first view.

What I am calling the "second" view might have two variants. The first variant can be imbedded in Robert Stalnaker's framework for pragmatics.[6] In this framework, a proposition is a function from possible words into truth values; the determinants of a proposition are a sentence and a (linguistic) context. An important contextual element is what the utterer of a sentence presupposes, or takes for granted. According to the first variant of the second view, a sentence of the form "*S* knows that *p*" does not determine a unique proposition. Rather, a proposition is determined by such a sentence together with the speaker's presuppositions concerning the relevant alternatives.[7] Skeptics and nonskeptics might make different presuppositions (both presuppositions being "legitimate"), and, if so, they are simply asserting or denying different propositions.

One trouble with this variant is its apparent implication that, if a speaker utters a knowledge sentence without presupposing a fully determinate set of alternatives, he does not assert or deny any proposition. That seems too strong. A second variant of the second view, then, is that sentences of the form "*S* knows that *p*" express vague or indeterminate propositions (if they express "propositions" at all), which can, but need not, be made more determinate by full specification of the alternatives. A person who *assents* to a knowledge sentence says that *S* discriminates the truth of *p* from relevant alternatives; but he may not have a distinct set of alternatives in mind. (Similarly, according to Paul Ziff, a person who says something is "good" says that it answers to *certain* interests;[8] but he may not have a distinct set of interests in mind.) Someone who *denies* a knowledge sentence more commonly has one or more alternatives in mind as relevant, because his denial may stem from a particular alternative *S* cannot rule out. But even the denier of a knowledge sentence need not have a full set of relevant alternatives in mind.

I am attracted by the second view under discussion, especially its second variant. In the remainder of the paper, however, I shall be officially neutral. In other words, I shall not try to settle the question of whether the semantic content of "know" contains rules that map the putative knower's situation into a unique set of relevant alternatives. I leave open the question of whether there is a "correct" set of relevant alternatives, and if so, what it is. To this extent, I also leave open the question of whether skeptics or their opponents are "right." In defending my analysis of "perceptually knows," however, I shall have to discuss particular examples. In treating these exam-

ples I shall assume some (psychological) regularities concerning the selection of alternatives. Among these regularities is the fact that speakers do not *ordinarily* think of "radical" alternatives, but are caused to think of such alternatives, and take them seriously, if the putative knower's circumstances call attention to them. Since I assume that radical or unusual alternatives are not *ordinarily* entertained or taken seriously, I may appear to side with the opponents of skepticism. My official analysis, however, is neutral on the issue of skepticism.

II

I turn now to the analysis of "perceptually knows." Suppose that Sam spots Judy on the street and correctly identifies her as Judy, i.e., believes she is Judy. Suppose further that Judy has an identical twin, Trudy, and the possibility of the person's being Trudy (rather than Judy) is a relevant alternative. Under what circumstances would we say that Sam *knows* it is Judy?

If Sam regularly identifies Judy as Judy and Trudy as Trudy, he apparently has some (visual) way of discriminating between them (though he may not know how he does it, i.e., what cues he uses). If he does have a way of discriminating between them, which he uses on the occasion in question, we would say that he *knows* it is Judy. But if Sam frequently mistakes Judy for Trudy, and Trudy for Judy, he presumably does not have a way of discriminating between them. For example, he may not have sufficiently distinct (visual) memory "schemata" of Judy and Trudy. So that, on a particular occasion, sensory stimulation from either Judy *or* Trudy would elicit a Judy-identification from him. If he happens to be right that it is Judy, this is just accidental. He doesn't *know* it is Judy.

The crucial question in assessing a knowledge attribution, then, appears to be the truth value of a counterfactual (or set of counterfactuals). Where Sam correctly identifies Judy as Judy, the crucial counterfactual is: "If the person before Sam were Trudy (rather than Judy), Sam would believe her to be Judy." If this counterfactual is true, Sam doesn't know it is Judy. If this counterfactual is false (and all other counterfactuals involving relevant alternatives are also false), then Sam may know it is Judy.

This suggests the following analysis of (non-inferential) perceptual knowledge.

> S (noninferentially) *perceptually knows that p* if and only if
> (1) S (noninferentially) perceptually believes that *p*,
> (2) *p* is true, and
> (3) there is no relevant contrary *q* of *p* such that, if *q* were true (rather than *p*), then S would (still) believe that *p*.

Restricting attention to relevant possibilities, these conditions assert in effect that the only situation in which S would believe that *p* is a situation in which *p* is true. In other words, S's believing that *p* is sufficient for the truth of *p*. This is essentially the analysis of noninferential knowledge proposed by D. M. Armstrong in *A Materialist Theory of the Mind* (though without any restriction to "relevant" alternatives), and refined and expanded in *Belief, Truth, and Knowledge*.[9]

This analysis is too restrictive. Suppose Oscar is standing in an open field containing Dack the dachshund. Oscar sees Dack and (noninferentially) forms a belief in (P):

> (P) The object over there is a dog.

Now suppose that (Q):

> (Q) The object over there is a wolf.

is a relevant alternative to (P) (because wolves are frequenters of this field). Further suppose that Oscar has a tendency to mistake wolves for dogs (he confuses them with malamutes, or German shepherds). Then if the object Oscar saw were Wiley the wolf, rather than Dack the dachshund, Oscar would (still) believe (P). This means that Oscar fails to satisfy the proposed analysis with respect to (P), since (3) is violated. But surely it is wrong to deny—for the indicated reasons—that Oscar *knows* (P) to be true. The mere fact that he would erroneously take a wolf to be a dog hardly shows that he doesn't know a *dachshund* to be a dog! Similarly, if someone looks at a huge redwood and correctly believes it to be a tree, he is not disqualified from knowing it to be a tree merely because there is a very small plant he would wrongly believe to be a tree, i.e., a bonsai tree.

The moral can be formulated as follows. If Oscar believes that a dog is present because of a certain way he is "appeared to," then this true belief fails to be knowledge if there is an alternative situation in which a non-dog produces the same belief by means of the same, or a very similar, appearance. But the wolf situation is not such an alternative: although it would produce in him the same belief, it would not be by means of the same (or a similar) appearance. An alternative that disqualifies a true belief from being perceptual knowledge must be a "perceptual equivalent" of the actual state of affairs.[10] A *perceptual equivalent* of an actual state of affairs is a possible state of affairs that would produce the same, or a sufficiently similar, perceptual experience.

The relation of perceptual equivalence must obviously be relativized to *persons* (or organisms). The presence of Judy and the presence of Trudy might be perceptual equivalents for Sam, but not for the twins' own mother (to whom the twins look quite different). Similarly, perceptual equivalence must be relativized to *times,* since perceptual discriminative capacities can be refined or enhanced with training or experience, and can deteriorate with age or disease.

How shall we specify alternative states of affairs that are candidates for being perceptual equivalents? First, we should specify the *object* involved. (I assume for simplicity that only one object is in question.) As the Judy-Trudy case shows, the object in the alternative state of affairs need not be identical with the actual object. Sometimes, indeed, we may wish to allow non-actual possible objects. Otherwise our framework will be unable in principle to accommodate some of the skeptic's favorite alternatives, e.g., those involving demons. If the reader's ontological sensibility is offended by talk of possible objects, I invite him to replace such talk with any preferred substitute.

Some alternative states of affairs involve the same object but different properties. Where the actual state of affairs involves a certain ball painted blue, an alternative might be chosen involving the same ball painted green. Thus, specification of an alternative requires not only an object, but properties of the object (at the time in question). These should include not only the property in the belief under scrutiny, or one of its contraries, but other properties as well, since the property in the belief (or one of its contraries) might not be sufficiently determinate to indicate what the resultant percept would be like. For full generality, let us choose a *maximal set of* (nonrelational) *properties.* This is a set that would exhaustively characterize an object (at a single time) in some possible world.[11]

An object plus a maximal set of (nonrelational) properties still does not fully specify a perceptual alternative. Also needed are relations between the object and the perceiver, plus conditions of the environment. One relation that can affect the resultant percept is *distance.* Another relational factor is *relative orientation,* both of object vis-à-vis perceiver and perceiver vis-à-vis object. The nature of the percept depends, for example, on which side of the object faces the perceiver, and on how the perceiver's bodily organs are oriented, or situated, vis-à-vis the object. Thirdly, the percept is affected by the current state of the *environment,* e.g., the illumination, the presence or absence of intervening objects, and the direction and velocity of the wind.

To cover all such elements, I introduce the notion of a *distance-orientation-environment* relation, for short, a *DOE relation.* Each such relation is a conjunction of relations or properties concerning distance, orientation, and environmental conditions. One DOE relation is expressed by the predicate "x is 20 feet from y, the front side of y is facing x, the eyes of x are open and focused in y's direction, no opaque object is interposed between x and y, and y is in moonlight."

Since the health of sensory organs can affect percepts, it might be argued that this should be included in these relations, thereby opening the condition of these organs to counterfactualization. For simplicity I neglect this complication. This does not mean that I don't regard the condition of sensory organs as open to counterfactualization. I merely omit explicit incorporation of this factor into our exposition.

We can now give more precision to our treatment of perceptual equivalents. Perceptual states of affairs will be specified by ordered triples, each consisting of (1) an object, (2) a maximal set of nonrelational properties, and (3) a DOE relation. If S perceives object b at t and if b has all the properties in a maximal set J and bears DOE relation R to S at t, then the actual state of affairs pertaining to this perceptual episode is represented by the ordered triple $<b,J,R>$. An

alternative state of affairs is represented by an ordered triple $<c,K,R^*>$, which may (but need not) differ from $<b,J,R>$ with respect to one or more of its elements.

Under what conditions is an alternative $<c,K,R^*>$ a perceptual equivalent of $<b,J,R>$ for person S at time t? I said that a perceptual equivalent is a state of affairs that would produce "the same, or a very similar" perceptual experience. That is not very committal. Must a perceptual equivalent produce exactly the same percept? Given our intended use of perceptual equivalence in the analysis of perceptual knowledge, the answer is clearly No. Suppose that a Trudy-produced percept would be qualitatively distinct from Sam's Judy-produced percept, but similar enough for Sam to mistake Trudy for Judy. This is sufficient grounds for saying that Sam fails to have knowledge. Qualitative identity of percepts, then, is too strong a requirement for perceptual equivalence.

How should the requirement be weakened? We must not weaken it too much, for the wolf alternative might then be a perceptual equivalent of the dachshund state of affairs. This would have the unwanted consequence that Oscar doesn't know Dack to be a dog.

The solution I propose is this. If the percept produced by the alternative state of affairs would not differ from the actual percept in any respect that is causally relevant to S's belief, this alternative situation is a perceptual equivalent for S of the actual situation. Suppose that a Trudy-produced percept would differ from Sam's Judy-produced percept to the extent of having a different eyebrow configuration. (A difference in shape between Judy's and Trudy's eyebrows does not ensure that Sam's percepts would "register" this difference. I assume, however, that the eyebrow difference would be registered in Sam's percepts.) But suppose that Sam's visual "concept" of Judy does not include a feature that reflects this contrast. His Judy-concept includes an "eyebrow feature" only in the sense that the absence of eyebrows would inhibit a Judy-classification. It does not include a more determinate eyebrow feature, though: Sam hasn't learned to associate Judy with distinctively shaped eyebrows. Hence, the distinctive "eyebrow shape" of his actual (Judy-produced) percept is not one of the percept-features that is causally responsible for his believing Judy to be present.

Assuming that a Trudy-produced percept would not differ from his actual percept in any *other* causally relevant way, the hypothetical Trudy-situation is a perceptual equivalent of the actual Judy-situation.

Consider now the dachshund-wolf case. The hypothetical percept produced by a wolf would differ from Oscar's actual percept of the dachshund in respects that *are* causally relevant to Oscar's judgment that a dog is present. Let me elaborate. There are various kinds of objects, rather different in shape, size, color, and texture, that would be classified by Oscar as a dog. He has a number of visual "schemata," we might say, each with a distinctive set of features, such that any percept that "matches" or "fits" one of these schemata would elicit a "dog" classification. (I think of a schema not as a "template," but as a set of more-or-less abstract—though iconic—features.[12] Now, although a dachshund and a wolf would each produce a dog-belief in Oscar, the percepts produced by these respective stimuli would differ in respects that are causally relevant to Oscar's forming a dog-belief. Since Oscar's dachshund-schema includes such features as having an elongated, sausagelike shape, a smallish size, and droopy ears, these features of the percept are all causally relevant, when a dachshund is present, to Oscar's believing that a dog is present. Since a hypothetical wolf-produced percept would differ in these respects from Oscar's dachshund-produced percept, the hypothetical wolf state of affairs is not a perceptual equivalent of the dachshund state of affairs for Oscar.

The foregoing approach requires us to relativize perceptual equivalence once again, this time to the belief in question, or the property believed to be exemplified. The Trudy-situation is a perceptual equivalent for Sam of the Judy-situation *relative to the property of being* (identical with) *Judy.* The wolf-situation is not a perceptual equivalent for Oscar of the dachshund-situation *relative to the property of being a dog.*

I now propose the following definition of perceptual equivalence:

If object *b* has the maximal set of properties *J* and is in DOE relation *R* to *S* at *t*, if *S* has some percept *P* at *t* that is perceptually caused by *b*'s having *J* and being in *R* to *S* at *t*, and if *P* noninferentially causes *S* to believe

(or sustains *S* in believing) of object *b* that it has property *F*, then $<c,K,R\,^*>$ is a perceptual equivalent of $<b,J,R>$ *for S at t relative to property F* if and only if

(1) if at *t* object *c* had *K* and were in R^* to *S*, then this would perceptually cause *S* to have some percept P^* at *t*,

(2) P^* would cause *S* noninferentially to believe (or sustain *S* in believing) of object *c* that it has *F*, and

(3) P^* would not differ from *P* in any respect that is causally relevant to *S*'s *F*-belief.

Since I shall analyze the *de re, relational,* or *transparent* sense of "perceptually knows," I shall want to employ, in my analysis, the *de re* sense of "believe." This is why such phrases as "believe . . . *of* object *b*" occur in the definition of perceptual equivalence. For present purposes, I take for granted the notion of (perceptual) *de re* belief. I assume, however, that the object *of which* a person perceptually believes a property to hold is the object he perceives, i.e., the object that "perceptually causes" the percept that elicits the belief. The notion of *perceptual causation* is another notion I take for granted. A person's percept is obviously caused by many objects (or events), not all of which the person is said to perceive. One problem for the theory of perception is to explicate the notion of perceptual causation, that is, to explain which of the causes of a percept a person is said to perceive. I set this problem aside here.[13] A third notion I take for granted is the notion of a (noninferential) *perceptual belief,* or perceptual "taking." Not all beliefs that are noninferentially caused by a percept can be considered perceptual "takings"; "indirectly" caused beliefs would not be so considered. But I make no attempt to delineate the requisite causal relation.

Several other comments on the definition of perceptual equivalence are in order. Notice that the definition is silent on whether *J* or *K* contains property *F*, i.e., whether *F* is exemplified either the actual or the alternative states of affairs. The relativization to *F* (in the definiendum) implies that an *F-belief* is produced in both situations, not that *F* is exemplified (in either or both situations). In applying the definition to cases of putative knowledge, we shall focus on cases where *F* belongs to *J* (so *S*'s belief is true in the actual situation) but does not belong to K (so S's belief is false in the counterfactual situation). But the definition of perceptual equivalence is silent on these matters.

Though the definition does not say so, I assume it is possible for object c to have all properties in K, and possible for c to be in R^* and S while having all properties in K. I do not want condition 1 to be vacuously true, simply by having an impossible antecedent.

It might seem as if the antecedent of (1) should include a further conjunct, expressing the supposition that object b is absent. This might seem necessary to handle cases in which, if c were in R^* to S, but b remained in its actual relation R to S, then b would "block" S's access to c. (For example, b might be an orange balloon floating over the horizon, and c might be the moon.) This can be handled by the definition as it stands, by construing R^*, where necessary, as including the absence of object b from the perceptual scene. (One cannot *in general* hypothesize that b is absent, for we want to allow object c to be identical with b.)

The definition implies that there is no temporal gap between each object's having its indicated properties and DOE relation and the occurrence of the corresponding percept. This simplification is introduced because no general requirement can be laid down about how long it takes for the stimulus energy to reach the perceiver. The intervals in the actual and alternative states may differ because the stimuli might be at different distances from the perceiver.

III

It is time to turn to the analysis of perceptual knowledge, for which the definition of perceptual equivalence paves the way. I restrict my attention to perceptual knowledge of the possession, by physical objects, of nonrelational properties. I also restrict the analysis to *noninferential* perceptual knowledge. This frees me from the complex issues introduced by inference, which require separate treatment.

It may be contended that all perceptual judgment is based on inference and, hence, that the proposed restriction reduces the scope of the

analysis to nil. Two replies are in order. First, although cognitive psychology establishes that percepts are affected by cognitive factors, such as "expectancies," it is by no means evident that these causal processes should be construed as inferences. Second, even if we were to grant that there is in fact no noninferential perceptual belief, it would still be of epistemological importance to determine whether noninferential perceptual knowledge of the physical world is conceptually possible. This could be explored by considering merely possible cases of noninferential perceptual belief, and seeing whether, under suitable conditions, such belief would count as knowledge.

With these points in mind, we may propose the following (tentative) analysis:

At t S non-inferentially perceptually knows of object b that it has property F if and only if

(1) for some maximal set of nonrelational properties J and some DOE relation R, object b has (all the members of) J at t and is in R to S at t,

(2) F belongs to J,

(3) (A) b's having J and being in R to S at t perceptually causes S at t to have some percept P,[14]

  (B) P noninferentially causes S and T to believe (or sustains S in believing) of object b that it has property F, and

  (C) there is no alternative state of affairs $<c,K,R^*>$ such that

  (i) $<c,K,R^*>$ is a relevant perceptual equivalent of $<b,J,R>$ for S at t relative to property F, and

  (ii) F does not belong to K.

Conditions 1 and 2 jointly entail the truth condition for knowledge: S knows b to have F (at t) only if b does have F (at t). Condition 3B contains the belief condition for knowledge, restricted, of course, to (noninferential) perceptual belief. The main work of the conditions is done by 3C. It requires that there be no relevant alternative that is (i) a perceptual equivalent to the actual state of affairs relative to property F, and (ii) a state of affairs in which the appropriate object lacks F (and hence S's F-belief is false).

How does this analysis relate to my theme of a "reliable discriminative mechanism"? A perceptual cognizer may be thought of as a two-part mechanism. The first part constructs percepts (a special class of internal states) from receptor stimulation. The second part operates on percepts to produce beliefs. Now, in order for the conditions of the analysans to be satisfied, each part of the mechanism must be sufficiently discriminating, or "finely tuned." If the first part is not sufficiently discriminating, patterns of receptor stimulation from quite different sources would result in the same (or very similar) percepts, percepts that would generate the same beliefs. If the second part is not sufficiently discriminating, then even if different percepts are constructed by the first part, the same beliefs will be generated by the second part. To be sure, even an undiscriminating bipartite mechanism may produce a belief that, luckily, is true; but there will be other, counterfactual, situations in which such a belief would be false. In this sense, such a mechanism is unreliable. What our analysis says is that S has perceptual knowledge if and only if not only does his perceptual mechanism produce true belief, but there are no relevant counterfactual situations in which the same belief would be produced via an equivalent percept and in which the belief would be false.

Let me now illustrate how the analysis is to be applied to the barn example, where there are facsimiles in Henry's district. Let S = Henry, b = the barn Henry actually sees, and F = the property of being a barn. Conditions 1 through 3B are met by letting J take as its value the set of all nonrelational properties actually possessed by the barn at t, R take as its value the actual DOE relation the barn bears to Henry at t, and P take as its value the actual (visual) percept caused by the barn. Condition 3C is violated, however. There *is* a relevant triple that meets subclauses (i) and (ii), i.e., the triple where c = a suitable barn facsimile, K = a suitable set of properties (excluding, of course, the property of being a barn), and $R^{\star}$ = approximately the same DOE relation as the actual one. Thus, Henry does not (noninferentially) perceptually *know* of the barn that it has the property of being a barn.

In the dachshund-wolf case, S = Oscar, b = Dack the dachshund, and F = being a dog. The first several conditions are again met. Is 3C met as well? There is a relevant alternative state of affairs in which Wiley the wolf is believed by Oscar to be a dog, but lacks that property. This state of affairs

doesn't violate 3C, however, since it isn't a *perceptual equivalent* of the actual situation relative to being a dog. So this alternative doesn't disqualify Oscar from knowing Dack to be a dog.

Is there another alternative that *is* a perceptual equivalent of the actual situation (relative to being a dog)? We can imagine a DOE relation in which fancy devices between Wiley and Oscar distort the light coming from Wiley and produce in Oscar a Dack-like visual percept. The question here, however, is whether this perceptual equivalent is *relevant*. Relevance is determined not only by the hypothetical object and its properties, but also by the DOE relation. Since the indicated DOE relation is highly unusual, this will count (at least for a nonskeptic) against the alternative's being relevant and against its disqualifying Oscar from knowing.[15]

The following "Gettierized" example, suggested by Marshall Swain, might appear to present difficulties. In a dark room there is a candle several yards ahead of S which S sees and believes to be ahead of him. But he sees the candle only indirectly, via a system of mirrors (of which he is unaware) that make it appear as if he were seeing it directly.[16] We would surely deny that S knows the candle to be ahead of him. (This case does not really fit our intended analysandum, since the believed property F is relational. This detail can be ignored, however.) Why? If we say, with Harman, that all perceptual belief is based on inference, we can maintain that S infers that the candle is ahead of him from the premise that he sees whatever he sees *directly*. This premise being false, S's knowing is disqualified on familiar grounds.

My theory suggests another explanation, which makes no unnecessary appeal to inference. We deny that S knows, I suggest, because the system of mirrors draws our attention to a perceptual equivalent in which the candle is *not* ahead of S, i.e., a state of affairs where the candle is behind S but reflected in a system of mirrors so that it appears to be ahead of him. Since the actual state of affairs involves a system of reflecting mirrors, we are impelled to count this alternative as relevant, and hence to deny that S knows.

Even in ordinary cases, of course, where S sees a candle directly, the possibility of reflecting mirrors constitutes a perceptual equivalent. In the ordinary case, however, we would not count this as relevant; we would not regard it as a "serious" possibility. The Gettierized case impels us to take it seriously because there the actual state of affairs involves a devious system of reflecting mirrors. So we have an explanation of why people are credited with knowing in ordinary perceptual cases but not in the Gettierized case.

The following is a more serious difficulty for our analysis. S truly believes something to be a tree, but there is a relevant alternative in which an electrode stimulating S's optic nerve would produce an equivalent percept, which would elicit the same belief. Since this is assumed to be a relevant alternative, it ought to disqualify S from knowing. But it doesn't satisfy our definition of a perceptual equivalent, first because the electrode would not be a perceptual cause of the percept (we would not say that S *perceives* the electrode), and second because S would not believe *of the electrode* (nor *of* anything else) that it is a tree. A similar problem arises where the alternative state of affairs would involve S's having a hallucination.

To deal with these cases, we could revise our analysis of perceptual knowledge as follows. (A similar revision in the definition of perceptual equivalence would do the job equally well.) We could reformulate 3C to say that there must neither be a relevant perceptual equivalent of the indicated sort (using our present definition of perceptual equivalence) *nor* a relevant alternative situation in which an equivalent percept occurs and prompts a *de dicto* belief that something has F, but where there is nothing that *perceptually* causes this percept and nothing *of which* F is believed to hold. In other words, knowledge can be disqualified by relevant alternative situations where S doesn't perceive anything and doesn't have any *de re* (F) belief at all. I am inclined to adopt this solution, but will not actually make this addition to the analysis.

Another difficulty for the analysis is this. Suppose Sam's "schemata" of Judy and Trudy have hitherto been indistinct, so Judy-caused percepts sometimes elicit Judy-beliefs and sometimes Trudy-beliefs, and similarly for Trudy-caused percepts. Today Sam falls down and hits his head. As a consequence a new feature is "added" to his Judy-schema, a mole-associated feature. From now on he will believe someone to be Judy only if he has the sort of percept that would be caused by a Judy-like person with a mole over the left eye. Sam is unaware that this change has taken place

and will remain unaware of it, since he isn't conscious of the cues he uses. Until today, neither Judy nor Trudy has had a left-eyebrow mole; but today Judy happens to develop such a mole. Thus, from now on Sam can discriminate Judy from Trudy. Does this mean that he will *know* Judy to be Judy when he correctly identifies her? I am doubtful.

A possible explanation of Sam's not knowing (on future occasions) is that Trudy-with-a-mole is a relevant perceptual equivalent of Judy. This is not Trudy's actual condition, of course, but it might be deemed a relevant possibility. I believe, however, that the mole case calls for a further restriction, one concerning the *genesis* of a person's propensity to form a certain belief as a result of a certain percept. A merely fortuitous or accidental genesis is not enough to support knowledge. I do not know exactly what requirement to impose on the genesis of such a propensity. The mole case intimates that the genesis should involve certain "experience" with objects, but this may be too narrow. I content myself with a very vague addition to our previous conditions, which completes the analysis:

(4) S's propensity to form an *F*-belief as a result of percept P has an appropriate genesis.

Of course this leaves the problem unresolved. But the best I can do here is identify the problem.

IV

A few words are in order about the intended significance of my analysis. One of its purposes is to provide an alternative to the traditional "Cartesian" perspective in epistemology. The Cartesian view combines a theory of knowledge with a theory of justification. Its theory of knowledge asserts that S knows that p at t only if S is (fully, adequately, etc.) justified at t in believing that p. Its theory of justification says that S is justified at t in believing that p only if either (A) p is self-warranting for S at t, or (B) p is (strongly, adequately, etc.) supported or confirmed by propositions each of which is self-warranting for S at t. Now propositions about the state of the external world at t are not self-warranting. Hence, if S knows any such proposition p at t, there must be some other propositions which strongly support *p* and which are self-warranting for *S* at *t*. These must be propositions about *S*'s mental state at *t* and perhaps some obvious necessary truths. A major task of Cartesian epistemology is to show that there is some such set of self-warranting propositions, propositions that support external-world propositions with sufficient strength.

It is impossible to canvass all attempts to fulfill this project; but none have succeeded, and I do not think that any will. One can conclude either that we have no knowledge of the external world or that Cartesian requirements are too demanding. I presuppose the latter conclusion in offering my theory of perceptual knowledge. My theory requires no justification for external-world propositions that derive entirely from self-warranting propositions. It requires only, in effect, that beliefs in the external world be suitably caused, where "suitably" comprehends a process or mechanism that not only produces true belief in the actual situation, but would not produce false belief in relevant counterfactual situations. If one wishes, one can so employ the term "justification" that belief causation of *this* kind counts as justification. In this sense, of course, my theory does require justification. But this is entirely different from the sort of justification demanded by Cartesianism.

My theory protects the possibility of knowledge by making Cartesian-style justification unnecessary. But it leaves a door open to skepticism by its stance on relevant alternatives. This is not a failure of the theory, in my opinion. An adequate account of the term "know" should make the temptations of skepticism comprehensible, which my theory does. But it should also put skepticism in a proper perspective, which Cartesianism fails to do.

In any event, I put forward my account of perceptual knowledge not primarily as an antidote to skepticism, but as a more accurate rendering of what the term "know" actually means. In this respect it is instructive to test my theory and its rivals against certain metaphorical or analogical uses of "know." A correct definition should be able to explain extended and figurative uses as well as literal uses, for it should explain how speakers arrive at the extended uses from the central ones. With this in mind, consider how tempting it is to say of an electric-eye door that it "knows" you are coming (at least that *something* is coming), or

"sees" you coming. The attractiveness of the metaphor is easily explained on my theory: the door has a reliable mechanism for discriminating between something being before it and nothing being there. It has a "way of telling" whether or not something is there: this "way of telling" consists in a mechanism by which objects in certain DOE relations to it have differential effects on its internal state. By contrast, note how artificial it would be to apply more traditional analyses of "know" to the electric-eye door, or to other mechanical detecting devices. How odd it would be to say that the door has "good reasons," "adequate evidence," or "complete justification" for thinking something is there; or that it has "the right to be sure" something is there. The oddity of these locutions indicates how far from the mark are the analyses of "know" from which they derive.

The trouble with many philosophical treatments of knowledge is that they are inspired by Cartesian-like conceptions of justification or vindication. There is a consequent tendency to overintellectualize or overrationalize the notion of knowledge. In the spirit of naturalistic epistemology,[17] I am trying to fashion an account of knowing that focuses on more primitive and pervasive aspects of cognitive life, in connection with which, I believe, the term "know" gets its application. A fundamental facet of animate life, both human and infra-human, is telling things apart, distinguishing predator from prey, for example, or a protective habitat from a threatening one. The concept of knowledge has its roots in this kind of cognitive activity.

Notes

[1]"A Causal Theory of Knowing" [Reading IV.2 in this volume].

[1a]The barn facsimile example was originally suggested to me as a puzzle by Carl Ginet.

[2]"An Analysis of Factual Knowledge," *Journal of Philosophy*, 65.6 (1968), 157–170. Reprinted in M. Roth and L. Galis, eds., *Knowing* (New York: Random House, 1970), 113–130.

[3]See, for example, Keith Lehrer and Thomas Paxson, Jr., "Knowledge: Undefeated Justified True Belief" and Peter D. Klein, "A Proposed Definition of Propositional Knowledge," *Journal of Philosophy*, 68.16 (1971), 471–482.

[4]*Thought* (Princeton: Princeton University Press, 1973), p. 152.

[5] *The Analysis of Mind* (London: George Allen and Unwin, 1921), pp. 159–160.

[6] "Pragmatics," in D. Davidson and G. Harman, eds., *Semantics of Natural Language* (Dordrecht: Reidel, 1972).

[7] Something like this is suggested by Fred Dretske, in "Epistemic Operators," *Journal of Philosophy,* 67.24 (1970), 1022. I should emphasize that Dretske himself uses the phrase "relevant alternative," probably its first occurrence.

[8] That "good" means *answers to certain interests* is claimed by Ziff in *Semantic Analysis* (Ithaca, N.Y.: Cornell University Press, 1960), chap. 6.

[9] *A Materialist Theory of the Mind* (New York: Humanities Press, 1968), pp. 189 ff., and *Belief, Truth and Knowledge* (Cambridge: Cambridge University Press, 1973), chaps. 12 and 13.

[10] My notion of a perceptual equivalent corresponds to Hintikka's notion of a "perceptual alternative." See "On the Logic of Perception," in N. S. Care and R. H. Grimm, eds., *Perception and Personal Identity* (Cleveland: The Press of Case Western Reserve University, 1969).

[11] I have in mind here purely qualitative properties. Properties like *being identical with Judy* would be given by the selected object. If the set of qualitative properties (at a given time) implied which object it is that has these properties, then specification of the object would be redundant, and we could represent states of affairs by ordered pairs of maximal sets of (qualitative) properties and DOE relations. Since this is problematic, however, I include specification of the object as well as the set of (qualitative) properties.

[12] For a discussion of iconic schemata, see Michael I. Posner, *Cognition: An Introduction* (Glenview, Ill.: Scott, Foresman, 1974), chap. 3.

[13] I take this problem up in "Perceptual Objects," forthcoming in *Synthese.*

[14] Should (3A) be construed as implying that *every* property in *J* is a (perceptual) cause of *P*? No. Many of *b*'s properties are exemplified in its interior, or at its backside. These are not causally relevant, at least in visual perception. (3A) must therefore be construed as saying that *P* is (perceptually) caused by *b*'s having (jointly) *all* the members of *J*, and leaving open which, among these members, are individually causally relevant. It follows, however, that (3A) does not require that *b*'s-having-*F*, in particular, is a (perceptual) cause of *P*, and this omission might be regarded as objectionable. "Surely," it will be argued, "*S* perceptually knows *b* to have *F* only if *b*'s-having-*F* (perceptually) causes the percept." The reason I omit this requirement is the following. Suppose *F* is the property of being a dog. Can we say that *b*'s-being-a-dog is a cause of certain light waves' being reflected? This is very dubious. It is the molecular properties of the surface of the animal that

are causally responsible for this transmission of light, and hence for the percept.

One might say that even if the percept needn't be (perceptually) caused by *b*'s-having-*F*, it must at least be caused by micro-structural properties of *b* that *ensure b*'s-having-*F*. As the dog example again illustrates, however, this is too strong. The surface properties of the dog that reflect the light waves do not *ensure* that the object is a dog, either logically or nomologically. Something could have that surface (on one side) and still have a non-dog interior and backside. The problem should be solved, I think, by reliance on whether there are relevant perceptual equivalents. If there are no relevant perceptual equivalents in which *K* excludes being a dog, then the properties of the actual object that are causally responsible for the percept suffice to yield knowledge. We need not require either that the percept be (perceptually) caused by *b*'s-having-*F*, nor by any subset of *J* that "ensures" *b*'s having-*F*.

[15] It is the "unusualness" of the DOE relation that inclines us not to count the alternative as relevant; it is not the mere fact that the DOE relation differs from the actual one. In general, our analysis allows knowledge to be defeated or disqualified by alternative situations in which the DOE relation differs from the DOE relation in the actual state of affairs. Our analysis differs in this respect from Fred Dretske's analysis in "Conclusive Reasons." Dretske's analysis, which ours resembles on a number of points, considers only those counterfactual situations in which everything that is "logically and causally independent of the state of affairs expressed by *P*" (p. 50) is the same as in the actual situation. (*P* is the content of *S*'s belief.) This implies that the actual DOE relation cannot be counterfactualized, but must be held fixed. (It may also imply—depending on what *P* is—that one cannot counterfactualize the perceived object nor the full set of properties *J*.) This unduly narrows the class of admissible alternatives. Many *relevant* alternatives, that do disqualify knowledge, involve DOE relations that differ from the actual DOE relation.

[16] Harman has a similar case, in *Thought,* pp. 22–23. In that case, however, *S* does not see the candle; it is not a cause of his percept. Given our causal requirement for perceptual knowledge, that case is easily handled.

[17] Cf. W. O. Quine, "Epistemology Naturalized," in *Ontological Relativity and Other Essays* (New York: Columbia University Press, 1969).

An early version of this paper was read at the 1972 Chapel Hill Colloquium. Later versions were read at the 1973 University of Cincinnati Colloquium, and at a number of other philosophy departments. For comments and criticism, I am especially indebted to Holly Goldman, Bruce Aune, Jaegwon Kim, Louis Loeb, and Kendall Walton.

Bibliography

Armstrong, D. M. *Belief, Truth and Knowledge.* Cambridge, MA: Cambridge University Press, 1973.

Audi, Robert. *Belief, Justification and Knowledge.* Belmont, CA: Wadsworth, 1988.

Baergen, Ralph. *Contemporary Epistemology.* Fort Worth, TX: Harcourt Brace, 1995. Chapter 5.

Dancy, Jonathan. *An Introduction to Contemporary Epistemology.* Oxford, England: Blackwell, 1985. Chapter 2.

Dancy, Jonathan, and Ernest Sosa, eds. *A Companion to Epistemology.* Oxford, England: Blackwell, 1992.

Everitt, Nicholas, and Alec Fisher. *Modern Epistemology.* New York: McGraw-Hill, 1995.

Fumerton, Richard. *Metaphysical and Epistemological Problems of Perception.* Lincoln: University of Nebraska, 1985.

Goodman, Michael, and Robert Snyder, eds. *Contemporary Readings in Epistemology.* Upper Saddle River, NJ: Prentice Hall, 1993.

Harman, Gilbert. *Thought.* Princeton, NJ: Princeton University Press, 1973.

Nozick, Robert. *Philosophical Explanations.* Cambridge, MA: Harvard University Press, 1981.

Pappas, George, ed. *Justification and Knowledge.* Dordrecht, Netherlands: Reidel, 1979.

Pappas, George, and Marshall Swain, eds. *Essays on Knowledge and Justification.* Ithaca, NY: Cornell University Press, 1978.

Pojman, Louis P. *What Can We Know? An Introduction to the Theory of Knowledge.* Belmont, CA: Wadsworth, 2000.

Roth, Michael, and Leon Galis, eds. *Knowing: Essays in the Theory of Knowledge.* New York: Random House, 1970.

Shope, Robert. *The Analysis of Knowledge.* Princeton, NJ: Princeton University Press, 1983.

Sosa, Ernest. *Knowledge in Perspective: Selective Essays in Epistemology.* Cambridge MA: Cambridge University Press, 1991.

Swain, Marshall. *Reasons and Knowledge.* Ithaca, NY: Cornell University Press, 1981.

Part V

Theories of Justification (I): Foundationalism and Coherentism

Now of the thinking states by which we grasp truth, some are unfailingly true; others admit of error-opinion, for example, and calculation, whereas scientific knowledge and intuition are always true; further, no other kind of thought except intuition is more accurate than scientific knowledge, whereas primary premises are more knowable than demonstrations, and all scientific knowledge is discursive. From these considerations it follows that there will be no scientific knowledge of the primary, and since, except intuition, nothing can be truer than scientific knowledge, it will be intuition that apprehends the primary premises.

ARISTOTLE
Posterial Analytics, II, 19

Until recently most epistemologists have held that some self-evident first principles are immediately known to the understanding and sufficient to build a complete system of knowledge. For Plato, these principles were the Forms, the knowledge of which was latent as innate Ideas within us. For Aristotle and Aquinas, they were the basic truths, such as the axioms of mathematics and logic, which are grasped immediately by the understanding. Aquinas wrote,

> Now a truth can come into the mind in two ways, namely, as known in itself, and as known through another. What is known in itself is like a principle, and is perceived immediately by the mind. And so the habit which perfects the intellect in

considering such a truth is called "understanding"; it is a firm and easy quality of mind which sees into principles. A truth, however, which is known through another is understood by the intellect, not immediately, but through an inquiry of reason of which it is the terminus. (*Summa Theologica*, Ia. Q84, a. 2)

René Descartes, in the first reading in Part II of this book, holds that knowledge of the existence and mental nature of the self is grasped noninferentially by the understanding. Furthermore, each person can have infallible knowledge of his or her psychological states, beliefs, and desires. For example, I can know infallibly that I am in pain, that I seem to see a tree in front of me, and that I believe that there is a tree in front of me, although I cannot know that there really is a tree in front of me. In addition, Descartes thought we had immediate knowledge of certain metaphysical truths such as that there must be as much reality in the total cause as in the effect—a proposition that enabled him to deduce the existence of a perfect divine being, who in turn guaranteed the veracity of our empirical beliefs. Self-evident truths were "clear and distinct," having a luminous aura about them that the intuition could not fail to grasp as obvious truth.

Empiricists such as John Locke believe we could have knowledge of physical objects, especially the primary qualities (as we saw in Part III.1).

What all these philosophers have in common is the theory that we can have immediate and infallible knowledge of first principles, or basic propositions, from which we can deduce further truths. The properly basic beliefs are known immediately through the *intuition* (sometimes called the "faculty of intuition"). All other knowledge is inferred deductively from these basic beliefs.

Two related notions are tied together in this notion of immediate and infallible or indubitable knowledge: self-evidence and incorrigibility. A proposition is self-evident just in the case that if one understands and considers it, one cannot help but believe and know it. It is obvious, luminous, certain. Examples of such propositions are the law of noncontradiction and basic truths of arithmetic such as $1 + 1 = 2$. A belief is incorrigible for someone S if and only if it's not possible for S to believe the proposition and the proposition be false. Examples are appearance statements such as "I seem to see a red object" and Descartes's *Cogito, ergo sum,* "I think, therefore I am." Both have been considered certain, but only propositions are self-evident. Incorrigibility is primarily a property of beliefs, but these terms often overlap. There is no clear consensus on their definitions.

This traditional view, that we may have infallible noninferential knowledge on which all other knowledge is based, we call *classical foundationalism.* Note the architectural metaphor "foundation." Descartes spoke of tearing down the superstructure and destroying the foundations of our epistemically unjustified house and of laying a new, infallible foundation with indubitable propositions, and thereupon erecting a solid and certain superstructure, a house of knowledge. As such, we may divide all beliefs into two kinds: basic beliefs and inferred beliefs. We may define the primary epistemic unit *properly basic belief* this way: "A belief that p is properly basic for a person S if and only if it is (1) basic (noninferential) for S and (2) properly so (justified noninferentially)." A nonbasic justified belief is one that is inferentially based on one or more properly basic beliefs.

The relationship is asymmetrical, in that the basic beliefs transfer justification and knowledge to the derived belief but not vice versa. The resulting treelike relationship is shown as follows:

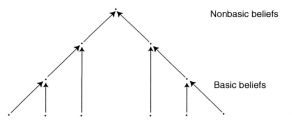

From indubitable first premises, Descartes deduced the existence of God as an omnibenevolent being whose nature excluded deception. Since God implanted our perceptual mechanisms within us, it will follow that we can know we are not being deceived when we believe things about objects in the world. Normally, if I seem to see a tree, I really do see one. Only under abnormal circumstances will I be deceived about such matters. Yet, because I can be deceived, I should withhold the attribution of knowledge to such empirical judgments.

Induction can never be a means of knowledge, but only of belief.

Contemporary philosophers found problems with Descartes's (1) arguments for the existence of God, (2) notion that "there must be at least as much reality in the total cause as in the effect," (3) notion of clear and distinct ideas, and (4) notion of infallibility (or incorrigibility). Held by many philosophers, but denied by others, it is generally conceded that Descartes fails to establish (1), (2), and (3) and that (4) is controversial. Whether our appearance beliefs—for example "I am in pain," "I seem to see a red object," and "I have a hot sensation"—are really infallible (or incorrigible) is a matter of debate.

Consider the statement, "I am in pain," uttered by me. If I believe that I am in pain, is it necessarily so? Do I infallibly know that I am in pain when I believe that I am? Consider this counterexample adapted from Keith Lehrer. A gullible woman who is having shoulder pains sees her physician who, believing the woman to be a hypochondriac, informs her that she is mistaken about these pains. "They really are acute tickles," he avers. "Acute tickles sometimes resemble pains, but they are really more pleasurable." The gullible woman believes the physician and the next day tells her husband that she is having tickling sensations in her left shoulder. Has she merely misnamed her experience or does her confusion disqualify the experience from being infallible (or incorrigible)?

Consider the statement "I am having a hot sensation," uttered by one who believes it with infallible certainty. Plausible counter-examples are available to this belief too. I once heard the following story about a fraternity initiation. The pledge was told that he was to be branded on his buttocks with a branding iron containing the Greek letters of his fraternity. The inductee saw the red hot iron pulled from the stove and heard it sizzling. He removed his pants and bared his backside to the fraternity members in anticipa-tion of the branding iron. Then an ice cold metal bar was applied to his backside. The pledge reported that for several seconds he felt an incredibly hot sensation.

Likewise, we may ask whether the appearance belief that I seem to see a red object is infallible or incorrigible. Could I be confused about colors so that I am really having an orange sensation? Or is seeming to see X sufficient to make such a belief incorrigible?

But even if these experiences can count as foundational in some sense, it would seem that classical foundationalism would restrict us to very little knowledge, for it can allow nothing but infallible or incorrigible beliefs in the foundations. Perhaps there are some self-evident, incorrigible truths, such as simple mathematical statements and truths of logic, as well as the *Cogito* (I think, therefore I am), but this doesn't give us enough of a foundation to build a sturdy superstructure. It doesn't even include empirical beliefs. For these and other reasons, most contemporary foundationalists have rejected classical foundationalism. However, in our readings Roderick Chisholm (V.1) and Timothy McGrew (V.4) set forth defenses of classical foundationalism, which McGrew defends against other versions of foundationalism.

Nevertheless, the trend has been for foundationalists to take on the label of "moderate" or "minimal" before "foundationalism." Such foundationalism accepts the foundational model of distinguishing basic from nonbasic beliefs but rejects the possibility of an infallible belief system and accepts fallibilism, the theory that many of our most cherished beliefs could be false.

The following are features of modest foundationalism:

1. An asymmetrical relationship exists between the foundations and the superstructure.

2. Doubts about any psychological beliefs (beliefs about our mental states, such as our desires) being indubitable or incorrigible are allowed.

3. Almost any belief can be basic for a person under certain circumstances. No particular type of content is required.

4. The foundational relationship is justification of belief rather than knowledge, although knowledge is the goal of believing.

5. Superstructure beliefs may be only inductively based on basic beliefs. That is, the transmission of justification from the basic to the nonbasic beliefs is more flexible than allowed by classical foundationalism.

6. Coherence is allowed some scope in the justification process. As an example, for Robert Audi, coherence plays a negative role in foundational structures. If someone shows that our belief set is incoherent, it cannot be justified. For Audi and William P. Alston, a justification of a belief can be "overdetermined." That is, it may be justified by appeal to properly basic beliefs, and it may also be justified by its cohering within a whole system of beliefs.

7. One must distinguish between *having* a justification for a belief and being able to *show* that one has such a justification. Moderate foundationalists argue that for the justification to obtain it is not necessary for a person to be able to show that he or she is justified.

The selection by Robert Audi (V.2) contains many of these points.

The Regress Problem

A driving force behind contemporary foundationalists is the problem of stopping the regress of inferential justification. Suppose you believe that eating vegetables will promote your health. I ask you why you believe that. You answer that your belief is based on your beliefs about nutrition. Vegetables have the kind of vitamins necessary for the proper maintenance of the human body. But suppose I ask you why you believe that vegetables contain the kind of vitamins necessary for the proper maintenance of the human body. Well, you'd either appeal to "common

knowledge" or start discussing chemistry and physiology. Where would the demand for a justification stop? Does it matter?

Structurally, your belief A that vegetables promote health is based on your belief B that vegetables contain necessary vitamins, which in turn is based on belief C having to do with chemistry and physiology. Or you could argue that A is based on D, inductive knowledge that vegetables generally promote physical health.

Another way of putting the matter is to say that we infer belief A from belief B and B from C and so on. Four kinds of such inference chains can be identified:

1. Belief A is itself inferred directly from belief B, which is unjustified.

2. Belief A owes its justification to belief B, which is based on belief C and so on *ad infinitum*.

3. Belief A owes its justification to belief B, which is based on belief C, which is based on belief A, doubling back in a circle.

4. Belief A owes its justification to belief B, which is based on a foundational or noninferential belief that needs no further justification.

There are problems with each type of chain.

Wittgenstein seems to have held the first option, because he remarked that "at the foundation of well-founded beliefs lies belief that is not founded." Perhaps contextualism (see the discussion later in this part introduction) fits this category, but it is hard to see, without more qualifications, how unjustified beliefs can yield a justified belief.

Regarding the infinite regress chain, it is difficult to believe that creatures like us have an infinite set of beliefs, and, even if we did, it would be impossible ever to show that such a justified belief was justified. Perhaps we have an infinite set of mathematical beliefs ("2 is greater than 1," "3 is larger than 2," and so forth), but it is doubtful whether the notion of an infinite set (or infinite sets of all our justified beliefs) has anything to commend it. No one has given a good argument for the infinite regress chain, though it hasn't been disproven, either.

The circular scheme is the model for coherentism. On the face of it, it seems to beg the question. For example, suppose you ask me why I believe in the Bible and I say, "Because it's inspired by God." Then you ask me why I believe in God, and I say, "I believe in God because the Bible says God exists." Arguing in a circle can be done by any fool and proves nothing. However, as we shall see, if the circle is big enough and the interrelations are intricate enough, many philosophers will accept something like the circular scheme. It is called *coherentism.*

The final pattern, which posits self-justified beliefs ("unmoved movers" to use Chisholm's phrase) at the base of every inferential chain, is the one foundationalists choose. Every justified belief either itself is a properly basic (justified) belief or ends in a chain of beliefs the last of which is self-justified. On the face of it, foundationalism seems the most satisfactory solution to the regress problem. It stops the chain of justification and does so in a way that does not beg the question.

Nonetheless, as noted in the readings, foundationalism has several problems. First, strong foundationalism contains too little content to sustain the edifice of knowledge; weaker foundationalism is too compromising to offer us justification. That is, classical foundationalism with its appeal to infallible knowledge doesn't seem adequate to yield much inferred knowledge or justified belief but tends toward skepticism about the external world, other minds, induction, and the like. Moderate or weak foundationalism, however, doesn't give us the strong justification, let alone knowledge, that we would like to have. In fact, as it compromises and accepts coherence constraints, it tends to become indistinguishable from moderate coherentism.

Second, the epistemic ascent argument set forth by Wilfrid Sellars and by Laurence BonJour (Reading V.3) maintains that foundationalism cannot explain, without appealing to an unwarranted stipulation, how a justification terminates. Let A represent the property of being a properly basic belief; then for a belief B to qualify as properly basic, the premises of the following justificatory argument must themselves be justified:

1. S's belief B has property A.
2. Beliefs having property A are highly likely to be true.
3. Therefore, S's belief B is highly likely to be true.

BonJour argues that for foundationalists to be justified in believing that B is properly basic, they must depend on this argument, so that their justification is not immediate or basic but inferential.

Foundationalists have attempted to set forth reasons why the ascent argument is not decisive against them.[1]

Coherentist Theories of Justification

There have always been coherence theories of truth, theories that claim that the truth resides in the absolute system of knowledge. Hegel, F. H. Bradley, and Brand Blanshard held the view that truth was defined not as correspondence of propositions with facts but as integrated and absolute wholes in which individual propositions received justification and relative truth credentials. Every true belief is entailed by every other proposition in the coherent system.

However, most contemporary coherentists, such as W. V. Quine, Wilfrid Sellars, Gilbert Harman, Keith Lehrer, and Laurence BonJour, reject the coherence theory of truth as an implausible metaphysical doctrine and adhere instead to a coherentist theory of justification. Individual beliefs are justified by the entire system of beliefs in which they cohere. All justification is inferential, so the notion of proper basicality is a contradiction in terms.

There are several versions of coherentism, but one important objection has been applied against all forms: the isolation objection. This objection states that the coherence of a theory is an inadequate justification of the theory, because by itself it doesn't supply the necessary criteria to distinguish it from illusory but consistent theories. Fairytales may sometimes be coherent, as may dreams and hallucinations. Astrology may be as coherent as astronomy, Newtonian physics as coherent as Einsteinian physics, but surely, the objection runs, we want to connect our theories with empirical data. Consistency may, generally, be a necessary condition for justification (although see Fumerton's critique in Reading V.6), but it is not a sufficient condition for justification.

In our readings, Jonathan Dancy defends both a coherence theory of truth and justification. He argues that coherentism gains in importance if it can connect truth and justification. Indeed, what is so great about justifying our beliefs if they do not connect with truth? According to Dancy, a proposition is true if and only if (iff) it is a member of a coherent set of propositions. Against the correspondence theory of truth, Dancy argues that there is no theory-free external point of view. He goes on to admit a certain apparent asymmetry between empirical observation and the resulting sensory beliefs. Nevertheless, what gives sensory beliefs their security is their internal coherence within one's belief-set.

Two insightful discussions end the section on the foundationalist-coherentist debate. Ernest Sosa's "The Raft and the Pyramid" closely analyzes the strengths and weaknesses of various forms of each of these theories. Susan Haack's "A Foundherentist Theory of Empirical Justification" attempts to combine foundational virtues—namely, the importance of experience for justification—with the virtues of coherentism, namely, the mutual support of our beliefs in the structure of justification.

Contextualism

Finally, an alternative to the foundationalist-coherentist controversy has recently been set forth by several philosophers, including Thomas Kuhn, Keith DeRose, David Lewis, and David Annis. Annis, whose reading concludes this part of the book, gives the most lucid description of this theory, called *contextualism,* and argues that justification is relative to social practices with differing norms. He distinguishes an issue context from an objector context. The *issue context* of a belief is the specific concern someone raises about it; the *objector context* refers to the group that raises objections to the believer about the belief in question. A belief is contextually basic for a person relative to an appropriate objector group at a specific time if that group lets the person hold the belief without supporting reasons. In different contexts, different beliefs take on proper basicality, but there is no general epistemic criterion for justifying beliefs independent of those arising from social practices and social approval.

Still in its infancy, contextualism has already been criticized as being unduly relativistic. We shall encounter another version of contextualism in David Lewis's "Elusive Knowledge" in Part VI of this work. Related epistemic theories appear in Part XI ("Challenges and Alternatives to Contemporary Epistemology").

Note

[1] See Roderick Chisholm, *Theory of Knowledge*, 3d ed. (Englewood Cliffs, NJ: Prentice-Hall, 1985), and Paul Moser, *Epistemic Justification* (Dordrecht, Netherlands: Reidel, 1985), chap. 4.

V.1 Contemporary Classical Foundationalism

RODERICK CHISHOLM

A biographical sketch of Roderick Chisholm (1916–1999) appears with Reading I.2. In this selection Chisholm takes it as given that we do have some knowledge and proceeds to argue for a version of foundationalism. He first inquires as to what grounds our beliefs. He argues that beliefs may be justified in three different ways. (1) They may be justified in virtue of the relation they bear to what is directly evident (our immediate experience); (2) they may be justified by certain relations they bear to each other; and (3) they may be justified by their own nature and thus independently of the relations they bear to other propositions.

The Directly Evident

One says "I know" when one is ready to give compelling grounds. "I know" relates to a possibility of demonstrating the truth. Whether someone knows something can come to light, assuming that he is convinced of it. But if what he believes is of such a kind that the grounds that he can give are no surer than his assertion, then he cannot say that he knows what he believes.

LUDWIG WITTGENSTEIN[1]

The nature of the good can be learned from experience only if the content of experience be first classified into good and bad, or grades of better and worse. Such classification or grading already involves the legislative application of the same principle which is sought. In logic, principles can be elicited by generalization from examples only if cases of valid reasoning have first been segregated by some criterion. It is this criterion which the generalization is required to disclose. In esthetics, the laws of the beautiful may be derived from experience only if the criteria of beauty have first been correctly applied.

C. I. LEWIS[2]

Reprinted from *Theory of Knowledge,* 2nd ed. (Englewood Cliffs, NJ.: Prentice-Hall, 1977), with permission of the publisher. [Notes edited.]

1. Socratic Questions

In investigating the theory of evidence from a philosophical—or Socratic—point of view, we make three general presuppositions.

We presuppose, first, that there *is* something that we know and we adopt the working hypothesis that *what* we know is pretty much that which, on reflection, we think we know. This may seem the wrong place to start. But where else *could* we start? . . .

We presuppose, second, that the things we know are justified for us in the following sense: *we* can know what it is, on any occasion, that constitutes our grounds, or reason, or evidence for thinking that we know. If I think that I know that there is now snow on the top of the mountain, then, as the quotation from Wittgenstein suggests, I am in a position to say what ground or reason I have for thinking that there is now snow on the top of the mountain. (Of course, from the fact that there is ground for thinking that there is now snow there, from the fact, say, that you have been there and seen it, it doesn't follow that *I* now have any ground or reason for the belief.)

And we presuppose, third, that if we do thus have grounds or reasons for the things we think we know, then there are valid general principles of evidence—principles stating the general conditions under which we may be said to have grounds or reasons for what we believe. And, as the quotation from Lewis above suggests, our concern, in investigating the theory of evidence, is to find out what these general principles are.

In order to formulate, or make explicit, our rules of evidence, we will do well to proceed as we do in logic, when formulating the rules of inference, or in moral philosophy, when formulating rules of action. We suppose that we have at our disposal certain instances which the rules should countenance or permit and other instances which the rules should reject or forbid; and we suppose that by investigating these instances we can formulate criteria which any instance must satisfy if it is to be accepted or permitted, as well as criteria which any instance must satisfy if it is to be rejected or forbidden. To obtain the instances we need if we are to formulate rules of evidence, we may proceed in the following way.

We consider certain things that we know to be true, or think we know to be true, or certain things which, upon reflection, we would be willing to call *evident*. With respect to each of these, we then try to formulate a reasonable answer to the question, "What justification do you have for thinking you know this thing to be true?" or "What justification do you have for counting this thing as something that is evident?" In beginning with what we think we know to be true, or with what, after reflection, we would be willing to count as being evident, we are assuming that the truth we are seeking is "already implicit in the mind which seeks it, and needs only to be elicited and brought to clear reflection."[3]

There are philosophers who point out, with respect to some things that are quite obviously known to be true, that questions concerning their justification "do not arise," for (they say) to express a doubt concerning such things is to "violate the rules of our language." But their objections do not apply to the type of question that we are discussing here; for these questions need not be taken to express any doubts or to indicate any attitude of skepticism. Designed only to elicit information, the questions are not challenges and they do not imply or presuppose that there is any ground for doubting, or for suspecting, that to which they pertain.[4] When Aristotle considered an invalid mood and asked himself "What is wrong with this?" he was trying to learn; he need not have been suggesting to himself that perhaps nothing was wrong with the mood.

It should be also noted that when we ask ourselves, concerning what we may think we know to be true, "What *justification* do I have for believing this?" or "What justification do I have for thinking I know that this is something that is true?" we are not asking any of the following questions: "What *further evidence* can I find in support of this?" "How did I *come to believe* this or find out that it is true?" "How would I go about *persuading* some other reasonable person that it is true?" We must not expect, therefore, that answers to these latter questions will be, *ipso facto*, answers to the questions that we are asking. Our questions are Socratic and therefore not at all of the type that one ordinarily asks.[5]

2. A Stopping Place?

In many instances the answers to our questions will take the following form: "What justifies me in thinking that I know that *a* is *F* is the fact that it is evident to me that *b* is *G*." For example: "What justifies me in thinking I know that he has that disorder is the fact that it is evident to me that he has those symptoms." Such an answer, therefore, presupposes an epistemic principle, what we might call a "rule of evidence." The rule would have the form:

If it is evident to me that *b* is *G*, then it is evident to me that *a* is *F*.

"If it *is* evident that he has those symptoms, then it is also evident that he has that disorder." And so we should distinguish the answer to our Socratic question from its epistemic presupposition. The answer to our Socratic question is a proposition to the effect that our justification for counting one thing as evident is the fact that something else is evident. And the epistemic presupposition of our answer is a rule of evidence: It is a proposition to the effect that if certain conditions obtain, then something may be said to be evident. One could say of such a rule that it tells us that one thing *serves to make another thing evident*.

This type of answer to our Socratic questions shifts the burden of justification from one claim to another. For we may now ask, "What justifies me in counting it as evident that *b* is *G*?" or "What justifies me in thinking I know that *b* is *G*?" And possibly we will formulate, once again, an answer of the first sort: "What justifies me in counting it as evident that *b* is *G* is the fact that it is evident that *c* is *H*." ("What justifies me in counting it as evident that he has those symptoms is the fact that it is evident that his temperature is recorded as being high. . . .") And this answer will presuppose still another rule of evidence: "If it is evident that c is H, then it is evident that b is G." How long can we continue in this way?

We might try to continue *ad indefinitum*, justifying each new claim that we elicit by still another claim. Or we might be tempted to complete a vicious circle: in such a case, having justified "a is F" by appeal to "b is G," and "b is G" by reference to "c is H," we would then justify "c is H" by reference to "a is F." But if we are rational beings, we will do neither of these things. For we will find that our Socratic questions lead us to a proper stopping place.

How are we to recognize such a stopping place?

Sextus Empiricus remarked that every object of apprehension seems to be apprehended either through itself or through another object.[6] Those things, if there are any, that are "apprehended through themselves" might provide us with a stopping place. But what could they be? The form of our Socratic questions suggests a way of finding an answer. Let us say provisionally that we have found a proper stopping place when the answer to our question may take the following form:

> What justifies me in thinking I know that a is F is simply the fact that a is F.

Whenever this type of answer is appropriate, we have encountered what is *directly evident*.

3. An Improper Stopping Place

At first consideration, one might suppose that those statements that correctly describe our "experience," or formulate our "perceptions" or "observations," are statements expressing what is directly evident in the sense described. But what is. expressed by such statements does not satisfy the criteria we have just set forth.

In answer to the question, "What is my justification for thinking I know that Mr. Smith is here?" one may say, "I see that he is here." But "I see that he is here" does not pick out the kind of stopping place we have just described in reply to the question, "What is my justification for counting it as evident that it is Mr. *Smith* that I see?" A reasonable man will *not* say, "What justifies me in count-

ing it as evident that I see Mr. Smith is simply the fact that I do see Mr. Smith." If he understands the Socratic question, he will say instead something like: "I know that Mr. Smith is a tall man with red hair; I see a tall man with red hair; I know that no one else satisfying that description would be in this room now. . . ." Each of these propositions in turn, including "I see a tall man with red hair," would be justified by reference to still other propositions. And this is true of any other perceptual proposition. Hence, we cannot say that what we know by means of perception or observation is itself something that is directly evident.

There are those who will say, "What justifies me in counting it as evident that Mr. Smith is here (or that I see Mr. Smith) is simply my present *experience*; but the experience itself cannot be said to be evident, much less to have evidence conferred upon it." But this reply seems clearly to make room for further Socratic questioning. For we may ask, "What justifies me in counting it as evident that my experience is of such a sort that experiences of that sort make it evident to me that Mr. Smith is here, or that I see that Mr. Smith is here?" And to this question one could reasonably reply in the way described above.

4. States That Present Themselves

The following quotation from Leibniz points to what is directly evident:

> Our direct awareness of our own existence and of our own thoughts provides us with the primary truths *a posteriori*, the primary truths of fact, or, in other words, our primary experiences; just as identical propositions constitute the primary truths *a priori*, the primary truths of reason, or, in other words, our primary insights. Neither the one nor the other is capable of being demonstrated and both can be called *immediate*— the former, because there is no mediation between the understanding and its objects, and the latter because there is no mediation between the subject and the predicate.[7]

We are here concerned with Leibniz's "primary truths of fact. . . ."

Thinking and believing provide us with paradigm cases of the directly evident. Consider a reasonable man who is thinking about a city he takes to be Albuquerque, or who believes that Albuquerque is in New Mexico, and suppose him to reflect on the philosophical question, "What is my justification for thinking that I know that I am thinking about a city I take to be Albuquerque, or that I believe that Albuquerque is in New Mexico?" (This strange question would hardly arise, of course, on any practical occasion, for the man is not asking, "What is my justification for thinking that Albuquerque is in New Mexico?" The question is a Socratic question and therefore a philosophical one.) The man could reply in this way: "My justification for thinking I know that I am thinking about a city I take to be Albuquerque, or that I believe that Albuquerque is in New Mexico, is simply the fact that I *am* thinking about a city I take to be Albuquerque, or that I *do* believe that it is in New Mexico." And this reply fits our formula for the directly evident:

What justifies me in thinking I know that *a* is *F* is simply the fact that *a* is *F*.

Our man has stated his justification for a proposition merely by reiterating that proposition. This type of justification is *not* appropriate to the questions that were previously discussed. Thus, in answer to "What justification do you have for counting it as evident that there can be no life on the moon?" it would be inappropriate—and presumptuous—simply to reiterate, "There can be no life on the moon." But we can state our justification for certain propositions about our *beliefs*, and certain propositions about our thoughts, merely by reiterating those propositions. They may be said, therefore, to pertain to what is directly evident.

Borrowing a technical term from Meinong, let us say that if there is something that is directly evident to a man, then there is some state of affairs that "presents itself to him." Thus, my believing that Socrates is mortal is a state of affairs that is "self-presenting" to me. If I do believe that Socrates is mortal, then, *ipso facto*, it is evident to me that I believe that Socrates is mortal; the state of affairs is "apprehended through itself."[8]

Other states that may be similarly self-presenting are those described by "thinking that one remembers that . . ." or "seeming to remember that . . ." (as distinguished from "remembering that . . ."), and "taking" or thinking that one perceives" (as distinguished from "perceiving").

Desiring, hoping, wondering, wishing, loving, hating may also be self-presenting. These states are what Leibniz intended by the term "thoughts" in the passage quoted above.

5. The Nature of Self-Presentation

Let us now try to characterize self-presentation more exactly. If seeming to have a headache is a state of affairs that is self-presenting for S at the present moment, then S does now seem to have a headache and, moreover, it is evident to him that he seems to have a headache.[9] And so we may formulate the definition this way:

D2.1 *h* is *self-presenting* for S at *t* = Df *h* occurs at *t*; and necessarily, if *h* occurs at *t*, then *h* is evident for S at *t*.

An alternative formulation would be this:

h is self-presenting for S at *t* = Df *h* is true at *t*; and necessarily, if *h* is true at *t*, then *h* is evident for S at *t*.

. . . For the moment, we will assume that they are interchangeable, sometimes saying that *states of affairs* are what is self-presenting and at other times saying that *propositions* are what is self-presenting.

We should note that what follows logically from what is self-presenting need not itself be self-presenting. It will be instructive to consider three different examples of this fact.

1. The proposition expressed by "I seem to have a headache" logically implies that expressed by "2 and 2 are 4." But even if the former is self-presenting, the latter is not. For the latter is not necessarily such that if it is true then it is evident for me; it could be true even if I didn't exist.

2. The proposition expressed by "I seem to have a headache" logically implies that expressed by "Either I seem to have a headache or all crows are black." But the latter proposition is not necessarily such that if it is true then it is evident to me; it could be true even if I didn't exist.

3. The proposition expressed by "I seem to have a headache" logically implies that expressed by "I exist." But the latter proposition is not necessarily such that, if it is true then it is evident for me; it could be true if I were asleep and such that nothing is evident to me.

The negations of self-presenting propositions will not be self-presenting, for they may all be true when no one exists and hence when nothing is evident. What of the proposition expressed by "I am thinking but I do not seem to see a dog." Is this necessarily such that, if it is true, then it is evident? No. For it could be true, even though I didn't have the concept of a dog and therefore didn't understand the proposition "I am thinking but I do not seem to see a dog." But if the proposition is one that could be true when I didn't understand it, then it is one that could be true without being evident to me. For, . . . a proposition cannot be evident to a person unless it is one that he is able to grasp or to understand. (More exactly, . . . if believing one proposition is more reasonable than believing another for any given person S, then S is able to grasp or understand the first proposition.)

One may object: "But isn't it directly evident to me now both that I am thinking and that I do not see a dog?" The answer is yes. But the concept of the directly evident is not the same as that of the self-presenting.

6. A Definition of the Directly Evident

The concept of the directly evident is considerably broader than that of the self-presenting. A self-presenting state of affairs for S is one which is necessarily such that, if it occurs, then it is evident to S. Hence we could say that the Cartesian statement "I am thinking" expresses what is self-presenting for S—provided he is thinking. For it would be impossible for S to be thinking unless it were evident to him that he was thinking. But what of the statement "There is someone who is thinking"? If we adhere to the tradition of Descartes and Leibniz, we will want to say that, if "I am thinking" expresses what is directly evident for S, then so, too, does "There is someone who is thinking." But the latter is not self-presenting by our definition above. For it is not *necessary* that, if there is someone who is thinking, then that fact is then evident to S. (If someone is thinking while S is asleep, the fact that someone is thinking need not be evident to S.) But, we may assume, it is not possible for anyone to accept the proposition he would express by "I am thinking" unless he also accepts the proposition that someone is thinking. And so let us say:

D2.2 *h* is *directly evident* for *S* = Df *h* is logically contingent; and there is an *e* such that (i) *e* is self-presenting for *S* and (ii) necessarily, whoever accepts *e* accepts *h*.

Those propositions which are themselves self-presenting, of course, will also be directly evident by this definition.

What of *negative* propositions? Isn't it directly evident to me that I do not now seem to see a dog? If such propositions were never directly evident, it would be difficult to see what would ever justify any contingent judgments of nonexistence. Yet we noted above that "I do not now seem to see a dog" cannot be said to be self-presenting— for it may be true without being evident. From what self-presenting proposition, then, may one deduce the proposition expressed by "I do not now seem to see a dog?" The answer would seem to be this: "I am considering the proposition that I seem to see a dog, and I do not seem to see a dog." (This example illustrates the fact that negative apprehension is more complex than positive apprehension.) . . .

The Indirectly Evident

1. The Justification of the Indirectly Evident

Those "truths of fact" that are known but are not directly evident may be said to be indirectly evident. Hence, whatever we know about "external objects," about other people, and about the past, may be said to be indirectly evident. In considering now our justification for what is thus only indirectly evident, we should remind ourselves of what was said . . . about the nature of the theory of evidence.

We said that the philosopher, in investigating the theory of evidence, makes three presuppositions. The first is that there is something that we know, and the philosopher takes it as a working hypothesis that what we know is pretty much that which, on reflection, we think we know. The second presupposition is that the things we know are so justified for us that *we* can know, on any occasion, what it is that constitutes our ground, reason, or evidence for what it is that we know. And the third presupposition is that, if we do thus have grounds or reasons for the things we think we know, then there are general principles of evidence which can be said to be satisfied by the things we think we know. Our hope is to formulate such principles.

What, then, of our justification for those propositions that are indirectly evident? We might say that they are justified in three different ways. (1) They may be justified by certain relations that they bear to what is *directly* evident. (2) They may be justified by certain relations that they bear to *each other*. And (3) they may be justified by *their own nature*, so to speak, and quite independently of the relations that they bear to anything else.

The term "foundationalism" is sometimes used for any view that emphasizes the first of these three ways. And the term "coherence theory" or "coherentism" is sometimes used for any view which emphasizes the second. But there is no use for these terms that is generally agreed upon and it may be well to avoid them.[10] And the truth of the matter, as we will see, would seem to be that what is indirectly evident may be justified in any one of these three ways.[11]

But aren't we overlooking the most obvious type of epistemic justification? Thus one might object: "The best justification we could have for a given proposition would be the fact that it comes from a *reliable source*. What could be more reasonable than accepting the deliverances of such a source—whether the source be an authority, or a computer, or a sense organ, or some kind of psychological faculty, or science itself?" The answer is, of course, that it is reasonable to put one's faith in a source which is such that one *knows* it to be reliable or one has good *ground or reason or evidence* for thinking it to be reliable. In investigating the theory of knowledge, we are concerned with the nature of the ground or reason or evidence that one might thus have for believing a source or an authority to be a reliable one. (Perhaps this latter point is best understood by reflecting upon the following hypothetical objection and how one might reply to it: "The best justification you can possibly have for accepting any given proposition is the fact that it is a member of the class of *true* propositions. And what could be more reasonable, after all, than restricting one's beliefs to propositions that are *true*?")

Let us begin, then, by considering the extent to which the indirectly evident might be justified by reference to what is directly evident. To what

extent can we say that our knowledge of what is indirectly evident is "based upon" or "known through" the directly evident? Are there certain epistemic principles or rules of evidence which, in application to what is directly evident, will yield whatever is indirectly evident? . . .

2. Confirmation

We begin by considering the nature of confirmation.

The technical expression "*e* confirms *h*" is used to express a relation which is such that, if it holds between a proposition *e* and a proposition *h*, then it holds necessarily between *e* and *h*. Since it holds necessarily, it is sometimes described as a *logical* relation. But it is also an *epistemic* relation. For it tells us, in effect, that knowledge of *e* would give one some reason for accepting *h*. Thus the relation that *e* bears to *h*, when *e* confirms *h*, is also sometimes expressed by saying "*h* has a certain positive probability in relation to *e*."[12]

But the relation is a puzzling one. For it may be that, although a given proposition *e* confirms another proposition *h*, the conjunction of *e* with certain *other* propositions will not confirm *h*. Indeed, it may be that the wider proposition will confirm the negation of *h*. And the wider propositions may be entirely consistent with the original proposition *e*. Consider, for example, the following propositions:

(h) John is a Democrat.

(e) Most of the people in this room are Democrats, and John is in this room.

(f) Most of the people on the left side of this room are not Democrats, and John is on the left side of this room.

(g) 45 of the 50 people who arrived on time are Democrats, and John arrived on time.

(i) 99 of the 100 people who voted for the measure are not Democrats, and John voted for the measure.

We may say that:

e confirms *h*
e-and-*f* confirms not-*h*
e-and-*f*-and-*g* confirms *h*
e-and-*f*-and-*g*-and-*i* confirms not-*h*.

The sense of the expression "*e* confirms *h*" might be put, somewhat loosely, by saying: "If *e* were the only thing you knew, or the only relevant evidence you had, then you would also have some reason for accepting *h*." Thus one could say: "If *e* above were the only evidence you had, then you would have some reason for accepting *h*; but if, in addition to *e*, *f* were also a part of your evidence, and if *e* and *f* were the only evidence you had, *then* you would have some reason for accepting not-*h*; . . . and so on."

The expression "*e tends to confirm h*," therefore, might be less misleading than "*e* confirms *h*," and we will use it in what follows. Let us say:

> D4.1 *e tends to confirm h* = Df Necessarily, for every *S*, if *e* is evident for *S* and if everything that is evident for *S* is entailed by *e*, then *h* has some presumption in its favor for *S*.

We have said that it is quite possible for it to be the case that, although (1) a certain proposition *e* tends to confirm a certain proposition *h*, nevertheless (2) there is a proposition *i* which is such that the conjunction, *e* and *i*, does not tend to confirm *h*. We might say in such a case that *i* would *defeat*, or *override*, the confirmation that *e* tends to provide. This concept could be defined simply as follows:

> D4.2 *i defeats* the confirmation that *e* tends to provide for *h* = Df (i) *e* tends to confirm *h*, and (ii) the conjunction, *e* and *i*, does not tend to confirm *h*.

Now we may turn to some of the basic principles of the theory of knowledge.

3. Perception and "Self-Presentation"

We may suppose, once again, that we are dealing with a rational person, *S*, who is conducting a critique of cogency of the kind we tried to describe at the beginning of [the section on the directly evident.] *S* asks himself, with respect to various things that he knows or thinks he knows, what his justification is for thinking that he knows those things. And, it will be recalled, he asks himself these questions not to discredit or cast doubt upon his knowledge, but in order to elicit certain general principles about the nature of knowledge and of evidence.

In answer to the question, "What is my justification for thinking that I know such and such?" *S*

may say: "My justification for thinking that I know such and such is the fact that I do know so and so." Let us express this briefly by saying: *S* justifies his claim or belief that he knows such and such by appeal to the proposition that he knows so and so.

. . . We will countenance the directly evident character of *S*'s "self-presenting states." The first of our epistemic principles is in fact a schema enabling us to abbreviate indefinitely many epistemic principles:

> (A) *S*'s being *F* is such that, if it occurs, then it is self-presenting to *S* that he is *F*.

We will imagine that, to replace "*F*," we have a list of various predicates, each of such a sort as to yield a description of a self-presenting state of *S*. Thus instances of principle A would be: "*S*'s being appeared to red is such that, if it occurs, then it is self-presenting to *S* that he is appeared to red"; "*S*'s being such that he wonders whether all men are mortal is such that, if it occurs, then it is self-presenting to *S* that he wonders whether all men are mortal."

And now . . . we may turn to perception. But we will single out two subspecies of perception and say, of the one, that it presents us with what is *reasonable*, and of the other, that it presents us with what is *evident*.

Our ordinary language makes difficulties for us at this point. For most perception words—for example, "perceive," "see," and "hear"—present us with certain problems of interpretation. How are we to interpret the sentences in which such words are followed by "that"-clauses? Consider, for example, "He perceives that a cat is on the roof," "He sees it sitting there," and "He hears it make a scratching noise." When we use our perception words in this way, do our sentences commit us to what is affirmed in their subordinate propositional clauses? Does "He perceives that a cat is on the roof" imply that there *is* a cat on the roof? Does "He sees that it is sitting there" imply that it is sitting there? And does "He hears it make a scratching noise" imply that there is something which is making a scratching noise?

The fact of the matter, unfortunately, is that the sentences are ambiguous. They may be taken either way. We may take the sentences in such a way that they do have such implications. Or we may take them in such a way that they do not. In the latter case, we may say, without contradiction,

"Well, *he* perceives that a cat is there, but obviously he is hallucinating once again; he is always seeing some cat or other that isn't really there."

There would be no point in trying to decide whether one or the other of these two uses is incorrect. But if we are going to talk about perception, we should decide how we will use the terms and make sure that, once we have decided to use them in one way, we don't *also* sometimes use them in the other.

Let us use our perception words, then, in the first way. "He perceives that there is a cat there" will imply, in our use, that there is a cat there. How, then, shall we describe the state of the man who is hallucinating—the man we considered above when we said, "*He* perceives that a cat is there, but obviously he is hallucinating once again"? The simplest procedure would be to say, "He *thinks* he perceives that a cat is there" or "He *believes* that he perceives that a cat is there."

An alternative to "He thinks (or believes) he perceives that a cat is there" would be, "He *takes* there to be a cat there." Such an alternative has some advantages over "He thinks (or believes) that he perceives," for the latter expression, in its ordinary use, may suggest a kind of higher order reflection *about* one's perceptions. Grammatically however, "He thinks (or believes) that he perceives" is more convenient, for it may be used with a "that"-clause, and it may be adapted to more specific perceptions, as "He believes that he sees" and "He believes that he hears." Hence we will use "believes that he perceives" in place of "takes." But when we say, "He believes that a cat is there," we will take it to mean simply that he has a spontaneous nonreflective experience, one that he would normally express by saying, "I perceive that. . . ."

5. Memory

. . .

The word "memory" presents us with a terminological difficulty analogous to that presented by "perception." Consider a case in which, as one might say, a man's memory has "deceived him": the man would have said, honestly and sincerely, that he remembered a certain event to have occurred; actually, the event did not occur at all. Such deceptions of memory are common; "we remember remembering things and later finding

them to be false." But if we say "what he remembered is false," the ordinary interpretation of the word "remember" will render what we say contradictory; hence, if we wish to take "remember" in this ordinary way, we must express the fact in question by saying, "What he *thought* he remembered is false." And of those cases where one's memory is not thus deceptive, we may say that "what he thought he remembered is true."

Let us introduce the expression "unveridical memory" and use it in the way we have just been using "unveridical perception." A person may be said to have an *unveridical memory* if he mistakenly thinks he remembers a certain thing. We may also say that he remembers that thing unveridically.

Since both memory and perception are capable of playing us false, we run a twofold risk when we appeal to the memory of a perception. Let us suppose that *S* defends his claim to know that "A cat was on the roof" by saying he thinks he remembers having perceived one there. The situation presents us with four possibilities. (1) The present memory and the past perception are both veridical: he did think he perceived a cat and what he saw was, in fact, a cat. (2) He correctly remembers having thought he saw a cat; but what he saw was not a cat. In this case, the fault lies with the past perception and not with the present memory. (3) He incorrectly remembers having thought he saw a cat; but what he really thought he saw, at the time, was a squirrel, and in fact it was a squirrel that he saw. In this case, the fault lies with the present memory and not with the past perception. (4) He incorrectly remembers having thought he saw a cat; but what he thought he saw, at the time, was a squirrel, and the perception was unveridical, for there was no squirrel there at all. In this case, the fault lies both with the present memory and the past perception. As we know, however, memory, by a kind of happy failure if not an act of dishonesty, may correct the past perception: The man thought he saw a squirrel but it was in fact a cat, and now he thinks he remembers that he thought he saw a cat. Ordinary language provides us with no clear way of distinguishing these different types of deception, and memory is likely to receive more blame than it deserves. But it would seem to be clear, in general, that we should assign a lower degree of evidence to the deliverances of memory.

Where we said, in effect, that one type of perceptual belief made something *reasonable*, and another type of perceptual belief made something *evident,* let us now replace "reasonable" and "evident," respectively, by "acceptable" and "reasonable." We may add, then, two principles pertaining to memory.

And so we will be saying, in effect, that if S seems to remember perceiving something to be F, then the proposition that he does remember perceiving something to be F is one that is reasonable for S. Our first principle pertaining to memory will be this:

> (D) For any subject S, if S believes, without ground for doubt, that he remembers perceiving something to be F, then the proposition that he does remember perceiving something to be F is one that is acceptable for S.

We may assume that, if the proposition that S would express in English by saying "I remember perceiving something to be F" is one that is acceptable for him, then so, too, is the proposition that he did perceive something to be F, as well as the proposition that something was F.

Perhaps there is reason to distinguish between "remembering perceiving" and "remembering having perceived." Thus one might be able to say "I remember having perceived someone leaving the bank" even though one cannot say, "I remember perceiving someone leaving the bank"; in such a case, presumably, the details of the perception have been forgotten and one remembers only that one *did* perceive. If this distinction is a tenable one, then we should note that principle D applies to remembering perceiving and need not apply to remembering having perceived.

We will assume, in effect, that, if the property being G is a sensible characteristic, then seeming to remember perceiving something to be G tends to make reasonable the propositions that one does remember perceiving something to be G, that one perceived something to be G, and that something was G. Our second principle pertaining to memory will be a schema, wherein the letter "F" may be replaced by any predicate (e.g., "red" or "blue") which connotes a sensible characteristic.

> (E) For any subject S, if S believes, without ground for doubt, that he remembers perceiving something to be F, then it is beyond reasonable doubt for S that he does remember perceiving something to be F.

Variants of these two principles have been suggested by other philosophers: Meinong held that our memory judgments, as he called them, possess "immediate presumptive evidence." Russell has said that every memory should "command a certain degree of credence." And Lewis said that "whatever is remembered, whether as explicit recollection or merely in the form of our sense of the past, is *prima facie* credible because so remembered."

There is still more that can be said in behalf of memory.

If our memories of sensible perceptions are reasonable, so, too, must be our memories of the "self-presenting states" discussed in [the section on The Directly Evident). Thus I may think that I remembered that I believed, or desired, or hoped, or loved, or that I undertook a certain thing, or that I was appeared to in a certain way. Don't such facts tend to make reasonable the propositions that I thus seem to remember? Let us add, therefore, another schematic principle. The expression "F" which appears in this principle may be replaced by any expression yielding a description of what we have called a self-presenting state:

> (F) For any subject S, if S believes, without ground for doubt, that he remembers being F, then it is beyond reasonable doubt for S that he does remember that he was F.

We have said that our perception of things in motion, or at rest, and our perception of events in temporal succession are sources of what is evident. In saying this, we have conceded the evident character of "fresh memory" or "proterasthesis"—our apprehension of the "immediate past." Whenever we perceive a thing to be in motion, or to be at rest, and whenever we perceive a succession of events, as we do when we listen to a melody or to a conversation, we perceive one event as being temporally prior to another. When we do perceive one event as being temporally prior, then we perceive the former as being past. Whether this apprehension of the immediate past is to be called "memory" may be a matter only of terminology. But if we do call it "memory," then we may say that what we thus remember, or think we remember, is something that is *evident.* . . .

. . . Our principles do not yet allow us to say, of Mr. *S*, that it is evident to him that a cat is on the roof.

We must return, then, to the concept of *confirmation*.

6. Confirmation and Concurrence

Appealing now to the concept of confirmation, and in particular to "*e* tends to confirm *h*," which was defined in section 2 above (D4.1), we will first note how to add to the class of propositions that have some positive epistemic status for our subject *S*.

Since whatever is evident is also reasonable and since whatever is reasonable is also acceptable, we may say that all of the propositions countenanced by the principles we have set forth are acceptable. We may now apply the concept of confirmation and say that if the conjunction of all of those propositions that are acceptable tends to confirm a given proposition, then that proposition has some presumption in its favor. Hence, we may add the following to our principles:

(G) If the conjunction of all those propositions *e* such that *e* is acceptable for *S* at *t* tends to confirm *h*, then *h* has some presumption in its favor for *S* at *t*.

The class of propositions that thus have some presumption in their favor for *S* may now include a vast number of inductive hypotheses and thus go considerably beyond the content of memory and perception. For example, they may include propositions about cats and roofs.

By applying Carneades' concept of *concurrence* to this expanded class of propositions, we are also able to expand the class of propositions that are to be countenanced as being *beyond reasonable doubt* for *S* at *t*.* When Carneades said that a set of propositions might be concurrent, he meant that each member of the set would support, and also be supported by, the other members of the set. We could say that any set of propositions that are mutually consistent and logically independent of each other is concurrent provided that each member of the set is confirmed by the conjunction of all the members of the set. More exactly:

D4.4 A is a set *of concurrent* propositions = Df *A* is a set of two or more propositions each of which is such that the conjunction of all the

others tends to confirm it and is logically independent of it.

There will conceivably be many sets of concurrent propositions among those propositions that now have some presumption in their favor for *S*. Let us consider, then, the following principle:

(H) Any set of concurring propositions, each of which has some presumption in its favor for *S*, is such that each of its members is beyond reasonable doubt for *S*.

In other words, if among the propositions having some presumption in their favor for *S*, there is a set related by mutual support, then each of those propositions is beyond reasonable doubt for *S*. This principle is somewhat bold, epistemically, but boldness is in order if we are to continue to hold that skepticism is false.

The following is an example, slightly oversimplified, of what might be such a concurrent set: "There is a cat on the roof today; there was one there yesterday; there was one there the day before yesterday; there was one there the day before that; and there is a cat on the roof almost every day." We may assume that the first statement expresses a present perception and, therefore, that it expresses what is reasonable (hence, also acceptable) by principle B; we may assume that the second, third, and fourth statements express certain memories and, therefore, that they express what is acceptable by principle D; and we may assume that the final statement is confirmed by the set of all of those statements that are empirically acceptable for *S* and, therefore, that it expresses what is acceptable by principle G. Each of the five propositions thus formulated may be said to be confirmed by the set of all the others. They are mutually consistent; hence, they are concurrent; and therefore, they are all reasonable by principle H.

Carneades had spoken of concurring presentations as hanging together like "links in a chain." But Meinong's figure may be more illuminating: "One may think of playing cards. No one of them is capable of standing by itself, but several of them leaned against each other, can serve to hold each other up." Each of the propositions in our concurrent set must be acceptable on its own if we are to derive reasonability from concurrence, just as each of the members of a house of cards must have its own degree of substance and rigidity if the house is not to collapse. (We may be reluctant to compare

---

*[Carneades of Cyrene (c. 213–129 B.C.).]

reasonability with a house of cards. In this event, Meinong has two other figures for us: the arch of a bridge, and a stack of weapons in the field.)

And finally, from our concurrent set of propositions—now reasonable as well as acceptable—we extract still another class of propositions; the members of this new class will be countenanced as being evident.

> (1) If *S* believes, without ground for doubt, that he perceives something to be *F*, and if the proposition that there is something that is *F* is a member of a set of concurrent propositions each of which is beyond reasonable doubt for *S*, then it is evident for *S* that he perceives something to be *F*.

This principle is even more audacious than principle H.

The set of concurrent propositions cited just above includes the perceptual proposition "A cat is on the roof." Hence, in virtue of principle I, and the definition of knowledge . . . we may be able to say, at last, that *S knows* that there is a cat on the roof.

7. Conclusion

Here, then, we have the beginning of a theory of evidence. It is by no means complete. Any complete theory would include the canons of inductive logic. And it would include many additional epistemic principles. Thus, in our formulation of the principles pertaining to perception and memory, we used the expression, "without ground for doubt"; we said in D4.3 that a person believes a proposition "without ground for doubt" provided he believes nothing that tends to confirm the negation of that proposition. Hence an adequate theory of evidence would set forth certain general principles concerning what propositions would tend to confirm that one is being deceived by one's senses or memory. But any adequate theory of evidence, I believe, would contain principles very much like those that we have set forth.

We said, at the beginning of this [section], that propositions that are not directly justified may be justified in one or another of three different ways. (1) They may be justified in virtue of the relation they bear to what is *directly evident*. (2) They may be justified by certain relations they bear to *each other*. And (3) they may be justified by

their own nature and thus quite independently of the relations they may bear to other propositions.

Looking back to the general principles we have formulated, we may now note the way in which all three phases of justification are here exemplified. (1) Every proposition we are justified in believing is justified, in part, because of some relation that it bears to the directly evident. (2) The reference to *concurrence* in our final two principles recognizes the importance of the mutual support that is provided, in part, by the logical relations that certain propositions bear to each other. And finally, (3) some propositions are such that, by their very nature, they tend to provide a justification for propositions about what one thinks one is perceiving and about what one thinks that one remembers.

Notes

[1] *On Certainty* (Oxford: Basil Blackwell, 1969), p. 32e.

[2] *Mind and the World-Order* (New York: Charles Scribner's Sons, 1929), p. 29; cf. his discussion of the "critique of cogency," in *The Ground and Nature of the Right* (New York: Columbia University Press, 1955), pp. 20–38.

[3] Lewis, *Mind and the World-Order*, p. 19.

[4] These remarks also apply to Leonard Nelson's statement, "If one asks whether one possesses objectively valid cognitions at all, one thereby presupposes that the objectivity of cognition is questionable at first . . ."; *Socratic Method and Critical Philosophy* (New Haven: Yale University Press, 1949), p. 190. One of the unfortunate consequences of the work of Descartes and, in the present century, the work of Bertrand Russell and Edmund Husserl, is the widely accepted supposition that questions about the justification for counting evident statements *as* evident must be *challenges* or expressions of *doubts*. See Bertrand Russell's *Problems of Philosophy* (New York: Holt, Rinehart & Winston, Inc., 1912) and his many other writings on the theory of knowledge, and E. Husserl's *Meditations Cartesiennes* (Paris: J. Vrin, 1931), also published as *Cartesianische Meditationen und Pariser Vorträge* (The Hague: Martinus Nijhoff, 1950). The objections to this approach to the concept of the evident were clearly put forth by A. Meinong; see his *Gesammelte Abhandlungen*, II (Leipzig: Johann Ambrosius Barth, 1913), p. 191. The papers by Nelson and Meinong that are here referred to are reprinted in *Empirical Knowledge: Readings from Contemporary Sources*, Roderick M. Chisholm and Robert J. Swartz, eds. (Englewood Cliffs, NJ.: Prentice Hall, Inc., 1973).

[5] According to Xenophon, Charicles said to Socrates: "You generally ask questions when you know quite well how the

matter stands; these are the questions you are not to ask."
[Memorabilia, 1, 2, 36]

[6]Sextus Empiricus, *Outlines of Pyrrhonism*, Book I, Chapter 6, in *Sextus Empiricus*, Vol. 1, The Loeb Classical Library (Cambridge: Harvard University Press, 1933).

[7]G. W. Leibniz, *New Essays Concerning Human Understanding* (La Salle, Ill.: Open Court Publishing Company, 1916), Book IV, Chapter 9.

[8]See A. Meinong, *On Emotional Presentation*, ed. and trans. M. S. Kalsi (Evanston: Northwestern University Press, 1972), sec. 1. Cf. Franz Brentano, *Psychology from an Empirical Standpoint* (London: Routledge & Kegan Paul, 1972), Chapter 2, sec. 2; C. J. Ducasse, "Propositions, Truth, and the Ultimate Criterion of Truth," *Philosophy and Phenomenological Research*, IV (1944), 317–340; William P. Alston, "Varieties of Privileged Access," in *Empirical Knowledge*, Chisholm and Swartz, eds., pp. 376–410; and Thomas J. Steel, "Knowledge and the Self-Presenting," in *Analysis and Metaphysics*, ed. Keith Lehrer (Dordrecht: D. Reidel, 1975), pp. 145–150.

[9]For other approaches to the concept of self-presentation, compare: Roderick Firth, "The Anatomy of Certainty," in *Empirical Knowledge*, Chisholm and Swartz, eds., pp. 203–223; Wilfrid Sellars, "Givenness and Explanatory Coherence," *Journal of Philosophy*, LXX (1973), 612–624; and Alston, "Varieties of Privileged Access," referred to above.

[10]Among the views that have been labeled "foundationalism" are also the following: (1) the view that some propositions are directly evident; (2) any view that makes the three presuppositions set forth above; (3) any view that raises the questions set forth at the beginning of this [section]. Compare the critique of "foundationalism" in F. L. Will, *Induction and Justification* (Ithaca: Cornell University Press, 1974). Distinction of several senses of "foundationalism" may be found in Mark Pastin, "C. I. Lewis's *Radical Phenomenalism*, Nous, IX (1975), 407–420; and William P. Alston, "Two Types of Foundationalism," *Journal of Philosophy*, LXXIII (1976), pp. 165–185.

[11]According to the theory of knowledge that is advocated by some contemporary philosophers, the view put forward in the present book is held to be one that over-emphasizes "foundationalism." Compare for example: F. L. Will, *Induction and Justification*; Keith Lehrer, *Knowledge* (London: Oxford University Press, 1974); Nicholas Rescher, *The Coherence Theory of Truth* (London: Oxford University Press, 1970); Wilfrid Sellars, *Science, Perception and Reality* (London: Routledge & Kegan Paul, 1963); "Empiricism and the Philosophy of Mind," in *Empirical Knowledge: Readings from Contemporary Sources*, R. M. Chisholm and R. J. Swartz, eds. (Englewood Cliffs, NJ.: Prentice-Hall, Inc., 1973); and "Givenness and Explanatory Coherence," *Journal of Philosophy*, LXX (1973), 612–624.

[12]For a general discussion of the epistemic significance of this relation, compare John Maynard Keynes, *A Treatise on Probability* (London: Macmillan Co., Ltd., 1952), Chapters I and 2. Compare Marsha Hanen, "Confirmation, Explanation and Acceptance," in *Analysis and Metaphysics*, ed. Keith Lehrer (Dordrecht: D. Reidel, 1975), pp. 93–128.

V.2 Contemporary Modest Foundationalism

ROBERT AUDI

Robert Audi is professor of philosophy at the University of Nebraska. In this essay Audi outlines the main theses of contemporary modest foundationalism, distinguishing it from classical foundationalism and arguing that it has "perhaps unexpected advantages" over other epistemic theories.

This essay was commissioned for the first edition of this anthology.

As I sit reading on a quiet summer evening, I sometimes hear a distinctive patter outside my open window. I immediately believe that it is raining. It may then occur to me that if I do not bring in the lawn chairs, the cushions will be soaked. But this I do not believe immediately, even if the thought strikes me in an instant; I believe it on the basis of my prior belief that it is raining. The first belief is perceptual, being grounded directly in what I hear. The second is inferential, being grounded not in what I perceive, but in what I believe: my belief that it is raining expresses a premise for my belief that the cushions will be soaked.

There are many beliefs of both kinds. Perception is a constant source of beliefs; and, from beliefs we have through perception, many arise inferentially. The latter, inferential beliefs, are then based on the former, perceptual beliefs. When I see a headlight beam cross my window and immediately believe, perceptually, that there is a bright light moving out there, I may, on the basis of that belief, come to believe, inferentially, that a car has turned into my driveway. From this proposition in turn I might infer that my doorbell is about to ring, and from that I might infer still further propositions. On the plausible assumption that knowledge implies belief, the same holds for knowledge: much of it is perceptually grounded, and much of it is inferential.[1] There is no definite limit on how many inferences one may draw in such a chain, and people differ in how many they tend to draw. Could it be, however, that despite the apparent obviousness of these points, there really *is* no non-inferential knowledge or belief, even in perceptual cases? Might every belief be based on some other and no belief be simply grounded in perception? If inference can take us forward indefinitely beyond perceptual beliefs, why may it not take us backward indefinitely from them? To see how this might occur, we must consider more systematically how beliefs arise, what justifies them, and when they are sufficiently well grounded to constitute knowledge.

I. The Sources of Belief and Knowledge

Imagine that when the rain began I had not trusted my ears. I might then have believed only that there was a pattering sound, and only on that basis, and after considering the situation, come to believe that it was raining. We need not stop here, however. For suppose I do not trust my sense of hearing at all. I might then believe only that it *seems* to me that there is a patter, and only on that basis believe that there is such a sound. All right, you may say, but surely this cannot go much further, and in fact there is no need to go even this far. But *can* we go further? What theoretical reason is there to stop at all? It is not as if we had to articulate all our beliefs. Little of what we believe is at any one time before our minds being inwardly voiced. Indeed, perhaps we can have an infinite number of beliefs, as some think we do in the case of arithmetic: we believe, it is said, such things as that 2 is larger than 1, that 3 is larger than 2, and so forth.[2] Another possibility is a cognitive circle: one believes p on the basis of q, q on the basis of r, and so on until one reaches some proposition, say z, which one believes on the basis of p. Debate about these matters continues on both the philosophy of mind and epistemology. In the philosophy of mind, the issue is whether a person's cognitive system can sustain an infinite set of beliefs or a circular cognitive chain; in epistemology, the main question is whether, even if it could, this would help in accounting for knowledge or justification.

The epistemological position associated with the view that even if there could be infinite or circular beliefs chains, they could not be sources of knowledge or justification, is foundationalism. Foundationalism is a long-established and leading view in epistemology; but despite the amount of attention it has received in the past fifteen to twenty years it has too rarely been carefully formulated and continues to be widely misunderstood.[3] Foundationalism is so called because it considers knowledge—and indeed justified belief, which is commonly regarded as a major part of knowledge—to be possible only through *foundational beliefs*. These beliefs are construed as non-inferential in the way perceptual beliefs are: based on experience rather than inference. The underlying idea is in part this: If knowledge or justified belief arises through inference, it requires belief of at least one premise, and that belief can produce knowledge or justified belief of a proposition inferred from the premise only if the premise belief is itself an instance of knowledge or at least justified. But if the premise belief is justified, it must be so by virtue of *something*—otherwise it would be self-justified, and hence a kind of foundational belief after all. If, however, experience cannot serve to justify it, then the belief must derive its justification from yet another set of premises, and the problem arises all over again: what justifies that set?

In the light of such points, the foundationalist concludes that if—as common sense would certainly have us suppose—some of our beliefs are justified or constitute knowledge, then some of our beliefs are justified, or constitute knowledge, simply because they arise (in a certain way) from experience. If we construe experience broadly enough to include logical reflection and rational intuition, then there appear to be at least four basic sources of knowledge and justified belief. Perception is one experiential source; consciousness is another and grounds, for example, my knowledge that I am thinking about the structure of justification; reflection is still another and is, for instance, the basis of my justified belief that if person A is older than B and B is older than C, then A is older than C. And memory is yet another source, because I can be justified in believing that, say, I left a light on simply by virtue of the sense of recalling my doing so.[4]

Particularly in the perceptual cases, the foundationalist tends to see experience as a mirror of nature.[5] This seems to foundationalists a good metaphor because it suggests at least two important points: first, that some experiences are *produced* by external states of the world, somewhat as light produces mirror images; and second, that (normally) the experiences in some way *match* their causes; for instance in the color and shape I sense in my visual field.[6] If I want to focus on one perceptual belief at a time, I might think of a thermometer model; it suggests both the causal connections just sketched, but also, perhaps even more than the mirror metaphor, *reliable* responses to the external world.[7] From this causal responsiveness perspective, it is at best unnatural to regard perceptual beliefs as inferential: they are not formed by inference from anything else believed, but directly reflect the objects and events that cause them. To assess foundationalism, then, we must consider whether all knowledge and all justified beliefs could arise from a regress or circle, or whether some must be non-inferential and in that sense

foundational, as where they originate in experience that reflects reality. Because even a finite circle can generate an infinite regress by repeated rotation around it, this is called the "epistemic regress problem." The foundationalist uses it to produce a supporting argument. That argument is my next concern.

II. The Epistemic Regress Argument

Let us start by formulating the regress problem more sharply and then proceed to state the regress argument which foundationalists propose as a partial solution to the problem.[8] First, suppose I have knowledge, even if only of something so simple as there being a patter outside my window. Could all my knowledge be inferential? Imagine that this is possible by virtue of an infinite epistemic regress—roughly, an infinite series of knowings, each based (inferentially) on the next. Just assume that a belief constituting inferential knowledge is based on knowledge of some other proposition, or at least on a further belief of another proposition; the further knowledge or belief might be based on knowledge of, or belief about, something still further, and so on. Call this sequence an *epistemic chain;* it is simply a chain of beliefs, with at least the first constituting knowledge, and each belief linked to the previous one by being based on it. A standard view is that there are just four kinds: an epistemic chain might be infinite or circular, hence in either case unending and in that sense regressive; third, it might terminate with a belief that is not knowledge; and fourth, it might terminate with a belief constituting direct knowledge. The epistemic regress problem is above all to assess these chains as possible sources (or at least carriers) of knowledge or justification.

The foundationalist response to the regress problem is to offer a regress argument favoring the fourth possibility as the only genuine one. The argument can be best formulated along these lines:

1.   If one has any knowledge, it occurs in an epistemic chain (possibly including the special case of a single link, such as a perceptual or *a priori* belief, which constitutes knowledge by virtue of being anchored directly in experience or reason).

2. The only possible kinds of epistemic chains are the four mutually exclusive kinds just sketched.

3. Knowledge can occur only in the last kind of chain.

4. Hence, if one has any knowledge, one has some direct knowledge.[9]

Some preliminary clarification is in order before we appraise this argument. First, the conclusion, being conditional, does not presuppose that there *is* any knowledge. This preserves neutrality with respect to skepticism, as is appropriate, because the issue concerns *conceptual* requirements for the possession of knowledge. The argument would have existential import, and so would not be purely conceptual, if it presupposed that there *is* knowledge and hence that at least one knower exists. Second, I take the first line of the argument to imply that inferential knowledge depends on at least one epistemic chain for its status *as* knowledge. I thus take the argument to imply the further conclusion that any inferential knowledge one has exhibits (inferential) *epistemic dependence* on some appropriate inferential connection, via some epistemic chain, to some non-inferential knowledge one has. Thus, the argument shows not only that if there is inferential knowledge, there *is* non-inferential knowledge; but also that if there is inferential knowledge, that very knowledge is *traceable* to some non-inferential knowledge as its foundation.

The second point suggests a third: if two epistemic chains should *intersect,* as where a belief that *p* is both foundationally grounded in experience and part of a circular chain, then if the belief is knowledge, that knowledge *occurs in* only the former chain, though the knowledge *qua belief* belongs to both chains. Knowledge, then, does not occur in a chain merely because the belief constituting it does. Fourth, the argument concerns the structure, not the content, of a body of knowledge and of its constituent epistemic chains. The argument may thus be used regardless of the purported items of knowledge to which one applies it in any particular person. It does not presuppose that, to have knowledge, there are specific things one must believe, or that a body of knowledge must have some one definite content.

A similar argument applies to justification. We simply speak of *justificatory chains* and proceed in a parallel way, substituting justification for knowledge. The conclusion would be that if there are any justified beliefs, there are some non-inferentially justified beliefs, and that if one has any inferentially justified belief, it shows (inferential) *justificatory dependence* on an epistemic chain appropriately linking it to some non-inferentially justified belief one has, that is, to a foundational belief. In discussing foundationalism, I shall often focus on justification.

Detailed assessment of the regress argument is impossible here. I shall simply comment on some important aspects of it to provide a better understanding of foundationalism and of some major objections to it.

The possibility of an infinite epistemic chain has seldom seemed to philosophers to be likely to solve the regress problem. Let me suggest one reason to think that it is doubtful that human beings are even capable of having infinite sets of beliefs. Recall the claim that we can have an infinite set of arithmetical beliefs, say that 2 is twice 1, that 4 is twice 2, and so on. Surely for a finite mind there will be some point or other at which the relevant proposition cannot be grasped. The required formulation (or entertaining of the proposition) would, at some point on the way "toward" infinity, become too lengthy to permit understanding it. Thus, even if we could read or entertain it part by part, when we got to the end we would be unable to remember enough of the first part to grasp and thereby believe what the formulation expresses. Granted, we could believe that the *formulation* just read expresses a truth; but this is not sufficient for believing the *truth* it expresses. That truth is a specific mathematical statement; believing, of a formulation we cannot even get before our minds or remember in toto, that it expresses *some* mathematical truth is not enough for believing, or even grasping, the true statement in question. Because we cannot understand the formulation as a whole, we cannot grasp that truth, and what we cannot grasp we cannot believe. I doubt that any other lines of argument show that we can have infinite sets of beliefs; nor, if we can, is it clear how infinite epistemic chains could account for any of our knowledge. I thus propose to consider only the other kinds of chain.

The possibility of a circular epistemic chain as a basis of knowledge has been taken much more seriously. The standard objection has been that such circularity is vicious, because you would ultimately have to know something on the basis of itself—say p on the basis of q, q on the basis of r, and r on the basis of p. A standard reply has been that if the circle is wide enough and its content sufficiently rich and coherent, the circularity is innocuous. I bypass this difficult matter, because I believe that coherentism as most plausibly formulated does not depend on circular chains.[10]

The third alternative, namely that an epistemic chain terminates in a belief which is not knowledge, has been at best rarely affirmed; and there is little plausibility in the hypothesis that knowledge can originate through a belief of a proposition that Person S does not know. If there are exceptions, it is where, although I do not know that p, I am justified, to *some* extent, in believing p, as in making a reasonable estimate that there are at least thirty books on a certain shelf. Here is a different case. Suppose it vaguely seems to me that I hear strains of music. If, on the basis of the resulting somewhat justified belief that there is music playing, I believe that my daughter has come home, and she has, do I know this? The answer is not clear. But that would not help anyone who claims knowledge can arise from belief which does not constitute knowledge. For it is equally unclear, and for the same sort of reason, whether my belief that there is music playing is *sufficiently* reasonable—say, in terms of how good my perceptual grounds are—to give me knowledge that music is playing. The stronger our tendency to say that I know she is home, the stronger our inclination to say that I do after all know that there are strains of music in the air. Notice something else. In the only cases where the third kind of chain seems likely to ground knowledge (or justification), there is a degree—apparently a substantial degree—of justification. If there can be an epistemic chain which ends with belief that is not knowledge only because it ends, in this way, with justification, then we are apparently in the general vicinity of knowledge. We seem to be at most a few degrees of justification away. Knowledge is not emerging from nothing, as it were (the picture originally painted by the third alternative) but from something characteristically much like it—justified true belief. There would thus be a foundation after all: not bedrock, but perhaps ground that is nonetheless firm enough to yield a foundation we can build on.

The fourth possibility is that epistemic chains that originate with knowledge end in non-inferential knowledge: knowledge not inferentially based on further knowledge (or further justified belief). That knowledge, in turn, is apparently grounded in experience, say in my auditory impression of music or my intuitive sense that if Person A is taller than B, then B is shorter than A. This non-inferential grounding of my knowledge can explain how it is (epistemically) direct: it arises non-inferentially—and so without any intermediary premise which must be known along the way—from (I shall assume) one of the four classical kinds of foundational material, namely, perception, memory, introspection, or reason.

Such direct grounding in experience (including reason) also seems to explain why a belief so grounded may be expected to be *true;* for experience seems to connect the beliefs they ground to the reality constituting their object, in such a way that what is believed about that reality tends to be the case. This, at least, seems to explain best why we have those beliefs. In any event, the ground-level knowledge could not be inferential; otherwise the chain would not end without a further link: every inference needs a premise. Let me illustrate all this. Normally when I know music is playing, that is just because I hear it; hence the chain grounding my knowledge that my daughter has come home is anchored in my auditory perception, which in turn reflects the musical reality represented by my knowledge and explains both my perception and, through that, my believing the proposition I know to be true.

The non-inferentially grounded epistemic chains in question may differ in many ways. They differ *compositionally,* in the sorts of beliefs constituting them, and *causally,* in the kind of causal relation holding between one belief and its successor. This relation, for instance, may or may not involve the predecessor belief's being necessary or sufficient for its successor: perhaps I would have believed, on grounds other than the music, my daughter was home, and perhaps not, depending on how many indications are accessible to me. Such chains also differ *structurally,* in the kind of *epistemic transmission* they show; it may be deductive, as where I infer a theorem from an axiom by rigorous rules of deductive inference, or inductive, as where I infer from a knife's good performance that other knives of that kind will also cut well; or the transmission of knowledge or justification may combine deductive and inductive elements. Epistemic chains also differ *foundationally,* in their ultimate grounds, the anchors of the chains; the grounds may, as illustrated, be perceptual or rational, and they may vary in justificational strength.

Different proponents of the fourth possibility have held various views about the character of the *foundational knowledge;* that is, the beliefs constituting the knowledge that makes up the final link and anchors the chain in experience or reason. Some, including Descartes, have thought that the appropriate beliefs must be infallible, or at least indefeasibly justified.[11] But in fact all that the fourth possibility requires is *non-inferential knowledge,* knowledge not (inferentially) based on other knowledge (or other justified belief). Non-inferential knowledge need not be of self-evident propositions, nor constituted by indefeasibly justified belief, the kind whose justification cannot be defeated. The case of introspective beliefs, which are paradigms of those that are non-inferentially justified, supports this view, and we shall see other reasons to hold it.

III. Fallibilist Foundationalism

If the regress argument is as important as I think in supporting and shaping epistemological foundationalism, then we can now formulate some foundationalist theses in the light of it. Let us start with two versions of what I shall call *generic foundationalism*. The first concerns knowledge:

I.   For any person, S, and any time, *t,* the structure of S's knowledge, at *t,* is foundational, and (thus) any inferential (hence non-foundational) knowledge S has depends on non-inferential (thus in a sense foundational) knowledge of S's.

The second position, regarding justification, is the thesis that

II.   For any S and any *t,* the structure of S's body of justified beliefs is, at *t,* foundational, and therefore any inferentially (hence non-foundationally) justified beliefs S has depend on non-inferentially (thus in a sense foundationally) justified beliefs of S's.

Different foundationalist theories may diverge in the kind and degree of dependence they assert. I especially want to contrast fallibilist (moderate) and strong foundationalist theses, particularly in the case of justification.

I take *fallibilist foundationalism,* as applied to justification, to be the inductivist thesis that

III.   For any S and any *t,* (a) the structure of S's body of justified beliefs is, at *t,* foundational in the sense indicated by thesis II; (b) the justification of S's foundational beliefs is at least typically defeasible; (c) the inferential transmission of justification need not be deductive: and (d) non-foundationally justified beliefs need not derive *all* their justification from foundational ones, but only enough so that they would remain justified if (other things remaining equal) any other justification they have (say, from coherence) were eliminated.[12]

This is fallibilistic in at least three ways: foundational beliefs may turn out to be unjustified or false or both; superstructure beliefs may be only inductively, hence fallibly, justified by foundational ones and hence can be false even when the latter are true; and the possibility of *discovering* error or lack of justification, even in foundational beliefs, is left open: they may be found to conflict either with other such beliefs with sufficiently well-supported superstructure beliefs. Even foundationalism as applied to knowledge can be fallibilistic; for granting that false propositions cannot be known, foundationalism about knowledge does not entail that someone's *grounds* for knowledge (at any level) are indefeasible. Perceptual grounds, for example, may be overridden; and one can fail (or cease) to know a proposition not because it is (or is discovered to be) false, but because one ceases to be justified in believing it.

Fallibilistic foundationalism contrasts markedly with what we might call *Cartesian foundationalism*. There are three main elements in that view. The first is *axiomatism* about foundations, the requirement (which goes back at least to Aristotle) of indubitable or clearly self-evident propositions as objects of the foundational beliefs: if I can rationally doubt that *p,* my belief of it is not strong enough to be a good foundation. The second is *deductivism* about transmission, the requirement that a superstructure belief—say, that *p*—can be justified by a foundational belief—say, that *q*—only if *p* is validly deducible from *q*. It is not enough that *p* is inductively supported by *q,* with however high probability, because then *p* could be false even if *q* is true. The third is a *second-order* requirement to the effect that, for any foundational knowledge or justified belief—for example, that one hears music—one can come to know or justifiedly believe that it *is* knowledge or justified belief; for instance, one can come to know that one does in fact know that there is music. I call this view Cartesian not because it is certain that Descartes held just this, but because something close to it is evident in his work and, almost equally important, this view has been associated with him in the literature about foundationalism. It is this third requirement that I am least confident he would hold; but in the *Meditations* there is no question that he is seeking foundations which one can *cite*, from a higher level of reflection, as certain and indubitable. For one thing, it is easier to understand the way he attempts to overcome skepticism in the way he does on the assumption that when he finds appropriate foundations, he supposes that they can be known or at least justifiedly taken to be such. Only then, he may have thought, can someone really know that the skeptic is wrong.

Fallibilist foundationalism, then, is far weaker than Cartesian foundationalism; and because the latter has been so influential in shaping philosophers' views of foundationalism in general, this point must be kept in mind in appraising the general foundationalist position. Moreover, we can construct weaker versions of foundationalism than III. For instance, one might hold only that justified foundational beliefs are necessary conditions for the existence of justified beliefs; this would allow coherence to be a necessary condition as well. One might even hold that justified foundational beliefs are not necessary but only sufficient, in which case one could have a mixed foundational theory that allows sources quite different from experience to produce justification. But I am not seeking a minimal formulation, or a mixed theory; my purpose has been only to set forth a plausible contemporary version of the theory, and, properly clarified, III will serve well as an indication of a kind of foundationalism that can be defended against the most plausible objections coherentists and others have—especially in recent decades—brought against it. Those objections have been treated elsewhere.[13] Here I shall simply point out some of the very general considerations supporting a fallibilist foundationalism.

First, the theory provides a plausible and reasonably straightforward solution to the regress problem. It selects what seems the best option among the four, and does not interpret that option in a way that makes knowledge or justification either impossible, as the skeptic would have it, or too easy to achieve, as they would be if they required no grounds at all or only grounds obtainable without the effort of observing, thinking, or in some other way taking account of experience.

Second, in working from the experiential and rational sources fallibilist foundationalism takes as basic to justification and knowledge, it accords with reflective common sense: the sorts of beliefs it says we are non-inferentially justified in holding, or can generally take to constitute non-inferential knowledge, are pretty much those which, on reflection, we think people are justified in holding, or in supposing to be knowledge, without any more than the evidence of the senses or of intuition. We do not, for instance, normally ask people for reasons to think it is raining when they can see clearly out an unobstructed window and say that it is; and if a person should give a reason, "I see it" is usually as good as any. *Prima facie*, in accepting it we are accepting an experiential, not an inferential, ground.

Third, fallibilist foundationalism is psychologically plausible, in two major ways: the account it suggests of the experiential and inferential genesis of many of our beliefs apparently fits what is known about their origins and development; and, far from positing infinite or circular belief chains, whose psychology is at least puzzling,[14] it allows (indeed encourages) a fairly simple account of the structure of cognition. Beliefs arise both from experience and from inference; some serve to unify others, especially those based on them; and their relative strengths, their changes, and their mutual interactions are all explicable within the moderate foundationalist assumptions suggested.

Fourth, fallibilist foundationalism serves to integrate our epistemology with our psychology and even biology, particularly in the crucial case of perceptual beliefs: what causally explains why we hold them—sensory experience—is also what justifies them. From an evolutionary point of view, moreover, many of the kinds of beliefs the theory takes to be non-inferentially justified—introspective and memorial beliefs as well as perceptual ones—are plainly essential to survival. We may need a map, and not merely a mirror, of the world to navigate it; but if experience does not generally mirror reality, we are in no position to move to the abstract level on which we can draw a good map. If a mirror without a map is insufficiently discriminating, a map without a mirror is insufficiently reliable.

Fifth, contrary to what has sometimes been thought about foundationalism in general, the fallibilist version is not dogmatic; on the contrary, it leads us to expect cognitive pluralism. Given that different people have different experiences, and that anyone's experiences change over time, people should be expected to differ from one another in their non-inferentially justified beliefs and, in their own case, across time; and given that logic does not dictate what is to be inferred from one's premises, people should be expected to differ considerably in their inferential beliefs as well. Logic does, to be sure, tell us what *may* be inferred, but it neither forces inferences nor, when we draw them, selects which among the permissible ones we will make. Particularly in the case of inductive inference, as where we infer a hypothesis as the best explanation of some puzzling event, our imagination comes into play; and even if we were to build from the same foundations as our neighbors, we would often produce quite different superstructures.

These points do not, of course, establish foundationalism; that is an immense task beyond any single essay. But they do bring out some perhaps unexpected advantages of a sufficiently moderate version of the theory, and I believe that, taken together with a balanced perspective on the problems besetting alternative theories—most notably coherentism—they strongly argue that a fallibilist foundationalism is a viable position to be reckoned with whatever may be someone's ultimate outlook in epistemology.

Notes

[1]That knowing a proposition implies believing it is not uncontroversial, but most epistemologists accept the implication. For defense of the implication, see e.g., Gilbert H. Harman, *Thought* (Princeton, NJ: Princeton University Press, 1973), and Robert Audi, *Belief, Justification, and Knowledge* (Belmont, CA: Wadsworth, 1988).

[2]See, e.g., Richard Foley, "Justified Inconsistent Beliefs," *American Philosophical Quarterly 16* (1979). I have criticized the infinite belief view in "Believing and Affirming," *Mind 91* (1982).

[3]For an indication of this misunderstanding see, e.g., William P. Alston, "Two Types of Foundationalism," *Journal of Philosophy 83* (1976), and my "The Architecture of Reason," *Proceedings and Addresses of the American*

Philosophical Association 62 (1988). This essay, like those, seeks to formulate foundationalism in a way that corresponds with plausible contemporary developments in the foundationalist tradition.

[4]Note that memory differs from the other three in this: it is apparently not a *basic* source of knowledge, as it is of justification; i.e., one cannot know something from memory unless one has *come* to know it in some other mode, e.g., through perception. This is discussed in Chapter 2 of my *Belief, Justification, and Knowledge* (Belmont, CA: Wadsworth, 1988). Cp. Carl Ginet, *Knowledge, Perception, and Memory* (Boston: Reidel, 1973) and George S. Pappas, "Suddenly He Knows," in Steven Luper-Foy, ed., The *Possibility of Knowledge: Nozick and His Critics* (Totowa, NJ: Rowman & Littlefield, 1987).

[5]The view that such experience is a mirror of nature is criticized at length by Richard Rorty in *Philosophy and the Mirror of Nature* (Princeton, NJ: Princeton University Press, 1979). He has in mind, however, a Cartesian version of foundationalism, which is not the only kind and which implies features of the "mirror" that are not entailed by the uses implied in this essay.

[6]This does not entail that there are *objects* in the visual field which have their own phenomenal colors and shapes; the point is only that there is some sense in which experiences *characterized by* color and shape (however that is to be analyzed) represent the colors and shapes apparently instantiated in the external world.

[7]This model comes from D. M. Armstrong. See especially *Belief, Truth and Knowledge* (Cambridge, England: Cambridge University Press, 1973). His theory of justification and knowledge is *reliabilist*, in taking both to be analyzable in terms of their being produced or sustained by reliable processes (such as tactile belief production), those that (normally) yield true beliefs more often than false. Foundationalism may, but need not, be reliabilist; and this essay is intended to be neutral with respect to the choice between reliabilist and internalist views. I have briefly sketched internalism in "Fallibilist Foundationalism and Holistic Coherentism," and I have assessed the controversy between the two kinds of theory in "Justification, Truth, and Reliability," *Philosophy and Phenomenal Research 49* (1988). For further discussion see Paul K. Moser, *Knowledge and Evidence* (New York: Cambridge University Press, 1989), and R. M. Chisholm, *Theory of Knowledge*, 3d ed. (Englewood Cliffs, NJ: Prentice-Hall, 1989).

[8]This section draws on my "Foundationalism, Coherentism, and Epistemological Dogmatism," *Philosophical Perspectives 2* (1988).

[9]The locus classicus of this argument is the *Posterior Analytics*, Book II. But while Aristotle's version agrees with the one given here insofar as his main conclusion is that "not all knowledge is demonstrative," he also says, "since the regress must end in immediate truths, those truths must be indemonstrable" (72b19–24), whereas I hold that direct knowledge does *not* require indemonstrability. There might

be appropriate premises; S's foundational belief is simply not based on them (I also question the validity of the inference in the second quotation, but I suspect Aristotle had independent grounds for its conclusion).

[10]In "Fallibilist Foundationalism and Holistic Coherentism," I set forth such a coherentism. As to circular versions, for some major difficulties they face see my "Psychological Foundationalism," *Monist 62* (1978).

[11]In Meditation I, e.g., Descartes says that "reason already persuades me that I ought no less carefully to withhold my assent from matters which are not entirely certain and indubitable than from those which appear to me manifestly to be false" (from the Haldane and Ross translation).

[12]Clause d needs the "other things being equal" clause because removal of justification from one source can affect justification from another even without being a basis of it; and the *level* of justification in question I take to be (as in

the counterpart formulation of coherentism) approximately that appropriate to knowledge. The formulation should hold, however, for any given level.

[13]For a reply to some of them, see my "Fallibilist Foundationalism and Holistic Coherentism," and for further defense of foundationalism and a wealth of relevant references, see Chisholm (1989) and Moser (1989).

[14]In "Psychological Foundationalism," *Monist 62* (1978), I argued that circular epistemic chains are at best deeply problematic; and in "Believing and Affirming," cited in note 2, I have explained some difficulties about the view that we have infinite sets of beliefs.

[15]Keith Lehrer, e.g., has maintained that foundationalism is dogmatic, in *Knowledge* (Oxford, England: Oxford University Press, 1974). I have replied to the dogmatism charge in general in "Foundationalism, Coherentism, and Epistemological Dogmatism," cited in note 8.

V.3 A Critique of Foundationalism

LAURENCE BONJOUR

Laurence BonJour is professor of philosophy at the University of Washington. After rehearsing the regress argument and foundationalism's claim to meet its challenge, BonJour distinguishes three different versions of foundationalism: (1) strong or classical foundationalism, which holds that basic beliefs yield knowledge and are infallible; (2) modest (strong) foundationalism, which holds that basic beliefs yield knowledge but are not infallible; and (3) weak foundationalism, which holds that the basic beliefs have a relatively low degree of warrant so that they need to be augmented by inferential relationships (coherence) with other minimally warranted beliefs. Weak foundationalism is a hybrid between strong foundationalism and coherence views.

At the core of the essay is BonJour's critique of foundationalism through what is sometimes called the *argument from epistemic ascent*. The argument says that regarding whatever feature we pick out as being the kind that yields proper basicality we need to ask for a justification of positing that feature, but if we do that we seem to be calling for additional justification, so that our basic beliefs aren't really foundational after all. Then BonJour takes up the two foundationalist attempts to answer this criticism: the externalist solution and the standard foundational solution, "givenness." He argues that neither is successful in meeting the problem.

Reprinted from the *American Philosophical Quarterly 15* (1978): 1–13, by permission of the editor and the author. Copyright 1978, *American Philosophical Quarterly*. [Notes edited.—Ed.]

The idea that empirical knowledge has, and must have, a *foundation* has been a common tenet of most major epistemologists, both past and present. There have been, as we shall see further below, many importantly different variants of this idea. But the common denominator among them, the central thesis of epistemological foundationism, as I shall understand it here, is the claim that certain empirical beliefs possess a degree of epistemic justification or warrant which does not depend, inferentially or otherwise, on the justification of other empirical beliefs, but is instead somehow immediate or intrinsic. It is these noninferentially justified beliefs, the unmoved (or self-moved) movers of the epistemic realm, as Chisholm has called them,[1] that constitute the foundation upon which the rest of empirical knowledge is alleged to rest.

In recent years, the most familiar foundationist views have been subjected to severe and continuous attack. But this attack has rarely been aimed directly at the central foundationist thesis itself, and new versions of foundationism have been quick to emerge, often propounded by the erstwhile critics themselves. Thus foundationism has become a philosophical hydra, difficult to come to grips with and seemingly impossible to kill. The purposes of this essay are, first, to distinguish and clarify the main dialectical variants of foundationism, by viewing them as responses to one fundamental problem which is both the main motivation and the primary obstacle for foundationism; and second, as a result of this discussion to offer schematic reasons for doubting whether any version of foundationism is finally acceptable.

The main reason for the impressive durability of foundationism is not any overwhelming plausibility attaching to the main foundationist thesis in itself, but rather the existence of one apparently decisive argument which seems to rule out all nonskeptical alternatives to foundationism, thereby showing that *some* version of foundationism must be true (on the assumption that skepticism is false). In a recent statement by Quinton, this argument runs as follows:

> If any beliefs are to be justified at all, . . . there must be some terminal beliefs that do not owe their . . . credibility to others. For a belief to be justified it is not enough for it to be accepted, let alone merely entertained: there must also be good reason for accepting

it. Furthermore, for an inferential belief to be justified the beliefs that support it must be justified themselves. There must, therefore, be a kind of belief that does not owe its justification to the support provided by others. Unless this were so no belief would be justified at all, for to justify any belief would require the antecedent justification of an infinite series of beliefs. The terminal . . . beliefs that are needed to bring the regress of justification to a stop need not be strictly self-evident in the sense that they somehow justify themselves. All that is required is that they should not owe their justification to any other beliefs.[2]

I shall call this argument the *epistemic regress argument,* and the problem which generates it, the *epistemic regress problem.* Since it is this argument which provides the primary rationale and argumentative support for foundationism, a careful examination of it will also constitute an exploration of the foundationist position itself. The main dialectical variants of foundationism can best be understood as differing attempts to solve the regress problem, and the most basic objection to the foundationist approach is that it is doubtful that any of these attempts can succeed. (In this essay, I shall be concerned with the epistemic regress argument and the epistemic regress problem only as they apply to empirical knowledge. It is obvious that an analogous problem arises also for *a priori* knowledge, but there it seems likely that the argument would take a different course. In particular, a foundationist approach might be inescapable in an account of *a priori* knowledge.)

I

This epistemic regress problem arises directly out of the traditional conception of knowledge as *adequately justified true belief*[3]—whether this be taken as a fully adequate definition of knowledge or, in light of the apparent counterexamples discovered by Gettier,[4] as merely a necessary but not sufficient condition. (I shall assume throughout that the elements of the traditional conception are at least necessary for knowledge.) Now the most natural way to justify a belief is by producing a justificatory argument: belief *A* is justified by citing some other (perhaps conjunctive) belief *B,* from which A is inferable in some acceptable way and which is thus offered as a reason for accepting A.[5] Call this *inferential justification*. It is clear, as Quinton points out in the passage quoted above, that for A to be genuinely justified by virtue of such a justificatory argument, B must itself be justified in some fashion; merely being inferable from an unsupported guess or hunch, e.g., would confer no genuine justification upon A.

Two further points about inferential justification, as understood here, must be briefly noted. First, the belief in question need not have been *arrived at* as the result of an inference in order to be inferentially justified. This is obvious, since a belief arrived at in some other way (e.g., as a result of wishful thinking) may later come to be maintained solely because it is now seen to be inferentially justifiable. Second, less obviously, a person for whom a belief is inferentially justified need not have explicitly rehearsed the justificatory argument in question to others or even to himself. It is enough that the inference be available to him if the belief is called into question by others or by himself (where such availability may itself be less than fully explicit) and that the availability of the inference be, in the final analysis, his reason for holding the belief. It seems clear that many beliefs which are quite sufficiently justified to satisfy the justification criterion for knowledge depend for their justification on inferences which have not been explicitly formulated and indeed which could not be explicitly formulated without considerable reflective effort (e.g., my current belief that this is the same piece of paper upon which I was typing yesterday).

Suppose then that belief A is (putatively) justified via inference, thus raising the question of how the justifying premise-belief B is justified. Here again the answer may be in inferential terms: B may be (putatively) justified in virtue of being inferable from some further belief C. But then the same question arises about the justification of C, and so on, threatening an infinite and apparently vicious regress of epistemic justification. Each belief is justified only if an epistemically prior belief is justified, and that epistemically prior belief is justified only if a still prior belief is justified, etc., with the apparent result that justification can never get started—and hence that there is no justification and no knowledge. The foundationist claim is that only through the adoption of some version of

foundationism can this skeptical consequence be avoided.

Prima facie, there seem to be only four basic possibilities with regard to the eventual outcome of this potential regress of epistemic justification: (i) the regress might terminate with beliefs for which no justification of any kind is available, even though they were earlier offered as justifying premises; (ii) the regress might proceed infinitely backwards with ever more new premise-beliefs being introduced and then themselves requiring justification; (iii) the regress might circle back upon itself, so that at some point beliefs which appeared earlier in the sequence of justifying arguments are appealed to again as premises; (iv) the regress might terminate because beliefs are reached which are justified—unlike those in alternative (i)—but whose justification does not depend inferentially on other empirical beliefs and thus does not raise any further issue of justification with respect to such beliefs. The foundationist opts for the last alternative. His argument is that the other three lead inexorably to the skeptical result, and that the second and third have additional fatal defects as well, so that some version of the fourth, foundationist alternative must be correct (assuming that skepticism is false).

With respect to alternative (i), it seems apparent that the foundationist is correct. If this alternative were correct, empirical knowledge would rest ultimately on beliefs which were, from an epistemic standpoint at least, entirely arbitrary and hence incapable of conferring any genuine justification. What about the other two alternatives?

The argument that alternative (ii) leads to a skeptical outcome has in effect already been sketched in the original formulation of the problem. One who opted for this alternative could hope to avoid skepticism only by claiming that the regress, though infinite, is not vicious; but there seems to be no plausible way to defend such a claim. Moreover, a defense of an infinite regress view as an account of how empirical knowledge is actually justified—as opposed to how it might in principle be justified—would have to involve the seemingly dubious thesis that an ordinary knower holds a literally infinite number of distinct beliefs. Thus it is not surprising that no important philosopher, with the rather uncertain exception of Peirce, seems to have advocated such a position.

Alternative (iii), the view that justification ultimately moves in a closed curve, has been historically more prominent, albeit often only as a dialectical foil for foundationism. At first glance, this alternative might seem even less attractive than the second. Although the problem of the knower having to have an infinite number of beliefs is no longer present, the regress itself, still infinite, now seems undeniably vicious. For the justification of each of the beliefs which figure in the circle seems now to presuppose *its own* epistemically prior justification: such a belief must, paradoxically, be justified before it can be justified. Advocates of views resembling alternative (iii) have generally tended to respond to this sort of objection by adopting a holistic conception of justification in which the justification of individual beliefs is subordinated to that of the closed systems of beliefs which such a view implies; the property of such systems usually appealed to as a basis for justification is internal *coherence*. Such coherence theories attempt to evade the regress problem by abandoning the view of justification as essentially involving a linear order of dependence (though a nonlinear view of justification has never been worked out in detail).[6] Moreover, such a coherence theory of empirical knowledge is subject to a number of other familiar and seemingly decisive objections. Thus alternative (iii) seems unacceptable, leaving only alternative (iv), the foundationist alternative, as apparently viable.

As thus formulated, the epistemic regress argument makes an undeniably persuasive case for foundationism. Like any argument by elimination, however, it cannot be conclusive until the surviving alternative has itself been carefully examined. The foundationist position may turn out to be subject to equally serious objections, thus forcing a reexamination of the other alternatives, a search for a further non-skeptical alternative, or conceivably the reluctant acceptance of the skeptical conclusion. In particular, it is not clear on the basis of the argument thus far whether and how foundationism can itself solve the regress problem; and thus the possibility exists that the epistemic regress argument will prove to be a two-edged sword, as lethal to the foundationist as it is to his opponents.

II

The most straightforward interpretation of alternative (iv) leads directly to a view which I will here call *strong foundationism*. According to strong foundationism, the foundational beliefs which terminate the regress of justification possess sufficient epistemic warrant, independently of any appeal to inference from (or coherence with) other empirical beliefs, to satisfy the justification condition of knowledge and qualify as acceptable justifying premises for further beliefs. Since the justification of these *basic beliefs*, as they have come to be called, is thus allegedly not dependent on that of any other empirical belief, they are uniquely able to provide secure starting-points for the justification of empirical knowledge and stopping-points for the regress of justification.

The position just outlined is in fact a fairly modest version of strong foundationism. Strong foundationists have typically made considerably stronger claims on behalf of basic beliefs. Basic beliefs have been claimed not only to have sufficient non-inferential justification to qualify as knowledge, but also to be *certain, infallible, indubitable,* or *incorrigible* (terms which are usually not very carefully distinguished). And most of the major attacks on foundationism have focused on these stronger claims. Thus it is important to point out that nothing about the basic strong foundationist response to the regress problem demands that basic beliefs be more than adequately justified. There might of course be other reasons for requiring that basic beliefs have some more exalted epistemic status or for thinking that in fact they do. There might even be some sort of indirect argument to show that such a status is a consequence of the sorts of epistemic properties which are directly required to solve the regress problem. But until such an argument is given (and it is doubtful that it can be), the question of whether basic beliefs are or can be certain, infallible, etc., will remain a relatively unimportant side-issue.

Indeed, many recent foundationists have felt that even the relatively modest version of strong foundationism outlined above is still too strong. Their alternative, still within the general aegis of the foundationist position, is a view which may be called *weak foundationism*. Weak foundationism accepts the central idea of foundationism—viz.

that certain empirical beliefs possess a degree of independent epistemic justification or warrant which does not derive inference or coherence relations. But the weak foundationist holds that these foundational beliefs have only a quite low degree of warrant, much lower than that attributed to them by even modest strong foundationism and insufficient by itself to satisfy the justification condition for knowledge or to qualify them as acceptable justifying premises for other beliefs. Thus this independent warrant must somehow be augmented if knowledge is to be achieved, and the usual appeal here is to coherence with other such minimally warranted beliefs. By combining such beliefs into larger and larger coherent systems, it is held, their initial, minimal degree of warrant can gradually be enhanced until knowledge is finally achieved. Thus weak foundationism, like the pure coherence theories mentioned above, abandons the linear conception of justification.[7]

Weak foundationism thus represents a kind of hybrid between strong foundationism and the coherence views discussed earlier, and it is often thought to embody the virtues of both and the vices of neither. Whether or not this is so in other respects, however, relative to the regress problem weak foundationism is finally open to the very same basic objection as strong foundationism, with essentially the same options available for meeting it. As we shall see, the key problem for any version of foundationism is whether it can itself solve the regress problem which motivates its very existence, without resorting to essentially *ad hoc* stipulation. The distinction between the two main ways of meeting this challenge both cuts across and is more basic than that between strong and weak foundationism. This being so, it will suffice to concentrate here on strong foundationism, leaving the application of the discussion to weak foundationism largely implicit.

The fundamental concept of strong foundationism is obviously the concept of a basic belief. It is by appeal to this concept that the threat of an infinite regress is to be avoided and empirical knowledge given a secure foundation. But how can there be any empirical beliefs which are thus basic? In fact, though this has not always been noticed, the very idea of an epistemically basic empirical belief is extremely paradoxical. For on what basis is such a belief to be justified, once appeal to further empirical beliefs is ruled out?

Chisholm's theological analogy, cited earlier, is most appropriate: a basic belief is in effect an epistemological unmoved (or self-moved) mover. It is able to confer justification on other beliefs, but apparently has no need to have justification conferred on it. But is such a status any easier to understand in epistemology than it is in theology? How can a belief impart epistemic "motion" to other beliefs unless it is itself in "motion"? And, even more paradoxically, how can a belief epistemically "move" itself?

This intuitive difficulty with the concept of a basic empirical belief may be elaborated and clarified by reflecting a bit on the concept of epistemic justification. The idea of justification is a generic one, admitting in principle of many specific varieties. Thus the acceptance of an empirical belief might be morally justified, i.e., justified as morally obligatory by reference to moral principles and standards; or pragmatically justified, i.e., justified by reference to the desirable practical consequences which will result from such acceptance; or religiously justified, i.e., justified by reference to specified religious texts or theological dogmas; etc. But none of these other varieties of justification can satisfy the justification condition for knowledge. Knowledge requires *epistemic* justification, and the distinguishing characteristic of this particular species of justification is, I submit, its essential or internal relationship to the cognitive goal of truth. Cognitive doings are epistemically justified, on this conception, only if and to the extent that they are aimed at this goal—which means roughly that one accepts all and only beliefs which one has good reason to think are true. To accept a belief in the absence of such a reason, however appealing or even mandatory such acceptance might be from other standpoints, is to neglect the pursuit of truth; such acceptance is, one might say, *epistemically irresponsible*. My contention is that the idea of being epistemically responsible is the core of the concept of epistemic justification.

A corollary of this conception of epistemic justification is that a satisfactory defense of a particular standard of epistemic justification must consist in showing it to be truth-conducive, i.e., in showing that accepting beliefs in accordance with its dictates is likely to lead to truth (and more likely than any proposed alternative). Without such a meta-justification, a proposed standard of epistemic justification lacks any underlying rationale. Why after all should an epistemically responsible inquirer prefer justified beliefs to unjustified ones, if not that the former are more likely to be true? To insist that a certain belief is epistemically justified, while confessing in the same breath that this fact about it provides no good reason to think that it is true, would be to render nugatory the whole concept of epistemic justification.

These general remarks about epistemic justification apply in full measure to any strong foundationist position and to its constituent account of basic beliefs. If basic beliefs are to provide a secure foundation for empirical knowledge, if inference from them is to be the sole basis for the justification of other empirical beliefs, then that feature, whatever it may be, in virtue of which a belief qualifies as basic must also constitute a good reason for thinking that the belief is true. If we let "F" represent this feature, then for a belief B to qualify as basic in an acceptable foundationist account, the premises of the following justificatory argument must themselves be at least justified:

(i)   Belief B has feature Φ.
(ii) Beliefs having feature Φ are highly likely to be true.
Therefore, B is highly likely to be true.

Notice further that while either premise taken separately might turn out to be justifiable on an *a priori* basis (depending on the particular choice of F), it seems clear that they could not both be thus justifiable. For B is *ex hypothesi* an empirical belief, and it is hard to see how a particular empirical belief could be justified on a purely *a priori* basis. And if we now assume, reasonably enough, that for B to be justified for a particular person (at a particular time) it is necessary, not merely that a justification for B exist in the abstract, but that the person in question be in cognitive possession of that justification, we get the result that B is not basic after all since its justification depends on that of at least one other empirical belief. If this is correct, strong foundationism is untenable as a solution to the regress problem (and an analogous argument will show weak foundationism to be similarly untenable).

The foregoing argument is, no doubt, exceedingly obvious. But how is the strong foundationist to answer it? *Prima facie,* there seem to be only two general sorts of answer which are even remotely plausible, so long as the strong foundationist remains within the confines of the traditional conception of knowledge, avoids tacitly embracing skepticism, and does not attempt the heroic task of arguing that an empirical belief could be justified on a purely *a priori* basis. First, he might argue that although it is indeed necessary for a belief to be justified and *a fortiori* for it to be basic that a justifying argument of the sort schematized above be in principle available in the situation, it is *not* always necessary that the person for whom the belief is basic (or anyone else) know or even justifiably believe that it is available; instead, in the case of basic beliefs at least, it is sufficient that the premises for an argument of that general sort (or for some favored particular variety of such argument) merely be *true,* whether or not that person (or anyone else) justifiably believes that they are true. Second, he might grant that it is necessary both that such justification exist and that the person for whom the belief is basic be in cognitive possession of it, but insist that his cognitive grasp of the premises required for that justification does not involve further empirical beliefs which would then require justification, but instead involves cognitive states of a more rudimentary sort which do not themselves require justification: *intuitions or immediate apprehensions.* I will consider each of these alternatives in turn.

III

The philosopher who has come the closest to an explicit advocacy of the view that basic beliefs may be justified even though the person for whom they are basic is not in any way in cognitive possession of the appropriate justifying argument is D. M. Armstrong. In his recent book, *Belief, Truth and Knowledge,* Armstrong presents a version of the epistemic regress problem (though one couched in terms of knowledge rather than justification) and defends what he calls an "Externalist" solution:

> According to 'Externalist' accounts of non-inferential knowledge, what makes a true non-inferential belief a case of *knowledge* is some natural relation which holds between the belief-state . . . and the situation which makes the belief true. It is a matter of a certain relation holding between the believer and the world [157].

Armstrong's own candidate for this "natural relation" is "that there must be a *law-like connection* between the state of affairs *Bap* [i.e. *a*'s believing that *p*] and the state of affairs that makes '*p*' true such that, given *Bap*, it must be the case that *p*." [166] A similar view seems to be implicit in Dretske's account of perceptual knowledge in *Seeing and Knowing*, with the variation that Dretske requires for knowledge not only that the relation in question obtain, but also that the putative knower *believe* that it obtains—though *not* that this belief be justified. In addition, it seems likely that various views of an ordinary-language stripe which appeal to facts about how language is learned either to justify basic belief or to support the claim that no justification is required would, if pushed, turn out to be positions of this general sort. Here I shall mainly confine myself to Armstrong, who is the only one of these philosophers who is explicitly concerned with the regress problem.

There is, however, some uncertainty as to how views of this sort in general and Armstrong's view in particular are properly to be interpreted. On the one hand, Armstrong might be taken as offering an account of how basic beliefs (and perhaps others as well) satisfy the adequate-justification condition for knowledge; while on the other hand, he might be taken as simply repudiating the traditional conception of knowledge and the associated concept of epistemic justification, and offering a surrogate conception in its place—one which better accords with the "naturalistic" world-view which Armstrong prefers. But it is only when understood in the former way that externalism (to adopt Armstrong's useful term) is of any immediate interest here, since it is only on that interpretation that it constitutes a version of foundationism and offers a direct response to the anti-foundationist argument set out above. Thus I shall mainly focus on this interpretation of externalism, remarking only briefly at the end of the present section on the alternative one.

Understood in this way, the externalist solution to the regress problem is quite simple: the person who has a basic belief need not be in possession of any justified reason for his belief and indeed, except in Dretske's version, need not even think that there is such a reason; the status of his belief as constituting knowledge (if true) depends solely on the external relation and not at all on his subjective view of the situation. Thus there are no further empirical beliefs in need of justification and no regress.

Now it is clear that such an externalist position succeeds in avoiding the regress problem and the anti-foundationist argument. What may well be doubted, however, is whether this avoidance deserves to be considered a *solution*, rather than an essentially *ad hoc* evasion, of the problem. Plainly the sort of "external" relation which Armstrong has in mind would, if known, provide a basis for a justifying argument along the lines sketched earlier, roughly as follows:

> **(i)**   Belief *B* is an instance of kind *K*.
> **(ii)**   Beliefs of kind *K* are connected in a law-like way with the sorts of states of affairs which would make them true, and therefore are highly likely to be true.
> Therefore, *B* is highly likely to be true.

But precisely what generates the regress problem in the first place is the requirement that for a belief *B* to be epistemically justified for a given person *P*, it is necessary, not just that there be justifiable or even true premises available in the situation which could in principle provide a basis for a justification of *B*, but that *P* himself know or at least justifiably believe some such set of premises and thus be in a position to employ the corresponding argument. The externalist position seems to amount merely to waiving this general requirement in cases where the justification takes a certain form, and the question is why this should be acceptable in these cases when it is not acceptable generally. (If it were acceptable generally, then it would seem that any true belief would be justified for any person, and the distinction between knowledge and true belief would collapse.) Such a move seems rather analogous to solving a regress of causes by simply stipulating that although most events must have a cause, events of a certain kind need not.

Whatever plausibility attaches to externalism seems to derive from the fact that if the external relation in question genuinely obtains, then *P* will not go wrong in accepting the belief, and it is, in a sense, not an accident that this is so. But it remains unclear how these facts are supposed to justify *P*'s acceptance of *B*. It is clear, of course, that an external observer who knew both that *P* accepted *B* and that there was a law-like connection between such acceptance and the truth of *B* would be in a position to construct an argument to justify *his own* acceptance of *B*. *P* could thus serve as a useful epistemic instrument, a kind of cognitive thermometer, for such an external observer (and in fact the example of a thermometer is exactly the analogy which Armstrong employs to illustrate the relationship which is supposed to obtain between the person who has the belief and the external state of affairs [166ff.]). But *P* himself has no reason at all for thinking that *B* is likely to be true. From his perspective, it *is* an accident that the belief is true.[8] And thus his acceptance of *B* is no more rational or responsible from an epistemic standpoint than would be the acceptance of a subjectively similar belief for which the external relation in question failed to obtain.[9]

Nor does it seem to help matters to move from Armstrong's version of externalism, which requires only that the requisite relationship between the believer and the world obtain, to the superficially less radical version apparently held by Dretske, which requires that *P* also believe that the external relation obtains, but does not require that this latter belief be justified. This view may seem slightly less implausible, since it at least requires that the person have some idea, albeit unjustified, of why *B* is likely to be true. But this change is not enough to save externalism. One way to see this is to suppose that the person believes the requisite relation to obtain on some totally irrational and irrelevant basis, e.g. as a result of reading tea leaves or studying astrological charts. If *B* were an ordinary, non-basic belief, such a situation would surely preclude its being justified, and it is hard to see why the result should be any different for an allegedly basic belief.

Thus it finally seems possible to make sense of externalism only by construing the externalist as simply abandoning the traditional notion of epistemic justification and along with it anything resembling the traditional conception of knowledge. (As already remarked, this may be precisely what the proponents of externalism intend to be doing, though most of them are not very clear on this point.) Thus consider Armstrong's final summation of his conception of knowledge:

Knowledge of the truth of particular matters of fact is a belief which must be true, where the "must" is a matter of law-like necessity.

Such knowledge is a reliable representation or "mapping" of reality [220].

Nothing is said here of reasons or justification or evidence or having the right to be sure. Indeed the whole idea, central to the western epistemological tradition, of knowledge as essentially the product of reflective, critical, and rational inquiry has seemingly vanished without a trace. It is possible of course that such an altered conception of knowledge may be inescapable or even in some way desirable, but it constitutes a solution to the regress problem or any problem arising out of the traditional conception of knowledge only in the radical and relatively uninteresting sense that to reject that conception is also to reject the problems arising out of it. In this essay, I shall confine myself to less radical solutions.

IV

The externalist solution just discussed represents a very recent approach to the justification of basic beliefs. The second view to be considered is, in contrast, so venerable that it deserves to be called the standard foundationist solution to the problem in question. I refer of course to the traditional doctrine of cognitive givenness, which has played a central role in epistemological discussions at least since Descartes. In recent years, however, the concept of the given, like foundationism itself, has come under serious attack. One upshot of the resulting discussion has been a realization that there are many different notions of givenness, related to each other in complicated ways, which almost certainly do not stand or fall together. Thus it will be well to begin by formulating the precise notion of givenness which is relevant in the present context and distinguishing it from some related conceptions.

In the context of the epistemic regress problem, givenness amounts to the idea that basic beliefs are justified by reference not to further *beliefs*, but rather to states of affairs in the world which are "immediately apprehended" or "directly presented" or "intuited." This justification by reference to non-cognitive states of affairs thus allegedly avoids the need for any further justification and thereby stops the regress. In a way, the basic gambit of givenism (as I shall call positions of this sort) thus resembles that of the externalist positions considered above. In both cases the justificatory appeal to further beliefs which generates the regress problem is avoided for basic beliefs by an appeal directly to the non-cognitive world; the crucial difference is that for the givenist, unlike the externalist, the justifying state of affairs in the world is allegedly apprehended *in some way* by the believer.

The givenist position to be considered here is significantly weaker than more familiar versions of the doctrine of givenness in at least two different respects. In the first place, the present version does not claim that the given (or, better, the apprehension thereof) is certain or even incorrigible. As discussed above, these stronger claims are inessential to the strong foundationist solution to the regress problem. If they have any importance at all in this context it is only because, as we shall see, they might be thought to be entailed by the only very obvious intuitive picture of how the view is supposed to work. In the second place, givenism as understood here does not involve the usual stipulation that only one's private mental and sensory states can be given. There may or may not be other reasons for thinking that this is in fact the case, but such a restriction is not part of the position itself. Thus both positions like that of C. I. Lewis, for whom the given is restricted to private states apprehended with certainty, and positions like that of Quinton, for whom ordinary physical states of affairs are given with no claim of certainty or incorrigibility being involved, will count as versions of givenism.

As already noted, the idea of givenness has been roundly criticized in recent philosophical discussion and widely dismissed as a piece of philosophical mythology. But much at least of this criticism has to do with the claim of certainty on behalf of the given or with the restriction to private, subjective states. And some of it at least has been mainly concerned with issues in the philosophy of mind which are only distantly related to our present epistemological concerns. Thus even if the objections offered are cogent against other and stronger versions of givenness, it remains unclear whether and how they apply to the more modest version at issue here. The possibility suggests itself that modest givenness may not be a myth, even if more ambitious varieties are, a result which would give the epistemological foundationist all he really needs, even though he has usually, in a spirit of philosophical greed, sought considerably more. In what follows, however, I shall sketch a line of argument which, if correct, will show that even modest givenism is an untenable position.

The argument to be developed depends on a problem within the givenist position which is surprisingly easy to overlook. I shall therefore proceed in the following way. I shall first state the problem in an initial way, then illustrate it by showing how it arises in one recent version of givenism, and finally consider whether any plausible solution is possible. (It will be useful for the purposes of this discussion to make two simplifying assumptions, without which the argument would be more complicated, but not essentially altered. First, I shall assume that the basic belief which is to be justified by reference to the given or immediately apprehended state of affairs is just the belief that this same state of affairs obtains. Second, I shall assume that the given or immediately apprehended state of affairs is not itself a belief or other cognitive state.)

Consider then an allegedly basic belief that-p which is supposed to be justified by reference to a given or immediately apprehended state of affairs that-p. Clearly what justifies the belief is not the state of affairs simpliciter, for to say that would be to return to a form of externalism. For the givenist, what justifies the belief is the *immediate apprehension* or *intuition* of the state of affairs. Thus we seem to have three items present in the situation: the belief, the state of affairs which is the object of the belief, and the intuition or immediate apprehension of that state of affairs. The problem to be raised revolves around the nature of the last of these items, the intuition or immediate apprehension (hereafter I will use mainly the former term). It *seems* to be a cognitive state, perhaps somehow of a more rudimentary sort than a belief, which involves the thesis or assertion that-p. Now if this is correct, it is easy enough to understand in a rough sort of way how an intuition can serve to justify a belief with this same assertive content. The problem is to understand why the intuition, involving as it does the cognitive thesis that-p, does not *itself* require justification. And if the answer is offered that the intuition is justified by reference to the state of affairs that-p, then the question will be why this would not require a second intuition or other apprehension of the state of affairs to justify the original one. For otherwise one and the same cognitive state must somehow constitute both an apprehension of the state of affairs and a justification of that very apprehension, thus pulling itself up by its own cognitive bootstraps. One is reminded here of Chisholm's claim that certain cognitive states justify themselves but that extremely paradoxical remark hardly constitutes an explanation of how this is possible.

If, on the other hand, an intuition is not a cognitive state and thus involves no cognitive grasp of the state of affairs in question, then the need for a justification for the intuition is obviated, but at the serious cost of making it difficult to see how the intuition is supposed to justify the belief. If the person in question has no cognitive grasp of that state of affairs (or of any other) by virtue of having such an intuition, then how does the intuition give him a *reason* for thinking that his belief is true or likely to be true? We seem again to be back to an externalist position, which it was the whole point of the category of intuition or givenness to avoid.

As an illustration of this problem, consider Quinton's version of givenism, as outlined in his book *The Nature of Things*. As noted above, basic beliefs may, according to Quinton, concern ordinary perceptible states of affairs and need not be certain or incorrigible. (Quinton uses the phrase "intuitive belief" as I have been using "basic belief" and calls the linguistic expression of an intuitive belief a "basic statement"; he also seems to pay very little attention to the difference between beliefs and statements, shifting freely back and forth between them, and I will generally follow him in this.) Thus "this book is red" might, in an appropriate context, be a basic statement expressing a basic or intuitive belief. But how are such basic statements (or the correlative beliefs) supposed to be justified? Here Quinton's account, beyond the insistence that they are not justified by reference to further beliefs, is seriously unclear. He says rather vaguely that the person is "aware" [129] or "directly aware" [139] of the appropriate state of affairs, or that he has "direct knowledge" [126] of it, but he gives no real account of the nature or epistemological status of this state of "direct awareness" or "direct knowledge," though it seems clear that it is supposed to be a cognitive state of some kind. (In particular, it is not clear what "direct" means, over and above "non-inferential.")

The difficulty with Quinton's account comes out most clearly in his discussion of its relation to the correspondence theory of truth:

> The theory of basic statements is closely connected with the correspondence theory of truth. In its classical form that theory holds that to each true statement, whatever its form may be, a fact of the same form corresponds. The theory of basic statements indicates the point at which correspondence is established, at which the system of beliefs makes its justifying contact with the world [139].

And further on he remarks that the truth of basic statements "is directly determined by their correspondence with fact" [143]. (It is clear that "determined" here means "epistemically determined.") Now it is a familiar but still forceful idealist objection to the correspondence theory of truth that if the theory were correct we could never know whether any of our beliefs were true, since we have no perspective outside our system of beliefs from which to see that they do or do not correspond. Quinton, however, seems to suppose rather blithely that intuition or direct awareness provides just such a perspective, from which we can in some cases apprehend both beliefs and the world and judge whether or not they correspond. And he further supposes that the issue of justification somehow does not arise for apprehensions made from this perspective, though without giving any account of how or why this is so.

My suggestion here is that no such account can be given. As indicated above, the givenist is caught in a fundamental dilemma: if his intuitions or immediate apprehensions are construed as cognitive, then they will be both capable of giving justification and in need of it themselves; if they are non-cognitive, then they do not need justification but are also apparently incapable of providing it. This, at bottom, is why epistemological givenness is a myth.

Once the problem is clearly realized, the only possible solution seems to be to split the difference by claiming that an intuition is a semi-cognitive or quasi-cognitive state, which resembles a belief in its capacity to confer justification, while differing from a belief in not requiring justification itself. In fact, some such conception seems to be implicit in most if not all givenist positions. But when stated thus baldly, this "solution" to the problem seems hopelessly contrived and *ad hoc*. If such a move is acceptable, one is inclined to expostulate, then once again any sort of regress could be solved in similar fashion. Simply postulate a final term in the regress which is sufficiently similar to the previous terms to satisfy, with respect to the penultimate term, the sort of need or impetus which originally generated the regress; but which is different enough from previous terms so as not itself to require satisfaction by a further term. Thus we would have semi-events, which could cause but need not be caused; semi-explanatia, which could explain but need not be explained; and semi-beliefs, which could justify but need not be justified. The point is not that such a move is always incorrect (though I suspect that it is), but simply that the nature and possibility of such a convenient regress-stopper needs at the very least to be clearly and convincingly established and explained before it can constitute a satisfactory solution to any regress problem.

The main account which has usually been offered by givenists of such semi-cognitive states is well suggested by the terms in which immediate or intuitive apprehensions are described: "immediate," "direct," "presentation," etc. The underlying idea here is that of *confrontation*: in intuition, mind or consciousness is directly confronted with its object, without the intervention of any sort of intermediary. It is in this sense that the object is *given* to the mind. The root metaphor underlying this whole picture is vision: mind or consciousness is likened to an immaterial eye, and the object of intuitive awareness is that which is directly before the mental eye and open to its gaze. If this metaphor were to be taken seriously, it would become relatively simple to explain how there can be a cognitive state which can justify but does not require justification. (If the metaphor is to be taken seriously enough to do the foundationist any real good, it becomes plausible to hold that the intuitive cognitive states which result would after all have to be infallible. For if all need for justification is to be precluded, the envisaged relation of confrontation seemingly must be conceived as too intimate to allow any possibility of error. To the extent that this is so, the various arguments which have been offered against the notion of infallible cognitive states count also against this version of givenism.)

Unfortunately, however, it seems clear that the mental eye metaphor will not stand serious scrutiny. The mind, whatever else it may be, is not an eye or, so far as we know, anything like an eye. Ultimately the metaphor is just far too simple to be even minimally adequate to the complexity of mental phenomena and to the variety of conditions upon which such phenomena depend. This is not to deny that there is considerable intuitive appeal to the confrontational model, especially as applied to perceptual consciousness, but only to insist that this appeal is far too vague in its import to adequately support the very specific sorts of epistemological results which the strong foundationist needs. In particular, even if empirical knowledge at some point involves some sort of confrontation or seeming confrontation, this by itself provides no clear reason for attributing epistemic justification or reliability, let alone certainty, to the cognitive states, whatever they may be called, which result.

Moreover, quite apart from the vicissitudes of the mental eye metaphor, there are powerful independent reasons for thinking that the attempt to defend givenism by appeal to the idea of a semi-cognitive or quasi-cognitive state is fundamentally misguided. The basic idea, after all, is to distinguish two aspects of a cognitive state, its capacity to justify other states and its own need for justification, and then try to find a state which possesses only the former aspect and not the latter. But it seems clear on reflection that these two aspects cannot be separated, that it is one and the same feature of a cognitive state, viz., its assertive content, which both enables it to confer justification on other states and also requires that it be justified itself. If this is right, then it does no good to introduce semi-cognitive states in an attempt to justify basic beliefs, since to whatever extent such a state is capable of conferring justification, it will to that very same extent require justification. Thus even if such states do exist, they are of no help to the givenist in attempting to answer the objection at issue here.

Hence the givenist response to the anti-foundationist argument seems to fail. There seems to be no way to explain how a basic cognitive state, whether called a belief or an intuition, can be directly justified by the world without lapsing back into externalism—and from there into skepticism. I shall conclude with three further comments aimed at warding off certain likely sorts of misunderstanding. First. It is natural in this connection to attempt to justify basic beliefs by appealing to *experience*. But there is a familiar ambiguity in the term "experience," which in fact glosses over the crucial distinction upon which the foregoing argument rests. Thus "experience" may mean either an *experiencing* (i.e., a cognitive state) or something *experienced* (i.e., an object of cognition). And once this ambiguity is resolved, the concept of experience seems to be of no particular help to the givenist. Second. I have concentrated, for the sake of simplicity, on Quinton's version of givenism in which ordinary physical states of affairs are among the things which are given. But the logic of the argument would be essentially the same if it were applied to a more traditional version like Lewis's in which it is private experiences which are given; and I cannot see that the end result would be different—though it might be harder to discern, especially in cases where the allegedly basic belief is a belief about another cognitive state. Third. Notice carefully that the problem raised here with respect to givenism is a logical problem (in a broad sense of "logical"). Thus it would be a mistake to think that it can be solved simply by indicating some sort of state which seems intuitively to have the appropriate sorts of characteristics; the problem is to understand how it is *possible* for any state to have those characteristics. (The mistake would be analogous to one occasionally made in connection with the free-will problem: the mistake of attempting to solve the logical problem of how an action can be not determined but also not merely random by indicating a subjective act of effort or similar state, which seems intuitively to satisfy such a description.)

Thus foundationism appears to be doomed by its own internal momentum. No account seems to be available of how an empirical belief can be genuinely justified in an epistemic sense, while avoiding all reference to further empirical beliefs or cognitions which themselves would require justification. How then is the epistemic regress problem to be solved? The natural direction to look for an answer is to the coherence theory of empirical knowledge and the associated non-linear conception of justification which were briefly mentioned above. But arguments by elimination are dangerous at best: there may be further alternatives which have not yet been formulated, and the possibility

still threatens that the epistemic regress problem may in the end be of aid and comfort only to the skeptic.

Notes

[1] Roderick M. Chisholm, *Theory of Knowledge*, 1st. ed., p. 30.

[2] Anthony Quinton, *The Nature of Things*, p. 119. This is an extremely venerable argument, which has played a central role in epistemological discussion at least since Artistotle's statement of it in the *Posterior Analytics*, Book I, ch. 2–3. (Some have found an anticipation of the argument in the *Theaetetus* at 209E–210B, but Plato's worry in that passage appears to be that the proposed definition of knowledge is circular, not that it leads to an infinite regress of justification.)

[3] "Adequately justified" because a belief could be justified to some degree without being sufficiently justified to qualify as knowledge (if true). But it is far from clear just how much justification is needed for adequacy. Virtually all recent epistemologists agree that certainty is not required. But the lottery paradox shows that adequacy cannot be understood merely in terms of some specified level of probability. (For a useful account of the lottery paradox, see Robert Ackermann, *Belief and Knowledge*, pp. 39–50). Armstrong, in *Belief, Truth and Knowledge*, argues that what is required is that one's reasons for the belief be "conclusive," but the precise meaning of this is less than clear. Ultimately, it may be that the concept of knowledge is simply too crude for refined epistemological discussion, so that it may be necessary to speak instead of degrees of belief and corresponding degrees of justification. I shall assume (perhaps controversially) that the proper solution to this problem will not affect the issues to be discussed here, and speak merely of the reasons or justification making the belief *highly likely* to be true, without trying to say exactly what this means.

[4] See Edmund Gettier, "Is Justified True Belief Knowledge?" [Reading IV.1—Ed.]. Also Ackermann, *Belief and Knowledge*, chap. 5, and the corresponding references.

[5] For simplicity, I will speak of inference relations as obtaining between beliefs rather than, more accurately, between the propositions which are believed. "Inference" is to be understood here in a very broad sense; any relation between two beliefs which allows one, if accepted, to serve as a good reason for accepting the other will count as inferential.

[6] The original statement of the non-linear view was by Bernard Bosanquet in *Implication and Linear Inference* (London, 1920). For more recent discussions, see Gilbert Harman, *Thought*; and Nicholas Rescher, "Foundationalism, Coherentism, and the Idea of Cognitive Systematization."

[7]For discussions of weak foundationism, see Bertrand Russell, *Human Knowledge*, part 2, chap. 2, and part 5, chaps. 6 and 7; Nelson Goodman, "Sense and Certainty," *Philosophical Review* 61 (1952): 160–167; Israel Scheffler, *Science and Subjectivity*, chap. 5; and Roderick Firth, "Coherence, Certainty, and Epistemic Priority."

[8]One way to put this point is to say that whether a belief is likely to be true or whether in contrast it is an accident that it is true depends significantly on how the belief is described. Thus it might be true of one and the same belief that it is "a belief connected in a law-like way with the state of affairs which it describes" and also that it is "a belief adopted on the basis of no apparent evidence"; and it might be likely to be true on the first description and unlikely to be true on the second. The claim here is that it is the believer's own conception which should be consid-ered in deciding whether the belief is justified. (Something analogous seems to be true in ethics: the moral worth of a person's action is correctly to be judged only in terms of that person's subjective conception of what he is doing and not in light of what happens, willy-nilly, to result from it.)

[9]Notice, however, that if beliefs standing in the proper external relation should happen to possess some subjec-tively distinctive feature (such as being spontaneous and highly compelling to the believer), and if the believer were to notice empirically, that beliefs having this feature were true a high proportion of the time, he would then be in a position to construct a justification for a new belief of that sort along the lines sketched at the end of section II. But of course a belief justified in that way would no longer be basic.

V.4 A Defense of Classical Foundationalism

TIMOTHY MCGREW

Tim McGrew is professor of philosophy at Western Michigan University. In this essay, he argues that moderate foundationalism faces a devastating criti-cism, and in consequence our best theory of knowledge is a version of strong foundationalism that requires certainty at the base of one's evidence tree but does not require certainty for knowledge at the higher levels. McGrew argues that such strong foundations are necessary, available, and sufficiently rich in content to overcome the skeptic's challenge.

Simple questions often have the most awkward consequences. One of the simplest questions that may be legitimately asked of our everyday judg-ments can be put in four short words: How do you know? And the remarkable thing about this ques-tion is that it can be iterated: In any normal situa-tion, an answer to the question will be some claim or set of claims that can reasonably be subjected to the same question all over again.

Any conversation in which one side sincerely asks this question and the other sincerely attempts to answer it is going to take one of a very limited number of forms. Either the conversation will go on forever, or it will stop. If it goes on forever, either the answerer comes back around in a circle, eventually repeating some of the claims that were initially called into question, or he goes on forever giving endless new reasons for believing the claims put forward earlier. If the conversation stops, either the answerer has just given up (an understandable reaction in everyday life!) or he has reached some claim so basic that he can fairly be said to be justified in believing it without having reasoned his way to it via other beliefs.

Foundationalism is the position that all justified empirical beliefs are either basic, in something like the final sense given above, or else have supporting lines of reasons that can be traced one way or another back to beliefs that are basic. It doesn't matter that no two sane people would have a conversation like this: The important point for foundationalists is that for justified beliefs the underlying reasons are there and *could* be produced, under ideal conditions, if necessary.[1] If we drew a diagram of such a conversation, it would have the form of an upside-down tree, branching out when two or more reasons support a belief at a given point. But ultimately every branch could be traced down to a belief that is basic, a point where that branch of the evidence tree comes to an end.

Foundationalists do not all agree among themselves about just what sort of justification the basic beliefs have to possess or about what sort of justifying relations enable us to reason our way from the foundations "up" to our everyday beliefs. Descartes, whose principal work *Meditations on First Philosophy* is a milestone of foundationalist thought, took a strong position on both points: The basic beliefs must be certainties, and the inference relations leading from those beliefs to higher-level beliefs must be deductively valid, allowing for no possibility of error at any step along the way. But the trend in recent decades has been to weaken both requirements, demanding only that the basic beliefs possess *some* degree of intrinsic plausibility rather than absolute certainty and allowing the use of various inference relations that are not airtight instead of insisting on deductive inference at every step. Robert Audi, a noted contemporary foundationalist, adopts this doubly modest position in reaction to the rather obvious deficiencies of the Cartesian position. Unlike the Cartesian, Audi can make room for justified belief regarding things of which we are not absolutely certain. And the

modest requirements he places on basic beliefs allow him to start with a wider set of grounds than the classical strong foundationalist has at his disposal, thereby (apparently) enhancing his chances of providing a really good justification for beliefs about the external world. In both ways, moderate foundationalism seems to be a more desirable position than its austere cousin.

What seems to have been overlooked, or at least left unexplored, is a position that separates the two parts of the strong Cartesian position. Audi is certainly right that nondeductive inference relations are necessary for us to arrive at interesting conclusions and that such inferences can have justificatory force. But in contrast to Audi's doubly moderate position, I think that Descartes is right about the need for certainties as the bases of empirical knowledge. Though much of our empirical knowledge is of course less than certain, there are compelling reasons to believe that our everyday empirical beliefs rest on a foundation of certainties.

Any attempt to revive strong foundationalism will have to answer three obvious questions: Are these strong foundations necessary? Are they available? And are they sufficient to ground empirical knowledge of the everyday sort?

Are Strong Foundations Necessary?

A Modest Proposal

If we can give a satisfactory answer to skeptical challenges without insisting on a foundation of empirical certainties, then it certainly makes sense to do so: We take on fewer responsibilities in this sort of argument if we start out making only more modest claims. But if fallible foundations turn out to be inadequate to stop the skeptical regress, then we will have to turn to strong foundationalism for a way out.

Moderate foundationalism, in its nonskeptical form, maintains that there is a knower S of whom the following claims are all true:

1. S has some basic (i.e., noninferentially justified) empirical beliefs.
2. S has some justified nonbasic empirical beliefs.

3. Every branch of an evidence tree supporting any of S's nonbasic empirical beliefs terminates in a basic empirical belief.

4. Some of S's basic empirical beliefs are less than certain for S.

The crucial point where moderate foundationalism differs from strong foundationalism is of course point 4; strong foundationalists will deny this claim while affirming the other three. To understand the motivation for strong foundationalism, consider the conversation we started with, picking up at the point where the imaginary conversationalists have gotten down to a basic belief.

KNOWER: . . . and I know that because I know that Z.

SKEPTIC: Okay, I can see that Z would be a good reason there—provided that you really know it. So now, of course, I have to ask: How . . .

KNOWER: Stop! You've asked that question dozens of times so far, but this time it won't work. Z is a *basic* belief: I am justified in believing it, but I don't have or need any argument for it.

SKEPTIC: What kind of crazy position is that? Can you really mean that you just stop somewhere and dig in your heels and refuse to give any further reasons?

KNOWER: No, not at all. What I'm saying is that Z is a belief that I'm *justified* in holding, not just that it's something I'd like to believe or that my peers let me get away with believing.

SKEPTIC: I guess I see where you're coming from, but now I have to ask: Are you *really* justified in holding Z? Anybody can say, "I'm justified in this belief," and sometimes it may actually be true. But is it true here?

The skeptic has a good point; this is a question all foundationalists have to answer. And this is just the point where things begin to get difficult for the moderate foundationalist.

Making It All Up

If I claim that I have met the Queen of England and you are in a skeptical mood, you may ask me how I know. The typical response for me would

be to give you my reasons, but nothing absolutely prevents me from saying, "Oh, I don't have reasons—I just believe that I've met her." But if I gave this response, you would quite reasonably conclude that I am some sort of nut; the belief that I've met a person of such prominence is not the sort of thing one can be justified in believing without having at least some reasons, even if they amount only to faded memories. Anyone who is allowed to get away with this sort of thing can end up claiming to be "justified" in literally any belief. And none of us will take him seriously, for a very good reason: In the absence of any evidence that he really is justified, he may as well be making it all up.

There is a tricky point here about what counts as "evidence" that a person is justified in holding a certain belief. Foundationalists all agree that in order to be justified in believing that P, where P is some belief that S has *inferred* from other beliefs, S needs to be justified in believing the premises from which P has been inferred. To know that S is justified in believing that P, then, I would need to know that S justifiably believes the premises on which it is based and also that the method of inference being used is a legitimate one—that the premises really do support S's belief that P. The second part of this can be put more crisply. Epistemologists speak of the connection between premises and conclusions as the sort of thing that can be expressed by an *epistemic principle* with a conditional form; roughly, if anyone makes such-and-such an inference from justified beliefs, then the person is justified in believing this proposition.

For basic beliefs, however, there are no such premises. In this case, the evidence will have to take the form of an epistemic principle regarding the way in which the belief is formed, a principle that states (roughly) that whenever anyone forms a belief in manner X, it is a justified belief. In neither case are we solely concerned with S's evidence for the truth of P; these epistemic principles come in only when we are looking for evidence for the truth of the claim that S *is justified in believing that* P. The individual in question doesn't necessarily have to know what the principle is; no one has to become a philosopher in order to know such mundane facts as "I have a headache." But the principle does have to be *true*. And someone who wants to know whether S's belief that he has a headache is really justified may reasonably hold out for an epistemic principle (whether known to S or not) that does *not* sound arbitrary and that indicates why that belief really is justified without any inferential support.

In the case at hand, this means that the skeptical question amounts to doubt that the supposedly basic beliefs really are underwritten by a true epistemic principle. It isn't enough to point out that they *might* be underwritten by a true principle; this would leave open the alternative that they are not, and the skeptic cannot lose this argument unless it can be shown that the alleged basic beliefs really do arise in such a way that one cannot fail to be justified in believing them.

Modesty on the Rocks

Moderate foundationalism holds that there are basic beliefs that are less than certain. For a wide range of concepts of justification, this amounts to saying that they are more or less probable but that this probability falls short of a 100 percent guarantee. But this raises an interesting question: Is there such a thing as probability, in the sense that counts for justification, that is *not* based on an inference from other beliefs?

Suppose you meet a friend on the sidewalk, and in the course of conversation he says, "It's probably going to rain today." What role does the word *probably* have in this sentence? That will depend on your friend; it could indicate a guarded utterance, meaning roughly "I think it will rain, but don't call me a liar if it turns out not to," or it could be an expression of confidence, meaning "I have virtually no doubt that it will rain." These paraphrases, however, do not bring out the epistemic significance of your friend's remark; to say that it will probably rain is (normally) to indicate that there are good, though not conclusive, reasons for believing that it will rain.[2] This is perfectly compatible with the implication that one does not wish to be held accountable for actions undertaken on one's testimony, or at the other extreme that one has great confidence; having good reasons is a paradigm case of well-placed confidence. But it goes beyond these mere psychological factors and focuses our attention on the feature that is critical for the discussion of modest foundationalism: Probability arises from a relation between the probable proposition and a body of evidence.

This simple fact about probability creates a fatal dilemma for moderate foundationalism. If there are basic beliefs that are merely probable, then they are not basic at all; they are inferred, probable in relation to some other beliefs that support them. The focus of our inquiry shifts back to the supporting beliefs, and the dilemma gets started there once again: Either they are basic or they are not. If they are not, we have to go back still further. If they are basic, then they cannot be merely probable.

Slipping Out the Backdoor

A natural response to this argument is disbelief. I know many things by memory, for example, but I'm far from certain of the things I remember. Surely memory is a fallible source of justified beliefs? Or what about faint perception? At the very edge of my hearing range, I seem to hear a low throb and the grinding of gravel—I think, but am not sure, that a car has turned into my driveway. Obviously, I am not certain of this. But if perception is a fallible source of justified basic beliefs, something must be wrong with this attack on moderate foundationalism.

Plausible as this response sounds, it is mistaken. In the memory case, there is something that I am absolutely certain about, namely, that I *seem* to have these memories. Doubt only arises at the point where I ask whether I am remembering *correctly*, but these doubts would not even make sense unless I could independently determine what I *seem* to remember. Something similar goes for the case of faint perception. What is absolutely certain in the perceptual case is that I really do have a certain sort of experience (which I am inclined to describe in the indicated fashion). This is the foundation: Even if I'm dreaming, it remains unshaken. What is uncertain is whether my instinctive conjecture about the cause of this experience is correct. Perception gives rise to many spontaneous beliefs—beliefs that I do not *try* to have and for which I am not normally conscious of any explicit argument. And these beliefs are undoubtedly fallible. But they are not basic.

It is important to stress this point: Strong foundationalists, no less than their moderate cousins, are free to use beliefs that arise from faint perception, fallible memory, and uncertain testimony in the process of justification. What they insist is that everyone who makes legitimate use of such beliefs, even if he is a moderate foundationalist (and therefore committed to denying the need to rely on certainties), is able to do so only because there is a deeper level at which there is something of which he is certain and on which the higher-level belief depends for its justification.

There is one other way to try to slip out the backdoor and evade the force of the argument against moderate foundationalism. We might try looking at perceptual beliefs simply as a class of beliefs that arise spontaneously and count up the number of times that they turn out to be correct. If a high proportion of the perceptual beliefs that I form spontaneously turn out to be true, isn't this evidence that my perceptual beliefs are highly likely to be true? And can't we then say that they are foundational, though merely probable, after all?

This response turns on an equivocation in the use of the word *probable*. In the sense in which this term (or something functionally equivalent) is needed for justification, it indicates something about the rationality of our beliefs. But as it is used in the preceding paragraph, *probable* hasn't got anything to do with rationality: it has to do with *success*. The frequency with which my beliefs turn out true doesn't say anything about my rationality: They may turn out to be true in virtue of factors that have nothing to do with the quality of my reasons. (Perhaps some brilliant and slightly twisted scientists have decided to prime my brain with spontaneous beliefs about high-energy physics.) It may strain our credulity to think that I could spontaneously produce a whole string of esoteric but true pronouncements about physics without knowing anything about the field, but this does not prove that I am really being rational; we are simply strongly inclined to think that I must have some evidence that I'm not letting on about. The mere fact that some beliefs arise spontaneously and are true does not mean that they are justified, much less basic in the sense that foundationalism requires.

So there is no way out of the dilemma: Strong foundations are necessary if we are to have justified inferred beliefs.

Are Strong Foundations Available?

Is there any empirical knowledge—knowledge of facts, rather than of mathematical and logical truths—that we literally cannot be wrong about? Strong foundationalism asserts that there is and that all the rest of our empirical knowledge is based on these secure beliefs. But the argument of the preceding section does not give us any assurance that these foundations exist. It could turn out that they are necessary but unavailable, and in that case, the skeptic would turn out to be right after all.

Headaches and Hamburgers

Imagine a situation in which you believe, for the normal sort of reasons, that you have a hamburger in your hands. Is there even the slightest possibility that you could be wrong about this? Although from a practical point of view it is hard to take doubts about this seriously, we have to admit that it is just barely possible that you could be mistaken. It is possible, for example, that you are having an exceptionally vivid dream; it seems there's a hamburger there, but you're really asleep in your bed with no hamburgers around. Scenarios like this show that however secure our normal empirical beliefs seem in practice, they are not quite certain. It is possible for us to hold these beliefs and be wrong about them.

By contrast, your belief that you have a headache isn't open to this sort of challenge. You may be awake or asleep, drunk or sober—it makes no difference. If you believe that you have a headache, you are *right*. What is more, your belief is *justified*. This is not at all like the bizarre case where you have (much to your surprise) a series of spontaneous true beliefs about linear accelerators while remaining clueless of physics. When it comes to your headache, you are aware without any inference or possibility of slippage of the very factors that make your belief a true one.

This same point can be extended to any sort of experience—not just headaches, but visual sensations, tactile perception, apparent memories, and even rushes of emotion. In each case, there is a level at which you cannot be wrong about your experience. It has just those qualities that you believe it to have. Someone who tries to argue that you do not have a headache may succeed in making your headache go *away* (though the reverse process is more likely to occur), but no one can make you not have a headache at the very time that you are attending to the experience. Headaches, unlike hamburgers, do not have any hidden features. There is a difference between seeming to have a hamburger and really having one, and we can imagine circumstances (however bizarre) under which the two could come apart. But if your doctor tells you that you merely *seem* to yourself to be in desperate pain and that you are in fact feeling fine, then it is time to find a new doctor.

Reference and Incorrigibility

Strong foundations, on the account we are developing, have a special property known as *incorrigibility*. Literally the term means "uncorrectability," but in epistemology it has a more technical meaning: For my belief in some contingent proposition p to be incorrigible entails that, necessarily, if I believe that p, then p is true. How can any contingent belief have this property? What kind of relation will guarantee the correctness of the belief?

The answer lies in *reference*. When I have a particular experience and express this fact to you, I am referring to something that I am directly aware of. Given the constraints of natural language, I am likely to try to use shared terms in order to convey to you the quality of the experience as I have it, but I do not have to describe it to myself in order to have the experience. Perhaps the closest linguistic construction to the belief I form is "I am experiencing *this*," where the italicized term picks out the experience in question by denoting it. A belief formed in this fashion cannot go wrong for a very simple reason: If there were nothing for the term *this* to refer to, it would not be possible to form the belief at all.

It is important, because of the use we have in mind for these foundations, that incorrigible beliefs have one other property. Besides being immune to error, they must be immune to being unjustified. Since they are supposed to function as basic beliefs, this means that there must be some intrinsic feature they possess that satisfies the minimal internal constraints on justified belief: The truth of the proposition must be not only guaranteed by our act of believing but also bound up in the proper way with our mode of access to the subject matter of these propositions. But from an internalist point of view, these constraints are satisfied by referentially formed beliefs. The relevant content is something that lies within the individual's field of awareness, and the very existence of that content is what makes the belief true. This is internal justification in the fullest sense that a basic belief can possibly have.

Objections and Replies

Every epistemological position has its critics, and strong foundationalism has more than most. Since these criticisms are largely responsible for the recent flight to moderate foundationalism, it is worth our while to address four of them here.

A fair number of critics of strong foundationalism confuse the classification of experiences with the content of those experiences. The first criticism we need to consider falls into this category. Bruce Aune advances an argument against strong foundations along the following lines:

1. All cognitively significant judgments involve predication.
2. All predication involves comparison.
3. All comparison relies on memory.
4. Memory is fallible.
5. Therefore, all cognitively significant judgments are fallible.

The conclusion of this argument is, of course, incompatible with strong foundationalism. The basic beliefs of strong foundationalism are supposed to be cognitively significant (otherwise, they can do no epistemic work), but they are also supposed to be certainties. If the argument works, it proves that strong foundations are entirely devoid of content.

In fact, it proves too much. If Aune's argument were sound, it would establish the impossibility of any cognitively significant judgments whatsoever. To make comparisons, we must have something to compare our present experiences to; we must already have had and named a similar experience. But how, then, does anyone's mental life get off the ground? There must be a *first* cognitively significant experience, and if later comparisons are possible at all, then it must be possible to assign to this first one some sort of description, even something as vague as "that unpleasant smell," in a noncomparative way.

Classifying our experiences into groups that have relevant similarities is a fallible business, if only because we have to remember what the earlier experiences were like in order to make the comparison and memory is a fallible thing. But this doesn't mean that our experiences have no distinctive characteristics or that we create their characteristics by an act of mental sorting. On the contrary, sorting and classification make no sense unless the things sorted have some definite characteristics on the basis of which the sorting can be done.

A second objection turns on the question of empirical evidence for or against basic beliefs. It is possible (for all we know) that a device could be constructed that would track neurological activity in your brain and give scientists excellent reason to believe that you are in a certain mental state—say, the state of feeling no pain. Suppose that such a cerebrescope were tested thousands of times without failing: When the device indicated that people were in pain, they confirmed it; and when it indicated that they were not, the test subjects also agreed. If this device were put on your head and indicated that you felt fine, could this count as evidence against your own belief that you have a splitting headache?

If the issue were a matter of piling up external evidence, it might. But in fact, you do not reason your way to the conclusion that you have a headache by noting your bloodshot eyes, the thermometer on the counter, and the bottle of aspirin clutched in your trembling hand. Your belief is formed referentially and cannot go wrong. To insist that a cerebrescope could give us evidence to the contrary is to miss the point about these beliefs. They are not up for grabs in a contest of evidence; because of the special way that they are formed, they are not sensitive to inductive evidence. Insisting that they are open to refutation is insisting that they are not, after all, incorrigible. And in this context that is question begging—even if the person urging for the test is wearing a lab coat.

A third objection is that our typical empirical beliefs simply don't seem to be based on first-person foundations. In fact, it is difficult for most people to look out over a garden and "see it as" a patchwork of colors, a pure visual experience without any level of interpretation imposed on it. In her recent book *Evidence and Inquiry*, Susan Haack takes this objection to be seriously damaging to any epistemology built on phenomenal data.[3]

At one level this observation is perfectly legitimate, but to use it as an objection to strong foundationalism confuses psychological priority with epistemic priority. It is certainly true that the first explicit thought we have when looking at a garden is of the real, three-dimensional physical garden, and it may be very difficult for us, unless we are professional artists, to create a mind-set in which we can look out over the garden and be aware only of a collage of colors. But it is likewise difficult for a reader to focus on a line of clear prose and see it as a pattern of dark and light regions on a page. Yet when we look at a child learning to read, it is obvious that this is precisely what is going on; and the development from a child to a mature reader is a continuous process. The moral we draw in the reading case is not that awareness of marks on the page is irrelevant to reading, but that increasing competence (mercifully) makes much of the process subconscious. Similarly, the answer to this challenge to strong foundationalism is that an adult's awareness of visual, tactile, and auditory stimuli is often subconscious but not therefore irrelevant to justification of empirical beliefs.

The fourth and most serious objection comes from a distinction between having a belief and having an experience. This objection is widely discussed but often presented in a confusing fashion, so it will help to lay it out in standard form:

1. If believing that I am having an experience, on the one hand, and actually having the experience, on the other, are not the same thing, then it is possible in principle for one of them to occur without the other occurring.

2. They are not the same thing.

3. Therefore, it is possible for me to have a belief that I am having a particular experience without actually having the experience, and hence for my belief to be wrong.

Multiple issues are lurking just beneath the premises here. First, it is important to remember that the strong foundationalist is only urging the incorrigibility of beliefs that are referentially formed. Since it is possible to believe the same *proposition* in multiple ways, we must distinguish between the content of beliefs and the way in which belief is formed and remember that the latter may be epistemically significant. One obvious case where this comes up is in cases of the same proposition believed at two different times in two different ways. Yesterday, when you believed that you had a headache, you formed the belief referentially. Today you believe *that you had a headache yesterday*. The same factors make both the earlier and the later belief true; but today you believe this truth not referentially but rather by inferring it from memory, written records, photographs of your flushed face, and the like. Strong foundationalists will not underwrite this latter belief as incorrigible.

Given this distinction, it could just turn out that the antecedent of premise 1 is false when applied to the sorts of beliefs that strong foundationalists have in mind. Since strong foundationalists are not demanding that all beliefs be explicit, they are free to construe belief in a modest way that is separable from and does not entail the existence of explicit verbalized judgment. Having an experience at all, on this view, might come out to be equivalent to having a tacit referential belief. There is some room for flexibility in the strong foundationalist position here.

But regardless of whether we take this line, there is a much greater problem with the argument: It is invalid. The error can be seen clearly if we look at the following parallel argument:

1. If being a bear and being an animal are not the same thing, then it is possible in principle for one of them to be instantiated without the other being instantiated.
2. They aren't the same thing.
3. Therefore, it is possible for there to be a bear that is not an animal.

The point is that the truth of premises 1 and 2 only guarantees that being a bear and being an animal can come apart *in one direction*. From the fact that we may have A without B, it does not follow that we may have B without A. Carried up to the objection above, this criticism amounts to pointing out that even if we were to allow that premise 1 is true because we may have experiences without forming tacit referential beliefs, it does not follow that it is possible for us to form referential beliefs without having the relevant experi-

ences. Indeed, the referential connection shows why this is not possible. And with that, the fourth objection to the availability of strong foundations collapses.

Are Strong Foundations Sufficient?

Merely showing that we do all have basic beliefs about which we cannot be wrong does not solve all our problems. A skeptic might well respond to the arguments presented so far with a shrug of his shoulders. "You've shown, I'll grant, that there are some empirical certainties—beliefs about which you cannot be wrong," he might say, "and that may be interesting for its own sake. But how are you going to reason your way from these first-person experiential statements to claims about a world of mind-independent objects? It's a long way from 'I seem to see something red' to 'Here's an apple.'"

This gap between appearance and reality is the final challenge that strong foundationalists confront. How can we move from the way things *seem* to justified beliefs about the way things *are*? There are really two parts to this difficulty. First, is there any way to form beliefs about mind-independent reality? And second, supposing that there is, can we have good reasons to believe in the existence of that reality? Can we really support realism about our surroundings on these first-person foundations? Both questions, according to strong foundationalists, can be given an affirmative answer.

The Means of Ascent

The form of reasoning we need is known as *explanatory inference*, or inference to the best explanation. In a wide range of situations—from criminology to medicine, particle physics to automotive repair—we attempt to find explanations that will unify and render comprehensible a welter of facts. Strong foundationalism can make use of this form of inference to address the skeptical challenge of ascending from first-person basic beliefs to a justified superstructure.

Explanatory inference enables us to have justified beliefs because of a simple but powerful feature of confirmation theory. Given a theory *T*, which is neither guaranteed nor ruled out by the known facts, and a belief *e*, which is also neither guaranteed nor ruled out by anything else we know, the following relationship holds:

> IC If *T* raises the probability of *e*, then *e* is evidence for (raises the probability of) *T*.

This principle of Incremental Confirmation is a deductive consequence of the axioms of probability theory, and although it is not necessary for a given individual to know IC in order to be justified by reasoning in accordance with it, the principle itself can be known a priori. Most people working in the field today acknowledge it as a workable definition of evidence.[4] When a scientist takes a new theory and derives an unexpected result from it, a result which turns out to be correct, there is strong reason to take the new theory seriously. This is, in outline, what happened when Einstein used the theory of relativity to predict that the apparent positions of certain stars during the full solar eclipse in 1919 would deviate from the apparent positions predicted by Newtonian physics.

Strong foundationalists can put the principle to work in the following fashion:

1. I have the surprising experience *E*.
2. But if there is a lawn in front of me, then of course I would have such experiences.

Therefore, it is more probable than before that

3. There is a lawn in front of me.

This argument is not deductive: The premises may be true while the conclusion in 3 is false. But it is not presented as a deductive argument; on the contrary, the argument is intended to be nondeductive. Strong foundationalists are not committed to the position that *all* justified beliefs are certainties! This is not a concession to moderate foundationalism; the merely probable beliefs at the higher levels do not run afoul of the dilemma presented in the first section because, unlike basic beliefs, they are *inferred*. It is precisely in our inferred beliefs that we would expect probability rather than certainty.

The general form of the simplified argument given here is this: Whenever we successfully anticipate and control our experiences on the basis of our theories, the theories gain in credibility. Even if we are not using exact numbers to quantify the degree of probability that a particular theory has, it remains true that under the conditions described the credibility of *T* given *e* is greater than the antecedent credibility of *T*. It is relatively simple to show that multiple lines of evidence supporting the same belief raise its credibility with dramatic speed. But this is precisely what we confront in daily life. The smell, sight, touch, and taste I have from a cheeseburger are all independent sensory clues that are well explained by the actual existence of a cheeseburger in my hands but not well explained by any rival hypothesis: They provide an overlapping and mutually reinforcing set of sensory evidence in favor of the belief that there really is a cheeseburger. Since we are constantly engaged in this sort of anticipation and control of our experience, the total confirmatory effect is overwhelming.

An important feature of this method of ascending from foundations—which is popular with moderate as well as with strong foundationalists—is that it leaves room for the introduction of new concepts. By contrast, any attempt to use pure rule-guided inductive extrapolation would not allow us to break outside of the circle of first-person experiences. From premises about falling apples, rule-guided extrapolation can at best give us a conclusion about more falling apples, or more vaguely about falling things. It permits us to omit concepts but not to introduce (for example) the notion of gravity as part of an explanation for why apples fall. Similarly, from premises of the form "I am experiencing like *this*," inductive extrapolation will at most permit us to infer conclusions of the form "In the future I will have similar experiences." Rule-guided extrapolation can only take the concepts involved in the premises and give us more of the same. But explanatory inference places no restrictions on the genesis of the concepts involved. The important epistemic feature is the relation between the hypothesis of realism on the one hand and our experience on the other. How the hypothesis arises is of no consequence.

Concept Empiricism and Concept Rationalism

This freedom accorded to us by explanatory inference would not get us very far if concept empiricism were true. According to concept empiricism, a position advocated somewhat inconsistently in Locke and with greater rigor by Hume, we cannot frame any concepts that are not given to us in experience. If all that we have is first-person experience, then we will never get around to a serious and independent third-person discourse; we will not be able to talk about objects except as a sort of shorthand for clumps of our individual experience.

This is a point on which phenomenalists and direct realists are in agreement. Where they disagree is just in the direction they take this principle. Phenomenalists, insisting that we are restricted to first-person data, maintain that we never get out and that realist talk about hamburgers is just a disguised way of talking about actual and possible experiences (visual, tactile, taste). Direct realists, insisting that we inhabit a world of real, mind-independent objects, demand that we must get our third-person concepts directly in experience: We must be *directly* aware of hamburgers. Many contemporary moderate foundationalists allow at least spontaneous beliefs about physical objects to stand as foundational; this position naturally lends itself to a form of direct realism.

Only indirect realists are blocked out by this principle. And this brings up an important point of contrast: Unlike its moderate cousin, strong foundationalism of the sort we have been investigating does not have any third-person physical-object statements among the basic empirical beliefs and is a version of indirect realism. Strong foundationalists are therefore committed to concept rationalism—the position that it is possible for us to create and employ concepts that go beyond experience.

There are good reasons to believe that concept empiricism is false. Empiricists have a notoriously hard time accounting for the genesis even of sensory concepts. Hume admitted in a moment of weakness that some sensory concepts could be formed without having been given in experience, as when we look at a spectrum from which one color has been omitted and our minds "fill in" the intermediate shade. So much the more with concepts like "electron" or "gravity" does it strain our credulity to be asked to believe that these are either given directly in experience (as direct realists insist) or else just shorthand for aspects of our experience (as phenomenalists maintain).

A possible misunderstanding needs to be blocked here. Concept rationalists are not committed to a strong belief-voluntarism. It is highly implausible to say that, unaided by experience, I could believe *that there are objects* by a sheer effort of will. Just forming the concept of a mind-independent object, however, isn't the same as believing that there really are such objects, any more than forming the concept of a unicorn puts me at odds with established zoological consensus. Concept rationalism is simply the position that, contrary to concept empiricists, we can sometimes have concepts that are not constructions from our sensory or introspective data. And the idea of a persisting material object is one such concept.

Two Kinds of Priority

In at least one respect, the metaphor of "foundations" can be misleading. When we think of the foundations of a house, it is obvious that the supporting bricks must be laid down earlier than those that rest on them; and once the house is built, the foundations cannot change without tearing the whole edifice down. If the analogy were perfect, we would expect that basic beliefs, in order to give any epistemic support to a higher-level empirical belief, must be formed before the higher-order belief is formed and must thereafter remain as its sole support. But as a picture of human knowledge this is paradoxical, for at least two reasons. First, the basic beliefs allowed us by strong foundationalism are momentary. They involve our present experience (including, of course, present memory experiences, present beliefs, etc.), but in a moment those experiences will be gone, replaced at best with experiences that are qualitatively similar. So the foundations seem to have vanished! Second, we often attempt to support something we already believe by acquiring *more* evidence for its truth. I believe that I have left my wallet in the car because of a memory of setting it on the seat beside me; then I go out to the car and actually have the experience that I describe as seeing the wallet on the seat. But if strong foundationalism is right, the only lines of reasoning that count as evidence are those that can be traced to basic beliefs. So we seem to be acquiring basic beliefs *after* we already believe the hypothesis in question. Can strong foundationalism account for this?

Failure to make a distinction between epistemic and chronological priority can make foundationalism, and particularly strong foundationalism, look hopelessly rigid. But when the distinction is made, the "paradoxical" consequences turn out to be tame. Strong foundationalism, like any theory of knowledge, is a position about justification *at a given point in time*. It is, if you like, a philosophical claim about "snapshots" of justified belief; it lays out conditions that must be met if one's belief that *P*, at time *t*, is to count as justified. Strong foundationalists are not committed to any further claims about the evolution of our belief systems *across time*. In particular, they are free to acknowledge that a purely experiential, first-person basis for knowledge will be constantly changing; old memories will fade, new experiences will offer fresh support for our beliefs, and so forth in a sort of cognitive "movie." Since this sort of development is not ruled out by foundationalism, we are free to acknowledge that many of our beliefs will actually predate, chronologically, our acquisition of the evidence that we *now* have to support them. What strong foundationalism requires is simply that our beliefs, to be justified at any given time, must *at that time* rest on a structure of supporting reasons that can be traced back *epistemically* to empirical certainties at their basis.

Restrictions

Even if we abandon concept empiricism, an objection to all forms of indirect realism remains to be addressed. According to this criticism, indirect realism locks us behind a veil of perceptions. We may *guess* that we inhabit a world of mind-independent objects, but how can we ever hope to check up on such a guess? If I doubt whether a newspaper has reported a politician's speech accurately, I can hunt down an audio clip and check it out for myself. But according to indirect realism we can never get at the world directly; we can never manage to get a firm grip on the objects that are supposedly causing our experiences. "To know that there was [such a causal connection]," Jonathan Bennett writes, "we should need independent access to empirical facts about the objective realm."[5] As a consequence, the objection runs, we can never tell whether our conjectures are correct. Indirect realism dooms us to skepticism.

In his article in defense of phenomenalism W. T. Stace parses out the intuition behind this objection by placing a restriction on our legitimate inferences that runs, roughly, as follows:

> *R*　　We can come to know that *A* causes *B* only if *A* is the sort of thing with which, at least some of the time, we can be directly acquainted.

This restriction (*R*) seems reasonable so long as the only mode of inference available to us is the method of cross-checking our perceptions against the facts themselves. If we can never, so to speak, grab the real world by the scruff of the neck and hold it up against our sensory experiences to see if they match, then it seems we can never have good reasons to believe facts about the world beyond our senses. But on a closer look, it turns out that *R* is in conflict with IC, the principle of incremental confirmation that we looked at earlier. According to that principle, *any* successful theory that meets the conditions spelled out can receive enhanced credibility for its successes.

And in point of fact, we constantly use IC in circumstances where *R* is violated, and it seems obvious that such reasoning can be justificatory. Consider black holes. By definition, their mass is so great that light cannot escape from them, so we cannot see them directly. Nevertheless, the behavior of nearby visible objects may give us excellent reason to believe that there is a black hole in a given region. We infer the existence of the black hole because it enables us to give a good causal explanation of the visible phenomena we do in fact observe. Or consider contemporary research on fundamental particles. Some of these particles are so small that it is not even theoretically possible to see them. To get around this difficulty, physicists use cloud chambers for studying nuclear transformations: They observe trails of water droplets that condense in the wake of a charged particle as it ionizes the water vapor through which it passes. If a theory predicts that a particular sort of particle will be produced in a given reaction, scientists look for its telltale vapor trail—a trail that is caused by the particle—rather than for the particle itself.

Of course, skeptics about empirical knowledge are likely to be skeptics about science. But the point is not that current scientific theories are true: It is that this mode of nondeductive inference is reasonable regardless of whether the particular conclusions we draw from it turn out to be correct. If skeptics want to attack realism, they had better find a means that does not rely on the dubious restriction *R*.

Rivals

A final obstacle to the use of strong foundations in defense of realism is one suggested by Descartes himself. All of our first-person experiences could, in principle, be brought about by an extremely powerful being (Descartes calls him a "deceiver of the utmost power and cunning") whose goal was to deceive us into thinking that we inhabit a physical world. Granting that the hypothesis of realism predicts our experience and is therefore confirmed by it, it seems that the hypothesis of an evil deceiver does so as well. The two theories are empirically equivalent; they offer us precisely the same expectations. Hence, they will apparently be confirmed in tandem, with the unhappy result that neither one can rise to more than a 50% credibility level no matter how much evidence we get. This isn't very encouraging.

The objection, if it goes through at all, demolishes all forms of foundationalism, weak as well as strong. Some philosophers have tried to block it by claiming that the idea of such a deceiver makes no sense or is conceptually incoherent, but this seems to violate our very strong intuition that it is at least *possible*, however unlikely, that we should be thus deceived. Foundationalists will need to tackle this one directly.

The best approach to this difficulty starts with a look at confirmation theory. Even when two theories both offer successful predictions and both rise in credibility as a result, they are not necessarily confirmed by the same amounts. In particular, if theory T_1 has a higher initial credibility than theory T_2, and they both raise the likelihood of an empirical truth e to the same extent, then it can be shown from the axioms of probability theory that T_1 will get a bigger "boost" from the successful prediction of e than T_2 does. The gap between their credibilities will widen in favor of the initially more credible theory with each successful confirmation.

And it would seem that the initial credibility of the existence of an evil deceiver is at least somewhat lower than that of ordinary realism. One reason for this is that in the deceiver scenario at least one thing is never represented to us by any sensation: the deceiver himself, who must stay "hidden" through this process if the Cartesian scenario is to remain empirically equivalent to realism. For this reason, there is no explanatory advantage to invoking the existence of the deceiver; we can (and do) manage to get around without hypothesizing his existence, and there is no empirical or scientific problem for which his existence could, in principle, be of the slightest interest to us. In the Cartesian scenario, we have not only the deceiver but also all of his individual mental states which are the causes of our particular experiences, not to mention the structure of whatever sort of (nondeceptive) world the deceiver actually inhabits. The existence of the deceiver over and above these particular causes of our experiences is a "fifth wheel." Though we may grant that his existence is logically possible, it is perfectly reasonable for us not to take it seriously since we have at hand a simpler, more plausible, and therefore better-confirmed explanation for our experience: that we inhabit a real world of mind-independent objects.

The Wider Picture

Why should anyone care what theory of knowledge is correct? Epistemology is pretty obviously *hard*, and at first blush it doesn't seem that any particular scientific achievement or practical course of action is likely to be affected by our choice of strong foundationalism over weak foundationalism or even some nonfoundational theory. Why should we rack our brains over theories that don't have any practical application?

The simple but sobering answer is that human beings have an overwhelming desire to know. Many of the scientific achievements we most admire have been brought about because people had a burning desire to figure out how things really work, to get it *right*. Any theory of knowledge that writes off these achievements as an illusion or an accident will have a catastrophic effect on our worldview. Closer to home, we would like to think that our beliefs about cars, houses, trees, and sidewalks are in some important sense better off than the beliefs of people who take their cues from astrologers and crystal balls. If a theory of knowledge offers no defense against the argument that we are all ultimately required to retreat to a point of unargued, unjustified commitment, then we are wrong: There is no ultimate epistemic difference between our beliefs and the beliefs of devout horoscope readers, and it is merely a historical accident that horoscope-readers are currently a minority of the population.

A sound and defensible theory of knowledge is our only *rational* line of defense against conceptual anarchy. This is the best and perhaps the only reason to take epistemology seriously; but it is also a sufficient one.

Notes

[1]Or at least, this is the form that foundationalism takes when it is advanced by an internalist. But since I find the case for epistemic internalism wholly convincing, I will take it for granted that we are speaking among internalists

here. There are also some complications that arise from the fact that a given individual may not be in a position to *articulate* all the reasons on which he is actually relying, but these do not affect the main point here. See the discussion in McGrew, *The Foundations of Knowledge* (Lanham, MD: Littlefield Adams Books, 1995), 3–8, for more details.

[2]See J. L. Mackie, *Truth, Probability and Paradox* (Oxford: Clarendon Press, 1973), 158ff., for a discussion of this point.

[3]Susan Haack, *Evidence and Inquiry* (Cambridge, MA: Blackwell, 1993), 107–108.

[4]Most, but not quite all. Peter Achinstein maintains in *The Nature of Explanation* (New York: Oxford University Press, 1983) that the condition is neither necessary nor sufficient. I find his arguments unpersuasive, but the dispute would take us far afield here.

[5]Jonathan Bennett, *Locke, Berkeley, Hume: Central Themes* (New York: Oxford University Press, 1971), 70.

V.5 A Defense of Coherentism

JONATHAN DANCY

Jonathan Dancy is professor of philosophy at the University of Keele and the author of several works in ethics and epistemology, including *Introduction to Contemporary Epistemology* from which this selection is taken. Dancy defends both a *coherence theory of truth,* which defines truth as a proposition belonging to a coherent set of propositions, and a *coherence theory of justification,* which holds that a belief is justified if and only if it is supported by the set of other propositions in the coherent system. Some coherentists, such as Keith Lehrer, accept justificatory coherence but reject the coherence theory of truth. Dancy argues that a strong case can be made for holding to both types of coherentism. He also argues that coherentism is compatible with empiricism.

Reprinted from Jonathan Dancy, *Introduction to Contemporary Epistemology* (Oxford: Basil Blackwell, 1985) by permission.

What Is Coherence?

In the last two chapters we have begun to treat our beliefs as a kind of interrelated theory, and the problem has been how the beliefs are related. There are of course many aspects of this question which we have not examined, but we have found reason to reject one answer to it. This is the view that the relation is crucially asymmetrical; that there is an asymmetrical distinction between evidence and theory under which evidence confirms and disconfirms theory in a way in which theory cannot confirm or disconfirm evidence. Foundationalism offers such a structure in its assertion that the direction of justification is all one-way, and in its claim that there are some comparatively fixed points in the structure, the basic beliefs. The notion of inference from fixed points clearly embodies the relevant asymmetries. The notion of inference itself is asymmetrical. It is possible to infer B from A without being able to infer A from B.

The notion of coherence, on which a more completely holistic theory is based, is intended to be symmetrical. But to know whether that intention is successful we need to know more exactly what coherentists mean by "coherent."

All coherentists agree that consistency is a necessary condition for coherence. Bradley added (Bradley, 1914 . . .)* that a coherent set should be complete or comprehensive in some sense. (We shall see why soon.) But consistency and completeness were not enough; they did not capture the feeling that a coherent set stuck together or fitted together in a special way. To capture this, classical coherentists use the notion of entailment (p entails q iff, given p, q *must* be true). Brand Blanshard wrote that in a fully coherent system "no proposition would be arbitrary, every proposition would be entailed by the others jointly and even singly, no proposition would stand outside the system" (Blanshard, 1939, vol. 2 . . .). But this account of coherence in terms of mutual entailment is disputed. Ewing suggested that it would be sufficient that each member of a coherent set be entailed by all the rest . . . and that anything further than this would be disastrous. Indeed, can we

make sense of the idea of a system within which each member entails all the rest?

Instead of answering this question directly, we can move towards it by considering an objection to any use of the notion of mutual entailment as the central element in a coherent set. That notion, as Blanshard uses it, is symmetrical enough. But entailment as traditionally understood is not a matter of degree. And this is important because coherentists want to give a sense to the notion that as one's belief-set grows, it improves (we hope); it becomes more coherent. And this is not just because it becomes more complete; completeness can hardly be a virtue in itself. And we cannot rely on the point that the relations of entailment only hold between members of a complete set, because this would not really capture the sense in which we aim, in expanding our belief-set, to make it more coherent. Since we are never likely to achieve a complete coherent set, the definition of coherence in terms of entailment has the consequence that nobody's beliefs are actually coherent at all. (Other problems with the appeal to entailment are explored in Rescher, 1973 . . .).

So if we are to have a coherence theory of justification, we need to give a good sense to the idea that justification can grow. An alternative account of coherence, offered in Lehrer (1974) and Sellars (1973), defines a coherent set as one which is consistent, complete and mutually explanatory. The idea here will be that, as the set increases in size, we can hope that each member of it is better explained by the rest. Explanations can improve in quality; this accounts for the growth of justification. And the notion of *mutual* explanation is clearly symmetrical, in the required sense.

Two comments could be made on this account of the coherent as the mutually explanatory. First, it seems that the requirement of completeness can be quietly dropped. This is because the need for completeness is already accounted for by the search for a higher degree of mutual explanatoriness. And it is just as well, because there is no really clear notion of completeness available here. We might perhaps suppose that a complete set contains every proposition or its contradictory. But this will be of no help unless we have a clear notion of "every proposition." In the same way, we have no clear idea of a perfect explanation, a point from which things cannot be improved. That point is at best one which we

---

*[Works cited in the text appear in the bibliography at the end of Part V.—Ed.]

approach without limit; there is no content to supposing that we might have reached it. So doubts about completeness make me happy to leave it out of the definition of coherence. (Other reasons will emerge later.)

The second point is that coherence is a property of a set of beliefs, not of the members. The set is coherent to the extent that the members are mutually explanatory and consistent. This will be important in what follows.

It may seem, then, that our account in terms of mutual explanation is an improvement on that which appeals to entailment to tie the coherent set together. But I think that the mutual explanation account restates rather than replaces Blanshard's use of entailment. For Blanshard's understanding of entailment is not the traditional one. Traditionally, "p entails q" is understood atomistically, as a feature of the individual meanings of p and q; given the meaning of p and that of q, if p is true then q must be, and this independently of considerations elsewhere in the system. This understanding of entailment is the basis of Rescher's complaint that where p entails q, q is a redundant member of the set; and hence that a coherent set is infected with mutual redundancy, contrary to Blanshard's stated intention. And it is the basis of our remark above that entailment is not a matter of degree. But Blanshard does not conceive of entailment in this way, as we would expect of anyone who is a holist in the theory of meaning. For him, entailment only occurs within a system; and since the system determines the meanings of p and of q, it determines the strength of the link between p and q. So as the system grows, that link can become stronger.

There is anyway an obvious intuitive link between entailment, as Blanshard sees it, and explanation. To explain q by appeal to p is to show why q should be true, given p. The explanation works to the extent that it shows that, given p, q must be true. Explanation thus reveals entailment, in Blanshard's sense. And like entailment, explanation should be viewed holistically rather than atomistically. So at the end of the day our two accounts of coherence collapse into each other.

Before we turn to the coherence theory of justification we need first to consider the coherence theory of truth; the two are closely connected.

The Coherence Theory of Truth

This theory holds that a proposition is true iff it is a member of a coherent set.

If we are doubtful about the possibility of a fully coherent set, we shall hold as coherentists classically did that truth is a matter of degree. Propositions are true to the extent that there is a coherent set of which they are members. Notice, however, that the theory does not identify truth with coherence. It gives no sense to the notion of a true set. Instead, it defines truth for members of sets. A proposition is true iff it is a member of a coherent set. Propositions cannot be coherent, in the required sense, and sets cannot be called true unless they are members of larger sets.

However, the theory does purport to offer a definition of truth. It does not restrict itself to telling us what circumstances would justify us in taking a proposition to be true. It might do this by claiming that we are justified in believing that p is true to the extent that doing so would increase the coherence of our belief-set. The coherentist does make this claim; he does offer a *criterial* account of truth, a theory about what are the criteria for truth. But he also offers an account of what truth itself is, a *definitional* account. The two accounts are supposed to fit together, as we shall see.

Many philosophers who have shown an interest in the coherence theory of truth have disputed the view that the theory offers a definition of truth on the grounds that, taken that way, the theory is manifestly false (e.g. Russell, 1907). It is manifestly false because no matter how tight our account of coherence we shall have to admit that there may be more than one coherent set of propositions. Nothing in the notion of coherence, as defined, gives us any right to say that there is a unique most coherent set. But it is obviously the case that there can be at most one complete set of truths. So truth cannot be defined in terms of coherence alone.

The situation might remind us of Quine's thesis of the underdetermination of theory by evidence. If there is more than one theory equally effective in handling the evidence, what are we to say about the different theories? Can we perhaps say that they are all true, or that all their members are true? It seems that we cannot. If our different coherent sets are all of them verging on complete, if they constitute complete but different descriptions of the world, how can we admit that all the parts of these different descriptions of the world are true? Surely if the descriptions are different, they are competing, and the prize they are competing for is the prize of *truth*. Hence only one of these competing sets can contain nothing but truths, and the coherence theory of truth is wrong.

This objection to the coherence theory of truth is standard. We can call it the plurality objection. It arouses extreme indignation amongst those who call themselves coherentists. Brand Blanshard writes (1939, Vol. 2 . . .):

> This objection, like so many other annihilating criticisms, would have more point if anyone had ever held the theory it demolishes. But if intended to represent the coherence theory as responsibly advocated, it is a gross misunderstanding.

Blanshard is arguing that the plurality objection fails to appreciate the empiricist character of his coherentism. For he takes it, as do other coherentists such as Bradley, that there is only one coherent set, and that this set is distinguished from all rivals by being empirically grounded. This is so, according to Bradley, because of the very aim of thought and enquiry, which is to discover the most systematic ordering of our experience (Bradley, 1914 . . .):

> My experience is solid . . . so far as in short it is a system. My object is to have a world as comprehensive and coherent as possible, and, in order to attain this object, I have not only to reflect but perpetually to have recourse to the materials of sense. I must go to this source both to verify the matter which is old and also to increase it by what is new. And in this way I must depend upon the judgements of perception.

What these coherentists are saying is that the enterprise is to start from the data of experience and to construct a set of beliefs around those data which will order the data in the most systematic (coherent) way. To do this we may need to reject *some* of the data, but we cannot reject them all because our very aim is to make sense of what we have as data. So the set of beliefs which we do construct *must* be empirically grounded, and this grounding in the data of experience guarantees

that there will be only one set which constitutes "the most systematic ordering."

This appeal to the need for an empirical grounding manages to exclude all the more fanciful putatively coherent sets of propositions from our reckoning. Thus, for instance, a perfect expansion of the Sherlock Holmes stories would not have to be counted as a true description of the world, despite its coherence. But unfortunately, even when we have ruled out all such coherent sets, there will be more than one remaining. For nothing in the appeal to the need to order the data of experience can make it the case that there need be one most systematic ordering. There may, for all we can do to prevent it, be more than one equally good way of "ordering" the data or of fitting them into an explanatory system, particularly when we remember that some of the data will be rejected on the way. This is, after all, just what the underdetermination of theory by evidence amounts to. So the plurality objection still has teeth.

The right defence against the plurality objection is offence. We should ask whether there is any other theory of truth, any other account of what truth is, which fares better. It emerges quickly that none of the standard theories of truth have the desired consequence that there can only be one set of truths. Certainly the traditional opponent of the coherence theory, the correspondence theory, faces the same difficulties. Correspondence theories try to erect an account of truth upon the undeniable remark that for a proposition to be true is for it to fit the facts. But as long as facts and true propositions are kept separate from each other, what is there to prevent there being two distinct sets of propositions which "fit the facts" equally well? We must either admit that the plurality objection is as effective against one theory as it is against another, and abandon the demand that "the truth" be somehow unique, or admit that though the truth must be unique, it is somehow not part of the role of the theory of truth to show this.

But perhaps the plurality objection still has a point. After all, the coherentist must admit that the competing theories are all true (since they are all equally coherent), while the correspondence theorist can say that one is true and the others false. The correspondence theorist has this advantage because he says that there is something beyond and distinct from the competing theories, the world, which can make it the case that one is true and the rest false. So the coherentist cannot really give a good sense to the notion that the different theories compete or are incompatible, it seems. And this is a weakness not shared by his opponent.

The reply to this comes in two parts. First we can say that for the coherentist each theory is incompatible with every other because one cannot embrace two theories at once, on pain of loss of coherence. So from the point of view of someone with a theory, every other theory is false because it cannot be added to the true theory. And second, it is only from the point of view of the world, a point of view external to any theory, that the correspondence theorist has an advantage. Only those people who hold no theory at all but view all theories from outside can give a sense to the notion of incompatibility between theories beyond that which the coherentist has already given. But there is no such thing as a theory-free, external, viewpoint. So the coherentist can give an account of what it is for two coherent theories to be incompatible, and there is no further account which only the correspondence theorist can give.

The Coherence Theory of Justification

This theory holds that a belief is justified to the extent to which the belief-set of which it is a member is coherent. Each belief is to be evaluated by appeal to the role it plays in the belief-set. If the coherence of the set would be increased by abandoning the belief and perhaps by replacing it by its opposite, the belief is not justified. If the set is more coherent with this belief as a member rather than with any alternative, the belief is justified. This notion of justification is relative to individual believers. The full account should be: if a's belief-set is more coherent with the belief that p as a member than without it or with any alternative, a is (or would be) justified in believing that p.

What is the link here between justification and truth? A belief-set with reasonable coherence will make each of its members justified. But that does not mean that they are all true. It may be that the belief-set cannot be further expanded; that after a

while the addition of further beliefs, however it may be done, always continues to decrease the coherence of the growing whole. In that case the members of the set are not all true, because they cannot all be members of a genuinely coherent whole. But they are still justified (for a). Equally a belief may be true, since the proposition which is its content is in fact a member of a coherent set, without that meaning that it is justified for a. So a belief can be true without being justified and justified without being true, on the coherence account. Justification can grow, but as it grows it need not be approaching truth. Of course as a belief-set grows and becomes more coherent, we have more and more reason to suppose that its members are true. But they may not be; indeed it is always quite probable that further expansion will require revision somewhere.

Despite the distinction between belief and justification, however, coherentists stress as a virtue of their theory that truth and justification are according to them all of a piece. The coherence of a belief-set goes to make its members justified; the coherence of a set of propositions, believed or not, goes to make its members true. The sense in which, on the theory, truth is one thing and justification another does not detract from the advantage of having a smooth link between justification and truth.

Suppose that, as Ewing . . . , Rescher . . . and Lehrer . . . suggest, we adopt a coherence theory of justification but reject the coherence theory of truth. (Perhaps we are impressed by the plurality objection.) We are left with a mystery. Surely our theory ought somehow to show why justification is worth having, why justified beliefs ought to be sought and adopted, and unjustified ones discarded. An obvious way of showing this is to show how or that justified beliefs are more likely to be true. If we take coherence as criterion both of truth and of justification, we have a good chance of being able to do this. The alternative is to suppose that justification is a matter of internal coherence, a question of fit between objects that are all of the same sort, while truth is a matter of the correspondence between propositions and objects of a different sort, facts or states of affairs. But then it would be difficult to find a reason for thinking that where the internal relation of justification is present, the external relation of truth is probably present too. So there is an enormous advantage in having theories of truth and justification that fit each other. The theory of truth ought to fit the epistemology and not be allowed to ride independent of it.

What are the objects which are linked by the relation of mutual explanation in a coherent set? In the coherence theory of truth they are propositions; in the coherence theory of justification they are propositions too. So when we talk of the justification of a's belief that p we are asking whether the proposition p forms, with other propositions which a believes, a promisingly coherent set. If it does, the truth of p is explained by appeal to the truth of those others. (A different approach is taken by Lehrer . . . , where he suggests that what needs to be explained is not the truth of p but rather the fact that a believes that p.) So in this respect also our theory of truth fits our theory of justification.

As well as this, coherentists would say we have more direct reasons to do without the asymmetries of foundationalism. We have seen no compelling reason to adopt those asymmetries yet . . . , and in the absence of such a reason we should take it that there is only one form of justification, the same for all beliefs. There are no fixed points by appeal to which other beliefs are assessed. Each belief is assessed in the same way, by considering the effect of its presence on the coherence of the whole. So there are no restrictions on what can be appealed to in support of what. The test, as Bradley says, is system and not any one-directional criterion of fitting the evidence.

Equally, in the event of a difficulty there are no antecedent requirements about where revision should be made. We have no independent reason to prefer to retain highly observational beliefs in preference to theoretical ones. The right revision is the one that results in the most coherent new whole, but we cannot tell in advance what sort of revision is most likely to achieve this.

Coherentists would claim that this holistic theory fits our actual practice far better than the more restrictive foundationalist account. In practice there are no taboos on what can be appealed to in support of what and no requirements about which sorts of statements should be retained in preference to others if there is a clash. We don't always preserve the observational at the expense of the theoretical. We do, for instance, suppose that you cannot be right when you say that this curtain looks orange to you, on the grounds that objects with the molecular structure of this curtain just don't look orange. Equally, we do support our observational beliefs by appeal to our theoretical ones (a weak form of foundationalism could perhaps admit this, of course . . .). So there is no theoretical need to accept the asymmetries, and our practice reveals that we don't do so anyway.

In this way coherentism makes a virtue of necessity. In the absence of fixed points and the lack of any clues about where revision should start, we know that at any time our belief-set is merely provisional. Revisions will be called for, and the need to revise may occur anywhere. This is a form of fallibilism. . . . Coherentists welcome it and claim that their approach reveals the strength of fallibilism; fallibilism is not an unfortunate defect but an essential part of the epistemological enterprise, the drive continually to revise in the search for greater coherence.

Further support for the theory comes from its ability to justify the principles of inference we use. Foundationalists suppose that we need not only basic beliefs but also principles of inference to take us from those beliefs to the more sophisticated superstructure. We understand, perhaps, what justifies the basic beliefs; but what justifies the principles of inference? The classic example of this question is our third sceptical argument . . . about induction. . . . But the inductive principle is not the only principle of inference at issue. Further principles might be:

1 If I seem to remember doing an action then (probably) I did the action. (Memory)
2 If others tell me that they observed an event, then (probably) the event did occur. (Testimony of others)
3 If it seems to me that a certain object is before me, then (probably) it is before me. (Perception)

Such principles cannot themselves be justified by appeal to basic beliefs, nor as conclusions of inferences from those beliefs. Foundationalists seem therefore to have to find yet a further form of justification for their principles of inference. Whether they can achieve this or not, coherentists face a much easier task. For them, principles of inference are of course necessary as one of the ways in which the coherent set is bound together. But they can be justified in the now familiar way, by appeal to the increase in coherence which results from the adoption of a principle. Use of a principle can be expected to increase the size of a belief-set, and is justified if the set increases in coherence as it increases in size. And if there are competing principles, as when we consider an alternative to 1 which includes a restriction to certain circumstances, then that alternative is justified whose use most increases the coherence of the whole. . . .

Another advantage of coherentism, suggested by Rescher . . . is that it directs attention away from the individual's struggle to construct his own epistemology, which is the classical conception of the epistemological enterprise . . . ; instead it gives a sense to the notion of knowledge as a social phenomenon, something that can be shared and which can increase by means of that sharing. This claim seems to depend on the ease with which coherentists can justify the use of principle 2. It is as if coherentists start from the traditional egocentric problem of what each of us is justified in believing. In this respect they don't diverge from the tradition except in failing to insist that the initial data are restricted to basic facts about one's own sensory states. However, the testimony of others can be used more or less immediately to increase the coherence of one's own belief-set, and so one can make an early move away from the egocentric predicament and think of oneself as a collaborator, even as one more likely to learn from others than to contribute to the sum total of knowledge (a sort of epistemological modesty). This falls short of supposing that knowledge is entirely a social phenomenon, as some would wish, but it approximates to that position despite taking the traditional starting point.

Coherentists also suppose that just as their approach provides a possible justification of induction, so it offers a general stance from which the sceptic can be defused, if not rebutted. . . .

Finally, [there is] a general reason for seeking a more complete holism in the theory of justification, to suit the adoption of a holistic theory of meaning. Coherentism is *the* holistic theory; it provides what is required.

These are the main advantages which coherentists would claim for their theory. We now turn to consider the central attack on coherentism. This is the complaint that coherentism and empiricism are incompatible.

4 The Role of Empirical Data

In [section] 2 we considered the plurality objection to the coherence theory of truth, and mentioned the standard reply. This is that one coherent set is picked out from the others by being empirically grounded. The enterprise of thought is to start from the data of experience and to construct a set of beliefs around those data which will order them in the most systematic way. But this empiricist approach seems to reveal a difficulty for coherentism as a theory of justification. For it appears to reintroduce a distinction between two sorts of justification. The coherentist should be a *monist* here; he should claim that justification is everywhere of the same sort. But doesn't the notion of empirical *data* introduce a form of pluralism? For the role of a datum seems unable to be captured by a theory whose sole concern is an internal relation between beliefs. A datum stands as such not because of any relation it bears to other beliefs, but because of its source. It has a claim to acceptance because it is part of our input, part of what experience is giving us.

Surely, then, we have to make room for the notion of someone's beliefs being justified, at least in part, by reference to something beyond the beliefs themselves; by reference, in fact, to his experience. But this amounts to abandoning our coherentist monism and resorting to the sort of asymmetry characteristic of foundationalism. Only foundationalism can give to sensory experience the sort of special role it must have in any empiricist account of the justification of experience. Empiricism and coherentism are incompatible.

The first question is why the coherentist should worry about this attack at all. He has been put in the position of maintaining that belief-sets which bear no relation to anyone's experience may have all the defining characteristics of coherence. But he would allow this only if he accepted the distinction between belief and experience; and this distinction is not one on which all interested parties will agree. Provided that we maintain with Kant that it is impossible to draw a suitable distinction between the cognitive and the sensory "elements" in sensory experience, or maintain that all experience is a form of cognition or judgement (i.e. acquisition of belief) rather than a form of sensation, we can construct a form of coherentism which does not fall foul of the argument. If a coherentist requires for justification that all cognitive elements be interconnected, there is no possibility that beliefs wholly disconnected from sensory experience might yet count as justified, once we take experience to be cognitive.

This defence, however important, is less than complete. For even if we accept that experience is a form of belief, we can still insist on a distinction between sensory beliefs and others (without yet specifying exactly how it is to be drawn), and with that distinction re-express the empiricist's point as the demand that the sensory beliefs support the others. But this is a demand for something beyond mere coherence, for the relevant notion of support is intended to be asymmetrical. It brings an asymmetry into the theory of justification in just the way that the coherentist is so keen to avoid. (And similar notions, for instance that our sensory beliefs are our evidence or our data, have the same effect.) The requirement that the sensory support the non-sensory amounts to the view that justification is one-way, from sensory to non-sensory, and hence to the view that justification takes two forms, first the justification of the non-sensory by the sensory, and second the (somehow different) justification of the sensory. And this is to abandon the essential monistic thesis of coherentism in favour of some form of foundationalism, limited though that form may yet turn out to be.

The coherentist might of course try to escape this attack by claiming that a mere distinction between sensory and non-sensory beliefs does not amount to any invidious asymmetry of the sort which is being foisted upon him. But I think that there is no escape for him this way. First, it is not the distinction itself which creates the asymmetry, but the demand that, so distinguished, the sensory beliefs support the non-sensory beliefs. Second, there seem to be good independent reasons why even a coherentist must ascribe to the sensory beliefs some special role in the epistemology of the individual. Not all these reasons are of equal weight, but I shall mention three.

First, those objects whose justification we are considering are belief-sets, and all the belief-sets with which we are familiar (our own and those of our contemporaries) are as a matter of fact empirically based. We have no cause to concern ourselves, therefore, with non-existent belief-sets which lack empirical grounding. Second, for a set

to count as a *belief*-set—for the propositional attitude concerned to be that of belief—it must be thought of as some sort of a response to an impinging environment. It isn't that beliefs which were wholly disconnected from experience would merely be unjustified; they wouldn't be beliefs at all. Third, it seems possible, although the question is to be determined empirically, i.e. by test, that an asymmetrical reliance on the experiential such as is expressed by thinking of our experience as our evidence would actually produce, from the same input, belief-sets with greater coherence, and if this is so there are reasons from within the coherentist approach itself for introducing an asymmetry into the account.

Given that there is to be this asymmetry, can the coherentist cope with it? We might try to do so by distinguishing between two sorts of security that beliefs can have, antecedent and subsequent. *Antecedent security* is security which a belief brings with it, which it has prior to any consideration of how well it fits with others or of the coherence of the set. We could hold that sensory beliefs have a degree of antecedent security in being prima facie reliable or justified; there will be greater degrees of antecedent security up to infallibility. *Subsequent security* is security which a belief acquires as a result of its contribution to the coherence of the set. All justified beliefs, on a coherence account, have a degree of subsequent security.

Coherentists would traditionally claim that no belief has any greater antecedent security than any other. We could call this position pure coherentism; an extreme form of it maintains that no beliefs have any antecedent security at all. But we might be persuaded by the argument above to suppose that sensory beliefs do have an antecedent security that others lack. If this "weak coherentism" is consistent, it would perhaps meet the demands of empiricism. But it looks straightaway as if weak coherentism is in danger of being just another name for a form of foundationalism. After all, prima facie reliability and such characteristics were mentioned in 4.3 as central to non-classical forms of foundationalism. Is it possible then to be an empiricist and accept an asymmetrical relation between sensory and other beliefs, without thereby becoming a foundationalist? In our discussion of Quine (7.2–3) it seemed that the empiricist insistence that our beliefs be grounded in experience should be somehow compatible with complete holism both in epistemology and in theory of meaning. Can we show in greater detail how this is possible?

5 Coherentism and Empiricism

The most fruitful coherentist approach can be found in the work of F. H. Bradley. Bradley is an empiricist, in this respect expressing himself as clearly as the most ardent could wish:

> I agree that we depend vitally on the sense-world, that our material comes from it, and that apart from it knowledge could not begin. To this world, I agree, we have forever to return, not only to gain new matter but to confirm and increase the old.
> (Bradley, 1914, p. 209)

Here we see Bradley ascribing to the "data of perception" or the "sense-world" an asymmetrical role in the individual's epistemology. In fact the asymmetry is complex. It is partly genetic; material *comes from* the sense-world, and without that world knowledge could not *begin*. And it has a continuing role, both in our need continually to return to previous "data of perception" and in our need to make sense of the continuing flow of new sensory life. This complex asymmetry is one which echoes (if I can reverse the temporal order) Quine's arguments for the verification theory of meaning; these were either genetic, as when he writes of the sort of meaning which is basic to the learning of one's language, or continuing, as when he writes of the sort of meaning that is basic to translation. . . .

Bradley is willing to accept that the sense-world plays a special role in epistemology, but he is unwilling to accept that that special role emerges in the sort of asymmetry which characterises foundationalism. . . :

> In order to begin my construction I take the foundation as absolute . . . But that my construction continues to rest on the beginnings of my knowledge is a conclusion which does not follow. For it is in another sense that my world rests upon the data of perception.
> [Ibid.]

Bradley holds that experience provides data (genetic asymmetry), but that the question

whether something which appears as datum should remain as accepted fact is one which is not even partially determined by its origin as datum. Data stand for acceptance into our world in the same way and by the same criteria as does any other proposition. The test in each case is what he calls "system," or in other words the question whether the coherence of our world is increased by their admission as accepted fact. In this respect there is no asymmetry; all propositions (in the sense, as it were, of proposals) that are justified receive a justification of exactly the same sort.

Is Bradley's position, accepting one asymmetry but rejecting another, consistent? One might say against it that even if we agree that all propositions, data and the rest, are justified by their contribution to system, there remains a crucial asymmetry which is not genetic. For the system had as a prime aim the need to make sense of the sense-world; even if in carrying out that aim we reject some elements of that world there remains an asymmetry in the purpose of systematisation. This asymmetry is revealed in the demand that by and large items which are taken to be data should be accepted. It is a point against any system that it requires too substantial a rejection of the "data of perception," whether or not the coherence of the system is thereby increased.

One could of course take the easy way out and argue that this objection is only valid against pure coherentism, which holds that all beliefs have equal antecedent security; it gets no grip on weak coherentism, which accepts that some beliefs have greater antecedent security than others and can thus offer an account of the necessity that by and large items that are taken to be data should survive epistemological scrutiny. But I think that this would be to miss the point. For the question really is whether this sort of antecedent security, if we are forced to admit it, amounts to an asymmetry in the account we give of justification and thus to a two-tier theory of justification such as only the foundationalist can provide. If it does, we have here an argument as effective against weak as against pure coherentism. So there are two separable questions here; does the necessity constitute some form of antecedent security for sensory beliefs, and, if so, does the antecedent security introduce an asymmetry which forces us to admit a two-tier theory of justification?

The antecedent security which sensory beliefs enjoy seems to amount to this, that we are to accept them as true if nothing counts against them. But don't we do this, and do so quite reasonably, for anything we are willing to count as belief? Any belief will remain until there is some reason to reject it. So *all* beliefs have an antecedent security, in this sense. And this does not introduce two forms of justification. There is no asymmetry created by accepting that all beliefs have some degree of antecedent security, provided that the antecedent security they enjoy is everywhere of the same sort.

But perhaps the problem is that different beliefs have different degrees of antecedent security, and that empiricists characteristically hold that sensory beliefs have *more* of it than others do. Can a coherentist make sense of this idea in his own terms? The problem seems to be that if one belief can be more secure than another in this way, this fact is independent of and prior to all considerations of coherence with other beliefs, and so reintroduces an asymmetry for which there can be no coherentist explanation.

The problem then is whether the coherentist *can* be an empiricist, not whether he *should* be one. And the empiricist is here distinguished by an attitude he takes towards his sensory beliefs; he demands more than another might before he is willing to reject them. But if this attitude is extrinsic to those beliefs themselves, and can without damaging distortion be seen as a further belief, it is a belief which the coherentist might share. And if he does share it, the required results will emerge. The removal of a sensory belief will create greater disturbance and require more to justify it, simply because the characteristic empiricist belief is part of the belief-set too. So this coherentist's sensory beliefs will have a greater degree of security, but it will be subsequent, not antecedent, security; for it is to be seen entirely in terms normally available to the coherentist, i.e. in terms of the internal coherence of his belief-set.

If this is right, pure coherentism is stronger than weak coherentism. If the weak coherentist is distinguished by his willingness to admit different degrees of antecedent security, his position is genuinely and unnecessarily weak.

The conclusion then is that coherentism is compatible with empiricism. Whether a coherentist *ought* to be an empiricist is a different question. . . . But the coherentist seems to have one promising avenue here. For him it is an empirical question whether at the end of the day a more coherent system will result from the adoption of the empiricist attitude to sensory beliefs; whether this form of empiricist stubbornness will eventually pay off. And this is the sort of way in which the coherentist *should* seek to justify empiricism.

V.6 A Critique of Coherentism

RICHARD FUMERTON

Richard Fumerton is professor of philosophy at the University of Iowa. In this essay, he argues that fundamental difficulties face any attempt to define justified belief in terms of coherence among beliefs. To be plausible, a coherence theory must embrace internalism, but a coherentist cannot give a reasonable account of our access to our own beliefs. Moreover, coherence seems at once neither sufficient nor necessary for the justification of our beliefs.

This essay was commissioned for the first edition of this anthology and was revised for this edition.

One of the most prominent attempts to avoid both skepticism and a vicious regress of justification without embracing foundationalism is the coherence theory of justification. Like the foundationalist, the coherence theorist usually accepts the principle that only justified beliefs can justify other beliefs; unlike the foundationalist, the coherence theorist wants also to assert that the only thing that can justify a belief is another set of beliefs. The crudest and most implausible version of a coherence theory simply endorses the legitimacy of circular reasoning, at least when the circles are "big" enough. I can justify my belief that P by appealing to E, justify my belief that E by appealing to F, justify my belief that F by appealing to G, and justify my belief that G by appealing once again to P. More sophisticated coherence theorists will point out that this caricature of a coherence theory overlooks its characteristic rejection of the notion of *linear* justification in favor of a *holistic* conception of justification. When we attempt to justify a belief by showing its coherence with other beliefs, we never appeal directly to P as the sole support of itself (as in the example just given). Rather, we try to justify our belief that P by appealing to the way in which P coheres with other propositions we believe, $Q, R, S,$ and T. We justify our belief that Q by appealing to its coherence with $P, R, S,$ and T; we justify our belief that S, by pointing out its coherence with $P, Q, R,$ and T; and so on. We try not so much to lift ourselves by our bootstraps as to give ourselves a helpful tug. Some find the analogy of a crossword puzzle useful in explaining how coherence contributes to justification.[1] The correctness of any given entry is confirmed by its "fit" with the other entries. But, one might object, each entry in the puzzle is also independently supported by a clue unrelated to the aforementioned fit. A better metaphor still might be a jigsaw puzzle created for masochists. The interlocking pieces are all precisely the same shape, and we are given only the task of creating a picture (we don't even know in advance what the picture is supposed to look like). If we succeed in constructing a nice neat picture out of the pieces, we can claim to be justified in placing the pieces where we did. Each piece's position is justified by the way in which it contributes to a picture given the arrangement of the other pieces.[2]

There are of course many different versions of a coherence theory of justification. Some coheren-

tists restrict their thesis to empirical beliefs; others allow a kind of privileged epistemic status to a subset of beliefs after which coherence is the sole source of justification. In what follows I comment primarily on pure coherentism and argue that the view is fundamentally flawed. Pure coherentism is the view that all beliefs are to be justified by virtue of their coherence with other beliefs. Most of the arguments apply equally, however, to versions of the view that attempt to locate coherence as the source of all *empirical* justification.

The first step in evaluating a coherence theory is to force the coherentist to make clear his criteria for coherence and his concept of truth and to explain how the two fit together. Perhaps the most natural theory of truth to complement a coherence theory of justification is a coherence theory of truth. If there is no more to an accurate picture of reality than a coherent picture of reality (think again of what would make our jigsaw puzzle "correct"), then justifying individual parts of the picture would most naturally be understood in terms of making the parts cohere. One cannot, however, simply assume that the coherence theorist of justification is presupposing a coherence theory of truth. Many who defend the coherence theory of justification explicitly reject coherence as a way of understanding truth. There are, however, some interesting problems that both coherence theories face, and it will be useful to examine them briefly.

The most obvious concern with a coherence theory of truth is that no concept of coherence developed so far has ruled out the possibility of two internally consistent, coherent systems of beliefs that are nevertheless incompatible. This possibility seems to force the proponent of a coherence theory of truth into either abandoning the law of noncontradiction or into relativizing the concept of truth. Because most coherentists are as fond of the law of noncontradiction as anyone else, presumably the most plausible alternative is to relativize truth. All of us who teach introductory philosophy classes remember how we cringe when hearing a student try to deflect the force of an objection by retreating to the position that the claim in question might not be "true for you even if it is true for me." It is almost always the case that such students really mean only to be referring to the fact that one and the same proposition can be rejected by one person and accepted by another. But the coherence theorist is probably committed to a more robust way of making sense of the student's plea for tolerance. Strictly speaking, one should not speak of a proposition's being true; one should only speak of its being true relative to a given system of beliefs, where I suppose one can distinguish as many different relativized concepts of truth as one can distinguish systems of beliefs.

This radical relativization of truth is paralleled by a radical subjectivity with respect to justification on a coherence theory of justification. It seems we can justify believing any proposition provided we "choose" the rest of our beliefs so to avoid incoherence. This "choice" between systems of beliefs seems completely and utterly arbitrary. One philosopher's *reductio* is often another philosopher's welcome consequence of a view, and to be sure many contemporary philosophers will embrace with open arms this radical subjectivity with respect to the concept of justification. Moreover, they will rightly protest my description of the dilemma as one of an arbitrary "choice" between beliefs. Fortunately for us, they should point out, we don't so much choose beliefs as find ourselves caused to have them. So we are not faced with the insurmountable problem of having to make a nonarbitrary choice between infinitely many internally coherent systems of beliefs. Our real-life decision is that of making (usually) relatively minor adjustments within a system that already exists, the core of which doesn't change much. Concerning the possibility of another kind of being with a radically different system of beliefs, all of which are justified relative to one another, the coherentist will probably allow such a possibility without flinching. It is worth remembering, after all, that the most radical foundationalist will probably allow that two beings might have radically different experiences, which justify each in believing propositions inconsistent with what the other believes.

Another more serious kind of problem, a regress problem, however, affects both coherence theories of truth and coherence theories of justification. It has always seemed to me that a coherence theory of truth is quite literally unintelligible because of a vicious metaphysical regress. The truth of P must be relativized to a system of beliefs—say, P, Q, R, and S. The truth of P relative to this system *consists* in the coherence of these beliefs. But one must remember that one of the reasons the coherence theorist rejects the realist's

notion of a fact making true a proposition (where a fact is supposed to be some feature of the world that exists independently of its being represented or pictured by some conscious being) is that the coherence theorist argues that a fact just *is* a proposition's being true. It is a joke to pretend to define P's truth in terms of P's corresponding to the fact that P for to refer to the fact that P is just another way of referring to P's being true. But the very statement of a coherence theory of truth seems to take as unproblematic the existence of *beliefs*—the fact that we believe certain propositions and reject others. But what is this fact of my believing P? Given the theory its being a fact that I believe P is just its being true that I believe P. But what makes it the case that I believe P? Given the theory its being true that I believe P must itself be defined in terms of coherence, presumably, coherence among beliefs in a set including the metabelief that I believe that P. But again, it will only be true that I have this metabelief "I believe that P" if meta-metabeliefs cohere in the relevant way. But how do we ever get anything that ends this regress to actually ground truth? How do we ever find the *source* of any truth? The coherence theorist of truth seems to help herself to a chunk of reality, belief systems, which, given the theory, the theorist has no right to use as metaphysical building blocks of anything. But without beliefs as something that exist independently of their being represented, there simply is nothing with which to "construct" reality. It would be like trying to put together a jigsaw puzzle without having any pieces with which to build.

If a coherence theory of truth faces a vicious ontological regress, a coherence theory of justification (combined, say, with a correspondence theory of truth) faces a vicious epistemological regress. Almost all coherence theorists explicitly or implicitly accept a version of *internalism*. Roughly, they accept the idea that the conditions that define a belief's being justified are conditions to which the believer has, or at least could have, access.[3] It is not enough that my beliefs actually do cohere in order for them to be justified. I must be aware of, or at least have the ability to be aware of, that coherence. Thus, for example, suppose I'm reading a math text with proofs far too complicated for me to follow. On a whim I decide to believe every fifth assertion on odd-numbered pages. Let us suppose that miraculously I end up with a complex set of mathematical beliefs that do in fact cohere beautifully even though the coherence is far too subtle and complex for me to grasp. Surely, if I am completely unaware of any of the logical or probabilistic connections among these beliefs, it is wildly implausible to suppose that these beliefs are justified *for me*.

But how exactly does a coherence theorist understand our access to beliefs and the coherence that holds between them? One could try to stay within the framework of a coherence theory and hold that our justification for believing that we have a certain belief is our awareness of a coherence between our metabelief that we believe P and other beliefs. But now we need to be aware of coherence between our meta-metabelief that we do in fact have the metabelief that P and other beliefs, and so on, *ad infinitum*.

Most coherentists seem to simply give themselves (illegitimately) knowledge of their beliefs (just as the coherence theorists of truth illegitimately give themselves beliefs as the building blocks of reality). One of the most sophisticated defenses of a coherence theory of justification for empirical beliefs, however, has been provided by Laurence BonJour in his book *The Structure of Empirical Knowledge*.[4] A confirmed internalist, BonJour, to his credit, was well aware of this problem and sought to deal with it by arguing that the coherence theorist needs a *doxastic presumption*. This amounts to the presumption that my beliefs about what I believe are correct. But when the smoke clears, it is obvious that BonJour must recognize that the belief constituting this presumption is an unjustified belief. He may protest it is in the nature of a presumption to deflect questions about justification, but one can be sure the skeptic will not be so easily deterred from asking the obviously relevant question concerning the epistemic status of my belief that I have these beliefs. And in his more candid moments, BonJour himself seems to recognize that his coherence theory combined with internalism yields comprehensive and radical skepticism with respect to empirical belief.[5]

In short, if one is going to be a coherence theorist, one had better abandon internalism. But if one abandons access requirements with respect to coherence, one's view is vulnerable to crushing counterexamples. Moreover, if one is going to be an externalist, there are surely more straightforward versions of the view (e. g., reliabilism) that

avoid some of the other problems facing coherentism, problems we are about to examine.

Even if one somehow succeeds in avoiding the regress problem just sketched, innumerable other technical difficulties face the coherence theory of justification. Most of those problems involve developing a plausible conception of coherence. BonJour (1985) argued that the coherence theorist must stress the importance of probabilistic connections among beliefs. Mere logical coherence is too weak. One can, after all, have a logically consistent set of beliefs that have nothing to do with one another. He also goes on to suggest (p. 97) that it would be far too strong to require that each belief in a system of beliefs be deducible from the rest, presumably because he thinks it would be too difficult to satisfy such a requirement. In fact, however, it is probably too *easy* to satisfy such a requirement, at least for someone lucky enough to have taken an introductory course in logic and who is disposed to make obvious inferences. Whenever I believe P and also believe Q, I will believe that P materially implies Q and that Q materially implies P.[6] But if this is so, then my belief that P will be entailed by my other beliefs (Q and Q materially implies P), my belief that Q will be entailed by my other beliefs (P and P materially implies Q), and my belief that P materially implies and is implied by Q will be entailed by my other beliefs (P and Q). But it is obvious that as long as my beliefs are logically consistent and I am a logician who understands material implication, I will undoubtedly trivially satisfy the very requirement that BonJour thought was too difficult a requirement to satisfy because of the very strong conception of coherence it presupposed. Ironically, belief systems in which every belief is entailed by the rest are a dime a dozen. It is actually harder to come by belief systems in which there are lots of nondeductive probabilistic connections.[7]

One might naturally object to the preceding argument by complaining that one's justification for believing P materially implies Q in the example is parasitic upon one's justification for believing P and Q and thus the former can hardly be used to bolster the justification of the latter. A *foundationalist* might quite correctly raise this objection, but it is difficult to see what business a coherentist has making this complaint given the coherentist's rejection of the concept of linear justification. In what sense is any belief's justification founded on or prior to another belief's justification?

Some coherence theorists will try to "tighten up" the relevant sort of coherence required for justification by turning to explanatory coherence as one particularly important sort of coherence that should be exemplified by a system of beliefs. Thus, for example, a belief might be said to be justified if it fits into a set of beliefs in which each belief is explained or explains "better" than it would in some alternative system of beliefs. The interpretation of such a view rests heavily on the criteria offered for determining good explanation, criteria that in this context will, of course, exclude reference to the truth of the explanans. I might, for example, endorse Hempel's famous D-N (deductive-nomological) model as capturing the formal structure of an explanation and construe the best explanatory system of beliefs as the system in which the most is explained with the fewest D-N explanations. (Crudely, a D-N explanation explains some phenomenon by describing antecedent conditions that laws of nature entail a proposition describing the phenomenon to be explained). Another question that must be answered involves the relevant comparison class of systems of beliefs referred to. Must my beliefs fare better than all possible systems of beliefs or merely all systems of beliefs that I have the conceptual capacity to entertain?[8]

Explanatory coherence may initially seem like a relevant criterion of justification, especially if one is inclined to think there is such a thing as reasoning to the best explanation construed as an alternative to inductive reasoning.[9] It is important to realize, however, that with an explanatory coherence theory of justification I cannot simply give myself unproblematically justified beliefs for which I can find plausible explanations. The explanandum beliefs must in turn be justified, presumably by virtue of the fact that they explain still other beliefs. But is it at all plausible to suppose that the justification for all your beliefs—your belief that you are in pain, for example—consists solely in the fact that it explains or is explained by other things you believe? When you feel a sudden stabbing pain in your back and believe (justifiably, of course), that it hurts, is it not just silly to suppose that your "hypothesis" is acceptable only because it fits best into some explanatory theory? As it turns out, I have such

pains occasionally and haven't a clue as to what is causing them, but that doesn't (and shouldn't) shake my conviction that my back hurts. Isn't it just obvious that there is a kind of direct awareness of the pain itself that needs to enter any plausible story of how we know that we are in pain? Furthermore, how does the theory accommodate justified beliefs in analytic truths, synthetic necessary truths (if there are any), and principles of reasoning? Do such beliefs even admit of explanatory coherence? And does an explanatory coherence theory help at all with the radical problem of subjectivity sketched earlier? Certainly if anything like a D-N model of explanation were correct, one would have no difficulty coming up with systems of beliefs that meet the formal requirements (again, excluding truth, of course) of adequate explanation, no matter what the content of those beliefs happened to be. If one uses criteria such as comprehensiveness and simplicity of explanations as a way of choosing between alternative explanations, you will have to deal with obvious counterintuitive consequences. If you want an example of an intuitively implausible system of beliefs with maximum explanatory power and simplicity, look at Berkeley's famous theory of perception: All our sensations come and go according to the will of God who has no need for the intermediary of material things. In any event, why should one prefer simpler explanations over more complex explanations? If simpler theories are true more often than complex theories, it is a contingent fact, and my belief that it is so could only be justified itself by its coherence with other beliefs. One cannot simply presuppose the truth of this belief in developing a coherence theory of justification.

Whatever else coherence involves, virtually all proponents of both coherence theories of justification and truth have always assumed that coherence *minimally* involves logical consistency. I argued earlier that logical coherence was too easy to come by to provide a useful criterion of justification. It may also be too *strong* a requirement for justified belief. Far from being sufficient for having a justified belief, coherence is not even necessary. Goldman has quite correctly argued that strictly speaking all one needs is *one* contradictory belief in one's belief system and each belief is inconsistent with the rest—the conjunction of anything with a contradiction is itself a contradiction.[10] A coherence theorist may be able to deal with this problem by insisting that justified beliefs need only cohere with those other beliefs that are logically *relevant*. It is true that everything is trivially entailed by a contradiction, but perhaps one can simply declare that this sort of entailment has nothing to do with genuine coherence (though I am not suggesting the full development of a "relevance" logic would be an easy task). But even if we meet the worry that a single contradiction might seem to contaminate the coherence of an entire system of beliefs, we are far from out of the woods.

In "Justified Inconsistent Beliefs," Richard Foley argues (quite correctly) by appealing to lotterylike examples that one can justifiably believe a number of propositions—*P, Q, R,* and *S*—such that the conjunction (*P* and *Q* and *R* and *S*) constitutes a contradiction.[11] If Persons A through J have an equal chance of winning a lottery, I can justifiably believe that A will lose, that B will lose, that C will lose, . . . and that J will lose, and also justifiably believe that either A or B or C, . . . or J will win. The propositions believed are inconsistent but are nevertheless each justifiably believed. The argument is simple, but it strikes at the very heart of the coherentist's intuitions. A foundationalist can easily accommodate the result. There is absolutely no reason why foundational knowledge might not make probable *P, Q, R,* and *S* without making probable the conjunction—as you may have discovered to your dismay during a period of heavy travel, the airline industry habitually engages in precisely this sort of reasoning when overbooking flights.

As would be expected of an argument so potentially decisive, its premises are not uncontroversial. A surprising number of philosophers think that there is a lottery *paradox*—something is wrong with allowing that someone could be justified in believing of each participant in the lottery that he will lose *and* that one of them will win. As a good foundationalist, I have never understood what the paradox is supposed to be, however. What reason is there for denying that one can have justified inconsistent beliefs regarding the outcome of the lottery?

In "A Solution to the Problem of Induction," John Pollock attempts to resolve the lottery "paradox."[12] His strategy is to grant that one has a prima facie reason for thinking that person A will lose the lottery while pointing out that one has

equally strong prima facie reasons for believing that B will lose, that C will lose, . . . and that J will lose. Furthermore, we also know that if B and C and . . . J lose, A will win. We are then in a position to present the following valid argument for the claim that

  1. A will win the lottery.
  2. B will lose.
  3. C will lose.

      .

      .

      .

  10. J will lose.
  11. If B will lose, and C will lose, and . . . J will lose, then A will win.
  12. Therefore, A will win.

The availability of this argument is supposed to balance our initial reason for thinking that A will lose, thus leaving us with no more reason to believe that A will lose than that he will win! It is hard for me to see how one could accept so paradoxical a solution to an alleged paradox. Pollock is assuming a principle that seems problematic, to say the least. To justifiably infer the conclusion of the preceding argument from its premises, one needs to be justified in believing the *conjunction* of its premises. And that one can justifiably believe of each of B through J that he will lose does not imply that one can justifiably believe that they *all* will. More generally, it just seems obviously fallacious to infer from the fact that I can justifiably believe *P* and justifiably believe *Q* that I can justifiably believe (*P* and *Q*).

In *Knowledge*, Keith Lehrer offers a highly sophisticated coherence theory of what he calls complete justification and discusses the lottery "paradox" within the framework of that theory.[13] There he appears to argue that an ideally rational person is interested in maximizing the number of true beliefs she has while minimizing the number of false beliefs. If one allows inconsistent beliefs in one's belief system, one is guaranteed to have at least one false belief, thus frustrating at least one of the ends of an ideal truth seeker. But as Lehrer would agree, the goal of the ideal epistemic agent is not just to avoid false beliefs—we can achieve that goal by refusing to believe anything. The rational person is also interested in arriving at true beliefs, and by purging ourselves of beliefs about the outcome of the lottery, we guarantee that we will forgo a great number of true beliefs. If A and B have the same set of beliefs excluding those concerning the outcome of the lottery and if A believes of each participant that he will lose while B withholds belief in these propositions, it is not hard to calculate that A is going to end up with a better "winning" percentage of true beliefs over false beliefs.

Summary

The only plausible coherence theories will require that a subject have access to relations of coherence before such relations will justify the subject's beliefs. A pure coherence theorist can give no plausible account of such access. Coherence among our beliefs is far too weak a requirement for our beliefs' being justified. It is also too strong a requirement. There seems little to recommend a coherence theory of justification.

Notes

[1] The metaphor is nicely employed by Susan Haack in *Evidence and Inquiry* (Oxford: Blackwell, 1993), 84–86, although she emphasizes that the metaphor illuminates only a *role* for coherence—it does not support a pure coherence theory of justification. [See Reading V.8 in this book.—Ed.]

[2] The metaphor of interchangeable pieces constrained only by common shape, with no specific picture to guide us is useful in appreciating the formidable task facing the coherentist. Coherence is the only thing analogous to the shape, and, of course, we have no *prior* idea what the world is supposed to "look" like when we try to represent it accurately with our belief system.

[3] I have argued in *Metaepistemology and Skepticism* (Lanham, MD: Rowman and Littlefield, 1995) that there

are significantly different versions of internalism. The strongest version of "access" internalism holds that everything that defines a belief's being justified is something to which the person holding that justified belief must have access. Such a view is too strong, I believe. A weaker form of access internalism holds only that when the justification for a belief depends on that belief's relations to other beliefs, one must have access to those relations—I call this view inferential access internalism. It is only the weaker view that my argument against coherence theories relies upon.

[4] Laurence BonJour, *The Structure of Empirical Knowledge* (Cambridge, MA: Harvard University Press, 1985).

[5] BonJour (1985); see particularly the last paragraph on p. 105. It should be noted in passing that BonJour has now renounced the coherence theory of justification in his latest work.

[6] For those who have not taken such a course, that statement that P materially implies Q is a statement whose truth can be defined in terms of the truth values of P and Q. It is false that P materially implies Q when P is true and Q is false. Otherwise, it is true.

[7] BonJour (1985) worries particularly about the apparent incoherence of a person's beliefs if that person's system of beliefs contains two subsets (call them x and y), which are themselves logically unrelated (p. 97). But the preceding point applies here again, of course. In addition to the beliefs that comprise x and the beliefs that comprise y, the subject can easily see that these subsets justify the beliefs that x materially implies y and that y materially implies x, and when we add these beliefs to the system we have logical entailment again.

[8] See Lehrer's discussion of this issue in *Knowledge* (Oxford: Clarendon Press, 1974), 161.

[9] A view I have challenged in "Induction and Reasoning to the Best Explanation," *Philosophy of Science 47* (1980).

[10] See Alvin Goldman, *Epistemology and Cognition* (Cambridge, MA: Harvard University Press, 1987), 197.

[11] Richard Foley, "Justified Inconsistent Beliefs," *American Philosophical Quarterly 16*, 1979, 247–258.

[12] John Pollock, "A Solution to the Problem of Induction," *Nous* 1984.

[13] Lehrer, 1974.

V.7 The Raft and the Pyramid: Coherence Versus Foundations in the Theory of Knowledge

Ernest Sosa

Ernest Sosa is professor of philosophy at Brown University. In this essay, Sosa compares the "solid security of the ancient foundationalist pyramid and the risky adventure of the new coherentist raft."

Contemporary epistemology must choose between the solid security of the ancient foundationalist pyramid and the risky adventure of the new coherentist raft. Our main objective will be to understand, as deeply as we can, the nature of the controversy and the reasons for and against each of the two options. But first of all we take note of two underlying assumptions.

1. Two Assumptions

(A1) Not everything believed is known, but nothing can be known without being at least believed (or accepted, presumed, taken for granted, or the like) in some broad sense. What additional requirements must a belief fill in order to be knowledge? There are surely at least the following two: (a) it must be true, and (b) it must be justified (or warranted, reasonable, correct, or the like).

(A2) Let us assume, moreover, with respect to the second condition A1(b): first, that it involves a normative or evaluative property; and, second, that the relevant sort of justification is that which pertains to knowledge: epistemic (or theoretical) justification. Someone seriously ill may have two sorts of justification for believing he will recover: the practical justification that derives from the contribution such belief will make to his recovery and the theoretical justification provided by the lab results, the doctor's diagnosis and prognosis, and so on. Only the latter is relevant to the question whether he knows.

Reprinted from *Midwest Studies in Philosophy, Vol. 5: Studies in Epistemology* (Minneapolis: University of Minnesota Press, 1980), 3–25, by permission of the author and the publisher. Copyright 1980, University of Minnesota Press.

2. Knowledge and Criteria

a. There are two key questions of the theory of knowledge:

   (i) What do we know?
   (ii) How do we know?

The answer to the first would be a list of bits of knowledge or at least of types of knowledge: of the self, of the external world, of other minds, and so on. An answer to the second would give criteria (or canons, methods, principles, or the like) that would explain how we know whatever it is that we do know.

b. In developing a theory of knowledge, we can begin either with a(i) or with a(ii). Particularism would have us begin with an answer to a(i) and only then take up a(ii) on the basis of that answer. Quite to the contrary, methodism would reverse that order. The particularist thus tends to be antiskeptical on principle. But the methodist is as such equally receptive to skepticism and to the contrary. Hume, for example, was no less a methodist than Descartes. Each accepted, in effect, that only the obvious and what is proved deductively on its basis can possibly be known.

c. What, then, is the obvious? For Descartes it is what we know by intuition, what is clear and distinct, what is indubitable and credible with no fear of error. Thus for Descartes basic knowledge is always an infallible belief in an indubitable truth. All other knowledge must stand on that basis through deductive proof. Starting from such criteria (canons, methods, etc.), Descartes concluded that knowledge extended about as far as his contemporaries believed.[1] Starting from similar criteria, however, Hume concluded that both science and common sense made claims far beyond their rightful limits.

d. Philosophical posterity has rejected Descartes's theory for one main reason: that it admits too easily as obvious what is nothing of the sort. Descartes's reasoning is beautifully simple: God exists; no omnipotent perfectly good being would descend to deceit; but if our common sense beliefs were radically false, that would represent deceit on His part. Therefore, our common sense beliefs must be true or at least cannot be radically false. But in order to buttress this line of reasoning and fill in details, Descartes appeals to various principles that appear something less than indubitable.

e. For his part, Hume rejects all but a minuscule portion of our supposed common sense knowledge. He establishes first that there is no way to prove such supposed knowledge on the basis of what is obvious at any given moment through reason or experience. And he concludes, in keeping with this methodism, that in point of fact there really is no such knowledge.

3. Two Metaphors: The Raft and the Pyramid

Both metaphors concern the body or system of knowledge in a given mind. But the mind is of course a more complex marvel than is sometimes supposed. Here I do not allude to the depths plumbed by Freud, nor even to Chomsky's. Nor need we recall the labyrinths inhabited by statesmen and diplomats, nor the rich patterns of some novels or theories. We need look no further than the most common, everyday beliefs. Take, for instance, the belief that driving tonight will be dangerous. Brief reflection should reveal that any of us with that belief will join to it several other closely related beliefs on which the given belief depends for its existence or (at least) its justification. Among such beliefs we could presumably find some or all of the following: that the road will be icy or snowy; that driving on ice or snow is dangerous; that it will rain or snow tonight; that the temperature will be below freezing; appropriate beliefs about the forecast and its reliability; and so on.

How must such beliefs be interrelated in order to help justify my belief about the danger of driving tonight? Here foundationalism and coherentism disagree, each offering its own metaphor.

Let us have a closer look at this dispute, starting with foundationalism.

Both Descartes and Hume attribute to human knowledge an architectonic structure. There is a nonsymmetric relation of physical support such that any two floors of a building are tied by that relation: one of the two supports (or at least helps support) the other. And there is, moreover, a part with a special status: the foundation, which is supported by none of the floors while supporting them all.

With respect to a body of knowledge K (in someone's possession), foundationalism implies that K can be divided into parts K_1, K_2, . . . such that there is some nonsymmetric relation R (analogous to the relation of physical support) which orders those parts in such a way that there is one—call it F—that bears R to every other part while none of them bears R in turn to F.

According to foundationalism, each piece of knowledge lies on a pyramid such as the following:

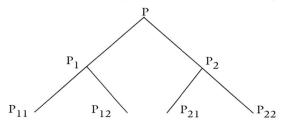

The nodes of such a pyramid (for a proposition P relative to a subject S and a time t) must obey the following requirements:

a. The set of all nodes that succeed (directly) any given node must serve jointly as a base that properly supports that node (for S at t).

b. Each node must be a proposition that S is justified in believing at t.

c. If a node is not self-evident (for S at t), it must have successors (that serve jointly as a base that properly supports that node).

d. Each branch of an epistemic pyramid must terminate.

For the foundationalist Descartes, for instance, each terminating node must be an indubitable proposition that S believes at t with no possibility of error. As for the nonterminal nodes, each of them represents inferential knowledge, derived by deduction from more basic beliefs.

Such radical foundationalism suffers from a fatal weakness that is twofold: (a) there are not so many perfectly obvious truths as Descartes thought; and (b) once we restrict ourselves to what is truly obvious in any given context, very little of one's supposed common sense knowledge can be proved on that basis. If we adhere to such radical foundationalism, therefore, we are just wrong in thinking we know so much.

Note that in citing such a "fatal weakness" of radical foundationalism, we favor particularism as against the methodism of Descartes and Hume. For we reject the methods or criteria of Descartes and Hume when we realize that they plunge us in a deep skepticism. If such criteria are incompatible with our enjoyment of the rich body of knowledge that we commonly take for granted, then as good particularists we hold on to the knowledge and reject the criteria.

If we reject radical foundationalism, however, what are we to put in its place? Here epistemology faces a dilemma that different epistemologists resolve differently. Some reject radical foundationalism but retain some more moderate form of foundationalism in favor of a radically different coherentism. Coherentism is associated with idealism—of both the German and the British variety—and has recently acquired new vigor and interest.

The coherentists reject the metaphor of the pyramid in favor of one that they owe to the positivist Neurath, according to whom our body of knowledge is a raft that floats free of any anchor or tie. Repairs must be made afloat, and though no part is untouchable, we must stand on some in order to replace or repair others. Not every part can go at once.

According to the new metaphor, what justifies a belief is not that it be an infallible belief with an indubitable object, nor that it have been proved deductively on such a basis, but that it cohere with a comprehensive system of beliefs.

4. A Coherentist Critique of Foundationalism

What reasons do coherentists offer for their total rejection of foundationalism? The argument that follows below summarizes much of what is alleged against foundationalism. But first we must distinguish between subjective states that incorporate a propositional attitude and those that do not. A propositional attitude is a mental state of someone with a proposition for its object: beliefs, hopes, and fears provide examples. By way of contrast, a headache does not incorporate any such attitude. One can of course be conscious of a headache, but the headache itself does not constitute or incorporate any attitude with a proposition for its object. With this distinction in the background, here is the anti-foundationalist argument, which has two lemmas—a(iv) and b(iii)—and a principal conclusion.

a. (i) If a mental state incorporates a propositional attitude, then it does not give us direct contact with reality, e.g., with pure experience, unfiltered by concepts or beliefs.

(ii) If a mental state does not give us direct contact with reality, then it provides no guarantee against error.

(iii) If a mental state provides no guarantee against error, then it cannot serve as a foundation for knowledge.

(iv) Therefore, if a mental state incorporates a propositional attitude, then it cannot serve as a foundation for knowledge.

b. (i) If a mental state does not incorporate a propositional attitude, then it is an enigma how such a state can provide support for any hypothesis, raising its credibility selectively by contrast with its alternatives. (If the mental state has no conceptual or propositional content, then what logical relation can it possibly bear to any hypothesis? Belief in a hypothesis would be a propositional attitude with the hypothesis itself as object. How can one depend logically for such a belief on an experience with no propositional content?)

(ii) If a mental state has no propositional content and cannot provide logical support for any hypothesis, then it cannot serve as a foundation for knowledge.

(iii) Therefore, if a mental state does not incorporate a propositional attitude, then it cannot serve as a foundation for knowledge.

c. Every mental state either does or does not incorporate a propositional attitude.

d. Therefore, no mental state can serve as a foundation for knowledge. (From a(iv), b(iii), and c.)

According to the coherentist critic, foundationalism is run through by this dilemma. Let us take a closer look.[2]

In the first place, what reason is there to think, in accordance with premise b(i), that only propositional attitudes can give support to their own kind? Consider practices—e.g., broad policies or customs. Could not some person or group be justified in a practice because of its consequences: that is, could not the consequences of a practice make it a good practice? But among the consequences of a practice may surely be found, for example, a more just distribution of goods and less suffering than there would be under its alternatives. And neither the more just distribution nor the lower degree of suffering is a propositional attitude. This provides an example in which propositional attitudes (the intentions that sustain the practice) are justified by consequences that are not propositional attitudes. That being so, is it not conceivable that the justification of belief that matters for knowledge be analogous to the objective justification by consequences that we find in ethics?

Is it not possible, for instance, that a belief that there is something red before one be justified in part because it has its origins in one's visual experience of red when one looks at an apple in daylight? If we accept such examples, they show us a source of justification that serves as such without incorporating a propositional attitude.

As for premise a(iii), it is already under suspicion from our earlier exploration of premise b(i). A mental state M can be nonpropositional and hence not a candidate for so much as truth, much less infallibility, while it serves, in spite of that, as a foundation of knowledge. Leaving that aside, let us suppose that the relevant mental state is indeed propositional. Must it then be infallible in order to serve as a foundation of justification and knowledge? That is so far from being obvious that it seems more likely false when compared with an analogue in ethics. With respect to beliefs, we may distinguish between their being true and their

being justified. Analogously, with respect to actions, we may distinguish between their being optimal (best of all alternatives, all things considered) and their being (subjectively) justified. In practical deliberation on alternatives for action, is it inconceivable that the most *eligible* alternative *not* be objectively the best, all things considered? Can there not be another alternative—perhaps a most repugnant one worth little if any consideration—that in point of fact would have a much better total set of consequences and would thus be better, all things considered? Take the physician attending to Frau Hitler at the birth of little Adolf. Is it not possible that if he had acted less morally, that would have proved better in the fullness of time? And if that is so in ethics, may not its likeness hold good in epistemology? Might there not be justified (reasonable, warranted) beliefs that are not even true, much less infallible? That seems to me not just a conceivable possibility, but indeed a familiar fact of everyday life, where observational beliefs too often prove illusory but no less reasonable for being false.

If the foregoing is on the right track, then the antifoundationalist is far astray. What has led him there?

As a diagnosis of the antifoundationalist argument before us, and more particularly of its second lemma, I would suggest that it rests on an Intellectualist Model of Justification.

According to such a model, the justification of belief (and psychological states generally) is parasitical on certain logical relations among propositions. For example, my belief (i) that the streets are wet, is justified by my pair of beliefs (ii) that it is raining, and (iii) that if it is raining, the streets are wet. Thus we have a structure such as this:

B(Q) is justified by the fact that B(Q) is grounded on (B(P), B(P⊃Q)).

And according to an Intellectualist Model, this is parasitical on the fact that

P and (P⊃Q) together logically imply Q.

Concerning this attack on foundationalism I will argue (a) that it is useless to the coherentist, since if the antifoundationalist dilemma impales the foundationalist, a form of it can be turned against the coherentist to the same effect; (b) that the dilemma would be lethal not only to foundationalism and coherentism but also to the very possibility of substantive epistemology; and (c) that a form of it would have the same effect on normative ethics.

(a) According to coherentism, what justifies a belief is its membership in a coherent and comprehensive set of beliefs. But whereas being grounded on B(P) and B(P⊃Q) is a property of a belief B(Q) that yields immediately the logical implication of Q and P and (P⊃Q) as the logical source of that property's justificatory power, the property of being a member of a coherent set is not one that immediately yields any such implication.

It may be argued, nevertheless, (i) that the property of being a member of a coherent set would supervene in any actual instance on the property of being a member of a particular set *a* that is in fact coherent, and (ii) that this would enable us to preserve our Intellectualist Model, since (iii) the justification of the member belief B(Q) by its membership in *a* would then be parasitical on the logical relations among the beliefs in *a* which constitute the coherence of that set of beliefs, and (iv) the justification of B(Q) by the fact that it is part of a coherent set would then be *indirectly* parasitical on logical relations among propositions after all.

But if such an indirect form of parasitism is allowed, then the experience of pain may perhaps be said to justify belief in its existence parasitically on the fact that P logically implies P! The Intellectualist Model seems either so trivial as to be dull, or else sharp enough to cut equally against both foundationalism and coherentism.

(b) If (i) only propositional attitudes can justify such propositional attitudes as belief, and if (ii) to do so they must in turn be justified by yet other propositional attitudes, it seems clear that (iii) there is no hope of constructing a complete epistemology, one which would give us, in theory, an account of what the justification of any justified belief would supervene on. For (i) and (ii) would rule out the possibility of a finite regress of justification.

(c) If only propositional attitudes can justify propositional attitudes, and if to do so they must in turn be justified by yet other propositional attitudes, it seems clear that there is no hope of constructing a complete normative ethics, one which would give us, in theory, an account of what the justification of any possible justified action would supervene upon. For the justification of an action presumably depends on the intentions it embeds and the justifi-

cation of these, and here we are already within the net of propositional attitudes from which, for the Intellectualist, there is no escape.

It seems fair to conclude that our coherentist takes his antifoundationalist zeal too far. His antifoundationalist argument helps expose some valuable insights but falls short of its malicious intent. The foundationalist emerges showing no serious damage. Indeed, he now demands equal time for a positive brief in defense of his position.

5. The Regress Argument

a. The regress argument in epistemology concludes that we must countenance beliefs that are justified in the absence of justification by other beliefs. But it reaches that conclusion only by rejecting the possibility in principle of an infinite regress of justification. It thus opts for foundational beliefs justified in some noninferential way by ruling out a chain or pyramid of justification that has justifiers, and justifiers of justifiers, and so on *without end*. One may well find this too short a route to foundationalism, however, and demand more compelling reasons for thus rejecting an infinite regress as vicious. We shall find indeed that it is not easy to meet this demand.

b. We have seen how even the most ordinary of everyday beliefs is the tip of an iceberg. A closer look below the surface reveals a complex structure that ramifies with no end in sight. Take again my belief that driving will be dangerous tonight, at the tip of an iceberg, (I), that looks like this:

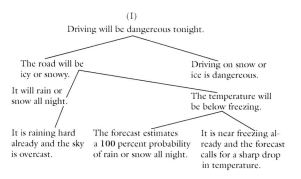

(I)
Driving will be dangerous tonight.

The road will be icy or snowy.

Driving on snow or ice is dangerous.

It will rain or snow all night.

The temperature will be below freezing.

It is raining hard already and the sky is overcast.

The forecast estimates a 100 percent probability of rain or snow all night.

It is near freezing already and the forecast calls for a sharp drop in temperature.

The immediate cause of my belief that driving will be hazardous tonight is the sound of raindrops on the windowpane. All but one or two members of the underlying iceberg are as far as they can be from my thoughts at the time. In what sense, then, do they form an iceberg whose tip breaks the calm surface of my consciousness?

Here I will assume that the members of (I) are beliefs of the subject, even if unconscious or subconscious, that causally buttress and thus justify his prediction about the driving conditions.

Can the iceberg extend without end? It may appear obvious that it cannot do so, and one may jump to the conclusion that any piece of knowledge must be ultimately founded on beliefs that are *not* (inferentially) justified or warranted by other beliefs. This is a doctrine of *epistemic foundationalism*.

Let us focus not so much on the *giving* of justification as on the *having* of it. *Can* there be a belief that is justified in part by other beliefs, some of which are in turn justified by yet other beliefs, and so on without end? Can there be endless regress of justification?

c. There are several familiar objections to such a regress:

(i) *Objection:* "It is incompatible with human limitations. No human subject could harbor the required infinity of beliefs." *Reply:* It is mere presumption to fathom with such assurance the depths of the mind, and especially its unconscious and dispositional depths. Besides, our object here is the nature of epistemic justification in itself and not only that of such justification as is accessible to humans. Our question is not whether humans could harbor an infinite iceberg of justification. Our question is rather whether *any* mind, no matter how deep, could do so. Or is it ruled out *in principle* by the very nature of justification?

(ii) *Objection:* "An infinite regress is indeed ruled out in principle, for if justification were thus infinite how could it possibly end? *Reply:* (i) If the end mentioned is *temporal,* then why must there be such an end? In the first place, the subject may be eternal. Even if he is not eternal, moreover, why must belief acquisition and justification

occur seriatim? What precludes an infinite body of beliefs acquired at a single stroke? Human limitations may rule this out for humans, but we have yet to be shown that it is precluded in principle, by the very nature of justification. (ii) If the end mentioned is justificatory on the other hand, then to ask how justification could possibly end is just to beg the question.

(iii) *Objection:* "Let us make two assumptions: first, that S's belief of q justifies his belief of p only if it works together with a justified belief on his part that q provides good evidence for p; and, second, that if S is to be justified in believing p on the basis of his belief of q and is to be justified in believing q on the basis of his belief of r, then S must be justified in believing that r provides good evidence for p via q. These assumptions imply that an actual regress of justification requires belief in an infinite proposition. Since no one (or at least no human) can believe an infinite proposition, no one (no human) can be a subject of such an actual regress."[3]

Reply: Neither of the two assumptions is beyond question, but even granting them both, it may still be doubted that the conclusion follows. It is true that each finitely complex belief of form "r provides good evidence for p via $q_1 \ldots q_n$" will *omit* how some members of the full infinite regress are epistemically tied to belief of p. But that seems irrelevant given the fact that for each member r of the regress, such that r is tied epistemically to belief of p, there *is* a finite belief of the required sort ("r provides good evidence for p via $q_1 \ldots q_n$") that ties the two together. Consequently, there is no apparent reason to suppose—even granted the two assumptions—that an infinite regress will require a single belief in an infinite proposition, and not just an infinity of beliefs in increasingly complex finite propositions.

(iv) *Objection:* "But if it is allowed that justification extend infinitely, then it is too easy to justify any belief at all or too many beliefs altogether. Take, for instance, the belief that there are perfect numbers greater than 100. And suppose a mind powerful enough to believe every member of the following sequence:

(*s1*)   There is at least one perfect number > 100
There are at least two perfect numbers > 100
"   three   "

If such a believer has no other belief about perfect numbers save the belief that a perfect number is a whole number equal to the sum of its whole factors, then surely he is *not* justified in believing that there are perfect numbers greater than 100. He is quite unjustified in believing any of the members of sequence (*s1*), in spite of the fact that a challenge to any can be met easily by appeal to its successor. Thus it cannot be allowed after all that justification extend infinitely, and an infinite regress is ruled out."

Reply: We must distinguish between regresses of justification that are actual and those that are merely potential. The difference is *not* simply that an actual regress is composed of actual beliefs. For even if all members of the regress are actual beliefs, the regress may still be *merely potential* in the following sense: while it is true that *if* any member *were* justified then its predecessors *would* be, still none is in fact justified. Anyone with our series of beliefs about perfect numbers in the absence of any further relevant information on such numbers would presumably be the subject of such a merely potential justificatory regress.

(v) *Objection:* "But defenders of infinite justificatory regresses cannot distinguish thus between actual regresses and those that are merely potential. There is no real distinction to be drawn between the two. For if any regress ever justifies the belief at its head, then every regress must always do so. But

obviously not every regress does so (as we have seen by examples), and hence no regress can do so."[4]

Reply: One can in fact distinguish between actual justificatory regresses and merely potential ones, and one can do so both abstractly and by examples.

What an actual regress has that a merely potential regress lacks is the property of containing only justified beliefs as members. What they both share is the property of containing no member without successors that would jointly justify it.

Recall our regress about perfect numbers greater than 100; i.e., there is at least one; there are at least two; there are at least three; and so on. Each member has a successor that would justify it, but no member is justified (in the absence of further information external to the regress). That is therefore a merely potential infinite regress. As for an actual regress, I see no compelling reason why someone (if not a human, then some more powerful mind) could not hold an infinite series of actually justified beliefs as follows:

(*s2*)   There is at least one even number.
There are at least two even numbers
"   three   "

It may be that no one could be the subject of such a series of justified beliefs unless he had a proof that there is a denumerable infinity of even numbers. But even if that should be so, it would not take away the fact of the infinite regress of potential justifiers, each of which is actually justified, and hence it would not take away the fact of the actual endless regress of justification.

The objection under discussion is confused, moreover, on the nature of the issue before us. Our question is *not* whether there can be an infinite potential regress, each member of which would be justified by its successors, such that the belief at its head is justified in virtue of its position there, at the head of such a regress. The existence and even the possibility of a single such regress with a belief at its head that was *not* justified in virtue of its position there would of course settle that question in the negative. Our question is, rather, whether there can be an actual infinite regress of justification, and the fact that a belief at the head of a potential regress might still fail to be justified despite its position does *not* settle this question. For even if there can be a merely potential regress with an unjustified belief at its head, that leaves open the possibility of an infinite regress, each member of which is justified by its immediate successors working jointly, where every member of the regress is in addition actually justified.

6. The Relation of Justification and Foundationalist Strategy

The foregoing discussion is predicated on a simple conception of justification such that a set of beliefs *b* conditionally justifies (*would* justify) a belief X iff, necessarily, if all members of *b* are justified then X is also justified (if it exists). The fact that on such a conception of justification actual endless regresses—such as (*s2*)—seem quite possible blocks a straightforward regress argument in favor of foundations. For it shows that an actual infinite regress cannot be dismissed out of hand.

Perhaps the foundationalist could introduce some relation of justification—presumably more complex and yet to be explicated—with respect to which it could be argued more plausibly that an actual endless regress is out of the question.

There is, however, a more straightforward strategy open to the foundationalist. For he *need not* object to the possibility of an endless regress of justification. His essential creed is the more positive belief that every justified belief must be at the head of a terminating regress. Fortunately, to affirm the universal necessity of a terminating regress is *not* to deny the bare possibility of a non-terminating regress. For a single belief can trail at once regresses of both sorts: one terminating and

one not. Thus the proof of the denumerably infinite cardinality of the set of evens may provide for a powerful enough intellect a *terminating* regress for each member of the *endless* series of justified beliefs:

(*s2*)   There is at least one even number
         There are at least two even numbers
         "   three   "

At the same time, it is obvious that each member of (*s2*) lies at the head of an actual endless regress of justification, on the assumption that each member is conditionally justified by its successor, which is in turn actually justified.

"Thank you so much," the foundationalist may sneer, "but I really do not need that kind of help. Nor do I need to be reminded of my essential creed, which I know as well as anyone. Indeed my rejection of endless regresses of justification is only a means of supporting my view that every justified belief must rest ultimately on foundations, on a terminating regress. You reject that strategy much too casually, in my view, but I will not object here. So we put that strategy aside. And now, my helpful friend, just what do we put in its place?"

Fair enough. How then could one show the need for foundations if an endless regress is not ruled out?

7. Two Levels of Foundationalism

a. We need to distinguish, first, between two forms of foundationalism: one *formal*, the other *substantive*. A type of *formal foundationalism* with respect to a normative or evaluative property F is the view that the conditions (actual and possible) within which F would apply can be specified in general, perhaps recursively. *Substantive foundationalism* is only a particular way of doing so, and coherentism is another.

Simpleminded hedonism is the view that:

(i) every instance of pleasure is good,
(ii) everything that causes something good is itself good, and
(iii) everything that is good is so in virtue of (i) or (ii) above.

Simpleminded hedonism is a type of formal foundationalism with respect to the good.

Classical foundationalism in epistemology is the view that:

(i) every infallible, indubitable belief is justified.

(ii) every belief deductively inferred from justified beliefs is itself justified, and

(iii) every belief that is justified is so in virtue of (i) or (ii) above.Classical foundationalism in epistemology is the view that:

Classical foundationalism is a type of formal foundationalism with respect to epistemic justification.

Both of the foregoing theories—simpleminded hedonism in ethics, and classical foundationalism in epistemology—are of course flawed. But they both remain examples of formal foundationalist theories.

b. One way of arguing in favor of formal foundationalism in epistemology is to formulate a convincing formal foundationalist theory of justification. But classical foundationalism in epistemology no longer has for many the attraction that it had for Descartes, nor has any other form of epistemic foundationalism won general acceptance. Indeed epistemic foundationalism has been generally abandoned, and its advocates have been put on the defensive by the writings of Wittgenstein, Quine, Sellars, Rescher, Aune, Harman, Lehrer, and others. It is lamentable that in our headlong rush away from foundationalism we have lost sight of the different types of foundationalism (formal vs. substantive) and of the different grades of each type. Too many of us now see it as a blur to be decried and avoided. Thus our present attempt to bring it all into better focus.

c. If we cannot argue from a generally accepted foundationalist theory, what reason is there to accept formal foundationalism? There is no reason to think that the conditions (actual and possible) within which an object is spherical are generally specifiable in nongeometric terms. Why should we think that the conditions (actual and possible) within which a belief is epistemically justified are generally specifiable in nonepistemic terms?

So far as I can see, the main reason for accepting formal foundationalism in the absence of an actual, convincing formal foundationalist theory is the very plausible idea that epistemic justification is subject to the supervenience that characterizes normative and evaluative properties generally.

Thus, if a car is a good car, then any physical replica of that car must be just as good. If it is a good car in virtue of such properties as being economical, little prone to break down, etc., then surely any exact replica would share all such properties and would thus be equally good. Similarly, if a belief is epistemically justified, it is presumably so in virtue of its character and its basis in perception, memory, or inference (if any). Thus any belief exactly like it in its character and its basis must be equally well justified. Epistemic justification is supervenient. The justification of a belief supervenes on such properties of it as its content and its basis (if any) in perception, memory, or inference. Such a doctrine of supervenience may itself be considered, with considerable justice, a grade of foundationalism. For it entails that every instance of justified belief is founded on a number of its nonepistemic properties, such as its having a certain basis in perception, memory, and inference, or the like.

But there are higher grades of foundationalism as well. There is, for instance, the doctrine that the conditions (actual and possible) within which a belief would be epistemically justified *can be specified* in general, perhaps recursively (and by reference to such notions as perception, memory, and inference).

A higher grade yet of formal foundationalism requires not only that the conditions for justified belief be specifiable, in general, but that they be specifiable by a simple, comprehensive theory.

d. Simpleminded hedonism is a formal foundationalist theory of the highest grade. If it is true, then in every possible world goodness supervenes on pleasure and causation in a way that is recursively specifiable by means of a very simple theory.

Classical foundationalism in epistemology is also a formal foundationalist theory of the highest grade. If it is true, then in every possible world epistemic justification supervenes on infallibility cum indubitability and deductive inference in a way that is recursively specifiable by means of a very simple theory.

Surprisingly enough, coherentism may also turn out to be formal foundationalism of the highest grade, provided only that the concept of coherence is itself both simple enough and free of any normative or evaluative admixture. Given these provisos, coherentism explains how epistemic justification supervenes on the nonepistemic in a theory of remarkable simplicity: a belief is justified if it has a place within a system of beliefs that is coherent and comprehensive.

It is a goal of ethics to explain how the ethical rightness of an action supervenes on what is not ethically evaluative or normative. Similarly, it is a goal of epistemology to explain how the epistemic justification of a belief supervenes on what is not epistemically evaluative or normative. If coherentism aims at this goal, that imposes restrictions on the notion of coherence, which must now be conceived innocent of epistemically evaluative or normative admixture. Its substance must therefore consist of such concepts as explanation, probability, and logical implication—with these conceived, in turn, innocent of normative or evaluative content.

e. We have found a surprising kinship between coherentism and substantive foundationalism, both of which turn out to be varieties of a deeper foundationalism. This deeper foundationalism is applicable to any normative or evaluative property F, and it comes in three grades. The *first* or lowest is simply the supervenience of F: the idea that whenever something has F its having it is founded on certain others of its properties which fall into certain restricted sorts. The *second* is the explicable supervenience of F: the idea that there are formulable principles that explain in quite general terms the conditions (actual and possible) within which F applies. The *third* and highest is the easily explicable supervenience of F: the idea that there is a *simple* theory that explains the conditions within which F applies. We have found the coherentist and the substantive foundationalist sharing a primary goal: the development of a formal foundationalist theory of the highest grade. For they both want a simple theory that explains precisely how epistemic justification supervenes, in general, on the nonepistemic. This insight gives us an unusual viewpoint on some recent attacks against foundationalism. Let us now consider as an example a certain simple form of argument distilled from the recent antifoundationalist literature.[5]

8. Doxastic Ascent Arguments

Several attacks on foundationalism turn on a sort of "doxastic ascent" argument that calls for closer scrutiny.[6] Here are two examples:

A. A belief B is foundationally justified for S in virtue of having property F only if S is justified in believing (1) that most at least of his beliefs with property F are true, and (2) that B has property F. But this means that belief B is not foundational after all, and indeed that the very notion of (empirical) foundational belief is incoherent.

It is sometimes held, for example, that perceptual or observational beliefs are often justified through their origin in the exercise of one or more of our five senses in standard conditions of perception. The advocate of doxastic ascent would raise a vigorous protest, however, for in his view the mere fact of such sensory prompting is impotent to justify the belief prompted. Such prompting must be coupled with the further belief that one's senses work well in the circumstances, or the like. For we are dealing here with *knowledge,* which requires not blind faith but *reasoned* trust. But now surely the further belief about the reliability of one's senses itself cannot rest on blind faith but requires its own backing of reasons, and we are off on the regress.

B. A belief B of proposition P is foundationally justified for S only if S is justified in believing that there are no factors present that would cause him to make mistakes on the matter of the proposition P. But, again, this means that belief B is not foundational after all and indeed that the notion of (empirical) foundational belief is incoherent.

From the vantage point of formal foundationalism, neither of these arguments seems persuasive. In the first place, as we have seen, what makes a belief foundational (formally) is its having a property that is nonepistemic (not evaluative in the epistemic or cognitive mode), and does not involve inference from other beliefs, but guarantees, via a necessary principle, that the belief in question is justified. A belief B is made foundational by having some such nonepistemic property that yields its justification. Take my belief that I am in pain in a context where it is caused by my being in pain. The property that my belief then has, of being a self-attribution of pain caused by one's own pain is, let us suppose, a nonepistemic property that yields the justification of any belief that has it. So my belief that I am in pain is in that context foundationally justified. Along with my belief that I am in pain, however, there come other beliefs that are equally well justified, such as my belief that I am in pain only if I am justified in believing that someone is in pain. Those who object to foundationalism as in A or B above are hence mistaken in thinking that their premises would refute foundationalism. The fact is that they would not touch it. For a belief is no less foundationally justified for having its justification yoked to that of another closely related belief.

The advocate of arguments like A and B must apparently strengthen his premises. He must apparently claim that the beliefs whose justification is entailed by the foundationally justified status of belief B must in some sense function as a *necessary source* of the justification of B. And this would of course preclude giving B foundationally justified status. For if the *being justified* of those beliefs is an *essential* part of the source of the justification of B, then it is ruled out that there be a wholly *non-epistemic* source of B's justification.

That brings us to a second point about A and B, for it should now be clear that these cannot be selectively aimed at foundationalism. In particular, they seem neither more nor less valid objections to coherentism than to foundationalism, or so I will now argue about each of them in turn.

A′. A belief X is justified for S in virtue of membership in a coherent set only if S is justified in believing (1) that most at least of his beliefs with the property of thus cohering are true, and (2) that X has that property.

Any coherentist who accepts A seems bound to accept A′. For what could he possibly appeal to as a relevant difference? But A′ is a quicksand of endless depth. (How is he justified in believing A′(1)? Partly through justified belief that *it* coheres? And what would justify *this*? And so on . . .)

B′. A belief X is justified for S only if S is justified in believing that there are no factors present that would cause him to make mistakes on the subject matter of that belief.

Again, any coherentist who accepts B seems bound to accept B′. But this is just another road to the quicksand. (For S is justified in believing that there are no such factors only if . . . and so on.)

Why are such regresses vicious? The key is again, to my mind, the doctrine of supervenience. Such regresses are vicious because they would be logically incompatible with the supervenience of epistemic

justification on such nonepistemic facts as the totality of a subject's beliefs, his cognitive and experiential history, and as many other nonepistemic facts as may seem at all relevant. The idea is that there is a set of such nonepistemic facts surrounding a justified belief such that no belief could possibly have been surrounded by those very facts without being justified. Advocates of A or B run afoul of such supervenience, since they are surely committed to the more general views derivable from either A or B by deleting "foundationally" from its first sentence. In each case the more general view would then preclude the possibility of supervenience, since it would entail that the source of justification always includes an *epistemic* component.

9. Coherentism and Substantive Foundationalism

a. The notions of coherentism and substantive foundationalism remain unexplicated. We have relied so far on our intuitive grasp of them. In this section we shall consider reasons for the view that substantive foundationalism is superior to coherentism. To assess these reasons, we need some more explicit account of the difference between the two.

By coherentism we shall mean any view according to which the ultimate sources of justification for any belief lie in relations among that belief and other beliefs of the subject: explanatory relations, perhaps, or relations of probability or logic.

According to substantive foundationalism, as it is to be understood here, there are ultimate sources of justification other than relations among beliefs. Traditionally these additional sources have pertained to the special content of the belief or its special relations to the subjective experience of the believer.

b. The view that justification is a matter of relations among beliefs is open to an objection from alternative coherent systems or detachment from reality, depending on one's perspective. From the latter perspective the body of beliefs is held constant and the surrounding world is allowed to vary, whereas from the former perspective it is the surrounding world that is held constant while the body of beliefs is allowed to vary.

In either case, according to the coherentist, there could be no effect on the justification for any belief.

Let us sharpen the question before us as follows. Is there reason to think that there is at least one system B′, alternative to our actual system of beliefs B, such that B′ contains a belief X with the following properties:

(i) in our present nonbelief circumstances we would not be justified in having belief X even if we accepted along with that belief (as our total system of beliefs) the entire belief system B′ in which it is embedded (no matter how acceptance of B′ were brought about); and

(ii) that is so despite the fact that belief X coheres within B′ at least as fully as does some actual justified belief of ours within our actual belief system B (where the justification of that actual justified belief is alleged by the coherentist to derive solely from its coherence within our actual body of beliefs B).

The coherentist is vulnerable to counterexamples of this sort right at the surface of his body of beliefs, where we find beliefs with minimal coherence, whose detachment and replacement with contrary beliefs would have little effect on the coherence of the body. Thus take my belief that I have a headache when I do have a splitting headache, and let us suppose that this *does* cohere within my present body of beliefs. (Thus I have no reason to doubt my present introspective beliefs, and so on. And if my belief does *not* cohere, so much the worse for coherentism, since my belief is surely justified.) Here then we have a perfectly justified or warranted belief. And yet such a belief may well have relevant relations of explanation, logic, or probability with at most a small set of other beliefs of mine at the time: say, that I am not free of headache, that I am in pain, that someone is in pain, and the like. If so, then an equally coherent alternative is not far to seek. Let everything remain constant, *including* the splitting headache, except for the following: replace the belief that I have a headache with the belief that I do *not* have a headache, the belief that I am in pain with the belief that I am *not* in pain, the belief that someone is in pain with the belief that someone is *not* in pain, and so on. I contend that my resulting hypothetical system of beliefs would cohere as fully as does my actual system of beliefs, and yet my hypothetical belief that I do *not* have a headache would not therefore be justified. What makes this difference concerning justification between my actual belief that I have a headache and the hypothetical belief that I am free of headache, each as coherent as the other within its own system, if not the actual splitting headache? But the headache is *not* itself a belief nor a relation among beliefs and is thus in no way constitutive of the internal coherence of my body of beliefs.

Some might be tempted to respond by alleging that one's belief about whether or not one has a headache is always *infallible*. But since we could devise similar examples for the various sensory modalities and propositional attitudes, the response given for the case of headache would have to be generalized. In effect, it would have to cover "peripheral" beliefs generally—beliefs at the periphery of one's body of beliefs, minimally coherent with the rest. These peripheral beliefs would all be said to be infallible. That is, again, a possible response, but it leads to a capitulation by the coherentist to the radical foundationalist on a crucial issue that has traditionally divided them: the infallibility of beliefs about one's own subjective states.

What is more, not all peripheral beliefs are about one's own subjective states. The direct realist is probably right that some beliefs about our surroundings are uninferred and yet justified. Consider my present belief that the table before me is oblong. This presumably coheres with such other beliefs of mine as that the table has the same shape as the piece of paper before me, which is oblong, and a different shape than the window frame here, which is square, and so on. So far as I can see, however, there is no insurmountable obstacle to replacing that whole set of coherent beliefs with an equally coherent set as follows: that the table before me is square, that the table has the same shape as the square window frame, and a different shape than the piece of paper, which is oblong, and so on. The important points are (a) that this replacement may be made without changing the rest of one's body of beliefs or any aspect of the world beyond, including one's present visual experience of something oblong, not square, as one looks at the table before one; and (b) that it is so, in part, because of the fact (c) that the subject need not have any beliefs about his present sensory experience.

Some might be tempted to respond by alleging that one's present experience is *self-intimating*, i.e., always necessarily taken note of and reflected in one's beliefs. Thus if anyone has visual experience of something oblong, then he believes that he has such experience. But this would involve a further important concession by the coherentist to the radical foundationalist, who would have been granted two of his most cherished doctrines: the infallibility of introspective belief and the self-intimation of experience.

10. The Foundationalist's Dilemma

The antifoundationalist zeal of recent years has left several forms of foundationalism standing. These all share the conviction that a belief can be justified not only by its coherence within a comprehensive system but also by an appropriate combination of observational content and origin in the use of the senses in standard conditions. What follows presents a dilemma for any foundationalism based on any such idea.

a. We may surely suppose that beings with observational mechanisms radically unlike ours might also have knowledge of their environment. (That seems possible even if the radical difference in observational mechanisms precludes overlap in substantive concepts and beliefs.)

b. Let us suppose that there is such a being, for whom experience of type f (of which we have no notion) has a role with respect to his beliefs of type f analogous to the role that our visual experience has with respect to our visual beliefs. Thus we might have a schema such as the following:

Human	*Extraterrestrial being*
Visual experience	f experience
Experience of something red	Experience of something F
Belief that there is something red before one	Belief that there is something F before one

c. It is often recognized that our visual experience intervenes in two ways with respect to our visual beliefs: as cause and as justification. But these are not wholly independent. Presumably, the justification of the belief that something here is red derives at least in part from the fact that it originates in a visual experience of something red that takes place in normal circumstances.

d. Analogously, the extraterrestrial belief that something here has the property of being F might be justified partly by the fact that it originates in a f experience of something F that takes place in normal circumstances.

e. A simple question presents the foundationalist's dilemma: regarding the epistemic principle that underlies our justification for believing that something here is red on the basis of our visual experience of something red, is it proposed as a fundamental principle or as a derived generalization? Let us compare the famous Principle of Utility of value theory, according to which it is best for that to happen which, of all the possible alternatives in the circumstances, would bring with it into the world the greatest balance of pleasure over pain, joy over sorrow, happiness over unhappiness, content over discontent, or the like. Upon this fundamental principle one may then base various generalizations, rules of thumb, and maxims of public health, nutrition, legislation, etiquette, hygiene, and so on. But these are all then derived generalizations which rest for their validity on the fundamental principle. Similarly, one may also ask, with respect to the generalizations advanced by our foundationalist, whether these are proposed as fundamental principles or as derived maxims or the like. This sets him face to face with a dilemma, each of whose alternatives is problematic. If his proposals are meant to have the status of secondary or derived maxims, for instance, then it would be quite unphilosophical to stop there. Let us turn, therefore, to the other alternative.

f. On reflection it seems rather unlikely that epistemic principles for the justification of observational beliefs by their origin in sensory experience could have a status more fundamental than that of derived generalizations. For by granting such principles fundamental status we would open the door to a multitude of equally basic principles with no unifying factor. There would be some for vision, some for hearing, etc., without even mentioning the corresponding extraterrestrial principles.

g. It may appear that there is after all an idea, however, that unifies our multitude of principles.

For they all involve sensory experience and sensible characteristics. But what is a sensible characteristic? Aristotle's answer appeals to examples: colors, shapes, sounds, and so on. Such a notion might enable us to unify perceptual epistemic principles under some more fundamental principle such as the following.

> If *s* is a sensible characteristic, then the belief that there is something with *s* before one is (prima facie) justified if it is based on a visual experience of something with *s* in conditions that are normal with respect to *s*.

h. There are at least two difficulties with such a suggestion, however, and neither one can be brushed aside easily. First, it is not clear that we can have a viable notion of sensible characteristics on the basis of examples so diverse as colors, shapes, tones, odors, and so on. Second, the authority of such a principle apparently derives from contingent circumstances concerning the reliability of beliefs prompted by sensory experiences of certain sorts. According to the foundationalist, our visual beliefs are justified by their origin in our visual experience or the like. Would such beliefs be equally well justified in a world where beliefs with such an origin were nearly always false?

i. In addition, finally, even if we had a viable notion of such characteristics, it is not obvious that fundamental knowledge of reality would have to derive causally or otherwise from sensory experience of such characteristics. How could one impose reasonable limits on extraterrestrial mechanisms for noninferential acquisition of beliefs? Is it not possible that such mechanisms need not always function through sensory experience of any sort? Would such beings necessarily be denied any knowledge of the surroundings and indeed of any contingent spatio-temporal fact? Let us suppose them to possess a complex system of true beliefs concerning their surroundings, the structures below the surface of things, exact details of history and geography, all constituted by concepts none of which corresponds to any of our sensible characteristics. What then? Is it not possible that their basic beliefs should all concern fields of force, waves, mathematical structures, and numerical assignments to variables in several dimensions? This is no doubt an exotic notion, but even so it still seems conceivable. And if it is in fact possible, what then shall we say of the noninferential beliefs of such beings? Would we have to concede the existence of special epistemic principles that can validate their noninferential beliefs? Would it not be preferable to formulate more abstract principles that can cover both human and extraterrestrial foundations? If such more abstract principles are in fact accessible, then the less general principles that define the human foundations and those that define the extraterrestrial foundations are both derived principles whose validity depends on that of the more abstract principles. In this the human and extraterrestrial epistemic principles would resemble rules of good nutrition for an infant and an adult. The infant's rules would of course be quite unlike those valid for the adult. But both would still be based on a more fundamental principle that postulates the ends of well-being and good health. What more fundamental principles might support both human and extraterrestrial knowledge in the way that those concerning good health and well-being support rules of nutrition for both the infant and adult?

11. Reliabilism: An Ethics of Moral Virtues and an Epistemology of Intellectual Virtues

In what sense is the doctor attending Frau Hitler justified in performing an action that brings with it far less value than one of its accessible alternatives? According to one promising idea, the key is to be found in the rules that he embodies through stable dispositions. His action is the result of certain stable virtues, and there are no equally virtuous alternative *dispositions* that, given his cognitive limitations, he might have embodied with equal or better total consequences, and that would have led him to infanticide in the circumstances. The important move for our purpose is the stratification of justification. Primary justification attaches to virtues and other dispositions, to stable dispositions to act, through their greater contribution of value when compared with alternatives. Secondary justification attaches to particular acts in virtue of their source in virtues or other such justified dispositions.

The same strategy may also prove fruitful in epistemology. Here primary justification would apply to *intellectual* virtues, to stable dispositions for belief acquisition, through their greater contribution toward getting us to the truth. Secondary justification would then attach to particular beliefs in virtue of their source in intellectual virtues or other such justified dispositions.[7]

That raises parallel questions for ethics and epistemology. We need to consider more carefully the concept of a virtue and the distinction between moral and intellectual virtues. In epistemology, there is reason to think that the most useful and illuminating notion of intellectual virtue will prove broader than our tradition would suggest and must give due weight not only to the subject and his intrinsic nature but also to his environment and to his epistemic community. This is a large topic, however, to which I hope some of us will turn with more space, and insight, than I can now command.[8]

Summary

1. *Two assumptions:* (A1) that for a belief to constitute knowledge it must be (a) true and (b) justified; and (A2) that the justification relevant to whether or not one knows is a sort of epistemic or theoretical justification to be distinguished from its practical counterpart.

2. *Knowledge and criteria.* Particularism is distinguished from methodism: the first gives priority to particular examples of knowledge over general methods or criteria, whereas the second reverses that order. The methodism of Descartes leads him to an elaborate dogmatism whereas that of Hume leads him to a very simple skepticism. The particularist is, of course, antiskeptical on principle.

3. *Two metaphors: the raft and the pyramid.* For the foundationalist every piece of knowledge stands at the apex of a pyramid that rests on stable and secure foundations whose stability and security do not derive from the upper stories or sections. For the coherentist a body of knowledge is a free-floating raft every plank of which helps directly or indirectly to keep all the others in place, and no plank of which would retain its status with no help from the others.

4. *A coherentist critique of foundationalism.* No mental state can provide a foundation for empirical knowledge. For if such a state is propositional, then it is fallible and hence no secure foundation. But if it is *not* propositional, then how can it possibly serve as a foundation for belief? How can one infer or justify anything on the basis of a state that, having no propositional content, must be logically dumb? An analogy with ethics suggests a reason to reject this dilemma. Other reasons are also advanced and discussed.

5. *The regress argument.* In defending his position, the foundationalist often attempts to rule out the very possibility of an infinite regress of justification (which leads him to the necessity for a foundation). Some of his arguments to that end are examined.

6. *The relation of justification and foundationalist strategy.* An alternative foundationalist strategy is exposed, one that does not require ruling out the possibility of an infinite regress of justification.

7. *Two levels of foundationalism.* Substantive foundationalism is distinguished from formal foundationalism, three grades of which are exposed: first, the supervenience of epistemic justification; second, its explicable supervenience; and, third, its supervenience explicable by means of a simple theory. There turns out to be a surprising kinship between coherentism and substantive foundationalism, both of which aim at a formal foundationalism of the highest grade, at a theory of the greatest simplicity that explains how epistemic justification supervenes on nonepistemic factors.

8. *Doxastic ascent arguments.* The distinction between formal and substantive foundationalism provides an unusual viewpoint on some recent attacks against foundationalism. We consider doxastic ascent arguments as an example.

9. *Coherentism and substantive foundationalism.* It is argued that substantive foundationalism is superior, since coherentism is unable to account adequately for the epistemic status of beliefs at the "periphery" of a body of beliefs.

10. *The foundationalist's dilemma.* All foundationalism based on sense experience is subject to a fatal dilemma.

11. *Reliabilism.* An alternative to foundationalism of sense experience is sketched.

Notes

[1]But Descartes's methodism was at most partial. James Van Cleve has supplied the materials for a convincing argument that the way out of the Cartesian circle is through a particularism of basic knowledge. See James Van Cleve, "Foundationalism, Epistemic Principles, and the Cartesian Circle." But this is, of course, compatible with methodism on inferred knowledge. Whether Descartes subscribed to such methodism is hard (perhaps impossible) to determine, since in the end he makes room for all the kinds of knowledge required by particularism. But his language when he introduces the method of hyperbolic doubt, and the order in which he proceeds, suggest that he did subscribe to such methodism.

[2]Cf. Laurence BonJour, "Holistic Coherentism," *Philosophical Studies 30* (1976); and, especially, Michael Williams, *Groundless Belief*; and Laurence BonJour, "A Critique of Foundationalism" [Reading V.3—Ed.].

[3]Cf. Richard Foley, "Inferential Justification and the Infinite Regress," *American Philosophical Quarterly* 15 (1978): 311–16.

[4]Cf. John Post, "Infinite Regresses of Justification and of Explanation," *Philosophical Studies* 34 (1980).

[5]The argument of this whole section is developed in greater detail in my paper "The Foundations of Foundationalism."

[6]For some examples of the influence of doxastic ascent arguments, see Wilfrid Sellars's writing in epistemology: "Empiricism and the Philosophy of Mind," especially section VIII, and particularly p. 168. Also I. T. Oakley, "An Argument for Skepticism Concerning Justified Belief," *American Philosophical Quarterly* 13 (1976): 221–28; and BonJour, "A Critique of Foundationalism" [Reading V.3—Ed.].

[7]This puts in a more traditional perspective the contemporary effort to develop a "causal theory of knowing." From our viewpoint, this effort is better understood not as an attempt to *define* propositional knowledge, but as an attempt to formulate fundamental principles of justification.

Cf. the work of D. Armstrong, *Belief, Truth, and Knowledge*, and that of F. Dretske, A. Goldman, and M. Swain, whose relevant already published work is included in *Essays on Knowledge and Justification*, ed. G. Pappas and M. Swain (Ithaca and London, 1978). But the theory is still under development by Goldman and by Swain, who have reached general conclusions about it similar to those suggested here, though not necessarily—so far as I know—for the same reasons or in the same overall context.

[8]I am indebted above all to Roderick Chisholm for his writings and for innumerable discussions. The main ideas in the present essay were first presented in a seminar of 1976–77 at the University of Texas. I am grateful to Anthony Anderson, David and Jean Blumenfeld, Laurence BonJour, and Martin Perlmutter, who made that seminar a valuable stimulus. Subsequent criticism by my colleague James Van Cleve has also been valuable and stimulating.

V.8 A Foundherentist Theory of Empirical Justification

Susan Haack

Susan Haack is professor of philosophy at the University of Miami. In this paper, Haack summarizes her theory of evidence—foundherentism. Like foundationalism and unlike coherentism, it allows the relevance of experience to empirical justification but, like coherentism and unlike foundationalism, requires neither privileged beliefs justified exclusively by experience nor any essentially one-directional notion of evidential support.

A Foundherentist Theory of Empirical Justification[1]

> Let us remember how common the folly is, of going from one faulty extreme into the opposite.[2]

Does the evidence presented establish beyond a reasonable doubt that the defendant did it? Given the evidence recently discovered by space scientists, am I justified in believing that bacterial life was once on Mars? Is scientific evidence especially authoritative, and if so, why? Should we take those advertisements claiming that the Holocaust never happened seriously, and if not, why not? Questions about what makes evidence better or worse, about what makes inquiry better or worse conducted, about disinterestedness and partiality are of real, daily—and sometimes of life-and-death—consequence.

Of late, however, cynicism about the very legitimacy of such questions has become the familiar philosophical theme of a whole chorus of voices, from enthusiasts of the latest developments in neuroscience, to radical self-styled neopragmatists, radical feminists and multiculturalists, and followers of (by now somewhat dated) Paris fashions.

This cynicism is unwarranted, but dealing with it requires something a bit more radical than epistemological business-as-usual. Evidence is often messy, ambiguous, and misleading; inquiry is often untidy, inconclusive, and biased by the inquirers' interests. However, it doesn't follow, as the cynics apparently suppose, that standards of good evidence and well-conducted inquiry are local, conventional, or mythical. And even halfway adequate understanding of the complexities of real-life evidence and the untidiness of real-life inquiry requires a reexamination of some of those comfortably familiar dichotomies that recent epistemology has relied upon—the logical versus the causal, internalism versus externalism, apriorism versus naturalism, and foundationalism versus coherentism.

Though the other dichotomies will also come under scrutiny, the main theme here will be that foundationalism and coherentism—the traditionally rival theories of justified belief—do not exhaust the options and that an intermediate theory is more plausible than either. I call it *foundherentism*.

The Case for Foundherentism

Foundationalist theories of empirical justification hold that an empirical belief is justified if and only if it is either a basic belief justified by the subject's experience[3] or else a derived belief justified, directly or indirectly, by the support of basic beliefs. Coherentist theories of empirical justification hold that a belief is justified if and only if it belongs to a coherent set of beliefs. In short, foundationalism requires a distinction of basic versus derived beliefs and an essentially one-directional notion of evidential support, whereas coherentism holds that beliefs can be justified only by mutual support among themselves.

The merit of foundationalism is that it acknowledges that a person's experience—what he sees, hears, etc.—is relevant to how justified he is in his beliefs about the world; its drawback is that it requires a privileged class of basic beliefs justified by experience alone but capable of supporting the rest of our justified beliefs, and ignores the pervasive interdependence among a person's beliefs. The merit of coherentism is that it acknowledges that pervasive interdependence and requires no distinction of basic and derived beliefs; its drawback is that it allows no role for the subject's experience.

Foundationalists, naturally, are keenly aware of the problems with coherentism. How could one possibly be justified in believing there's a dog in the yard, they ask, if what one sees, hears, and smells plays no role? And isn't the coherentist's talk of mutual support among beliefs just a euphemism for what is really a vicious circle in which what supposedly justifies the belief that p is the belief that q, and what justifies the belief that q the belief that r, . . . and what justifies the belief that z is the belief that p?

Coherentists, naturally, are no less keenly aware of the problems with foundationalism. What sense does it make to suppose that someone could have a justified belief that there's a dog in the yard, they ask, except in the context of the rest of his beliefs about dogs? Besides, why should we suppose that there *are* any beliefs both justified by experience alone and capable of supporting the rest of our justified beliefs? After all, foundationalists can't even agree among themselves whether the basic beliefs are about observable physical objects, along the lines of "There's a brown dog," or are about the subject's experience, along the lines of "It now seems to me that I see what looks like a brown dog" or "I am appeared to brownly." And anyway, only propositions, not events, can stand in logical relations to other propositions; so how *could* a subject's experience justify those supposedly basic beliefs?

As the two styles of theory have evolved, with each party trying to overcome the difficulties the other thinks insuperable, they have come closer together.

Strong foundationalism requires that basic beliefs be fully justified by the subject's experience; pure foundationalism requires that derived beliefs be justified exclusively by the support, direct or indirect, of basic beliefs. But weak foundationalism requires only that basic beliefs be justified to some degree by experience; and impure foundationalism, though requiring all derived beliefs to get some support from basic beliefs, allows mutual support among derived beliefs to raise their degree of justification.

Uncompromisingly egalitarian forms of coherentism hold that only overall coherence matters, so that every belief in a coherent set is equally justified. But moderated, inegalitarian forms of coherentism give a subject's beliefs about his present experience a distinguished initial status or give a special standing to beliefs which are spontaneous rather than inferential in origin.

In a way, these moderated forms of foundationalism and coherentism lean in the right direction, but the leaning destabilizes them.

Weak foundationalism concedes that basic beliefs need not be fully justified by experience alone; but then what reason remains to deny that they could get more (or less) justified by virtue of their relations to other beliefs? Impure foundationalism concedes that there can be mutual support among derived beliefs; but then what reason remains to insist that more pervasive mutual support is unacceptable? And weak, impure foundationalism allows both (1) that basic beliefs are less than fully justified by experience and (2) that derived beliefs may be mutually supportive; but now the insistence that derived beliefs can give no support to basic beliefs looks arbitrary, and the distinction of basic and derived beliefs pointless.[4]

Moderated, inegalitarian coherentism concedes that some beliefs are distinguished by their perceptual content or "spontaneous" origin; but

isn't this implicitly to concede that justification is not after all a relation exclusively among beliefs, that input from experience is essential?

Not surprisingly, these fancier forms of foundationalism and compromising kinds of coherentism, though more sophisticated than their simpler ancestors, tend to be ambiguous and unstable. On the foundationalist side, for example, under pressure of just the kinds of difficulty my analysis identifies, C. I. Lewis moves from a pure to an impure foundationalism and then briefly to a kind of protofoundherentism.[5] And on the coherentist side, under pressure of just the kind of difficulty my analysis identifies, Laurence BonJour tries to guarantee experiential input by adding an "Observation Requirement"—which, however, is ambiguous. On one interpretation, it is genuinely coherentist but doesn't allow the relevance of experience; on the other, it allows the relevance of experience but isn't genuinely coherentist.[6] (BonJour now acknowledges that, after all, coherentism won't do.)[7]

Neither of the traditionally rival theories can be made satisfactory without sacrificing its distinctive character. The obvious conclusion—though those still wedded to the old dichotomy will doubtless continue to resist it—is that we need a new approach which allows the relevance of experience to empirical justification, but without postulating any privileged class of basic beliefs or requiring that relations of support be essentially one directional: in other words, a foundherentist theory.

Explication of Foundherentism

The details get complicated, but the main ideas are simple. A foundherentist account will acknowledge (like foundationalism) that how justified a person is in an empirical belief must depend in part on his experience—my version will give a role both to sensory experience and to introspective awareness of one's own mental states. As coherentists point out, though experience can stand in causal relations to beliefs, it can't stand in logical relations to propositions. But what this shows is not that experience is irrelevant to empirical justification but that justification is a double-aspect concept, partly causal as well as partly logical in character.

A foundherentist account will acknowledge (like coherentism) that there is pervasive mutual support among a person's justified beliefs. As foundationalists point out, a belief can't be justified by a vicious circle of reasons. What this shows, however, is not that mutual support is illegitimate but that we need a better understanding of the difference between legitimate mutual support and vicious circularity; my version will rely on an analogy between the structure of evidence and a crossword puzzle.

Of course, the viability of the foundherentist approach doesn't depend on my being completely successful in articulating it. No doubt there could be other versions of foundherentism falling within these general contours but differing in their details.

I take as my starting point the following vague but very plausible, formulation: "A is more or less justified, at t, in believing that p, depending on how good his evidence is."

By starting from here, I take for granted, first, that justification comes in degrees: a person may be more or less justified in believing something. (I also assume that a person may be more justified in believing some things than he is in believing others.)

I also take for granted, second, that the concepts of evidence and justification are internally connected: how justified a person is in believing something depends on the quality of his evidence with respect to that belief.

I assume, third, that justification is personal: one person may be more justified in believing something than another is in believing the same thing because one person's evidence may be better than another's. (But though justification is personal, it is not subjective. How justified A is in believing that p depends on how good *his*, A's, evidence is. But how justified A is in believing that p doesn't depend on how good A *thinks* his evidence is; and anyone who believed the same thing on the same evidence would be justified to the same degree.)

And I assume, fourth, that justification is relative to a time: a person may be more justified in believing something at one time than at another because his evidence at one time may be better than his evidence at another.

"A is more/less justified, at t, in believing that p, depending on how good his evidence is." Obviously, the main tasks are to explain "his evidence" and "how good." The double-aspect character of the concept of justification is already in play; for "his," in "his evidence," is a causal notion, whereas "how good" is logical or quasi-logical in character.

The concept of justification is causal as well as logical across the board;[8] its causal aspect is not restricted to experiential evidence alone. Quite generally, how justified someone is in believing something depends not only on *what* he believes, but on *why* he believes it. For example, if two people both believe the accused is innocent, one because he has evidence that she was 100 miles from the scene of the crime at the relevant time, the other because he thinks she has an honest face, the former is more justified than the latter. In short, degree of justification depends on the quality of the evidence that actually causes the belief in question.

The word "belief" is ambiguous. Sometimes it refers to a mental state, someone's believing something [an S-belief];[9] sometimes it refers to the content of what is believed, a proposition [a C-belief]. "A's evidence" needs to be tied somehow to what causes A's S-belief, but must also be capable of standing in logical or quasi-logical relations to the C-belief, the proposition believed.

The idea is to begin by characterizing A's S-evidence with respect to p—this will be a set of states of A causally related to his S-belief that p—and then to use this as the starting point of a characterization of A's C-evidence with respect to p; this will be a set of propositions capable of standing in logical or quasi-logical relations to the C-belief that p.

If A initially came to believe that the rock-rabbit is the closest surviving relative of the elephant because a fellow tourist told him he read this somewhere, and later still believes it, but now because he has learned all the relevant biological details, he is more justified at the later time than at the earlier. So, if they are different, "A's S-evidence with respect to p" should relate to the causes of A's S-belief that p at the time in question rather than to what prompted it in the first place.

What goes on in people's heads is very complicated. There will likely be some factors inclining A toward believing that p, and others pulling against it. Perhaps, for example, A believes that Tom Grabit stole the book because his seeing Grabit leave the library with a shifty expression and a suspicious bulge under his sweater exerts a stronger positive pull than his belief that it is possible that Tom Grabit has a light-fingered identical twin exerts in the opposite direction. Both sustaining and inhibiting factors are relevant to degree of justification, so both will be included in A's S-evidence.

In this vector of forces [the causal nexus of A's S-belief that p], besides A's present experience and present memory traces of his past experience, and other S-beliefs of his, such factors as his wishes, hopes, and fears will often play a role. But A's desire not to believe ill of his students, say, or his being under the influence of alcohol, though they may affect whether or with what degree of confidence he believes that Grabit stole the book, aren't themselves part of his evidence with respect to that proposition.

So "A's S-evidence with respect to p" will refer to those experiential and belief-states of A's which belong, at the time in question, to the causal nexus of A's S-belief that p. The phrase "with respect to" signals the inclusion of both positive, sustaining, and negative, inhibiting evidence [respectively, A's S-evidence for p, and A's S-evidence against p]. A's S-evidence with respect to p will include other beliefs of his [A's S-reasons with respect to p]; and his perceptions, his introspective awareness of his own mental goings-on, and memory traces of his earlier perceptual and introspective states [A's experiential S-evidence with respect to p].

The part about memory needs amplifying. A's experiential S-evidence may include present memory traces of past experience, such as his remembering seeing his car keys on the dresser. This corresponds to the way we talk of A's remembering seeing, hearing, reading, and so on. We also talk of A's remembering that p, meaning that he earlier came to believe that p and has not forgotten it. How justified A is in such persisting beliefs will depend on how good his evidence is—his evidence at the time in question, that is. A person's evidence for persisting beliefs will normally include memory traces of past perceptual experience; my belief that my high school English teacher's name was "Miss Wright," for instance, is now sustained by my remembering hearing and seeing the name used by myself and others.

Testimonial evidence, in a broad sense—what a person reads, what others tell him—enters the picture by way of his hearing or seeing, or remembering hearing or seeing, what someone else says or writes. Of course, A's hearing B say that p won't contribute to his, A's, believing that p, unless A understands B's language. But if A believes that p in part because B told him that p, how justified A is in believing that p will depend in part on how justified A is in thinking B honest and reliable. But I anticipate.

A's S-evidence with respect to p is a set of states of A causally related to his S-belief that p. But in the part of the theory that explains what makes evidence better or worse, "evidence" will have to mean "C-evidence" and refer to a set of propositions. The two aspects interlock: A's C-evidence with respect to p will be a set of propositions, and how good it is will depend on those propositions' logical or quasi-logical relations to p; but *which* propositions A's C-evidence with respect to p consists of depends on which of A's S-beliefs and perceptual (etc.) states belong to the causal nexus of the S-belief in question.

A's C-reasons with respect to p, obviously enough, should be the C-beliefs—that is, the propositions—which are the contents of his S-reasons. For example, if one of A's S-reasons with respect to p is his S-belief that female cardinal birds are brown, the corresponding C-reason will be the proposition that female cardinal birds are brown.

But what about A's experiential C-evidence? My proposal is that "A's experiential C-evidence with respect to p" refer to propositions to the effect that A is in the perceptual/introspective/memory states which constitute his experiential S-evidence with respect to p. Since a perceptual (etc.) state can't be part of the causal nexus of A's S-belief that p unless A is *in* that state, these propositions are all true. But they need not be propositions that A believes.[10]

So A's experiential C-evidence has a distinctive status. A's C-reasons may be true or may be false, and A may be more or less justified, or not justified at all, in believing them. But A's experiential C-evidence consists of propositions all of which are, *ex hypothesi*, true, and with respect to which, the question of justification doesn't arise. (This is the foundherentist way of acknowledging that the ultimate evidence for empirical beliefs is experience—very different from the forced and unnatural way in which foundationalism tries to acknowledge it, by requiring basic *beliefs* justified by experience alone.)

In line with the way we ordinarily talk about the evidence of the senses—"Why do I think there's a cardinal in the oak tree? Well, I can see the thing; that distinctive profile is clear, though the light's not too good, and it's quite far away, so I can't really see the color"—I suggest a characterization of A's experiential C-evidence in terms of propositions to the effect that A is in the sort of perceptual state a normal subject would be in when seeing this or that in these or those circumstances. For example, if A's experiential S-evidence with respect to p is his perceptual state, its looking to him as it would to a normal observer seeing a female cardinal bird at a distance of forty feet in poor light, the corresponding experiential C-evidence will be a proposition to the effect that A is in the kind of perceptual state a normal observer would be in when looking at a female cardinal bird in those circumstances.

Built into my account of experiential evidence is a conception of perception as, in a certain sense, direct. This is not to deny that perception involves complicated neurophysiological goings-on. Nor is it to deny that the judgments causally sustained by the subject's experience are interpretative, that they depend on his background beliefs as well—which, on the contrary, is a key foundherentist thought. It is only to assert that in normal perception we interact with physical things and events around us, which look a certain way to all normal observers under the same circumstances.

You may be wondering why I include the subject's sensory and introspective experience as evidence, but not, say, his extra-sensory perceptual (ESP) experience. Well, the task here is descriptive—to articulate explicitly what is implicit when we say that A has excellent reasons for believing that p, that B is guilty of wishful thinking, that C has jumped to an unjustified conclusion, and so on. As those phrases "excellent reasons" and "guilty of wishful thinking" indicate, his other beliefs should be included as part of a subject's evidence but his wishes should not. Actually, I think it most unlikely there is such a thing as ESP, but it is excluded because—unlike sensory experience, for which we even have the phrase "the evidence of the senses"—it has no role in the implicit conception of evidence I am trying to make explicit.

The concepts of better and worse evidence, of more and less justified belief, are evaluative; so, after the descriptive task of explication, there will be the ratificatory question, whether our standards of better and worse evidence really are, as we hope and believe they are, indicative of truth. But that comes later.

The present task is to explicate "how good" in "how good A's C-evidence is." What factors raise and what lower degree of justification?

Foundationalists often think of the structure of evidence on the model of a mathematical proof, a model which understandably makes them leery of the idea of mutual support. My approach will be informed by the analogy of a crossword puzzle—where there is undeniably pervasive mutual support among entries but, equally undeniably, no vicious circle. The clues are the analog of experiential evidence, already-completed intersecting entries the analog of reasons. As how reasonable a crossword entry is depends both on the clues and on other intersecting entries, the idea is, so how justified an empirical belief is depends on experiential evidence and reasons working together.

Perhaps needless to say, an analogy is only an analogy, not an argument. Its role is only to suggest ideas, which then have to stand on their own feet. And there are always disanalogies; there will be nothing in my theory analogous to the solution to today's crossword puzzle which appears in tomorrow's newspaper, for instance, nor any analog of the designer of a crossword puzzle.

But the analogy does suggests a very plausible multidimensional answer to the question, What makes a belief more or less justified? How reasonable a crossword entry is depends on how well it is supported by the clue and any already-completed intersecting entries; how reasonable those other entries are, independent of the entry in question; and how much of the crossword has been completed. How justified A is in believing that p, analogously, depends on how well the belief in question is supported by his experiential evidence and reasons [supportiveness]; how justified his reasons are, independent of the belief in question [independent security]; and how much of the relevant evidence his evidence includes [comprehensiveness].

On the first dimension, A's C-evidence may be conclusive for p, conclusive against p, supportive-but-not-conclusive of p, undermining-but-not-conclusive against p, or indifferent with respect to p/with respect to not-p.

Foundationalists often take for granted that evidence is conclusive just in case it deductively implies the proposition in question, but this isn't quite right. Inconsistent premisses deductively imply any proposition whatever, but inconsistent evidence isn't conclusive evidence for anything—let alone conclusive evidence for everything! Think, for example, of a detective whose evidence is (1) the murder was committed by a lefthanded person, (2) either Smith or Brown did it, (3) Smith is lefthanded, and (4) Brown is righthanded. Though this deductively implies that Smith did it, it certainly isn't conclusive evidence for that belief (let alone conclusive evidence for the belief that Smith did it *and* conclusive evidence for the belief that Brown did it *and* conclusive evidence for the belief that extraterrestrials did it!).

Deductive implication is necessary but not sufficient for conclusiveness. Evidence E is conclusive for p just in case the result of adding p to E [the p-extrapolation of E] is consistent, and the result of adding not-p to E [the not-p-extrapolation of E] is inconsistent. E is conclusive against p just in case its p-extrapolation is inconsistent and its not-p-extrapolation consistent. But if E itself is inconsistent, both its p-extrapolation and its not-p-extrapolation are also inconsistent, so E is indifferent with respect to p.

Often, though, evidence is not conclusive either way, nor yet inconsistent and hence indifferent, but supports the belief in question, or its negation, to some degree. Suppose the detective's evidence is (1) the murder was committed by a lefthanded person, (2) either Smith or Brown did it, (3) Smith is lefthanded, (4) Brown is lefthanded, and (5) Smith recently saw the victim, Mrs. Smith, in a romantic restaurant holding hands with Brown. Though not conclusive, this evidence is supportive to some degree of the belief that Smith did it—for, if he did, we have some explanation of why.

The example suggests that supportiveness depends on whether and how much adding p to E makes a better explanatory story. But a better explanatory story than what? Conclusiveness is a matter of the superiority of p over its negation with respect to consistency. But if p is potentially explanatory of E or some component of E, it is not to be expected that not-p will be too. So I construe supportiveness as depending on the superiority of p over its rivals with respect to explanatory

integration; where a rival of p is any proposition adding which to E improves its explanatory integration to some degree, and which, given E, is incompatible with p.

The word "integration" was chosen to indicate that E may support p either because p explains E or some component of E or vice versa—that there is "mutual reinforcement between an explanation and what it explains."[11] (Thus, the concept of explanatory integration is closer kin to the coherentist concept of explanatory coherence than to the foundationalist concept of inference to the best explanation.)

Usually, as conclusiveness of evidence is taken to be the province of deductive logic, supportiveness of evidence is taken to be the province of inductive logic. But at least if "logic" is taken in its now-usual narrow sense, as depending on form alone, this looks to be a mistake. Explanation requires generality, kinds, laws—a motive for the murder, a mechanism whereby smoking tobacco causes cancer, and so forth. If so, explanatoriness, and hence supportiveness, requires a vocabulary that classifies things into real kinds; and hence depends on content, not on form alone. (Hempel drew the moral, many years ago now, from the "grue" paradox).[12] But there is supportive-but-not-conclusive evidence, even if there is no formal inductive logic.

Supportiveness alone does not determine degree of justification, which also depends on independent security and comprehensiveness. Suppose our detective's evidence is (1) the murder was committed by a lefthanded person, (2) either Smith or Brown did it, (3) Smith is righthanded, but (4) Brown is lefthanded. The detective's evidence is conclusive that Brown did it; nevertheless, he is not well justified in believing this unless, among other things, he is justified in believing that the murder was committed by a lefthanded person, that either Smith or Brown did it, and so on.

The idea of independent security is easiest to grasp in the context of the crossword analogy. In a crossword, how reasonable an entry is depends in part on its fit with intersecting entries and hence on how reasonable those entries are, independently of the entry in question. Similarly, how justified a person is in believing something depends in part on how well it is supported by his other beliefs and hence on how justified he is in believing those reasons, independently of the belief in question.

It is that last phrase—in my theory as with a crossword puzzle—that averts the danger of a vicious circle. The reasonableness of the entry for 3 down may depend in part on the reasonableness of the intersecting entry for 5 across—independent of the support given to the entry for 5 across by the entry for 3 down. Similarly, how justified A is in believing that p may depend in part on how justified he is in believing that q—independent of the support given his belief that q by his belief that p.

And, though "justified" appears on the right-hand side of the independent security clause, there is no danger of an infinite regress—any more than with a crossword puzzle. As in the case of a crossword eventually we reach the clues, so with empirical justification eventually we reach experiential evidence. And experiential C-evidence does not consist of other C-beliefs of the subject, but of propositions all of which are, *ex hypothesi*, true, and with respect to which the question of justification doesn't arise. This is not to deny that, as crossword clues may be cryptic, experiential evidence may be ambiguous or misleading; on the contrary, my account of experiential C-evidence is intended to recognize that it often is. It is only to say that the question of justification arises with respect to a person's beliefs, but not with respect to his experiences.

How reasonable a crossword entry is depends not only on how well it is supported by the clue and other intersecting entries, and on how reasonable those other entries are, but also on how much of the crossword has been completed. Thus, degree of justification depends not only on supportiveness and independent security but also on comprehensiveness—on how much of the relevant evidence the subject's evidence includes.

Comprehensiveness promises to be even tougher to spell out than supportiveness and independent security; the crossword analogy isn't much help here, and neither is the nearest analog in the literature, the total evidence requirement on inductions, which refers not to the totality of relevant evidence but to the totality of relevant available evidence. And then there is the further problem that relevance itself comes in degrees.

I am assuming, however, that (degree of) relevance is an objective matter. Naturally, whether I think your handwriting is relevant to your trustworthiness depends on whether I believe in graphology; but whether it *is* relevant depends on whether graphology is *true*.

As this reveals—though relevance, and hence comprehensiveness, is objective—judgments of relevance, and hence judgments of comprehensiveness are perspectival; that is, they depend on the background beliefs of the person making them. The same goes for judgments of supportiveness and independent security. How supportive you or I judge E to be with respect to p, for example, will depend on what rivals of p we happen to be able to think of; but how supportive E *is* of p does not. Quality of evidence is objective, but judgments of quality of evidence are perspectival.

Because quality of evidence is multidimensional, we should not necessarily expect a linear ordering of degrees of justification. For example, A's evidence with respect to p might be strongly supportive but weak on comprehensiveness, while his evidence with respect to q might be strong on comprehensiveness but only weakly supportive. Nor, a fortiori, does it look realistic to aspire to anything as ambitious as a numerical scale of degrees of justification. But something can be said about what is required for A to be justified to *any* degree in believing that p.

One necessary condition is that there *be* such a thing as A's C-evidence with respect to p. If A's S-belief that p is caused simply by a blow to the head (or by one of those belief-inducing pills philosophers are fond of imagining), A isn't justified to any degree in believing that p. Since it is the justification of empirical beliefs that is at issue, another necessary condition is that A's C-evidence should include some experiential C-evidence—present experiential evidence or memory traces of what he earlier saw, heard, read, etc. This is my analog of BonJour's Observation Requirement, obviously much more at home in foundherentism than his requirement was in his coherentist theory. (It is not meant to rule out the possibility that some of a person's beliefs may not be sustained directly by experiential evidence, not even by memory traces, but rely on other beliefs and their experiential evidence—as in an unconventional crossword puzzle some entries might have no clues of their own but rely on other entries and their clues.)[13] A third necessary condition is that A's C-evidence with respect to p should meet minimal conditions of supportiveness, independent security, and comprehensiveness; for example, it should be better than indifferent in terms of supportiveness. Jointly, these necessary conditions look to be sufficient.

What about the upper end of the scale? Our ordinary use of phrases like "A is completely justified in believing that *p*" is vague and context-dependent, depending *inter alia* on whether it is A's particular business to know whether *p*, and how important it is to be right about whether *p*; perhaps it also runs together strictly epistemological with ethical concerns. This vague concept [*complete* justification] is useful for practical purposes—and for the statement of Gettier-type paradoxes. In other philosophical contexts, however, "A is completely justified in believing that *p*" is used in a context-neutralized, optimizing way, requiring conclusiveness, maximal independent security, and full comprehensiveness of evidence [COMPLETE justification].

The account sketched here has been personal, that is, focused firmly on our friend A. But this is not to deny that in even the most ordinary of our everyday beliefs we rely extensively on testimonial evidence. And where the sciences are concerned, reliance on others' evidence—and hence on the interpretation of others' words and judgments of others' reliability—is absolutely pervasive. (This reveals that not only the social sciences but also the natural sciences presuppose the possibility of interpreting others' utterances: for example, an astronomer's reliance on others' reports of observations.)

Anyhow, thinking about evidence in the sciences prompts me to ask whether it is possible to extrapolate from my account of "A is more or less justified in believing that *p*" to a concept of justification applicable to groups of people. It might be feasible to do this by starting with the degree of justification of a hypothetical subject whose evidence includes all the evidence of each member of the group, and then discount this by some measure of the degree to which each member of the group is justified in believing that other members are competent and honest.

The Ratification of Foundherentism

Thus far, the task has been to articulate our standards of better and worse evidence, of more and less justified belief. But what do I mean by "our"? And what assurance can I give that a belief's being justified, by those standards, is any indication that it is true?

When I speak of "our" standards of better and worse evidence, I emphatically do not mean to suggest that these standards are local or parochial, accepted in "our," as opposed to "their," community. Rather, I see these standards—essentially, how well a belief is anchored in experience and how tightly it is woven into an explanatory mesh of beliefs—as rooted in human nature, in the cognitive capacities and limitations of all normal human beings.

It is sure to be objected that the evidential standards of different times, cultures, communities, or scientific paradigms differ radically. However, I think this supposed variability is at least an exaggeration and quite possibly altogether an illusion, the result of mistaking the perspectival character of judgments of evidential quality for radical divergence in standards of better and worse evidence.

Because judgments of the quality of evidence are perspectival, people with radically different background beliefs can be expected to differ significantly in their judgments of degree of justification. It doesn't follow that there are no shared standards of evidence. If we think of the constraints of experiential anchoring and explanatory integration rather than of specific judgments of the relevance, supportiveness, etc., of this or that evidence, I believe we will find commonality rather than divergence.

Again, the point is easier to see in the context of the crossword puzzle analogy. Suppose you and I are both doing the same crossword puzzle and have filled in some long central entry differently. You think, given your solution to that long central entry, that the fact that 14 down ends in a "T" is evidence in its favor; I think, given my solution to that long central entry, that the fact that it ends in a "D" is evidence in its favor. Nevertheless, we are both trying to fit the entry to its clue and to other already-completed entries. Now suppose you and I are both on an appointments committee. You think the way this candidate writes his "g"s indicates that he is not to be trusted; I think graphology is bunk and scoff at your "evidence." Because of a disagreement in background beliefs, we disagree about what evidence is relevant. Nevertheless, we are both trying to assess the supportiveness, independent security, and comprehensiveness of the evidence with respect to the proposition that the candidate is trustworthy.

But even if I am wrong about this, even if there really are radically divergent standards of evidential quality, it wouldn't follow that there are no objective indications of truth; *variability* of standards does not, in and of itself, imply *relativity* of standards.[14] So those epistemic relativists who have inferred that, since judgments of justification vary from community to community, there can be no objectively correct standards of better and worse evidence have committed a non sequitur as well as relying on a dubious premiss.

As for those who have succumbed to epistemic relativism because they have given up on the concept of truth, I have room here only to say that theirs seems to me an entirely factitious despair.[15] In any case, all that will be required of the concept of truth in what follows is that a proposition or statement is true just in case things are as it says.

Supposing—as I believe, and so do you—that we humans are fallible, limited, but inquiring creatures who live in a world which is largely independent of us and what we believe about it, but in which there are kinds, laws, regularities; and supposing—as I believe, and so do you—that our senses are a source, though by no means an infallible source, of information about things and events in the world around us and that introspection is a source, though by no means an infallible source, of information about our own mental goings-on. Then, if any indication of how things are is possible for us, how well our beliefs are anchored in our experience and knit into an explanatory mesh is such an indication. (And supposing—as I believe, and so, probably, do you— we have no other sources of information about the world and ourselves, no ESP or clairvoyance or the like, then this is the only indication we can have of how things are.)

That last paragraph was nothing like an a priori ratification of foundherentism, for those "supposing" clauses are empirical in character. Assumptions about human cognitive capacities and limitations are *built into* our standards of evidential quality; so the truth-indicativeness of those standards depends on the truth of those empirical assumptions. But neither was that last paragraph

much like the appeals to psychology or cognitive science on which some epistemological naturalists of a more extreme stripe than mine propose to rely, for the assumptions referred to in my "supposing" clauses, though empirical, are of such generality as to be rather philosophical than scientific in character.

Those assumptions would surely be presupposed by any conceivable scientific experiment. But they are well integrated with what the sciences of cognition have to tell us about the mechanisms of perception and introspection, and of when and why they are more or less reliable, and with what the theory of evolution suggests about how we came to have the sort of information-detecting apparatus we do. As one would hope, the epistemological part of my crossword puzzle—the part where the entries are themselves about crosswords—interlocks snugly with other parts.

But what am I to say to those readers familiar with Descartes's failed attempt to prove "what I clearly and distinctly perceive is true," who are bound to suspect that I must be arguing in a circle? After pointing out that I have not offered a ratificatory argument in which some premiss turns out to be identical with the conclusion, nor an argument relying on a certain mode of inference to arrive at the conclusion that this very mode of inference is a good one—only that, to borrow Peirce's words, by now "the reader will, I trust, be too well-grounded in logic to mistake mutual support for a vicious circle of reasoning."[16]

And what am I to say to readers worried about the evil demon, who are bound to object that I have not ruled out the possibility that our senses are not a source of information about the external world at all? After pointing out that since, *ex hypothesi*, his machinations would be absolutely undetectable, if there were an evil demon *no* truth indication would be possible for us—only that my claim is a conditional one: that, if any truth indication is possible for us, the foundherentist criteria are truth-indicative. (I could discharge the antecedent and arrive at a categorical conclusion by adopting a definition of truth along Peircean lines, as the opinion that would survive all possible experiential evidence and the fullest logical scrutiny, but I prefer the more cautious and more realist strategy.)

Determined skeptics won't be persuaded; but determined skeptics never are! And the rest of you may notice that foundherentism enables us to side-step another dichotomy which has—if you'll pardon the pun—bedeviled recent epistemology: *either* a hopeless obsession with hyperbolic skepticism *or* a hopeless relativism or tribalism preoccupied with "our (local, parochial) epistemic practices." Foundherentism, I believe, provides a more realistic picture of our epistemic condition— a robustly fallibilist picture which, without sacrificing objectivity, acknowledges something of how complex and confusing evidence can be.

Notes

[1] This brief statement of foundherentism is based primarily on my *Evidence and Inquiry: Towards Reconstruction in Epistemology* (Oxford: Blackwell, 1993), especially Chaps. 1, 4, and 10. I have also drawn on material from earlier articles of mine, especially "Theories of Knowledge: An Analytic Framework," *Proceedings of the Aristotelian Society 83*, 1982–1983, 143–157 (where foundherentism was first introduced); "C. I. Lewis," in *American Philosophy*, ed. Marcus Singer, Royal Institute of Philosophy Lecture Series, 19, Cambridge University Press, Cambridge, 1985, 215–239; and "Rebuilding the Ship While Sailing on the Water," in *Perspectives on Quine*, ed. R. Barrett and R. Gibson (Oxford: Blackwell, 1990), 111–127 (where some of the key ideas of foundherentism were developed). I have drawn as well on material from the symposium on *Evidence and Inquiry* published in *Philosophy and Phenomenological Research 56.3*, 1996, 611–657; and from the debate with BonJour to appear in *Synthese* for July 1997.

[2] Thomas Reid, *Essays on the Intellectual Powers* (1785), in *Thomas Reid: Inquiry and Essays*, ed. R. E. Beanblossom and K. Lehrer (Indianapolis: Hackett, 1983), 6.4.

[3] I restrict my attention here to experientialist forms of foundationalism, ignoring, e.g., foundationalist theories of a priori knowledge.

[4] My characterization of foundationalism is quite standard; cf. for example, Alston's in E. Sosa and J. Dancy, eds., *Companion to Epistemology* (Oxford: Blackwell, 1992), 144; or Sosa's in "The Raft and the Pyramid," *Midwest Studies in Philosophy 5*, 1980, 23–24. But matters have been confused because, in "Can Empirical Knowledge Have a Foundation?" *American Philosophical Quarterly 15*, 1978, 1–13, and *The Structure of Empirical Knowledge* (Cambridge, MA: Harvard University Press, 1986), 28, BonJour uses "weak foundationalism" to refer a style of theory that is both weak *and* impure, in my sense, and in

addition allows mutual support among basic beliefs and— apparently—allows "basic" beliefs to get support from "derived" beliefs. As my scare quotes indicate, once one directionality has been so completely abandoned, it is unclear that the theory really qualifies as foundationalist at all; certainly, the basic/derived distinction has become purely *pro forma*. See also Haack, "Reply to BonJour," *Synthese*, July 1997.

[5] See Haack, *Evidence and Inquiry*, Chap. 2 for details.

[6] See Haack, *Evidence and Inquiry*, Chap. 3 for details.

[7] Laurence BonJour, "Haack on Justification and Experience," *Synthese*, July 1997.

[8] An idea I first began to work out in "Epistemology *with* a Knowing Subject," *Review of Metaphysics 32.2*, 1979, 309–336.

[9] Expressions introduced in square brackets are my new, technical terms or special, technical uses of familiar terms.

[10] So my theory is not straightforwardly externalist, since A's S-evidence must consist of states of A—states, furthermore, of which A can be aware; but neither is it straightforwardly internalist, since A's experiential C-evidence consists of propositions A need not believe or even conceive.

[11] W. V. Quine, and J. Ullian, *The Web of Belief* (New York: Random House, 1970), 79.

[12] N. Goodman, "The New Riddle of Induction," in *Fact, Fiction and Forecast*, 2d ed. (Indianapolis: Bobbs-Merrill, 1965), 59–83; C. G. Hempel, "Postscript on Confirmation," in *Aspects of Scientific Explanation* (New York: Free Press, 1965), 47–52.

[13] In case a desperate foundationalist is tempted to try seizing on this in hopes of salvaging the derived/basic distinction, let me point out that beliefs without direct experiential evidence could contribute to the support of beliefs with direct experiential evidence, and that this maneuver would identify no plausible *kind* of belief as basic/as derived—think, e.g., of a scientist whose belief that electrons are composed thus and so is sustained by what he sees in the bubble chamber.

[14] See also Haack "Reflections on Relativism: From Momentous Tautology to Seductive Contradiction," *Nous*, Supplement, 1996, 297–315, and in James E. Tomberlin, ed., *Philosophical Perspectives 10: Metaphysics* (Oxford: Blackwell, 1996), 297–315 and Haack, *Manifesto of a Passionate Moderate: Unfashionable Essays* (Chicago: University of Chicago Press, 1998), 149–66.

[15] I have more to say in "Confessions of an Old-Fashioned Prig," in Haack, *Manifesto of a Passionate Moderate: Unfashionable Essays*, 7–30.

[16] C. S. Peirce, *Collected Papers*, eds. C. Hartshorne, P. Weiss, and A. Burks (Cambridge, MA: Harvard University Press, 1931–1958), 6.315.

V.9 A Contextual Theory of Epistemic Justification

David Annis

David Annis is professor of philosophy at Ball State University. In this essay, Annis offers an alternative to the foundationalist-coherentist controversy: "contextualism." This theory rejects both the idea of intrinsically basic beliefs in the foundational sense and the thesis that coherence is sufficient for justification. He argues that justification is relative to the varying norms of social practices.

I. Foundationalism, Coherentism, and Contextualism

Foundationalism is the theory that every empirical statement which is justified ultimately must derive at least some of its justification from a special class of basic statements which have at least some degree of justification independent of the support such statements may derive from other statements. Such *minimal* foundationalism does not require certainty or incorrigibility; it does not deny the revisability of *all* statements, and it allows an important role for intrasystematic justification or coherence.[1] The main objections to foundationalism have been (a) the denial of the existence of basic statements and (b) the claim that even if such statements were not mythical, such an impoverished basis would never justify all the various statements we normally take to be justified.

Opposed to foundationalism has been the coherence theory of justification. According to coherentism a statement is justified if and only if it coheres with a certain kind of system of statements. Although there has been disagreement among coherentists in explaining what coherence is and specifying the special system of statements, the key elements in these explanations have been consistency, connectedness, and comprehensiveness. The chief objection to the theory has been that coherence within a consistent and comprehensive set of statements is not sufficient for justification.[2] Theorists of epistemic justification have tended to stress foundationalism and coherentism

and in general have overlooked or ignored a third kind of theory, namely, *contextualism*. The contextualist denies that there are basic statements in the foundationalist's sense and that coherence is sufficient for justification. According to contextualism both theories overlook contextual parameters essential to justification. In what follows I develop a version of a contextualist theory.[3]

II. The Basic Model—Meeting Objections

The basic model of justification to be developed here is that of a person's being able to meet certain objections. The objections one must meet and whether or not they are met are relative to certain goals. Since the issue is that of epistemic justification, the goals are epistemic in nature. With respect to one epistemic goal, accepting some statement may be reasonable, whereas relative to a different goal it may not be. Two of our epistemic goals are having true beliefs and avoiding having false beliefs. Other epistemic goals such as simplicity, conservation of existing beliefs, and maximization of explanatory power will be assumed to be subsidiary to the goals of truth and the avoidance of error.[4]

Given these goals, if a person S claims that some statement h is true, we may object (A) that S is not in a position to know that h or (B) that h is false. Consider (A). Suppose we ask S how he knows that h and he responds by giving us various reasons $e_1, e_2, \ldots, e_n$ for the truth of h. We may object that one of his reasons e_1–e_n is false, e_1–e_n does not provide adequate support for h, S's specific reasoning from e_1–e_n to h is fallacious, or that there is evidence i such that the conjunction of

Reprinted from the *American Philosophical Quarterly* 15 (1978): 213–19, by permission of the author and the editor. Copyright 1978, *American Philosophical Quarterly*.

e_1–e_n and i does not provide adequate support for h. These objections may be raised to his reasons for e_1–e_n as well as to his responses to our objections.

There are also cases where a person is not required to give reasons for his claim that h is true. If S claims to see a brown book across the room, we usually do not require reasons. But we may still object that the person is not in a position to know by arguing, for example, that the person is not reliable in such situations. So even in cases where we do not in general require reasons, objections falling into categories (A) or (B) can be raised.

But it would be too strong a condition to require a person to be able to meet all *possible* objections falling into these categories. In some distant time new evidence may be discovered as the result of advances in our scientific knowledge which would call into question the truth of some statement h. Even though we do not in fact have that evidence now, it is logically possible that we have it, so it is a possible objection to h now. If the person had to meet the objection, he would have to be in a different and better epistemic position than the one he is presently in, that is, he would have to have new evidence in order to respond to the objection. The objectors also would have to be in a better position to raise the objection. But the objections to be raised and answered should not require the participants to be in a new epistemic position. What is being asked is whether the person in his present position is justified in believing h. Thus the person only has to answer *current* objections, that is, objections based on the current evidence available.

Merely uttering a question that falls into one of our categories does not make it an objection S must answer. To demand a response the objection must be an expression of a *real* doubt. According to Peirce, doubt is an uneasy and dissatisfied state from which we struggle to free ourselves. Such doubt is the result of "some surprising phenomenon, some experience which either disappoints an expectation, or breaks in upon some habit of expectation."[5] As Dewey puts it, it is only when "jars, hitches, breaks, blocks, . . . incidents occasioning an interruption of the smooth straight forward course of behavior" occur that doubt arises.[6] Thus for S to be held accountable for answering an objection, it must be a manifestation of a real doubt where the doubt is occasioned by a real life situation. Assuming that the subjective probabilities a person assigns reflect the person's actual epistemic attitudes and that these are

the product of his confrontation with the world, the above point may be expressed as follows. S is not required to respond to an objection if *in general* it would be assigned a low probability by the people questioning S.

If an objection must be the expression of a real doubt caused by the jars of a real life situation, then such objections will be primarily *local* as opposed to *global*. Global objections call into question the totality of beliefs held at a certain time or a whole realm of beliefs, whereas local objections call into question a specific belief. This is not to say that a real situation might not occur that would prompt a global objection. If having experienced the nuclear radiation of a third world war, there were a sudden and dramatic increase in the error rate of perceptual beliefs of the visual sort, we would be more hesitant about them as a class.

It must be assumed that the objecting audience has the epistemic goals of truth and the avoidance of error. If they were not critical truth seekers, they would not raise appropriate objections. To meet an objection i, S must respond in such a way as to produce within the objecting group a general but not necessarily universal rejection of i or at least the general recognition of the diminished status of i as an objection. In the latter case S may, for example, point out that although i might be true, it only decreases the support of e_i (one of his reasons for believing h) a very small amount, and hence he is still justified in believing h. There are of course many ways in which S can handle an objection. He might indicate that it is not of the type (A) or (B) and so is not relevant. He may respond that it is just an *idle* remark not prompted by real doubt; that is, there is no reason for thinking that it is true. He may ask the objector for his reasons, and he can raise any of the objections of the type (A) or (B) in response. Again the give and take is based on real objections and responses.

III. The Social Nature of Justification

When asking whether S is justified in believing h, this has to be considered relative to an *issue-context*. Suppose we are interested in whether Jones, an ordinary non-medically trained person, has the general information that polio is caused by a virus. If his response to our question is that he remembers the paper reporting that Salk said it was, then this is good enough. He has performed adequately given the issue-context. But suppose the context is an examination for the M.D. degree. Here we expect a lot more. If the candidate simply said what Jones did, we would take him as being very deficient in knowledge. Thus relative to one issue-context a person may be justified in believing *h* but not justified relative to another context.

The issue-context is what specific issue involving *h* is being raised. It determines the level of understanding and knowledge that *S* must exhibit, and it determines an appropriate objector-group. For example in the context of the examination for the M.D. degree, the appropriate group is not the class of ordinary non-medically trained people, but qualified medical examiners.

The importance (value or utility) attached to the outcome of accepting *h* when it is false or rejecting *h* when it is true is a component of the issue-context. Suppose the issue is whether a certain drug will help cure a disease in humans without harmful effects. In such a situation we are much more demanding than if the question were whether it would help in the case of animals. In both cases the appropriate objector-group would be the same, namely, qualified researchers. But they would require quite a bit more proof in the former case. Researchers do in fact strengthen or weaken the justificatory conditions in relation to the importance of the issue. If accepting *h* when *h* is false would have critical consequences, the researcher may increase the required significance level in testing *h*.

Man is a social animal, and yet when it comes to the justification of beliefs philosophers tend to ignore this fact. But this is one contextual parameter that no adequate theory of justification can overlook. According to the contextualist model of justification sketched above, when asking whether some person *S* is justified in believing *h,* we must consider this relative to some specific issue-context which determines the level of understanding and knowledge required. This in turn determines the appropriate objector-group. For *S* to be justified in believing *h* relative to the issue-context, *S* must be able to meet all current objections falling into (A) and (B) which express a real doubt of the qualified objector-group where the objectors are critical truth seekers. Thus social information—the beliefs, information, and theories of others—plays

an important part in justification, for it in part determines what objections will be raised, how a person will respond to them, and what responses the objectors will accept.

Perhaps the most neglected component in justification theory is the *actual* social practices and norms of justification of a culture or community of people. Philosophers have looked for universal and a priori principles of justification. But consider this in the context of scientific inquiry. There certainly has been refinement in the methods and techniques of discovery and testing in science. Suppose that at a time *t* in accordance with the best methods then developed for discovery and testing in a scientific domain by critical truth seekers, *S* accepts theory *T*. It is absurd to say that *S* is not justified in accepting *T* since at a later time a refinement of those techniques would lead to the acceptance of a different theory. Thus relative to the standards at *t,* *S* is justified in accepting *T*.

The same conclusion follows if we consider a case involving two different groups existing at the same time instead of two different times as in the above example. Suppose *S* is an Earth physicist and accepts *T* on the basis of the best methods developed by Earth physicists at *t*. Unknown to us the more advanced physicists on Twin Earth reject *T*. *S* is still justified in accepting *T*.

To determine whether *S* is justified in believing *h* we must consider the actual standards of justification of the community of people to which he belongs. More specifically we determine whether *S* is justified in believing *h* by specifying an issue-context raised within a community of people *G* with certain social practices and norms of justification. This determines the level of understanding and knowledge *S* is expected to have and the standards he is to satisfy. The appropriate objector-group is a subset of *G*. To be justified in believing *h, S* must be able to meet their objections in a way that satisfies their practices and norms.

It follows that justification theory must be *naturalized*. In considering the justification of beliefs we cannot neglect the actual social practices and norms of justification of a group. Psychologists, sociologists, and anthropologists have started this study, but much more work is necessary.[7]

The need to naturalize justification theory has been recognized in recent philosophy of science. Positivists stressed the *logic* of science—the structure of theories, confirmation, explanation—in abstraction from science as actually carried on. But much of the main thrust of recent philosophy of science is that such an approach is inadequate. Science as *practiced* yields justified beliefs about the world. Thus the study of the actual practices, which have changed through time, cannot be neglected. The present tenor in the philosophy of science is thus toward a historical and methodological realism.[8]

From the fact that justification is relative to the social practices and norms of a group, it does not follow that they cannot be criticized nor that justification is somehow subjective. The practices and norms are epistemic and hence have as their goals truth and the avoidance of error. Insofar as they fail to achieve these goals they can be criticized. For example the Kpelle people of Africa rely more on the authority of the elders than we do. But this authority could be questioned if they found it led to too many false perceptual beliefs. An objection to a practice must of course be real; that is, the doubt must be the result of some jar or hitch in our experience of the world. Furthermore such objections will always be local as opposed to global. Some practice or norm and our experiences of the world yield the result that another practice is problematic. A real objection presupposes some other accepted practice. This however does not commit us to some form of subjectivism. Just as there is no theory-neutral observation language in science, so there is no standard-neutral epistemic position that one can adopt. But in neither case does it follow that objectivity and rational criticism are lost.[9]

IV. The Regress Argument

Philosophers who have accepted foundationalism have generally offered a version of the infinite regress argument in support of it. Two key premises in the argument are the denial of a coherence theory of justification and the denial that an infinite sequence of reasons is sufficient to justify a belief. But there is another option to the conclusion of the argument besides foundationalism. A contextualist theory of the sort offered above stops the regress and yet does not require basic statements in the foundationalist's sense.

Suppose that the Joneses are looking for a red chair to replace a broken one in their house. The issue-context is thus not whether they can discern subtle shades of color. Nor is it an examination in physics where the person is expected to have detailed knowledge of the transmission of light and color perception. Furthermore nothing of great importance hinges on a correct identification. Mr. Jones, who has the necessary perceptual concepts and normal vision, points at a red chair a few feet in front of him and says "here is a red one." The appropriate objector-group consists of normal perceivers who have general knowledge about the standard conditions of perception and perceptual error. In such situations which we are all familiar with, generally, there will be no objections. His claim is accepted as justified. But imagine that someone objects that there is a red light shining on the chair so it may not be red. If Jones cannot respond to this objection when it is real, then he is not in an adequate cognitive position. But suppose he is in a position to reply that he knows about the light and the chair is still red since he saw it yesterday in normal light. Then we will accept his claim.

A belief is *contextually basic* if, given an issue-context, the appropriate objector-group does not require the person to have reasons for the belief in order to be in a position to have knowledge. If the objector-group requires reasons, then it is not basic in the context. Thus in the first situation above Jones's belief that there is a red chair here is contextually-basic, whereas it is not basic in the second situation.

Consider the case either where the objector-group does not require S to have reasons for his belief that h in order to be in a position to have knowledge and where they accept his claim, or the case where they require reasons and accept his claim. In either case there is no regress of reasons. If an appropriate objector-group, the members of which are critical truth seekers, have no real doubts in the specific issue-context, then the person's belief is justified. The belief has withstood the test of verifically motivated objectors.

V. Objections to the Theory

There are several objections to the contextualist theory offered, and their main thrust is that the conditions for justification imposed are too stringent. The objections are as follows. First according to the theory offered, to be justified in believing *h* one must be able to meet a restricted class of objections falling into categories (A) and (B). But this ignores the distinction between *being* justified and *showing* that one is justified. To be justified is just to satisfy the principles of justification. To show that one is justified is to demonstrate that one satisfies these principles, and this is much more demanding.[10] For example *S* might have evidence that justifies his belief that *h* even though he is not able to articulate the evidence. In this case *S* would not be able to show that he was justified.

Second, if to be justified in believing *h* requires that one be able to meet the objection that *h* is false, then the theory ignores the distinction between truth and justification. A person can be justified in believing a statement even though it is false.

Finally the theory requires *S* to be in a position to answer all sorts of objections from a variety of perspectives. But this again is to require too much. For example assume that two scientists in different countries unaware of each other's work perform a certain experiment. The first scientist, S_1, gets one result and concludes that *h*. The second scientist, S_2, does not get the result (due to incorrect measurements). To require of S_1 that he be aware of S_2's experiment and be able to refute it is to impose an unrealistic burden on him in order for his belief to be justified. It is to build a *defeasibility* requirement into the justification condition. One approach to handling the Gettier problem has been to add the condition that in order to have knowledge, besides having justified true belief, the justification must not be defeated. Although there have been different characterizations of defeasibility, a core component or unrestricted version has been that a statement *i* defeats the justification evidence *e* provides *h* just in case *i* is true and the conjunction of *i* and *e* does not provide adequate support for *h*.[11] But according to the contextualist theory presented in order for *S* to be justified in believing *h*, he must be able to meet the objection that there is defeating evidence.

In reply to the first objection, the theory offered does not ignore the distinction between being justified and showing that one is justified. It is not required of *S* that he be able to state the standards of justification and demonstrate that he satisfies them. What is required is that he be able to meet real objections. This may *sometimes* require

him to discuss standards, but not always. Furthermore the example given is not a counterexample since it is not a case of justified belief. Consider a case where relative to an issue-context we would expect *S* to have reasons for his belief that *h*. Suppose when asked how he knows or what his reasons are he is not able to say anything. We certainly would not take him as justified in his belief. We may not be able to articulate all our evidence for *h*, but we are required to do it for some of the evidence. It is not enough that we have evidence for *h*; it must be *taken* by us as evidence, and this places us "in the logical space of reasons, of justifying and being able to justify what one says."[12]

The first point in response to the next objection is that *epistemic* justification makes a claim to knowledge. To be *epistemically* justified in believing *h* is to be in a position to know *h*. Furthermore if the goals of epistemic justification are truth and the avoidance of error, then one *ought not* accept false statements. From an epistemic point of view to do so is objectionable. Hence the falsity of *h* at least counts against the person's being justified.

However, the contextualist account offered does not ignore the distinction between truth and justification. Meeting an objection does not entail showing the objection is false. It only requires general agreement on the response. So the objection may still be true. Thus *S* may be justified in believing *h* since he can meet the objection when *h* is in fact false. Furthermore an objection in order to require a response has to be the expression of a real doubt. Since it is possible for verifically motivated objectors not to be aware of the falsity of *h*, this objection will not be raised, so *S* may be justified in believing *h* even though it is false.

The situation is complex, however, since there are cases where the falsity of *h* implies *S* is not justified in believing *h*. Suppose that Jones is at a party and wonders whether his friend Smith is there. Nothing of great importance hinges on his presence; he simply wonders whether he is there. Perhaps he would not mind a chat with Smith. He looks about and asks a few guests. They have not seen him there. In such a situation Jones is justified in believing Smith is not there.

Imagine now that Jones is a police officer looking for Smith, a suspected assassin, at the party. Merely looking about casually and checking with a few guests is certainly not adequate. If Smith turns out to be hiding in one of the closets, we will not conclude that Jones was justified in his belief only it turned out false. He displayed gross negligence in not checking more thoroughly. There are cases where relative to an issue-context we require the person S to put himself in such an epistemic position that h will not turn out to be false. In this case the falsity of h is *non-excusable*. To be justified in believing h in non-excusable cases, S must be able to meet the objection that h is false. This is not required in excusable cases.

Assume that h is some very complicated scientific theory and S puts himself in the very best evidential position at the time. Even if the truth of h is very important, the falsity of h is excusable. The complexity of the issue and the fact that S put himself in the best position possible excuses S from the falsity of h, so he is still justified. But not all excusable cases involve a complex h nor being in the best position possible. Suppose that Smith has an identical twin brother but the only living person who knows this is the brother. Furthermore there are no records that there was a twin brother. If Jones returns a book to Smith's house and mistakenly gives it to the brother (where the issue-context is simply whether he returned the borrowed book and nothing of great importance hinges on to whom he gave it), he is still justified in his belief that he gave it to his friend Smith. Although Jones could have put himself in a better position (by asking questions about their friendship), there was no reason for him in the context to check further. People did not generally know about the twin brother, and Smith did not notice any peculiar behavior. Given the issue-context, members of the appropriate objector-group would not *expect* Jones to check further. So he evinces no culpability when his belief turns out to be false. Excusability thus depends on the issue-context and what the appropriate objector-group, given their standards of justification and the information available, expect of S.

Part of assimilating our epistemic standards, as is the case with both legal and moral standards, is learning the conditions of excusability. Such conditions are highly context-dependent, and it would be extremely difficult if not impossible to formulate rules to express them. In general we learn the conditions of excusability case by case. One need only consider moral and legal negligence to realize the full complexity of excuses, an area still to be studied despite Austin's well-known plea a number of years ago.

In response to the third objection it should be noted that epistemic justification is not to be taken lightly. Accepting h in part determines what other things I will believe and do. Furthermore I can infect the minds of others with my falsehoods and thus affect their further beliefs and actions. So to be epistemically justified requires that our claims pass the test of criticism. This point has motivated some philosophers to build a defeasibility requirement into the conditions of justification.[13]

The contextualist theory presented above, however, does not do this. There may be a defeating statement i, but S need meet this objection only if the objector-group raises it. For them to raise it, i must be the expression of real doubt. But it is perfectly possible for verifically motivated people to be unaware of i.

Furthermore the concept of epistemic excusability applies to defeating evidence. Suppose there is defeating evidence i. S may still be justified in his belief that h in the issue-context, even though he is unable to meet the objection. Relative to the issue-context, the appropriate objector-group with their standards of justification and available information may not expect of S that he be aware of i. Perhaps the issue involving h is very complicated. Thus his failure to meet the defeating evidence is excusable.

In the experiment case we can imagine issue-contexts where we would expect the first scientist to know of the experiment of the other scientist. But not all issue-contexts demand this. Nevertheless we may still require that he be in a position to say something about the other experiment if informed about it. For example he might indicate that he knows the area well, has performed the experiment a number of times and gotten similar results, it was performed under carefully controlled conditions, so he has every reason for believing that the experiment is replicable with similar results. Thus there must be something wrong with the other experiment. Requiring the scientist to be able to respond in the *minimal* way seems not to be overly demanding.

VI. Summary

Contextualism is an alternative to the traditional theories of foundationalism and coherentism. It denies the existence of basic statements in the foundationalist's sense (although it allows contextually basic statements), and it denies that coherence as it traditionally has been explained is sufficient for justification. Both theories overlook contextual parameters essential to justification, such as the issue-context and thus the value of *h*, social information, and social practices and norms of justification. In particular, the social nature of justification cannot be ignored.

Notes

[1] For a discussion of minimal foundationalism see William P. Alston, "Has Foundationalism Been Refuted?"; James W. Cornman, "Foundationalism versus Nonfoundational Theories of Empirical Justification"; David B. Annis, "Epistemic Foundationalism."

[2] Recent discussions of coherentism are found in Keith Lehrer, *Knowledge*, chaps. 7–8; Nicholas Rescher, "Foundationalism, Coherentism, and the Idea of Cognitive Systematization" and his *The Coherence Theory of Truth*. Criticism of Lehrer's coherence theory is to be found in Cornman, "Foundational Versus Nonfoundational Theories of Empirical Justification," and in my review of Lehrer in *Philosophia* 6 (1976): 209–13. Criticism of Rescher's version is found in Mark Pastin's "Foundationalism Redux," unpublished, an abstract of which appears in *The Journal of Philosophy* 61 (1974): 709–10.

[3] Historically the key contextualists have been Peirce, Dewey, and Popper. But contextualist hints, suggestions, and theories are also to be found in Robert Ackermann, *Belief and Knowledge;* Bruce Aune, *Knowledge, Mind and Nature;* John Austin, *Sense and Sensibilia* (London, 1962);

Isaac Levi, *Gambling with Truth* (New York, 1967); Stephen Toulmin, *The Uses of Argument* (London, 1958) and *Human Understanding* (Princeton, New Jersey, 1972); Carl Wellman, *Challenge and Response: Justification in Ethics* (Carbondale, Illinois, 1971); F. L. Will, *Induction and Justification;* Ludwig Wittgenstein, *Philosophical Investigations* (New York, 1953) and *On Certainty*.

[4] For a discussion of epistemic goals see Levi, *Gambling with Truth*.

[5] C. S. Peirce, *Collected Papers,* vol. 6, ed. Charles Hartshorne and Paul Weiss (Harvard, 1965), p. 469.

[6] John Dewey, *Knowing and the Known* (Boston, 1949), p. 315. See also Wittgenstein's *On Certainty*.

[7] See, for example, Michael Cole et al., *The Cultural Context of Learning and Thinking* (New York, 1971).

[8] For a discussion of the need to naturalize justification theory in the philosophy of science, see Frederick Suppe, "Afterword—1976" in the 2nd edition of his *The Structure of Scientific Theories* (Urbana, Illinois, 1977).

[9] See Frederick Suppe's "The Search for Philosophic Understanding of Scientific Theories" and his "Afterword–1976" in *The Structure of Scientific Theories* for a discussion of objectivity in science and the lack of a theory-neutral observation language.

[10] Alston discusses this distinction in "Has Foundationalism Been Refuted?" See also his "Two Types of Foundationalism."

[11] The best discussion of defeasibility is Marshall Swain's "Epistemic Defeasibility."

[12] Wilfrid Sellars, *Science, Perception and Reality,* p. 169.

[13] Carl Ginet, "What Must Be Added to Knowing to Obtain Knowing That One Knows?," *Synthese* 21 (1970): 163–86.

Bibliography

Alston, William. "Concepts of Epistemic Justification." *Monist 68* (1985). Reprinted in his book *Epistemic Justification: Essays in the Theory of Knowledge*. Ithaca, NY: Cornell University Press, 1990.

Alston, William. "Two Types of Foundationalism." *Journal of Philosophy 73* (1976). Also in his book *Epistemic Justification: Essays in the Theory of Knowledge*. Ithaca, NY: Cornell University Press, 1990.

Armstrong, D. M. *Belief, Truth and Knowledge.* Cambridge: Cambridge University Press, 1973.

Ayer, A. J. *The Foundations of Empirical Knowledge.* New York: St. Martin's Press, 1955.

Baergen, Ralph. *Contemporary Epistemology.* Fort Worth, TX: Harcourt Brace, 1955. Chapter 5.

Blanshard, Brand. *The Nature of Thought.* London: Allen & Unwin, 1939.

BonJour, Laurence. *The Structure of Empirical Knowledge.* Cambridge, MA: Harvard University Press, 1985.

Bradley, F. H. *Essays on Truth and Reality.* Oxford: Oxford University Press, 1914.

Butchvarov, Panayot. *The Concept of Knowledge.* Evanston, IL: Northwestern University Press, 1970.

Chisholm, Roderick. *The Foundations of Knowing.* Minneapolis, MN: University of Minnesota Press, 1982.

Chisholm, Roderick, and Robert Schwartz, eds. *Empirical Knowledge.* Englewood Cliffs, NJ: Prentice-Hall, 1973.

Dancy, Jonathan, and Ernest Sosa, eds. *A Companion to Epistemology.* Oxford: Blackwell, 1992.

Everitt, Nicholas, and Alec Fisher. *Modern Epistemology.* New York: McGraw-Hill, 1995.

Ewing, A. C. *Idealism: A Critical Survey.* London: Methuen, 1934.

Foley, Richard. *The Theory of Epistemic Rationality.* Cambridge, MA: Harvard University Press, 1987.

Goldman, Alan H. *Empirical Knowledge.* University of California Press, 1988.

Goldman, Alvin. *Epistemology and Cognition.* Cambridge, MA: Harvard University Press, 1986.

Goodman, Michael, and Robert Snyder, eds. *Contemporary Readings in Epistemology.*

Upper Saddle River, NJ: Prentice Hall, 1993.

Haack, Susan. *Evidence and Inquiry: Towards Reconstruction in Epistemology.* Oxford: Blackwell, 1993.

Lehrer, Keith. *Knowledge.* Oxford, England: Clarendon Press, 1974.

Lehrer, Keith. *Theory of Knowledge.* Boulder, CO: Westview, 1990.

Lewis, C. I. *An Analysis of Knowledge and Valuation.* La Salle, IL: Open Court, 1946.

McGrew, Timothy J. *The Foundations of Knowledge.* Lanham, MD: Littlefield Adams, 1995.

Moser, Paul. *Empirical Justification.* Boston, MA: Reidel, 1985.

Moser, Paul, ed. *Empirical Knowledge.* Totowa, NJ: Rowman & Littlefield, 1986.

Pappas, George, ed. *Justification and Knowledge,* Dordrecht, Netherlands: Reidel, 1979.

Pappas, George, and Marshall Swain, eds. *Essays on Knowledge and Justification.* Ithaca, NY: Cornell University Press, 1978.

Pojman, Louis P. *What Can We Know? An Introduction to the Theory of Knowledge,* 2nd ed. Belmont, CA: Wadsworth, 2001.

Pollock, John. *Contemporary Theories of Knowledge.* Totowa, NJ: Rowman & Littlefield, 1986.

Quine, W. V. *Two Dogmas of Empiricism.* Cambridge, MA: Harvard University Press, 1958.

Rescher, Nicholas. *The Coherence Theory of Truth.* Oxford, England: Clarendon Press, 1973.

Russell, Bertrand. "On the Nature of Truth." *Proceedings of the Aristotelian Society.* 1906–1907.

Sellars, Wilfrid. *Science, Perception and Reality.* London: Routledge & Kegan Paul, 1963.

Sellars, Wilfrid. "Givenness and Explanatory Coherence." *Journal of Philosophy 70* (1973).

Sosa, Ernest. "The Foundations of Foundationalism." *Nous 14* (1980).

Sosa, Ernest. *Knowledge in Perspective: Selective Essays in Epistemology.* Cambridge: Cambridge University Press, 1991.

Steup, Matthias. *An Introduction to Contemporary Epistemology.* Upper Saddle River, NJ: Prentice Hall, 1996.

Van Cleve, James. "Foundationalism, Epistemic Principles and the Cartesian Circle." *Philosophical Review 88* (1979). Ridgeview, 1988.

Part VI

Theories of Justification (II): Externalism and Internalism

Bishop James Ussher (1581–1656), Primate of All Ireland, calculated the genealogies in the Bible and determined that the creation of the heavens and Earth, as well as the first humans, took place in the year 4004 B.C.E (October 23 at noon), about 6,000 years ago. Modern science totally rejects Ussher's theory. The fossil record, the dating of the age of rocks that posits the Earth is about 5 billion years old, the evidence from astronomy that the universe is at least 15 billion years old, our best evidence for evolutionary theory—all purport to refute Bishop Ussher's conclusions. But suppose Ussher is right about the age of the universe and the Genesis account of Creation is accurate so that all our evidence for evolution and the longevity of the universe is systematically misleading. The radioisotope tests for dating organic materials do not function reliably after about 5,500 years. The fossils of dinosaurs were hidden in Earth by a malicious demon to mislead unbelievers. Our evidence for an ancient universe is fraudulent but is such that finite minds like ours could never comprehend the truth unaided by revelation. If we had not sinned, our noetic devices would have processed all this information reliably, but as it is, sin has corrupted our belief-forming mechanisms so that they are unreliable about such matters. Only through conversion,

wherein divine grace sets our mechanisms back in proper working order, can we become knowledgeable of the hidden truth.

According to internalists, or *justificationists*, as long as we are following the best evidence available to us, we are justified in believing the evolutionary account and the creationists are unjustified in their lucky true belief. The externalists (*reliabilists*) argue that this is not the case. As long as a reliable process causes creationists to believe the way they do, they have knowledge as well as justification.

Actually, there are two kinds of externalists: reliabilists and naturalists, the former (D. M. Armstrong, and Alvin Goldman in reading VI.1) hold that reliable processes are justifactory. Naturalists, such as W. V. Quine in the third reading, reject the notion of justification altogether. Knowledge is a matter of having beliefs caused in the proper way. The idea of justification implies normativity, but as we are not responsible for our beliefs, the idea of evaluation is misplaced.

There are several advantages to externalism. It defeats the skeptic, dissolves the problems of induction and other minds, and makes sense of perceptual knowledge.

Externalism defeats skepticism. Since knowledge is defined as true beliefs caused in the proper manner, it doesn't matter whether the subject can give an account of his or her beliefs or is even conscious of those beliefs. In a similar vein, externalism dissolves the problem of induction and other minds because these beliefs are seen as being caused by reliable processes.

With regard to perception, we often cannot give an account of our beliefs. We may not even know why we hold them. Suppose you come to dinner at my home, and after dinner I take you into another room and give you a quiz. "Do you know what color the walls in the dining room were and what pictures were hanging on them?" I ask. You pause, for you don't remember even noticing the walls or the pictures, but you correctly say, "The walls were red and a couple of pictures of Oxford were on one wall and a Renoir picture was on the other." "How did you know that?" I ask. You admit that you don't know how you knew. Your perceptual mechanisms picked up the information, stored it in your mind or brain, and let you retrieve it at the appropriate moment. Were you justified in believing that the walls were red and that pictures of Oxford were on one wall? What if you thought you were only guessing? What if you didn't really believe what you said, but only said what came to your mind unbidden via the unconscious?

The externalist says you knew the color of the walls and what pictures were hanging there, just as long as a reliable mechanism caused your beliefs. The internalist has trouble with this sort of case and either says it is a borderline case of justification or is an unjustified true belief.

But there are weaknesses with externalism. First of all, exactly what is to count as a reliable belief-forming mechanism is vague. What percentage of true beliefs must the process be able to produce before it is admitted to be reliable? The major problem, however, is that it seems to dissolve the notion of normativity. Knowledge is more than simply having true beliefs or properly caused beliefs. A long tradition, going back to Plato in the *Theaetetus,*

holds that knowledge requires the ability to give reasons, a justification. Appropriate causation of a belief seems necessary but not sufficient for justification, for we can imagine counterexamples where a belief that *p* has been properly caused, but where we would not want to say that the subject knew *p*. Laurence BonJour offers the following counterexample:

> Samantha believes herself to have the power of clairvoyance, though she has no reason for or against this belief. One day she comes to believe, for no apparent reason, that the President is in New York City. She maintains this belief, appealing to her alleged clairvoyance power, even though she is at the same time aware of a massive amount of apparently cogent evidence, consisting of news reports, press releases, allegedly live television pictures, and so on, indicating that the President is at that time in Washington, D.C. Now the President is in fact in New York City, the evidence to the contrary being part of a massive official hoax mounted in the face of an assassination threat. Moreover, Samantha does in fact have completely reliable clairvoyant power under the conditions which were then satisfied, and her belief about the President did result from the operation of that power.[1]

In this case the reliability requirement is met, but we would hesitate to say that Samantha knows that the president is in New York or is justified in her belief.

Likewise, even if it turned out that Bishop Ussher was right in dating the creation of the heavens and Earth to the year 4004 B.C.E. and that present-day creationists had their correct beliefs formed in reliable ways (their belief-forming mechanisms were unconsciously tied into information patterns going back to Creation, though they didn't have good reasons to believe this), as long as they weren't able to give good reasons for their beliefs, we would deny that they were epistemically justified in their beliefs.

Finally, reliabilists seem to be driven to giving counterfactual accounts of knowing and so are heirs to all the problems inherent in such accounts, as well as specifying the relevant belief-forming mechanism in specific cases.

In the first reading, Alvin Goldman develops a causal account of foundational justification called "historical reliabilism," in contrast with the traditional "current time slice" theories of justification. Current time slice or synchronic theories view the justificatory status of a belief as a function of what is true for the believer at the time of the believing. Historical reliabilism holds that the justificatory status is a function of the belief's prior history, specifically of whether it was produced in the right way. Goldman's theory is objectivist and externalist.

In the second reading, Keith Lehrer nicely maps out the geography of the internalist–externalist debate and argues against Goldman's account and for internalism.

In the third reading, W. V. Quine argues for a more radical version of externalism than Goldman and the reliabilists. According to Quine, normative epistemology is an outmoded enterprise that must be turned over to psychology. With the failure of Rudolf Carnap's project for constructing a foundational system of knowledge and with our understanding of the indeterminacy of translation, all hope of reviving the "old epistemology" is fruitless. What is left is a descriptive inquiry into the relationship between sensory inputs and the "torrential output," our picture of the world.

In the fourth reading, Earl Conee and Richard Feldman examine the central thesis of reliability theories: that a belief is justified if and only if it is produced by a process that reliably leads to true beliefs. They argue that such a theory must clearly identify the nature of these reli-

able processes. However, it turns out that seemingly insuperable problems attend any attempt to identify these processes. In particular, any given token process may be assessed under many types. So process reliabilism, the most prominent of externalist theories, turns out to be at best incomplete.

Matthias Steup, in our next reading, defends an account of internalism that, directly opposed to externalism, is both deontological and evidentialist. Contrary to externalists, Steup holds that we do have epistemic duties and that believing does have a volitional element.

In our sixth reading, Hilary Kornblith's "Naturalistic Epistemology and Its Critics," is valuable for two reasons. First, it sums up and assesses the current debate between naturalistic epistemologists and their critics. Second, it provides an account of how naturalism can preserve the goals of traditional epistemology: describing justification and knowledge, meeting the skeptical challenge, and providing advice on how to enlarge the set of true beliefs and knowledge while minimizing the set of false ones.

Our seventh reading, "Elusive Knowledge," is a subtle defense of externalist contextualism. David Lewis deals with the frustration of applying our normal epistemic standards to commonsense knowledge claims, noting that our standards seem to dissolve clear instances of knowledge. He proposes a solution that would solve this problem. In our final reading John Greco defends agent reliabilism as a form of virtue epistemology.

Let us turn to our first reading, the groundbreaking article by Alvin Goldman, "Reliabilism: What Is Justified Belief?"

Note

[1] Laurence BonJour, *The Structure of Empirical Knowledge* (Cambridge, MA: Harvard University Press, 1985), 38.

VI.1 Reliabilism: What Is Justified Belief?

ALVIN I. GOLDMAN

Alvin I. Goldman is professor of philosophy at the University of Arizona. Two of his earlier essays appear in Part IV. This essay is a successor to these earlier causal accounts in which Goldman argues that (1) all present versions of internalism are plagued with insuperable obstacles, (2) the absence of a causal requirement is common to each of these inadequate principles, and (3) the theory that best satisfies the causal requirement is an external version of justification—namely, "reliabilism," which defines the justificatory status of a belief in terms of the reliability of the process that caused it. The reliability of a process consists in its tendency to produce true beliefs rather than false ones. This is an externalist and objective theory of justification because the agent need not have access to the causal mechanisms that produce justified beliefs.

The aim of this essay is to sketch a theory of justified belief. What I have in mind is an explanatory theory, one that explains in a general way why certain beliefs are counted as justified and others as unjustified. Unlike some traditional approaches, I do not try to prescribe standards for justification that differ from, or improve upon, our ordinary standards. I merely try to explicate the ordinary standards, which are, I believe, quite different from those of many classical, e.g., "Cartesian," accounts.

Many epistemologists have been interested in justification because of its presumed close relationship to knowledge. This relationship is intended to be preserved in the conception of justified belief presented here. In previous papers on knowledge,[1] I have denied that justification is necessary for knowing, but there I had in mind "Cartesian" accounts of justification. On the account of justified belief suggested here, it *is* necessary for knowing, and closely related to it.

The term "justified," I presume, is an evaluative term, a term of appraisal. Any correct definition or synonym of it would also feature evaluative terms. I assume that such definitions or synonyms might be given, but I am not interested in them. I want a set of *substantive* conditions that

specify when a belief is justified. Compare the normal term "right." This might be defined in other ethical terms or phrases, a task appropriate to meta-ethics. The task of normative ethics, by contrast, is to state substantive conditions for the rightness of actions. Normative ethics tries to specify non-ethical conditions that determine when an action is right. A familiar example is act-utilitarianism, which says an action is right if and only if it produces, or would produce, at least as much net happiness as any alternative open to the agent. These necessary and sufficient conditions clearly involve no ethical notions. Analogously, I want a theory of justified belief to specify in non-epistemic terms when a belief is justified. This is not the only kind of theory of justifiedness one might seek, but it is one important kind of theory and the kind sought here.

In order to avoid epistemic terms in our theory, we must know which terms are epistemic. Obviously, an exhaustive list cannot be given, but here are some examples: "justified," "warranted," "has (good) grounds," "has reason (to believe)," "knows that," "sees that," "apprehends that," "is probable" (in an epistemic or inductive sense), "shows that," "establishes that," and "ascertains that." By contrast, here are some sample nonepistemic expressions: "believes that," "is true," "causes," "it is necessary that," "implies," "is deducible from," and "is probable" (either in the frequency sense or the propensity sense). In general, (purely) doxastic, metaphysi-

Reprinted from *Justification and Knowledge*, ed. G. S. Pappas (Dordrecht: D. Reidel, 1979), 1–23, by permission of the author and the publisher. Copyright 1979, D. Reidel Publishing Company.

cal, modal, semantic, or syntactic expressions are not epistemic.

There is another constraint I wish to place on a theory of justified belief, in addition to the constraint that it be couched in non-epistemic language. Since I seek an explanatory theory, i.e., one that clarifies the underlying source of justificational status, it is not enough for a theory to state "correct" necessary and sufficient conditions. Its conditions must also be appropriately deep or revelatory. Suppose, for example, that the following sufficient condition of justified belief is offered: "If S senses redly at t and S believes at t that he is sensing redly, then S's belief at t that he is sensing redly is justified." This is not the kind of principle I seek; for, even if it is correct, it leaves unexplained *why* a person who senses redly and believes that he does, believes this justifiably. Not every state is such that if one is in it and believes one is in it, this belief is justified. What is distinctive about the state of sensing redly, or "phenomenal" states in general? A theory of justified belief of the kind I seek must answer this question, and hence it must be couched at a suitably deep, general, or abstract level.

A few introductory words about my *explicandum* are appropriate at this juncture. It is often assumed that whenever a person has a justified belief, he knows that it is justified and knows what the justification is. It is further assumed that the person can state or explain what his justification is. On this view, a justification is an argument, defense, or set of reasons that can be given in support of a belief. Thus, one studies the nature of justified belief by considering what a person might *say* if asked to defend, or justify, his belief. I make none of these sorts of assumptions here. I leave it an open question whether, when a belief *is* justified, the believer *knows* it is justified. I also leave it an open question whether, when a belief is justified, the believer can *state* or *give* a justification for it. I do not even assume that when a belief is justified there is something "possessed" by the believer which can be called a "justification." I do assume that a justified belief gets its status of being justified from some processes or properties that make it justified. In short, there must be some justification-conferring processes or properties. But this does not imply that there must be an argument, or reason, or anything else, "possessed" at the time of belief by the believer.

I

A theory of justified belief will be a set of principles that specify truth-conditions for the schema [S's belief in p at time t is justified], i.e., conditions for the satisfaction of this schema in all possible cases. It will be convenient to formulate candidate theories in a recursive or inductive format, which would include (A) one or more base clauses, (B) a set of recursive clauses (possibly null), and (C) a closure clause. In such a format, it is permissible for the predicate "is a justified belief" to appear in recursive clauses. But neither this predicate, nor any other epistemic predicate, may appear in (the antecedent of) any base clause.[2]

Before turning to my own theory, I want to survey some other possible approaches to justified belief. Identification of problems associated with other attempts will provide some motivation for the theory I shall offer. Obviously, I cannot examine all, or even very many, alternative attempts. But a few sample attempts will be instructive.

Let us concentrate on the attempt to formulate one or more adequate base-clause principles.[3] Here is a classical candidate:

(1)   If S believes p at t, and p is indubitable for S (at t), then S's belief in p at t is justified.

To evaluate this principle, we need to know what "indubitable" means. It can be understood in at least two ways. First, "p is indubitable for S" might mean: "S has no *grounds* for doubting p." Since "ground" is an epistemic term, however, principle (1) would be inadmissible in this reading, for epistemic terms may not legitimately appear in the antecedent of a base-clause. A second interpretation would avoid this difficulty. One might interpret "p is indubitable for S" psychologically, i.e., as meaning "S is psychologically incapable of doubting p." This would make principle (1) admissible, but would it be correct? Surely not. A religious fanatic may be psychologically incapable of doubting the tenets of his faith, but that doesn't make his belief in them justified. Similarly, during the Watergate affair, someone may have been so blinded by the aura of the presidency that even after the most damaging evidence against Nixon had emerged he was still incapable of doubting Nixon's veracity. It doesn't follow that his belief in Nixon's veracity was justified.

A second candidate base-clause principle is this:

(2)   If S believes p at t and p is self-evident, then S's belief in p at t is justified.

To evaluate this principle, we again need an interpretation of its crucial term, in this case "self-evident." On one standard reading, "evident" is a synonym for "justified." "*Self*-evident" would therefore mean something like "directly justified," "intuitively justified," or "non-derivatively justified." On this reading "self-evident" is an epistemic phrase, and principle (2) would be disqualified as a base-clause principle.

However, there are other possible readings of "p is self-evident" on which it isn't an epistemic phrase. One such reading is: "It is impossible to understand p without believing it."[4] According to this interpretation, trivial analytic and logical truths might turn out to be self-evident. Hence, any belief in such a truth would be a justified belief, according to (2).

What does "it is *impossible* to understand p without believing it" mean? Does it mean "*humanly* impossible"? That reading would probably make (2) an unacceptable principle. There may well be propositions which humans have an innate and irrepressible disposition to believe, e.g., "Some events have causes." But it seems unlikely that people's inability to refrain from believing such a proposition makes every belief in it justified.

Should we then understand "impossible" to mean "impossible in principle," or "logically impossible"? If that is the reading given, I suspect that (2) is a vacuous principle. I doubt that even trivial logical or analytic truths will satisfy this definition of "self-evident." Any proposition, we may assume, has two or more components that are somehow organized or juxtaposed. To understand the proposition one must "grasp" the components and their juxtaposition. Now in the case of *complex* logical truths, there are (human) psychological operations that suffice to grasp the components and their juxtaposition but do not suffice to produce a belief that the proposition is true. But can't we at least *conceive* of an analogous set of psychological operations even for simple logical truths, operations which perhaps are not in the repertoire of human cognizers but which might be in the repertoire of some conceivable beings? That is, can't we conceive of psychological operations that

would suffice to grasp the components and componential-juxtaposition of these simple propositions but do not suffice to produce *belief* in the propositions? I think we can conceive of such operations. Hence, for any proposition you choose, it will be possible for it to be understood without being believed.

Finally, even if we set these two objections aside, we must note that self-evidence can at best confer justificational status on relatively few beliefs, and the only plausible group are beliefs in necessary truths. Thus, other base-clause principles will be needed to explain the justificational status of beliefs in contingent propositions.

The notion of a base-clause principle is naturally associated with the idea of "direct" justifiedness, and in the realm of contingent propositions first-person-current-mental-state propositions have often been assigned this role. In Chisholm's terminology, this conception is expressed by the notion of a "*self-presenting*" state or proposition. The sentence "I am thinking," for example, expresses a self-presenting proposition. (At least I shall *call* this sort of content a "proposition," though it only has a truth value given some assignment of a subject who utters or entertains the content and a time of entertaining.) When such a proposition is true for person S at time t, S is justified in believing it at t: in Chisholm's terminology, the proposition is "evident" for S at t. This suggests the following base-clause principle:

(3)   If p is a self-presenting proposition, and p is true for S at t, and S believes p at t, then S's belief in p at t is justified.

What, exactly, does "self-presenting" mean? In the second edition of *Theory of Knowledge*, Chisholm offers this definition: "*h* is self-presenting for S at t = df. h is true at t; and necessarily, if h is true at t, then h is evident for S at t."[5] Unfortunately, since "evident" is an epistemic term, "self-presenting" also becomes an epistemic term on this definition, thereby disqualifying (3) as a legitimate base-clause. Some other definition of self-presentingness must be offered if (3) is to be a suitable base-clause principle.

Another definition of self-presentation readily comes to mind. "Self-presentation" is an approximate synonym of "self-intimation," and a proposition may be said to be self-intimating if and only if whenever it is true of a person that person believes it. More precisely, we may give the following definition:

> (SP)   Proposition p is self-presenting if and only if: necessarily, for any S and any t, if p is true for S at t, then S believes p at t.

On this definition, "self-presenting" is clearly not an epistemic predicate, so (3) would be an admissible principle. Moreover, there is initial plausibility in the suggestion that it is *this* feature of first-person-current-mental-state propositions—viz., their truth guarantees their being believed—that makes beliefs in them justified.

Employing this definition of self-presentation, is principle (3) correct? This cannot be decided until we define self-presentation more precisely. Since the operator "necessarily" can be read in different ways, there are different forms of self-presentation and correspondingly different versions of principle (3). Let us focus on two of these readings: a "*nomological*" reading and a "*logical*" reading. Consider first the nomological reading. On this definition a proposition is self-presenting just in case it is nomologically necessary that if p is true for S at t, then S believes p at t.[6]

Is the nomological version of principle (3)—call it "(3_N)"—correct? Not at all. We can imagine cases in which the antecedent of (3_N) is satisfied, but we would not say that the belief is justified. Suppose, for example, that p is the proposition expressed by the sentence "I am in brain-state B," where "B" is shorthand for a certain highly specific neural state description. Further suppose it is a nomological truth that anyone in brain-state B will ipso facto *believe* he is in brain-state B. In other words, imagine that an occurrent belief with the content "I am in brain-state B" is realized whenever one is in brain-state B.[7] According to (3_N), any such belief is justified. But that is clearly false. We can readily imagine circumstances in which a person goes into brain-state B and therefore has the belief in question, though this belief is by no means justified. For example, we can imagine that a brain-surgeon operating on S artificially induced brain-state B. This results, phenomenologically, in S's suddenly believing—out of the blue—that he is in brain-state B, without any relevant antecedent beliefs. We would hardly say, in such a case, that S's belief that he is in brain-state B is justified.

Let us turn next to the logical version of (3)—call it "(3_L)"—in which a proposition is defined as

self-presenting just in case it is logically necessary that if p is true for S at t, then S believes p at t. This stronger version of principle (3) might seem more promising. In fact, however, it is no more successful than (3_N). Let p be the proposition "I am awake" and assume that it is logically necessary that if this proposition is true for some person S and time t, then S believes p at t. This assumption is consistent with the further assumption that S frequently believes p when it is false, e.g., when he is dreaming. Under these circumstances, we would hardly accept the contention that S's belief in this proposition is always justified. Nor should we accept the contention that the belief is justified when it is *true*. The truth of the proposition logically guarantees that the belief is *held,* but why should it guarantee that the belief is *justified?*

The foregoing criticism suggests that we have things backwards. The idea of self-presentation is that truth guarantees belief. This fails to confer justification because it is compatible with there being belief without truth. So what seems necessary—or at least sufficient—for justification is that belief should guarantee truth. Such a notion has usually gone under the label of "*infallibility*" or "*incorrigibility.*" It may be defined as follows:

> (INC)   Proposition p is incorrigible if and only if: necessarily, for any S and any t, if S believes p at t, then p is true for S at t.

Using the notion of incorrigibility, we may propose principle (4).

> (4)   If p is an incorrigible proposition, and S believes p at t, then S's belief in p at t is justified.

As was true of self-presentation, there are different varieties of incorrigibility, corresponding to different interpretations of "necessarily." Accordingly, we have different versions of principle (4). Once again, let us concentrate on a nomological and a logical version, (4_N) and (4_L) respectively.

We can easily construct a counterexample to (4_N) along the lines of the belief-state/brain-state counterexample that refuted (3_N). Suppose it is nomologically necessary that if anyone believes he is in brain-state B then it is true that he is in brain-state B, for the only way this belief-state is realized is through brain-state B itself. It follows that "I am in brain-state B" is a nomologically incorrigible proposition. Therefore, according to (4_N), whenever anyone believes this proposition at any time, that belief is justified. But we may again construct a brain-surgeon example in which someone comes to have such a belief but the belief isn't justified.

Apart from this counterexample, the general point is this. Why should the fact that S's believing p guarantees the truth of p imply that S's belief is justified? The nature of the guarantee might be wholly fortuitous, as the belief-state/brain-state example is intended to illustrate. To appreciate the point, consider the following related possibility. A person's mental structure might be such that whenever he believes that p will be true (of him) a split second later, then p is true (of him) a split second later. This is because, we may suppose, his believing it brings it about. But surely we would not be compelled in such a circumstance to say that a belief of this sort is justified. So why should the fact that S's believing p guarantees the truth of p *precisely at the time of belief* imply that the belief is justified? There is no intuitive plausibility in this supposition.

The notion of *logical* incorrigibility has a more honored place in the history of conceptions of justification. But even principle (4_L), I believe, suffers from defects similar to those of (4_N). The mere fact that belief in p logically guarantees its truth does not confer justificational status on such a belief.

The first difficulty with (4_L) arises from logical or mathematical truths. Any true proposition of logic or mathematics is logically necessary. Hence, any such proposition p is logically incorrigible, since it is logically necessary that, for any S and any t, if S believes p at t then p is true (for S at t). Now assume that Nelson believes a certain very complex mathematical truth at time t. Since such a proposition is logically incorrigible, (4_L) implies that Nelson's belief in this truth at t is justified. But we may easily suppose that this belief of Nelson is not at all the result of proper mathematical reasoning, or even the result of appeal to trustworthy authority. Perhaps Nelson believes this complex truth because of utterly confused reasoning, or because of hasty and ill-founded conjecture. Then his belief is not justified, contrary to what (4_L) implies.

The case of logical or mathematical truths is admittedly peculiar, since the truth of these propositions is assured independently of any beliefs. It might seem, therefore, that we can better capture the idea of "belief logically guaranteeing truth" in cases where the propositions in question are *con-tingent*. With this in mind, we might restrict (4_L) to *contingent* incorrigible propositions. Even this amendment cannot save (4_L), however, since there are counterexamples to it involving purely contingent propositions.

Suppose that Humperdink has been studying logic—or, rather, pseudo-logic—from Elmer Fraud, whom Humperdink has no reason to trust as a logician. Fraud has enunciated the principle that any disjunctive proposition consisting of at least 40 distinct disjuncts is very probably true. Humperdink now encounters the proposition p, a contingent proposition with 40 disjuncts, the 7th disjunct being "I exist." Although Humperdink grasps the proposition fully, he doesn't notice that it is entailed by "I exist." Rather, he is struck by the fact that it falls under the disjunction rule Fraud has enunciated (a rule I assume Humperdink is not *justified* in believing). Bearing this in mind, Humperdink forms a belief in p. Now notice that p is logically incorrigible. It is logically necessary that if anyone believes p, then p is true (of him at that time). This simply follows from the fact that, first, a person's believing anything entails that he exists, and second, "I exist" entails p. Since p is logically incorrigible, principle (4_L) implies that Humperdink's belief in p is justified. But surely, given our example, that conclusion is false. Humperdink's belief in p is not at all justified.

One thing that goes wrong in this example is that while Humperdink's belief in p logically implies its truth, Humperdink doesn't *recognize* that his believing it implies its truth. This might move a theorist to revise (4_L) by adding the requirement that S "recognize" that p is logically incorrigible. But this, of course, won't do. The term "recognize" is obviously an epistemic term, so the suggested revision of (4_L) would result in an inadmissible base-clause.

II

Let us try to diagnose what has gone wrong with these attempts to produce an acceptable base-clause principle. Notice that each of the foregoing attempts confers the status of "justified" on a belief without restriction on *why* the belief is held, i.e., on what *causally initiates* the belief or *causally sustains* it. The logical versions of principles (3) and (4), for example, clearly place no restriction on causes of belief. The same is true of the nomological versions of (3) and (4), since nomological requirements can be satisfied by simultaneity or cross-sectional laws, as illustrated by our brain-state/belief-state examples. I suggest that the absence of causal requirements accounts for the failure of the foregoing principles. Many of our counterexamples are ones in which the belief is caused in some strange or unacceptable way, e.g., by the accidental movement of a brain-surgeon's hand, by reliance on an illicit, pseudo-logical principle, or by the blinding aura of the presidency. In general, a strategy for defeating a noncausal principle of justifiedness is to find a case in which the principle's antecedent is satisfied but the belief is caused by some faulty belief-forming process. The faultiness of the belief-forming process will incline us, intuitively, to regard the belief as unjustified. Thus, correct principles of justified belief must be principles that make causal requirements, where "cause" is construed broadly to include sustainers as well as initiators of belief (i.e., processes that determine, or help to overdetermine, a belief's continuing to be held).[8]

The need for causal requirements is not restricted to base-clause principles. Recursive principles will also need a causal component. One might initially suppose that the following is a good recursive principle: "If S justifiably believes q at t, and q entails p, and S believes p at t, then S's belief in p at t is justified." But this principle is unacceptable. S's belief in p doesn't receive justificational status simply from the fact that p is entailed by q and S justifiably believes q. If what causes S to believe p at t is entirely different, S's belief in p may well not be justified. Nor can the situation be remedied by adding to the antecedent the condition that S justifiably believes that q entails p. Even if he believes this, and believes q as well, he might not put these beliefs together. He might believe p as a result of some other wholly extraneous considerations. So once again, conditions that fail to require appropriate causes of a belief don't guarantee justifiedness.

Granted that principles of justified belief must make reference to causes of belief, what kinds of causes confer justifiedness? We can gain insight into this problem by reviewing some faulty processes of belief-formation, i.e., processes whose belief-outputs would be classed as unjusti-

fied. Here are some examples: confused reasoning, wishful thinking, reliance on emotional attachment, mere hunch or guesswork, and hasty generalization. What do these faulty processes have in common? They share the feature of *unreliability:* they tend to produce *error* a large proportion of the time. By contrast, which species of belief-forming (or belief-sustaining) processes are intuitively justification-conferring? They include standard perceptual processes, remembering, good reasoning, and introspection. What these processes seem to have in common is *reliability:* the beliefs they produce are generally true. My positive proposal, then, is this. The justificational status of a belief is a function of the reliability of the process or processes that cause it, where (as a first approximation) reliability consists in the tendency of a process to produce beliefs that are true rather than false.

To test this thesis further, notice that justifiedness is not a purely categorical concept, although I treat it here as categorical in the interest of simplicity. We can and do regard certain beliefs as more justified than others. Furthermore, our intuitions of comparative justifiedness go along with our beliefs about the comparative reliability of the belief-causing processes.

Consider perceptual beliefs. Suppose Jones believes he has just seen a mountain-goat. Our assessment of the belief's justifiedness is determined by whether he caught a brief glimpse of the creature at a great distance, or whether he had a good look at the thing only 30 yards away. His belief in the latter sort of case is (*ceteris paribus*) more justified than in the former sort of case. And, if his belief is true, we are more prepared to say he *knows* in the latter case than in the former. The difference between the two cases seems to be this. Visual beliefs formed from brief and hasty scanning, or where the perceptual object is a long distance off, tend to be wrong more often than visual beliefs formed from detailed and leisurely scanning, or where the object is in reasonable proximity. In short, the visual processes in the former category are less reliable than those in the latter category. A similar point holds for memory beliefs. A belief that results from a hazy and indistinct memory impression is counted as less justified than a belief that arises from a distinct memory impression, and our inclination to classify those beliefs as "*knowledge*" varies in the same way. Again, the reason is associated with the comparative reliability of the processes. Hazy and indistinct memory impressions are generally less reliable indicators of what actually happened, so beliefs formed from such impressions are less likely to be true than beliefs formed from distinct impressions. Further, consider beliefs based on inference from observed samples. A belief about a population that is based on random sampling, or on instances that exhibit great variety, is intuitively more justified than a belief based on biased sampling, or on instances from a narrow sector of the population. Again, the degree of justifiedness seems to be a function of reliability. Inferences based on random or varied samples will tend to produce less error or inaccuracy than inferences based on non-random or non-varied samples.

Returning to a categorical concept of justifiedness, we might ask just *how* reliable a belief-forming process must be in order that its resultant beliefs be justified. A precise answer to this question should not be expected. Our conception of justification is *vague* in this respect. It does seem clear, however, that *perfect* reliability isn't required. Belief-forming processes that *sometimes* produce error still confer justification. It follows that there can be justified beliefs that are false.

I have characterized justification-conferring processes as ones that have a "tendency" to produce beliefs that are true rather than false. The term "tendency" could refer either to *actual* long-run frequency, or to a "propensity," i.e., outcomes that would occur in merely *possible* realizations of the process. Which of these is intended? Unfortunately, I think our ordinary conception of justifiedness is vague on this dimension too. For the most part, we simply assume that the "observed" frequency of truth versus error would be approximately replicated in the actual long-run, and also in relevant counterfactual situations, i.e., ones that are highly "realistic" or conform closely to the circumstances of the actual world. Since we ordinarily assume these frequencies to be roughly the same, we make no concerted effort to distinguish them. Since the purpose of my present theorizing is to capture our ordinary conception of justifiedness, and since our ordinary conception is vague on this matter, it is appropriate to leave the theory vague in the same respect.

We need to say more about the notion of a belief-forming "*process.*" Let us mean by a "process" a *functional operation* or procedure, i.e., something that generates a *mapping* from certain states—"inputs"—into other states—"outputs." The outputs in the present case are states of believing this or that proposition at a given moment. On this interpretation, a process is a *type* as opposed to a *token*. This is fully appropriate, since it is only types that have statistical properties such as producing truth 80 percent of the time; and it is precisely such statistical properties that determine the reliability of a process. Of course, we also want to speak of a process as *causing* a belief, and it looks as if types are incapable of being causes. But when we say that a belief is caused by a given process, understood as a functional procedure, we may interpret this to mean that it is caused by the particular *inputs* to the process (and by the intervening events "through which" the functional procedure carries the inputs into the output) on the occasion in question.

What are some examples of belief-forming "processes" construed as functional operations? One example is reasoning processes, where the inputs include antecedent beliefs and entertained hypotheses. Another example is functional procedures whose inputs include desires, hopes, or emotional states of various sorts (together with antecedent beliefs). A third example is a memory process, which takes as input beliefs or experiences at an earlier time and generates as output beliefs at a later time. For example, a memory process might take as input a belief *at* t_1 that Lincoln was born in 1809 and generate as output a belief *at* t_n that Lincoln was born in 1809. A fourth example is perceptual processes. Here it isn't clear whether inputs should include states of the environment, such as the distance of the stimulus from the cognizer, or only events within or on the surface of the organism, e.g., receptor stimulations. I shall return to this point in a moment.

A critical problem concerning our analysis is the degree of generality of the process-types in question. Input-output relations can be specified very broadly or very narrowly, and the degree of generality will partly determine the degree of reliability. A process-type might be selected so narrowly that only one instance of it ever occurs, and hence the type is either completely reliable or completely unreliable. (This assumes that reliability is a function of *actual* frequency only.) If such narrow process-types were selected, beliefs that are intuitively unjustified might be said to result from perfectly reliable processes, and beliefs that are intuitively justified might be said to result from perfectly unreliable processes.

It is clear that our ordinary thought about process-types slices them broadly, but I cannot at present give a precise explication of our intuitive principles. One plausible suggestion, though, is that the relevant processes are *content-neutral*. It might be argued, for example, that the process of *inferring p whenever the Pope asserts p* could pose problems for our theory. If the Pope is infallible, this process will be perfectly reliable; yet we would not regard the belief-outputs of this process as justified. The content-neutral restriction would avert this difficulty. If relevant processes are required to admit as input beliefs (or other states) with *any* content, the aforementioned process will not count, for its input beliefs have a restricted propositional content, viz., "*the Pope* asserts *p*."

In addition to the problem of "generality" or "abstractness" there is the previously mentioned problem of the "*extent*" of belief-forming processes. Clearly, the causal ancestry of beliefs often includes events outside the organism. Are such events to be included among the "inputs" of belief-forming processes? Or should we restrict the extent of belief-forming processes to "*cognitive*" events, i.e., events within the organism's nervous system? I shall choose the latter course, though with some hesitation. My general grounds for this decision are roughly as follows. Justifiedness seems to be a function of how a cognizer deals with his environmental input, i.e., with the goodness or badness of the operations that register and transform the stimulation that reaches him. ("Deal with," of course, does not mean *purposeful* action, nor is it restricted to *conscious* activity). A justified belief is, roughly speaking, one that results from cognitive operations that are, generally speaking, good or successful. But "*cognitive*" operations are most plausibly construed as operations of the cognitive faculties, i.e., "information-processing" equipment *internal* to the organism.

With these points in mind, we may now advance the following base-clause principle for justified belief.

(5)   If *S*'s believing *p* at *t* results from a reliable cognitive belief-forming process (or set of processes), then *S*'s belief in *p* at *t* is justified.

Since "reliable belief-forming process" has been defined in terms of such notions as belief, truth, statistical frequency, and the like, it is not an epistemic term. Hence, (5) is an admissible base-clause.

It might seem as if (5) promises to be not only a successful base clause, but the only principle needed whatever, apart from a closure clause. In other words, it might seem as if it is a necessary as well as a sufficient condition of justifiedness that a belief be produced by reliable cognitive belief-forming processes. But this is not quite correct, given our provisional definition of "reliability."

Our provisional definition implies that a reasoning process is reliable only if it generally produces beliefs that are true, and similarly, that a memory process is reliable only if it generally yields beliefs that are true. But these requirements are too strong. A reasoning procedure cannot be expected to produce true belief if it is applied to false premises. And memory cannot be expected to yield a true belief if the original belief it attempts to retain is false. What we need for reasoning and memory, then, is a notion of "*conditional reliability*." A process is conditionally reliable when a sufficient proportion of its output-beliefs are true *given that its input-beliefs are true.*

With this point in mind, let us distinguish *belief-dependent* and *belief-independent* cognitive processes. The former are processes *some* of whose inputs are belief-states.[9] The latter are processes *none* of whose inputs are belief-states. We may then replace principle (5) with the following two principles, the first a base-clause principle and the second a recursive-clause principle.

(6_A)   If *S*'s belief in *p* at *t* results ("immediately") from a belief-independent process that is (unconditionally) reliable, then *S*'s belief in *p* at *t* is justified.

(6_B)   If *S*'s belief in *p* at *t* results ("immediately") from a belief-dependent process that is (at least) conditionally reliable, and if the beliefs (if any) on which this process operates in producing *S*'s belief in *p* at *t* are themselves justified, then *S*'s belief in *p* at *t* is justified.[10]

If we add to (6_A) and (6_B) the standard closure clause, we have a complete theory of justified belief. The theory says, in effect, that a belief is justified if and only if it is "*well-formed*," i.e., it has an ancestry of reliable and/or conditionally reliable cognitive operations. (Since a dated belief may be over-determined, it may have a number of distinct ancestral trees. These need not all be full of reliable or conditionally reliable processes. But at least one ancestral tree must have reliable or conditionally reliable processes throughout.)

The theory of justified belief proposed here, then, is an *Historical* or *Genetic* theory. It contrasts with the dominant approach to justified belief, an approach that generates what we may call (borrowing a phrase from Robert Nozick) "*Current Time-Slice*" theories. A Current Time-Slice theory makes the justificational status of a belief wholly a function of what is true of the cognizer *at the time* of belief. An Historical theory makes the justificational status of a belief depend on its prior history. Since my Historical theory emphasizes the reliability of the belief-generating processes, it may be called "*Historical Reliabilism.*"

The most obvious examples of Current Time-Slice theories are "Cartesian" Foundationalist theories, which trace all justificational status (at least of contingent propositions) to current mental states. The usual varieties of Coherence theories, however, are equally Current Time-Slice views, since they too make the justificational status of a belief wholly a function of *current* states of affairs. For Coherence theories, however, these current states include all other beliefs of the cognizer, which would not be considered relevant by Cartesian Foundationalism. Have there been other Historical theories of justified belief? Among contemporary writers, Quine and Popper have Historical epistemologies, though the notion of "justification" is not their avowed *explicandum*. Among historical writers, it might seem that Locke and Hume had Genetic theories of sorts. But I think that their Genetic theories were only theories of ideas, not of knowledge or justification. Plato's theory of recollection, however, is a good example of a Genetic theory of knowing.[11] And it might be argued that Hegel and Dewey had Genetic epistemologies (if Hegel can be said to have had a clear epistemology at all).

The theory articulated by (6_A) and (6_B) might be viewed as a kind of "Foundationalism" because of its recursive structure. I have no objection to this label, as long as one keeps in mind how dif-

ferent this "diachronic" form of Foundationalism is from Cartesian, or other "synchronic" varieties of, Foundationalism.

Current Time-Slice theories characteristically assume that the justificational status of a belief is something which the cognizer is able to know or determine at the time of belief. This is made explicit, for example, by Chisholm.[12] The Historical theory I endorse makes no such assumption. There are many facts about a cognizer to which he lacks "privileged access," and I regard the justificational status of his beliefs as one of those things. This is not to say that a cognizer is necessarily ignorant, at any given moment, of the justificational status of his current beliefs. It is only to deny that he necessarily has, or can get, knowledge or true belief about this status. Just as a person can know without knowing that he knows, so he can have justified belief without knowing that it is justified (or believing justifiably that it is justified).

A characteristic case in which a belief is justified though the cognizer doesn't know that it's justified is where the original evidence for the belief has long since been forgotten. If the original evidence was compelling, the cognizer's original belief may have been justified, and this justificational status may have been preserved through memory. But since the cognizer no longer remembers how or why he came to believe, he may not know that the belief is justified. If asked now to justify his belief, he may be at a loss. Still, the belief *is* justified, though the cognizer can't demonstrate or establish this.

The Historical theory of justified belief I advocate is connected in spirit with the causal theory of knowing I have presented elsewhere.[13] I had this in mind when I remarked near the outset of the essay that my theory of justified belief makes justifiedness come out closely related to knowledge. Justified beliefs, like pieces of knowledge, have appropriate histories; but they may fail to be knowledge either because they are false or because they founder on some other requirement for knowing of the kind discussed in the post-Gettier knowledge-trade.

There is a variant of the Historical conception of justified belief that is worth mentioning in this context. It may be introduced as follows. Suppose S has a set B of beliefs at time t_0, and some of these beliefs are *un*justified. Between t_0 and t_1 he reasons from the entire set B to the conclusion p, which he then accepts at t_1. The reasoning procedure he uses is a very sound one, i.e., one that is conditionally reliable. There is a sense or respect in which we are tempted to say that S's belief in p at t_1 is "justified." At any rate, it is tempting to say that the *person* is justified in believing p at t. Relative to his antecedent cognitive state, he did as well as could be expected: the *transition* from his cognitive state at t_0 to his cognitive state at t_1 was entirely sound. Although we may acknowledge this brand of justifiedness—it might be called "*Terminal-Phase Reliabilism*"—it is not a kind of justifiedness so closely related to knowing. For a person to know proposition p, it is not enough that the *final phase* of the process that leads to his belief in p be sound. It is also necessary that some entire history of the process be sound (i.e., reliable or conditionally reliable).

Let us return now to the Historical theory. In the next section, I shall adduce reasons for strengthening it a bit. Before looking at these reasons, however, I wish to review two quite different objections to the theory.

First, a critic might argue that *some* justified beliefs do not derive their justificational status from their causal ancestry. In particular, it might be argued that beliefs about one's current phenomenal states and intuitive beliefs about elementary logical or conceptual relationships do not derive their justificational status in this way. I am not persuaded by either of these examples. Introspection, I believe, should be regarded as a form of retrospection. Thus, a justified belief that I am "now" in pain gets its justificational status from a relevant, though brief, causal history.[14] The apprehension of logical or conceptual relationships is also a cognitive process that occupies time. The psychological process of "seeing" or "intuiting" a simple logical truth is very fast, and we cannot introspectively dissect it into constituent parts. Nonetheless, there are mental operations going on, just as there are mental operations that occur in *idiots savants,* who are unable to report the computational processes they in fact employ.

A second objection to Historical Reliabilism focuses on the reliability element rather than the causal or historical element. Since the theory is intended to cover all possible cases, it seems to imply that for any cognitive process C, if C is reliable in possible world W, then any belief in W that results from C is justified. But doesn't this permit

easy counterexamples? Surely we can imagine a possible world in which wishful thinking is reliable. We can imagine a possible world where a benevolent demon so arranges things that beliefs formed by wishful thinking usually come true. This would make wishful thinking a reliable process in that possible world, but surely we don't want to regard beliefs that result from wishful thinking as justified.

There are several possible ways to respond to this case, and I am unsure which response is best, partly because my own intuitions (and those of other people I have consulted) are not entirely clear. One possibility is to say that in the possible world imagined, beliefs that result from wishful thinking *are* justified. In other words, we reject the claim that wishful thinking could never, intuitively, confer justifiedness.[15]

However, for those who feel that wishful thinking couldn't confer justifiedness even in the world imagined, there are two ways out. First, it may be suggested that the proper criterion of justifiedness is the propensity of a process to generate beliefs that are true *in a non-manipulated environment,* i.e., an environment in which there is no purposeful arrangement of the world either to accord or conflict with the beliefs that are formed. In other words, the suitability of a belief-forming process is only a function of its success in "*natural*" situations, not situations of the sort involving benevolent or malevolent demons or any other such manipulative creatures. If we reformulate the theory to include this qualification, the counterexample in question will be averted.

Alternatively, we may reformulate our theory, or reinterpret it, as follows. Instead of construing the theory as saying that a belief in possible world W is justified if and only if it results from a cognitive process that is reliable in W, we may construe it as saying that a belief in possible world W is justified if and only if it results from a cognitive process that is reliable in *our world*. In short, our conception of justifiedness is derived as follows. We note certain cognitive processes in the actual world, and form beliefs about which of these are reliable. The ones we believe to be reliable are then regarded as justification-conferring processes. In reflecting on hypothetical beliefs, we deem them justified if and only if they result from processes already picked out as justification-conferring, or processes very similar to those. Since wishful thinking is not among these processes, a belief formed in a possible world *W* by wishful thinking would not be deemed justified, even if wishful thinking is reliable *in W*. I am not sure that this is a correct reconstruction of our intuitive conceptual scheme, but it would accommodate the benevolent demon case, at least if the proper thing to say in that case is that the wishful-thinking-caused beliefs are unjustified.

Even if we adopt this strategy, however, a problem still remains. Suppose that wishful thinking turns out to be reliable *in the actual world!*[16] This might be because, unbeknownst to us at present, there is a benevolent demon who, lazy until now, will shortly start arranging things so that our wishes come true. The long-run performance of wishful thinking will be very good, and hence even the new construal of the theory will imply that beliefs resulting from wishful thinking (in *our* world) are justified. Yet this surely contravenes our intuitive judgment on the matter.

Perhaps the moral of the case is that the standard format of a "conceptual analysis" has its shortcomings. Let me depart from that format and try to give a better rendering of our aim and the theory that tries to achieve that aim. What we really want is an *explanation* of why we count, or would count, certain beliefs as justified and others as unjustified. Such an explanation must refer to our *beliefs* about reliability, not to the actual *facts*. The reason we *count* beliefs as justified is that they are formed by what we *believe* to be reliable belief-forming processes. Our beliefs about which belief-forming processes are reliable may be erroneous, but that does not affect the adequacy of the explanation. Since we *believe* that wishful thinking is an unreliable belief-forming process, we regard beliefs formed by wishful thinking as unjustified. What matters, then, is what we *believe* about wishful thinking, not what is *true* (in the long run) about wishful thinking. I am not sure how to express this point in the standard format of conceptual analysis, but it identifies an important point in understanding our theory.

III

Let us return, however, to the standard format of conceptual analysis, and let us consider a new objection that will require some revisions in the theory advanced until now. According to our theory, a belief is justified in case it is caused by a process that is in fact reliable, or by one we generally believe to be reliable. But suppose that although one of *S*'s beliefs satisfies this condition, *S* has no reason to believe that it does. Worse yet, suppose *S* has reason to believe that his belief is caused by an *un*reliable process (although *in fact* its causal ancestry is fully reliable). Wouldn't we deny in such circumstances that *S*'s belief is justified? This seems to show that our analysis, as presently formulated, is mistaken.

Suppose that Jones is told on fully reliable authority that a certain class of his memory beliefs are almost all mistaken. His parents fabricate a wholly false story that Jones suffered from amnesia when he was seven but later developed *pseudo*-memories of that period. Though Jones listens to what his parents say and has excellent reason to trust them, he persists in believing the ostensible memories from his seven-year-old past. Are these memory beliefs justified? Intuitively, they are not justified. But since these beliefs result from genuine memory and original perceptions, which are adequately reliable processes, our theory says that these beliefs are justified.

Can the theory be revised to meet this difficulty? One natural suggestion is that the actual reliability of a belief's ancestry is not enough for justifiedness; in addition, the cognizer must be *justified in believing* that the ancestry of his belief is reliable. Thus one might think of replacing (6_A), for example, with (7). (For simplicity, I neglect some of the details of the earlier analysis.)

(7)   If *S*'s belief in *p* at *t* is caused by a reliable cognitive process, and *S* justifiably believes at *t* that his *p*-belief is so caused, then *S*'s belief in *p* at *t* is justified.

It is evident, however, that (7) will not do as a base clause, for it contains the epistemic term "justifiably" in its antecedent.

A slightly weaker revision, without this problematic feature, might next be suggested, viz.,

(8)   If *S*'s belief in *p* at *t* is caused by a reliable cognitive process, and *S* believes at *t* that his *p*-belief is so caused, then *S*'s belief in *p* at *t* is justified.

But this won't do the job. Suppose that Jones believes that his memory beliefs are reliably caused despite all the (trustworthy) contrary testimony of his parents. Principle (8) would be satisfied, yet we wouldn't say that these beliefs are justified.

Next, we might try (9), which is stronger than (8) and, unlike (7), formally admissible as a base clause.

> (9) If S's belief in p at t is caused by a reliable cognitive process, and S believes at t that his p-belief is so caused, and this meta-belief is caused by a reliable cognitive process, then S's belief in p at t is justified.

A first objection to (9) is that it wrongly precludes unreflective creatures—creatures like animals or young children, who have no beliefs about the genesis of their beliefs—from having justified beliefs. If one shares my view that justified belief is, at least roughly, *well-formed* belief, surely animals and young children can have justified beliefs.

A second problem with (9) concerns its underlying rationale. Since (9) is proposed as a substitute for (6_A), it is implied that the reliability of a belief's own cognitive ancestry does not make it justified. But, the suggestion seems to be, the reliability of a *meta-belief*'s ancestry confers justifiedness on the first-order belief. Why should that be so? Perhaps one is attracted by the idea of a "trickle-down" effect: if an $n + 1$-level belief is justified, its justification trickles down to an n-level belief. But even if the trickle-down theory is correct, it doesn't help here. There is no assurance from the satisfaction of (9)'s antecedent that the meta-belief itself is *justified*.

To obtain a better revision of our theory, let us re-examine the Jones case. Jones has strong evidence against certain propositions concerning his past. He doesn't *use* this evidence, but if he *were* to use it properly, he would stop believing these propositions. Now the proper use of evidence would be an instance of a (conditionally) reliable process. So what we can say about Jones is that he *fails* to use a certain (conditionally) reliable process that he could and should have used. Admittedly, had he used this process, he would have "worsened" his doxastic states: he would have replaced some true beliefs with suspension of judgment. Still, he couldn't have known this in the case in question. So he failed to do something which, epistemically, he should have done. This

diagnosis suggests a fundamental change in our theory. The justificational status of a belief is not only a function of the cognitive process *actually* employed in producing it, it is also a function of processes that could and should be employed.

With these points in mind, we may tentatively propose the following revision of our theory, where we again focus on a base-clause principle but omit certain details in the interest of clarity.

> (10) If S's belief in p at t results from a reliable cognitive process, and there is no reliable or conditionally reliable process available to S which, had it been used by S in addition to the process actually used, would have resulted in S's not believing p at t, then S's belief in p at t is justified.

There are several problems with this proposal. First, there is a technical problem. One cannot use an additional belief-forming (or doxastic-state-forming) process *as well as* the original process if the additional one would result in a different doxastic state. One wouldn't be using the original process at all. So we need a slightly different formulation of the relevant counterfactual. Since the basic idea is reasonably clear, however, I won't try to improve on the formulation here. A second problem concerns the notion of "*available*" belief-forming (or doxastic-state-forming) processes. What is it for a process to be "available" to a cognizer? Were scientific procedures "available" to people who lived in pre-scientific ages? Further-more, it seems implausible to say that all "available" processes ought to be used, at least if we include such processes as gathering *new* evidence. Surely a belief can sometimes be justified even if additional evidence-gathering would yield a different doxastic attitude. What I think we should have in mind here are such additional processes as calling previously acquired evidence to mind, assessing the implications of that evidence, etc. This is admittedly somewhat vague, but here again our ordinary notion of justifiedness is vague, so it is appropriate for our analysans to display the same sort of vagueness.

This completes the sketch of my account of justified belief. Before concluding, however, it is essential to point out that there is an important use of "justified" which is not captured by this account but can be captured by a closely related one.

There is a use of "justified" in which it is not implied or presupposed that there is a *belief* that is justified. For example, if *S* is trying to decide whether to believe *p* and asks our advice, we may tell him that he is "justified" in believing it. We do not thereby imply that he *has* a justified *belief,* since we know he is still suspending judgment. What we mean, roughly, is that he *would* or *could* be justified if he were to believe *p*. The justificational status we ascribe here cannot be a function of the causes of *S*'s believing *p*, for there is no belief by *S* in *p*. Thus, the account of justifiedness we have given thus far cannot explicate *this* use of "justified." (It doesn't follow that this use of "justified" has no connection with causal ancestries. Its proper use may depend on the causal ancestry of the cognizer's cognitive state, though not on the causal ancestry of his believing *p*.)

Let us distinguish two uses of "justified": an *ex post* use and an *ex ante* use. The *ex post* use occurs when there exists a belief, and we say of *that belief* that it is (or isn't) justified. The *ex ante* use occurs when no such belief exists, or when we wish to ignore the question of whether such a belief exists. Here we say of the *person,* independent of his doxastic state vis-à-vis *p*, that *p* is (or isn't) suitable for him to believe.[17]

Since we have given an account of *ex post* justifiedness, it will suffice if we can analyze *ex ante* justifiedness in terms of it. Such an analysis, I believe, is ready at hand. *S* is *ex ante* justified in believing *p* at *t* just in case his total cognitive state at *t* is such that from that state he could come to believe *p* in such a way that this belief would be *ex post* justified. More precisely, he is *ex ante* justified in believing *p* at *t* just in case a reliable belief-forming operation is available to him such that the application of that operation to his total cognitive state at *t* would result, more or less immediately, in his believing *p* and this belief would be *ex post* justified. Stated formally, we have the following:

(11)   Person *S* is *ex ante* justified in believing *p* at *t* if and only if there is a reliable belief-forming operation available to *S* which is such that if *S* applied that operation to this total cognitive state at *t*, *S* would believe *p* at *t*-plus-delta (for a suitably small delta) and that belief would be *ex post* justified.

For the analysans of (11) to be satisfied, the total cognitive state at *t* must have a suitable causal ancestry. Hence, (11) is implicitly an Historical account of *ex ante* justifiedness.

As indicated, the bulk of this essay was addressed to *ex post* justifiedness. This is the appropriate analysandum if one is interested in the connection between justifiedness and knowledge, since what is crucial to whether a person *knows* a proposition is whether he has an actual *belief* in the proposition that is justified. However, since many epistemologists are interested in *ex ante* justifiedness, it is proper for a general theory of justification to try to provide an account of that concept as well. Our theory does this quite naturally, for the account of *ex ante* justifiedness falls out directly from our account of *ex post* justifiedness.[18]

Notes

[1] "A Causal Theory of Knowing"; "Innate Knowledge," in S. P. Stich, ed., *Innate Ideas* (Berkeley: University of California Press, 1975); and "Discrimination and Perceptual Knowledge."

[2] Notice that the choice of a recursive format does not prejudice the case for or against any particular theory. A recursive format is perfectly general. Specifically, an explicit set of necessary and sufficient conditions is just a special case of a recursive format, i.e., one in which there is no recursive clause.

[3] Many of the attempts I shall consider are suggested by material in William P. Alston, "Varieties of Privileged Access."

[4] Such a definition (though without the modal term) is given, for example, by W. V. Quine and J. S. Ullian in *The Web of Belief,* p. 21. Statements are said to be self-evident just in case "to understand them is to believe them."

[5] Page 22.

[6] I assume, of course, that "nomologically necessary" is *de re* with respect to "*S*" and "*t*" in this construction. I shall not focus on problems that may arise in this regard, since my primary concerns are with different issues.

[7] This assumption violates the thesis that Davidson calls "The Anomalism of the Mental." Cf. "Mental Events" in L. Foster and J. W. Swanson, eds., *Experience and Theory* (Amherst: University of Massachusetts Press, 1970). But it is unclear that this thesis is a necessary truth. Thus, it seems fair to assume its falsity in order to produce a counterexample. The example neither entails nor precludes the mental–physical identity theory.

[8] Keith Lehrer's example of the gypsy lawyer is intended to show the inappropriateness of a causal requirement. (See *Knowledge,* pp. 124–25.) But I find this example unconvincing. To the extent that I clearly imagine that the

lawyer fixes his belief solely as a result of the cards, it seems intuitively wrong to say that he *knows*—or has a *justified belief*—that his client is innocent.

[9]This definition is not exactly what we need for the purposes at hand. As Ernest Sosa points out, introspection will turn out to be a belief-dependent process, since sometimes the input into the process will be a belief (when the introspected content is a belief). Intuitively, however, introspection is not the sort of process which may be merely conditionally reliable. I do not know how to refine the definition so as to avoid this difficulty, but it is a small and isolated point.

[10]It may be objected that principles (6_A) and (6_B) are jointly open to analogues of the lottery paradox. A series of processes composed of reliable but less-than-perfectly-reliable processes may be extremely unreliable. Yet applications of (6_A) and (6_B) would confer justifiedness on a belief that is caused by such a series. In reply to this objection, we might simply indicate that the theory is intended to capture our ordinary notion of justifiedness, and this ordinary notion has been formed without recognition of this kind of problem. The theory is not wrong *as* a theory of the ordinary (naive) conception of justifiedness. On the other hand, if we want a theory to do more than capture the ordinary conception of justifiedness, it might be possible to strengthen the principles to avoid lottery-paradox analogues.

[11]I am indebted to Mark Pastin for this point.

[12]Cf. *Theory of Knowledge*, 2nd ed., pp. 17, 114–16.

[13]Cf. "A Causal Theory of Knowing." The reliability aspect of my theory also has its precursors in earlier papers of mine on knowing: "Innate Knowledge" and "Discrimination and Perceptual Knowledge."

[14]The view that introspection is retrospection was taken by Ryle, and before him (as Charles Hartshorne points out to me) by Hobbes, Whitehead, and possibly Husserl.

[15]Of course, if people in world *W* learn *inductively* that wishful thinking is reliable, and regularly base their beliefs on this inductive inference, it is quite unproblematic and straightforward that their beliefs are justified. The only interesting case is where their beliefs are formed *purely* by wishful thinking, without using inductive inference. The suggestion contemplated in this paragraph of the text is that, in the world imagined, even pure wishful thinking would confer justifiedness.

[16]I am indebted here to Mark Kaplan.

[17]The distinction between *ex post* and *ex ante* justifiedness is similar to Roderick Firth's distinction between *doxastic* and *propositional* warrant. See his "Are Epistemic Concepts Reducible to Ethical Concepts?" in Alvin I. Goldman and Jaegwon Kim, eds., *Values and Morals, Essays in Honor of William Frankena, Charles Stevenson, and Richard Brandt* (Dordrecht: D. Reidel, 1978).

[18]Research on this essay was begun while the author was a fellow of the John Simon Guggenheim Memorial Foundation and of the Center for Advanced Study in the Behavioral Sciences. I am grateful for their support. I have received helpful comments and criticism from Holly S. Goldman, Mark Kaplan, Fred Schmitt, Stephen P. Stich, and many others at several universities where earlier drafts of the paper were read.

VI.2 A Critique of Externalism

KEITH LEHRER

Keith Lehrer is professor of philosophy at the University of Arizona. We have already encountered his defense of skepticism (Reading II.4) and his analysis of knowledge (Reading IV.4). In this selection from his book *Theory of Knowledge,* Lehrer argues against all forms of externalism, both reliabilism, which transforms properly caused beliefs into justification (as is the case with Goldman, Reading VI.1), and the more radical naturalism that repudiates justification as necessary for knowledge (see Quine, Reading VI.3). But it is the justificatory type of externalism that Lehrer concentrates on. After identifying the strength of externalism as defeating the threat of skepticism, Lehrer sets forth two fundamental objections to externalism: (1) Possession of correct information is inadequate for knowledge, and (2) we may be justified in a belief even when it has not been caused (or sustained) by a reliable process. Note the idea of trustworthiness in Lehrer's account.

Our analysis of complete and undefeated justification in terms of coherence and truth within an acceptance system brings us into conflict with an important competing theory of knowledge called *externalism*. The fundamental doctrine of externalism is that what must be added to true belief to obtain knowledge is the appropriate connection between belief and truth. An earlier account presented by Goldman affirmed that the appropriate connection is causal. This is a very plausible sort of account of perceptual knowledge. The fact that I see something, the hand I hold before me, for example, causes me to believe that I see a hand. The fact that my seeing a hand causes me to believe I see a hand results, it is claimed, in my knowing that I see a hand. According to such an analysis, it is the history of my belief, a matter of external causation, rather than coherence with some internal system, that yields knowledge. The central tenet of externalism is that some relationship to the external world accounting for the truth of our belief suffices to convert true belief to knowledge without our having any idea of that relationship. It is not our conception of how we are related to a fact that yields knowledge but simply our being so related to it.

The early analysis, though providing a plausible account of perceptual knowledge, was a less plausible account of our knowledge of generalities, that men do not become pregnant, for example, or that neutrinos have a zero rest mass, or that there is no largest prime number. For here the nature of the required causal relationship between what is believed and the belief of it evades explication. That objection is, however, one of detail. Later analyses of others, and of Goldman himself, aim at preserving the thesis of externalism that some relationship of the belief to what makes it true yields knowledge, whether we have any idea of that rela-

tionship or not. Armstrong and Dretske have argued that the relationship should be construed as nomological, one resulting from some law of nature connecting the belief with what makes it true. This account is closely connected with the proposal of Nozick that belief track truth in a sense explicated, in part, by the counterfactual claim that the person would not have believed what she did if it were not for the truth of the belief. Goldman now claims that justified belief must be the result of a belief-forming process that reliably yields truth. Beliefs resulting from such a process are justified, he contends, while other externalists deny that justification is necessary for knowledge. They all agree, however, that a belief resulting from a certain kind of process or relationship connecting belief with truth can yield knowledge without the sustenance or support of any other beliefs or system of beliefs.

Naturalism

Assuming that the required relationship is something like causation, externalist theories are *naturalistic*. What is a naturalistic theory? It is one in which all the terms used in the analysis are ones that describe phenomena of nature, such as causation, for example, or that can be reduced to such terms. Hume's theory of belief was naturalistic in this sense. He restricted his account of human knowledge to relations of causation, contiguity, and resemblance. It was, however, Quine who introduced the term *epistemology naturalized* and suggested that inquiry into the nature of human knowledge be restricted to accounts of how belief arises and is altered. Other philosophers have adopted the term to refer simply to all those accounts of knowledge couched in naturalistic vocabulary or reducible to such a vocabulary. The early account of Goldman considered above according to which S knows that p if and only if S's believing that p is caused in the appropriate way by the fact that p is, in this extended sense, an example of epistemology naturalized. Other early naturalistic accounts offered by Armstrong and Dretske rested on the assumption that the conversion relation was based on nomological rather than causal relations, that is, relations articulated in laws of nature. Dretske's basic idea was that the reasons we have for believing what we do should be nomologically connected with the truth of what is believed, that is, that it should be a law of nature that a person having such reasons for believing what she does will have a true belief. Assuming a naturalistic account of having a reason which Dretske supplies, such an account is also naturalistic.

One interesting aspect of some externalistic theories which naturalize epistemology is the way in which they attempt to avoid the problems of foundationalism. According to Dretske or Nozick, for example, there is no need either to justify beliefs or posit self-justified beliefs blindly because, contrary to the traditional analysis, the justification of beliefs is not required to convert true beliefs into knowledge. Beliefs or true beliefs having the appropriate sort of naturalistic external relationships to the facts are, as a result of such relationship, converted into knowledge without being justified. It is the way true beliefs are connected to the world that makes them knowledge rather than the way in which we might attempt to justify them. Notice how plausible this seems for perceptual beliefs. It is the way my belief that I see a bird is related to the facts, for example, when my seeing a bird causes the belief that I do, which accounts for my knowing that I see a bird, rather than some justification I have for that belief. What matters for knowledge is how the belief arises, not how I might reason on behalf of it. The traditional analysis says that knowledge is true belief coupled with the right sort of justification. One sort of externalist analysis says that knowledge is true belief coupled with the right sort of naturalistic relation. It is plausible to assume that the naturalistic relationship will be one concerning how the belief arises, in short, the natural history of the belief. Looked at in this way, the justification requirement can be eliminated altogether in favor of the right sort of historical account.

The Advantages of Externalism

Before turning to details and objections, it is useful to notice the advantages of externalism. First of all, according to some externalists, the need for justification and a theory of justification is eliminated as a component of an analysis of knowledge. On such an account, it is admitted that inference may play some role in the natural history of a true belief, but it is also possible to hold that some beliefs are noninferential. They are beliefs arising from experience without the intervention of inference. This may be offered as an account of what the foundationalist was searching for, but in the wrong place. True beliefs that arise in the appropriate way from experience are knowledge because of the way they arise. There is no need to affirm that such beliefs are self-justified to maintain that they convert to knowledge. We might think of such beliefs as naturalized basic beliefs. Such basic beliefs might, of course, serve as the premises for inferring other beliefs and such inference might convert those beliefs to knowledge as well. It is the history of the belief rather than some sort of justification of the belief that converts it to knowledge.

A Reply to Skepticism

It is helpful, as well, to notice how neatly this sort of theory deals with traditional and modern forms of skepticism. The skeptic, confronted with a commonsense perceptual claim, that I see a tree, for example, has traditionally raised some skeptical doubt, the Cartesian one, for example, that we might be deceived by an evil demon who supplies us with deceptive sensations which lead us to believe we see external objects when we do not see them at all. Or consider the case of a small object, a "braino," implanted in our brain which, when operated by a computer, provides us with sensory states which are all produced by the computer influencing the brain rather than by the external objects we believe to exist. In neither case, affirms the skeptic, do I know I see a tree. The reply is simple. If my beliefs are, indeed, produced by the demon or by the braino, then they are false and I am ignorant. On the other hand, if the beliefs are true and produced in the appropriate way, then I do know.

To this the skeptic is wont to reply that I only know that I see a tree if I know that it is not the demon or the braino that produces my belief and, furthermore, to insist that I do not know this. Why do I not know that there is no demon or braino? I do not know so because my experience would be exactly the same if there were; that is what the demon and braino do, produce exactly the same experiences as I would have if I were to see a tree. I have no evidence whatever against these skeptical hypotheses and, therefore, the skeptic concludes, I do not know them to be false. The reply of the externalist is simple. I do not need to *know* that the skeptical hypotheses are false to know that I see a tree, though, of course, the skeptical hypotheses must *be* false. Otherwise, my belief that I see a tree will be false. All that is necessary is that my belief be true and that it arise in the appropriate way, that it have a suitable history, for knowledge to arise. If my belief is true and has arisen in the appropriate way, then I know that I see a tree, even if I do not know that the conflicting skeptical hypotheses are false. I might never have considered such skeptical machinations. Confronted with them, I might be astounded by them and find them so bizarre as not to be worthy of consideration.

The skeptic might retort that I cannot so easily escape the clutches of skepticism. For example, she might suggest that when I claim to know that I am seeing a car, a Mazda RX7, for example, I must have the information required to tell a Mazda RX7 from cars of another sort, and lacking such information, I do not know that I see a Mazda RX7. Hence, I must know that the car is not a Toyota MR2 or a Porsche 944, which bear some resemblance to a Mazda RX7. Going on, the skeptic might argue that to know that I see a Mazda RX7, I must have the information required to tell seeing a Mazda RX7 from experiences of another sort, those supplied by the demon or braino, and lacking such information, I do not know that I am seeing a Mazda RX7, or even that I am seeing a car. So, the skeptic concludes, just as I must know that the car I am seeing is not of another manufacture, so I must know that my experiences are not of skeptical manufacture. That, she insists, is precisely what I do not know. Skepticism wins.

Relevant Alternatives: A Reply to the Skeptic

The reply of the externalist is a combination of counterassertion and explanation. The counterassertion is that my true belief that I see a tree

arising in the way it does is knowledge, even if I do not know that it has arisen in that way rather than in the way the skeptic suggests. If the skeptical hypothesis is true and the belief has not arisen in the way I suppose, then I lack knowledge, but if it has arisen in the way I suppose, then I have knowledge, even if I do not know competing hypotheses about the origin of the belief to be false. It does not matter whether I know that the belief originated in the appropriate manner. All that matters is that it have originated in that way. Then I know. The explanation about the Mazda, for example, is that there will be some cases, but not all, in which some information excluding other alternatives, will be necessary for knowledge. The alternative that I am seeing a Porsche 944 and not a Mazda RX7 is a relevant alternative. The alternative that I am being deceived by an evil demon or a braino is not. What is the difference? My information about what a Mazda RX7 looks like must be sufficient to enable me to distinguish it from other cars, and that information plays a role in the formation of my belief that I am seeing a Mazda RX7. In other cases, particularly those suggested by the skeptic in which there is no such distinguishing information, no such information enters into the appropriate origination of the belief. Where the distinguishing information is a necessary component in the suitable generation of the belief, the alternatives to be distinguished from the truth are relevant, but where it is not a necessary component, the alternatives are not relevant ones. To be sure, a skeptic might find the distinction between relevant and irrelevant alternatives capricious and question-begging as a counterargument. Nevertheless, the initial reply to the skeptic to the effect that true belief originating in the appropriate manner is knowledge, even if we do not know the skeptical hypotheses to be false, is a straightforward consequence of epistemology naturalized whether or not it satisfies the demands of the skeptic.

Knowing That One Knows: Rejection of Deductive Closure

There remains, of course, the question whether I know that I know that I see a tree when I do not know that the skeptical hypotheses are false. If I know that I see a tree, then it follows that the skeptical hypotheses concerning the demon and braino are false. It follows, first of all, from the fact that if I know that I see a tree, then I do see a tree, and, therefore, my experiences are not a result of demonic bewitchment or computer wizardry. It follows, further, from my knowing that I see a tree that my belief originates in the appropriate natural way and not from the demon or braino. In short, it follows both from the fact known and from the knowing of the fact that the skeptical hypotheses are false.

Some naturalists in epistemology would deny that I know that the skeptical hypotheses are false or that I need to know this in order to know that I know that I see a tree. They do this by denying what they call a *deductive closure* condition, namely, the condition that if I know that p and that q is a logical consequence of knowing that p, then I, therefore, know that q. Thus, I might know that p, and know that q is a consequence of knowing that p, even though I do not know that q.

The denial of closure is directly relevant to replying to the skeptic. I might know that I see a tree, know that the falsity of the demon hypothesis is a consequence of my seeing a tree, even though I do not know that the demon hypothesis is false. If, however, I might know that I see a tree without knowing that the demon hypothesis is false, then might I also know that I know that I see a tree without knowing that the demon hypothesis is false? On the naturalist account, it appears that we may answer in the affirmative. If I can know something without knowing what I know to be the consequences of it, then I can know that I know something without knowing what I know to be the consequences of my knowing it.

The falsity of the demon hypothesis is something I know to be a consequence of my knowing that I see a tree, but I may, nevertheless, know that I see a tree without knowing what I know to be a consequence of my knowing it, to wit, the falsity of the demonic hypothesis. Once we deny the closure condition, we may agree with the skeptic that the falsity of the skeptical hypotheses is a necessary condition of what we know, while cheerfully admitting that we do not know that the skeptical hypotheses are false. Such are the joys of naturalism and rejection of the closure condition. Given that the appropriate origination of a true belief converts it to knowledge, it becomes obvious that the closure condition must be rejected. My true belief that I see a tree may originate in the appropriate way without a belief in the logical consequences of that true belief originating in the appropriate way. Indeed, I might fail to believe in the truth of the logical consequences. It may strike one as odd that a person should know that she sees a tree, know that the falsity of the skeptical hypothesis is a consequence, and yet fail to know the skeptical hypothesis to be false. The oddity is in the eye of the epistemologist, however, for there is no logical contradiction in this position.

The Naturalistic Relation

The advantages of naturalism are robust, but the theory must be true, not merely advantageous, to solve the problems with which we began. To ascertain whether the theory is true, we must have some account of the naturalistic relationship that is supposed to convert true belief into knowledge. Before proceeding to consideration of such accounts, however, let us consider the rejection of the justification condition. At least one defender of epistemology naturalized, Goldman in his later work, is inclined to argue that the notion of justification is a naturalistic notion. One might be a naturalist about justification and maintain that justification is reducible to some naturalistic relationship. In fact, a philosopher eager to connect the naturalistic analysis with the traditional one might argue that a person has the requisite sort of justification for knowledge if and only if true belief arises in the appropriate naturalistic manner. This would provide us with a naturalistic reduction of justification. Thus, the externalist theory can be construed as a naturalistic account of justification or as a repudiation of a nonnaturalistic account of justification. As we shall see later, however, there are objections to externalist accounts of justification that might lead an externalist to prefer the repudiation strategy.

What exactly is the external relationship that converts true belief into knowledge? It is typical of epistemological theories to take some sort of example as a paradigm of knowledge, to fine-tool the theory to fit that sort of example and, at least at the outset, to ignore less felicitous examples whose subsequent consideration necessitates rather substantial modification of the theory. That is the history of externalism. The paradigm example is perception. In the case of perception, it is indeed very plausible to contend that what converts perceptual belief into knowledge is the way that the belief arises in perceptual experience. My belief that I see a tree is converted into knowledge by being caused by my actually seeing a tree. Another kind of example is communication. You tell me that Holly Smith is Department Head and that causes me to believe that Holly Smith is Department Head. Do I know that Holly Smith is Department Head as a result of this causation? It might be contended, and has been, that if my informant knows that what he tells me is true, then I know because he knows and his communication caused me to believe this. Of course, his knowing remains to be explicated. The assumption is that there is a causal chain beginning with the fact that Holly Smith is Department Head and ending with my believing it which accounts for my knowing it.

Thus, following Goldman's early proposal, we might consider the following as characteristic of externalistic theories which eliminate the justification condition.

(CK)   S knows that p if and only if S believes that p and this belief is caused in the appropriate way by the fact that p.

This account leaves us with the need to explain the difference between being caused in an appropriate way and being caused in a way that is not appropriate. Typical cases of perception provide a model of the appropriate kind of causation.

Dretske has suggested that when x is something S perceives, then

(DK)   S knows that x is F if and only if S's belief that x is F is caused or causally sustained by the information that x is F received from the source x by S.

Dretske's analysis, though restricted to perceptual knowledge, highlights two needed qualifications recognized by other authors as well. The first is that the belief need not be caused but only causally sustained by the information that p. This is necessary because the originating causation of a belief might involve an error which is corrected by subsequent information one receives.

If I see two men in the distance, I might take the one on the left to be Buchanan and believe that I see Buchanan when, in fact, it is not Buchanan, as I note when I move closer, but Harnish instead. At the same time, I note that the other man, the one on the right, is Buchanan and that Buchanan and Harnish are dressed in such a way that each appears to be the other in preparation for Tolliver's Halloween party. My belief that I see Buchanan was caused by my seeing Harnish dressed as Buchanan, and I continue to hold that belief subsequently when I receive the further information which corrects my mistake about the man on the right but sustains my belief that I see Buchanan and, indeed, that I saw him earlier, though I did not recognize him. Moreover, on this sort of account the appropriate kind of causal relation is explicated in terms of receiving information from a source.

The foregoing analyses are, however, too restricted in scope to provide us with a general analysis of knowledge. There is more to knowledge than perceptual knowledge, and not all knowledge that p can be supposed to be caused by the fact that p. The most obvious example is general knowledge, my knowledge that all human beings die, for example. That fact includes the fact of death of as yet unborn humans which cannot now cause me to believe that all humans die or causally sustain that belief. Our knowledge that all neutrinos have zero rest mass is yet more difficult to account for on such a model, since no one has ever perceived a neutrino at rest. Assuming there to be mathematical knowledge, for example, that integers are infinite, the causal theory seems inappropriate. The integers appear to lie outside the temporal order and to be incapable of causing anything.

Accounts of knowledge in terms of causation or the receipt of information fail to provide an account of our knowledge of general and theoretical truths. Moreover, it is easy to see that externalism in no way requires such a restrictive conception of the external relationship. Causal or information-receiving analyses of knowledge have the virtue of explicating knowledge in a way that explains the connection between truth and belief, between reality and thought, and provides an answer to skepticism. We may, however, maintain the connection between truth and belief without committing ourselves to a restrictive causal connection. Instead, we may require that the *history* of the belief connect the belief with truth.

There are two popular accounts of how the history of a belief might connect the belief with truth. The first and perhaps best known is the later account of Goldman according to which true belief is converted to knowledge *via* justification when the belief is the result of a reliable belief-forming process. Goldman's basic idea, which he has modified and refined, is as follows:

> If *S*'s believing that *p* at *t* results from a reliable cognitive belief-forming process (or set of processes), then *S*'s belief in *p* at *t* is justified.

The refinements include an account of reliable rules, methods, and processes. The other account, offered by Nozick, requires that a belief must track truth in order to convert to knowledge in the sense that the person would believe that *p* if *p* were true and would not believe that *p* if *p* were not true.

The two theories share some advantages. Both retain the reply to the skeptic considered above. They both accomplish this without assuming that we have any guarantee that our beliefs are true, moreover. That my belief is the outcome of a reliable belief-forming process does not presuppose that I have any guarantee of the truth of the belief. Similarly, I might believe that something is true when I would not have believed it, had it not been true even though I have no guarantee that this is so. Thus, given either account of knowledge, the skeptic may be answered while allowing, what seems obvious, that we are fallible in the way in which we form our beliefs, even those converting to knowledge. The result is a fallibilistic epistemology without the postulation of self-justified beliefs.

Objections to Externalism: Information Without Knowledge

There is, however, a general objection to all externalist theories which is as simple to state as it is fundamental. It is that a person who has no idea that her beliefs are caused or causally sustained by a reliable belief-forming process might fail to know because of her ignorance of this. Alternatively, the person who has no idea that she would not have believed what she did had it not been true might fail to know because of her ignorance of that. Any purely externalist account faces the fundamental objection that a person totally ignorant of the external factors connecting her belief with truth, might be ignorant of the truth of her belief as a result. All externalist theories share a common defect, to wit, that they provide accounts of the possession of information rather than of the attainment of knowledge. The appeal of such theories is their naturalistic character. They assimilate knowledge to other natural causal relationships between objects. Our attainment of knowledge is just one natural relationship between facts among all the rest. It is a relationship of causality, or nomological correlation, or frequency correlation, or counterfactual dependence. But this very attractive feature of such theories is their downfall. The relationship in question may suffice for the recording of information, but if we are ignorant of the relationship, we lack knowledge. As in our refutation of foundationalism, what is missing from the accounts of externalists is the needed supplementation of background information. To convert the specified relationships into knowledge, we need the additional information of the existence of those relationships. Such additional information is, how-ever, precisely the sort of information required for coherence and complete justification.

The general problem with externalism can be seen most graphically by considering the analogy proposed by Armstrong. He suggested that the right model of knowledge is a thermometer. The relationship between the reading on a thermometer and the temperature of the object illustrates the theories mentioned above. Suppose that the thermometer is an accurate one and that it records a temperature of 104 degrees for some oil it is used to measure. We can say, with Armstrong, that there is a nomological connection between the temperature and the thermometer reading, with Dretske that the thermometer receives the information, with Nozick that the thermometer would not record a temperature of 104 degrees if it were not true that the oil was at 104 degrees, and with Goldman that the reading is the outcome of a reliable temperature-recording process. The problem with the analogy is that the thermometer is obviously ignorant of the temperature it records. The question is—why?

One might be inclined to suggest that the thermometer is ignorant of temperature only because it lacks the capacity of thought. If, contrary to fact, the thermometer could entertain the thought that the oil is 104 degrees, would that suffice? Would the thermometer know that the temperature is 104 degrees? What are we to say of this fanciful thought experiment? One might protest, of course, that it is too farfetched to turn the philosophical lathe. The thermometer does record information accurately, however, and, given the capacity for thought, it may be said that the thermometer not only contains the information but possesses that information as well. But our thoughtful thermometer does not *know* that the temperature of the oil is 104 degrees as a result of thinking that this is so. The reason is that it might have no idea that it is an accurate temperature-recording device. If it has no idea that this is so, then, even if it thinks the temperature of the oil is 104 degrees when it records that temperature, it has no idea that the recorded temperature is correct. To obtain the benefits of these reflections, however, it is necessary to move to the human case.

Suppose a person, whom we shall name Mr. Truetemp, undergoes brain surgery by an experimental surgeon who invents a small device which is both a very accurate thermometer and a computational device capable of generating thoughts. The device, call it a tempucomp, is implanted in Truetemp's head so that the very tip of the device, no larger than the head of a pin, sits unnoticed on his scalp and acts as a sensor to transmit information about the temperature to the computational system in his brain. This device, in turn, sends a message to his brain causing him to think of the temperature recorded by the external sensor. Assume that the tempucomp is very reliable, and so his thoughts are correct temperature thoughts. All told, this is a reliable belief-forming process. Now imagine, finally, that he has no idea that the tempucomp has been inserted in his brain, is only slightly puzzled about why he thinks so obsessively about the temperature, but never checks a thermometer to determine whether these thoughts about the temperature are correct. He accepts them unreflectively, another effect of the tempucomp. Thus, he thinks and accepts that the temperature is 104 degrees. It is. Does he know that it is? Surely not. He has no idea whether he or his thoughts about the temperature are reliable. What he accepts, that the temperature is 104 degrees, is correct, but he does not know that his thought is correct. His thought that the temperature is 104

degrees is correct information, but he does not know this. Though he records the information because of the operations of the tempucomp, he is ignorant of the facts about the tempucomp and about his temperature telling reliability. Yet, the sort of causal, nomological, statistical, or counterfactual relationships required by externalism may all be present. Does he know that the temperature is 104 degrees when the thought occurs to him while strolling in Pima Canyon? He has no idea why the thought occurred to him or that such thoughts are almost always correct. He does not, consequently, know that the temperature is 104 degrees when that thought occurs to him.

The preceding example is not presented as a decisive objection against externalism and should not be taken as such. It is possible to place some constraint on relationships or processes converting belief to knowledge to exclude production by the tempucomp. The fundamental difficulty remains, however. It is that more than the possession of correct information is required for knowledge. One must have some way of knowing that the information is correct. Consider another example. Someone informs me that Professor Haller is in my office. Suppose I have no idea whether the person telling me this is trustworthy. Even if the information I receive is correct and I believe what I am told, I do not know that Haller is in my office, because I have no idea of whether the source of my information is trustworthy. The nomological, statistical, or counterfactual relationships or processes may be trustworthy, but I lack this information.

When we considered the distinction between belief and acceptance in the third chapter, we noted the argument to the effect that a person who receives the information that p and believes that p as a result may fail to know that p. The reason is that the person may not know that the information she thus receives and believes is correct information. If a person does not know that the information, that p, which she receives is correct information, then she does not know that p. All forms of externalism fail to deal with this problem adequately. To know that the information one possesses is correct, one requires background information about that information. One requires information about whether the received information is trustworthy or not, and lacking such information, one falls short of knowledge. This is a line of argumentation we have already encountered, in earlier chapters. A necessary condition of knowledge is coherence with background information, with an acceptance system, informing us of the trustworthiness of the information we possess.

Externalism and Justification

Some forms of externalism repudiate justification as a condition of knowledge, according to Nozick and Dretske, for example. Such accounts may provide an interesting account of what it is like for belief to constitute correct information or to track truth, but they provide no account of knowledge. The reason is that no one knows that what she accepts is true when it would have been just as reasonable for her to have accepted the opposite on the basis of her information. A necessary normative condition of a person knowing that p is that it be more reasonable for her to accept that p than to accept the denial of p on the basis of her information. This condition implies the need for a justification condition of the sort we have proposed.

One may, as Goldman illustrates, combine externalism with the affirmation of a justification condition, but such an account, if it takes account of background information in an acceptable manner, will introduce a coherence factor. Goldman insists, for example, that a justified belief resulting from a reliable belief-forming process must not be undermined by other evidence the subject possesses. The condition requiring that the belief not be undermined by other evidence is a kind of negative coherence condition to the effect that the belief not be incoherent with background information. Nevertheless, the source of justification on this account is the reliability of the belief-forming process, that is, the fact that the belief has the sort of history frequently producing true beliefs. As a result of providing a justification condition, a normative constraint is supplied.

The objection raised against externalism in general still applies to such a theory, however. A person totally ignorant of the reliability of the process producing his belief would not know that what he believes is true, even if he had no information that would undermine his belief. The example of Mr. Truetemp illustrates this perfectly. He has no evidence that his thoughts about the

temperature are incorrect. Had he taken time to consider evidence, he would have discovered that his thoughts about the temperature are correct, but he did not consider any evidence concerning the matter, and that is why he does not know that his thoughts about the temperature are correct.

Take a more commonplace example. If I read a thermometer at the local gas station, and it says that the temperature is 104 degrees, I do not know simply from reading the thermometer that the temperature is 104 degrees. I may not have any evidence that it is untrustworthy, but the competitor to the effect that gas station thermometers are often inaccurate is not one I can beat or neutralize, at least not without inquiring about the thermometer. Whether or not the belief-forming process is reliable, which perhaps it is, I do not know whether the information about the temperature is trustworthy or not. Indeed, I may have no view on the matter. I may believe what I see out of habit, but this is not knowledge. This is a central problem for externalism, to wit, that ignorance of our reliability or of other external relationships leaves us ignorant of whether our information is trustworthy. Trust sharpens the epistemic blade.

The Invincibility Objection

There is another objection to historical reliabilism that leads to an important lesson. The objection raised by Cohen is that if we are deceived in such a way that we are invincibly ignorant of the deception, we are justified in what we believe, nonetheless. Cohen's example was the Cartesian demon who deceives us in all our perceptual beliefs. The details of the deception may vary, but let us suppose that the demon clouds our senses and supplies us with deceptive sensory data leading us to believe that we perceive the world though we actually perceive nothing at all. Since our perceptual beliefs are virtually all erroneous, the process that produces them is not reliable. Yet, Cohen suggests, we are certainly justified in our beliefs. We may have done the best we could to ensure that we were not deceived, attended to what we observe with the greatest circumspection, and noticed no error. Having done the best we could, indeed, the best anyone could do, we are certainly justified in believing what we do.

The intuition is reinforced by noting the difference between two people, one who examines his sensory data with the sort of care that would keep him virtually free from error in normal circumstances, and one who forms perceptual beliefs so casually that he would frequently err under the best of circumstances. The former puts together all his information and concludes that he is seeing the path of an alpha particle in a cloud chamber. The other believes this because some person, whom he knows to be scientifically ignorant, has told him that this is what he is seeing. We would wish to say that the former but not the latter was justified in believing that he sees the path of an alpha particle in a cloud chamber, even though both beliefs are produced by processes that are unreliable, given the interventions of the demon.

Externalism might be modified to meet the objection, and Goldman has suggested more than one way. The example shows that it is internal factors, not external ones, that make us justified and explain the difference between the circumspect and casual observers above. The sort of justification appealed to in the example is personal justification as explicated in the last chapter. The circumspect observer wins the justification round arising when the skeptic claims that casual observations are often in error by replying that his observation is circumspect and not casual. The casual observer loses that round to the skeptic.

The Absentminded Demon

There is, however, an important lesson to be learned from reliabilism. It is that the sort of justification required for knowledge is not entirely an internal matter, either. On the contrary, the needed form of justification depends on the appropriate match between what one accepts about how one is related to the world and what is actually the case. To see this, consider a minor amendment in the preceding example in which the demon, in a moment of cosmic absentmindedness, forgets for a moment to cloud our senses, with the result that we really perceive what we think we do. If this moment is one that occurs very briefly as we suddenly awake and is immediately followed by further slumber to conceal the demonic error, we might believe we perceive what, in this instance, we actually do perceive. I might perceive my hand

for the first time and believe I see a hand, only to lose consciousness after this formidable event. Do I know that I see a hand in that brief moment? I believe I do, but, since such beliefs are almost all false, I am almost totally untrustworthy in such matters as is everybody else, though accepting myself to be worthy of trust.

I am as much deceived about my trustworthiness in this case as I would be when confronted with a convincing liar who tells me almost all falsehoods about some party he attended except for one fact which, in a moment of absentmindedness, he accurately conveyed, namely, that he arrived before the host. If I accept all that he tells me and also that he is a trustworthy source of information about the event, I may be personally justified in accepting all that he says, but I do not know that the one truth he has conveyed is a truth. I do not know that he arrived before the host. The reason is that my assumption that my informant is trustworthy is in error, even if he has told me the truth in this one instance, and this error is sufficient to deprive me of the sort of justification I require for knowledge. This is the truth about justification contained in reliabilism.

Complete Justification and Reliabilism

The account that we have offered of complete justification in the last chapter is sufficient to deal with the sort of problem we have just considered. To be personally justified in accepting what another says, one must accept that the person is trustworthy, for, otherwise, the skeptic can win the justification game by claiming that informants are sometimes untrustworthy, or more directly, that the informant from whom I received the information is an untrustworthy informant. Thus, to be personally justified, I must accept that the informant is trustworthy. Since that is false, however, I will not be justified in accepting that my informant arrived before the host on the basis of my verific system, what is left of my acceptance system when all errors are deleted. I will not be verifically justified, and so I will not be completely justified either. Hence, the account offered above incorporates the reliabilist insight and explains how we fail to obtain knowledge when the source of information is unreliable.

The appeal of reliabilism and the other forms of externalism may, moreover, be easily understood in terms of the coherence theory and the account of complete justification contained therein. To oversimplify a bit, personal justification depends on our background information about the relationship of acceptance to the truth of what is accepted, about nomological or statistical correlations, about counterfactual dependence, or about reliable processes. This information is contained in my acceptance system. I know that I see my cat sitting on papers on the desk. I accept that I would not believe that I see a cat if it were not true that I see him. I accept that my believing I see a cat is correlated with my seeing a cat, though I would not put it that way. I accept that always, or almost always, I see a cat when I think I see one because my accepting that I see a cat results from a reliable process. It is my acceptance of these things that converts merely accepting that I see a cat into personal justification, into victory in the justification game. For that victory to be converted into complete justification, however, what I accept about these things must also be true. The conversion of mere acceptance into personal justification depends on my accepting the things about myself whose bare existence the externalist mistakenly assumes to be sufficient to convert true belief into knowledge. The conversion also depends, as the externalist says it does, on these things I accept about myself being true. The error of externalism is to fail to notice that the subject of knowledge must accept that the externalist conditions hold true. The insight of externalism is the claim that the conditions must, indeed, hold true.

Causation and Justification: The Basing Relation

The truth contained in reliabilism is, however, concealed by an error. What a person originally believes as a result of prejudice may later be accepted on the basis of scientific evidence. Therefore, the reliabilist must be in error when he claims that it is what originates a belief that converts it into a justified belief and knowledge. This is, in effect, to confuse the *reason* a person has for

believing something with the *cause* of his believing it. The confusion is such a common one that we might name it the *causal fallacy*.

It is easy to see how the fallacy arises. When a person's justification for her belief is based on evidence, then she believes what she does *because* of the evidence. This suggests a causal account of what is involved when the justification of a belief is based on evidence. It suggests that the notion of a justification being based on evidence should be explicated in causal terms. Following this proposal, a person's justification for her belief is based on certain evidence if and only if her belief is causally related in some specified way to the evidence. How to specify the exact way in which the belief must be causally related to the evidence would remain a problem on this approach, but it would be a problem of detail rather than of principle. All such theories must be rejected, however.

Often the evidence on which a justification is based does causally explain the existence of the belief, and it may even be admitted that sometimes the belief is justified because of the way in which it is causally explained by the evidence. Nevertheless, it is also possible for a justified belief to be causally independent of the evidence that justifies it. Indeed, it may well be that the evidence in no way explains why the person holds the belief, even though her justification for the belief is based on the evidence. The evidence that justifies a person's belief may be evidence she acquired because she already held the belief, rather than the other way round. This is to be expected, since it is common sense to distinguish between the reasons that justify a belief and the causes that produce it. The causes of belief are various, and, though the reasons we have for a belief sometimes cause the belief to arise, the belief may also arise from some other cause than having the reasons that justify it. Having the reasons we do may justify the belief, however, even though they have no causal influence upon the belief at all.

An example will illustrate. It is easy to imagine the case of someone who comes to believe something for the wrong reason and, consequently, cannot be said to be justified in his belief, but who, as a result of his belief, uncovers some evidence which completely justifies his belief. Suppose that a man, Mr. Raco, is racially prejudiced and, as a result, believes that the members of some race are susceptible to some disease to which members of his race are not susceptible. This belief, we may imagine, is an unshakable conviction. It is so strong a conviction that no evidence to the contrary would weaken his prejudiced conviction, and no evidence in favor would strengthen it. Now imagine that Mr. Raco becomes a doctor and begins to study the disease in question. Imagine that he reads all that is known about the disease and discovers that the evidence, which is quite conclusive, confirms his conviction. The scientific evidence shows that only members of the race in question are susceptible to the disease. We may imagine as well that Mr. Raco has become a medical expert perfectly capable of understanding the canons of scientific evidence, though, unfortunately, he becomes no less prejudiced as a result of this. Nevertheless, he understands and appreciates the evidence as well as any medical expert and, as a result, has reason for his belief that justifies it. He has discovered that his conviction is confirmed by the scientific evidence. He knows that only members of the other race are susceptible to the disease in question. Yet, the reasons that justify him in this belief do not causally explain the belief. The belief is the result of prejudice, not reason, but it is confirmed by reason which provides the justification for the belief. Prejudice gives Mr. Raco conviction, but reason gives him justification.

Harman and others, most notably Marshall Swain and Alvin Goldman, have suggested that a belief is based on evidence only if the evidence conditionally or partially explains the belief. The idea is that, even if the belief is not originated by the evidence on which it is based, it must be causally sustained by the evidence. Again, in the typical case, this will be true. Usually, the reasons a person has for a belief can be expected to have some causal influence on the belief, even if they do not originate that belief. It is, unfortunately, difficult to evaluate the claim that the reasons that justify a belief must always partially explain or causally sustain the belief because a sufficiently precise account of partial explanation and causal sustenance is lacking. There appears to be no better reason for supposing that the evidence that justifies a belief must partially explain or causally sustain the belief than for supposing that it must originate it. The explanation for this is that we may suppose that the evidence justifying Mr. Raco's beliefs does not in any way explain or causally sustain his belief. What explains and sustains his belief is his prejudice. His

belief is neither strengthened nor explained by his discovering the evidence for it. His prejudice gives him the strongest level of conviction, and the evidence adds nothing to the strength of it.

One might, however, suggest that his conviction is conditionally or counterfactually explained or sustained by the evidence, nonetheless. It might be proposed that if Mr. Raco were not to believe what he does out of prejudice, he would believe it as a result of the evidence. This is again likely, but it need not be so. Imagine that Mr. Raco is so dependent on his prejudice that if he were to cease to believe what he does out of prejudice, he would become quite mad and become uninfluenced by reason. To avoid such an objection one might propose, as Swain did, that to say the belief is sustained by the evidence is only to say that if Mr. Raco were not to believe what he does out of prejudice but were to continue to believe it nonetheless, then he would believe it as a result of the evidence. Perhaps this is to be expected, but must it be so? Again suppose that were Mr. Raco to cease to believe what he does out of prejudice, he would become quite mad and uninfluenced by reason; then were he to believe the same thing though not out of prejudice, he would believe it as a result of madness.

The point is the one with which he began. Though evidence ordinarily has some influence over belief or would have if other factors were to lose their influence, this is really incidental to justification. The analogy between justification and validity explains why. If a person validly deduces a conclusion from something he knows, this may cause him to believe the conclusion or influence his belief in the conclusion. But the validity of the inference does not depend on this causal influence. If valid deduction had no influence whatever on whether a person believed the conclusion, that would not undermine the validity of the inference. Similarly, if someone justifies some conclusion on the basis of something he knows, this may cause him to believe the conclusion or influence his belief in the conclusion. The justification of his conclusion, however, does not depend on the causal influence. Thus, a person may justify a second belief in terms of a first belief and the justification of the second belief may be based on the first without the second belief being causally influenced thereby.

The preceding discussion rests on a distinction between explaining why a person believes something, on the one hand, and explaining how he knows it, on the other. When a person knows that his belief is true, the explanation of why he believes what he does may have something to do with his having the evidence he does, but it need not. The explanation may rest on political, erotic, or other extraneous influences, but the explanation of how a person knows that his belief is true, when the justification of the belief is based on evidence, must be in terms of the evidence. It is how a person knows that is explained by evidence. Why he believes what he does may be explained by anything whatever. Therefore, a justification of a belief that is known to be true is based on certain evidence if and only if his having that evidence explains how he knows that the belief is true. The evidence explains how the person knows, moreover, if and only if the evidence justifies the person's belief. The manner in which evidence justifies a belief is explained in the account of complete justification in the last chapter. Evidence that justifies a belief consists of that part of the acceptance system of a person which yields complete justification.

The idea of evidence explaining how a person knows may be further clarified by recalling once again that our primary concern is to provide a theory to explain how people know that the information that they possess is correct. If the evidence that a person has justifies her belief that p, then the evidence explains how she knows that the information that p is correct. She knows this from the evidence. Similarly, if a person is asked how she knows that p, her reply will be to justify the claim that p in terms of her evidence. It is appeal to her evidence that shows that she knows and how she knows. Thus, a justification based on evidence explains how a person knows that p if that justification would be a correct answer to the question "How do you know that p?"

Reliability and the Justification Game

The example of Mr. Raco, a person originally believing out of racial prejudice that the members of some race suffer a disease which members of other races do not suffer and later accepting this on the basis of scientific evidence, shows that a belief need not be produced or, as the example further indicated, even sustained by the evidence that justifies accepting it. Reliability enters into justification not by originating belief but by backing acceptance in the justification game. Consider the justification game played by the prejudiced man before obtaining the scientific information.

CLAIMANT: The members of that race suffer a disease to which members of other races are not susceptible.

SKEPTIC: You believe what you do as the result of prejudice.

CLAIMANT: It is more reasonable for me to accept that I do not believe what I do as a result of prejudice than to accept that I believe what I do as a result of prejudice. (I am quite unprejudiced concerning members of the race in question, it is just that they are inferior.)

This personal justification would fail to convert into verific and complete justification. The claimant's error concerning his prejudice would disqualify this move in the verific justification game.

After acquiring the scientific information, the claimant is in a position to neutralize the claim of the skeptic in the justification game by making the following reply to the claim of the skeptic above:

CLAIMANT: It is as reasonable for me to accept that I believe what I do out of prejudice and that the best scientific evidence shows that what I thus believe is, in fact, true than to accept merely that I believe what I do out of prejudice. (In the standard medical reference work concerning this disease, it is stated that only members of the race in question are susceptible to the disease. This has been confirmed by recent studies cited in . . .)

This move succeeds in the verific justification game. The claimant wins the round, and his move cannot be disqualified. Whatever his moral failings, as a result of obtaining scientific understanding, he is victorious in the justification game. He is, therefore, personally and verifically justified in accepting what he does.

The preceding reflections illustrate the point that the evidence which justifies a person in accepting something must explain how the person knows that p rather than why he believes it. The scientific evidence explains how the person knows by explaining how he is victorious in the justification game. Usually, what makes a person victorious in the justification game is closely connected to what makes him believe what he does. But the connection is not essential to justification. As a result, the reliability essential to justification is not the reliability of the process which produces or causally sustains belief. What is essential is the reliability or trustworthiness of the evidence for what we accept to guide us to acceptance of what is true rather than false. The trustworthiness of the evidence makes us trustworthy in the matter, whatever our general defects. In epistemology as in life generally, you do not have to be perfect in order to be justified.

Externalism, Foundationalism, and Coherence: An Ecumenical Reconsideration

The foregoing articulation of the coherence theory of justification suggests that there is some merit in the foundation theory and in externalism which we have preserved in our theory. It is, therefore, time to turn from criticism to ecumenicalism. The foundation theory held some introspective, perceptual, and memory beliefs to be self-justified. We argued that the justification of all such beliefs depends on background information concerning our trustworthiness in such matters. Thus, it is coherence with such information in our acceptance system that produces the justification. Nevertheless, we concede that some beliefs are justified without inference because we accept ourselves to be trustworthy in such matters, and that a principle of our trustworthiness is needed to convert mere acceptance into justified acceptance.

Moreover, though the principle of our trustworthiness must cohere with what we accept about our successes and failures in past epistemic employments, the principle of our own trustworthiness provides its own personal justification. We are, at least in part, personally justified in accepting that we are trustworthy precisely because we accept that we are. If we did not accept that we were trustworthy, there would be an unbeatable skeptical challenge to any claim we made in the justification game, to wit, that we are untrustworthy in what we accept. To beat that move, we must accept that we are trustworthy. So, there appears

to be at least one thing that we accept, one important and fundamental thing, that is self-justified as the foundationalist contended, even if it is not those introspective, perceptual, and memory beliefs that he most favors. To be personally justified one must accept some principle of trustworthiness which is, in part, self-justified.

To be verifically and completely justified as well, some principle of trustworthiness we accept must be true. Otherwise, the skeptical challenge that we are not trustworthy in what we accept would not be beaten in the verific justification game. The insight of externalism is the contention that there must be some truth connection between our accepting something and the truth of what we accept. It is our acceptance of our trustworthiness and the correctness of what we thus accept that yields the truth connection.

Externalism is motivated by the doubt about whether what we accept can supply the truth connection. The reason for the doubt is the assumption that it is psychologically unrealistic to suppose that beliefs about our beliefs are necessary for knowledge. Such higher order beliefs about beliefs are not, of course, necessary for receiving and relaying information. Even a thermometer is capable of that. Such beliefs are, however, necessary for knowledge. Is it unrealistic to suppose that people believe themselves to be trustworthy? Some unrealistic theory of belief may yield that consequence, but our theory of acceptance avoids it. The mental state of acceptance is a functional state, one that plays a role in thought, inference, and action. We think, infer, and act in a way manifesting our trust in what we accept.

Thus, it is appropriate and not at all unrealistic to suppose that, in addition to the other things we accept, we accept our own trustworthiness as well. We have supplied the truth that supplies the truth connection required by the externalist in the form of a self-justified principle of our own trustworthiness. We cannot be accused of chauvinism in claiming that complete justification is the result of coherence with an acceptance system incorporating the principle. Unless we are trustworthy in what we accept, neither we nor our adversaries can be justified in what we accept and we must all concede the day to the skeptic. If we are trustworthy, as we accept ourselves to be, what we accept will cohere with our acceptance system and our verific system to yield complete justification. The attainment of knowledge, like so many other benefits in life, rests on self-trust.

VI.3 Epistemology Naturalized

W. V. QUINE

W. V. Quine (1908–2000) for many years was professor of philosophy at Harvard University. Quine argues that epistemology centered in normative justification is dead. Because foundationalism (especially Carnap's ambitious effort) has failed as an attempt to ground our knowledge claims, we should give up traditional epistemology altogether and concentrate on empirical psychology. Whereas "old epistemology aspired to contain . . . natural science . . . epistemology in its new setting, conversely, is contained in natural science, as a chapter of psychology." The new epistemology-psychology turns into the descriptive examination of the relation "between the meager input [of sensory stimulation] and the torrential output [our three-dimensional picture of the world]." With the demise of "old epistemology" go all concerns about normativity or justification.

Quine begins his essay with an examination of the twofold goal of traditional epistemology: (1) the conceptual reduction, whereby physical terms are reduced to terms referring to phenomenal features of sensory experience; and (2) a doctrinal reduction, whereby truths about the physical world are *correctly* obtained from sensory experience. Quine argues that the twofold goal failed and that there is no "correct" or normative function left.

Epistemology is concerned with the foundations of science. Conceived thus broadly, epistemology includes the study of the foundations of mathematics as one of its departments. Specialists at the turn of the century thought that their efforts in this particular department were achieving notable success: mathematics seemed to reduce altogether to logic. In a more recent perspective this reduction is seen to be better describable as a reduction to logic and set theory. This correction is a disappointment epistemologically, since the firmness and obviousness that we associate with logic cannot be claimed for set theory. But still the success achieved in the foundations of mathematics remains exemplary by comparative standards, and we can illuminate the rest of epistemology somewhat by drawing parallels to this department.

Studies in the foundations of mathematics divide symmetrically into two sorts, conceptual and doctrinal. The conceptual studies are concerned with meaning, the doctrinal with truth. The conceptual studies are concerned with clarifying concepts by defining them, some in terms of others. The doctrinal studies are concerned with establishing laws by proving them, some on the basis of others. Ideally the more obscure concepts would be defined in terms of the clearer ones so as to maximize clarity, and the less obvious laws would be proved from the more obvious ones so as to maximize certainty. Ideally the definitions would generate all the concepts from clear and distinct ideas, and the proofs would generate all the theorems from self-evident truths.

The two ideals are linked. For, if you define all the concepts by use of some favored subset of them, you thereby show how to translate all theorems into these favored terms. The clearer these terms are, the likelier it is that the truths couched in them will be obviously true, or derivable from obvious truths. If in particular the concepts of mathematics were all reducible to the clear terms of logic, then all the truths of mathematics would go over into truths of logic; and surely the truths of logic are all obvious or at least potentially obvious, i.e., derivable from obvious truths by individually obvious steps.

This particular outcome is in fact denied us, however, since mathematics reduces only to set

Reprinted from *Ontological Relativity and Other Essays* (Columbia University Press, 1969) by permission.

theory and not to logic proper. Such reduction still enhances clarity, but only because of the interrelations that emerge and not because the end terms of the analysis are clearer than others. As for the end truths, the axioms of set theory, these have less obviousness and certainty to recommend them than do most of the mathematical theorems that we would derive from them. Moreover, we know from Gödel's work that no consistent axiom system can cover mathematics even when we renounce self-evidence. Reduction in the foundations of mathematics remains mathematically and philosophically fascinating, but it does not do what the epistemologist would like of it: it does not reveal the ground of mathematical knowledge, it does not show how mathematical certainty is possible.

Still there remains a helpful thought, regarding epistemology generally, in that duality of structure which was especially conspicuous in the foundations of mathematics. I refer to the bifurcation into a theory of concepts, or meaning, and a theory of doctrine, or truth; for this applies to the epistemology of natural knowledge no less than to the foundations of mathematics. The parallel is as follows. Just as mathematics is to be reduced to logic, or logic and set theory, so natural knowledge is to be based somehow on sense experience. This means explaining the notion of body in sensory terms; here is the conceptual side. And it means justifying our knowledge of truths of nature in sensory terms; here is the doctrinal side of the bifurcation.

Hume pondered the epistemology of natural knowledge on both sides of the bifurcation, the conceptual and the doctrinal. His handling of the conceptual side of the problem, the explanation of body in sensory terms, was bold and simple: he identified bodies outright with the sense impressions. If common sense distinguishes between the material apple and our sense impressions of it on the ground that the apple is one and enduring while the impressions are many and fleeting, then, Hume held, so much the worse for common sense; the notion of its being the same apple on one occasion and another is a vulgar confusion.

Nearly a century after Hume's *Treatise*, the same view of bodies was espoused by the early American philosopher Alexander Bryan Johnson.[1] "The word iron names an associated sight and feel," Johnson wrote.

What then of the doctrinal side, the justification of our knowledge of truths about nature? Here, Hume despaired. By his identification of bodies with impressions he did succeed in construing some singular statements about bodies as indubitable truths, yes; as truths about impressions, directly known. But general statements, also singular statements about the future, gained no increment of certainty by being construed as about impressions.

On the doctrinal side, I do not see that we are further along today than where Hume left us. The Humean predicament is the human predicament. But on the conceptual side there has been progress. There the crucial step forward was made already before Alexander Bryan Johnson's day, although Johnson did not emulate it. It was made by Bentham in his theory of fictions. Bentham's step was the recognition of contextual definition, or what he called paraphrasis. He recognized that to explain a term we do not need to specify an object for it to refer to, nor even specify a synonymous word or phrase; we need only show, by whatever means, how to translate all the whole sentences in which the term is to be used. Hume's and Johnson's desperate measure of identifying bodies with impressions ceased to be the only conceivable way of making sense of talk of bodies, even granted that impressions were the only reality. One could undertake to explain talk of bodies in terms of talk of impressions by translating one's whole sentence about bodies into whole sentences about impressions, without equating the bodies themselves to anything at all.

This idea of contextual definition, or recognition of the sentence as the primary vehicle of meaning, was indispensable to the ensuing developments in the foundations of mathematics. It was explicit in Frege, and it attained its full flower in Russell's doctrine of singular descriptions as incomplete symbols.

Contextual definition was one of two resorts that could be expected to have a liberating effect upon the conceptual side of the epistemology of natural knowledge. The other is resort to the resources of set theory as auxiliary concepts. The epistemologist who is willing to eke out his austere ontology of sense impressions with these set-theoretic auxiliaries is suddenly rich: he has not just his impressions to play with, but sets of them, and sets of sets, and so on up. Constructions in the foundations of mathematics have shown that such set-theoretic aids are a powerful addition; after all, the entire glossary of concepts of classical mathematics is constructible from them. Thus equipped, our epistemologist may not need either to identify bodies with impressions or to settle for contextual definition; he may hope to find in some subtle construction of sets upon sets of sense impressions a category of objects enjoying just the formula properties that he wants for bodies.

The two resorts are very unequal in epistemological status. Contextual definition is unassailable. Sentences that have been given meaning as wholes are undeniably meaningful, and the use they make of their component terms is therefore meaningful, regardless of whether any translations are offered for those terms in isolation. Surely Hume and A. B. Johnson would have used contextual definition with pleasure if they had thought of it. Recourse to sets, on the other hand, is a drastic ontological move, a retreat from the austere ontology of impressions. There are philosophers who would rather settle for bodies outright than accept all these sets, which amount, after all, to the whole abstract ontology of mathematics.

This issue has not always been clear, however, owing to deceptive hints of continuity between elementary logic and set theory. This is why mathematics was once believed to reduce to logic, that is, to an innocent and unquestionable logic, and to inherit these qualities. And this is probably why Russell was content to resort to sets as well as to contextual definition when in *Our Knowledge of the External World* and elsewhere he addressed himself to the epistemology of natural knowledge, on its conceptual side.

To account for the external world as a logical construct of sense data—such, in Russell's terms, was the program. It was Carnap, in his *Der logische Aufbau der Welt* of 1928, who came nearest to executing it.

This was the conceptual side of epistemology; what of the doctrinal? There the Humean predicament remained unaltered. Carnap's constructions, if carried successfully to completion, would have enabled us to translate all sentences about the world into terms of sense data, or observation, plus logic and set theory. But the mere fact that a sentence is *couched* in terms of observation, logic, and set theory does not mean that it can be *proved* from observation sentences by logic and set the-

ory. The most modest of generalizations about observable traits will cover more cases than its utterer can have had occasion actually to observe. The hopelessness of grounding natural science upon immediate experience in a firmly logical way was acknowledged. The Cartesian quest for certainty had been the remote motivation of epistemology, both on its conceptual and its doctrinal side; but that quest was seen as a lost cause. To endow the truths of nature with the full authority of immediate experience was as forlorn a hope as hoping to endow the truths of mathematics with the potential obviousness of elementary logic.

What then could have motivated Carnap's heroic efforts on the conceptual side of epistemology, when hope of certainty on the doctrinal side was abandoned? There were two good reasons still. One was that such constructions could be expected to elicit and clarify the sensory evidence for science, even if the inferential steps between sensory evidence and scientific doctrine must fall short of certainty. The other reason was that such constructions would deepen our understanding of our discourse about the world, even apart from questions of evidence; it would make all cognitive discourse as clear as observation terms and logic and, I must regretfully add, set theory.

It was sad for epistemologists, Hume and others, to have to acquiesce in the impossibility of strictly deriving the science of the external world from sensory evidence. Two cardinal tenets of empiricism remained unassailable, however, and so remain to this day. One is that whatever evidence there *is* for science *is* sensory evidence. The other, to which I shall return, is that all inculcation of meanings of words must rest ultimately on sensory evidence. Hence the continuing attractiveness of the idea of a *logischer Aufbau* in which the sensory content of discourse would stand forth explicitly.

If Carnap had successfully carried such a construction through, how could he have told whether it was the right one? The question would have had no point. He was seeking what he called a *rational reconstruction*. Any construction of physicalistic discourse in terms of sense experience, logic, and set theory would have been seen as satisfactory if it made the physicalistic discourse come out right. If there is one way there are many, but any would be a great achievement.

But why all this creative reconstruction, all this make-believe? The stimulation of his sensory receptors is all the evidence anybody has had to go on, ultimately, in arriving at his picture of the world. Why not just see how this construction really proceeds? Why not settle for psychology? Such a surrender of the epistemological burden to psychology is a move that was disallowed in earlier times as circular reasoning. If the epistemologist's goal is validation of the grounds of empirical science, he defeats his purpose by using psychology or other empirical science in the validation. However, such scruples against circularity have little point once we have stopped dreaming of deducing science from observations. If we are out simply to understand the link between observation and science, we are well advised to use any available information, including that provided by the very science whose link with observation we are seeking to understand.

But there remains a different reason, unconnected with fears of circularity, for still favoring creative reconstruction. We should like to be able to *translate* science into logic and observation terms and set theory. This would be a great epistemological achievement, for it would show all the rest of the concepts of science to be theoretically superfluous. It would legitimize them—to whatever degree the concepts of set theory, logic, and observation are themselves legitimate—by showing that everything done with the one apparatus could in principle be done with the other. If psychology itself could deliver a truly translational reduction of this kind, we should welcome it; but certainly it cannot, for certainly we did not grow up learning definitions of physicalistic language in terms of a prior language of set theory, logic, and observation. Here, then, would be good reason for persisting in a rational reconstruction: we want to establish the essential innocence of physical concepts, by showing them to be theoretically dispensable.

The fact is, though, that the construction which Carnap outlined in *Der logische Aufbau der Welt* does not give translational reduction either. It would not even if the outline were filled in. The crucial point comes where Carnap is explaining how to assign sense qualities to positions in physical space and time. These assignments are to be made in such a way as to fulfill, as well as possible, certain desiderata which he states, and with growth of experience the assignments are to be revised to suit. This plan, however illuminating,

does not offer any key to *translating* the sentences of science into terms of observation, logic, and set theory.

We must despair of any such reduction. Carnap had despaired of it by 1936, when, in "Testability and Meaning,"[2] he introduced so-called *reduction forms* of a type weaker than definition. Definitions had shown always how to translate sentences into equivalent sentences. Contextual definition of a term showed how to translate sentences containing the term into equivalent sentences lacking the term. Reduction forms of Carnap's liberalized kind, on the other hand, do not in general give equivalences; they give implications. They explain a new term, if only partially, by specifying some sentences which are implied by sentences containing the term, and other sentences which imply sentences containing the term.

It is tempting to suppose that the countenancing of reduction forms in this liberal sense is just one further step of liberalization comparable to the earlier one, taken by Bentham, of countenancing contextual definition. The former and sterner kind of rational reconstruction might have been represented as a fictitious history in which we imagined our ancestors introducing the terms of physicalistic discourse on a phenomenalistic and set-theoretic basis by a succession of contextual definitions. The new and more liberal kind of rational reconstruction is a fictitious history in which we imagine our ancestors introducing those terms by a succession rather of reduction forms of the weaker sort.

This, however, is a wrong comparison. The fact is rather that the former and sterner kind of rational reconstruction, where definition reigned, embodied no fictitious history at all. It was nothing more nor less than a set of directions—or would have been, if successful—for accomplishing everything in terms of phenomena and set theory that we now accomplish in terms of bodies. It would have been a true reduction by translation, a legitimation by elimination. *Definire est eliminare.* Rational reconstruction by Carnap's later and looser reduction forms does none of this.

To relax the demand for definition, and settle for a kind of reduction that does not eliminate, is to renounce the last remaining advantage that we supposed rational reconstruction to have over straight psychology; namely, the advantage of translational reduction. If all we hope for is a reconstruction that links science to experience in explicit ways short of translation, then it would seem more sensible to settle for psychology. Better to discover how science is in fact developed and learned than to fabricate a fictitious structure to a similar effect.

The empiricist made one major concession when he despaired of deducing the truths of nature from sensory evidence. In despairing now even of translating those truths into terms of observation and logico-mathematical auxiliaries, he makes another major concession. For suppose we hold, with the old empiricist Peirce, that the very meaning of a statement consists in the difference its truth would make to possible experience. Might we not formulate, in a chapter-length sentence in observational language, all the difference that the truth of a given statement might make to experience, and might we not then take all this as the translation? Even if the difference that the truth of the statement would make to experience ramifies indefinitely, we might still hope to embrace it all in the logical implications of our chapter-length formulation, just as we can axiomatize an infinity of theorems. In giving up hope of such translation, then, the empiricist is conceding that the empirical meanings of typical statements about the external world are inaccessible and ineffable.

How is this inaccessibility to be explained? Simply on the ground that the experiential implications of a typical statement about bodies are too complex for finite axiomatization, however lengthy? No; I have a different explanation. It is that the typical statement about bodies has no fund of experiential implications it can call its own. A substantial mass of theory, taken together, will commonly have experiential implications; this is how we make verifiable predictions. We may not be able to explain why we arrive at theories which make successful predictions, but we do arrive at such theories.

Sometimes also an experience implied by a theory fails to come off; and then, ideally, we declare the theory false. But the failure falsifies only a block of theory as a whole, a conjunction of many statements. The failure shows that one or more of those statements is false, but it does not show which. The predicted experiences, true and false, are not implied by any one of the component statements of the theory rather than another. The

component statements simply do not have empirical meanings, by Peirce's standard, but a sufficiently inclusive portion of theory does. If we can aspire to a sort of *logischer Aufbau der Welt* at all, it must be to one in which the texts slated for translation into observational and logico-mathematical terms are mostly broad theories taken as wholes, rather than just terms or short sentences. The translation of a theory would be a ponderous axiomatization of all the experiential difference that the truth of the theory would make. It would be a queer translation, for it would translate the whole but none of the parts. We might better speak in such a case not of translation but simply of observational evidence for theories; and we may, following Peirce, still fairly call this the empirical meaning of the theories.

These considerations raise a philosophical question even about ordinary unphilosophical translation, such as from English into Arunta or Chinese. For, if the English sentences of a theory have their meaning only together as a body, then we can justify their translation into Arunta only together as a body. There will be no justification for pairing off the component English sentences with component Arunta sentences, except as these correlations make the translation of the theory as a whole come out right. Any translations of the English sentences into Arunta sentences will be as correct as any other, so long as the net empirical implications of the theory as a whole are preserved in translation. But it is to be expected that many different ways of translating the component sentences, essentially different individually, would deliver the same empirical implications for the theory as a whole; deviations in the translation of one component sentence could be compensated for in the translation of another component sentence. Insofar, there can be no ground for saying which of two glaringly unlike translations of individual sentences is right.[3]

For an uncritical mentalist, no such indeterminacy threatens. Every term and every sentence is a label attached to an idea, simple or complex, which is stored in the mind. When on the other hand we take a verification theory of meaning seriously, the indeterminacy would appear to be inescapable. The Vienna Circle espoused a verification theory of meaning but did not take it seriously enough. If we recognize with Peirce that the meaning of a sentence turns purely on what would count as evidence for its truth, and if we recognize with Duhem that theoretical sentences have their evidence not as single sentences but only as larger blocks of theory, then the indeterminacy of translation of theoretical sentences is the natural conclusion. And most sentences, apart from observation sentences, are theoretical. This conclusion, conversely, once it is embraced, seals the fate of any general notion of propositional meaning or, for that matter, state of affairs.

Should the unwelcomeness of the conclusion persuade us to abandon the verification theory of meaning? Certainly not. The sort of meaning that is basic to translation, and to the learning of one's own language, is necessarily empirical meaning and nothing more. A child learns his first words and sentences by hearing and using them in the presence of appropriate stimuli. These must be external stimuli, for they must act both on the child and on the speaker from whom he is learning.[4] Language is socially inculcated and controlled; the inculcation and control turn strictly on the keying of sentences to shared stimulation. Internal factors may vary *ad libitum* without prejudice to communication as long as the keying of language to external stimuli is undisturbed. Surely one has no choice but to be an empiricist so far as one's theory of linguistic meaning is concerned.

What I have said of infant learning applies equally to the linguist's learning of a new language in the field. If the linguist does not lean on related languages for which there are previously accepted translation practices, then obviously he had no data but the concomitances of native utterance and observable stimulus situation. No wonder there is indeterminacy of translation—for of course only a small fraction of our utterances report concurrent external stimulation. Granted, the linguist will end up with unequivocal translations of everything; but only by making many arbitrary choices—arbitrary even though unconscious—along the way. Arbitrary? By this I mean that different choices could still have made everything come out right that is susceptible in principle to any kind of check.

Let me link up, in a different order, some of the points I have made. The crucial consideration behind my argument for the indeterminacy of translation was that a statement about the world does not always or usually have a separable fund of empirical consequences that it can call its own.

That consideration served also to account for the impossibility of an epistemological reduction of the sort where every sentence is equated to a sentence in observational and logico-mathematical terms. And the impossibility of that sort of epistemological reduction dissipated the last advantage that rational reconstruction seemed to have over psychology.

Philosophers have rightly despaired of translating everything into observational and logico-mathematical terms. They have despaired of this even when they have not recognized, as the reason for this irreducibility, that the statements largely do not have their private bundles of empirical consequences. And some philosophers have seen in this irreducibility the bankruptcy of epistemology. Carnap and the other logical positivists of the Vienna Circle had already pressed the term "metaphysics" into pejorative use, as connoting meaninglessness; and the term "epistemology" was next. Wittgenstein and his followers, mainly at Oxford, found a residual philosophical vocation in therapy: in curing philosophers of the delusion that there were epistemological problems.

But I think that at this point it may be more useful to say rather that epistemology still goes on, though in a new setting and a clarified status. Epistemology, or something like it, simply falls into place as a chapter of psychology and hence of natural science. It studies a natural phenomenon, viz., a physical human subject. This human subject is accorded a certain experimentally controlled input—certain patterns of irradiation in assorted frequencies, for instance—and in the fullness of time the subject delivers as output a description of the three-dimensional external world and its history. The relation between the meager input and the torrential output is a relation that we are prompted to study for somewhat the same reasons that always prompted epistemology; namely, in order to see how evidence relates to theory, and in what ways one's theory of nature transcends any available evidence.

Such a study could still include, even, something like the old rational reconstruction, to whatever degree such reconstruction is practicable; for imaginative constructions can afford hints of actual psychological processes, in much the way that mechanical simulations can. But a conspicuous difference between old epistemology and the epistemological enterprise in this new psychological setting is that we can now make free use of empirical psychology.

The old epistemology aspired to contain, in a sense, natural science; it would construct it somehow from sense data. Epistemology in its new setting, conversely, is contained in natural science, as a chapter of psychology. But the old containment remains valid too, in its way. We are studying how the human subject of our study posits bodies and projects his physics from his data, and we appreciate that our position in the world is just like this. Our very epistemological enterprise, therefore, and the psychology wherein it is a component chapter, and the whole of natural science wherein psychology is a component book—all this is our own construction or projection from stimulations like those we were meting out to our epistemological subject. There is thus reciprocal containment, though containment in different senses: epistemology in natural science and natural science in epistemology.

This interplay is reminiscent again of the old threat of circularity, but it is all right now that we have stopped dreaming of deducing science from sense data. We are after an understanding of science as an institution or process in the world, and we do not intend that understanding to be any better than the science which is its object. This attitude is indeed one that Neurath was already urging in Vienna Circle days, with his parable of the mariner who has to rebuild his boat while staying afloat in it.

One effect of seeing epistemology in a psychological setting is that it resolves a stubborn old enigma of epistemological priority. Our retinas are irradiated in two dimensions, yet we see things as three-dimensional without conscious inference. Which is to count as observation—the unconscious two-dimensional rejection or the conscious three-dimensional apprehension? In the old epistemological context the conscious form had priority, for we were out to justify our knowledge of the external world by rational reconstruction, and that demands awareness. Awareness ceased to be demanded when we gave up trying to justify our knowledge of the external world by rational reconstruction. What to count as observation now can be settled in terms of the stimulation of sensory receptors, let consciousness fall where it may.

The Gestalt psychologists' challenge to sensory atomism, which seemed so relevant to episte-

mology forty years ago, is likewise deactivated. Regardless of whether sensory atoms or Gestalten are what favor the forefront of our consciousness, it is simply the stimulations of our sensory receptors that are best looked upon as the input to our cognitive mechanism. Old paradoxes about unconscious data and inference, old problems about chains of inference that would have to be completed too quickly—these no longer matter.

In the old anti-psychologistic days the question of epistemological priority was moot. What is epistemologically prior to what? Are Gestalten prior to sensory atoms because they are noticed, or should we favor sensory atoms on some more subtle ground? Now that we are permitted to appeal to physical stimulation, the problem dissolves; A is epistemologically prior to B if A is causally nearer than B to the sensory receptors. Or, what is in some ways better, just talk explicitly in terms of causal proximity to sensory receptors and drop the talk of epistemological priority.

Around 1932 there was debate in the Vienna Circle over what to count as observation sentences, or *Protokollsätze*. One position was that they had the form of reports of sense impressions. Another was that they were statements of an elementary sort about the external world, e.g., "A red cube is standing on the table." Another, Neurath's, was that they had the form of reports of relations between percipients and external things: "Otto now sees a red cube on the table." The worst of it was that there seemed to be no objective way of settling the matter: no way of making real sense of the question.

Let us now try to view the matter unreservedly in the context of the external world. Vaguely speaking, what we want of observation sentences is that they be the ones in closest causal proximity to the sensory receptors. But how is such proximity to be gauged? The idea may be rephrased this way: observation sentences are sentences which, as we learn language, are most strongly conditioned to concurrent sensory stimulation rather than to stored collateral information. Thus let us imagine a sentence queried for our verdict as to whether it is true or false, queried for our assent or dissent. Then the sentence is an observation sentence if our verdict depends only on the sensory stimulation present at the time.

But a verdict cannot depend on present stimulation to the exclusion of stored information. The very fact of our having learned the language evinces much storing of information, and of information without which we should be in no position to give verdicts on sentences however observational. Evidently then we must relax our definition of observation sentence to read thus: a sentence is an observation sentence if all verdicts on it depend on present sensory stimulation and on no stored information beyond what goes into understanding the sentence.

This formulation raises another problem: how are we to distinguish between information that goes into understanding a sentence and information that goes beyond? This is the problem of distinguishing between analytic truth, which issues from the mere meanings of words, and synthetic truth, which depends on more than meanings. Now I have long maintained that this distinction is illusory. There is one step toward such a distinction, however, which does make sense: a sentence that is true by mere meanings of words should be expected, at least if it is simple, to be subscribed to by all fluent speakers in the community. Perhaps the controversial notion of analyticity can be dispensed with, in our definition of observation sentence, in favor of this straightforward attribute of community-wide acceptance.

This attribute is of course no explication of analyticity. The community would agree that there have been black dogs, yet none who talk of analyticity would call this analytic. My rejection of the analyticity notion just means drawing no line between what goes into the mere understanding of the sentences of a language and what else the community sees eye-to-eye on. I doubt that an objective distinction can be made between meaning and such collateral information as is community-wide.

Turning back then to our task of defining observation sentences, we get this: an observation sentence is one on which all speakers of the language give the same verdict when given the same concurrent stimulation. To put the point negatively, an observation sentence is one that is not sensitive to differences in past experience within the speech community.

This formulation accords perfectly with the traditional role of the observation sentence as the court of appeal of scientific theories. For by our definition the observation sentences are the sentences on which all members of the community will agree under uniform stimulation. And what is the criterion of membership in the same community? Simply, general fluency of dialogue. This criterion admits of degrees, and indeed we may usefully take the community more narrowly for some studies than for others. What count as observation sentences for a community of specialists would not always so count for a larger community.

There is generally no subjectivity in the phrasing of observation sentences, as we are now conceiving them; they will usually be about bodies. Since the distinguishing trait of an observation sentence is intersubjective agreement under agreeing stimulation, a corporeal subject matter is likelier than not.

The old tendency to associate observation sentences with a subjective sensory subject matter is rather an irony when we reflect that observation sentences are also meant to be the intersubjective tribunal of scientific hypotheses. The old tendency was due to the drive to base science on something firmer and prior in the subject's experience; but we dropped that project.

The dislodging of epistemology from its old status of first philosophy loosed a wave, we saw, of epistemological nihilism. This mood is reflected somewhat in the tendency of Polányi, Kuhn, and the late Russell Hanson to belittle the role of evidence and to accentuate cultural relativism. Hanson ventured even to discredit the idea of observation, arguing that so-called observations vary from observer to observer with the amount of knowledge that the observers bring with them. The veteran physicist looks at some apparatus and sees an x-ray tube. The neophyte, looking at the same place, observes rather "a glass and metal instrument replete with wires, reflectors, screws, lamps, and pushbuttons." One man's observation is another man's closed book or flight of fancy. The notion of observation as the impartial and objective source of evidence for science is bankrupt. Now my answer to the x-ray example was already hinted a little while back: what counts as an observation sentence varies with the width of community considered. But we can also always get an absolute standard by taking in all speakers of the language, or most. It is ironical that philosophers, finding the old epistemology untenable as a whole, should react by repudiating a part which has only now moved into clear focus.

Clarification of the notion of observation sentence is a good thing, for the notion is fundamental in two connections. These two correspond to the duality that I remarked upon early in this essay: the duality between concept and doctrine, between knowing what a sentence means and knowing whether it is true. The observation sentence is basic to both enterprises. Its relation to doctrine, to our knowledge of what is true, is very much the traditional one: observation sentences are the repository of evidence for scientific hypotheses. Its relation to meaning is fundamental too, since observation sentences are the ones we are in a position to learn to understand first, both as children and as field linguists. For observation sentences are precisely the ones that we can correlate with observable circumstances of the occasion of utterance or assent, independently of variations in the past histories of individual informants. They afford the only entry to a language.

The observation sentence is the cornerstone of semantics. For it is, as we just saw, fundamental to the learning of meaning. Also, it is where meaning is firmest. Sentences higher up in theories have no empirical consequences they can call their own; they confront the tribunal of sensory evidence only in more or less inclusive aggregates. The observation sentence, situated at the sensory periphery of the body scientific, is the minimal verifiable aggregate; it has an empirical content all its own and wears it on its sleeve.

The predicament of the indeterminacy of translation has little bearing on observation sentences. The equating of an observation sentence of our language to an observation sentence of another language is mostly a matter of empirical generalization; it is a matter of identity between the range of stimulations that would prompt assent to the one sentence and the range of stimulations that would prompt assent to the other.

It is no shock to the preconceptions of old Vienna to say that epistemology now becomes semantics. For epistemology remains centered as always on evidence, and meaning remains centered as always on verification; and evidence is verification. What is likelier to shock preconceptions is that meaning, once we get beyond observation

sentences, ceases in general to have any clear applicability to single sentences; also that epistemology merges with psychology, as well as with linguistics.

This rubbing out of boundaries could contribute to progress, it seems to me, in philosophically interesting inquiries of a scientific nature. One possible area is perceptual norms. Consider, to begin with, the linguistic phenomenon of phonemes. We form the habit, in hearing the myriad variations of spoken sounds, of treating each as an approximation to one or another of a limited number of norms—around thirty altogether—constituting so to speak a spoken alphabet. All speech in our language can be treated in practice as sequences of just those thirty elements, thus rectifying small deviations. Now outside the realm of language also there is probably only a rather limited alphabet of perceptual norms altogether, toward which we tend unconsciously to rectify all perceptions. These, if experimentally identified, could be taken as epistemological building blocks, the working elements of experience. They might prove in part to be culturally variable, as phonemes are, and in part universal.

Again there is the area that the psychologist Donald T. Campbell calls evolutionary epistemology. In this area there is work by Hüseyin Yilmaz, who shows how some structural traits of color perception could have been predicted from survival value. And a more emphatically epistemological topic that evolution helps to clarify is induction, now that we are allowing epistemology the resources of natural science.

Notes

[1]A. B. Johnson, *A Treatise on Language* (New York, 1836; Berkeley, 1947).

[2]Carnap, *Philosophy of Science* 3 (1936): 419–71; 4 (1937): 1–40.

[3]See Quine, *Ontological Relativity* (New York, 1969), pp. 2ff.

[4]See ibid., p. 28.

VI.4 The Generality Problem for Reliabilism

EARL CONEE AND RICHARD FELDMAN

Earl Conee and Richard Feldman are professors of philosophy at Rochester University. In this essay they argue that the most dominant form of externalism, process reliabilism, has an insuperable problem: It fails to identify the processes involved in producing justification, and, hence, knowledge.

I. Introduction

A. Reliabilism and the Generality Problem

The central idea of process reliability theories of epistemic justification is this:

RJ.   A belief is justified if and only if it is produced by a process that reliably leads to true beliefs.[1]

A fully articulated reliabilist theory must identify with sufficient clarity the nature of the processes it invokes. In doing so, the theory confronts what has come to be known as "the generality problem."[2]

A simple example will show the nature of the problem. Suppose that Smith has good vision and is familiar with the visible differences among common species of trees. Smith looks out a house window one sunny afternoon and sees a plainly visible nearby maple tree. She forms the belief that there is a maple tree near the house. Assuming everything else in the example is normal, this belief is justified and Smith knows that there is a maple tree near the house. Process reliabilist theories reach the right verdict about this case only if it is true that the process that caused Smith's belief is reliable. And one might think that the process is obviously reliable. However, before accepting this conclusion, we should think carefully about exactly what that process is and what its reliability consists in.

Light reflects from the tree and its surroundings into Smith's eyes. Optic neural events result, and these produce further neural events within Smith's brain. Particular concrete occurrences, involving sensory neural stimulation in combination with complex standing conditions in Smith's brain, result in Smith forming the belief. This concrete sequence of events is the process that caused the belief. So, if we take the process that must be reliable to be composed of causally active events that bring about the belief, then reliabilism requires for justification that a sequence of concrete events is reliable.

However, reliability is a kind of tendency. The notion of reliability applies straightforwardly only to enduring mechanisms, such as an eye or a whole visual system, and to repeatable types of processes, such as the type: visually initiated belief formation. Reliability does not apply in any obvious way to the particular sequence of concrete events that caused Smith's belief on this occasion. Each event in the sequence happens only once and the sequence causes whatever beliefs result just on that occasion. Process reliabilists who realize this have sought the requisite reliability in the *types* of process of which particular causal sequences are tokens.[3]

As many reliabilists have recognized, each token process that causes a particular belief is of numerous different types of widely varying reliability. The token event sequence in our example of seeing the maple tree is an instance of the following types, among others: visually initiated belief-forming process, process of a retinal image of such-and-such specific characteristics leading to a belief that there is a maple tree nearby, process of relying on a leaf shape to form a tree-classifying judgment, perceptual process of classifying by species a tree located behind a solid obstruction, etc. The number of types is unlimited. They are as numerous as the properties had by the belief-forming process. Thus, process reliability theories confront the question of which type must be reliable for the resulting belief to be justified. It is

Reprinted from *Philosophical Studies,* 1998 by permission.

clear that the answer to this question will significantly affect the implications of the theory. For instance, while visually formed beliefs in general seem to be fairly reliable, processes that use a characteristically maple-leafish visual experience to judge that a maple tree is near seem much more highly reliable, and perceptual processes leading to a belief that a tree, which is behind a solid obstruction, is of a particular species seem generally unreliable, in spite of the fact that in some of their instances, such as the present case, the obstruction is transparent. The process token is of endlessly many other types as well, types of extremely varied reliability. So, which type has to be sufficiently reliable?

Process reliabilists must solve this generality problem. A solution identifies the type whose reliability determines whether a process token yields justification.[4] This type is "the relevant type" for that token. Thus, it is not the causally active process token that has to be sufficiently reliable, according to reliabilists. It is the relevant type of the process. We need to know what determines this sort of relevance.

Without a specification of the relevant type, process reliabilism is radically incomplete. Only when a bearer of reliability has been identified does the theory have any implications about the justification of beliefs in particular cases. Philosophers often overlook this. They purport to determine whether or not a given belief is justified according to reliabilism using nothing more than one description of the process causing the belief. No such inference is acceptable. The theory must first be elaborated at least enough to imply exactly what process type has to be reliable in the case in question. A fully general reliabilist theory of justification has to do this for all cases in which there is a fact of the matter.

A second necessary task for process reliabilists is to specify which situations of a process type's operation determine whether or not the type is reliable. Strength of reliability might be settled by the frequency with which the process actually produces true beliefs or rather by its truth-to-falsehood output ratio in certain counterfactual circumstances. The generality problem arises no matter how this question about reliability is answered. William Alston's sensible specification of what determines the reliability of a process type will do for present purposes:

R. A process type is reliable if and only if it would yield a high proportion of truths over a wide range of situations of the sort we typically encounter.[5]

B. Necessary Conditions for a Solution to the Generality Problem

A solution to the generality problem must meet the following three conditions.

First, it must be principled. Given the multiplicity of belief-forming process types and their variations in reliability, it is easy to make *ad hoc* case-by-case selections of types that match our intuitions. But case-by-case selections of relevant types does not constitute working out a reliabilist theory of justification.

The claim that the reliability of "the relevant type" of the belief-forming process is what determines a belief's justification is analogous to the claim that "the suitable type" of a horse is what produces victory in a horse race. On its own, the phrase "the suitable type of horse" tells us nothing about what makes horses win races. If we are offered only case-by-case choices of "suitability-making properties," choices made on the basis of knowing which horses are the winners, then the claim is no closer to having any definite content. Clearly, a general basis for identifying suitability is required for the claim to say more than just that something or other makes each winning horse win its race. Analogously, we have an informative reliabilist theory of knowledge or justification only after we are told what determines the relevant type.

Although a solution must be principled, it need not state necessary and sufficient conditions for relevance that are either precise or always determinate. Claims to the effect that a belief is "epistemically justified" might be vague and they might be context-sensitive in various ways. A solution must be universal only in that it must specify the relevant type whenever there are definite facts about justification.

The second requirement for solving the generality problem is that the rule must make defensible epistemic classifications. Stating a general rule of relevance that merely assigns some type or other to each process token does not constitute an adequate solution to the generality problem. The types identified must have a reliability that is plausibly correlated with the justification of the resulting beliefs.

Finally, a solution must remain true to the spirit of the reliabilist approach. We are addressing process reliability theories.[6] So, the rule of relevance must somehow implement the basic idea that it is the reliability of a process of belief formation, specified in non-epistemic terms, that settles the epistemic status of the belief. Process reliabilists characteristically think that a belief is justified because the workings of the process that produced it (or sustained it) are sufficiently conducive to generating true beliefs. A solution to the generality problem would specify those workings so as to bear out this idea. A solution thus cannot identify the relevant type for a process in a way that merely smuggles a non-reliabilist epistemic evaluation into the characterization of relevant types. For instance, one could develop a form of "reliabilism" that just restates an evidentialist theory of justification in a roundabout way. Pseudoreliabilism of this sort holds that there are only two relevant types of belief-forming process. One type is "belief based on adequate evidence" and the other type is "belief based on inadequate evidence." Assuming that the first of these is reliable and the second is not, this version of reliabilism will get plausible results (or at least results that an evidentialist would find plausible).[7] But this theory is only verbally a version of reliabilism. It mentions the processes of belief formation only in order to characterize the quality of the evidence for the belief. This is obviously incompatible with the spirit of process reliabilism.

C. Our Thesis

Our thesis is that the prospects for a solution to the generality problem for process reliabilism are worse than bleak. We will investigate the merits of approaches exemplified by several recent proposals. There is no significant progress in any of these approaches, singly or in combination. The basic process reliabilist idea just does not pan out.

It is reasonable to look for a solution to the generality problem in three places: common sense, science, and context. Common sense is the likeliest source. As we shall soon see, Alvin Goldman's early account of reliabilism draws much of its initial attraction from the *prima facie* correlation between justified beliefs and beliefs produced by common sense types of processes that are probably reliable. Goldman immediately realized that some refinement of these common sense types is needed, for reasons that we shall illustrate below. But at first glance the thought is appealing that common sense process types like "careful perception," "vivid memory," and the like are reliable. So, it makes sense to pursue the reliabilist idea that these types of process produce justified beliefs because of their reliability. In contrast, common sense belief-forming process types like "guessing" seem to be unreliable and seem to yield unjustified beliefs.

If, as we shall argue, common sense types will not do, then the next likeliest source of relevance is scientific classification. Scientific types of belief-forming processes are types that correspond to the predicates that enter into the laws and explanations of science. We shall next investigate the possibility of solving the generality problem by identifying relevant types with these scientific types.

Another reasonable thought is that different types are relevant to justification in different contexts, just as different comparison classes determine the application of terms like "small" and "far" in different contexts and just as different reference classes determine the truth value of probability judgments in different contexts. Thus, we shall consider next the merits of contextualist solutions to the generality problem.

We shall argue that none of these approaches works out. This might raise the concern that our way of posing of the generality problem for reliabilism is somehow ill conceived. It might be thought that the relevant types are obvious when the question is properly understood, or that no general solution is actually needed. We shall take up this line of thinking as well.

That exhausts the reasonable philosophical approaches to the generality problem. If they all fail, then so does process reliabilism.

II. Common Sense Types

In his pioneering defense of process reliabilism, Alvin Goldman appeals to common sense process types in an effort to convey the plausibility of the theory. He writes,

> . . . what kinds of cause confer justifiedness? We can gain some insight into this problem by reviewing some faulty processes of belief-formation, i.e., processes whose belief-outputs would be classed as unjustified. Here are some examples: confused reasoning, wishful thinking, reliance on emotional attachment, mere hunch or guesswork, and hasty generalization. What do these faulty processes have in common? They share the feature of *unreliability*: they tend to produce *error* a large proportion of the time. By contrast, which species of belief-forming (or belief-sustaining) processes are intuitively justification-conferring? They include standard perceptual processes, remembering, good reasoning, and introspection. What these processes seem to have in common is *reliability*.[8]

Thinking of reliabilism in terms of these types gives the theory its initial appeal.

However, common sense types have two liabilities as the basis for a solution to the generality problem. First, there are far too many common sense types to provide a unique identification of the relevant type for each process token. In our initial example, Smith's visually formed maple tree belief results from a process instantiating all the following common sense types: visual process, perceptual process, tree-identifying process, daytime process, indoor process, etc., etc. These types differ widely in their reliability. So, we still need to be told which one determines the justificatory status of the resulting belief.

The other main problem with the types Goldman mentions is that not all beliefs resulting from any one such type are even approximately equally justified. Consider another common sense type that Goldman refers to, brief and hasty scanning. Sometimes, on the basis of brief and hasty scanning we can get extremely well-justified beliefs, as when we see in a glance that there is a tree in the backyard. Other times brief and hasty scanning does not yield a justified belief, as when the belief concerns exactly how many leaves are on the tree. Simple common sense classifications are thus too broad to make the right epistemic distinctions among beliefs.

In a recent discussion of the generality problem, William Alston sometimes calls what he proposes as the relevant types "habits" of belief formation.[9] Likewise, Charles Wallis appeals to "strategies" of belief formation.[10] Habit and strategy are common sense classifications of some of the ways we form beliefs. In classifying trees by species, an expert naturalist has identifying routines that differ considerably from those of novice and ill-informed tree classifiers. Even though all of them may judge by experiencing the same views of the trees, the expert is better justified. So there is some initial plausibility in the idea that it is the "routine," the "habit of mind," the "strategy," employed in forming a given belief that determines its level of justification.[11] This suggests:

> H.   The relevant type for any belief-forming process token is the habit of mind, or belief-forming strategy, that it instantiates.

For a large class of cases, it is doubtful that (H) serves to identify a single relevant type. This is because many process tokens are instances of more than one habit. Smith, our maple tree identifier, may have a habit of concentrating while making careful visual judgments, a habit of calling to mind types of trees known to be in the area when making species classifications, and a habit of counting points on leaves for identifying deciduous trees. Some of her belief-forming process tokens result from the employment of all three habits. So there would be no such thing as "the habit" employed on those occasions, and thus no relevant type by the present proposal.

There are, furthermore, cases in which justified beliefs are formed in a way that is in no intuitive sense "habitual," or "routine," or "strategy-employing." For instance, Smith might happen to notice a cardinal on a branch of the maple tree, and be thereby justified in believing that a cardinal is there. She is not employing any strategy, or habit, or routine, in forming this belief. Thus, a theory that requires a high enough reliability for the relevant type here would conclude that the belief is not justified, since there is no habit or strategy that is either reliable or unreliable. Yet in many such cases the belief clearly is justified.

Also, the same belief-forming habit can produce some justified beliefs and some unjustified ones. Jones might make a habit of judging the theme of a philosophy article by reading only its concluding paragraph. Sometimes the theme is clearly presented there and Jones will be justified. Other times the final paragraph does not make clear the point of the paper and Jones will not gain justification by employing this procedure.

Another approach using common sense classifications would be to hold that the solution to the generality problem is to classify together processes that produce equally general beliefs:

> G.   Two process tokens are of the same relevant type if and only if they generate beliefs at the same level of generality.

(G) has no promise as a solution to the generality problem. The problem of finding the relevant type does not reduce to that of finding the right level of generality for the contents of the resulting beliefs. It is often not clear what "level of generality" a belief has. But if there is any merit in the approach that (G) represents, then two judgments will be at the same level of generality if their contents consist in classifying an individual by species. Thus, the following visually based beliefs are all at the same level of generality: this is a mountain goat, this is a giraffe, this is a crocodile, this is an alligator. (G) implies that all such classificatory beliefs result from the same relevant type, and hence all are equally justified. But clearly this is not so. For instance, some such beliefs are based on more justifying perceptible features than others. To ordinary observers, nearby giraffes are pretty obvious, while nearby crocodiles are easily mistaken for alligators. Processes generating equally general beliefs are not all equally justifying.

A similar idea would be to distinguish processes in terms of the identity of their particular output beliefs, so that the different beliefs just mentioned would result from different relevant types of processes. This has numerous unacceptable results too, however. Clearly there are both justified and unjustified examples of belief in the same proposition.

There is no reason to think that any appeal to simple common sense types will solve the generality problem. Their main liability is that they are too broad to differentiate properly among the justification levels of our various beliefs. Other types can be constructed by conjoining together the broad common sense classifications that we have been discussing. These can be much narrower, for

instance: visual process causing a belief that classifies by species a close, unobstructed, opaque object, in bright sunlight. But the members of such types still vary in their degree of justification depending on such things as whether the viewer is familiar with the visual appearance of the species from the viewing angle, has normal vision, is intoxicated, is expecting visual trickery, is emotionally distraught, etc. There is no good reason to believe that even such narrow kinds will include only equally justified beliefs, however elaborately they are specified, as long as they use only common sense non-epistemic categories.[12]

Common sense types thus do not stand scrutiny as candidates to provide a satisfactory solution to the generality problem.

III. Scientific Types

It is in keeping with the "naturalistic" spirit of reliabilist theories to look for classifying help from natural science. One tempting line of thought is that reliabilists can count on cognitive psychology to identify the types of belief-forming processes that will be useful to their theory. Suggestions of such a view can be found in writings by Alston, Goldman and Ralph Baergen.[13]

A. Natural Kinds

Alston's mention of habits of mind is not his theoretical proposal for coping with the generality problem. Rather, he suggests that belief-forming process tokens belong to natural kinds and that these kinds are the types to which reliabilists ought appeal. He writes:

> With a process token, as with any other particular, any of its properties can be said to be correlated with a type to which it belongs . . . Even if it is true that you and I belong to indefinitely many classes, such as *objects weighing more than ten pounds, objects that exist in the twentieth century, objects mentioned in this paper*, etc. etc., it is still the case that membership in the class of human beings is fundamental for *what we are* in a way that those others are not, just because it is the *natural kind* to which we belong. I

shall suggest that something analogous is true of belief-forming processes—that there are fundamental considerations that mark out, for each such process token, a type that is something like its "natural kind."[14]

Although this is not Alston's final account of the matter, it is important to see that more is needed. Merely citing the fact that each belief-forming process falls into a natural kind does not provide an adequate rule of relevance. To see this, note the inadequacy of the following solution to the generality problem:

> NS1 The relevant type for any belief forming process token is the natural kind to which it belongs.

Process tokens do belong to natural kinds. Still, there is no good reason to think that each token belongs to just a single natural kind, and hence no reason to think that (NS1) provides a solution to the generality problem. What the natural kinds of belief-forming processes are is up for grabs, but every belief-forming process token is categorized in multiple ways by laws in each of several sciences. These all seem to be natural kinds of the process, according to current science. Reasonable candidates for natural kinds of a typical visual belief-forming process include electrochemical process, organic process, perceptual process, visual process, and facial-recognition process. All belief-forming process tokens are thus in a multiplicity of natural kinds. So (NS1) does not single out a relevant type for any such process. These natural kinds differ widely in their reliability. So, (NS1) does not solve the generality problem.

B. Psychological Realism

Process tokens thus belong to numerous natural kinds. Alston contends, however, that for each belief-forming process token there is only one type that is "psychologically real." His suggestion is that this type is the relevant type.

According to Alston, every process token instantiates what he calls a "function." He stipulates that this term is to have its mathematical sense. In the case of beliefs formed on the basis of perceptual experience, these functions take as inputs features of experience to which we are responsive and yield beliefs as outputs. Alston is aware that each particular input/output pair is in the extension of many mathematical functions, but he claims that there is only one such function that any belief-forming process actually is an "activation" of. Only this one is psychologically real.[15]

The intended solution to the generality problem seems to be:

> NS2 The relevant type for any process token is the natural psychological kind corresponding to the function that is actually operative in the formation of the belief.

(NS2) does narrow the set of candidates for relevant types. Furthermore, psychology does aspire to provide psychological explanations of at least all normally acquired beliefs.[16] If this aspiration is met, there will be psychological types of belief-forming process for all such beliefs.

If (NS2) provides a solution to the generality problem, it must be that there is only one actually operative "psychologically real" type for each belief-forming process. In apparent support of this, while discussing the application of (NS2) to beliefs resulting from vision, Alston emphasizes that there is a fact about which elements of a visual scene a person responds to in forming a belief about what is present. Thus, in our example about Smith and the maple tree, Smith might form her belief on the basis of noticing certain features of leaf shape. The token process therefore goes from these input features to that belief. In other examples, when presented with the same scene Smith might pick up on features such as the tree's overall shape or bark texture, rather than leaf shape. These considerations show that the relevant type in the original case must be one that corresponds to a function having as an input/output pair the leaf-shape features to which Smith responds and the belief that she forms.

This may limit somewhat the candidates for relevant types, but in Smith's case there still are numerous overlapping functional relations, and corresponding psychological process types, that include the input/output pair that we have identified. There is a very narrow function that goes from just the leaf shape that Smith notices as input to just the output of Smith's particular belief that a maple tree is nearby. There is another function, one that maps a variety of fairly similar inputs, including the particular shape that Smith noticed, onto some belief or other to the effect that there is a maple tree nearby, including the belief Smith forms. There is a broader function, one that maps a variety of somewhat similar inputs, all involving visual shapes, onto either the belief that there is a maple tree nearby or the belief that there is an oak tree nearby or the belief that there is an elm tree nearby, etc. There are still broader types that include this pair, as well as inputs involving other sensory cues. In many cases, all these functional causal relations, and many others as well, would be actually operative in forming Smith's belief. Smith's disposition to form the particular belief that she did on the basis of the particular shape that she saw is part of these broader classifying dispositions. The one event of belief-formation manifests them all. Thus, in this and other typical cases, there are a multitude of actually operative psychological types.

An example from another domain may help to make this point clear. Suppose that a certain pot of water at sea level is brought to a boil. There occurred a certain sequence of concrete events leading to the boiling of the water. This sequence instantiates any number of types, all "physically real." We can identify these types in terms of the functions that describe their final stage. At any given pressure, there is a function that maps water onto a certain temperature—its boiling point. This corresponds to the process "bringing water to a boil at sea-level atmospheric pressure." There is a broader type, "bringing water to a boil." The function corresponding to this second type takes water and varying pressures as inputs, and yields a boiling point for water at each temperature. A still broader function takes as inputs triples of temperatures, pressures, and types of liquid and yields the boiling point for each. This corresponds to the type "bringing liquids to a boil." The token process in our example is an instance of all these types. It is not the case that only one is "physically real." All of them accurately characterize what occurred in the pot. Similarly, far too many functions are "psychologically real." They all correspond to natural psychological kinds. So, (NS2) fails to identify the relevant type.

C. Maximum Specificity and Narrow Causal Types

Alston also suggests that his psychological realism implies, or at least is compatible with, a different specification of relevant types, one that relies on completely causally specific functions. He assumes that "the functions in question are maximally specific, in that any difference in input that is registered by the function indicates a different function."[17] Making use of this idea of maximal specificity is one way of trying to make good on the idea that only one function is "operative" in the formation of any belief.[18]

In any case where a person forms a belief on the basis of a perceptual experience, some features of the experience contribute to a belief-forming causal sequence that starts with the experience. Other features of the experience play no causal role in belief formation. The same goes for subsequent events in the sequence leading to the belief. Some features of these events help to cause the belief, others do not. The maximum specificity proposal is the idea that the relevant type includes all and only process tokens with the same causal features: they all begin with experiences with the same causally active features, are followed by subsequent events with the same causal features, and have the same belief as output. At one time, Alvin Goldman suggested a very similar solution to the generality problem.[19] We can formulate this proposal as follows:

> NS3   The relevant type for any belief forming process token t is the natural kind that includes all and only those tokens sharing with t all the same causally contributory features from the input experience to the resulting belief.[20]

(NS3) does yield a unique type for each process token. But the reliabilist theory of justification that employs (NS3) is seriously defective. (NS3) classifies into the same relevant type only beliefs that share *all* internal causal predecessors. Thus, on the reasonable assumption that the content of any normally formed belief is causally determined by its antecedent psychological causes, according to (NS3) each relevant type can have only one content for its output belief.[21] This makes trouble in cases in which the proposition believed dictates the truth-ratio of all process types leading only to it. In such cases the reliability of the relevant type is settled by the mere identity of the belief. Thus, the relevant type of a process leading to any necessary truth must be perfectly reliable. The relevant type of any process leading to any necessary falsehood must be perfectly unreliable. Also perfectly reliable would be the relevant types of all processes leading to any self-confirming belief, such as the belief that someone believes something.

The problems for reliabilist theories built on (NS3) are not confined to beliefs in necessities, impossibilities, or the relatively unusual beliefs just mentioned. Suppose that Jones looks very carefully at a tree and forms the belief that it is a beech on the basis of seeing features which are in fact distinctive to beech trees. As long as experience of such features happens to help to prompt Jones to believe that it is a beech tree, it does not matter to (NS3) why they do so. It can be for good reasons, for bad reasons, or for no reason at all. Recall (R), which tells us that the reliability of a type is determined by the long run truth-ratio of its output when it functions under normal conditions. In the normal worlds used to evaluate the reliability of Jones's tree-identifying process, nothing other than a beech tree presents Jones with exactly the features that initiate the causal process leading to his belief.[22] This by itself is enough for the theory to imply that Jones's belief is justified, regardless of how much information he happens to have about the look of beech trees. Since the highly specific causal factors that led to his belief in fact are indicative of only beech trees, his belief must be justified, according to this theory. In the worlds that determine the reliability of the relevant type, only beeches cause the sort of experience that led to his belief that a beech tree is nearby. So this maximally specific type is maximally reliable. Reliabilist theories based on (NS3) thus are unable to distinguish the epistemic status of lucky guesses that happen to be based on distinctive features from expert judgments based on well-understood classifications.

An additional problem is that (NS3) yields a version of reliabilism that is not in keeping with the spirit of process reliabilism. As we have just seen, (NS3) often renders irrelevant the details of the process intervening between an input and a resulting belief. In particular, suppose that Jones and Smith both respond to the same features of a visual input with the belief that there is an elm tree present. Suppose that this input will occur only when there is an elm tree present—it is a distinctive look of an elm leaf, say, the visual appearance of a particular quantity of tiny notches around its

edge. Finally, suppose that Smith knows what she is seeing, while Jones is applying some ridiculous and unjustified sort of numerology to the topic. Jones plucks from thin air the idea that the magic number for elms is nine. Jones gets a nine for the tree whose leaf he beholds by counting the number of those distinctive elm notches along the edge of a leaf, and dividing by six, his "tree number." Given (NS3), the relevant types for their processes are maximally specific. These types are thoroughly reliable since nothing other than an elm would cause just that input in any significant fraction of nearby worlds. The fact that one of the two knows what elms look like and the other does not and the fact that one process goes through a silly application of superstitious nonsense do not affect the reliability of the maximally specific types (NS3) specifies.[23] It is just this sort of difference that process reliabilism is supposed to make matter: it is supposed to be sensitive to the possibility that the process one person uses is not generally reliable while the one the other uses is generally reliable, even if in the case at hand both people happen to begin their processes by noticing what is in fact an extremely reliable indicator of the right answer. In other words, process reliability theories are supposed to appeal to much broader relevant types.

D. Categories from Science

Ralph Baergen discusses several examples, explaining what reliabilists might say about them. By generalizing from his remarks it is possible to devise one more way reliabilists might appeal to science to solve the generality problem. This is a second way of attempting to cash out Alston's remark that only one process type is "actually operative" in belief formation.

One example, discussed in the literature by Richard Feldman, concerns a person who sees something on a distant hill.[24] She forms the belief that what she sees is an animal and the belief that it is a mountain goat. Feldman points out that the more general belief may well be better justified than the more specific one. So, he concludes that reliabilists must find a way to distinguish between the types of processes that cause the beliefs.

Baergen proposes a way to do this.[25] He appeals to David Marr's theory of vision, which holds that in classifying objects on the basis of visual perception, we generate a model of the object which "is compared to descriptions in a sort of catalogue. This catalogue is arranged in levels, so that rough categorizations take place at the lower levels, followed by more fine-grained discriminations at higher levels."[26] Baergen suggests that we make use of this idea in identifying relevant types:

> Our account of processes might well reflect this by saying that rough categorizations are generated by different process[es] than those yielding fine-grained categorizations. Applied to Feldman's case, the mountain-goat-belief is generated by a different process than that which generated the animal-belief, for they involve different levels of categorization. Also, the process that generated the animal-belief is likely to be more reliable, for there are likely to be fewer nearby situations in which this generates a false belief than there are for the mountain-goat process. So, Reliabilism *can* provide intuitively correct results here.[27]

No doubt reliabilists can state a rule of relevance that produces the intuitively correct results "here." But reliabilism needs a fully general rule. Baergen reports part of a theory of vision that implies that perceptual classifications result from processes that are organized by levels of generality of the resulting beliefs. He suggests that reliabilists can identify relevant types in some way that plays on this fact. However, Baergen does not make clear how to build upon this example to develop a general account of relevant types.

One possibility, suggested by Baergen's use of psychology, is that the relevant types are the types that are invoked by the best psychological theories of belief-formation. The idea here is that while any token belongs to numerous types that are psychologically real, only one of those types will enter in the best psychological theory that explains the resulting belief. That type is the relevant type. Marr's theory may have been used to illustrate how this might apply in the case of visual belief-formation.

> NS4   The relevant type for any belief-forming process token t is the psychological kind that is part of the best psychological explanation of the belief that results from t.

It may be that Alston had something like (NS4) in mind when he said that only one type was "actually operative."

(NS4) rests on the dubious assumption that there is a unique "best" psychological explanation for each belief. The value of an explanation depends upon the use to which it is put. A very specific and narrow explanation might have greater value for some purposes, while a broader explanation might have greater value for other purposes.[28]

Even if (NS4) did identify unique types, it would not be possible to evaluate its implications for process reliabilism without knowing what those types are. There is no particular reason to think that the types that are of greatest value for psychological explanation are uniformly helpful to reliabilist theories of justification.

To see why types that are particularly useful for psychological explanation might not be of much help to reliabilists, consider the types Baergen mentions. His proposal ties the relevant types for classificatory beliefs based on visual perception to the level of generality of the resulting belief, and he suggests, plausibly, that a type that produces relatively general beliefs is more reliable than types that produce more specific beliefs. A version of process reliabilism making use of this idea would thus make all more general classificatory beliefs better justified than more specific classifications. That is an unacceptable result. Sometimes, a belief applying a broader classification is less well justified than is a belief applying a narrower one. For instance, a person may know at a glance that a thing she sees is a whale, but be less well justified in her belief that it is a mammal. So the generality of a visually based classificatory belief does not determine a relevant type that yields a satisfactory version of reliabilism. There is, then, no reason to think that the particular scientific classifications Baergen mentions yield types that are entirely helpful to reliabilism.

Although science does provide the tools to narrow the candidates for relevant types, there is no good reason to think that scientific classifications provide the tools for solving the generality problem.

IV. Solutions Without a Necessary and Sufficient Condition

Some philosophers have responded to the generality problem by explicitly denying that the problem requires a general resolution. We will examine two such responses in this section.

A. Constraints

Frederick Schmitt proposes five constraints on which process types are relevant, and then appeals to the constraints in describing problem cases.[29] According to Schmitt, "relevant processes are cognitive processes."[30] His constraints require, among other things, that relevant types are salient, that they are folk psychological process types, and that tokens of the same type are intrinsically similar.

These constraints are not meant to compose what Schmitt calls a "criterion of relevance": a necessary and sufficient condition for relevant types. Schmitt believes that no such criterion is needed. Instead, the constraints are supposed to identify the sorts of factors that we take to matter when we make judgments about justification.

To explain why no criterion of relevance is needed, Schmitt writes:

> [W]e have intuitions about which processes are relevant. In judging whether a subject is justified in an inferential belief, we check to see which inferential process the subject exercises—e.g., whether it is induction from sufficiently many instances or affirming the consequent. We have the intuition that these are the relevant processes to consider. In the case of perceptual belief, we check which environmental conditions obtain—whether it is sunny or foggy—and whether the subject is careful and attentive in perception or quick and distracted. Here again we have intuitions about which processes are relevant. Reliabilism may explain why perceptual or inferential beliefs are justified or unjustified by relying on these intuitions.[31]

The existence of these intuitions does not relieve process reliabilists of the responsibility to provide an explanation of their invocation of relevance. Granting that the intuitions exist, the question that we have been asking remains to be answered: According to reliabilism, which type must be reliable for a particular belief to be justified?

Furthermore, Schmitt is mistaken about exactly what intuitions we do have. Schmitt says

that "we have intuitions about which processes are relevant." Since Schmitt is addressing the generality problem, this claim seems intended to imply that "relevant" in the reliabilist use of "the relevant type of the process" has some intuitive application to examples. But that is not so. The reliabilist use of "the relevant type" is entirely technical. The expression might as well have been "the type that determines justification according to the philosophical theory known as 'reliabilism.'" No one has pre-theoretic intuitions about this topic. Rather, people have intuitions about which features in examples determine a belief's epistemic status. It is up to reliability theorists to assign reference to "relevant type" from scratch.

The existence of intuitions about which factors are relevant to justification does not eliminate reliabilism's need for a theory of relevant types. The constraints Schmitt describes do not do this on their own. They provide a variety of conflicting criteria. In his discussion of cases, Schmitt gives the constraints differing weights so as to achieve the desired result.[32] Perhaps one can, by weighing one factor heavily in one case, a different factor heavily in another, manipulate the constraints in a way that seems to give reliabilism acceptable results. But this is no victory for reliabilism. One could equally well say that the justification of a belief is a function of epistemically irrelevant factors such as the duration of the token of the cognitive process that caused it, the distance of the proximate external cause of the process from the center of the earth, and the amount of energy the process consumed. By *ad hoc* weighting of these factors, one could get acceptable results. The theory, nevertheless, has no merit.

A set of flexible constraints does not solve the generality problem. There are, of course, terms in our language whose application is governed by a set of flexible and varying factors. For example, when we say that someone is a "good athlete," there are a variety of factors that enter into our evaluations. They might include speed, strength, and endurance, among other things. But there is no fixed weight uniformly given to these factors. In different contexts these different factors may be weighed differently and it would be a mistake to ask for some fixed ranking of the importance of these various factors in evaluations of athletic ability. Although Schmitt does not say this, it is possible that he intends to propose that evaluations of processes as reliable work in somewhat the same way.[33] We turn in the next section to a proposal along these lines.

B. Context

Mark Heller contends that the demand for "a general principle for selecting the correct level of generality [for relevant types] . . . is unreasonable."[34] He thinks that contextual factors determine relevant types and thereby solve the generality problem. Heller elaborates his claims about the role of context as follows:

> "Reliable" is a perfectly ordinary word that in perfectly ordinary situations is applied to tokens which are instances of several types, where those types have different degrees of reliability. Yet we somehow manage to use this word without difficulty in ordinary discourse.[35]

Heller says that the primary task of his paper is to defend the claim that "reliable" is richly sensitive to the evaluator's context. This much is unobjectionable. The word "reliable" surely is context sensitive. That is, whether or not a thing is accurately called "reliable" depends in part upon the standards set by the context of the ascription. These standards vary, depending for instance on how important it is to rely on the thing that is said to be reliable. This is at most a first step toward solving the generality problem. We need to see how context sensitivity helps with the identification of the relevant type.[36]

Heller does not claim just that the standards for the application of "reliable" are context dependent. He makes the further claim that we readily understand applications of "reliable" to process tokens that are instances of many types. Thus, when a person says "That process is reliable," the person can refer to a process token and say something true. The person's statement is true provided the contextually determined type for that token is truly said to be "reliable" in the context of attribution. If Heller is right, then context determines two features of our predications of "reliable" to tokens. One has to do with the standard for the strength of reliability required for the term to apply in the context. That feature is of no help in determining the relevant type. The other feature

has to do with the identification of the type that must meet those standards. We will refer to these latter types as "contextually determined types." Thus, a phrase of the form "the process leading to S's belief that p" is supposed to have, relative to a context, a contextually determined type.

A solution to the generality problem can be constructed from these thoughts. The proposal that we shall formulate combines Heller's contentions about the context dependence of the word "reliable" with the epistemic contextualist view that the standards for assessing the truth value of knowledge and justification attributions are dependent on the attributor's context.[37]

> C   In any context, C, if a person says something of the form "S knows p" or "S is justified in believing p," the relevant type of the belief-forming process is the contextually determined type for the phrase "the process leading to S's belief that p" relative to context C.

(C) embodies the idea that the description "the process leading to S's belief that p" has a contextually determined process type. (C) puts that idea to the service of reliabilism by identifying contextually determined types with the relevant types needed to fill out reliabilist theories of knowledge and justification.

A fundamental objection to (C) is that contextual factors do not typically yield one determinate process type for the phrase "the process leading to S's belief that p." As a result, reliabilist theories built upon principle (C) will not yield the correct truth value for many clearly determinate attributions of knowledge or justification.

There are some situations in which phrases referring to process tokens apparently work in the way Heller describes. For example, suppose Jones says, "I have three ways to start my old jalopy: first, shifting into gear while rolling it down a hill; second, jump-starting it; and third, praying and then turning the key." Only the first two usually work. Suppose that Jones then starts his car by jump-starting it. He remarks:

> P.   "The process by which I just started my car is reliable."

Here, Jones's explicit mention of the three types serves to limit drastically the types under consideration. The token mentioned in (P) is of one of those types only. So, this is a case in which "reliable" is explicitly predicated of a process token and we have no problem in understanding what type must be reliable for the predication to be true.

In typical knowledge attributions, however, no contextual narrowing of candidate process types occurs. If it did, then when a person said that someone knows something, there would typically be a range of contextually salient process types such that the token process leading to the person's belief instantiated only one. But this is plainly not the case for most knowledge attributions. Ordinarily, no class of types of belief-forming processes will have been made contextually salient. And nothing else about typical contexts isolates any one type. So, it is just not true that in the context of knowledge attributions there are contextually determined types for the phrase "the process that caused this belief."

To see that this is so, consider our initial example in which Smith comes to know that there is a maple tree nearby by seeing it there. Suppose that Jones, who is sitting in the room with Smith, says:

K. "Smith knows that there is a maple tree nearby."

If Heller's version of reliabilism is to work, there must be, relative to the context of Jones's remark, some contextually determined type for the phrase "the process that caused Smith's belief." What would that type be? Nothing beyond the speaker's intentions seems to narrow the candidate pool in this sort of example. Perhaps Jones would be thinking of something like perception of familiar objects at a reasonable distance, or perhaps to something narrower, such as visual perception of familiar well-lit trees from a reasonable distance. Perhaps Jones would not have any type of belief-forming process in mind. After all, he did not say anything about belief-forming processes and there is no reason to think that he is having any thoughts about them. So, there is no reason to think that in this sort of mundane example, there is such a thing as the contextually determined type for the phrase "the process that caused Smith's belief." Moreover, there is no reason to think that the truth value of Jones's attribution of knowledge to Smith depends in any way on which, if any, of these types Jones has in mind.

Furthermore, even if an attributor of knowledge does have some belief-forming process types in mind, the attributor's thoughts do not identify relevant types in a way that is uniformly helpful to reliabilists. An attributor of knowledge may be mistaken about the reasons for a person's belief, and thus may be thinking about process types that the subject's token process does not even exemplify. For example, suppose that Jones witnesses Smith identify a bird as being of a certain species after Smith has had only the briefest glimpse of it under poor lighting conditions. Jones says that Smith's belief is unjustified and so Smith lacks knowledge. Jones does have in mind some process type for Smith's belief, something like forming a bird classifying belief on the basis of a brief glimpse in poor lighting conditions. Suppose, however, that Smith has formed her belief on the basis of hearing the bird's song, an identification method that Jones has not even thought of. Moreover, Smith does have knowledge as a result. If process reliabilism is anywhere close to the truth about knowledge and justification, it is the reliability of some process type that Smith actually underwent that matters here. So, the generality problem must be solved by appeal to facts about the processes actually involved in the formation of the belief, not by appeal to the possibly mistaken thoughts about those processes in the minds of knowledge attributors.

(C) is incorrect. There simply are no contextually determined types in many, perhaps most, typical contexts in which knowledge and justification claims have a clear truth value. It is true that context helps to determine the standards a process type must meet to be correctly described as "reliable." But the attributor's context comes nowhere near to picking out a relevant type of each belief-forming process, and the process types that are salient to the attributor can be entirely irrelevant to the truth of knowledge claims.

This section has focused on common sense types of belief-forming processes. There are also the many scientific types that classify each belief-forming process. It is clear that nothing about typical contexts of attribution of knowledge or justification uniformly singles out one of them. Since our minds are rarely scientifically orientated, speakers' intentions are even less likely to narrow down the scientific types. Nothing else about a context of utterance does so either. Thus, context does not solve the generality problem.

VI. Conclusion

That is the full variety of existing approaches to disposing of the generality problem. In the absence of a brand new idea about relevant types, the problem looks insoluble. Consequently, process reliability theories of justification and knowledge look hopeless.[38]

Notes

[1]Some authors discuss process reliability accounts of knowledge rather than accounts of epistemic justification. No point will be made below that turns on the differences between knowledge and justification.

[2]Alvin Goldman in "What Is Justified Belief?" in G. S. Pappas, ed. *Justification and Knowledge* (Dordrecht, Holland, 1979) and *Epistemology and Cognition* (Cambridge, MA: Harvard University Press, 1986) defends process reliabilist accounts of epistemic justification. In those works he recognizes the existence of the generality problem. See especially "What Is Justified Belief?", pp. 11, and *Epistemology and Cognition*, pp. 49–51. The problem is emphasized in Richard Feldman's "Reliability and Justification," *The Monist* 68 (1985): 159–174. It is also discussed by John Pollock in "Reliability and Justified Belief," *Canadian Journal of Philosophy* 14 (1984): 103–114. For responses to the problem, see the works of William Alston, Ralph Baergen, Mark Heller, Frederick Schmitt, Ernest Sosa, and Charles Wallis cited and discussed below.

[3]It is possible to construct a version of process reliabilism which is only about process tokens and does not confront the generality problem. It faces a considerable problem in making sense of the claim that a token sequence of events has some tendency toward producing beliefs whose truth-ratio would constitute its "reliability." Furthermore, the problems that affect (NS3) below, in virtue of a type having just one belief content in its outputs, also affect reliability theories that locate a sort of reliability in process tokens.

[4]There may not always be a fact of the matter. In the examples used here the belief is either definitely justified or definitely unjustified. The reliability of relevant types for process tokens that lead to beliefs whose epistemic status is unclear will be of less value to present concerns, since such cases are less useful in assessing epistemological theories.

[5]"How to Think About Reliability," *Philosophical Topics* (Spring 1995): 1–29. The proposal mentioned here appears on p. 10. This proposal has problematic features, but it conveys a useable idea of the sort of reliability to which a reliabilist is most likely to appeal.

[6]Reliabilist theories that make use of the reliability of indicators or mechanisms of belief-formation are thus not our topic. But the problems for the theory of relevance (NS3) below carry over straightforwardly to many reliable indicator theories. Also, there is a problem similar to the generality problem concerning "the mechanism" that produces a given belief. When a visual judgment relies on only black-and-white discrimination, is the person's whole visual apparatus the relevant mechanism, or is it the black-and-white sensitive portion of that apparatus, or is it only the active part of that portion? Does "the mechanism" for remembered beliefs include parts of the brain active in forming the belief, or just parts active in storing it and recovering it? These questions may have answers that are attractive to reliabilists, but as with the generality problem, the challenge is to identify a principle that implies all and only the correct answers to such questions.

[7]The results of this theory may be implausible in "demon worlds" in which a demon sees to it that believing in accord with one's evidence does not reliably lead to truths. Whether this is a decisive objection to this version of reliabilism depends in part on how reliability is measured. The objection as it is often described makes the challengeable assumption that a process is reliable in a world only if it regularly leads to truths in that world. In contrast, see for instance William Alston's proposal, stated as (R) above. It does not imply that unreliability in a demon world entails a lack of justification. What (R) makes decisive is roughly the truth-ratio of belief-production in more typical situations.

[8]"What Is Justified Belief?" pp. 10–11.

[9]"How to Think About Reliability," pp. 13f.

[10]Charles Wallis, "Truth-Ratios, Process, Task, and Knowledge," *Synthese* 98 (1994): 243–269. See especially p. 266. Wallis relies on belief-forming strategies as part of his response to problems that he discusses for reliability theories of knowledge. It is not clear that he is attempting to solve the generality problem that is the topic of this essay. One reason for this unclarity is that Wallis is working on a concept of knowledge that is relativized to the specification of a task, unlike the traditional concept which is our topic. In any case, we do not intend to attribute to him a simple reliance on strategies as a full solution.

[11]What follows is a possible solution to the generality problem, suggested by some of Alston's language, that merits a brief look. It is not what Alston proposes. His proposals will be taken up shortly.

[12]In "What Is Justified Belief?" Goldman calls attention to a distinction between belief-forming processes that take beliefs as inputs and processes that form beliefs entirely on the basis of things other than beliefs. Defenders of reliabilism have not used this distinction in their efforts to solve the generality problem. Goldman's use of the distinction complicates the theory for good reason. But it does nothing to isolate relevant types. We see no gain in addressing here any of the more complicated versions of reliabilism that employ the distinction.

[13]Alston's and Baergen's implementations of this idea are discussed below. Goldman mentions this sort of approach in *Epistemology and Cognition*, p. 50.

[14]"How to Think About Reliability," p. 11.

[15]"How to Think About Reliability," Section VI.

[16]Philosophers often invoke examples in which beliefs result from blows to the head or tumors. It may be that such beliefs do not result from any *psychological* belief-forming process type. Perhaps the explanations of such beliefs must come from a different science or perhaps psychology must be inclusive enough to account for them too, simply because they are mental effects. If some beliefs lack any psychological cause, that would present a problem for (NS2), since even these beliefs can be assessed for justification, and hence they must have a relevant type.

[17]"How to Think About Reliability," p. 26.

[18]Throughout this section, when we speak of maximally specific functions or types, we mean the maximally specific *psychological* functions or types.

[19]*Epistemology and Cognition*, p. 50.

[20]Theories can differ over exactly what counts as the input. The process type could begin at the surface of the skin, or farther in at some point where conscious experience begins, or farther out in an external cause of the experience. Alston favors perceptual experiences as the initial step (pp. 12f). He does not defend this selection. No point made here depends on any particular beginning for the causal sequence that constitutes the process.

[21]Strictly speaking, the assumption may imply only that the "narrow" content of the beliefs resulting from a given relevant type will be the same. No point made here depends on the difference between narrow and broad content. Also, see note 16 above concerning the completeness of psychological explanation.

[22]It is safe to assume that many of our clear vivid experiences of complex ordinary things like trees are produced only by these same ordinary things in all situations of the sort we typically encounter. Holograms, hallucinations, and perfect pictures are, at most, highly atypical.

[23]One might think that the fact that Jones relies on unjustified background beliefs has some bearing on this example. That thought seems right. But (NS3) ignores this fact and suggests nothing about how to make use of it in defending a process reliabilist theory. See note 12.

[24]"Reliability and Justification," *The Monist* 68 (1985): 159–174. The example is discussed on pp. 164f.

[25]Ralph Baergen, *Contemporary Epistemology* (Harcourt Brace, Fort Worth, 1995), p. 99. Contrary to what Baergen says, Feldman does not assert that the processes are of the same type. He merely points out the undesirable consequence of the proposition that they are of the same type. It is notable that this sort of example shows that common sense process types, like the visual belief forming process, do not produce beliefs of equal justification even when relativized to a fully detailed specification of the external circumstances.

[26]*Contemporary Epistemology*, p. 100.

[27]*Contemporary Epistemology*, p. 100.

[28]Compare the water boiling example above. There seems to be no reason to think that the explanation at one level of generality is necessarily better than an explanation at any other level.

[29]*Knowledge and Belief* (Routledge, Chapman, and Hall, New York, 1992), Chapter VI.

[30]*Knowledge and Belief*, p. 169.

[31]*Knowledge and Belief*, pp. 141–142.

[32]For example, Schmitt says about an example that one constraint, which favors a broad relevant type, outweighs two others that favor a narrower type (p. 171). In another case, the existence of two constraints favoring a narrower type is said to outweigh one pointing in a different direction (p. 157).

[33]Schmitt does say that relevance is a "messy, more contextual affair" than some might think (p. 159).

[34]"The Simple Solution to the Problem of Generality," *Nous* 29 (1995): 501–515. The quotation is from p. 502.

[35]"The Simple Solution to the Problem of Generality," p. 502.

[36]Ernest Sosa suggests a contextualist response to the generality problem in *Knowledge in Perspective: Selected Essays in Epistemology* (Cambridge, Cambridge University Press, 1991). Sosa suggests in a programmatic way that relevant types are ones that can "be usefully generalized upon by us as the epistemic community of the believer" (p. 284). Sosa does not elaborate upon this idea, which is a small part of a complex theory. What he does say does not seem to identify a unique type, since multiple types may be "usefully generalized upon."

[37]Although the following thesis is suggested by much of what Heller writes, it goes beyond the explicit proposals in Heller's paper. Also, it makes no use of passages suggesting that a relevant alternatives approach to a theory of knowledge solves the generality problem. We see no plausibility in this latter suggestion on its own, and no way incorporate into it the central theme of Heller's paper concerning the importance for solving the generality problem of the context-sensitivity of "reliable."

[38]An earlier version of this paper was presented at a symposium at the American Philosophical Association in December 1996. We are grateful to William Alston for his comments. We are also grateful to Ralph Baergen and John Bennett for comments on earlier drafts.

VI.5 A Defense of Internalism

MATTHIAS STEUP

Matthias Steup is professor of philosophy at St. Cloud State University. He is
the author of several works in epistemology, including *An Introduction to
Contemporary Epistemology* (1996). Here is his abstract.

In this paper I present and defend an account of epistemic justification
that is internalist, deontological, and evidentialist. According to my account,
epistemic justification is nearly always recognizable on reflection. This makes
it internalist. It is deontological because I take epistemic justification to be a
matter of epistemic duty fulfillment, and it is evidentialist because the content of our epistemic duties is to believe in accord with the evidence. I
defend this account against three objections: (1) Whether a belief is justified
or not is frequently not recognizable on reflection; (2) epistemic justification
cannot be a function of duty fulfillment because belief is involuntary; and (3)
deontological justification does not amount to genuine epistemic justification
because it is not truth-conductive.

Internalism and Direct Recognizability

In this paper I shall set forth what I take to be a
plausible version of internalism and defend it
against objections. According to internalism, the
things that make beliefs justified or unjustified—
"J-factors," as we may call them—must, in some
sense, be internal to the subject. The perhaps
strictest way to internalize J-factors is to limit them
to beliefs. My own view is that the constraint internalists place on J-factors is more plausibly construed in terms of cognitive accessibility. What
qualifies as a J-factor must be something that is
cognitively accessible to us in such a way that we
can always tell whether what we believe is justified
or not. Following Chisholm, then, I take internalism to be the view that J-factors must be *directly*
recognizable, that is, recognizable *on reflection*.[1]

I begin by trying to explain what I mean by
the phrase "recognizable on reflection." When we
recognize something on reflection, the knowledge
we obtain in this way is neither exclusively a priori
nor exclusively introspective. Rather, typically it
will be both a priori and introspective. Consider an
example. Suppose you are asking yourself whether
you're justified in believing that you had corn
flakes for breakfast. It's important not to misun-
derstand this question. The question is not
whether you *could* acquire the information needed
to believe justifiably that you had corn flakes for
breakfast. If you're not sure, perhaps you could
call somebody with whom you had breakfast and
acquire relevant information this way. Perhaps you
could find out some other way. But that's not
what you are interested in when you ask yourself
that question. Rather, what you're interested in is
this: Am I *now, given the knowledge and justified
background beliefs I have in this situation*, justified
in believing that I had corn flakes for breakfast? To
answer this question, you may make use of everything you can know and justifiably believe at the
time denoted by "now."

You might make use of what you now remember about today's morning, of the visual images
you can recall from when you were having breakfast, and of bits of conversation you may have had
during breakfast. If you thus appeal to your memories, the knowledge you obtain through reflection will be, at least in part, introspective. But
reflection is likely to involve an a priori element as
well. You might consider what logical and epistemic connections obtain between what you can
now remember about this morning and the belief

---

in question, and appeal to general principles about these connections. And if we assume that epistemic principles, if known, are known a priori, it follows that reflection involves an a priori element whenever an appeal to epistemic principles is involved. Reflection, then, is a process that is typically both introspective and a priori: introspective because access to J-factors such as memorial and perceptual states is introspective and a priori because, as internalists assume, epistemic principles are knowable only a priori.

The question "Am I now justified in believing that *p*?" is relative, then, to a certain body of information, the content of which is fixed by the temporal indexical "now." Once the relevant body of information changes, the reference of "now" changes, and the question becomes a different one. It follows from this that the question can indeed be answered *only* through reflection. Suppose you do call somebody up who had breakfast with you and ask that person what you were having this morning when you had breakfast together. Obviously, whether you are justified in believing "I had corn flakes for breakfast" *after* that phone call is a different question than the question of whether you were justified in believing this *before* the phone call. Thus, if you ask the question before the phone call, and then try to answer it by making the phone call, you are really confusing two different questions:

1. Am I now justified in believing I had corn flakes for breakfast?
2. Did I have corn flakes for breakfast?

Though these two question are quite similar, they differ in one important respect: You can answer (2), but not (1), by acquiring further relevant information. You can answer (2) by asking somebody else and receiving information you did not have before you asked. But you cannot answer (1) by receiving information you do not have at the time you're asking the question. Rather, (1) can only be answered on the basis of what you can know and justifiably believe at the time denoted by "now."

According to the kind of internalism I shall defend, then, the things that render beliefs justified or unjustified must be recognizable on reflection. They must be such that you do not need to gather further information, let alone launch an empirical research program, to become aware of them. According to this view, *wishful thinking* is among the things that qualify as J-factors. When a belief of yours is rendered unjustified because it's grounded in wishful thinking, you can tell this because there are two things you can recognize on reflection: (1) My belief is grounded in wishful thinking; (2) beliefs grounded in wishful thinking are unjustified. A second example: *Perceptual experiences* are among the things that qualify as J-factors. When a belief of yours is justified by an undefeated perceptual experience, you can tell that it is justified because there are, once again, two things you can recognize on reflection: (1) My belief is supported by an undefeated perceptual experience; (2) beliefs that are supported in this way are justified. A third example: According to internalism, the *reliability* of cognitive processes does not qualify as a J-factor. Whether your beliefs are produced by reliable cognitive processes is not always recognizable on reflection, for you might need further information to determine whether they are thus produced.

So internalism, as I understand it, is a view about the nature of justification: J-factors must be recognizable on reflection. When evaluating a belief's epistemic credentials at a certain time, what makes this belief either justified or unjustified must be *recognizable at that time*, that is, must be recognizable without having to rely on any information not available at that time. If J-factors are thus constrained, epistemic justification becomes transparent: Its presence or absence can nearly always be determined. Consequently, in advocating internalism, I take it that the following is true: For any proposition *p*, a rational person can nearly always recognize, on reflection, whether she is, or would be, justified in believing that *p*.[2]

Internalism and Deontology

My reason for placing a direct recognizability constraint on J-factors is that I take the concept of epistemic justification to be a *deontological* one. I believe that epistemic justification is analogous to moral justification in the following sense: Both kinds of justification belong to the family of deontological concepts, concepts such as permission, prohibition, obligation, blame, and responsibility.

An act that is morally justified is an act that is morally permissible, an act for which one cannot be justly blamed, or an act the agent was not obliged to refrain from performing. I conceive of epistemic justification in an analogous way. A belief that is epistemically justified is a belief that is epistemically permissible, a belief for which the subject cannot justly be blamed, or a belief the subject is not obliged to drop.[3]

If one takes the concept of epistemic justification to be a deontological one and thus takes epistemic justification to be a matter of individual responsibility, the internalist constraint that J-factors must be recognizable on reflection is pretty much an unavoidable consequence. In ethics, it is particularly clear, and, as Linda Zagzebski has pointed out, nearly unquestioned, that responsibility and duty fulfillment demand direct recognizability.[4] Thus, among ethical theories we do not find a straightforward analog to externalism in epistemology. No one defends the view that what makes an *action* morally justified or unjustified is something the agent cannot directly recognize.[5] Rather, what makes actions justified or unjustified must be, at least ordinarily, directly recognizable. Likewise, if epistemic justification is analogous to the justification of actions in being deontological, then what makes beliefs epistemically justified or unjustified must be, at least ordinarily, directly recognizable.

Even though there is then an undeniably close link between justification, duty fulfillment, and the recognizability of justification, I do not think the link is tight enough to warrant, in any obvious way, the conclusion that justification, moral or epistemic, is *always* directly recognizable. There are at least three types of cases in which, one could plausibly argue, justification, or the lack of it, cannot be recognized on reflection. First, there are cases of culpable ignorance. If there are certain things I ought to know but have either forgotten or never bothered to learn, then, so it might be argued, it is possible that, as a result of my ignorance, I do or believe certain things I am not justified in doing or believing—although, given my ignorance, this is not something I can recognize at the time in question. Second, it might be argued that, in both ethics and epistemology, there are certain cases of conflicting reasons where it is extremely hard to find out what one would be justified in doing or believing, cases in which one

might not be able to recognize at all what one would be justified in doing or believing. Third, one could argue that there are agents whose character, through moral and epistemic neglect, is so deformed that they simply cannot see their moral or epistemic failings.[6]

Now, I'm not sure that any of these cases provides us with a compelling reason to deny that justification, moral or epistemic, can always be recognized. Nevertheless, I shall grant the point in question and define internalism as the view that J-factors are *nearly* always recognizable, where the difference between "nearly always" and an unqualified "always" is determined by the extent to which the three cases in question actually occur. Internalism, even if qualified in this way, still differs significantly from externalism with regard to the extent to which epistemic justification is directly recognizable. For if the reliability of cognitive processes is included among the things that are J-factors (or is perhaps even viewed as the only J-factor), then situations in which justification is not directly recognizable are much more widespread than under the kind of internalism I am defending here.

Internalism and the Analysis of Knowledge

To appreciate the strength of the internalist position, it is essential to understand how internalists approach—indeed, must approach—the analysis of knowledge. Now, the analysis of knowledge can be carried out in two different ways: Some philosophers analyze knowledge by incorporating a condition specifically designed to handle the Gettier problem; some do not. Few epistemologists would object to the following two necessary conditions: What is known must be (1) true and (2) something that is believed. Beyond that, however, there is a lot of disagreement. I believe that, in addition to the truth and belief conditions, two more conditions are required: What is known must be a true belief that is (3) justified and (4) lacks the features that are definitive of Gettier-type situations. I shall use the term "degettierized" to refer to this fourth condition of knowledge.

Those epistemologists who dispense with the degettierization condition would say that, in addition to (1) and (2), only *one* further condition is needed. This condition will have to specify what "epistemizes" true belief, that is, what carries a true belief all the way toward knowledge. It will have to accomplish both of the things the justification condition and the degettierization condition are supposed to accomplish. Alvin Plantinga is one of those who favor the latter of these approaches.[7] He defines *warrant* as that which epistemizes true belief, and he thus views internalism as the view that warrant is essentially a matter of justification—typically, deontologically conceived. His own view is that epistemization is an external affair. Consequently, warrant—the property that epistemizes true belief—has nothing to do with justification.

Now, I do not take justification to be that which epistemizes true belief, and I don't think other internalists do. Rather, I take justification in conjunction with degettierization to be what epistemizes true belief because, unlike Plantinga, I think that the analysis of knowledge must include a degettierization condition. I would, therefore, agree with Plantinga that epistemization—the process that turns true belief into knowledge—is an external affair. And I think most other internalists would, too. After all, internalism about justification is to be distinguished from internalism about knowledge. For two reasons, the latter kind of internalism must be rejected. First, taking the concept of justification to be deontological justifies placing a direct recognizability constraint on justification. It does not justify placing this constraint on knowledge. Second, internalism about knowledge is untenable because two necessary conditions of knowledge are clearly external: truth and degettierization. It is obviously false that, with regard to any proposition *p,* I can nearly always find out on reflection whether *p* is true or not.[8] And whether a belief is degettierized or not (whether I am in a Gettier-type situation or not) is not recognizable on reflection either.

To see why the fourth condition of knowledge is external, consider a Gettier case. Suppose I look out my office window and see a squirrel climbing up a tree. This is nothing extraordinary, and I spontaneously believe "There's a squirrel out there." My belief is justified, for it is based on undefeated perceptual evidence. Alas, what I take

to be a squirrel is a hologram projected by a crazy professor from the Electrical Engineering Department. This hologram is so perfect that, without close examination, it would be impossible to tell that it's not a real squirrel but just a clever squirrel-like image. Suppose further there's actually a squirrel out there, but it is sitting quietly behind a large branch, and I can't see it from my current vantage point. My belief, then, is not only justified but also true, for there really is a squirrel out there. Yet it isn't knowledge. Now, can I tell on reflection that my present situation involves a factor that stands in the way of knowledge? Obviously not. If I were to reflect on whether or not I know there's a squirrel out there, I would have no reason at all to conclude that I do not know.[9]

This point will apply to all Gettier cases, irrespective of their specific features. For by definition, Gettier cases are cases in which there is an element hidden from me: My belief is true just because of some lucky accident. Suppose this element was not hidden from me. Suppose it was either known to me or recognizable on reflection. Well, this couldn't be reconciled with an essential feature of Gettier cases: What I believe must be justified. But if the justification condition is met, then that element—whatever it is—by virtue of which my belief is merely accidentally true must not be directly recognizable to me at the time in question. So if one is in a Gettier case, one can't tell on reflection that this is so. And since being in a Gettier case is something that can happen, it follows that whether the fourth condition—the degettierization condition—is met or not is not always directly recognizable.[10]

I take it, then, that knowledge involves two internal and two external conditions. The two internal conditions are belief and justification.[11] The two external conditions are truth and degettierization. Externalists take knowledge to be less internal than that. Extreme externalists might say that none of the necessary conditions of knowledge is internal. Moderate externalists might acknowledge the internal nature of belief but deny that epistemic justification is deontological and thus internal. Now, as I pointed out above, to justify this denial, Plantinga's point—turning true belief into knowledge is an external matter—will not suffice, for internalists do not contest this point. Rather, when externalists attempt to demonstrate that justification is not internal, they must try to show that turning a *true and degetierized* belief into knowledge is an external matter. And to show this, they would have to establish that deontological justification is not a necessary condition of knowledge. But if we take into account what, according to the kind of internalism I advocate, deontological justification amounts to, we will see that it is not easy to establish this.

With regard to the content of our epistemic duties, internalists can take a variety of different positions. Since I cannot go into a discussion of their respective merits, I shall merely indicate what I take to be the most plausible view. Our epistemic duty is to believe in accord with our evidence: believe p only if p is supported by our evidence, disbelieve p only if p is contradicted by our evidence, and suspend judgment about p if our evidence neither supports nor contradicts p. Now, does a person's evidence meet the internalist constraint that J-factors be recognizable on reflection? This depends on what we count as evidence. In my view, what qualifies as evidence is the following: perceptual, introspective, memorial states and states of rationally comprehending abstract matters, such as conceptual, arithmetical, or geometric connections, and of course beliefs. Items such as these qualify as J-factors, for whether or not they obtain is directly recognizable.

If we view internalism in this way, then the assertion that deontological justification is not a necessary condition of knowledge amounts to the following claim: It's possible to know something without directly recognizable supporting evidence. On the face of it, this seems to be an implausible view. Nevertheless, there is space for discussion here. After all, little children, cats, and dogs can plausibly be said to have knowledge of their environment. And if we study the behavior of rats, earthworms, and amoebas, it would appear that knowledge can be attributed even to rather primitive organisms. But surely, when we talk about rats, earthworms, and amoebas, the idea that such creatures can have directly recognizable evidence is rather far-fetched. And thus it would appear that knowledge without justification—that is, without the kind of justification that depends on having evidence—is possible after all.[12]

My reply to this objection is that, in my philosophical concern with knowledge, what I am interested in is not the kind of knowledge exemplified by higher and lower animals, but rather the kind of

knowledge *humans* are capable of having. And that kind of knowledge is, I take it, qualitatively different from the kind of knowledge attainable by rats, earthworms, and amoebas. It is what Ernest Sosa calls "reflective" knowledge: the kind of knowledge that can itself become the object of knowledge. Humans can evaluate their evidence, assess whether or not what they believe is justified, and thus come to recognize when they know and when they do not. Little children and animals can't do that. Their response to their environment is, as Sosa would put it, "thermometer-like."[13] They can register features of their environment, but they do not have any capacity for discriminating between justified and unjustified beliefs and cases of knowledge and of ignorance. Reflective knowledge, then, is beyond their ken, for they can't attain knowledge of their epistemic states. But it is that kind of knowledge—knowledge that can be recognized *as* knowledge—that, according to internalism, requires the kind of justification that involves both epistemic duty fulfillment and having evidence.[14]

The kind of internalism I am defending, then, can be summarized thus. Epistemic justification is the kind of justification that, when it comes in a sufficiently high degree, turns a true and degetierized belief into reflective knowledge. It is deontological and evidentialist in nature and nearly always directly recognizable. In the remainder of this paper, I shall address three objections to this account: (1) It is false that epistemic justification is nearly always directly recognizable; (2) epistemic justification is not deontological because belief is not under our voluntary control; and (3) epistemic justification is not deontological because it is not truth-conducive.

Evidentialism, Deontology, and Direct Recognizability

Let us compare internalism, as I conceive of it, with one version of externalism: reliabilism. First, reliabilism is not a deontological view. According to it, whether one's beliefs are justified does not depend on epistemic duty fulfillment but on whether one's beliefs are produced by reliable cognitive processes. Second, reliabilism is opposed to internalism with regard to the recognizability of epistemic justification: J-factors need not be directly recognizable. Third, reliabilism is not evidentialist: If reliable belief production is both necessary and sufficient for justified belief, then having evidence is neither necessary nor sufficient for epistemic justification.

Reliabilists, then, reject my view that we can nearly always tell whether what we believe is justified or not. It seems to me, however, at bottom, our disagreement about the recognizability of justification is really indicative of another, more fundamental disagreement. I don't wish to dispute that, *if* we think about epistemic justification the way *reliabilists* do, there are plenty of cases in which it's not directly recognizable whether what one believes is justified or not. And that's because reliabilists reject deontology and evidentialism, which I endorse. Likewise, reliabilists should agree that, *if* we think about epistemic justification as being deontological and evidentialist, then there are much fewer cases in which it's not directly recognizable whether what one believes is justified or not. The recognizability of epistemic justification is a function of what makes beliefs justified or unjustified, and since internalists and externalists disagree about that, they of course disagree about the extent to which epistemic justification is directly recognizable.

Externalists might argue, however, that even granting deontology and evidentialism, internalists are too optimistic about direct recognizability. In other words, internalism suffers from incoherence: the internalist constraint that J-factors must nearly always be directly recognizable is inconsistent with deontology and evidentialism, since the latter two features allow in fact for massive failure of direct recognizability.

To substantiate this challenge, externalists would have to argue that at least one of the following two types of cases frequently occurs: (1) cases in which one has evidence *for p* without being able to recognize that one has evidence *for p*; (2) cases in which one has evidence *against p* without being able to recognize that one has evidence against *p*. Above, I indicated that internalists might be willing to concede the existence of certain cases in which justification is not directly recognizable. Externalists could try to show that there are even more such cases than one might think initially, thus bit by bit expanding the extent to which epistemic justification is not directly recognizable.

I don't think it likely this project will meet with success. Any such case must be, as I explained above, a case premised on deontology and evidentialism, or else the disagreement about it will merely be a reflection of an underlying, deeper disagreement about the nature of epistemic justification. But as long as externalist critics work within the constraints of deontology and evidentialism, I don't think it will be easy for them to succeed in producing cases in which a belief's justificational status is not directly recognizable. It won't be easy for them because direct recognizability is *built into* the concept of *having evidence*. Evidence that's not directly recognizable simply is not evidence a person has. It is not a person's epistemic duty to believe in accord with such evidence (evidence there is but which one does not have), and thus such evidence is irrelevant with regard to a belief's justificational status. In short, if we understand evidentialism to be the view that a belief is justified if and only if the subject meets her epistemic duty by *having* (undefeated) evidence for that belief and if we agree that evidence not directly recognizable is not evidence one has, then it will be difficult indeed to describe possible cases that are consistent with deontology and evidentialism but are cases in which epistemic justification or the lack of it is not directly recognizable.

Deontological Justification and Doxastic Involuntarism

According to William Alston, having justified beliefs cannot be a matter of epistemic duty fulfillment because beliefs are not under our voluntary control. His argument can be summed up thus:

1. If a belief is deontologically justified or unjustified, it is under the subject's voluntary control.

2. Beliefs are never under our voluntary control.

3. Therefore, beliefs are never deontologically justified or unjustified.

Let's begin with a preliminary point. I grant that beliefs are never under our *direct* voluntary control. Doing *x* is under my direct voluntary control when a mere act of will suffices to do *x*. For example, raising my arm is under my direct voluntary control; turning on the light is not. It is, however, indirectly under my voluntary control. I can get up and flip the switch, which I can bring about through a series of bodily motions each of which is under my direct voluntary control. Now, if the argument were concerned merely with direct voluntary control; it would have to be rejected immediately. Obviously, for an action to be deontological justified or unjustified, it need not be under our direct voluntary control. Why, then, should we place a much stricter condition on deontological justification with regard to belief?

What is at issue, rather, is *indirect* voluntary control. But is it true that belief is never under our indirect voluntary control? More than just a few epistemologists think it is.[15] I must confess that I find this quite baffling, for I think there is no question at all that we do enjoy a great deal of indirect control over what we believe. Consider unjustified beliefs. To say that we don't have even indirect control over unjustified beliefs is to say that, at those times when we have an unjustified belief, there is nothing we can do to get rid of it. This, I think, is clearly false. We can assess the epistemic credentials of what we believe; we can weigh the evidence. Since this is something we can do, it is within our power, at least a good deal of the time, to recognize that what we believe is unjustified and, on the basis of such reflection, to quit believing what we unjustifiably believe.

Unfortunately, Alston's argument is not effectively rebutted by pointing this out. Opponents of deontology might as well grant that unjustified beliefs are frequently under our indirect voluntary control, for it seems fairly clear, at least initially, that most of our justified beliefs are *not* under our indirect voluntary control. Consider, for example, perceptual beliefs about our environment. If you see that it's raining and thus believe that it's raining, you're simply stuck with that belief. The same point can be made about the entire array of beliefs that are grounded in excellent sensory, memorial, introspective, or intuitional evidence. Such beliefs can quite plausibly be thought of as involuntary. And if they are indeed involuntary, it would then seem to follow that at best only *some* of our beliefs are deontologically justified or unjustified. But that's a disastrous consequence. It would mean that the type of theory I'm defending here is of very limited applicability and thus relevance.

It seems to me there are two effective ways to rebut Alston's argument. To begin with, Richard Feldman challenges the first premise. Granting that *moral* obligations require voluntary control, he points out that not all types of obligation are like moral obligations in this respect. For example, one can have a legal obligation to repay a debt even when one is unable to do this. Why, then, should we think that epistemic obligation is analogous to moral obligation? Given that there are many different types of obligation, and that not all of these require voluntary control, wouldn't it be more plausible to assume that, with regard to voluntary control, there is an important disanalogy between moral and epistemic obligation?[16]

I agree with Feldman that the first premise ought to be challenged, but, unlike Feldman, I am inclined to argue that not even moral obligation demands voluntary control—at least if by voluntary control we mean what Alston means by that concept. According to Alston, I have voluntary control over doing x at t if and only if, at t, I can do x and refrain from doing x.[17] If this is what we mean by voluntary control, then I think it is not at all clear that we can have a moral obligation to do x only if we have voluntary control over doing x.

Consider an example: Picture yourself at your favorite restaurant having dinner. At the table next to you, there is somebody who bothers you by talking and laughing in an overly loud manner. Now, let's grant that you are morally obliged to refrain from sticking your knife into that person's hand. According to the thesis in question, for you to be under this obligation, it must be the case that you *can* stick a knife in his hand. But can you? I do not mean to deny that, under certain circumstances, you can. But can you in the situation I am asking you to consider? And in the situation I'm asking you to consider, although you clearly are bothered by the man, you do not harbor violent emotions toward him. You don't feel even the slightest impulse to get up, take your knife, and drive it into the man's hand. Let's say, then, that you have absolutely no reason *for* sticking a knife in the unpleasant guest's hand and indeed plenty of decisive moral and prudential reasons *against* it. Could you, notwithstanding these reasons, get up and do so anyhow? I do not think there is a coherent account of what would be going on if, *under exactly the circumstances we are imagining*, you got up and stuck a knife in the man's hand.

Whatever that sort of behavior would be, it would not be an *action* of yours. And if it was an action, it would not take place exactly under the circumstances we are imagining.[18]

The significance of the knife example is this: You are morally obliged to refrain from sticking a knife in the man's hand although this is something you couldn't do anyhow in the situation in question. Examples like this one, as well as others, show that it's a mistake to assume that deontological status—an action or a belief's being permissible, forbidden, or obligatory—depends on voluntary control over it, where voluntary control over doing x at t requires of the subject that she can, at t, do x and refrain from doing x.[19] Yet I do not wish to dismiss the intuition that deontological status and voluntary control are conceptually linked. Let us therefore explore whether we can conceive of voluntary control in some other way.

It seems to me that, when we use the concept of voluntary control in its ordinary sense, sticking a knife in a person's hand is just the sort of thing over which we do take ourselves to have voluntary control. So what we really mean by "voluntary control" is perhaps not the ability to act in a certain way and refrain from acting in that way *at one and the same time*, but rather the ability to act in a certain way, or to refrain from acting in that way, depending on which way of acting is supported by our reasons. On this view, voluntary action is action that is responsive to our reasons.[20]

To make sense of this, consider again the situation in the restaurant. According to our ordinary view of things, it's unproblematic to say you are obliged to refrain from sticking a knife in the man's hand because we assume that it's under your voluntary control to do that sort of thing or not. And by that latter claim, we mean that you can stick a knife in the man's hand in response to a reason to do so and that you can refrain from sticking a knife in the man's hand in response to a reason to refrain from doing so. On this account, sticking a knife in somebody's hand is an action that's under my voluntary control if I can perform it, or refrain from performing it, in response to reasons for or against performing it.

I am sympathetic toward this concept of voluntary control.[21] However, if this is what we mean by that concept, the second premise of the argument displayed above must be rejected. If voluntariness does indeed consist in responsiveness to

reasons, then it would be rather odd to maintain that, while what we *do* is under our voluntary control, what we *believe* is not. Consider again what we mean when we identify voluntariness with responsiveness to reasons and take sticking a knife in somebody's hand to be under our voluntary control. What we mean is this: Should I have a suitable reason, it is the sort of thing I can do. Now, this might be otherwise. Perhaps my fear of blood or my inhibition to harm somebody is so great that I couldn't stick a knife in somebody's hand even if I had an extremely good reason to do so. In that case, sticking a knife in a person's hand is not the sort of thing over which I have voluntary control. But if I am not that kind of a person, if I can indeed respond to suitable reasons for sticking a knife in somebody's hand by going ahead and doing it, then it is something that is under my voluntary control.

Now consider a belief that is as a good a candidate for the status of being involuntary as any: my belief that it's raining when I see that it's raining. When we consider this belief, it certainly looks as though we do not have voluntary control over it. It did not come about as the result of a decision, nor could I effectively decide to drop this belief. The impression of involuntariness, however, arises only if we apply a different yardstick: if, now that we are considering *belief* instead of *action*, we switch from our current concept of voluntary control back to our previous one. Let us refer to voluntary control as defined by Alston as *narrow* and to the modified concept I subsequently introduced as *broad*. In the situation we are considering—I see and thus believe that it's raining—I do *not* enjoy narrow voluntary control over the belief that it's raining. But we agreed already that making deontological status dependent on narrow voluntary control is too restrictive, at least as far as action is concerned. Now, I do not think there is any justification for treating deontological status differently for actions and beliefs, to require merely broad voluntary control for deontological status of actions but narrow voluntary control for deontological status of belief. Let us therefore reconsider the voluntariness of my belief "It's raining," making sure that the concept of voluntary control we are working with is not narrow but broad.

The question, then, is the following: Can I, in response to suitable reasons, refrain from believing that it's raining when I take myself to see that it's raining? I don't see any reason to assume that I couldn't. For example, if I see that it's raining but then come to learn from a reliable source that under the present circumstances I am very likely to hallucinate that it's raining, I might drop this belief. My belief that it's raining, then, is a belief I can retain or drop in response to reasons for or against retaining it. Hence, it is a belief over which I have—in an indirect way—voluntary control. Of course, it could be otherwise. My ability to drop this belief in response to suitable reasons might be impeded by a funny drug, hypnosis, a brain lesion, and other bizarre phenomena. If this were the case, my belief that it's raining would be involuntary. Absent such bizarre phenomena, however, I am perfectly capable of responding to a suitable reason by dropping this belief. Thus, according to our revised concept of voluntariness, whether or not to believe it's raining is something that is indirectly under my voluntary control.

Note that treating the voluntariness of belief in this way is analogous to the way we treated the voluntariness of actions above. As long as you do not have any good reason for sticking a knife in somebody's hand, you can't do it. But suppose you are supplied with a pretty good reason to do that sort of thing. Well, if in *that* case you can do it, then you have voluntary control over whether or not to stick a knife in somebody's hand. Likewise, if you can stop believing that it's raining when supplied with a suitable reason, then you have voluntary control over whether or not to believe that it's raining.

If we conceive of voluntary belief as belief that is responsive to our reasons, the extent of involuntary belief will be rather small. What can prevent us from adjusting our beliefs to our reasons are things like the following: brain lesions, phobias, neurotic compulsions and inhibitions, various forms of paranoia, the effects of drugs, and other similar things. Things like that, when present and causally active in the right way, render beliefs as well as actions involuntary. But under normal circumstances, we act and form beliefs in response to the reasons we have and modify our behavior and change our beliefs when our reasons change. Under normal circumstances then, our beliefs are just as voluntary as our actions.[22]

The upshot of my discussion is that advocates of the involuntarism argument face a dilemma.

They must base their argument either on Alston's narrow concept of voluntary control or on the broad conception I outlined above, or something similar to it. Depending on which alternative they prefer, either the argument's first or second premise must be considered dubious. I do not think, therefore, that the argument from doxastic involuntarism amounts to an obstacle to deontological accounts of epistemic justification.

Deontological Justification and Truth-Conduciveness

According to Alston, there is a second reason why epistemic justification is not deontological. Deontological justification is not truth-conducive. It does nothing toward turning true beliefs into knowledge and thus does not amount to epistemic justification.[23] This point, Alston argues, can be established by considering a case of cultural isolation. Here's an account of the kind of case Alston has in mind. Imagine a tribe whose members engage in doxastic habits that are not conducive to the acquisition of knowledge. Beliefs formed as the result of these habits have no tendency to be true. To the extent they are true, this is just a matter of luck. Consequently, the beliefs under consideration are not epistemically justified. They could never amount to knowledge. According to Alston, however, they are deontologically justified, for the tribe members cannot be blamed for they way they form their beliefs. This is so because in this tribe traditional intellectual practices are never critically questioned. Nor has the tribe, through contact with other cultures, ever been externally exposed to criticism of its intellectual procedures. Given these circumstances, the tribe members, according to Alston, are blame free.

How does Alston's cultural isolation objection raise a problem for internalism? Obviously, even if Alston were right about the type of case he has in mind, his objection would not establish that deontological justification is not necessary for knowledge. Even if it were true that deontologically justified beliefs fall sometimes short of being knowledge, it wouldn't follow that there are cases of knowledge without deontological justification. Nevertheless, the objection has bite. Alston's point, I take it, is not that occasionally deontological justification falls short of being epistemic justification. Rather, the point of his example is to highlight a general phenomenon: Deontological justification does nothing toward epistemization. It is true that deontologically justified beliefs are often also epistemically justified. But when this is so, it's not the case that these beliefs are epistemically justified *because* they are deontologically justified. Rather, the former status is an unrelated concomitant of the latter status. Now, if this is true, then we must wonder why deontological justification should be necessary for knowledge. Presumably, what enters into the analysis of knowledge as a necessary condition ought to be something that, in one way or another, contributes to the process the result of which is knowledge. So, if deontological justification does not contribute at all to that process, one may legitimately have doubts about its place in the analysis of knowledge.

I do not think, however, that Alston's cultural isolation case establishes the point in question. First of all, Alston does not mention any specific beliefs that are formed as a result of the epistemically questionable doxastic habits. Nor does he explain exactly which epistemically questionable practices lead to the beliefs that, according to him, are deontologically justified but do not enjoy genuine epistemic justification. This leaves his objection a bit vague and nebulous, and I suspect there is a reason for this. Once we attempt to pin down the kind of beliefs Alston has in mind and fill in all the details required for explaining why such beliefs are deontologically justified without having what genuine epistemizing justification requires, we will see that it's not at all easy to give a specific example of the case Alston has in mind.

According to Alston, deontological justification depends on what can reasonably be expected of one.[24] Keeping this in mind, let's consider some candidates for beliefs that do not enjoy genuine epistemic justification but might be deontologically justified. First, suppose the tribe members engage in *wishful thinking*. Now, are there conceivable circumstances under which it cannot be reasonably expected of an adult capable of rational thinking to avoid wishful thinking? I don't think so. Any adult capable of rational thought can see that, when the objective is knowledge, wishful thinking is not a good way of meeting this objective. To put the matter the other way around, if I

were to encounter an adult who does not see that wishful thinking is an unsuitable means of acquiring knowledge, I would have to wonder whether that person is fully rational.

Second, suppose the tribe members engage in *generalizing from small and nonrepresentative samples*. Here I am prepared to make the same point: It can reasonably be expected of fully rational adults to see that truth seeking and the pursuit of knowledge impose the duty to avoid such a doxastic practice. The same applies to doxastic conduct such as *jumping to conclusions, trusting false authorities*, and *ignoring relevant background information*. Indeed, I think it applies to *whatever* renders beliefs epistemically unjustified. I do not think it is therefore possible to construe cases in which deontological justification diverges from the kind of justification that contributes to the process of epistemization. There cannot be divergence here because the connection between the pursuit of truth and knowledge, and the doxastic practices conducive to that goal is *transparent*. Any adult fully capable of rational thought can see which doxastic conduct is instrumental in reaching this goal and which doxastic conduct is not. Consequently, there are no cases in which a subject enjoys, in believing that *p*, deontological justification vis-à-vis the goal of attaining knowledge, but is at the same time not epistemically justified in believing that *p*.[25]

Reliabilists will not accept my position on this matter. According to them, for a belief to be justified it must be based on a reliable ground.[26] And whether a belief is based on a reliable ground is something that is frequently not recognizable on reflection. Hence, from the reliabilist point of view, it can easily happen that a belief is deontologically but not epistemically justified. I think, however, that it is not only unnecessary but indeed counterintuitive to place a reliability constraint on justification. It seems to me that this constraint is motivated by the expectation that epistemic justification—when things go right—turns beliefs into knowledge. And since a belief based on an unreliable ground cannot amount to knowledge, justification must involve reliability.

This line of reasoning, however, is not compelling. Its intuitive appeal arises from the conceptual link between knowledge and reliability. I accept this link. Without reliability there can't be knowledge. But from this link, it doesn't follow that reliability has to enter into the analysis of knowledge via the justification condition. After all, there is an alternative. Reliability could—and I think should—enter the analysis of knowledge through the fourth condition, whose job is to degettierize justified true belief.[27] It is therefore possible to retain reliability within the analysis of knowledge without imposing it as a necessary condition on justification.

Conclusion

In this paper, I have tried to defend an approach to epistemology that is deontological, evidentialist, and internalist. This approach, it seems to me, successfully withstands the objections externalists have raised against it. Moreover, as I have indicated in the previous paragraph, it can be defended against externalist objections without dismissing the intuitive appeal behind these objections. The intuitive appeal of externalism lies in the fact that knowledge is to a large extent external. One way of doing justice to its externality is to make epistemic justification an external affair. This, I think, is preserving one important intuition by sacrificing another: the intuition that justification is, by its very nature, an internal matter.[28] It would be better to preserve both of these intuitions. And both of them are preserved when we combine an internalist justification condition with an externalist degettierization condition.[29] This is, in my opinion, the right approach to analyzing knowledge.[30]

Notes

[1]For passages in which Chisholm expresses his internalist point of view, see Roderick Chisholm, *Theory of Knowledge*, 2d ed. (Englewood Cliffs, NJ: Prentice Hall, 1977), p. 17; and *Theory of Knowledge*, 3d. ed. (Englewood Cliffs, NJ: Prentice Hall, 1989), pp. 62, 76.

[2]What I have said about recognizing justification on reflection amounts to no more than a brief sketch. Adequate treatment of this topic would call for a full-length paper.

[3]For statements of the deontological view of epistemic justification, see Chisholm, *Theory of Knowledge*, 2d ed., p. 14; Carl Ginet, *Knowledge, Perception, and Memory* (Dordrecht: Reidel, 1975) p. 28, and Laurence BonJour, *The Structure of Empirical Knowledge* (Cambridge, MA: Harvard University Press, 1985), p. 8.

[4]See Linda Zagzebski, *Virtues of the Mind: An Inquiry into the Nature of Virtue and the Ethical Foundations of Knowledge* (Cambridge: Cambridge University Press, 1996), pp. 41ff.

[5]The point in question is that in ethics it is hard to find an externalist theory of moral *justification*. With regard to moral *rightness*, the situation is of course different. Certainly, straightforward construals of utilitarianism make an action's rightness epistemically external to the agent. But, it seems to me, even the hardiest consequentialists should acknowledge that, if an action's moral rightness is determined by its consequences, it's rightness cannot be the same thing as its status of being justified or unjustified, where this status is a matter of personal responsibility or duty fulfillment.

[6]For cases of that kind, see James Montmarquet, "Epistemic Virtue," *Mind 96* (1987).

[7]See Alvin Plantinga, *Warrant and Proper Function* (Oxford: Oxford University Press, 1993).

[8]This is so for two reasons. First, justification is fallible. Sometimes, I have perfectly good reasons to consider true what is in fact false. Under such circumstances, I cannot recognize on reflection that what I believe is not true but false. Second, there are numerous times when I just don't have enough evidence, or no evidence at all, to tell whether the proposition I'm considering is true. In such cases, I need more information, which is to say that I can't tell on reflection whether the proposition in question is true.

[9]This is not to say, of course, that I couldn't find out. But the point is that, in order to find out, I need further information. Without that further information, I cannot *now* tell that in fact I do not know.

[10]I am not, however, saying that it's *never* directly recognizable *whether* one is in a Gettier situation. For when one knows that *p,* one can directly recognize that, with regard to *p,* one is *not* in a Gettier situation.

[11]I'm inclined to say that we can nearly always tell, for a given proposition *p,* whether we believe *p* or not. Thus, I take belief to be an internalist concept. For doubts about the direct recognizability of belief, see Jaegwon Kim, *Philosophy of Mind* (Boulder, CO: Westview Press, 1996), p. 18.

[12]For an argument to the effect that knowledge does not require justification, see Alston's essay "Justification and Knowledge" in his *Epistemic Justification* (Ithaca, NY: Cornell University Press, 1989), pp. 172–182.

[13]See Ernest Sosa, *Knowledge in Perspective: Selected Essays in Epistemology* (Cambridge: Cambridge University Press, 1991), particularly "Reliabilism and Intellectual Virtue," pp. 131–145.

[14]I do not mean to suggest that knowing that one knows that *p* is necessary for reflective knowledge of *p.* This view would be much too restrictive. Rather, I conceive of human, or reflective, knowledge as the kind of knowledge

one has when knowing that one knows is an epistemic state the agent can attain.

[15] See, for example, Alston, *Epistemic Justification*, essays 4 and 5; Jonathan Bennett, "Why Is Belief Involuntary?" *Analysis 50* (1990), pp. 87–107; and Richard Feldman, "Epistemic Obligation," in *Philosophical Perspectives 2*, ed. James Tomberline (Atascadero, CA: Ridgeview, 1988).

[16] See Feldman, "Epistemic Obligation."

[17] See Alston, *Epistemic Justification*, p. 123.

[18] For a position on this matter similar to the one I am suggesting here, see Peter Van Inwagen "When Is the Will Free?" in T. O'Connor, ed. *Agents, Causes, and Events* (Oxford: Oxford University Press, 1985).

[19] Other examples: Can you stop making mortgage payments when you have no reason at all for doing so? Can you capriciously, without any reason (good or bad) whatever, refrain from teaching a class you are scheduled to teach?

[20] For a concept of voluntariness along these lines, see Bennett, "Why Is Belief Involuntary?"

[21] However, I do not wish to identify *free* action with voluntary action. Whether actions over which we have voluntary control are examples of free—causally undetermined —actions is a further question that I cannot address in the present context.

[22] A solution along these lines is set forth in Matthais Steup, *An Introduction to Epistemology* (Upper Saddle River, NJ: Prentice Hall, 1996), pp. 77ff.

[23] See Alston, *Epistemic Justification*, p. 95.

[24] See Alston, *Epistemic Justification*, p. 146.

[25] In reply to my argument that rational agents can always tell whether what they believe is justified by their evidence, Alston accuses me of cultural insensitivity. See Alston, *Epistemic Justification*, p. 146. His point is that, while the standards of epistemic justification do not vary from culture to culture, the standards of deontological justification do. But he merely asserts that they do. He does not provide examples to support his view. Thus, I am left wondering what he has in mind. Does he mean to suggest that, in some cultures, but not in others, agents have an epistemic duty to refrain from wishful thinking or jumping to conclusions? Exactly which epistemic duties are such that agents have them in some but not in other cultures? In the absence of such examples, I do not see that my own view is any more "insensitive" to cultural differences than Alston's own.

[26] See Alston's paper "Concepts of Epistemic Justification," in *Epistemic Justification*, pp. 81–114.

[27] I'm not suggesting, however, that a reliability requirement suffices to preclude Gettier cases. Rather, I believe the connection works the other way around. Whatever constraint has the effect of ruling out gettierization also has the effect of ensuring that the belief in question was formed in a reliable manner.

[28] This intuition finds its perhaps most forceful expression in the evil-demon challenge to reliabilism. In an evil-demon world, a world in which reality is radically different from what the inhabitants of this world take it to be, perception is an unreliable cognitive process. But isn't it counterintuitive to judge, based on this reason, that perceptual beliefs in this world are bound to be unjustified? For statements of the evil-demon objection to reliabilism, see Stewart Cohen, "Justification and Truth," *Philosophical Studies 46* (1984), pp. 281f.; and Carl Ginet, "Contra Reliabilism," *Monist 68* (1985), p. 178.

[29] Here, I can only assert the idea that the demand for reliability can be met in the degettierization condition. Its justification would have to be carried out elsewhere.

[30] I developed some of the ideas expressed in this paper when I was writing a commentary on Alvin Goldman's paper "Internalism Exposed." His paper and my commentary were presented at the Central Division Meeting of the American Philosophical Association in Pittsburgh, April 25, 1997. I wish to thank Goldman for an extended and stimulating e-mail correspondence on the internalism-externalism controversy. My own understanding of this issue was aided by his clear and incisive account of the problems internalists face. For helpful comments, I also wish to thank Carl Ginet.

VI.6 Naturalistic Epistemology and Its Critics

Hilary Kornblith

Hilary Kornblith is professor of philosophy at the University of Vermont and the author of several works in epistemology, including *Inductive Inference and Its Natural Ground* (1993) and "A Conservative Approach to Social Epistemology" (1994).

    In this essay Kornblith both surveys the debate between naturalistic and traditional approaches to epistemology and defends naturalism from its traditionalist critics. He outlines the naturalist criticism of traditional foundationalism, arguing that strong foundationalism simply fails to give us more than a "slight" set of secure beliefs and that the attempts to broaden foundationalism ends up with unimpressive results. Naturalism can preserve the basic goals of traditional epistemology: (1) to give us an account of what knowledge and justification are; (2) to extend our knowledge, meeting the skeptical challenge; and (3) to provide epistemic advice. He responds to criticisms that naturalism ignores the skeptic and normativity.

The naturalistic approach to epistemology has undergone substantial development in the last several years. Here I present the state of the art, as well as an account of the most important criticisms to date.

I

Let me begin with a few socio-historical remarks. One of the proximate causes of current interest in naturalistic epistemology traces to W. V. Quine's 1969 paper, "Epistemology Naturalized."[1] Quine there argued for a new approach to epistemological questions. Traditional epistemology, as Quine viewed it, was a failed research program. Philosophers from Descartes to the present day have sought to put knowledge on its "proper foundation." Showing that knowledge has a proper foundation would require a set of beliefs which enjoy a special epistemological status: Depending on one's preferred foundational view, these beliefs are certain, infallible, incorrigible, indubitable, prima facie justified, or the like. They are justified but not in virtue of their relations to other beliefs. For many philosophers, beliefs about one's own

sense experience were said to enjoy this special status. Other beliefs, if they are to be justified at all, must somehow derive their justification from foundational beliefs. A proper epistemological theory would give an account of the special property which foundational beliefs enjoy; it would demonstrate that an important class of beliefs actually have the preferred property; a set of epistemic principles, themselves enjoying a special epistemic status, would then be shown to be justification-transmitting; and these principles, when applied to the foundational beliefs, would generate the remainder of the class of justified beliefs. We could thereby show the extent of our knowledge, as well as, simultaneously, display its epistemic credentials.

    The foundationalist program is undeniably attractive. As practiced by Descartes, for example, it serves to unify a number of distinct epistemological projects. First, it gives us an account of what knowledge and justification are. Second, by showing that a large number of beliefs meet the appropriate epistemic standards, it demonstrates the extent of our knowledge and thereby provides a response to the skeptic. Third, it provides us with epistemic advice, i.e., a set of instructions to follow if we wish to be more accurate in arriving at our beliefs. Each of these projects seems, on its face, well worth pursuing. Foundationalism seems to provide a method for simultaneously addressing all three.

Reprinted from *Philosophical Topics*, vol. 23:1 (spring 1995) by permission.

Now Quine, as I've said, sees the history of epistemology up to 1969 as the history of a failed research program: Foundationalism has simply failed to deliver the goods.[2] The years since 1969 have not, to my mind, provided reasons for reversing Quine's verdict. Foundationalism has faced serious difficulties at every turn. The class of foundational beliefs has proven to be extremely elusive. Those who favor extremely strong requirements on foundations, such as incorrigibility or infallibility, have not clearly demonstrated that *any* beliefs at all meet the favored standard. At best, the class of beliefs meeting such requirements is so slight as to provide insufficient support for the vast majority of beliefs which, pretheoretically, seem to be justified. Those who favor very strong requirements on the foundations thus find themselves in a difficult situation: They must severely narrow the class of beliefs which are claimed to enjoy the special epistemological status; but in so doing, they thereby make far more difficult any attempt to respond to the skeptic on that basis. One might, at this point, simply embrace skepticism, but this is a very high price for holding on to the foundationalist account of knowledge and justification.

The obvious solution here is to weaken one's requirements on foundational belief. This makes far easier the project of deriving a substantial edifice of knowledge from the favored foundation, but the weaker the foundation, the less impressive the edifice. If foundational beliefs have very little going for them epistemically, the fact that we can derive lots of other beliefs from them tells us little of interest. Moreover, even foundational accounts placing weak requirements on the privileged class of beliefs have run into substantial difficulties in deriving an interesting superstructure of knowledge. So long as substantial constraints are placed on the principles by which the superstructure is derived, the task of providing a foundationalist reconstruction of knowledge proves extraordinarily difficult.

Now one might also loosen up the requirements on the epistemic principles by which the superstructure is derived. Once again, the looser these requirements, the less impressive is the fact that one can generate a large body of beliefs answering to them. But long before one starts loosening up on these requirements, it should start dawning on one that one's commitment to foundationalism is no longer doing a great deal of epistemological work. All of this loosening up of standards is driven by one's pretheoretical commitments—the view that, in the end, we do have a great deal of knowledge. But so long as we hold on to this pretheoretical commitment, foundationalism itself is not really addressing any of the three epistemological projects with which we began. The first project, saying what constitutes knowledge, is addressed only formally by foundationalism; all the content in one's account is now being driven by the desire to make our ordinary commitments meet whatever criteria we eventually endorse. The second project, answering the skeptic, has now been trivialized, because we are endorsing an account of knowledge in virtue of the very fact that it permits a response to skepticism. The ability to reject skepticism is not so much an interesting result—as it would have been for Descartes, had his project worked out—it is instead something which we built in from the beginning, a constraint on what we would even count as an adequate account of knowledge. Finally, the desire for substantive epistemic advice is shortchanged as well.[3] When our pretheoretical ideas about what we are justified in believing are put in the driver's seat, the only epistemic advice which results is to keep believing what we pretheoretically believed. The idea that epistemology might give us some instruction about how better to get at the truth is thereby abandoned.

If foundationalism is an idea which simply failed to work out, what should we put in its place? Quine's suggestion is enigmatic:

> [E]pistemology still goes on, though in a new setting and a clarified status. Epistemology, or something like it, simply falls into place as a chapter of psychology and hence of natural science.[4]

This suggestion of Quine's has seemed to many to amount to nothing more than changing the subject.[5] Epistemology has historically been interested in normative questions: What should we believe? Under what conditions are we justified in believing something? Psychology, on the other hand, seems to have no interest in such questions. Instead, it attempts to provide an accurate description of the mechanisms by which beliefs are produced, retained, and modified. But the descriptive enterprise, it seems, is no more a substitute for the normative one than an account of how people act is a substitute for a study of the right and the good. After all, people sometimes arrive at beliefs in ways which are just crazy. While it is perfectly appropriate for psychology to describe these and other ways of arriving at beliefs, without editorial comment, a proper epistemological theory must do more. Some have thus seen Quine's argument for naturalizing epistemology as little more than a non sequitur: Foundationalism was a bad solution to the normative questions epistemology traditionally asked; so we should stop asking those questions and do psychology instead.[6]

I do not wish to get involved here in the details of Quine exegesis, but this much, I believe, is quite safe to say. There are ways of interpreting Quine which do not have him offering obviously dreadful arguments; both good sense and charity, therefore, suggest that we should explore such interpretations. In particular, there are two aspects of Quine's program of naturalizing epistemology which we will need to examine: First, there is the rejection of the a priori and, along with it, the conception of epistemology as first philosophy; second, there is the idea that skeptical questions arise from within science. Let me say a bit about each of these.

Famously, Quine has argued for the rejection of the analytic-synthetic distinction and, with it, the very idea of a priori truth. One source of Quine's rejection of a priority is his holism: No statement is immune to rational revision; sufficiently large changes in our body of beliefs can force changes even in beliefs which appeared to be held independently of any empirical evidence. The notion of a priori truth is thus empty. But once we reject the idea of a priori truth, Descartes' conception of epistemology as first philosophy must be rejected as well. On Descartes' view, epistemology is logically prior to science. First, we must figure out how properly to arrive at our beliefs; this is the business of epistemology. It must be investigated independently of any of our empirical beliefs, for until we figure out how properly to arrive at such beliefs, the empirical beliefs we currently have, and upon which we might be tempted to rely in forming our epistemological theory, are nothing more than a potential source of misinformation. Once we have our epistemological theory in place, we may then put it to use in arriving at empirical beliefs. Epistemology thus precedes science; it tells us how science is properly done.

But if there are no a priori truths, then this conception of epistemology is misguided. Epistemology cannot precede science; it must, instead, be viewed as continuous with science. Moreover, as Quine argues, the very idea of responding to skepticism in the way Descartes envisioned misunderstands the skeptical problematic. Skeptical problems arise from within science. It is because science shows us how various aspects of our common-sense view of the world may be mistaken that we come to raise the question of whether we might be entirely mistaken in the way we view the world. But because this question arises from within science, it is perfectly appropriate to draw on the resources of science to answer it.

There are many ways in which this approach to epistemology might be filled out. What I want to do here is describe a project which flows naturally from the suggestions Quine made in "Epistemology Naturalized," a project which fits well with much of the research going on today under that heading. But before I turn to an account of a viable naturalistic project for epistemology, I will need to discuss another important influence on the development of naturalism: the work of Alvin Goldman.

II

Alvin Goldman's first paper in epistemology, "A Causal Theory of Knowing,"[7] appeared in 1967, and if one were to read it side by side with Quine's "Epistemology Naturalized," one might easily get the impression that Goldman's approach to epistemology and Quine's approach have nothing to do with one another. Goldman is engaged in a project of giving an analysis of the concept of knowledge; Quine rejects the very idea of conceptual analysis. Goldman, as he announces in his first paragraph, is moved by a desire to solve the Gettier problem; Quine has shown little interest in this problem.[8] Nevertheless, the project which Goldman inaugurated with "A Causal Theory of Knowing," while different from Quine's in nontrivial ways, also has deep affinities with Quinean naturalism.

Goldman proposed that knowledge that p is properly analyzed as belief that p caused by the fact that p. Thus, on this account, when I know that there is a table in front of me, my belief that there is such a table is caused by the fact that there is a table. Goldman revised and developed this account in "Discrimination and Perceptual Knowledge,"[9] identifying perceptual knowledge with true belief which is the product of a discriminatory capacity. To know that there is a table before one, one must be able to discriminate between situations in which there is a table and those in which no table is present. This account was then further developed to provide an account of justified belief: [10] A belief is justified just in case it is reliably produced, that is, just in case it is the product of a psychological process which tends to produce true beliefs.

Although Goldman was engaging in conceptual analysis, and in that respect was very much in tune with epistemologists of the sixties and seventies who had no sympathy whatsoever with naturalism, his proposed analyses of knowledge and justification nevertheless marked a radical break with tradition. On traditional accounts, a person is justified in holding a belief just in case a good argument for the belief is, in some suitable sense, available to that person.[11] Theorists disagreed about precisely what was to count as a good argument. On Goldman's view, however, a person is justified in holding a belief just in case the belief is produced in the right sort of way; the person in question need have no idea at all about how the belief is produced, nor need any sort of argument for the belief be available to the person. Being justified is a property some beliefs have in virtue of their causal history, not in virtue of the believer's grasp of some kind of justificatory argument.

It is this feature of Goldman's account which led many philosophers to suggest that Goldman was, not so much addressing traditional epistemological questions in a distinctive way, but rather changing the topic and ignoring the traditional questions. It is no coincidence that Goldman's account, like Quine's, tended to evoke this kind of response. But the similarity between the two is far deeper than that. If Goldman was changing the topic—and I will want to say something about that—then the direction in which Goldman was moving the focus of epistemological discussion was very similar to the direction in which Quine was also moving the focus of epistemological discussion.

Remember that on Quine's view, a proper naturalistic epistemology becomes "a chapter of psychology." Similarly, on Goldman's account, if we are to investigate the features of our beliefs in virtue of which they are justified, what is required is a detailed understanding of the psychological mechanisms by which our beliefs are produced.[12] Justified beliefs are ones which are produced by mechanisms which are well-adapted to the kinds of environments in which human beings tend to be found. The good-making features of these psychological mechanisms need not be such that they would tend to produce true beliefs in every possible world; rather, they need only be well-adapted to this world. Thus, for example, just as our perceptual mechanisms tend to provide us with a rich and accurate understanding of many features of the world around us, without being well-adapted to every possible environment, the appropriate approach to understanding human inference would have us examine the kinds of inferences which would allow for an accurate understanding of our world, not those inferences which could not help but provide an accurate understanding of any possible world. Carrying out Goldman's program would thus have us investigate the kinds of psychological mechanisms which are found in human beings and would have us examine the extent to which they operate well in human environments, providing an accurate understanding of the world.[13] This is, of course, a thoroughly empirical study.

Now this is not to say that Goldman and Quine would entirely agree on the proper conduct of epistemology. They would not. Goldman's epistemology still retains substantial connections with the tradition of conceptual analysis, a tradition which Quine entirely repudiates. On Goldman's view, conceptual analysis is the vehicle by which we are provided with an account of knowledge and justification. An understanding of which beliefs are justified, however, and an account of the ways in which our epistemic practice may be improved require careful empirical investigation. In addition, the kinds of psychology to which Goldman and Quine would assign a good deal of epistemological work are importantly different. On Goldman's view, it is cognitive science which will do the lion's share of the work here. Quine's deep skepticism about intentional notions, however, has him defer to a behaviorally oriented psychology.

In the end, however, what Goldman and Quine have in common is, to my mind at least, far more important than their differences. If they are even roughly right, then at least much of epistemology becomes an empirical discipline, continuous with the sciences. This marks a substantial change in how epistemology is done.

I will now turn to providing a sketch of how such an empirical epistemology might be carried out, together with an account of the relationship between this approach to epistemology and the kinds of concerns which, traditionally, have motivated epistemologists.

III

The kind of approach to epistemological questions I favor shares with Quine a skepticism about the very idea of conceptual analysis, but shares with Goldman a commitment to the research program of cognitive psychology. I see a proper naturalistic epistemology as empirical all the way down, and yet, at the same time, I believe that there is a great deal of continuity between any such epistemology and the traditional projects which have motivated epistemologists for centuries.

On my view, knowledge is a natural phenomenon, and it is this natural phenomenon that is the subject matter of epistemology—not the concept of knowledge, but knowledge itself. Analyzing our concept of knowledge, to the extent that we can make sense of such a project, is no more useful than analyzing the ordinary concept of, say, aluminum. The ordinary concept of aluminum is of little interest for two reasons. First, most people are largely ignorant of what makes aluminum the kind of stuff it is, and so their concept of aluminum will tell us little about the stuff itself. Second, most people have many misconceptions about aluminum, and so their concepts of aluminum will reflect this misinformation as well. There are interesting anthropological questions about the ordinary concept of aluminum, but precisely because this concept is as much a reflection of ignorance and misinformation as it is a reflection of anything about aluminum, those who have an interest in aluminum are ill-advised to study our concept of it.

Now the same may be said, I believe, of knowledge. Epistemologists ought to be interested in the study of knowledge itself. If we sub-

stitute a study of the ordinary concept of knowledge, we are getting at knowledge only indirectly; knowledge is thereby filtered through a good deal of ignorance about the phenomenon, as well as a good deal of misinformation. Better to examine the phenomenon of human knowledge in its natural setting and leave an examination of ordinary concepts to cognitive anthropology. The same may of course be said about justification and related epistemological notions.

The phenomenon of knowledge is ubiquitous. It may be found in simple perceptual situations, where an epistemic agent confronts a table in good light and in clear viewing conditions, as well as in the more complex interactions between agent and environment found in the scientific laboratory. I am assuming that there is a single phenomenon here to be studied, that these clear-cut cases of knowledge constitute a natural kind and not some grue-like hodgepodge or, like the class of individuals thought to be witches, a largely heterogeneous group whose few commonalities are entirely different from what they are ordinarily taken to be. If this assumption is mistaken, then the very idea of knowledge is based on a mistake, and it requires either elimination or radical revision. But the defeasibility of this project—its assumption that knowledge and justification and other allied epistemic notions constitute natural kinds—is not just a feature of a naturalistic epistemology; it is a feature of any epistemology whatsoever. If epistemic kinds are merely gerrymandered and grue-like, or if they presuppose a radically false theory and are witch-like, they thereby lose their interest. I see no reason to think, at the present time, that epistemic notions have this undesirable feature.

I will thus assume that, at least pretheoretically, there is a robust phenomenon of human knowing and that this phenomenon is susceptible to investigation. We may try to figure out what the phenomenon consists in; what it is that makes these cases instances of a single kind. We may ask about the extent of the phenomenon and the conditions that make it possible. And we may ask how to improve human performance; how we might go about gaining more knowledge. Let us examine each of these projects in turn.

Just as Plato was interested in what knowledge is, the naturalistic epistemologist is also concerned with the phenomenon of human knowledge and what it is which makes the various instances of it instances of a single kind. There is a sociological and deflationary answer which might be given to this question: What instances of knowledge have in common is that they play a certain social role; they provide assurance which is backed by socially recognized experts. It seems to me clear enough that instances of knowledge do answer to some such characterization, but what makes the sociological account deflationary is the suggestion that this is all that instances of knowledge have in common, that there is nothing more to knowledge than the social role it plays. If something along these lines is correct, then knowledge turns out to be a far more shallow and less interesting kind than philosophers have traditionally thought it to be.

The account of knowledge which Goldman offers makes knowledge a more interesting and deeper kind. On Goldman's account, knowledge is reliably produced true belief. Such an account does not conflict with the suggestion that knowledge plays a certain social role; instead, by offering a deeper account of what makes something an item of knowledge, Goldman's account seeks to explain how it is that items of knowledge are well suited to play the social role they in fact play. At the same time, Goldman is committed to the view that the social forces which play a role in the production of belief genuinely are, by and large, conducive to truth. Our social institutions, and in particular, our scientific institutions, are so structured as to produce true belief; they are not merely vehicles for the dissemination of belief of whatever sort or vehicles for the concentration and perpetuation of political power, as some would have it. An account such as Goldman's must therefore show how the social arrangement of scientific institutions lends itself to playing this truth-connected role. In particular, it must be shown that various features of our social institutions which seem to conflict with getting at the truth nevertheless play a role, by and large, in producing true belief. Accordingly, Goldman—and others of a like turn of mind, such as Philip Kitcher—have devoted considerable attention to this project.[14]

It might be thought that these claims about our social institutions are really detachable from the view that knowledge is reliably produced true belief.[15] Couldn't one hold that knowledge has some such essential connection with truth and yet remain neutral on the claim about the connection between our social institutions and truth? In the end, I do not think that these two views are so neatly detachable, at least not for a naturalist. If one insists on insulating claims about the nature of knowledge from claims about the social practices and institutions in which knowledge is embodied, then one is giving up the view of knowledge as a natural phenomenon susceptible to empirical investigation, which, to my mind, is a crucial constituent of the naturalistic approach. It is the investigation of knowledge as a phenomenon in the world which distinguishes naturalism from other approaches to knowledge. It is this feature as well which lends substance to the various claims made about knowledge; without tying knowledge to the world in this way, we would leave nothing for our account to answer to.

By the same token, the naturalist who favors a Goldman-style account of knowledge and justification is committed to explaining how it is that the psychological mechanisms by which beliefs are produced, modified, and retained are, on the whole, conducive to the production of true belief. This empirical investigation of the reliability of belief production is not in any way trivial. While it is certainly true that this investigation is itself carried out by using the very mechanisms of belief production whose reliability is in question, this does not assure that the investigation will confirm the overall reliability of our mechanisms of belief production.[16] Indeed, this kind of investigation typically results in a better understanding of the ways in which such mechanisms may go wrong. In addition, there is no reason to think that every mechanism of belief production must be reliable; there may well be mechanisms which, by and large, tend to produce false beliefs. There is, indeed, a good deal of evidence that some mechanisms of belief production are like this.

This empirical investigation of the mechanisms of belief production at both the level of the individual and at the level of the group allows us to begin to answer the question of how knowledge is possible. The possibility of human knowledge is examined from two different perspectives. On the one hand, we wish to know what it is about us that allows us to understand the world. On the other hand, we wish to know what it is about the world that allows it to be known. What is required, in the end, is an account of how the various presuppositions

tions of our mechanisms of belief acquisition, both individual and social, dovetail with various features of the world so that the resulting beliefs tend to get things right. I will provide two brief illustrations of how such an account proceeds.[17]

First, consider the familiar visual illusion in which a series of lights are turned on and off in succession so as to give the impression of motion. Highway signs frequently trade on this illusion. One of the interesting facts about this phenomenon, and about visual illusions of motion generally, is that even when we know how the illusion is produced, and, in this case, that there is no motion at all, we are still presented with an impression of motion. What seems to be going on in this case is the following. The visual system is so constructed as to assume a world populated, for the most part, by three-dimensional objects with more or less stable boundaries. Given a series of impressions of a sort which might be caused by such objects, the visual system automatically imposes an interpretation on them consistent with that assumption. Because the assumption is in fact true of our world, that is, because our world is largely made up of three-dimensional objects with more or less stable boundaries, the visual system works quite quickly and, for the most part, accurately. The assumption built into the system, however, is not true of every possible world, and, were we placed in an environment largely populated by objects violating the assumption, the beliefs produced by the visual system would tend to be mistaken. The presuppositions of our visual system match, or roughly match, certain pervasive features of the world, and it is in virtue of that approximate match that we are able reliably to gain information about the world. We should not expect our epistemology to discover techniques of belief acquisition which would work in any world whatsoever. Instead, we should expect to discover processes like the one embodied in the visual system which are tailored to contingent though pervasive features of the actual world.

We may examine our native inferential tendencies in the same way. As Tversky and Kahneman[18] have illustrated in great detail, human beings have a natural tendency to draw conclusions about a population of objects on the basis of extremely small samples, indeed, often on the basis of a single case. This is a dramatic violation of the law of large numbers. As Tversky and Kahneman argue, we ought to draw conclusions about a population only when we have a fairly large sample on which to base a conclusion; to do otherwise is simply irrational. Tversky and Kahneman draw the obvious conclusion. Human beings are built to reason badly.

This inferential tendency, however, must be evaluated in light of the environments in which it is operative. We ought to be asking, not whether it would work well in any possible environment, but whether it works well in the environments in which human beings tend to be found. I have argued, in fact, that this tendency serves us well and that it does so precisely because, on the whole, it tends to produce true beliefs.

Drawing conclusions about a population on the basis of a single sample will work well when the populations are largely uniform with respect to the traits which are projected. Thus, for example, if I conclude that all copper conducts electricity after noting that a single sample of copper conducts electricity, I will not go wrong. In general, if we tend to project essential features of natural kinds, the tendency to generalize quickly will be a reliable one. What is needed here in order to evaluate our inferential tendency is an examination of the structure of human concepts and an understanding of the features of kinds which tend to be projected. Work in conceptual development indicates that from the beginning, children assume that the observable properties of objects do not determine kind membership and that, instead, there are unobservable features of objects which are essential to the kinds of which they are members. In short, it is a feature of human conceptual structure that we take for granted that natural kinds have Lockean real essences. If natural kinds do have Lockean real essences, as I have argued they do, and if we are even roughly attuned to the essential properties of kinds, as I have argued we are, then the tendency to make inferences about a population on the basis of small samples is broadly reliable. Once again, we see the respects in which features of our psychology track pervasive though contingent features of the world. It is this sort of fit which makes knowledge possible.

The search for principles of reasoning which would world well in any possible world was, to my mind, a mistake. A proper explanation of the possibility of human knowledge will not appeal to such principles of reasoning but rather to principles like the ones just illustrated, ones whose reliability is deeply contingent and whose success can only be explained by demonstrating the fit between features of the world and features of the principles themselves. It is for this reason that epistemology becomes an empirical discipline, continuous with the sciences, and it is for this reason that epistemology must draw so heavily on work in psychology.

This project of explaining how human knowledge is possible also provides the basis for empirically informed epistemic advice. If we wish to give advice to agents on how to improve their belief acquisition, we need to know where agents are most liable to err and what kinds of psychological processes may in fact be realized. It is of little use to tell human agents, for example, to make all of their beliefs consistent, given that checking our entire body of beliefs for consistency is not within our power. Even attempting to gain as much consistency in our beliefs as we can is not good advice, for our efforts are far better spent in other kinds of cognitive management. The empirical examination of processes of belief acquisition will thus give us the information which is needed to advise agents on where their efforts are best employed. Those who are interested in cognitive improvement should thus be interested in this project.

The naturalistic project thus provides a way of unifying the three epistemological projects undertaken by Descartes: giving an account of what knowledge is; explaining how knowledge is possible; and providing useful epistemic advice. The way in which these projects are unified is, of course, quite different from the way in which Descartes attempted to unify them. Indeed, the project of explaining how knowledge is possible is interpreted in such a different way by naturalists and Cartesians that many will want to claim that the subject here has simply been changed. Descartes wished to answer the total skeptic; the naturalistic account of how knowledge is possible does not even attempt to address that kind of challenge. As naturalists see it, however, what was legitimate in the skeptical challenge is, in fact, addressed by the naturalistic project. What remains unanswered has proven to be a fruitless research project and is thus best abandoned. Naturalists may be proven wrong here by being shown that a response to the Cartesian skeptic would in some way be illuminating.

Whatever one thinks of the challenge presented by the Cartesian skeptic, there is something powerful in the unifying vision presented by epistemological naturalists, just as there was something powerful in the unifying vision presented by Descartes. The three epistemological projects which have been described are surely worthy of pursuit. The fact that empirical work is required in order to pursue them hardly makes them less worthy of our attention, although I recognize that many will think that this makes them appear less philosophical. It is interesting to note, however, that more traditional and a priori approaches to epistemological questions have not been able to provide such a unifying account, at least once one rejects some of Descartes' more implausible claims. The project of providing constructive epistemic advice, so central to Descartes' conception of epistemology, has been largely abandoned by traditional epistemologists, for they recognize that a priori means alone are insufficient to the task.[19] But the remaining projects, when divorced from their connection with epistemic advice, arguably lose much of their interest.[20] Why should we care about having justified beliefs, for example, when justification is so understood that making our beliefs justified will not make it more likely that they be true? Much of what motivated Descartes' epistemological work is now pursued in a different manner by epistemological naturalists. Much of the more traditional epistemology, which is so much influenced by Descartes' methods, has abandoned his concerns.

I am not arguing that we should pursue the naturalistic approach because, in the end, it is more nearly continuous with the history of epistemological endeavors than a priori work in epistemology. By my lights, being continuous with the history of epistemological endeavors is not automatically a good thing. Rather, I am arguing that many of the concerns which were central to Descartes' project are still rightly viewed as legitimate ones, and the fact that a priori work in epistemology does not properly address them counts against that project. The real issue here should not be, "Which kind of work is more nearly continuous with what actually concerned Descartes and the other late, great epistemologists?" Instead, we need to ask, "What kind of questions about knowledge are worthy of our pursuit?" The naturalistic approach has, I believe, clearly identified a set of such questions and has shown us how they may be productively addressed. That is, to my mind, a real achievement.

IV

Naturalistic epistemologists do not claim merely to be addressing some of the legitimate questions in the field; rather, it is claimed that the naturalistic approach addresses all of the legitimate questions and that there is nothing left for more traditional approaches to deal with. It will come as no surprise then that naturalism has met with more than a few challenges. Indeed, as the naturalistic approach has become better established, more epistemologists have registered their doubts about the project. I will briefly summarize the main lines of criticism and sketch the sorts of reply which are available to the naturalist.

One objection which has arisen repeatedly is that a naturalistic epistemology cannot be both "a chapter of psychology" and, simultaneously, a normative enterprise. Insofar as epistemology is absorbed by empirical science, it thereby becomes merely descriptive. But a central project of epistemology involves developing epistemic advice; and this normative dimension of epistemology must therefore be bypassed. Epistemology without normativity, it is argued, is just *Hamlet* without the Prince of Denmark.[21]

I myself am quite sympathetic with the suggestion that the normative dimension of epistemological inquiry is essential to it. The idea that a naturalistic epistemology is thoroughly empirical, however, does not in any way rob it of its normative force. As I have already indicated, the project of providing useful epistemic advice must be empirically informed, for we need to know what kinds of errors human beings are most liable to make if we are to give advice where it is most needed, and we must know what kinds of advice are humanly followable if we are to provide advice which can address our shortcomings. That empirical information is essential to the task of providing epistemic advice in this way is undeniable.

The disagreement, however, does not end here. Some will see the empirical project I have described as merely applied epistemology; on some accounts, it is no part of philosophy at all.

Rather, the project I have described cannot get going, it will be urged, without a prior account of how we ought, ideally, to arrive at our beliefs. This is the proper business of epistemology. The empirical work only comes in when we try to figure out how far human beings tend to be from the ideal and when we try to figure out the best strategies for remedial work, that is, for getting individuals as close to the ideal as is humanly possible. Some a priori work having to do with ideals of reasoning, however, is required before any of the empirical work can be done.[22] Whatever one may want to call the empirical work, surely the a priori project just described is part of epistemology.

Now obviously those, such as Quine, who reject the very idea of a priority are not going to be moved by this kind of argument, nor should they. But important as I believe the issue of a priority to be in the debate between naturalists and their critics, we need not raise that issue here. I will suppose, for the sake of argument, that there is such a thing as a priori knowledge. What I want to suggest on behalf of naturalism is that even if there were such knowledge, it could not play the role just described in launching the project of devising useful epistemic advice.

The objection just considered supposes that we have available some useful notion of ideal reasoning which can be arrived at a priori. Such an account will abstract away from various human limitations, including limits on memory, attention, life span, and so on. Now this account cannot abstract from all human limitations. After all, if we allow superhuman intellectual abilities, then reasoning itself becomes entirely unnecessary: A creature with no intellectual limitations would be able to intuit truths directly. The very necessity of reasoning is itself a sign of our intellectual limits. So suppose that we hold fixed a certain class of beliefs which can be arrived at without reasoning—say, perceptual beliefs as well as some others—and we then ask what further beliefs might be inferred from them by way of ideal reasoning. What is to constrain this notion of the ideal? What is to give it content?

The problem with appealing to the notion of a priori principles of good reasoning in order to constrain this conception of an ideal is that such principles—assuming there to be such—may make no contact at all with the project of providing useful epistemic advice. Human beings are innately disposed to reason in certain ways, and these innate dispositions may be extremely reliable in the actual world even without being identical to, or even close approximations to, any principles which are a priori reasonable. When we reason reliably, the only epistemic advice which is called for is to keep doing what we are already doing, however the principles that we are innately disposed to apply may compare with a priori principles. Similarly, when we reason badly, when principles of reasoning which we are innately disposed to apply are unreliable, what we wish to replace these principles with are ones which we can act in accord with in such a way as to regularly arrive at true beliefs in *the actual world*. We needn't be concerned about whether such principles are a priori knowable. Even if it should turn out that the way in which such principles achieve their reliability can only be understood a posteriori, perhaps because they trade on some contingent though pervasive feature of the world, these would still be the kind of principles which we would want to recommend. More than this, principles which we know a priori to be reliable when we abstract away from human limitations may turn out to be very bad principles to reason in accord with once those limitations are factored back in. Empirical work on human reasoning has shown these concerns to be more than merely imaginary. The apriorist notion of the ideal, naturalists will want to argue, turns out, as a matter of empirical fact, to be irrelevant to the project of offering epistemic advice. Indeed, it thus seems a misnomer to call it any kind of ideal at all.[23]

I thus conclude that the objection against naturalism we have been considering—that in making epistemology thoroughly empirical, it loses all normative force—is entirely without merit. First, there is a clear respect in which an empirical theory of reasoning may have normative force; the mere fact that it is empirical does not, by itself, rob the theory of normative consequences. And second, there is reason to think that if any account is robbed of normative force here, it is, not the empirical theory, but the theory which deprives itself of empirical input. It is the antinaturalist, I believe, who must be concerned that his theory is irrelevant to normative concerns.[24]

Let me turn then to a different objection to naturalism, an objection which Laurence BonJour has presented quite forcefully.[25] BonJour presents an argument against naturalism which, he says,

"seems . . . as obvious and compelling as any in the whole of philosophy. . . ."[26] Let me quote Bon-Jour at length:

I will assume here, without worrying about the details, that the fact that a belief is a report of direct observation or experience constitutes an adequate reason for thinking it to be true. But what about the non-observational or non-experiential beliefs? If we are to have any reason for thinking these latter beliefs to be true, such a reason must apparently either (i) depend on an inference of some sort from some of the directly observational beliefs or (ii) be entirely independent of direct observation. A reason of sort (ii) is plainly *a priori*. And a reason of sort (i) can only be cogent if its corresponding conditional, a conditional statement having the conjunction of the directly observational premises as antecedent and the proposition that is the content of the non-observational belief as a consequent, is something that we in turn have a reason to think to be true. But the reason for thinking that this latter, conditional statement is true can again only be *a priori*: if, as we may assume, all relevant observations are already included in the antecedent, they can offer no support to the claim that *if* that antecedent is true, then something further is true. Thus if, as the naturalist claims, there are no *a priori* reasons for thinking anything to be true . . . the inevitable result is that we have no reason for thinking that any of our beliefs whose content transcends direct observation are true.

This is epistemological disaster in itself, but a further consequence is that the vast majority of claims about the nature of the world, the nature and reliability of human psychological processes, etc., upon which naturalized epistemology so lovingly focuses, are things that we have no reason at all for thinking to be true—as, indeed, are the very theses that epistemology must be naturalized or that traditional epistemology is untenable. . . . In this way, naturalized epistemology is *self-referentially inconsistent*: its own epistemological claims exclude the possibility of there being any cogent reason for thinking that those claims are true.[27]

But this argument is not conclusive.

Let us put aside, for the sake of argument, as BonJour does, worries about the notion of direct observation. BonJour explicitly assumes that if an observation statement O is to provide good reason for believing some further claim T, then the conditional "If O, then T" must itself be a claim which the agent has good reason to believe. But naturalists would deny this premise. Naturalists believe that human beings are so provided by nature that they are inclined to make certain kinds of inferences which are in fact reliable, long before they have evidence that those inferences are reliable. On the naturalistic account, such inferences constitute cases of good reasoning. Thus, for example, children and animals may reason quite well without having the evidence, or in some cases even the conceptual repertoire, which would license those inferences. This is not to say that such evidence is inevitably and for all time out of their reach. Nonhuman animals are unlikely to be able to assess the reliability of their own inferences. But children do grow up, and when they are in a position to raise the question of the reliability of their own inferences, they are also in a position to gather evidence on the issue and, in some cases, resolve it. This project of evaluating one's own inferences by means of the inferential machinery under evaluation, as I earlier argued, is not an idle exercise. There are circumstances under which such an investigation would reveal deep problems in the inferential machinery. Passing this kind of test, then, although it is not a guarantee against all conceivable challenges, is informative.

What could BonJour's complaint here be? It cannot be that a priori assurances, if we had them, would quiet the total skeptic, for, on BonJour's own account, a priori reasoning gives us no such definitive refutation; rather what it does, at best, is make it reasonable to believe that the skeptic is mistaken. But in this respect, it is not at all clear that the naturalist is worse off. BonJour is simply taking for granted certain constraints on good reasoning which the naturalist rejects.[28] So there is a substantive dispute here as to what good reasoning consists in, not, as BonJour portrays things, a simple case of self-referential inconsistency. Contrary to what BonJour suggests, naturalism is not self-refuting.

These are, to my mind, the two most important objections to naturalism available in the literature. At this point, the dispute between naturalists and antinaturalists will turn on the fruits of their theories. What each side needs to show is that it has a productive research program available, a program of research which will be genuinely illuminating. It is in this that the future of epistemology will be determined.[29]

Notes

[1] W. V. Quine, "Epistemology Naturalized," in his *Ontological Relativity and Other Essays* (New York: Columbia University Press, 1969).

[2] While Quine focuses exclusively on foundationalism, there is reason to think that the naturalist critique applies equally well to coherentism, at least as traditionally conceived. See my "Beyond Foundationalism and the Coherence Theory," *Journal of Philosophy 77* (1980): 597–612.

[3] This last point is made especially forcefully in Stephen Stich, *The Fragmentation of Reason* (Cambridge, Mass.: MIT Press, 1990), and in Mark Kaplan, "Epistemology Denatured," *Midwest Studies in Philosophy 19* (1994): 350–365.

[4] Quine, op. cit., 82.

[5] See especially Barry Stroud, *The Significance of Philosophical Skepticism* (Oxford: Oxford University Press, 1984), and Jaegwon Kim, "What Is 'Naturalized Epistemology'?" *Philosophical Perspectives 2* (1988): 381–405.

[6] See Kim, op. cit., Stroud, op. cit., and Elliott Sober, "Psychologism," *Journal for the Theory of Social Behavior 8* (1978): 165–191.

[7] Alvin Goldman, "A Causal Theory of Knowing," *Journal of Philosophy 64* (1967): 357–72.

[8] The only mention of the Gettier problem in the Quinean corpus with which I am familiar is to be found in *Quiddities* (Cambridge, Mass.: Harvard University Press, 1987). Quine there suggests that "the best we can do is give up the notion of knowledge as a bad job and make do rather with its separate ingredients" (ibid., 109).

[9] Alvin Goldman, "Discrimination and Perceptual Knowledge,'" *Journal of Philosophy 73* (1976): 771–91.

[10] In Alvin Goldman, "What Is Justified Belief?" in George Pappas, ed., *Justification and Knowledge* (Dordrecht: Reidel, 1979), 1–23. The account is further developed in great detail in his *Epistemology and Cognition* (Cambridge, Mass.: Harvard University Press, 1986).

[11] I argue that this is the proper way to view the central difference between reliabilism, on the one hand, and foundationalism and the coherence theory, on the other, in Kornblith, op. cit.

[12] This empirical investigation takes the place of the search for epistemic principles connecting the foundation of

knowledge with its superstructure. While the foundationalist account requires that these connecting epistemic principles enjoy a privileged epistemological status, the investigation of these psychological mechanisms is simply a part of empirical science.

[13]This is one, though only one, of the defining features of James Gibson's approach to psychology. See especially his *The Senses Considered as Perceptual Systems* (Boston: Houghton Mifflin Co., 1966) and *The Ecological Approach to Visual Perception* (Boston: Houghton Mifflin Co., 1979).

[14]For Goldman's work here, see the papers in part 3 of his *Liaisons: Philosophy Meets the Cognitive and Social Sciences* (Cambridge, Mass.: MIT Press, 1993). For Kitcher's work, see "The Division of Cognitive Labor," *Journal of Philosophy* 87 (1990): 5–22; "Socializing Knowledge," *Journal of Philosophy* 88 (1991): 675–76; "Authority, Deference and the Role of Individual Reason," in Ernan McMullin, ed., *The Social Dimension of Scientific Knowledge* (South Bend, Ind.: Notre Dame University Press, 1992); and *The Advancement of Science* (Oxford: Oxford University Press, 1993). My own view on this matter is further developed in "A Conservative Approach to Social Epistemology," in Frederick Schmitt, ed., *Socializing Epistemology: The Social Dimensions of Knowledge* (Lanham, Md.: Rowman and Littlefield, 1994), 93–110.

[15]Miriam Solomon argues that they are in "Is There an Invisible Hand of Reason?" (forthcoming).

[16]This point is nicely defended in Michael Friedman, "Truth and Confirmation," *Journal of Philosophy* 76 (1979): 361–382 and in Philip Kitchner. "The Naturalists Return," *Philosophical Review* 101 (1992): 53–114.

[17]This approach, and the two illustrations, are developed in detail in my *Inductive Inference and Its Natural Ground* (Cambridge, Mass.: MIT Press, 1993).

[18]Tversky and Kahneman, "Belief in the Law of Small Numbers," *Psychological Bulletin* 2 (1971): 105–110.

[19]Thus, see, for example, BonJour's remarks about the meliorative project in epistemology in his "Against Naturalized Epistemology," *Midwest Studies in Philosophy* 19 (1994): 283–300.

[20]Here I am echoing Kaplan, op. cit., and Stich, op. cit., although Kaplan attempts to use this perspective to argue against naturalism.

[21]See especially Kim, op. cit., and Stroud, op. cit.

[22]BonJour, op. cit., defends this approach.

[23]I believe that this kind of response can be developed to answer the challenge to naturalism presented in Kaplan, op. cit., but a full reply to Kaplan must await another occasion. See my "Cogent Arguments for Naturalism: A Reply to Kaplan" (in preparation).

[24]There is another way of construing the worry about normativity, and this has to do with the alleged fact-value gap. I address this challenge to naturalism in my "Epistemic Normativity," *Synthese* 94 (1993): 357–376. For a different attempt to defend naturalism on this score, see James Maffie, "Naturalism and the Normativity of Epistemology," *Philosophical Studies* 59 (1990): 87–103.

[25]See BonJour, op. cit.

[26]Ibid., 24.

[27]Ibid., 22–23.

[28]BonJour does argue for these constraints elsewhere (see his *The Structure of Empirical Knowledge* [Cambridge, Mass.: Harvard University Press, 1985]), but this argument too is open to challenge. Indeed, BonJour himself acknowledges there that his account of what counts as good reason forces him to total skepticism. So he can hardly complain that the naturalist is worse off in this respect. Indeed, it seems clear that the naturalist is far better off here, for the naturalist does not endorse the account of good reasoning which leads to the skeptical conclusion.

[29]Earlier versions of this paper were presented at a symposium on naturalism at the Eastern Division Meeting of the American Philosophical Association in December 1994, where Sandra Rosenthal commented, and at Brigham Young University. I am indebted to audiences at both of these presentations. I am also indebted to David Christensen, Derk Pereboom, Miriam Solomon, and Bill Talbott for very helpful comments on a previous draft of this paper.

VI.7 Elusive Knowledge

DAVID LEWIS

David Lewis (1921–2001) was professor of philosophy at Princeton University and the author of several works in metaphysics and philosophy of language. In this article he considers several puzzles of epistemology, including the Gettier problem, the lottery paradox (no matter how much evidence, I can't be said to know that my ticket won't win), and the situation where a child "knows" the right answer but doesn't think he knows it. Lewis observes that common sense ensures us that we do have a lot of knowledge, but when we apply epistemic standards to these claims, our knowledge seems to vanish, hence the title "Elusive Knowledge." He proposes a solution, the formula of which is "Subject *S knows* proposition *P* iff *P* holds in every possibility left uneliminated by *S*'s evidence; equivalently, iff *S*'s evidence eliminates every possibility in which not-*P*." Most of the article is an elucidation of that thesis.

We know a lot. I know what food penguins eat. I know that phones used to ring, but nowadays squeal, when someone calls up. I know that Essendon won the 1993 Grand Final. I know that here is a hand, and here is another.

We have all sorts of everyday knowledge, and we have it in abundance. To doubt that would be absurd. At any rate, to doubt it in any serious and lasting way would be absurd; and even philosophical and temporary doubt, under the influence of argument, is more than a little peculiar. It is a Moorean fact that we know a lot. It is one of those things that we know better than we know the premises of any philosophical argument to the contrary.

Besides knowing a lot that is everyday and trite, I myself think that we know a lot that is interesting and esoteric and controversial. We know a lot about things unseen: tiny particles and pervasive fields, not to mention one another's underwear. Sometimes we even know what an author meant by his writings. But on these ques-

tions, let us agree to disagree peacefully with the champions of "post-knowledgeism." The most trite and ordinary parts of our knowledge will be problem enough.

For no sooner do we engage in epistemology—the systematic philosophical examination of knowledge—than we meet a compelling argument that we know next to nothing. The skeptical argument is nothing new or fancy. It is just this: it seems as if knowledge must be by definition infallible. If you claim that *S* knows that *P*, and yet you grant that *S* cannot eliminate a certain possibility in which not-*P*, it certainly seems as if you have granted that *S* does not after all know that *P*. To speak of fallible knowledge, of knowledge despite uneliminated possibilities of error, just *sounds* contradictory.

Blind Freddy can see where this will lead. Let your paranoid fantasies rip—CIA plots, hallucinogens in the tap water, conspiracies to deceive, old Nick himself—and soon you find that uneliminated possibilities of error are everywhere. Those possibilities of error are farfetched, of course, but possibilities all the same. They bite into even our most everyday knowledge. We never have infallible knowledge.

Never—well, hardly ever. Some say we have infallible knowledge of a few simple, axiomatic necessary truths; and of our own present experience. They say that I simply cannot be wrong that a part of a part of something is itself a part of that

Reprinted from "Elusive Knowledge" in *Australasian Journal of Philosophy*, vol. 74:4 (December 1996) by permission.

Thanks to many for valuable discussions of this material. Thanks above all to Peter Unger; and to Stewart Cohen, Michael Devitt, Alan Hajek, Stephen Hetherington, Denis Robinson, Ernest Sosa, Robert Stalnaker, Jonathan Vogel, and a referee for this Journal. Thanks also to the Boyce Gibson Memorial Library and to Ormond College.

thing; or that it seems to me now (as I sit here at the keyboard) exactly as if I am hearing clicking noises on top of a steady whirring. Some say so. Others deny it. No matter; let it be granted, at least for the sake of the argument. It is not nearly enough. If we have only that much infallible knowledge, yet knowledge is by definition infallible, then we have very little knowledge indeed—not the abundant everyday knowledge we thought we had. That is still absurd.

So we know a lot; knowledge must be infallible; yet we have fallible knowledge or none (or next to none). We are caught between the rock of fallibilism and the whirlpool of scepticism. Both are mad!

Yet fallibilism is the less intrusive madness. It demands less frequent corrections of what we want to say. So, if forced to choose, I choose fallibilism. (And so say all of us.) We can get used to it, and some of us have done. No joy there—we know that people can get used to the most crazy philosophical sayings imaginable. If you are a contented fallibilist, I implore you to be honest, be naive, hear it afresh. "He knows, yet he has not eliminated all possibilities of error." Even if you've numbed your ears, doesn't this overt, explicit fallibilism *still* sound wrong?

Better fallibilism than scepticism; but it would be better still to dodge the choice. I think we can. We will be alarmingly close to the rock, and also alarmingly close to the whirlpool, but if we steer with care, we can—just barely—escape them both.

Maybe epistemology is the culprit. Maybe this extraordinary pastime robs us of our knowledge. Maybe we do know a lot in daily life; but maybe when we look hard at our knowledge, it goes away. But only when we look at it harder than the sane ever do in daily life; only when we let our paranoid fantasies rip. That is when we are forced to admit that there always are uneliminated possibilities of error, so that we have fallible knowledge or none.

Much that we say is context-dependent, in simple ways or subtle ways. Simple: "it's evening" is truly said when, and only when, it is said in the evening. Subtle: it could well be true, and not just by luck, that Essendon played rottenly, the Easybeats played brilliantly, yet Essendon won. Different contexts evoke different standards of evaluation. Talking about the Easybeats we apply lax standards, else we could scarcely distinguish their better days from their worse ones. In talking about Essendon, no such laxity is required. Essendon won because play that is rotten by demanding standards suffices to beat play that is brilliant by lax standards.

Maybe ascriptions of knowledge are subtly context-dependent, and maybe epistemology is a context that makes them go false. Then epistemology would be an investigation that destroys its own subject matter. If so, the sceptical argument might be flawless, when we engage in epistemology—and only then![1]

If you start from the ancient idea that justification is the mark that distinguishes knowledge from mere opinion (even true opinion), then you well might conclude that ascriptions of knowledge are context-dependent because standards for adequate justification are context-dependent. As follows: opinion, even if true, deserves the name of knowledge only if it is adequately supported by reasons; to deserve that name in the especially demanding context of epistemology, the arguments from supporting reasons must be especially watertight; but the special standards of justification that this special context demands never can be met (well, hardly ever). In the strict context of epistemology we know nothing, yet in laxer contexts we know a lot.

But I myself cannot subscribe to this account of the context-dependence of knowledge, because I question its starting point. I don't agree that the mark of knowledge is justification.[2] First, because justification is not sufficient: your true opinion that you will lose the lottery isn't knowledge, whatever the odds. Suppose you know that it is a fair lottery with one winning ticket and many losing tickets, and you know how many losing tickets there are. The greater the number of losing tickets, the better is your justification for believing you will lose. Yet there is no number great enough to transform your fallible opinion into knowledge—after all, you just might win. No justification is good enough—or none short of a watertight deductive argument, and all but the sceptics will agree that this is too much to demand.[3]

Second, because justification is not always necessary. What (non-circular) argument supports our reliance on perception, on memory, and on testimony?[4] And yet we do gain knowledge by these means. And sometimes, far from having supporting arguments, we don't even know how we know. We once had evidence, drew conclusions, and thereby gained knowledge; now we have forgotten our reasons, yet still we retain our knowledge. Or we know the name that goes with the face, or the sex of the chicken, by relying on subtle visual cues, without knowing what those cues may be.

The link between knowledge and justification must be broken. But if we break that link, then it is not—or not entirely, or not exactly—by raising the standards of justification that epistemology destroys knowledge. I need some different story.

To that end, I propose to take the infallibility of knowledge as my starting point.[5] Must infallibilist epistemology end in scepticism? Not quite. Wait and see. Anyway, here is the definition. Subject S *knows* proposition P iff P holds in every possibility left uneliminated by VI.4 The Generality Problem for S's evidence; equivalently, iff S's evidence eliminates every possibility in which not-P.

The definition is short, the commentary upon it is longer. In the first place, there is the proposition, P. What I choose to call "propositions" are individuated coarsely, by necessary equivalence. For instance, there is only one necessary proposition. It holds in every possibility; hence in every possibility left uneliminated by S's evidence, no matter who S may be and no matter what his evidence may be. So the necessary proposition is known always and everywhere. Yet this known proposition may go unrecognised when presented in impenetrable linguistic disguise, say as the proposition that every even number is the sum of two primes. Likewise, the known proposition that I have two hands may go unrecognised when presented as the proposition that the number of my hands is the least number n such that every even number is the sum of n primes. (Or if you doubt the necessary existence of numbers, switch to an example involving equivalence by logic alone.) These problems of disguise shall not concern us here. Our topic is modal, not hyperintensional, epistemology.[6]

Next, there are the possibilities. We needn't enter here into the question whether these are concrete, abstract constructions, or abstract simples. Further, we needn't decide whether they must always be maximally specific possibilities, or whether they need only be specific enough for the purpose

at hand. A possibility will be specific enough if it cannot be split into sub-cases in such a way that anything we have said about possibilities, or anything we are going to say before we are done, applies to some sub-cases and not to others. For instance, it should never happen that proposition P holds in some but not all sub-cases; or that some but not all sub-cases are eliminated by S's evidence.

But we do need to stipulate that they are not just possibilities as to how the whole world is; they also include possibilities as to which part of the world is oneself, and as to when it now is. We need these possibilities *de se et nunc* because the propositions that may be known include propositions *de se et nunc*.[7] Not only do I know that there are hands in this world somewhere and somewhen. I know that I have hands, or anyway I have them *now*. Such propositions aren't just made true or made false by the whole world once and for all. They are true for some of us and not for others, or true at some times and not others, or both.

Further, we cannot limit ourselves to "real" possibilities that conform to the actual laws of nature, and maybe also to actual past history. For propositions about laws and history are contingent, and may or may not be known.

Neither can we limit ourselves to "epistemic" possibilities for S—possibilities that S does not know not to obtain. That would drain our definition of content. Assume only that knowledge is closed under strict implication. (We shall consider the merits of this assumption later.) Remember that we are not distinguishing between equivalent propositions. Then knowledge of a conjunction is equivalent to knowledge of every conjunct. P is the conjunction of all propositions not-W, where W is a possibility in which not-P. That suffices to yield an equivalence: S knows that P iff, for every possibility W in which not-P, S knows that not-W. Contraposing and canceling a double negation: iff every possibility which S does not know not to obtain is one in which P. For short: iff P holds throughout S's epistemic possibilities. Yet to get this far, we need no substantive definition of knowledge at all! To turn this into a substantive definition, in fact the very definition we gave before, we need to say one more thing: S's epistemic possibilities are just those possibilities that are uneliminated by S's evidence.

So, next, we need to say what it means for a possibility to be eliminated or not. Here I say that the uneliminated possibilities are those in which the subject's entire perceptual experience and memory are just as they actually are. There is one possibility that actually obtains (for the subject and at the time in question); call it *actuality*. Then a possibility *W* is *uneliminated* iff the subject's perceptual experience and memory in *W* exactly match his perceptual experience and memory in actuality. (If you want to include other alleged forms of basic evidence, such as the evidence of our extrasensory faculties, or an innate disposition to believe in God, be my guest. If they exist, they should be included. If not, no harm done if we have included them conditionally.)

Note well that we do not need the "pure sense-datum language" and the "incorrigible protocol statements" that for so long bedeviled foundationalist epistemology. It matters not at all whether there are words to capture the subject's perceptual and memory evidence, nothing more and nothing less. If there are such words, it matters not at all whether the subject can hit upon them. The given does not consist of basic axioms to serve as premises in subsequent arguments. Rather, it consists of a match between possibilities.

When perceptual experience *E* (or memory) eliminates a possibility *W*, that is not because the prepositional content of the experience conflicts with *W*. (Not even if it is the narrow content.) The propositional content of our experience could, after all, be false. Rather, it is the existence of the experience that conflicts with *W*: *W* is a possibility in which the subject is not having experience *E*. Else we would need to tell some fishy story of how the experience has some sort of infallible, ineffable, purely phenomenal propositional content . . . Who needs that? Let *E* have propositional content *P*. Suppose even—something I take to be an open question—that *E* is, in some sense, fully characterized by *P*. Then I say that *E* eliminates *W* iff *W* is a possibility in which the subject's experience or memory has content different from *P*. I do not say that *E* eliminates *W* iff *W* is a possibility in which *P* is false.

Maybe not every kind of sense perception yields experience; maybe, for instance, the kinaesthetic sense yields not its own distinctive sort of sense-experience but only spontaneous judgements about the position of one's limbs. If this is true, then the thing to say is that kinaesthetic evidence eliminates all possibilities except those that

exactly resemble actuality with respect to the subject's spontaneous kinaesthetic judgements. In saying this, we would treat kinaesthetic evidence more on the model of memory than on the model of more typical senses.

Finally, we must attend to the word "every." What does it mean to say that every possibility in which not-*P* is eliminated? An idiom of quantification, like "every," is normally restricted to some limited domain. If I say that every glass is empty, so it's time for another round, doubtless I and my audience are ignoring most of all the glasses there are in the whole wide world throughout all of time. They are outside the domain. They are irrelevant to the truth of what was said.

Likewise, if I say that every uneliminated possibility is one in which *P*, or words to that effect, I am doubtless ignoring some of all the uneliminated alternative possibilities that there are. They are outside the domain, they are irrelevant to the truth of what was said.

But, of course, I am not entitled to ignore just any possibility I please. Else true ascriptions of knowledge, whether to myself or to others, would be cheap indeed. I may properly ignore some uneliminated possibilities; I may not properly ignore others. Our definition of knowledge requires a *sotto voce* proviso. *S knows* that *P* iff *S*'s evidence eliminates every possibility in which not-*P*—Psst!—except for those possibilities that we are properly ignoring.

Unger suggests an instructive parallel.[8] Just as *P* is known iff there are no uneliminated possibilities of error, so likewise a surface is flat iff there are no bumps on it. We must add the proviso: Psst!—except for those bumps that we are properly ignoring. Else we will conclude, absurdly, that nothing is flat. (Simplify by ignoring departures from flatness that consist of gentle curvature.)

We can restate the definition. Say that we *presuppose* proposition *Q* iff we ignore all possibilities in which not-*Q*. To close the circle: we *ignore* just those possibilities that falsify our presuppositions. *Proper* presupposition corresponds, of course, to proper ignoring. Then *S* knows that *P* iff *S*'s evidence eliminates every possibility in which not-*P* —Psst!—except for those possibilities that conflict with our proper presuppositions.[9]

The rest of (modal) epistemology examines the *sotto voce* proviso. It asks: what may we properly presuppose in our ascriptions of knowledge?

Which of all the uneliminated alternative possibilities may not properly be ignored? Which ones are the "relevant alternatives"?—relevant, that is, to what the subject does and doesn't know?[10] In reply, we can list several rules.[11] We begin with three prohibitions: rules to tell us what possibilities we may not properly ignore.

First, there is the *Rule of Actuality*. The possibility that actually obtains is never properly ignored; actuality is always a relevant alternative; nothing false may properly be presupposed. It follows that only what is true is known, wherefore we did not have to include truth in our definition of knowledge. The rule is "externalist"—the subject himself may not be able to tell what is properly ignored. In judging which of his ignorance are proper, hence what he knows, we judge his success in knowing—not how well he tried.

When the Rule of Actuality tells us that actuality may never be properly ignored, we can ask: *whose* actuality? Ours, when we ascribe knowledge or ignorance to others? Or the subject's? In simple cases, the question is silly. (In fact, it sounds like the sort of pernicious nonsense we would expect from someone who mixes up what is true with what is believed.) There is just one actual world, we the ascribers live in that world, the subject lives there too, so the subject's actuality is the same as ours.

But there are other cases, less simple, in which the question makes perfect sense and needs an answer. Someone may or may not know who he is; someone may or may not know what time it is. Therefore I insisted that the propositions that may be known must include propositions *de se et nunc;* and likewise that the possibilities that may be eliminated or ignored must include possibilities *de se et nunc.* Now we have a good sense in which the subject's actuality may be different from ours. I ask today what Fred knew yesterday. In particular, did he then know who he was? Did he know what day it was? Fred's actuality is the possibility *de se et nunc* of being Fred on September 19th at such-and-such possible world; whereas my actuality is the possibility *de se et nunc* of being David on September 20th at such-and-such world. So far as the world goes, there is no difference: Fred and I are worldmates, his actual world is the same as mine. But when we build subject and time into the possibilities *de se et nunc*, then his actuality yesterday does indeed differ from mine today.

What is more, we sometimes have occasion to ascribe knowledge to those who are off at other possible worlds. I didn't read the newspaper yesterday. What would I have known if I had read it? More than I do in fact know. (More and less: I do in fact know that I left the newspaper unread, but if I had read it, I would not have known that I had left it unread.) I-who-did-not-read-the-newspaper am here at this world, ascribing knowledge and ignorance. The subject to whom I am ascribing that knowledge and ignorance, namely I-as-I-would-have-been-if-I-had-read-the-newspaper, is at a different world. The worlds differ in respect at least of a reading of the newspaper. Thus the ascriber's actual world is not the same as the subject's. (I myself think that the ascriber and the subject are two different people: the subject is the ascriber's otherworldly counterpart. But even if you think the subject and the ascriber are the same identical person, you must still grant that this person's actuality *qua* subject differs from his actuality *qua* ascriber.)

Or suppose we ask modal questions about the subject: what must he have known, what might he have known? Again we are considering the subject as he is not here, but off at other possible worlds. Likewise if we ask questions about knowledge of knowledge: what does he (or what do we) know that he knows?

So the question "whose actuality?" is not a silly question after all. And when the question matters, as it does in the cases just considered, the right answer is that it is the subject's actuality, not the ascriber's, that never can be properly ignored.

Next, there is the *Rule of Belief.* A possibility that the subject believes to obtain is not properly ignored, whether or not he is right to so believe. Neither is one that he ought to believe to obtain—one that evidence and arguments justify him in believing—whether or not he does so believe.

That is rough. Since belief admits of degree, and since some possibilities are more specific than others, we ought to reformulate the rule in terms of degree of belief, compared to a standard set by the unspecificity of the possibility in question. A possibility may not be properly ignored if the subject gives it, or ought to give it, a degree of belief that is sufficiently high, and high not just because the possibility in question is unspecific.

How high is "sufficiently high"? That may depend on how much is at stake. When error would be especially disastrous, few possibilities may be properly ignored. Then even quite a low degree of belief may be "sufficiently high" to bring the Rule of Belief into play. The jurors know that the accused is guilty only if his guilt has been proved beyond reasonable doubt.[12]

Yet even when the stakes are high, some possibilities still may be properly ignored. Disastrous though it would be to convict an innocent man, still the jurors may properly ignore the possibility that it was the dog, marvelously well-trained, that fired the fatal shot. And, unless they are ignoring other alternatives more relevant than that, they may rightly be said to know that the accused is guilty as charged. Yet if there had been reason to give the dog hypothesis a slightly less negligible degree of belief—if the world's greatest dog-trainer had been the victim's mortal enemy—then the alternative would be relevant after all.

This is the only place where belief and justification enter my story. As already noted, I allow justified true belief without knowledge, as in the case of your belief that you will lose the lottery. I allow knowledge without justification, in the cases of face recognition and chicken sexing. I even allow knowledge without belief, as in the case of the timid student who knows the answer but has no confidence that he has it right, and so does not believe what he knows.[13] Therefore any proposed converse to the Rule of Belief should be rejected. A possibility that the subject does not believe to a sufficient degree, and ought not to believe to a sufficient degree, may nevertheless be a relevant alternative and not properly ignored.

Next, there is the *Rule of Resemblance*. Suppose one possibility saliently resembles another. Then if one of them may not be properly ignored, neither may the other. (Or rather, we should say that if one of them may not properly be ignored *in virtue of rules other than this rule,* then neither may the other. Else nothing could be properly ignored; because enough little steps of resemblance can take us from anywhere to anywhere.) Or suppose one possibility saliently resembles two or more others, one in one respect and another in another, and suppose that each of these may not properly be ignored (in virtue of rules other than this rule). Then these resemblances may have an additive effect, doing more together than any one of them would separately.

We must apply the Rule of Resemblance with care. Actuality is a possibility uneliminated by the subject's evidence. Any other possibility W that is likewise uneliminated by the subject's evidence thereby resembles actuality in one salient respect: namely, in respect of the subject's evidence. That will be so even if W is in other respects very dissimilar to actuality—even if, for instance, it is a possibility in which the subject is radically deceived by a demon. Plainly, we dare not apply the Rules of Actuality and Resemblance to conclude that any such W is a relevant alternative—that would be capitulation to scepticism. The Rule of Resemblance was never meant to apply to *this* resemblance! We seem to have an *ad hoc* exception to the Rule, though one that makes good sense in view of the function of attributions of knowledge. What would be better, though, would be to find a way to reformulate the Rule so as to get the needed exception without *ad hoc*ery. I do not know how to do this.

It is the Rule of Resemblance that explains why you do not know that you will lose the lottery, no matter what the odds are against you and no matter how sure you should therefore be that you will lose. For every ticket, there is the possibility that it will win. These possibilities are saliently similar to one another: so either every one of them may be properly ignored, or else none may. But one of them may not properly be ignored: the one that actually obtains.

The Rule of Resemblance also is the rule that solves the Gettier problems: other cases of justified true belief that are not knowledge.[14]

(1) I think that Nogot owns a Ford, because I have seen him driving one; but unbeknownst to me he does not own the Ford he drives, or any other Ford. Unbeknownst to me, Havit does own a Ford, though I have no reason to think so because he never drives it, and in fact I have often seen him taking the tram. My justified true belief is that one of the two owns a Ford. But I do not know it; I am right by accident. Diagnosis: I do not know, because I have not eliminated the possibility that Nogot drives a Ford he does not own whereas Havit neither drives nor owns a car. This possibility may not properly be ignored. Because, first, actuality may not properly be ignored; and, second, this possibility saliently resembles actuality. It resembles actuality perfectly so far as Nogot is concerned; and it resembles actuality well so far

as Havit is concerned, since it matches actuality both with respect to Havit's carless habits and with respect to the general correlation between carless habits and carlessness. In addition, this possibility saliently resembles a third possibility: one in which Nogot drives a Ford he owns while Havit neither drives nor owns a car. This third possibility may not properly be ignored, because of the degree to which it is believed. This time, the resemblance is perfect so far as Havit is concerned, rather good so far as Nogot is concerned.

(2) The stopped clock is right twice a day. It says 4:39, as it has done for weeks. I look at it at 4:39; by luck I pick up a true belief. I have ignored the unelimated possibility that I looked at it at 4:22 while it was stopped saying 4:39. That possibility was not properly ignored. It resembles actuality perfectly so far as the stopped clock goes.

(3) Unbeknownst to me, I am travelling in the land of the bogus barns; but my eye falls on one of the few real ones. I don't know that I am seeing a barn, because I may not properly ignore the possibility that I am seeing yet another of the abundant bogus barns. This possibility saliently resembles actuality in respect of the abundance of bogus barns and the scarcity of real ones, hereabouts.

(4) Donald is in San Francisco, just as I have every reason to think be is. But, bent on deception, he is writing me letters and having them posted to me by his accomplice in Italy. If I had seen the phoney letters, with their Italian stamps and postmarks, I would have concluded that Donald was in Italy. Luckily, I have not yet seen any of them. I ignore the unelimated possibility that Donald has gone to Italy and is sending me letters from there. But this possibility is not properly ignored, because it resembles actuality both with respect to the fact that the letters are coming to me from Italy and with respect to the fact that those letters come, ultimately, from David. So I don't know that Donald is in San Francisco.

Next, there is the *Rule of Reliability*. This time, we have a presumptive rule about what *may* be properly ignored; and it is by means of this rule that we capture what is right about causal or reliabilist theories of knowing. Consider processes whereby information is transmitted to us: perception, memory, and testimony. These processes are fairly reliable.[15] Within limits, we are entitled to take them

for granted. We may properly presuppose that they work without a glitch in the case under consideration. Defeasibly—*very* defeasibly!—a possibility in which they fail may properly be ignored.

My visual experience, for instance, depends causally on the scene before my eyes, and what I believe about the scene before my eyes depends in turn on my visual experience. Each dependence covers a wide and varied range of alternatives.[16] Of course, it is possible to hallucinate—even to hallucinate in such a way that all my perceptual experience and memory would be just as they actually are. That possibility never can be eliminated. But it can be ignored. And if it is properly ignored—as it mostly is—then vision gives me knowledge. Sometimes, though, the possibility of hallucination is not properly ignored; for sometimes we really do hallucinate. The Rule of Reliability may be defeated by the Rule of Actuality. Or it may be defeated by the Rules of Actuality and of Resemblance working together, in a Gettier problem: if I am not hallucinating, but unbeknownst to me I live in a world where people mostly do hallucinate and I myself have only narrowly escaped, then the unelimated possibility of hallucination is too close to actuality to be properly ignored.

We do not, of course, presuppose that nowhere ever is there a failure of, say, vision. The general presupposition that vision is reliable consists, rather, of a standing disposition to presuppose, concerning whatever particular case may be under consideration, that we have no failure in that case.

In similar fashion, we have two permissive *Rules of Method*. We are entitled to presuppose—again, very defeasibly—that a sample is representative; and that the best explanation of our evidence is the true explanation. That is, we are entitled properly to ignore possible failures in these two standard methods of neo-deductive inference. Again, the general rule consists of a standing disposition to presuppose reliability in whatever particular case may come before us.

Yet another permissive rule is the *Rule of Conservatism*. Suppose that those around us normally do ignore certain possibilities, and it is common knowledge that they do. (They do, they expect each other to, they expect each other to expect each other to, . . .) Then—again, very defeasibly!—these generally ignored possibilities may properly be ignored. We are permitted, defeasibly, to adopt the usual and mutually expected presuppositions of those around us.

(It is unclear whether we need all four of these permissive rules. Some might be subsumed under others. Perhaps our habits of treating samples as representative, and of inferring to the best explanation, might count as normally reliable processes of transmission of information. Or perhaps we might subsume the Rule of Reliability under the Rule of Conservatism, on the ground that the reliable processes whereby we gain knowledge are familiar, are generally relied upon, and so are generally presupposed to be normally reliable. Then the only extra work done by the Rule of Reliability would be to cover less familiar—and merely hypothetical?—reliable processes, such as processes that relied on extrasensory faculties. Likewise *mutatis mutandis,* we might subsume the Rules of Method under the Rule of Conservatism. Or we might instead think to subsume the Rule of Conservatism under the Rule of Reliability, on the ground that what is generally presupposed tends for the most part to be true, and the reliable processes whereby this is so are covered already by the Rule of Reliability. Better redundancy than incompleteness, though. So, leaving the question of redundancy open, I list all four rules.)

Our final rule is the *Rule of Attention*. But it is more a triviality than a rule. When we say that a possibility *is* properly ignored, we mean exactly that; we do not mean that it *could have been* properly ignored. Accordingly, a possibility not ignored at all is *ipso facto* not properly ignored. What is and what is not being ignored is a feature of the particular conversational context. No matter how farfetched a certain possibility may be, no matter how properly we might have ignored it in some other context, if in *this* context we are not in fact ignoring it but attending to it, then for us now it is a relevant alternative. It is in the contextually determined domain. If it is an uneliminated possibility in which not-P, then it will do as a counter-example to the claim that P holds in every possibility left uneliminated by S's evidence. That is, it will do as a counter-example to the claim that S knows that P.

Do some epistemology. Let your fantasies rip. Find uneliminated possibilities of error everywhere. Now that you are attending to them, just as I told you to, you are no longer ignoring them, properly or otherwise. So you have landed in a context with an enormously rich domain of potential counter-examples to ascriptions of knowledge. In such an extraordinary context, with such a rich domain, it never can happen (well, hardly ever) that an ascription of knowledge is true. Not an ascription of knowledge to yourself (either to your present self or to your earlier self, untainted by epistemology); and not an ascription of knowledge to others. That is how epistemology destroys knowledge. But it does so only temporarily. The pastime of epistemology does not plunge us forevermore into its special context. We can still do a lot of proper ignoring; a lot of knowing; and a lot of true ascribing of knowledge to ourselves and others, the rest of the time.

What is epistemology all about? The epistemology we've just been doing, at any rate, soon became an investigation of the ignoring of possibilities. But to investigate the ignoring of them was *ipso facto* not to ignore them. Unless this investigation of ours was an altogether atypical sample of epistemology, it will be inevitable that epistemology must destroy knowledge. That is how knowledge is elusive. Examine it, and straightway it vanishes.

Is resistance useless? If you bring some hitherto ignored possibility to our attention, then straightway we are not ignoring it at all, so *a fortiori* we are not properly ignoring it. How can this alteration of our conversational state be undone? If you are persistent, perhaps it cannot be undone—at least not so long as you are around. Even if we go off and play backgammon, and afterward start our conversation afresh, you might turn up and call our attention to it all over again.

But maybe you called attention to the hitherto ignored possibility by mistake. You only suggested that we ought to suspect the butler because you mistakenly thought him to have a criminal record. Now that you know he does not—that was the *previous* butler—you wish you had not mentioned him at all. You know as well as we do that continued attention to the possibility you brought up impedes our shared conversational purposes. Indeed, it may be common knowledge between you and us that we would all prefer it if this possibility could be dismissed from our attention. In that case we might quickly strike a tacit agreement to speak just as if we were ignoring it; and after just a little of that, doubtless it really would be ignored.

Sometimes our conversational purposes are not altogether shared, and it is a matter of conflict whether attention to some far-fetched possibility would advance them or impede them. What if some far-fetched possibility is called to our attention not by a sceptical philosopher, but by counsel for the defence? We of the jury may wish to ignore it, and wish it had not been mentioned. If we ignored it now, we would bend the rule of cooperative conversation; but we may have good reason to do exactly that. (After all, what matters most to us as jurors is not whether we can truly be said to know; what really matters is what we should believe to what degree, and whether or not we should vote to convict.) We would ignore the far-fetched possibility if we could—but can we? Perhaps at first our attempted ignoring would be make-believe ignoring, or self-deceptive ignoring; later, perhaps, it might ripen into genuine ignoring. But in the meantime, do we know? There may be no definite answer. We are bending the rules, and our practices of context-dependent attributions of knowledge were made for contexts with the rules unbent.

If you are still a contented fallibilist, despite my plea to hear the sceptical argument afresh, you will probably be discontented with the Rule of Attention. You will begrudge the sceptic even his very temporary victory. You will claim the right to resist his argument not only in everyday contexts, but even in those peculiar contexts in which he (or some other epistemologist) busily calls your attention to far-fetched possibilities of error. Further, you will claim the right to resist without having to bend any rules of cooperative conversation. I said that the Rule of Attention was a triviality: that which is not ignored at all is not properly ignored. But the Rule was trivial only because of how I had already chosen to state the *sotto voce* proviso. So you, the contented fallibist, will think it ought to have been stated differently. Thus, perhaps: "Psst!—except for those possibilities we *could* properly have ignored." And then you will insist that those far-fetched possibilities of error that we attend to at the behest of the sceptic are nevertheless possibilities we could properly have ignored. You will say that no amount of attention can, by itself, turn them into relevant alternatives.

If you say this, we have reached a standoff. I started with a puzzle: how can it be, when his conclusion is so silly, that the sceptic's argument is so irresistible? My Rule of Attention, and the version of the proviso that made that Rule trivial, were built to explain how the sceptic manages to sway us—why his argument seems irresistible, however temporarily. If you continue to find it eminently resistible in all contexts, you have no need of any such explanation. We just disagree about the explanandum phenomenon.

I say *S* knows that *P* iff *P* holds in every possibility left uneliminated by *S*'s evidence—Psst!—except for those possibilities that *we* are properly ignoring. "We" means: the speaker and hearers of a given context; that is, those of us who are discussing *S*'s knowledge together. It is our ignorings, not *S*'s own ignorings, that matter to what we can truly say about *S*'s knowledge. When we are talking about our own knowledge or ignorance, as epistemologists so often do, this is a distinction without a difference. But what if we are talking about someone else?

Suppose we are detectives; the crucial question for our solution of the crime is whether *S* already *knew*, when he bought the gun, that he was vulnerable to blackmail. We conclude that he did. *We* ignore various far-fetched possibilities, as hard-headed detectives should. But *S* does not ignore them. *S* is by profession a sceptical epistemologist. He never ignores much of anything. If it is our own ignorings that matter to the truth of our conclusion, we may well be right that *S* already knew. But if it is *S*'s ignorings that matter, then we are wrong, because *S* never knew much of anything. I say we may well be right; so it is our own ignorings that matter, not *S*'s.

But suppose instead that we are epistemologists considering what *S* knows. If we are well-informed about *S* (or if we are considering a well-enough specified hypothetical case), then if *S* attends to a certain possibility, we attend to *S*'s attending to it. But to attend to *S*'s attending to it is *ipso facto* to attend to it ourselves. In that case, unlike the case of the detectives, the possibilities we are properly ignoring must be among the possibilities that *S* himself ignores. We may ignore fewer possibilities than *S* does, but not more.

Even if *S* himself is neither sceptical nor an epistemologist, he may yet be clever at thinking up far-fetched possibilities that are uneliminated by his evidence. Then again, we well-informed epistemologists who ask what S knows will have to attend to the possibilities that S thinks up. Even if S's idle cleverness does not lead S himself to draw sceptical conclusions, it nevertheless limits the knowledge that we can truly ascribe to him when attentive to his state of mind. More simply: his cleverness limits his knowledge. He would have known more, had he been less imaginative.[17]

Do I claim you can know P just by presupposing it?! Do I claim you can know that a possibility W does not obtain just by ignoring it? Is that not what my analysis implies, provided that the presupposing and the ignoring are proper? Well, yes. And yet I do not claim it. Or rather, I do not claim it for any specified P or W. I have to grant, in general, that knowledge just by presupposing and ignoring *is* knowledge; but it is an *especially* elusive sort of knowledge, and consequently it is an unclaimable sort of knowledge. You do not even have to practice epistemology to make it vanish. Simply *mentioning* any particular case of this knowledge aloud or even in silent thought, is a way to attend to the hitherto ignored possibility, and thereby render it no longer ignored, and thereby create a context in which it is no longer true to ascribe the knowledge in question to yourself or others. So, just as we should think, presuppositions alone are not a basis on which to *claim* knowledge.

In general, when S knows that P some of the possibilities in which not-P are eliminated by S's evidence and others of them are properly ignored. There are some that can be eliminated, but cannot properly be ignored. For instance, when I look around the study without seeing Possum the cat, I thereby eliminate various possibilities in which Possum is in the study; but had those possibilities not been eliminated, they could not properly have been ignored. And there are other possibilities that never can be eliminated, but can properly be ignored. For instance, the possibility that Possum is on the desk but has been made invisible by a deceiving demon falls normally into this class (though not when I attend to it in the special context of epistemology).

There is a third class: not-P possibilities that might either be eliminated or ignored. Take the far-fetched possibility that Possum has somehow managed to get into a closed drawer of the desk—maybe he jumped in when it was open, then I closed it without noticing him. That possibility could be eliminated by opening the drawer and making a thorough examination. But if uneliminated, it may nevertheless be ignored, and in many contexts that ignoring would be proper. If I look all around the study, but without checking the closed drawers of the desk, I may truly be said to know that Possum is not in the study—or at any rate, there are many contexts in which that may truly be said. But if I did check all the closed drawers, then I would know *better* that Possum is not in the study. My knowledge would be better in the second case because it would rest more on the elimination of not-P possibilities, less on the ignoring of them.[18,19]

Better knowledge is more stable knowledge: it stands more chance of surviving a shift of attention in which we begin to attend to some of the possibilities formerly ignored. If, in our new shifted context, we ask what knowledge we may truly ascribe to our earlier selves, we may find that only the better knowledge of our earlier selves still deserves the name. And yet, if our former ignorings were proper at the time, even the worse knowledge of our earlier selves could truly have been called knowledge in the former context.

Never—well, hardly ever—does our knowledge rest entirely on elimination and not at all on ignoring. So hardly ever is it quite as good as we might wish. To that extent, the lesson of scepticism is right—and right permanently, not just in the temporary and special context of epistemology.[20]

What is it all for? Why have a notion of knowledge that works in the way I described? (Not a compulsory question. Enough to observe that we do have it.) But I venture the guess that it is one of the messy short-cuts—like satisficing, like having indeterminate degrees of belief—that we resort to because we are not smart enough to live up to really high, perfectly Bayesian, standards of rationality. You cannot maintain a record of exactly which possibilities you have eliminated so far, much as you might like to. It is easier to keep track of which possibilities you have eliminated if you—Psst!—ignore many of all the possibilities there are. And besides, it is easier to list some of the propositions that are true in *all* the uneliminated, unignored possibilities than it is to find propositions that are true in *all and only* the uneliminated, unignored possibilities.

If you doubt that the word "know" bears any real load in science or in metaphysics, I partly agree. The serious business of science has to do not with knowledge *per se*, but rather, with the elimination of possibilities through the evidence of perception, memory, etc., and with the changes that one's belief system would (or might or should) undergo under the impact of such eliminations. Assumptions of knowledge to yourself or others are a very sloppy way of conveying very incomplete information about the elimination of possibilities. It is as if you had said:

> The possibilities eliminated, whatever else they may also include, at least include all the not-*P* possibilities; or anyway, all of those except for some we are presumably prepared to ignore just at the moment.

The only excuse for giving information about what really matters in such a sloppy way is that at least it is easy and quick! But it *is* easy and quick; whereas giving full and precise information about which possibilities have been eliminated seems to be extremely difficult, as witness the futile search for a "pure observation language." If I am right about how assumptions of knowledge work, they are a handy but humble approximation. They may yet be indispensable in practice, in the same way that other handy and humble approximations are.

If we analyse knowledge as a modality, as we have done, we cannot escape the conclusion that knowledge is closed under (strict) implication.[21] Dretske has denied that knowledge is closed under implication; further, he has diagnosed closure as the fallacy that drives arguments for scepticism. As follows: the proposition that I have hands implies that I am not a handless being, and *a fortiori* that I am not a handless being deceived by a demon into thinking that I have hands. So, by the closure principle, the proposition that I know I have hands implies that I know that I am not handless and deceived. But I don't know that I am not handless and deceived—for how can I eliminate that possibility? So, by *modus tollens*, I don't know that I have hands. Dretske's advice is to resist scepticism by denying closure. He says that although having hands *does* imply not being handless and deceived,

yet knowing that I have hands *does not* imply knowing that I am not handless and deceived. I do know the former, I do not know the latter.[22]

What Dretske says is close to right, but not quite. Knowledge *is* closed under implication. Knowing that I have hands *does* imply knowing that I am not handless and deceived. Implication preserves truth—that is, it preserves truth in any given, fixed context. But if we switch contexts midway, all bets are off. I say (1) pigs fly; (2) what I just said had fewer than three syllables (true); (3) what I just said had fewer than four syllables (false). So "less than three" does not imply "less than four"? No! The context switched midway, the semantic value of the context-dependent phrase "what I just said" switched with it. Likewise in the sceptical argument the context switched midway, and the semantic value of the context-dependent word "know" switched with it. The premise "I know that I have hands" was true in its everyday context, where the possibility of deceiving demons was properly ignored. The mention of that very possibility switched the context midway. The conclusion "I know that I am not handless and deceived" was false in *its* context, because that was a context in which the possibility of deceiving demons was being mentioned, hence was not being ignored, hence was not being properly ignored. Dretske gets the phenomenon right, and I think he gets the diagnosis of scepticism right; it is just that he misclassifies what he sees. He thinks it is a phenomenon of logic, when really it is a phenomenon of pragmatics. Closure, rightly understood, survives the test. If we evaluate the conclusion for truth not with respect to the context in which it was uttered, but instead with respect to the different context in which the premise was uttered, then truth is preserved. And if, *per impossibile,* the conclusion could have been said in the same unchanged context as the premise, truth would have been preserved.

A problem due to Saul Kripke turns upon the closure of knowledge under implication. *P* implies that any evidence against *P* is misleading. So, by closure, whenever you know that *P*, you know that any evidence against *P* is misleading. And if you know that evidence is misleading, you should pay it no heed. Whenever we know—and we know a lot, remember—we should not heed any evidence tending to suggest that we are wrong. But that is absurd. Shall we dodge the conclusion by denying closure? I think not. Again, I diagnose a change of context. At first, it was stipulated that S knew, whence it followed that S was properly ignoring all possibilities of error. But as the story continues, it turns out that there is evidence on offer that points to some particular possibility of error. Then, by the Rule of Attention, that possibility is no longer properly ignored, either by S himself or by we who are telling the story of S. The advent of that evidence destroys S's knowledge, and thereby destroys S's licence to ignore the evidence lest he be misled.

There is another reason, different from Dretske's, why we might doubt closure. Suppose two or more premises jointly imply a conclusion. Might not someone who is compartmentalized in his thinking—as we all are?—know each of the premises but fail to bring them together in a single compartment? Then might he not fail to know the conclusion? Yes; and I would not like to plead idealization-of-rationality as an excuse for ignoring such cases. But I suggest that we might take not the whole compartmentalized thinker, but rather each of his several overlapping compartments, as our 'subjects.' That would be the obvious remedy if his compartmentalization amounted to a case of multiple personality disorder; but maybe it is right for milder cases as well.

A compartmentalized thinker who indulges in epistemology can destroy his knowledge, yet retain it as well. Imagine two epistemologists on a bushwalk. As they walk, they talk. They mention all manner of far-fetched possibilities of error. By attending to these normally ignored possibilities they destroy the knowledge they normally possess. Yet all the while they know where they are and where they are going! How so? The compartment in charge of philosophical talk attends to far-fetched possibilities of error. The compartment in charge of navigation does not. One compartment loses its knowledge, the other retains its knowledge. And what does the entire compartmentalized thinker know? Not an altogether felicitous question. But if we need an answer, I suppose the best thing to say is that S knows that P iff any one of S's compartments knows that P. Then we can say what we would offhand want to say: yes, our philosophical bushwalkers still know their whereabouts.

Context-dependence is not limited to the ignoring and non-ignoring of far-fetched possibilities. Here is another case. Pity poor Bill! He squanders all his spare cash on the pokies, the races, and the lottery. He will be a wage slave all his days. We know he will never be rich. But if he wins the lottery (if he wins big), then he will be rich. Contrapositively: his never being rich, plus other things we know, imply that he will lose. So, by closure, if we know that he will never be rich, we know that he will lose. But when we discussed the case before, we concluded that we cannot know that he will lose. All the possibilities in which Bill loses and someone else wins saliently resemble the possibility in which Bill wins and the others lose; one of those possibilities is actual; so by the Rules of Actuality and of Resemblance, we may not properly ignore the possibility that Bill wins. But there is a loophole: the resemblance was required to be salient. Salience, as well as ignoring, may vary between contexts. Before, when I was explaining how the Rule of Resemblance applied to lotteries, I saw to it that the resemblance between the many possibilities associated with the many tickets was sufficiently salient. But this time, when we were busy pitying poor Bill for his habits and not for his luck, the resemblance of the many possibilities was not so salient. At that point, the possibility of Bill's winning was properly ignored; so then it was true to say that we knew he would never be rich. Afterward I switched the context. I mentioned the possibility that Bill might win, wherefore that possibility was no longer properly ignored. (Maybe there were two separate reasons why it was no longer properly ignored, because maybe I also made the resemblance between the many possibilities more salient.) It was true at first that we knew that Bill would never be rich. And at that point it was also true that we knew he would lose—but that was only true so long as it remained unsaid! (And maybe unthought as well.) Later, after the change in context, it was no longer true that we knew he would lose. At that point, it was also no longer true that we knew he would never be rich.

But wait. Don't you smell a rat? Haven't I, by my own lights, been saying what cannot be said? (Or whistled either.) If the story I told was true, how have I managed to tell it? In trendyspeak, is there not a problem of reflexivity? Does not my story deconstruct itself?

I said: S knows that P iff S's evidence eliminates every possibility in which not-P—Psst!—except for those possibilities that we are properly ignoring.

That "psst" marks an attempt to do the impossible—to mention that which remains unmentioned. I am sure you managed to make believe that I had succeeded. But I could not have done.

And I said that when we do epistemology, and we attend to the proper ignoring of possibilities, we make knowledge vanish. First we do know, then we do not. But I had been doing epistemology when I said that. The uneliminated possibilities were *not* being ignored—not just then. So by what right did I say even that we used to know?[23]

In trying to thread a course between the rock of fallibilism and the whirlpool of scepticism, it may well seem as if I have fallen victim to both at once. For do I not say that there are all those uneliminated possibilities of error? Yet do I not claim that we know a lot? Yet do I not claim that knowledge is, by definition, infallible knowledge?

I did claim all three things. But not all at once! Or if I did claim them all at once, that was an expository shortcut, to be taken with a pinch of salt. To get my message across, I bent the rules. If I tried to whistle what cannot be said, what of it? I relied on the cardinal principle of pragmatics, which overrides every one of the rules I mentioned: interpret the message to make it make sense—to make it consistent, and sensible to say.

When you have context-dependence, ineffability can be trite and unmysterious. Hush! [moment of silence] I might have liked to say, just then, "All of us are silent." It was true. But I could not have said it truly, or whistled it either. For by saying it aloud, or by whistling, I would have rendered it false.

I could have said my say fair and square, bending no rules. It would have been tiresome, but it could have been done. The secret would have been to resort to "semantic ascent." I could have taken great care to distinguish between (1) the language I use when I talk about knowledge, or whatever, and (2) the second language that I use to talk about the semantic and pragmatic workings of the first language. If you want to hear my story told that way, you probably know enough to do the job for yourself. If you can, then my informal presentation has been good enough.

Notes

[1] The suggestion that ascriptions of knowledge go false in the context of epistemology is to be found in Barry Stroud, "Understanding Human Knowledge in General" in Marjorie Clay and Keith Lehrer (eds.), *Knowledge and Skepticism* (Boulder: Westview Press, 1989); and in Stephen Hetherington, "Lacking Knowledge and Justification by Theorising About Them" (lecture at the University of New South Wales, August 1992). Neither of them tells the story just as I do, however it may be that their versions do not conflict with mine.

[2] Unless, like some, we simply define "justification" as "whatever it takes to turn true opinion into knowledge" regardless of whether what it takes turns out to involve argument from supporting reasons.

[3] The problem of the lottery was introduced in Henry Kyburg, *Probability and the Logic of Rational Belief* (Middletown, CT: Wesleyan University Press, 1961), and in Carl Hempel, "Deductive-Nomological vs. Statistical Explanation" in Herbert Feigl and Grover Maxwell (eds.), *Minnesota Studies in the Philosophy of Science,* Vol. II (Minneapolis: University of Minnesota Press, 1962). It has been much discussed since, as a problem both about knowledge and about our everyday, non-quantitative concept of belief.

[4] The case of testimony is less discussed than the others; but see C. A. J. Coady, *Testimony: A Philosophical Study* (Oxford: Clarendon Press, 1992) pp. 79–129.

[5] I follow Peter Unger, *Ignorance: A Case for Scepticism* (New York: Oxford University Press, 1975). But I shall not let him lead me into scepticism.

[6] See Robert Stalnaker, *Inquiry* (Cambridge, MA: MIT Press, 1984) pp. 59–99.

[7] See my "Attitudes *De Dicto* and *De Se*," *The Philosophical Review* 88 (1979) pp. 513–543; and R. M. Chisholm, "The Indirect Reflexive" in C. Diamond and J. Teichman (eds.), *Intention and Intentionality: Essays in Honour of G. E. M. Anscombe* (Brighton: Harvester, 1979).

[8] Peter Unger, *Ignorance,* chapter II. I discuss the case, and briefly foreshadow the present paper, in my "Scorekeeping in a Language Game," *Journal of Philosophical Logic* 8 (1979) pp. 339–359, esp. pp. 353–355.

[9] See Robert Stalnaker, "Presuppositions," *Journal of Philosophical Logic* 2 (1973) pp. 447–457; and "Pragmatic Presuppositions" in Milton Munitz and Peter Unger (eds.), *Semantics and Philosophy* (New York: New York University Press, 1974). See also my "Scorekeeping in a Language Game."

The definition restated in terms of presupposition resembles the treatment of knowledge in Kenneth S. Ferguson, *Philosophical Scepticism* (Cornell University doctoral dissertation, 1980).

[10] See Fred Dretske, "Epistemic Operators," *The Journal of Philosophy* 67 (1970) pp. 1007–1022, and "The Pragmatic Dimension of Knowledge," *Philosophical Studies* 40 (1981) pp. 363–378; Alvin Goldman, "Discrimination and Perceptual Knowledge," *The Journal of Philosophy* 73 (1976) pp. 771–791; G. C. Stine, "Skepticism, Relevant Alternatives, and Deductive Closure," *Philosophical Studies*

29 (1976) pp. 249–261; and Stewart Cohen, "How to Be a Fallibilist," *Philosophical Perspectives* 2 (1988) pp. 91–123.

[11]Some of them, but only some, taken from the authors just cited.

[12]Instead of complicating the Rule of Belief as I have just done, I might equivalently have introduced a separate Rule of High Stakes saying that when error would be especially disastrous, few possibilities are properly ignored.

[13]A. D. Woozley, "Knowing and Not Knowing," *Proceedings of the Aristotelian Society* 53 (1953) pp. 151–172; Colin Radford, "Knowledge—By Examples," *Analysis* 27 (1966) pp. 1–11.

[14]See Edmund Gettier, "Is Justified True Belief Knowledge?," *Analysis* 23 (1963) pp. 121–123. Diagnoses have varied widely. The four examples below come from: (1) Keith Lehrer and Thomas Paxson Jr., "Knowledge: Undefeated True Belief," *The Journal of Philosophy* 66 (1969) pp. 225–237; (2) Bertrand Russell, *Human Knowledge: Its Scope and Limits* (London: Allen and Unwin, 1948) p. 154; (3) Alvin Goldman, "Discrimination and Perceptual Knowledge," op. cit.; (4) Gilbert Harman, *Thought* (Princeton, NJ: Princeton University Press 1973) p. 143.

Though the lottery problem is another case of justified true belief without knowledge, it is not normally counted among the Gettier problems. It is interesting to find that it yields to the same remedy.

[15]See Alvin Goldman, "A Causal Theory of Knowing," *The Journal of Philosophy* 64 (1967) pp. 357–372; D. M. Armstrong, *Belief, Truth and Knowledge* (Cambridge: Cambridge University Press, 1973).

[16]See my "Veridical Hallucination and Prosthetic Vision," *Australasian Journal of Philosophy* 58 (1980) pp. 239–249. John Bigelow has proposed to model knowledge-delivering processes generally on those found in vision.

[17]See Catherine Elgin, "The Epistemic Efficacy of Stupidity," *Synthese* 74 (1988) pp. 297–311. The "efficacy" takes many forms; some to do with knowledge (under various rival analyses), some to do with justified belief. See also Michael Williams, *Unnatural Doubts:*

Epistemological Realism and the Basis of Scepticism (Oxford: Blackwell, 1991) pp. 352–355, on the instability of knowledge under reflection.

[18]Mixed cases are possible: Fred properly ignores the possibility W_1 which Ted eliminates; however Ted properly ignores the possibility W_2 which Fred eliminates. Ted has looked in all the desk drawers but not the file drawers, whereas Fred has checked the file drawers but not the desk. Fred's knowledge that Possum is not in the study is better in one way, Ted's is better in another.

[19]To say truly that X is known, I must be properly ignoring any uneliminated possibilities in which not-X; whereas to say truly that Y is better known than X, I must be attending to some such possibilities. So I cannot say both in a single context. If I say "X is known, but Y is better known," the context changes in mid-sentence: some previously ignored possibilities must stop being ignored. That can happen easily. Saying it the other way around—"Y is better known than X, but even X is known"—is harder, because we must suddenly start to ignore previously unignored possibilities. That cannot be done, really; but we could bend the rules and make believe we had done it, and no doubt we would be understood well enough. Saying "X is flat, but Y is flatter" (that is, "X has no bumps at all, but Y has even fewer or smaller bumps") is a parallel case. And again, "Y is flatter, but even X is flat" sounds clearly worse—but not altogether hopeless.

[20]Thanks here to Stephen Hetherington. While his own views about better and worse knowledge are situated within an analysis of knowledge quite unlike mine, they withstand transplantation.

[21]A proof-theoretic version of this closure principle is common to all "normal' modal logics: if the logic validates an inference from zero or more premises to a conclusion, then also it validates the inference obtained by prefixing the necessary operator to each premise and to the conclusion. Further, this rule is all we need to take us from classical sentential logic to the least normal modal logic. See Brian Chellas, *Modal Logic: An Introduction* (Cambridge: Cambridge University Press, 1980) p. 114.

[22]See Stalnaker, *Inquiry,* pp. 79–99.

V1.8 Virtues in Epistemology

JOHN GRECO

John Greco is associate professor of philosophy at Fordham University and the author of several works in epistemology, including *Putting Skeptics in Their Place* (Cambridge University Press). In this essay he defends a version of reliabilism, which he identifies with a kind of Aristotelian intellectual virtue theory. Part One reviews some recent history of epistemology, focusing on ways in which the intellectual virtues have been invoked to address a range of traditional and nontraditional concerns. Greco argues that a reliabilist understanding of the intellectual virtues is best suited for constructing an account of knowledge. Part Two explores three problems for an account of knowledge: skepticism, Gettier cases, and the value of knowledge problem.

What is a virtue in epistemology? In the broadest sense, a virtue is an excellence of some kind. In epistemology, the relevant kind of excellence will be "intellectual." But then what is an intellectual virtue? Some philosophers have understood intellectual virtues to be broad cognitive abilities or powers. On this view, intellectual virtues are innate faculties or acquired habits that enable a person to arrive at truth and avoid error in some relevant field. For example, Aristotle defined "intuitive reason" as the ability to grasp first principles, and he defined "science" as the ability to demonstrate further truths from these first principles.[1] Some contemporary authors add accurate perception, reliable memory, and various kinds of good reasoning to the list of intellectual virtues. These authors follow Aristotle in the notion that intellectual virtues are cognitive abilities or powers, but they loosen the requirements for what count as such.[2]

Other authors have understood the intellectual virtues quite differently, however. On their view intellectual virtues are more like personality traits than cognitive abilities or powers. For example, intellectual courage is a trait of mind that allows one to persevere in one's ideas. Intellectual open-mindedness is a trait of mind that allows one to be receptive to the ideas of others. Among these authors, however, there is

disagreement about why such personality traits count as virtues. Some think it is because they are truth-conducive, increasing one's chances of arriving at true beliefs while avoiding false beliefs.[3] Others think that such traits are virtues independently of their connection to truth—they would be virtues even if they were not truth-conducive at all.[4]

Who is right about the nature of the intellectual virtues? One might think that this is a matter of semantics—that different authors have simply decided to use the term "intellectual virtue" in different ways. In the essay that follows I will argue that there is some truth to this analysis. However, it is not the whole truth. This is because epistemologists invoke the notion of an intellectual virtue for specific reasons, in the context of addressing specific problems in epistemology. In effect, they make claims that under- standing the intellectual virtues in a certain way allows us to solve those problems. And of course claims like that are substantive, not merely terminological. In Part One of this essay I will review some recent history of epistemology, focussing on ways in which the intellectual virtues have been invoked to solve specific epistemological problems. The purpose of this part is to give a sense of the contemporary landscape that has emerged, and to clarify some of the disagreements among those who invoke the virtues in epistemology. In Part Two I will explore some epistemological problems in greater detail. The purpose of this part is

Reprinted from *The Oxford Handbook of Epistemology*, ed. Paul Moser (Oxford University Press, 2002) by permission of the author and the publisher.

to defend a particular approach in virtue episte-mology by displaying its power in addressing these problems.

Part One. History and Landscape

1. Sosa's Virtue Perspectivism

The intellectual virtues made their contemporary debut in a series of papers by Ernest Sosa.[5] In those papers Sosa is primarily concerned with two problems in the theory of knowledge. The first is the debate between foundationalism and coheren-tism. The second is a series of objections that have been raised against reliabilism.

a. FOUNDATIONALISM AND COHERENTISM. Foundationalism and coherentism are positions regarding the structure of knowledge. According to foundationalism, knowledge is like a pyramid: A solid foundation of knowledge grounds the entire structure, providing the support required by knowledge at the higher levels. According to coherentism, knowledge is like a raft: Different parts of the structure are tied together via relations of mutual support, with no part of the whole play-ing a more fundamental role than do others.[6] Let us use the term "epistemic justification" to name whatever property it is that turns mere true belief into knowledge. We may then define "pure coher-entism" as holding that only coherence con-tributes to epistemic justification, and we may define "pure foundationalism" as holding that coherence does not contribute to epistemic justifi-cation at all. In the papers that introduce the notion of an intellectual virtue, Sosa argues that neither pure coherentism nor pure foundational-ism can be right.

Against pure coherentism is the well-known objection that there can be highly coherent belief-systems that are nevertheless largely divorced from reality. But then coherence cannot be the only thing that matters for epistemic justification. Sosa presses this basic point in various ways. For one, consider the victim of Descartes' evil demon. By hypothesis, the victim's beliefs are as coherent as our own. That is, they are members of a coherent system of beliefs, tied together by a great number and variety of logical and quasi-logical relations.

Suppose that by chance some few of those beliefs are also true. Surely they do not amount to knowl-edge, although both true and coherent.[7]

Another way that Sosa argues the point is to highlight the importance of experience for epi-stemic justification. Consider that any human being will have perceptual beliefs with few con-nections to other beliefs in her total belief system. For example, my perceptual belief that there is a bird outside my window has few logical relations to other beliefs that I have. But then one can gen-erate counterexamples to pure coherentism by means of the following recipe. First, replace my belief that there is a bird outside my window with the belief that there is squirrel outside my window. Second, make whatever few other changes are nec-essary to preserve coherence. For example, replace my belief that I seem to see a bird with the belief that I seem to see a squirrel. Clearly, the overall coherence of the new belief system will be about the same as that of the first. This is because coher-ence is entirely a function of relations among beliefs, and those relations are about the same in the two systems. But it seems wrong that the new belief about the squirrel is as well justified as the old belief about the bird, for my sensory experi-ence is still such that I seem to see a bird, and do not seem to see a squirrel. Again, coherence can-not be the only thing that contributes to epistemic justification.[8]

However, there is an equally daunting prob-lem for pure foundationalism, although the way to see it is less direct. Consider how foundationalism might account for my knowledge that there is a bird outside the window. Since the knowledge in question is perceptual, it is plausible to say that it is grounded in sensory experience. Specifically, it is plausible to say that my belief that there is a bird outside the window is epistemically justified because it is grounded in a visual experience of a particular phenomenal quality. What is more, this explains the difference in epistemic status between my belief about the bird and the belief about the squirrel above. In the latter case, there is no grounding in sensory experience of a relevant sort. But here a problem lurks. Consider the founda-tionalist epistemic principle invoked above, that is, that a particular sort of sensory experience, with a particular phenomenal quality, justifies the belief that there is a bird outside the window. Is this to be understood as a fundamental principle about epistemic justification, or is it to be understood as an instance of some more general principle? If we say the former, then there would seem to be an infinite number of such principles, with no hope for unity among them. In effect, we would be committed to saying that such principles, in all their number and variety, merely state brute facts about epistemic justification. This is hardly a satisfying position. The more attractive view is that such principles are derived. But then there is more work to be done. Something more fundamental about epistemic justification remains to be explained.

This is where the notion of an intellectual virtue is useful, Sosa argues. Virtues in general are excellences of some kind; more specifically, they are innate or acquired dispositions to achieve some end. Intellectual virtues, Sosa argues, will be dispositions to achieve the intellectual ends of grasping truths and avoiding falsehoods. This notion of an intellectual virtue can be used to give a general account of epistemic justification as follows:

> A belief $B(p)$ is epistemically justified for a person S (that is, justified in the sense required for knowledge) if and only if $B(p)$ is produced by one or more intellectual virtues of S.

This account of justification, Sosa argues, allows us to explain the unifying ground of the foundationalist's epistemic principles regarding perceptual beliefs. Specifically, such principles describe various intellectually virtuous dispositions. Thus human beings are gifted with perceptual powers or abilities; that is, dispositions to reliably form beliefs about the environment on the basis of sensory inputs of various modalities. Such abilities are relative to circumstances and environment, but they are abilities nonetheless. The foundationalist's epistemic principles relating perceptual beliefs to their experiential grounds can now be understood as describing or explicating these various abilities.[9]

And the payoff does not end there. For it is possible to give similar accounts of other sources of justification traditionally recognized by foundationalism. Because they are reliable, such faculties as memory, introspection and logical intuition count as intellectual virtues, and therefore give rise to epistemic justification for their respective products. In a similar fashion, various kinds of deductive and inductive reasoning reliably take one from true belief to further true belief, and hence count as virtues in their own right. By defining epistemic justification in terms of intellectual virtue, Sosa argues, we get a unified account of all the sources of justification traditionally recognized by foundationalism.[10]

Once the foundationalist makes this move, however, pure foundationalism becomes untenable. We said that perception, memory and the like are sources of epistemic justification because they are intellectual virtues. But now coherence has an equal claim to be an intellectual virtue, and hence an equal claim to be a source of epistemic justification. The intellectual virtues were characterized as cognitive abilities or powers; as dispositions that reliably give rise to true belief under relevant circumstances and in a relevant environment. We may now think of coherence—or more exactly, coherence-seeking reason—as just such a power. In our world, in normal circumstances, coherence-seeking reason is also a reliable source of true belief and hence a source of epistemic justification.[11]

Finally, Sosa argues, we are now in a position to recognize two kinds of knowledge. First, there is "animal knowledge," enjoyed by any being whose true beliefs are the products of intellectual virtue. But second, there is "reflective knowledge," which further requires a coherent perspective on one's beliefs and their source in intellectual virtue. We may also label the latter kind of knowledge "human knowledge," recognizing that the relevant sort of reflective coherence is a distinctively human virtue. More exactly,

> S has animal knowledge regarding p only if
> 1. p is true, and
> 2. S's belief B(p) is produced by one or more intellectual virtues of S.

> S has reflective knowledge regarding p only if
> 1. p is true,
> 2. S's belief $B(p)$ is produced by one or more intellectual virtues of S, and
> 3. S has a true perspective on $B(p)$ as being produced by one or more intellectual virtues, where such perspective is itself produced by an intellectual virtue of S.[12]

b. RELIABILISM.   Let us define generic reliabilism as follows.

A belief $B(p)$ is epistemically justified for S if and only if $B(p)$ is the outcome of a sufficiently reliable cognitive process, that is, a process that is sufficiently truth-conducive.[13]

Generic reliabilism is a powerful view. For one, it accounts for a wide range of our pre-theoretical intuitions regarding which beliefs have epistemic justification. Thus reliabilism explains why beliefs caused by perception, memory, introspection, logical intuition, and sound reasoning are epistemically justified, and it explains why beliefs caused by hallucination, wishful thinking, hasty generalization, and other unreliable processes are not. The view also provides a powerful resource against well-known skeptical arguments. For example, a variety of skeptical arguments trade on the assumption that our cognitive faculties must be vindicated as reliable in order to count as sources of epistemic justification. Because it seems impossible to provide such vindication in a noncircular way, a broad skeptical conclusion threatens. Generic reliabilism cuts off this kind of skeptical reasoning at its roots, with the idea that epistemic justification requires *de facto* reliability rather than vindicated reliability: The difference between knowledge and mere opinion is that the former is grounded in cognitive processes that are in fact reliable in this world.[14]

The view is powerful, but subject to a variety of problems. One of these is that reliability seems insufficient for epistemic justification. To see why, consider the following case. Suppose that S suffers from a rare sort of brain lesion, one effect of which is to cause the victim to believe that he has a brain lesion. However, S has no evidence that he has such a condition, and even has evidence against it. We can imagine, for example, that he has just been given a clean bill of health by competent neurologists. It seems clear that S's belief that he has a brain lesion is unjustified, although (by hypothesis) it has been caused by a highly reliable cognitive process.[15]

The forgoing case seems to show that reliability is not sufficient for epistemic justification. A second case seems to show that reliability is not necessary for epistemic justification. Consider again Descartes' victim of an evil demon. We said that, by hypothesis, the victim's belief system is as coherent as our own. We may now add that the victim bases her beliefs on her experience as we do, and reasons to new beliefs as we do. Clearly, the

victim's beliefs cannot amount to knowledge, because she is the victim of massive deception. But still, it seems wrong to say that her beliefs are not justified at all. Let us follow Sosa and call this "the new evil demon problem" for reliabilism. According to simple reliabilism, epistemic justification is entirely a matter of reliability. But the demon victim's beliefs are not reliably formed. The problem for reliabilism is to explain why the victim's beliefs are nevertheless justified.[16]

Sosa argues that both of the above problems can be solved by invoking the notion of an intellectual virtue. Consider the case of the epistemically serendipitous brain lesion. What the case shows is that not all reliable cognitive processes give rise to epistemic justification. On the contrary, the reliabilist must place some kind of restriction on the kind of processes that do so. Sosa's suggestion is that the relevant processes are those which are grounded in the knower's intellectual virtues; that is, her cognitive abilities or powers. Because the belief about the brain lesion does not arise in this way, making this move allows the reliabilist to deny that the belief is epistemically justified.[17]

Now consider the new evil demon problem. Clearly the beliefs of the demon victim are not reliably formed, and therefore lack something important for knowledge. But notice that there are two ways that a belief can fail by way of reliability. One way is that something goes wrong "from the skin inward." For example, the subject might fail to respond appropriately to her sensory experience, or might fail to reason appropriately from her beliefs. Another way to go wrong, however, is "from the skin outward." Perhaps there is no flaw to be found downstream from experience and belief, but one's cognitive faculties are simply not fitted for one's environment. It is this second way that the demon victim fails. Internally speaking, she is in as good working order as we are. Externally speaking, however, her epistemic condition is a disaster. But then there is a straightforward sense in which even the victim's beliefs are internally justified, Sosa argues. Namely, they are beliefs that result from intellectual virtues.

We saw earlier that Sosa endorses the following account of epistemic justification.

A belief $B(p)$ is epistemically justified for a person S if and only if $B(p)$ is produced by one or more intellectual virtues of S.

According to Sosa, we need only add that whether a cognitive faculty counts as a virtue is relative to an environment. The victim's perception and reasoning powers are not reliable in her demon environment, and hence are not virtues relative to her world. But those same faculties are reliable, and therefore do count as virtues, relative to the actual world. Accordingly, we have a sense in which the demon victim's beliefs are internally justified although not reliably formed. In fact, Sosa argues, they are internally justified in every respect relevant for animal knowledge.[18]

Finally, it is possible to define a further kind of internal justification associated with reflective knowledge. Remember that reflective knowledge requires a perspective on one's beliefs and their sources in intellectual virtue. The victim of a deceiving demon might also enjoy such a perspective, together with the broad coherence that this entails. This perspective and coherence provides the basis for a further kind of internal justification, Sosa argues.[19]

2. Moral Models of Intellectual Virtue

According to Sosa, an intellectual virtue is a reliable cognitive ability or power. Coherence-seeking reason is thus an intellectual virtue if reliable, but so are perception, memory, and introspection. Other philosophers have argued against this characterization of the intellectual virtues, however. For example, James Montmarquet's account differs from Sosa's in at least three major respects.[20]

First, cognitive powers such as perception and reason do not count as intellectual virtues at all according to Montmarquet. Rather, on his view the virtues are conceived as personality traits, or qualities of character, such as intellectual courage and intellectual carefulness. In this way the intellectual virtues are analogous to the moral virtues, such as moral temperance and moral courage.

Second, Montmarquet argues that it is a mistake to characterize the intellectual virtues as reliable, or truth-conducive. This is because we can conceive of possible worlds, such as Descartes' demon world, where the beliefs of intellectually virtuous persons are almost entirely false. But traits such as intellectual courage and intellectual carefulness would remain virtues even in such a world, Montmarquet argues. Likewise, we can conceive

of worlds where intellectual laziness and carelessness reliably produce true beliefs. But again, traits like laziness and carelessness would remain vices even in such worlds. Therefore, Montmarquet concludes, the intellectual virtues cannot be defined in terms of their reliability. Montmarquet's alternative is to define the virtues in terms of a desire for truth. According to this model, the intellectual virtues are those personality traits that a person who desires the truth would want to have.

Finally, on Montmarquet's view the exercise and nonexercise of the intellectual virtues are under our control, and are therefore appropriate objects of praise and blame. When one faces a truck approaching at high speed, one cannot help but perceive accordingly. However, one can control whether one takes a new idea seriously, or considers a line of argument carefully. Hence we have a third way in which Montmarquet's account of the intellectual virtues departs from Sosa's.

It is clear that Montmarquet's account of the intellectual virtues has affinities with Aristotle's account of the moral virtues. Hence Montmarquet thinks of the intellectual virtues as personality traits or qualities; he emphasizes the importance of proper motivation, and he holds that the exercise of the virtues is under our control. A philosopher who follows Aristotle's model of the moral virtues even more closely is Linda Zagzebski. In fact, Zagzebski criticizes Aristotle for maintaining a strong distinction between the intellectual and moral virtues, arguing that the former are best understood as a subset of the latter. (*VM*, esp. 137–58) [See note 3. Ed.]

According to Zagzebski, all virtues are acquired traits of character that involve both a motivational component and a reliable success component. Hence, all moral virtues involve a general motivation to achieve the good, and are reliably successful in doing so. All intellectual virtues involve a general motivation to achieve true belief, and are reliably successful in doing so. But since the true is a component of the good, Zagzebski argues, intellectual virtues can be understood as a subset of the moral virtues. In addition to their general motivation and reliability, each virtue can be defined in terms of its specific or characteristic motivational structure. For example, moral courage is the virtue according to which a person is motivated to risk danger when something of value is at stake, and is reliably successful at doing so. Benevolence is the virtue according to which a person is motivated to bring about the well-being of others, and is reliably successful at doing so. Likewise, intellectual courage is the virtue according to which a person is motivated to be persevering in her own ideas, and is reliably successful at doing so. (*VM*, esp. 165–97)

One advantage of understanding the intellectual virtues this way, Zagzebski argues, is that it allows the following account of knowledge. First, Zagzebski defines an "act of intellectual virtue."

> An act of intellectual virtue *A* is an act that arises from the motivational component of *A*, is something a person with virtue *A* would (probably) do in the circumstances, is successful in achieving the end of the *A* motivation, and is such that the agent acquires a true belief through these features of the act. (*VM*, 270)

We may then define knowledge as follows:

> *S* has knowledge regarding *p* if and only if
> 1. *p* is true, and
> 2. *S*'s true belief *B*(*p*) arises out of acts of intellectual virtue.

Since the truth condition is redundant in the above definition, we may say alternatively:

> *S* has knowledge regarding *p* if and only if *S*'s believing *p* arises out of acts of intellectual virtue. (*VM*, esp. 264–73)

Even more so than Montmarquet, Zagzebski adopts Aristotle's account of the moral virtues as her model for understanding the intellectual virtues. Thus on her account (a) the intellectual virtues are understood as acquired traits of character, (b) their acquisition is partly under our control, (c) both their possession and exercise are appropriate objects of moral praise, and (d) both their lack and nonexercise can be appropriate objects of moral blame. It is noteworthy that Zagzebski's account departs from Sosa's on all of these points. Thus for Sosa the intellectual virtues are cognitive abilities rather than character traits; they need not be acquired, and their acquisition and use need not be under one's control. On Sosa's account, the possession and exercise of the intellectual virtues are grounds for praise, but this need not be praise of a moral sort.

Hence we praise people for their keen perception and sound reasoning, but this is more like praise for an athlete's prowess than like praise for a hero's courage.

On the face of things, therefore, there would seem to be a significant disagreement over the nature of the intellectual virtues. But at this point it might be suggested that the issue is merely terminological. What Zagzebski means by a virtue is something close to what Aristotle means by a moral virtue, and therefore natural cognitive powers such as perception and memory do not count as virtues on her meaning of the tem. Sosa has adopted a different sense of the term, however, according to which anything that has a function has virtues. In this sense, a virtue is a characteristic excellence of some sort, and reliable perception and reliable memory qualify as intellectual excellences. But to see this as a terminological dispute obscures a substantive one. This comes out if we recall that both Sosa and Zagzebski offer accounts of knowledge in terms of their respective notions of intellectual virtue. The substantive question is now this: Which account of the intellectual virtues better serves this purpose? Sosa also invokes the intellectual virtues to address the dispute between foundationalism and coherentism over the structure of knowledge. Here we may ask again: Which notion of the intellectual virtues is best suited for this purpose?

Once the question regarding the nature of the intellectual virtues is framed this way, however, it seems clear that Zagzebski's account is too strong. Consider first the idea that knowledge arises out of acts of intellectual virtue. On Zagzebski's account, this means that knowledge must manifest dispositions that both (a) involve a certain motivational structure and (b) involve relevant kinds of voluntary control. But neither of these requirements seems necessary for knowledge.

Consider a case of simple perceptual knowledge: You are crossing the street in good light, you look to your left, and you see that a large truck is moving quickly toward you. It would seem that you know that there is a truck moving toward you independently of any control, either over the ability to perceive such things in general, or over this particular exercise of that ability. Neither is it required that one have a motivation to be open-minded, careful, or the like. On the contrary, it would seem that you know that there is a truck coming toward you even if you are motivated *not* to be open-minded, careful, or the like. . . .

It seems clear that an account of the intellectual virtues modeled on Aristotle's account of the moral virtues is apt for addressing a variety of epistemological concerns. It is a mistake, however, to generalize from such concerns to an account of knowledge per se. As we have seen, the moral model is ill suited for that purpose, since it will result in an account of knowledge that is too strong.

3. WISDOM AND UNDERSTANDING. Perhaps one place where the moral model is useful is in accounts of "higher grade" epistemic achievements such as wisdom and understanding. According to Zagzebski, wisdom has clear moral dimensions. Thus wisdom unifies the knowledge of the wise person, but also her desires and values. This is why it is impossible for wisdom to be misused, she argues, and why it is incoherent to talk of a person that is wise but immoral. Also, wisdom is achieved only through extensive life experience, and hence takes time to acquire. Therefore, Zagzebski argues, wisdom is best understood on a moral model of the intellectual virtues, either because it is such a virtue itself, or because it is the product of such virtues. (*VM*, 22–3) This seems plausible, especially if we mean wisdom to include practical wisdom, or wisdom regarding how one ought to live. But again, it would be a mistake to generalize from an account of wisdom to an account of knowledge per se. I suggest that Zagzebski's account of wisdom is plausible precisely because we think that wisdom is harder to achieve than knowledge. The stronger conditions implied by Zagzebski's account therefore seem more appropriate here than in a general account of knowledge.

I have argued that Zagzebski's position benefits from a distinction between knowledge and wisdom. By maintaining this distinction, it is possible to resist putting conditions on knowledge per se that are appropriate only for knowledge of a higher grade. In a similar fashion, Sosa's position benefits from a distinction between knowledge and understanding.[21] To see how this is so, it is useful to notice a tension in Sosa's thinking.

Recall that Sosa makes a distinction between animal knowledge and reflective knowledge. One has animal knowledge as long as one's true belief has its source in a reliable cognitive faculty. One

has reflective knowledge only if one's first-order belief also fits into a coherent perspective, which perspective must include a belief that one's first-order belief has its reliable source. Sometimes Sosa writes as if animal knowledge is real knowledge, while reflective knowledge amounts to a higher achievement still.[22] In other places Sosa's evaluation of animal knowledge is less enthusiastic. Hence he calls it "servomechanic" and "mere animal" knowledge, and in one place suggests that the label is "metaphorical."[23] Either way, however, it is clear that Sosa thinks animal knowledge is of a lesser kind than reflective knowledge.

The tension is now this: As we saw above, Sosa holds that the virtue of coherence is its reliability. Like perception, memory and introspection, reason-seeking coherence makes its contribution to epistemic justification and knowledge because it is reliable. But then why should reflective knowledge be of a higher kind than animal knowledge? If the difference between animal and reflective knowledge is a coherent perspective, and if the value of coherence is its reliability, it would seem that the distinction between animal knowledge and reflective knowledge is at most a difference in degree rather than in kind. Moreover, we have no good reason to think that a person with reflective knowledge will always be more reliable than a person with only animal knowledge; that is, it seems clearly possible that the cognitive virtues of a person without an epistemic perspective could be more reliable than the cognitive virtues of a person with it. But then reflective knowledge is not necessarily higher than animal knowledge, even in degree.

Here is a different problem for Sosa's view. Suppose we take what seems to be Sosa's considered position, which is that human knowledge is reflective knowledge. On this view a broad skepticism threatens, because it seems clear that in a typical case most people lack the required epistemic perspective; that is, in the typical case most people lack beliefs about the source of their first-order belief, and whether that source is reliable. For example, in most cases where I have a belief that there is a bird outside my window, I do not have further beliefs about the source of that belief, or about the reliability of that source. Sosa's response to this kind of objection is to stress that the required epistemic perspective need only be implicit. Thus he writes,

[A person judging shapes on a screen] is justified well enough in taking it that, in his circumstances, what looks to have a certain shape does have that shape. He implicitly trusts that connection, as is revealed by his inferential 'habit' of moving from experiencing the look to believing the seen object to have the corresponding shape. So the 'belief' involved is a highly implicit belief, manifested chiefly in such a 'habit'. . . .[24]

But it is important to maintain a distinction between (a) implicit beliefs and (b) habits or dispositions for forming beliefs. One reason we need the distinction is because often there are such dispositions where there are no such beliefs. For example, simple pattern recognition in perception involves dispositions of amazing subtlety and complexity—that is, dispositions to go from perceptual cues to beliefs about external stimuli.[25] But it is highly implausible to attribute *beliefs* about such perceptual cues, and about their connections to external stimuli, to perceivers. It is implausible to attribute such beliefs to adult perceivers, not to mention small children and animals. But all perceivers, small children and animals included, have the relevant dispositions to form perceptual beliefs.

Moreover, there is a second reason for Sosa to insist on the distinction between implicit beliefs and dispositions for forming beliefs. For without it, his distinction between animal knowledge and reflective knowledge collapses. Recall that even animal knowledge requires a source in reliable cognitive abilities or powers; that is, it requires a source in intellectual virtues. But the virtues required for animal knowledge just are dispositions for forming beliefs. If we identify such dispositions with a perspective on one's beliefs, then there will be no difference between animal and reflective knowledge. Therefore, Sosa's position seems to result in skepticism regarding reflective knowledge. In order to maintain a distinction between animal and reflective knowledge at all, we must understand one's epistemic perspective to involve beliefs about one's first-order beliefs and their sources, and not just dispositions for forming first-order beliefs. But then it is implausible that human beings typically have an epistemic perspective, and therefore implausible that human beings typically have reflective knowledge.

In the preceding paragraphs we have identified two problems for Sosa's position. First, Sosa's distinction between animal and reflective knowledge seems unmotivated, given his claim that the virtue of coherence is its reliability. If that claim is correct, then there is no good reason for thinking that reflective knowledge is of a higher kind than animal knowledge, or that the two belong to significantly different kinds at all. Second, if we do maintain the distinction, then the result seems to be a broad skepticism with respect to reflective (or human) knowledge. This is because most human beings fail to have the required epistemic perspective. Both these problems can be solved, however, if we recognize two plausible claims: (a) that there is a distinction in kind between knowledge and understanding and (b) that coherence has a distinctive value through its contribution to understanding. The first problem is solved because this allows us to make a principled distinction between nonreflective knowledge and reflective knowledge: In virtue of its greater coherence through an epistemic perspective, reflective knowledge involves a kind of understanding that nonreflective knowledge lacks. The second problem is solved because this allows us to drop the requirement of an epistemic perspective for human knowledge: Nonreflective knowledge is real knowledge, and even real human knowledge. Reflective knowledge is of a higher grade and of a rarer sort, involving a special kind of understanding. On this view we still get a skeptical conclusion regarding reflective knowledge, because it will still be the case that few human beings have the kind of perspective that reflective knowledge requires. But the sting is taken out of this conclusion if we recognize that it is a special kind of understanding, rather than knowledge per se, that people so often lack. We never thought that such understanding was widespread in the first place, and so a skeptical conclusion in this regard is just what we would expect.[26]

In effect, I am making the same diagnosis of Sosa's account of knowledge as I did of Zagzebski's, and I am suggesting the same solution. In both cases I have argued that the requirements they put on knowledge are too strong, and that therefore their accounts have unattractive skeptical results. And in both cases the solution is to distinguish between knowledge per se and some epistemic value of a higher grade. This allows us to weaken the requirements on knowledge so as to make it generally attainable, and at the same time recognize the intellectual virtues that Zagzebski and Sosa want to emphasize.

However, one question remains: Why should the special kind of understanding involved in an epistemic perspective constitute a distinctive epistemic value? Granting that understanding is a distinctive epistemic value over and above knowledge per se, and granting that coherence contributes to that distinctive value, why should the particular sort of understanding involved in an epistemic perspective constitute a distinctive epistemic value all of its own? Consider that understanding has traditionally been understood in terms of knowledge of causes. Thus understanding involves knowledge of why things exist, how they work, and how they are related. This is why it is plausible that coherence contributes to understanding: coherence in general, and especially explanatory coherence, contributes to a grasp of exactly these matters. But then why should reflective knowledge, or understanding regarding the sources of one's first-order beliefs, be considered a distinctive kind of understanding, with its own distinctive epistemic value? Why should it be different from understanding about how humans came to exist, or what causes plants to grow, or how the mind is related to the body? Obviously, reflective knowledge is distinctive by virtue of its subject matter—it concerns one's first-order beliefs and their source in reliable cognitive faculties. But the relevant question concerns why reflective knowledge is distinctive *epistemically*. Why should reflective knowledge be of a different *epistemic* kind than coherent understanding regarding other things?

It seems to me that there is no good answer to this question. On the contrary, the above considerations show that reflective knowledge is not a distinctive epistemic kind at all. The important distinction is not between animal knowledge and reflective knowledge, but between knowledge per se and understanding per se.

Part Two. A Virtue Account of Knowledge

In Part One, we saw that different virtue theorists defend different, seemingly incompatible accounts of the intellectual virtues. In this context I argued

for an irenic conclusion: that different kinds of intellectual virtue or excellence are best suited to address different issues in epistemology. In particular, I argued (1) that a minimalist notion of the intellectual virtues, in which the virtues are conceived as reliable cognitive abilities or powers, is best suited for an account of knowledge; and (2) that stronger notions of the intellectual virtues are best suited to address a range of other issues.

In Part Two, I will pursue the idea that a minimalist, reliabilist notion of the intellectual virtues is useful for constructing an account of knowledge. I will do so by addressing three important issues for a theory of knowledge: the challenge of skepticism, Gettier problems, and the problem of explaining why knowledge is more valuable than mere true belief. By defining knowledge in terms of the intellectual virtues so conceived, it is possible to adequately address all three of these issues. But first it will be helpful to make some general comments about virtue, epistemic justification, and knowledge.

1. Agent Reliabilism

Recall generic reliabilism and the conditions it lays down for epistemic justification:

> A belief $B(p)$ is epistemically justified if and only if $B(p)$ is the outcome of a sufficiently reliable cognitive process.

We saw that these conditions are too weak, as is demonstrated by the case of the epistemically serendipitous brain lesion. The lesson to be learned from that case is that not all reliable cognitive processes give rise to epistemic justification and knowledge. Such considerations gave rise to an account in terms of intellectual virtue.

> A belief $B(p)$ is epistemically justified for a person S if and only if $B(p)$ is produced by one or more intellectual virtues of S; that is, by one or more of S's cognitive abilities or powers.

Here the key is to make the cognitive agent the seat of reliability, thereby moving from generic reliabilism to agent reliabilism. By restricting the relevant processes to those grounded in the knower's abilities or powers, we effectively disallow strange and fleeting processes, including brain lesions and the like, from giving rise to epistemic justification.

Recall also that this way of thinking allows an account of internal justification, or the kind of justification enjoyed even by the victim of Descartes' evil demon. Thus Sosa suggested:

> A belief $B(p)$ is epistemically justified for S relative to environment E if and only if $B(p)$ is produced by one or more cognitive dispositions that are intellectual virtues in E.

Notice that on this account the beliefs of the demon's victim are as justified as ours, so long as we relativize to the same environment. This kind of justification is "internal" because it is entirely a function of factors "from the skin inward," or better, "from the mind inward." This is insured by relativizing justification to external environments.

Finally, it is possible to define a sense of subjective justification, or a sense in which a belief is justified from the knower's own point of view. We have already seen that knowledge must be reliably formed. Many have had the intuition that, in addition to this, a knower must be aware that her belief is reliably formed. One way to cash out such awareness is to require an epistemic perspective on the relevant belief, but I have argued that an account in these terms is too strong for a requirement on knowledge. Nevertheless, a kind of awareness of reliability is manifested in the very dispositions that constitute one's cognitive abilities: The fact that a person interprets experience one way rather than another, or draws one inference rather than another, manifests an awareness of sorts that some relevant evidence is a reliable indication of some relevant truth. Or at least this is so if the person is trying to form her beliefs accurately in the first place—if the person is in the normal mode of trying to believe what is true, as opposed to what is convenient, or comforting, or politically correct. We may use these considerations to define a sense of subjective justification that is not too strong to be a requirement on knowledge.

> A belief $B(p)$ is subjectively justified for S if and only if $B(p)$ is produced by cognitive dispositions that S manifests when S is motivated to believe what is true.

In cases of knowledge such dispositions will also be virtues, since they will be objectively reliable in addition to being well motivated. But even in cases where S is not reliable, she may nevertheless have justified beliefs in this sense, since her believing may nevertheless manifest well-motivated dispositions.

Because the notion of intellectual virtue employed in the above definitions is relatively weak, the account of epistemic justification and knowledge that results is relatively weak as well: there is no strong motivation condition, no control condition, and no condition requiring an epistemic perspective. In the sections that follow, I will argue that this minimalist approach is just what is needed in a theory of knowledge.

2. Skepticism[27]

A number of skeptical arguments have been prominent in the theory of knowledge. These arguments constitute philosophical problems in the following sense: They begin from premises that seem eminently plausible, and proceed by seemingly valid reasoning to conclusions that are outrageously implausible. On this view, skeptical arguments present a theoretical problem rather than a practical problem. The task for a theory of knowledge is to identify some mistake in the skeptical argument and to replace it with something more adequate. Two of the most difficult of these problems come from Hume. The first concerns our knowledge of unobserved matters of fact. The second concerns our knowledge of empirical facts in general.

a. SKEPTICISM ABOUT UNOBSERVED MATTERS OF FACT. According to Hume's first argument, we can know nothing about the world that we do not currently observe. For example, I can't know that my next sip of coffee will taste like coffee, or even that my cat will not sprout wings and fly away.

Here is how Hume's reasoning goes. First, he points out that everything we believe about unobserved matters of fact depends on previous observations. Thus I believe that coffee tastes a certain way because I have tasted coffee before, and I believe that cats do not have wings or fly because I have had previous dealings with cats. But such beliefs depend on an additional assumption as well, Hume argues. For my observations about coffee and cats are relevant only if I assume that things such as coffee and cats act in regular ways. In other words, I must assume that my previous observations of things give some indication of their future behavior. But how is that assumption to be justified? Hume argues that it cannot be, and that therefore all our beliefs about unobserved matters of fact are themselves unjustified.

Well, why can't the assumption be justified? Hume's answer is straightforward: The assumption is itself a belief about unobserved matters of fact, and so any attempt to justify it must fall into circular reasoning. Consider that I can justify my assumption that things act in regular ways only by relying on previous observations—I have observed that they do. But these observations of past regular behavior are relevant for establishing additional regular behavior only if I assume the very thing I am trying to establish—that things behave in regular ways!

Hume's argument can be put more formally as follows.

1.   All our beliefs about unobserved matters of fact depend for their evidence on (a) previous observations and (b) the assumption (Al) that observed cases are a reliable indication of unobserved cases; that things behave (and will continue to behave) in regular ways.
2.   But (Al) is itself a belief about an unobserved matter of fact.
3.   Therefore, assumption (Al) depends for its evidence on (Al).(1,2)
4.   Circular reasoning does not give rise to justification.
5.   Therefore, (Al) is unjustified.(3,4)
6.   Therefore, all our beliefs about unobserved matters of fact depend for their evidence on an unjustified assumption.(1,5)
7.   Beliefs that depend for their evidence on an unjustified assumption are themselves unjustified
8.   Therefore, none of our beliefs about unobserved matters of fact are justified.(6,7)

b. Skepticism about the World.   Here is another argument from Hume—this one concerning all our knowledge of matters of fact about the world, whether observed or unobserved. The argument belongs to a family of skeptical arguments, all of which claim (a) that our knowledge of the world depends on how things appear through the senses and (b) that there is no good inference from the

way things appear to the way things actually are. Here is the argument put formally

1.   All of our beliefs about the world depend, at least in part, on the way things appear to us via the senses.
2.   The nature of this dependency is broadly evidential—the fact that things in the world appear a certain way is often our reason for thinking that they are that way.
3.   Therefore, if I am to know how things in the world actually are, it must be via some good inference from how things appear to me.(1,2)
4.   But there is no good inference from the way things appear to the way things are.
5.   Therefore, I cannot know how things in the world actually are.(3,4)

This argument is a powerful one. Premises (1) and (2) say only that our beliefs about the world depend for their evidence on the way things appear to us. That seems undeniable. Premise (4) is the only remaining independent premise, and there are excellent reasons for accepting it. One reason mirrors the first argument from Hume above. Specifically, our beliefs about the world depend for their evidence on (a) sensory appearances but also (b) an assumption (A2) that the way things appear is a reliable indication of the way things are. But assumption (A2) is itself a belief about the world, and so any attempt to justify it would depend on that very assumption. Hence there can be no noncircular inference from sensory appearances to reality.

Here is a second reason in favor of premise (4). Even if a noncircular inference from appearances to reality were possible in principle, no such inference would be psychologically plausible. In other words, it would not be plausible that such an inference is actually used when we form beliefs about objects on the basis of sensory appearances. This is because an inference takes us from belief to belief, but we do not typically have beliefs about appearances. In the typical case, we form our beliefs about objects in the world without forming beliefs about appearances at all, much less inferring beliefs about the world from beliefs about appearances.

c. Where the Skeptical Arguments Go Wrong.   Notice that the two skeptical arguments from Hume cannot be dismissed on the usual grounds. For example, neither argument demands certainty for knowledge, nor does either depend on a controversial metaphysics. On the contrary, the various premises of Hume's arguments are consistent with innocent assumptions about the standards for knowledge, the ontology of appearances, the relationship between mind and world, and the like.[28] The real problem is that circular reasoning cannot give rise to knowledge, and our reasoning about things in the world, whether observed or unobserved, seems to be circular. Once again, the task for a theory of knowledge is to identify the mistake in the arguments. *Something* in the arguments is not innocent, and an adequate theory of knowledge should explain what that it is.

Agent reliabilism provides such explanations. Consider first Hume's argument concerning our beliefs about unobserved matters of fact. That argument begins with the claim that all such beliefs depend on an assumption: that observed cases are a reliable indication of unobserved cases. Another way to put Hume's claim is as follows: that our evidence for unobserved matters of fact must always contain some such assumption among its premises. But why does Hume think that? I suggest that Hume's claim is based on a widespread but mistaken assumption about knowledge and evidence. Namely, that there must be a necessary relation between an item of knowledge and the evidence that grounds it. In cases of deductive knowledge the relation will be logical. But even inductive knowledge, Hume thinks, must involve some quasi-logical relation. That is why our evidence for beliefs about unobserved matters of fact needs a premise about observed cases being a reliable indication of unobserved cases: It is only through some such premise that a quasi-logical relation, this time a probability relation, is established.

Agent reliabilism allows a straightforward diagnosis of this line of reasoning: It is a mistake to think that there must be a necessary relation between evidence and knowledge. On the contrary, knowledge requires evidence that is *in fact* reliable, as opposed to evidence that is necessarily reliable. More exactly, knowledge requires that the knower be in fact reliable in the way that she forms her beliefs on the basis of her evidence. But if that is right, then Hume is wrong to think that our beliefs about unobserved matters of fact depend on assumption (A1) for their evidence.

Agent reliabilism also explains where Hume's second skeptical argument goes wrong. That argument begins with the claim that beliefs about the world depend on the way things appear for their evidence, and concludes from this that knowledge of the world requires a good inference from appearances to reality. But this line of reasoning depends on an implicit assumption: that sensory appearances ground beliefs about the world by means of an *inference*. This assumption is mistaken, however, and agent reliabilism explains why.

Let us define an inference as a movement from premise-beliefs to a conclusion-belief on the basis of their contents and according to a general rule. According to agent reliabilism, this is one way that a belief can be evidentially grounded, since using a good inference-rule is one way that a belief can be reliably formed. But that is not the only way that an evidential relation can be manifested—not every movement in thought constitutes an inference from premise-beliefs to a conclusion-belief according to a general rule. For example, the movement from sensory appearances to belief does not. When one forms a perceptual belief about the world, it is not the case that one first forms a belief about how things appear, and then infers that the way things appear is probably the way things are. Rather, the process is more direct than that. In a typical case of perception, one reliably moves from appearances to reality without so much as a thought about the appearances themselves, and without doing anything like following a rule of inference. Put simply, our perceptual powers are not reasoning powers.

It might be objected that the present point is merely a verbal one—I have rejected the assumption that the evidence of sensory appearances is inferential, but only by employing a restricted sense of "inference." But this objection misses a more substantive point. Namely, that not all movements in thought can be evaluated by the criteria governing inferences in the narrower sense defined above. In particular, to ask whether there is a good inference from sensory appearances to reality misunderstands the way that sensory appearances function as evidence for our beliefs about the world. This is the mistake that Hume's second argument makes, and agent reliabilism explains why it is a mistake.

4. Gettier Problems[29]

According to agent reliabilism, knowledge is true belief produced by the intellectual virtues of the believer, where intellectual virtues are understood to be reliable cognitive abilities or powers. This account of knowledge explains a wide range of our pre-theoretical intuitions regarding which cases do and do not count as knowledge. For example, the account continues to have the advantages of reliabilism: It explains why beliefs resulting from perception, memory, introspection, logical intuition, and sound reasoning typically count as knowledge, and it explains why beliefs resulting from hallucination, wishful thinking, and other unreliable processes do not. Moreover, the account handles cases that have been deemed problematic for generic reliabilism, such as the case of the serendipitous brain lesion, and the case described in the new evil demon problem. Nevertheless, more needs to be said in light of certain other cases. Specifically, in this section I will argue that agent reliabilism has the resources to address a wide range of "Gettier problems."

In 1963, Edmund Gettier wrote a short paper purporting to show that knowledge is not true justified belief. His argument proceeded by way of two counterexamples, each of which seemed to show that a belief could be both true and justified and yet not amount to knowledge. Here are two examples that are in the spirit of Gettier's originals.

> *Case 1.* On the basis of excellent reasons, S believes that her co-worker, Mr. Nogot, owns a Ford: Nogot testifies that he owns a Ford, and this is confirmed by S's own relevant observations. From this S infers that someone in her office owns a Ford. As it turns out, S's evidence is misleading and Nogot does not in fact own a Ford. However, another person in S's office, Mr. Havit, does own a Ford, although S has no reason for believing this.[30]

> *Case 2.* Walking down the road, S seems to see a sheep in the field and on this basis believes that there is a sheep in the field. However, due to an unusual trick of light, S has mistaken a dog for a sheep, and so what she sees is not a sheep at all. Nevertheless, unsuspected by S, there is a sheep in another part of the field.[31]

In both of these cases the relevant belief seems justified, at least in senses of justification that emphasize the internal or the subjective, and in both cases the relevant belief is true. Yet in neither case would we be inclined to judge that the person in question has knowledge.

These examples show that internal and/or subjective justification is not sufficient for knowledge. Put another way, they show that knowledge requires some stronger relation between belief and truth. From the perspective of a virtue theory, there is a natural way to think of this stronger relation, for it is natural to distinguish between (a) achieving some end by luck or accident and (b) achieving the end through the exercise of one's abilities (or virtues). This suggests the following difference between Gettier cases and cases of knowledge. In Gettier cases, S believes the truth, but it is only by accident that she does so. In cases of knowledge, however, it is no accident that S believes the truth. Rather, in cases of knowledge S believes the truth as the result of her own cognitive abilities—her believing the truth can be credited to her, as opposed to dumb luck or blind chance.

This suggestion is on the right track, but more needs to be said. Here is why. I said that the difference between Gettier cases and cases of knowledge is that in the latter, but not the former, it is to S's credit that she believes the truth. Put another way, in cases of knowledge S is responsible for believing the truth, because she believes it as the result of her own cognitive abilities. But in the Gettier cases above, S does exercise her cognitive abilities, and this is partly why she believes the truth. Hence it is not clear that Gettier cases and cases of knowledge can be distinguished as I have suggested—it is not clear why it is appropriate to credit S with true belief in cases of knowledge, and appropriate to deny credit in Gettier cases. Again, more needs to be said.[32]

The first thing to note is that attributions of credit imply attributions of causal responsibility. As I suggested above, to give S credit for her true belief is to say that she "is responsible" for her believing the truth—that her believing the truth "is the result" of her own abilities or virtues. This is in fact a general phenomenon. According to Aristotle, actions deserving moral credit "proceed from a firm and unchangeable character.[33] When we give credit for an athletic feat, we imply that it is the result of athletic ability, as opposed to good luck, or cheating, or a hapless opponent. In all such cases, an attribution of credit implies an attribution of causal responsibility for the action in question—it implies that the cause of the action is relevant abilities (or virtues) in the actor.

The second thing to note is that attributions of causal responsibility display an interesting pragmatics. Specifically, when we say that Y occurs because X occurs, or that Y's occurring is due to X's occurring, we mark out X's occurring as a particularly important or salient part of the causal story behind Y's occurring. For example, to say that the fire occurred because of the explosion is not to say that the explosion caused the fire all by itself. Rather, it is to say that the explosion is a particularly important part, perhaps the most important part, of the whole story. Or to change the example: To say that the fire occurred because of S's negligence is not to say that S's negligence caused the fire all by itself. Rather, it is to say that S's negligence is a particularly salient part, perhaps the most salient part, of the set of relevant factors that caused the fire.

What determines salience? Any number of things might, but two kinds of consideration are particularly important for present purposes. First, salience is often determined by what is *abnormal* in the case. For example, we will say that sparks caused the fire if the presence of sparks in the area is not normal. That explanation misfires, however, if we are trying to explain the cause of a fire in a welding shop, where sparks are flying all the time. Second, salience is often determined by our *interests and purposes*. If the thing to be explained is smoke coming from the engine, for example, we will look for the part that needs to be replaced. Here it is perfectly appropriate to say that the cause of the smoke is the malfunctioning carburetor, although clearly a faulty carburetor cannot cause smoke all by itself.

And now the important point is this: Since attributions of credit imply attributions of causal responsibility, the former inherit the pragmatics of the latter. Specifically, to say that S's believing the truth is to her credit is to say that S's cognitive abilities, her intellectual virtues, are an important part of the causal story regarding how S came to believe the truth. It is to say that S's cognitive abilities are a particularly salient part, perhaps the most salient part, of the total set of relevant causal factors.

We may now return to the diagnosis of Gettier problems that was suggested earlier. There I said that in Gettier cases S believes the truth, but it is only by accident that she does so. This was opposed to cases of knowledge, where it is to S's credit that she believes the truth, because she does so as the result of her own cognitive abilities. However, this diagnosis led to the following question: Why is it appropriate to credit S with true belief in cases of knowledge, but not in the two Gettier cases above, given that in all these cases S's abilities are part of the causal story regarding how S came to have a true belief? We now have an answer to that question: In cases of knowledge, but not in Gettier cases, S's abilities are a *salient* part of the causal story regarding how S came to have a true belief. It is plausible, in fact, that our cognitive abilities have a kind of "default" salience, owing to our interests and purposes as information-sharing beings. In Gettier cases, however, this default salience is trumped by something abnormal in the case. For example, someone in the office owns a Ford, but it is not the person S thinks it is. There is a sheep in the field, but it is not in the place that S is looking. In these cases it is only good luck that S ends up with a true belief, which is to say that S's believing the truth cannot be put down to her abilities.

These considerations suggest the following account of knowledge.

S has knowledge regarding p if and only if

1. S's belief $B(p)$ is *subjectively* justified in the following sense: $B(p)$ is produced by cognitive dispositions that S manifests when S is motivated to believe what is true,

2. S's belief $B(p)$ is *objectively* justified in the following sense: $B(p)$ is produced by one or more intellectual virtues of S; that is, by one or more of S's cognitive abilities or powers, and

3. S believes the truth regarding p *because* S believes p out of intellectual virtue. Alternatively: The intellectual virtues that result in S's believing the truth regarding p are an important necessary part of the total set of causal factors that give rise to S's believing the truth regarding p.

If we stipulate that intellectual virtues involve a motivation to believe the truth, we may collapse the above account as follows.

S has knowledge regarding *p* if and only if *S* believes the truth regarding *p* because *S* believes *p* out of intellectual virtue.[34]

5. The Value Problem

In recent work Linda Zagzebski has called attention to the value problem for knowledge.[35] An adequate account of knowledge, she points out, ought to explain why knowledge is more valuable than mere true belief. The account of knowledge presented above readily suggests an answer to that problem.

Recall Aristotle's distinction between (a) achieving some end by luck or accident and (b) achieving the end through the exercise of one's abilities (or virtues). It is only the latter kind of action, Aristotle argues, that is both intrinsically valuable and constitutive of human flourishing. "Human good," he writes, "turns out to be activity of soul exhibiting excellence."[36] In this discussion Aristotle is clearly concerned with intellectual virtue as well as moral virtue: His position is that the successful exercise of one's intellectual virtues is both intrinsically good and constitutive of human flourishing.

If this is correct then there is a clear difference in value between knowledge and mere true belief. In cases of knowledge, we achieve the truth through the exercise of our own cognitive abilities or powers, which are a kind of intellectual virtue. Moreover, we can extend the point to include other kinds of intellectual virtue as well. It is plausible, for example, that the successful exercise of intellectual courage is also intrinsically good, and also constitutive of the best intellectual life. And of course there is a long tradition that says the same about wisdom and the same about understanding. On the view I am suggesting, there are a plurality of intellectual virtues, and their successful exercise gives rise to a plurality of epistemic goods. The best intellectual life—intellectual flourishing, so to speak—is rich with all of these.[37]

Notes

[1]Aristotle, *Nicomachean Ethics*, Book VI.

[2]For example, see Ernest Sosa, *Knowledge in Perspective* (Cambridge: Cambridge University Press, 1991); Alvin

Goldman, "Epistemic Folkways and Scientific Epistemology," in his *Liaisons: Philosophy Meets the Cognitive and Social Sciences* (Cambridge, MA: MIT Press, 1992); and John Greco, "Virtues and Vices of Virtue Epistemology," *Canadian Journal of Philosophy* 23 (1993).

[3]For example, see Linda Zagzebski, *Virtues of the Mind* (Cambridge: Cambridge University Press, 1996). Hereafter VM.

[4]For example, see James Montmarquet, "Epistemic Virtue," *Mind* 96 (1987); and James Montmarquet, *Epistemic Virtue and Doxastic Responsibility* (Lanham, MD: Rowman and Littlefield, 1993).

[5]See especially "The Raft and the Pyramid: Coherence versus Foundations in the Theory of Knowledge," *Midwest Studies in Philosophy* V (1980); "Epistemology Today: A Perspective in Retrospect," *Philosophical Studies* 40 (1981); "The Coherence of Virtue and the Virtue of Coherence: Justification in Epistemology," *Synthese* 64 (1985); and "Knowledge and Intellectual Virtue," *The Monist* 68 (1985), all reprinted in *Knowledge in Perspective*. See also "Reliabilism and Intellectual Virtue" and "Intellectual Virtue in Perspective," both in *Knowledge in Perspective*. Below all page numbers for these works correspond to *Knowledge in Perspective*.

[6]See especially "The Raft and the Pyramid."

[7]See, for example, "The Foundations of Foundationalism," pp. 157–8.

[8]This argument is developed in "The Raft and the Pyramid," pp. 184–6.

[9]See "The Raft and the Pyramid," pp. 186–9.

[10]See "Epistemology Today" and "The Coherence of Virtue and the Virtue of Coherence."

[11]See especially "The Coherence of Virtue and the Virtue of Coherence."

[12]See especially "Knowledge and Intellectual Virtue" and "Intellectual Virtue in Perspective." At present I characterize the two kinds of knowledge in terms of necessary conditions only. This is because Sosa thinks that other conditions are necessary to make the set sufficient. I discuss further conditions on knowledge in Part Two of this essay, in the section on Gettier problems.

[13]See, for example, David Armstrong, *Belief, Truth and Knowledge* (Cambridge: Cambridge University Press, 1973); Fred Dretske, "Conclusive Reasons," *Australasian Journal of Philosophy* 49 (1971); and Alvin Goldman, "What Is Justified Belief" in George Pappas, ed., *Justification and Knowledge* (Dordrecht: D. Reidel Publishing, 1979).

[14]For more on the relation between skepticism and reliabilism, see Part Two of this essay.

[15]This example is due to Alvin Plantinga, *Warrant: The Current Debate* (Oxford: Oxford University Press, 1993), p. 199.

[16]This problem is due to Keith Lehrer and Stewart Cohen, "Justification, Truth and Coherence," *Synthese* 55 (1983).

[17]See "Proper Functionalism and Virtue Epistemology," *Nous* 27 (1993). Relevant sections of this paper are reprinted as "Three Forms of Virtue Epistemology," in Guy Axtell, ed., *Knowledge, Belief and Character* (Lanham, MD: Rowman and Littlefield, 2000).

[18]Sosa develops these ideas in "Reliabilism and Intellectual Virtue"; and "Intellectual Virtue in Perspective." See also "Goldman's Reliabilism and Virtue Epistemology," forthcoming in *Philosophical Topics*.

[19]See especially "Intellectual Virtue in Perspective."

[20]See "Epistemic Virtue" and *Epistemic Virtue and Doxastic Responsibility*.

[21]So argues Stephen Grimm in "Ernest Sosa, Knowledge and Understanding," *Philosophical Studies* 106 (2001). In the next two paragraphs I am indebted to Grimm's paper.

[22]See, for example, "Perspectives in Virtue Epistemology: A Response to Dancy and BonJour," *Philosophical Studies* 78 (1995), p. 233. Reprinted in Axtell (2000). See also "How to Resolve the Pyrrhonian Problematic: A Lesson form Descartes," *Philosophical Studies* 85 (1997), where Sosa endorses Descartes' distinction between unreflective *cognitio* and reflective *scientia*.

[23]For example, see "Intellectual Virtue in Perspective," pp. 274–5.

[24]"Virtue Perspectivism: A Response to Foley and Fumerton," *Philosophical Issues, 5, Truth and Rationality* (1994), pp. 44–5. Sosa is responding to an objection from Richard Foley, "The Epistemology of Sosa," same volume.

[25]See, for example, J. Hochberg, *Perception* (Englewood Cliffs, N.J.: Prentice Hall, 1978).

[26]Richard Fumerton makes a similar point in "Achieving Epistemic Ascent," in John Greco, ed., *Sosa and his Critics* (Oxford: Blackwell Publishers, 2003).

[27]In this section I draw on material from *Putting Skeptics in Their Place* (New York: Cambridge University Press, 2000); and from "Agent Reliabilism," *Philosophical Perspectives, 13, Epistemology* (1999).

[28]I defend this claim at length in *Putting Skeptics in Their Place*. See especially Chapter Four.

[29]In this section I draw on material from "Knowledge as Credit for True Belief," in Michael DePaul and Linda Zagzebski, eds., *Intellectual Virtue: Perspectives from Ethics and Epistemology* (Oxford: Oxford University Press, 2002).

[30]The example is from Keith Lehrer, "Knowledge, Truth and Evidence," *Analysis* 25 (1965).

[31]The example is slightly revised from Roderick Chisholm, *Theory of Knowledge,* 2nd edition (Englewood Cliffs, NJ: Prentice Hall, Inc., 1977), p. 105.

[32]The remarks that follow are indebted to Joel Feinberg's insightful discussions of moral blame. See his "Problematic Responsibility in Law and Morals"; "Action and Responsibility"; and "Causing Voluntary Actions." All collected in *Doing and Deserving: Essays in the Theory of Responsibility* (Princeton: Princeton University Press, 1970).

[33]*Nicomachean Ethics*, II4. Feinberg argues that all attributions of moral responsibility imply that the action in question proceeds from character. This is probably too strong, since a person can be appropriately blamed for action out of character. Nevertheless, there is a special sort of moral responsibility, with which Aristotle is concerned, that does imply this. See *Doing and Deserving*, p. 126.

[34]A number of authors have defended the idea that, in cases of knowledge, one believes the truth because one believes out of intellectual virtue. See Ernest Sosa, "Beyond Skepticism, to the Best of our Knowledge," *Mind* 97 (1988), and *Knowledge in Perspective*; Linda Zagzebski, *Virtues of the Mind,* and "What is Knowledge?" in John Greco and Ernest Sosa, eds. *The Blackwell Guide to Epistemology* (Oxford: Blackwell Publishers, 1999); and Wayne Riggs, "Reliability and the Value of Knowledge," *Philosophy and Phenomenological Research,* forthcoming.

[35]Zagzebski raises the problem in *Virtues of the Mind*, pp. 300–2, and in a more extended way in "From Reliabilism to Virtue Epistemology," *Proceedings of the Twentieth World Congress of Philosophy, Volume V. Epistemology* (1999). This paper is reprinted in expanded form in Axtell (2000). For further discussion of the value problem from a virtue perspective, see Zagzebski, "The Search for the Source of Epistemic Good," in Greco (2003); Sosa, "The Place of Truth in Epistemology," in DePaul and Zagzebski (2002); and Wayne Riggs, "Reliability and the Value of Knowledge."

[36]*Nicomachean Ethics*, I.7.

[37]I am indebted to many people for their comments on earlier versions of this material, including Robert Audi, Stephen Grimm, and Wayne Riggs. I would especially like to thank Ernest Sosa and Linda Zagzebski for many discussions on relevant topics.

Bibliography

Armstrong, David M. *Belief, Truth, and Knowledge*. Cambridge: Cambridge University Press, 1973.

Almeder, Robert. "On Naturalizing Epistemology." *American Philosophical Quarterly 27,* no. 4 (October 1990).

Alston, William. *Epistemic Justification*. Ithaca, NY: Cornell University Press, 1989.

Baergen, Ralph. *Contemporary Epistemology*. Fort Worth, TX: Harcourt Brace, 1995. Chapter 5.

Bennett, Jonathan. "Why Is Belief Involuntary?" *Analysis 50* (1990), 87–107.

Chisholm, Roderick. *The Foundations of Knowing*. Minneapolis: University of Minnesota Press, 1957.

Chisholm, Roderick. *Theory of Knowledge,* 2d ed. Englewood Cliffs, NJ: Prentice Hall, 1977.

Chisholm, Roderick. *Theory of Knowledge,* 3d ed. Englewood Cliffs, NJ: Prentice Hall, 1989.

Cohen, Stewart. "Justification and Truth." *Philosophical Studies 46* (1984).

Dancy, Jonathan, and Ernest Sosa, eds. *A Companion to Epistemology*. Oxford: Blackwell, 1992.

Dretske, Fred. *Knowledge and the Flow of Information*. Cambridge, MA: MIT Press, 1981.

Everitt, Nicholas, and Alec Fisher. *Modern Epistemology*. New York: McGraw-Hill, 1995.

Feldman, Richard. "Reliabilism and Justification." *Monist 68* (1985).

Feldman, Richard. "Epistemic Obligation." In *Philosophical Perspectives. Vol. 2: Epistemology,* edited by James Tomberlin. Atascadero, CA: Ridgeview, 1988.

Feldman, Richard and Earl Conee. "Evidential-ism." *Philosophical Studies 48* (1985).

French, P., T. Uehling, and H. Wettstein, eds. *Midwest Studies in Philosophy, Vol. XIX.* Notre Dame, IN: University of Notre Dame Press, 1994.

Goldman, Alvin I. *Epistemology and Cognition*. Cambridge, MA: Harvard University Press. 1985. Chapter 5.

Goldman, Alvin. "Strong and Weak Justification." *Philosophical Perspectives. Vol. 2: Epistemology,* edited by James Tomberlin. Atascadero, CA: Ridgeview, 1988.

Goldman, Alvin. "Epistemic Folkways and Scientific Epistemology." In *Liaisons: Philosophy Meets the Cognitive and Social Sciences.* Cambridge, MA: MIT Press, 1991.

Goodman, Michael, and Robert Snyder, eds. *Contemporary Readings in Epistemology.* Upper Saddle River, NJ: Prentice Hall, 1993.

Kim, Jaegwon. *Philosophy of Mind*. Boulder, CO: Westview Press, 1996.

Kitcher, Philip. "The Naturalists Return." *Philosophical Review 101* (1992).

Kornblith, Hilary, ed., *Naturalized Epistemology.* Cambridge, MA: MIT Press, 1985.

Kornblith, Hilary. *Inductive Inference and Its Natural Ground: An Essay in Naturalistic Epistemology.* Cambridge, MA: MIT Press, 1993.

Montmarquet, James. "Epistemic Virtue." *Mind 96* (1987), 482–497.

Moser, Paul. *Epistemic Justification*. Chapter 4. Dordrecht, Netherlands: Reidel, 1985.

Pappas, George, ed. *Justification and Knowledge.* Dordrecht, Netherlands: Reidel, 1979.

Plantinga, Alvin. *Warrant and Proper Function.* Oxford: Oxford University Press, 1993.

Plantinga, Alvin. *Warrant: The Current Debate.* Oxford: Oxford University Press, 1993.

Pojman, Louis P. *What Can We Know? An Introduction to the Theory of Knowledge,* 2nd. ed. Belmont, CA: Wadsworth, 2000. Chapters 8–10.

Pollock, John L. *Contemporary Theories of Knowledge.* Totowa, NJ: Rowman & Littlefield, 1986.

Quine, W. V. *Ontological Relativity and Other Essays.* New York: Columbia University Press, 1969.

Sosa, Ernest. *Knowledge in Perspective: Selective Essays in Epistemology.* Cambridge: Cambridge University Press, 1991.

Steup, Matthias. *An Introduction to Contemporary Epistemology.* Upper Saddle River, NJ: Prentice Hall, 1996. Chapters 8 and 9.

Stroud, Barry. *The Significance of Skepticism.* Oxford: Clarendon Press, 1984. Chapter 6.

Swain, Marshall. *Reasons and Knowledge.* Ithaca, NY: Cornell University Press, 1981.

Tomberlin, James, ed. *Philosophical Perspectives. Vol. 2: Epistemology.* Atascadero, CA: Ridgeview, 1988. This volume contains several essays relevant to this part of the book.

Van Inwagen, Peter. "When Is the Will Free?" In T. O'Connor (ed.), *Agents, Causes, and Events.* Oxford: Oxford University Press, 1985.

Zagzebski, Linda. *Virtues of the Mind: An Inquiry into the Nature of Virtue and the Ethical Foundations of Knowledge.* Cambridge: Cambridge University Press, 1996.

Part VII

A Priori Knowledge

Classifications and Definitions

The problem of synthetic a priori knowledge involves epistemological, metaphysical, and semantic considerations. The terms *a priori* and *a posteriori* are Latin expressions developed by scholastic philosophers in the Middle Ages. A priori literally means "from what is prior," and a posteriori means "from what is posterior." Leibniz (1646–1716) used a posteriori to signify contingent truths of fact, truths about what is discoverable by experience, and used a priori to signify truths of reason, truths that depend on the principle of identity (A = A), which the mind could discover without the aid of the senses. Immanuel Kant (1724–1804) further refined these notions to refer to judgments depending on empirical experience and judgments that do not, respectively. He further combined a priori knowledge with synthetic propositions giving rise to the present problem: is there synthetic a priori knowledge? For Kant, synthetic a priori knowledge is knowledge that is not derived from particular sensations but is presupposed in all our experience. It is logically necessary (that is, it could not be otherwise; it is true in all possible worlds), whereas synthetic a posteriori knowledge is contingent (that is, it could have been otherwise and is not true in all possible worlds).

A classification of the relevant concepts is as follows:

A. Epistemological categories
  1. *A priori* knowledge does not depend on evidence from sense experience (Plato's innate Ideas and Leibniz's "truths of reason"); for example, mathematics and logic.
  2. *A posteriori* knowledge depends on evidence from sense experience (Plato's "appearance" and Leibniz's "truths of fact")—empirical knowledge.
B. Metaphysical categories
  1. *Necessary truths* "are" true in all possible worlds (for example, the statement that "God exists" according to the ontological argument).
  2. *Contingent truths* "are" true in the actual world but not in all possible worlds (for example, the fact that you exist and were born after January 1, 1800).
C. Semantical categories
  1. *Analytic*—predicate is *contained* in the subject, explicative, not ampliative (for example, "All mothers are women").

2. *Synthetic*—predicate is not contained in the subject but adds something to the subject, ampliative, not explicative (for example, "Mary is a mother").

Combinations

If we combine these categories, using the epistemological and the semantic as the dominant ones (and subordinating the metaphysical categories), we arrive at the chart at the bottom of the page.

Kant rejected the idea of analytic a posteriori knowledge because the very idea of an analytic judgment depends solely on the relations of the concepts involved and is discoverable by determining whether its denial entails a contradiction. That is, the analytic makes no reference to experience, whereas the a posteriori depends on experience.

Generally, rationalists assert, while empiricists deny, the existence of synthetic a priori

knowledge. That is, while empiricists believe experience is the basis of all our knowledge, except analytic truths, the rationalist holds that reason can discover truths that are neither empirical nor analytic. For a radical rationalist such as Kant, all knowledge is grounded in self-evident, a priori, nonempirical knowledge.

The essential claim of those who hold to synthetic a priori knowledge is that *the mind can grasp connections between ideas (concepts) that are not strictly analytically related.*

The Kantian Theory About Synthetic A Priori Knowledge

The primary question of Kant's *Critique of Pure Reason* is, How are synthetic a priori judgments possible? Ewing has shown that Kant makes four claims about synthetic a priori judgments:

1. They are logically necessary—wholes that determine their own parts.

	Analytic	Synthetic
	Entailments Identity statements Tautologies Definitions	**Mathematics** 5 + 7 = 12
		Exclusionary Nothing red is green.
	Examples "All bachelors are unmarried." "All bodies are extended."	**Presuppositions of Experience** Space, time, and causality
A Priori		**Moral Judgments** The categorical imperative "It is always wrong to torture for the fun of it."
		The Laws of Logic The principle of noncontradiction
		Metaphysical God's existence Freedom of the will
		Examples
A Posteriori	None	All empirical statements: "All bodies are heavy." "All copper conducts electricity." "John is a bachelor."

2. They are not derivable from particular sensations (although empirical experience is the trigger to cause them to arise).

3. They are presupposed in all of our experience.

4. They are contributed by our minds.

Our synthetic a priori "knowledge" is merely of the presuppositions or conditions of experience, and, as such, only of the *appearance* of the world to us, constructed as we are. We can have no a priori knowledge of the reality (the *Ding an Sich*). As red-tinted glasses cause us to see the world in shades of red, so the constraints of synthetic a priori categories cause us to experience the world causally, temporally, and spatially.

As mentioned earlier, all a priori knowledge is necessary and has universal application. It is true in all possible worlds, whereas statements known a posteriori are contingent. They could have turned out to be false rather than true.

In the second reading in this part of the book, A. J. Ayer gives a conventionalist critique of the notion of the synthetic a priori. He argues that all the supposed a priori knowledge can be reduced to analytic truths.

Nevertheless, there is reason to hold to the idea of synthetic a priori knowledge. A. C. Ewing sets forth some considerations in its favor in the third reading. Knowledge of mathematical, logical, and other statements can best be construed as a priori. Furthermore, there is a transcendental argument in its favor: Ayer's very statement that "there can be no synthetic *a priori* truths" is itself a synthetic a priori statement, so that if it's true, it's false. Even if all other cases are doubtful, the laws of logic seem to function as synthetic a priori truths. The principle of noncontradiction is necessary for the very possibility of thought, including the thought of the principle itself. Its denial is self-refuting, because to deny the principle depends on the very principle it is denying: If the principle of

noncontradiction is not true, then the denial of its denial is just as valid as the denial itself.

A key to the distinction between analytic and synthetic a priori judgments is found in the notion of *containment*. When I say all bachelors are unmarried, we understand that the idea of "unmarried" is already present or contained in the notion of "bachelor," so I have not added anything to the concept of "bachelor." But when I say that if something is red it is not green, the notion of "not being green" does not seem to be contained in the concept "red," yet I do not need to look and see that the proposition is true. I can understand it immediately, using reason alone. The proposition "If something is red, it is not green" is not an analytic proposition but neither is it an empirical proposition. It is a necessary truth, known a priori. It is a *synthetic* a priori judgment.

But some philosophers doubt that the notion of *containment* is sturdy enough to bear the weight of the analytic-synthetic distinction. W. V. Quine, in his classic essay "Two Dogmas of Empiricism (Reading VII.4), argues that *containment* is a vague metaphor, and that its vagueness spreads over the entire analytic-synthetic distinction. The separating line between the analytic and the a priori is so unclear that we might well throw out the analytic-synthetic distinction itself.

H. P. Grice and P. F. Strawson take issue with Quine's rejection of the analytic-synthetic distinction, arguing that there is a presumption in its favor. They argue both that the rejection of the distinction leads to absurd consequences and that we don't need a formal definition of synonymy for it to make sense.

In our next reading, Roderick Chisholm surveys and defends the traditional theses about synthetic a priori and analytic knowledge.

Our final reading by Saul Kripke breaks with the long tradition of identifying a priori knowledge with necessary truth. Kripke argues that we can have a posteriori necessary truth and nonnecessary a priori knowledge.

VII.1 *A Priori* Knowledge

Immanuel Kant

Immanuel Kant (1724–1804), who was born into a deeply pietistic Lutheran family in Königsberg, Germany, lived in that town his entire life, and taught at the University of Königsberg. He lived a duty-bound, methodical life, so regular that citizens were said to have set their clocks by his walks. Kant is one of the premier philosophers in the Western tradition. In his monumental work *The Critique of Pure Reason* (1781), he inaugurated a revolution in the theory of knowledge.

Kant began as a rationalist but on reading Hume was struck with the cogency of his argument. Hume "woke me from my dogmatic slumbers," Kant wrote, and henceforth accepted the idea that all our knowledge begins with experience. But Kant thought that Hume had made an invalid inference in concluding that all our knowledge arises from experience. Kant sought to demonstrate that the rationalists had an invaluable insight, which had been lost in their flamboyant speculation, that something determinate in the mind causes us to know what we know.

Kant argued that the mind is so structured and empowered that it imposes interpretive categories on our experience, so we do not simply experience the world, as the empiricists alleged, but interpret it through the constitutive mechanisms of the mind. This is sometimes called Kant's Copernican revolution.

In this selection, Kant makes his famous distinction between a priori and a posteriori knowledge. A priori knowledge is what we know *prior* to experience. It is opposed to a posteriori knowledge, which is based *on* experience. For Hume, all knowledge of matters of fact is a posteriori and only analytic statements (such as mathematical truths or statements such as "All mothers are women") are known a priori. Kant rejects this formula. For him it is possible to have a priori knowledge of matters of fact. "But though all our knowledge begins with experience, it does not follow that it all arises out of experience." Indeed, he thinks that mathematical truth is not analytic but synthetic (the predicate adds something to the subject) and that there is other synthetic a priori knowledge, such as our knowledge of time, space, causality, and the moral law. The schema looks like this:

	A Priori	A Posteriori
Analytic	Tautologies and entailments ("All bachelors are unmarried.")	None
Synthetic	Causality, space, and time (5 + 7 = 12, the moral law)	Empirical judgments (There are people in this room.")

After a brief selection from the preface of the *Critique of Pure Reason* (1781), we turn to the preamble of Kant's *Prolegomena to Any Future Metaphysic* (1783).

Translated by Paul Carus, *Kant's Prolegomena* (Chicago 1902). Some notes omitted.

Until now we have assumed that all our knowledge must conform to objects. But every attempt to extend our knowledge of objects by establishing something in regard to them *a priori,* by means of concepts, has, on this assumption, ended in failure. Therefore, we must see whether we may have better success in our metaphysical task if we begin with the assumption that objects must conform to our knowledge. In this way we would have knowledge of objects *a priori.* We should then be proceeding in the same way as Copernicus in his revolutionary hypothesis. After he failed to make progress in explaining the movements of the heavenly bodies on the supposition that they all revolved around the observer, he decided to reverse the relationship and made the observer revolve around the heavenly body, the sun, which was at rest. A similar experiment can be done in metaphysics with regard to the intuition of objects. If our intuition must conform to the constitution of the object, I do not see how we could know anything of the object *a priori,* but if the object of sense must conform to the constitution of our faculty of intuition, then *a priori* knowledge is possible. [From the Preface of *Critique of Pure Reason* (1781), my translation.]

Prolegomena: Preamble on the Peculiarities of All Metaphysical Knowledge

§1. Of the Sources of Metaphysics

If it becomes desirable to organize any knowledge as science, it will be necessary first to determine accurately those peculiar features which no other science has in common with it, constituting its peculiarity; otherwise the boundaries of all sciences become confused, and none of them can be treated thoroughly according to its nature.

The peculiar characteristic of a science may consist of a simple difference of object, or of the sources of knowledge, or of the kind of knowledge, or perhaps of all three conjointly. On these, therefore, depends the idea of a possible science and its territory.

First, as concerns the sources of metaphysical knowledge, its very concept implies that they cannot be empirical. Its principles (including not only its maxims but its basic notions) must never be derived from experience. It must not be physical but metaphysical knowledge, namely, knowledge lying beyond experience. It can therefore have for its basis neither external experience, which is the source of physics proper, nor internal, which is the basis of empirical psychology. It is therefore *a priori* knowledge, coming from pure understanding and pure reason.

But so far metaphysics would not be distinguishable from pure mathematics; it must therefore be called *pure philosophical* knowledge; and for the meaning of this term I refer to the *Critique of the Pure Reason,*[1] where the distinction between these two employments of reason is sufficiently explained. So far concerning the sources of metaphysical knowledge.

§2. Concerning the Kind of Knowledge Which Can Alone Be Called Metaphysical

a. On the Distinction between Analytical and Synthetical Judgments in General.—The peculiarity of its sources demands that metaphysical knowledge must consist of nothing but *a priori* judgments. But whatever be their origin or their logical form, there is a distinction in judgments, as to their content, according to which they are either merely *explicative,* adding nothing to the content of knowledge, or *expansive,* increasing the given knowledge. The former may be called *analytical,* the latter *synthetical,* judgments.

Analytical judgments express nothing in the predicate but what has been already actually thought in the concept of the subject, though not so distinctly or with the same (full) consciousness. When I say: "All bodies are extended," I have not amplified in the least my concept of body, but have only analyzed it, as extension was really thought to belong to that concept before the judgment was made, though it was not expressed. This judgment is therefore analytical. On the contrary, this judgment, "All bodies have weight," contains in its predicate something not actually thought in the universal concept of body; it amplifies my knowledge by adding something to my concept, and must therefore be called synthetical.

b. The Common Principle of All Analytical Judgments Is the Law of Contradiction.—All analytical judgments depend wholly on the law of contradiction, and are in their nature *a priori* cognitions, whether the concepts that supply them with matter be empirical or not. For the predicate of an affirmative analytical judgment is already contained in the concept of the subject, of which it cannot be denied without contradiction. In the same way its opposite is necessarily denied of the subject in an analytical, but negative, judgment, by the same law of contradiction. Such is the nature of the judgments: "All bodies are extended," and "No bodies are unextended (that is, simple)."

For this very reason all analytical judgments are *a priori* even when the concepts are empirical, as, for example, "Gold is a yellow metal"; for to know this I require no experience beyond my concept of gold as a yellow metal. It is, in fact, the very concept, and I need only analyze it without looking beyond it.

c. Synthetical Judgments Require a Different Principle from the Law of Contradiction.—There are synthetical *a posteriori* judgments of empirical origin; but there are also others which are certain *a priori,* and which spring from pure understanding and reason. Yet they both agree in this, that they cannot possibly spring from the principle of analysis, namely, the law of contradiction, alone. They require a quite different principle from which they may be deduced, subject, of course, always to the law of contradiction, which must never be violated, even though everything cannot be deduced from it. I shall first classify synthetical judgments.

1. *Judgments of Experience* are always synthetical. For it would be absurd to base an analytical judgment on experience, as our concept suffices for the purpose without requiring any testimony from experience. That body is extended is a judgment established *a priori,* and not an empirical judgment. For before appealing to experience, we already have all the conditions of the judgment in the concept, from which we have but to elicit the predicate according to the law of contradiction, and thereby to become conscious of the necessity of the judgment, which experience could not in the least teach us.

2. *Mathematical Judgments* are all synthetical. This fact seems hitherto to have altogether escaped the observation of those who have analyzed human reason; it even seems directly opposed to all their

conjectures, though it is incontestably certain and most important in its consequences. For as it was found that the conclusions of mathematicians all proceed according to the law of contradiction (as is demanded by all apodictic certainty), men persuaded themselves that the fundamental principles were known from the same law. This was a great mistake, for a synthetical proposition can indeed be established by the law of contradiction, but only by presupposing another synthetical proposition from which it follows, but never by that law alone.

First of all, we must observe that all strictly mathematical judgments are *a priori,* and not empirical, because they carry with them necessity, which cannot be obtained from experience. But if this be not conceded to me, very good; I shall confine my assertion to *pure mathematics,* the very notion of which implies that it contains pure *a priori* and not empirical knowledge.

It must at first be thought that the proposition $7 + 5 = 12$ is a mere analytical judgment, following from the concept of the sum of seven and five, according to the law of contradiction. But on closer examination it appears that the concept of the sum of $7 + 5$ contains merely their union in a single number, without its being at all thought what the particular number is that unites them. The concept of twelve is by no means thought by merely thinking of the combination of seven and five; and, analyze this possible sum as we may, we shall not discover twelve in the concept. We must go beyond these concepts, by calling to our aid some intuition which corresponds to one of the concepts—that is, either our five fingers or five points (as Segner has it in his *Arithmetic*)—and we must add successively the units of the five given in the intuition to the concept of seven. Hence our concept is really amplified by the proposition $7 + 5 = 12$, and we add to the first concept a second concept not thought in it. Arithmetical judgments are therefore synthetical, and the more plainly according as we take larger numbers; for in such cases it is clear that, however closely we analyze our concepts without calling intuition to our aid, we can never find the sum by such mere dissection.

Just as little is any principle of geometry analytical. That a straight line is the shortest path between two points is a synthetical proposition. For my concept of straight contains nothing of quantity, but only a quality. The concept "shortest" is therefore altogether additional and cannot be obtained by any analysis of the concept "straight line." Here, too, intuition must come to aid us. It alone makes the synthesis possible. What usually makes us believe that the predicate of such apodictic judgments is already contained in our concept, and that the judgment is therefore analytical, is the duplicity of the expression. We must think a certain predicate as attached to a given concept, and necessity indeed belongs to the concepts. But the question is not what we must join in thought *to* the given concept, but what we actually think together with and in it, though obscurely; and so it appears that the predicate belongs to this concept necessarily indeed, yet not directly but indirectly by means of an intuition which must be present.

Some other principles, assumed by geometers, are indeed actually analytical, and depend on the law of contradiction; but they only serve, as identical propositions, as a method of concatenation, and not as principles—for example $a = a$, the whole is equal to itself, or $a + b > a$, the whole is greater than its part. And yet even these, though they are recognized as valid from mere concepts, are admitted in mathematics only because they can be represented in some intuition.

The essential and distinguishing feature of pure mathematical knowledge among all other *a priori* knowledge is that it cannot at all proceed from concepts, but only by means of the construction of concepts.[2] As therefore in its propositions it must proceed beyond the concept to that which its corresponding intuition contains, these propositions neither can, nor ought to, arise analytically, by dissection of the concept, but are all synthetical.

I cannot refrain from pointing out the disadvantage resulting to philosophy from the neglect of this easy and apparently insignificant observation. Hume being prompted to cast his eye over the whole field of *a priori* cognitions in which human understanding claims such mighty possessions (a calling he felt worthy of a philosopher) heedlessly severed from it a whole, and indeed its most valuable, province, namely, pure mathematics; for he imagined its nature or, so to speak, the state constitution of this empire depended on totally different principles, namely, on the law of contradiction alone; and although he did not divide judgments in this manner formally and universally as I have done here, what he said was equivalent to this: that mathematics contains only analytical, but metaphysics synthetical, *a priori* propositions. In this, however, he was greatly mistaken, and the mistake had a decidedly injurious effect upon his whole conception. But for this, he would have extended his question concerning the origin of our synthetical judgments far beyond the metaphysical concept of causality and included in it the possibility of mathematics *a priori* also, for this latter he must have assumed to be equally synthetical. And then he could not have based his metaphysical propositions on mere experience without subjecting the axioms of mathematics equally to experience, a thing which he was far too acute to do. The good company into which metaphysics would thus have been brought would have saved it from the danger of a contemptuous illtreatment, for the thrust intended for it must have reached mathematics, which was not and could not have been Hume's intention. Thus that acute man would have been led into considerations which must needs be similar to those that now occupy us, but which would have gained inestimably by his inimitably elegant style.

3. *Metaphysical Judgments,* properly so called, are all synthetical. We must distinguish judgments pertaining to metaphysics from metaphysical judgments properly so called. Many of the former are analytical, but they only afford the means for metaphysical judgments, which are the whole end of the science and which are always synthetical. For if there be concepts pertaining to metaphysics (as, for example, that of substance), the judgments springing from simple analysis of them also pertain to metaphysics, as, for example, substance is that which only exists as subject, etc.; and by means of several such analytical judgments we seek to approach the definition of the concepts. But as the analysis of a pure concept of the understanding (the kind of concept pertaining to metaphysics) does not proceed in any different manner from the dissection of any other, even empirical, concepts, not belonging to metaphysics (such as, air is an elastic fluid, the elasticity of which is not destroyed by any known degree of cold), it follows that the concept indeed, but not the analytical judgment, is properly metaphysical. This science has something peculiar in the production of its *a priori* cognitions, which must therefore be distinguished from the features it has in common with other rational knowledge. Thus the judgment that all

the substance in things is permanent is a synthetical and properly metaphysical judgment.

If the *a priori* concepts which constitute the materials and tools of metaphysics have first been collected according to fixed principles, then their analysis will be of great value; it might be taught as a particular part (as a *philosophia definitiva*), containing nothing but analytical judgments pertaining to metaphysics, and could be treated separately from the synthetical which constitute metaphysics proper. For indeed these analyses are not of much value except in metaphysics, that is, as regards the synthetical judgments which are to be generated by these previously analyzed concepts.

The conclusion drawn in this section then is that metaphysics is properly concerned with synthetical propositions *a priori,* and these alone constitute its end, for which it indeed requires various dissections of its concepts, namely, analytical judgments, but wherein the procedure is not different from that in every other kind of knowledge, in which we merely seek to render our concepts distinct by analysis. But the generation of *a priori* knowledge by intuition as well as by concepts, in fine, of synthetical propositions *a priori,* especially in philosophical knowledge, constitutes the essential subject of metaphysics.

§3. A Remark on the General Division of Judgment into Analytical and Synthetical

This division is indispensable, as concerns the critique of human understanding, and therefore deserves to be called classical in such critical investigation, though otherwise it is of little use. But this is the reason why dogmatic philosophers, who always seek the sources of metaphysical judgments in metaphysics itself, and not apart from it in the pure laws of reason generally, altogether neglected this apparently obvious distinction. Thus the celebrated Wolff and his acute follower Baumgarten came to seek the proof of the principle of sufficient reason, which is clearly synthetical, in the principle of contradiction. In Locke's *Essay,* however, I find an indication of my division. For in the fourth book (Chapter III, §9, seq.), having discussed the various connections of representations in judgments, and their sources, one of which he makes "identity or contradiction" (analytical judgments)

and another the coexistence of ideas in a subject (synthetical judgments), he confesses (§10) that our (*a priori*) knowledge of the latter is very narrow and almost nothing. But in his remarks on this species of knowledge, there is so little of what is definite and reduced to rules that we cannot wonder if no one, not even Hume, was led to make investigations concerning this sort of proposition. For such general and yet definite principles are not easily learned from other men, who have had them only obscurely in their minds. One must hit on them first by one's own reflection; then one finds them elsewhere, where one could not possibly have found them at first because the authors themselves did not know that such an idea lay at the basis of their observations. Men who never think independently have nevertheless the acuteness to discover everything, after it has been once shown them, in what was said long since, though no one was ever able to see it there before.

§4. The General Question of the Prolegomena: Is Metaphysics at All Possible?

Were a metaphysics which could maintain its place as a science really in existence, could we say: "Here is metaphysics; learn it and it will convince you irresistibly and irrevocably of its truth"? This question would then be useless, and there would only remain that other question (which would rather be a test of our acuteness than a proof of the existence of the thing itself): "How is the science possible, and how does reason come to attain it?" But human reason has not been so fortunate in this case. There is no single book to which you can point as you do to Euclid, and say: "This is metaphysics; here you may find the noblest objects of this science, the knowledge of a highest being and of a future existence, proved from principles of pure reason." We can be shown indeed many propositions, demonstrably certain and never questioned; but these are all analytical, and rather concern the materials and the scaffolding for metaphysics than the extension of knowledge, which is our proper object in studying it (§2). Even supposing you produce synthetical judgments (such as the law of sufficient reason, which you have never proved, as you ought to, from pure reason *a priori,* though we gladly concede its truth), you lapse, when you try to employ them for your principal purpose, into such doubtful assertions that in all ages one metaphysics has contradicted another, either in its assertions or their proofs, and thus has itself destroyed its own claim to lasting assent. Nay, the very attempts to set up such a science are the main cause of the early appearance of skepticism, a mental attitude in which reason treats itself with such violence that it could never have arisen save from complete despair of ever satisfying its most important aspirations. For long before men began to inquire into nature methodically, they consulted abstract reason, which had to some extent been exercised by means of ordinary experience; for reason is ever present, while laws of nature must usually be discovered with labor. So metaphysics floated to the surface, like foam, which dissolved the moment it was scooped off. But immediately there appeared a new supply on the surface, to be ever eagerly gathered up by some; while others, instead of seeking in the depths the cause of the phenomenon, thought they showed their wisdom by ridiculing the idle labor of their neighbors.

Weary therefore of dogmatism, which teaches us nothing, and of skepticism, which does not even promise us anything—even the quiet state of a contented ignorance—disquieted by the importance of knowledge so much needed, and rendered suspicious by long experience of all knowledge which we believe we possess or which offers itself in the name of pure reason, there remains but one critical question on the answer to which our future procedure depends, namely, "Is metaphysics at all possible?" But this question must be answered, not by sceptical objections to the asseverations of some actual system of metaphysics (for we do not as yet admit such a thing to exist), but from the conception, as yet only problematical, of a science of this sort.

In the *Critique of Pure Reason* I have treated this question synthetically, by making inquiries into pure reason itself and endeavoring in this source to determine the elements as well as the laws of its pure use according to principles. The task is difficult and requires a resolute reader to penetrate by degrees into a system based on no data except reason itself, and which therefore seeks, without resting upon any fact, to unfold knowledge from its original germs. The *Prolegomena,* however, are designed for prepara-

tory exercises; they are intended to point out what we have to do in order to make a science actual if it is possible, rather than to propound it. The *Prolegomena* must therefore rest upon something already known as trustworthy, from which we can set out with confidence and ascend to sources as yet unknown, the discovery of which will not only explain to us what we knew but exhibit a sphere of many cognitions which all spring from the same sources. The method of prolegomena, especially of those designed as a preparation for future metaphysics, is consequently analytical.

But it happens, fortunately, that though we cannot assume metaphysics to be an actual science, we can say with confidence that there is actually given certain pure *a priori* synthetical cognitions, pure mathematics and pure physics; for both contain propositions which are unanimously recognized, partly apodictically certain by mere reason, partly by general consent arising from experience and yet as independent of experience. We have therefore at least some uncontested synthetical knowledge *a priori* and need not ask *whether* it be possible, for it is actual, but *how* it is possible, in order that we may deduce from the principle which makes the given knowledge possible the possibility of all the rest.

§5. The General Problem: How Is Knowledge from Pure Reason Possible?

We have already learned the significant distinction between analytical and synthetical judgments. The possibility of analytical propositions was easily comprehended, being entirely founded on the law of contradiction. The possibility of synthetical *a posteriori* judgments, of those which are gathered from experience, also requires no particular explanations, for experience is nothing but a continued synthesis of perceptions. There remain therefore only synthetical propositions *a priori,* of which the possibility must be sought or investigated, because they must depend upon other principles than the law of contradiction.

But here we need not first establish the possibility of such propositions so as to ask whether they are possible. For there are enough of them which indeed are of undoubted certainty; and, as our present method is analytical, we shall start from the fact that such synthetical but purely rational knowledge actually exists; but we must now inquire into the ground of this possibility and ask *how* such knowledge is possible, in order that we may, from the principles of its possibility, be enabled to determine the conditions of its use, its sphere and its limits. The real problem upon which all depends, when expressed with scholastic precision, is therefore: "How are synthetic propositions *a priori* possible?"

For the sake of popular understanding I have above expressed this problem somewhat differently, as an inquiry into purely rational knowledge, which I could do for once without detriment to the desired insight, because, as we have only to do here with metaphysics and its sources, the reader will, I hope, after the foregoing reminders, keep in mind that when we speak of knowing by pure reason we do not mean analytical but synthetical knowledge.[3]

Metaphysics stands or falls with the solution of this problem; its very existence depends upon it. Let anyone make metaphysical assertions with ever so much plausibility, let him overwhelm us with conclusions; but if he has not previously proved able to answer this question satisfactorily, I have a right to say: This is all vain, baseless philosophy and false wisdom. You speak through pure reason and claim, as it were, to create cognitions *a priori* not only by dissecting given concepts, but also by asserting connections which do not rest upon the law of contradiction, and which you claim to conceive quite independently of all experience; how do you arrive at this, and how will you justify such pretensions? An appeal to the consent of the common sense of mankind cannot be allowed, for that is a witness whose authority depends merely upon rumor. Says Horace:

"Quodcunque ostendis mihi sic,
incredulus odi."[4]

The answer to this question is as indispensable as it is difficult; and although the principal reason that it was not sought long ago is that the possibility of the question never occurred to anybody, there is yet another reason, namely, that a satisfactory answer to this one question requires a much more persistent, profound, and painstaking reflection than the most diffuse work on metaphysics, which on its first appearance promised immortal fame to its author. And every intelligent reader,

when he carefully reflects what this problem requires, must at first be struck with its difficulty, and would regard it as insoluble and even impossible did there not actually exist pure synthetical cognitions *a priori*. This actually happened to David Hume, though he did not conceive the question in its entire universality as is done here and as must be done if the answer is to be decisive for all metaphysics. For how is it possible, says that acute man, that when a concept is given me I can go beyond it and connect with it another which is not contained in it, in such a manner as if the latter *necessarily* belonged to the former? Nothing but experience can furnish us with such connections (thus he concluded from the difficulty which he took to be impossibility), and all that vaunted necessity or, what is the same thing, knowledge assumed to be *a priori* is nothing but a long habit of accepting something as true, and hence of mistaking subjective necessity for objective.

Should my reader complain of the difficulty and the trouble which I shall occasion him in the solution of this problem, he is at liberty to solve it himself in an easier way. Perhaps he will then feel under obligation to the person who has undertaken for him a labor of so profound research and will rather feel some surprise at the facility with which, considering the nature of the subject, the solution has been attained. Yet it has cost years of work to solve the problem in its whole universality (using the term in the mathematical sense, namely, for that which is sufficient for all cases), and finally to exhibit it in the analytical form, as the reader will find it here.

All metaphysicians are therefore solemnly and legally suspended from their occupations till they shall have adequately answered the question, "How are synthetic cognitions *a priori* possible?" For the answer contains the only credentials which they must show when they have anything to offer us in the name of pure reason. But if they do not possess these credentials, they can expect nothing else of reasonable people, who have been deceived so often, than to be dismissed without further inquiry.

If they, on the other hand, desire to carry on their business, not as a science, but as an art of wholesome persuasion suitable to the common sense of man, this calling cannot in justice be denied them. They will then speak the modest language of a rational belief; they will grant that they are not allowed even to conjecture, far less to know, anything which lies beyond the bounds of all possible experience, but only to assume (not for speculative use, which they must abandon, but for practical use only) the existence of something possible and even indispensable for the guidance of the understanding and of the will in life. In this manner alone can they be called useful and wise men, and the more so as they renounce the title of metaphysicians. For the latter profess to be speculative philosophers; and since, when judgments *a priori* are under discussion, poor probabilities cannot be admitted (for what is declared to be known *a priori* is thereby announced as necessary), such men cannot be permitted to play with conjectures, but their assertion must be either science or nothing at all.

It may be said that the entire transcendental philosophy, which necessarily precedes all metaphysics, is nothing but the complete solution of the problem here propounded, in systematic order and completeness, and hence we have hitherto never had any transcendental philosophy. For what goes by its name is properly a part of metaphysics, whereas the former science is intended only to constitute the possibility of the latter and must therefore precede all metaphysics. And it is not surprising that when a whole science, deprived of all help from other sciences and consequently in itself quite new, is required to answer a single question satisfactorily, we should find the answer troublesome and difficult, nay, even shrouded in obscurity.

As we now proceed to this solution according to the analytical method, in which we assume that such cognitions from pure reason actually exist, we can only appeal to two sciences of theoretical knowledge (which alone is under consideration here), namely, pure mathematics and pure natural science. For these alone can exhibit to us objects in intuition, and consequently (if there should occur in them a cognition *a priori*) can show the truth or conformity of the cognition to the object *in concreto,* that is, its actuality, from which we could proceed to the ground of its possibility by the analytical method. This facilitates our work greatly for here universal considerations are not only applied to facts, but even start from them, while in a synthetic procedure they must strictly be derived *in abstracto* from concepts.

But in order to rise from these actual and, at the same time, well-grounded pure cognitions *a priori* to a possible knowledge of the kind as we are seeking, namely, to metaphysics as a science, we must comprehend that which occasions it—I mean the mere natural, though in spite of its truth still suspect, cognition *a priori* which lies at the basis of that science, the elaboration of which without any critical investigation of its possibility is commonly called metaphysics. In a word, we must comprehend the natural conditions of such a science as a part of our inquiry, and thus the transcendental problem will be gradually answered by a division into four questions:

1. How is pure mathematics possible?
2. How is pure natural science possible?
3. How is metaphysics in general possible?
4. How is metaphysics as a science possible?

It may be seen that the solution of these problems, though chiefly designed to exhibit the essential matter of the *Critique,* has yet something peculiar, which for itself alone deserves attention. This is the search for the sources of given sciences in reason itself, so that its faculty of knowing something *a priori* may by its own deeds be investigated and measured. By this procedure these sciences gain, if not with regard to their contents, yet as to their proper use; and while they throw light on the higher question concerning their common origin, they give, at the same time, an occasion better to explain their own nature.

Notes

[1] *Critique of Pure Reason,* "Methodology," Ch. I, Sec. 2.

[2] *Critique of Pure Reason,* "Methodology," Ch. I, Sec. 1.

[3] It is unavoidable that, as knowledge advances, certain expressions which have become classical after having been used since the infancy of science will be found inadequate and unsuitable, and a newer and more appropriate application of the terms will give rise to confusion. [This is the case with the term "analytical."] The analytical method, so far as it is opposed to the synthetical, is very different from one that consists of analytical propositions; it signifies only that we start from what is sought, as if it were given, and ascend to the only conditions under which it is possible. In this method we often use nothing but synthetical propositions, as in mathematical analysis, and it were better to term it the *regressive* method, in contradistinction to the *synthetic* or *progressive.* A principal part of logic too is distinguished by the name of analytic, which here signifies the logic of truth in contrast to dialectic, without considering whether the cognitions belonging to it are analytical or synthetical.

[4] ["To all that which thou provest me thus, I refuse to give credence, and hate"—*Epistle* II, 3, 188.]

VII.2 An Empiricist Critique of *A Priori* Knowledge

A. J. Ayer

A. J. Ayer (1910–1989) was for many years professor of philosophy at Oxford University. In this essay from his early work, *Language, Truth, and Logic,* Ayer argues that we have no reason to believe in synthetic a priori truth. All the candidates for such knowledge can be explained either as tautologies or as analytic truth.

. . . Having admitted that we are empiricists, we must now deal with the objection that is commonly brought against all forms of empiricism; the objection, namely, that it is impossible on empiricist principles to account for our knowledge of necessary truths. For, as Hume conclusively showed, no general proposition whose validity is subject to the test of actual experience can ever be logically certain. No matter how often it is verified in practice, there still remains the possibility that it will be confuted on some future occasion. The fact that a law has been substantiated in $n - 1$ cases affords no logical guarantee that it will be substantiated in the nth case also, no matter how large we take n to be. And this means that no general proposition referring to a matter of fact can ever be shown to be necessarily and universally true. It can at best be a probable hypothesis. And this, we shall find, applies not only to general propositions, but to all propositions which have a factual content. They can none of them ever become logically certain. This conclusion, which we shall elaborate later on, is one which must be accepted by every consistent empiricist. It is often thought to involve him in complete scepticism; but this is not the case. For the fact that the validity of a proposition cannot be logically guaranteed in no way entails that it is irrational for us to believe it. On the contrary, what is irrational is to look for a guarantee where none can be forthcoming; to demand certainty where probability is all that is obtainable. We have already remarked upon this, in referring to the work of Hume. And we

shall make the point clearer when we come to treat of probability, in explaining the use which we make of empirical propositions. We shall discover that there is nothing perverse or paradoxical about the view that all the "truths" of science and common sense are hypotheses; and consequently that the fact that it involves this view constitutes no objection to the empiricist thesis.

Where the empiricist does encounter difficulty is in connection with the truths of formal logic and mathematics. For whereas a scientific generalization is readily admitted to be fallible, the truths of mathematics and logic appear to everyone to be necessary and certain. But if empiricism is correct no proposition which has a factual content can be necessary or certain. Accordingly the empiricist must deal with the truths of logic and mathematics in one of the two following ways: he must say either that they are not necessary truths, in which case he must account for the universal conviction that they are; or he must say that they have no factual content, and then he must explain how a proposition which is empty of all factual content can be true and useful and surprising.

If neither of these courses proves satisfactory, we shall be obliged to give way to rationalism. We shall be obliged to admit that there are some truths about the world which we can know independently of experience; that there are some properties which we can ascribe to all objects, even though we cannot conceivably observe that all objects have them. And we shall have to accept it as a mysterious inexplicable fact that our thought has this power to reveal to us authoritatively the nature of objects which we have never observed. Or else we must accept the Kantian explanation which, apart from the epistemological difficulties which we have already touched on, only pushes the mystery a stage further back.

This selection is Chapter IV, except for small omissions, of Ayer's *Language, Truth and Logic*, published in Great Britain by Victor Gollancz, Ltd., in 1936, and in the United States by Dover Publications, Inc. It is here reprinted with the kind permission of the publishers. Notes omitted.

It is clear that any such concession to rationalism would upset the main argument of this book. For the admission that there were some facts about the world which could be known independently of experience would be incompatible with our fundamental contention that a sentence says nothing unless it is empirically verifiable. And thus the whole force of our attack on metaphysics would be destroyed. It is vital, therefore, for us to be able to show that one or other of the empiricist accounts of the propositions of logic and mathematics is correct. If we are successful in this, we shall have destroyed the foundations of rationalism. For the fundamental tenet of rationalism is that thought is an independent source of knowledge, and is moreover a more trustworthy source of knowledge than experience; indeed some rationalists have gone so far as to say that thought is the only source of knowledge. And the ground for this view is simply that the only necessary truths about the world which are known to us are known through thought and not through experience. So that if we can show either that the truths in question are not necessary or that they are not "truths about the world," we shall be taking away the support on which rationalism rests. We shall be making good the empiricist contention that there are no "truths of reason" which refer to matters of fact.

The course of maintaining that the truths of logic and mathematics are not necessary or certain was adopted by Mill. He maintained that these propositions were inductive generalizations based on an extremely large number of instances. The fact that the number of supporting instances was so very large accounted, in his view, for our believing these generalizations to be necessarily and universally true. The evidence in their favor was so strong that it seemed incredible to us that a contrary instance should ever arise. Nevertheless it was in principle possible for such generalizations to be confuted. They were highly probable, but, being inductive generalizations, they were not certain. The difference between them and the hypotheses of natural science was a difference in degree and not in kind. Experience gave us very good reason to suppose that a "truth" of mathematics or logic was true universally; but we were not possessed of a guarantee. For these "truths" were only empirical hypotheses which had worked particularly well in the past; and, like all empirical hypotheses, they were theoretically fallible.

I do not think that this solution of the empiricist's difficulty with regard to the propositions of logic and mathematics is acceptable. In discussing it, it is necessary to make a distinction which is perhaps already enshrined in Kant's famous dictum that, although there can be no doubt that all our knowledge begins with experience, it does not follow that it all arises out of experience. When we say that the truths of logic are known independently of experience, we are not of course saying that they are innate, in the sense that we are born knowing them. It is obvious that mathematics and logic have to be learned in the same way as chemistry and history have to be learned. Nor are we denying that the first person to discover a given logical or mathematical truth was led to it by an inductive procedure. It is very probable, for example, that the principle of the syllogism was formulated not before but after the validity of syllogistic reasoning had been observed in a number of particular cases. What we are discussing, however, when we say that the logical and mathematical truths are known independently of experience, is not a historical question concerning the way in which these truths were originally discovered, nor a psychological question concerning the way in which each of us comes to learn them, but an epistemological question. The contention of Mill's which we reject is that the propositions of logic and mathematics have the same status as empirical hypotheses; that their validity is determined in the same way. We maintain that they are independent of experience in the sense that they do not owe their validity to empirical verification. We may come to discover them through an inductive process; but once we have apprehended them we see that they are necessarily true, that they hold good for every conceivable instance. And this serves to distinguish them from empirical generalizations. For we know that a proposition whose validity depends upon experience cannot be seen to be necessarily and universally true.

In rejecting Mill's theory, we are obliged to be somewhat dogmatic. We can do no more than state the issue clearly and then trust that his contention will be seen to be discrepant with the relevant logical facts. The following considerations may serve to show that of the two ways of dealing with logic and mathematics which are open to the empiricist, the one which Mill adopted is not the one which is correct.

The Irrefutability of the Propositions of Mathematics and Logic

The best way to substantiate our assertion that the truths of formal logic and pure mathematics are necessarily true is to examine cases in which they might seem to be confuted. It might easily happen, for example, that when I came to count what I had taken to be five pairs of objects, I found that they amounted only to nine. And if I wished to mislead people I might say that on this occasion twice five was not ten. But in that case I should not be using the complex sign "$2 \times 5 = 10$" in the way in which it is ordinarily used. I should be taking it not as the expression of a purely mathematical proposition, but as the expression of an empirical generalization, to the effect that whenever I counted what appeared to me to be five pairs of objects I discovered that they were ten in number. This generalization may very well be false. But if it proved false in a given case, one would not say that the mathematical proposition "$2 \times 5 = 10$" had been confuted. One would say that I was wrong in supposing that there were five pairs of objects to start with, or that one of the objects had been taken away while I was counting, or that two of them had coalesced, or that I had counted wrongly. One would adopt as an explanation whatever empirical hypothesis fitted in best with the accredited facts. The one explanation which would in no circumstances be adopted is that ten is not always the product of two and five.

To take another example: if what appears to be a Euclidean triangle is found by measurement not to have angles totalling 180 degrees, we do not say that we have met with an instance which invalidates the mathematical proposition that the sum of the three angles of a Euclidean triangle is 180 degrees. We say that we have measured wrongly, or, more probably, that the triangle we have been measuring is not Euclidean. And this is our procedure in every case in which a mathematical truth might appear to be confuted. We always preserve its validity by adopting some other explanation of the occurrence.

The same thing applies to the principles of formal logic. We may take an example relating to the so-called law of excluded middle, which states that a proposition must be either true or false, or,

in other words, that it is impossible that a proposition and its contradictory should neither of them be true. One might suppose that a proposition of the form "x has stopped doing y" would in certain cases constitute an exception to this law. For instance, if my friend has never yet written to me, it seems fair to say that it is neither true nor false that he has stopped writing to me. But in fact one would refuse to accept such an instance as an invalidation of the law of excluded middle. One would point out that the proposition "My friend has stopped writing to me" is not a simple proposition, but the conjunction of the two propositions "My friend wrote to me in the past" and "My friend does not write to me now": and, furthermore, that the proposition "My friend has not stopped writing to me" is not, as it appears to be, contradictory to "My friend has stopped writing to me," but only contrary to it. For it means "My friend wrote to me in the past, and he still writes to me." When, therefore, we say that such a proposition as "My friend has stopped writing to me" is sometimes neither true nor false, we are speaking inaccurately. For we seem to be saying that neither it nor its contradictory is true. Whereas what we mean, or anyhow should mean, is that neither it nor its apparent contradictory is true. And its apparent contradictory is really only its contrary. Thus we preserve the law of excluded middle by showing that the negating of a sentence does not always yield the contradictory of the proposition originally expressed.

There is no need to give further examples. Whatever instance we care to take, we shall always find that the situations in which a logical or mathematical principle might appear to be confuted are accounted for in such a way as to leave the principle unassailed. And this indicates that Mill was wrong in supposing that a situation could arise which would overthrow a mathematical truth. The principles of logic and mathematics are true universally simply because we never allow them to be anything else. And the reason for this is that we cannot abandon them without contradicting ourselves, without sinning against the rules which govern the use of language, and so making our utterances self-stultifying. In other words, the truths of logic and mathematics are analytic propositions or tautologies. In saying this we are making what will be held to be an extremely controversial statement, and we must now proceed to make its implications clear.

The Nature of Analytic Propositions

The most familiar definition of an analytic proposition, or judgment, as he called it, is that given by Kant. He said that an analytic judgment was one in which the predicate B belonged to the subject A as something which was covertly contained in the concept of A. He contrasted analytic with synthetic judgments, in which the predicate B lay outside the subject A, although it did stand in connection with it. Analytic judgments, he explains, "add nothing through the predicate to the concept of the subject, but merely break it up into those constituent concepts that have all along been thought in it, although confusedly." Synthetic judgments, on the other hand, "add to the concept of the subject a predicate which has not been in any wise thought in it, and which no analysis could possibly extract from it." Kant gives "all bodies are extended" as an example of an analytic judgment, on the ground that the required predicate can be extracted from the concept of "body," "in accordance with the principle of contradiction"; as an example of a synthetic judgment, he gives "all bodies are heavy." He refers also to "7 + 5 = 12" as a synthetic judgment, on the ground that the concept of twelve is by no means already thought in merely thinking the union of seven and five. And he appears to regard this as tantamount to saying that the judgment does not rest on the principle of contradiction alone. He holds, also, that through analytic judgments our knowledge is not extended as it is through synthetic judgments. For in analytic judgments "the concept which I already have is merely set forth and made intelligible to me."

I think that this is a fair summary of Kant's account of the distinction between analytic and synthetic propositions, but I do not think that it succeeds in making the distinction clear. For even if we pass over the difficulties which arise out of the use of the vague term "concept," and the unwarranted assumption that every judgment, as well as every German or English sentence, can be said to have a subject and a predicate, there remains still this crucial defect. Kant does not give one straightforward criterion for distinguishing between analytic and synthetic propositions; he gives two distinct criteria, which are by no means equivalent. Thus his ground for holding that the proposition "7 + 5 = 12" is synthetic is, as we have seen, that the subjective intension of "7 + 5" does not comprise the subjective intension of "12"; whereas his ground for holding that "all bodies are extended" is an analytic proposition is that it rests on the principle of contradiction alone. That is, he employs a psychological criterion in the first of these examples, and a logical criterion in the second, and takes their equivalence for granted. But, in fact, a proposition which is synthetic according to the former criterion may very well be analytic according to the latter. For, as we have already pointed out, it is possible for symbols to be synonymous without having the same intensional meaning for anyone: and accordingly from the fact that one can think of the sum of seven and five without necessarily thinking of twelve, it by no means follows that the proposition "7 + 5 = 12" can be denied without self-contradiction. From the rest of his argument, it is clear that it is this logical proposition, and not any psychological proposition, that Kant is really anxious to establish. His use of the psychological criterion leads him to think that he has established it, when he has not.

I think that we can preserve the logical import of Kant's distinction between analytic and synthetic propositions, while avoiding the confusions which mar his actual account of it, if we say that a proposition is analytic when its validity depends solely on the definitions of the symbols it contains, and synthetic when its validity is determined by the facts of experience. Thus, the proposition "There are ants which have established a system of slavery" is a synthetic proposition. For we cannot tell whether it is true or false merely by considering the definitions of the symbols which constitute it. We have to resort to actual observation of the behavior of ants. On the other hand, the proposition "Either some ants are parasitic or none are" is an analytic proposition. For one need not resort to observation to discover that there either are or are not ants which are parasitic. If one knows what is the function of the words "either," "or," and "not," then one can see that any proposition of the form "Either p is true or p is not true" is valid, independently of experience. Accordingly, all such propositions are analytic.

It is to be noticed that the proposition "Either some ants are parasitic or none are" provides no information whatsoever about the behavior of ants, or, indeed, about any matter of fact.

And this applies to all analytic propositions. They none of them provide any information about any matter of fact. In other words, they are entirely devoid of factual content. And it is for this reason that no experience can confute them.

When we say that analytic propositions are devoid of factual content, and consequently that they say nothing, we are not suggesting that they are senseless in the way that metaphysical utterances are senseless. For, although they give us no information about any empirical situation, they do enlighten us by illustrating the way in which we use certain symbols. Thus if I say, "Nothing can be colored in different ways at the same time with respect to the same part of itself," I am not saying anything about the properties of any actual thing; but I am not talking nonsense. I am expressing an analytic proposition, which records our determination to call a color expanse which differs in quality from a neighboring color expanse a different part of a given thing. In other words, I am simply calling attention to the implications of a certain linguistic usage. Similarly, in saying that if all Bretons are Frenchmen, and all Frenchmen Europeans, then all Bretons are Europeans, I am not describing any matter of fact. But I am showing that in the statement that all Bretons are Frenchmen, and all Frenchmen Europeans, the further statement that all Bretons are Europeans is implicitly contained. And I am thereby indicating the convention which governs our usage of the words "if" and "all."

We see, then, that there is a sense in which analytic propositions do give us new knowledge. They call attention to linguistic usages, of which we might otherwise not be conscious, and they reveal unsuspected implications in our assertions and beliefs. But we can see also that there is a sense in which they may be said to add nothing to our knowledge. For they tell us only what we may be said to know already. Thus, if I know that the existence of May Queens is a relic of tree-worship, and I discover that May Queens still exist in England, I can employ the tautology "If p implies q, and p is true, q is true" to show that there still exists a relic of tree-worship in England. But in saying that there are still May Queens in England, and that the existence of May Queens is a relic of tree-worship, I have already asserted the existence in England of a relic of tree-worship. The use of the tautology does, indeed, enable me to make this concealed assertion explicit. But it does not provide me with any new knowledge, in the sense in which empirical evidence that the election of May Queens had been forbidden by law would provide me with new knowledge. If one had to set forth all the information one possessed, with regard to matters of fact, one would not write down any analytic propositions. But one would make use of analytic propositions in compiling one's encyclopedia, and would thus come to include propositions which one would otherwise have overlooked. And, besides enabling one to make one's list of information complete, the formulation of analytic propositions would enable one to make sure that the synthetic propositions of which the list was composed formed a self-consistent system. By showing which ways of combining propositions resulted in contradictions, they would prevent one from including incompatible propositions and so making the list self-stultifying. But in so far as we had actually used such words as "all" and "or" and "not" without falling into self-contradiction, we might be said already to know what was revealed in the formulation of analytic propositions illustrating the rules which govern our usage of these logical particles. So that here again we are justified in saying that analytic propositions do not increase our knowledge. . . .

The Propositions of Geometry

The mathematical propositions which one might most pardonably suppose to be synthetic are the propositions of geometry. For it is natural for us to think, as Kant thought, that geometry is the study of the properties of physical space, and consequently that its propositions have factual content. And if we believe this, and also recognize that the truths of geometry are necessary and certain, then we may be inclined to accept Kant's hypothesis that space is the form of intuition of our outer sense, a form imposed by us on the matter of sensation, as the only possible explanation of our *a priori* knowledge of these synthetic propositions. But while the view that pure geometry is concerned with physical space was plausible enough in Kant's day, when the geometry of Euclid was the only geometry known, the subsequent invention of non-Euclidean geometries has shown it to be mistaken. We see now that the axioms of a geometry are simply definitions, and that the theorems of a geometry are simply the logical consequences of these definitions. A geometry is not in itself about physical space; in itself it cannot be said to be "about" anything. But we can use a geometry to reason about physical space. That is to say, once we have given the axioms a physical interpretation, we can proceed to apply the theorems to the objects which satisfy the axioms. Whether a geometry can be applied to the actual physical world or not, is an empirical question which falls outside the scope of the geometry itself. There is no sense, therefore, in asking which of the various geometries known to us are false and which are true. In so far as they are all free from contradiction, they are all true. What one can ask is which of them is the most useful on any given occasion, which of them can be applied most easily and most fruitfully to an actual empirical situation. But the proposition which states that a certain application of a geometry is possible is not itself a proposition of that geometry. All that the geometry itself tells us is that if anything can be brought under the definitions, it will also satisfy the theorems. It is therefore a purely logical system, and its propositions are purely analytic propositions.

It might be objected that the use made of diagrams in geometrical treatises shows that geometrical reasoning is not purely abstract and logical, but depends on our intuition of the properties of figures. In fact, however, the use of diagrams is not essential to completely rigorous geometry. The diagrams are introduced as an aid to our reason. They provide us with a particular application of the geometry, and so assist us to perceive the more general truth that the axioms of the geometry involve certain consequences. But the fact that most of us need the help of an example to make us aware of those consequences does not show that the relation between them and the axioms is not a purely logical relation. It shows merely that our intellects are unequal to the task of carrying out very abstract processes of reasoning without the assistance of intuition. In other words, it has no bearing on the nature of geometrical propositions, but is simply an empirical fact about ourselves. Moreover, the appeal to intuition, though generally of psychological value, is also a source of danger to the geometer. He is tempted to make assumptions which are accidentally true of the particular figure he is taking as an illustration, but do not follow from his axioms. It has, indeed, been shown that Euclid himself was guilty of this, and consequently that the presence of the figure is essential to some of his proofs. This shows that his system is not, as he presents it, completely rigorous, although of course it can be made so. It does not show that the presence of the figure is essential to a truly rigorous geometrical proof. To suppose that it did would be to take as a necessary feature of all geometries what is really only an incidental defect in one particular geometrical system.

We conclude, then, that the propositions of pure geometry are analytic. And this leads us to reject Kant's hypothesis that geometry deals with the form of intuition of our outer sense. For the ground for this hypothesis was that it alone explained how the propositions of geometry could be both true *a priori* and synthetic: and we have seen that they are not synthetic. Similarly our view that the propositions of arithmetic are not synthetic but analytic leads us to reject the Kantian hypothesis that arithmetic is concerned with our pure intuition of time, the form of our inner sense. And thus we are able to dismiss Kant's transcendental aesthetic without having to bring forward the epistemological difficulties which it is commonly said to involve. For the only argument which can be brought in favor of Kant's theory is that it alone explains certain "facts." And now we have found that the "facts" which it purports to explain are not facts at all. For while it is true that we have *a priori* knowledge of necessary propositions, it is not true, as Kant supposed, that any of these necessary propositions are synthetic. They are without exception analytic propositions, or, in other words, tautologies.

We have already explained how it is that these analytic propositions are necessary and certain. We saw that the reason why they cannot be confuted in experience is that they do not make any assertion about the empirical world. They simply record our determination to use words in a certain fashion. We cannot deny them without infringing the conventions which are presupposed by our very denial, and so falling into self-contradiction. And this is the sole ground of their necessity. As Wittgenstein puts it, our justification for holding that the world could not conceivably disobey the laws of logic is simply that we could not say of an unlogical world how it would look. And just as the validity of an analytic proposition is independent of the nature of the external world, so is it independent of the nature of our minds. It is perfectly conceivable that we should have employed different linguistic conventions from those which we actually do employ. But whatever these conventions might be, the tautologies in which we recorded them would always be necessary. For any denial of them would be self-stultifying.

We see, then, that there is nothing mysterious about the apodictic certainty of logic and mathematics. Our knowledge that no observation can ever confute the proposition "7 + 5 = 12" depends simply on the fact that the symbolic expression "7 + 5" is synonymous with "12," just as our knowledge that every oculist is an eye-doctor depends on the fact that the symbol "eye-doctor" is synonymous with "oculist." And the same explanation holds good for every other *a priori* truth.

How Can Tautologies Be Surprising?

What is mysterious at first sight is that these tautologies should on occasion be so surprising, that there should be in mathematics and logic the possibility of invention and discovery. As Poincaré says: "If all the assertions which mathematics puts forward can be derived from one another by formal logic, mathematics cannot amount to anything more than an immense tautology. Logical inference can teach us nothing essentially new, and if everything is to proceed from the principle of identity, everything must be reducible to it. But can we really allow that these theorems which fill so many books serve no other purpose than to say in a round-about fashion 'A = A'?" Poincaré finds this incredible. His own theory is that the sense of invention and discovery in mathematics belongs to it in virtue of mathematical induction, the principle that what is true for the number 1, and true for $n + 1$ when it is true for n, is true for all numbers. And he claims that this is a synthetic *a priori* principle. It is, in fact, *a priori*, but it is not synthetic. It is a defining principle of the natural numbers, serving to distinguish them from such numbers as the infinite cardinal numbers, to which it cannot be applied. Moreover, we must remember that discoveries can be made, not only in arithmetic, but

also in geometry and formal logic, where no use is made of mathematical induction. So that even if Poincaré were right about mathematical induction, he would not have provided a satisfactory explanation of the paradox that a mere body of tautologies can be so interesting and so surprising.

The true explanation is very simple. The power of logic and mathematics to surprise us depends, like their usefulness, on the limitations of our reason. A being whose intellect was infinitely powerful would take no interest in logic and mathematics. For he would be able to see at a glance everything that his definitions implied, and, accordingly, could never learn anything from logical inference which he was not fully conscious of already. But our intellects are not of this order. It is only a minute proportion of the consequences of our definitions that we are able to detect at a glance. Even so simple a tautology as "$91 \times 79 = 7189$" is beyond the scope of our immediate apprehension. To assure ourselves that "7189" is synonymous with "91×79" we have to resort to calculation, which is simply a process of tautological transformation—that is, a process by which we change the form of expressions without altering their significance. The multiplication tables are rules for carrying out this process in arithmetic, just as the laws of logic are rules for the tautological transformation of sentences expressed in logical symbolism or in ordinary language. As the process of calculation is carried out more or less mechanically, it is easy for us to make a slip and so unwittingly contradict ourselves. And this accounts for the existence of logical and mathematical "falsehoods," which otherwise might appear paradoxical. Clearly the risk of error in logical reasoning is proportionate to the length and the complexity of the process of calculation. And in the same way, the more complex an analytic proposition is, the more chance it has of interesting and surprising us.

It is easy to see that the danger of error in logical reasoning can be minimized by the introduction of symbolic devices, which enable us to express highly complex tautologies in a conveniently simple form. And this gives us an opportunity for the exercise of invention in the pursuit of logical enquiries. For a well-chosen definition will call our attention to analytic truths, which would otherwise have escaped us. And the framing of definitions which are useful and fruitful may well be regarded as a creative act.

Having thus shown that there is no inexplicable paradox involved in the view that the truths of logic and mathematics are all of them analytic, we may safely adopt it as the only satisfactory explanation of their *a priori* necessity. And in adopting it we vindicate the empiricist claim that there can be no *a priori* knowledge of reality. For we show that the truths of pure reason, the propositions which we know to be valid independently of all experience, are so only in virtue of their lack of factual content. To say that a proposition is true *a priori* is to say that it is a tautology. And tautologies, though they may serve to guide us in our empirical search for knowledge, do not in themselves contain any information about any matter of fact.

VII.3 In Defense of *A Priori* Knowledge

A. C. EWING

A. C. Ewing (1899–1973) was for many years Lecturer in Moral Science at Cambridge University. In this selection from his book *The Fundamental Questions of Philosophy,* Ewing tries to meet Ayer's objections (Reading VII.2) and argues for the existence of synthetic a priori knowledge. He argues that deductive inferences as well as mathematical truths are synthetic a priori truths and that the statement that there is no synthetic a priori knowledge is itself a synthetic a priori judgment.

Meaning of the Distinction; "A Priori" Character of Mathematics

In the theory of knowledge, the first point that confronts us is the sharp distinction between two kinds of knowledge which have been called respectively *a priori* and empirical. Most of our knowledge we obtain by observation of the external world (sense-perception) and of ourselves (introspection). This is called empirical knowledge. But some knowledge we can obtain by simply thinking. That kind of knowledge is called *a priori*. Its chief exemplifications are to be found in logic and mathematics. In order to see that 5 + 7 = 12 we do not need to take five things and seven things, put them together, and then count the total number. We can know what the total number will be simply by thinking.

Another important difference between *a priori* and empirical knowledge is that in the case of the former we do not see merely that something, S, is in fact P, but that it must be P and why it is P. I can discover that a flower is yellow (or at least produces sensations of yellow) by looking at it, but I cannot thereby see why it is yellow or that it must be yellow. For anything I can tell it might equally well have been a red flower. But with a truth such as that 5 + 7 = 12 I do not see merely that it is a fact but that it must be a fact. It would be quite absurd to suppose that 5 + 7 might have been equal to 11 and just happened to be equal to 12, and I can see that the nature of 5 and 7 constitutes a fully adequate and intelligible reason why their sum should be 12 and not some other number. It is indeed conceivable

This selection is part of Chapter II of *The Fundamental Problems of Philosophy* (1951). It is reprinted here with the permission of Routledge and Kegan Paul, London.

that some of the things which make the two groups of 5 and 7 might, when they were put together, fuse like drops of water, or even vanish, so that there were no longer 12 things; but what is inconceivable is that there could *at the same time* be 5 + 7 things of a certain kind at once in a certain place and yet less than 12 things of that kind in that place. Before some of the things fused or vanished they would be 5 + 7 in number and also 12 in number, and after the fusion or disappearance they would be neither 5 + 7 nor 12. When I say in this connection that something is inconceivable, I do not mean merely or primarily that we cannot conceive it—this is not a case of a mere psychological inability like the inability to understand higher mathematics. It is a positive insight: we definitely see it to be impossible that certain things could happen. This we do not see in the case of empirical propositions which are false: they are not true but might for anything we know have been true. It is even conceivable, so far as we can see, that the fundamental laws of motion might have been quite different from what they are, but we can see that there could not have been a world which contradicted the laws of arithmetic. This is expressed by saying that empirical propositions are *contingent,* but true *a priori* propositions *necessary.* What we see to be necessary is not indeed that arithmetic should apply to the universe. It is conceivable that the universe might have been constituted entirely of a homogeneous fluid, and then, since there would have been no distinction between different things, it is difficult to see how arithmetic could have applied to it. What we do see is that arithmetic must be true of whatever can be numbered at all.

We must not be misled here by the fact that in order to come to understand arithmetic we originally required examples. Once we have learned the beginnings of arithmetic in the kindergarten with the help of examples, we do not need examples any more to grasp it, and we can see the truth of many arithmetic propositions, e.g., that 3112 + 2467 = 5579, of which we have never had examples. We have probably never taken 3112 things and 2467 things, put them together and counted the resulting set, but we still know that this is what the result of the counting would be. If it were empirical knowledge, we could not know it without counting. The examples are needed, not to prove anything, but only in order to enable us to come to understand in the first instance what is meant by number.

In geometry we indeed stand more in need of examples than in arithmetic, though I think this is only a psychological matter. In arithmetic we only need examples at the most elementary stage, but in geometry most people need a drawn figure, or at least an image of one in their minds, to see the validity of most proofs. But we must distinguish between an illustration and the basis of a proof. If the particular figure were not merely an illustration but the basis of the theorem, the latter would have to be proved by measuring it, but a measurement with a ruler or protractor never figures in Euclid's proofs. That the proof is not really based on the figure drawn is shown by the fact that we can still follow a proof concerning the properties of right-angled triangles even if the figure used to illustrate it is so badly drawn that it is obviously not a right-angled triangle at all. Again, if geometry were empirical, it would be a very hazardous speculation from the single example before us on the blackboard to conclude that all triangles had a property. It might be an individual idiosyncrasy of some triangles and not others. These considerations should be conclusive of themselves, but we might add that recent developments in geometry have had the effect of much loosening the connection between geometrical proofs and the empirical figure. It is possible to work out non-Euclidean geometries where we cannot depend on figures.

The "*A Priori*" in Logic

Another important field for *a priori* knowledge is logic. The laws of logic must be known *a priori* or not at all. They certainly are not a matter for empirical observation, and the function of logical argument is just to give us conclusions which we have not discovered by observation. The argument would be superfluous if we had observed them already. We are able to make inferences because there is sometimes a logical connection between one or more propositions (the premise or premises) and another proposition, the conclusion, such that the latter must be true if the former is. Then, if we know the former, we can assert the latter on the strength of it, thus anticipating any experience. To take an example, there is a story that Mr. X., a man of high reputation and great social standing, had been asked to preside at a big social function. He was late in coming, and so a Roman Catholic priest was asked to make a speech to pass the time till his arrival. The priest told various anecdotes, including one which recorded his embarrassment when as confessor he had to deal with his first penitent and the latter confessed to a particularly atrocious murder. Shortly afterwards Mr. X. arrived, and in his own speech he said: "I see Father ———— is here. Now, though he may not recognize me, he is an old friend of mine, in fact I was his first penitent." It is plain that such an episode would enable one to infer that Mr. X. had committed a murder without having observed the crime. The form of inference involved: The first penitent was a murderer, Mr. X. was the first penitent, therefore Mr. X. was a murderer—is of the famous kind to which logicians have given the name of *syllogism*. The importance of syllogisms has often been exaggerated, but they are as important as any kind of inference, and we cannot deny that in many cases a syllogism has given people information of which they were not in any ordinary sense aware before they used the syllogism and which they did not acquire by observation. Inference is only possible because there are special connections between the propositions involved such that one necessarily follows from others. It is a chief function of logic to study these connections, of which that expressed in the syllogism is by no means the only one.

(A *syllogism* consists of three propositions, two forming the *premises* and the other the *conclusion*. Each proposition can be expressed by a subject and predicate connected by the verb to be, the *copula,* and if we call everything which stands as either subject or predicate a *term,* there must be three and only three terms in the syllogism. The one common to the two premises is called the *middle term,* and it is on this common element that the inference depends. The other two, having been connected by means of it, occur without it in the conclusion. Thus in the usual example of the syllogism—All men are mortal, Socrates is a man, ∴ Socrates is mortal—man is the middle term connecting Socrates with mortality so that we could, even if he had not already died, know that he was mortal.)

Other Cases of the *"A Priori"*

A priori knowledge, while most prominent in mathematics and logic, is not limited to these subjects. For instance, we can see *a priori* that the same surface cannot have two different colors all over at the same time, or that a thought cannot have a shape. Philosophers have been divided into *rationalists* and *empiricists* according to whether they stressed the *a priori* or the empirical element more. The possibility of metaphysics depends on *a priori* knowledge, for our experience is quite inadequate to enable us to make on merely empirical grounds any sweeping generalizations of the kind the metaphysician desires. The term *a priori* covers both self-evident propositions, i.e. those which are seen to be true in their own right, and those which are derived by inference from propositions themselves self-evident.

The Linguistic Theory of the *"A Priori"* and the Denial That *"A Priori"* Propositions or Inferences Can Give New Knowledge

At the present time even empiricist philosophers recognize the impossibility of explaining away *a priori* propositions as merely empirical generalizations, but they are inclined to the view that *a priori* propositions and *a priori* reasoning are merely concerned with language, and so cannot tell us anything new about the real world. Thus it is said that, when we make an inference, the conclusion is just part of the premises expressed in different language.[1] If so, inference would be of use merely for clarifying our language and would involve no real advance in knowledge. Some inferences are of this type, e.g. A is a father, therefore A is male. But are they all? That would be hard indeed to square with the *prima facie* novelty of many conclusions. Take, for instance, the proposition that the square on the hypotenuse of a right-angled triangle is equal to the sum of the squares on the other two sides. Such a proposition can be inferred from the axioms and postulates of Euclid, but it certainly does not seem to be included in their meaning. Otherwise we should know it as soon as we understood the axioms and postulates. The example I gave of the murder discovered by a logical argument seems to be another case of a fact not known at all beforehand by the reasoner which is discovered by his reasoning. Extreme empiricist philosophers contend that this appearance of novelty is really illusory, and that in some sense we knew the conclusion all along; but they have never succeeded in making clear in what sense we did so. It is not enough to say that the conclusion is implicit in the premises. "Implicit" means "implied by," and of course a conclusion is implied by its premises, if the inference is correct at all. But this admission leaves quite open the question whether or not a proposition can follow from a different one which does not contain it as part of itself; and since we obviously can by deductive inference come to know things which we did not know before in any ordinary sense of "know," we must treat the empiricist's claim as unjustified till he has produced a clearly defined sense of "implicit in" or "contained in" which leaves room for that novelty in inference which we all cannot help really admitting. In any ordinary sense of "know" the conclusion is not in the cases I have mentioned known prior to the inference, and since the premises are and indeed must be known before we know the conclusion, it is therefore in no ordinary sense of "part" part of the premises.

It is indeed sometimes said that the premises include the conclusion in a confused form, but it is obvious that the beginner in geometry cannot be said to be aware of Pythagoras's theorem even in a confused form though he may know all the premises from which it can be deduced. Nor does awareness of the propositions that A was B's first penitent and that B's first penitent was a murderer include even confusedly the awareness that A was a murderer as long as the premises are not combined. When they are combined therefore something new appears that was not present to consciousness before in any way; there is a new discovery. We can also show by definite logical argument that the interpretation we are discussing does not enable one to avoid the admission of novelty in inference. For, what is it to know something in a confused form? It is surely to know some general attributes present in a whole but not others. To be aware of p even confusedly must involve discriminating some general attributes in p, and those are given in the

premises, which are admittedly understood in some degree. If we do not discriminate any attributes, the confusion is too great for argument to be possible at all. Now it is admitted that, when we reach the conclusion, we do discriminate attributes which we did not discriminate before, even if they are alleged to have been contained in the confused whole which was present to our minds before we started inferring. It is further admitted that the conclusion follows necessarily from the premises. Therefore the general attributes which we discriminated at the time when we knew only the premises and not the conclusion must be linked with the attributes we discriminate afterwards in such a way that the latter follow necessarily from the former. So we still have to admit that sheer *a priori* inference can enable us to discover new attributes. In some cases it may take a good while to draw the inference, in other cases it may be practically instantaneous as soon as the premises are known and combined, but whether it takes a long or a short time to draw the inference cannot be relevant to the principle.

Nevertheless, the view that inference cannot yield new conclusions dies hard, and so it will not be superfluous to bring further arguments. (1) "This has shape" admittedly follows logically from "this has size" and vice versa. If the view I am criticizing were true, "this has size" would, therefore, have to include in its meaning "this has shape," and "this has shape" would also have to include in its meaning "this has size." But this would only be possible if the two sentences meant exactly the same thing, which they obviously do not. (2) Take an argument such as—Montreal is to the north of New York, New York is to the north of Washington, therefore Montreal is to the north of Washington. If the view I am discussing is true, the conclusion is part of the premises. But it is not part of either premise by itself, otherwise both premises would not be needed. So the only way in which it could be part of both together would be if it were divisible into two propositions one of which was part of the first and the other part of the second. I defy anybody to divide it in this way. (3) The proposition "Socrates was a philosopher" certainly entails the proposition "if Socrates had measles some philosophers have had measles," but it cannot be that the second proposition is included in the first. For the first proposition certainly does not include the notion of measles.

What is really the same view is often expressed by saying that all *a priori* propositions are "analytic." A distinction has commonly been drawn between *analytic* propositions, in which the predicate is in the notion of the subject already formed before the proposition is asserted, so that the proposition gives no new information, and *synthetic* propositions in which the predicate is not so contained and which are thus capable of giving new information.[2] Analytic propositions are essentially verbal, being all true by definition, e.g. all fathers are male. As an example of a synthetic proposition we could take any proposition established by experience such as "I am cold" or "It is snowing," but empiricists often assert that there are no synthetic *a priori* propositions. That this view cannot be justified may be shown at once. The proposition that there are no synthetic *a priori* propositions, since it cannot be established by empirical observations, would be, if justified, itself a synthetic *a priori* proposition, and we cannot affirm it as a synthetic *a priori* proposition that there are no synthetic *a priori* propositions. We may therefore dismiss off-hand any arguments for the theory. Such arguments, whatever they were, would have to involve synthetic *a priori* propositions. Further, the view must be false if it is ever true that the conclusion of an inference is not part of its premises. For, if the proposition—S is Q—ever follows validly from—S is P, the proposition—all that is SP is SQ, must be true *a priori*. But, unless the concept Q is part of the concept SP, the proposition—all that is SP is SQ—cannot be analytic. Therefore our arguments against the view that in all valid inferences the conclusion is part of the premises expressed in different language are also arguments against the view that all *a priori* propositions are analytic.

The analytic view seems plausible when we are concerned with the simplest propositions of logic and arithmetic, but we must not assume that a proposition is analytic because it is obvious. Though it may be very difficult to determine precisely where analytic propositions end and synthetic propositions begin, we cannot use this as a ground for denying the latter. It is very difficult to say precisely where blue ends and green begins, since the different shades run into each other imperceptibly, but we cannot therefore argue that all blue is really green. Taking arithmetic, even if there is a good deal of plausibility in saying that

2 + 2 is included in the meaning of "4," there is none in saying 95 – 91 or (216/2) – [(287 + 25)/3] are so included. Yet, if the analytic view were true, all the infinite numerical combinations which could be seen *a priori* to be equal to 4 would have to be included in the meaning of "4."

Some empiricists, without committing themselves to the view that all *a priori* propositions are analytic, still say these are a matter of arbitrary choice or verbal convention. They are influenced here by a modern development in the view of geometry. It used to be held that the axioms of Euclid expressed a direct insight into the nature of physical space, but this is denied by modern scientists, and the view is taken that they are arbitrary postulates which geometricians make because they are interested in what would follow *if* they were true. Whether they are true or not is then a matter of empirical fact to be decided by science. But, even if this suggests that the premises of our *a priori* arguments may be arbitrary postulates, this does not make the subsequent steps arbitrary. From the postulates of Euclid it follows that the three angles of a triangle are equal to two right angles. If the original postulates are arbitrary, it is not certain that the conclusion is true of the real world; but it is still not an arbitrary matter that it follows from the postulates. The postulates may well be false, but there can be no doubt that *if* they were true the conclusions must be so, and it is in this hypothetical working out of the consequences of postulates which may not be true that pure geometry consists. The *a priori* necessity of pure geometry is not therefore in the least invalidated by modern developments. What is *a priori* is that the conclusions follow from the axioms and postulates, and this is not at all affected by the (empirical) discovery that not all the axioms and postulates exactly apply to the physical world. (Applied Euclidean geometry is possible in practice because it is an empirical fact that they approximately apply. The divergencies only show themselves when we consider unusually great velocities or distances.)

If not only the postulates but the successive stages in the inference were themselves arbitrary, we might just as well infer from the same premises that the angles of a triangle were equal to a million right angles or to none at all. All point in inference would be lost. Dictators may do a great deal, but they cannot alter the laws of logic and mathematics; these laws would not change even if by a system of intensive totalitarian education every human being were persuaded to fall in with a world dictator's whim in the matter and believe they were different from what they are. Nor can they change with alterations in language, though they may be expressed differently. That the truth of *a priori* propositions does not just depend on the nature of language can be easily seen when we consider that, even if we do not know any Fijian or Hottentot, we can know that also in these languages and not only in the languages we know the proposition 5 + 7 = 12 must be true. It is of course true that by altering the meaning of the words we could make the proposition we expressed by "5 + 7 = 12" false, e.g. if I used "12" in a new sense to mean what other people mean by "11," but then it would be a different proposition. I could play the same trick with empirical propositions and say truly, e.g., that "fire does not burn" or "there is an elephant in this room" if I used "burn" to mean "drown" or "elephant" to mean "table." This does not in the least impair the obviousness of the contrary propositions established by experience. Finally, as we argued above that the proposition that there can be no synthetic *a priori* propositions would itself, if justified, have to be a synthetic *a priori* proposition, so we may argue that the proposition that all *a priori* propositions are a matter of arbitrary linguistic convention would, if true, have to be itself a matter of arbitrary linguistic convention. It therefore could not be vindicated by any argument and would be merely a matter of a new usage of words arbitrarily established by the persons who assert it, since it certainly does not express the usual meaning of "*a priori* propositions." So we must reject any attempt to explain away the *a priori* as a genuine source of new knowledge. If the attempt had succeeded, we should have had to admit that philosophy in anything like its old sense was impossible, for philosophy clearly cannot be based merely on observation.

The views we have been criticizing contain the following elements of truth. (1) *A priori* propositions can be seen to be true and the con-

clusions of an inference seen to follow from their premises without any further observation, provided we understand the meaning of the words used. But to say that q follows from p once we understand the meaning of the words is not to say that q is part of the meaning of the words used to express p. "Follow from" and "be part of" are not synonyms. (2) If q follows from p you cannot assert p and deny q without contradicting yourself, but this is only to say that in that case the denial of q implies the denial of p. It is not to say that q is part of what you assert when you assert p, unless we already assume that what is implied is always part of what implies it, i.e. beg the question at issue. (3) An *a priori* proposition cannot be fully understood without being seen to be true. It may be impossible to understand something fully without understanding something else not included in it at all, so it may still be synthetic.

People have been inclined to deny synthetic *a priori* propositions because they could not see how one characteristic could necessarily involve another, but that this could not happen would be itself a synthetic *a priori* metaphysical proposition. People have also thought that it was necessary to give some sort of explanation of *a priori* knowledge, and could not see how this could be done except in terms of language. To this I should reply that there is no reason to suppose that *a priori* knowledge requires some special explanation any more than does our ability to attain knowledge empirically by observation. Why not take it as an ultimate fact? Human beings certainly cannot explain everything, whether there is ultimately an explanation for it or not.

Notes

[1] This theory is not applied to *inductive* inference.

[2] This definition would have to be amended slightly to suit modern logicians who (I think, rightly) deny that all propositions are of the subject-predicate form, but this would not alter the principle though importing a complication of detail with which we need not deal here.

VII.4 Two Dogmas of Empiricism

W. V. QUINE

W. V. Quine (1908–2000) argues against two fundamental theses of empiricism: the analytic-synthetic distinction and the belief that individual observation statements are the fundamental unit of meaning. In the first part of this essay, he seeks to undermine the distinction between analytic and synthetic statements that underlies both the Kantian project and contemporary empiricism. One version of the argument appeals to the notion of *containment:* the predicate term is contained in the subject. Quine contends that the notion of *containment* is a vague metaphor and that its vagueness spreads over the entire analytic-synthetic distinction. Furthermore, the concept of analyticity rests on the concept of synonymy, on having the same meaning. That is, if it is analytic that "A bachelor is an unmarried male" this is because the terms "bachelor" and "unmarried male" are already synonymous. But, Quine argues, to say that these terms are synonymous is to presuppose that they are analytic. Hence, the argument is circular.

In the second part of this essay, Quine attacks the notion of radical reductionism, which is tied to the verification theory of meaning and assumes that individual observation statements are the basic unit of meaning. Quine rejects this atomistic view, holding instead a "pragmatic coherentism." That is, all our beliefs form a holistic web, so that individual statements are never confirmed or falsified in isolation but only with reference to the holistic web. The most successful system of beliefs is that of science because it allows us to make correct predictions. This workability of our belief system is the pragmatic aspect of epistemology.

Modern empiricism has been conditioned in large part by two dogmas. One is a belief in some fundamental cleavage between truths which are *analytic,* or grounded in meanings independently of matters of fact, and truths which are *synthetic,* or grounded in fact. The other dogma is *reductionism:* the belief that each meaningful statement is equivalent to some logical construct upon terms which refer to immediate experience. Both dogmas, I shall argue, are ill-founded. One effect of abandoning them is, as we shall see, a blurring of the supposed boundary between speculative metaphysics and natural science. Another effect is a shift toward pragmatism.

W. V. Quine, "Two Dogmas of Empiricism," reprinted by permission of the publishers from *A Logical Point of View,* 2nd. Edition, Rev., by W. V. Quine, Cambridge, Massachusetts: Harvard University Press, © 1953, 1961, 1980 by the President and Fellows of Harvard College; © 1981 by W. V. Quine. Notes have been deleted.

1. Background for Analyticity

Kant's cleavage between analytic and synthetic truths was foreshadowed in Hume's distinction between relations of ideas and matters of fact, and in Leibniz's distinction between truths of reason and truths of fact. Leibniz spoke of truths of reason as true in all possible worlds. Picturesqueness aside, this is to say that the truths of reason are those which could not possibly be false. In the same vein we hear analytic statements defined as statements whose denials are self-contradictory. But this definition has small explanatory value; for the notion of self-contradictoriness, in the quite broad sense needed for this definition of analyticity, stands in exactly the same need of clarification as does the notion of analyticity itself. The two notions are the two sides of a single dubious coin.

Kant conceived of an analytic statement as one that attributes to its subject no more than is already conceptually contained in the subject. This formulation has two shortcomings: it limits itself to statements of subject-predicate form, and it appeals to a notion of containment which is left at a metaphorical level. But Kant's intent, evident more from the use he makes of the notion of analyticity than from his definition of it, can be restated thus: a statement is analytic when it is true by virtue of meanings and independently of fact. Pursuing this line, let us examine the concept of *meaning* which is presupposed.

Meaning, let us remember, is not to be identified with naming. Frege's example of "Evening Star" and "Morning Star," and Russell's of "Scott" and "the author of *Waverley*," illustrate that terms can name the same thing but differ in meaning. The distinction between meaning and naming is no less important at the level of abstract terms. The terms "9" and "the number of the planets" name one and the same abstract entity but presumably must be regarded as unlike in meaning; for astronomical observation was needed, and not mere reflection on meanings, to determine the sameness of the entity in question.

The above examples consist of singular terms, concrete and abstract. With general terms, or predicates, the situation is somewhat different but parallel. Whereas a singular term purports to name an entity, abstract or concrete, a general term does not; but a general term is *true* of an entity, or of each of many, or of none. The class of all entities of which a general term is true is called the *extension* of the term. Now paralleling the contrast between the meaning of a singular term and the entity named, we must distinguish equally between the meaning of a general term and its extension. The general terms "creature with a heart" and "creature with kidneys," for example, are perhaps alike in extension but unlike in meaning.

Confusion of meaning with extension, in the case of general terms, is less common than confusion of meaning with naming in the case of singular terms. It is indeed a commonplace in philosophy to oppose intension (or meaning) to extension, or, in a variant vocabulary, connotation to denotation.

The Aristotelian notion of essence was the forerunner, no doubt, of the modern notion of intension or meaning. For Aristotle it was essential in men to be rational, accidental to be two-legged. But there is an important difference between this attitude and the doctrine of meaning. From the latter point of view it may indeed be conceded (if only for the sake of argument) that rationality is involved in the meaning of the word "man" while two-leggedness is not; but two-leggedness may at the same time be viewed as involved in the meaning of "biped" while rationality is not. Thus from the point of view of the doctrine of meaning it makes no sense to say of the actual individual, who is at once a man and a biped, that his rationality is essential and his two-leggedness accidental or vice versa. Things had essences, for Aristotle, but only linguistic forms have meanings. Meaning is what essence becomes when it is divorced from the object of reference and wedded to the word.

For the theory of meaning a conspicuous question is the nature of its objects: what sort of things are meanings? A felt need for meant entities may derive from an earlier failure to appreciate that meaning and reference are distinct. Once the theory of meaning is sharply separated from the theory of reference, it is a short step to recognizing as the primary business of the theory of meaning simply the synonymy of linguistic forms and the analyticity of statements; meanings themselves, as obscure intermediary entities, may well be abandoned.

The problem of analyticity then confronts us anew. Statements which are analytic by general philosophical acclaim are not, indeed, far to seek. They fall into two classes. Those of the first class, which may be called *logically true,* are typified by:

(1) No unmarried man is married.

The relevant feature of this example is that it not merely is true as it stands, but remains true under any and all reinterpretations of "man" and "married." If we suppose a prior inventory of *logical* particles, comprising "no," "un-," "not," "if," "then," "and," etc., then in general a logical truth is a statement which is true and remains true under all reinterpretations of its components other than the logical particles.

But there is also a second class of analytic statements, typified by:

(2) No bachelor is married.

The characteristic of such a statement is that it can be turned into a logical truth by putting synonyms for synonyms; thus (2) can be turned into (1) by putting "unmarried man" for its synonym "bachelor." We still lack a proper characterization of this second class of analytic statements, and therewith of analyticity generally, inasmuch as we have had in the above description to lean on a notion of "synonymy" which is no less in need of clarification than analyticity itself.

Our problem, however, is analyticity; and here the major difficulty lies not in the first class of analytic statements, the logical truths, but rather in the second class, which depends on the notion of synonymy.

2. Definition

There are those who find it soothing to say that the analytic statements of the second class reduce to those of the first class, the logical truths, by *definition;* "bachelor," for example, is *defined* as "unmarried man." But how do we find that "bachelor" is defined as "unmarried man"? Who defined it thus, and when? Are we to appeal to the nearest dictionary, and accept the lexicographer's formulation as law? Clearly this would be to put the cart before the horse. The lexicographer is an empirical scientist, whose business is the recording of antecedent facts; and if he glosses "bachelor" as "unmarried man" it is because of his belief that there is a relation of synonymy between those forms, implicit in general or preferred usage prior to his own work. The notion of synonymy presupposed here has still to be clarified, presumably in terms relating to linguistic behaviour. Certainly the "definition" which is the lexicographer's report of an observed synonymy cannot be taken as the ground of the synonymy.

Definition is not, indeed, an activity exclusively of philologists. Philosophers and scientists frequently have occasion to "define" a recondite term by paraphrasing it into terms of a more familiar vocabulary. But ordinarily such a definition, like the philologist's, is pure lexicography affirming a relation of synonymy antecedent to the exposition in hand.

Just what it means to affirm synonymy, just what the interconnections may be which are necessary and sufficient in order that two linguistic forms be properly describable as synonymous, is far from clear; but, whatever these interconnections may be, ordinarily they are grounded in usage. Definitions reporting selected instances of synonymy come then as reports upon usage.

There is also, however, a variant type of definitional activity which does not limit itself to the reporting of pre-existing synonymies. I have in mind what Carnap calls *explication*—an activity to which philosophers are given, and scientists also in their more philosophical moments. In explication the purpose is not merely to paraphrase the definiendum into an outright synonym, but actually to improve upon the definiendum by refining or supplementing its meaning. But even explication, though not merely reporting a pre-existing synonymy between definiendum and definiens, does rest, nevertheless, on *other* pre-existing synonymies. The matter may be viewed as follows. Any word worth explicating has some contexts which, as wholes, are clear and precise enough to be useful; and the purpose of explication is to preserve the usage of these favoured contexts while sharpening the usage of other contexts. In order that a given definition be suitable for purposes of explication, therefore, what is required is not that the definiendum in its antecedent usage be synonymous with the definiens, but just that each of these favoured contexts of the definiendum, taken as a whole in its antecedent usage, be synonymous with the corresponding context of the definiens.

Two alternative definientia may be equally appropriate for the purposes of a given task of explication and yet not be synonymous with each other; for they may serve interchangeably within the favoured contexts but diverge elsewhere. By cleaving to one of these definientia rather than the other, a definition of explicative kind generates, by fiat, a relation of synonymy between definiendum and definiens which did not hold before. But such a definition still owes its explicative function, as seen, to pre-existing synonymies.

There does, however, remain still an extreme sort of definition which does not hark back to prior synonymies at all: namely, the explicitly conventional introduction of novel notations for purposes of sheer abbreviation. Here the definiendum becomes synonymous with the definiens simply because it has been created expressly for the purpose of being synonymous with the definiens. Here we have a really transparent case of synonymy created by definition; would that all species of synonymy were as intelligible. For the rest, definition rests on synonymy rather than explaining it.

The word "definition" has come to have a dangerously reassuring sound, owing no doubt to its frequent occurrence in logical and mathematical writings. We shall do well to digress now into a brief appraisal of the role of definition in formal work.

In logical and mathematical systems either of two mutually antagonistic types of economy may be striven for, and each has its peculiar practical utility. On the one hand, we may seek economy of practical expression—ease and brevity in the statement of multifarious relations. This sort of economy calls usually for distinctive concise notations for a wealth of concepts. Second, however, and oppositely, we may seek economy in grammar and vocabulary; we may try to find a minimum of basic concepts such that, once a distinctive notation has been appropriated to each of them, it becomes possible to express any desired further concept by mere combination and iteration of our basic notations. This second sort of economy is impractical in one way, since a poverty in basic idioms tends to a necessary lengthening of discourse. But it is practical in another way: it greatly simplifies theoretical discourse *about* the language, through minimizing the terms and the forms of construction wherein the language consists.

Both sorts of economy, though prima facie incompatible, are valuable in their separate ways. The custom has consequently arisen of combining both sorts of economy by forging in effect two languages, the one a part of the other. The inclusive language, though redundant in grammar and vocabulary, is economical in message lengths, while the part, called primitive notation, is economical in grammar and vocabulary. Whole and part are correlated by rules of translation whereby each idiom not in primitive notation is equated to some complex built up of primitive notation. These rules of translation are the so-called *definitions* which appear in formalized systems. They are best viewed not as adjuncts to one language but as correlations between two languages, the one a part of the other.

But these correlations are not arbitrary. They are supposed to show how the primitive notations can accomplish all purposes, save brevity and convenience, of the redundant language. Hence the definiendum and its definiens may be expected, in each case, to be related in one or another of the three ways lately noted. The definiens may be a faithful paraphrase of the definiendum into the narrower notion, preserving a direct synonymy as of antecedent usage; or the definiens may, in the spirit of explication, improve upon the antecedent usage of the definiendum; or finally, the definiendum may be a newly created notation, newly endowed with meaning here and now.

In formal and informal work alike, thus, we find that definition—except in the extreme case of the explicitly conventional introduction of new notations—hinges on prior relations of synonymy. Recognizing then that the notion of definition does not hold the key to synonymy and analyticity, let us look further into synonymy and say no more of definition.

3. Interchangeability

A natural suggestion, deserving close examination, is that the synonymy of two linguistic forms consists simply in their interchangeability in all contexts without change of truth value—interchangeability, in Leibniz's phrase, *salva veritate*. Note that synonyms so conceived need not even be free from vagueness, as long as the vaguenesses match.

But it is not quite true that the synonyms "bachelor" and "unmarried man" are everywhere interchangeable *salva veritate*. Truths which become false under substitution of "unmarried man" for "bachelor" are easily constructed with the help of "bachelor of arts" or "bachelor's buttons"; also with the help of quotation, thus:

"Bachelor" has less than ten letters.

Such counter-instances can, however, perhaps be set aside by treating the phrases "bachelor of arts" and "bachelor's buttons" and the quotation " 'bachelor' " each as a single indivisible word and then stipulating that the interchangeability *salva veritate* which is to be the touchstone of synonymy is not supposed to apply to fragmentary occurrences inside of a word. This account of synonymy supposing it acceptable on other counts, has indeed the drawback of appealing to a prior conception of "word" which can be counted on to present difficulties of formulation in its turn. Nevertheless, some progress might be claimed in having reduced the problem of synonymy to a problem of wordhood. Let us pursue this line a bit, taking "word" for granted.

The question remains whether interchangeability *salva veritate* (apart from occurrences within words) is a strong enough condition for synonymy, or whether, on the contrary, some heteronymous expressions might be thus interchangeable. Now let us be clear that we are not concerned here with synonymy in the sense of complete identity in psychological associations or poetic quality; indeed no two expressions are synonymous in such a sense. We are concerned only with what may be called *cognitive* synonymy. Just what this is cannot be said without successfully finishing the present study; but we know something about it from the need which arose for it in connection with analyticity in §1. The sort of synonymy needed there was merely such that any analytic statement could be turned into a logical truth by putting synonyms for synonyms. Turning the tables and assuming analyticity, indeed, we could explain cognitive synonymy of terms as follows (keeping to the familiar example): to say that "bachelor" and "unmarried man" are cognitively synonymous is to say no more nor less than that the statement:

(3)   All and only bachelors are unmarried men is analytic.

What we need is an account of cognitive synonymy not presupposing analyticity—if we are to explain analyticity conversely with help of cognitive synonymy as undertaken in §1. And indeed such an independent account of cognitive synonymy is at present up for consideration, namely, interchangeability *salva veritate* everywhere except within words. The question before us, to resume the thread at last, is whether such interchangeability is a sufficient condition for cognitive synonymy. We can quickly assure ourselves that it is, by examples of the following sort. The statement:

(4)   Necessarily all and only bachelors are bachelors

is evidently true, even supposing "necessarily" so narrowly construed as to be truly applicable only to analytic statements. Then, if "bachelor" and "unmarried man" are interchangeable *salva veritate,* the result:

(5)   Necessarily all and only bachelors are unmarried men

of putting "unmarried man" for an occurrence of "bachelor" in (4) must, like (4), be true. But to say that (5) is true is to say that (3) is analytic, and

hence that "bachelor" and "unmarried man" are cognitively synonymous.

Let us see what there is about the above argument that gives it its air of hocus-pocus. The condition of interchangeability *salva veritate* varies in its force with variations in the richness of the language at hand. The above argument supposes we are working with a language rich enough to contain the adverb "necessarily," this adverb being so construed as to yield truth when and only when applied to an analytic statement. But can we condone a language which contains such an adverb? Does the adverb really make sense? To suppose that it does is to suppose that we have already made satisfactory sense of "analytic." Then what are we so hard at work on right now?

Our argument is not flatly circular, but something like it. It has the form, figuratively speaking, of a closed curve in space.

Interchangeability *salva veritate* is meaningless until relativized to a language whose extent is specified in relevant respects. Suppose now we consider a language containing just the following materials. There is an indefinitely large stock of one-place predicates (for example, "F" where "Fx" means that x is a man) and many-place predicates (for example, "G" where "Gxy" means that x loves y), mostly having to do with extra-logical subject-matter. The rest of the language is logical. The atomic sentences consist each of a predicate followed by one or more variables "x," "y," etc.; and the complex sentences are built up of the atomic ones by truth functions ("not," "and," "or," etc.) and quantification. In effect such a language enjoys the benefits also of descriptions and indeed singular terms generally, these being contextually definable in known ways. Even abstract singular terms naming classes, classes of classes, etc., are contextually definable in case the assumed stock of predicates includes the two-place predicate of class membership. Such a language can be adequate to classical mathematics and indeed to scientific discourse generally, except in so far as the latter involves debatable devices such as contrary-to-fact conditionals or modal adverbs like "necessarily." Now a language of this type is extensional, in this sense: any two predicates which agree extensionally (that is, are true of the same objects) are interchangeable *salva veritate.*

In an extensional language, therefore, interchangeability *salva veritate* is no assurance of cognitive synonymy of the desired type. That "bachelor" and "unmarried man" are interchangeable *salva veritate* in an extensional language assures us of no more than that (3) is true. There is no assurance here that the extensional agreement of "bachelor" and "unmarried man" rests on meaning rather than merely on accidental matters of fact, as does the extensional agreement of "creature with a heart" and "creature with kidneys."

For most purposes extensional agreement is the nearest approximation to synonymy we need care about. But the fact remains that extensional agreement falls far short of cognitive synonymy of the type required for explaining analyticity in the manner of §1. The type of cognitive synonymy required there is such as to equate the synonymy of "bachelor" and "unmarried man" with the analyticity of (3), not merely with the truth of (3).

So we must recognize that interchangeability *salva veritate,* if construed in relation to an extensional language, is not a sufficient condition of cognitive synonymy in the sense needed for deriving analyticity in the manner of §1. If a language contains an intensional adverb "necessarily" in the sense lately noted, or other particles to the same effect, then interchangeability *salva veritate* in such a language does afford a sufficient condition of cognitive synonymy; but such a language is intelligible only in so far as the notion of analyticity is already understood in advance.

The effort to explain cognitive synonymy first, for the sake of deriving analyticity from it afterward as in §1, is perhaps the wrong approach. Instead we might try explaining analyticity somehow without appeal to cognitive synonymy. Afterward we could doubtless derive cognitive synonymy from analyticity satisfactorily enough if desired. We have seen that cognitive synonymy of "bachelor" and "unmarried man" can be explained as analyticity of (3). The same explanation works for any pair of one-place predicates, of course, and it can be extended in obvious fashion to many-place predicates. Other syntactical categories can also be accommodated in fairly parallel fashion. Singular terms may be said to be cognitively synonymous when the statement of identity formed by putting "=" between them is analytic. Statements may be said simply to be cognitively synonymous when their biconditional (the result of joining them by "if and only if") is analytic. If we care to lump all categories into a single formu-

lation, at the expense of assuming again the notion of "word" which we appealed to early in this section, we can describe any two linguistic forms as cognitively synonymous when the two forms are interchangeable (apart from occurrences within "words") *salva* (no longer *veritate* but) *analyticitate*. Certain technical questions arise, indeed, over cases of ambiguity or homonymy; let us not pause for them, however, for we are already digressing. Let us rather turn our backs on the problem of synonymy and address ourselves anew to that of analyticity.

4. Semantical Rules

Analyticity at first seemed most naturally definable by appeal to a realm of meanings. On refinement, the appeal to meanings gave way to an appeal to synonymy or definition. But definition turned out to be a will-o'-the-wisp, and synonymy turned out to be best understood only by dint of a prior appeal to analyticity itself. So we are back at the problem of analyticity.

I do not know whether the statement "Everything green is extended" is analytic. Now does my indecision over this example really betray an incomplete understanding, an incomplete grasp of the "meanings," of "green" and "extended"? I think not. The trouble is not with "green" or "extended," but with "analytic."

It is often hinted that the difficulty in separating analytic statements from synthetic ones in ordinary language is due to the vagueness of ordinary language and that the distinction is clear when we have a precise artificial language with explicit "semantical rules." This, however, as I shall now attempt to show, is a confusion.

The notion of analyticity about which we are worrying is a purported relation between statements and languages: a statement S is said to be *analytic* for a language $L,$ and the problem is to make sense of this relation generally, that is, for variable "S" and "L." The gravity of this problem is not perceptibly less for artificial languages than for natural ones. The problem of making sense of the idiom "S is analytic for $L,$" with variable "S" and "$L,$" retains its stubbornness even if we limit the range of the variable "L" to artificial languages. Let me now try to make this point evident.

For artificial languages and semantical rules we look naturally to the writings of Carnap. His semantical rules take various forms, and to make my point I shall have to distinguish certain of the forms. Let us suppose, to begin with, an artificial language L_0 whose semantical rules have the form explicitly of a specification, by recursion or otherwise, of all the analytic statements of L_0. The rules tell us that such and such statements, and only those, are the analytic statements of L_0. Now here the difficulty is simply that the rules contain the word "analytic," which we do not understand! We understand what expressions the rules attribute analyticity to, but we do not understand what the rules attribute to those expressions. In short, before we can understand a rule which begins "A statement S is analytic for language L_0 if and only if . . . ," we must understand the general relative term "analytic for"; we must understand "S is analytic for L" where "S" and "L" are variables.

Alternatively we may, indeed, view the so-called rule as a conventional definition of a new simple symbol "analytic-for-L_0," which might better be written untendentiously as "K" so as not to seem to throw light on the interesting word "analytic." Obviously any number of classes K, M, N, etc. of statements of L_0 can be specified for various purposes or for no purpose; what does it mean to say that K, as against M, N, etc., is the class of the "analytic" statements of L_0?

By saying what statements are analytic for L_0 we explain "analytic-for-L_0" but not "analytic," not "analytic for." We do not begin to explain the idiom "S is analytic for L" with variable "S" and "L" even if we are content to limit the range of "L" to the realm of artificial languages.

Actually we do know enough about the intended significance of "analytic" to know that analytic statements are supposed to be true. Let us then turn to a second form of semantical rule, which says not that such and such statements are analytic but simply that such and such statements are included among the truths. Such a rule is not subject to the criticism of containing the ununderstood word "analytic"; and we may grant for the sake of argument that there is no difficulty over the broader term "true." A semantical rule of this second type, a rule of truth, is not supposed to specify all the truths of the language; it merely stipulates, recursively or otherwise, a certain multitude of statements which, along with others

unspecified, are to count as true. Such a rule may be conceded to be quite clear. Derivatively, afterward, analyticity can be demarcated thus: a statement is analytic if it is (not merely true but) true according to the semantical rule.

Still there is really no progress. Instead of appealing to an unexplained word "analytic," we are now appealing to an unexplained phrase "semantical rule." Not every true statement which says that the statements of some class are true can count as a semantical rule—otherwise *all* truths would be "analytic" in the sense of being true according to semantical rules. Semantical rules are distinguishable, apparently, only by the fact of appearing on a page under the heading "Semantical Rules"; and this heading is itself then meaningless.

We can say indeed that a statement is *analytic-for-L_0* if and only if it is true according to such and such specifically appended "semantical rules," but then we find ourselves back at essentially the same case which was originally discussed: "S is analytic-for-L_0 if and only if. . . ." Once we seek to explain "S is analytic for L" generally for variable "L" (even allowing limitation of "L" to artificial languages), the explanation "true according to the semantical rules of L" is unavailing; for the relative term "semantical rule of" is as much in need of clarification, at least, as "analytic for."

It may be instructive to compare the notion of semantical rule with that of postulate. Relative to a given set of postulates, it is easy to say what a postulate is: it is a member of the set. Relative to a given set of semantical rules, it is equally easy to say what a semantical rule is. But given simply a notation, mathematical or otherwise, and indeed as thoroughly understood a notation as you please in point of the translations or truth conditions of its statements, who can say which of its true statements rank as postulates? Obviously the question is meaningless—as meaningless as asking which points in Ohio are starting-points. Any finite (or effectively specifiable infinite) selection of statements (preferably true ones, perhaps) is as much *a* set of postulates as any other. The word "postulate" is significant only relative to an act of enquiry; we apply the word to a set of statements just in so far as we happen, for the year or the moment, to be thinking of those statements in relation to the statements which can be reached from them by some set of transformations to which we have seen fit to direct our attention.

Now the notion of semantical rule is as sensible and meaningful as that of postulate, if conceived in a similarly relative spirit—relative, this time, to one or another particular enterprise of schooling unconversant persons in sufficient conditions for truth of statements of some natural or artificial language L. But from this point of view no one signalization of a subclass of the truths of L is intrinsically more a semantical rule than another; and, if "analytic" means "true by semantical rules," no one truth of L is analytic to the exclusion of another.

It might conceivably be protested that an artificial language L (unlike a natural one) is a language in the ordinary sense *plus* a set of explicit semantical rules—the whole constituting, let us say, an ordered pair; and that the semantical rules of L then are specifiable simply as the second component of the pair L. But, by the same token and more simply, we might construe an artificial language L outright as an ordered pair whose second component is the class of its analytic statements; and then the analytic statements of L become specifiable simply as the statements in the second component of L. Or better still, we might just stop tugging at our bootstraps altogether.

Not all the explanations of analyticity known to Carnap and his readers have been covered explicitly in the above considerations, but the extension to other forms is not hard to see. Just one additional factor should be mentioned which sometimes enters: sometimes the semantical rules are in effect rules of translation into ordinary language, in which case the analytic statements of the artificial language are in effect recognized as such from the analyticity of their specified translations in ordinary language. Here certainly there can be no thought of an illumination of the problem of analyticity from the side of the artificial language.

From the point of view of the problem of analyticity the notion of an artificial language with semantical rules is a *feu follet par excellence*. Semantical rules determining the analytic statements of an artificial language are of interest only in so far as we already understand the notion of analyticity; they are of no help in gaining this understanding.

Appeal to hypothetical languages of an artificially simple kind could conceivably be useful in clarifying analyticity, if the mental or behavioural or cultural factors relevant to analyticity—whatever they may be—were somehow sketched into the simplified model. But a model which takes analyticity merely as an irreducible character is unlikely to throw light on the problem of explicating analyticity.

It is obvious that truth in general depends on both language and extra-linguistic fact. The statement "Brutus killed Caesar" would be false if the world had been different in certain ways, but it would also be false if the word "killed" happened rather to have the sense of "begat." Thus one is tempted to suppose in general that the truth of a statement is somehow analysable into a linguistic component and a factual component. Given this supposition, it next seems reasonable that in some statements the factual component should be null; and these are the analytic statements. But, for all its a priori reasonableness, a boundary between analytic and synthetic statements simply has not been drawn. That there is such a distinction to be drawn at all is an unempirical dogma of empiricists, a metaphysical article of faith.

5. The Verification Theory and Reductionism

In the course of these sombre reflections we have taken a dim view first of the notion of meaning, then of the notion of cognitive synonymy, and finally of the notion of analyticity. But what, it may be asked, of the verification theory of meaning? This phrase has established itself so firmly as a catchword of empiricism that we should be very unscientific indeed not to look beneath it for a possible key to the problem of meaning and the associated problems.

The verification theory of meaning, which has been conspicuous in the literature from Peirce onward, is that the meaning of a statement is the method of empirically confirming or infirming it. An analytic statement is that limiting case which is confirmed no matter what.

As urged in §1, we can as well pass over the question of meanings as entities and move straight to sameness of meaning, or synonymy. Then what the verification theory says is that statements are synonymous if and only if they are alike in point of method of empirical confirmation or infirmation.

This is an account of cognitive synonymy not of linguistic forms generally, but of statements. However, from the concept of synonymy of statements we could derive the concept of synonymy for other linguistic forms, by considerations somewhat similar to those at the end of §3. Assuming the notion of "word," indeed, we could explain any two forms as synonymous when the putting of the one form for an occurrence of the other in any statement (apart from occurrences within "words") yields a synonymous statement. Finally, given the concept of synonymy thus for linguistic forms generally, we could define analyticity in terms of synonymy and logical truth as in §1. For that matter, we could define analyticity more simply in terms of just synonymy of statements together with logical truth; it is not necessary to appeal to synonymy of linguistic forms other than statements. For a statement may be described as analytic simply when it is synonymous with a logically true statement.

So, if the verification theory can be accepted as an adequate account of statement synonymy, the notion of analyticity is saved after all. However, let us reflect. Statement synonymy is said to be likeness of method of empirical confirmation or infirmation. Just what are these methods which are to be compared for likeness? What, in other words, is the nature of the relation between a statement and the experiences which contribute to or detract from its confirmation?

The most naive view of the relation is that it is one of direct report. This is *radical reductionism.* Every meaningful statement is held to be translatable into a statement (true or false) about immediate experience. Radical reductionism, in one form or another, well antedates the verification theory of meaning explicitly so called. Thus Locke and Hume held that every idea must either originate directly in sense experience or else be compounded of ideas thus originating; and taking a hint from Tooke we might rephrase this doctrine in semantical jargon by saying that a term, to be significant at all, must be either a name of a sense datum or a compound of such names or an abbreviation of such a compound. So stated, the doctrine remains ambiguous as between sense data as sensory events and sense data as sensory qualities; and it remains vague as to the admissible ways of compounding. Moreover, the doctrine is unnecessarily and intolerably restrictive in the term-by-term critique which it imposes. More reasonably, and without yet exceeding the limits of what I have called radical reductionism, we may take full statements as our significant units—thus demanding that our statements as wholes be translatable into sense-datum language, but not that they be translatable term by term.

This emendation would unquestionably have been welcome to Locke and Hume and Tooke, but historically it had to await an important reorientation in semantics—the reorientation whereby the primary vehicle of meaning came to be seen no longer in the term but in the statement. This reorientation, explicit in Frege ((1), §60), underlies Russell's concept of incomplete symbols defined in use; also it is implicit in the verification theory of meaning, since the objects of verification are statements.

Radical reductionism, conceived now with statements as units, set itself the task of specifying a sense-datum language and showing how to translate the rest of significant discourse, statement by statement, into it. Carnap embarked on this project in the *Aufbau.*

The language which Carnap adopted as his starting-point was not a sense-datum language in the narrowest conceivable sense, for it included also the notations of logic, up through higher set theory. In effect, it included the whole language of pure mathematics. The ontology implicit in it (that is, the range of values of its variables) embraced not only sensory events but classes, classes of classes, and so on. Empiricists there are who would boggle at such prodigality. Carnap's starting-point is very parsimonious, however, in its extra-logical or sensory part. In a series of constructions in which he exploits the resources of modern logic with much ingenuity, Carnap succeeds in defining a wide array of important additional sensory concepts which, but for his constructions, one would not have dreamed were definable on so slender a basis. He was the first empiricist who, not content with asserting the reducibility of science to terms of immediate experience, took serious steps toward carrying out the reduction.

If Carnap's starting-point is satisfactory, still his constructions were, as he himself stressed, only a fragment of the full programme. The construction of even the simplest statements about the physical world was left in a sketchy state. Carnap's suggestions on this subject were, despite their sketchiness, very suggestive. He explained spatio-temporal point-instants as quadruples of real numbers and envisaged assignment of sense qualities to point-instants according to certain canons. Roughly summarized, the plan was that qualities should be assigned to point-instants in such a way as to achieve the laziest world compatible with our experience. The principle of least action was to be our guide in constructing a world from experience.

Carnap did not seem to recognize, however, that his treatment of physical objects fell short of reduction not merely through sketchiness, but in principle. Statements of the form "Quality q is at point-instant $x;y;z;t$" were, according to his canons, to be apportioned truth values in such a way as to maximize and minimize certain overall features, and with growth of experience the truth values were to be progressively revised in the same spirit. I think this is a good schematization (deliberately over-simplified, to be sure) of what science really does; but it provides no indication, not even the sketchiest, of how a statement of the form "Quality q is at $x;y;z;t$" could ever be translated into Carnap's initial language of sense data and logic. The connective "is at" remains an added undefined connective; the canons counsel us in its use but not in its elimination.

Carnap seems to have appreciated this point afterward; for in his later writings he abandoned all notion of the translatability of statements about the physical world into statements about immediate experience. Reductionism in its radical form has long since ceased to figure in Carnap's philosophy.

But the dogma of reductionism has, in a subtler and more tenuous form, continued to influence the thought of empiricists. The notion lingers that to each statement, or each synthetic statement, there is associated a unique range of possible sensory events such that the occurrence of any of them would add to the likelihood of truth of the statement, and that there is associated also another unique range of possible sensory events whose occurrence would detract from that likelihood. This notion is of course implicit in the verification theory of meaning.

The dogma of reductionism survives in the supposition that each statement, taken in isolation from its fellows, can admit of confirmation or infirmation at all. My counter-suggestion, issuing essentially from Carnap's doctrine of the physical world in the *Aufbau,* is that our statements about the external world face the tribunal of sense experience not individually but only as a corporate body.

The dogma of reductionism, even in its attenuated form, is intimately connected with the other dogma—that there is a cleavage between the analytic and the synthetic. We have found ourselves led, indeed, from the latter problem to the former through the verification theory of meaning. More directly, the one dogma clearly supports the other in this way: as long as it is taken to be significant in general to speak of the confirmation and infirmation of a statement, it seems significant to speak also of a limiting kind of statement which is vacuously confirmed, *ipso facto,* come what may; and such a statement is analytic.

The two dogmas are, indeed, at root identical. We lately reflected that in general the truth of statements does obviously depend both upon language and upon extra-linguistic fact; and we noted that this obvious circumstance carries in its train, not logically but all too naturally, a feeling that the truth of a statement is somehow analysable into a linguistic component and a factual component. The factual component must, if we are empiricists, boil down to a range of confirmatory experiences. In the extreme case where the linguistic component is all that matters, a true statement is analytic. But I hope we are now impressed with how stubbornly the distinction between analytic and synthetic has resisted any straightforward drawing. I am impressed also, apart from prefabricated examples of black and white balls in an urn, with how baffling the problem has always been of arriving at any explicit theory of the empirical confirmation of a synthetic statement. My present suggestion is that it is nonsense, and the root of much nonsense, to speak of a linguistic component and a factual component in the truth of any individual statement. Taken collectively, science has its double dependence upon language and experience; but this duality is not significantly traceable into the statements of science taken one by one.

The idea of defining a symbol in use was, as remarked, an advance over the impossible term-by-term empiricism of Locke and Hume. The statement, rather than the term, came with Frege to be recognized as the unit accountable to an empiricist critique. But what I am now urging is that even in taking the statement as unit we have drawn our grid too finely. The unit of empirical significance is the whole of science.

6. Empiricism Without the Dogmas

The totality of our so-called knowledge or beliefs, from the most casual matters of geography and history to the profoundest laws of atomic physics or even of pure mathematics and logic, is a man-made fabric which impinges on experience only along the edges. Or, to change the figure, total science is like a field of force whose boundary conditions are experience. A conflict with experience at the periphery occasions readjustments in the interior of the field. Truth values have to be redistributed over some of our statements. Re-evaluation of some statements entails re-evaluation of others, because of their logical interconnections—the logical laws being in turn simply certain further statements of the system, certain further elements of the field. Having re-evaluated one statement we must re-evaluate some others, which may be statements logically connected with the first or may be the statements of logical connections themselves. But the total field is so underdetermined by its boundary conditions, experience, that there is much latitude of choice as to what statements to re-evaluate in the light of any single contrary experience. No particular experiences are linked with any particular statements in the interior of the field, except indirectly through considerations of equilibrium affecting the field as a whole.

If this view is right, it is misleading to speak of the empirical content of an individual statement—especially if it is a statement at all remote from the experiential periphery of the field. Furthermore, it becomes folly to seek a boundary between synthetic statements, which hold contingently on experience, and analytic statements, which hold come what may. Any statement can be held true come what may, if we make drastic enough adjustments elsewhere in the system. Even a statement very close to the periphery can be held true in the face of recalcitrant experience by pleading hallucination or by amending certain statements of the kind called logical laws. Conversely, by the same token, no statement is immune to revision.

Revision even of the logical law of the excluded middle has been proposed as a means of simplifying quantum mechanics; and what difference is there in principle between such a shift and the shift whereby Kepler superseded Ptolemy, or Einstein Newton, or Darwin Aristotle?

For vividness I have been speaking in terms of varying distances from a sensory periphery. Let me try now to clarify this notion without metaphor. Certain statements, though *about* physical objects and not sense experience, seem peculiarly germane to sense experience—and in a selective way: some statements to some experiences, others to others. Such statements, especially germane to particular experiences, I picture as near the periphery. But in this relation of "germaneness" I envisage nothing more than a loose association reflecting the relative likelihood, in practice, of our choosing one statement rather than another for revision in the event of recalcitrant experience. For example, we can imagine recalcitrant experiences to which we would surely be inclined to accommodate our system by re-evaluating just the statement that there are brick houses on Elm Street, together with related statements on the same topic. We can imagine other recalcitrant experiences to which we would be inclined to accommodate our system by re-evaluating just the statement that there are no centaurs, along with kindred statements. A recalcitrant experience can, I have urged, be accommodated by any of various alternative re-evaluations in various alternative quarters of the total system; but, in the cases which we are now imagining, our natural tendency to disturb the total system as little as possible would lead us to focus our revisions upon these specific statements concerning brick houses or centaurs. These statements are felt, therefore, to have a sharper empirical reference than highly theoretical statements of physics or logic or ontology. The latter statements may be thought of as relatively centrally located within the total network, meaning merely that little preferential connection with any particular sense data obtrudes itself.

As an empiricist I continue to think of the conceptual scheme of science as a tool, ultimately, for predicting future experience in the light of past experience. Physical objects are conceptually imported into the situation as convenient intermediaries—not by definition in terms of experience, but simply as irreducible posits comparable, epistemologically, to the gods of Homer. For my part I do, *qua* lay physicist, believe in physical objects and not in Homer's gods; and I consider it a scientific error to believe otherwise. But in point of epistemological footing the physical objects and the gods differ only in degree and not in kind. Both sorts of entities enter our conception only as cultural posits. The myth of physical objects is epistemologically superior to most in that it has proved more efficacious than other myths as a device for working a manageable structure into the flux of experience.

Positing does not stop with macroscopic physical objects. Objects at the atomic level are posited to make the laws of macroscopic objects, and ultimately the laws of experience, simpler and more manageable; and we need not expect or demand full definition of atomic and subatomic entities in terms of macroscopic ones, any more than definition of macroscopic things in terms of sense data. Science is a continuation of common sense, and it continues the common-sense expedient of swelling ontology to simplify theory.

Physical objects, small and large, are not the only posits. Forces are another example; and indeed we are told nowadays that the boundary between energy and matter is obsolete. Moreover, the abstract entities which are the substance of mathematics—ultimately classes and classes of classes and so on up—are another posit in the same spirit. Epistemologically these are myths on the same footing with physical objects and gods, neither better nor worse except for differences in the degree to which they expedite our dealings with sense experiences.

The overall algebra of rational and irrational numbers is underdetermined by the algebra of rational numbers, but is smoother and more convenient; and it includes the algebra of rational numbers as a jagged or gerrymandered part. Total science, mathematical and natural and human, is similarly but more extremely underdetermined by experience. The edge of the system must be kept squared with experience; the rest, with all its elaborate myths or fictions, has as its objective the simplicity of laws.

Ontological questions, under this view, are on a par with questions of natural science. Consider the question whether to countenance classes as entities. This, as I have argued elsewhere, is the question whether to quantify with respect to variables which take classes as values. Now Carnap (6) has main-

tained that this is a question not of matters of fact but of choosing a convenient language form, a convenient conceptual scheme or framework for science. With this I agree, but only on the proviso that the same be conceded regarding scientific hypotheses generally. Carnap ((6), p. 32 n) has recognized that he is able to preserve a double standard for ontological questions and scientific hypotheses only by assuming an absolute distinction between the analytic and the synthetic; and I need not say again that this is a distinction which I reject.

The issue over there being classes seems more a question of convenient conceptual scheme; the issue over there being centaurs, or brick houses on Elm Street, seems more a question of fact. But I have been urging that this difference is only one of degree, and that it turns upon our vaguely pragmatic inclination to adjust one strand of the fabric of science rather than another in accommodating some particular recalcitrant experience. Conservatism figures in such choices, and so does the quest for simplicity.

Carnap, Lewis, and others take a pragmatic stand on the question of choosing between language forms, scientific frameworks; but their pragmatism leaves off at the imagined boundary between the analytic and the synthetic. In repudiating such a boundary I espouse a more thorough pragmatism. Each man is given a scientific heritage plus a continuing barrage of sensory stimulation; and the considerations which guide him in warping his scientific heritage to fit his continuing sensory promptings are, where rational, pragmatic.

Bibliographical References

Carnap, Rudolf (1), *Der logische Aufbau der Welt* (Berlin, 1928).

——— (2), *The Logical Syntax of Language* (New York: Harcourt Brace, and London: Kegan Paul, 1937). Translation, with extensions, of *Logische Syntax der Sprache* (Vienna: Springer, 1934).

——— (3), *Meaning and Necessity* (Chicago: University of Chicago Press, 1947).

——— (4), *Logical Foundations of Probability* (Chicago: University of Chicago Press, 1950).

——— (5), "Testability and Meaning," *Philosophy of Science,* 3 (1936), 419–71; 4 (1937), 1–40 (reprinted, New Haven: Graduate Philosophy Club, Yale University, 1950).

——— (6), "Empiricism, Semantics, and Ontology," *Revue internationale de philosophie,* 4 (1950), 20–40. Reprinted in Linsky.

Duhem, Pierre, *La Théorie physique: son objet et sa structure* (Paris, 1906).

Frege, Gottlob (1), *Foundations of Arithmetic* (New York: Philosophical Library, 1950).

VII.5 In Defense of a Dogma

H. P. Grice and Peter F. Strawson

Until their recent retirements, H. P. Grice was a fellow at St. John's College, Oxford University, and Peter F. Strawson was professor of philosophy at Oxford University. In this essay, Grice and Strawson seek to rebut Quine's contention that the analytic synthetic distinction is invalid (see Reading VII.4). They argue against Quine that if the idea of synonymy is meaningless, then so is the idea of having meaning at all. Grice and Strawson argue that Quine has failed to make his case that the notion of analyticity is obscure.

In his article "Two Dogmas of Empiricism," Professor Quine advances a number of criticisms of the supposed distinction between analytic and synthetic statements, and of other associated notions. It is, he says, a distinction which he rejects. We wish to show that his criticisms of the distinction do not justify his rejection of it. . . .

Is there . . . a presumption in favor of the distinction's existence? Prima facie, it must be admitted that there is. An appeal to philosophical tradition is perhaps unimpressive and is certainly unnecessary. But it is worth pointing out that Quine's objection is not simply to the words "analytic" and "synthetic," but to a distinction which they are supposed to express, and which at different times philosophers have supposed themselves to be expressing by means of such pairs of words

or phrases as "necessary" and "contingent," "a priori" and "empirical," "truth of reason" and "truth of fact"; so Quine is certainly at odds with a philosophical tradition which is long and not wholly disreputable. But there is no need to appeal only to tradition; for there is also present practice. We can appeal, that is, to the fact that those who use the terms "analytic" and "synthetic" do to a very considerable extent agree in the applications they make of them. They apply the term "analytic" to more or less the same cases, withhold it from more or less the same cases, and hesitate over more or less the same cases. This agreement extends not only to cases which they have been *taught* so to characterize, but to new cases. In short, "analytic" and "synthetic" have a more or less established philosophical *use*; and this seems to suggest that it is absurd, even senseless, to say that there is no such distinction. For, in general, if a pair of contrasting expressions are habitually and generally

From *The Philosophical Review* 65 (1965). Notes have been deleted.

used in application to the same cases, *where these cases do not form a closed list*, this is a sufficient condition for saying that there are *kinds* of cases to which the expressions apply; and nothing more is needed for them to mark a distinction.

In view of the possibility of this kind of argument, one may begin to doubt whether Quine really holds the extreme thesis which his words encourage one to attribute to him. It is for this reason that we made the attribution tentative. For on at least one natural interpretation of this extreme thesis, when we say of something true that it is analytic and of another true thing that it is synthetic, it simply never is the case that we thereby mark a distinction between them. And this view seems terribly difficult to reconcile with the fact of an established philosophical usage (i.e., of general agreement in application in an open class). For this reason, Quine's thesis might be better represented not as the thesis that there is *no difference at all* marked by the use of these expressions, but as the thesis that the nature of, and reasons for, the difference or differences are totally misunderstood by those who use the expressions, that the stories they tell themselves *about* the difference are full of illusion.

We think Quine might be prepared to accept this amendment. If so, it could, in the following way, be made the basis of something like an answer to the argument which prompted it. Philosophers are notoriously subject to illusion, and to mistaken theories. Suppose there were a particular mistaken theory about language or knowledge, such that, seen in the light of this theory, some statements (or propositions or sentences) appeared to have a characteristic which no statements really have, or even, perhaps, which it does not make sense to suppose that any statement has, and which no one who was not consciously or subconsciously influenced by this theory would ascribe to any statement. And suppose that there were other statements which, seen in this light, did not appear to have this characteristic, and others again which presented an uncertain appearance. Then philosophers who were under the influence of this theory would tend to mark the supposed presence or absence of this characteristic by a pair of contrasting expressions, say "analytic" and "synthetic." Now in these circumstances it still could not be said that there was no distinction at all being marked by the use of these expressions, for there would be at least the distinction we have just described (the distinction, namely, between those

statements which appeared to have and those which appeared to lack a certain characteristic), and there might well be other assignable differences too, which would account for the difference in appearance; but it certainly could be said that *the* difference these philosophers supposed themselves to be marking by the use of the expressions simply did not exist, and perhaps also (supposing the characteristic in question to be one which it was absurd to ascribe to any statement) that these expressions, as so used, were senseless or without meaning. We should only have to suppose that such a mistaken theory was very plausible and attractive, in order to reconcile the fact of an established philosophical usage for a pair of contrasting terms with the claim that *the* distinction which the terms purported to mark did not exist at all, though not with the claim that there simply did not exist a difference of any kind between the classes of statements so characterized. We think that the former claim would probably be sufficient for Quine's purposes. But to establish such a claim on the sort of grounds we have indicated evidently requires a great deal more argument than is involved in showing that certain explanations of a term do not measure up to certain requirements of adequacy in philosophical clarification— and not only more argument, but argument of a very different kind. For it would surely be too harsh to maintain that the *general* presumption is that philosophical distinctions embody the kind of illusion we have described. On the whole, it seems that philosophers are prone to make too few distinctions rather than too many. It is their assimilations, rather than their distinctions, which tend to be spurious.

So far we have argued as if the prior presumption in favor of the existence of the distinction which Quine questions rested solely on the fact of an agreed *philosophical* usage for the terms "analytic" and "synthetic." A presumption with only this basis could no doubt be countered by a strategy such as we have just outlined. But, in fact, if we are to accept Quine's account of the matter, the presumption in question is not only so based. For among the notions which belong to the analyticity-group is one which Quine calls "cognitive synonymy," and in terms of which he allows that the notion of analyticity could at any rate be formally explained. Unfortunately, he adds, the notion of cognitive synonymy is just as unclarified as that of analyticity. To say that two expressions x and y are cognitively synonymous seems to correspond, at any rate roughly, to what we should ordinarily express by saying that x and y have the same meaning or that x means the same as y. If Quine is to be consistent in his adherence to the extreme thesis, then it appears that he must maintain not only that the distinction we suppose ourselves to be marking by the use of the terms "analytic" and "synthetic" does not exist, but also that the distinction we suppose ourselves to be marking by the use of the expressions "means the same as," "does not mean the same as" does not exist either. At least, he must maintain this insofar as the notion of *meaning the same as,* in its application to predicate-expressions, is supposed to differ from and go beyond the notion of *being true of just the same objects as.* (This latter notion—which we might call that of "coextensionality"—he is prepared to allow to be intelligible, though, as he rightly says, it is not sufficient for the explanation of analyticity.) Now since he cannot claim this time that the pair of expressions in question (viz., "means the same," "does not mean the same") is the special property of philosophers, the strategy outlined above of countering the presumption in favor of their marking a genuine distinction is not available here (or is at least enormously less plausible). Yet the denial that the distinction (taken as different from the distinction between the coextensional and the non-coextensional) really exists, is extremely paradoxical. It involves saying, for example, that anyone who seriously remarks that "bachelor" means the same as "unmarried man" but that "creature with kidneys" does not mean the same as "creature with a heart"—supposing the last two expressions to be coextensional—*either* is not in fact drawing attention to any distinction at all between the relations between the members of each pair of expressions *or* is making a philosophical mistake about the nature of the distinction between them. In either case, what he says, taken as he intends it to be taken, is senseless or absurd. More generally, it involves saying that it is always senseless or absurd to make a statement of the form "Predicates x and y in fact apply to the same objects, but do not have the same meaning." But the paradox is more violent than this. For we frequently talk of the presence or absence of relations of synonymy between kinds of expressions—e.g., conjunctions, particles of many kinds, whole sentences—where there does not appear to be any obvious substitute for the ordinary notion of synonymy, in the

way in which coextensionality is said to be a substitute for synonymy of predicates. Is all such talk meaningless? Is all talk of correct or incorrect *translation* of sentences of one language into sentences of another meaningless? It is hard to believe that it is. But if we do successfully make the effort to believe it, we have still harder renunciations before us. If talk of sentence-synonymy is meaningless, then it seems that talk of sentences having a meaning at all must be meaningless too. For if it made sense to talk of a sentence having a meaning, or meaning something, then presumably it would make sense to ask "What does it mean?" And if it made sense to ask "What does it mean?" of a sentence, then sentence-synonymy could be roughly defined as follows: Two sentences are synonymous if and only if any true answer to the question "What does it mean?" asked of one of them, is a true answer to the same question, asked of the other. We do not, of course, claim any clarifying power for this definition. We want only to point out that if we are to give up the notion of sentence-synonymy as senseless, we must give up the notion of sentence-significance (of a sentence having meaning) as senseless too. But then perhaps we might as well give up the notion of sense. . . .

We have argued so far that there is a strong presumption in favor of the existence of the distinction, or distinctions, which Quine challenges—a presumption resting both on philosophical and on ordinary usage—and that this presumption is not in the least shaken by the fact, if it is a fact, that the distinctions in question have not been, in some sense, adequately clarified. It is perhaps time to look at what Quine's notion of adequate clarification is.

The main theme of his article can be roughly summarized as follows. There is a certain circle or family of expressions, of which "analytic" is one, such that if any one member of the circle could be taken to be satisfactorily understood or explained, then other members of the circle could be verbally, and hence satisfactorily, explained in terms of it. Other members of the family are: "self-contradictory" (in a broad sense), "necessary," "synonymous," "semantic rule," and perhaps (but again in a broad sense) "definition." The list could be added to. Unfortunately each member of the family is in as great need of explanation as any other. We give some sample quotations:

"The notion of self-contradictoriness (in the required broad sense of inconsistency) stands in exactly the same need of clarification as does the notion of analyticity itself." Again, Quine speaks of "a notion of synonymy which is in no less need of clarification than analyticity itself." Again, of the adverb "necessarily," as a candidate for use in the explanation of synonymy, he says, "Does the adverb *really make sense?* To suppose that it does is to suppose that we have already *made satisfactory sense* of 'analytic.'" To make "satisfactory sense" of one of these expressions would seem to involve two things. (1) It would seem to involve providing an explanation which does not incorporate any expression belonging to the family-circle. (2) It would seem that the explanation provided must be of the same general character as those rejected explanations which do incorporate members of the family-circle (i.e., it must specify some feature common and peculiar to all cases to which, for example, the word "analytic" is to be applied; it must have the same general form as an explanation beginning, "a statement is analytic if and only if . . ."). It is true that Quine does not explicitly state the second requirement; but since he does not even consider the question whether any other kind of explanation would be relevant, it seems reasonable to attribute it to him. If we take these two conditions together, and generalize the result, it would seem that Quine requires of a satisfactory explanation of an expression that it should take the form of a pretty strict definition but should not make use of any member of a group of interdefinable terms to which the expression belongs. We may well begin to feel that a satisfactory explanation is hard to come by. The other element in Quine's position is one we have already commented on in general, before enquiring what (according to him) is to count as a satisfactory explanation. It is the step from "We have not made satisfactory sense (provided a satisfactory explanation) of *x*" to "*x* does not make sense."

It would seem fairly clearly unreasonable to insist *in general* that the availability of a satisfactory explanation in the sense sketched above is a necessary condition of an expression's making sense. It is perhaps dubious whether *any* such explanations can *ever* be given. (The hope that they can be is, or was, the hope of reductive analysis in general.) Even if such explanations can be given in some cases, it would be pretty generally agreed that there [are]

other cases in which they cannot. One might think, for example, of the group of expressions which includes "morally wrong," "blameworthy," "breach of moral rules," etc.; or of the group which includes the propositional connectives and the words "true" and "false," "statement," "fact," "denial," "assertion." Few people would want to say that the expressions belonging to either of these groups were senseless on the ground that they have not been formally defined (or even on the ground that it was impossible formally to define them) except in terms of members of the same group. It might, however, be said that while the unavailability of a satisfactory explanation in the special sense described was not a *generally* sufficient reason for declaring that a given expression was senseless, it was a sufficient reason in the case of the expressions of the analyticity group. But anyone who said this would have to advance a reason for discriminating in this way against the expressions of this group. The only plausible reason for being harder on these expressions than on others is a refinement on a consideration which we have already had before us. It starts from the point that "analytic" and "synthetic" themselves are technical philosophical expressions. To the rejoinder that other expressions of the family concerned, such as "means the same as" or "is inconsistent with," or "self-contradictory," are not at all technical expressions, but are common property, the reply would doubtless be that, to qualify for inclusion in the family circle, these expressions have to be used in specially adjusted and precise senses (or pseudo-senses) which they do not ordinarily possess. It is the fact, then, that all the terms belonging to the circle are *either* technical terms *or* ordinary terms used in specially adjusted senses, that might be held to justify us in being particularly suspicious of the claims of members of the circle to have any sense at all, and hence to justify us in requiring them to pass a test for significance which would admittedly be too stringent if generally applied. This point has some force, though we doubt if the special adjustments spoken of are in every case as considerable as it suggests. (This seems particularly doubtful in the case of the word "inconsistent"—a perfectly good member of the non-technician's meta-logical vocabulary). But though the point has some force, it does not have whatever force would be required to justify us in insisting that the expressions concerned should pass exactly that test for significance which is in question. The fact, if it is a fact, that the expressions cannot be explained in precisely the way which Quine seems to require, does not mean that they cannot be explained at all. There is no need to try to pass them off as expressing innate ideas. They can be and are explained, though in other and less formal ways than that which Quine considers. (And the fact that they are so explained fits with the facts, first, that there is a generally agreed philosophical use for them, and second, that this use is technical or specially adjusted.) To illustrate the point briefly for one member of the analyticity family, let us suppose we are trying to explain to someone the notion of *logical impossibility* (a member of the family which Quine presumably regards as no clearer than any of the others) and we decide to do it by bringing out the contrast between logical and natural (or causal) impossibility. We might take as our examples the logical impossibility of a child of three's being an adult, and the natural impossibility of a child of three's understanding Russell's Theory of Types. We might instruct our pupil to imagine two conversations one of which begins by someone (X) making the claim:

(1) My neighbor's three-year-old child understands Russell's Theory of Types

and the other of which begins by someone (Y) making the claim:

(1′) "My neighbor's three-year-old child is an adult."

It would not be inappropriate to reply to X, taking the remark as a hyperbole:

(2) "You mean the child is a particularly bright lad."

If X were to say:

(3) "No, I mean what I say—he really does understand it,"

one might be inclined to reply:

(4) "I don't believe you—the thing's impossible."

But if the child were then produced, and did (as one knows he would not) expound the theory correctly, answer questions on it, criticize it, and so on, one would in the end be forced to acknowledge that the claim was literally true and that the child was a prodigy. Now consider one's reaction to Y's claim. To begin with, it might be somewhat similar to the previous case. One might say:

(2′) "You mean he's uncommonly sensible or very advanced for his age."

If Y replies:

(3′) "No, I mean what I say,"

we might reply:

(4′) "Perhaps you mean that he won't grow any more, or that he's a sort of freak, that he's already fully developed."

Y replies:

(5′) "No, he's not a freak, he's just an adult."

At this stage—or possibly if we are patient, a little later—we shall be inclined to say that we just don't understand what Y is saying, and to suspect that he just does not know the meaning of some of the words he is using. For unless he is prepared to admit that he is using words in a figurative or unusual sense, we shall say, not that we don't believe him, but that his words have *no* sense. And whatever kind of creature is ultimately produced for our inspection, it will not lead us to say what Y said was literally true, but at most to say that we now see what he meant. As a summary of the difference between the two imaginary conversations, we might say that in both cases we would tend to begin by supposing that the other speaker was using words in a figurative or unusual or restricted way; but in the face of his repeated claim to be speaking literally, it would be appropriate in the first case to say that we did not believe him and in the second case to say that we did not understand him. If, like Pascal, we thought it prudent to prepare against very long chances, we should in the first case know what to prepare for; in the second, we should have no idea.

We give this as an example of just one type of informal explanation which we might have recourse to in the case of one notion of the analyticity group. (We do not wish to suggest it is the only type.) Further examples, with different though connected types of treatment, might be necessary to teach our pupil the use of the notion of logical impossibility in its application to more complicated cases—if indeed he did not pick it up from the one case. Now of course this type of explanation does not yield a formal statement of necessary and sufficient conditions for the application of the notion concerned. So it does not fulfill one of the conditions which Quine seems to require of a satisfactory explanation. On the other hand, it does appear to fulfill the other. It breaks out of the family circle. The distinction in which we ultimately come to rest is that between not believing something and not understanding something; or between incredulity yielding to conviction, and incomprehension yielding to comprehension. It would be rash to maintain that *this* distinction does not need clarification; but it would be absurd to maintain that it does not exist. In the face of the availability of this informal type of explanation for the notions of the analyticity group, the fact that they have not received another type of explanation (which it is dubious whether *any* expressions *ever* receive) seems a wholly inadequate ground for the conclusion that the notions are pseudo-notions, that the expressions which purport to express them have no sense. To say this is not to deny that it would be philosophically desirable, and a proper object of philosophical endeavor, to find a more illuminating general characterization of the notions of this group than any that has been so far given. But the question of how, if at all, this can be done is quite irrelevant to the question of whether or not the expressions which belong to the circle have an intelligible use and mark genuine distinctions.

So far we have tried to show that sections 1 to 4 of Quine's article—the burden of which is that the notions of the analyticity group have not been satisfactorily explained—do not establish the extreme thesis for which he appears to be arguing. . . .

There are two further points worth making which arise out of the first two sections.

(1) One concerns what Quine says about *definition* and *synonymy*. He remarks that definition does not, as some have supposed, "hold the key to synonymy and analyticity," since "definition—except in the extreme case of the explicitly conventional introduction of new notations—hinges on prior relations of synonymy." But now consider what he says of these extreme cases. He says: "Here the definiendum becomes synonymous with the definiens simply because it has been expressly created for the purpose of being synonymous with the definiens. Here we have a really transparent case of synonymy created by definition; would that all

species of synonymy were as intelligible." Now if we are to take these words of Quine seriously, then his position *as a whole* is incoherent. It is like the position of a man to whom we are trying to explain, say, the idea of one thing fitting into another thing, or two things fitting together, and who says: "I can understand what it means to say that one thing fits into another, or that two things fit together, in the case where one was specially made to fit the other; but I cannot understand what it means to say this in any other case." Perhaps we should not take Quine's words here too seriously. But if not, then we have the right to ask him exactly what state of affairs he thinks *is* brought about by explicit definition, what relation between expressions *is* established by this procedure, and why he thinks it unintelligible to suggest that the same (or a closely analogous) state of affairs, or relation, should exist in the absence of this procedure. For our part, we should be inclined to take Quine's words (or some of them) seriously, and reverse his conclusions; and maintain that the notion of synonymy by explicit convention would be unintelligible if the notion of synonymy by usage were not presupposed. There cannot be law where there is no custom, or rules where there are not practices (though perhaps we can understand better what a practice is by looking at a rule).

(2) The second point arises out of a paragraph . . . of Quine's [article]. We quote:

> I do not know whether the statement "Everything green is extended" is analytic. Now does my indecision over this example really betray an incomplete understanding, an incomplete grasp, of the "meanings" of "green" and "extended"? I think not. The trouble is not with "green" or "extended," but with "analytic."

If, as Quine says, the trouble is with "analytic," then the trouble should doubtless disappear when "analytic" is removed. So let us remove it, and replace it with a word which Quine himself has contrasted favorably with "analytic" in respect of perspicuity—the word "true." Does the indecision at once disappear? We think not. The indecision over "analytic" (and equally, in this case, the indecision over "true") arises, of course, from a further indecision: viz., that which we feel when confronted with such questions as "Should we count a *point* of green light as *extended* or not?" As is frequent enough in such cases, the hesitation arises from the fact that the boundaries of application of words are not determined by usage in all possible directions. But the example Quine has chosen is particularly unfortunate for his thesis, in that it is only too evident that our hesitations are not *here* attributable to obscurities in "analytic." It would be possible to choose other examples in which we should hesitate between "analytic" and "synthetic" and have few qualms about "true." But no more in these cases than in the sample case does the hesitation necessarily imply any obscurity in the notion of analyticity; since the hesitation would be sufficiently accounted for by the same or a similar kind of indeterminacy in the relations between the words occurring within the statement about which the question, whether it is analytic or synthetic, is raised.

VII.6 Truths of Reason

RODERICK CHISHOLM

For a biographical sketch of Roderick Chisholm, see Reading V.1.

In this selection, Chisholm explicates the meaning of a priori propositions (once we understand the proposition, we see that it is true), and defends the analytic–synthetic distinction, and the notion of synthetic a priori knowledge.

> There are also two kinds of truths: those of reasoning and those of fact. The truths of reasoning are necessary, and their opposite is impossible. Those of fact, however, are contingent, and their opposite is possible. When a truth is necessary, we can find the reason by analysis, resolving the truth into simpler ideas and simpler truths until we reach those that are primary.
>
> Leibniz, *Monadology* 33

A Traditional Metaphysical View

Reason, according to one traditional view, functions as a source of knowledge. This view, when it is clearly articulated, may be seen to involve a number of metaphysical presuppositions and it is, therefore, unacceptable to many contemporary philosophers. But the alternatives to this view, once *they* are clearly articulated, may be seen to be at least problematic and to imply an extreme form of skepticism.

According to this traditional view, there are certain *truths of reason* and some of these truths of reason can be known *a priori*. These truths pertain to certain abstract or eternal objects—things such as properties, numbers, and propositions or states of affairs, things that would exist even if there weren't any contingent things such as persons and physical objects. To present the traditional view, we will first illustrate such truths and then we will try to explain what is meant by saying that we know some of these truths *a priori*.

Reprinted from *Theory of Knowledge* (Englewood Cliffs, NJ: Prentice-Hall, 1989) by permission. Notes have been edited.

Some of the truths of reason concern what we might call relations of "inclusion" and "exclusion" that obtain among various properties. The relation of *inclusion* among properties is illustrated by these facts: The property of being square includes that of being rectangular, and that of being red includes that of being colored. The relation of *exclusion* is exemplified by these facts: The property of being square excludes that of being circular, and that of being red excludes that of being blue. To say that one property excludes another, therefore, is to say more than that the one fails to include the other. Being red fails to include being heavy, but it does not exclude being heavy; if it excluded being heavy, as it excludes being blue, then nothing could be both red and heavy.[1]

Other examples of such inclusion and exclusion are these: Being both red and square includes being red and excludes being circular; being both red and warm-if-red includes being warm; being both nonwarm and warm-if-red excludes being red.

These relations are all such that they hold *necessarily*. And they would hold, therefore, even if there weren't any contingent things.

One can formulate more general truths about the relations of inclusion and exclusion. For example, every property *F* and every property *G* is such that *F*'s excluding *G* includes *G*'s excluding *F*; *F*'s excluding *G* includes *F*'s including not-*G*; *F* excludes non-*F*, and includes *F*-or-*G*. And such truths as these are necessary.

States of affairs or propositions are analogous to properties. Like properties, they are related by inclusion and exclusion; for example, "some men being Greeks" includes, and is included by, "some Greeks being men," and excludes "no Greeks being men." States of affairs, like properties, may be compound; for example, "some men being Greek and Plato being Roman"; "Socrates being wise or Xantippe being wise." The conjunctive state of affairs, "Socrates being a man and all men being mortal," includes "Socrates being mortal" and excludes "no men being mortal." Such truths about states of affairs are examples of truths of logic. And such truths, according to the traditional doctrine, are all necessary. They would hold even if there had been no Socrates or Greeks or men.

Other truths of reason are those of mathematics; for example, the truths expressed by "2 and 3 are 5" and "7 and 5 are 12."

Not All Knowledge of Necessity Is *A Posteriori*

When it is said that these truths of reason are known (or are capable of being known) "*a priori*," what is meant may be suggested by contrasting them with what is known "*a posteriori*." A single example may suggest what is intended when it is said that these truths may be known without being known *a posteriori*.

Corresponding to "Being red excludes being blue," which is a truth about properties, the following general statement is a truth about individual things: "Necessarily, every individual thing, past, present, or future, is such that if it is red then it is not blue." If the latter truth were known *a posteriori*, then it would be justified by some induction or inductions; our evidence presumably would consist in the fact that a great variety of red things and a great variety of nonblue things have been observed in the past, and that up to now, no red things have been blue. We might thus inductively confirm "Every individual thing, past, present, or future, is such that if it is red then it is not blue." Reflecting upon this conclusion, we may then go on to make still another step. We will proceed to the further conclusion, "Being red excludes being blue," and then deduce, "Necessarily, every individual thing, past, present, or future, is such that if it is red then it is not blue."

Thus, there might be said to be three steps involved in an inductive justification of "Necessarily, being red excludes being blue": (1) the accumulation of instances—"This red thing is not blue," "That blue thing is not red," and so on—along with the summary statement, "No red thing observed up to now has been blue"; (2) the inductive inference from these data to "Every individual thing, past, present, and future, is such that if it is red then it is not blue"; (3) the step from this inductive conclusion to "Being red excludes being blue," or "Necessarily, every individual thing, past, present, or future, is such that if it is red then it is not blue."

Why *not* say that such "truths of reason" are thus known *a posteriori*?

For one thing, some of these truths pertain to properties that have never been exemplified. If we take "square," "rectangular," and "circular" in the precise way in which these words are usually interpreted in geometry, we must say that nothing is square, rectangular, or circular; things in nature, as Plato said, "fall short" of having such properties. Hence, to justify "Necessarily, being square includes being rectangular and excludes being circular," we cannot even take the first of the three steps illustrated above; there being no squares, we cannot collect instances of squares that are rectangles and squares that are not circles.

For another thing, application of induction would seem to presuppose a knowledge of the "truths of reason." In setting out to confirm an inductive hypothesis, we must be able to recognize what its consequences would be. Ordinarily, to recognize these we must apply deduction; we take the hypothesis along with other things that we know and we see what is then implied. All of this, it would seem, involves apprehension of truths of reason—such truths as may be suggested by "For all states of affairs, p and q, the conjunctive state of affairs, composed of p and of either not-p or q, includes q," and "All A's being B excludes some A's not being B." Hence, even if we are able to justify some of the "truths of reason" by inductive procedures, any such justification will presuppose others, and we will be left with some "truths of reason" which we have not justified by means of induction.

And finally, the last of the three steps described above—the step from the inductive generalization "Every individual thing, past, present, and future, is such that if it is red then it is not blue" to "Being red excludes being blue," or "Necessarily, every individual thing, past, present, and future, is such that if it is red then it is not blue"—remains obscure.

How do we reach this final step? What justifies us in saying that *necessarily*, every individual thing, past, present, and future, is such that if it is red then it is not blue? The English philosopher, William Whewell, wrote that the mere accumulation of instances cannot afford the slightest ground for the necessity of a generalization upon those instances. "Experience," he said, "can observe and record what has happened; but she cannot find, in any case, or in any accumulation of cases, any reason for what *must* happen. She may see objects side by side, but she cannot see a reason why they must ever be side by side. She finds certain events to occur in succession; but the succession supplies, in its occurrence, no reasons for its recurrence; she

contemplates external objects; but she cannot detect any internal bond, which indissolubly connects the future with the past, the possible with the real. To learn a proposition by experience, and to see it to be necessarily true, are two altogether different processes of thought. . . . If anyone does not clearly comprehend this distinction of necessary and contingent truths, he will not be able to go along with us in our researches into the foundations of human knowledge; nor indeed, to pursue with success any speculation on the subject."[2]

Intuitive Induction

Plato suggested that in order to acquire a knowledge of necessity, we should turn away from "the twilight of becoming and perishing" and contemplate the world of "the absolute and eternal and immutable."[3] According to Aristotle, however, and to subsequent philosophers in the tradition with which we are here concerned, one way of obtaining the requisite intuition is to consider the particular things of this world.

As a result of perceiving a particular blue thing, or a number of particular blue things, we may come to know what it is for a thing to be blue, and thus, we may be said to know what the property of being blue is. And as a result of perceiving a particular red thing, or a number of particular red things, we may come to know what it is for a thing to be red, and thus, to know what the property of being red is. Then, having this knowledge of what it is to be red and of what it is to be blue, we are able to see that being red excludes being blue, and that this is necessarily so.

Thus, Aristotle tells us that as a result of perceiving Callias and a number of other particular men, we come to see what it is for a thing to have the property of being human. And then, by considering the property of being human, we come to see that being human includes being animal, and that this is necessarily so.[4]

Looking to these examples, we may distinguish four stages:

1. There is the perception of the individual things—in the one case, the perception of the particular red things and blue things, and in the other, the perception of Callias and the other particular men.

2. There is a process of abstraction—we come to see what it is for a thing to be red and for a thing to be blue, and we come to see what it is for a thing to be a man.

3. There is the intuitive apprehension of certain relations holding between properties—in the one case, apprehension of the fact that being red excludes being blue, and in the other, apprehension of the fact that being rational and animal includes being animal.

4. Once we have acquired this intuitive knowledge, then, *ipso facto,* we also know the truth of reason expressed by "Necessarily, everything is such that if it is red then it is not blue" and "Necessarily, everything is such that if it is human then it is animal."

Aristotle called this process "induction." But since it differs in essential respects from what subsequently came to be known as "induction," some other term, say, "intuitive induction," may be less misleading.

If we have performed an "intuitive induction" in the manner described, then we may say that by contemplating the relation between properties we are able to know that being red excludes being blue and thus to know that *necessarily,* everything is such that if it is red then it is not blue. And we can say, therefore, that the universal generalization, as well as the proposition about properties, is known *a priori.* The order of justification thus differs from that of the enumerative induction considered earlier, where one attempts to justify the statement about properties by reference to a generalization about particular things.

There is a superficial resemblance between "intuitive induction" and "induction by simple enumeration," since in each case, we start with particular instances and then proceed beyond them. Thus, when we make an induction by enumeration, we may proceed from "This *A* is *B*," "That *A* is *B*," and so on, to "In all probability, all *A*'s are *B*'s," or to "In all probability, the next *A* is *B*." But in an induction by enumeration, the function of the particular instances is to *justify* the conclusion. If we find subsequently that our perceptions of the particular instances were unveridical, say, that the things we took to be *A*'s were not *A*'s at all, then the inductive argument would lose whatever force it may have had. In an "intuitive induction," however, the particular perceptions are only incidental to the conclusion. This may be seen in the following way.

Let us suppose that the knowledge expressed by the two sentences "Necessarily, being red excludes being blue" and "Necessarily, being human includes being animal" is arrived at by intuitive induction; and let us suppose further that in each case, the process began with the perception of certain particular things. Neither conclusion depends for its *justification* upon the particular perceptions which led to the knowledge concerned. As Duns Scotus put it, the perception of the particular things is only the "occasion" of acquiring the knowledge. If we happen to find our perception was unveridical, this finding will have no bearing upon the result. "If the senses from which these terms were received were all false, or what is more deceptive, if some were false and others true, I still maintain that the intellect would not be deceived about such principles. . . ."[5] If what we take to be Callias is not a man at all, but only a clever imitation of a man, then, if the imitation is clever enough, our deceptive experience will still be an occasion for contemplating the property of being human—the property of being both rational and animal—and thus, for coming to know that being human includes being animal.

Leibniz thus observes: ". . . if I should discover any demonstrative truth, mathematical or other, while dreaming (as might in fact be), it would be just as certain as if I had been awake. This shows us how intelligible truth is independent of the truth of the existence outside of us of sensible and material things."[6]

It may be, indeed, that to perform an intuitive induction—i.e., to "abstract" a certain property, contemplate it, and then see what it includes and excludes—we need only to *think* of some individual thing as having that property. By thinking about a blue thing and a red thing, for example, we may come to see that being blue excludes being red. Thus, Ernst Mach spoke of "experiments in the imagination."[7] And E. Husserl, whose language may have been needlessly Platonic, said, "The Eidos, the *pure essence,* can be exemplified intuitively in the data of experience, data of perception, memory, and so forth, but just as readily *also in the mere data of fancy.* . . ."[8]

According to this traditional account, then, once we have acquired some concepts (once we know, with respect to certain attributes, just *what* it is for something to have those attributes), we will also be in a position to know just *what* it is for a proposition or state of affairs to be necessary—to be necessarily such that it is true or necessarily such that it obtains. Then, by contemplating or reflecting upon certain propositions or states of affairs, we will be able to see that *they* are necessary.

This kind of knowledge has traditionally been called *a priori*.

Axioms

Speaking very roughly, we might say that one mark of an *a priori* proposition is this: once you understand it, you see that it is true. We might call this the traditional conception of the *a priori*. Thus Leibniz remarks: "You will find in a hundred places that the Scholastics have said that these propositions are evident, *ex terminis,* as soon as the terms are understood. . . ."9

If we say an *a priori* proposition is one such that "once you understand it then you see that it is true," we must take the term "understand" in a somewhat rigid sense. You couldn't be said to "understand" a proposition, in the sense intended, unless you can grasp *what* it is for that proposition to be true. The properties or attributes that the proposition implies—those that would be instantiated if the proposition were true—must be properties or attributes that you can grasp in the sense that we have tried to explicate. To "understand" a proposition, in the sense intended, then, it is not enough merely to be able to say what *sentence* in your language happens to express that proposition. The proposition must be one that you have contemplated and reflected upon.

One cannot *accept* a proposition, in the sense in which we have been using the word "accept," unless one also *understands* that proposition. We might say, therefore, that an *a priori* proposition is one such that, if you accept it, then it becomes certain for you. (For if you accept it, then you understand it, and as soon as you understand it, it becomes certain for you.) This account of the *a priori*, however, would be somewhat broad. We know some *a priori* propositions on the basis of others and these propositions are not themselves such that, once they are understood, then they are certain.

But let us begin by trying to characterize more precisely those *a priori* propositions which are not known on the basis of any *other* propositions.

Leibniz said that these propositions are the "first lights." He wrote: "The immediate apperception of our existence and of our thoughts furnishes us with the first truths *a posteriori,* or of fact, i.e., the *first experiences,* as the identical propositions contain the first truths *a priori,* or of reason, i.e., the *first lights.* Both are incapable of proof, and may be called *immediate.* . . ."

The traditional term for those *a priori* propositions which are "incapable of proof" is *axiom.* Thus Frege wrote: "Since the time of antiquity an axiom has been taken to be a thought whose truth is known without being susceptible to demonstration by a logical chain of reasoning."10 In *one* sense, of course, every true proposition *h* is capable of proof, for there will always be other true propositions from which we can derive *h* by means of some principle of logic. What did Leibniz and Frege mean, then, when they said that an axiom is "incapable of proof"?

The answer is suggested by Aristotle. An axiom, or "basic truth," he said, is a proposition "which has no other proposition prior to it"; there is no proposition which is "better known" than it is. We could say that if one proposition is "better known" than another, then accepting the one proposition is more reasonable than accepting the other. Hence, if an axiomatic proposition is one such that no other proposition is better known than it is, then it is one that is certain. (It will be recalled that we characterized *certainty* in Chapter 1. We there said that a proposition *h* is *certain* for a person *S*, provided that *h* is evident for *S* and provided that there is no other proposition *i* which is such that it is *more* reasonable for *S* to accept *i* than it is for him to accept *h*.) Hence Aristotle said that an axiom is a "primary premise." Its ground does not lie in the fact that it is seen to follow from *other* propositions. Therefore we cannot prove such a proposition by making use of any premises that are "better known" than it is. (By "a proof," then, Aristotle, Leibniz, and Frege meant more than "a valid derivation from premises that are true.")

Let us now try to say what it is for a proposition or state of affairs to be an *axiom:*

D3.1   *h* is an *axiom* = Df *h* is necessarily such that (i) it is true and (ii) for every *S*, if *S* accepts *h*, then *h* is certain for *S*.

The following propositions among countless others may be said to be axioms in our present sense of the term:

If some men are Greeks, then some Greeks are men.

If Jones is ill and Smith is away, then Jones is ill.

The sum of 5 and 3 is 8.

The product of 4 and 2 is 8.

For most of us, i.e., for those of us who really *do* consider them, they may be said to be *axiomatic* in the following sense.

D3.2   *h* is *axiomatic* for *S* = Df (i) *h* is an axiom and (ii) *S* accepts *h*.

We may assume that any conjunction of axioms is itself an axiom. But it does not follow from this assumption that any conjunction of propositions which are axiomatic for a subject *S* is itself axiomatic for *S*. If two propositions are axiomatic for *S* and if *S* does not accept their conjunction, then the conjunction is not axiomatic for *S*. (Failure to accept their conjunction need not be a sign that *S* is unreasonable. It may be a sign merely that the conjunction is too complex an object for *S* to grasp.)

We have suggested that our knowledge of what is axiomatic is a subspecies of our *a priori* knowledge, that is to say, some of the things we know *a priori* are *not* axiomatic in the present sense. They are *a priori* but they are not what Aristotle called "primary premises."

What would be an example of a proposition that is *a priori* for *S* but not axiomatic for *S*? Consider the last two axioms on our list above; i.e.,

The sum of 5 and 3 is 8.

The product of 4 and 2 is 8.

Let us suppose that their conjunction is also an axiom and that *S* accepts this conjunction; therefore the conjunction is axiomatic for *S*. Let us suppose further that the following proposition is axiomatic for *S:*

If the sum of 5 and 3 is 8 and the product of 4 and 2 is 8, then the sum of 5 and 3 is the product of 4 and 2.

We will say that, if, in such a case, *S* accepts the proposition

The sum of 5 and 3 is the product of 4 and 2

then that proposition is *a priori* for *S*. Yet the proposition may not be one which is such that it is

certain for anyone who accepts it. It may be that one can consider *that* proposition without thereby seeing that it is true.

There are various ways in which we might now attempt to characterize this broader concept of the *a priori*. Thus we might say: "You know a proposition *a priori* provided you accept it and it is implied by propositions that are axiomatic for you." But this would imply that *any* necessary proposition that you happen to accept is one that you know *a priori* to be true. (Any necessary proposition *h* is implied by any axiomatic proposition *e*. Indeed any necessary proposition *h* is implied by *any* proposition *e*—whether or not *e* is axiomatic and whether or not *e* is true or false. For if *h* is necessary, then, it is necessarily true that, for any proposition *e*, either *e* is false or *h* is true. And to say "*e* implies *h*" is to say it is necessarily true that either *e* is false or *h* is true.) *Some* of the necessary propositions that we accept may *not* be propositions that we know *a priori*. They may be such that, if we know them, we know them *a posteriori*—on the basis of authority. Or they may be such that we cannot be said to know them at all.

To capture the broader concept of the *a priori*, we might say that a proposition is known *a priori* provided it is axiomatic that the proposition follows from something that is axiomatic. But let us say, more carefully:

D3.3   *h* is known *a priori* by *S* = Df There is an *e* such that (i) *e* is axiomatic for *S*, (ii) the proposition, *e* implies *h*, is axiomatic for *S*, and (iii) *S* accepts *h*.

We may add that a person knows a proposition *a posteriori* if he knows the proposition but doesn't know it *a priori*. . . .

A Priori and A Posteriori

Kant had said, . . . that "necessity is a mark of the *a priori*." We may accept Kant's dictum, if we take it to mean that what is known *a priori* is necessary.

But is it possible to know a necessary proposition to be true and not to know this *a priori*? In other words, can we know some necessary propositions *a posteriori*?

A possible example of a proposition that is known *a posteriori* and is yet necessary might be a logical theorem which one accepts on the ground that reputable logicians assert it to be true. Whether there are in fact any such propositions depends upon two things, each of them somewhat problematic.

The first is that such a proposition cannot be said to be *known* to be true unless such testimonial evidence is sufficient for knowledge. And this is a question we cannot discuss in the present book.

The second is that such a proposition cannot be said to be known to be true unless it is one that the man *accepts*. But when a man, as we say, accepts a theorem on the basis of authority and not on the basis of demonstration, is it the theorem *itself* that he accepts or is it what Brentano calls a "surrogate" for the theorem? If a man reads a logical text, finds there a formula which expresses a certain logical principle, and then, knowing that the author is reputable, concludes that the formula is true, it may well be that the man does *not* accept the logical principle. What he accepts is, rather, the contingent proposition to the effect that a certain formula in a book expresses a logical principle that is true.

But if we waive these difficulties, then perhaps we may say that there is an analytic *a posteriori*—or at least that some of the logical truths that we know are such that we know them only *a posteriori*.

But even if some of the things we know *a posteriori* are logically true, there is at least this additional epistemic relation holding between the necessary and the *a priori*:

If a man knows—or someone once knew—*a posteriori* that a certain necessary proposition is true, then *someone* knows *a priori* that some necessary proposition is true. If the first man bases his knowledge on the testimony of authority, and if this authority in turn bases his knowledge upon the testimony of some other authority, then sooner or later there will be an "ultimate authority" who knows some proposition *a priori*.

Skepticism with Respect to the *A Priori*

Let us now consider a skeptical objection to what we have been saying.

"You have said what it is for a proposition to be axiomatic for a person and you have given examples of propositions which, you say, are axiomatic for you and presumably for others. But how do you know that those propositions are axiomatic? How do you know that they satisfy the terms of your definitions?

"If you really do know that they are axiomatic, then you must have some *general principle* by means of which you can apply your definitions. There must be something about your experience that guarantees these propositions for you and you must *know* that it guarantees them. But what could the principle be?

"The most you can say, surely, is that such propositions just *seem* to be true, or that when you reflect on them you find you cannot doubt them and that you cannot help but accept them. But, as the history of science makes clear, such facts as these provide no guarantee that the propositions in question are true. Notoriously, there have been ever so many false propositions which reasonable people have found they couldn't doubt. And some of these may well have been taken as axiomatic. Consider the logical paradoxes, for example. People found they couldn't help but believe certain propositions, and as a result they became entangled in contradictions."

The objection may be summarized as follows:

1. You cannot know that a given proposition is axiomatic for you unless the proposition is one such that, when you contemplate it, you have a kind of experience—say, a strong feeling of conviction— that provides you with a guarantee that the proposition is true. But

2. there is no experience which will provide such a guarantee. Therefore

3. you cannot really know, with respect to any proposition that it is one that is axiomatic.

Is this a valid argument? The conclusion certainly follows from the premises. And, knowing the history of human error, we can hardly question the second of the two premises. But what of the first premise? If we cannot find any reason to accept the first premise, then we do not need to accept the conclusion. How, then, would the skeptic defend his first premise?

There is a certain more general principle to which the skeptic might appeal in the attempt to defend the first premise. I will call this principle the *generalizability thesis* and formulate it as follows. "You cannot *know* that any given proposition p is true unless you also know two other things. The first of these things will be a certain more *general* proposition q; q will not imply p but it will specify the conditions under which propositions of a certain type are true. And the second thing will be a proposition r, which enables you to *apply* this general proposition to p. In other words, r will be a proposition to the effect that the first proposition p satisfies the conditions specified in the second proposition q."

But if the generalizability thesis is true, no one knows anything. Consider the application of the thesis to a single proposition p. According to the thesis, if we know p, then we know two further propositions—a general proposition q and a proposition r that applies q to p. Applying the generalizability thesis to each of the two propositions, q and r, we obtain four more propositions; applying it to each of them, we obtain eight more propositions; . . . and so on *ad indefinitum*. The generalizability thesis implies, therefore, that we cannot know any proposition to be true unless we know all the members of such an infinite hierarchy of propositions. And therefore it implies that we cannot know any proposition to be true.

The skeptic may reply: "But in *objecting* to my general principle, you are presupposing that we *do* know something. And this begs the question." The proper rejoinder is: "But in *affirming* your general principle, you are presupposing that we *don't* know anything. And *that* begs the question."

The general reply to a skepticism that addresses itself to an entire area of knowledge can only be this: we do have the knowledge in question, and therefore, any philosophical theory implying that we do not is false. This way of looking at the matter may seem especially plausible in the present instance. It is tempting to say of skepticism, with respect to the truths of reason, what Leonard Nelson said of skepticism, with respect to the truths of mathematics. The advocate of such a skepticism, Nelson said, has invited us to "sacrifice the clearest and most lucid knowledge that we possess—indeed, the *only* knowledge that is clear and lucid *per se*. I prefer to strike the opposite course. If a philosophy, no matter how attractive or plausible or ingenious it may be, brings me into conflict with mathematics, I conclude that not mathematics but my philosophy is on the wrong track."[11] There is certainly no *better* ground for skepticism with respect to our knowledge of the

truths of reason than there is for skepticism with respect to our knowledge of physical things.

And so what of the skeptic's question, "How do you know that the proposition that 2 and 4 are 6 is one that is axiomatic?" Let us recall what we said in connection with his earlier question about self-presenting states. The question was: "How do you know that seeming to have a headache is a self-presenting state?" In dealing with that question, we avoided falling into the skeptic's trap. We said that the only possible answer to such a question is that we *do* know that seeming to have a headache is self-presenting state. We should follow a similar course in the present case.

"Linguisticism"

It has been suggested that the sentences giving rise to the problem of the synthetic *a priori* are really "postulates about the meanings of words" and, therefore, that they do not express what is synthetic *a priori*. But if the suggestion is intended literally, then it would seem to betray the confusion between use and mention that we encountered earlier. A *postulate* about the meaning of the word "red," for example, or a sentence expressing such a postulate, would presumably mention the word "red." It might read, "The word 'red' may be taken to refer to a certain color," or perhaps, "Let the word 'red' be taken to refer to a certain color." But, "Everything that is red is colored," although it uses the words "red" and "colored," does not mention them at all. It is not the case, therefore, that, "Red is a color," refers only to words and the ways in which they are used.

A popular conception of the truths of reason is the view according to which they are essentially "linguistic." Many have said, for example, that the sentences formulating the truths of logic are "true in virtue of the rules of language" and, hence, that they are "true in virtue of the way in which we use words."[12] What could this possibly mean?

The two English *sentences*, "Being round excludes being square," and, "Being rational and animal includes being animal," plausibly could be said to "owe their truth," in part, to the way in which we use words. If we used "being square" to refer to the property of being heavy and not to that of being square, then the first sentence (provided the other words in it had their present use) would be false instead of true. And if we used the word "and" to express the relation of disjunction instead of conjunction, then the second sentence (again, provided that the other words in it had their present use) would also be false instead of true. But as W. V. Quine has reminded us, "even so factual a sentence as 'Brutus killed Caesar' owes its truth not only to the killing but equally to our using the component words as we do."[13] Had "killed," for example, been given the use that "was survived by" happens to have, then, other things being the same, "Brutus killed Caesar" would be false instead of true.

It might be suggested, therefore, that the truths of logic and other truths of reason stand in this peculiar relationship to language: they are true "*solely* in virtue of the rules of our language" or "*solely* in virtue of the ways in which we use words." But if we take the phrase "solely in virtue of" in the way in which it would naturally be taken, then the suggestion is obviously false.

To say of a sentence that it is true *solely* in virtue of the ways in which we use words or that it is true *solely* in virtue of the rules of our language, would be to say that the only condition that needs to obtain in order for the sentence to be true is that we use words in certain ways or that there be certain rules pertaining to the way in which words are to be used. But let us consider what conditions must obtain if the English sentence, "Being round excludes being square," is to be true. One such condition is indicated by the following sentence which we may call "T":

> The English sentence, "Being square excludes being round," is true, if and only if, being square excludes being round.

Clearly, the final part of T, the part following the second "if," formulates a necessary condition for the truth of the English sentence, "Being round excludes being square," but it refers to a relationship among properties and not to rules of language or ways in which we use words. Hence we cannot say that the *only* conditions that need to obtain in order for, "Being round excludes being square," to be true is that we use words in certain ways or that there be certain rules pertaining to the ways in which words are to be used; and therefore, the sentence cannot be said to be true solely in virtue of the ways in which we use words.

There would seem to be no clear sense, therefore, in which the *a priori* truths of reason can be said to be primarily "linguistic."

Analyzing the Predicate Out of the Subject

The terms "analytic" and "synthetic" were introduced by Kant in order to contrast two types, of categorical judgment. It will not be inaccurate to interpret "judgment," in Kant's sense, to mean the same as what we mean by "proposition." The terms "analytic" and "synthetic" are used in much of contemporary philosophy to refer instead to the types of *sentence* that express the types of judgment to which Kant referred. And perhaps Kant's view is best expressed by reference to sentences: an analytic *judgment* or *proposition* is one that is expressible in a certain type of *sentence*. But what type of sentence?

An analytic judgment, according to Kant, is a judgment in which "the predicate adds nothing to the concept of the subject." If I judge that all squares are rectangles, then, in Kant's terminology, the concept of the subject of my judgment is the property of being square, and the concept of the predicate is the property of being rectangular. Kant uses the term "analytic," since, he says, the concept of the predicate helps to "break up the concept of the subject into those constituent concepts that have all along been thought in it." Since being square is the conjunctive property of being equilateral and rectangular, the predicate of the judgment expressed by "All squares are rectangular" may be said to "analyze out" what is contained in the subject. An analytic judgment, then, may be expressed in the form of an explicit redundancy: e.g., "Everything is such that if it is both equilateral and rectangular then it is rectangular." To deny such an explicit redundancy would be to affirm a *contradictiso in adjecto,* for it would be to judge that there are things which both have and do not have a certain property—in the present instance, that there is something that both is and is not rectangular. Hence, Kant said that "the common principle of all analytic judgments is the law of contradiction."[14]

What might it mean to say, with respect to a sentence of the form "Everything that is an *S* is a

P" that the predicate-term can be analyzed out of the subject-term?

One thing that might be meant is this: that what the sentence expresses can *also* be expressed in a sentence in which the predicate-term is the same as the subject term. Thus the predicate of "Everything that is a man is a rational animal" could be said to be analyzed out of the subject, since what the sentence expresses can also be expressed by saying "Everything that is a rational animal is a rational animal." But not all of the traditional examples of propositions that are analytic may be expressed in sentences wherein the subject term and the predicate-term are the same.

Consider the sentence:

1. All squares are rectangles.

What this sentence expresses may also be put as:

2. Everything that is an equilateral thing and a rectangle is, a rectangle.

Sentence (2) provides us with a paradigm case of a sentence in which the predicate-term ("a rectangle") may be said to be analyzed out of the subject-term ("an equilateral thing and a rectangle").

We may note that, in sentence (2), the predicate-term is *also* part of the subject-term. Shall we say, then, that the predicate of a sentence is *analyzed out* of the subject if the predicate is the same as the subject or if the subject is a conjunction of two terms one of which is the predicate? This definition would be somewhat broad, for it would require us to say that in the following sentence the predicate is analyzed out of the subject:

3. Everything that is a square and a rectangle is a rectangle.

But (3) does not exhibit the type of analysis that is to be found in (2). Thus in (3) the subject-term ("a square and a rectangle") is redundant (given "a square" in the subject we don't *need* to add "a rectangle"), but in (2) the subject-term ("an equilateral thing and a rectangle") is not redundant.

We could say, somewhat more exactly, that a predicate-term is *analyzed out* of a subject-term provided the subject-term is such that either it is itself the predicate-term or it is a conjunction of independent terms one of which is the predicate-term. But what is it for two terms to be "independent"?

We may say, of certain pairs of terms in a given language, that one of the terms *logically*

implies the other in that language. Thus in English "square" logically implies "rectangle," and "red thing" logically implies "colored thing." These terms may be said to be such that in English they are *true of,* or *apply to,* certain things. And the English language is necessarily such that "rectangle" applies to everything that "square" applies to, and it is also necessarily such that "colored thing" applies to everything that "red" applies to. To say, then, "*T logically implies R* in language *L*" is to say this: *L* is necessarily such that *R* applies in *L* to all those things to which *T* applies in *L*.

Now we may say what it is for two terms to be *independent*—what it is for two terms to be logically independent of each other in a given language.

Two terms are *logically independent* of each other in a given language provided only that the terms and their negations are such that no one of them logically implies the other in that language. Thus "red thing" and "square" are logically independent in English, for the four terms, "red thing," "square," "nonred thing," and "nonsquare" are such that no one of them implies the other in English.

We can now say, somewhat more exactly, what it is for the predicate-term *P*, of a sentence in a given language *L*, to be *analyzed out* of the subject-term *S*. First of all, the sentence will be an "All *S* is *P*" sentence; that is to say, the sentence will be necessarily such that it is true in *L*, if and only if, for every *x*, if *S* applies to *x* in *L*, then *P* applies to *x* in *L*. And second, either the subject-term *S* is itself the same as *P* or it is a conjunction of logically independent terms one of which is *P*.

Finally, we may define the Kantian sense of "analytic proposition" as follows: A proposition is analytic provided only it may be expressed in a sentence in which the predicate-term is analyzed out of the subject-term.

To see how the definitions may be applied, consider the following sentences, each of which may be said to express an analytic proposition, in the traditional sense of the term "analytic":

All fathers are parents.
No bachelors are married.
All dogs are dogs or cats.

What these three sentences express in English may also be put as follows:

Everything that is a male and a parent is a parent.

Everything that is a male human and a thing that is unmarried is a thing that is unmarried.

Everything that is (i) a dog or a cat and (ii) a dog or a noncat is a dog or a cat.

The last three sentences are sentences in which the predicate is analyzed out of the subject. And therefore the propositions expressed by the first sentences are all analytic.

The Synthetic *A Priori*

Kant raised the question: Is there a synthetic *a priori*? Are there synthetic propositions that we know *a priori* to be true?

If we construe "analytic proposition" in the way in which we have tried to spell out (by reference to the predicate of a sentence being "analyzed out of" the subject), and if, as many philosophers do, we take "synthetic proposition" to mean the same as "proposition which is not analytic," then Kant's question may not be particularly interesting. For, it would seem, there are many propositions which we know *a priori* and which are not analytic, in this restricted sense of the term "analytic." Among them are such propositions as:

If there are more than 7 dogs, then there are more than 5 dogs.
If there are either dogs or cows but no cows, then there are dogs.
If all men are mortal and Socrates is a man then Socrates is mortal.

But when philosophers ask whether there are synthetic propositions that we know *a priori* to be true, they are not usually thinking of such propositions as these. They are thinking rather of propositions which can be expressed naturally in English in the form "All *S* are *P*." Given what we have said about the nature of analytic propositions, we may put the question, "Is there a synthetic *a priori?*" somewhat more exactly as follows:

Are there any propositions which are such that: (i) they are known by us *a priori;* (ii) they can be expressed in English in the form "Everything

which is *S* is *P*"; and yet (iii) they are *not* such that in English their predicate-terms can be analyzed out of their subject-terms?

Let us consider, then, certain possible examples of "the synthetic *a priori*," so conceived.

1. One important candidate for the synthetic *a priori* is the knowledge that might be expressed by saying either "Being square includes being a shape" or "Necessarily, everything that is square is a thing that has a shape." The sentence "Everything that is square is a thing that has a shape" recalls our paradigmatic "Everything that is square is a rectangle." In the case of the latter sentence, we were able to "analyze the predicate out of the subject": We replaced the subject-term "square" with a conjunctive term, "equilateral thing and a rectangle," and were thus able to express our proposition in the form:

Everything that is an *S* and a *P* is a *P*

where the terms replacing "*S*" and "*P*" are such that neither is implied by the other or by the negation of the other. But can we do this with "Everything that is square has a shape"?

The problem is to fill in the blank in the following sentence:

Everything that is a _____ and a thing that has a shape is a thing that has a shape

in the appropriate way. This means we should find a term such that: (i) the resulting sentence will express what is expressed by "Everything that is square has a shape"; (ii) the term will neither imply nor be implied by "thing that has a shape"; and (iii) the negation of our term will neither imply nor be implied by "thing that has a shape." With what term, then, can we fill the blank?

We might try "either a square or a thing that does not have a shape," thus obtaining "Everything that is (i) either a square or a thing that does not have a shape and (ii) a thing that has a shape is a thing that has a shape." But the sentence thus obtained is not one in which the predicate is analyzed out of the subject. The two terms making up the subject, namely (i) "either a square or a thing that does not have a shape" and (ii) "a thing that has a shape," are such that, in our language, any negation of the second logically implies the first (i.e., "not such as to be a thing that has a shape" logically implies "either a square or a thing that does not have a shape"). We do not have a sentence, therefore, in which the predicate can be said to be analyzed out of the subject; for the two terms making up the subject are not logically independent in our language.

What if we fill in the blank by "square," thus obtaining "Everything that is a square and a thing that has a shape is a thing that has a shape"? This will not help us, for the two terms making up the subject—"square" and "a thing that has a shape"—are such that, in our language, the first logically implies the second; hence they are not logically independent of each other; and therefore the sentence is not one in which the predicate is analyzed out of the subject. And if we drop the second term from the subject, as we can without any loss, we will be back where we started.

And so we have not found a way of showing that "Everything that is square has a shape" is analytic. But the sentence expresses what we know *a priori* to be true. And therefore, it would seem, there is at last some presumption in favor of the proposition that there is a synthetic *a priori*.

There are indefinitely many other propositions presenting essentially the same difficulties as "Everything that is square has a shape." Examples are: "Everything red is colored"; "Everyone who hears something in C-sharp minor hears a sound." The sentences express what is known *a priori*, but no one has been able to show that they are analytic.

It has been suggested that the sentences giving rise to the problem of the synthetic *a priori* are really "postulates about the meanings of words," and therefore, that they do not express what is synthetic *a priori*. But if the suggestion is intended literally, then it would seem to betray the confusion between use and mention that we encountered earlier. A postulate about the meaning of the word "red," for example, or a sentence expressing such a postulate, would personally mention the word "red." It might read, "The word 'red' may be taken to refer to a certain color," or perhaps, "Let the word 'red' be taken to refer to a certain color." But "Everything that is red is colored," although it uses the words "red" and "colored," doesn't mention them at all. Thus, there would seem to be no clear sense in which it could be said really to be a "meaning postulate" or to refer in any way to words and how they are used.

2. What Leibniz called the "disparates" furnish us with a second candidate for the synthetic *a priori*. These are closely related to the type of sentence just considered, but involve problems that are essentially different. An example of a sentence concerned with disparates would be our earlier "Being red excludes being blue" or (alternatively put) "Nothing that is red is blue." Philosophers have devoted considerable ingenuity to trying to show that "Nothing that is red is blue" can be expressed as a sentence that is analytic, but so far as I have been able to determine, all of these attempts have been unsuccessful. Again, it is recommended that the reader try to re-express "Nothing that is red is blue" in such a way that the predicate may be "analyzed out" of the subject in the sense we have described above.

3. It has also been held, not without plausibility, that certain ethical sentences express what is synthetic *a priori*. Thus, Leibniz, writing on what he called the "supersensible element" in knowledge, said: ". . . but *to return to necessary truths,* it is generally true that we know them only by this natural light, and not at all by the experience of the senses. For the senses can very well make known, in some sort, what is, but they cannot make known what *ought to be* or what could not be otherwise." Or consider the sentence, "All pleasures, as such, are intrinsically good, or good in themselves, whenever and wherever they may occur." If this sentence expresses something that is known to be true, then what it expresses must be synthetic *a priori*. To avoid this conclusion, some philosophers deny that sentences about what is intrinsically good, or good in itself, *can* be known to be true.

An Untenable Dualism?

But many philosophers now believe that the distinction between the analytic and the synthetic has been shown to be untenable; we should consider what reasons there might be for such a belief. Ordinarily, it is defended by reference to the following facts. (1) In drawing a distinction between analytic and synthetic sentences, one must speak of *necessity,* as we have done, or employ concepts, e.g., that of *synonymy,* that can be explicated only by reference to necessity. Thus we have spoken of a language being *necessarily* such that, if a given term applies to a thing in that language, then a certain other term also applies to that thing in that language. (2) There is no reliable way of telling, merely by observing a man's behavior, whether the language he then happens to be using is one which is *necessarily* such that if a given term applies to something in that language then a certain other term applies to that thing in that language. And (3) it is not possible, by reference merely to linguistic behavior, to say what it is for a language to be *necessarily* such that, for two given terms, if the one applies to something in that language then the other also applies to that thing in that language.[15]

But these three propositions, even if they are true, are not sufficient to yield the conclusion (4) that the distinction between the analytic and the synthetic is untenable. If we attempt to formulate the additional premise that would be needed to make the argument valid, we will see that it must involve a philosophical generalization—a generalization concerning what conditions must obtain if the distinction between the analytic and the synthetic is to be tenable. And how would the generalization be defended? This question should be considered in the light of what we have said about skepticism and the problem of the criterion. Of the philosophical generalizations that would make the above argument valid, none of them, so far as I know, has ever been defended. It is not accurate, therefore, to say that the distinction between the analytic and the synthetic has been *shown* to be untenable.

Notes

[1] "Being red excludes being blue" should not be taken to rule out the possibility of a thing being red in one part and blue in another; it tells us only that being red in one part at one time excludes being blue in exactly that same part at exactly that same time. The point might be put even more exactly by saying that it is necessarily true that anything that is red has a part that is not blue.

[2] William Whewell, *Philosophy of the Inductive Sciences Founded upon Their History, I* (London: J. W. Parker & Son, 1840), pp. 59–61.

[3] *Republic* 479, 508.

[4] *Posterior Analytics,* 100a–100b.

[5] *Philosophical Writings,* ed. and trans. Alan Wolter (New York: Thomas Nelson & Sons, 1962), p. 109 (the Nelson philosophical texts); cf. p. 103.

[6] *The Philosophical Works of Leibniz,* ed. G. M. Duncan (New Haven: The Tuttle, Morehouse & Taylor Co., 1908), p. 161.

[7] *Erkenntnis und Irrtum* (Leipzig: Felix Meiner, 1905), pp. 180ff.

[8] E. Husserl, *Ideas: General Introduction to Phenomenology* (New York: The Macmillan Company, 1931), p. 57.

[9] G. W. Leibniz, *New Essays Concerning Human Understanding,* Book IV, Chapter 7 (Open Court edition), p. 462. Compare Alice Ambrose and Morris Lazerowitz, *Fundamentals of Symbolic Logic* (New York: Holt, Rinehart and Winston, Inc., 1962): "A proposition is said to be true *a priori* if its truth can be ascertained by examination of the proposition alone or if it is deductible from propositions whose truth is so ascertained, and by examination of nothing else. . . . Understanding the words used in expressing these propositions is sufficient for determining that they are true" p. 17.

[10] Gottlob Frege, *Kleine Schriften* (Hildesheim: Georg Olms Verlagsbuchhandlung, 1967), p. 262.

[11] Leonard Nelson, *Socratic Method and Critical Philosophy* (New Haven: Yale University Press, 1949), p. 184.

[12] See Anthony Quinton, "The *A Priori* and the Analytic," in Robert Sleigh, ed., *Necessary Truth* (Englewood Cliffs, NJ: Prentice-Hall, Inc., 1972), pp. 89–109.

[13] W. V. Quine, "Carnap and Logical Truth," *The Philosophy of Rudolf Carnap,* P. A. Schilpp, ed. (La Salle, IL: Open Court Publishing Co., 1963), p. 386.

[14] *Prolegomena to Any Further Metaphysics,* sec. 2.

[15] Cf. W. V. Quine, "Two Dogmas of Empiricism," in *From a Logical Point of View,* esp. pp. 20–37, and Morton White, "The Analytic and the Synthetic: An Untenable Dualism," in *Semantics and the Philosophy of Language,* ed. Leonard Linsky (Urbana: University of Illinois Press, 1952), pp. 272–286.

VII.7 A Priori Knowledge, Necessity, and Contingency

SAUL A. KRIPKE

Saul Kripke was educated at Harvard and is professor of philosophy at Princeton University. He is the author of several important works in metaphysics and philosophy of language, including *Naming and Necessity* from which this selection is taken.

Typically, as with Leibniz and Kant, rationalists have asserted that all a priori knowledge must be of necessary truth (propositions true in all possible worlds). Kripke argues against this thesis. Necessity is not a necessary condition for a priori contingent knowledge. Anytime we stipulate a definition of a term (his illustration is that of stipulating that the length of a certain bar in Paris is one meter long), we can know a priori the truth of the definition. If we define "water" as the molecular structure of H_2O, then we can know a priori that water is H_2O.

Philosophers have talked (and, of course, there has been considerable controversy in recent years over the meaningfulness of these notions) about various categories of truth, which are called "a priori," "analytic," "necessary"—and sometimes even "certain" is thrown into this batch. The terms are often used as if *whether* there are things answering to these concepts is an interesting question, but we might as well regard them all as meaning the same thing. Now, everyone remembers Kant (a bit) as making a distinction between "a priori" and "analytic." So maybe this distinction is still made. In contemporary discussion very few people, if any, distinguish between the concepts of statements being a priori and their being necessary. At any rate I shall *not* use the terms "a priori" and "necessary" interchangeably here.

Consider what the traditional characterizations of such terms as "a priori" and "necessary" are. First the notion of a prioricity is a concept of epistemology. I guess the traditional characterization from Kant goes something like: a priori truths are those which can be known independently of any experience. This introduces another problem before we get off the ground, because there's another modality in the characterization of "a priori," namely, it is supposed to be something which *can* be known independently of any experience.

That means that in some sense it's *possible* (whether we do or do not in fact know it independently of any experience) to know this independently of any experience. And possible for whom? For God? For the Martians? Or just for people with minds like ours? To make this all clear might involve a host of problems all of its own about what sort of possibility is in question here. It might be best therefore, instead of using the phrase "a priori truth," to the extent that one uses it at all, to stick to the question of whether a particular person or knower knows something a priori or believes it true on the basis of a priori evidence.

I won't go further too much into the problems that might arise with the notion of a prioricity here. I will say that some philosophers somehow change the modality in this characterization from *can* to *must*. They think that if something belongs to the realm of a priori knowledge, it couldn't possibly be known empirically. This is just a mistake. Something may belong in the realm of such statements that *can* be known a priori but still may be known by particular people on the basis of experience. To give a really common-sense example: anyone who has worked with a computing machine knows that the computing machine may give an answer to whether such and such a number is prime. No one has calculated or proved that the number is prime; but the machine has given the answer: this number is prime. We, then, if we believe that the number is prime, believe it on the basis of our knowledge of the laws of physics, the construction of the machine, and so on. We therefore do not believe this on the basis of purely a priori evidence. We believe it (if anything is a posteriori at all) on the basis of a posteriori evidence. Nevertheless, maybe this could be known a priori by someone who made the requisite calculations. So "*can* be known a priori" doesn't mean "*must* be known a priori."

The second concept which is in question is that of necessity. Sometimes this is used in an epistemological way and might then just mean a priori. And of course, sometimes it is used in a physical way when people distinguish between physical and logical necessity. But what I am concerned with here is a notion which is not a notion of epistemology but of metaphysics, in some (I hope) non-pejorative sense. We ask whether something might have been true, or might have been false. Well, if something is false, it's obviously not necessarily true. If it is true, might it have been otherwise? Is it possible that, in this respect, the world should have been different from the way it is? If the answer is "no," then this fact about the world is a necessary one. If the answer is "yes," then this fact about the world is a contingent one. This in and of itself has nothing to do with anyone's knowledge of anything. It's certainly a philosophical thesis, and not a matter of obvious definitional equivalence, either that everything a priori is necessary or that everything necessary is a priori. Both concepts may be vague. That may be another problem. But at any rate they are dealing with two different domains, two different areas, the epistemological and the metaphysical. Consider, say, Fermat's last theorem—or the Goldbach conjecture. The Goldbach conjecture says that an even number greater than 2 must be the sum of two prime numbers. If this is true, it is presumably necessary, and, if it is false, presumably necessarily false. We are taking the classical view of mathematics here and assume that in mathematical reality it is either true or false.

If the Goldbach conjecture is false, then there is an even number, n, greater than 2, such that for no primes p_1 and p_2, both $<n$, does $n = p_1 + p_2$. This fact about n, if true, is verifiable by direct computation, and thus is necessary if the results of arithmetical computations are necessary. On the other hand, if the conjecture is true, then every even number exceeding 2 is the sum of two primes. Could it then be the case that, although in fact every such even number is the sum of two primes, there might have been such an even number which was not the sum of two primes? What would that mean? Such a number would have to be one of 4, 6, 8, 10, . . .; and, by hypothesis, since we are assuming Goldbach's conjecture to be true, each of these can be shown, again by direct computation, to be the sum of two primes. Goldbach's conjecture, then, cannot be contingently true or false; whatever truth-value it has belongs to it by necessity.

But what we can say, of course, is that right now, as far as we know, the question can come out either way. So, in the absence of a mathematical proof deciding this question, none of us has any a priori knowledge about this question in either direction. We don't know whether Goldbach's conjecture is true or false. So right now we certainly don't know anything a priori about it.

Perhaps it will be alleged that we *can* in principle know a priori whether it is true. Well, maybe we can. Of course an infinite mind which can search through all the numbers can or could. But I don't know whether a finite mind can or could. Maybe there just is no mathematical proof whatsoever which decides the conjecture. At any rate this might or might not be the case. Maybe there is a mathematical proof deciding this question; maybe every mathematical question is decidable by an intuitive proof or disproof. Hilbert thought so; others have thought not; still others have thought the question unintelligible unless the notion of intuitive proof is replaced by that of formal proof in a single system. Certainly no one formal system decides all mathematical questions, as we know from Gödel. At any rate, and this is the important thing, the question is not trivial; even though someone said that it's necessary, if true at all, that every even number is the sum of two primes, it doesn't follow that anyone knows anything a priori about it. It doesn't even seem to me to follow without some further philosophical argument (it is an interesting philosophical question) that anyone *could* know anything a priori about it. The "could," as I said, involves some other modality. We mean that even if no one, perhaps even in the future, knows or will know a priori whether Goldbach's conjecture is right, in principle there is a way, which *could* have been used, of answering the question a priori. This assertion is not trivial.

The terms "necessary" and "a priori," then, as applied to statements, are *not* obvious synonyms. There may be a philosophical argument connecting them, perhaps even identifying them; but an argument is required, not simply the observation that the two terms are clearly interchangeable. (I will argue below that in fact they are not even coextensive—that necessary a posteriori truths, and probably contingent a priori truths, both exist.)

I think people have thought that these two things must mean the same for these reasons:

First, if something not only happens to be true in the actual world but is also true in all possible worlds, then, of course, just by running through all the possible worlds in our heads, we ought to be able with enough effort to see, if a statement is necessary, that it is necessary, and thus know it a priori. But really this is not so obviously feasible at all.

Second, I guess it's thought that, conversely, if something is known a priori it must be necessary, because it was known without looking at the world. If it depended on some contingent feature of the actual world, how could you know it without looking? Maybe the actual world is one of the possible worlds in which it would have been false. This depends on the thesis that there can't be a way of knowing about the actual world without looking that wouldn't be a way of knowing the same thing about every possible world. This involves problems of epistemology and the nature of knowledge; and of course it is very vague as stated. But it is not really *trivial* either. More important than any particular example of something which is alleged to be necessary and not a priori or a priori and not necessary, is to see that the notions are different, that it's not trivial to argue on the basis of something's being something which maybe we can only know a posteriori, that it's not a necessary truth. It's not trivial, just because something is known in some sense a priori, that what is known is a necessary truth.

Another term used in philosophy is "analytic." Here it won't be too important to get any clearer about this in this talk. The common examples of analytic statements, nowadays, are like "bachelors are unmarried." Kant (someone just pointed out to me) gives as an example "gold is a yellow metal," which seems to me an extraordinary one, because it's something I think that can turn out to be false. At any rate, let's just make it a matter of stipulation

that an analytic statement is, in some sense, true by virtue of its meaning and true in all possible worlds by virtue of its meaning. Then something which is analytically true will be both necessary and a priori. (That's sort of stipulative.)

Another category I mentioned was that of certainty. Whatever certainty is, it's clearly not obviously the case that everything which is necessary is certain. Certainty is another epistemological notion. Something can be known, or at least rationally believed, a priori, without being quite certain. You've read a proof in the math book; and, though you think it's correct, maybe you've made a mistake. You often do make mistakes of this kind. You've made a computation, perhaps with an error.

Let's use some terms quasi-technically. Let's call something a *rigid designator* if in every possible world it designates the same object, a *non-rigid* or *accidental designator* if that is not the case. Of course we don't require that the objects exist in all possible worlds. Certainly Nixon might not have existed if his parents had not gotten married, in the normal course of things. When we think of a property as essential to an object we usually mean that it is true of that object in any case where it would have existed. A rigid designator of a necessary existent can be called *strongly rigid*.

One of the intuitive theses I will maintain in these talks is that *names* are rigid designators. Certainly they seem to satisfy the intuitive test: although someone other than the US President in 1970 might have been the US President in 1970 (e.g. Humphrey might have), no one other than Nixon might have been Nixon. In the same way, a designator rigidly designates a certain object if it designates that object wherever the object exists; if, in addition, the object is a necessary existent, the designator can be called *strongly rigid*. For example, "the President of the US in 1970" designates a certain man, Nixon; but someone else (e.g. Humphrey) might have been the President in 1970, and Nixon might not have; so this designator is not rigid.

In these lectures I will argue, intuitively, that proper names are rigid designators, for although the man (Nixon) might not have been the President, it is not the case that he might not have been Nixon (though he might not have been *called* "Nixon"). Those who have argued that to make sense of the notion of rigid designator, we must antecedently make sense of "criteria of transworld identity" have precisely reversed the cart and the horse; it is *because* we can refer (rigidly) to Nixon, and stipulate that we are speaking of what might have happened to *him* (under certain circumstances), that "transworld identifications" are unproblematic in such cases.[1]

The tendency to demand purely qualitative descriptions of counterfactual situations has many sources. One, perhaps, is the confusion of the epistemological and the metaphysical, between a prioricity and necessity. If someone identifies necessity with a prioricity, and thinks that objects are named by means of uniquely identifying properties, he may think that it is the properties used to identify the object which, being known about it a priori, must be used to identify it in all possible worlds, to find out which object is Nixon. As against this, I repeat: (1) Generally, things aren't "found out" about a counterfactual situation, they are stipulated; (2) possible worlds need not be given purely qualitatively, as if we were looking at them through a telescope. And we will see shortly that the properties an object has in every counterfactual world have nothing to do with properties used to identify it in the actual world.

Above I said that the Frege–Russell view that names are introduced by description could be taken either as a theory of the meaning of names (Frege and Russell seemed to take it this way) or merely as a theory of their reference. Let me give an example, not involving what would usually be called a "proper name," to illustrate this. Suppose someone stipulates that 100 degrees centigrade is to be the temperature at which water boils at sea level. This isn't completely precise because the pressure may vary at sea level. Of course, historically, a more precise definition was given later. But let's suppose that this were the definition. Another sort of example in the literature is that one metre is to be the length of S where S is a certain stick or bar in Paris. (Usually people who like to talk about these definitions then try to make "the length of" into an "operational" concept. But it's not important.)

Wittgenstein says something very puzzling about this. He says: "There is one thing of which one can say neither that it is one metre long nor that it is not one metre long, and that is the standard metre in Paris. But this is, of course, not to

ascribe any extraordinary property to it, but only to mark its peculiar role in the language game of measuring with a metre rule."[2] This seems to be a very "extraordinary property," actually, for any stick to have. I think he must be wrong. If the stick is a stick, for example, 39.37 inches long (I assume we have some different standard for inches), why isn't it one metre long? Anyway, let's suppose that he is wrong and that the stick is one metre long. Part of the problem which is bothering Wittgenstein is, of course, that this stick serves as a standard of length and so we can't attribute length to it. Be this as it may (well, it may not be), is the statement "Stick S is one metre long," a necessary truth? Of course its length might vary in time. We could make the definition more precise by stipulating that one metre is to be the length of S at a fixed time t_0. Is it then a necessary truth that stick S is one metre long at time t_0? Someone who thinks that everything one knows a priori is necessary might think: "This is the *definition* of a metre. By definition, stick S is one metre long at t_0. That's a necessary truth." But there seems to me to be no reason so to conclude, even for a man who uses the stated definition of "one metre." For he's using this definition not to *give the meaning* of what he called the "metre," but to *fix the reference*. (For such an abstract thing as a unit of length, the notion of reference may be unclear. But let's suppose it's clear enough for the present purposes.) He uses it to fix a reference. There is a certain length which he wants to mark out. He marks it out by an accidental property, namely that there is a stick of that length. Someone else might mark out the same reference by another accidental property. But in any case, even though he uses this to fix the reference of his standard of length, a metre, he can still say, "if heat had been applied to this stick S at t_0, then at t_0 stick S would not have been one metre long."

Well, why can he do this? Part of the reason may lie in some people's minds in the philosophy of science, which I don't want to go into here. But a simple answer to the question is this: Even if this is the *only* standard of length that he uses,[3] there is an intuitive difference between the phrase "one metre" and the phrase "the length of S at t_0." The first phrase is meant to designate rigidly a certain length in all possible worlds, which in the actual world happens to be the length of the stick S at t_0. On the other hand "the length of S at t_0" does not designate anything rigidly. In some counterfactual situations the stick might have been longer and in some shorter, if various stresses and strains had been applied to it. So we can say of this stick, the same way as we would of any other of the same substance and length, that if heat of a given quantity had been applied to it, it would have expanded to such and such a length. Such a counterfactual statement, being true of other sticks with identical physical properties, will also be true of this stick. There is no conflict between that counterfactual statement and the definition of "one metre" as "the length of S at t_0," because the "definition," properly interpreted, does *not* say that the phrase "one metre" is to be *synonymous* (even when talking about counterfactual situations) with the phrase "the length of S at t_0," but rather that we have *determined the reference* of the phrase "one metre" by stipulating that "one metre" is to be a *rigid* designator of the length which is in fact the length of S at t_0. So this does *not* make it a necessary truth that S is one metre long at t_0. In fact, under certain circumstances, S would not have been one metre long. The reason is that one designator ("one metre") is rigid and the other designator ("the length of S at t_0") is not.

What then, is the *epistemological* status of the statement "Stick S is one metre long at t_0," for someone who has fixed the metric system by reference to stick S? It would seem that he knows it a priori. For if he used stick S to fix the reference of the term "one metre," then as a result of this kind of "definition" (which is not an abbreviative or synonymous definition), he knows automatically, without further investigation, that S is one metre long.[4] On the other hand, even if S is used as the standard of a metre, the *metaphysical* status of "S is one metre long" will be that of a contingent statement, provided that "one metre" is regarded as a rigid designator: under appropriate stresses and strains, heatings or coolings, S would have had a length other than one metre even at t_0. (Such statements as "Water boils at 100 degrees centigrade, at sea level" can have a similar status.) So in this sense, there are contingent a priori truths. More important for present purposes, though, than accepting this example as an instance of the contingent a priori, is its illustration of the distinction between "definitions" which fix a reference and those which give a synonym.

In the case of names one might make this distinction too. Suppose the reference of a name is given by a description or a cluster of descriptions. If the name *means the same* as that description or cluster of descriptions, it will not be a rigid designator. It will not necessarily designate the same object in all possible worlds, since other objects might have had the given properties in other possible worlds, unless (of course) we happened to use essential properties in our description. So suppose we say, "Aristotle is the greatest man who studied with Plato." If we used that as a *definition*, the name "Aristotle" is to mean "the greatest man who studied with Plato." Then of course in some other possible world that man might not have studied with Plato and some other man would have been Aristotle. If, on the other hand, we merely use the description to *fix the referent* then that man will be the referent of "Aristotle" in all possible worlds. The only use of the description will have been to pick out to which man we mean to refer. But then, when we say counterfactually "suppose Aristotle had never gone into philosophy at all," we need not mean "suppose a man who studied with Plato, and taught Alexander the Great, and wrote this and that, and so on, had never gone into philosophy at all," which might seem like a contradiction. We need only mean, "suppose that *that man* had never gone into philosophy at all."

It seems plausible to suppose that, in some cases, the reference of a name is indeed fixed *via* a description in the same way that the metric system was fixed. When the mythical agent first saw Hesperus, he may well have fixed his reference by saying, "I shall use 'Hesperus' as a name of the heavenly body appearing in yonder position in the sky." He then fixed the reference of "Hesperus" by its apparent celestial position. Does it follow that it is part of the *meaning* of the name that Hesperus has such and such position at the time in question? Surely not: if Hesperus had been hit earlier by a comet, it might have been visible at a different position at that time. In such a counterfactual situation we would say that Hesperus would not have occupied that position, but not that Hesperus would not have been Hesperus. The reason is that "Hesperus" rigidly designates a certain heavenly body and "the body in yonder position" does not—a different body, or no body might have been in that position, but no other body might have been Hesperus (though another body, not Hesperus, might have been *called* "Hesperus"). Indeed, as I have said, I will hold that names are always rigid designators.

I guess the main thing I'll talk about now is identity statements between names. But I hold the following about the general case. First, that characteristic theoretical identifications like "Heat is the motion of molecules," are not contingent truths but necessary truths, and here of course I don't mean just physically necessary, but necessary in the highest degree—whatever that means. (Physical necessity *might* turn out to be necessity in the highest degree. But that's a question which I don't wish to prejudge. At least for this sort of example, it might be that when something's physically necessary, it always is necessary *tout court*.) Second, that the way in which these have turned out to be necessary truths does not seem to me to be a way in which the mind-brain identities could turn out to be either necessary or contingently true. So this analogy has to go. It's hard to see what to put in its place. It's hard to see therefore how to avoid concluding that the two are actually different.

Let me go back to the more mundane case about proper names. This is already mysterious enough. There's a dispute about this between Quine and Ruth Barcan Marcus.[5] Marcus says that identities between names are necessary. If someone thinks that Cicero is Tully, and really uses "Cicero" and "Tully" as names, he is thereby committed to holding that his belief is a necessary truth. She uses the term "mere tag." Quine replies as follows, "We may tag the planet Venus, some fine evening, with the proper name "Hesperus." We may tag the same planet again, some day before sunrise, with the proper name "Phosphorus." When we discover that we have tagged the same planet twice our discovery is empirical. And not because the proper names were descriptions."[6] First, as Quine says when we discovered that we tagged the same planet twice, our discovery was empirical. Another example I think Quine gives in another book is that the same mountain seen from Nepal and from Tibet, or something like that, is from one angle called "Mt. Everest" (you've heard of that); from another it's supposed to be called "Gaurisanker." It can actually be an empirical discovery that Gaurisanker is Everest. (Quine says that the exam-

ple is actually false. He got the example from Erwin Schrödinger. You wouldn't think the inventor of wave mechanics got things that wrong. I don't know where the mistake is supposed to come from. One could certainly imagine this situation as having been the case; and it's another good illustration of the sort of thing that Quine has in mind.)

What about it? I wanted to find a good quote on the other side from Marcus in this book but I am having trouble locating one. Being present at that discussion, I remember[7] that she advocated the view that if you really have names, a good dictionary should be able to tell you whether they have the same reference. So someone should be able, by looking in the dictionary, to say that Hesperus and Phosphorus are the same. Now this does not seem to be true. It does seem, to many people, to be a consequence of the view that identities between names are necessary. Therefore the view that identity statements between names are necessary has usually been rejected. Russell's conclusion was somewhat different. He did think there should never be any empirical question whether two names have the same reference. This isn't satisfied for ordinary names, but it is satisfied when you're naming your own sense datum, or something like that. You say, "Here, this, and that (designating the same sense datum by both demonstratives)." So you can tell without empirical investigation that you're naming the same thing twice; the conditions are satisfied. Since this won't apply to ordinary cases of naming, ordinary "names" cannot be genuine names.

What should we think about this? First, it's true that someone can use the name "Cicero" to refer to Cicero and the name "Tully" to refer to Cicero also, and not know that Cicero is Tully. So it seems that we do not necessarily know a priori that an identity statement between names is true. It doesn't follow from this that the statement so expressed is a contingent one if true. This is what I've emphasized in my first lecture. There is a very strong feeling that leads one to think that, if you can't know something by a priori ratiocination, then it's got to be contingent: it might have turned out otherwise; but nevertheless I think this feeling is wrong.

Let's suppose we refer to the same heavenly body twice, as "Hesperus" and "Phosphorus." We say: Hesperus is that star over there in the evening; Phosphorus is that star over there in the morning.

Actually, Hesperus is Phosphorus. Are there really circumstances under which Hesperus wouldn't have been Phosphorus? Supposing that Hesperus is Phosphorus, let's try to describe a possible situation in which it would not have been. Well, it's easy. Someone goes by and he calls two *different* stars "Hesperus" and "Phosphorus." It may even be under the same conditions as prevailed when we introduced the names "Hesperus" and "Phosphorus." But are those circumstances in which Hesperus is not Phosphorus or would not have been Phosphorus? It seems to me that they are not.

Now, of course I'm committed to saying that they're not, by saying that such terms as "Hesperus" and "Phosphorus," when used as names, are rigid designators. They refer in every possible world to the planet Venus. Therefore, in that possible world too, the planet Venus is the planet Venus and it doesn't matter what any other person has said in this other possible world. How should *we* describe this situation? He can't have pointed to Venus twice, and in the one case called it "Hesperus" and in the other "Phosphorus," as we did. If he did so, then "Hesperus is Phosphorus" would have been true in that situation too. He pointed maybe neither time to the planet Venus—at least one time he didn't point to the planet Venus, let's say when he pointed to the body he called "Phosphorus." Then in that case we can certainly say that the name "Phosphorus" might not have referred to Phosphorus. We can even say that in the very position when viewed in the morning that we found Phosphorus, it might have been the case that Phosphorus was not there—that something else was there, and that even, under certain circumstances it would have been *called* "Phosphorus." But that still is not a case in which Phosphorus was not Hesperus. There might be a possible world in which, a possible counterfactual situation in which, "Hesperus" and "Phosphorus" weren't names of the things they in fact are names of. Someone, if he did determine their reference by identifying descriptions, might even have used the very identifying descriptions we used. But still that's not a case in which Hesperus wasn't Phosphorus. For there couldn't have been such a case, given that Hesperus is Phosphorus.

Now this seems very strange because in advance, we are inclined to say, the answer to the question whether Hesperus is Phosphorus might have turned out either way. So aren't there really two possible worlds—one in which Hesperus was Phosphorus, the other in which Hesperus wasn't Phosphorus—in advance of our discovering that these were the same? First, there's one sense in which things might turn out either way, in which it's clear that that doesn't imply that the way it finally turns out isn't necessary. For example, the four-colour theorem might turn out to be true and might turn out to be false. It might turn out either way. It still doesn't mean that the way it turns out is not necessary. Obviously, the "might" here is purely "epistemic"—it merely expresses our present state of ignorance, or uncertainty.

But it seems that in the Hesperus–Phosphorus case, something even stronger is true. The evidence I have before I know that Hesperus is Phosphorus is that I see a certain star or a certain heavenly body in the evening and call it "Hesperus," and in the morning and call it "Phosphorus." I know these things. There certainly is a possible world in which a man should have seen a certain star at a certain position in the evening and called it "Hesperus" and a certain star in the morning and called it "Phosphorus"; and should have concluded—should have found out by empirical investigations—that he names two different stars, or two different heavenly bodies. At least one of these stars or heavenly bodies was not Phosphorus, otherwise it couldn't have come out that way. But that's true. And so it's true that given the evidence that someone has antecedent to his empirical investigation, he can be placed in a sense in exactly the same situation, that is a qualitatively identical epistemic situation, and call two heavenly bodies "Hesperus" and "Phosphorus," without their being identical. So in that sense we can say that it might have turned out either way. Not that it might have turned out either way as to Hesperus's being Phosphorus. Though for all we knew in advance, Hesperus wasn't Phosphorus, that couldn't have turned out any other way, in a sense. But being put in a situation where we have exactly the same evidence, qualitatively speaking, it could have turned out that Hesperus was not Phosphorus; that is, in a counterfactual world in which "Hesperus" and "Phosphorus" were not used in the way that we use them, as names of this planet, but as names of some other objects, one could have had qualitatively identical evidence and concluded that "Hesperus" and "Phosphorus" named two different objects.[8] But we, using the names as we do right now, can say in advance, that if Hesperus and Phosphorus are one and the same, then in no other possible world can they be different. We use "Hesperus" as the name of a certain body and "Phosphorus" as the name of a certain body. We use them as names of those bodies in all possible worlds. If, in fact, they are the *same* body, then in any other possible world we have to use them as a name of that object. And so in any other possible world it will be true that Hesperus is Phosphorus. So two things are true: first, that we do not know a priori that Hesperus is Phosphorus, and are in no position to find out the answer except empirically. Second, this is so because we could have evidence qualitatively indistinguishable from the evidence we have and determine the reference of the two names by the positions of two planets in the sky, without the planets being the same.

Of course, it is only a contingent truth (not true in every other possible world) that the star seen over there in the evening is the star seen over there in the morning, because there are possible worlds in which Phosphorus was not visible in the morning. But that contingent truth shouldn't be identified with the statement that Hesperus is Phosphorus. It could only be so identified if you thought that it was a necessary truth that Hesperus is visible over there in the evening or that Phosphorus is visible over there in the morning. But neither of those are necessary truths even if that's the way we pick out the planet. These are the contingent marks by which we identify a certain planet and give it a name.

We have concluded that an identity statement between names, when true at all, is necessarily true, even though one may not know it a priori. Suppose we identify Hesperus as a certain star seen in the evening and Phosphorus as a certain star, or a certain heavenly body, seen in the morning; then there may be possible worlds in which two different planets would have been seen in just those positions in the evening and morning. However, at least one of them, and maybe both, would not have been Hesperus, and then that would not have been a situation in which Hesperus was not Phosphorus. It might have been a situation in which the planet seen in this position in the evening was not the planet seen in this position in the morning; but that

is not a situation in which Hesperus was not Phosphorus. It might also, if people gave the names "Hesperus" and "Phosphorus" to these planets, be a situation in which some planet other than Hesperus was called "Hesperus." But even so, it would not be a situation in which Hesperus itself was not Phosphorus.[9]

Some of the problems which bother people in these situations, as I have said, come from an identification, or as I would put it, a confusion, between what we can know a priori in advance and what is necessary. Certain statements—and the identity statement is a paradigm of such a statement on my view—if true at all must be necessarily true. One does know a priori, by philosophical analysis, that if such an identity statement is true it is necessarily true.

Notes

[1] Of course I don't imply that language contains a name for every object. Demonstratives can be used as rigid designators, and free variables can be used as rigid designators of unspecified objects. Of course when we specify a counterfactual situation, we do not describe the whole possible world, but only the portion which interests us.

[2] *Philosophical Investigations*, §50.

[3] Philosophers of science may see the key to the problem in a view that "one metre" is a "cluster concept." I am asking the reader hypothetically to suppose that the "definition" given is the *only* standard used to determine the metric system. I think the problem would still arise.

[4] Since the truth he knows is contingent, I choose *not* to call it "analytic," stipulatively requiring analytic truths to be both necessary and a priori.

[5] Ruth Barcan Marcus, "Modalities and Intensional Languages" (comments by W. V. Quine, plus discussion), *Boston Studies in the Philosophy of Science* (Dordrecht: Reidel, 1963), pp. 77–116.

[6] [Ibid.] p. 101.

[7] [Ibid.] p. 115.

[8] There is a more elaborate discussion of this point in the third lecture, in *Naming and Necessity*, where its relation to a certain sort of counterpart theory is also mentioned.

[9] Recall that we describe the situation in our language, not the language that the people in that situation would have used. Hence we must use the terms "Hesperus" and "Phosphorus" with the same reference as in the actual world. The fact that people in that situation might or might not have used these names for different planets is irrelevant. So is the fact that they might have done so using the very same descriptions as we did to fix their references.

Bibliography

Baergen, Ralph. *Contemporary Epistemology.* Fort Worth, TX: Harcourt Brace, 1995. Chapter 8.

Carruthers, Peter. *Human Knowledge and Human Nature.* Oxford: Oxford University Press, 1992.

Dancy, Jonathan, and Ernest Sosa, eds. *A Companion to Epistemology.* Oxford: Blackwell, 1992.

Goodman, Michael, and Robert Snyder, eds. *Contemporary Readings in Epistemology.* Upper Saddle River, NJ: Prentice Hall, 1993. Chapter 3.

Harris, J. F., and R. H. Severens, eds. *Analyticity: Selected Readings.* Chicago: Quadrangle Books, 1970.

Kitcher, Philip. "A Priori Knowledge." *Philosophical Review 76,* 1980.

Kitcher, Philip. "Aprioricity and Necessity." *Australasian Journal of Philosophy 58,* 1988.

Kripke, Saul. *Naming and Necessity.* Cambridge, MA: Harvard University Press, 1980.

Moser, Paul K., ed. *A Priori Knowledge.* Oxford: Oxford University Press. 1987.

Pap, Arthur. *The A Priori in Physical Theory.* New York: King's Crown Press, 1946.

Plantinga, Alvin. *The Nature of Necessity.* Oxford: Clarendon Press, 1974.

Sleigh, R. C., ed. *Necessary Truths.* Englewood Cliffs, NJ: Prentice Hall, 1972.

Steup, Matthias. *An Introduction to Contemporary Epistemology.* Upper Saddle River, NJ: Prentice Hall, 1996. Chapter 3.

Stitch, Stephen, ed. *Innate Ideas.* Berkeley: University of California Press, 1975.

Part VIII

The Justification of Induction

From a single experience, we sometimes make an inductive leap to the many; from *some* experiences of a certain kind, we often make a leap to judgments about *all* experiences of that kind. A child puts a hand on a red-hot stove and pulls away in pain and thereby learns never to put a hand on such a stove again. Another child forgets to look to the left when crossing a street and barely misses getting run down by a speeding vehicle, thereby learning never to cross the street without looking in both directions first. People who get food poisoning from eating a certain kind of mushroom learn never to eat that variety again. From the fact that some people have died, we infer that all people eventually die. From experiencing vegetables nourishing and cigarettes causing cancer, we generalize that vegetables always nourish and cigarettes always tend to cause cancer. From limited past experience, we generalize that water always boils at sea level at 100 degrees Celsius, that the Sun continues to rise, that the laws of motion and gravity always function.

From limited experiences, we generalize about future experiences. The food we eat, the friends we keep, the chairs we unthinkingly trust to support us, the way we walk, the buildings and trees we steer clear of, the clothes we wear, the sentences we speak, the cars we drive and the ways we drive them, the rules we obey, and the laws of nature we rely on all bear testimony to our faith in the principle of induction with its probability functions. Probability, said Locke, is

the guide to life. We cannot, experience tells us, live without it. Our existence as well as science itself is based on the principle of induction that tells us to reason from past frequencies to future likelihoods, from the limited known of the past and present to the unknown of the past, present, and future.

But though inductive probability is psychologically inescapable, we have trouble providing a rational justification for it. What argument is there for our belief that the laws of motion and the law of gravity will continue to exist next year or the year after? Why don't the laws of nature die or grow old and fragile like people or the laws of society? How do we know that the Sun will rise tomorrow or the week after? or that vegetables will continue to nourish us and cigarettes continue to cause cancer, rather than just the reverse? Why do we assume that the future will be like the past and present?

It was David Hume (1711–1776) who first raised the problem of *induction,* although he never used that term. Hume pointed out that the contrary of every matter of fact is always logically possible, because, unlike the truths of reason (logic and mathematics), it is never contradictory to deny a matter of fact. It is not logically necessary that Earth is now rotating or revolving around the Sun, nor that it will do so tomorrow. These are mere contingent truths. "That the Sun will not rise tomorrow is no less intelligible a proposition, and implies no more a contradiction than the affirmation that it will rise." And if the Sun's not rising is possible, what reason do we have for thinking it won't actually happen?

What is our justification for our belief regarding matters of fact? Hume asks. He replies that we justify that belief by our belief in causal laws and relationships. We believe that a causal order rooted in nature's laws operates to produce all that is. But what is the foundation of all our reasoning concerning cause and effect? "Experience," Hume replies. All our experience corroborates such relations. But, Hume relentlessly continues, "What is the foundation of all conclusions from experience?" His reply: "In reality, all arguments from experience are founded on the similarity which we discover among natural objects, and by which we are induced to expect effects similar to those which we have found to follow from such objects." Only a fool or a lunatic would pretend to dispute this faith in causality based on experience.

But experience "only shows us a number of uniform effects, resulting from certain objects and teaches us that those particular objects, at that particular time, were endowed with such powers and forces, when a new object, endowed with similar sensible qualities, is produced, we expect similar powers and forces, and look for a like effect. From a body of like color and consistence with bread we expect like nourishment and support. But this surely is a step or progress of the mind, which wants to be explained."

Reasoning from the proposition "I have always found so and so to happen in the past" to the proposition "So and so will continue to happen in the future" is a great leap that stands in need of justification.

We must admit, contends Hume, "that the inference is not intuitive; neither is it demonstrative. Of what nature is it then? To say it is experiential is begging the question. For all inferences from experience suppose, as their foundation, that the future will resemble the past. . . . It is impossible, therefore, that any argument from experience can prove this resem-

blance of the past to the future; since all these arguments are founded on the supposition of that resemblance."

Why may not the future turn out to be quite different from the past? "What logic, what processes of argument secure you against this supposition?"

Hume shows that our belief that the future would be like the past was based on our belief in the uniformity of nature, which in turn was based on our past experience, which is an inadequate premise for arguing for the future. The argument "The uniformity of nature has been reliable in the past so it will likely be reliable in the future" is not a sound deductive argument, because the conclusion contains more information than the premises. Inductive generalizations are, in the words of C. E. Peirce, "ampliative"—adding more data than the premises contain.

Hume's point is that we cannot justify the principle of induction via either a deductive or an inductive argument. Here is what he has in mind. Suppose we attempt to justify the principle of induction by means of a deductive argument. What premises should we use? Well, whatever they are, they must be known to be true. But because we do not know the future, the premises must be confined to the present and past. And because a valid deductive argument may not include in the conclusion any claims or information not already implicit in the premises, this argument can only include statements about the past and the present, not the future. But it is just the future that we are concerned with, so deductive arguments all fail to justify the principle of induction.

Suppose we try to justify the principle of induction by means of an inductive argument. We argue that the principle of induction has had a high probability of success until now, so we may conclude that it probably will continue to have a high probability of success in the future. But, the skeptic asks, what justifies us making the leap from the past to the future? A belief in the uniformity of nature? But, he (or she) continues, how do we know that the uniformity of nature will function in the future? Because it always has in the past, we respond. But now we are going around in circles, for we are appealing to the very principle that we would establish through induction—the principle of induction—and thus are begging the question.

Therefore neither a deductive nor an inductive argument establishes the principle of induction. In our second reading, Russell elaborates and interprets Hume's argument.

Since Hume's time there have been many attempts to justify induction. The general consensus says Hume is correct that no deductive argument can establish the truth of induction. But three other types of argumentation *have* enjoyed popularity: *sophisticated inductivism, pragmatic arguments,* and the *dissolution argument.* Each is represented in the readings in this part of the book. In "Will the Future Be Like the Past?" (Reading VIII.3) Frederick Will uses the metaphor of a contained expanse that successfully moves on to new territory to argue that there is something correct about using higher-order inductivism to establish lower-order induction. Hans Reichenbach in "The Pragmatic Justification of Induction" (Reading VIII.4) argues that the principle of induction is the only game in town. If this principle doesn't bring successful predictions, nothing will. In "Dissolving the Problem of Induction," Peter Strawson (Reading VIII.5) argues that it is a mistake to try to justify what is presupposed by the idea of justification itself.

In the final reading, Nelson Goodman goes one up on Hume. Instead of solving Hume's riddle, he sets forth a new riddle of induction, that of distinguishing between proper and improper projectable properties; that is, properties we are warranted in projecting into the future. To illustrate his problem, Goodman asks us to imagine a new color word *grue,* which is defined in terms of our old color words *green* and *blue.* An object is grue if and only if it is green at some time t before the year 2000 or blue at some time t during or after the year 2000.

All the emeralds we have so far observed have been observed before 2000, and so are grue. So, using the principle that the future will be like the past, we conclude that the emeralds we see after 2000 will be grue. But a grue emerald after 2000 is, by definition, blue. So the greenness of emeralds so far inductively supports the nongreenness of emeralds in the future, but that is a paradox.

We might protest that the grue and the green emerald seem exactly the same and that we see no reason whatsoever for imagining the property grue. But, avers Goodman, the point is that this intuitive judgment needs to be justified in terms of distinguishing between legitimate projectable regularities and illegitimate ones. Inductive logic itself doesn't do that for us. What does? Goodman's challenge is for new rules by which to sort out what is justifiably projectable and what is not.

VIII.1 The Problem of Induction

DAVID HUME

The Scottish philosopher David Hume (1711–1776) pointed out the problem of justifying our belief in induction in *An Enquiry Concerning Human Understanding* (1748) from which this selection is taken. Within the context of a discussion of causality, Hume argues that there is no way of proving or establishing as probable that the future will resemble the past. You cannot use a deductive argument, for a sound deductive argument disallows claims in the conclusion that are not found in the premises and the premises only contain information about the past and present, not the future. You cannot establish the principle of the induction by appealing to inductive experience, for that is assuming exactly the point in question: the validity of induction. Hume admits that we all take the principle of induction for granted and use it successfully every day, but philosophical curiosity prompts him to wonder at the difficulty of justifying the principle.

Sceptical Doubts Concerning the Operations of the Understanding

Part I

All the objects of human reason or enquiry may naturally be divided into two kinds, to wit, *Relations of Ideas,* and *Matters of Fact.* Of the first kind are the sciences of Geometry, Algebra, and Arithmetic; and in short, every affirmation which is either intuitively or demonstratively certain. *That the square of the hypotenuse is equal to the squares of the two sides,* is a proposition which expresses a relation between these figures. *That three times five is equal to the half of thirty,* expresses a relation between these numbers. Propositions of this kind are discoverable by the mere operation of thought, without dependence on what is anywhere existent in the universe. Though there never were a circle or triangle in nature, the truths demonstrated by Euclid would for ever retain their certainty and evidence.

Matters of fact, which are the second objects of human reason, are not ascertained in the same manner; nor is our evidence of their truth, however great, of a like nature with the foregoing. The con-

trary of every matter of fact is still possible; because it can never imply a contradiction, and is conceived by the mind with the same facility and distinctness, as if ever so comfortable to reality. *That the sun will not rise tomorrow* is no less intelligible a proposition, and implies no more contradiction than the affirmation, *that it will rise.* We should in vain, therefore, attempt to demonstrate its falsehood. Were it demonstratively false, it would imply a contradiction, and could never be distinctly conceived by the mind.

It may, therefore, be a subject worthy of curiosity, to enquire what is the nature of that evidence which assures us of any real existence and matter of fact, beyond the present testimony of our senses, or the records of our memory. This part of philosophy, it is observable, has been little cultivated, either by the ancients or moderns; and therefore our doubts and errors, in the prosecution of so important an enquiry, may be the more excusable; while we march through such difficult paths without any guide or direction. They may even prove useful, by exciting curiosity, and destroying that implicit faith and security, which is the bane of all reasoning and free enquiry. The discovery of defects in the common philosophy, if any such there be, will not, I presume, be a discouragement, but rather an incitement, as is usual, to attempt something more full and satisfactory than has yet been proposed to the public.

Reprinted from *An Enquiry Concerning Human Understanding* (1748).

All reasonings concerning matter of fact seem to be founded on the relation of *Cause and Effect.* By means of that relation alone we can go beyond the evidence of our memory and senses. If you were to ask a man, why he believes any matter of fact, which is absent; for instance, that his friend is in the country, or in France; he would give you a reason; and this reason would be some other fact; as a letter received from him, or the knowledge of his former resolutions and promises. A man finding a watch or any other machine in a desert island, would conclude that there had once been men in that island. All our reasonings concerning fact are of the same nature. And here it is constantly supposed that there is a connection between the present fact and that which is inferred from it. Were there nothing to bind them together, the inference would be entirely precarious. The hearing of an articulate voice and rational discourse in the dark assures us of the presence of some person: Why? because these are the effects of the human make and fabric, and closely connected with it. If we anatomize all the other reasonings of this nature, we shall find that they are founded on the relation of cause and effect, and that this relation is either near or remote, direct or collateral. Heat and light are collateral effects of fire, and the one effect may justly be inferred from the other.

If we would satisfy ourselves, therefore, concerning the nature of that evidence, which assures us of matters of fact, we must enquire how we arrive at the knowledge of cause and effect. . . .

This proposition, *that causes and effects are discoverable, not by reason but by experience,* will readily be admitted with regards to such objects, as we remember to have once been altogether unknown to us; since we must be conscious of the utter inability, which we then lay under, of foretelling what would arise from them. Present two smooth pieces of marble to a man who has no tincture of natural philosophy; he will never discover that they will adhere together in such a manner as to require great force to separate them in a direct line, while they make so small a resistance to a lateral pressure. Such events, as bear little analogy to the common course of nature, are also readily confessed to be known only by experience; nor does any man imagine that the explosion of gunpowder, or the attraction of a loadstone, could ever be discovered by arguments *a priori.* In like manner, when an effect is supposed to depend upon an intricate machinery or secret structure of parts, we make no difficulty in attributing all our knowledge of it to experience. Who will assert that he can give the ultimate reason, why milk or bread is proper nourishment for a man, not for a lion or a tiger?

But the same truth may not appear, at first sight, to have the same evidence with regard to events, which have become familiar to us from our first appearance in the world, which bear a close analogy to the whole course of nature, and which are supposed to depend on the simple qualities of objects, without any secret structure of parts. We are apt to imagine that we could discover these effects by the mere operation of our reason, without experience. We fancy, that were we brought on a sudden into this world, we could at first have inferred that one Billiard-ball would communicate motion to another upon impulse; and that we needed not to have waited for the event, in order to pronounce with certainty concerning it. Such is the influence of custom, that, where it is strongest, it not only covers our natural ignorance, but even conceals itself, and seems not to take place, merely because it is found in the highest degree.

But to convince us that all the laws of nature, and all the operations of bodies without exception, are known only by experience, the following reflections may, perhaps, suffice. Were any object presented to us, and were we required to pronounce concerning the effect, which will result from it, without consulting past observation; after what manner, I beseech you, must the mind proceed in this operation? It must invent or imagine some event, which it ascribes to the object as its effect; and it is plain that this invention must be entirely arbitrary. The mind can never possibly find the effect in the supposed cause, by the most accurate scrutiny and examination. For the effect is totally different from the cause, and consequently can never be discovered in it. Motion in the second Billiard-ball is a quite distinct event from motion in the first; nor is there anything in the one to suggest the smallest hint of the other. A stone or piece of metal raised into the air, and left without any support, immediately falls: but to consider the matter *a priori,* is there anything we discover in this situation which can beget the idea of a downward, rather than an upward, or any other motion, in the stone or metal?

And as the first imagination or invention of a particular effect, in all natural operations, is arbitrary, where we consult not experience; so must we also esteem the supposed tie or connection between the cause and effect, which binds them together, and renders it impossible that any other effect could result from the operation of that cause. When I see, for instance, a Billiard-ball moving in a straight line towards another; even suppose motion in the second ball should by accident be suggested to me, as the result of their contact or impulse; may I not conceive, that a hundred different events might as well follow from that cause? May not both these balls remain at absolute rest? May not the first ball return in a straight line, or leap off from the second in any line or direction? All these suppositions are consistent and conceivable. Why then should we give the preference to one, which is no more consistent or conceivable than the rest? All our reasonings *a priori* will never be able to show us any foundation for this preference.

In a word, then, every effect is a distinct event from its cause. It could not, therefore, be discovered in the cause, and the first invention or conception of it, *a priori,* must be entirely arbitrary. And even after it is suggested, the conjunction of it with the cause must appear equally arbitrary; since there are always many other effects, which, to reason, must seem fully as consistent and natural. In vain, therefore, should we pretend to determine any single event, or infer any cause of effect, without the assistance of observation and experience. . . .

Part II

But we have not yet attained any tolerable satisfaction with regard to the question first proposed. Each solution still gives rise to a new question as difficult as the foregoing, and leads us on to farther enquiries. When it is asked, *What is the nature of all our reasonings concerning matter of fact?* the proper answer seems to be, that they are founded on the relation of cause and effect. When again it is asked, *What is the foundation of all our reasonings and conclusions concerning that relation?* it may be replied in one word, Experience. But if we still carry on our sifting humor, and ask, *What is the foundation of all conclusions from experience?* this implies a new question, which may be of more

difficult solution and explication. Philosophers, that give themselves airs of superior wisdom and sufficiency, have a hard task when they encounter persons of inquisitive dispositions, who push them from every corner to which they retreat, and who are sure at last to bring them to some dangerous dilemma. The best expedient to prevent this confusion, is to be modest in our pretensions; and even to discover the difficulty ourselves before it is objected to us. By this means, we may make a kind of merit of our very ignorance.

I shall content myself, in this section, with an easy task, and shall pretend only to give a negative answer to the question here proposed. I say then, that, even after we have experience of the operations of cause and effect, our conclusions from that experience are *not* founded on reasoning, or any process of the understanding. This answer we must endeavor both to explain and to defend. . . .

In reality, all arguments from experience are founded on the similarity which we discover among natural objects, and by which we are induced to expect effects similar to those which we have found to follow from such objects. And though none but a fool or madman will ever pretend to dispute the authority of experience, or to reject that great guide of human life, it may surely be allowed a philosopher to have so much curiosity at least as to examine the principle of human nature, which gives this mighty authority to experience, and makes us draw advantage from that similarity which nature has placed among different objects. From causes which appear *similar* we expect similar effects. This is the sum of all our experimental conclusions. Now it seems evident that, if this conclusion were formed by reason, it would be as perfect at first, and upon one instance, as after ever so long a course of experience. But the case is far otherwise. Nothing so like as eggs; yet no one, on account of this appearing similarity, expects the same taste and relish in all of them. It is only after a long course of uniform experiments in any kind, that we attain a firm reliance and security with regard to a particular event. Now where is that process of reasoning which, from one instance, draws a conclusion, so different from that which it infers from a hundred instances that are nowise different from that single one? This question I propose as much for the sake of information, as with an intention of raising difficulties. I cannot find, I cannot imagine any such reasoning. But I keep my mind still open to instruction, if any one will vouchsafe to bestow it on me.

Should it be said that, from a number of uniform experiments, we *infer* a connection between the sensible qualities and the secret powers; this, I must confess, seems the same difficulty, couched in different terms. The question still recurs, on what process of argument this inference is founded? Where is the medium, the interposing ideas, which join propositions so very wide of each other? It is confessed that the color, consistence, and other sensible qualities of bread appear not, of themselves, to have any connection with the secret powers of nourishment and support. For otherwise we could infer these secret powers from the first appearance of these sensible qualities, without the aid of experience; contrary to the sentiment of all philosophers, and contrary to plain matter of fact. Here, then, is our natural state of ignorance with regard to the powers and influence of all objects. How is this remedied by experience? It only shows us a number of uniform effects, resulting from certain objects, and teaches us that those particular objects, at that particular time, were endowed with such powers and forces. When a new object, endowed with similar sensible qualities, is produced, we expect similar powers and forces, and look for a like effect. From a body of like color and consistence with bread we expect like nourishment and support. But this surely is a step or progress of the mind, which wants to be explained. When a man says, *I have found, in all past instances, such sensible qualities conjoined with such secret powers:* And when he says, *Similar sensible qualities will always be conjoined with similar secret powers,* he is not guilty of a tautology, nor are these propositions in any respect the same. You say that the one proposition is an inference from the other. But you must confess that the inference is not intuitive; neither is it demonstrative: Of what nature is it, then? To say it is experimental, is begging the question. For all inferences from experience suppose, as their foundation, that the future will resemble the past, and that similar powers will be conjoined with similar sensible qualities. If there be any suspicion that the course of nature may change, and that the past may be no rule for the future, all experience becomes useless, and can give rise to no inference or conclusion. It is impossible, therefore, that any arguments from experience can prove this resemblance of the past to the future; since all these arguments are founded on the supposition of that resemblance. Let the course of things be allowed hitherto ever so regular; that alone, without some new argument or inference, proves not that, for the future, it will continue so. In vain do you pretend to have learned the nature of bodies from your past experience. Their secret nature, and consequently all their effects and influence, may change, without any change in their sensible qualities. This happens sometimes, and with regard to some objects: Why may it [not] happen always, and with regard to all objects? What logic, what process of argument secures you against this supposition? My practice, you say, refutes my doubts. But you mistake the purport of my question. As an agent, I am quite satisfied in the point; but as a philosopher, who has some share of curiosity, I will not say scepticism, I want to learn the foundation of this inference. No reading, no enquiry has yet been able to remove my difficulty, or give me satisfaction in a matter of such importance. Can I do better than propose the difficulty to the public, even though, perhaps, I have small hopes of obtaining a solution? We shall, at least, by this means, be sensible of our ignorance, if we do not augment our knowledge.

I must confess that a man is guilty of unpardonable arrogance who concludes, because an argument has escaped his own investigation, that therefore it does not really exist. I must also confess that, though all the learned, for several ages, should have employed themselves in fruitless search upon any subject, it may still, perhaps, be rash to conclude positively that the subject must, therefore, pass all human comprehension. Even though we examine all the sources of our knowledge, and conclude them unfit for such a subject, there may still remain a suspicion, that the enumeration is not complete, or the examination not accurate. But with regard to the present subject, there are some considerations which seem to remove all this accusation of arrogance or suspicion of mistake.

It is certain that the most ignorant and stupid peasants—nay infants, nay even brute beasts—improve by experience, and learn the qualities of natural objects, by observing the effects which result from them. When a child has felt the sensation of pain from touching the flame of a candle, he will be careful not to put his hand near any candle; but will expect a similar effect from a cause which is similar in its sensible qualities and appearance. If you assert, therefore, that the understanding of the child is led into this conclusion by any process of argument or ratiocination, I may justly require you to produce that argument; nor have you any pretense to refuse so equitable a demand. You cannot say that the argument is abstruse, and may possibly escape your enquiry; since you confess that it is obvious to the capacity of a mere infant. If you hesitate, therefore, a moment, or if, after reflection, you produce any intricate or profound argument, you, in a manner, give up the question, and confess that it is not reasoning which engages us to suppose the past resembling the future, and to expect similar effects from causes which are, to appearance, similar. This is the proposition which I intended to enforce in the present section. If I be right, I pretend not to have made any mighty discovery. And if I be wrong, I must acknowledge myself to be indeed a very backward scholar; since I cannot now discover an argument which, it seems, was perfectly familiar to me long before I was out of my cradle.

Sceptical Solution of These Doubts

Part I

. . . Nature will always maintain her rights, and prevail in the end over any abstract reasoning whatsoever. Though we should conclude, for instance, as in the foregoing section, that, in all reasonings from experience, there is a step taken by the mind which is not supported by any argument or process of the understanding; there is no danger that these reasonings, on which almost all knowledge depends, will ever be affected by such a discovery. If the mind be not engaged by argument to make this step, it must be induced by some other principle of equal weight and authority; and that principle will preserve its influence as long as human nature remains the same. What that principle is may well be worth the pains of enquiry.

Suppose a person, though endowed with the strongest faculties of reason and reflection, to be brought on a sudden into this world; he would, indeed, immediately observe a continual succession of objects, and one event following another, but he would not be able to discover anything farther. He would not, at first, by any reasoning, be able to reach the idea of cause and effect; since the particular powers, by which all natural operations are performed, never appear to the senses; nor is it reasonable to conclude, merely because one event, in one instance, precedes another, that therefore the one is the cause, the other the effect. Their conjunction may be arbitrary and casual. There may be no reason to infer the existence of one from the appearance of the other. And in a word, such a person, without more experience, could never employ his conjecture or reasoning concerning any matter of fact, or be assured of anything beyond what was immediately present to his memory and senses.

Suppose, again, that he has acquired more experience, and has lived so long in the world as to have observed familiar objects or events to be constantly conjoined together; what is the consequence of this experience? He immediately infers the existence of one object from the appearance of the other. Yet he has not, by all his experience, acquired any idea or knowledge of the secret power by which the one object produces the other; nor is it, by any process of reasoning, he is engaged to draw this inference. But still he finds himself determined to draw it: And though he should be convinced that his understanding has no part in the operation, he would nevertheless continue in the same course of thinking. There is some other principle which determines him to form such a conclusion.

This principle is Custom or Habit. For wherever the repetition of any particular act or operation produces a propensity to renew the same act or operation, without being impelled by any reasoning or process of the understanding, we always say, that this propensity is the effect of *Custom*. By employing that word, we pretend not to have given the ultimate reason of such a propensity. We only point out a principle of human nature, which is universally acknowledged, and which is well known by its effects. Perhaps we can push our enquiries no farther, or pretend to give the cause of this cause; but must rest contented with it as the ultimate principle, which we can assign, of all our conclusions from experience. It is sufficient satisfaction, that we can go so far, without repining at the narrowness of our faculties because they will carry us no farther. And it is certain we here advance a very intelligible proposition at least, if not a true one, when we assert that, after the constant conjunction of two objects—heat and flame, for instance, weight and solidity—we are determined by custom alone to expect the one from the appearance of the other. This hypothesis seems even the only one which explains the difficulty, why we draw, from a thousand instances, an inference which we are not able to draw from one instance, that is, in no respect, different from them. Reason is incapable of any such variation. The conclusions which it draws from considering one circle are the same which it would form upon surveying all the circles in the universe. But no man, having seen only one body move after being impelled by another, could infer that every other body will move after a like impulse. All inferences from experience, therefore, are effects of custom, not of reasoning.

Custom, then, is the great guide of human life. It is that principle alone which renders our experience useful to us, and makes us expect, for the future, a similar train of events with those which have appeared in the past. Without the influence of custom, we should be entirely ignorant of every matter of fact beyond what is immediately present to the memory and senses. We should never know how to adjust means to ends, or to employ our natural powers in the production of any effect. There would be an end at once of all action, as well as of the chief part of speculation.

But here it may be proper to remark, that though our conclusions from experience carry us beyond our memory and senses, and assure us of matters of fact which happened in the most distant places and most remote ages, yet some fact must always be present to the senses or memory, from which we may first proceed in drawing these conclusions. A man, who should find in a desert country the remains of pompous buildings, would conclude that the country had, in ancient times, been cultivated by civilized inhabitants, but did nothing of this nature occur to him, he could never form such an inference. We learn the events of former ages from history; but then we must

peruse the volumes in which this instruction is contained, and thence carry up our inferences from one testimony to another, till we arrive at the eyewitnesses and spectators of these distant events. In a word, if we proceed not upon some fact, present to the memory or senses, our reasonings would be merely hypothetical; and however the particular links might be connected with each other, the whole chain of inferences would have nothing to support it, nor could we ever, by its means, arrive at the knowledge of any real existence. If I ask why you believe any particular matter of fact, which you relate, you must tell me some reason; and this reason will be some other fact, connected, with it. But as you cannot proceed after this manner, *in infinitum,* you must at last terminate in some fact, which is present to your memory or senses; or must allow that your belief is entirely without foundation.

What, then, is the conclusion of the whole matter? A simple one; though, it must be confessed, pretty remote from the common theories of philosophy. All belief of matter of fact or real existence is derived merely from some object, present to the memory or senses, and a customary conjunction between that and some other object. Or in other words; having found in many instances, that any two kinds of objects—flame and heat, snow and cold—have always been conjoined together, if flame or snow be presented anew to the senses, the mind is carried by custom to expect heat or cold, and to *believe* that such a quality does exist, and will discover itself upon a nearer approach. This belief is the necessary result of placing the mind in such circumstances. It is an operation of the soul, when we are so situated, as unavoidable as to feel the passion of love, when we receive benefits; or hatred, when we meet with injuries. All these operations are a species of natural instincts, which no reasoning or process of the thought and understanding is able either to produce or to prevent.

VIII.2 On Induction

BERTRAND RUSSELL

Bertrand Russell (1872–1970), one of the greatest philosophers in the twentieth century, in his pithy *Problems of Philosophy* (1912), offers the clearest elaboration of Hume's problem that we can have no knowledge of the past. At best, arguments supporting the principle of induction give us justification for past futures but not future futures. He points out that fundamental laws of science are in question in Hume's challenge and that the principle is as unproved as it is undeniable.

In almost all our previous discussions we have been concerned in the attempt to get clear as to our data in the way of knowledge of existence. What things are there in the universe whose existence is known to us owing to our being acquainted with them? So far, our answer has been that we are acquainted with our sense-data, and, probably, with ourselves. These we know to exist. And past sense-data which are remembered are known to have existed in the past. This knowledge supplies our data.

But if we are to be able to draw inferences from these data—if we are to know of the existence of matter, of other people, of the past before our individual memory begins, or of the future, we must know general principles of some kind by means of which such inferences can be drawn. It must be known to us that the existence of some one sort of thing, A, is a sign of the existence of some other sort of thing, B, either at the same time as A or at some earlier or later time, as, for example, thunder is a sign of the earlier existence of lightning. If this were not known to us, we could never extend our knowledge beyond the sphere of our private experience; and this sphere, as we have seen, is exceedingly limited. The question we have now to consider is whether such an extension is possible, and if so, how it is effected.

Let us take as an illustration a matter about which none of us, in fact, feel the slightest doubt. We are all convinced that the sun will rise tomorrow. Why? Is this belief a mere blind outcome of past experience, or can it be justified as a reasonable belief? It is not easy to find a test by which to judge whether a belief of this kind is reasonable or not, but we can at least ascertain what sort of general beliefs would suffice, if true, to justify the judgement that the sun will rise to-morrow, and the many other similar judgements upon which our actions are based.

It is obvious that if we are asked why we believe that the sun will rise to-morrow, we shall naturally answer, "Because it always has risen every day." We have a firm belief that it will rise in the future, because it has risen in the past. If we are challenged as to why we believe that it will continue to rise as heretofore, we may appeal to the laws of motion: the earth, we shall say, is a freely rotating body, and such bodies do not cease to rotate unless something interferes from outside, and there is nothing outside to interfere with the earth between now and to-morrow. Of course it might be doubted whether we are quite certain that there is nothing outside to interfere, but this is not the interesting doubt. The interesting doubt is as to whether the laws of motion will remain in operation until to-morrow. If this doubt is raised, we find ourselves in the same position as when the doubt about the sunrise was first raised.

The *only* reason for believing that the laws of motion will remain in operation is that they have operated hitherto, so far as our knowledge of the past enables us to judge. It is true that we have a greater body of evidence from the past in favour of the laws of motion than we have in favour of the sunrise, because the sunrise is merely a particular case of fulfilment of the laws of motion, and there are countless other particular cases. But the real question is: Do *any* number of cases of a law being fulfilled in the past afford evidence that it will be fulfilled in the future? If not, it becomes plain that we have no ground whatever for expecting the sun

Reprinted from *The Problems of Philosophy* (Oxford, England: Oxford University Press, 1912) by permission of the publisher.

to rise to-morrow, or for expecting the bread we shall eat at our next meal not to poison us, or for any of the other scarcely conscious expectations that control our daily lives. It is to be observed that all such expectations are only *probable;* thus we have not to seek for a proof that they *must* be fulfilled, but only for some reason in favour of the view that they are *likely* to be fulfilled.

Now in dealing with this question we must, to begin with, make an important distinction, without which we should soon become involved in hopeless confusions. Experience has shown us that, hitherto, the frequent repetition of some uniform succession or coexistence has been a *cause* of our expecting the same succession or coexistence on the next occasion. Food that has a certain appearance generally has a certain taste, and it is a severe shock to our expectations when the familiar appearance is found to be associated with an unusual taste. Things which we see become associated, by habit, with certain tactile sensations which we expect if we touch them; one of the horrors of a ghost (in many ghost-stories) is that it fails to give us any sensations of touch. Uneducated people who go abroad for the first time are so surprised as to be incredulous when they find their native language not understood.

And this kind of association is not confined to men; in animals also it is very strong. A horse which has been often driven along a certain road resists the attempt to drive him in a different direction. Domestic animals expect food when they see the person who usually feeds them. We know that all these rather crude expectations of uniformity are liable to be misleading. The man who has fed the chicken every day throughout its life at last wrings its neck instead, showing that more refined views as to the uniformity of nature would have been useful to the chicken.

But in spite of the misleadingness of such expectations, they nevertheless exist. The mere fact that something has happened a certain number of times causes animals and men to expect that it will happen again. Thus our instincts certainly cause us to believe that the sun will rise tomorrow, but we may be in no better a position than the chicken which unexpectedly has its neck wrung. We have therefore to distinguish the fact that past uniformities *cause* expectations as to the future, from the question whether there is any reasonable ground for giving weight to such expectations after the question of their validity had been raised.

The problem we have to discuss is whether there is any reason for believing in what is called "the uniformity of nature." The belief in the uniformity of nature is the belief that everything that has happened or will happen is an instance of some general law to which there are *no* exceptions. The crude expectations which we have been considering are all subject to exceptions, and therefore liable to disappoint those who entertain them. But science habitually assumes, at least as a working hypothesis, that general rules which have exceptions can be replaced by general rules which have no exceptions. "Unsupported bodies in air fall" is a general rule to which balloons and aeroplanes are exceptions. But the laws of motion and the law of gravitation, which account for the fact that most bodies fall, also account for the fact that balloons and aeroplanes can rise; thus the laws of motion and the law of gravitation are not subject to these exceptions.

The belief that the sun will rise to-morrow might be falsified if the earth came suddenly into contact with a large body which destroyed its rotation; but the laws of motion and the law of gravitation would not be infringed by such an event. The business of science is to find uniformities, such as the laws of motion and the law of gravitation, to which, so far as our experience extends, there are no exceptions. In this search science has been remarkably successful, and it may be conceded that such uniformities have held hitherto. This brings us back to the question: Have we any reason, assuming that they have always held in the past, to suppose that they will hold in the future?

It has been argued that we have reason to know that the future will resemble the past, because what was the future has constantly become the past, and has always been found to resemble the past, so that we really have experience of the future, namely of times which were formerly future, which we may call past futures. But such an argument really begs the very question at issue. We have experience of past futures, but not of future futures, and the question is: Will future futures resemble past futures? This question is not to be answered by an argument which starts from past futures alone. We have therefore still to seek for some principle which shall enable us to know that the future will follow the same laws as the past.

The reference to the future in this question is not essential. The same question arises when we apply the laws that work in our experience to past things of which we have no experience—as, for example, in geology, or in theories as to the origin of the Solar System. The question we really have to ask is: "When two things have been found to be often associated, and no instance is known of the one occurring without the other, does the occurrence of one of the two, in a fresh instance, give any good ground for expecting the other?" On our answer to this question must depend the validity of the whole of our expectations as to the future, the whole of the results obtained by induction, and in fact practically all the beliefs upon which our daily life is based.

It must be conceded, to begin with, that the fact that two things have been found often together and never apart does not, by itself, suffice to *prove* demonstratively that they will be found together in the next case we examine. The most we can hope is that the oftener things are found together, the more probable it becomes that they will be found together another time, and that, if they have been found together often enough, the probability will amount *almost* to certainty. It can never quite reach certainty, because we know that in spite of frequent repetitions there sometimes is a failure at the last, as in the case of the chicken whose neck is wrung. Thus probability is all we ought to seek.

It might be urged, as against the view we are advocating, that we know all natural phenomena to be subject to the reign of law, and that sometimes, on the basis of observation, we can see that only one law can possibly fit the facts of the case. Now to this view there are two answers. The first is that, even if *some* law which has no exceptions applies to our case, we can never, in practice, be sure that we have discovered that law and not one to which there are exceptions. The second is that the reign of law would seem to be itself only probable, and that our belief that it will hold in the future, or in unexamined cases in the past, is itself based upon the very principle we are examining.

The principle we are examining may be called the *principle of induction,* and its two parts may be stated as follows:

(*a*) When a thing of a certain sort A has been found to be associated with a thing of a certain other sort B, and has never been found dissociated from a thing of the sort B, the greater the number of cases in which A and B have been associated, the greater is the probability that they will be associated in a fresh case in which one of them is known to be present;

(*b*) Under the same circumstances, a sufficient number of cases of association will make the probability of a fresh association nearly a certainty, and will make it approach certainty without limit.

As just stated, the principle applies only to the verification of our expectation in a single fresh instance. But we want also to know that there is a probability in favour of the general law that things of the sort A are *always* associated with things of the sort B, provided a sufficient number of cases of association are known, and no cases of failure of association are known. The probability of the general law is obviously less than the probability of the particular case, since if the general law is true, the particular case must also be true, whereas the particular case may be true without the general law being true. Nevertheless the probability of the general law is increased by repetitions, just as the probability of the particular case is. We may therefore repeat the two parts of our principle as regards the general law, thus:

(*a*) The greater the number of cases in which a thing of the sort A has been found associated with a thing of the sort B, the more probable it is (if no cases of failure of association are known) that A is always associated with B;

(*b*) Under the same circumstances, a sufficient number of cases of the association of A with B will make it nearly certain that A is always associated with B, and will make this general law approach certainty without limit.

It should be noted that probability is always relative to certain data. In our case, the data are merely the known cases of coexistence of A and B. There may be other data, which *might* be taken into account, which would gravely alter the probability. For example, a man who had seen a great many white swans might argue, by our principle, that on the data it was *probable* that all swans were white, and this might be a perfectly sound argument. The argument is not disproved by the fact that some swans are black, because a thing may very well happen in spite of the fact that some data render it improbable. In the case of the swans, a man might know that color is a very variable characteristic in many species of animals, and that, therefore, an induction as to color is peculiarly liable to error. But this knowledge would be a fresh datum, by no means proving that the probability relatively to our previous data had been wrongly estimated. The fact, therefore, that things often fail to fulfill our expectations is no evidence that our expectations will not *probably* be fulfilled in a given case or a given class of cases. Thus our inductive principle is at any rate not capable of being *disproved* by an appeal to experience.

The inductive principle, however, is equally incapable of being *proved* by an appeal to experience. Experience might conceivably confirm the inductive principle as regards the cases that have been already examined; but as regards unexamined cases, it is the inductive principle alone that can justify any inference from what has been examined to what has not been examined. All arguments which, on the basis of experience, argue as to the future or the unexperienced parts of the past or present, assume the inductive principle; hence we can never use experience to prove the inductive principle without begging the question. Thus we must either accept the inductive principle on the ground of its intrinsic evidence, or forego all justification of our expectations about the future. If the principle is unsound, we have no reason to expect the sun to rise tomorrow, to expect bread to be more nourishing than a stone, or to expect that if we throw ourselves off the roof we shall fall. When we see what looks like our best friend approaching us, we shall have no reason to suppose that his body is not inhabited by the mind of our worst enemy or of some total stranger. All our conduct is based upon associations which have worked in the past, and which we therefore regard as likely to work in the future; and this likelihood is dependent for its validity upon the inductive principle.

The general principles of science, such as the belief in the reign of law, and the belief that every event must have a cause, are as completely dependent upon the inductive principle as are the beliefs of daily life. All such general principles are believed because mankind have found innumerable instances of their truth and no instances of their falsehood. But this affords no evidence for their truth in the future, unless the inductive principle is assumed.

Thus all knowledge which, on the basis of experience tells us something about what is not experienced, is based upon a belief which experience can neither confirm nor confute, yet which, at least in its more concrete applications, appears to be as firmly rooted in us as many of the facts of experience. The existence and justification of such beliefs—for the inductive principle, as we shall see, is not the only example—raises some of the most difficult and most debated problems of philosophy.

VIII.3 Will the Future Be Like the Past?

FREDERICK L. WILL

Frederick Will was for many years professor of philosophy at the University of Illinois. After a brief exposition of Hume's argument that we cannot establish conclusions about the future with certainty and after a description of Maynard Keynes's attempt to justify induction, Will argues that we can have knowledge "about nature's behavior and how the future will resemble the past." Will asks us to imagine our world as an enclosure beyond which no one can go or make observations. Outside the enclosure is the land of the future. The Humean skeptic is like the person in a static enclosure, but the correct analogy is that of an ever-expanding enclosure with a constantly receding border so that as our predictions of the future are realized, we obtain knowledge of nature's laws and the future. Because the new territory brought into the enclosure constantly conforms to induction, we have that reason to trust induction.

Hume's Scepticism

The standard argument for complete inductive scepticism, for the belief that inductive procedures have no rational and no empirical justification whatever, is the one stated in a small variety of ways in the writings of Hume. If one consults these writings in search of an answer to the question of inductive validity one finds the same clear answer argued first in technical detail in the *Treatise*, secondly compressed into a few non-technical paragraphs in the *Abstract of a Treatise of Human Nature*, and thirdly, presented again in a non-technical but somewhat fuller version in a chapter in the *Enquiry Concerning Human Understanding*. There is no basis whatever for any conclusion concerning future matters, according to this argument; there is no way whatever in which such conclusions can be established to be certainly true or even probable. For in the first place no such conclusion can be demonstrated by reasoning alone, since they are all conclusions about matters of fact, and since it is the case that the denial of any assertion of a matter of fact is not self-contradictory. But if one gives up the rationalistic aspiration to demonstrate propositions about matters of fact or existence *a priori*, and turns instead to experience, this road, though apparently more promising at first, likewise ends by leading one exactly nowhere. Clearly no statement about future matters of fact can be established by observation. Future things cannot be observed. Any event or state of affairs which can be observed is by definition not in the future. The only recourse which remains therefore is the inductive procedure of employing present or past observations and inferring therefrom the nature of the future. But this procedure to which we are all forced, or rather, to which we all should be forced, if we did not, in company with the animals, use it naturally from birth, is in the light of close analysis completely indefensible. For such reasoning assumes, and is quite invalid without the assumption, that the future will be like the past.

> . . . all inferences from experience suppose, as their foundation, that the future will resemble

the past, and that similar powers will be conjoined with similar sensible qualities. If there be any suspicion that the course of nature may change, and that the past may be no rule for the future, all experience becomes useless, and can give rise to no inference or conclusion. (*Enquiry*, Section IV.)

Will the future "resemble the past"? Or be "conformable to the past"? These are the ways in which in the *Enquiry* Hume expresses the question concerning the uniformity of nature, restricting to its reference toward the future the question which already had been asked in broader terms in the *Treatise*. There, without the temporal restriction, it is argued that the principle of inductive conclusions, the principle upon which reason would proceed if reason determined us in these matters, is *"that instances, of which we have had no experience, must resemble those, of which we have had experience, and that the course of nature continues always uniformly the same."* (Bk. I, Pt. III, Sect. VI.)

However the principle is stated, the argument about it remains the same. It is indispensable, if inductive conclusions are to be justified; but just as it is absolutely indispensable, so, and this is the measure of our logical misfortune, it cannot be established as certain or as probable in any way. It cannot be established by any demonstrative argument. For it is clearly an assertion of a matter of fact, and therefore the kind of assertion whose denial is non-contradictory and conceivable.

> That there are no demonstrative arguments in the case seems evident; since it implies no contradiction that the course of nature may change, and that an object, seemingly like those which we have experienced, may be attended with different or contrary effects. May I not clearly and distinctly conceive that a body, falling from the clouds, and which, in all other respects, resembles snow, has yet the taste of salt or the feeling of fire? Is there any more intelligible proposition than to affirm, that all the trees will flourish in December and January, and decay in May and June? Now whatever is intelligible, and can be distinctly conceived, implies no contradiction and can never be proved false by any demonstrative argument or abstract reasoning *a priori*. (*Enquiry*, Sect. IV. Cf. *Treatise, loc. cit.*)

Reprinted from *Mind* (Oxford, England: Oxford University Press, 1947) by permission. Notes omitted.

Any further doubts about the doubtfulness of this principle which is the main-spring of inductive inference are quickly disposed of. No one who understands the principle with its reference to unobserved instances will suggest that it can be simply observed to be true. It is still true that one cannot observe the future, or the unobserved generally. And, finally, no one who has a sound logical conscience and appreciates the indispensability of the principle to induction generally will tolerate the suggestion that the principle may be established by inductions from experience. Such a process would be circular.

> It is impossible, therefore, that any arguments from experience can prove this resemblance of the past to the future; since all these arguments are founded on the supposition of that resemblance.

And again:

> . . . all our experimental conclusions proceed upon the supposition that the future will be conformable to the past. To endeavour, therefore, the proof of this last supposition by probable arguments, or arguments regarding existence, must be evidently going in a circle, and taking that for granted, which is the very point in question. (*Enquiry*, Sect. IV.)

On this point the *Treatise* (*loc. cit.*) and the *Abstract* speak with one voice. One final quotation from the latter may serve to summarise the conclusion.

> 'Tis evident that *Adam* with all his science, would never have been able to *demonstrate,* that the course of nature must continue uniformly the same, and that the future must be conformable to the past. What is possible can never be demonstrated to be false; and 'tis possible the course of nature may change, since we can conceive such a change. Nay, I will go farther, and assert, that he could not so much as prove by any *probable* arguments, that the future must be conformable to the past. All probable arguments are built on the supposition, that there is this conformity betwixt the future and the past, and therefore can never prove it. This conformity is a *matter of fact,* and if it must be proved, will admit of no proof but from experience. But our experience in the past can be a proof of nothing for the future, but upon a supposition, that there is a resemblance betwixt them. This therefore is a point, which can admit of no proof at all, and which we take for granted without any proof. (*Abstract,* 1938 ed., p. 15.)

Is Inductive Reasoning Really Circular?

. . . It would be more promising in respect to logical neatness and precision for one to consider the alleged circularity of all inductive procedure, which is the central point of the above argument, while using as test case some specific scientific law or principle rather than some affirmation as vague and imprecise as that the future will resemble the past. But, for the purpose of analyzing the sceptic's views and meeting the arguments by which these views have been defended, such a procedure would have this deficiency, that no matter what specific scientific generalisation were chosen, one reply which would be sure to be made would consist of an appeal beyond this generalisation to some general beliefs about uniformity, some general Principle of Uniformity which, it would be urged, is assumed somehow in the inductive establishment of this and other scientific generalisations. Since the sceptical argument has been presented in terms of general Principles of Uniformity, and it is in these terms that it is alleged to demonstrate the logical circularity of all inductive reasoning, it seems worth while to attempt to deal with this argument, if one can, in the same terms—in terms of some alleged Principle of Uniformity for which it has been claimed in recent philosophy that it does serve as a wide and basic inductive assumption.

In his *Treatise on Probability*, J. M. Keynes attempts to formulate a set of principles which, if assumed to be true of a given area of subject-matter, would justify, in accordance with the principles of probability, the employment of inductive methods in that area. One of the principles which he discusses, the simplest and at the same time the one for which it seems, at first view, most plausible to contend that it may serve as a broad inductive assumption, is the one to which he gave the name of the "Principle of the Uniformity of Nature." This Principle affirms that nature is uniform in a specific way; and that is in respect to position in space and time. "It involves," writes Keynes, "the assertion of a generalised judgment of irrelevance, namely, of the irrelevance of mere position in time and space to generalisations which have no reference to particular positions in time and space." (P. 226. *Cf.* also pp. 255–256, 263, 276.) It is this principle, he argues, which

> . . . supplies the answer, if it is correct, to the criticism that the instances, on which generalisations are based, are all alike in being past, and that any generalisation, which is applicable to the future, must be based, for this reason, upon imperfect analogy. We judge directly that the resemblance between instances, which consists in their being past, is in itself irrelevant, and does not supply a valid ground for impugning a generalisation. (p. 256)

It is, however, difficult to interpret this so-called Principle in such a way that it makes a statement which is both definite and is not at the same time refuted in some areas of experience. Keynes observes that what this Principle affirms is "that the same total cause always produces the same effect" (p. 248), and this is so; but the difficulty here is that of giving a definite meaning to the important adjective "same" as it applies to causes and effects. Unless there is a specifiable meaning applicable to causes in all fields, the formula "same cause—same effect" is not a univocal principle affirming the presence of a specific kind of uniformity in every area of natural phenomena. Yet, when one sets out to specify just what kind of sameness is meant when this formula is employed, one discovers that there is a great variety of interpretations of this word in different fields of inquiry, and that what determines whether a given set of circumstances is regarded as the same cause, for example, varies from field to field, depending upon the nature of the subject-matter as that is revealed in the various generalisations which are regarded as established for that subject-matter. These generalisations exhibit among themselves great differences in scope and precision, as well as in the degree of confidence with which they are accepted. They include, for example, the generali-

sations about the coherence and constancy of properties which are involved in our belief in and distinctions among various kinds of material objects. And they include the more precise generalisations, frequently expressed in the form of mathematical equations, which would normally be referred to as "scientific laws," as well as broader generalisations formulated in various accepted Principles and Theories. When this is understood, when one sees that in the employment of the Principle of Uniformity what determines the kind of sameness to which the Principle affirms that differences in mere position in space and time are irrelevant is the specific generalisations, the laws, principles, and so on, which have been established in that field, one is in a better position to understand this so-called Principle and its alleged employment as a general inductive assumption. In any given field the Principle of Uniformity states that mere differences in space and time are irrelevant in just this sense, that there are certain generalisations, true of this field, which describe the conditions under which certain objects exist and events occur, and in which differences in mere position in space and time make little or no detectable difference. That this is so, accordingly, is not an inductive assumption in that field in the sense that it is specified and made before all inductive inquiry in the field. It is an inductive assumption in the more usual sense that conclusions of previous experience and inquiries are available for employment in any field as bases for further investigation in that field.

The primary purpose here is not to elucidate and specify the variations of meaning which such a Principle or formula must undergo if it is to be understood as applying to the great variety of fields in which inductive inquiry is carried on, to the great variety in the kinds of uniformity which the generalisations in these fields describe. The primary purpose is to inquire whether the sceptics are right in insisting that it is impossible to provide a genuine evidence for beliefs about uniformity or whether, on the contrary, it is possible to furnish empirical evidence for these beliefs which, in its employment, does not involve circular reasoning. It is granted that what the Principle of Uniformity affirms in any field, if "Principle" it may be called, is that there is uniformity in that field in this sense and no other; that there are certain specific generalisations which apply to that field and in which mere differences of position in time and space are regarded as irrelevant. In the light of this interpretation of uniformity the question briefly is, how can such a broad affirmation be confirmed or verified by induction without circularity?

For purposes of simplicity, in order to secure the clearest statement of the argument in the fewest words, it will be useful in what follows to abbreviate the statement of this Principle of Uniformity and also to consider it only in reference to time. If it can be shown that what the Principle affirms concerning the irrelevance of time in specific generalisations can be confirmed inductively, it can also be shown in exactly the same way that it is possible to confirm the Principle in its spatial reference also. So abbreviated and restricted, the Principle asserts that, in the specific way just defined, differences in time make no difference. Can this interpretation of the assertion that the future will resemble the past be confirmed? What, if any, is the evidence for it?

It follows directly from the interpretation which has just been given of this principle what the evidence for it must be. If the Principle affirms no more for any given area of fact than the validity in that area of certain generalisations which are uniform with respect to space and time, then the evidence for the Principle must be whatever evidence there is for these particular generalisations. This includes all the observations in the past and present which confirm the presence in that area of the uniformities of which these general statements speak. Belief in the uniformity in a given area is not something which is specifiable apart from the laws, principles, and other generalisations regarded as established in that area, but is itself belief in just the kind of uniformities which these generalisations describe and define. If it is correct, then, to say of any generalisation, *e.g.* of any scientific law, that it is confirmed or verified by empirical evidence, is it not correct to say that, to that extent, there is evidence for belief in the uniformity of nature?

Past and Future

The sceptic's answer to this question repeats that final rejoinder of Hume. Granted that there is empirical evidence which has been used to establish various scientific laws, all that it is evidence for, he insists, is the assertion that *in the past* these laws were true, that in the past differences in time have made no difference. This evidence is absolutely worthless for inferences which speak about the future unless it is possible to assume that the future will be like the past. But stop! That is part of what one is trying to show, that is, that mere differences in temporal position, whether past or future, make no difference in these laws of nature. That the future will be like the past means, among other things, that in the future these laws will hold, that in this specific respect differences in time will make no difference. This cannot be inductively confirmed, the sceptic is saying, because any inductive argument for it assumes it and is therefore, as evidence, completely valueless.

One major source of the plausibility of the sceptic's reasoning lies in the analogies which knowing the future easily suggests and in terms of which one is apt to think and be misled. Is this not, one may ask, like any case of sampling? And must one not take care, when reasoning inductively from samples, that one's samples are fair? If a scientist reasons concerning the behaviour of oxygen, nitrogen, or hydrogen on Mars, if such elements there be on Mars, on the basis of the known behaviour of these elements on the earth, he is assuming that in some respects the samples of the elements on the other planet are like those we have here. Similarly in reasoning about the future behaviour of these elements on the basis of present and past behaviour one must assume that future samples of these elements will be like present and past ones. Now if it is the case that past samples may be regarded as evidence about future ones only upon such an assumption, then no examination of past samples, however extensive, can be regarded as yielding evidence for the assumption itself. Any reasoning which did attempt to employ such samples as evidence for the assumption would be forced to use the assumption as a principle in the reasoning and would therefore beg the whole question at issue.

A physical representation of the kind of analogy presented here might be as follows: Suppose that there was somewhere in the world an enclosure beyond which it was impossible for anyone ever to go or to make any observations. Nothing could be seen, heard, or in any other way perceived beyond the border. The territory beyond the enclosure, forever barred from human perception, is the land of Future. The territory within the enclosure is the land of Present and Past, but since it is overwhelmingly the latter, it all goes under the name of Past. Now suppose that someone within the enclosure is interested in some proposition about the way things behave beyond the enclosure, say, a simple and homely proposition about chickens, to the effect that beyond the enclosure roosters fight more than hens. And he wonders what evidence, if any, there is for this proposition. Of course he cannot observe this to be true. He must base it upon his observation in the land of Past; and if he does base it upon the observed fact that roosters in the land of Past fight more than hens, he must assume that in this respect chickens beyond the enclosure behave like chickens within it, so that, knowing that in the latter area roosters are the more pugnacious, he may employ this knowledge as evidence that things are this way also in the former area. This is an assumption which no empirical evidence, confined as it must be to evidence in Past, can be employed to support. Any attempt to support it with such evidence must itself assume that in respect to the phenomena involved differences between Past and Future are negligible; and since that is exactly what the reasoning is attempting to establish, the process is patently circular.

This is the kind of metaphor which makes friends, and influences people, in this case, to draw the wrong conclusions. There are several faults in the analogy. The chief one is that, as represented, the border between Past and Future is stationary, while in the temporal situation it is not. To duplicate the temporal situation in this respect the analogy should represent the border as constantly moving, revealing as it does constantly, in territory which has hitherto been Future, hens and roosters similar as regards difference in disposition to those already observed in Past. The matter of evidence for the proposition about hens and roosters is then also different. If this proposition is in a position analogous to the beliefs about uniformity which are represented in modern scientific laws, the situation is something like this. Previously inhabitants in Past had drawn more sweeping conclusions concerning the difference between the disposition to fight of male and female chickens. They have discovered recently that in respect to young chicks and pullets this generalisation did not hold. They have therefore revised the proposition to exclude

all the known negative instances and speak only and more surely of the behaviour of hens and roosters, meaning by these latter terms just fully grown and developed female and male chickens.

So far as there is any record, chickens in Past have verified this rule; so far as there is any record, every chicken revealed by the ever-receding border has likewise verified it; so far as there is any record there has not been one negative instance. Is it not the case that the inhabitants of Past do have evidence for the proposition that all chickens obey this rule, those already in Past, which they call "Past-chickens," and those also which are not yet in Past but which will be subsequently revealed by the moving border, and which they call not unnaturally "Future-chickens"? They have a vast number of positive instances of the rule, and no negative instances, except those in respect to which the rule has already been revised. In view of the present evidence that in all cases, year after year and century after century, the progressively revealed chickens have verified and do verify this rule, must one not conclude that the inhabitants of past do have evidence for this proposition, and that anyone is wrong who says that they have actually no evidence one way or other?

The sceptic, however, is still prepared to argue his case, and his argument, in terms of the present analogy, has a now familiar ring. That the inhabitants of Past have no evidence whatsoever about the behaviour of Future-chickens, he will insist; and as grounds he will point out that although the border does progressively recede and reveal chickens like those previously observed in Past, these are really not Future-chickens. By the very fact that they have been revealed they are no longer Future-chickens, but are now Past-chickens. Observation of them is not observation of Future-chickens, and any attempt to reason from such observation to conclusions about Future-chickens must therefore assume that Future-chickens are like Past-chickens. For the inhabitants of Past, in these efforts to know the land beyond the border, this is both an inescapable and unknowable presumption.

What should one say of an argument of this kind? Only through some logical slip, one feels strongly, would it be possible to arrive at such a conclusion. One would have thought that the receding border was a matter upon which the inhabitants of Past may legitimately congratulate themselves in the light of their interest in learning what Future-chickens, when they become Past, are going to be like. If the border had not yet begun to recede they would indeed be in an unfortunate position for securing such knowledge. But happily this is not the case. The border is constantly receding. And granting that it will constantly recede, revealing always more of the land of Future, and even granting also that this means that there is an inexhaustible area to be revealed, the inhabitants of Past are in the fortunate position that with the progressive recession they may learn more and more about chickens, Past and Future. They may derive hypotheses from their experience of what has already been revealed and proceed further to test these by the progressive revelations of Future, in the light of which they may be confirmed, refuted, or revised. The sceptic's argument amounts to the assertion that all this apparent good fortune is really illusory and that the sorry Pastians are actually in no better position with respect to knowing about Future-chickens and Future-things generally than they would be if the border never moved at all. For the movement of the border does not reveal Future-chickens, since Future is by definition the land beyond the border. No matter how much or how little is revealed, by the very fact that it is revealed and on this side of the border it is not Future but Past, and therefore, since the land of Future always is beyond observation, no empirical method can produce any evidence that what is in that land is in any way similar to what is not. That this rendering of the sceptic's position, though in the language of the above metaphor, is undistorted and fair may be seen by consulting the words of an illustrious modern sceptic and follower of Hume, Bertrand Russell. In his chapter, "On Induction," in *The Problems of Philosophy*, Russell expressed the matter in this fashion:

> It has been argued that we have reason to know that the future will resemble the past, because what was the future has constantly become the past, and has always been found to resemble the past, so that we really have experience of the future, namely of times which were formerly future, which we may call past futures. But such an argument really begs the very question at issue. We have experience of past futures, but not of future futures, and the question is: Will future futures resemble past futures? This question

is not to be answered by an argument which starts from past futures alone. We have therefore still to seek for some principle which shall enable us to know that the future will follow the same laws as the past.

This is the central difficulty urged by Hume, Russell, and others in arguing that there can never be any empirical evidence that the future will be like the past. Empirically, in Russell's language, it is possible to have evidence only that this has been true of past and possibly present futures, not that it will be true of future futures. It is the situation in the land of Past all over again. There are generalisations which are constantly being confirmed by experience. But every time a confirming instance occurs it is nullified as evidence by the argument that it is not really a confirming instance at all. For by the fact that it has occurred it is an instance of a past future, and therefore it tells nothing whatever about future futures. In treating of the land of Past it was suggested that there is involved in arguing in this manner a logical slip or error. It remains to investigate how this is the case.

Suppose that in 1936, to take but a short span of time, a man says that in the above-defined sense the future will be like the past. In 1936, if he could somehow have shown that 1937 would be like 1936, this would have been evidence for his statement, as even a sceptic would admit. But in 1937, when he does establish that 1937 is like 1936, it has somehow ceased to be evidence. So long as he did not have it, it was evidence; as soon as he gets it it ceases to be. The constant neutralisation of the evidence which is effected in this argument is effected by the same kind of verbal trick which children play upon one another in fun. Child A asks child B what he is going to do to-morrow. B replies that he is going to play ball, go swimming, or what not. Thereupon A says, "You can't do that."

B: Why not?

A: Because to-morrow never comes. When to-morrow comes it won't be to-morrow; it will be to-day. You can never play to-morrow; you can only play to-day.

Again, if a prophet announces that next year will bring a utopia, and if each succeeding year, when the predicted utopia does not come, he defends himself by pointing out that he said "next year" and that obviously this is not next year, no reasonable person would pay much attention to him. Such a person would realise, on a moment's reflection, that the prophet is being deceptive with the word "next." In 1936 "next year" means "1937"; in 1937 it means "1938." Since every year "next year" means a different year, a year yet to come, what the prophet says can never be verified or disproved. If in 1936 he meant by this phrase 1937, as he sensibly should, then this statement can be verified or refuted in 1937. But if, when 1937 comes, he insists that he did not mean 1937, but "next year," and if in 1938 he again insists that he did not mean that year, and so on, then what he seems to be meaning by "next year" is the $n + 1$th year where n is the ever-progressing number of the present year. No one should alter his present activities or his plans for the future on the basis of such a prediction, for, of course, it really is not a prediction. While in the form of a statement about the future it does not say anything about the future, anything which could possibly be true or false in the infinity of time, if infinity it is, which yet remains to transpire. For what the prophet is saying is that utopia will come next year, and by his own interpretation of the words "next year" he is affirming that next year will never come. In other words, at the time which never comes, and hence when nothing occurs, a utopia will occur. This is not even sensible speech; it is a contradiction.

In a similar though less simple way those who employ the sceptical argument about uniformity to show that there is no evidence whatever for any statement about the future are being themselves deceived and are deceiving others by their use of expressions like "next," "future," "future future," and "past future." The man who said in 1936 that the future would be like the past, that mere differences in temporal position make no difference in the behaviour of nature which is described in scientific laws, meant, as he sensibly should, that this was true of the years 1937, 1938, and so on. He said something of the form "all A's are B's" and it has been possible since 1936 to examine the A's of 1937 to 1946 and to see whether what he said is confirmed or disproved by the available evidence. If, however, now that it is 1946, and all this evidence is in, he should remark that since it is 1946 the years 1937–46 are no longer future and therefore have ceased to be evidence for the proposition, then he is guilty of using, or rather abusing the word "future" in the way in which the prophet in the previous example was abusing the word "next." For the only basis for his contention that the observed A's are not confirming evidence, or what is that same thing, that they are confirming instances only if one assumes quite circularly that the future is like the past, is in his illusive use of the word "future." Time does pass, and, because it does, the present is a constantly changing one; and the point of reference for the use of words like "future" and "past" is accordingly different. The correct conclusion to be drawn from the fact that time passes is that the future is constantly being revealed and that, in consequence, we have had and shall have the opportunity to learn more and more accurately what the laws of nature's behaviour are and how therefore the future will be like the past. But this sceptical man has his eyes fixed in fatal fascination upon the movement of time, the constantly changing present. And seeing that, as the present changes, what was once future is not now future, but present, and will shortly be past, he is led to draw the conclusion that after all, for any present whatever, the future is forever hidden behind a veil.

VIII.4 The Pragmatic Justification of Induction

HANS REICHENBACH

Hans Reichenbach (1891–1953) was born in Germany, taught at the University of Berlin, and was professor of philosophy at the University of California, Los Angeles, from 1938 until his death.

   Reichenbach agrees with Hume that neither a deductive nor an inductive demonstration for inductive inference is possible. Nevertheless, we have good practical reasons for trusting induction. Our situation is like that of a cancer patient who will die unless he undergoes an operation. The operation may not succeed, but it's his only hope for continued life. Likewise, the principle of induction is our only hope for guidance in life and in science. Living by inductive principles is our best bet, for if there are laws of nature and we follow them, we will be able to predict and, to a degree, control the future. If there are no such laws, it doesn't matter what we do, for nature will prove to be lawless and chaotic.

The nontautological character of induction has been known a long time; Bacon had already emphasized that it is just this character to which the importance of induction is due. If inductive inference can teach us something new, in opposition to deductive inference, this is because it is not a tautology. This useful quality has, however, become the center of the epistemological difficulties of induction. It was David Hume who first attacked the principle from this side; he pointed out that the apparent constraint of the inductive inference, although submitted to by everybody, could not be justified. We believe in induction; we even cannot get rid of the belief when we know the impossibility of a logical demonstration of the validity of inductive inference; but as logicians we must admit that this belief is a deception—such is the result of Hume's criticism. We may summarize his objections in two statements:

   1.   We have no logical demonstration for the validity of inductive inference.

   2.   There is no demonstration a posteriori for the inductive inference; any such demonstration would presuppose the very principle which it is to demonstrate.

These two pillars of Hume's criticism of the principle of induction have stood unshaken for two centuries, and I think they will stand as long as there is a scientific philosophy. . . .

   Inductive inference cannot be dispensed with because we need it for the purpose of action. To deem the inductive assumption unworthy of the assent of a philosopher, to keep a distinguished reserve, and to meet with a condescending smile the attempts of other people to bridge the gap between experience and prediction is cheap self-deceit; at the very moment when the apostles of such a higher philosophy leave the field of theoretical discussion and pass to the simplest actions of daily life, they follow the inductive principle as surely as does every earth-bound mind. In any action there are various means to the realization of our aim; we have to make a choice, and we decide in accordance with the inductive principle. Although there is no means which will produce with certainty the desired effect, we do not leave the choice to chance but prefer the means indicated by the principle of induction. If we sit at the wheel of a car and want to turn the car to the right, why do we turn the wheel to the right? There is no certainty that the car will follow the wheel; there are indeed cars which do not always so behave. Such cases are fortunately exceptions. But if we should not regard the inductive prescription and consider the effect of a turn of the

Reprinted from *Experience and Prediction* (University of Chicago Press, 1938) by permission of the author.

wheel as entirely unknown to us, we might turn it to the left as well. I do not say this to suggest such an attempt; the effects of skeptical philosophy applied in motor traffic would be rather unpleasant. But I should say a philosopher who is to put aside his principles any time he steers a motor-car is a bad philosopher.

It is no justification of inductive belief to show that it is a habit. It is a habit; but the question is whether it is a good habit, where "good" is to mean "useful for the purpose of actions directed to future events." If a person tells me that Socrates is a man, and that all men are mortal, I have the habit of believing that Socrates is mortal. I know, however, that this is a good habit. If anyone had the habit of believing in such a case that Socrates is not mortal, we could demonstrate to him that this was a bad habit. The analogous question must be raised for inductive inference. If we should not be able to demonstrate that it is a good habit, we should either cease using it or admit frankly that our philosophy is a failure.

Science proceeds by induction and not by tautological transformations of reports. [Francis] Bacon is right about Aristotle; but the *novum organon* [i.e., induction as opposed to deduction] needs a justification as good as that of the *organon*. Hume's criticism was the heaviest blow against empiricism; if we do not want to dupe our consciousness of this by means of the narcotic drug of aprioristic rationalism, or the soporific of skepticism, we must find a defense for the inductive inference which holds as well as does the formalistic justification of deductive logic.

§39. The Justification of the Principle of Induction

We shall now begin to give the justification of induction which Hume thought impossible. In the pursuit of this inquiry, let us ask first what has been proved, strictly, by Hume's objections.

Hume started with the assumption that a justification of inductive inference is only given if we can show that inductive inference must lead to success. In other words, Hume believed that any justified application of the inductive inference presupposes a demonstration that the conclusion is true. It is this assumption on which Hume's criticism is based. His two objections directly concern only the question of the truth of the conclusion; they prove that the truth of the conclusion cannot be demonstrated. The two objections, therefore, are valid only in so far as the Humean assumption is valid. It is this question to which we must turn: Is it necessary, for the justification of inductive inference, to show that its conclusion is true?

A rather simple analysis shows us that this assumption does not hold. Of course, if we were able to prove the truth of the conclusion, inductive inference would be justified; but the converse does not hold: a justification of the inductive inference does not imply a proof of the truth of the conclusion. The proof of the truth of the conclusion is only a sufficient condition for the justification of induction, not a necessary condition.

The inductive inference is a procedure which is to furnish us the best assumption concerning the future. If we do not know the truth about the future, there may be nonetheless a best assumption about it, i.e., a best assumption relative to what we know. We must ask whether such a characterization may be given for the principle of induction. If this turns out to be possible, the principle of induction will be justified.

An example will show the logical structure of our reasoning. A man may be suffering from a grave disease; the physician tells us: "I do not know whether an operation will save the man, but if there *is* any remedy, it is an operation." In such a case, the operation would be justified. Of course, it would be better to know that the operation will save the man; but, if we do not know this, the knowledge formulated in the statement of the physician is a sufficient justification. If we cannot realize the sufficient conditions of success, we shall at least realize the necessary conditions. If we were able to show that the inductive inference is a necessary condition of success, it would be justified; such a proof would satisfy any demands which may be raised about the justification of induction.

Now obviously there is a great difference between our example and induction. The reasoning of the physician presupposes inductions; his knowledge about an operation as the only possible means of saving a life is based on inductive generalizations, just as are all other statements of empirical character. But we wanted only to illustrate the logical structure of our reasoning. If we want to regard such a reasoning as a justification of the principle of induction, the character of induction as a necessary condition of success must be demonstrated in a way which does not presuppose induction. Such a proof, however, can be given.

If we want to construct this proof, we must begin with a determination of the aim of induction. It is usually said that we perform inductions with the aim of foreseeing the future. This determination is vague; let us replace it by a formulation more precise in character:

The aim of induction is to find series of events whose frequency of occurrence converges toward a limit.

We choose this formulation because we found that we need probabilities and that a probability is to be defined as the limit of a frequency; thus our determination of the aim of induction is given in such a way that it enables us to apply probability methods. If we compare this determination of the aim of induction with determinations usually given, it turns out to be not a confinement to a narrow aim but an expansion. What we usually call "foreseeing the future" is included in our formulation as a special case; the case of knowing with certainty for every event *A* the event *B* following it would correspond in our formulation to a case where the limit of the frequency is of the numerical value 1. Hume thought of this case only. Thus our inquiry differs from that of Hume in so far as it conceives the aim of induction in a generalized form. But we do not omit any possible applications if we determine the principle of induction as the means of obtaining the limit of a frequency. If we have limits of frequency, we have all we want, including the case considered by Hume; we have then the laws of nature in their most general form, including both statistical and so-called causal laws—the latter being nothing but a special case of statistical laws, corresponding to the numerical value 1 of the limit of the frequency. We are entitled, therefore, to consider the determination of the limit of a frequency as the aim of the inductive inference.

Now it is obvious that we have no guaranty that this aim is at all attainable. The world may be so disorderly that it is impossible for us to construct series with a limit. Let us introduce the term "predictable" for a world which is sufficiently ordered to enable us to construct series with a limit. We must admit, then, that we do not know whether the world is predictable. . . .

These considerations lead, however, to a more precise formulation of the logical structure of the inductive inference. We must say that, if there is any method which leads to the limit of the frequency, the inductive principle will do the same; if there is a limit of the frequency, the inductive principle is a sufficient condition to find it. If we omit now the premise that there is a limit of the frequency, we cannot say that the inductive principle is the necessary condition of finding it because there are other methods using a correction c_n. There is a set of equivalent conditions such that the choice of one of the members of the set is necessary if we want to find the limit; and, if there is a limit, each of the members of the set is an appropriate method for finding it. We may say, therefore, that the *applicability* of the inductive principle is a necessary condition of the existence of a limit of the frequency.

The decision in favor of the inductive principle among the members of the set of equivalent means may be substantiated by pointing out its quality of embodying the smallest risk; after all, this decision is not of a great relevance, as all these methods must lead to the same value of the limit if they are sufficiently continued. It must not be forgotten, however, that the method of clairvoyance is not, without further ado, a number of the set because we do not know whether the correction c_n occurring here is submitted to the condition of convergence to zero. This must be proved first, and it can only be proved by using the inductive principle, viz., a method known to be a member of the set: this is why clairvoyance, in spite of all occult pretensions, is to be submitted to the control of scientific methods, i.e., by the principle of induction.

It is in the analysis expounded that we see the solution of Hume's problem. Hume demanded too much when he wanted for a justification of the inductive inference a proof that its conclusion is true. What his objections demonstrate is only that such a proof cannot be given. We do not perform, however, an inductive inference with the pretension of obtaining a true statement. What we obtain is a wager; and it is the best wager we can lay because it corresponds to a procedure the applicability of which is the necessary condition of the possibility of predictions. To fulfill the conditions sufficient for the attainment of true predictions does not lie in our power; let us be glad that we are able to fulfil at least the conditions necessary for the realization of this intrinsic aim of science. . . .

. . . With this result the application of the system of scientific inductions finds a justification similar to, and even better than, that of the single induction: *the system of scientific inductions is the best posit we know concerning the future.*

We found that the posits of the highest level are always blind posits; thus the system of knowledge, as a whole, is a blind posit. Posits of the lower levels have appraised weights; but their serviceableness depends on the unknown weights of the posits of higher levels. The uncertainty of knowledge as a whole therefore penetrates to the simplest posits we can make—those concerning the events of daily life. Such a result seems unavoidable for any theory of prediction. We have no certainty as to foreseeing the future. We do not know whether the predictions of complicated theories, such as the quantum theory or the theory of albumen molecules, will turn out to be true; we do not even know whether the simplest posits concerning our immediate future will be confirmed, whether they concern the sun's rising or the persistence of the conditions of our personal environment. There is no principle of philosophy to warrant the reliability of such predictions; that is our answer to all attempts made within the history of philosophy to procure for us such certainty, from Plato, through all varieties of theology, to Descartes and Kant. In spite of that, we do not renounce prediction; the arguments of skeptics like Hume cannot shake our resolution: at least to *try* predictions. We know with certainty that among all procedures for foreseeing the future, known to us as involving success if success is possible, the procedure of concatenated inductions is the best. We try it as our best posit in order to have our chance—if we do not succeed, well, then our trial was in vain.

Is this to say that we are to renounce any belief in success? There is such a belief; everyone has it when he makes inductions; does our solution of the inductive problem oblige us to dissuade him from this firm belief?

This is not a philosophical but a social question. As philosophers we know that such a belief is not justifiable; as sociologists we may be glad that there is such a belief. Not everyone is likely to act according to a principle if he does not believe in success; thus belief may guide him when the postulates of logic turn out to be too weak to direct him.

Yet our admission of this belief is not the attitude of the skeptic who, not knowing a solution of his own, permits everyone to believe what he wants. We may admit the belief because we know that it will determine the same actions that logical analysis would determine. Though we cannot justify the belief, we can justify the logical structure of the inference to which it fortunately corresponds as far as the practical results are concerned. This happy coincidence is certainly to be explained by Darwin's idea of selection; those animals were to survive whose habits of belief corresponded to the most useful instrument for foreseeing the future. There is no reason to dissuade anybody from doing with belief something which he ought to do in the same way if he had no belief.

This remark does not merely apply to the belief in induction as such. There are other kinds of belief which have crystallized round the methods of expanding knowledge. Men of scientific research are not always of so clear an insight into philosophical problems as logical analysis would require: they have filled up the world of research work with mystic concepts; they talk of "instinctive presentiments," of "natural hypotheses," and one of the best among them told me once that he found his great theories because he was convinced of the harmony of nature. If we were to analyze the discoveries of these men, we would find that their way of proceeding corresponds in a surprisingly high degree to the rules of the principle of induction, applied however to a domain of facts where average minds did not see their traces. In such cases, inductive operations are imbedded within a belief which as to its intension differs from the inductive principle, although its function within the system of operations of knowledge amounts to the same. The mysticism of scientific discovery is nothing but a superstructure of images and wishes; the supporting structure below is determined by the inductive principle.

I do not say this with the intention to discredit the belief—to pull the superstructure down. On the contrary, it seems to be a psychological law that discoveries need a kind of mythology; just as the inductive inference may lead us in certain cases to the preference of methods different from it, it may lead us also to the psychological law that sometimes those men will be best in making inductions who believe they possess other guides. The philosopher should not be astonished at this.

This does not mean that I should advise him to share any of these kinds of belief. It is the philosopher's aim to know what he does; to understand thought operations and not merely to apply them instinctively, automatically. He wants to look through the superstructure and to discover the supporting structure. Belief in induction, belief in a uniformity of the world, belief in a mystic harmony between nature and reason—they belong, all of them, to the superstructure; the solid foundation below is the system of inductive operations. The difficulty of a logical justification of these operations misled philosophers to seek a justification of the superstructure, to attempt an ontological justification of inductive belief by looking for necessary qualities of the world which would insure the success of inductive inferences. All such attempts will fail—because we shall never be able to give a cogent proof of any material presumption concerning nature. The way toward an understanding of the step from experience to prediction lies in the logical sphere; to find it we have to free

ourselves from one deep-rooted prejudice: from the presupposition that the system of knowledge is to be a system of true propositions. If we cross out this assumption within the theory of knowledge, the difficulties dissolve, and with them dissolves the mystical mist lying above the research methods of science. We shall then interpret knowledge as a system of posits, or wagers; with this the question of justification assumes as its form the question whether scientific knowledge is our best wager. Logical analysis shows that this demonstration can be given, that the inductive procedure of science is distinguished from other methods of prediction as leading to the most favorable posits. Thus we wager on the predictions of science and wager on the predictions of practical wisdom: we wager on the sun's rising tomorrow, we wager that food will nourish us tomorrow, we wager that our feet will carry us tomorrow. Our stake is not low; all our personal existence, our life itself, is at stake. To confess ignorance in the face of the future is the tragic duty of all scientific philosophy; but, if we are excluded from knowing true predictions, we shall be glad that at least we know the road toward our best wagers.

VIII.5 Dissolving the Problem of Induction

PETER F. STRAWSON

Peter Strawson until his retirement was professor of philosophy at Oxford University. Ludwig Wittgenstein, who influenced Strawson's thought, wrote that his aim in philosophy was "to show the fly the way out of the fly-bottle . . . aiming at *complete* clarity, [which] means that philosophical problems should *completely* disappear" (*Philosophical Investigations,* sections 309, 133). Strawson applies this therapeutic model of philosophy to the problem and argues that just as the questions of whether deductive arguments in general are valid or the law is legal, show that the questioner fails to understand the concepts in question, the question whether induction is justified shows that the questioner does not understand what induction is all about. Induction is precisely our standard of empirical rationality. "Every successful method or recipe for finding out about the unobserved must be one which has inductive support; for to say that a recipe is successful is to say that it has been repeatedly applied with success."

What reason have we to place reliance on inductive procedures? Why should we suppose that the accumulation of instances of As which are Bs, however various the conditions in which they are observed, gives any good reason for expecting the next A we encounter to be a B? It is our habit to form expectations in this way; but can the habit be rationally justified? When this doubt has entered our minds it may be difficult to free ourselves from it. For the doubt has its source in a confusion; and some attempts to resolve the doubt preserve the confusion; and other attempts to show that the doubt is senseless seem altogether too facile. The root-confusion is easily described; but simply to describe it seems an inadequate remedy against it. So the doubt must be examined again and again, in the light of different attempts to remove it.

If someone asked what grounds there were for supposing that deductive reasoning was valid, we might answer that there were in fact no grounds for supposing that deductive reasoning was always valid; sometimes people made valid inferences, and sometimes they were guilty of logical fallacies. If he said that we had misunderstood his question, and that what he wanted to know was what grounds there were for regarding deduction *in general* as a valid method of argument, we should have to answer that his question was without sense, for to say that an argument, or a form or method of argument, was valid or invalid would *imply* that it was deductive; the concepts of validity and invalidity had application only to individual deductive arguments or forms of deductive argument. Similarly, if a man asked what grounds there were for thinking it reasonable to hold beliefs arrived at inductively, one might at first answer that there were good and bad inductive arguments, that sometimes it was reasonable to hold a belief arrived at inductively and sometimes it was not. If he, too, said that his question had been misunderstood, that he wanted to know whether induction in general was a reasonable method of inference, then we might well think his question senseless in the same way as the question whether deduction is in general valid; for to call a particular belief reasonable or unreasonable is to apply inductive standards, just as to call a particular

Reprinted from *Introduction to Logical Theory* (New York: John Wiley & Sons, 1952 by permission of the publisher.

argument valid or invalid is to apply deductive standards. The parallel is not wholly convincing; for words like "reasonable" and "rational" have not so precise and technical a sense as the word "valid." Yet it is sufficiently powerful to make us wonder how the second question could be raised at all, to wonder why, in contrast with the corresponding question about deduction, it should have seemed to constitute a genuine problem.

Suppose that a man is brought up to regard formal logic as the study of the science and art of reasoning. He observes that all inductive processes are, by deductive standards, invalid; the premises never entail the conclusions. Now inductive processes are notoriously important in the formation of beliefs and expectations about everything which lies beyond the observation of available witnesses. But an *invalid* argument is an *unsound* argument; an *unsound* argument is one in which *no good reason* is produced for accepting the conclusion. So if inductive processes are invalid, if all the arguments we should produce, if challenged, in support of our beliefs about what lies beyond the observation of available witnesses are unsound, then we have no good reason for any of these beliefs. This conclusion is repugnant. So there arises the demand for a justification, not of this or that particular belief which goes beyond what is entailed by our evidence, but a justification of induction in general. And when the demand arises in this way it is, in effect, the demand that induction shall be shown to be really a kind of deduction; for nothing less will satisfy the doubter when this is the route to his doubts.

Tracing this, the most common route to the general doubt about the reasonableness of induction, shows how the doubt seems to escape the absurdity of a demand that induction in general shall be justified by inductive standards. The demand is that induction should be shown to be a rational process; and this turns out to be the demand that one kind of reasoning should be shown to be another and different kind. Put thus crudely, the demand seems to escape one absurdity only to fall into another. Of course, inductive arguments are not deductively valid; if they were, they would be deductive arguments. Inductive reasoning must be assessed, for soundness, by inductive standards. Nevertheless, fantastic as the wish for induction to be deduction may seem, it is only in terms of it that we can understand some of the attempts that have been made to justify induction.

VIII

The first kind of attempt I shall consider might be called the search for the supreme premise of inductions. In its primitive form it is quite a crude attempt; and I shall make it cruder by caricature. We have already seen that for a particular inductive step, such as "The kettle has been on the fire for ten minutes, so it will be boiling by now," we can substitute a deductive argument by introducing a generalization (e.g., "A kettle always boils within ten minutes of being put on the fire") as an additional premise. This manoeuvre shifted the emphasis of the problem of inductive support on to the question of how we established such generalizations as these, which rested on grounds by which they were not entailed. But suppose the manoeuvre could be repeated. Suppose we could find one supremely general proposition, which taken in conjunction with the evidence for any accepted generalization of science or daily life (or at least of science) would entail that generalization. Then, so long as the status of the supreme generalization could be satisfactorily explained, we could regard all sound inductions to unqualified general conclusions as, at bottom, valid deductions. The justification would be found, for at least these cases. The most obvious difficulty in this suggestion is that of formulating the supreme general proposition in such a way that it shall be precise enough to yield the desired entailments, and yet not obviously false or arbitrary. Consider, for example, the formula: "For all f, g, wherever n cases of $f. g$, and no cases of $f.\sim g$, are observed, then all cases of f are cases of g." To turn it into a sentence, we have only to replace "n" by some number. But what number? If we take the value of "n" to be 1 or 20 or 500, the resulting statement is obviously false. Moreover, the choice of any number would seem quite arbitrary; there is no privileged number of favourable instances which we take as decisive in establishing a generalization. If, on the other hand, we phrase the proposition vaguely enough to escape these objections—if, for example, we phrase it as "Nature is uniform"—then it becomes too vague to provide the desired entailments. It

should be noticed that the impossibility of framing a general proposition of the kind required is really a special case of the impossibility of framing precise rules for the assessment of evidence. If we could frame a rule which would tell us precisely when we had *conclusive* evidence for a generalization, then it would yield just the proposition required as the supreme premise.

> Even if these difficulties could be met, the question of the status of the supreme premise would remain. How, if a non-necessary proposition, could it be established? The appeal to experience, to inductive support, is clearly barred on pain of circularity. If, on the other hand, it were a necessary truth and possessed, in conjunction with the evidence for a generalization, the required logical power to entail the generalization (e.g., if the latter were the conclusion of a hypothetical syllogism, of which the hypothetical premise was the necessary truth in question), then the evidence would entail the generalization independently, and the problem would not arise: a conclusion unbearably paradoxical. In practice, the extreme vagueness with which candidates for the role of supreme premise are expressed prevents their acquiring such logical power, and at the same time renders it very difficult to classify them as analytic or synthetic: under pressure they may tend to tautology; and, when the pressure is removed, assume an expansively synthetic air.

> In theories of the kind which I have here caricatured the ideal of deduction is not usually so blatantly manifest as I have made it. One finds the "Law of the Uniformity of Nature" presented less as the suppressed premise of crypto-deductive inferences than as, say, the "presupposition of the validity of inductive reasoning."

X

Let us turn from attempts to justify induction to attempts to show that the demand for a justification is mistaken. We have seen already that what lies behind such a demand is often the absurd wish that induction should be shown to be some kind of deduction—and this wish is clearly traceable in the two attempts at justification which we have examined. What other sense could we give to the demand? Sometimes it is expressed in the form of a request for proof that induction is a *reasonable* or *rational* procedure, that we have *good grounds* for placing reliance upon it. Consider the uses of the phrases "good grounds," "justification," "reasonable," &c. Often we say such things as "He has *every justification* for believing that *p*"; "I have *very good reasons* for believing it"; "There are *good grounds* for the view that *q*"; "There is *good evidence* that *r*." We often talk, in such ways as these, of justification, good grounds or reasons or evidence for certain beliefs. Suppose such a belief were one expressible in the form "Every case of *f* is a case of *g*." And suppose someone were asked what he meant by saying that he had good grounds or reasons for holding it. I think it would be felt to be a satisfactory answer if he replied: "Well, in all my wide and varied experience I've come across innumerable cases of *f* and never a case of *f* which wasn't a case of *g*." In saying this, he is clearly claiming to have *inductive* support, *inductive* evidence, of a certain kind, for his belief; and he is also giving a perfectly proper answer to the question, what he meant by saying that he had ample justification, good grounds, good reasons for his belief. It is an analytic proposition that it is reasonable to have a degree of belief in a statement which is proportional to the strength of the evidence in its favour; and it is an analytic proposition, though not a proposition of mathematics, that, other things being equal, the evidence for a generalization is strong in proportion as the number of favourable instances, and the variety of circumstances in which they have been found, is great. So to ask whether it is reasonable to place reliance on inductive procedures is like asking whether it is reasonable to proportion the degree of one's convictions to the strength of the evidence. Doing this is what "being reasonable" *means* in such a context.

As for the other form in which the doubt may be expressed, viz., "Is induction a justified, or justifiable, procedure?", it emerges in a still less favourable light. No sense has been given to it, though it is easy to see why it seems to have a sense. For it is generally proper to inquire of *a particular belief,* whether its adoption is justified;

and, in asking this, we are asking whether there is good, bad, or any, evidence for it. In applying or withholding the epithets "justified," "well founded," &c., in the case of specific beliefs, we are appealing to, and applying, inductive standards. But to what standards are we appealing when we ask whether the application of inductive standards is justified or well grounded? If we cannot answer, then no sense has been given to the question. Compare it with the question: Is the law legal? It makes perfectly good sense to inquire of a particular action, of an administrative regulation, or even, in the case of some states, of a particular enactment of the legislature, whether or not it is legal. The question is answered by an appeal to a legal system, by the application of a set of legal (or constitutional) rules or standards. But it makes no sense to inquire in general whether the law of the land, the legal system as a whole, is or is not legal. For to what legal standards are we appealing?

The only way in which a sense might be given to the question, whether induction is in general a justified or justifiable procedure, is a trivial one which we have already noticed. We might interpret it to mean "Are all conclusions, arrived at inductively, justified?," i.e., "Do people always have adequate evidence for the conclusions they draw?" The answer to this question is easy, but uninteresting: it is that sometimes people have adequate evidence, and sometimes they do not.

XI

It seems, however, that this way of showing the request for a general justification of induction to be absurd is sometimes insufficient to allay the worry that produces it. And to point out that "forming rational opinions about the unobserved on the evidence available" and "assessing the evidence by inductive standards" are phrases which describe the same thing, is more apt to produce irritation than relief. The point is felt to be "merely a verbal" one; and though the point of this protest is itself hard to see, it is clear that something more is required. So the question must be pursued further. First, I want to point out that there is something a little odd about talking of "the inductive method," or even "the inductive policy," as if it were just one possible method among others of arguing from the observed to the unobserved, from the available evidence to the facts in question. If one asked a meteorologist what method or methods he used to forecast the weather, one would be surprised if he answered: "Oh, just the inductive method." If one asked a doctor by what means he diagnosed a certain disease, the answer "By induction" would be felt as an impatient evasion, a joke, or a rebuke. The answer one hopes for is an account of the tests made, the signs taken account of, the rules and recipes and general laws applied. When such a specific method of prediction or diagnosis is in question, one can ask whether the method is justified in practice; and here again one is asking whether its employment is inductively justified, whether it commonly gives correct results. This question would normally seem an admissible one. One might be tempted to conclude that, while there are many different specific methods of prediction, diagnosis, &c., appropriate to different subjects of inquiry, all such methods could properly be called "inductive" in the sense that their employment rested on inductive support; and that, hence, the phrase "non-inductive method of finding out about what lies deductively beyond the evidence" was a description without meaning, a phrase to which no sense had been given; so that there could be no question of justifying our selection of one method, called "the inductive," of doing this.

However, someone might object: "Surely it is possible, though it might be foolish, to use methods utterly different from accredited scientific ones. Suppose a man, whenever he wanted to form an opinion about what lay beyond his observation or the observation of available witnesses, simply shut his eyes, asked himself the appropriate question, and accepted the first answer that came into his head. Wouldn't this be a non-inductive method?" Well, let us suppose this. The man is asked: "Do you usually get the right answer by your method?" He might answer: "You've mentioned one of its drawbacks; I never do get the right answer; but it's an extremely easy method."

One might then be inclined to think that it was not a method of finding things out at all. But suppose he answered: Yes, it's usually (always) the right answer. Then we might be willing to call it a method of finding out, though a strange one. But, then, by the very fact of its success, it would be an inductively supported method. For each application of the method would be an application of the general rule, "The first answer that comes into my head is generally (always) the right one"; and for the truth of this generalization there would be the inductive evidence of a long run of favourable instances with no unfavourable ones (if it were "always"), or of a sustained high proportion of successes to trials (if it were "generally").

So every successful method or recipe for finding out about the unobserved must be one which has inductive support; for to say that a recipe is successful is to say that it has been repeatedly applied with success; and repeated successful application of a recipe constitutes just what we mean by inductive evidence in its favour. Pointing out this fact must not be confused with saying that "the inductive method" is justified by its success, justified because it works. This is a mistake, and an important one. I am not seeking to "justify the inductive method," for no meaning has been given to this phrase. *A fortiori,* I am not saying that induction is justified by its success in finding out about the unobserved. I am saying, rather, that any successful method of finding out about the unobserved is necessarily justified by induction. This is an analytic proposition. The phrase "successful method of finding things out which has no inductive support" is self-contradictory. Having, or acquiring, inductive support is a necessary condition of the success of a method.

Why point this out at all? First, it may have a certain therapeutic force, a power to reassure. Second, it may counteract the tendency to think of "the inductive method" as something on a par with specific methods of diagnosis or prediction and therefore, like them, standing in need of (inductive) justification.

VIII.6 The New Riddle of Induction

Nelson Goodman

Nelson Goodman until his retirement was professor of philosophy at Harvard University. In this selection, taken from his book *Fact, Fiction and Forecast,* Goodman argues that beside Hume's puzzle over induction, there is a second problem: What are the rules for deciding which properties are projectable into the future? Why does seeing another black raven confirm our hypothesis that all ravens are black or that the next raven we see will be black but the seeing of three bachelors in a room not count as evidence that tomorrow we will see three bachelors in this room? Inventing a new color term *grue,* made up from our color terms *green* and *blue,* Goodman illustrates the problem of projectability.

Confirmation of a hypothesis by an instance depends rather heavily upon features of the hypothesis other than its syntactical form. That a given piece of copper conducts electricity increases the credibility of statements asserting that other pieces of copper conduct electricity, and thus confirms the hypothesis that all copper conducts electricity. But the fact that a given man now in this room is a third son does not increase the credibility of statements asserting that other men now in this room are third sons, and so does not confirm the hypothesis that all men now in this room are third sons. Yet in both cases our hypothesis is a generalization of the evidence statement. The difference is that in the former case the hypothesis is a *lawlike* statement; while in the latter case, the hypothesis is a merely contingent or accidental generality. Only a statement that is *lawlike*—regardless of its truth or falsity or its scientific importance—is capable of receiving confirmation from an instance of it; accidental statements are not. Plainly, then, we must look for a way of distinguishing lawlike from accidental statements.

So long as what seems to be needed is merely a way of excluding a few odd and unwanted cases that are inadvertently admitted by our definition of confirmation, the problem may not seem very hard or very pressing. We fully expect that minor

Reprinted from *Fact, Fiction and Forecast* (Cambridge, MA: Harvard University Press, 1984) by permission. Notes have been edited. © 1979, 1982 by Nelson Goodman.

defects will be found in our definition and that the necessary refinements will have to be worked out patiently one after another. But some further examples will show that our present difficulty is of a much graver kind.

Suppose that all emeralds examined before a certain time t are green.[1] At time t, then, our observations support the hypothesis that all emeralds are green; and this is in accord with our definition of confirmation. Our evidence statements assert that emerald a is green, that emerald b is green, and so on; and each confirms the general hypothesis that all emeralds are green. So far, so good.

Now let me introduce another predicate less familiar than "green." It is the predicate "grue" and it applies to all things examined before t just in case they are green but to other things just in case they are blue. Then at time t we have, for each evidence statement asserting that a given emerald is green, a parallel evidence statement asserting that that emerald is grue. And the statements that emerald a is grue, that emerald b is grue, and so on, will each confirm the general hypothesis that all emeralds are grue. Thus according to our definition, the prediction that all emeralds subsequently examined will be green and the prediction that all will be grue are alike confirmed by evidence statements describing the same observations. But if an emerald subsequently examined is grue, it is blue and hence not green. Thus although we are well aware which of the two incompatible predictions is genuinely confirmed, they are equally well confirmed according to our present definition. Moreover, it is clear that if we simply choose an appropriate predicate, then on the basis of these same observations we shall have equal confirmation, by our definition, for any prediction whatever about other emeralds—or indeed about anything else.[2] As in our earlier example, only the predictions subsumed under lawlike hypotheses are genuinely confirmed; but we have no criterion as yet for determining lawlikeness. And now we see that without some such criterion, our definition not merely includes a few unwanted cases, but is so completely ineffectual that it virtually excludes nothing. We are left once again with the intolerable result that anything confirms anything. This difficulty cannot be set aside as an annoying detail to be taken care of in due course. It has to be met before our definition will work at all.

Nevertheless, the difficulty is often slighted because on the surface there seem to be easy ways of dealing with it. Sometimes, for example, the problem is thought to be much like the paradox of the ravens. We are here again, it is pointed out, making tacit and illegitimate use of information outside the stated evidence: the information, for example, that different samples of one material are usually alike in conductivity, and the information that different men in a lecture audience are usually not alike in the number of their older brothers. But while it is true that such information is being smuggled in, this does not by itself settle the matter as it settles the matter of the ravens. There the point was that when the smuggled information is forthrightly declared, its effect upon the confirmation of the hypothesis in question is immediately and properly registered by the definition we are using. On the other hand, if to our initial evidence we add statements concerning the conductivity of pieces of other materials or concerning the number of older brothers of members of other lecture audiences, this will not in the least affect the confirmation, according to our definition, of the hypothesis concerning copper or of that concerning other lecture audiences. Since our definition is insensitive to the bearing upon hypotheses of evidence so related to them, even when the evidence is fully declared, the difficulty about accidental hypotheses cannot be explained away on the ground that such evidence is being surreptitiously taken into account.

A more promising suggestion is to explain the matter in terms of the effect of this other evidence not directly upon the hypothesis in question but *in*directly through other hypotheses that *are* confirmed, according to our definition, by such evidence. Our information about other materials does by our definition confirm such hypotheses as that all pieces of iron conduct electricity, that no pieces of rubber do, and so on; and these hypotheses, the explanation runs, impart to the hypothesis that all pieces of copper conduct electricity (and also to the hypothesis that none do) the character of lawlikeness—that is, amenability to confirmation by direct positive instances when found. On the other hand, our information about other lecture audiences *dis*confirms many hypotheses to the effect that all the men in one audience are third sons, or that none are; and this strips any character of lawlikeness from the hypothesis that all (or the hypothesis that none) of the men in *this* audience are third sons. But clearly if this course is to be followed, the circumstances under which hypotheses are thus related to one another will have to be precisely articulated.

The problem, then, is to define the relevant ways in which such hypotheses must be alike. Evidence for the hypothesis that all iron conducts electricity enhances the lawlikeness of the hypothesis that all zirconium conducts electricity, but does not similarly affect the hypothesis that all the objects on my desk conduct electricity. Wherein lies the difference? The first two hypotheses fall under the broader hypothesis—call it "*H*"—that every class of things of the same material is uniform in conductivity; the first and third fall only under some such hypothesis as—call it "*K*"—that every class of things that are either all of the same material or all on a desk is uniform in conductivity. Clearly the important difference here is that evidence for a statement affirming that one of the classes covered by *H* has the property in question increases the credibility of any statement affirming that another such class has this property; while nothing of the sort holds true with respect to *K*. But this is only to say that *H* is lawlike and *K* is not. We are faced anew with the very problem we are trying to solve: the problem of distinguishing between lawlike and accidental hypotheses.

The most popular way of attacking the problem takes its cue from the fact that accidental hypotheses seem typically to involve some spatial or temporal restriction, or reference to some particular individual. They seem to concern the people in some particular room, or the objects on some particular person's desk; while lawlike hypotheses characteristically concern all ravens or all pieces of copper whatsoever. Complete generality is thus very often supposed to be a sufficient condition of lawlikeness; but to define this complete generality is by no means easy. Merely to require that the hypothesis contain no term naming, describing, or indicating a particular thing or location will obviously not be enough. The troublesome hypothesis that all emeralds are grue contains no such term; and where such a term does occur, as in hypotheses about men in *this room,* it can be suppressed in favor of some predicate (short or long, new or old) that contains no such term but applies only to exactly the same things. One might think, then, of excluding not only hypotheses that actually contain terms for specific individuals but also all hypotheses that are equivalent to others that do contain such terms. But, as we have just seen, to exclude only hypotheses of which *all* equivalents contain such terms is to exclude nothing. On the other hand, to exclude all hypotheses that have *some* equivalent containing such a term is to exclude everything; for even the hypothesis

All grass is green

has as an equivalent

All grass in London or elsewhere is green.

The next step, therefore, has been to consider ruling out predicates of certain kinds. A syntactically universal hypothesis is lawlike, the proposal runs, if its predicates are "purely qualitative" or "non-positional."[3] This will obviously accomplish nothing if a purely qualitative predicate is then conceived either as one that is equivalent to some expression free of terms for specific individuals, or as one that is equivalent to no expression that contains such a term; for this only raises again the difficulties just pointed out. The claim appears to be rather that at least in the case of a simple enough predicate we can readily determine by direct inspection of its meaning whether or not it is purely qualitative. But even aside from obscurities in the notion of "the meaning" of a predicate, this claim seems to me wrong. I simply do not know how to tell whether a predicate is qualitative or positional, except perhaps by completely begging the question at issue and asking whether the predicate is "well-behaved"—that is, whether simple

syntactically universal hypotheses applying it are lawlike.

This statement will not go unprotested. "Consider," it will be argued, "the predicates 'blue' and 'green' and the predicate 'grue' introduced earlier, and also the predicate 'bleen' that applies to emeralds examined before time *t* just in case they are blue and to other emeralds just in case they are green. Surely it is clear," the argument runs, "that the first two are purely qualitative and the second two are not; for the meaning of each of the latter two plainly involves reference to a specific temporal position." To this I reply that indeed I do recognize the first two as well-behaved predicates admissible in lawlike hypotheses, and the second two as ill-behaved predicates. But the argument that the former but not the latter are purely qualitative seems to me quite unsound. True enough, if we start with "blue" and "green," then "grue" and "bleen" will be explained in terms of "blue" and "green" and a temporal term. But equally truly, if we start with "grue" and "bleen," then "blue" and "green" will be explained in terms of "grue" and "bleen" and a temporal term; "green," for example, applies to emeralds examined before time *t* just in case they are grue, and to other emeralds just in case they are bleen. Thus qualitativeness is an entirely relative matter and does not by itself establish any dichotomy of predicates. This relativity seems to be completely overlooked by those who contend that the qualitative character of a predicate is a criterion for its good behavior.

Of course, one may ask why we need worry about such unfamiliar predicates as "grue" or about accidental hypotheses in general, since we are unlikely to use them in making predictions. If our definition works for such hypotheses as are normally employed, isn't that all we need? In a sense, yes; but only in the sense that we need no definition, no theory of induction, and no philosophy of knowledge at all. We get along well enough without them in daily life and in scientific research. But if we seek a theory at all, we cannot excuse gross anomalies resulting from a proposed theory by pleading that we can avoid them in practice. The odd cases we have been considering are clinically pure cases that, though seldom encountered in practice, nevertheless display to best advantage the symptoms of a widespread and destructive malady.

We have so far neither any answer nor any promising clue to an answer to the question what distinguishes lawlike or confirmable hypotheses from accidental or non-confirmable ones; and what may at first have seemed a minor technical difficulty has taken on the stature of a major obstacle to the development of a satisfactory theory of confirmation. It is this problem that I call the new riddle of induction.

Notes

[1]Although the example used is different, the argument to follow is substantially the same as that set forth in my note "A Query on Confirmation" [*Journal of Philosophy,* XLIII (1946), 383–385.]

[2]For instance, we shall have equal confirmation, by our present definition, for the prediction that roses subsequently examined will be blue. Let "emerose" apply just to emeralds examined before time *t,* and to roses examined later. Then all emeroses so far examined are grue, and this confirms the hypothesis that all emeroses are grue and hence the prediction that roses subsequently examined will be blue. The problem raised by such antecedents has been little noticed, but is no easier to meet than that raised by similarly perverse consequents.

[3]Carnap took this course in his paper "On the Application of Inductive Logic," *Philosophy and Phenomenological Research,* vol. 8 (1947), pp. 133–47, which is in part a reply to my "A Query on Confirmation." The discussion was continued in my note "On Infirmities of Confirmation Theory," *Philosophy and Phenomenological Research,* vol. 8 (1947), pp. 149–51; and in Carnap's "Reply to Nelson Goodman," same journal, same volume, pp. 461–2.

Bibliography

Goodman, Nelson. *Fact, Fiction and Forecast.* Cambridge, MA: Harvard University Press, 1955.

Jeffrey, Richard. *The Logic of Decision,* 2d ed. Chicago: University of Chicago Press, 1983.

Kyburg, Henry E., Jr. *Probability and the Logic of Rational Belief.* Middletown, CT: Wesleyan University Press, 1961.

Mackie, J. L. "A Defense of Induction." In *Logic and Knowledge.* Oxford: Clarendon Press, 1995.

Mill, John Stuart. *System of Logic,* 10th ed. London: Longman's Green, 1879.

Reichenbach, Hans. *Experience and Prediction.* Chicago: University of Chicago Press, 1938.

Skyrms, Brian. *Choice and Chance.* Belmont, CA: Wadsworth, 1986.

Stove, D. C. *Probability and Hume's Inductive Scepticism.* Oxford: Clarendon Press, 1973.

Strawson, P. F. *Introduction to Logical Theory.* New York: Wiley, 1952.

Swinburne, Richard, ed. *The Justification of Induction.* Oxford: Oxford University Press, 1974.

Will, Frederick. *Induction and Justification.* Ithaca, NY: Cornell University Press, 1973.

Part IX

Scientific Method, Justification, and the Demarcation Problem

Science has a privileged status in our society. We hold that it is a more reliable enterprise for attaining truth or justified belief than other methodological enterprises. Hence, we afford it a special place in our educational curricula and honor our scientists as great benefactors of society. The names of Nicholas Copernicus, Galileo, Isaac Newton, Charles Darwin, and Albert Einstein are among the most revered in contemporary Western society, having replaced the names of the saints in the Middle Ages as the paragons of cosmic success.

Philosophy of science attempts to understand how our theories about nature and the world are justified. What methods assure that a theory is deserving of the honorific name of *science*—a justified theory about the way nature or the universe works. The traditional view, still taught in schools, is that science proceeds by observations that generate hypotheses about the way nature works, which in turn must be tested by experiments and eventually, through trial and error, lead to proven theories—knowledge of the laws of nature. This traditional view of scientific method has been shown to be both too broad and too narrow. It is too broad because almost any theory could pass muster, including astrology, witchcraft, and myth, because they are based on observation and testing. The view is too narrow because it excludes justified belief in most established theories, for virtually no theory has been proved beyond all doubt on the basis of observation and experiment. Certainly atomic and subatomic physics elude our observational grasp. An example of the point that theories are underdetermined by the evidence is Copernicus's heliocentrism, which replaced Ptolemaic geocentrism, not because of conclusive observational evidence, but because it was simpler, not needing a plethora of planetary epicycles. This traditional view is critically examined by Carl Hempel in our second reading on scientific hypotheses.

So we return to the question of what demarcates science from nonscience and nonsense. What method renders our theoretical beliefs about the workings of nature justified?

The readings in this part of our work deal with this question. Early in the 20th century a group of philosophers and scientists in Vienna, Austria, was consumed with the project of reducing all meaningful discourse to a language of science. Let us examine their answer to our question.

Logical Positivism

Logical positivism is the name given in 1931 by A. E. Bluimberg and Herbert Feigl to a set of philosophical doctrines put forward by the Vienna Circle. From 1907 to the early 1930s, these philosophers and scientists—led by Moritz Schlick and Rudolf Carnap, but also including Frederick Waissmann, Kurt Godel, and Otto Neurath—sought to promote the ideas of the British empiricists—such as David Hume and Bertrand Russell—and the Czech thinker Ernest Mach who held that science consists fundamentally in the description of experience. They hoped to produce a scientifically based philosophy, eliminating all transcendental metaphysics and emphasizing the importance of mathematics and theoretical physics.

Central to their program was the *verification principle*, that the meaning of a sentence is the method of verifying the proposition it expresses—i.e., a proposition names a set of sensory experiences that are together equivalent to the proposition's being true. Essentially, they agreed with David Hume's famous statement, "If we take in hand any volume of divinity or school metaphysics, for instance, let us ask, *Does it contain any abstract reasoning concerning quantity or number?* No. *Does it contain any experimental reasoning concerning matter of fact or existence?* No. Commit it then to the flames; for it can contain nothing but sophistry and illusion."[1]

Mathematical and logical propositions were meaningful as tautologies. Ethical statements are not really assertions at all. Ethical statements such as "Killing people is wrong" are meaningless emotional ejaculations (read, "Killing people—Boo!"). Theology consists of nonsense because there is no way to verify its claims, e.g., that God exists and that He dwells in eternity beyond time.

Although the Vienna Circle dissolved in the early 1930s, its ideas spread to England and America. The classic expression of their ideas in English is A. J. Ayer's *Language, Truth and Logic* (1935), written as his doctoral dissertation after an extended stay in Austria with the members of the Vienna Circle. A segment is

reproduced in Reading IX.1, and we have already seen the chapter on the A Priori in Reading VII.2. In the United States logical positivism was combined with pragmatism by W. V. Quine and Carl Hempel. Quine went beyond the positivists, arguing for the subordination of epistemology to psychology (see "Epistemology Naturalized," Reading VI.3), the elimination of the analytic/synthetic distinction (see "Two Dogmas of Empiricism," Reading VII.4), and even the elimination of *meaning* altogether. Hempel's theory is contained in Reading IX.2.

Falsification and the Demise of Logical Positivism

Logical positivism was seen by many, including its proponents, as destructive of philosophy. Its only role was to serve science by revealing the deep structure of our statements, i.e., by showing that philosophical problems are merely confusions. In the words of Ludwig Wittgenstein, the role of this new philosophy was to deliver us from "the bewitchment of our intellect," a bewitchment caused by philosophy. It was to help the fly get out of the fly bottle.

Gradually, a strong reaction arose against logical positivism. It was pointed out that its own verification principle was unscientific because it could not be empirically verified. When Carnap sought to correct its formulation to read that a proposition is meaningful only if it is possible to confirm it, it was noted that this would let in transcendental metaphysics, say, in the sentence, "Either it is raining or the absolute is perfect." Hilary Putnam gave the example, "There is a gold mountain one mile high and no one knows it," as a counterexample to theological positivist's dicta.

A series of rival theories about the nature and method of science grew up as a response to the demise of logical positivism.

In our third reading "Science: Conjectures and Refutations," Karl Popper argues that the criterion for scientific method is not verification, but *falsification*, or more accurately, the process of setting forth bold conjectures and then attempting to refute them. A theory is scientific only if one can specify in advance a crucial experiment that would falsify it. If one cannot (or will not) specify how to falsify it, it is not a scientific theory. Popper rejects induction as the proper method of science and sets forth a broad theory about how science grows, asymptotically approaching truth.

Our fourth reading, by the Hungarian-English philosopher Imre Lakatos, argues that Popper's criterion is an improvement on the traditional method and verificationism but is nevertheless overly simplistic. Popper ignores the remarkable resilience of scientists to invent *ad hoc* hypotheses[2] in order to save their theories. His view is that theories should be seen as research programs: some programs are progressive and lead to new, more fruitful, and unexpected theories, whereas others are degenerate, leading to dead ends, and so should be abandoned.

In our final reading the Austrian-American philosopher Paul Feyerabend argues that the privileged status enjoyed by science is undeserved. Science is essentially just another ideology with its own biases. It is a myth with no more special authority or rational method than a religion. Recognizing this, we ought to demote it from its social pinnacle. Feyerabend's critique anticipates some of the points made in Richard Rorty's essay "Dismantling Truth: Solidarity versus Objectivity" (Reading XI.4).

Notes

[1] David Hume, *An Enquiry Concerning Human Understanding* (Oxford University Press, 1975), p. 165.

[2] An *ad hoc* hypothesis is a hypothesis invented, not because it has evidence in its favor, but simply to save a theory that is threatened, but is deemed worthy of salvage. One example is the invention of planetary epicycles devised to save Ptolemaic astronomy from the criticisms of the Copernican revolution in the 16th century. Another is the hypothesis that sin has done epistemic damage to our noetic structure in order to save the theory that human beings have natural knowledge of God but do not realize it. Popper and Lakatos give other examples in their articles in this section.

IX.1 The Verification Method and the Elimination of Metaphysics

A. J. AYER

Alfred Jules Ayer (1910–1989) was born in London, the son of immigrant parents. He attended Eton and Christ Church, Oxford University, where he studied under Gilbert Ryle. When he was 26 he traveled to Vienna to meet Moritz Schlick, the leader of the Vienna Circle, a group of logical positivists. On his return to Oxford he wrote his most famous book, *Language, Truth and Logic,* a selection of which is reprinted here. He later became a professor at University College, London University, before returning to Oxford in 1960 to take up the Wykeham Professorship of Logic, where he taught until a short time before his death in 1989. A lifelong athiest, he astounded the public several months before his death with a report of a mystical experience. His heart stopped for four minutes, during which time "I was confronted by a red light, exceedingly bright, and also very painful, even when I turned away from it. I was aware that this light was responsible for the government of the universe."*

Ayer was England's most prominent logical positivist. That philosophy, which had its roots in Hume's Empiricism, like Hume rejected metaphysics as nonsense. Its driving idea was that for a sentence to be meaningful, it must be verifiable in principle by experience. So my statement that atoms exist, though not observable by human senses, could conceivably be true if we had instruments to bring them to human consciousness. We must somehow be able to point to it. But moral and theological statements cannot be verified. Statements such as "Telling the truth is good" or "Killing innocents is bad" can't be observed. That is, we can observe a lie or a killing, but we can't observe the "goodness" or "badness" which are predicated of these subject terms. Ayer would reduce the value sentences to emotive expressions, such as "Telling the truth—Hurrah!" and "Killing innocents— Boo!" Theological assertions such as "God exists" are simply nonsense because they fail to express the conditions under which one could verify such claims. In the first selection given below Ayer sets

forth to eliminate all metaphysical discourse. In the second selection he critiques ethics and theology.

The Abolition of Metaphysics

Preface to First Edition

The views which are put forward in this treatise derive from the doctrines of Bertrand Russell and Wittgenstein, which are themselves the logical outcome of the empiricism of Berkeley and David Hume. Like Hume, I divide all genuine propositions into two classes: those which, in his terminology, concern "relations of ideas," and those which concern "matters of fact." The former class comprises the *a priori* propositions of logic and pure mathematics, and these I allow to be necessary and certain only because they are analytic. That is, I maintain that the reason why these propositions cannot be confuted in experience is that they do not make any assertion about the empirical world, but simply record our determination to use symbols in a certain fashion. Propositions concerning empirical matters of fact, on the other hand, I hold to be hypotheses, which can be probable but never certain. And in giving an

---

*"What I Saw When I Was Dead . . ." *Spectator* July 16, 1988, reprinted in *The Philosophy of A. J. Ayer*, ed. L. E. Hahn (Open Court, 1992) p. 48.

Reprinted from A. J. Ayer, *Language, Truth and Logic* (Dover Press, 1952) by permission of Dover Publications.

account of the method of their validation I claim also to have explained the nature of truth.

To test whether a sentence expresses a genuine empirical hypothesis, I adopt what may be called a modified verification principle. For I require of an empirical hypothesis, not indeed that it should be conclusively verifiable, but that some possible sense-experience should be relevant to the determination of its truth or falsehood. If a putative proposition fails to satisfy this principle, and is not a tautology, then I hold that it is metaphysical, and that, being metaphysical, it is neither true nor false but literally senseless. It will be found that much of what ordinarily passes for philosophy is metaphysical according to this criterion, and, in particular, that it can not be significantly asserted that there is a nonempirical world of values, or that men have immortal souls, or that there is a transcendent God.

As for the propositions of philosophy themselves, they are held to be linguistically necessary, and so analytic. And with regard to the relationship of philosophy and empirical science, it is shown that the philosopher is not in a position to furnish speculative truths, which would, as it were, compete with the hypotheses of science, nor yet to pass *a priori* judgements upon the validity of scientific theories, but that his function is to clarify the propositions of science by exhibiting their logical relationships, and by defining the symbols which occur in them. Consequently I maintain that there is nothing in the nature of philosophy to warrant the existence of conflicting philosophical "schools." And I attempt to substantiate this by providing a definitive solution of the problems which have been the chief sources of controversy between philosophers in the past.

The view that philosophizing is an activity of analysis is associated in England with the work of G. E. Moore and his disciples. But while I have learned a great deal from Professor Moore, I have reason to believe that he and his followers are not prepared to adopt such a thoroughgoing phenomenalism as I do, and that they take a rather different view of the nature of philosophical analysis. The philosophers with whom I am in the closest agreement are those who compose the "Viennese circle," under the leadership of Moritz Schlick, and are commonly known as logical positivists. And of these I owe most to Rudolf Carnap. Further, I wish to acknowledge my indebtedness

to Gilbert Ryle, my original tutor in philosophy, and to Isaiah Berlin, who have discussed with me every point in the argument of this treatise, and made many valuable suggestions, although they both disagree with much of what I assert. . . .

Chapter 1: The Elimination of Metaphysics

The traditional disputes of philosophers are, for the most part, as unwarranted as they are unfruitful. The surest way to end them is to establish beyond question what should be the purpose and method of a philosophical enquiry. And this is by no means so difficult a task as the history of philosophy would lead one to suppose. For if there are any questions which science leaves it to philosophy to answer, a straightforward process of elimination must lead to their discovery.

We may begin by criticising the metaphysical thesis that philosophy affords us knowledge of a reality transcending the world of science and common sense. Later on, when we come to define metaphysics and account for its existence, we shall find that it is possible to be a metaphysician without believing in a transcendent reality; for we shall see that many metaphysical utterances are due to the commission of logical errors, rather than to a conscious desire on the part of their authors to go beyond the limits of experience. But it is convenient for us to take the case of those who believe that it is possible to have knowledge of a transcendent reality as a starting-point for our discussion. The arguments which we use to refute them will subsequently be found to apply to the whole of metaphysics.

One way of attacking a metaphysician who claimed to have knowledge of a reality which transcended the phenomenal world would be to enquire from what premises his propositions were deduced. Must he not begin, as other men do, with the evidence of his senses? And if so, what valid process of reasoning can possibly lead him to the conception of a transcendent reality? Surely from empirical premises nothing whatsoever concerning the properties, or even the existence, of anything super-empirical can legitimately be inferred. But this objection would be met by a denial on the part of the metaphysician that his assertions were ultimately based on the evidence of his senses. He would say that he was endowed with a faculty of intellectual intuition which enabled him to know facts that could not be known through sense-experience. And even if it could be shown that he was relying on empirical premises, and that his venture into a nonempirical world was therefore logically unjustified, it would not follow that the assertions which he made concerning this non-empirical world could not be true. For the fact that a conclusion does not follow from its putative premise is not sufficient to show that it is false. Consequently one cannot overthrow a system of transcendent metaphysics merely by criticising the way in which it comes into being. What is required is rather a criticism of the nature of the actual statements which comprise it. And this is the line of argument which we shall, in fact, pursue. For we shall maintain that no statement which refers to a "reality" transcending the limits of all possible sense-experience can possibly have any literal significance; from which it must follow that the labours of those who have striven to describe such a reality have all been devoted to the production of nonsense.

It may be suggested that this is a proposition which has already been proved by Kant. But although Kant also condemned transcendent metaphysics, he did so on different grounds. For he said that the human understanding was so constituted that it lost itself in contradictions when it ventured out beyond the limits of possible experience and attempted to deal with things in themselves. And thus he made the impossibility of a transcendent metaphysic not, as we do, a matter of logic, but a matter of fact. He asserted, not that our minds could not conceivably have had the power of penetrating beyond the phenomenal world, but merely that they were in fact devoid of it. And this leads the critic to ask how, if it is possible to know only what lies within the bounds of sense-experience, the author can be justified in asserting that real things do exist beyond, and how he can tell what are the boundaries beyond which the human understanding may not venture, unless he succeeds in passing them himself. As Wittgenstein says, "in order to draw a limit to thinking, we should have to think both sides of this limit,"[1] a truth to which Bradley gives a special twist in maintaining that the man who is ready to prove that metaphysics is impossible is a brother metaphysician with a rival theory of his own.[2]

Whatever force these objections may have against the Kantian doctrine, they have none whatsoever against the thesis that I am about to set forth. It cannot here be said that the author is himself overstepping the barrier he maintains to be impassable. For the fruitlessness of attempting to transcend the limits of possible sense-experience will be deduced, not from a psychological hypothesis concerning the actual constitution of the human mind, but from the rule which determines the literal significance of language. Our charge against the metaphysician is not that he attempts to employ the understanding in a field where it cannot profitably venture, but that he produces sentences which fail to conform to the conditions under which alone a sentence can be literally significant. Nor are we ourselves obliged to talk nonsense in order to show that all sentences of a certain type are necessarily devoid of literal significance. We need only formulate the criterion which enables us to test whether a sentence expresses a genuine proposition about a matter of fact, and then point out that the sentences under consideration fail to satisfy it. And this we shall now proceed to do. We shall first of all formulate the criterion in somewhat vague terms, and then give the explanations which are necessary to render it precise.

The criterion which we use to test the genuineness of apparent statements of fact is the criterion of verifiability. We say that a sentence is factually significant to any given person, if, and only if, he knows how to verify the proposition which it purports to express—that is, if he knows what observations would lead them, under certain conditions, to accept the proposition as being true, or reject it as being false. If, on the other hand, the putative proposition is of such a character that the assumption of its truth, or falsehood, is consistent with any assumption whatsoever concerning the nature of his future experience, then, as far as he is concerned, it is, if not a tautology, a mere pseudoproposition. The sentence expressing it may be emotionally significant to him; but it is not literally significant. And with regard to questions the procedure is the same. We enquire in every case what observations would lead us to answer the question, one way or the other; and, if none can be discovered, we must conclude that the sentence under consideration does not, as far as we are concerned, express a genuine question, however strongly its grammatical appearance may suggest that it does.

As the adoption of this procedure is an essential factor in the argument of this book, it needs to be examined in detail.

In the first place, it is necessary to draw a distinction between practical verifiability, and verifiability in principle. Plainly we all understand, in many cases believe, propositions which we have not in fact taken steps to verify. Many of these are propositions which we could verify if we took enough trouble. But there remain a number of significant propositions, concerning matters of fact, which we could not verify even if we chose; simply because we lack the practical means of placing ourselves in the situation where the relevant observations could be made. A simple and familiar example of such a proposition is the proposition that there are mountains on the farther side of the moon. No rocket has yet been invented which would enable me to go and look at the farther side of the moon, so that I am unable to decide the matter by actual observation. But I do know what observations would decide it for me, if, as is theoretically conceivable, I were once in a position to make them. And therefore I say that the proposition is verifiable in principle, if not in practice, and is accordingly significant. On the other hand, such a metaphysical pseudo-proposition as "the Absolute enters into, but is itself incapable of, evolution and progress," is not even in principle verifiable. For one cannot conceive of an observation which would enable one to determine whether the Absolute did, or did not, enter into evolution and progress. Of course it is possible that the author of such a remark is using English words in a way in which they are not commonly used by English-speaking people, and that he does, in fact, intend to assert something which could be empirically verified. But until he makes us understand how the proposition that he wishes to express would be verified, he fails to communicate anything to us. And if he admits, as I think the author of the remark in question would have admitted, that his words were not intended to express either a tautology or a proposition which was capable, at least in principle, of being verified, then it follows that he has made an utterance which has no literal significance even for himself.

A further distinction which we must make is the distinction between the "strong" and the "weak" sense of the term "verifiable." A proposition is said to be verifiable, in the strong sense of the term, if, and only if, its truth could be conclusively established in experience. But it is verifiable, in the weak sense, if it is possible for experience to render it probable. In which sense are we using the term when we say that a putative proposition is genuine only if it is verifiable?

It seems to me that if we adopt conclusive verifiability as our criterion of significance, as some positivists have proposed, our argument will prove too much. Consider, for example, the case of general propositions of law—such propositions, namely, as "arsenic is poisonous"; "all men are mortal"; "a body tends to expand when it is heated." It is of the very nature of these propositions that their truth cannot be established with certainty by any finite series of observations. But if it is recognised that such general propositions of law are designed to cover an infinite number of cases, then it must be admitted that they cannot, even in principle, be verified conclusively. And then, if we adopt conclusive verifiability as our criterion of significance, we are logically obligated to treat these general propositions of law in the same fashion as we treat the statements of the metaphysician.

In face of this difficulty, some positivists have adopted the heroic course of saying that these general propositions are indeed pieces of nonsense, albeit an essentially important type of nonsense. But here the introduction of the term "important" is simply an attempt to hedge. It serves only to mark the authors' recognition that their view is somewhat too paradoxical, without in any way removing the paradox. Besides, the difficulty is not confined to the case of general propositions of law, though it is there revealed most plainly. It is hardly less obvious in the case of propositions about the remote past. For it must surely be admitted that, however strong the evidence in favour of historical statements may be, their truth can never become more than highly probable. And to maintain that they also constituted an important, or unimportant, type of nonsense would be unplausible, to say the very least. Indeed, it will be our contention that no proposition, other than a tautology, can possibly be anything more than a probable hypothesis. And if this is correct, the principle that a sentence can be factually significant only if it expresses what is conclusively verifiable is self-stultifying as a criterion of significance. For it leads to the conclusion that it is impossible to make a significant statement of fact at all.

Nor can we accept the suggestion that a sentence should be allowed to be factually significant if, and only if, it expresses something which is definitely confutable by experience. Those who adopt this course assume that, although no finite series of observations is ever sufficient to establish the truth of a hypothesis beyond all possibility of doubt, there are crucial cases in which a single observation, or series of observations, can definitely confute it. But, as we shall show later on, this assumption is false. A hypothesis cannot be conclusively confuted any more than it can be conclusively verified. For when we take the occurrence of certain observations as proof that a given hypothesis is false, we presuppose the existence of certain conditions. And though, in any given case, it may be extremely improbable that this assumption is false, it is not logically impossible. We shall see that there need be no self-contradiction in holding that some of the relevant circumstances are other than we have taken them to be, and consequently that the hypothesis has not really broken down. And if it is not the case that any hypothesis can be definitely confuted, we cannot hold that the genuineness of a proposition depends on the possibility of its definite confutation.

Accordingly, we fall back on the weaker sense of verification. We say that the question that must be asked about any putative statement of fact is not, Would any observations make its truth or falsehood logically certain? but simply, Would any observations be relevant to the determination of its truth or falsehood? And it is only if a negative answer is given to this second question that we conclude that the statement under consideration is nonsensical.

To make our position clearer, we may formulate it in another way. Let us call a proposition which records an actual or possible observation an experiential proposition. Then we may say that it is the mark of a genuine factual proposition, not that it should be equivalent to an experiential proposition, or any finite number of experiential propositions, but simply that some experiential propositions can be deduced from it in conjunction with certain other premises without being deducible from those other premises alone.

This criterion seems liberal enough. In contrast to the principle of conclusive verifiability, it clearly does not deny significance to general propositions or to propositions about the past. Let us see what kinds of assertion it rules out.

A good example of the kind of utterance that is condemned by our criterion as being not even false but nonsensical would be the assertion that the world of sense-experience was altogether unreal. It must, of course, be admitted that our senses do sometimes deceive us. We may, as the result of having certain sensations, expect certain other sensations to be obtainable which are, in fact, not obtainable. But, in all such cases, it is further sense-experience that informs us of the mistakes that arise out of sense-experience. We say that the senses sometimes deceive us, just because the expectations to which our sense-experiences give rise do not always accord with what we subsequently experience. That is, we rely on our senses to substantiate or confute the judgements which are based on our sensations. And therefore the fact that our perceptual judgements are sometimes found to be erroneous has not the slightest tendency to show that the world of sense-experience is unreal. And, indeed, it is plain that no conceivable observation, or series of observations, could have any tendency to show that the world revealed to us by sense-experience was unreal. Consequently, anyone who condemns the sensible world as a world of mere appearance, as opposed to reality, is saying something which, according to our criterion of significance, is literally nonsensical.

An example of a controversy which the application of our criterion obliges us to condemn as fictitious is provided by those who dispute concerning the number of substances that there are in the world. For it is admitted both by monists, who maintain that reality is one substance, and by pluralists, who maintain that reality is many, that it is impossible to imagine any empirical situation which would be relevant to the solution of their dispute. But if we are told that no possible observation could give any probability either to the assertion that reality was one substance or to the assertion that it was many, then we must conclude that neither assertion is significant. We shall see later on that there are genuine logical and empirical questions involved in the dispute between monists and pluralists. But the metaphysical question concerning "substance" is ruled out by our criterion as spurious.

A similar treatment must be accorded to the controversy between realists and idealists, in its metaphysical aspect. A simple illustration, which I have made use of in a similar argument elsewhere, will help to demonstrate this. Let us suppose that a picture is discovered and the suggestion made that it was painted by Goya. There is a definite procedure for dealing with such a question. The experts examine the picture to see in what way it resembles the accredited works of Goya, and to see if it bears any marks which are characteristic of a forgery; they look up contemporary records for evidence of the existence of such a picture, and so on. In the end, they may still disagree, but each one knows what empirical evidence would go to confirm or discredit his opinion. Suppose, now, that these men have studied philosophy, and some of them proceed to maintain that this picture is a set of ideas in the perceiver's mind, or in God's mind, others that it is objectively real. What possible experience could any of them have which would be relevant to the solution of this dispute one way or the other? In the ordinary sense of the term "real," in which it is opposed to "illusory," the reality of the picture is not in doubt. The disputants have satisfied themselves that the picture is real, in this sense, by obtaining a correlated series of sensations of sight and sensations of touch. Is there any similar process by which they could discover whether the picture was real, in the sense in which the term "real" is opposed to "ideal"? Clearly there is none. But, if that is so, the problem is fictitious according to our criterion. This does not mean that the realist-idealist controversy may be dismissed without further ado. For it can legitimately be regarded as a dispute concerning the analysis of existential propositions, and so as involving a logical problem which, as we shall see, can be definitively solved. What we have just shown is that the question at issue between idealists and realists becomes fictitious when, as is often the case, it is given a metaphysical interpretation.

There is no need for us to give further examples of the operation of our criterion of significance. For our object is merely to show that philosophy, as a genuine branch of knowledge, must be distinguished from metaphysics. We are not now concerned with the historical question how much of what has traditionally passed for phi-losophy is actually metaphysical. We shall, however, point out later on that the majority of the "great philosophers" of the past were not essentially metaphysicians, and thus reassure those who would otherwise be prevented from adopting our criterion by considerations of piety.

As to the validity of the verification principle . . . it will be shown that all propositions which have factual content are empirical hypotheses; and that the function of an empirical hypothesis is to provide a rule for the anticipation of experience. And this means that every empirical hypothesis must be relevant to some actual, or possible, experience, so that a statement which is not relevant to any experience is not an empirical hypothesis, and accordingly has no factual content. But this is precisely what the principle of verifiability asserts.

It should be mentioned here that the fact that the utterances of the metaphysician are non-sensical does not follow simply from the fact that they are devoid of factual content. It follows from that fact, together with the fact that they are not *a priori* propositions. . . . *a priori* propositions, which have always been attractive to philosophers on account of their certainty, owe this certainty to the fact that they are tautologies. We may accordingly define a metaphysical sentence as a sentence which purports to express a genuine proposition, but does, in fact, express neither a tautology nor an empirical hypothesis. And as tautologies and empirical hypotheses form the entire class of significant propositions, we are justified in concluding that all metaphysical assertions are nonsensical. Our next task is to show how they come to be made.

The use of the term "substance," to which we have already referred, provides us with a good example of the way in which metaphysics mostly comes to be written. It happens to be the case that we cannot, in our language, refer to the sensible properties of a thing without introducing a word or phrase which appears to stand for the thing itself as opposed to anything which may be said about it. And, as a result of this, those who are infected by the primitive superstition that to every name a single real entity must correspond assume that it is necessary to distinguish logically between the thing itself and any, or all, of its sensible properties. And so they employ the term "substance" to refer to the thing itself. But from the fact that we happen to employ a single word to refer to a thing, and make that word the grammatical subject of the sentences in which we refer to the sensible appearances of the thing, it does not by any means follow that the thing itself is a "simple entity," or that it cannot be defined in terms of the totality of its appearances. It is true that in talking of "its" appearances we appear to distinguish the thing from the appearances, but that is simply an accident of linguistic usage. Logical analysis shows that what makes these "appearances" the "appearances of" the same thing is not their relationship to an entity other than themselves, but their relationship to one another. The metaphysician fails to see this because he is misled by a superficial grammatical feature of his language.

A simpler and clearer instance of the way in which a consideration of grammar leads to metaphysics is the case of the metaphysical concept of Being. The origin of our temptation to raise questions about Being, which no conceivable experience would enable us to answer, lies in the fact that, in our language, sentences which express existential propositions and sentences which express attributive propositions may be of the same grammatical form. For instance, the sentences "Martyrs exist" and "Martyrs suffer" both consist of a noun followed by an intransitive verb, and the fact that they have grammatically the same appearance leads one to assume that they are of the same logical type. It is seen that in the proposition "Martyrs suffer," the members of a certain species are credited with a certain attribute, and it is sometimes assumed that the same thing is true of such a proposition as "Martyrs exist." If this were actually the case, it would, indeed, be as legitimate to speculate about the Being of martyrs as it is to speculate about their suffering. But, as Kant pointed out, existence is not an attribute. For, when we ascribe an attribute to a thing, we covertly assert that it exists: so that if existence were itself an attribute, it would follow that all positive existential propositions were tautologies, and all negative existential propositions self-contradictory; and this is not the case. So that those who raise questions about Being which are based on the assumption that existence is an attribute are guilty of following grammar beyond the boundaries of sense.

A similar mistake has been made in connection with such propositions as "Unicorns are fictitious." Here again the fact that there is a superficial grammatical resemblance between the English sentences "Dogs are faithful" and "Unicorns are fictitious," and between the corresponding sentences in other languages, creates the assumption that they are of the same logical type. Dogs must exist in order to have the property of being faithful, and so it is held that unless unicorns in some way existed they could not have the property of being fictitious. But, as it is plainly self-contradictory to say that fictitious objects exist, the device is adopted of saying that they are real in some nonempirical sense—that they have a mode of real being which is different from the mode of being of existent things. But since there is no way of testing whether an object is real in this sense, as there is for testing whether it is real in the ordinary sense, the assertion that fictitious objects have a special non-empirical mode of real being is devoid of all literal significance. It comes to be made as a result of the assumption that being fictitious is an attribute. And this is a fallacy of the same order as the fallacy of supposing that existence is an attribute, and it can be exposed in the same way.

In general, the postulation of real non-existent entities results from the superstition, just now referred to, that, to every word or phrase that can be the grammatical subject of a sentence, there must somewhere be a real entity corresponding. For as there is no place in the empirical world for many of these "entities," a special non-empirical world is invoked to house them. To this error must be attributed, not only the utterances of a Heidegger, who bases his metaphysics on the assumption that "Nothing" is a name which is used to denote something peculiarly mysterious, but also the prevalence of such problems as those concerning the reality of propositions and universals whose senselessness, though less obvious, is no less complete.

These few examples afford a sufficient indication of the way in which most metaphysical assertions come to be formulated. They show how easy it is to write sentences which are literally nonsensical without seeing that they are nonsensical. And thus we see that the view that a number of the traditional "problems of philosophy" are metaphysical, and consequently fictitious, does not involve any incredible assumptions about the psychology of philosophers.

Among those who recognise that if philosophy is to be accounted a genuine branch of knowledge it must be defined in such a way as to distinguish it from metaphysics, it is fashionable to speak of the metaphysician as a kind of misplaced poet. As his statements have no literal meaning, they are not subject to any criteria of truth or falsehood: but they may still serve to express, or arouse, emotion, and thus be subject to ethical or aesthetic standards. And it is suggested that they may have considerable value, as means of moral inspiration, or even as works of art. In this way, an attempt is made to compensate the metaphysician for his extrusion from philosophy.

I am afraid that this compensation is hardly in accordance with his deserts. The view that the metaphysician is to be reckoned among the poets appears to rest on the assumption that both talk nonsense. But this assumption is false. In the vast majority of cases the sentences which are produced by poets do have literal meaning. The difference between the man who uses language scientifically and the man who uses it emotively is not that the one produces sentences which are incapable of arousing emotion, and the other sentences which have no sense, but that the one is primarily concerned with the expression of true propositions, the other with the creation of a work of art. Thus, if a work of science contains true and important propositions, its value as a work of science will hardly be diminished by the fact that they are inelegantly expressed. And similarly, a work of art is not necessarily the worse for the fact that all the propositions comprising it are literally false. But to say that many literary works are largely composed of falsehoods is not to say that they are composed of pseudopropositions. It is, in fact, very rare for a literary artist to produce sentences which have no literal meaning. And where this does occur, the sentences are carefully chosen for their rhythm and balance. If the author writes nonsense, it is because he considers it most suitable for bringing about the effects for which his writing is designed.

The metaphysician, on the other hand, does not intend to write nonsense. He lapses into it through being deceived by grammar, or through committing errors of reasoning, such as that which leads the view that the sensible world is unreal. But it is not the mark of a poet simply to make mistakes of this sort. There are some, indeed, who would see in the fact that the metaphysician's utterances are senseless a reason against the view that they have aesthetic value. And, without going so far as this, we may safely say that it does not constitute a reason for it.

It is true, however, that although the greater part of metaphysics is merely the embodiment of humdrum errors, there remain a number of metaphysical passages which are the work of genuine mystical feeling; and they may more plausibly be held to have moral or aesthetic value. But, as far as we are concerned, the distinction between the kind of metaphysics that is produced by a philosopher who has been duped by grammar, and the kind that is produced by a mystic who is trying to express the inexpressible, is of no great importance: what is important to us is to realise that even the utterances of the metaphysician who is attempting to expound a vision are literally senseless; so that henceforth we may pursue our philosophical researches with as little regard for them as for the more inglorious kind of metaphysics which comes from a failure to understand the workings of our language.

Notes

[1] *Tractatus Logico-Philosophicus,* Preface.

[2] Bradley, *Appearance and Reality,* 2nd ed., p. 1.

IX.2 The Scientific Method of Hypothesis Testing

CARL HEMPEL

> Carl Hempel (1907–1997), a German-born philosopher, joined the Vienna
> Circle and became a logical positivist. He spent many years as professor of
> philosophy at Princeton University. Hempel was the leading advocate of the
> deductive-nomological model, which holds scientific explanation as deduc-
> tively valid arguments proceeding from general laws and initial conditions to
> the phenomena to be explained (*explananda*). He argued that a symmetry
> existed between explanation and prediction, where the only difference is tem-
> poral. In explanation the *explanandum* has already occurred, whereas in pre-
> diction, what you are predicting is still to come. In the following selection,
> using a famous medical case from the 1840s in which the Hungarian physi-
> cian Ignaz Semmelweis discovered the cause of puerperal fever (childbed
> fever), Hempel outlined his general theory of explanation.

As a simple illustration of some important aspects of scientific inquiry let us consider Semmelweis' work on childbed fever. Ignaz Semmelweis, a physician of Hungarian birth, did this work during the years from 1844 to 1848 at the Vienna General Hospital. As a member of the medical staff of the First Maternity Division in the hospital, Semmelweis was distressed to find that a large pro-portion of the women who were delivered of their babies in that division contracted a serious and often fatal illness known as puerperal fever or childbed fever. In 1844, as many as 260 out of 3,157 mothers in the First Division, or 8.2 per-cent, died of the disease; for 1845, the death rate was 6.8 percent, and for 1846, it was 11.4 percent. These figures were all the more alarming because in the adjacent Second Maternity Division of the same hospital, which accommodated almost as many women as the First, the death toll from childbed fever was much lower: 2.3, 2.0, and 2.7 percent for the same years. In a book that he wrote later on the causation and the prevention of childbed fever, Semmelweis describes his efforts to resolve the dreadful puzzle.[1]

He began by considering various explana-tions that were current at the time; some of these he rejected out of hand as incompatible with well-established facts; others he subjected to specific tests.

One widely accepted view attributed the rav-ages of puerperal fever to "epidemic influences," which were vaguely described as "atmospheric-cosmic-telluric changes" spreading over whole dis-tricts and causing childbed fever in women in confinement. But how, Semmelweis reasons, could such influences have plagued the First Division for years and yet spared the Second? And how could this view be reconciled with the fact that while the fever was raging in the hospital, hardly a case occurred in the city of Vienna or in its surroundings: a genuine epidemic, such as cholera, would not be so selective. Finally, Semmelweis notes that some of the women admit-ted to the First Division, living far from the hospi-tal, had been overcome by labor on their way and had given birth in the street: yet despite these adverse conditions, the death rate from childbed fever among these cases of "street birth" was lower than the average for the First Division.

On another view, overcrowding was a cause of mortality in the First Division. But Semmelweis points out that in fact the crowding was heavier in the Second Division, partly as a result of the des-perate efforts of patients to avoid assignment to the notorious First Division. He also rejects two similar conjectures that were current, by noting that there were no differences between the two Divisions in regard to diet or general care of the patients.

Reprinted from *Philosophy of Natural Science* (Prentice-Hall, 1996), by permission.

In 1846, a commission that had been appointed to investigate the matter attributed the prevalence of illness in the First Division to injuries resulting from rough examination by the medical students, all of whom received their obstetrical training in the First Division. Semmelweis notes in refutation of this view that (*a*) the injuries resulting naturally from the process of birth are much more extensive than those that might be caused by rough examination; (*b*) the midwives who received their training in the Second Division examined their patients in much the same manner but without the same ill effects; (*c*) when, in response to the commission's report, the number of medical students was halved and their examinations of the women were reduced to a minimum, the mortality, after a brief decline, rose to higher levels than ever before.

Various psychological explanations were attempted. One of them noted that the First Division was so arranged that a priest bearing the last sacrament to a dying woman had to pass through five wards before reaching the sickroom beyond: the appearance of the priest, preceded by an attendant ringing a bell, was held to have a terrifying and debilitating effect upon the patients in the wards and thus to make them more likely victims of childbed fever. In the Second Division, this adverse factor was absent, since the priest had direct access to the sickroom. Semmelweis decided to test this conjecture. He persuaded the priest to come by a roundabout route and without ringing of the bell, in order to reach the sick chamber silently and unobserved. But the mortality in the First Division did not decrease.

A new idea was suggested to Semmelweis by the observation that in the First Division the women were delivered lying on their backs; in the Second Division, on their sides. Though he thought it unlikely, he decided "like a drowning man clutching at a straw," to test whether this difference in procedure was significant. He introduced the use of the lateral position in the First Division, but again, the mortality remained unaffected.

At last, early in 1847, an accident gave Semmelweis the decisive clue for his solution of the problem. A colleague of his, Kolletschka, received a puncture wound in the finger, from the scalpel of a student with whom he was performing an autopsy, and died after an agonizing illness during which he displayed the same symptoms that Semmelweis had observed in the victims of childbed fever. Although the role of microorganisms in such infections had not yet been recognized at the time, Semmelweis realized that "cadaveric matter" which the student's scalpel had introduced into Kolletschka's blood stream had caused his colleague's fatal illness. And the similarities between the course of Kolletschka's disease and that of the women in his clinic led Semmelweis to the conclusion that his patients had died of the same kind of blood poisoning: he, his colleagues, and the medical students had been the carriers of the infectious material, for he and his associates used to come to the wards directly from performing dissections in the autopsy room, and examine the women in labor after only superficially washing their hands, which often retained a characteristic foul odor.

Again, Semmelweis put his idea to a test. He reasoned that if he were right, then childbed fever could be prevented by chemically destroying the infectious material adhering to the hands. He therefore issued an order requiring all medical students to wash their hands in a solution of chlorinated lime before making an examination. The mortality from childbed fever promptly began to decrease, and for the year 1848 it fell to 1.27 percent in the First Division, compared to 1.33 in the Second.

In further support of his idea, or of his *hypothesis*, as we will also say, Semmelweis notes that it accounts for the fact that the mortality in the Second Division consistently was so much lower: the patients there were attended by midwives, whose training did not include anatomical instruction by dissection of cadavers.

The hypothesis also explained the lower mortality among "street births": women who arrived with babies in arms were rarely examined after admission and thus had a better chance of escaping infection.

Similarly, the hypothesis accounted for the fact that the victims of childbed fever among the newborn babies were all among those whose mothers had contracted the disease during labor; for then the infection could be transmitted to the baby before birth, through the common bloodstream of mother and child, whereas this was impossible when the mother remained healthy.

Further clinical experiences soon led Semmelweis to broaden his hypothesis. On one occasion, for example, he and his associates, having carefully disinfected their hands, examined first a woman in labor who was suffering from a festering cervical cancer; then they proceeded to examine twelve other women in the same room, after only routine washing without renewed disinfection. Eleven of the twelve patients died of puerperal fever. Semmelweis concluded that childbed fever can be caused not only by cadaveric material, but also by "putrid matter derived from living organisms."

We have seen how, in his search for the cause of childbed fever, Semmelweis examined various hypotheses that had been suggested as possible answers. How such hypotheses are arrived at in the first place is an intriguing question which we will consider later. First, however, let us examine how a hypothesis, once proposed, is tested.

Sometimes, the procedure is quite direct. Consider the conjectures that differences in crowding, or in diet, or in general care account for the difference in mortality between the two divisions. As Semmelweis points out, these conflict with readily observable facts. There are no such differences between the divisions; the hypotheses are therefore rejected as false.

But usually the test will be less simple and straightforward. Take the hypothesis attributing the high mortality in the First Division to the dread evoked by the appearance of the priest with his attendant. The intensity of that dread, and especially its effect upon childbed fever, are not as directly ascertainable as are differences in crowding or in diet, and Semmelweis uses an indirect method of testing. He asks himself: Are there any readily observable effects that should occur if the hypothesis were true? And he reasons: *If* the hypothesis were true, *then* an appropriate change in the priest's procedure should be followed by a decline in fatalities. He checks this implication by a simple experiment and finds it false, and he therefore rejects the hypothesis.

Similarly, to test his conjecture about the position of the women during delivery, he reasons: *If* this conjecture should be true, *then* adoption of the lateral position in the First Division will reduce the mortality. Again, the implication is shown false by his experiment, and the conjecture is discarded.

In the last two cases, the test is based on an argument to the effect that *if* the contemplated

hypothesis, say H, is true, *then* certain observable events (e.g., decline in mortality) should occur under specified circumstances (e.g., if the priest refrains from walking through the wards, or if the women are delivered in lateral position); or briefly, if H is true, then so is I, where I is a statement describing the observable occurrences to be expected. For convenience, let us say that I is inferred from, or implied by, H; and let us call I a *test implication of the hypothesis H*. (We will later give a more accurate description of the relation between I and H.)

In our last two examples, experiments show the test implication to be false, and the hypothesis is accordingly rejected. The reasoning that leads to the rejection may be schematized as follows:

a]
If H is true, then so is I.
But (as the evidence shows) I is not true.
H is not true.

Any argument of this form, called *modus tollens* in logic,[2] is deductively valid; that is, if its premises (the sentences above the horizontal line) are true, then its conclusion (the sentence below the horizontal line) is unfailingly true as well. Hence, if the premises of (a) are properly established, the hypothesis H that is being tested must indeed be rejected.

Next, let us consider the case where observation or experiment bears out the test implication I. From his hypothesis that childbed fever is blood poisoning produced by cadaveric matter, Semmelweis infers that suitable antiseptic measures will reduce fatalities from the disease. This time, experiment shows the test implication to be true. But this favorable outcome does not conclusively prove the hypothesis true, for the underlying argument would have the form

b]
If H is true, then so is I.
(As the evidence shows) I is true.
H is true.

And this mode of reasoning, which is referred to as *the fallacy of affirming the consequent*, is deductively invalid, that is, its conclusion may be false even if its premises are true.[3] This is in fact illustrated by Semmelweis' own experience. The initial version of his account of childbed fever as a form of blood poisoning presented infection with cadaveric matter essentially as the one and only source of the disease; and he was right in reasoning that if this hypothesis should be true, then destruction of cadaveric particles by antiseptic washing should reduce the mortality. Furthermore, his experiment did show the test implication to be true. Hence, in this case, the premises of (*b*) were both true. Yet, his hypothesis was false, for as he later discovered, putrid material from living organisms, too, could produce childbed fever.

Thus, the favorable outcome of a test, i.e., the fact that a test implication inferred from a hypothesis is found to be true, does not prove the hypothesis to be true. Even if many implications of a hypothesis have been borne out by careful tests, the hypothesis may still be false. The following argument still commits the fallacy of affirming the consequent:

c]
$$\begin{array}{l} \text{If } H \text{ is true, then so are } I_1, I_2, \ldots, I_n. \\ \text{(As the evidence shows) } I_1, I_2, \ldots, I_n, \\ \underline{\text{are all true.}} \\ H \text{ is true.} \end{array}$$

This, too, can be illustrated by reference to Semmelweis' final hypothesis in its first version. As we noted earlier, his hypothesis also yields the test implications that among cases of street births admitted to the First Division, mortality from puerperal fever should be below the average for the Division, and that infants of mothers who escape the illness do not contract childbed fever; and these implications, too, were borne out by the evidence—even though the first version of the final hypothesis was false.

But the observation that a favorable outcome of however many tests does not afford conclusive proof for a hypothesis should not lead us to think that if we have subjected a hypothesis to a number of tests and all of them have had a favorable outcome, we are no better off than if we had not tested the hypothesis at all. For each of our tests might conceivably have had an unfavorable outcome and might have led to the rejection of the hypothesis. A set of favorable results obtained by testing different test implications, $I_1, I_2, \ldots, I_n$, of a hypothesis, shows that as far as these particular implications are concerned, the hypothesis has been borne out; and while this result does not afford a complete proof of the hypothesis, it provides at least some support, some partial corroboration or confirmation for it. The extent of this support will depend on various aspects of the hypothesis and of the test data.

The idea that in scientific inquiry, inductive inference from antecedently collected data leads to appropriate general principles is clearly embodied

in the following account of how a scientist would ideally proceed:

> If we try to imagine how a mind of superhuman power and reach, but normal so far as the logical processes of its thought are concerned, . . . would use the scientific method, the process would be as follows: First, all facts would be observed and recorded, *without selection* or *a priori* guess as to their relative importance. Secondly, the observed and recorded facts would be analyzed, compared, and classified, *without hypothesis or postulates* other than those necessarily involved in the logic of thought. Third, from this analysis of the facts generalizations would be inductively drawn as to the relations, classificatory or causal, between them. Fourth, further research would be deductive as well as inductive, employing inferences from previously established generalizations.[4]

This passage distinguishes four stages in an ideal scientific inquiry: (1) observation and recording of all facts, (2) analysis and classification of these facts, (3) inductive derivation of generalizations from them, and (4) further testing of the generalizations. The first two of these stages are specifically assumed not to make use of any guesses or hypotheses as to how the observed facts might be interconnected; this restriction seems to have been imposed in the belief that such preconceived ideas would introduce a bias and would jeopardize the scientific objectivity of the investigation.

But the view expressed in the quoted passage—I will call it the *narrow inductivist conception of scientific inquiry*—is untenable, for several reasons. A brief survey of these can serve to amplify and to supplement our earlier remarks on scientific procedure.

First, a scientific investigation as here envisaged could never get off the ground. Even its first phase could never be carried out, for a collection of all the facts would have to await the end of the world, so to speak; and even all the facts up to now cannot be collected, since there are an infinite number and variety of them. Are we to examine, for example, all the grains of sand in all the deserts and on all the beaches, and are we to record their shapes, their weights, their chemical composition, their distances from each other, their constantly changing temperature, and their equally changing distance from the center of the moon? Are we to record the floating thoughts that cross our minds in the tedious process? The shapes of the clouds overhead, the changing color of the sky? The construction and the trade name of our writing equipment? Our own life histories and those of our fellow investigators? All these, and untold other things, are, after all, among "all the facts up to now."

Perhaps, then, all that should be required in the first phase is that all the relevant facts be collected. But relevant to what? Though the author does not mention this, let us suppose that the inquiry is concerned with a specified *problem*. Should we not then begin by collecting all the facts—or better, all available data—relevant to that problem? This notion still makes no clear sense. Semmelweis sought to solve one specific problem, yet he collected quite different kinds of data at different stages of his inquiry. And rightly so; for what particular sorts of data it is reasonable to collect is not determined by the problem under study, but by a tentative answer to it that the investigator entertains in the form of a conjecture or hypothesis. Given the conjecture that mortality from childbed fever was increased by the terrifying appearance of the priest and his attendant with the death bell, it was relevant to collect data on the consequences of having the priest change his routine; but it would have been totally irrelevant to check what would happen if doctors and students disinfected their hands before examining their patients. With respect to Semmelweis' eventual contamination hypothesis, data of the latter kind were clearly relevant, and those of the former kind totally irrelevant.

Empirical "facts" or findings, therefore, can be qualified as logically relevant or irrelevant only in reference to a given hypothesis, but not in reference to a given problem.

Suppose now that a hypothesis H has been advanced as a tentative answer to a research problem: what kinds of data would be relevant to H? Our earlier examples suggest an answer: A finding is relevant to H if either its occurrence or its nonoccurrence can be inferred from H. Take Torricelli's hypothesis, for example. As we saw, Pascal inferred from it that the mercury column in a barometer should grow shorter if the barometer were carried up a mountain. Therefore, any finding to the effect that this did indeed happen in a particular case is relevant to the hypothesis; but so would be the

finding that the length of the mercury column had remained unchanged or that it had decreased and then increased during the ascent, for such findings would refute Pascal's test implication and would thus disconfirm Torricelli's hypothesis. Data of the former kind may be called positively, or favorably, relevant to the hypothesis; those of the latter kind negatively, or unfavorably, relevant.

In sum, the maxim that data should be gathered without guidance by antecedent hypotheses about the connections among the facts under study is self-defeating, and it is certainly not followed in scientific inquiry. On the contrary, tentative hypotheses are needed to give direction to a scientific investigation. Such hypotheses determine, among other things, what data should be collected at a given point in a scientific investigation.

It is of interest to note that social scientists trying to check a hypothesis by reference to the vast store of facts recorded by the U.S. Bureau of the Census, or by other data-gathering organizations, sometimes find to their disappointment that the values of some variable that plays a central role in the hypothesis have nowhere been systematically recorded. This remark is not, of course, intended as a criticism of data gathering: those engaged in the process no doubt try to select facts that might prove relevant to future hypotheses; the observation is simply meant to illustrate the impossibility of collecting "all the relevant data" without knowledge of the hypotheses to which the data are to have relevance.

The second stage envisaged in our quoted passage is open to similar criticism. A set of empirical "facts" can be analyzed and classified in many different ways, most of which will be unilluminating for the purposes of a given inquiry. Semmelweis could have classified the women in the maternity wards according to criteria such as age, place of residence, marital status, dietary habits, and so forth; but information on these would have provided no clue to a patient's prospects of becoming a victim of childbed fever. What Semmelweis sought were criteria that would be significantly connected with those prospects; and for this purpose, as he eventually found, it was illuminating to single out those women who were attended by medical personnel with contaminated hands; for it was with this characteristic, or with the corresponding class of patients, that high mortality from childbed fever was associated.

Thus, if a particular way of analyzing and classifying empirical findings is to lead to an explanation of the phenomena concerned, then it must be based on hypotheses about how those phenomena are connected; without such hypotheses, analysis and classification are blind.

Our critical reflections on the first two stages of inquiry as envisaged in the quoted passage also undercut the notion that hypotheses are introduced only in the third stage, by inductive inference from antecedently collected data. But some further remarks on the subject should be added here.

Induction is sometimes conceived as a method that leads, by means of mechanically applicable rules, from observed facts to corresponding general principles. In this case, the rules of inductive inference would provide effective canons of scientific discovery; induction would be a mechanical procedure analogous to the familiar routine for the multiplication of integers, which leads, in a finite number of predetermined and mechanically performable steps, to the corresponding product. Actually, however, no such general and mechanical induction procedure is available at present; otherwise, the much studied problem of the causation of cancer, for example, would hardly have remained unsolved to this day. Nor can the discovery of such a procedure ever be expected. For—to mention one reason—scientific hypotheses and theories are usually couched in terms that do not occur at all in the description of the empirical findings on which they rest, and which they serve to explain. For example, theories about the atomic and subatomic structure of matter contain terms such as 'atom', 'electron', 'proton', 'neutron', 'psi-function', etc.; yet they are based on laboratory findings about the spectra of various gases, tracks in cloud and bubble chambers, quantitative aspects of chemical reactions, and so forth—all of which can be described without the use of those "theoretical terms." Induction rules of the kind here envisaged would therefore have to provide a mechanical routine for constructing, on the basis of the given data, a hypothesis or theory stated in terms of some quite novel concepts, which are nowhere used in the description of the data themselves. Surely, no general mechanical rule of procedure can be expected to achieve this. Could there be a general rule, for example, which, when applied to the data

available to Galileo concerning the limited effectiveness of suction pumps, would, by a mechanical routine, produce a hypothesis based on the concept of a sea of air?

To be sure, mechanical procedures for inductively "inferring" a hypothesis on the basis of given data may be specifiable for situations of special, and relatively simple, kinds. For example, if the length of a copper rod has been measured at several different temperatures, the resulting pairs of associated values for temperature and length may be represented by points in a plane coordinate system, and a curve may be drawn through them in accordance with some particular rule of curve fitting. The curve then graphically represents a general quantitative hypothesis that expresses the length of the rod as a specific function of its temperature. But note that this hypothesis contains no novel terms; it is expressible in terms of the concepts of temperature and length, which are used also in describing the data. Moreover, the choice of "associated" values of temperature and length as data already presupposes a guiding hypothesis; namely, that with each value of the temperature, exactly one value of the length of the copper rod is associated, so that its length is indeed a function of its temperature alone. The mechanical curve-fitting routine then serves only to select a particular function as the appropriate one. This point is important; for suppose that instead of a copper rod, we examine a body of nitrogen gas enclosed in a cylindrical container with a movable piston as a lid, and that we measure its volume at several different temperatures. If we were to use this procedure in an effort to obtain from our data a *general* hypothesis representing the volume of the gas as a function of its temperature, we would fail, because the volume of a gas is a function both of its temperature and of the pressure exerted upon it, so that at the same temperature, the given gas may assume different volumes.

Thus, even in these simple cases, the mechanical procedures for the construction of a hypothesis do only part of the job, for they presuppose an antecedent, less specific hypothesis (i.e., that a certain physical variable is a function of one single other variable), which is not obtainable by the same procedure.

There are, then, no generally applicable "rules of induction," by which hypotheses or theories can be mechanically derived or inferred from empirical data. The transition from data to theory requires creative imagination. Scientific hypotheses and theories are not *derived* from observed facts, but *invented* in order to account for them. They constitute guesses at the connections that might obtain between the phenomena under study, at uniformities and patterns that might underlie their occurrence. "Happy guesses"[5] of this kind require great ingenuity, especially if they involve a radical departure from current modes of scientific thinking, as did, for example, the theory of relativity and quantum theory. The inventive effort required in scientific research will benefit from a thorough familiarity with current knowledge in the field. A complete novice will hardly make an important scientific discovery, for the ideas that may occur to him are likely to duplicate what has been tried before or to run afoul of well-established facts or theories of which he is not aware.

Nevertheless, the ways in which fruitful scientific guesses are arrived at are very different from any process of systematic inference. The chemist Kekulé, for example, tells us that he had long been trying unsuccessfully to devise a structural formula for the benzene molecule when, one evening in 1865, he found a solution to his problem while he was dozing in front of his fireplace. Gazing into the flames, he seemed to see atoms dancing in snakelike arrays. Suddenly, one of the snakes formed a ring by seizing hold of its own tail and then whirled mockingly before him. Kekulé awoke in a flash: he had hit upon the now famous and familiar idea of representing the molecular structure of benzene by a hexagonal ring. He spent the rest of the night working out the consequences of this hypothesis.[6]

This last remark contains an important reminder concerning the objectivity of science. In his endeavor to find a solution to his problem, the scientist may give free rein to his imagination, and the course of his creative thinking may be influenced even by scientifically questionable notions. Kepler's study of planetary motion, for example, was inspired by his interest in a mystical doctrine about numbers and a passion to demonstrate the music of the spheres. Yet, scientific objectivity is safeguarded by the principle that while hypotheses and theories may be freely invented and *proposed* in science, they can be *accepted* into the body of scientific knowledge only if they pass critical scrutiny, which includes in particular the checking of suitable test implications by careful observation or experiment.

Interestingly, imagination and free invention play a similarly important role in those disciplines whose results are validated exclusively by deductive reasoning; for example, in mathematics. For the rules of deductive inference do not afford mechanical rules of discovery, either. As illustrated by our statement of *modus tollens* above, those rules are usually expressed in the form of general schemata, any instance of which is a deductively valid argument. If premises of the specified kind are given, such a schema does indeed specify a way of proceeding to a logical consequence. But for any set of premises that may be given, the rules of deductive inference specify an infinity of validly deducible conclusions. Take, for example, one simple rule represented by the following schema:

$$\frac{p}{p \text{ or } q}$$

It tells us, in effect, that from the proposition that p is the case, it follows that p or q is the case, where p and q may be any propositions whatever. The word 'or' is here understood in the "nonexclusive" sense, so that 'p or q' is tantamount to 'either p or q or both p and q'. Clearly, if the premise of an argument of this type is true, then so must be the conclusion; hence, any argument of the specified form is valid. But this one rule alone entitles us to infer infinitely many different consequences from any one premise. Thus, from 'the Moon has no atmosphere', it authorizes us to infer any statement of the form 'The Moon has no atmosphere, or q', where for 'q' we may write any statement whatsoever, no matter whether it is true or false; for example, 'the Moon's atmosphere is very thin', 'the Moon is uninhabited', 'gold is denser than silver', 'silver is denser than gold', and so forth. (It is interesting and not difficult to prove that infinitely many different statements can be formed in English; each of these may be put in the place of the variable 'q'.) Other rules of deductive inference add, of course, to the variety of statements derivable from one premise or set of premises. Hence, if we are given a set of statements as premises, the rules of deduction give no direction to our inferential procedures. They do not single out one statement as "the" conclusion to be derived from our premises, nor do they tell us how to obtain interesting or systematically important conclusions; they provide no mechanical routine, for example, for deriving significant mathematical theorems from given postulates. The discovery of important, fruitful mathematical theorems, like the discovery of important, fruitful theories in empirical science, requires inventive ingenuity; it calls for imaginative, insightful guessing. But again, the interests of scientific objectivity are safeguarded by the demand for an *objective validation* of such conjectures. In mathematics, this means proof by deductive derivation from axioms. And when a mathematical proposition has been proposed as a conjecture, its proof or disproof still requires inventiveness and ingenuity, often of a very high caliber; for the rules of deductive inference do not even provide a general mechanical procedure for constructing proofs or disproofs. Their systematic role is rather the modest one of serving as *criteria of soundness for arguments* offered as proofs: an argument will constitute a valid mathematical proof if it proceeds from the axioms to the proposed theorem by a chain of inferential steps each of which is valid according to one of the rules of deductive inference. And to check whether a given argument is a valid proof in this sense is indeed a purely mechanical task.

Scientific knowledge, as we have seen, is not arrived at by applying some inductive inference procedure to antecedently collected data, but rather by what is often called "the method of hypothesis," i.e., by inventing hypotheses as tentative answers to a problem under study, and then subjecting these to empirical test. It will be part of such test to see whether the hypothesis is borne out by whatever relevant findings may have been gathered before its formulation; an acceptable hypothesis will have to fit the available relevant data. Another part of the test will consist in deriving new test implications from the hypothesis and checking these by suitable observations or experiments. As we noted earlier, even extensive testing with entirely favorable results does not establish a hypothesis conclusively, but provides only more or less strong support for it. Hence, while scientific inquiry is certainly not inductive in the narrow sense we have examined in some detail, it may be said to be *inductive in a wider sense*, inasmuch as it involves the acceptance of hypotheses on the basis of data that afford no deductively conclusive evidence for it, but lend it only more or less strong "inductive support," or confirmation. And any "rules of induction" will have to be conceived, in analogy to the rules of deduction, as canons of validation rather than of discovery. Far from generating a hypothesis that accounts for given empirical findings, such rules will presuppose that both the empirical data forming the "premises" of the "inductive argument" and a tentative hypothesis forming its "conclusion" are *given*. The rules of induction would then state criteria for the soundness of the argument. According to some theories of induction, the rules would determine the strength of the support that the data lend to the hypothesis, and they might express such support in terms of probabilities.

Notes

[1]The story of Semmelweis' work and of the difficulties he encountered forms a fascinating page in the history of medicine. A detailed account, which includes translations and paraphrases of large portions of Semmelweis' writings, is given in W. J. Sinclair, *Semmelweis: His Life and His Doctrine* (Manchester, England: Manchester University Press, 1909). Brief quoted phrases in this chapter are taken from this work. The highlights of Semmelweis' career are recounted in first chapter of P. de Kruif, *Men Against Death* (New York: Harcourt, Brace & World, Inc., 1932).

[2]For details, see another volume in this series: W. Salmon, *Logic*, pp., 24–25.

[3]See Salmon, *Logic*, pp. 27–29.

[4]A. B. Wolfe, "Functional Economics," in *The Trend of Economics,* ed. R. G. Tugwell (New York: Alfred A. Knopf, Inc., 1924), p. 450 (italics are quoted).

[5]This characterization was given already by William Whewell in his work *The Philosophy of the Inductive Sciences*, 2nd ed. (London: John W. Parker, 1847); II, 41. Whewell also speaks of "invention" as "part of induction" (p. 46). In the same vein, K. Popper refers to scientific hypotheses and theories as "conjectures"; see, for example, the essay "Science: Conjectures and Refutations" in his book, *Conjectures and Refutations* (New York and London: Basic Books, 1962). Indeed, A. B. Wolfe, whose narrowly inductivist conception of ideal scientific procedure was quoted earlier, stresses that "the limited human mind" has to use "a greatly modified procedure," requiring scientific imagination and the selection of data on the basis of some "working hypothesis" (p. 450 of the essay cited in note 4).

[6]Cf. the quotations from Kekulé's own report in A. Findlay, *A Hundred Years of Chemistry,* 2nd ed. (London: Gerald Duckworth & Co., 1948), p. 37; and W. I. B., Beveridge, *The Art of Scientific Investigation,* 3rd ed. (London: William Heinemann, Ltd., 1957), p. 56.

IX.3   Science: Conjectures and Refutations

Karl Popper

Karl Popper (1902–1994), an Austrian-born philosopher, spent most of his career at the London School of Economics. In this selection, Popper rejects the positivist thesis that only what can be verified is cognitively meaningful. Even metaphysics can be meaningful. What is irrational is refusing to treat one's theories as hypotheses that must be subjected to critical scrutiny. The single criterion for science is *falsifiability*. We can never prove universal propositions (e.g., 'All swans are white' or 'all men are mortal'), for there might always be an exception. Rationality consists of trying to falsify universal theories, that is, attempting to refute bold theories, finding the lethal exception. Popper accuses both Marxism and Freudianism of being *pseudo sciences* because they fail to search for or take into account disconfirming evidence. The best we can attain is a fallibilism in which we hold our theories as experimental, always seeking to qualify them with the use of evidence. We must put forth bold conjectures complemented by bold attempts at refutation, thus asymptotically approaching the truth.

There could be no fairer destiny for any . . . theory than that it should point the way to a more comprehensive theory in which it lives on, as a limiting case.

Albert Einstein

Mr. Turnbull had predicted evil consequences, . . . and was now doing the best in his power to bring about the verification of his own prophecies.

Anthony Trollope

I

When I received the list of participants in this course and realized that I had been asked to speak to philosophical colleagues I thought, after some hesitation and consultation, that you would probably prefer me to speak about those problems which interest me most, and about those developments with which I am most intimately acquainted. I therefore decided to do what I have never done before: to give you a report on my own work in the philosophy of science since the

autumn of 1919 when I first began to grapple with the problem "*When should a theory be ranked as scientific?*" or "*Is there a criterion for the scientific character or status of a theory?*"

The problem which troubled me at the time was neither "When is a theory true?" nor "When is a theory acceptable?" My problem was different. I *wished to distinguish between science and pseudo-science*, knowing very well that science often errs, and that pseudo-science may happen to stumble on the truth.

I knew, of course, the most widely accepted answer to my problem: that science is distinguished from pseudo-science—or from "metaphysics"—by its *empirical method*, which is essentially *inductive*, proceeding from observation or experiment. But this did not satisfy me. On the contrary, I often formulated my problem as one of distinguishing between a genuinely empirical method and a non-empirical or even a pseudo-empirical method—that is to say, a method which, although it appeals to observation and experiment, nevertheless does not come up to scientific standards. The latter method may be exemplified by astrology, with its stupendous mass of empirical evidence based on observation—on horoscopes and on biographies.

But as it was not the example of astrology which led me to my problem I should perhaps briefly describe the atmosphere in which my prob-

This was a lecture given at Peterhouse, Cambridge, in 1953. Copyright © 1965 by Karl Popper. Notes edited.

lem arose and the examples by which it was stimulated. After the collapse of the Austrian Empire there had been a revolution in Austria: The air was full of revolutionary slogans and ideas, and new and often wild theories. Among the theories which interested me Einstein's theory of relativity was no doubt by far the most important. Three others were Marx's theory of history, Freud's psychoanalysis, and Alfred Adler's so-called "individual psychology."

There was a lot of popular nonsense talked about these theories, and especially about relativity (as still happens even today), but I was fortunate in those who introduced me to the study of this theory. We all—the small circle of students to which I belonged—were thrilled with the result of Eddington's eclipse observations, which in 1919 brought the first important confirmation of Einstein's theory of gravitation. It was a great experience for us, and one which had a lasting influence on my intellectual development.

The three other theories I have mentioned were also widely discussed among students at that time. I myself happened to come into personal contact with Alfred Adler, and even to cooperate with him in his social work among the children and young people in the working-class districts of Vienna where he had established social guidance clinics.

It was during the summer of 1919 that I began to feel more and more dissatisfied with these three theories—the Marxist theory of history, psychoanalysis, and individual psychology; and I began to feel dubious about their claims to scientific status. My problem perhaps first took the simple form, "What is wrong with Marxism, psychoanalysis, and individual psychology? Why are they so different from physical theories, from Newton's theory, and especially from the theory of relativity?"

To make this contrast clear I should explain that few of us at the time would have said that we believed in the *truth* of Einstein's theory of gravitation. This shows that it was not my doubting the *truth* of those other three theories which bothered me, but something else. Yet neither was it that I merely felt mathematical physics to be more *exact* than the sociological or psychological type of theory. Thus what worried me was neither the problem of truth, at that stage at least, nor the problem of exactness or measurability. It was rather that I

felt that these other three theories, though posing as sciences, had in fact more in common with primitive myths than with science; that they resembled astrology rather than astronomy.

I found that those of my friends who were admirers of Marx, Freud, and Adler were impressed by a number of points common to these theories and especially by their apparent *explanatory power*. These theories appeared to be able to explain practically everything that happened within the fields to which they referred. The study of any of them seemed to have the effect of an intellectual conversion or revelation, opening your eyes to a new truth hidden from those not yet initiated. Once your eyes were thus opened you saw confirming instances everywhere: The world was full of *verifications* of the theory. Whatever happened always confirmed it. Thus its truth appeared manifest; and unbelievers were clearly people who did not want to see the manifest truth, who refused to see it, either because it was against their class interest, or because of their repressions which were still "unanalysed" and crying aloud for treatment.

The most characteristic element in this situation seemed to me the incessant stream of confirmations, of observations which "verified" the theories in question; and this point was constantly emphasized by their adherents. A Marxist could not open a newspaper without finding on every page confirming evidence for his interpretation of history, not only in the news, but also in its presentation—which revealed the class bias of the paper—and especially of course in what the paper did not say. The Freudian analysts emphasized that their theories were constantly verified by their "clinical observations." As for Adler, I was much impressed by a personal experience. Once, in 1919, I reported to him a case which to me did not seem particularly Adlerian, but which he found no difficulty in analyzing in terms of his theory of inferiority feelings, although he had not even seen the child. Slightly shocked, I asked him how he could be so sure. "Because of my thousandfold experience," he replied; whereupon I could not help saying, "And with this new case, I suppose, your experience has become thousand-and-onefold."

What I had in mind was that his previous observations may not have been much sounder than this new one; that each in its turn had been interpreted in the light of "previous experience," and at the same time counted as additional confirmation. What, I asked myself, did it confirm? No more than that a case could be interpreted in the light of the theory. But this meant very little, I reflected, since every conceivable case could be interpreted in the light of Adler's theory, or equally of Freud's. I may illustrate this by two very different examples of human behavior: that of a man who pushes a child into the water with the intention of drowning it, and that of a man who sacrifices his life in an attempt to save the child. Each of these two cases can be explained with equal ease in Freudian and in Adlerian terms. According to Freud the first man suffered from repression (say, of some component of his Oedipus complex), while the second man had achieved sublimation. According to Adler the first man suffered from feelings of inferiority (producing perhaps the need to prove to himself that he dared to commit some crime), and so did the second man (whose need was to prove to himself that he dared to rescue the child). I could not think of any human behavior which could not be interpreted in terms of either theory. It was precisely this fact—that they always fitted, that they were always confirmed—which in the eyes of their admirers constituted the strongest argument in favor of these theories. It began to dawn on me that this apparent strength was in fact their weakness.

With Einstein's theory the situation was strikingly different. Take one typical instance—Einstein's prediction, just then confirmed by the findings of Eddington's expedition. Einstein's gravitational theory had led to the result that light must be attracted by heavy bodies (such as the sun), precisely as material bodies were attracted. As a consequence it could be calculated that light from a distant fixed star whose apparent position was close to the sun would reach the earth from such a direction that the star would seem to be slightly shifted away from the sun; or, in other words, that stars close to the sun would look as if they had moved a little away from the sun, and from one another. This is a thing which cannot normally be observed since such stars are rendered invisible in daytime by the sun's overwhelming brightness; but during an eclipse it is possible to take photographs of them. If the same constellation is photographed at night one can measure the distances on the two photographs, and check the predicted effect.

Now the impressive thing about this case is the risk involved in a prediction of this kind. If observation shows that the predicted effect is definitely absent, then the theory is simply refuted. The theory is *incompatible with certain possible results of observation*—in fact with results which everybody before Einstein would have expected. This is quite different from the situation I have previously described, when it turned out that the theories in question were compatible with the most divergent human behavior, so that it was practically impossible to describe any human behavior that might not be claimed to be a verification of these theories.

These considerations led me in the winter of 1919–20 to conclusions which I may now reformulate as follows.

1. It is easy to obtain confirmations, or verifications, for nearly every theory—if we look for confirmations.

2. Confirmations should count only if they are the result of *risky predictions*; that is to say, if, unenlightened by the theory in question, we should have expected an event which was incompatible with the theory—an event which would have refuted the theory.

3. Every 'good' scientific theory is a prohibition: It forbids certain things to happen. The more a theory forbids, the better it is.

4. A theory which is not refutable by any conceivable event is non-scientific. Irrefutability is not a virtue of a theory (as people often think) but a vice.

5. Every genuine test of a theory is an attempt to falsify it, or to refute it. Testability is falsifiability; but there are degrees of testability: Some theories are more testable, more exposed to refutation, than others; they take, as it were, greater risks.

6. Confirming evidence should not count *except when it is the result of a genuine test of the theory*; and this means that it can be presented as a serious but unsuccessful attempt to falsify the theory. (I now speak in such cases of "corroborating evidence.")

7. Some genuinely testable theories, when found to be false, are still upheld by their admirers—for example by introducing *ad hoc* some auxiliary assumption, or by reinterpreting the theory *ad hoc* in such a way that it escapes refutation. Such a procedure is always possible, but it rescues the theory from refutation only at the price of destroying, or at least lowering, its scientific status. (I later described such a rescuing operation as a *conventionalist twist* or a *conventionalist stratagem.*)

One can sum up all this by saying that the criterion of the scientific status of a theory is its falsifiability, or refutability, or testability.

II

I may perhaps exemplify this with the help of the various theories so far mentioned. Einstein's theory of gravitation clearly satisfied the criterion of falsifiability. Even if our measuring instruments at the time did not allow us to pronounce on the results of the tests with complete assurance, there was clearly a possibility of refuting the theory.

Astrology did not pass the test. Astrologers were greatly impressed, and misled, by what they believed to be confirming evidence—so much so that they were quite unimpressed by any unfavorable evidence. Moreover, by making their interpretations and prophecies sufficiently vague they were able to explain away anything that might have been a refutation of the theory had the theory and the prophecies been more precise. In order to escape falsification they destroyed the testability of their theory. It is a typical soothsayer's trick to predict things so vaguely that the predictions can hardly fail, that they become irrefutable.

The Marxist theory of history, in spite of the serious efforts of some of its founders and followers, ultimately adopted this soothsaying practice. In some of its earlier formulations (for example, in Marx's analysis of the character of the "coming social revolution") their predictions were testable, and in fact falsified. Yet instead of accepting the refutations the followers of Marx reinterpreted both the theory and the evidence in order to make them agree. In this way they rescued the theory from refutation; but they did so at the price of adopting a device which made it irrefutable. They thus gave a "conventionalist twist" to the theory; and by this stratagem they destroyed its much advertised claim to scientific status.

The two psychoanalytic theories were in a different class. They were simply non-testable, irrefutable. There was no conceivable human behavior which could contradict them. This does not mean that Freud and Adler were not seeing certain things correctly: I personally do not doubt that much of what they say is of considerable importance and may well play its part one day in a psychological science which is testable. But it does mean that those "clinical observations" which analysts naively believe confirm their theory cannot do this any more than the daily confirmations which astrologers find in their practice. And as for Freud's epic of the Ego, the Super-ego, and the Id, no substantially stronger claim to scientific status can be made for it than for Homer's collected stories from Olympus. These theories describe some facts, but in the manner of myths. They contain most interesting psychological suggestions, but not in a testable form.

At the same time I realized that such myths may be developed and become testable, that historically speaking all—or very nearly all—scientific theories originate from myths, and that a myth may contain important anticipations of scientific theories. Examples are Empedocles' theory of evolution by trial and error, or Parmenides' myth of the unchanging block universe in which nothing ever happens and which, if we add another dimension, becomes Einstein's block universe (in which, too, nothing ever happens, since everything is, four-dimensionally speaking, determined and laid down from the beginning). I thus felt that if a theory is found to be non-scientific, or "metaphysical" (as we might say), it is not thereby found to be unimportant, or insignificant, or "meaningless," or "nonsensical." But it cannot claim to be backed by empirical evidence in the scientific sense—although it may easily be, in some genetic sense, the "result of observation."

(There were a great many other theories of this pre-scientific or pseudo-scientific character, some of them, unfortunately, as influential as the Marxist interpretation of history; for example, the racialist interpretation of history—another of those impressive and all-explanatory theories which act upon weak minds like revelations.)

Thus the problem which I tried to solve by proposing the criterion of falsifiability was neither a problem of meaningfulness or significance, nor a problem of truth or acceptability. It was the problem of drawing a line (as well as this can be done) between the statements, or systems of statements, of the empirical sciences, and all other statements—whether they are of a religious or of a metaphysical character, or simply pseudo-scientific. Years later—it must have been in 1928 or 1929—I called this first problem of mine the *problem of demarcation*. The criterion of falsifiability is a solution to this problem of demarcation, for it says that statements or systems of statements, in order to be ranked as scientific, must be capable of conflicting with possible, or conceivable, observations.

III

Today I know, of course, that this *criterion of demarcation*—the criterion of testability, or falsifiability, or refutability—is far from obvious; for even now its significance is seldom realized. At that time, in 1920, it seemed to me almost trivial, although it solved for me an intellectual problem which had worried me deeply, and one which also had obvious practical consequences (for example, political ones). But I did not yet realize its full implications, or its philosophical significance. When I explained it to a fellow student of the Mathematics Department (now a distinguished mathematician in Great Britain), he suggested that I should publish it. At the time I thought this absurd; for I was convinced that my problem, since it was so important for me, must have agitated many scientists and philosophers who would surely have reached my rather obvious solution. That this was not the case I learnt from Wittgenstein's work, and from its reception; and so I published my results thirteen years later in the form of a criticism of Wittgenstein's *criterion of meaningfulness*.

Wittgenstein, as you all know, tried to show in the *Tractatus* (see, for example, his propositions 6.53; 6.54; and 5) that all so-called philosophical or metaphysical propositions were actually non-propositions or pseudo-propositions, that they were senseless or meaningless. All genuine (or meaningful) propositions were truth functions of the elementary or atomic propositions which described "atomic facts," i.e., facts which can in principle be ascertained by observation. In other words, meaningful propositions were fully reducible to elementary or atomic propositions which were simple statements describing possible states of affairs, and which could in principle be established or rejected by observation. If we call a statement an "observation statement" not only if it states an actual observation but also if it states anything that *may* be observed, we shall have to say (according to the *Tractatus*, 5 and 4.52) that every genuine proposition must be a truth-function of, and therefore deducible from, observation statements. All other apparent propositions will be meaningless pseudo-propositions; in fact they will be nothing but nonsensical gibberish.

This idea was used by Wittgenstein for a characterization of science, as opposed to philosophy. We read (for example in 4.11, where natural science is taken to stand in opposition to philosophy): "The totality of true propositions is the total natural science (or the totality of the natural sciences)." This means that the propositions which belong to science are those deducible from true observation statements; they are those propositions which can be *verified* by true observation statements. Could we know all true observation statements, we should also know all that may be asserted by natural science.

This amounts to a crude verifiability criterion of demarcation. To make it slightly less crude, it could be amended thus: "The statements which may possibly fall within the province of science are those which may possibly be verified by observation statements; and these statements, again, coincide with the class of *all* genuine or meaningful statements." For this approach, then, *verifiability, meaningfulness, and scientific character all coincide*.

I personally was never interested in the so-called problem of meaning; on the contrary, it appeared to me a verbal problem, a typical pseudo-problem. I was interested only in the problem of demarcation, i.e., in finding a criterion of the scientific character of theories. It was just this interest which made me see at once that Wittgenstein's verifiability criterion of meaning was intended to play the part of a criterion of demarcation as well, and which made me see that, as such, it was totally inadequate, even if all misgivings about the dubious concept of meaning were set aside. For Wittgenstein's criterion of demarcation—to use my own terminology in this context—is verifiability, or deducibility from observation statements. But this criterion is too narrow (*and* too wide): It excludes from science practically everything that is, in fact, characteristic of it (while failing in effect to exclude astrology). No scientific theory can ever be deduced from observation statements, or be described as a truth-function of observation statements.

All this I pointed out on various occasions to Wittgensteinians and members of the Vienna Circle. In 1931–2 I summarized my ideas in a largish book (read by several members of the Circle but never published, although part of it was incorporated in my *Logic of Scientific Discovery*); and in 1933 I published a letter to the Editor of *Erkenntnis* in which I tried to compress into two pages my ideas on the problems of demarcation and induction. In this letter and elsewhere I described the problem of meaning as a pseudo-problem, in contrast to the problem of demarcation. But my contribution was classified by members of the Circle as a proposal to replace the verifiability criterion of *meaning* by a falsifiability criterion of *meaning*—which effectively made nonsense of my views.[1] My protests that I was trying to solve, not their pseudo-problem of meaning, but the problem of demarcation, were of no avail.

My attacks upon verification had some effect, however. They soon led to complete confusion in the camp of the verificationist philosophers of sense and nonsense. The original proposal of verifiability as the criterion of meaning was at least clear, simple, and forceful. The modifications and shifts which were now introduced were the very opposite. This, I should say, is now seen even by the participants. But since I am usually quoted as one of them I wish to repeat that although I created this confusion I never participated in it. Neither falsifiability nor testability were proposed by me as criteria for meaning; and although I may plead guilty to having introduced both terms into the discussion, it was not I who introduced them into the theory of meaning.

Criticism of my alleged views was widespread and highly successful. I have yet to meet a criticism of my views. Meanwhile, testability is being widely accepted as a criterion of demarcation.

IV

I have discussed the problem of demarcation in some detail because I believe that its solution is the key to most of the fundamental problems of the philosophy of science. . . . [B]ut only one of them—the *problem of induction*—can be discussed here at any length.

I had become interested in the problem of induction in 1923. Although this problem is very closely connected with the problem of demarcation, I did not fully appreciate the connection for about five years.

I approached the problem of induction through Hume. Hume, I felt, was perfectly right in pointing out that induction cannot be logically justified. He held that there can be no valid logical arguments allowing us to establish *"that those instances, of which we have had no experience, resemble those, of which we have had experience."* Consequently, *"even after the observation of the frequent or constant conjunction of objects, we have no reason to draw any inference concerning any object beyond those of which we have had experience."* For "shou'd it be said that we have experience"—experience teaching us that objects constantly conjoined with certain other objects continue to be so conjoined—then, Hume says, "I wou'd renew my question, *why from this experience we form any conclusion beyond those past instances, of which we have had experience.*" In other words, an attempt to justify the practice of induction by an appeal to experience must lead to an *infinite regress*. As a result we can say that theories can never be inferred from observation statements, or rationally justified by them.

I found Hume's refutation of inductive inference clear and conclusive. But I felt completely dissatisfied with his psychological explanation of induction in terms of custom or habit.

It has often been noticed that this explanation of Hume's is philosophically not very satisfactory. It is, however, without doubt intended as a *psychological* rather than a philosophical theory; for it tries to give a causal explanation of a psychological fact—*the fact that we believe in laws*, in statements asserting regularities or constantly conjoined kinds of events—by asserting that this fact is due to (i.e., constantly conjoined with) custom or habit. But even this reformulation of Hume's theory is still unsatisfactory; for what I have just called a "psychological fact" may itself be described as a custom or habit—the custom or habit of believing in laws or regularities; and it is neither very surprising nor very enlightening to hear that such a custom or habit must be explained as due to, or conjoined with, a custom or habit (even though a different one). Only when we remember that the words "custom" and "habit" are used by Hume, as they are in ordinary language, not merely to *describe* regular behavior, but rather to *theorize about its origin* (ascribed to frequent repetition), can we reformulate his psychological theory in a more satisfactory way. We can then say that, like other habits, *our habit of believing in laws is the product of frequent repetition*—of the repeated observation that things of a certain kind are constantly conjoined with things of another kind. . . .

This shows that there is an infinite regress involved in Hume's psychological theory.

Hume, I felt, had never accepted the full force of his own logical analysis. Having refuted the logical idea of induction he was faced with the following problem: How do we actually obtain our knowledge, as a matter of psychological fact, if induction is a procedure which is logically invalid and rationally unjustifiable? There are two possible answers: (1) We obtain our knowledge by a noninductive procedure. This answer would have allowed Hume to retain a form of rationalism. (2) We obtain our knowledge by repetition and induction, and therefore by a logically invalid and rationally unjustifiable procedure, so that all apparent knowledge is merely a kind of belief—belief based on habit. This answer would imply that even scientific knowledge is irrational, so that rationalism is absurd, and must be given up. (I shall not discuss here the age-old attempts, now again fashionable, to get out of the difficulty by asserting that though induction is of course logically invalid if we mean by *logic* the same as *deductive logic*, it is not irrational by its own standards, as may be seen from the fact that every reasonable man applies it *as a matter of fact*. It was Hume's great achievement to break this uncritical identification of the question of fact—*quid facti?*—and the question of justification or validity—*quid juris?* . . .

It seems that Hume never seriously considered the first alternative. Having cast out the logical theory of induction by repetition he struck a bargain with common sense, meekly allowing the reentry of induction by repetition, in the guise of a psychological theory. I proposed to turn the tables upon this theory of Hume's. Instead of explaining our propensity to expect regularities as the result of repetition, I proposed to explain repetition-for-us as the result of our propensity to expect regularities and to search for them.

Thus I was led by purely logical considerations to replace the psychological theory of induction by the following view. Without waiting, passively, for repetitions to impress or impose regularities upon us, we actively try to impose regularities upon the world. We try to discover similarities in it, and to interpret it in terms of laws invented by us. Without waiting for premises we jump to conclusions. These may have to be discarded later, should observation show that they are wrong.

This was a theory of trial and error—of *conjectures and refutations*. It made it possible to understand why our attempts to force interpretations upon the world were logically prior to the observation of similarities. Since there were logical reasons behind this procedure, I thought that it would apply in the field of science also; that scientific theories were not the digest of observations, but that they were inventions—conjectures boldly put forward for trial, to be eliminated if they clashed with observations; with observations which were rarely accidental but as a rule undertaken with the definite intention of testing a theory by obtaining, if possible, a decisive refutation.

V

The belief that science proceeds from observation to theory is still so widely and so firmly held that my denial of it is often met with incredulity. I have even been suspected of being insincere—of denying what nobody in his senses can doubt.

But in fact the belief that we can start with pure observations alone, without anything in the nature of a theory, is absurd; as may be illustrated by the story of the man who dedicated his life to natural science, wrote down everything he could observe, and bequeathed his priceless collection of observations to the Royal Society to be used as inductive evidence. This story should show us that though beetles may profitably be collected, observations may not.

Twenty-five years ago I tried to bring home the same point to a group of physics students in Vienna by beginning a lecture with the following instructions: "Take pencil and paper; carefully observe, and write down what you have observed!" They asked, of course, what I wanted them to observe. Clearly the instruction "Observe!" is absurd. (It is not even idiomatic, unless the object of the transitive verb can be taken as understood.) Observation is always selective. It needs a chosen object, a definite task, an interest, a point of view, a problem. And its description presupposes a descriptive language, with property words; it presupposes similarity and classifications, which in its turn presupposes interests, points of view, and problems. "A hungry animal," writes Katz, "divides the environment into edible and inedible things. An animal in flight sees roads to escape and hiding places. . . . Generally speaking, objects change . . . according to the needs of the animal." We may add that objects can be classified, and can become similar or dissimilar, only in this way—by being related to needs and interests. This rule applies not only to animals but also to scientists. For the animal a point of view is provided by its needs, the task of the moment, and its expectations; for the scientist by his theoretical interests, the special problem under investigation, his conjectures and anticipations, and the theories which he accepts as a kind of background: his frame of reference, his "horizon of expectations."

The problem "Which comes first, the hypothesis (H) or the observation (O)" is soluble, as is the problem "Which comes first, the hen (H) or the egg (O)." The reply to the latter is "An earlier kind of egg"; to the former, "An earlier kind of hypothesis." It is quite true that any particular hypothesis we choose will have been preceded by observations—the observations, for example, which it is designed to explain. But these observations, in their turn, presupposed the adoption of a frame of reference, a frame of expectations, a frame of theories. If they were significant, if they created a need for explanation and thus gave rise to the invention of a hypothesis, it was because they could not be explained within the old theoretical framework, the old horizon of expectations. There is no danger here of an infinite regress. Going back to more and more primitive theories and myths we shall in the end find unconscious, *inborn* expectations.

The theory of inborn *ideas* is absurd, I think; but every organism has inborn *reactions* or *responses*; and among them, responses adapted to impending events. These responses we may describe as "expectations" without implying that

these "expectations" are conscious. The newborn baby "expects," in this sense, to be fed (and, one could even argue, to be protected and loved). In view of the close relation between expectation and knowledge we may even speak in quite a reasonable sense of "inborn knowledge." This "knowledge" is not, however, *valid a priori*; an inborn expectation, no matter how strong and specific, may be mistaken. (The newborn child may be abandoned, and starve.)

Thus we are born with expectations; with "knowledge" which, although not *valid a priori*, is *psychologically or genetically a priori*, i.e., prior to all observational experience. One of the most important of these expectations is the expectation of finding a regularity. It is connected with an inborn propensity to look out for regularities, or with a *need* to *find* regularities, as we may see from the pleasure of the child who satisfies this need.

This "instinctive" expectation of finding regularities, which is psychologically *a priori*, corresponds very closely to the "law of causality" which Kant believed to be part of our mental outfit and to be *a priori* valid. One might thus be inclined to say that Kant failed to distinguish between psychologically *a priori* ways of thinking or responding and *a priori* valid beliefs. But I do not think that his mistake was quite as crude as that. For the expectation of finding regularities is not only psychologically *a priori*, but also logically *a priori*: It is logically prior to all observational experience, for it is prior to any recognition of similarities, as we have seen; and all observation involves the recognition of similarities (or dissimilarities). But in spite of being logically *a priori* in this sense the expectation is not valid *a priori*. For it may fail: We can easily construct an environment (it would be a lethal one) which, compared with our ordinary environment, is so chaotic that we completely fail to find regularities. (All natural laws could remain valid: Environments of this kind have been used in the animal experiments mentioned in the next section.)

Thus Kant's reply to Hume came near to being right; for the distinction between an *a priori* valid expectation and one which is both genetically and logically prior to observation, but not *a priori* valid, is really somewhat subtle. But Kant proved too much. In trying to show how knowledge is possible, he proposed a theory which had the unavoidable consequence that our quest for knowledge must necessarily succeed, which is clearly mistaken. When Kant said, "Our intellect does not draw its laws from nature but imposes its laws upon nature," he was right. But in thinking that these laws are necessarily true, or that we necessarily succeed in imposing them upon nature, he was wrong. Nature very often resists quite successfully, forcing us to discard our laws as refuted; but if we live we may try again.

To sum up this logical criticism of Hume's psychology of induction we may consider the idea of building an induction machine. Placed in a simplified "world" (for example, one of sequences of colored counters), such a machine may through repetition "learn," or even "formulate," laws of succession which hold in its "world." If such a machine can be constructed (and I have no doubt that it can) then, it might be argued, my theory must be wrong; for if a machine is capable of performing inductions on the basis of repetition, there can be no logical reasons preventing us from doing the same.

The argument sounds convincing, but it is mistaken. In constructing an induction machine we, the architects of the machine, must decide *a priori* what constitutes its "world"; what things are to be taken as similar or equal; and what *kind* of "laws" we wish the machine to be able to "discover" in its "world." In other words we must build into the machine a framework determining what is relevant or interesting in its world: The machine will have its "inborn" selection principles. The problems of similarity will have been solved for it by its makers who thus have interpreted the "world" for the machine.

VI

Our propensity to look out for regularities, and to impose laws upon nature, leads to the psychological phenomenon of *dogmatic thinking* or, more generally, dogmatic behavior: We expect regularities everywhere and attempt to find them even where there are none; events which do not yield to these attempts we are inclined to treat as a kind of 'background noise'; and we stick to our expectations even when they are inadequate and we ought to accept defeat. This dogmatism is to some extent necessary. It is demanded by a situation which can only be dealt with by forcing our conjectures upon the world. Moreover, this dogmatism allows us to approach a good theory in stages, by way of approximations: If we accept defeat too easily, we may prevent ourselves from finding that we were very nearly right.

It is clear that this *dogmatic attitude*, which makes us stick to our first impressions, is indicative of a strong belief; while a *critical attitude*, which is ready to modify its tenets, which admits doubt and demands tests, is indicative of a weaker belief. Now according to Hume's theory, and to the popular theory, the strength of a belief should be a product of repetition; thus it should always grow with experience, and always be greater in less primitive persons. But dogmatic thinking, an uncontrolled wish to impose regularities, a manifest pleasure in rites and in repetition as such, are characteristic of primitives and children; and increasing experience and maturity sometimes create an attitude of caution and criticism rather than of dogmatism.

I may perhaps mention here a point of agreement with psychoanalysis. Psychoanalysts assert that neurotics and others interpret the world in accordance with a personal set pattern which is not easily given up, and which can often be traced back to early childhood. A pattern or scheme which was adopted very early in life is maintained throughout, and every new experience is interpreted in terms of it; verifying it, as it were, and contributing to its rigidity. This is a description of what I have called the dogmatic attitude, as distinct from the critical attitude, which shares with the dogmatic attitude the quick adoption of a schema of expectations—a myth, perhaps, or a conjecture of hypothesis—but which is ready to modify it, to correct it, and even to give it up. I am inclined to suggest that most neuroses may be due to a partially arrested development of the critical attitude; to an arrested rather than a natural dogmatism; to resistance to demands for the modification and adjustment of certain schematic interpretations and responses. This resistance in its turn may perhaps be explained, in some cases, as due to an injury or shock, resulting in fear and in an increased need for assurance or certainty, analogous to the way in which an injury to a limb makes us afraid to move it, so that it becomes stiff. (It might even be argued that the case of the limb is not merely analogous to the dogmatic response, but an instance of it.) The explanation of any concrete case will have to take into account the weight of the difficulties involved in making the necessary adjustments—difficulties which may be considerable, especially in a complex and changing world: We know from experiments on animals that varying degrees of neurotic behavior may be produced at will by correspondingly varying difficulties.

I found many other links between the psychology of knowledge and psychological fields which are often considered remote from it—for example, the psychology of art and music; in fact, my ideas about induction originated in a conjecture about the evolution of Western polyphony. But you will be spared this story.

VII

My logical criticism of Hume's psychological theory, and the considerations connected with it (most of which I elaborated in 1926–7, in a thesis entitled "On Habit and Belief in Laws"), may seem a little removed from the field of the philosophy of science. But the distinction between dogmatic and critical thinking, or the dogmatic and the critical attitude, brings us right back to our central problem. For the dogmatic attitude is clearly related to the tendency to *verify* our laws and schemata by seeking to apply them and to confirm them, even to the point of neglecting refutations, whereas the critical attitude is one of readiness to change them—to test them, to refute them, to *falsify* them, if possible. This suggests that we may identify the critical attitude with the scientific attitude, and the dogmatic attitude with the one which we have described as pseudo-scientific.

It further suggests that genetically speaking the pseudo-scientific attitude is more primitive than, and prior to, the scientific attitude, that it is a pre-scientific attitude. And this primitivity or priority also has its logical aspect. For the critical attitude is not so much opposed to the dogmatic attitude as superimposed upon it: Criticism must be directed against existing and influential beliefs in need of critical revision—in other words, dogmatic beliefs. A critical attitude needs for its raw material, as it were, theories or beliefs which are held more or less dogmatically.

Thus science must begin with myths and with the criticism of myths—neither with the collection of observations, nor with the invention of experiments, but with the critical discussion of myths, and of magical techniques and practices. The scientific tradition is distinguished from the pre-scientific tradition in having two layers. Like the latter, it passes on its theories; but it also passes on a critical attitude toward them. The theories are passed on, not as dogmas, but rather with the challenge to discuss them and improve upon them. This tradition is Hellenic: It may be traced back to Thales, founder of the first *school* (I do not mean "of the first *philosophical* school," but simply "of the first school") which was not mainly concerned with the preservation of a dogma. . . .

The critical attitude, the tradition of free discussion of theories with the aim of discovering their weak spots so that they may be improved upon, is the attitude of reasonableness, of rationality. It makes far-reaching use of both verbal argument and observation—of observation in the interest of argument, however. The Greeks' discovery of the critical method gave rise at first to the mistaken hope that it would lead to the solution of all the great old problems; that it would establish certainty; that it would help to *prove* our theories, to *justify* them. But this hope was a residue of the dogmatic way of thinking; in fact nothing can be justified or proved (outside of mathematics and logic). The demand for rational proofs in science indicates a failure to keep distinct the broad realm of rationality and the narrow realm of rational certainty: It is an untenable, an unreasonable demand.

Nevertheless, the role of logical argument, of deductive logical reasoning, remains all-important for the critical approach; not because it allows us to prove our theories, or to infer them from observation statements, but because only by purely deductive reasoning is it possible for us to discover what our theories imply, and thus to criticize them effectively. Criticism, I said, is an attempt to find the weak spots in a theory, and these, as a rule, can be found only in the more remote logical consequences which can be derived from it. It is here that purely logical reasoning plays an important part in science.

Hume was right in stressing that our theories cannot be validly inferred from what we can know to be true—neither from observations nor from anything else. He concluded from this that our belief in them was irrational. If *belief* means here our inability to doubt our natural laws and the constancy of natural regularities, then Hume is again right: This kind of dogmatic belief has, one might say, a physiological rather than a rational basis. If, however, the term *belief* is taken to cover our critical acceptance of scientific theories—a *tentative* acceptance combined with an eagerness to revise the theory if we succeed in designing a test which it cannot pass—then Hume was wrong. In such an acceptance of theories there is nothing irrational. There is not even anything irrational in relying for practical purposes upon well-tested theories, for no more rational course of action is open to us.

Assume that we have deliberately made it our task to live in this unknown world of ours, to adjust ourselves to it as well as we can, to take advantage of the opportunities we can find in it, and to explain it, *if* possible (we need not assume that it is), and as far as possible, with the help of laws and explanatory theories. *If we have made this our task, then there is no more rational procedure than the method of trial and error—of conjecture and refutation,* of boldly proposing theories, of trying our best to show that these are erroneous, and of accepting them tentatively if our critical efforts are unsuccessful.

From the point of view here developed, all laws, all theories remain essentially tentative, or conjectural, or hypothetical, even when we feel unable to doubt them any longer. Before a theory has been refuted we can never know in what way it may have to be modified. That the sun will always rise and set within twenty-four hours is still proverbial as a law established by induction beyond reasonable doubt. It is odd that this example is still in use, though it may have served well enough in the days of Aristotle and Pytheas of Massalia—the great traveler who for centuries was called a liar because of his tales of Thule, the land of the frozen sea and the *midnight sun.*

The method of trial and error is not, of course, simply identical with the scientific or critical approach—with the method of conjecture and refutation. The method of trial and error is applied not only by Einstein but, in a more dogmatic fashion, by the amoeba also. The difference lies not so much in the trials as in a critical and constructive attitude towards errors; errors which the scientist

consciously and cautiously tries to uncover in order to refute his theories with searching arguments, including appeals to the most severe experimental tests which his theories and his ingenuity permit him to design.

The critical attitude may be described as the conscious attempt to make our theories, our conjectures, suffer in our stead in the struggle for the survival of the fittest. It gives us a chance to survive the elimination of an inadequate hypothesis—when a more dogmatic attitude would eliminate it by eliminating us. (There is a touching story of an Indian community which disappeared because of its belief in the holiness of life, including that of tigers.) We thus obtain the fittest theory within our reach by the elimination of those which are less fit. (By "fitness" I do not mean merely "usefulness" but truth. . . .) I do not think that this procedure is irrational or in need of any further rational justification. . . .

I may summarize some of my conclusions as follows:

1. Induction, i.e., inference based on many observations, is a myth. It is neither a psychological fact, nor a fact of ordinary life, nor one of scientific procedure.

2. The actual procedure of science is to operate with conjectures: to jump to conclusions—often after one single observation (as noticed, for example, by Hume and Born).

3. Repeated observations and experiments function in science as *tests* of our conjectures or hypothesis, i.e., as attempted refutations.

4. The mistaken belief in induction is fortified by the need for a criterion of demarcation which, it is traditionally but wrongly believed, only the inductive method can provide.

5. The conception of such an inductive method . . . implies a faulty demarcation.

6. None of this is altered in the least if we say that induction makes theories only probable rather than certain. . . .

IX

If, as I have suggested, the problem of induction is only an instance or facet of the problem of demarcation, then the solution to the problem of demarcation must provide us with a solution to the problem of induction. This is indeed the case, I believe, although it is perhaps not immediately obvious.

For a brief formulation of the problem of induction we can turn . . . to Born, who writes: ". . . no observation or experiment, however extended, can give more than a finite number of repetitions"; therefore, "the statement of a law—B depends on A—always transcends experience. Yet this kind of statement is made everywhere and all the time, and sometimes from scanty material.

In other words, the logical problem of induction arises from (a) Hume's discovery (so well expressed by Born) that it is impossible to justify a law by observation or experiment, since it "transcends experience"; (b) the fact that science proposes and uses laws "everywhere and all the time." (Like Hume, Born is struck by the "scanty material," i.e., the few observed instances upon which the law may be based.) To this we have to add (c) *the principle of empiricism*, which asserts that in science only observation and experiment may decide upon the *acceptance or rejection* of scientific statements, including laws and theories.

These three principles, (a), (b), and (c), appear at first sight to clash; and this apparent clash constitutes the *logical problem of induction.*

Faced with this clash, Born gives up (c), the principle of empiricism (as Kant and many others, including Bertrand Russell, have done before him), in favor of what he calls a "metaphysical principle"; a metaphysical principle which he does not even attempt to formulate; which he vaguely describes as a "code or rule of craft"; and of which I have never seen any formulation which even looked promising and was not clearly untenable.

But in fact the principles (a) to (c) do not clash. We can see this the moment we realize that the acceptance by science of a law or of a theory is *tentative only;* which is to say that all laws and theories are conjectures, or tentative *hypotheses* (a position which I have sometimes called "hypotheticism"); and that we may reject a law or theory on the basis of new evidence, without necessarily discarding the old evidence which originally led us to accept it.

The principle of empiricism (c) can be fully preserved, since the fate of a theory, its acceptance or rejection, is decided by observation and experiment—by the result of tests. So long as a theory stands up to the severest tests we can design, it is accepted; if it does not, it is rejected. But it is never inferred, in any sense, from the empirical evidence. There is neither a psychological nor a logical induction. *Only the falsity of the theory can be inferred from empirical evidence, and this inference is a purely deductive one.*

Hume showed that it is not possible to infer a theory from observation statements; but this does not affect the possibility of refuting a theory by observation statements. The full appreciation of this possibility makes the relation between theories and observations perfectly clear.

This solves the problem of the alleged clash between the principles (a), (b), and (c), and with it Hume's problem of induction.

X

Thus the problem of induction is solved. But nothing seems less wanted than a simple solution to an age-old philosophical problem. Wittgenstein and his school hold that genuine philosophical problems do not exist, from which it clearly follows that they cannot be solved. Others among my contemporaries do believe that there are philosophical problems, and respect them, but they seem to respect them too much; they seem to believe that they are insoluble, if not taboo, and they are shocked and horrified by the claim that there is a simple, neat, and lucid, solution to any of them. If there is a solution it must be deep, they feel, or at least complicated.

However this may be, I am still waiting for a simple, neat, and lucid criticism of the solution which I published first in 1933 in my letter to the Editor of *Erkenntnis,* and later in *The Logic of Scientific Discovery.*

Of course, one can invent new problems of induction, different from the one I have formulated and solved. (Its formulation was half its solution.) But I have yet to see any reformulation of the problem whose solution cannot be easily obtained from my old solution. I am now going to discuss some of these reformulations.

One question which may be asked is this: How do we really jump from an observation statement to a theory?

Although this question appears to be psychological rather than philosophical, one can say something positive about it without invoking psychology. One can say first that the jump is not from an observation statement, but from a problem-situation, and that the theory must allow us *to explain* the observations which created the problem (that is, *to deduce* them from the theory strengthened by other accepted theories and by other observation statements, the so-called initial conditions). This leaves, of course, an immense number of possible theories, good and bad; and it thus appears that our question has not been answered.

But this makes it fairly clear that when we asked our question we had more in mind than "How do we jump from an observation statement to a theory?" The question we had in mind was, it now appears, "How do we jump from an observation statement to a *good* theory?" But to this the answer is: by jumping first to *any* theory and then testing it, to find whether it is good or not; i.e., by repeatedly applying the critical method, eliminating many bad theories, and inventing many new ones. Not everybody is able to do this; but there is no other way.

Other questions have sometimes been asked. The original problem of induction, it was said, is the problem of *justifying* induction, i.e., of justifying inductive inference. If you answer this problem by saying that what is called an "inductive inference" is always invalid and therefore clearly not justifiable, the following new problem must arise: How do you justify your method of trial and error? Reply: the method of trial and error is a *method of eliminating false theories* by observation statements; and the justification for this is the purely logical relationship of deducibility, which allows us to assert the falsity of universal statements if we accept the truth of singular ones.

Another question sometimes asked is this: Why is it reasonable to prefer non-falsified statements to falsified ones? To this question some involved answers have been produced, for example, pragmatic answers. But from a pragmatic point of view the question does not arise, since false theories often serve well enough: Most formulas used in engineering or navigation are known to be false, although they may be excellent approximations and easy to handle; and they are used with confidence by people who know them to be false.

The only correct answer is the straightforward one: because we search for truth (even though we can never be sure we have found it), and because the falsified theories are known or believed to be false, while the non-falsified theories may still be true. Besides, we do not prefer *every* non-falsified theory—only one which, in the light of criticism, appears to be better than its competitors, which solves our problems, which is well tested, and of which we think, or rather conjecture or hope (considering other provisionally accepted theories), that it will stand up to further tests.

It has also been said that the problem of induction is "Why is it *reasonable* to believe that the future will be like the past?" and that a satisfactory answer to this question should make it plain that such a belief is, in fact, reasonable. My reply is that it is reasonable to believe that the future will be very different from the past in many vitally important respects. Admittedly it is perfectly reasonable to *act* on the assumption that it will, in many respects, be like the past, and that well-tested laws will continue to hold (since we can have no better assumption to act upon); but it is also reasonable to believe that such a course of action will lead us at times into severe trouble, since some of the laws upon which we now heavily rely may easily prove unreliable. (Remember the midnight sun!) One might even say that to judge from past experience, and from our general scientific knowledge, the future will *not* be like the past, in perhaps most of the ways which those have in mind who say that it will. Water will sometimes not quench thirst, and air will choke those who breathe it. An apparent way out is to say that the future will be like the past *in the sense that the laws of nature will not change*, but this is begging the question. We speak of a "law of nature" only if we think that we have before us a regularity which does not change; and if we find that it changes, then we shall not continue to call it a "law of nature." Of course our search for natural laws indicates that we hope to find them, and that we believe that there are natural laws, but our belief in any particular natural law cannot have a safer basis than our unsuccessful critical attempts to refute it.

I think that those who put the problem of induction in terms of the *reasonableness* of our beliefs are perfectly right if they are dissatisfied with a Humean, or post-Humean, skeptical despair of reason. We must indeed reject the view that a belief in science is as irrational as a belief in primitive magical practices—that both are a matter of accepting a "total ideology," a convention or a tradition based on faith. But we must be cautious if we formulate our problem, with Hume, as one of the reasonableness of our *beliefs*. We should split this problem into three—our old problem of demarcation, or of how to *distinguish* between science and primitive magic; the problem of the rationality of the scientific or critical *procedure*, and of the role of observation within it; and lastly the problem of the rationality of our *acceptance* of theories for scientific and for practical purposes. To all these three problems solutions have been offered here.

One should also be careful not to confuse the problem of the reasonableness of the scientific procedure and the (tentative) acceptance of the results of this procedure—i.e., the scientific theories—with the problem of the rationality or otherwise *of the belief that this procedure will succeed*. In practice, in practical scientific research, this belief is no doubt unavoidable and reasonable, there being no better alternative. But the belief is certainly unjustifiable in a theoretical sense, as I have argued. . . . Moreover, if we could show, on general logical grounds, that the scientific quest is likely to succeed, one could not understand why anything like success has been so rare in the long history of human endeavors to know more about our world. . . .

Notes

[1]Wittgenstein's example of a nonsensical pseudo-proposition is: "Socrates is identical." Obviously, "Socrates is not identical" must also be nonsense. Thus the negation of any nonsense will be nonsense, and that of a meaningful statement will be meaningful. *But the negation of a testable (or falsifiable) statement need not be testable*, as was pointed out, first in my *L.Sc.D.*, (e.g., pp. 38 f.) and later by my critics. The confusion caused by taking testability as a criterion of meaning rather than of demarcation can easily be imagined.

IX.4 Science and Pseudoscience

IMRE LAKATOS

Imre Lakatos (1922–1974), a Hungarian-born philosopher, spent most of his career at the London School of Economics. He began as a disciple of Popper but gradually broke from Popper's theory of falsification, deeming it only part of the truth about scientific method. In place of the criterion of falsification, Lakatos developed a notion of scientific progress: That is, a research program is scientific if it leads to fruitful and interesting further projects. It need not be the true theory, only a challenging and progressive one, hopefully in the direction of truth. If it fails to generate new experiments and projects, it is a degenerate project, worthy of being discarded. Whereas approaching the truth is a worthy goal, we cannot know that our theories are true, but we can provide increasing justification through a process of innovative hypothesis invention and testing.

Man's respect for knowledge is one of his most peculiar characteristics. Knowledge in Latin is *scientia*, and science came to be the name of the most respectable kind of knowledge. But what distinguishes knowledge from superstition, ideology or pseudoscience? The Catholic Church excommunicated Copernicans, the Communist Party persecuted Mendelians on the ground that their doctrines were pseudoscientific. The demarcation between science and pseudoscience is not merely a problem of armchair philosophy: it is of vital social and political relevance.

Many philosophers have tried to solve the problem of demarcation in the following terms: a statement constitutes knowledge if sufficiently many people believe it sufficiently strongly. But the history of thought shows us that many people were totally committed to absurd beliefs. If the strength of beliefs were a hallmark of knowledge, we should have to rank some tales about demons, angels, devils, and of heaven and hell as knowledge. Scientists, on the other hand, are very sceptical even of their best theories. Newton's is the most powerful theory science has yet produced, but Newton himself never believed that bodies attract each other at a distance. So no degree of commitment to beliefs makes them knowledge. Indeed, the hallmark of scientific behavior is a certain scepticism even towards one's most cherished theories. Blind commitment to a theory is not an intellectual virtue: it is an intellectual crime.

Thus a statement may be pseudoscientific even if it is eminently "plausible" and everybody believes in it, and it may be scientifically valuable even if it is unbelievable and nobody believes in it. A theory may even be of supreme scientific value even if no one understands it, let alone believes it.

The cognitive value of a theory has nothing to do with its psychological influence on people's minds. Belief, commitment, understanding are states of the human mind. But the objective, scientific value of a theory is independent of the human mind which creates it or understands it. Its scien-

From "The Methodology of Scientific Research," *Philosophical Papers*, Vol. 1, Imre Lakatos (New York: Cambridge University Press, copyright 1977), pp. 1–7. Reprinted by permission of Cambridge University Press. This paper was written in early 1973 and was originally delivered as a radio lecture. It was broadcast by the Open University on 30 June 1973.

tific value depends only on what objective support these conjectures have in facts. As Hume said:

> If we take in our hand any volume; of divinity, or school metaphysics, for instance; let us ask, does it contain any abstract reasoning concerning quantity or number? No. Does it contain any experimental reasoning concerning matter of fact and existence? No. Commit it then to the flames. For it can contain nothing but sophistry and illusion.

But what is "experimental" reasoning? If we look at the vast seventeenth-century literature on witchcraft it is full of reports of careful observations and sworn evidence—even of experiments. Glanvill, the house philosopher of the early Royal Society, regarded witchcraft as the paradigm of experimental reasoning. We have to define experimental reasoning before we start Humean book burning.

In scientific reasoning, theories are confronted with facts; and one of the central conditions of scientific reasoning is that theories must be supported by facts. Now how exactly can facts support theory?

Several different answers have been proposed. Newton himself thought that he proved his laws from facts. He was proud of not uttering mere hypotheses: he only published theories proven from facts. In particular, he claimed that he deduced his laws from the "phenomena" provided by Kepler. But his boast was nonsense, since according to Kepler, planets move in ellipses, but according to Newton's theory, planets would move in ellipses only if the planets did not disturb each other in their motion. But they do. This is why Newton had to devise a perturbation theory from which it follows that no planet moves in an ellipse.

One can today easily demonstrate that there can be no valid derivation of a law of nature from any finite number of facts; but we still keep reading about scientific theories being proved from facts. Why this stubborn resistance to elementary logic?

There is a very plausible explanation. Scientists want to make their theories respectable, deserving of the title "science," that is, genuine knowledge. Now the most relevant knowledge in the seventeenth century, when science was born, concerned God, the Devil, Heaven and Hell. If one got one's conjectures about matters of divinity wrong, the consequence of one's mistake was eternal damnation. Theological knowledge cannot be fallible: it must be beyond doubt. Now the Enlightenment thought that we were fallible and ignorant about matters theological. There is no scientific theology and, therefore, no theological knowledge. Knowledge can only be about Nature, but this new type of knowledge had to be judged by the standards they took over straight from theology: it had to be proven beyond doubt. Science had to achieve the very certainty which had escaped theology. A scientist, worthy of the name, was not allowed to guess: he had to prove each sentence he uttered from facts. This was the criterion of scientific honesty. Theories unproven from facts were regarded as sinful pseudoscience, heresy in the scientific community.

It was only the downfall of Newtonian theory in this century which made scientists realize that their standards of honesty had been utopian. Before Einstein most scientists thought that Newton had deciphered God's ultimate laws by proving them from the facts. Ampère, in the early nineteenth century, felt he had to call his book on his speculations concerning electromagnetism: *Mathematical Theory of Electrodynamic Phenomena Unequivocally Deduced from Experiment*. But at the end of the volume he casually confesses that some of the experiments were never performed and even that the necessary instruments had not been constructed!

If all scientific theories are equally unprovable, what distinguishes scientific knowledge from ignorance, science from pseudoscience?

One answer to this question was provided in the twentieth century by "**inductive** logicians." Inductive logic set out to define the probabilities of different theories according to the available total evidence. If the mathematical probability of a theory is high, it qualifies as scientific; if it is low or even zero, it is not scientific. Thus the hallmark of scientific honesty would be never to say anything that is not at least highly probable. **Probabilism** has an attractive feature: instead of simply providing a black-and-white distinction between science and pseudoscience, it provides a continuous scale from poor theories with low probability to good theories with high probability. But, in 1934, Karl Popper, one of the most influential philosophers of our time, argued that the mathematical probability of all theories, scientific or pseudoscientific, given **any** amount of evidence is zero. If Popper is

right, scientific theories are not only equally unprovable but also equally improbable. A new demarcation criterion was needed and Popper proposed a rather stunning one. A theory may be scientific even if there is not a shred of evidence in its favor, and it may be pseudoscientific even if all the available evidence is in its favor. That is, the scientific or nonscientific character of a theory can be determined independently of the facts. A theory is "scientific" if one is prepared to specify in advance a crucial experiment (or observation) which can falsify it, and it is pseudoscientific if one refuses to specify such a "potential falsifier." But if so, we do not demarcate scientific theories from pseudoscientific ones, but rather scientific method from non-scientific method. Marxism, for a Popperian, is scientific if the Marxists are prepared to specify facts which, if observed, make them give up Marxism. If they refuse to do so, Marxism becomes a pseudoscience. It is always interesting to ask a Marxist, what conceivable event would make him abandon his Marxism. If he is committed to Marxism, he is bound to find it immoral to specify a state of affairs which can falsify it. Thus a proposition may petrify into pseudoscientific dogma or become genuine knowledge, depending on whether we are prepared to state observable conditions which would refute it.

Is, then, Popper's falsifiability criterion the solution to the problem of demarcating science from pseudoscience? No. For Popper's criterion ignores the remarkable tenacity of scientific theories. Scientists have thick skins. They do not abandon a theory merely because facts contradict it. They normally either invent some rescue hypothesis to explain what they then call a mere **anomaly** or, if they cannot explain the anomaly, they ignore it, and direct their attention to other problems. Note that scientists talk about anomalies, recalcitrant instances, not refutations. History of science, of course, is full of accounts of how crucial experiments allegedly killed theories. But such accounts are fabricated long after the theory had been abandoned. Had Popper ever asked a Newtonian scientist under what experimental conditions he would abandon Newtonian theory, some Newtonian scientists would have been exactly as nonplussed as are some Marxists.

What, then, is the hallmark of science? Do we have to capitulate and agree that a scientific revolution is just an irrational change in commitment, that it is a religious conversion? Tom Kuhn, a distinguished American philosopher of science, arrived at this conclusion after discovering the naïvety of Popper's falsificationism. But if Kuhn is right, then there is no explicit demarcation between science and pseudoscience, no distinction between scientific progress and intellectual decay, there is no objective standard of honesty. But what criteria can he then offer to demarcate scientific progress from intellectual degeneration?

In the last few years I have been advocating a methodology of scientific research programs, which solves some of the problems which both Popper and Kuhn failed to solve.

First, I claim that the typical descriptive unit of great scientific achievements is not an isolated hypothesis but rather a research program. Science is not simply trial and error, a series of conjectures and refutations. "All swans are white" may be falsified by the discovery of one black swan. But such trivial trial and error does not rank as science. Newtonian science, for instance, is not simply a set of four conjectures—the three laws of mechanics and the law of gravitation. These four laws constitute only the "hard core" of the Newtonian program. But this hard core is tenaciously protected from refutation by a vast "protective belt" of auxiliary hypotheses. And, even more importantly, the research program also has a "heuristic," that is, a powerful problem-solving machinery, which, with the help of sophisticated mathematical techniques, digests anomalies and even turns them into positive evidence. For instance, if a planet does not move exactly as it should, the Newtonian scientist checks his conjectures concerning atmospheric refraction, concerning propagation of light in magnetic storms, and hundreds of other conjectures which are all part of the program. He may even invent a hitherto unknown planet and calculate its position, mass and velocity in order to explain the anomaly.

Now, Newton's theory of gravitation, Einstein's relativity theory, quantum mechanics, Marxism, Freudianism, are all research programs, each with a characteristic hard core stubbornly defended, each with its more flexible protective belt and each with its elaborate problem-solving machinery. Each of them, at any stage of its development, has unsolved problems and undigested anomalies. All theories, in this sense, are born refuted and die refuted. But are they equally good?

Until now I have been describing what research programs are like. But how can one distinguish a scientific or progressive program from a pseudo-scientific or degenerating one?

Contrary to Popper, the difference cannot be that some are still unrefuted, while others are already refuted. When Newton published his *Principia*, it was common knowledge that it could not properly explain even the motion of the moon; in fact, lunar motion refuted Newton. Kaufmann, a distinguished physicist, refuted Einstein's relativity theory in the very year it was published. But all the research programs I admire have one characteristic in common. They all predict novel facts, facts which had been either undreamt of, or have indeed been contradicted by previous or rival programs. In 1686, when Newton published his theory of gravitation, there were, for instance, two current theories concerning comets. The more popular one regarded comets as a signal from an angry God warning that He will strike and bring disaster. A little known theory of Kepler's held that comets were celestial bodies moving along straight lines. Now according to Newtonian theory, some of them moved in hyperbolas or parabolas never to return; others moved in ordinary ellipses. Halley, working in Newton's program, calculated on the basis of observing a brief stretch of a comet's path that it would return in seventy-two years' time; he calculated to the minute when it would be seen again at a well-defined point of the sky. This was incredible. But seventy-two years later, when both Newton and Halley were long dead, Halley's comet returned exactly as Halley predicted. Similarly, Newtonian scientists predicted the existence and exact motion of small planets which had never been observed before. Or let us take Einstein's program. This program made the stunning prediction that if one measures the distance between two stars in the night and if one measures the distance between them during the day (when they are visible during an eclipse of the sun), the two measurements will be different. Nobody had thought to make such an observation before Einstein's program. Thus, in a progressive research program, theory leads to the discovery of hitherto unknown novel facts. In degenerating programs, however, theories are fabricated only in order to accommodate known facts. Has, for instance, Marxism ever predicted a stunning novel fact successfully? Never! It has some famous unsuccessful predictions. It predicted the absolute impoverishment of the working class. It predicted that the first socialist revolution would take place in the industrially most developed society. It predicted that socialist societies would be free of revolutions. It predicted that there will be no conflict of interests between socialist countries. Thus the early predictions of Marxism were bold and stunning but they failed. Marxists explained all their failures: they explained the rising living standards of the working class by devising a theory of imperialism; they even explained why the first socialist revolution occurred in industrially backward Russia. They "explained" Berlin 1953, Budapest 1956, Prague 1968. They "explained" the Russian-Chinese conflict. But their auxiliary hypotheses were all cooked up after the event to protect Marxian theory from the facts. The Newtonian program led to novel facts; the Marxian lagged behind the facts and has been running fast to catch up with them.

To sum up. The hallmark of empirical progress is not trivial verifications: Popper is right that there are millions of them. It is no success for Newtonian theory that stones, when dropped, fall towards the earth, no matter how often this is repeated. But so-called "refutations" are not the hallmark of empirical failure, as Popper has preached, since all programs grow in a permanent ocean of anomalies. What really count are dramatic, unexpected, stunning predictions: a few of them are enough to tilt the balance; where theory lags behind the facts, we are dealing with miserable degenerating research programs.

Now, how do scientific revolutions come about? If we have two rival research programs, and one is progressing while the other is degenerating, scientists tend to join the progressive program. This is the rationale of scientific revolutions. But while it is a matter of intellectual honesty to keep the record public, it is not dishonest to stick to a degenerating program and try to turn it into a progressive one.

As opposed to Popper the methodology of scientific research programs does not offer instant rationality. One must treat budding programs leniently: programs may take decades before they get off the ground and become empirically progressive. Criticism is not a Popperian quick kill, by refutation. Important criticism is always constructive: there is no refutation without a better theory. Kuhn is wrong in thinking that scientific revolutions are sudden, irrational changes in vision. The history of science refutes both Popper and Kuhn: on close inspection both Popperian crucial experiments and Kuhnian revolutions turn out to be myths: what normally happens is that progressive research programs replace degenerating ones.

The problem of demarcation between science and pseudoscience has grave implications also for the institutionalization of criticism. Copernicus's theory was banned by the Catholic Church in 1616 because it was said to be pseudoscientific. It was taken off the index in 1820 because by that time the Church deemed that facts had proved it and therefore it became scientific. The Central Committee of the Soviet Communist Party in 1949 declared Mendelian genetics pseudoscientific and had its advocates, like Academician Vavilov, killed in concentration camps; after Vavilov's murder Mendelian genetics was rehabilitated; but the Party's right to decide what is science and publishable and what is pseudoscience and punishable was upheld. The new liberal Establishment of the West also exercises the right to deny freedom of speech to what it regards as pseudoscience, as we have seen in the case of the debate concerning race and intelligence. All these judgments were inevitably based on some sort of demarcation criterion. This is why the problem of demarcation between science and pseudoscience is not a pseudo-problem of armchair philosophers: it has grave ethical and political implications.

IX.5 Science as Myth

Paul Feyerabend

Paul Feyerabend (1924–1994), Austrian-American philosopher of science, was for many years a professor of philosophy at the University of California, Berkeley. His most famous work is *Against Method* (1988), from which this selection is taken. Feyerabend argues that science contains no special, let alone superior, method to other disciplines and that its high position in our society is a fraud. In a truly democratic society people would be free to choose their epistemology and not be coerced to treat science with special reverence. Therefore, just as there is a separation of church and state in our democratic society, there should be a separation of science and state.

Science is much closer to myth than a scientific philosophy is prepared to admit. It is one of the many forms of thought that have been developed by man, and not necessarily the best. It is conspicuous, noisy, and impudent, but it is inherently superior only for those who have already decided in favor of a certain ideology, or who have accepted it without ever having examined its advantages and its limits. And as the accepting and rejecting of ideologies should be left to the individual it follows that the separation of state and *church* must be complemented by the separation of state and *science*, that most recent, most aggressive, and most dogmatic religious institution. Such a separation may be our only chance to achieve a humanity we are capable of, but have never fully realized. . . .

The rise of modern science coincides with the suppression of non-Western tribes by Western invaders. The tribes are not only physically suppressed, they also lose their intellectual independence and are forced to adopt the bloodthirsty religion of brotherly love—Christianity. The most intelligent members get an extra bonus: they are introduced into the mysteries of Western Rationalism and its peak—Western Science. Occasionally this leads to an almost unbearable tension with tradition (Haiti). In most cases the tradition disappears without the trace of an argument; one simply becomes a slave both in body and in mind. Today this development is gradually reversed—with great reluctance, to be sure, but it is reversed. Freedom is regained, old traditions are

rediscovered, both among the minorities in Western countries and among large populations in non-Western continents. *But science still reigns supreme.* It reigns supreme because its practitioners are *unable to understand*, and *unwilling to condone*, different ideologies, because they have the *power* to enforce their wishes, and because they *use* this power just as their ancestors used *their* power to force Christianity on the peoples they encountered during their conquests. Thus, while an American can now choose the religion he likes, he is still not permitted to demand that his children learn magic rather than science at school. There is a separation between state and church; there is no separation between state and science.

And yet science has no greater authority than any other form of life. Its aims are certainly not more important than are the aims that guide the lives in a religious community or in a tribe that is united by a myth. At any rate, [scientists] have no business restricting the lives, the thoughts, the education of the members of a free society where everyone should have a chance to make up his own mind and to live in accordance with the social beliefs he finds most acceptable. The separation between state and church must therefore be complemented by the separation between state and science.

We need not fear that such a separation will lead to a breakdown of technology. There will always be people who prefer being scientists to being the masters of their fate and who gladly submit to the meanest kind of (intellectual and institutional) slavery provided they are paid well and provided also there are some people around who examine their work and sing their praise. Greece

Against Method (London: Verso, 1975). Reprinted with permission.

developed and progressed because it could rely on the services of unwilling slaves. We shall develop and progress with the help of the numerous *willing* slaves in universities and laboratories who provide us with pills, gas, electricity, atom bombs, frozen dinners and, occasionally, with a few interesting fairy-tales. We shall treat these slaves well, we shall even listen to them, for they have occasionally some interesting stories to tell, but we shall *not* permit them to impose their ideology on our children in the guise of 'progressive' theories of education. We shall not permit them to teach the fancies of science as if they were the only factual statements in existence. This separation of science and state may be our only chance to overcome the hectic barbarism of our scientific-technical age and to achieve a humanity we are capable of, but have never fully realized. Let us, therefore, . . . review the arguments that can be adduced for such a procedure.

The image of 20th-century science in the minds of scientists and laymen is determined by technological miracles such as color television, the moon shots, the infra-red oven, as well as by a somewhat vague but still quite influential rumor, or fairy-tale, concerning the manner in which these miracles are produced.

According to the fairy-tale the success of science is the result of a subtle, but carefully balanced combination of inventiveness and control. Scientists have *ideas*. And they have special *methods* for improving ideas. The theories of science have passed the test of method. They give a better account of the world than ideas which have not passed the test.

The fairy-tale explains why modern society treats science in a special way and why it grants it privileges not enjoyed by other institutions.

Ideally, the modern state is ideologically neutral. Religion, myth, prejudices *do* have an influence, but only in a roundabout way, through the medium of politically influential *parties*. Ideological principles *may* enter the governmental structure, but only via a majority vote, and after a lengthy discussion of possible consequences. In our schools the main religions are taught as *historical phenomena*. They are taught as parts of the truth only if the parents insist on a more direct mode of instruction. It is up to them to decide about the religious education of their children. The financial support of ideologies does not exceed the financial support granted to parties and to private groups. State and ideology, state and church, state and myth, are carefully separated.

State and science, however, work closely together. Immense sums are spent on the improvement of scientific ideas. Bastard subjects such as the philosophy of science, which have not a single discovery to their credit, profit from the boom of the sciences. Even human relations are dealt with in a scientific manner, as is shown by education programs, proposals for prison reform, army training, and so on. Almost all scientific subjects are compulsory subjects in our schools. While the parents of a six-year-old child can decide to have him instructed in the rudiments of Protestantism, or in the rudiments of the Jewish faith, or to omit religious instruction altogether, they do not have a similar freedom in the case of the sciences. Physics, astronomy, history *must* be learned. They cannot be replaced by magic, astrology, or by a study of legends. . . .

The reason for this special treatment of science is, of course, our little fairy-tale: if science has found a method that turns ideologically contaminated ideas into true and useful theories, then it is indeed not mere ideology, but an objective measure of all ideologies. It is then not subjected to the demand for a separation between state and ideology.

But the fairy-tale is false, as we have seen. There is no special method that guarantees success or makes it probable. Scientists do not solve problems because they possess a magic wand—methodology, or a theory of rationality—but because they have studied a problem for a long time, because they know the situation fairly well, because they are not too dumb (though that is rather doubtful nowadays when almost anyone can become a scientist), and because the excesses of one scientific school are almost always balanced by the excesses of some other school. (Besides, scientists only rarely solve their problems, they make lots of mistakes, and many of their solutions are quite useless.) Basically there is hardly any difference between the process that leads to the announcement of a new scientific law and the process preceding passage of a new law in society: one informs either all citizens or those immediately concerned, one collects 'facts' and prejudices, one discusses the matter, and one finally votes. But while a democracy makes some effort to *explain* the process so that everyone can understand it, scientists either *conceal* it, or *bend* it, to make it fit their sectarian interests.

No scientist will admit that voting plays a role in his subject. Facts, logic, and methodology alone decide—this is what the fairy-tale tells us. But how do facts decide? What is their function in the advancement of knowledge? We cannot *derive* our theories from them. We cannot give a *negative* criterion by saying, for example, that good theories are theories which can be refuted, but which are not yet contradicted by any fact. A principle of falsification that removes theories because they do not fit the facts would have to remove the whole of science (or it would have to admit that large parts of science are irrefutable). The hint that a good theory *explains more* than its rivals is not very realistic either. True: new theories often predict new things—but almost always at the expense of things already known. Turning to logic we realize that even the simplest demands *are not* satisfied in scientific practice, and *could not be* satisfied, because of the complexity of the material. The ideas which scientists use to present the known and to advance into the unknown are only rarely in agreement with the strict injunctions of logic or pure mathematics, and the attempt to make them conform would rob science of the elasticity without which progress cannot be achieved. We see: facts alone are not strong enough for making us accept, or reject, scientific theories, the range they leave to thought is *too wide*; logic and methodology eliminate too much, they are *too narrow*. In between these two extremes lies the ever-changing domain of human ideas and wishes. And a more detailed analysis of successful moves in the game of science ('successful' from the point of view of the scientists themselves) shows indeed that there is a wide range of freedom that *demands* a multiplicity of ideas and *permits* the application of democratic procedures (ballot-discussion-vote) but that is actually closed by power politics and propaganda. *This is where the fairy-tale of a special method assumes its decisive function*. It conceals the freedom of decision which creative scientists and the general public have even inside the most rigid and the most advanced parts of science by a recitation of 'objective' criteria, and it thus protects the big-shots (Nobel Prize winners; heads of laboratories, of organizations such as the AMA, of special schools; 'educators'; etc.) from the masses (laymen; experts in non-scientific fields; experts in

other fields of science): only those citizens count who were subjected to the pressures of scientific institutions (they have undergone a long process of education), who succumbed to these pressures (they have passed their examinations), and who are now firmly convinced of the truth of the fairy-tale. This is how scientists have deceived themselves and everyone else about their business, but without any real disadvantage: they have more money, more authority, more sex appeal than they deserve, and the most stupid procedures and the most laughable results in their domain are surrounded with an aura of excellence. It is time to cut them down in size, and to give them a more modest position in society. . . .

Modern science . . . is not at all as difficult and as perfect as scientific propaganda wants us to believe. A subject such as medicine, or physics, or biology appears difficult only because it is taught badly, because the standard instructions are full of redundant material, and because they start too late in life. During the war, when the American Army needed physicians within a very short time, it was suddenly possible to reduce medical instruction to half a year (the corresponding instruction manuals have disappeared long ago, however. Science may be simplified during the war. In peacetime the prestige of science demands greater complication.) And how often does it not happen that the proud and conceited judgment of an expert is put in its proper place by a layman! Numerous inventors built 'impossible' machines. Lawyers show again and again that an expert does not know what he is talking about. Scientists, especially physicians, frequently come to different results so that it is up to the relatives of the sick person (or the inhabitants of a certain area) to decide *by vote* about the procedure to be adopted. How often is science improved, and turned into new directions by non-scientific influences! It is up to us, it is up to the citizens of a free society to either accept the chauvinism of science without contradiction or to overcome it by the counterforce of public action. Public action was used against science by the Communists in China in the fifties, and it was again used, under very different circumstances, by some opponents of evolution in California in the seventies. Let us follow their example and let us free society from the strangling hold of an ideologically petrified science just as our ancestors freed *us* from the strangling hold of the One True Religion!

Bibliography

Ayer, A. J. *Logical Positivism*. Free Press, 1959.

Feyerabend, Paul. *Against Method*. Verso, 1975.

Hanson, N. R. *Patterns of Discovery*. Cambridge University Press, 1958.

Hempel, Carl. *Philosophy of Natural Science*. Prentice-Hall, 1966.

Kitcher, Phillip. *Abusing Science*. MIT Press, 1982.

Kuhn, Thomas. *The Structure of Scientific Revolutions*. University of Chicago Press, 1971.

Lakatos, Imre. *Philosophical Papers*. London: Verso, 1977.

Lakatos, Imre and Alan Musgrave. *Criticism and the Growth of Knowledge*. Cambridge University Press, 1970.

Lipton, Peter. *Inference to the Best Explanation*. London: Routledge, 1993.

Laudan, Larry. *Science and Hypothesis*. Dordrecht: D. Reidel, 1981.

Polkinghorne, John. *Reason and Reality; The Relationship between Science and Theology*. Valley Forge, PA: Trinity Press International, 1991.

Popper, Karl. *Conjectures and Refutations*. Harper & Row, 1968.

Quine, V. W. and J. S. Ulian. *The Web of Belief*. Random House, 1970.

Schick, Theodore, ed. *Readings in the Philosophy of Science*. Mayfield Publishing Co., 2000.

Part X The Ethics of Belief

Our passional nature not only lawfully may, but must, decide an option between propositions, whenever it is a genuine option that cannot by its nature be decided on intellectual grounds; for to say under such circumstances, "Do not decide, but leave the question open," is itself a passional decision,—just like deciding yes or no,—and is attended with the same risk of losing truth.

WILLIAM JAMES
The Will to Believe

It is wrong always, everywhere, and for anyone, to believe anything upon insufficient evidence.

W. K. CLIFFORD
"The Ethics of Belief," *Lectures and Essays*

Do we have a moral duty to believe propositions to the degree that the evidence supports them? What sorts of duties are there in relation to believing? To have a duty to do something implies we *can* do it—but is believing within our power? Or is it forced on us? More generally, what is the relationship between the will and belief? Can we obtain beliefs directly on willing to have them? Can we only obtain beliefs indirectly via the will: willing a belief and then actively participating in a process that will be likely to bring about that belief?

The readings in this part of the book deal with the various sorts of duties we may be said to have regarding belief acquisition. Three types of duties are found in the literature. First, there are *epistemic duties*, duties to believe according to the evidence or duties to inculcate the sort of belief-forming mechanisms that will ensure justified beliefs. This is echoed in John Locke's dictum in our first reading that "the one unerring mark by which a man may know whether he is a lover of truth for truth's sake is the not entertaining any proposition with greater assurance than the proofs it is built upon will warrant."

Second, there is the view that holds that we have *moral duties* to believe according to the available evidence. There is something morally wrong about violating an epistemic duty to believe according to the evidence. This view is put forward by Clifford in the second reading: "It is wrong always, everywhere, and for anyone, to believe anything upon insufficient evidence."

Finally, there are *pragmatic* or *prudential* duties, duties to believe propositions insofar as they lead to the best outcomes. Hume, Mill, James, and H. H. Price hold this view. Price sets forth the thesis this way:

> Even if it were in our power to be wholly rational all of the time, it still would not follow that there is anything morally blameworthy about assenting unreasonably (against the evidence or without regard to the evidence) or that we ought to be chastised for doing so. There is nothing wicked about such assents. It is however true, and important, that unreasonable assent is contrary to our *long term interest*. It is to our long term interest to believe true propositions rather than false ones. And if we assent reasonably (i.e. in accordance with the evidence), it is likely that in the long run the propositions we believe will be more often true than false (*Belief,* p. 238).

The only "ought" regarding belief acquisition is a prudential one. A person is free to seek whatever goals he or she desires: happiness, salvation, convenience, esthetic pleasure, and so forth. It is simply in one's long-term interest generally to seek to have true beliefs.

The question whether we *ought* to believe propositions for such and such reasons raises the prior question of whether we *can* believe propositions simply by willing to do so. The doctrine that we can obtain beliefs directly on willing to believe them is called "volitionalism" or "voluntarism." I generally use the former term. In the readings, Clifford, James, and Meiland all accept volitionalism, whereas I doubt it. But even if we reject volitionalism, this does not entail a rejection of the view that we have epistemic duties or moral duties with regard to doxastic states, for we may be able to

influence or obtain beliefs *indirectly* via certain processes, such as autosuggestion, hypnotism, focusing on aspects of evidence, developing better belief-forming mechanisms, and the like. We have already mentioned our first reading, Locke's critique of enthusiasm, in which he argues that we ought never believe anything against the light of reason.

In the second reading, "The Ethics of Belief," the British philosopher W. K. Clifford (1845–1879) assembles reason's roadblock to pragmatic justifications for acquiring beliefs not fully supported by the evidence. Clifford argues that there is an ethics to believing that makes all believing without sufficient evidence immoral. Pragmatic justifications are not justifications at all but counterfeits of genuine justifications, which must always be based on evidence.

Clifford illustrates his thesis with the example of a shipowner who sends an emigrant ship to sea. He knows that the ship is old and not well built, but he fails to have the ship inspected. Dismissing from his mind all doubts and suspicions of the unseaworthiness of the vessel, he trusts in Providence to care for it. In this way, the shipowner acquires a sincere and comfortable conviction of its safety. After the ship sinks, killing all the passengers, he collects his insurance money without a trace of guilt.

Clifford comments that although the shipowner sincerely believed that all was well with the ship, his sincerity in no way exculpates him because "he had no right to believe on such evidence as was before him." We have an obligation to get ourselves in a position where we will only believe propositions on sufficient evidence. Furthermore, it is not a valid objection to say that what the shipowner had an obligation to do was *act* in a certain way (inspect the ship), not *believe* in a certain way. Although he *does* have an obligation to inspect the ship, the objection overlooks the function of believing as action guiding. "No man holding a strong belief on one side of a question, or even wishing to hold a belief on one side, can investigate it with such fairness and completeness as if he were really in doubt and unbiased; so that the existence of a belief not founded on fair inquiry unfits a man for the performance of this necessary duty." The general conclusion is that it is always wrong for anyone to believe anything on insufficient evidence.

The classic response to Clifford's ethics of belief is William James's "The Will to Believe" (1896), the third reading in this part of the book. James argues that life would be greatly impoverished if we confined our beliefs to such a Scrooge-like epistemology as Clifford proposes. In everyday life, where the evidence for important propositions is often unclear, we must live by faith or cease to act at all. Although we may not make leaps of faith just anywhere, sometimes practical considerations force us to make a decision regarding propositions that do not have their truth value written on their faces.

In "The Sentiment of Rationality" (1879), James defines "faith" as "a belief in something concerning which doubt is still theoretically possible; and as the test of belief is willingness to act, one may say that faith is the readiness to act in a cause the prosperous issue of which is not certified to us in advance." In "The Will to Believe," he speaks of "belief" as a live, momentous hypothesis, on which we cannot avoid a decision, for not to choose is in effect to choose against the hypothesis. There is a good illustration of this notion of faith in "The Sentiment of Rationality." A mountain climber in the Alps finds himself in a position from which he can only escape by means of an enormous leap. If he tries to calculate the evidence,

only believing on sufficient evidence, he will be paralyzed by emotions of fear and mistrust, and hence be lost. Without evidence of being able to perform this feat successfully, the climber would be better off getting himself to believe that he can and will make the leap. "In this case . . . the part of wisdom clearly is to believe what one desires; for the belief is one of the indispensable preliminary conditions of the realization of its object. *There are then cases where faith creates its own verification.*"

James claims that religion may be just such a genuine option for many people, and where it is, the individual has the right to believe the better story rather than the worse. To do so, one must will to believe what the evidence alone is inadequate to support.

In the fourth reading, "What Ought We to Believe?" Jack Meiland argues that pragmatic reasons may override epistemic reasons in belief formation, so it is sometimes permissible and even our moral duty to believe against the evidence. Loyalty to a friend or fear of disastrous psychological consequences may be sufficient reasons for rejecting the available evidence in forming beliefs.

In the final reading, I first argue against volitionalism on two grounds: First, it is psychologically aberrant and conceptually incoherent, so our ability to obtain beliefs directly on willing to have them is at best a rare phenomenon. Second, in opposition to Meiland, I argue that we do have moral duties to believe according to the best evidence in the sense that we can indirectly get ourselves in the position where the best justified belief is likely to obtain.

X.1 Of Enthusiasm

JOHN LOCKE

A biographical sketch of John Locke (1632–1704) appears before Reading III.1.
    Locke held that since God was a god of truth, he would never require that we believe anything against the natural light of reason—though some mysteries (e.g., immortality) are beyond our understanding. Religious people, who have ample grounds for believing in God, must beware lest they allow their imagination and passion to run away with them. Reason and faith are compatible, so every claim to faith must be supported with evidence. That is, we must be lovers of truth, believing propositions according to their supporting evidence. Locke wrote in a letter to Anthony Collins, "To love the truth for truth's sake is the principal part of human perfection in this world, and the seed-plot of all other virtues" (29 October 1703). Lady Masham wrote of Locke, "He was always, in the greatest and in the smallest affairs of human life, as well as in speculative opinions, disposed to follow reason, whosoever suggested it; he being ever a faithful servant, I had almost said a slave, to truth; never abandoning her for anything else, and following her for her own sake purely."[1]
    Locke's use of *enthusiasm* contains the negative connotations that word held for many philosophers and theologians of his day, including Bishop Butler, Jonathan Swift, Henry More, and Bishop Warburton. Leibniz wrote, "Enthusiasm was originally a good term. Just as *sophism* properly indicates an exercise of wisdom, so enthusiasm signifies that there is a divinity in us. But these men having consecrated their passions, fancies, dreams, and even their anger, as something divine, *enthusiasm* began to signify a mental disturbance attributed to the influence of some divinity. . . . Since then, we attribute it to those who believe without foundation that their impulses come from God."[2]

1. He that would seriously set upon the search of truth, ought in the first place to prepare his mind with a love of it. For he that loves it not, will not take much pains to get it, nor be much concerned when he misses it. There is nobody in the commonwealth of learning, who does not profess himself a lover of truth; and there is not a rational creature that would not take it amiss to be thought otherwise of. And yet for all this, one may truly say, that there are very few lovers of truth for truths sake, even amongst those who persuade themselves that they are so. How a man may know whether he be so in earnest, is worth inquiry: And I think there is one unerring mark of it, viz. the not entertaining any proposition with greater assurance than the proofs it is built upon will warrant. Whoever goes beyond this measure of assent, it is plain receives not the truth in the love of it; loves not truth for truth's sake, but for some other bye end. For the evidence that any proposition is true (except such as are self-evident) lying only in the proofs a man has of it, whatsoever degrees of assent he affords it beyond the degrees of that evidence, it is plain that all the surplusage of assurance is owing to some other affection, and not to the love of truth: It being as impossible, that the love of truth should carry my assent above the evidence there is to me that it is true, as that the love of truth should make me assent to any proposition for the sake of that evidence, which it has not, that it is true; which is in effect to love it as a truth, because it is possible or probable that it may not be true. In any truth that gets not possession of our minds by the irresistible light of self-evidence, or by the force of demonstration, the arguments that gain it assent

Reprinted from *An Essay Concerning Human Understanding*, Book IV.19 (1689).

are the vouchers and gage of its probability to us; and we can receive it for no other, than such as they deliver it to our understandings. Whatsoever credit or authority we give to any proposition, more than it receives from the principles and proofs it supports itself upon, is owing to our inclinations that way, and is so far a derogation from the love of truth as such: Which, as it can receive no evidence from our passions or interests, so it should receive no tincture from them.

2. The assuming an authority of dictating to others, and a forwardness to prescribe to their opinions, is a constant concomitant of this bias and corruption of our judgments. For how almost can it be otherwise, but that he should be ready to impose on another's belief, who has already imposed on his own? Who can reasonably expect arguments and conviction from him, in dealing with others, whose understanding is not accustomed to them in his dealing with himself? Who does violence to his own faculties, tyrannizes over his own mind, and usurps the prerogative that belongs to truth alone, which is to command assent by only its own authority, i.e. by and in proportion to that evidence which it carries with it.

3. Upon this occasion I shall take the liberty to consider a third ground of assent [the first two are reason and revelation—Ed.], which with some men has the same authority, and is as confidently relied on as either faith or reason; I mean enthusiasm: Which laying by reason, would set up revelation without it. Whereby in effect it takes away both reason and revelation, and substitutes in the room of it the ungrounded fancies of a man's own brain, and assumes them for a foundation both of opinion and conduct.

4. Reason is natural revelation, whereby the eternal father of light, and fountain of all knowledge, communicates to mankind that portion of truth which he has laid within the reach of their natural faculties: Revelation is natural reason enlarged by a new set of discoveries communicated by God immediately, which reason vouches the truth of, by the testimony and proofs it gives, that they come from God. So that he that takes away reason, to make way for revelation, puts out the light of both, and does much the same, as if he would persuade a man to put out his eyes, the better to receive the remote light of an invisible star by a telescope.

5. Immediate revelation being a much easier way for men to establish their opinions and regulate their conduct, than the tedious and not always successful labor of strict reasoning, it is no wonder that some have been very apt to pretend to revelation, and to persuade themselves that they are under the peculiar guidance of heaven in their actions and opinions, especially in those of them which they cannot account for by the ordinary methods of knowledge and principles of reason. Hence we see that in all ages, men, in whom melancholy has mixed with devotion, or whose conceit of themselves has raised them into an opinion of a greater familiarity with God, and a nearer admittance to his favor than is afforded to others, have often flattered themselves with a persuasion of an immediate intercourse with the Deity, and frequent communications from the Divine Spirit. God, I own, cannot be denied to be able to enlighten the understanding, by a ray darted into the mind immediately from the fountain of light; this they understand he has promised to do, and who then has so good a title to expect it as those who are his peculiar people, chosen by him, and depending on him?

6. Their minds being thus prepared, whatever groundless opinion comes to settle itself strongly upon their fancies, is an illumination from the spirit of God, and presently of divine authority: And whatsoever odd action they find in themselves a strong inclination to do, that impulse is concluded to be a call or direction from heaven, and must be obeyed; it is a commission from above, and they cannot err in executing it.

7. This I take to be properly enthusiasm, which, though founded neither on reason nor divine revelation, but rising from the conceits of a warmed or over-weening brain, works yet, where it once gets footing, more powerfully on the persuasions and actions of men, than either of those two, or both together: Men being most forwardly obedient to the impulses they receive from themselves; and the whole man is sure to act more vigorously, where the whole man is carried by a natural motion. For strong conceit, like a new principle, carries all easily with it, when got above common sense, and freed from all restraint of reason, and check of reflection, it is heightened into a divine authority, in concurrence with our own temper and inclination.

8. Though the odd opinions and extravagant actions enthusiasm has run men into, were enough to warn them against this wrong principle, so apt to misguide them both in their belief and conduct; yet the love of something extraordinary, the ease and glory it is to be inspired, and be above the common and natural ways of knowledge, so flatters many men's laziness, ignorance, and vanity, that when once they are got into this way of immediate revelation, of illumination without search, and of certainty without proof, and without examination, it is a hard matter to get them out of it. Reason is lost upon them, they are above it: They see the light infused into their understandings, and cannot be mistaken; it is clear and visible there, like the light of bright sunshine; shows itself, and needs no other proof but its own evidence: They feel the hand of God moving them within, and the impulses of the spirit, and cannot be mistaken in what they feel. . . .

9. This is the way of talking of these men: They are sure, because they are sure: And their persuasions are right, because they are strong in them. For, when what they say is stripped of the metaphor of seeing and feeling, this is all it amounts to: And yet these similes so impose on them, that they serve them for certainty in themselves, and demonstration to others.

10. But to examine a little soberly this internal light, and this feeling on which they build so much. These men have, they say, clear light, and they see; they have awakened sense, and they feel; this cannot, they are sure, be disputed them. For when a man says he sees or feels, nobody can deny it him, that he does so. But here let me ask: This seeing, is it the perception of the truth of the proposition, or of this, that it is a revelation from God? This feeling, is it a perception of an inclination or fancy to do something, or of the spirit of God moving that inclination? These are two very different perceptions, and must be carefully distinguished, if we would not impose upon ourselves. I may perceive the truth of a proposition, and yet not perceive that it is an immediate revelation from God. I may perceive the truth of a proposition in Euclid, without its being or my perceiving it to be a revelation: Nay, I may perceive I came not by this knowledge in a natural way, and so may conclude it revealed, without perceiving that it is a revelation from God; because there be spirits, which, without being

divinely commissioned, may excite those ideas in me, and lay them in such order before my mind, that I may perceive their connection. So that the knowledge of any proposition coming into my mind, I know not how, is not a perception that it is from God. Much less is a strong persuasion, that it is true, a perception that it is from God, or so much as true. But however it be called light and seeing, I suppose it is at most but belief and assurance: And the proposition taken for a revelation, is not such as they know to be true, but take to be true. For where a proposition is known to be true, revelation is needless: And it is hard to conceive how there can be a revelation to any one of what he knows already. If therefore it be a proposition which they are persuaded, but do not know, to be true, whatever they may call it, it is not seeing, but believing. For these are two ways, whereby truth comes into the mind, wholly distinct, so that one is not the other. What I see I know to be so by the evidence of the thing itself: What I believe I take to be so upon the testimony of another: But this testimony I must know to be given, or else what ground have I of believing? I must see that it is God that reveals this to me, or else I see nothing. The question then here is, how do I know that God is the revealer of this to me; that this impression is made upon my mind by his Holy Spirit, and that therefore I ought to obey it? If I know not this, how great soever the assurance is that I am possessed with, it is groundless; whatever light I pretend to, it is but enthusiasm. For whether the proposition supposed to be revealed, be in itself evidently true, or visibly probable, or by the natural ways of knowledge uncertain, the proposition that must be well grounded, and manifested to be true, is this, that God is the revealer of it, and that what I take to be a revelation is certainly put into my mind by him, and is not an illusion dropped in by some other spirit, or raised by my own fancy. For if I mistake not, these men receive it for true, because they presume God revealed it. Does it not then stand them upon, to examine upon what grounds they presume it to be a revelation from God? or else all their confidence is mere presumption: And this light, they are so dazzled with, is nothing but an *ignis fatuus* that leads them constantly round in this circle; it is a revelation, because they firmly believe it, and they believe it, because it is a revelation.

11. In all that is of divine revelation, there is need of no other proof but that it is an inspiration from God: For he can neither deceive nor be deceived. But how shall it be known that any proposition in our minds is a truth infused by God; a truth that is revealed to us by him, which he declares to us, and therefore we ought to believe? Here it is that enthusiasm fails of the evidence it pretends to. For men thus possessed boast of a light whereby they say they are enlightened, and brought into the knowledge of this or that truth. But if they know it to be a truth, they must know it to be so, either by its own self-evidence to natural reason, or by the rational proofs that make it out to be so. If they see and know it to be a truth, either of these two ways, they in vain suppose it to be a revelation. For they know it to be true the same way, that any other man naturally may know that it is so without the help of revelation. For thus all the truths, of what kind soever, that men uninspired are enlightened with, came into their minds, and are established there. If they say they know it to be true because it is a revelation from God, the reason is good: But then it will be demanded how they know it to be a revelation from God. If they say, by the light it brings with it, which shines bright in their minds, and they cannot resist: I beseech them to consider whether this be any more than what we have taken notice of already, viz. that it is a revelation, because they strongly believe it to be true. For all the light they speak of is but a strong, though ungrounded persuasion of their own minds, that it is a truth. For rational grounds from proofs that it is a truth, they must acknowledge to have none; for then it is not received as a revelation, but upon the ordinary grounds that other truths are received: And if they believe it to be true because it is a revelation, and have no other reason for its being a revelation, but because they are fully persuaded without any other reason that it is true; they believe it to be a revelation, only because they strongly believe it to be a revelation; which is a very unsafe ground to proceed on, either in our tenets or actions. And what readier way can there be to run ourselves into the most extravagant errors and miscarriages, than thus to set up fancy for our supreme and sole guide, and to believe any proposition to be true, any action to be right, only because we believe it to be so? The strength of our persuasions is no evidence at all of their own rectitude: Crooked things may be as stiff and inflexible as straight: And men may be as positive and peremptory in error as in truth. How come else the untractable zealots in different and opposite parties? For if the light, which every one thinks he has in his mind, which in this case is nothing but the strength of his own persuasion, be an evidence that it is from God, contrary opinions have the same title to be inspirations; and God will be not only the father of lights, but of opposite and contradictory lights, leading men contrary ways; and contradictory propositions will be divine truths, if an ungrounded strength of assurance be an evidence, that any proposition is a divine revelation.

12. This cannot be otherwise, whilst firmness of persuasion is made the cause of believing, and confidence of being in the right is made an argument of truth. St. Paul himself believed he did well, and that he had a call to it when he persecuted the Christians, whom he confidently thought in the wrong: But yet it was he, and not they, who were mistaken. Good men are men still, liable to mistakes; and are sometimes warmly engaged in errors, which they take for divine truths, shining in their minds with the clearest light.

13. Light, true light, in the mind is, or can be nothing else but the evidence of the truth of any proposition; and if it be not a self-evident proposition, all the light it has, or can have, is from the clearness and validity of those proofs, upon which it is received. To talk of any other light in the understanding is to put ourselves in the dark, or in the power of the Prince of darkness, and by our own consent to give ourselves up to delusion to believe a lie. For if strength of persuasion be the light, which must guide us; I ask how shall any one distinguish between the delusions of Satan, and the inspirations of the Holy Ghost? He can transform himself into an angel of light. And they who are led by this son of the morning, are as fully satisfied of the illumination, i.e. are as strongly persuaded, that they are enlightened by the spirit of God, as any one who is so: They acquiesce and rejoice in it, are acted by it: And nobody can be more sure, nor more in the right (if their own strong belief may be judge) than they.

14. He therefore that will not give himself up to all the extravagancies of delusion and error, must bring this guide of his light within to the trial. God, when he makes the prophet, does not unmake the man. He leaves all his faculties in the natural state, to enable him to judge of his inspirations, whether they be of divine original or no. When he illuminates the mind with supernatural light, he does not extinguish that which is natural. If he would have us assent to the truth of any proposition, he either evidences that truth by the usual methods of natural reason, or else makes it known to be a truth which he would have us assent to, by his authority; and convinces us that it is from him, by some marks which reason cannot be mistaken in. Reason must be our last judge and guide in every thing. I do not mean that we must consult reason, and examine whether a proposition revealed from God can be made out by natural principles, and if it cannot, that then we may reject it: But consult it we must, and by it examine, whether it be a revelation from God or no. And if reason finds it to be revealed from God, reason then declares for it, as much as for any other truth, and makes it one of her dictates. Every conceit that thoroughly warms our fancies must pass for an inspiration, if there be nothing but the strength of our persuasions, whereby to judge of our persuasions: If reason must not examine their truth by something extrinsic to the persuasions themselves, inspirations and delusions, truth and falsehood, will have the same measure, and will not be possible to be distinguished.

15. Thus we see the holy men of old, who had revelations from God, had something else besides that internal light of assurance in their own minds, to testify to them that it was from God. They were not left to their own persuasions alone, that those persuasions were from God; but had outward signs to convince them of the author of those revelations. And when they were to convince others, they had a power given them to justify the truth of their commission from heaven, and by visible signs to assert the divine authority of a message they were sent with. Moses saw the bush burn without being consumed, and heard a voice out of it. This was something besides finding an impulse upon his mind to go to Pharaoh, that he might bring his brethren out of Egypt: And yet he thought not this enough to authorize him to go with that message, till God, by another miracle of his rod turned into a serpent, had assured him of a power to testify his mission, by the same miracle repeated before them, whom he was sent to. Gideon was sent by an angel to deliver Israel from the Midianites, and yet he desired a sign to convince him that this commission was from God. These, and several the like instances to be found among the prophets of old, are enough to show that they thought not an inward seeing or persuasion of their own minds, without any other proof, a sufficient evidence that it was from God; though the scripture does not every where mention their demanding or having such proofs.

16. In what I have said I am far from denying that God can, or doth sometimes enlighten men's minds in the apprehending of certain truths, or excite them to good actions by the immediate influence and assistance of the holy spirit, without any extraordinary signs accompanying it. But in such cases too we have reason and scripture, unerring rules to know whether it be from God or no. Where the truth embraced is consonant to the revelation in the written word of God, or the action conformable to the dictates of right reason or holy writ, we may be assured that we run no risk in entertaining it as such; because though perhaps it be not an immediate revelation from God, extraordinarily operating on our minds, yet we are sure it is warranted by that revelation which he has given us of truth. . . .

Notes

[1] Quoted in A. S. Pringle-Pattison's edition of *An Essay Concerning Human Understanding* by John Locke (Oxford University Press, 1924), p. 359.

[2] Op. cit., p. 360.

X.2 The Ethics of Belief

W. K. CLIFFORD

In this essay, the British philosopher W. K. Clifford (1845–1879) sets forth a classic version of evidentialism, arguing that there is an ethics to believing that makes all believing without sufficient evidence immoral. Pragmatic justifications are not justifications at all but counterfeits of genuine justifications, which must always be based on evidence. It is never morally permissible to violate our epistemic duties. Clifford opens his essay with the illustration of a shipowner who violates his epistemic duty and thus causes a disaster.

A shipowner was about to send to sea an emigrant ship. He knew that she was old, and not over-well built at the first; that she had seen many seas and climes, and often had needed repairs. Doubts had been suggested to him that possibly she was not seaworthy. These doubts preyed upon his mind and made him unhappy; he thought that perhaps he ought to have her thoroughly overhauled and refitted, even though this should put him to great expense. Before the ship sailed, however, he succeeded in overcoming these melancholy reflections. He said to himself that she had gone safely through so many voyages and weathered so many storms that it was idle to suppose she would not come safely home from this trip also. He would put his trust in Providence, which could hardly fail to protect all these unhappy families that were leaving their fatherland to seek for better times elsewhere. He would dismiss from his mind all ungenerous suspicions about the honesty of builders and contractors. In such ways he acquired a sincere and comfortable conviction that his vessel was thoroughly safe and seaworthy; he watched her departure with a light heart, and benevolent wishes for the success of the exiles in their strange new home that was to be; and he got his insurance money when she went down in midocean and told no tales.

What shall we say of him? Surely this, that he was verily guilty of the death of those men. It is admitted that he did sincerely believe in the soundness of his ship; but the sincerity of his conviction can in no wise help him, because *he had no right to believe on such evidence as was before him.*

Reprinted from W. K. Clifford's *Lectures and Essays,* 1879.

He had acquired his belief not by honestly earning it in patient investigation, but by stifling his doubts. And although in the end he may have felt so sure about it that he could not think otherwise, yet inasmuch as he had knowingly and willingly worked himself into that frame of mind, he must be held responsible for it.

Let us alter the case a little, and suppose that the ship was not unsound after all; that she made her voyage safely, and many others after it. Will that diminish the guilt of her owner? Not one jot. When an action is once done, it is right or wrong forever; no accidental failure of its good or evil fruits can possibly alter that. The man would not have been innocent, he would only have been not found out. The question of right or wrong has to do with the origin of his belief, not the matter of it; not what it was, but how he got it; not whether it turned out to be true or false, but whether he had a right to believe on such evidence as was before him.

There was once an island in which some of the inhabitants professed a religion teaching neither the doctrine of original sin nor that of eternal punishment. A suspicion got abroad that the professors of this religion had made use of unfair means to get their doctrines taught to children. They were accused of wresting the laws of their country in such a way as to remove children from the care of their natural and legal guardians; and even of stealing them away and keeping them concealed from their friends and relations. A certain number of men formed themselves into a society for the purpose of agitating the public about this matter. They published grave accusations against individual citizens of the highest position and character, and did all in their power to injure those citizens in the exercise of their professions. So great was the noise they made, that a Commission was appointed to investigate the facts; but after the Commission had carefully inquired into all the evidence that could be got, it appeared that the accused were innocent. Not only had they been accused on insufficient evidence, but the evidence of their innocence was such as the agitators might easily have obtained, if they had attempted a fair inquiry. After these disclosures the inhabitants of that country looked upon the members of the agitating society, not only as persons whose judgment was to be distrusted, but also as no longer to be counted honorable men. For although they had sincerely and conscientiously believed in the charges they had made, *yet they had no right to believe on such evidence as was before them.* Their sincere convictions, instead of being honestly earned by patient inquiring, were stolen by listening to the voice of prejudice and passion.

Let us vary this case also, and suppose, other things remaining as before, that a still more accurate investigation proved the accused to have been really guilty. Would this make any difference in the guilt of the accusers? Clearly not; the question is not whether their belief was true or false, but whether they entertained it on wrong grounds. They would no doubt say, "Now you see that we were right after all; next time perhaps you will believe us." And they might be believed, but they would not thereby become honorable men. They would not be innocent, they would only be not found out. Every one of them, if he chose to examine himself *in foro conscientiae,* would know that he had acquired and nourished a belief, when he had no right to believe on such evidence as was before him; and therein he would know that he had done a wrong thing.

It may be said, however, that in both of these supposed cases it is not the belief which is judged to be wrong, but the action following upon it. The shipowner might say, "I am perfectly certain that my ship is sound, but still I feel it my duty to have her examined, before trusting the lives of so many people to her." And it might be said to the agitator, "However convinced you were of the justice of your cause and the truth of your convictions, you ought not to have made a public attack upon any man's character until you had examined the evidence on both sides with the utmost patience and care."

In the first place, let us admit that, so far as it goes, this view of the case is right and necessary; right, because even when a man's belief is so fixed that he cannot think otherwise, he still has a choice in regard to the action suggested by it, and so cannot escape the duty of investigating on the ground of the strength of his convictions; and necessary, because those who are not yet capable of controlling their feelings and thoughts must have a plain rule dealing with overt acts.

But this being premised as necessary, it becomes clear that it is not sufficient, and that our previous judgment is required to supplement it. For it is not possible so to sever the belief from the action it suggests as to condemn the one without condemning the other. No man holding a strong belief on one side of a question, or even wishing to hold a belief on one side, can investigate it with such fairness and completeness as if he were really in doubt and unbiased; so that the existence of a belief not founded on fair inquiry unfits a man for the performance of this necessary duty.

Nor is that truly a belief at all which has not some influence upon the actions of him who holds it. He who truly believes that which prompts him to an action has looked upon the action to lust after it, he has committed it already in his heart. If a belief is not realized immediately in open deeds, it is stored up for the guidance of the future. It goes to make a part of that aggregate of beliefs which is the link between sensation and action at every moment of all our lives, and which is so organized and compacted together that no part of it can be isolated from the rest, but every new addition modifies the structure of the whole. No real belief, however trifling and fragmentary it may seem, is ever truly insignificant; it prepares us to receive more of its like, confirms those which resembled it before, and weakens others; and so gradually it lays a stealthy train in our inmost thoughts, which may some day explode into overt action, and leave its stamp upon our character forever.

And no one man's belief is in any case a private matter which concerns himself alone. Our lives are guided by that general conception of the course of things which has been created by society for social purposes. Our words, our phrases, our forms and processes and modes of thought, are common property, fashioned and perfected from age to age; an heirloom which every succeeding generation inherits as a precious deposit and a sacred trust to be handed on to the next one, not unchanged but enlarged and purified, with some clear marks of its proper handiwork. Into this, for good or ill, is woven every belief of every man who has speech of his fellows. An awful privilege, and an awful responsibility, that we should help to create the world in which posterity will live.

In the two supposed cases which have been considered, it has been judged wrong to believe on insufficient evidence, or to nourish belief by suppressing doubts and avoiding investigation. The reason of this judgment is not far to seek: it is that in both these cases the belief held by one man was of great importance to other men. But for as much as no belief held by one man, however seemingly trivial the belief, and however obscure the believer, is ever actually insignificant or without its effect on the fate of mankind, we have no choice but to extend our judgment to all cases of belief whatever. Belief, that sacred faculty which prompts the decisions of our will, and knits into harmonious working all the compacted energies of our being, is ours not for ourselves, but for humanity. It is rightly used on truths which have been established by long experience and waiting toil, and which have stood in the fierce light of free and fearless questioning. Then it helps to bind men together, and to strengthen and direct their common action. It is desecrated when given to unproved and unquestioned statements, for the solace and private pleasure of the believer; to add a tinsel splendor to the plain straight road of our life and display a bright mirage beyond it; or even to drown the common sorrows of our kind by a self-deception which allows them not only to cast down, but also to degrade us. Whoso would deserve well of his fellows in this matter will guard the purity of his belief with a very fanaticism of jealous care, lest at any time it should rest on an unworthy object, and catch a stain which can never be wiped away.

It is not only the leader of men, statesman, philosopher, or poet, that owes this bounden duty to mankind. Every rustic who delivers in the village alehouse his slow, infrequent sentences, may help to kill or keep alive the fatal superstitions which clog his race. Every hard-worked wife of an artisan may transmit to her children beliefs which shall knit society together, or rend it in pieces. No simplicity of mind, no obscurity of station, can escape the universal duty of questioning all that we believe.

It is true that this duty is a hard one, and the doubt which comes out of it is often a very bitter thing. It leaves us bare and powerless where we thought that we were safe and strong. To know all about anything is to know how to deal with it under all circumstances. We feel much happier and more secure when we think we know precisely what to do, no matter what happens, than when we have lost our way and do not know where to turn. And if we have supposed ourselves to know all about anything, and to be capable of doing what is fit in regard to it, we naturally do not like to find that we are really ignorant and powerless, that we have to begin again at the beginning, and try to learn what the thing is and how it is to be dealt with—if indeed anything can be learned about it. It is the sense of power attached to a sense of knowledge that makes men desirous of believing, and afraid of doubting.

This sense of power is the highest and best of pleasures when the belief on which it is founded is a true belief, and has been fairly earned by investigation. For then we may justly feel that it is common property, and holds good for others as well as for ourselves. Then we may be glad, not that I have learned secrets by which I am safer and stronger, but that *we men* have got mastery over more of the world; and we shall be strong, not for ourselves, but in the name of Man and in his strength. But if the belief has been accepted on insufficient evidence, the pleasure is a stolen one. Not only does it deceive ourselves by giving us a sense of power which we do not really possess, but it is sinful, because it is stolen in defiance of our duty to mankind. That duty is to guard ourselves from such beliefs as from a pestilence, which may shortly master our own body and then spread to the rest of the town. What would be thought of one who, for the sake of a sweet fruit, should deliberately run the risk of bringing a plague upon his family and his neighbors?

And, as in other such cases, it is not the risk only which has to be considered; for a bad action is always bad at the time when it is done, no matter what happens afterwards. Every time we let ourselves believe for unworthy reasons, we weaken our powers of self-control, of doubting, of judicially and fairly weighing evidence. We all suffer severely enough from the maintenance and support of false beliefs and the fatally wrong actions which they lead to, and the evil born when one such belief is entertained is great and wide. But a greater and wider evil arises when the credulous character is maintained and supported, when a habit of believing for unworthy reasons is fostered and made permanent. If I steal money from any person, there may be no harm done by the mere transfer of possession; he may not feel the loss, or it may prevent him from using the money badly. But I cannot help doing this great wrong towards Man, that I make myself dishonest. What hurts society is not that it should lose its property, but that it should become a den of thieves; for then it must cease to be society. This is why we ought not to do evil that good may come; for at any rate this great evil has come, that we have done evil and are made wicked thereby. In like manner, if I let myself believe anything on insufficient evidence, there may be no great harm done by the mere belief; it may be true after all, or I may never have occasion to exhibit it in outward acts. But I cannot help doing this great wrong toward Man, that I make myself credulous. The danger to society is not merely that it should believe wrong things, though that is great enough; but that it should become credulous, and lose the habit of testing things and inquiring into them; for then it must sink back into savagery.

The harm which is done by credulity in a man is not confined to the fostering of a credulous character in others, and consequent support of false beliefs. Habitual want of care about what I believe leads to habitual want of care in others about the truth of what is told to me. Men speak the truth to one another when each reveres the truth in his own mind and in the other's mind; but how shall my friend revere the truth in my mind when I myself am careless about it, when I believe things because I want to believe them, and because they are comforting and pleasant? Will he not learn to cry, "Peace," to me, when there is no peace? By such a course I shall surround myself with a thick atmosphere of falsehood and fraud, and in that I must live. It may matter little to me, in my cloud-castle of sweet illusions and darling lies; but it matters much to Man that I have made my neighbors ready to deceive. The credulous man is father to the liar and the cheat; he lives in the bosom of this his family, and it is no marvel if he should become even as they are. So closely are our duties knit together, that whoso shall keep the whole law, and yet offend in one point, he is guilty of all.

To sum up: *it is wrong always, everywhere, and for anyone, to believe anything upon insufficient evidence.* If a man, holding a belief which he was taught in childhood or persuaded of afterwards, keeps down and pushes away any doubts which arise about it in his mind, purposely avoids the reading of books and the company of men that call in question or discuss it, and regards as impious those questions which cannot easily be asked without disturbing it—the life of that man is one long sin against mankind.

X.3 The Will to Believe

WILLIAM JAMES

William James (1842–1910), an American philosopher and psychologist, was born in New York City and educated at Harvard. He was the brother of Henry James, the novelist. William James struggled through much of his life with ill health. He was assailed by doubts over freedom of the will and the existence of God, and he developed the philosophy of pragmatism in part as a response to these difficulties. His principal works are *The Principles of Psychology* (1890), *The Varieties of Religious Experience* (1902), and *The Will to Believe* (1897), from which this selection is taken.

This essay has been regarded as the classic response to Clifford's ethics of belief (see the previous reading). James argues that life would be greatly impoverished if we confined our beliefs to such a Scrooge-like epistemology as Clifford proposes. In everyday life, where the evidence for important propositions is often unclear, we must live by faith or cease to act at all. Although we may not make leaps of faith just anywhere, sometimes practical considerations force us to make a decision regarding propositions that do not have their truth value written on their faces. "Belief" is defined as a live, momentous optional hypothesis, on which we cannot avoid a decision, for not to choose is in effect to choose against the hypothesis. James claims that religion may be such an optional hypothesis for many people, and where it is, the individual has the right to believe the better story rather than the worse. To do so, he or she must will to believe what the evidence alone is inadequate to support.

I

Let us give the name of hypothesis to anything that may be proposed to our belief; and just as the electricians speak of live and dead wires, let us speak of any hypothesis as either *live* or dead. A live hypothesis is one which appeals as a real possibility to him to whom it is proposed. If I ask you to believe in the Mahdi, the notion makes no electric connection with your nature—it refuses to scintillate with any credibility at all. As an hypothesis it is completely dead. To an Arab, however (even if he be not one of the Mahdi's followers), the hypothesis is among the mind's possibilities: It is alive. This shows that deadness and liveness in an hypothesis are not intrinsic properties, but relations to the individual thinker. They are measured by his willingness to act.

The maximum of liveness in an hypothesis means willingness to act irrevocably. Practically, that means belief; but there is some believing tendency wherever there is willingness to act at all.

Next, let us call the decision between two hypotheses an *option*. Options may be of several kinds. They may be first, *living* or *dead;* secondly, *forced* or *avoidable;* thirdly, *momentous* or *trivial;* and for our purposes we may call an option a *gen-*

Reprinted from William James, *The Will to Believe* (New York: Longmans, Green & Co., 1897).

uine option when it is of a forced, living, and momentous kind.

1. A living option is one in which both hypotheses are live ones. If I say to you: "Be a theosophist or be a Mohammedan," it is probably a dead option, because for you neither hypothesis is likely to be alive. But if I say: "Be an agnostic or be a Christian," it is otherwise: trained as you are, each hypothesis makes some appeal, however small, to your belief.

2. Next, if I say to you: "Choose between going out with your umbrella or without it," I do not offer you a genuine option, for it is not forced. You can easily avoid it by not going out at all. Similarly, if I say, "Either love me or hate me," "Either call my theory true or call it false," your option is avoidable. You may remain indifferent to me, neither loving nor hating, and you may decline to offer any judgment as to my theory. But if I say, "Either accept this truth or go without it," I put on you a forced option, for there is no standing place outside of the alternative. Every dilemma based on a complete logical disjunction, with no possibility of not choosing, is an option of this forced kind.

3. Finally, if I were Dr. Nansen and proposed to you to join my North Pole expedition, your option would be momentous; for this would probably be your singular opportunity, and your choice now would either exclude you from the North Pole sort of immortality altogether or put at least the chance of it into your hands. He who refuses to embrace a unique opportunity loses the prize as surely as if he tried and failed. *Per contra,* the option is trivial when the opportunity is not unique, when the stake is insignificant, or when the decision is reversible if it later prove unwise. Such trivial options abound in the scientific life. A chemist finds an hypothesis live enough to spend a year in its verification: he believes in it to that extent. But if his experiments prove inconclusive either way, he is quit for his loss of time, no vital harm being done.

It will facilitate our discussion if we keep all these distinctions well in mind.

II

The next matter to consider is the actual psychology of human opinion. When we look at certain facts, it seems as if our passional and volitional nature lay at the root of all our convictions. When we look at others, it seems as if they could do nothing when the intellect had once said its say. Let us take the latter facts up first.

Does it not seem preposterous on the very face of it to talk of our opinions being modifiable at will? Can our will either help or hinder our intellect in its perceptions of truth? Can we, by just willing it, believe that Abraham Lincoln's existence is a myth, and that the portraits of him in *McClure's Magazine* are all of some one else? Can we, by any effort of our will, or by any strength of wish that it were true, believe ourselves well and about when we are roaring with rheumatism in bed, or feel certain that the sum of the two one-dollar bills in our pocket must be a hundred dollars? We can say any of these things, but we are absolutely impotent to believe them; and of just such things is the whole fabric of the truths that we do believe is made up—matters of fact, immediate or remote, as Hume said, and relations between ideas, which are either there or not there for us if we see them so, and which if not there cannot be put there by any action of our own.

In Pascal's *Thoughts* there is a celebrated passage known in literature as Pascal's wager. In it he tries to force us into Christianity by reasoning as if our concern with truth resembled our concern with the stakes in a game of chance. Translated

freely his words are these: You must either believe or not believe that God is—which will you do? Your human reason cannot say. A game is going on between you and the nature of things which at the day of judgment will bring out either heads or tails. Weigh what your gains and your losses would be if you should stake all you have on heads, or God's existence: if you win in such case, you gain eternal beatitude; if you lose, you lose nothing at all. If there were an infinity of chances, and only one for God in this wager, still you ought to stake your all on God; for though you surely risk a finite loss by this procedure, any finite loss is reasonable, even a certain one is reasonable, if there is but the possibility of infinite gain. Go, then, and take holy water, and have masses said; belief will come and stupefy your scruples. . . . Why should you not? At bottom, what have you to lose?

You probably feel that when religious faith expresses itself thus, in the language of the gaming-table, it is put to its last trumps. Surely Pascal's own personal belief in masses and holy water had far other springs; and this celebrated page of his is but an argument for others, a last desperate snatch at a weapon against the hardness of the unbelieving heart. We feel that a faith in masses and holy water adopted wilfully after such a mechanical calculation would lack the inner soul of faith's reality; and if we were ourselves in the place of the Deity, we should probably take particular pleasure in cutting off believers of this pattern from their infinite reward. It is evident that unless there be some pre-existing tendency to believe in masses and holy water, the option offered to the will by Pascal is not a living option. Certainly no Turk ever took to masses and holy water on its account; and even to us Protestants these means of salvation seem such foregone impossibilities that Pascal's logic, invoked for them specifically, leaves us unmoved. As well might the Mahdi write to us, saying, "I am the Expected One whom God has created in his effulgence. You shall be infinitely happy if you confess me; otherwise you shall be cut off from the light of the sun. Weigh, then, your infinite gain if I am genuine against your finite sacrifice if I am not!" His logic would be that of Pascal; but he would vainly use it on us, for the hypothesis he offers us is dead. No tendency to act on it exists in us to any degree.

The talk of believing by our volition seems, then, from one point of view, simply silly. From

X.3 The Will to Believe 521

another point of view it is worse than silly, it is vile. When one turns to the magnificent edifice of the physical sciences, and sees how it was reared; what thousands of disinterested moral lives of men lie buried in its mere foundations; what patience and postponement, what choking down of preference, what submission to the icy laws of outer fact are wrought into its very stones and mortar; how absolutely impersonal it stands in its vast augustness—then how besotted and contemptible seems every little sentimentalist who comes blowing his voluntary smoke-wreaths, and pretending to decide things from out of his private dream! Can we wonder if those bred in the rugged and manly school of science should feel like spewing such subjectivism out of their mouths? The whole system of loyalties which grow up in the schools of science go dead against its toleration; so that it is only natural that those who have caught the scientific fever should pass over to the opposite extreme, and write sometimes as if the incorruptibly truthful intellect ought positively to prefer bitterness and unacceptableness to the heart in its cup.

> It fortifies my soul to know
> That though I perish, Truth is so

sings Clough, while Huxley exclaims: "My only consolation lies in the reflection that, however bad our posterity may become, so far as they hold by the plain rule of not pretending to believe what they have no reason to believe, because it may be to their advantage so to pretend [the word 'pretend' is surely here redundant], they will not have reached the lowest depth of immorality." And that delicious *enfant terrible* Clifford writes: "Belief is desecrated when given to unproved and unquestioned statements for the solace and private pleasure of the believer. . . . Whoso would deserve well of his fellows in this matter will guard the purity of his belief with a very fanaticism of jealous care, lest at any time it should rest on an unworthy object, and catch a stain which can never be wiped away. . . . If [a] belief has been accepted on insufficient evidence [even though the belief be true, as Clifford on the same page explains] the pleasure is a stolen one. . . . It is sinful because it is stolen in defiance of our duty to mankind. That duty is to guard ourselves from such beliefs as from a pestilence which may shortly master our own body and then spread to the rest of the town. . . . It is wrong always, everywhere, and for every one, to believe anything upon insufficient evidence."

III

All this strikes one as healthy, even when expressed, as by Clifford, with somewhat too much of robustious pathos in the voice. Free will and simple wishing do seem, in the matter of our credences, to be only fifth wheels to the coach. Yet if any one should thereupon assume that intellectual insight is what remains after wish and will and sentimental preference have taken wing, or that pure reason is what then settles our opinions, he would fly quite as directly in the teeth of facts.

It is only our already dead hypotheses that our willing nature is unable to bring to life again. But what has made them dead for us is for the most part a previous action of our willing nature of an antagonistic kind. When I say "willing nature," I do not mean only such deliberate volitions as may have set up habits of belief that we cannot now escape from—I mean all such factors of belief as fear and hope, prejudice and passion, imitation and partisanship, the circumpressure of our caste and set. As a matter of fact, we find ourselves believing, we hardly know how or why. Mr. Balfour gives the name of "authority" to all those influences, born of the intellectual climate, that make hypotheses possible or impossible for us, alive or dead. Here in this room, we all of us believe in molecules and the conservation of energy, in democracy and necessary progress, in Protestant Christianity and the duty of fighting for "the doctrine of the immortal Monroe," all for no reasons worthy of the name. We see into these matters with no more inner clearness, and probably with much less, than any disbeliever in them might possess. His unconventionality would probably have some grounds to show for its conclusions; but for us, not insight, but the *prestige* of the opinions, is what makes the spark shoot from them and light up our sleeping magazines of faith. Our reason is quite satisfied, in nine hundred and ninety-nine cases out of every thousand of us, if it can find a few arguments that will do to recite in case our credulity is criticized by some one else. Our faith is faith in some one else's faith, and in the greatest matters this is the most the case. . . .

Evidently, then our non-intellectual nature does influence our convictions. There are passional tendencies and volitions which run before and others which come after belief, and it is only the latter that are too late for the fair; and they are not too late when the previous passional work has been already in their own direction. Pascal's argument, instead of being powerless, then seems a regular clincher, and is the last stroke needed to make our faith in masses and holy water complete. The state of things is evidently far from simple; and pure insight and logic, whatever they might do ideally, are not the only things that really do produce our creeds.

IV

Our next duty, having recognized this mixedup state of affairs, is to ask whether it be simply reprehensible and pathological, or whether, on the contrary, we must treat it as a normal element in making up our minds. The thesis I defend is, briefly stated, this: *Our passional nature not only lawfully may, but must, decide an option between propositions, whenever it is a genuine option that cannot by its nature be decided on intellectual grounds; for to say, under such circumstances, "Do not decide, but leave the question open," is itself a passional decision—just like deciding yes or no—and is attended with the same risk of losing the truth. . . .*

VII

One more point, small but important, and our preliminaries are done. There are two ways of looking at our duty in the matter of opinion—ways entirely different, and yet ways about whose difference the theory of knowledge seems hitherto to have shown very little concern. *We must know the truth;* and *we must avoid error*—these are our first and great commandments as would-be knowers; but they are not two ways of stating an identical commandment, they are two separable laws. Although it may indeed happen that when we believe the truth A, we escape as an incidental consequence from believing the falsehood B, it hardly ever happens that by merely disbelieving B we necessarily believe A. We may in escaping B fall into believing other falsehoods, C or D, just as bad as B; or we may escape B by not believing anything at all, not even A.

Believe truth! Shun error!—these, we see, are two materially different laws; and by choosing between them we may end by coloring differently our whole intellectual life. We may regard the chase for truth as paramount, and the avoidance of error as secondary; or we may, on the other hand, treat the avoidance of error as more imperative, and let truth take its chance. Clifford, in the instructive passage which I have quoted, exhorts us to the latter course. Believe nothing, he tells us, keep you mind in suspense forever, rather than by closing it on insufficient evidence incur the awful risk of believing lies. You, on the other hand, may think that the risk of being in error is a very small matter when compared with the blessings of real knowledge, and be ready to be duped many times in your investigation rather than postpone indefinitely the chance of guessing true. I myself find it impossible to go with Clifford. We must remember that these feelings of our duty about either truth or error are in any case only expressions of our passional life. Biologically considered, our minds are as ready to grind out falsehood as veracity, and he who says, "Better go without belief forever than believe a lie!" merely shows his own preponderant private horror of becoming a dupe. He may be critical of many of his desires and fears, but this fear he slavishly obeys. He cannot imagine any one questioning its binding force. For my own part, I have also a horror of being duped; but I can believe that worse things than being duped may happen to a man in this world: so Clifford's exhortation has to my ears a thoroughly fantastic sound. It is like a general informing his soldiers that it is better to keep out of battle forever than to risk a single wound. Not so are victories either over enemies or over nature gained. Our errors are surely not such awfully solemn things. In a world where we are so certain to incur them in spite of all our caution, a certain lightness of heart seems healthier than this excessive nervousness on their behalf. At any rate, it seems the fittest thing for the empiricist philosopher.

VIII

And now, after all this introduction, let us go straight at our question. I have said, and now repeat it, that not only as a matter of fact do we find our passional nature influencing us in our opinions, but that there are some options between opinions in which this influence must be regarded both as an inevitable and as a lawful determinant of our choice.

I fear here that some of you my hearers will begin to scent danger, and lend an inhospitable ear. Two first steps of passion you have indeed had to admit as necessary—we must think so as to avoid dupery, and we must think so as to gain truth; but the surest path to those ideal consummations, you will probably consider, is from now onwards to take no further passional step.

Well, of course, I agree as far as the facts will allow. Wherever the option between losing truth and gaining it is not momentous, we can throw the chance of *gaining truth* away, and at any rate save ourselves from any chance of *believing falsehood,* by not making up our minds at all till objective evidence has come. In scientific questions, this is almost always the case; and even in human affairs in general, the need of acting is seldom so urgent that a false belief to act on is better than no belief at all. Law courts, indeed, have to decide on the best evidence attainable for the moment, because a judge's duty is to make law as well as to ascertain it, and (as a learned judge once said to me) few cases are worth spending much time over: the great thing is to have them decided on *any* acceptable principle, and got out of the way. But in our dealings with objective nature we obviously are recorders, not makers, of the truth; and decisions for the mere sake of deciding promptly and getting on to the next business would be wholly out of place. Throughout the breadth of physical nature facts are what they are quite independently of us, and seldom is there any such hurry about them that the risks of being duped by believing a premature theory need be faced. The questions here are always trivial options, the hypotheses are hardly living (at any rate not living for us spectators), the choice between believing truth or falsehood is seldom forced. The attitude of sceptical balance is therefore the absolutely wise one if we would escape mistakes. What difference, indeed, does it make to most of us whether we have or have not a theory of the Röntgen rays, whether we believe or not in mind-stuff, or have a conviction about the causality of conscious states? It makes no difference. Such options are not forced on us. On every account it is better not to make them, but still keep weighing reasons *pro et contra* with an indifferent hand.

I speak, of course, here of the purely judging mind. For purposes of discovery such indifference is to be less highly recommended, and science would be far less advanced than she is if the passionate desires of individuals to get their own faiths confirmed had been kept out of the game. See for example the sagacity which Spencer and Weismann now display. On the other hand, if you want an absolute duffer in an investigation, you must, after all, take the man who has no interest whatever in its results: he is the warranted incapable, the positive fool. The most useful investigator, because the most sensitive observer, is always he whose eager interest in one side of the question is balanced by an equally keen nervousness lest he become deceived. Science has organized this nervousness into a regular *technique,* her so-called method of verification; and she has fallen so deeply in love with the method that one may even say she has ceased to care for truth by itself at all. It is only truth as technically verified that interests her. The truth of truths might come in merely affirmative form, and she would decline to touch it. Such truth as that, she might repeat with Clifford, would be stolen in defiance of her duty to mankind. Human passions, however, are stronger than technical rules. "*Le cœur a ses raisons,*" as Pascal says, "*que la raison ne connait pas,*" and however indifferent to all but the bare rules of the game the umpire, the abstract intellect, may be, the concrete players who furnish him the materials to judge of are usually, each one of them, in love with some pet "live hypothesis" of his own. Let us agree, however, that wherever there is no forced option, the dispassionately judicial intellect with no pet hypothesis, saving us, as it does, from dupery at any rate, ought to be our ideal.

The question next arises: Are there not somewhere forced options in our speculative questions, and can we (as men who may be interested at least as much in positively gaining truth as in merely escaping dupery) always wait with impunity till the coercive evidence shall have arrived? It seems *a priori* improbable that the truth should be so nicely adjusted to our needs and powers as that. In the great boarding-house of nature, the cakes and the butter and the syrup seldom come out so even and leave the plates so clean. Indeed, we should view them with scientific suspicion if they did.

IX

Moral questions immediately present themselves as questions whose solution cannot wait for sensible proof. A moral question is a question not of what sensibly exists, but of what is good, or would be good if it did exist. Science can tell us what exists; but to compare the *worths,* both of what exists and of what does not exist, we must consult not science, but what Pascal calls our heart. . . .

Turn now from these wide questions of good to a certain class of questions of fact, questions concerning personal relations, states of mind between one man and another. *Do you like me or not?*—for example. Whether you do or not depends, in countless instances, on whether I meet you halfway, am willing to assume that you must like me, and show you trust and expectation. The previous faith on my part in your liking's existence is in such cases what makes your liking come. But if I stand aloof, and refuse to budge an inch until I have objective evidence, until you shall have done something apt, as the absolutists say, *ad extorquendum assensum meum,* ten to one your liking never comes. How many women's hearts are vanquished by the mere sanguine insistence of some man that they *must* love him! He will not consent to the hypothesis that they cannot. The desire for a certain kind of truth here brings about that special truth's existence; and so it is in innumerable cases of other sorts. . . . *And where faith in a fact can help create the fact,* that would be an insane logic which should say that faith running ahead of scientific evidence is the "lowest kind of immorality" into which a thinking being can fall. Yet such is the logic by which our scientific absolutists pretend to regulate our lives!

X

In truths dependent on our personal action, then, faith based on desire is certainly a lawful and possibly an indispensable thing.

But now, it will be said, these are all childish human cases, and have nothing to do with great cosmical matters, like the question of religious faith. Let us then pass on to that. Religions differ so much in their accidents that in discussing the religious question we must make it very generic

and broad. What then do we now mean by the religious hypothesis? Science says things are; morality says some things are better than other things; and religion says essentially two things.

First, she says that the best things are the more eternal things, the overlapping things, the things in the universe that throw the last stone, so to speak, and say the final word. "Perfection is eternal"—this phrase of Charles Secrétan seems a good way of putting this first affirmation of religion, an affirmation which obviously cannot yet be verified scientifically at all.

The second affirmation of religion is that we are better off even now if we believe her first affirmation to be true.

Now, let us consider what the logical elements of this situation are *in case the religious hypothesis in both its branches be really true.* (Of course, we must admit that possibility at the outset. If we are to discuss the question at all, it must involve a living option. If for any of you religion be a hypothesis that cannot, by any living possibility, be true, then you need go no farther. I speak to the "saving remnant" alone.) So proceeding, we see, first, that religion offers itself as a *momentous* option. We are supposed to gain, even now, by our belief, and to lose by our non-belief, a certain vital good. Secondly, religion is a *forced* option, so far as that good goes. We cannot escape the issue by remaining sceptical and waiting for more light, because, although we do avoid error in that way *if religion be untrue,* we lose the good, *if it be true,* just as certainly as if we positively chose to disbelieve. It is as if a man should hesitate indefinitely to ask a certain woman to marry him because he was not perfectly sure that she would prove an angel after he brought her home. Would he not cut himself off from that particular angel-possibility as decisively as if he went and married some one else? Scepticism, then, is not avoidance of option; it is option of a certain particular kind of risk. *Better risk loss of truth than chance of error*—that is your faith-vetoer's exact position. He is actively playing his stake as much as the believer is; he is backing the field against the religious hypothesis, just as the believer is backing the religious hypothesis against the field. To preach scepticism to us as a duty until "sufficient evidence" for religion be found, is tantamount therefore to telling us, when in presence of the religious hypothesis, that to yield to our fear of its being error is wiser and better than to yield to our hope that it may be true. It is not intellect against all passions, then; it is only intellect with one passion laying down its law. And by what, forsooth, is the supreme wisdom of this passion warranted? Dupery for dupery, what proof is there that dupery through hope is so much worse than dupery through fear? I, for one, can see no proof; and I simply refuse obedience to the scientist's command to imitate his kind of option, in a case where my own stake is important enough to give me the right to choose my own form of risk. If religion be true and the evidence for it be still insufficient, I do not wish, by putting your extinguisher upon my nature (which feels to me as if it had after all some business in this matter), to forfeit my sole chance in life of getting upon the winning side—that chance depending, of course, on my willingness to run the risk of acting as if my passional need of taking the world religiously might be prophetic and right.

All this is on the supposition that it really may be prophetic and right, and that, even to us who are discussing the matter, religion is a live hypothesis which may be true. Now, to most of us religion comes in a still further way that makes a veto on our active faith even more illogical. The more perfect and more eternal aspect of the universe is represented in our religions as having personal form. The universe is no longer a mere *It* to us, but a *Thou*, if we are religious; and any relation that may be possible from person to person might be possible here. For instance, although in one sense we are passive portions of the universe, in another we show a curious autonomy, as if we were small active centers on our own account. We feel, too, as if the appeal of religion to us were made to our own active goodwill, as if evidence might be forever withheld from us unless we met the hypothesis halfway to take a trivial illustration: just as a man who in a company of gentlemen made no advances, asked a warrant for every concession, and believed no one's word without proof, would cut himself off by such churlishness from all the social rewards that a more trusting spirit would earn—so here, one who should shut himself up in snarling logicality and try to make the gods extort his recognition willy-nilly, or not get it at all, might cut himself off forever from his only opportunity of making the gods' acquaintance. This feeling, forced on us we know not whence that by obstinately believing that there are

gods (although not to do so would be so easy both for our logic and our life) we are doing the universe the deepest service we can, seems part of the living essence of the religious hypothesis. If the hypothesis *were* true in all its parts, including this one, then pure intellectualism, with its veto on our making willing advances, would be an absurdity; and some participation of our sympathetic nature would be logically required. I therefore, for one, cannot see my way to accepting the agnostic rules for truth-seeking, or wilfully agree to keep my willing nature out of the game. I cannot do so for this plain reason, that *a rule of thinking which would absolutely prevent me from acknowledging certain kinds of truth if those kinds of truth were really there, would be an irrational rule.* That for me is the long and short of the formal logic of the situation, no matter what the kinds of truth might materially be.

I confess I do not see how this logic can be escaped. But sad experience makes me fear that some of you may still shrink from radically saying with me *in abstracto,* that we have the right to believe at our own risk any hypothesis that is live enough to tempt our will. I suspect, however, that if this is so, it is because you have gone away from the abstract logical point of view altogether, and are thinking (perhaps without realizing it) of some particular religious hypothesis which for you is dead. The freedom to "believe what we will" you apply to the case of some patent superstition; and the faith you think of is the faith defined by the schoolboy when he said, "Faith is when you believe something that you know ain't true." I can only repeat that this is misapprehension. *In concreto,* the freedom to believe can only cover living options which the intellect of the individual cannot by itself resolve; and living options never seem absurdities to him who has them to consider. When I look at the religious question as it really puts itself to concrete men, and when I think of all the possibilities which both practically and theoretically it involves, then this command that we shall put a stopper on our heart, instincts, and courage, and *wait*—acting of course meanwhile more or less as if religion were not true—till doomsday, or till such time as our intellect and senses working together may have raked in evidence enough—this command, I say, seems to me the queerest idol ever manufactured in the philosophic cave. Were we scholastic absolutists, there might be more excuse. If we had an infallible intellect with its objective certitudes, we might feel ourselves disloyal to such a perfect organ of knowledge in not trusting to it exclusively, in not waiting for its releasing word. But if we are empiricists, if we believe that no bell in us tolls to let us know for certain when truth is in our grasp, then it seems a piece of idle fantasticality to preach so solemnly our duty of waiting for the bell. Indeed we *may* wait if we will—I hope you do not think that I am denying that— but if we do so, we do so at our peril as much as if we believed. In either case we *act,* taking our life in our hands. No one of us ought to issue vetoes to the other, nor should we bandy words of abuse. We ought, on the contrary, delicately and profoundly to respect one another's mental freedom: then only shall we bring about the intellectual republic; then only shall we have that spirit of inner tolerance without which all our outer tolerance is soulless, and which is empiricism's glory; then only shall we live and let live, in speculative as well as in practical things.

I began by a reference to Fitz-James Stephen; let me end by a quotation from him. "What do you think of yourself? What do you think of the world?

. . . These are questions with which all must deal as it seems good to them. They are riddles of the Sphinx, and in some way or other we must deal with them. . . . In all important transactions of life we have to take a leap in the dark. . . . If we decide to leave the riddles unanswered, that is a choice; if we waver in our answer, that, too, is a choice: but whatever choice we make, we make it at our peril. If a man chooses to turn his back altogether on God and the future, no one can prevent him; no one can show beyond reasonable doubt that he is mistaken. If a man thinks otherwise and acts as he thinks, I do not see that any one can prove that he is mistaken. Each must act as he thinks best; and if he is wrong, so much the worse for him. We stand on a mountain pass in the midst of whirling snow and blinding mist, through which we get glimpses now and then of paths which may be deceptive. If we stand still we shall be frozen to death. If we take the wrong road we shall be dashed to pieces. We do not certainly know whether there is any right one. What must we do? 'Be strong and of a good courage.' Act for the best, hope for the best, and take what comes.

. . . If death ends all, we cannot meet death better."

X.4 What Ought We to Believe?

JACK MEILAND

Jack Meiland is professor of philosophy at the University of Michigan. In this selection he argues that we have no special duties to believe according to the evidence, but that every epistemic state must be judged from the perspective of our moral duties. The only ethics of belief are ethical concerns *per se*. In every prospective belief acquisition, we need to ask not what the evidence demands, but what our moral commitments demand.

Lady Britomart: Barbara, I positively forbid you to listen to your father's abominable wickedness. And you, Adolphus, ought to know better than to go about saying that wrong things are true. What does it matter whether they are true if they are wrong?

Undershaft: What does it matter whether they are wrong if they are true?

GEORGE BERNARD SHAW
Major Barbara, Act III

One of the cornerstones of modern Western thought is the doctrine that belief ought to be based solely on sufficient evidence. John Passmore puts it in this way:

> Modern philosophy was founded on the doctrine, uncompromisingly formulated by Descartes, that to think philosophically is to accept as true only that which recommends itself to Reason. To be unphilosophical, in contrast, is to be seduced by the enticements of Will, which beckons men beyond the boundaries laid down by Reason into the wilderness of error. In England, Locke had acclimatized this Cartesian ideal. There is "one unerring mark," he wrote, "by which a man may know whether he is a lover of truth for truth's sake:" namely "*the not entertaining any proposition with greater assurance than the proofs it is built upon will warrant.*" Nineteenth-century agnosticism reaffirmed this Lockean dictum, with a striking degree of moral fervor. The *locus classicus* is a passage in W. K. Clifford's "The Ethics of Belief:" "It is wrong everywhere and for anyone, to believe anything upon insufficient evidence."[1]

Of course, this doctrine has a more ancient pedigree than Passmore indicates. One way of interpreting Plato's Socrates yields this same ideal about belief:

> Socrates astonished, fascinated and exasperated his fellow Athenians. He seems to have been, as nearly as possible, the completely rational man. What is reasonable to believe is what the evidence warrants; what is reasonable to do is what is conducive to the highest good. How could this be otherwise? Furthermore, how could you not believe and act according to the dictates of reason; are you not, after all, a rational being?[2]

The doctrine expressed in these passages is a normative doctrine. It tell us what is reasonable or rational, and it urges us to do the reasonable or rational thing as it is here described. We may put this doctrine in the following way: belief in a factual issue may legitimately be based only (solely and wholly) on considerations of evidential fact. Let us call this doctrine "evidentialism."[3] Expressed in normative principles, this doctrine is: (i) one ought not to believe on insufficient evidence; (ii) one ought to believe whatever is backed by sufficient evidence. I want to examine this normative doctrine about belief.

I

Suppose that Jones and Smith have been business partners and exceptionally close friends for more than thirty-five years. One day Jones discovers a discrepancy in the business's accounts. Upon investigation he comes into the possession of evidence which is sufficient (in anyone's eyes) to justify the belief that Smith has been secretly syphoning off money from the business. Now Jones is in the following predicament. He is, and knows that he is, the type of person who is unable to conceal his feelings and beliefs from others. He thus knows that if he decides that Smith has indeed been stealing money from the firm, it will definitely affect his behavior toward Smith. Even if Jones tries to conceal his belief, he knows that he will inevitably act in a remote, cold, censorious and captious manner toward Smith and that eventually both the friendship and the business partnership will break up. Jones decides that this price is too high and therefore decides not to believe that Smith stole money from the firm. In fact, he goes farther: he decides that Smith did not steal money from the firm.

I take this to be a clear violation of the normative principle that one should believe whatever is backed by sufficient evidence (where it is, of course, understood that this principle assumes that the person has this evidence and is aware of the relation between this evidence and the proposition in question). Other realistic examples of this sort are not hard to find. Take the classical case in which a wife finds a blonde hair on her husband's coat, a handkerchief with lipstick on it in his pocket, a scrap of paper with a phone number scrawled on it, and so on until everyone would agree that the evidence is sufficient that the husband has been seeing another woman. However, the wife believes that their marriage is basically sound and can weather this storm. Like Jones, she

Reprinted from "What Ought We to Believe? or the Ethics of Belief Revisited," *American Philosophical Quarterly,* vol. 17, 1980 by permission.

knows that she cannot conceal her suspicions and hence decides to believe that her husband is not being unfaithful to her. And let us further suppose that in these two examples, things turn out as hoped. The money stops disappearing, and Jones and Smith remain fast friends and partners for many years thereafter. The husband eventually stops seeing the other woman, becomes more attentive to his wife, and the marriage continues stronger than ever for many years. In these circumstances, it does *not* seem to me right to say that Jones and the wife should have believed Smith and the husband to be guilty just because there was sufficient evidence to justify these beliefs. And even if the partnership and the marriage did not last, I think that Jones and the wife were *not* wrong (as W. K. Clifford puts it) to hold beliefs (that Smith and the husband were innocent) on the basis of insufficient evidence. Moreover, these beliefs do not seem to me to be unreasonable or irrational in the least. If things do turn out as Jones and the wife hope, then some very precious things—a strong friendship, a good marriage—will have been preserved by their having certain beliefs even though the evidence is insufficient.

Thus, the doctrine of evidentialism—that belief should be determined solely by factual evidence—seems to me in general to be unacceptable.

One objection that is likely to arise is this. "Jones and the wife did not have to believe that Smith and the husband were innocent in order to achieve the results they desired. Instead, Jones and the wife could have believed them to be guilty, or at least suspected them of guilt, and yet ignored these beliefs or suspicions. This would preserve the evidentialist principle about belief and at the same time secure the desirable results." This objection simply ignores an important feature of the case, namely that Jones and the wife just are not people who can ignore these things. We all know people who are unable to dissemble about matters close to their hearts. So I do not take these examples to be at all unrealistic, and this objection can be safely dismissed.

Two more interesting objections are these. First, it may be claimed that Jones and the wife are engaging in "rationalization," and that rationalizing is a very bad practice. Hence, we should not consider them to have done the right thing in adopting these beliefs. However, I do not think that they are engaging in this practice, at least if we understand rationalization to be the practice of holding certain beliefs because they are expedient by allowing the person to mask his or her true motivations from him or herself. In these examples, Jones and the wife are very clear about their motivations: they are adopting certain beliefs in order to save their friendship or marriage. Second, it might be objected that Jones and the wife are engaging in self-deception. They are deceiving themselves about the true nature of Smith's behavior or the husband's behavior by deliberately adopting these beliefs. I think that this charge lacks force too, for the reasons just given. They know that the evidence is sufficient for the belief that Smith and the husband are guilty and they are not hiding this fact from themselves. But suppose that we accept, for the sake of argument, that they are deceiving themselves about this matter. I believe that this only shifts the question—from whether it is wrong to believe on the basis of insufficient evidence to the question of whether self-deception is always wrong.

II

Another, quite different, sort of objection runs as follows: "Your position treats believing as though it were some kind of voluntary action, as though one could decide to believe *p* or not to believe *p*. But in fact, believing is not voluntary. One either does believe *p* or does not believe *p* depending on whether the facts or information at one's disposal coerce one into believing. Since believing is not a voluntary matter, we cannot decide whether or not to believe *p*." I think that this is an important objection because it does bring out that feature of my position, namely that I take belief to be, in some cases at least, a voluntary matter. But one thing to notice initially is that my position shares this feature with the evidentialist position as exemplified by Passmore's quotation from Clifford. When Clifford says that it is wrong to believe on the basis of insufficient evidence, I take him to be making a moral judgment. (Passmore also takes Clifford in this way—hence Passmore's talk about "moral fervor.") If we accept that "ought" implies "can," then Clifford has no business telling us that we ought to believe only on the basis of sufficient evidence unless he too thinks that belief is in these cases a voluntary matter. Hence the above objection is an objection to both the evidentialist position and my own position. Evidentialists should take note of this.

In order to deal with this objection, we must distinguish various situations in which belief occurs. The kind of situation with which we are principally concerned is that in which the evidence is sufficient. I take "sufficient" here to mean that the evidence justifies the belief. If the wife believed that her husband is deceiving her solely on the basis of a handkerchief with lipstick on it, we would say that her belief is not justified. There are many other reasonable explanations of why he has a handkerchief with lipstick on it in his pocket, and thus the evidence is not sufficient to justify her belief. This belief is not a reasonable one if this is the only evidence for it. On the other hand, if the wife discovers her husband in the arms of another woman, we would probably say that the evidence is more than sufficient. We would say that the evidence is incontrovertible or conclusive. Here the belief is not only justified but almost forced upon the wife. Now, in this discussion I am considering only cases which lie between these two extremes— that is, situations in which the belief is reasonable or justified on the evidence but in which one is not forced to have that belief by the "evidence."

Given these distinctions, we can see that the objector is telling us this: every situation in which the evidence is sufficient is a situation in which belief is forced upon the person. The objector is denying that there is a middle ground between unreasonable (unjustified) belief on the one hand and forced belief on the other hand. I believe that the objector is wrong. Consider this case: a jury, having heard the evidence, convicts a person of a crime; the defendant's attorney, however, remains dubious of the verdict and, after several years of further investigation, turns up conclusive evidence of his client's innocence; nevertheless, at the time of the trial, everyone (including the defense attorney) who had followed the trial closely believed the jury's verdict to be fair and eminently justified. Now, my point here is *not* that a belief can be justified (be supported by sufficient evidence) and yet turn out to be false. Instead, my point is that a person (in this example, the defense attorney) can be in possession of evidence which everyone (including himself) agrees is sufficient to justify a certain belief (that his client is guilty), that this person can be fully aware of how the evidence is related to that belief (thus ruling out cases in which the person is unaware that the evidence justifies the belief), and yet not have that belief or indeed have the contradictory belief. The defense attorney agrees that the evidence is sufficient and that the trial was perfectly fair, and yet he continues to believe that his client is innocent. Sufficient evidence does not result in some logical or psychological necessity which forces the belief in question upon the person. If the evidence is conclusive and the person realizes this, then perhaps that person must hold that belief. But this is not so if the evidence is less than conclusive, for example sufficient.

III

The problem with which I am dealing in this paper is a problem about facts and values. But it is not the much-discussed problem of whether solely factual statements can justify value statements. Instead, it is the problem of whether value considerations can justify, or help to justify, beliefs about purely factual matters. This question about facts, values, and the justification of belief is just as important as the problem of justifying value statements. As Passmore has pointed out, the view that beliefs about factual matters should be based solely on factual material is a cornerstone of modern rationality. I have tried to show that this modern presupposition is mistaken. Indeed, since I believe that Jones and the wife are being eminently rational in believing "against" the evidence, I think that this modern presupposition is itself irrational.

Why is this modern presupposition (which I have called "evidentialism") about the connection between evidence and belief so wide-spread and pervasive? Some important reasons are not hard to discover.

Probably the most important reason is this. Many people probably feel that if any other factor (than factual evidence) were allowed to be influential in determining belief, belief could become an intensely subjective matter, and people would be out of touch with the real world. People would live in fantasy worlds with very undesirable results. Mere survival would become precarious; and, more generally, people would not be able to achieve the results that they desire. If there is a sabertoothed tiger outside one's cave, and if one does not believe that the tiger is there, one is very likely to be eaten up. This yields a clear application of the principle of the survival of the fittest, with the fittest in this case being those who believe that which is supported by evidence (for example, the low growling noise outside the cave, the previous signs of a tiger in the neighborhood, and so on). Thus, the modern presupposition that we are examining has this strong practical basis.

But if we support this modern presupposition by giving it a practical basis, this has a very important implication, namely that this presupposition is therefore open to a critique based also on "practical" reasons. In particular, we could base such a critique on value considerations which also fall into the realm of the practical, and there would be no possibility that such a critique would be irrelevant. I have tried to suggest the outlines of such a critique in this paper.

This general point about the kinds of considerations which are relevant in evaluating this modern presupposition is put forward with admirable clarity and force by Ralph Barton Perry:

> This being the case, belief becomes a question of conduct. Shall I or shall I not induce in others or in myself beliefs which do not have full evidential warrant? . . . It is clear that over and above the theoretical justification of belief there is here implied a *practical maxim* to the effect that I *ought to promote only beliefs that are theoretically justified,* that is, beliefs that are formally correct and empirically verified. . . . It is extremely difficult to persuade the scientist, trained as he is to accept the compulsions of mathematics and experimentation, to see that the *right* of these compulsions to exclusive control over belief is not itself to be established by such compulsions. . . . It is clear, then, that the inculcation of belief by the employment of its non-evidential causes, on the one hand, and the scrupulous restriction of belief within the limits of evidential proof, on the other, are practical alternatives.[4]

IV

Someone might want to object to what I have said by arguing that in my description of my two cases, I have overlooked some other beliefs which Jones and the wife have and which do obey the principle

that one ought to believe whatever has sufficient evidence. For example, one might say of the wife that she believes that if she believes that her husband has not been unfaithful to her, then she will be happier and her marriage might be saved. Now, this belief is one about which it is plausible to say that she has sufficient evidence for it. She need only consult her own feelings and certain general principles (almost truisms) about the behavior of errant husbands. And this is the belief on which she is acting. So she is still acting in an eminently rational way while nevertheless following the principle of sufficient evidence as the sole warrant of belief.

Let us call this more complex belief "B_1." That is, B_1 is the belief that if she believes that her husband has not been unfaithful to her, then she will be happier and her marriage might be saved. Notice that B_1 itself mentions another belief which we will call B_2, namely the belief that her husband has not been unfaithful to her. Let us admit, for the sake of argument, that the wife has sufficient evidence for B_1 and, moreover, believes B_1 on the basis of that evidence. However, it is clear that the wife will actually gain the desirable results of happiness and a rescued marriage only if she does believe B_2—that her husband has not been unfaithful to her—as well. B_1 alone is not sufficient to bring about these desirable results. Consequently, whatever other beliefs she may have on the basis of sufficient evidence, she ought to believe that her husband has not been unfaithful to her—and *that* belief still does not have the backing of sufficient evidence. Thus, it is still the case that her most reasonable or rational course of action in this case is to hold a belief "against" the evidence.

V

Our topic in this paper may appropriately be called "the Ethics of Belief." But there are at least two different projects that can appropriately bear this title. In this and the following sections, I want to specify my project more exactly by differentiating it from another project which has received some attention in the past and then to explain my position by contrasting it with another position in this same area.

One project in the area of the Ethics of Belief is that of *defining* epistemic terms—terms such as "believe," "know," "evident" and so on—by using value, ethical, or "practical" concepts. Thus, A. J. Ayer has attempted to define "knows" in terms of "has a right to be sure." And Roderick Chisholm has attempted to define "evident" in terms of the notion of obligation.[5]

Another, and quite different, project in this area is an inquiry into the question of whether we have rights or obligations to believe certain propositions where these rights or obligations are determined by value, ethical, or "practical" factors. I am engaged here only in this second type of project. If epistemic terms are definable by the use of value or "practical" concepts, perhaps it would follow that we have rights or duties to believe or to refrain from believing. If so, then these two types of projects would not be logically independent of one another. However, my claim is that however these epistemic terms are to be defined, what we are justified in believing, what it is reasonable to believe, depends at least partly on value and "practical" factors. Thus, I am not concerned with defining epistemic terms but only with the factors that determine these rights and duties. I believe that carrying out this second type of project does not logically imply any position concerning the definition of epistemic terms.[6]

VI

In order to see more perspicuously exactly what position I wish to defend and how I defend it, I will first fill in more completely the evidentialist position as it is held or would be agreed to by a great many philosophers, scientists, and other intellectuals today. The evidentialist position maintains that there exists what we might call "purely evidential warrant." That is, evidentialism maintains that a person can be justified or not justified in believing p simply on the basis of the evidence alone. In an excellent article on C. I. Lewis' ethics of belief, Chisholm formulates the following "practical syllogism:"

> Anyone having just the evidence in question is warranted in accepting the conclusion.
> I am in the position of having just that evidence.
> Therefore I am justified in accepting the conclusion.[7]

This syllogism illustrates evidentialism very well. Evidentialism agrees that a person can have a right (or even an obligation) to believe p, but this right (or obligation) is said to arise solely from the relation between the evidence and the conclusion. There will, of course, be differences among the holders of evidentialism as to the amount and kind of evidence needed and about just what the evidence does or does not justify. For example, one evidentialist might say that one has a right to believe p only if the evidence is sufficient, while another evidentialist might say that one has a right to believe p just as long as he does not have sufficient evidence for not-p. But evidentialists are firmly united in believing that there is an objective justificatory relation between evidence and conclusion which by itself warrants belief and which is the same for everyone (see the major premise of Chisholm's "practical syllogism" quoted above) regardless of any "personal" or "subjective" factors pertaining to the believer.

Evidentialists are united in another doctrine too. They hold that it is not correct to call the act of believing p "right" or "wrong" because of the content of the belief. Suppose that there is a belief which many people find distasteful, disgusting, or even vile—for example, the Nazi belief that some people are racially inferior to others. Many evidentialists would criticize people who hold this belief for holding it—saying that it is wrong of these people to believe this—but they would make this criticism solely on the grounds that there is insufficient evidence for this belief. When they say that it is wrong to hold this belief, this can be a moral evaluation. That is, they can be saying that it is morally wrong to hold this Nazi belief. But such evaluation is always based on the relation between evidence and conclusion, not on the content of the belief itself. To put this in another way, evidentialists would maintain that it is morally wrong to hold this Nazi belief but only (for example) on the grounds that it is morally wrong to hold *any* belief for which there is insufficient evidence.

Evidentialism also includes another very important doctrine. Suppose that a person holds this Nazi belief and puts it into practice by, for example, agitating for the deportation of certain racial groups. Evidentialism would allow a person to condemn this action morally, but it would not allow a person to condemn the belief because it led to this agitation. Evidentialism holds that there is a chasm between belief and action such that moral condemnation of the action which stems from that belief does not reach across this chasm and apply to the holding of the belief too. This chasm is founded on the idea that the only factor relevant to the holding of factual beliefs is evidence. It is also founded on the idea that facts have no moral or value character in themselves, and that consequently the holding of factual beliefs should have no such moral character (except in so far as it may be a moral matter to believe on the basis of evidence).

My cases of Jones and Smith, and the husband and wife, are designed specifically to show that this chasm does not exist. The specific feature which I have expressly built into these cases is that Jones and the wife are people whose beliefs automatically or involuntarily influence their actions. They are people who, as we say, cannot in the long run hide their feelings, attitudes, and beliefs. There are such people. But I do not want my case to rest on the existence of a few such people. I think that we are all people like this with respect to some beliefs and some attitudes. Few of us are consummate dissemblers. Many things are not that important to us, and about these things we can hide our true feelings and perhaps fool all of the people all of the time. But I think that for each of us there are some things which we probably cannot hide in the long run. What this shows is that there are cases of a not uncommon sort in which the alleged gap between belief and action simply does not exist. These are cases which the evidentialist position simply cannot handle correctly. The evidentialist position hold that one is morally responsible for actions but not for beliefs (except possibly on a purely epistemic basis). But our cases are cases in which having a certain belief is tantamount to behaving in certain ways. Moreover, if I am right, adopting those beliefs is a voluntary matter.[8] Consequently, moral responsibility and moral predication in general should cross the alleged chasm between behavior and belief. By this I mean that if that behavior is behavior which one ought to prevent oneself from engaging in, and if one can (as I claim) prevent this behavior by adopting a certain belief, then one ought to adopt that belief, apart from the epistemic warrant or lack thereof for that belief. Here I am not concerned about what kind of "ought" this is (nor am I concerned as to whether it represents obligation). It may be a

moral "ought"; it may be prudential; it may be of some other kind. I believe that the argument holds for all of the various kinds of "oughts."

Because evidentialism cannot handle cases like these correctly, I believe that we need a new theory about what we ought to believe.

VII

Another way of seeing the inadequacy of evidentialism is as follows. Evidentialism rests squarely on the notion of "purely evidential warrant." It holds that if there are some types of things which ought or ought not to be believed, this should be determined solely by the state of the evidence. (Consider again Chisholm's major premise: "Anyone having just the evidence in question is warranted in accepting the conclusion.") This seems clearly wrong to me. It seems to me that the justification of belief must depend, at least in part, on the believer's situation. To see this, let's go back to our husband and wife case and add a private detective hired by the wife to investigate her husband's activities. It is easy to imagine a situation in which the detective succeeds in gathering evidence on the basis of which we would say that it is reasonable for him to believe that the husband is seeing another woman. But the very same evidence may not justify the wife in believing this. Because of the relationship between husband and wife in this case, the wife should not lightly or too quickly believe that about her husband. And this is not—or not only—because if she did believe it, she would then act in certain ways. It is not only a matter of not acting hastily; she should also not believe hastily either. Her situation in life requires that she be very careful about this—more careful than, say, her neighbors or her husband's employer or even the private detective. That she and her husband have had a good marriage, full of mutual trust and confidence for fifteen years, requires that any belief on her part that her husband is seeing another woman be based on very, very substantial evidence. Evidentialists will reply that they agree with this and that in fact evidentialism gains support by being able to account for what I have just said. The evidentialist account would be as follows: through living with her husband for fifteen years, the wife has accumulated much evidence that he is not the type of man who would betray his wife with another woman; this is why the wife should not lightly decide that he is unfaithful; but this is sheerly a matter of the weight of evidence on both sides, as evidentialism requires. This account, while formally satisfactory from the evidentialist point of view, strikes me as lacking a proper appreciation of the human reality of this situation. I believe that she has a duty to her husband, arising from their commitment to one another over a long period, to require a stronger basis for belief in his treachery than does, say, the private detective. We might even say "she owes him that." It is not a matter of her having much evidence to the contrary. Instead, it is a matter of obligation toward someone to whom she has been very close.

VIII

At this point, someone might say that my position is ambiguous as between the following two alternatives:

(I) The (weaker) thesis that extra-factual considerations can sometimes be allowed to count as legitimately influencing or determining belief.

(II) The (stronger) thesis that extra-factual considerations should always count (to some extent) in the holding of beliefs.

I think that my position does seem ambiguous as between these because neither of these alternatives exactly captures my position. On the one hand, I want to hold that there can be cases in which what a person should believe is determined solely by the state of the factual evidence. On the other hand, I want to hold that in *all* cases, extra-factual considerations are relevant.

To see what I mean here, suppose that we add another person to our case of the husband and wife. This person has no special relationship to either the husband or the wife and (let us try to imagine) is investigating the question of the husband's infidelity from a totally detached, disinterested point of view. (Perhaps this is just one of a number of cases of suspected infidelity which this person is investigating as part of a research project in social psychology.) In such a case, it seems that this investigator's belief about the supposed infidelity should be determined solely by the factual evidence.

I would agree with this. But I think that in order to judge that this is so, one must find out that this investigator has no special relationship to these people and in general that his situation does not require that he take extra-factual considerations into account. Perhaps we can put this by saying that one role which extra-factual matters should have in the determination of belief is that extra-factual matters should decide whether the person's belief is to be determined solely by factual evidence. Thus, I agree with the weaker thesis (I) that extra-factual considerations should sometimes legitimately influence belief, with its implication that in other cases only the factual evidence should determine belief. Our instance of the detached investigator is one of the latter cases. But I also agree with the stronger thesis (II) that extra-factual considerations should always count (to some extent) in the holding of beliefs, since I believe that extra-factual considerations must always be consulted in order to decide what factors should determine a person's beliefs in a given case.

In saying that there are cases in which a person's beliefs should be determined solely by factual evidence, I may seem to be conceding to the evidentialist everything he wants. For in such cases at least, I seem to be allowing the existence of a purely evidential warranting relation. This question will be taken up further in the next section. But here I think we can see immediately that my position has not merged with that of the evidentialist. Consider again Chisholm's syllogism, and in particular its major premise: "*Anyone* having just the evidence in question is warranted in accepting the conclusion." This is unacceptable to me. The wife and the investigator may have exactly the same factual evidence, and yet one may be thereby warranted in accepting that the husband has been unfaithful while the other is not so warranted.

It is *no* part of my purpose to claim that the state of the evidence never has any bearing on whether a given belief is justified. In that sense, I agree that there is such a thing as purely evidential warrant (where this means only that the evidence has a bearing on whether the belief is justified). What I deny is that evidence by itself can justify belief without consideration of and control by value and situational factors. Even when we are dealing with the case of the detached investigator, we can know that this is such a case, a case in which evidence should determine belief, only by considering value and situational factors. Thus, value and situational factors control the bearing of the evidence in *all* cases. Some cases will be such that the decision will be to allow the evidence to determine belief. And this might give rise to the *mistaken* doctrine that *every* case is a case of this sort. That is, it might give rise to the mistaken doctrine that there is such a thing as purely evidential warrant in the sense in which the evidence is supposed to justify belief apart from any other factor. This is mistaken because simply in order to identify those cases in which evidence should be allowed to determine belief, we must employ value and situational factors.

But, it may be objected, this position ignores certain obvious data which demonstrate a direct, basic, and underivative relationship between evidence and proposition regardless of value and situational factors. Suppose, the objector might continue, that a blonde hair is found on the husband's coat and that this is the total evidence available. The objector would say that it would be unreasonable for anyone, regardless of values or situation, to believe that the husband was seeing another woman. Thus, he would conclude, there is a basic and independent relationship between evidence and proposition which determines the reasonableness, or at least the unreasonableness, of belief. I think that this objection is mistaken, however, because even here one may imagine a situation in which the person should believe that the husband is seeing another woman—a situation in which the stakes are extremely high and the time available very short so that the person ought to go on what evidence he has available, however slim that evidence is. Here again, the case is controlled by value and situational factors.

Finally, it must be pointed out that I am urging that extra-factual considerations impinge on the holding of beliefs in *two* different, though related, ways. First, extra-factual considerations (such as the wife's relationship to her husband, as contrasted with the investigator's lack of relationship to either of them) determine which factors should influence belief. For example, they determine whether a given case is one in which belief should be determined solely by factual evidence. Now, let us suppose that we have a case in which

it is decided that belief should *not* be controlled solely by factual evidence. What other factors, then, should influence belief? Here is the second way in which extra-factual considerations should bear on belief: They should influence the selection of a particular belief from the alternative beliefs available. So we may put the matter in this way: extra-factual considerations should be consulted in every case to see which factor should determine belief; and in some of these cases extra-factual considerations will themselves be among the factors that should influence belief. In the case of the wife, her relationship of fifteen years standing to her husband shows that evidence alone (unless it is conclusive) should not determine belief; and her desire to continue the marriage turns out to be one of the factors that should influence what she does believe. In the case of the detached investigator, the lack of special situational factors shows that his belief should be determined by evidence alone.

IX

But more still needs to be said about the role, if any, of the idea of purely evidential warrant in the position I am defending here. Does this position allow a role for this idea? It may seem to some readers that in the previous section I was explicitly denying any role to this notion while nevertheless secretly allowing it a place. Let's begin our discussion of this matter with the following objection: "You seem to deny that there is such a thing as purely evidential warrant, a relation between evidence and conclusion which exists independently of extra-factual considerations, since you claim that extra-factual considerations are relevant in every case. Yet, on the other hand, you do allow that we may, in many or all cases, describe exactly what evidence a person has for a given proposition. Surely, then, talk of purely evidential warrant can find a home here. For on the basis of such a description of the evidence, we can go on to talk about how much support this person has for a belief that this proposition is true. This evidence provides support for that belief. And that is all that one means when talking about 'purely evidential warrant.'"

This objection is important and must be taken seriously because it will help us to clarify the issues here. What I have said so far in this paper may seem ambiguous as between the following two possibilities: (1) I could be denying that there is such a thing as purely evidential warrant; or (2) I could be saying that there is such a thing as purely evidential warrant but that it never determines by itself what we ought to believe.

I believe that the problem here arises from a fundamental ambiguity in the notion of "purely evidential warrant" itself. This notion is a compound notion, and we must separate its parts in order to understand what is going on here. These parts are as follows: (1) the evidential component; (2) the warranting component. When E is evidence for C, E stands in a certain relationship to C. Philosophers will differ over the correct analysis of this evidential relationship. For example, Carnap believed that the notion of evidence was captured by his concept of "degree of confirmation" and thus that the evidential relationship is a logical relationship between two statements or propositions. In any case, if we accept the broad distinction between fact and value now employed in so many areas of philosophy, I think that it is clear that the evidential relation is a factual relation between propositions. (I am, of course, using "factual" in a way in which logical relations between propositions are "factual" relations. In other contexts, it would be important to contrast "logical" and "factual.") But the warranting relation is not a factual relation, in this sense of the term "factual." When we talk about one or more propositions as warranting belief in another proposition, we are talking about the reasonableness, the rationality, or the "oughtness" of believing that latter proposition on the basis of the former propositions. Warranting will be different things on different occasions. On one occasion, one proposition may warrant belief in another in the sense of making it reasonable or justified for a person to believe the latter. On another occasion, we may feel that one proposition warrants belief in another in the sense that the person *ought* to believe the latter on the basis of the former. But whatever warranting is on a given occasion, it always falls on the "value" side of the fact-value dichotomy. It has to do with "reasonableness," "justification," and "oughtness."

The important consequence of this is that if one accepts some fairly strong form of the fact-value dichotomy, then it follows that the existence of an evidential relation between two propositions

does not imply anything *by itself* about the way in which the first proposition does or does not warrant belief in the second proposition. In order to move from the existence of an evidential relation to the existence of a warranting relation, we require some "bridging" principles, some principles which license this move. Now, my position is that these "bridge" principles are practical principles, in a broad sense of the term "practical." They are principles which mention or have some other connection with values and ends.

We began this section by noting that what I have said in this paper may seem ambiguous as between two possibilities: (1) denying that there is such a thing as "purely evidential warrant"; (2) admitting that there is such a thing but denying that it ever determines by itself what we ought to believe. Now this ambiguity can be cleared up. I do agree, with the evidentialists, that there often is a relation between two propositions which we may call the *evidential* relation and which exists independently of value and situational factors. But it does not follow from this that belief in the proposition for which there is evidence (even sufficient evidence) is thereby *warranted*. This does not follow unless we adopt some "practical" bridging principle which allows this to follow. So while there is a "purely *evidential* relation"—a relation between propositions which is "purified" of dependence on values and ends—there is no "purely evidential *warranting* relation." For the warranting relation will depend on a practical bridge principle and thus not be independent of values and ends. Warranting has and must have a practical basis.

But even if we were to agree on this point, there still is the question of what bridge principles to adopt. Several possibilities suggest themselves immediately:

P_1: If S has sufficient evidence for C, then S ought (absolutely) to believe C.
P_2: If S has sufficient evidence for C, then S ought (prima-facie) to believe C.

Earlier in this paper, I have tried to show that P_1 is not an acceptable principle. This is what my cases of Jones and the wife are principally intended to show. These cases do *not* show that P_2 is unacceptable. P_2 is a plausible principle and one which many people will be inclined to adopt. Nevertheless—and here my earlier point arises again—P_2 (or whatever bridge principle we do adopt) needs to be justified by a practical argument.

Now, let us suppose that we do justify P_2 by a practical argument and that we accept P_2 on this basis. This means that even sufficient evidence provides only a prima facie reason for believing C. What, then, could "outweigh" sufficient evidence in a particular case such that one on balance ought not to believe C? My answer is that extra-factual considerations can bring about this result. The cases of Jones and the wife again show this, too. Thus, we can see that the practical bears on the question "What ought we to believe?" at several crucial points. First, the practical bears on the justification of bridge principles which determine in general the relation between evidence and belief— that is, which determine in general how evidence is to be weighed in deciding what to believe. Second, since P_1 is not a satisfactory principle, practical factors will also be involved in decisions about particular beliefs in particular cases. Here, the potential believer's values, ends, and situation will have a definite bearing on whether he or she ought to adopt a particular belief.

Notes

[1] John Passmore, *A Hundred Years of Philosophy* (Harmondsworth, 1968), p. 95.

[2] Dorothy Walsh, *Literature and Knowledge* (Middletown, Conn., 1969), p. 21.

[3] I owe the term "evidentialism" to Nicholas Rescher.

[4] Ralph Barton Perry, "The Right to Believe," in *In the Spirit of William James* (Bloomington, Ind., 1958), pp. 178 and 181. Incidentally, it should be apparent that my position in this paper is very different from that of William James in his essay "The Will to Believe." James would appear to allow factors other than factual evidence to determine belief only when the evidence is not sufficient, whereas I am arguing here that extra-factual considerations should sometimes do so even when there is sufficient evidence to justify belief on one side or the other. There are other very large differences as well between our positions.

[5] A. J. Ayer, *The Problem of Knowledge* (London, 1954), pp. 31–35; Roderick Chisholm, "Evidence as Justification," *The Journal of Philosophy,* vol. 58 (1961), pp. 739–748. These attempts have been criticised by Herbert Heidelberger, "On Defining Epistemic Expressions," *The Journal of Philosophy,* vol. 60 (1963), pp. 344–348.

[6] In his book *Perceiving: A Philosophical Study* (Ithaca, 1957, p. 15) Chisholm attempts to define various epistemic notions in terms of the idea of something's being "worthy of one's belief." Roderick Firth criticises this attempt, in part by showing that it leads to the result that a certain view is ruled out *a priori* by Chisholm's definitions.

[7] Roderick Chisholm, "Lewis' Ethics of Belief," in Paul Schilpp (ed.), *The Philosophy of C. I. Lewis* (LaSalle, 1968), p. 226.

[8] In addition to the arguments for voluntarism about beliefs given earlier in this paper, see the splendid arguments for voluntarism given by Roderick Chisholm in "Lewis' Ethics of Belief," *op. cit.,* pp. 223–227. A different view is taken by Bernard Williams in "Deciding to Believe," in Howard Kiefer and Milton Munitz (eds.), *Language, Belief, and Metaphysics* (Albany, 1970), p. 106.

X.5 Believing, Willing, and the Ethics of Belief

LOUIS P. POJMAN

In this essay I try to do three things. In the introduction I give an overview of various relations between acts of the will and belief acquisitions. In Part I, I argue against the thesis that we can obtain beliefs directly on willing to have them. There is something both psychologically aberrant and conceptually incoherent about obtaining and sustaining beliefs through acts of will. In

Part II, I argue that while we can obtain beliefs indirectly via the will, there is a prima facie duty not to do so. I argue that Meiland's thesis to the contrary is incorrect. I use the term *volit* to mean the act of obtaining a belief directly on willing to have it.

Introduction: Varieties of Volitionalism

It is a widely held view that we can obtain beliefs and withhold beliefs directly on performing an act of the will. This thesis is sometimes identified with the view that believing is a basic act, an act that is under our direct control. Descartes holds a *global* version of this thesis: the will is limitless in relation to belief acquisition and we must be directly responsible for our beliefs, especially our false beliefs, for otherwise we could draw the blasphemous conclusion that God is responsible for them.[1] Kierkegaard at times seems to hold this thesis. Sometimes a less global or *local* version of this doctrine is held, asserting that only some beliefs are under our direct control—those beliefs that are not irresistible or forced on us. Aquinas, Locke, Newman, James, Pieper, Chisholm, and Meiland are representatives of this position, holding that we may *volit* (obtain a belief directly on willing it) just in case the evidence is not sufficient or irresistible in forming a belief.[2] I call the thesis that some or all of our beliefs are basic acts of will "direct volitionalism." I contrast this view with the thesis that some beliefs arise indirectly from basic acts, acts of will, and intentions—a thesis I call "indirect volitionalism."

I want to make another distinction at the outset regarding the relation of believing to willing in belief acquisition: the distinction between *de*scribing volitional acts and *pre*scribing them. I call those types of volitionalism *descriptive* that merely describe the process of coming to believe through *voliting* (obtaining a belief directly on willing to have it). I call those types of volitionalism *prescriptive* that include a normative element. Direct prescriptive volitionalism states that it is permissible or obligatory to acquire certain beliefs directly by willing to have them. Indirect prescriptive volitionalism states that it is permissible or obligatory to take the necessary steps to acquire beliefs based on nonepistemic considerations. A schematic representation of the various theses I have in mind appears at the bottom of this page.

This schema is not meant to be an exhaustive set of relations between believing and willing, but to capture the central theses regarding that relationship in the history of philosophy.

Direct volitionalism has to do with the nature of believing and the type of control that we have over our belief states; prescriptive volitionalism has to do with the ethics of belief, with our duties in

	Direct	Indirect
Descriptive	1. One can acquire beliefs directly simply by willing to believe certain propositions.	2. One can acquire beliefs indirectly by willing to believe propositions and then taking the necessary steps to bring it about that one believes in the propositions.
Prescriptive	3. One can acquire beliefs directly by willing to believe propositions, and one is justified in so doing.	4. One can acquire beliefs indirectly by willing to believe propositions as described in thesis 2, and one is justified in purposefully bringing it about that one acquires beliefs in this way.

This is a revised version of "Believing and Willing" (*Canadian Journal of Philosophy, 15*, no. 1, 1985) and chapters XIII and XIV of *Religious Belief and the Will* (London: Routledge & Kegan Paul, 1986).

regard to the acquisition and sustainment of beliefs. In what follows I discuss these two types of volitionalism both in their direct and indirect forms, contrasting them with the standard mode of belief acquisition. In Part I, I first set forth the criteria a fully successful volitional belief acquisition would need to meet and show why we should be skeptical about whether any instances obtain, and then offer two arguments against direct descriptive volitionalism: the phenomenological argument, which proceeds on the basis of an introspective account of the nature of belief acquisition, and the "logic of belief" argument, which shows a conceptual connection between believing and nonvolitional states. In Part II, I turn to indirect prescriptive volitionalism and the ethics of belief and argue that we have a duty not to get ourselves to believe against the evidence.

I   Direct Volitionalism

What role does the will play in forming a belief? Is belief formation in some sense within our direct control? Or does the judgment come naturally as a spontaneous response to the total evidence (including background information and assumptions)? If receiving evidence in entertaining propositions is like placing weights on balanced scales, can the will influence the outcome? In the standard model of belief acquisition, the judgment is not a separate act but simply the result of the weighing process. It is as though the weighing process exhibited the state of evidence, and then the mind simply registered the state of the scales. In the volitional model, the judgment is a special action over and above the weighing process. It is as though the mind recognized the state of the scales but were allowed to choose whether to accept that state or to influence it by putting a mental finger on one side or the other, depending on desire. The nonvolitionalist need not deny that desire unconsciously influences our belief acquisitions, but does resist the notion that beliefs can be formed by conscious acts of will. And the volitionalist need not maintain that such volits can occur any time one wants them to. There may be times when it is impossible to move the weights through any effort of the will. Here the analogy with freedom of the will is apposite. Just as the metaphysi-

cal libertarian need not claim that every act is within our control, but only some significant acts; likewise, the doxastic libertarian need not claim that every belief is within our control, but only some significant beliefs. It is sometimes possible to place the mental finger on the doxastic scales and influence the formation of a judgment or belief.

In what follows I seek to show that problems affect the volitional notion of belief formation. Although it is not possible to prove that no one *ever* volits or that it is impossible to do so (as Bernard Williams mistakenly claims), I offer two arguments to undermine the thesis that we acquire beliefs by consciously willing to have them. I also indicate the legitimate role the will does play in belief acquisition. My first argument is called "the phenomenological argument against direct descriptive volitionalism." It involves an introspective analysis of the phenomena of belief acquisition, showing that there is something psychologically aberrant about the notion of voliting. The second argument, the "logic of belief" argument against direct descriptive volitionalism, demonstrates a conceptual connection between belief and truth, that there is something incoherent about holding that a particular belief is held decisively on the basis of wanting to have that belief.

The Phenomenological Argument Against Direct Descriptive Volitionalism

First of all we must understand what is involved in direct volitionalism (in this section "volitionalism" stands for "direct descriptive volitionalism" unless otherwise stated). The following features seem necessary and jointly sufficient conditions for a minimally interesting thesis of volitionalism:

1. *The acquisition is a basic act.* That is, some of our beliefs are obtained by acts of will directly on being willed. Believing itself need not be an action—it may be dispositional. The volitionalist need not assert that *all* belief acquisitions occur via the fiat of the will, only that *some* of them do.

2. *The acquisition must be done in full consciousness of what one is doing.* The paradigm cases of acts of will are those in which the agent deliberates over two courses of action and decides on one of them. However, acts of will may take place with greater or lesser awareness. Here our notion

of will is ambiguous between two meanings: "desiring" and "deciding." Sometimes by "act of will" we mean simply a desire that manifests itself in action, such as my being hungry and finding myself going to the refrigerator or tired and finding myself heading for bed. We are not always aware of our desires or intentions. There is difference between this type of willing and the sort where we are fully aware of a decision to perform an act. If we obtain beliefs via the will in the weaker sense of desiring of which we are only dimly aware, how can we ever be sure that it was really an act of will that caused the belief directly rather than the will simply being an accompaniment of the belief? That is, there is a difference between willing to believe and believing willingly. The latter case is not an instance of acquiring a belief by fiat of the will, only the former is. To make his or her case, the volitionalist must assert that the acts of will that produce beliefs are decisions of which we are fully aware.

3. *The belief must be acquired independently of evidential considerations.* That is, the evidence is not decisive in forming the belief. Perhaps the belief may be influenced by evidence (testimony, memory, inductive experience, and the like), so that the leap of faith cannot occur just any time over any proposition, but only over propositions that have some evidence in their favor but are still inadequately supported by that evidence. They have an initial subjective probability of, or just under, 0.5. According to Descartes, we ought to withhold belief in such situations where the evidence is exactly equal, whereas with Kierkegaard religious and existential considerations may justify leaps of believing even when the evidence is weighted against the proposition in question. William James prescribes such leaps only when the option is forced, living, and momentous. It may not be possible to volit in the way Kierkegaard prescribes without a miracle of grace, as he suggests, but the volitionalist would have to assert that volitional belief goes beyond all evidence at one's disposal and hence the believer must acquire the belief through an act of choice that goes beyond evidential considerations. Recurring to our earlier metaphor of the weights, it is possible to place our volitional finger on the mental scales of evidence assessment, tipping them one way or the other.

In sum, then, a volit is an act of will whereby I acquire a belief directly on willing to have the belief, and it is an act made in full consciousness and independently of evidential considerations. The act of acquiring a belief may itself not be a belief but a way of moving from mere entertainment of a proposition to its acceptance.

There is much to be said in favor of volitionalism. It seems to extend the scope of human freedom to an important domain, and it seems to fit our experience of believing where we are conscious of having made a choice. The teacher who sees that the evidence against a pupil's honesty is great and yet decides to trust him, believing that somehow he is innocent in spite of the evidence, and the theist who believes in God in spite of insufficient evidence, both seem to be everyday examples confirming our inclination toward a volitional account of belief formation. We suspect, at times, that many of our beliefs, while not formed through *fully* conscious volits, have been formed through *half-aware* desires, for on introspection we note that past beliefs have been acquired in ways that could not have taken the evidence seriously into consideration. Volitionalism seems a good explanatory theory to account for a great deal of our cognitive experience.

Nonetheless, certain considerations may make us question whether on reflection volitionalism is the correct account of our situation. I argue that it is not the natural way in which we acquire beliefs, and that while it may not be logically impossible that some people volit, it seems psychologically odd and even conceptually incoherent. In this section I shall look at the psychology of belief acquisition and in the next the logic of that experience. I turn then to the phenomenological argument against volitionalism, which schematically goes something like this:

1. Phenomenologically speaking, acquiring a belief is a happening in which the world forces itself on a subject.

2. A happening in which the world forces itself upon a subject is not a thing the subject does (is not a basic act) or chooses.

3. Therefore, phenomenologically speaking, acquiring a belief is not something a subject does or chooses.

This describes the standard mode of belief acquisition and, it will be urged, is the way all beliefs occur. The first premise appeals to our introspective data and assumes that acquiring a belief has a spontaneous, unbidden, involuntary, or forced aspect attached to it. The second premise merely points out the active—passive distinction—that there is a difference between doing something and having something happen to oneself. Hence, the conclusion states that as a happening believing is not something one does or chooses. The phenomenological argument asks us to look within ourselves to see if acquiring a belief is not different from entertaining a proposition, the latter of which can be done at will. The first premise is based on the view that beliefs are psychological states about states of affairs. They are, to use Cambridge University philosopher Frank Ramsey's metaphor, mappings in the mind by which we steer our lives. As such the states of affairs that beliefs represent exist independently of the mind; they exist independently of whether we want them to exist. Insofar as beliefs presume to represent the way the world is, and hence serve as effective guides to action, the will seems superfluous. Believing seems more like seeing than looking, falling than jumping, catching a cold than catching a ball, getting drunk than taking a drink, blushing than smiling, getting a headache than giving one to someone else. Indeed, this involuntary, passive aspect seems true on introspection of most propositional attitudes: anger, envy, fearing, suspecting, doubting, though not necessarily of imagining or entertaining a proposition, where an active element may often be present.

The heart of the argument is in the first premise, and that premise can only be established by considering a number of different types of belief acquisition to see if they all exhibit this passive or nonvolitional feature: having the world force itself on one. Although such an investigation might never end, I can, at least, consider typical cases of belief formation of various types. Let me begin with perceptual beliefs. If I am in a normal physiological condition and open my eyes, I cannot help but see certain things; for example, this piece of white paper in front of me. It seems intuitively obvious that I don't have to choose, before I believe I see it, to have a belief that I see this piece of white paper. Here "seeing is believing." This is not to deny a certain active element in perception. I can explore my environment, focus in on certain features, turn from others. I can direct my perceptual mechanism, but once I do this the perceptions I obtain come of themselves whether or not I will to have them. I may even have an aversion to white paper and not want to have such a perception. Likewise, if I am in a normal physiological state and someone nearby turns on loud music, I hear it. I cannot help believing that I hear it. Belief is forced on me.

Consider, next, memorial beliefs. The typical instances of believing what I seem to remember require no special choosings. I may choose to search my memory for the name of my friend's wife, but what I finally come up with, what I seem to remember, comes of itself, has its own weight attached to it. I do not *choose* to believe my memory report that my friend's wife's name is Pam. Normally, I *cannot help* believing it. There may be times when we only faintly recollect, but the fact that we only weakly believe our memory reports does not imply a volitional element in the belief formation. Although there are times (especially when considering events in the distant past or in childhood) when we are not sure whether what we seem to remember actually occurred, even here it seems that it is typically the evidence of the memory that impresses us sufficiently to tip the scales of judgment one way or the other.

This analysis can be extended to abstract and logical beliefs. Very few volitionalists affirm that we choose to believe that the law of noncontradiction has universal application or that "2 + 2 = 4." These sorts of beliefs seem almost undeniably nonvolitional, and some volitionalists would even withhold the designation "belief" from them, classifying them as cases of knowledge *simpliciter*. In any case, all agree that in these cases if one understands what is being asserted, one is compelled to believe (or know) these propositions. They are paradigms of doxastic happenings that force themselves on us regardless of whether we will to believe them.

A similar process is at work regarding theoretical beliefs, including scientific, religious, ideological, political, and moral beliefs. Given a whole network of background beliefs, some views or theories are simply going to win out in our noetic structure over others. We sometimes find ourselves forced to accept theories that conflict with and even overthrow our favorite explanations. Accepting a theory as the best explanation, or as probably true, doesn't entail that we must act on it. We may believe an explanation to be true but find it so unedifying or personally revulsive that we are at a loss for what action to take. Such might be the case when a libertarian finds herself forced by argument to accept the doctrine of determinism or when a person loses his religious faith. After *"perestroika"* and the recent anticommunist revolution in the Soviet Union, I saw two bright Russian law students weeping. When asked why they were weeping, one student said, "We were taught that communism was the truth which would win out over capitalism. We've been proved wrong, and we don't know what to do." When doxastic revolutions break out, chaos results, and we suddenly find ourselves without relied-on anchors to stabilize us or maps to guide us.

We can also accept a theory as the best explanation among a set of weak hypotheses without believing it. There is an attitude of accepting a proposition, acting on it as an experimental hypothesis, without assenting to its truth. A behavioral analysis would conflate such acceptance with belief, but there is no reason to accept behaviorism. Sometimes we accept a theory little by little as evidence from various parts of it makes sense to us. At other times, it is as though we suddenly saw the world differently—what was once a cosmic duck is now seen as a cosmic rabbit. The term "seeing" is appropriate, because even as we do not choose what we see when we look at an object (although we can focus on part of it, neglect another part, and so forth), so we do not choose to believe a theory and thereby come to believe it. Rather, we cannot do otherwise in these cases. Nothing I have said, of course, is meant to deny that the will plays an indirect role in acquiring such beliefs.

Finally, and most importantly, there is the matter of testimony beliefs that arise on the basis of reports of others. This is the kind of belief emphasized by Pieper and Meiland. Certainly, this seems a more complex type of believing than perceptions or memory beliefs. Often we read reports in newspapers or hear rumors or predictions and hesitate before siding one way or the other. Sometimes the news seems shocking or threatening to our whole noetic structure. Here one may have the phenomenal feel, at first glance, that a decision is being made by the agent. For example, I hear a report that someone I know well and esteem highly has cheated his company of $50,000. The evidence seems the sort I normally credit as reliable, but I somehow resist accepting

it. Have I willed to withhold belief or disbelief? I don't think so. Although I am stunned by the evidence, I have a great deal of background evidence, which I cannot immediately express in detail but which I have within my noetic structure, subconsciously, but which plays a role in putting the fresh data into a larger perspective.

Perhaps I find myself believing willingly that, in spite of the evidence, my friend is innocent. Does this "believing willingly" against the evidence constitute an act of will? I don't think so. Here the reader will recall the distinction between (1) willing to believe and thereby believing and (2) believing willingly, where one feels drawn toward a belief state and willingly goes along with it. One can identify with and feel good about what one comes to believe, but in neither case is the will directly causative. In addition, there is the experience of viewing the objective evidence as roughly counterbalanced, but where one feels inclined one way or the other. Here something like our intuitions or unconscious processes play a decisive role in belief formation, but these are not things we have direct control over. Within our noetic structure are dispositional beliefs and dispositions to believe that influence belief formation. There is no need to appeal to acts of will to explain instances of anomalous belief acquisition.

Normally, however, I find myself immediately and automatically assenting to testimony. If I am lost in a new neighborhood and looking for a supermarket, I may ask someone for directions. Under favorable circumstances, I will believe what she tells me because I have learned through experience that normally people will give reliable directions if they can. Even if I have to deliberate about the testimony, wondering whether the witness is credible, I don't come to a conclusion on the basis of willing to believe one way or the other but because the complex factors in the situation incline me one way or the other. One of these factors may be my wants and wishes that influence my focus; but once the belief comes, it comes as produced by the evidence and not by the choice.

It may be that given enough time and resources we can come to believe almost anything indirectly by willing the appropriate means and acting on them. For example, we believe that the world is spherical and not flat, and no amount of effort seems sufficient to overturn this belief; but perhaps if we had good prudential reasons to do so (for example, if someone offered us a million dollars if we could get ourselves to believe that the world was flat), we might go to a hypnotist, take drugs, or use elaborate autosuggestion until we actually acquired the belief.

Perhaps the volitionalist will respond that there is really little difference between a case of autosuggestion and a case of voliting. Consider the following cases, which progressively tend toward a state of successful autosuggestive belief acquisition:

1. It might be virtually impossible for anyone to use autosuggestion to come to believe that one does not exist.

2. It may take several days for the average person to get him or herself to believe through autosuggestion that the earth is flat.

3. It may take several hours to get oneself to believe that one's spouse is faithful where there is good evidence to the contrary.

4. It may only take several minutes for a garden-variety racist to get into a state of believing that people of another race are full human beings.

5. It may take some people only a few seconds to acquire the belief that the tossed coin will come up heads.

6. With practice, some people could get themselves, in an imperceptively short amount of time, to acquire the belief that the tossed coin will come up heads.

7. Some masters at autosuggestion may be able to acquire beliefs about tossed coins without any time intervening between the volition and the belief formation.

Perhaps it is strange, stupid, or even perversely immoral to engage in such autosuggestive belief acquisition, but Cases 2 and 5 seem psychologically possible (leave aside for the moment the likely damage to our belief-forming mechanisms and our noetic structure as a whole). It is conceivable that 6 and 7 obtain. In throwing dice, one sometimes has the feeling that the lucky (unlucky) number will turn up in a way that resembles this sort of phenomenon. Perhaps there are some people who can believe some propositions at will the way people can blush, wiggle their ears, and sneeze as basic acts. If 7 is psychologically possible, then the first premise and the conclusion of the phenomenological argument must be altered to take account of

these anomalies, so that the revised argument would read as follows:

1. Acquiring a belief is *typically* a happening in which the world forces itself upon a subject.

2. And happenings in which the world forces itself on a subject are not things the subject does or chooses.

3. Therefore, acquiring a belief is not *typically* something a subject does or chooses.

However, while we can never entirely rule out such behavior, it seems dubious whether we actually do perform such acts. It is hard to know whether such a case would be a case of imagining a state of affairs or believing a proposition, for the distinction is blurred at this point. At some point, to imagine that p becomes a belief that p. For most of us, most of the time, however, such belief acquisitions are not possible. Consider the proposition "This coin will land heads." Do you have any sense of yes-ness or no-ness, assent or dissent, regarding it? Or suppose that the local torturer holds out his two fists and says to you, "If you choose the fist with the penny in it, you will receive $100,000, but if you pick the empty fist, you will be tortured for the next week. The only stipulation on your choosing the correct fist is that when you choose it, you must not only point to it but *believe* that the coin is in that hand and not in the other (a lie detector will monitor your reaction)." I take it that most of us would be in for some hard times.

The last illustration nicely brings out the difference between acting and believing. It is relatively easy to *do* crazy things if there are practical grounds for them. We can easily act when the evidence is equally balanced (for example, call heads while the coin is in the air), but believing is typically more passive in nature, not a doing, but a guide to doing. The phenomenological argument shows that volitionalism is abnormal and bizarre, but it does not rule out the possibility of acquiring beliefs by voliting.

Another possible use of the will regarding belief acquisition needs to be addressed: the veto phenomenon. Some philosophers (Locke and Holyer) hold that the will can act as a veto on belief inclinations, halting would-be beliefs in the process of formation. This is a negative type of volition, for it does not claim that we can actually attain beliefs by the fiat of the will, only that we can prevent some from getting hold of us by putting up a doxastic roadblock just in the nick of time. What seems to occur is this:

1. S entertains proposition *p* (this is sometimes under our direct control).

2. S is inclined to believe that *p* or S suspects that *p* (this is not normally under our control).

3. The veto phenomenon occurs by raising doubts, suspending judgment, or "tabling" the proposition under focus.

4. S looks at further evidence or looks at the old evidence in a fresh light and forms a judgment. (Although the "looking" is under our direct control, the "seeing" or judgment is not.)

Is the veto event under our direct control, or is it caused by a counterclaim, a sense that there is counterevidence, or a sense that there is something wrong with our first inclination? For example, I am interviewing Candidate A for a vacant position in our department and have a strong inclination to believe her to be the right person for the job, but I suddenly remember that we still have two candidates to interview and realize that my inclination to believe that "A is *the* best candidate for the job" is founded on insufficient evidence. I must modify the proposition to state that she is a good candidate. Here it seems that another belief (that there are other good candidates still to be interviewed) comes into play and forces the other belief aside. No act of will is present to my consciousness. But even if I do feel a will to believe or withhold judgment in these sorts of cases, it doesn't follow that the will causes the belief. It may well be an accompaniment. Nevertheless, there are other types of vetoing where I may clearly prevent a belief from forming on the basis of the evidence. Consider the situation where John tells Joan that her father has embezzled some money from his company, and before he is finished presenting the evidence Joan stops him, crying, "Stop it, please, I can't bear to hear any more!" It seems plausible to suppose that something analogous to her stopping John from providing the incriminating evidence that would cause a belief to form, may also occur within us when we begin to consider evidence for a position we deplore. We may inwardly turn away from the evidence, focus on something else, and so fail to form a belief in the matter. This seems a case of self-deception, but in any case, the veto power seems to be sometimes under our direct control. Nevertheless, it does not show that we actually can acquire beliefs by voliting, but shows only that the will has a negative role to play in preventing beliefs from fixing themselves in us.

Cartesia

Although our analysis hasn't ruled out the possibility of voliting, it does support the claim that there is something peculiar about the phenomenon. If voliters exist, they are like people who can wiggle their ears, blush, vomit, or regulate their heartbeats at will. But unlike these volitional phenomena, believing at will seems to involve a conceptual confusion. Typically, I take it, believing is representational in nature, purporting to mirror our world and our relations with the world, so that every instance of volitional–nonrepresentational believing deviates from that relationship in a fundamental way. To see this better, imagine a society, Cartesia, whose members all volit. They attain beliefs as we engage in coughing, both voluntarily and involuntarily. Regarding every proposition, voliting will be a serious consideration. When a member of Cartesia hears that her spouse has been unfaithful, she must ask herself, not simply what the evidence is for this charge but whether she has an obligation to believe that her spouse is faithful in spite of sufficient evidence. Such people have no difficulty in making Kierkegaardian leaps of faith against sufficient evidence, let alone where the evidence is counterbalanced. For example, when they throw coins up into the air, they form convictions about the way the coins will land. No doubt they will have a strong normative component regarding voliting in order to regulate the activity. There will have to be elaborate classification systems covering obligatory volits, permissible volits, little white volits, immoral volits, and illegal volits punishable by the state.

Such a society is hard to imagine, but in it there would have to be a distinction between voliting-type beliefs and nonvoliting-type beliefs. The latter alone would be treated as reliable for action guidance, voliting types of belief being tolerated mainly in the private domain, where no public issue is at stake. In other words, the nonvoliting belief acquisitions would be treated very much the way beliefs are treated in our society, as action guides, which as such should be reliable mirrors of the evidence.

Perhaps we can give an evolutionary account of the nonvolitional nature of belief acquisition. To survive, animals need a fairly accurate and spontaneous representation of the world. The cat's action of catching the mouse and the primitive human's running away from the bear would not be aided by intervening volits between the representations of the mouse and the bear and the beliefs that the representations were accurate, nor would it be helpful for us to have to decide to believe our perceptions under normal conditions. Basically, we are credulous creatures. For most believings, most of the time, *contra* Descartes and Kierkegaard, the will has nothing to do with the matter. Beliefs come naturally as that which purports to represent the way the world is so that our actions may have a reliable map by which to steer.

The "Logic of Belief" Argument Against Volitionalism

The phenomenological argument gets its force by attacking the second characteristic of an act of voliting: the act must be done in full consciousness. If my analysis is correct, voliting must be a highly abnormal phenomenon, if it exists in any positive form at all. However, I have not ruled out the possibility of some people voliting. In this sense, my analysis has resembled Hume's account in which it is a contingent matter that we do not obtain beliefs by fiat of the will. A second argument will now be advanced that attacks volitionalism primarily on the basis of its third characteristic: that it must be done independently of evidential or truth considerations (I use these terms synonymously to stand for evidence in the broad sense of the term, including the self-evidence of basic beliefs). I call this argument the "logic of belief" argument. It states that the notion of volitional believing involves a conceptual confusion, that it is broadly a logical mistake. It argues there is something incoherent in stating one can obtain or sustain a belief in full consciousness *simply* by a basic act of the will; that is, by purposefully disregarding the evidence connection. This strategy does not altogether rule out the possibility of obtaining beliefs by voliting in less than full consciousness (not truly voliting), but asserts that when full consciousness enters

the "belief" will wither from one's noetic structure. One cannot believe in full consciousness "that p and I believe that p for other than truth considerations." If you understand that to believe p is to believe p is true and *wishing never makes it so*, then there is simply no epistemic reason for believing p. Suppose I say I believe I have $1,000,000 in my checking account, and suppose when you point out to me that there is no reason to believe this, I respond, "I know that there is not the slightest reason to suppose there is $1,000,000 in my checking account, but I believe it anyway, simply because I want to." If you were convinced I was not joking, you would probably conclude I was insane or didn't know what I was talking about.

If I said that I somehow find myself believing I have $1,000,000 but don't know why, we might suppose a memory trace of having deposited $1,000,000 into my account, or evidence to that effect in the guise of an intuition, caused my belief. But you would be stumped if I denied that and said, "No, I don't have any memory trace regarding placing $1,000,000 into my account. In fact, I'm sure I never placed $1,000,000 into the account. I just find it good to believe it's there, so I have chosen to believe it."

The point is that because beliefs just are about the way the world is and are made true (or false) depending on the way the world is, it is a confusion to believe that any given belief is true simply on the basis of being willed. As soon as the believer, assuming he (or she) understands these basic concepts, discovers the basis of his belief—as being caused by the will alone—he must drop the belief. In this regard, saying, "I believe p but only because I want to believe it," has the same incoherence attached to it as G. E. Moore's paradoxical "I believe p but it is false that p." Structurally, neither are strictly logical contradictions, but both show an incoherence that might be called broadly contradictory.

Robert Audi has objected that my argument only has merit if one supposes the believer is rational, for an irrational believer could continue to believe that p in some other sense. However, I think that there is something wrong with describing irrational persons as having a belief here at all. There is a fundamental confusion lurking in their noetic structure that disqualifies them from having that notion ascribed to them in the full sense of the word. That is, it is not necessarily the case that, just because S believes he believes *p*, S *actually* believes *p*, especially if he (or she) also consciously believes not-*p* at the same time. Although we can have contradictory beliefs without knowing that we do, it is hard to understand what a fully conscious contradictory belief would be. In like manner, the fully conscious voliter isn't believing anything when he (or she) believes he has acquired a belief simply by voliting. It is as though he were saying, "To believe anything is to believe it because of some evidence (even self-evidence) E, but to believe what I am now believing is believed nonevidentially." What is being believed?

My formulation builds minimal understanding of the concept of belief and truth or evidence into its premises, but if the reader is sympathetic to Audi's criticism, we can modify our formula to apply only to rational believing (leaving aside whether irrational believing *in this sense* is possible).

But even if the believer can believe it is his (or her) will causing the belief in cases of doxastic incontinence, the argument would show the believer could not believe that his belief was being caused or sustained in the right way. The rational believer, in full consciousness, would see there must be a truth connection between states of affairs and the belief by virtue of which the belief is true, so the will is essentially unnecessary for the belief—although it may be necessary in order to get into a proper state of mind where he will be able to perceive the evidence perspicuously. Just as there is an instrumental relation between opening one's eyes and seeing whatever one sees, but an intrinsic relation between states of affairs in the world and what one sees, so likewise there is only an instrumental relationship between willing to believe *p* and believing *p*, whereas there is an intrinsic relationship between state of affairs S by virtue of which *p* is true and my belief that *p*. Once the believer realizes willing never makes it so, he or she must give up the belief the will is decisively or intrinsically sustaining the belief *p*, although he may believe there is an instrumental relationship. At least, the believer will not be able to believe that the will *alone* is causing him to believe *p*, but that the evidence is the deciding factor.

There is a clear difference between acting, which is volitional, and acquiring a belief, which is not volitional but an event or a happening.

Believing is evidential, in that to believe *p* is to presuppose that I have evidence for *p* or that *p* is self-evident or evident to the senses. I need not have a developed concept of evidence to believe this. Children do not have a full concept of belief, but they tacitly suppose something like this. On reflection, rational adults seem to recognize the connection between a belief and objective states of affairs. In a sense, belief that *p* seems to imply the thought of a causal chain stretching back from the belief to a primary relationship with the world and so faithfully representing the world. We may have more or less confidence about the preciseness of the way our beliefs represent the world, but some degree seems implicit in every belief state.

Another way to make this same point about the evidentiality of belief is to define propositional belief in terms of a subjective probability index. All believing is believing to a degree of confidence. You may test the approximate degree to which you believe a proposition by imagining how surprised you would be if you found out that the particular belief in question turned out to be false. Suppose we had a way of quantifying the strength of our beliefs by means of a "belief meter." The meter has two rubber balls wired to it, which, when the balls are squeezed, measures the pressure of the squeezes. The subject holds a ball in each hand and is instructed to squeeze the ball in his (or her) right hand when he believes the proposition, and to squeeze the ball in his left hand when he believes the proposition to be false, and to refrain from squeezing when he believes the proposition to be neither true nor false. In addition, the subject is instructed to squeeze the appropriate ball with a pressure appropriate to the *degree* with which he believes the proposition in question. A certain amount of experimentation may be necessary to work the correlations out, but accuracy will be approximated by the help of a truth serum. In this way we might be able to quantify our beliefs into a subjective probability index. For example, it might turn out that Ann discovers she only believes God exists to a probability of 0.6, whereas she believes it will rain today to a probability of 0.8. It might also turn out that Ann discovers she had deceived herself into thinking she had a deep conviction about God's existence, whereas she really only weakly believes in God's existence. (Of course, she could doubt the reliability of the belief meter, but we may suppose it has an excellent track record.)

In principle, I see no reason against the possibility of rough belief quantification just described, but the point is that we already have a satisfactory notion of subjective probability in terms of the relative degrees with which we believe propositions. If believing were the result of our immediate willings, it would not be about the probability of states of affairs obtaining, but simply about our desires. It would be the case that I could come to a judgment that the probability of p on the evidence E was 0.5 and via a volit conclude it was 0.6. Could I in full consciousness make such a leap? It seems as possible as believing "2 + 2 = 4" and then deliberately at the same time believing "2 + 2 = 5."

It may be objected that this argument implies we must have a concept of probability, but I think we all do have a notion of degrees of belief that entails a rough notion of subjective probability in the manner described. If this argument is sound, the interesting thing is that not only can we not volit a belief, but we cannot even volit a change in the degree with which we believe a proposition. We cannot increase the strength of our belief that p from 0.6 to 0.65 simply by a fiat of the will.

The "logic of belief" argument has not ruled out the logical possibility of voliting but simply rules out as logically odd (in the wider sense of the term) the possibility of acquiring a belief in full consciousness by a fiat of the will without regard to truth considerations. It does not rule out the possibility of obtaining the belief in less than full consciousness or indirectly. The phenomena in these cases seem similar to that of self-deception, where one is not fully aware of what one truly believes. Once someone discovers that he (or she) has self-deceived himself, the logic of the discovery seems to entail the giving up of the false "belief" (the belief the person thought he or she had on a conscious level). Likewise, once someone realizes that the only basis for believing that p is the wanting p to be true, the belief must wither. Hence, if someone could come to have a belief through directly willing to have it, once he (or she) reflected on the acquisition and discovered its illegitimate origin, the person would give it up (unless, of course, he now had evidence for it). He would see on reflection that the purported belief reflects only the content of his will. It has the same status as a product of the imagination.

Consider this similarity between imagining and willing to believe. Take for example, vivid imaginer Imogene, who gets so carried away with her imagination that she sometimes believes her imagination reports. While sitting bored to death in her logic class, she fantasizes that she is swimming in the Bahamas or is being embraced by Warren Beatty. She imagines these things so vividly that for the moment she believes that they are really happening, until the teacher rudely calls on her and breaks the spell of her daydream, thus shattering her transient "beliefs." Perhaps many of our beliefs formed through the imagination are more subtle than this, and that we never discover; but when we do discover that a belief has its basis in the imagination, we discard it as worthless—and we do so automatically and not by a volit. But voliting and imagining seem to display the very same logic regarding belief acquisition. Both are acquired independently of evidential considerations.

Of course, it is possible that a person may regard his or her wants about reality as counting as *evidence* for propositions. For example, someone might say, "I have found that whenever I want a proposition to be true, amazingly it generally turns out to be so." Here wanting would indirectly cause belief, not by voliting, but rather by being regarded as reliable evidence, a type of credible testimony. It would still be the case that what causes the believer to believe is evidential and not simply the will's fiat.

If my analysis is correct, there is a deep conceptual confusion in self-consciously believing of any proposition that it has originated through a volit and/or that what sustains one's belief is one's will.[3]

I conclude that voliting seems both psychologically aberrant and conceptually confused. It is psychologically problematic because the feature of demanding full consciousness attaches to acts of will. It is conceptually confused because it neglects the evidential aspect of conscious belief acquisition and sustainment.

II Indirect Volitionalism and the Ethics of Belief

Indirectly believing does involve the will. I have argued that we cannot normally believe anything at all simply by willing to do so, for believing aims at truth and is not a basic act or a direct product of the will. If we could believe whatever we chose to believe simply by willing to do so, belief would not be about reality but about our wants. Nevertheless, the will does play an important indirect role in believing. Many of the beliefs that we arrive at are finally the results of our policy decisions. Although believing itself is not an act, our acts determine the sorts of beliefs we end up with. It is primarily because we judge that our beliefs are to some significant degree the indirect results of our actions that we speak of being responsible for them. Although we cannot be said to be directly responsible for them, as though they were actions, we can be said to be indirectly responsible for many of them. If we had chosen differently, if we had been better moral agents, paid attention to the evidence, and so forth, we would have different beliefs than we in fact do have.

To be sure, we are not responsible for all our beliefs, and the degree of responsibility seems to vary in proportion to the amount of evidence available at different times and our ability to attend properly to that evidence. For example, the person who pays attention to a certain matter often comes to have more accurate beliefs than the inattentive person. Attention is generally within our direct control. As long as we agree that the inattentive person could have acted differently, could have been attentive if he (or she) had really wanted to, we can conclude that the inattentive person is responsible for not having the true beliefs he might have had. In the same way we can conclude that the attentive person is responsible for the beliefs he or she has.

Being (indirectly) responsible for our beliefs indicates that praise and blame attach indirectly to our epistemic states, that indirectly beliefs are morally assessable. It may be that I have many beliefs I ought not to have. If I had been a better person, learned to investigate certain matters with the right categories, I might now be endowed with a more accurate system of beliefs and believe many of my present beliefs in different degrees of confidence from my present state of belief.

Many philosophers reject the notion of an ethics of belief. Mill, James, and Meiland believe that there are no special doxastic moral duties. Hume and Price argue that there are only counsels of prudence. Price puts it thus:

But even if it were in our power to be wholly rational all of the time, it still would not follow that there is anything morally blameworthy about assenting unreasonably (against the evidence or without regard to the evidence) or that we ought to be chastised for doing so. There is nothing wicked about such assents. It is however true, and important, that unreasonable assent is contrary to our *long term interest*. It is to our long term interest to believe true propositions rather than false ones. And if we assent reasonably (i.e. in accordance with the evidence), it is likely that in the long run the propositions we believe will be more often true than false.[4]

The only "ought" regarding belief acquisition is a prudential ought. A person is free to seek whatever goals he (or she) desires: happiness, salvation, convenience, aesthetic pleasure, and so forth. It is simply in your long-term best interest generally to seek to have true beliefs. However, if you find yourself inclined to sacrifice truth for some other goal, you have every right to do so. We may call this the *libertarian view of doxastic responsibility*. It affirms that believing is a purely private matter. Mill says that each person must be accorded "absolute freedom of opinion on all subjects practical and speculative."[5]

One may readily recognize the virtues of this position. Not many of us want to see totalitarian thought reforms, brainwashing, and government intervention into personal beliefs, in order to help others acquire "true beliefs." The libertarian position is right to emphasize human autonomy with regard to our private selves, and it may even be the case that it is a good thing to have a plurality of opinions in a society. Nevertheless, libertarian-prudentialist doctrine is false: *It sells the truth short*. It does so on two counts: it underestimates the significance of truth for the individual him- or herself, and it ignores the social dimension of truth seeking. Personhood, involving a high degree of autonomy, entails respect for highly justified beliefs. Socially, truth seeking is important, for unless a society has accurate information many of its goals are not likely to be reached. I develop these ideas in the following analysis.

Perhaps the clearest account of a volitional stance on the ethics of belief is Jack Meiland's article "What Ought We to Believe," in which

Meiland argues that not only is it sometimes morally *permissible* to believe against the evidence, but that it is sometimes morally *obligatory* to do so. In all cases of belief acquisition "extra-factual considerations are relevant."[6] After presenting Meiland's position against a strict evidentialism and in favor of prescriptive volitional belief acquisition, I show what is wrong with Meiland's position, showing that what is new is not true and what is true is not new. Specifically, I contend there is a more moderate form of evidentialism that escapes Meiland's criticisms and thus provides a middle way between the two extremes of rigid evidentialism and volitionalism. I outline what such a moderate evidentialism with regard to the ethics of belief looks like.

Rigid evidentialism states, following Meiland's interpretation, that one ought to believe propositions if and only if they are backed by sufficient evidence. This position, which, according to Meiland, is found in Descartes, Locke, Clifford, and Chisholm, is largely impervious to subjective factors in belief formation. Chisholm's formulation is cited as a clear expression of this position:

1.   Anyone having just the evidence in question is warranted in accepting the conclusion.
2.   I am in a position of having that evidence.
3.   Therefore, I am justified in accepting the conclusion. (p. 19)

On this account, everyone is epistemically required to come to the same conclusion, given the same evidence. The argument for this position can be spelled out as follows. Suppose Person A is justified on Evidence E in believing that *p*. Suppose, further, that Person B has exactly the same evidence as A has but believes that not-*p*. On the face of it, it seems contradictory to say that although A is justified in believing *p* on E, B is justified in believing not-*p* on E. This suggests that E both justifies belief *p* and not-*p*, but this defies our very notion of justification. Hence, the evidentialist concludes that not both A and B can be justified in believing what they believe on E. If A is justified in believing *p* on E, then B is not, and vice versa. Yet anyone who has the evidence A has is in the same state of being justified as A is, whether he or she knows it or not.

What this argument for evidentialism neglects is a notion of the larger context into which apparently similar evidence comes. Just as a farmer, a

real estate dealer, and an artist, all looking at the "same" field, may not see the same field, so evidence always is relative to a person's individuating background beliefs, capacities to interpret data, and expectations. Meiland, rightly, points out that subjective factors play a strong role in our interpretation of evidence and in the formation of beliefs, but oversteps the evidence when he interprets this subjectivism to include direct volitionalism, the acquisition of beliefs through conscious choices. Classical evidentialism may be too rigid in its notion of justification. It neglects psychological factors, which enter into every belief acquisition. All believing is believing from a perspective, and any type of evidentialism that neglects this perspectival element may be designated "rigid" in that it lacks a proper appreciation for the complexity of evidence gathering and assembling.

A second important feature of Meiland's position on the ethics of belief is his subsuming epistemic duties under the heading of general ethical duties. That is, we have no special epistemic duties that are not already covered by ethical principles *simpliciter*. If we claim that someone has a duty to believe some proposition, we must give moral reasons for that duty, not epistemic ones. Meiland argues on utilitarian grounds that it is often morally required that we act against so-called epistemic requirements of believing according to sufficient evidence. Here Meiland holds a stronger position than James, Chisholm, or Nathanson, who allow for voliting only when the evidence is insufficient, as a sort of a tie breaker.[7] Meiland maintains that we are sometimes obligated to get ourselves to believe propositions even when we have sufficient evidence to the contrary. However, he does not go as far as Kierkegaard in allowing for believing against even conclusive evidence. When we have conclusive evidence, it is not in our power to believe against the evidence.

The sort of sufficient evidence for a proposition against which we may believe is illustrated in the example of the wife who finds lipstick on her husband's handkerchief, a blonde strand of hair on his suit, and a crumpled piece of paper with a telephone number on it in a woman's handwriting in his pocket. This would constitute sufficient evidence (on the rigid evidentialist account) that the husband is having an affair with another woman and would normally cause the wife to believe that her husband was being unfaithful. However, the wife may have good reason for rejecting the evidence even though she admits it is sufficient to justify belief in her husband's unfaithfulness. She rejects the belief, however, for pragmatic reasons. Suppose the wife closely examines the evidence and decides that if she comes to believe what it points to (or continues to believe that her husband is unfaithful), their marriage will be ruined and great unhappiness will ensue. If, however, she can get herself to believe that her husband is faithful, in spite of the evidence to the contrary, the marriage probably will be saved. She reasons that her husband will very likely get over his infatuation and return to his marital commitment. Suppose she has good evidence for this second belief. Should she not acquire the belief in her husband's faithfulness, in hope of saving her marriage? Perhaps she also justifiably believes that undergoing this volitional process, of somehow acquiring a belief by willing to have it despite the evidence, will do no permanent damage to her noetic structure. After acquiring the belief and letting the belief direct her actions, the marriage will be saved; and after the marriage is saved, she will recall the process she underwent to save the marriage. Now, however, she will be in a position to live with the unwelcome evidence and even speak openly with her husband about it. Given these factors, is not the wife morally obligated to take steps to obtain the belief in her husband's faithfulness?

Unlike the usual volitionalist strategy of advocating voluntary believing only in extreme cases, Meiland makes the rather daring claim that in every case of believing where there is insufficient evidence or sufficient evidence for an unwelcome proposition, extrafactual considerations are relevant considerations (p. 21). Although Meiland believes that believing is within the direct control of our will (except where there is conclusive evidence), he is content to let his case rest on the possibility that we may indirectly cause ourselves to believe against the evidence.

I have four objections to Meiland's position on the ethics of belief: (1) his notion of evidentialism is overly rigid and ignores a broader form of evidentialism that obviates the need for a volitional alternative in most cases of believing; (2) a minor criticism is that Meiland fails to make clear why we may have an obligation to believe against the evidence when it is sufficient but may not have an obligation to believe against the evidence when it

is conclusive; (3) his position undervalues the importance of having reliable belief-forming mechanisms and misconstrues the nature of belief acquisitions; and (4) if Meiland's position is interpreted by the principle of charity into making merely the weak claim that sometimes we have a moral duty to override our duty of seeking to have true, justified beliefs, then there is nothing new in his position. Let us look briefly at each of these criticisms.

First, Meiland is correct in criticizing the Clifford-Chisholm line of evidentialism, which focuses on a nonperspectival relationship between evidence and justification. This position seems to neglect or underemphasize the point that evidence is person-relative, so that each person views the data with a different noetic endowment. The Aristotelian and the nominalist who hear the argument from contingency for the existence of God, will each view its soundness differently. But, given their different worldviews, each may well be justified in coming to the belief he does. Although there may be such a thing as *propositional warrant,* which provides objective evidence for a given proposition, justification has mainly to do with what is reasonable for a given person to believe, given his or her noetic structure, background beliefs, ability to pay attention, ability to weigh evidence impartially, ability to interpret the evidence according to certain rules, and the like. A person living in the Middle Ages may well have been warranted in believing that the earth is flat, even though there may have been objective evidence to support the proposition that it is round, evidence that anyone in an ideal situation would have.

Meiland posits an unnecessary dichotomy between objective (sufficient) evidence and subjective factors where the will determines the belief. The only alternatives are not rigid evidentialism and volitionalism. Simply because objective evidence is not the only necessary factor in belief acquisition does not mean that the will can or should decide the matter. One must take into account such subjective factors as unconscious wants and past learning that have been internalized so that we are not aware of the information processing our subconscious self is undertaking. For example, chicken sexers, while failing the strong evidentialist's test of being able to give an account of their evidence, nevertheless probably have evidence for the reliable judgments they consistently make. Given their high success rate in identifying the sex of chicks, it is more reasonable to say that they know but cannot tell us even themselves how they know the chick's sex than to attribute their success to acts of the will (or simply luck).

I am suggesting that a more moderate version of evidentialism includes a recognition of subjective factors in belief acquisition without admitting that the will directly causes belief or that it should cause it indirectly. We don't need to bring in volitions to account for the subjective element in belief formation. An alternative interpretation of one of Meiland's examples will illustrate what I mean. Imagine a defense attorney who agrees with the prosecution and the jury that there is sufficient evidence against his client but, who, nevertheless, continues to believe in his client's innocence despite the evidence. His belief is vindicated years later. This is supposed to show that the attorney has a right to believe his client is innocent in spite of the evidence where there are pragmatic grounds for doing so. I doubt the will is directly involved here at all, and I believe the attorney's belief can be accounted for through my modified version of evidentialism. The attorney, Smith, hears and sees all the evidence E against his client, Brown. He concludes on the basis of E that Brown is probably guilty. But he pauses, introspects, and senses some resistance from within to that conclusion. He finds himself with a tendency to reject the first conclusion in favor of a belief that Brown is innocent. Perhaps for a time he vacillates between two belief tendencies, or he experiences undulating alternate belief states. When he is in court or looking at the evidence in private, he feels a subtle certainty that Brown is guilty, but when he faces Brown, looks him in the eye, and speaks to him, he senses that he must be wrong in believing the evidence that points to Brown's guilt. Perhaps we can say (following Price) Smith half-believes Brown is innocent and half-believes he is guilty, the belief states alternating so frequently that he cannot fully make up his mind. Perhaps the feeling Brown is innocent finally wins out in the battle of Smith's mind. Meiland would explain this alternation and conclusion as making a decision to believe. I doubt whether this description is correct and suggest it is more likely Smith's previous experience with people, especially defendants, both innocent and guilty, has caused him to form reliable beliefs about characteristic features and behaviors of the

guilty and innocent, including the "seemingly innocent" and the "seemingly guilty." He is unaware of this large repository of internalized evidence and cannot formulate it. Here, we want to say Smith's reliability at judging character and legal evidence warrants our saying he has internalized skills and sets of inductive generalizations (for example, judging from certain characteristic looks on innocent faces to a conclusion of particular innocence) that cause individual belief occurrences. Smith has data and skills that the jury does not, that a less competent attorney does not, and that the judge may not have.

One can generalize from this case and say with regard to any proposition, p, and for any person S, that if S finds himself (or herself) believing p, the belief that p is *prima facie* evidence for p itself relative to S; that is, S is *prima facie* justified in believing p. It may not be very strong justification, and S may be forced to weaken his hold on p when he cannot defend p, but it is some evidence, enough to start with. Furthermore, to the extent that S finds himself a reliable judge in a given area, to exactly that extent is he justified in holding on to a belief tenaciously in the light of evidence to the contrary. Modified evidentialism accepts intuitive judgments as playing an evidential role in believing. If my account of evidentialism is correct, then the motivation for much of Meiland's volitionalism is dissipated. Simply saying that subjective factors enter into our belief acquisitions is not sufficient to justify volitionalism, for in a sense all believing involves subjective factors that are causative in belief formation. (This leads to the second criticism of Meiland's position.)

The *second* criticism of Meiland's position focuses on his distinctions among insufficient evidence, sufficient evidence, and conclusive evidence in relation to the ability to volit. According to Meiland, it is only possible to volit (or indirectly get ourselves into a belief state through volitional means) when the evidence is not conclusive. Hence, it can only be morally required that we volit in those cases. But unless we reduce "conclusive evidence" to the trivially true definiens "that which we cannot will ourselves not to believe," we seem to have a problem; for if I have a moral obligation to believe (through volitional means) against sufficient evidence, why can I not have an obligation to believe (via those same means) against conclusive evidence? The answer cannot be simply that it is easier to do this in the first case. It may be that we must spend more time and effort getting ourselves to believe against conclusive evidence, going to a better hypnotist or whatever, but if our utilitarian cost–benefit analysis specifies that the psychic price is worth paying (for example, we may be able to save our children's sanity or lives by keeping our marriage together by believing that our spouses are faithful even though we catch them in bed committing adultery), then, on Meiland's analysis, we should pay that price. I see no criterion to distinguish between believing against evidence where it is only sufficient and believing against the evidence where it is conclusive. If Meiland responds that there is a likelihood that such manipulations would mess up the subject's mind, we should respond, "What makes you so confident this isn't what happens in every case of purposefully getting ourselves to believe against or in the absence of sufficient evidence?" This leads to the most serious criticism of volitional positions on the ethics of belief.

Third, my main criticism of positions like Meiland's (including William James's) has to do with the importance of having well-justified beliefs and truth seeking in general. We generally believe these two concepts are closely related, so the best way to assure ourselves of having true beliefs is to seek to develop one's belief-forming mechanisms in such ways as to become good judges of various types of evidence, attaining the best possible justification of our beliefs. The value of having the best justified beliefs possible can be defended both on deontological grounds with regard to the individual and on teleological or utilitarian grounds regarding the society as a whole. The deontological argument is connected with our notion of autonomy. To be an autonomous person is to have a high degree of warranted beliefs available on which to base one's actions. There is a tendency to lower freedom of choice as one shrinks the repertoire of well-justified beliefs regarding a plan of action, and because it is a generally accepted moral principle that it is wrong to lessen autonomy or personhood, it is wrong to lessen the degree of justification of one's beliefs on important matters. Hence, there is a general presumption against beliefs by willing to have them. Cognitive voliting is a sort of lying or cheating in that it enjoins believing against what has the best guarantee of

being the truth. When a friend or doctor lies to a terminally ill patient about her condition, the patient is deprived of the best evidence available for making decisions about her limited future. She is being treated less than fully autonomously. Although a form of paternalism may sometimes be justified, there is always a presumption against it and in favor of truth telling. We even say that the patient has a right to know what the evidence points to. Cognitive voliting is a sort of lying to oneself, which, as such, decreases one's own freedom and personhood. It is a type of doxastic suicide that may only be justified in extreme circumstances. If there is something intrinsically wrong about lying (making it *prima facie* wrong), there is also something intrinsically wrong with cognitive voliting, either directly or indirectly. Whether it be Pascal, James, Meiland, Newman, or Kierkegaard, all prescriptive volitionalists (consciously or not) seem to undervalue the principle of truthfulness and its relationship to personal autonomy.

The utilitarian, or teleological, argument against cognitive voliting is fairly straightforward. General truthfulness is a desideratum without which society cannot function. Without it, language itself would not be possible, because it depends on faithful use of words and sentences to stand for appropriately similar objects and states of affairs. Communication depends on a general adherence to accurate reporting. More specifically, it is very important that a society have true beliefs with regard to important issues, so that actions based on beliefs have a firm basis.

The doctor who cheated her way through medical school and who, as a consequence, lacks appropriate beliefs about certain symptoms, may endanger a patient's health. A politician who fails to take into consideration the amount of pollution being given off by large corporations that support his candidacy, may endanger the lives and health of his constituents. Even the passer-by who gives wrong information to a stranger who asks directions may seriously inconvenience the stranger. Here Clifford's point about believing against the evidence is well taken, despite its "all-too-robustious" tone (as James describes it). The shipowner who failed to make necessary repairs on his vessel and "chose" to believe that it was seaworthy, is guilty of the deaths of the passengers. "He had no right to believe on such evidence as was before him."[8] It is because beliefs are action guiding, maps by which we steer, and as such tend to cause actions, that society has a keen interest in our having the best-justified beliefs possible regarding important matters.

Nevertheless, Meiland might reply, while there may be a general duty to seek to have well-justified beliefs, there may be many cases where other considerations override our duty to believe according to the evidence. In fact, these cases may be so numerous that one is tempted to conclude (as Meiland does) that "extrafactual considerations" are relevant to every case of belief acquisition (and, following this logic, relevant to every case of maintaining each of our beliefs). The trouble with this response is that it ignores the sort of intention skill that truth seeking is. It is dispositional, a habit. If it is to be effective at all, it must be deeply engrained within us, so it is not at all easy to dispense with. The wife, if she has been properly brought up as a truth seeker, may simply not be able to believe against the evidence without going through elaborate conditioning processes that might seriously affect her personality and even her personal identity.

Furthermore, our beliefs do not exist in isolation from each other, so that to overthrow one belief may have reverberations throughout our entire noetic structure, affecting many of our other beliefs. Getting oneself to believe against the evidence that supports a belief that p, may upset our other justified beliefs q, r, and s, which in turn may affect still other beliefs. Cognitive voliting, as Bernard Williams has pointed out, "is like a revolutionary movement trying to extirpate the last remains of the *ancien regime*. The man gets rid of this belief that his son is dead, and then there is some belief which strongly implies that his son is dead, and that has to be got rid of. It might be that a project of this kind tends in the end to involve total destruction of the world of reality, to lead to paranoia."[9] After the wife succeeds in believing her husband is innocent, what is the effect of this on her noetic structure? What happens every time she looks at the suit on which the strand of hair was found or sees a handkerchief? What happens every time she sees a strand of blonde hair? every time she sees her husband talking to a blonde? every time she sees a telephone number? Must she repress memories and deny this is important evidence against her spouse's faithfulness? Do we have enough control over our knowledge about our unconscious selves to be able to predict the final result of volitional believing on our personality and character?

The utilitarian argument against volitional manipulation of our belief mechanisms might be stated this way.

1. Voliting is morally justified only if we have adequate evidence (acquired nonvolitionally) that it will result in better consequences than if we abstain from voliting.

2. But our noetic structure is such that we almost never do have adequate evidence it will produce better consequences.

3. Therefore, voliting is almost never morally justified.

We almost never know how we will be affected by frustrating and manipulating our normal belief-forming mechanisms. Our subconscious realm, where normal beliefs are formed, seems very complex, so that in attempting to influence it over one matter, we may cause unpredictable chain reactions within our noetic structure.

Of course, Meiland might well reply that if, on reflection, the cost is going to be this great, we ought not believe against sufficient evidence in most cases. Perhaps this is a satisfactory reply, and perhaps our main difference is merely one of emphasis: Meiland arguing against rigid evidentialism that makes objective justification an absolute duty and I arguing for a presumption of truth seeking, making it a very high moral duty. These are not incompatible views. However, I think there is more to our difference than this. The difference is rooted in two different views on how evidence is processed and of the possibility of consciously willing to have certain beliefs against what is taken to be good evidence. Meiland simply believes we have more control over our beliefs than I believe we do, and this difference results in a difference about the relevancy of volitional strategies.

Meiland has a pragmatic justification of belief that goes like this:

1. A has sufficient evidence for p (there is a strong inclination on A's part to believe p or A does believe p), but A also has nonevidential reasons for believing not-p.

2. A decides, after reflection, that it is morally permissible or obligatory to get himself into a position where he believes not-p.

3. A takes whatever steps are necessary in order to get into that position, and presumably, A comes to believe not-*p*.

There is something odd about this argument, for it raises the fundamental question (considered in Section I) of whether a rational person can consciously carry out a cognitive volit or sustain a belief while knowing that he or she has obtained the belief solely through a fiat of the will. For example, what happens when the wife, in Meiland's example, reflects on her belief that her husband is innocent? She looks at her belief and looks at the way it was brought about. Can she go on believing her husband is innocent despite the sufficient evidence to the contrary? There seems to be something incoherent about the phenomena of consciously acquiring or sustaining a belief regardless of the perceived evidence against the belief. This brings me to my final criticism of Meiland's position.

Fourth, Meiland may escape all my objections by arguing that while it is always relevant in principle to take pragmatic considerations into account in acquiring (and sustaining) beliefs, it may hardly ever be our actual duty. He may defend his flank by saying he merely wants to show that truth seeking (as the rigid evidentialist conceives of it) is not an absolute moral duty but is overridable in some instances. But if this is all he is saying, his position surely loses much of its brashness and excitement. It may be true, but it is hardly new. Most moral systems since W. D. Ross and including such unlikely bedfellows as Richard Brandt, William Frankena, R. M. Hare, and J. L. Mackie would agree that there are few, if any, moral absolutes, and that truth seeking is not a moral absolute (nonoverridable) but a strong *prima facie* duty. Meiland's position must be stronger than this to be interesting, but if it is stronger than this, it seems implausible.

Criteria for Morally Prescriptive Indirect Volitionalism

Let me conclude this essay by offering a set of criteria by which to decide when it is morally permissible to indirectly volit. I agree with Meiland against Clifford, Gale, and others who contend we ought never under any circumstances to get ourselves to believe anything where the evidence alone doesn't warrant it. Aiming at having all true or justified beliefs seems to be a moral duty, but not an absolute one. Under some conditions it might be overridden by other duties. Although instances of morally justified voliting (indirectly) are probably rare, there may be some. Meiland's example of the wife concerned with saving her marriage may indeed be such a case. Another may be the following. Suppose I gain some information about you that causes me to act in a way you perceive as harmful to your interests and suppose that I have obtained this information in a morally unacceptable way, say, by reading your diary or private correspondence, and that I would not have had this information had I not read this material. Suppose, further, there is a competent psychiatrist who can bring it about, at minimum risk, that I totally forget the information I possess about your private life. Or suppose there is a psychologically harmless pill that will do this same thing. Is it obvious that you would not have a right to demand I take the necessary steps to forget the memory belief I have? Perhaps a certain type of forgiveness involves getting ourselves, through autosuggestion, to forget in part the seriousness of the acts against us. Of course, self-creating beliefs seem the best examples of what may be morally permissible in this area. Suppose you must swim two miles to shore in order to save your life. You have never swum so far and have good evidence you can't do it. However, you reason that if you can get yourself to believe you can swim two miles, the confidence will somehow produce a physiological state giving you a better chance of swimming two miles (although not quite a 50 percent chance). Would you not be justified in getting yourself into that place?

If at times it is morally permissible or even obligatory to volit a belief against sufficient evidence, what conditions must be met? I suggest the following: a prudential condition and two utilitarian conditions (a general and a specific).

1. *A prudential requirement.* The justified volit would have to involve a nonvolitional cost–benefit analysis that might be undermined if the agent were not a dispositional evidentialist. The act must be seen as possible and worth doing on the evidence available. There must be some morally acceptable benefit that outweighs the cost involved in getting the new belief by voliting.

2. *A general utility requirement.* Others must not be significantly harmed by this act, or their harm must not outweigh the benefits that would accrue to the agent, and the benefits must be normally acceptable. Again, the leap is parasitical on evidentialism, for a mistake may be dangerous. For example, if I get myself to believe the world will end shortly (for religious reasons) and then I become secretary of the interior, I may treat the environment so poorly as to hasten the end of the world.

3. *The chain of deception requirement.* This is a special instance of the utility requirement. In getting yourself into a state S where you will believe *p*, which you presently do not believe on the evidence, you will be responsible for a chain of unnecessary false reports. That is, if you were to tell others *p* was the case, you would be lying. Although the self that actually reports *p* will not be lying, that self is spreading a falsehood (or reporting falsely), becoming an unreliable witness and starting a possible chain of false reports. In essence, in willing to deceive your future self, who will sincerely report to others, you are taking on the responsibility for deceiving others. As the beginning of a chain of misinformation, only the most extreme grounds would seem to justify the volit.

If, however, you can make a cost–benefit analysis in the most rigorously evidentialist fashion and can determine that the volit is both psychologically possible and worth the cost of deceiving yourself and possibly others, then perhaps the volit is justified. If you are sure you are not going to bring harm to others or lessen their autonomy significantly and that you will not harm your children by being an unreliable witness, then you might well be justified in acquiring a belief by willing to have it and doing what is necessary to bring it about. But who can be so certain, given the uncertainty of how all these factors will work out in life? James's stranded mountain climber at the edge of the gorge certainly seems to be, for his options are limited. The person who read your diary may also be justified in trying to forget his or her belief. Perhaps the hermit who lives alone on an island is justified, though perhaps he or she has an obligation to place a sign on the dock, warning people who approach that they trespass at their own risk, for the inhabitant has engaged regularly in voliting and may seriously misinform them on certain matters. For the rest of us, almost all the time, indirect

voliting will not be a relevant consideration, but will be an imprudent and immoral act. Because truth matters, and because we can take steps to acquire habits making true beliefs more likely, there is an ethics of belief.

Notes

[1]Descartes, *Meditations,* trans. E. Haldane and G. R. T. Ross (Cambridge, England: Cambridge University Press, 1911), Meditation IV and Replies, p. 175.

[2]Thomas Aquinas, *Summa Theologica* Part II, Q. 4, Art. 2; Søren Kierkegaard, *Philosophical Fragments,* trans. D. Swenson (Princeton, NJ: Princeton University Press, 1962), p. 104; John Henry Newman, *An Essay in Aid of a Grammar of Assent* (Westminster, MD: Christian Classics, 1973), p. 232; William James, "The Will to Believe" in *Essays in Pragmatism* (New York: Haefner, 1969) [Reading X.3 in this anthology]; Joseph Pieper, *Belief and Faith* (New York: Pantheon Press, 1956), p. 25f; Roderick Chisholm, "Lewis' Ethics of Belief" in Paul Schilpp, ed., *The Philosophy of C. I. Lewis* (Peru, IL: Open Court, 1968); Jack Meiland, "What Ought We to Believe" (*American Philosophical Quarterly, 17,* no. 1 (January 1980), 15–24; and Robert Holyer, "Belief and Will Revisited" (*Dialogue,* 1983).

[3]There is one final objection to my thesis that we do not (normally) acquire beliefs by voliting. This objection centers on the phenomenon of self-creative or self-verifying beliefs, the activity described by William James in his classic essay "The Will to Believe," whereby one's deciding to believe is causally operative in creating a state of affairs that makes the belief true. This, the objector claims, seems like a normal case of volitionalism. Suppose you are going to play a game of chess. Your using autosuggestion to get into a state of mind where you believe you will win actually plays a causal role in your winning (it may, of course, have the reverse effect through causing overconfidence). James's own example (with my filling out an interpretation) is of a man trapped at the edge of a crevasse, overlooking a yawning gorge. He calculates that a successful leap is improbable, but it will increase in probability in proportion to his convincing himself that he must get himself to believe what an impartial look at the evidence will not allow. So he volits the belief. Or consider a student who loves philosophy and whose self-identity is centered on the goal of being a good philosopher. She doubts whether she will ever become such, but believes that her chances of becoming good will be increased by believing that she will reach that goal. So she apparently volits and believes without sufficient evidence that she will become a good philosopher. Because of this confidence, she succeeds where she would have otherwise failed. These sort of cases have been used as counterexamples to my arguments against volitionalism.

Two things can be said about such cases. The first is that they are not counterexamples to the thesis that we cannot acquire beliefs by fiat of the will. It seems reasonable to say that a deliberation process went on in each of these cases in which the will *indirectly* caused belief by refocusing the mind on favorable evidence rather than on the unfavorable evidence. No volit is necessary.

For example, caught as I am before the yawning gorge, I ask myself, how in the world am I to attain the presumably necessary belief (which I don't have) that I can jump the gorge. I cannot just acquire it by a fiat, so I hit on the idea of thinking of all the successful long jumps I made in grammar school. I then imagine myself a great Olympic track star. Perhaps a little self-hypnosis helps here. I focus on appropriate successes (real or imaginary), block out negative thoughts (if I can), and finally self-deceive myself to the point where I believe that I believe that I can leap over the crevasse. But all this illustrates is a case of indirect volitional control, not direct control over believing. I have a goal, plan a policy of action, and indirectly come to attain that goal.

The second thing to say is that this example seems to be an instance where a form of self-deception has salutary effects.

[4] H. H. Price, *Belief* (London: Allen & Unwin, 1967), p. 238.

[5] John Stuart Mill, *On Liberty* (London: 1859). Mill continues, "the appropriate region of human liberty . . . comprises liberty of conscience in the most comprehensive sense: Liberty of thought and feeling, absolute freedom of opinion on all subjects practical and speculative, scientific, moral or theological." The statement is ambiguous, seeming to conflate the right to be protected from doxastic coercion and the right to manipulate our minds as we see fit.

[6] Jack Meiland, "What Ought We to Believe, or the Ethics of Belief Revisited," *American Philosophical Quarterly 17* (January 1980), 15–24. Reprinted in this anthology (the preceding reading).

[7] Chisholm, "Lewis' Ethics of Belief"; Stephen Nathanson, "The Ethics of Belief," in *Philosophy and Phenomenological Research,* 1982.

[8] W. K. Clifford, "The Ethics of Belief," in *Lectures and Essays,* 2d ed. (London: Macmillan, 1866) (Reading X.1 in this anthology).

[9] Bernard Williams, "Deciding to Believe," in *Problems of the Self* (Cambridge, England: Cambridge University Press, 1972).

Bibliography

Alston, William. "The Deontological Conception of Epistemic Justification." In William Alston, *Epistemic Justification*. Ithaca, NY: Cornell University Press, 1989.

Chisholm, Roderick. *Perceiving*. Ithaca, NY: Cornell University Press, 1957.

Firth, Roderick. "Are Epistemic Concepts Reducible to Ethical Concepts?" In A. I. Goldman and J. Kim, eds., *Values and Morals*. Dordrecht, Netherlands: Reidel, 1978.

Heil, John. "Doxastic Agency." *Philosophical Studies 43* (1983).

Pojman, Louis. *Religious Belief and the Will*. London: Routledge & Kegan Paul, 1986.

Steup, Mathias, ed. *Knowledge, Truth, and Duty*. Oxford University Press, 2000.

Williams, Bernard. *Problems of the Self*. Cambridge, MA: Cambridge University Press, 1972.

Part XI

Challenges and Alternatives to Contemporary Epistemology

Is knowledge essentially social or individualistic? Is the Cartesian ("egocentric") paradigm a false model of knowing? Are truth and reality relative to agents or communities? Is all justification intrinsically perspectival or contextual, or can we transcend social contexts and understand things impartially? Is the sex of the knower relevant to the process of acquiring knowledge, or is it irrelevant? Is knowledge political? These are some of the questions asked in the writings included in this part of our book.

In the past twenty or thirty years, the paradigms of traditional epistemology have been called into question. The Cartesian model of the solitary individual constructing a house of truth upon the foundations of clear and distinct ideas has been attacked and rejected by a large segment of the epistemic community. In its place a model has arisen wherein our cognitive interdependence puts individuality in doubt altogether. Our community is part of our noetic structures, deeply rooted in our unconscious, if not conscious minds. Social knowledge—the product of group effort, which no one person may completely understand—replaces the egocentric quest for certainty. Even knowledge of good and evil are transformed by the group. The feminist epistemologist Anne Seller illustrates this with regard to her experience with the question of the morality of abortion in the 1970s:

For example, as the abortion debate developed in the seventies, women developed an understanding that they, rather than their biology, could determine their roles in society. This gave the issue a new symbolic importance in terms of who controls our lives, changed the terms of the debate from one about crime to one about rights, and led reformers to identify themselves as women rather than reformers. None of this could have happened if the unspeakable had not become speakable:

> As one early activist put it: "I was alone at first, but every time I gave a speech I was no longer alone because people came from everywhere saying, 'You've said what I felt, but I didn't know how to say it.'" (Luker, 1984)

She might have added that she was no longer mad or bad, although she was not necessarily right.[1]

For Seller, beliefs are valid and become knowledge, relative to one's political community. She does not want to leave things there, allowing for the Nazi and sexist to vindicate their beliefs via their groups, but she has no argument, except faith that they would live better lives if they altered those beliefs.

As a feminist epistemologist, Seller represents a growing number of women who seek to fuse the political with the epistemic. On the surface, it seems that those two subjects are incompatible. The political has to do with gaining power, with changing social arrangements, whereas epistemology has to do with the search for truth and justification. Politics are partial, whereas the condition for pursuing truth is impartiality. As Seller puts it, "My philosophical education taught me to follow reason wherever it went and to distrust political considerations. My experience as a feminist has taught me to stick by my political commitments even when I appear to have lost the argument."[2] Similarly, rejecting a notion of strong objectivity, Sandra Harding has developed the notion of *standpoints,* social perspectives from which we view the world in nonhierarchical modes.[3]

Philosophers have always recognized a social aspect to knowledge. Our parents and teachers condition and educate us to see things in certain ways and to ignore others. Language itself biases our perspective. We rely on testimony for our knowledge of the past and on experts for our knowledge of material beyond our grasp. But the traditional picture was that of the egocentric knower using reason to decide on when to defer to authority or the testimony of others. He or she was, in the last analysis, responsible for his or her beliefs.[4]

This position is under attack from oppositional epistemologists and thinkers, including three of the philosophers in our readings—Helen Longino, Lorraine Code, and Richard Rorty. It is defended by the other two, Susan Haack and Margarita Garcia Levin.

Feminist epistemology is the vector where diverse values of oppositional epistemology converge. In our readings, Longino calls into question the traditional epistemic virtues of consistency, simplicity, explanatory power and generality, impartial search for pure knowledge, and fruitfulness of experiment and in their place erects a loose confederation of oppositional virtue, novelty,

ontological heterogeneity, complexity or mutuality of interaction, applicability to human need, decentralization of power, and universal empowerment, which is democratic and egalitarian. Rejecting the god's-eye view of a comprehensive or global metaphysic, she opts for *local* epistemology, that which serves the cognitive needs of women and the oppressed in special communities.

Code, in our first reading, supports epistemological relativism to the extent that knowledge, truth, and reality "can be understood only in relation to particular sets of cultural or social circumstances, to a theoretical framework, a specifiable range of perspectives, a conceptual scheme, or a form of life." She seeks to separate this from subjectivism, which asserts that knowledge and truth are relative to individuals (rather than culture). However, her position is that the sex of the knower is one of a set of "subjective factors constitutive of received conceptions of knowledge and of what it means to be a knower." She argues that we can never identify the necessary and sufficient conditions for knowledge in the formula "S knows that p" until we pay as much attention to S as we pay to p.

On the other hand, in our third reading Haack argues that feminist epistemology is at best a mere passing fad and at worst a dangerous intellectual apartheid of the sexes. There is no special feminist knowledge or way of knowing. Confusing politics and epistemology is a version of confusing facts with values.

Rorty in our fourth reading seeks to dissolve the very notions of objective truth, as some kind of correspondence with reality, and science, as the systematic attempt to know reality. Ultimately, there is no separation between the sciences and the humanities. In our fifth reading, Levin defends the case for traditional rational objectivity against the attacks by oppositional thinkers.

In our final reading Karl Popper sets forth an evolutionary-Platonic theory of knowledge.

Notes

[1]Anne Seller, "Realism Versus Relativism: Towards a Politically Adequate Epistemology," in *Feminist Perspectives in Philosophy,* eds., M. Griffiths and M. Whitford (Bloomington: Indiana University Press, 1988). Seller defines relativism as the view "that every woman's experience is valid, not false, illusory or mistaken, and that all ways of making sense of the world are equally valid." She modifies this, relativizing truth claims to groups.

[2]Seller, ibid.

[3]Sandra Harding, *The Science Question in Feminism* (Ithaca, NY: Cornell University Press, 1986).

[4]See Richard Foley, "Egoism in Epistemology," in *Socializing Epistemology,* ed. Frederick Schmitt (Lantham, MD: Rowman and Littlefield, 1994) for a defense of this position.

XI.1 Is the Sex of the Knower Epistemologically Significant?

LORRAINE CODE

Lorraine Code is professor of philosophy at York University in Canada and the author of several works in feminist philosophy, including *What Can She Know? Feminist Theory and the Construction of Knowledge* (1991) from which the present selection is taken.

Code asks, What assumptions are made when we use the statement "S knows that *p*"? She proceeds to develop a version of epistemic relativism in which "knowledge, truth or even 'reality' can be understood only in relation to particular sets of cultural or social circumstances, to a theoretical framework, a specifiable range of perspectives, a conceptual scheme, or a form of life." Even the criteria of truth and falsity, as well as the standards of rationality, are relative. There is no universal, unchanging framework for settling conflicting knowledge claims. She argues that traditional mainstream epistemology has been "malestream," done from the white European, elitist, male perspective. However, even this perspective is not one essential property, but a social construct.

The Question

A question that focuses on the knower, as the title of this chapter does, claims that there are good reasons for asking who that knower is. Uncontroversial as such a suggestion would be in ordinary conversa-

tions about knowledge, academic philosophers commonly treat "the knower" as a featureless abstraction. Sometimes, indeed, she or he is merely a place holder in the proposition "S knows that p." Epistemological analyses of the proposition tend to focus on the "knowing that," to determine conditions under which a knowledge claim can legitimately be made. Once discerned, it is believed, such conditions will hold across all possible utterances of the proposition. Indeed, throughout the history of modern philosophy the central "problem of knowledge" has been to determine necessary and sufficient conditions for the possibility and justification of knowledge claims. Philosophers have sought ways of establishing a relation of correspondence between knowledge and "reality" and/or ways of establishing the coherence of particular knowledge claims within systems of already-established truths. They have proposed methodologies for arriving at truth, and criteria for determining the validity of claims to the effect that "S knows that p." Such endeavors are guided by the putatively self-evident principle that truth once discerned, knowledge once established, claim their status *as* truth and knowledge by virtue of a grounding in or coherence within a permanent, objective, ahistorical, and circumstantially neutral framework or set of standards.

The question "Who is S?" is regarded neither as legitimate nor as relevant in these endeavors. As inquirers into the nature and conditions of human knowledge, epistemologists commonly work from the assumption that they need concern themselves only with knowledge claims that meet certain standards of *purity*. Questions about the circumstances of knowledge acquisition serve merely to clutter and confuse the issue with contingencies and other impurities. The question "Who is S?" is undoubtedly such a question. If it matters who S is, then it must follow that something peculiar to S's character or nature could bear on the validity of the knowledge she or he claims: that S's *identity* might count among the conditions that make that knowledge claim possible. For many philosophers, such a suggestion would undermine the cherished assumption that knowledge can—and should—be evaluated on its own merits. More seriously still, a proposal that it matters who the knower is looks suspiciously like a move in the direction of epistemological relativism. For many philosophers, an endorsement of relativism signals the end of knowledge and of epistemology.

Broadly described, epistemological relativists hold that knowledge, truth, or even "reality" can be understood only in relation to particular sets of cultural or social circumstances, to a theoretical framework, a specifiable range of perspectives, a conceptual scheme, or a form of life. Conditions of justification, criteria of truth and falsity, and standards of rationality are likewise relative: there is no universal, unchanging framework or scheme for rational adjudication among competing knowledge claims.

Critics of relativism often argue that relativism entails incommensurability: that a relativist cannot evaluate knowledge claims comparatively. This argument is based on the contention that epistemological relativism entails conceptual relativism: that it contextualizes language just as it contextualizes knowledge, so that there remains no "common" or neutral linguistic framework for discussion, agreement, *or* disagreement. Other critics maintain that the very concept "knowledge" is rendered meaningless by relativism: that the only honest—and logical—move a relativist can make is once and for all to declare her or his skepticism. Where there are no universal standards, the argument goes, there can be no knowledge worthy of the name. Opponents often contend that relativism is simply incoherent because of its inescapable self-referentiality. Relativism, they argue, is subject to the same constraints as every other claim to knowledge and truth. Any claim for the truth of relativism must itself be relative to the circumstances of the claimant; hence relativism itself has no claim to objective or universal truth. In short, relativism is often perceived as a denial of the very possibility of epistemology.

Now posing the question "Who is S?"—that is, "Who is the knowing subject?"—does indeed count as a move in the direction of relativism, and my intention in posing it is to suggest that the answer has epistemological import. But I shall invoke certain caveats to demonstrate that such a move is not the epistemological disaster that many theorists of knowledge believe it to be.

It is true that, on its starkest construal, relativism may threaten to slide into subjectivism, into a position for which knowledge claims are indistinguishable from expressions of personal opinion, taste, or bias. But relativism need not be construed so starkly, nor do its *limitations* warrant exclusive emphasis. There are advantages to endorsing a measure of epistemological relativism that make of it an enabling rather than a constraining position. By no means the least of these advantages is the fact that relativism is one of the more obvious means of avoiding reductive explanations, in terms of drastically simplified paradigms of knowledge, monolithic explanatory modes, or privileged, decontextualized positions. For a relativist, who contends that there can be many valid ways of knowing any phenomenon, there is the possibility of taking several constructions, many perspectives into account. Hence relativism keeps open a range of interpretive possibilities. At the same time, because of the epistemic choices it affirms, it creates stringent accountability requirements of which knowers have to be cognizant. Thus it introduces a moral-political component into the heart of epistemological enquiry.

There probably is no absolute authority, no practice of all practices or scheme of all schemes. Yet it does not follow that conceptual schemes, practices, and paradigms are radically idiosyncratic or purely subjective. Schemes, practices, and paradigms evolve out of communal projects of inquiry. To sustain viability and authority, they must demonstrate their adequacy in enabling people to negotiate the everyday world and to cope with the decisions, problems, and puzzles they encounter daily. From the claim that no single scheme has absolute explanatory power, it does not follow that all schemes are equally valid. Knowledge is qualitatively variable: some knowledge is *better* than other knowledge. Relativists are in a good position to take such qualitative variations into account and to analyze their implications.

Even if these points are granted, though, it would be a mistake to believe that posing the "Who is S?" question indicates that the circumstances of the knower are *all* that counts in knowledge evaluation. The point is, rather, that understanding the circumstances of the knower makes possible a more *discerning* evaluation. The claim that certain of those circumstances are epistemologically significant—the sex of the knower, in this instance—by no means implies that they are definitive, capable of bearing the entire burden of justification and evaluation. This point requires special emphasis. Claiming epistemological significance for the sex of the knower might seem tantamount to a dismissal, to a contention that S made such a claim only because of his or her sex. Dismissals of this sort, both of women's knowledge *and* of their claims to be knowers in any sense of the word, are only too common throughout the history of western thought. But claiming that the circumstances of the knower are not epistemologically definitive is quite different from claiming that they are of no epistemological consequence. The position I take in this book is that the sex of the knower is one of a cluster of *subjective* factors (i.e., factors that pertain to the circumstances of cognitive agents) constitutive of

received conceptions of knowledge and of what it means to be a knower. I maintain that subjectivity and the specificities of cognitive agency can and must be accorded central epistemological significance, yet that so doing does not commit an inquirer to outright subjectivism. Specificities count, and they require a place in epistemological evaluation, but they cannot tell the whole story.

Knowers and the Known

The only thing that is clear about S from the standard proposition "S knows that p" is that S is a (would-be) knower. Although the question "Who is S?" rarely arises, certain assumptions about S as knower permeate epistemological inquiry. Of special importance for my argument is the assumption that knowers are self-sufficient and solitary individuals, at least in their knowledge-seeking activities. This belief derives from a long and venerable heritage, with its roots in Descartes's quest for a basis of perfect certainty on which to establish his knowledge. The central aim of Descartes's endeavors is captured in this claim: "I shall have the right to conceive high hopes if I am happy enough to discover one thing only which is certain and indubitable." That "one thing," Descartes believed, would stand as the fixed, pivotal, Archimedean point on which all the rest of his knowledge would turn. Because of its systematic relation to that point, his knowledge would be certain and indubitable.

Most significant for this discussion is Descartes's conviction that his quest will be conducted in a private, introspective examination of the contents of his own mind. It is true that, in the last section of the *Discourse on the Method*, Descartes acknowledges the benefit "others may receive from the communication of [his] reflection," and he states his belief that combining "the lives and labours of many" is essential to progress in scientific knowledge. It is also true that this individualistically described act of knowing exercises the aspect of the soul that is common to and alike in all knowers: namely, the faculty of reason. Yet his claim that knowledge seeking is an introspective activity of an individual mind accords no relevance either to a knower's embodiment or to his (or her) intersubjective relations. For each knower, the Cartesian route to knowledge is through private, abstract thought, through the efforts of reason unaided either by the senses or by consultation with other knowers. It is this individualistic, self-reliant, private aspect of Descartes's philosophy that has been influential in shaping subsequent epistemological ideals.

Reason is conceived as autonomous in the Cartesian project in two ways, then. Not only is the quest for certain knowledge an independent one, undertaken separately by each rational being, but it is a journey of reason alone, unassisted by the senses. For Descartes believed that sensory experiences had the effect of distracting reason from its proper course.

The custom of formulating knowledge claims in the "S knows that p" formula is not itself of Cartesian origin. The point of claiming Cartesian inspiration for an assumption implicit in the formulation is that the knower who is commonly presumed to be the subject of that proposition is modeled, in significant respects, on the Cartesian pure inquirer. For epistemological purposes, all knowers are believed to be alike with respect both to their cognitive capacities and to their methods of achieving knowledge. In the empiricist tradition this assumption is apparent in the belief that simple, basic observational data can provide the foundation of knowledge just because perception is invariant from observer to observer, in standard observation conditions. In fact, a common way of filling the places in the "S knows that p" proposition is with substitutions such as "Peter knows that the door is open" or "John knows that the book is red." It does not matter who John or Peter is. . . .

In some recent epistemological discussion, emphasis has shifted away from simple perceptual claims toward processes of evaluating the "warranted assertability" of more complex knowledge claims. In such contexts it does make sense to analyze the degree or extent of the knowledge claimed. Yet claims of the simple, perceptual sort are still most commonly cited as exemplary. They are assumed to have an all-or-nothing character; hence they seem not to admit of qualitative assessment. Granting them exemplary status implies that, for knowledge in general, it is appropriate to ask about neither the circumstances of the knowing process nor who the knower is. There would be no point to the suggestion that her or his identity might bear on the *quality* of the knowledge under discussion.

Proposing that the sex of the knower is significant casts doubt both on the autonomy of reason and on the (residual) exemplary status of simple observational knowledge claims. The suggestion that reason might function differently according to whose it is and in what circumstances its capacities are exercised implies that the manner of its functioning is dependent, in some way, on those circumstances, not independent from them. Simple perceptual examples are rendered contestable for their tendency to give a misleading impression of how knowledge is constructed and established and to suppress diversities in knowledge acquisition that derive from the varied circumstances—for example, the sex—of different knowers.

Just what am I asking, then, with this question about the epistemological *significance* of the sex of the knower? First, I do not expect that the question will elicit the answer that the sex of the knower is pertinent among conditions for the existence of knowledge, in the sense that taking it into account will make it possible to avoid skepticism. Again, it is unlikely that information about the sex of the knower could count among criteria of evidence or means of justifying knowledge claims. Nor is it prima facie obvious that the sex of the knower will have a legitimate bearing on the qualitative judgments that could be made about certain claims to know. Comparative judgments of the following kind are not what I expect to elicit: that if the knower is female, her knowledge is likely to be better grounded; if the knower is male, his knowledge will likely be more coherent.

In proposing that the sex of the knower is epistemologically significant, I am claiming that the scope of epistemological inquiry has been too narrowly defined. My point is not to denigrate projects of establishing the best foundations possible or of developing workable criteria of coherence. I am proposing that even if it is not possible (or not *yet* possible) to establish an unassailable foundationalist or coherentist position, there are numerous questions to be asked about knowledge whose answers matter to people who are concerned to know well. Among them are questions that bear not just on criteria of evidence, justification, and warrantability, but on the "nature" of cognitive agents: questions about their character; their material, historical, cultural circumstances;

their interests in the inquiry at issue. These are questions about how credibility is established, about connections between knowledge and power, about the place of knowledge in ethical and aesthetic judgments, and about political agendas and the responsibilities of knowers. I am claiming that all of these questions are epistemologically significant.

The Sex of the Knower

What, then, of the sex of the knower? In the rest of this chapter . . . I examine some attempts to give content to the claim that the sex of the knower *is* epistemologically significant. Many of these endeavors have been less than satisfactory. Nonetheless, I argue that the claim itself is accurate.

Although it has rarely been spelled out prior to the development of feminist critiques, it has long been tacitly assumed that S is male. Nor could S be just any man, the apparently infinite substitutability of the "S" term notwithstanding. The S who could count as a model, paradigmatic knower has most commonly—if always tacitly—been an adult (but not *old*), white, reasonably affluent (latterly middle-class) educated man of status, property, and publicly acceptable accomplishments. In theory of knowledge he has been allowed to stand for all men.[1] This assumption does not merely derive from habit or coincidence, but is a manifestation of engrained philosophical convictions. Not only has it been taken for granted that knowers properly so-called are male, but when male philosophers have paused to note this fact, as some indeed have done, they have argued that things are as they should be. Reason may be alike in all men, but it would be a mistake to believe that "man," in this respect, "embraces woman." Women have been judged incapable, for many reasons, of achieving knowledge worthy of the name. It is no exaggeration to say that anyone who wanted to *count* as a knower has commonly had to be male.

In the *Politics,* Aristotle observes: "The freeman rules over the slave after another manner from that in which the male rules over the female, or the man over the child; although the parts of the soul are present in all of them, they are present in different degrees. For the slave has no delibera-

tive faculty at all; the woman has, but it is without authority, and the child has, but it is immature."[2] Aristotle's assumption that a woman will naturally be ruled by a man connects directly with his contention that a woman's deliberative faculty is "without authority." Even if a woman could, in her sequestered, domestic position, acquire deliberative skills, she would remain reliant on her husband for her sources of knowledge and information. She must be ruled by a man because, in the social structure of the *polis,* she enjoys neither the autonomy nor the freedom to put into visible practice the results of the deliberations she may engage in, in private. If she can claim no authority for her rational, deliberative endeavors, then her chances of gaining recognition as a knowledgeable citizen are seriously limited, whatever she may do.

Aristotle is just one of a long line of western thinkers to declare the limitations of women's cognitive capacities.[3] Rousseau maintains that young men and women should be educated quite differently because of women's inferiority in reason and their propensity to be dragged down by their sensual natures. For Kierkegaard, women are merely aesthetic beings: men alone can attain the (higher) ethical and religious levels of existence. And for Nietzsche, the Apollonian (intellectual) domain is the male preserve, whereas women are Dionysian (sensuous) creatures. Nineteenth-century philosopher and linguist Wilhelm von Humboldt, who writes at length about women's knowledge, sums up the central features of this line of thought as follows: "A sense of truth exists in [women] quite literally as a sense: . . . their nature also contains a lack or a failing of analytic capacity which draws a strict line of demarcation between ego and world; therefore, they will not come as close to the ultimate investigation of truth as man." The implication is that women's knowledge, if ever the products of their projects deserve that label, is inherently and inevitably *subjective*— in the most idiosyncratic sense—by contrast with the best of men's knowledge.

Objectivity, quite precisely construed, is commonly regarded as a defining feature of knowledge per se. So if women's knowledge is declared to be *naturally* subjective, then a clear answer emerges to my question. The answer is that if the would-be knower is female, then her sex is indeed epistemologically significant, for it disqualifies her as a knower in the fullest sense of that term. Such disqualifications will operate differently for women of different classes, races, ages, and allegiances, but in every circumstance they will operate asymmetrically for women and for men. . . .

The presuppositions I have just cited claim more than the rather simple fact that many kinds of knowledge and skill have, historically, been inaccessible to women on a purely practical level. It is true, historically speaking, that even women who were the racial and social "equals" of standard male knowers were only rarely able to become learned. The thinkers I have cited (and others like them) claim to find a rationale for this state of affairs through appeals to dubious "facts" about women's natural incapacity for rational thought. Yet deeper questions still need to be asked: Is there knowledge that is, quite simply, inaccessible to members of the female, or the male, sex? Are there kinds of knowledge that only men, or only women, can acquire? Is the sex of the knower crucially determining in this respect, across all other specificities? The answers to these questions should not address only the *practical* possibilities that have existed for members of either sex. Such practical possibilities are the constructs of complex social arrangements that are themselves constructed out of historically specific choices, and are, as such, open to challenge and change.

Knowledge, as it achieves credence and authoritative status at any point in the history of the male-dominated mainstream, is commonly held to be a product of the individual efforts of human knowers. References to Pythagoras's theorem, Copernicus's revolution, and Newtonian and Einsteinian physics signal an epistemic community's attribution of pathbreaking contributions to certain of its individual members. The implication is that *that* person, singlehandedly, has effected a leap of progress in a particular field of inquiry. In less publicly spectacular ways, other cognitive agents are represented as contributors to the growth and stability of public knowledge.

Now any contention that such contributions are the results of independent endeavor is highly contestable. As I argue elsewhere, a complex of historical and other sociocultural factors produces the conditions that make "individual" achievement possible, and "individuals" themselves are socially constituted. The claim that individual men are the creators of the authoritative (often Kuhn-

paradigm-establishing) landmarks of western intellectual life is particularly interesting for the fact that the contributions—both practical and substantive—of their lovers, wives, children, servants, neighbors, friends, and colleagues rarely figure in analyses of their work.

The historical attribution of such achievements to specific cognitive agents does, nonetheless, accord a significance to individual efforts which raises questions pertinent to my project. It poses the problem, in another guise, of whether aspects of human specificity could, in fact, constitute conditions for the existence of knowledge or determine the kinds of knowledge that a knower can achieve. It would seem that such incidental physical attributes as height, weight, or hair color would not count among factors that would determine a person's capacities to know (though the arguments that skin color *does* count are too familiar). It is not necessary to consider how much Archimedes weighed when he made his famous discovery, nor is there any doubt that a thinner or a fatter person could have reached the same conclusion. But in cultures in which sex differences figure prominently in virtually every mode of human interaction, being female or male is far more fundamental to the construction of subjectivity than are such attributes as size or hair color. So the question is whether femaleness or maleness are the kinds of subjective factor (i.e., factors about the circumstances of a knowing subject) that are constitutive of the form and content of knowledge. Attempts to answer this question are complicated by the fact that sex/gender does not function uniformly and universally, even in western societies. Its implications vary across class, race, age, ability, and numerous other interwoven specificities. A separated analysis of sex/gender, then, always risks abstraction and is limited in its scope by the abstracting process. Further, the question seems to imply that sex and gender are themselves constants, thus obscuring the processes of *their* sociocultural construction. Hence the formulation of adequately nuanced answers is problematic and necessarily partial.

Even if it should emerge that gender-related factors play a crucial role in the construction of knowledge, then, the inquiry into the epistemological significance of the sex of the knower would not be complete. The task would remain of considering whether a distinction between "natural" and socialized capacity can retain any validity. The equally pressing question as to how the hitherto devalued products of *women's* cognitive projects can gain acknowledgment as "knowledge" would need to be addressed so as to uproot entrenched prejudices about knowledge, epistemology, and women. "The epistemological project" will look quite different once its tacit underpinnings are revealed.

Reclaiming "the Feminine"

Whether this project could or should emerge in a *feminist epistemology* is quite another question. Investigations that start from the conviction that the sex of the knower *is* epistemologically significant will surely question received conceptions of the nature of knowledge and challenge the hegemony of mainstream epistemologies. Some feminist theorists have maintained that there are distinctively female—or feminine—ways of knowing: neglected ways, from which the label "knowledge," traditionally, is withheld. Many claim that a recognition of these "ways of knowing" should prompt the development of new, rival, or even separate epistemologies. Others have adopted Mary O'Brien's brilliant characterization of mainstream epistemology as "malestream," claiming that one of the principal manifestations of its hegemony is its suppression of female—or "feminine" knowledge. In this section I sketch some classic and more recent arguments in favor of feminine "ways of knowing" and offer a preliminary analysis of their strengths and shortcomings.

Claims that there are specifically female or feminine ways of knowing often find support in the contention that women's significantly different experiences (different, that is, from men's experiences) lead them to know "the world" differently (i.e., from the ways men do). A putatively different female consciousness, in turn, generates different theories of knowledge, politics, metaphysics, morality, and aesthetics. Features of women's experiences commonly cited are a concern with the concrete, everyday world; a connection with objects of experience rather than an objective distance from them; a marked affective tone; a respect for the environment; and a readiness to listen perceptively and responsibly to a variety of "voices" in

the environment, both animate and inanimate, manifested in a tolerance of diversity.

Many of these features are continuous with the attributes with which the dominant discourse of affluent western societies characterizes a good mother. Indeed, one of the best-known advocates of a caring, maternal approach both to knowledge and to a morality based on that knowledge is Sara Ruddick, in her now-classic article "Maternal Thinking." Maternal thinking, Ruddick believes, grows out of the *practice* of caring for and establishing an intimate connection with another being—a growing child. That practice is marked by a "unity of reflection, judgment and emotion . . . [which is] . . . no more relative to its particular reality (the growing child) than the thinking that arises from scientific, religious, or other practice" is relevant to scientific or religious matters alone. Just as scientific or religious thought can structure a knower's characteristic approach to experiences and knowledge in general, Ruddick believes that attitudes and skills developed in the attentive and painstaking practices of caring for infants and small children are generalizable across cognitive domains.

Ruddick's celebration of values traditionally associated with mothering and femininity is not the first such in the history of feminist thought. Among nineteenth-century American feminists, both Margaret Fuller and Matilda Gage praised women's intuition as a peculiarly insightful capacity. Fuller, for example, believed that women have an intuitive perception that enables them to "seize and delineate with unerring discrimination" the connections and links among the various life forms that surround them. In this respect, she maintains, women are superior to men. And Gage believed that women have unique intellectual capacities, manifested especially in an intuitive faculty that does not "need a long process of ratiocination" for its operations. Both Fuller and Gage, albeit in quite different contexts, advocate legitimizing this suppressed and undervalued faculty whose deliverances, they believe, are attuned to and hence better able to reveal the secrets of nature and (for Gage) of spirituality, than masculine ratiocinative practices.

This nineteenth-century belief in the powers of female intuition is echoed in the work of two of the best-known twentieth-century radical feminists, Shulamith Firestone and Mary Daly. For

Firestone, there are two sharply contrasting modes or styles of response to experience: an "aesthetic response," which she links to femaleness and characterizes as "subjective, intuitive, introverted, wishful, dreamy or fantastic, concerned with the subconscious (the *id*), emotional, even temperamental (hysterical)"; and a technological response, which she describes as masculine: "objective, logical, extroverted, realistic, concerned with the conscious mind (the ego), rational, mechanical, pragmatic and down-to-earth, stable." Firestone's claim is not that the aesthetic (= the feminine) should dominate, but that there should be a fusion between the two modes. To overcome patriarchal domination, she believes, it is vital for the aesthetic principle to manifest itself in all cultural and cognitive activity and for technology to cease operating to exclude affectivity. . . .

Some theorists maintain that research into the lateralization of brain function reveals "natural" female-male cognitive differences. The findings of this research are frequently interpreted to indicate that in men, "left-brain" functions predominate, whereas "right-brain" functioning is better developed in women. Evidence that women have better verbal skills and fine motor coordination, whereas men are more adept at spatial skills, mathematics, and abstract thinking, is cited as proof of the existence of female and male cognitive differences. Depending on the political orientation of the inquirer, such findings are read either as confirmations of male supremacy and female inferiority or as indications of a need to revalue "the feminine." Among the celebratory interpretations are Gina Covina's claim that women, whom she describes as more "rightbrained" than men, deal with experience "in a diffuse non-sequential way, assimilating many different phenomena simultaneously, finding connections between separate bits of information." By contrast, men, whom she labels "leftbrained," engage typically in thinking that is "focused narrowly enough to squeeze out human or emotional considerations . . . [and to enable] . . . men to kill (people, animals, plants, natural processes) with free consciousnesses." For Covina, there are "natural" female-male differences. They are marked not just descriptively but evaluatively.

If brain-lateralization studies, or theories like Daly's and Firestone's, can be read as demonstrations of women's and men's *necessarily* different cognitive capacities, then my title question requires

an affirmative answer. But it is not clear that such conclusions follow unequivocally. Consider the fact that allegedly sex-specific differences are not observable in examinations of the structure of the brain itself, and that in small children "both hemispheres appear to be equally proficient." At most, then, it would seem, the brain may come to control certain processes in sexually differentiated ways. Evidence suggests that the brain *develops* its powers through training and practice. Brains of creatures presented with a wide variety of tasks and stimuli develop strikingly greater performance capacities than brains of creatures kept in impoverished environments. As Ruth Bleier points out, "the biology of the brain itself is shaped by the individual's environment and experiences."

Bleier notes the difficulty of assessing the implications of lateralization research. She observes that there are just as many studies that find no sex differences as there are studies that do, and that variability within each sex is greater than variability between them. Janet Sayers suggests that it is as plausible to argue that sex differences in the results of tests to measure spatial ability are the results of sex-specific strategies that subjects adopt to deal with the tests themselves as it is to attribute them to differences in brain organization. She points out that there is no conducive demonstration that differences in brain organization actually "*cause* sex differences in spatial ability." It is not easy to see, then, how these studies can plausibly support arguments about general differences in male and female cognitive abilities or about women's incapacity to enter such specific domains as engineering and architecture, where spatial abilities figure largely.

These are just some of the considerations that recommend caution in interpreting brain-lateralization studies. Differences in female and male brain functioning are just as plausibly attributable to sociocultural factors such as the sex-stereotyping of children's activities or to differing parental attitudes to children of different sexes, even from earliest infancy. It would be a mistake to rely on the research in developing a position about the epistemological significance of the sex of the knower, especially as its results are often elaborated and interpreted to serve political ends.

Now Fuller, Gage, Ruddick, Firestone, Daly, and Covina evidently believe—albeit variously—in the effectiveness of *evaluative reversals* of alleged differences as a fundamental revolutionary move. Philosophers should acknowledge the superiority of feminine ideals in knowledge acquisition as much as in social life and institutions, and masculine ways of thought should give way, more generally, to feminine ways. These recommendations apply to theoretical content and to methodology, to rules for the conduct of inquiry, and to principles of justification and legitimation.

The general thesis that inspires these recommendations is that women have an edge in the development and exercise of just those attributes that merit celebration as feminine: in care, sensitivity, responsiveness and responsibility, intuition and trust. There is no doubt that these traits are commonly represented as constitutive of femininity. Nor is there much doubt that a society that valued them might be a better society than one that denigrates and discourages them. But these very traits are as problematic, both theoretically and practically, as they are attractive. It is not easy to separate their appeal from the fact that women—at least women of prosperous classes and privileged races—have been encouraged to cultivate them throughout so long a history of oppression and exploitation that they have become marks of acquiescence in powerlessness. Hence there is a persistent tension in feminist thought between a laudable wish to celebrate "feminine" values as tools for the creation of a better social order and a fear of endorsing those same values as instruments of women's continued oppression.

My recurring critique, throughout this book, of theoretical appeals to an *essential* femininity is one I engage in from a position sensitive to the pull of both sides in this tension. By "essentialism" I mean a belief in an essence, an inherent, natural, eternal female nature that manifests itself in such characteristics as gentleness, goodness, nurturance, and sensitivity. These are some of women's more positive attributes. Women are also represented, in essentialist thought, as naturally less intelligent, more dependent, less objective, more irrational, less competent, more scatterbrained than men: indeed, essential femaleness is commonly defined against a masculine standard of putatively *human* essence.

Essentialist attributions work both normatively and descriptively. Not only do they purport to describe how women essentially *are,* they are commonly enlisted in the perpetuation of

women's (usually inferior) social status. Yet essentialist claims are highly contestable. Their diverse manifestations across class, race, and ethnicity attest to their having a sociocultural rather than a "natural" source. Their deployment as instruments for keeping women in their place means that caution is always required in appealing to them—even though they often appear to designate women's *strengths.* Claims about masculine essence need also to be treated with caution, though it is worth noting that they are less commonly used to oppress men. Essential masculine aggressiveness, sexual needs, and ego-enhancing requirements are often added, rather, to reasons why women should remain subservient. Perhaps there are some essential female or male characteristics, but claims that there are always need to be evaluated and analyzed. The burden of proof falls on theorists who appeal to essences, rather than on those who resist them.

As I have noted, some of the thinkers I have cited advocate an evaluative reversal, in a tacit acceptance of stereotypical, essentialist conceptions of masculinity and femininity. To understand the import of the tension in feminist thought, these stereotypes need careful analysis. The issues of power and theoretical hegemony that are inextricably implicated in their maintenance need likewise to be analyzed. As an initial step toward embarking on this task I offer, in the remainder of this section, a critical analysis of [two] landmark articles that engage with malestream epistemology with the intention of revealing grounds for feminist opposition to its traditional structures. . . .

(ii) In another early, landmark article, "The Social Function of the Empiricist Conception of Mind," Sandra Harding confronts stereotypes of femininity from a different direction. Her thesis is that "the empiricist model of mind supports social hierarchy by implicitly sanctioning 'underclass' stereotypes." Emphasizing the passivity of knowers in Humean empiricism, Harding contends, first, that classical empiricism can allow no place for creativity, for historical self-consciousness, or for the adoption of a critical stance. Second, she discerns a striking similarity between "the Humean mind" and stereotypical conceptions of women's minds: "formless, passive, and peculiarly receptive to direction from outside."[4] Her intention is to show that an espousal of empiricist theory, combined with an uncritical acceptance of feminine stereotypes, legitimates manipulative and controlling treatment of women in the social world. There are striking echoes, as Harding herself notes, with the Aristotelian view of woman's lack of rational authority: a lack that, for Aristotle, likewise justifies women's inferior social position.

Present-day empiricists would no doubt contend that Harding's equation of empiricism with a "passive" epistemology and theory of mind has little validity, given the varieties of contemporary empiricism in its transformations under the influence of philosophers such as Quine. Yet even if Harding has drawn only a caricature of "the Humean mind," her account has a heuristic value in highlighting certain tendencies of orthodox, classical empiricism. Empiricism, and its latter-day positivist offspring, could indeed serve, either as a philosophy of mind or as a theory of knowledge, to legitimate under the guise of objectivity and impartial neutrality just the kinds of social practice feminists are concerned to eradicate. The impartiality of empiricist analysis, the interchangeability of its subjects of study, work to provide rationalizations for treating people as "cases" or "types," rather than as active, creative cognitive agents. Such rationalizations are common in positivistic social science.

More intriguing is a "double standard" Harding discerns in classical empiricist thought. The *explicit* picture of the Humean inquirer, she maintains, is of a person who is primarily passive, receptive, and hence manipulable. Yet the very existence of Hume's own philosophy counts as evidence that he himself escapes that characterization. His intellectual activity is marked by "a critical attitude, firm purposes and a willingness to struggle to achieve them, elaborate principles of inquiry and hypotheses to be investigated, clarity of vision, precision, and facility at rational argument." This description of the *implicit* Humean inquirer, Harding notes, feeds into standard gender stereotypes, in which men come across as "effective historical agents" while women are incapable of historical agency.

Harding accuses the promulgators of the classical empiricist conception of mind of false consciousness. Their own theoretical activity exempts *their* minds from the very model for which they claim universal validity: the contention that no one is a self-directed agent, everyone is a blank tablet, cannot apply to the authors themselves. Hence the empiricists presuppose a we/they structure in which "they" indeed are as the theory describes them, but "we," by virtue of our theoretical creativity, escape the description. In consequence, "the empiricist model of mind . . . functions as a self-fulfilling *prescription* beneficial to those already in power: treat people as if they are passive and need direction from others, and they will become or remain able to be manipulated and controlled." Harding maintains that the implicit distinction between active empiricist theorist and passive ordinary inquirer maps onto the stereotypical active male/passive female distinction and acts to legitimate the social and political consequences of that stereotype in androcentered power structures.

Now it is not easy to show that Harding is right either to find an implicit "double standard" in Humean thought or to suggest that demarcations of the two "kinds" of knower are appropriately drawn along sexual lines. Hume himself may have meant merely to distinguish a philosopher at his most sophisticated from an ordinary "vulgar" thinker. His elitism may have been intellect- or class-related, rather than sex-related. If Harding is right, however, the Humean "double standard" would suggest that the sex of the knower is epistemologically significant, in that it designates men alone as capable of active, creative, critical knowing—and of constructing epistemological theories. By contrast, women are capable only of receiving and shuffling information. Even if she is mistaken in her Humean attributions, then, the parallels Harding draws between the intellectual elitism that empiricism can create and sexual elitism find ample confirmation in the social world. The common relegation of women to low-status forms of employment, which differ from high-status employment partly in the kinds of knowledge, expertise, and cognitive authority they require, is just one confirming practice.

What ensures Harding's paper a place in the history of feminist critiques of philosophy is less the detail of its Hume interpretation than its articulation of the political implications of metaphysical theses. In the face of challenges such as these, which have been more subtly posed both in Harding's later work and elsewhere as feminist thought has increased in sophistication, the neutrality of such theses can never be taken for granted. Should it be declared, the onus is on its declarers to demonstrate the validity of their claims. So despite the flaws in Harding's analysis, her article supports my contention that the sex of the knower is epistemologically significant. If metaphysical theories are marked by the maleness of their creators, then theories of knowledge informed by them cannot escape the marking. Whether the case can be made that both theoretical levels are thus marked, without playing into sexual stereotypes, is a difficult question, but the evidence points compellingly toward the conclusion that the sex of a philosopher informs his theory-building.

(iii) The influence of stereotypically sex-specific traits on conceptions of the proper way to do philosophy is instructively detailed in Janice Moulton's analysis of "The Adversary Method," as she perceptively names it. Moulton shows that a subtle conceptual "conflation of aggression and competence"[5] has produced a paradigm for philosophical inquiry that is modeled on adversarial confrontation between opponents. This conflation depends, above all, on an association of aggression with such positive qualities as energy, power, and ambition: qualities that count as prerequisites for success in the white, middle-class, male professional world. Moulton questions the validity of this association in its conferral of normative status on styles of behavior stereotypically described as male. Yet what is most seriously wrong with the paradigm, she argues, is not so much its maleness as its constitutive role in the production of truncated philosophical problems, inquiries, and solutions.

The adversarial method is most effective, Moulton claims, in structuring isolated disagreements about specific theses and arguments. Hence it depends for its success on the artificial isolation of such claims and arguments from the contexts that occasion their articulation. Adversarial argument aims to show that an opponent is wrong, often by attacking conclusions implicit in, or potentially consequent on, his basic or alleged premises. Under the adversarial paradigm, the point is to confront the most extreme opposing position, with the object of showing that one's own position is defensible even against such stark opposition. Exploration, explanation, and understanding are lesser goals. The irony, Moulton claims, is that the adversarial paradigm produces

bad reasoning, because it leads philosophers to adopt the mode of reasoning best suited to defeat an opponent—she uses "counterexample reasoning" to illustrate her point—as the paradigmatic model for reasoning as such. Diverse modes of reasoning which might be more appropriate to different circumstances, tend to be occluded, as does the possibility that a single problem might be amenable to more than one approach.

Moulton's analysis lends support to the contention that the sex of significant at the "metaepistemological" level where the legitimacy of epistemological problems is established. The connection between aggressive cognitive styles and stereotypes of masculine behavior is now a commonplace of feminist thought. Moulton's demonstration of such behavior constitutes the dominate mode—the paradigm—in philosophy, which has so long claimed to stand outside "the commonplace," is compelling. She shows that mainstream philosophy bears the marks of its androcentric derivation out of a stereotypically constructed masculinity, whatever the limitations of that construction are.

Like all paradigms, the adversarial method has a specific location in intellectual history. While it demarcates the kinds of puzzle a philosopher can legitimately consider, a recognition of its historical specificity shows that this is not how philosophy has always been done nor how it must, of necessity, be done. In according the method (interim) paradigm status, Moulton points to the historical contingency of its current hegemony. The fact that many feminist philosophers report a sense of dissonance between the supposed gender neutrality of the method and their own feminine gender puts the paradigm under serious strains. Such strains create the space and the possibilities for developing alternative methodological approaches. Whether the sex of the knower will be methodologically and/or epistemologically significant in such approaches must for now, remain an open question.

Knowledge, Methodology, and Power

The adversarial method is but one manifestation of a complex interweaving of power and knowledge which sustains the hegemony of mainstream epistemology. Like the empiricist theory of the mind, it presents a public demeanor of neutral inquiry, engaged in the disinterested pursuit of truth. Despite its evident interest in triumphing over opponents, it would be unreasonable to condemn this disinterest as merely a pose. There is no reason to believe that practitioners whose work is informed by these methodological assumptions have ruthlessly or tyrannically adopted a theoretical stance for the express purpose of engaging in projects that thwart the intellectual pursuit of women or of other marginalized philosophers. Could such a purpose be discerned, the task of revealing the epistemological significance of the sex of the knower would be easy. Critics could simply offer such practitioners a clear demonstration of the errors of their ways and hope that, with a presumption of goodwill on their part, they would abandon the path of error for that of truth and fairness.

Taking these practitioners at their word, acknowledging the sincerity of their convictions about their neutral, objective, impartial engagement in the pursuit of truth, reveals the intricacy of this task. Certain sets of problems, by virtue of their complexity or their intrinsic appeal, often become so engrossing for researchers that they override and occlude other contenders for attention. Reasons for this suppression are often subtle and not always specifically articulable. Nor is it clear that the exclusionary process is wholly conscious. A network of sociopolitical relationships and intellectual assumptions creates an invisible system of acceptance and rejection, discourse and silence, ascendancy and subjugation within and around disciplines. Implicit cultural presuppositions work with the personal idiosyncrasies of intellectual authorities to keep certain issues from placing high on research agendas. Critics have to learn how to notice their absence.

In "The Discourse on Language," Michel Foucault makes the astute observation that "within its own limits, every discipline recognizes true and false propositions, but it repulses a whole teratology of learning."[6] The observation captures some of the subtleties involved in attempting to understand the often imperceptible workings of hegemonic, usually masculine power in mainstream philosophy. A discipline defines itself both by what it excludes (repulses) and by what it includes. But the self-definition process removes what is excluded (repulsed) from view so that it is not straightforwardly available for assessment, criticism, and analysis. Even in accepting mainstream avowals of neutral objectivity, critics have to learn to see what is repulsed by the disciplinarily imposed limits on methodology and areas of inquiry. The task is not easy. It is much easier to seek the flaws in existing structures and practices and to work at eradicating them than it is to learn to perceive what is not there to be perceived.

Feminist philosophy simply did not exist until philosophers learned to perceive the near-total absence of women in philosophical writings from the very beginning of western philosophy, to stop assuming that "man" could be read as a generic term. Explicit denigrations of women, which became the focus of philosophical writing in the early years of the contemporary women's movement, were more readily perceptible. The authors of derogatory views about women in classical texts clearly needed power to be able to utter their pronouncements with impunity: a power they claimed from a "received" discourse that represented women's nature in such a way that women undoubtedly merited the negative judgments that Aristotle or Nietzsche made about them. Women are now in a position to recognize and refuse these overt manifestations of contempt.

The covert manifestations are more intransigent. Philosophers, when they have addressed the issue at all, have tended to group philosophy with science as the most gender-neutral of disciplines. But feminist critiques reveal that this alleged neutrality masks a bias in favor of institutionalizing stereotypical masculine values into the fabric of the discipline—its methods, norms, and contents. In so doing, it suppresses values, styles, problems, and concerns stereotypically associated with femininity. Thus, whether by chance or by design, it creates a hegemonic philosophical practice in which the sex of the knower is, indeed, epistemologically significant.

Notes

[1]To cite just one example: in *The Theory of Epistemic Rationality* (Cambridge: Harvard University Press, 1987), Richard Foley appeals repeatedly to the epistemic judgments of people who are "like the rest of us" (p. 108). He contrasts their beliefs with beliefs that seem "crazy or bizarre or outlandish . . . beliefs to most of the rest of us"

(p. 114), and argues that an account of rational belief is plausible only if it can be presented from "some nonweird perspective" (p. 140). Foley contends that "an individual has to be at least minimally like us in order for charges of irrationality even to make sense" (p. 240). Nowhere does he address the question of who "we" are.

[2]Aristotle, *Politics*, trans. Benjamin Jowett, in *The Basic Works of Aristotle*, ed. Richard McKeon (New York: Random House, 1941), 1260b.

[3]It would be inaccurate, however, to argue that this line is unbroken. Londa Schiebinger demonstrates that in the history of science—and, by implication, the history of the achievement of epistemic authority—there were many periods when women's intellectual achievements were not only recognized but respected. The "long line" I refer to is the dominant, historically most visible one. Schiebinger, *The Mind Has No Sex? Women in the Origins of Modern Science* (Cambridge: Harvard University Press, 1989).

[4]Sandra Harding, "The Social Function of the Empiricist Conception of Mind," *Metaphilosophy* 10 (January 1979): 39, 42.

[5]Janice Moulton, "A Paradigm of Philosophy: The Adversary Method," in Sandra Harding and Merrill B. Hintikka, eds., *Discovering Reality* (Dordrecht: Reidel, 1983), p. 151.

[6]Michel Foucault, "The Discourse on Language," in *The Archaeology of Knowledge*, trans. Alan Sheridan (New York: Pantheon, 1972), p. 223.

XI.2 Feminist Epistemology as a Local Epistemology

Helen E. Longino

Helen Longino teaches philosophy and women's studies at the University of Minnesota. She is the author of *Science as Social Knowledge* (Princeton University Press, 1990) and coeditor of *Feminism and Science* (Oxford University Press, 1996) and of *Gender and Scientific Authority* (University of Chicago Press, 1996). Her essays on topics in philosophy of science, feminist science studies, and feminist epistemology have been published in many journals, including *Philosophy of Science*, *The Journal of Philosophy*, *Signs*, and *Hypatia*.

Feminist epistemology has both critical and constructive dimensions. Whereas the critical dimension is concerned with demonstrating masculine bias in traditional epistemological analyses, the constructive dimension is concerned with carving out space for specifically feminist forms of inquiry. This paper is an exercise in constructive analysis: identifying scientific values feminists have embraced and analyzing their relation to feminist inquiry in general and to more traditional scientific values. It argues that both the feminist and the traditional scientific values have political dimensions and that what these are depends on features of the context in which the values are deployed. The feminist values are also provisional and partial and, as the framework of a normative epistemology, are local. To the extent that any set of cognitive values is subordinated to a goal of inquiry, the paper suggests, any normative epistemology will be local. General philosophical epistemology ought then to be understood as interpretive rather than normative.

I

Introductory Remarks. The very idea of feminist epistemology throws some philosophers into near apoplexy. Partly this is social and psychological: an aversion to the revisionist challenges of feminism abetted by a healthy if residual misogyny. Partly this is intellectual: how could a politically and intellectually partial form of inquiry have anything to say about epistemology, which is or ought to be about very general questions concerning the nature of knowledge? The former is worth noting, but not discussing; the second, however, goes to the heart of what feminist epistemology is. This essay pursues one line of thought in feminist epistemology with a view to sorting out the relation between it and general epistemology, and between it and other approaches in feminist theory of knowledge.

First I should note what feminist epistemology is not. It is not the study or defence of feminine intuition, of "women's ways of knowing," of subjectivism; it is not an embrace of irrationality or of Protagorean relativism. Although feminist philosophers have celebrated the female subject, have argued for the constructive role of emotion in knowledge, and have criticized standard accounts of objectivity and rationality, attacks on feminist epistemology tend to ignore the arguments feminists offer and instead go after straw women. As they misrepresent the feminist work they purport to criticize, they do not deserve any kind of detailed response, but do impose on feminists a burden yet again to say what we mean. Also, contrary to the apparent view of many of its detractors, feminist epistemology encompasses a number of different directions of analysis some of which are, others of which are not, mutually compatible. In addition, themes and positions in feminist epistemology overlap with themes and positions in philosophy generally. Thus some of the tensions within feminist epistemological thought are mirrored by tensions in other areas of philosophy, while some are peculiar to it. For example, many commentators take feminist epistemology to be a species of naturalized and social epistemology, but just as there are ways of naturalizing and ways of socializing epistemology, so there are ways of doing feminist epistemology.

Feminist epistemology has both critical and constructive dimensions. Critical dimensions include the demonstration of forms of masculine bias at the heart of philosophical analyses of such topics as objectivity, reason, knowledge, and rationality. Constructive dimensions include carving out a space for specifically feminist programs in inquiry, identifying or defending epistemic guidelines of feminist inquiry. Among constructive programs feminist standpoint theory and feminist empiricism have been the most visible, but feminist forms of pragmatism are also finding favour. (See Lloyd 1984, Code 1991, 1995, Harding 1986, 1991, Rooney 1994, 1995, Anderson 1995, Solomon 1995, also Alcoff and Potter 1993, Lennon and Whitford 1994.)*

Most feminist epistemologies (those named above) have been feminist adaptations of extant philosophical orientations. Another way to start thinking about feminist epistemology is to consider what feminists engaged in inquiry, in the production of knowledge, have to say about knowledge, to investigate whether and how they think feminist practices of inquiry might differ from standard practices. Feminists standing back from and reflecting on their practices have had quite a bit to say about moral dimensions of practices of inquiry; about the development of mutual respect among researchers, about the desirability of cooperation as opposed to competition among researchers, about the desirability of respect for, even love of, the objects of one's research, be these social or natural, about issues of responsibility. (See Hubbard 1990, Martin 1988, Birke 1984, Stanley 1990.) Feminists in the course of working through particular research programs, whether empirical or analytical, have also defended, elaborated, or invoked a variety of cognitive or theoretical values, desirable characteristics of the outcomes of inquiry. Thinking about these values and the roles they do or might play in inquiry, can initiate a chain of reflections leading to a somewhat unorthodox, but ultimately, I believe, quite fruitful, characterization of epistemology. I will discuss some of the values that have been endorsed by feminist thinkers and their relation to traditional epistemic values and

[*See the bibliography at the end of this part for the references to these citations.—Ed.]

move from this discussion to a consideration of the relation between an epistemology focused on feminist cognitive values and general philosophical epistemology and between this form of feminist reflection on knowledge and other, perhaps more familiar, directions in feminist epistemology.

II

Feminist Values in Inquiry. In a series of earlier papers, I have explored a set of values individually and severally invoked by feminist researchers (Longino 1994, 1996). They probably do not exhaust the values that feminist researchers do or could endorse but they do exhibit a suitable range. To simplify matters, I treat these as theoretical virtues, i.e. as characteristics of theories, models, or hypotheses, that are taken as counting *prima facie* and *ceteris paribus* in favour of their acceptance. The virtues I have discussed in this capacity include empirical adequacy, novelty, ontological heterogeneity, complexity or mutuality of interaction, applicability to human needs, and decentralization of power or universal empowerment. While empirical adequacy is held in common by feminist and non-feminist researchers, the remaining five contrast intriguingly with more commonly touted values of consistency with theories in other domains, simplicity, explanatory power and generality, fruitfulness or refutability. I shall briefly say something about each of the feminist virtues, excluding empirical adequacy.

Feminists endorse the novelty of theoretical or explanatory principle as protection against unconscious perpetuation of the sexism and androcentrism of traditional theorizing or of theorizing constrained by a desire for consistency with accepted explanatory models. The novelty envisioned is not the novelty of discovery of new entities (like the top quark) predicted by theory but rather of frameworks of understanding. For example, some feminist scholars have criticized the articulation of female centred models of evolution by feminist primatologists as remaining too much within the framework of sociobiology, and thus, perpetuating other noxious values of that theoretical approach. Novelty, thus understood, is contrary to the value of conservatism as propounded by Quine or of consistency with theories in other

domains as described by Kuhn. The embrace of novelty may be conjoined with a hope of ultimately seeing or engineering an overturning of the theories with which a new view is inconsistent, or with merely making salient aspects of experience or reality hidden or marginalized by presently accepted theory.

Feminists who endorse heterogeneity as a virtue indicate a preference for theories and models that preserve the heterogeneity in the domain under investigation, or that, at least, do not eliminate it on principle. An approach to inquiry that requires uniform specimens may facilitate generalization, but it runs the risk of missing important differences—so the male of a species comes to be taken as paradigmatic for the species (as in "Gorillas are solitary animals; a typical individual travels only with a female and her/their young"). Or, via the concept of male dominance, males are treated as the only causally effective agents in a population. The embrace of heterogeneity extends beyond human and animal behaviour, however, and is also invoked in the context of genetic and biochemical processes. Feminist researchers have resisted unicausal accounts of development in favour of accounts in which quite different factors play causal roles. Heterogeneity is thus opposed to ontological simplicity and to the associated explanatory virtue of unification. Under the guidance of these latter virtues, similarities between, rather than differences in, the phenomena would be stressed.

Mutuality or reciprocity of interaction, sometimes more generally complexity of interaction, is something of a processual companion to the virtue of ontological heterogeneity. While heterogeneity of ontology tolerates the existence of different kinds of things, complexity, mutuality, reciprocity characterize their interactions. Feminists endorsing this virtue express a preference for theories representing interactions as complex and involving not just joint, but also mutual and reciprocal relationships among factors. They explicitly reject theories or explanatory models that attempt to identify one causal factor in a process, whether that be a dominant animal or a "master molecule" like DNA. This virtue favours accounts of fertilization, or gametic fusion, for example, which treat the process as an interaction between egg and sperm, rather than the active sperm acting on the passive egg.

Many feminists also endorse the idea that science should be "for the people," that research that alleviates human needs, especially those traditionally attended by women, such as care of the young, weak, and infirm or feeding the hungry, should be preferred over research for military purposes or for knowledge's sake. While not rejecting curiosity altogether as an appropriate aim of research, these feminists place a greater emphasis on the pragmatic dimension of knowledge, but only in connection with the final virtue in this collection—decentralization of power. Thus forms of knowledge and its application in technologies which empower beneficiaries are preferred to those which produce or reproduce dependence relations. Both the feminist pragmatic virtues and their traditional contraries, fruitfulness and refutability, have to do with the expansion of a theoretical approach in an empirical direction. But the relevance of the empirical in the traditional view is within a self-enclosed research context. Applicability and empowerment, by contrast, are directed to the social and practical milieu outside the research context.

III

Feminist and Traditional Cognitive Values. One might ask why the virtues I've just sketched should be given equal status with the more traditional epistemic virtues with which they contrast. But this question begs another—what is the status of the traditional epistemic virtues? While these are quite frequently invoked as factors closing the gap between evidence and hypotheses revealed by underdetermination arguments, it's not at all evident that they are capable of discriminating between the more and less probable, let alone between the true and the false. Consistency with theories in other domains, for example, only has epistemic value if we suppose these other theories to be true. While they presumably are empirically adequate, additional considerations in favour of their truth will have to consist of other assumptions or theoretical virtues. The probative value of consistency, then, is relative to the truth of the theories with which consistency is recommended.

Simplicity and explanatory power fare no better. While there is an understandable preference for simpler theories when contrasted with theories or models loaded with entities and processes and relationships that do not add to the predictive

capacities of the theory, it is not clear that simplicity generally can carry epistemic weight. As is well known, simplicity can be interpreted in different ways. The interpretation contrasting with the alternative virtue of heterogeneity is ontological—the fewer entities the better, or no more entities than are required to explain the phenomena. As a caution of prudence this has much to recommend it, and it may even be a useful heuristic. But for simplicity as an epistemic standard there are at least three problems:

i.   This formulation begs the question what counts as an adequate explanation. Is an adequate explanation an account sufficient to generate predictions or an account of underlying processes, and, if explanation is just retrospective prediction, then must it be successful at individual or population levels? Either the meaning of simplicity will be relative to one's account of explanation, thus undermining the capacity of simplicity to function as an independent epistemic value, or the insistence on simplicity will dictate what gets explained and how.

ii.   We have no a priori reason to think the universe simple, i.e. composed of very few kinds of thing (as few as the kinds of elementary particles, for example) rather than of many different kinds of thing. Nor is there or could there be empirical evidence for such a view.

iii.   The degree of simplicity or variety in one's theoretical ontology may be dependent on the degree of variety one admits into one's description of the phenomena. If one imposes uniformity on the data by rejecting anomalies, then one is making a choice for a certain kind of account. If the view that the boundaries of our descriptive categories are conventional is correct, then there is no epistemological fault in this, but neither is there virtue.

Explanatory power and generality also lose their epistemic allure under close examination. Indeed the greater the explanatory power and generality of a theory, i.e. the greater the variety of phenomena brought under its explanatory umbrella, the less likely it is to be (literally) true. Its explanatory strength is purchased at the cost of truth, which lies in the details and may be captured through the filling in of an indefinite series of *ceteris paribus* clauses (Cartwright 1983). Explanatory power and generality may constitute good reasons for accepting a model or theory if one places value on unifying theoretical frameworks, but this is a value distinct from truth and has to be defended on other grounds. Mutuality or reciprocity of influence in an explanatory model is less likely to be generalizable than a linear or unicausal model which permits the incorporation of the explanation of an effect into an explanation of its cause. The explanations of multiple interacting causal factors branch out rather than coalescing. Rather than a vertically ordered hierarchy culminating in a master theory or master science, one is confronted with a horizontally ordered network of models.

Finally, what Kuhn called fruitfulness and the feminist pragmatic virtues are not really contraries in their epistemic relevance. Fruitfulness of a theory is its ability to generate problems for research. This can be given a somewhat narrower interpretation as refutability, that is, having (falsifiable) empirical consequences. This does not argue for the truth of a theory, but for its tractability, that is for its capacity to have empirical data brought to bear on it. Both refutability and fruitfulness may be less intrinsic features of a theory, than a matter of the instruments available for producing relevant data, as well as other theoretical and empirical developments in associated fields that make articulation of the theory possible. The feminist pragmatic virtues do not reject the importance of empirical consequences but seek them in certain areas: in the world of human life as well as in the laboratory. The most politically loaded of the feminist virtues requires in addition that the mode of applicability involve empowerment of the many rather than the concentration of power among the few. Some thinkers about the sciences have rejected altogether the distinction between pure and applied science that lies behind the treatment of refutability or fruitfulness as a virtue, i.e. as a criterion of theory evaluation or selection. (Cf. Latour 1989) Contemporary science, on this view, is better understood as technoscience, inquiry into nature that is inseparable from its technological infrastructures and outcomes. Within this framework, the feminist pragmatic virtues could be understood not as a rejection of "pure science" but as a recognition of the technologically driven nature of science and a call for certain technological infrastructures and outcomes over others. Rejecting the conventional distinction between pure and applied science facilitates the rejection of the idea that scientists bear no responsibility for how their work is used. Thus the feminist pragmatic virtues can be a vehicle for bringing considerations of social responsibility back into the centre of scientific inquiry.

While all of these points could be further developed, I have, for each of the more mainstream epistemic values, indicated why their epistemic status is no greater than that of the alternatives advocated by feminist researchers and philosophers. This raises the question why, in spite of repeated demonstrations of the weakness of their probative value, philosophers persist in invoking them. Although I have elsewhere argued that the standard virtues have in certain contexts of their use both material and ideological sociopolitical consequences, I am inclined to think that these are (for the most part) unintended by most advocates of the traditional virtues and that their attraction lies elsewhere. One might start by noting that the traditional virtues do characterize classical Newtonian mechanics. They may have acquired their normative status by association in a framework that took physics as the model of science. I don't think, however, that this, even if on the right track, can be the whole of the story.

One might well ask of the alternative virtues I have described what makes them feminist. I think this is the wrong question. They are, after all, not advocated exclusively by feminists, but also by other oppositional scientists. They serve as alternatives for a larger (or different) scientific community than the feminist one. The question ought to be: what recommends the alternative virtues to feminists? As I have suggested elsewhere, what *ought* to recommend these virtues to feminists is that they (do or could) serve feminist cognitive goals. What makes feminists feminist is the desire to dismantle the oppression and subordination of women. This requires identification of the mechanisms and institutions of female oppression and subordination, that is, the mechanisms and institutions of gender. The cognitive goal of feminist researchers therefore, is to reveal the operation of gender, by making visible both the activities of those gendered female and the processes whereby they are made invisible, and by identifying the mechanisms whereby female gendered agents are subordinated. What ought to recommend these virtues to feminists, then, is that inquiry regulated by these values and theories characterized by these virtues are more likely to reveal gender than inquiry guided by the mainstream virtues. (For account of how this might work in particular contexts, see Longino (1994, 1996).) There is undoubtedly more to be said here as well, including consideration of other possible theoretical virtues, other cognitive aims, and the relations of these virtues to other (non-cognitive) values endorsed by feminists and to values endorsed by other communities of inquiry.

IV

Epistemological Reflections. What can these virtues tell us about the prospects for a normative feminist epistemology based on them? First of all, although the virtues have been endorsed by feminists (although not by all feminists) and can be discerned at work in feminist appraisal, their subordination to a broader cognitive goal means that they are not in and of themselves feminist theoretical virtues, or to put it another way, such subordination means that these alternative virtues will not necessarily be a part of a feminist epistemological kit. They have no intrinsic standing as feminist theoretical virtues or virtues for feminists, but only a provisional one. For as long as and to the extent that their regulative role can promote the goal of revealing gender, and as long as revealing gender remains the primary goal of feminist inquiry, they can serve as norms or standards of feminist inquiry. It is possible, however, that in different contexts they would not promote feminist cognitive goals, or that those goals themselves might change in such a way that other cognitively regulative norms would be called for. Indeed, to the extent that feminists dissent from the virtues, they may either be urging a change of feminist cognitive goals or claiming that the goals are not served by the virtues discussed here. There could be multiple sets of feminist cognitive virtues corresponding to different conceptions of what feminist cognitive goals are or should be. The concept of gender has itself changed as a consequence of feminist inquiry. Recognizing the disunity both of gender and of forms of gender subordination might require either a change in cognitive aim or a change in the virtues.

Secondly, the normative claim of these values/virtues is limited to the community sharing

the primary goal. On those who do not share it these virtues have no claim. To generalize this point, the alternative virtues are only binding in those communities sharing a cognitive goal that is advanced by those virtues. Their normative reach is, thus, local. In emphasizing the provisionality and locality of alternative virtues, this account contrasts quite sharply with accounts offered or implied by advocates of the traditional virtues which, as (purely) epistemic are represented as universally binding. I've indicated above the sorts of arguments that would cast doubt on such a claim. What is missing is the articulation of a cognitive goal that would ground the traditional virtues. If the structure of justification is the same as that for the alternative virtues, then the traditional virtues, no less than the alternative ones, are only provisional and locally binding. Both feminist and nonfeminist critics of mainstream science have argued that its goal is domination and control. This constitutes an interpretation of the practices of mainstream science. If it is a correct interpretation, then the traditional virtues would need to be evaluated relative to that cognitive aim. If it is not the goal of scientific practice, but is promoted by the traditional virtues, this would suggest a reexamination of the latter's status relative to the (real) goal of mainstream practice.

I've argued elsewhere (as have others) that the underdetermination argument necessitates a move away from individualism in philosophy of science and epistemology. To summarize my own version of such arguments: in light of the semantic gap between hypotheses and the statements describing data, the latter acquire evidential relevance for hypotheses only in light of background assumptions. Justificatory practices must therefore include not only the testing of hypotheses against data, but the subjection of background assumptions (and reasoning and data) to criticism from a variety of perspectives. Thus, intersubjective discursive interaction is added to interaction with the material world under investigation as components of methodology. From a normative point of view this means articulating conditions for effective criticism, typically specifying structural features of a discursive community that ensure the effectiveness of the critical discourse taking place within it. I have suggested four such conditions: (a) the provision of venues for the articulation of criticism, (b) uptake (rather than mere toleration) of criticism, (c) public standards to which discursive interactions are referenced, (d) equality of intellectual authority for all (qualified) members of the community.

Within this scheme the traditional and alternative virtues constitute partially overlapping, but distinctive sets of public community standards. That is, they serve to regulate discourse in their respective communities. They can be criticized or challenged relative to the cognitive aims they are taken to advance or to other values assigned higher priority and they can in turn serve as grounds for critique. Nor is criticism limited to intra-community discourse. The areas of overlap or intersection make possible critical interaction among as well as within communities. Generalizing from what I've earlier argued, the public standards that I argue must be a component feature of an objective or reliable scientific community will be binding only on those who share the overall cognitive goal that grounds those standards and who agree that the standards do indeed advance that cognitive goal. Such agreement must itself be the outcome of critical discursive interactions in a context satisfying conditions of effective criticism. As the virtues understood as public standards are subordinated to the advancement of a specific cognitive aim which may change, they must be understood as provisional. As they are binding only on those who share that aim, they must be understood as partial. This way of thinking about knowledge and inquiry involves a shift in attention away from the outcomes or products of inquiry, whether these are theories or beliefs, to the processes or dynamics of knowledge production. The ideal state is not the having of a single best account, but the existence of a plurality of theoretical orientations that both make possible the elaboration of particular models of the phenomenal world and serve as resources for criticism of each other.

I've already indicated why the feminist or any set of alternative theoretical virtues could not be superseded by the traditional virtues. Two further objections must be addressed. One might ask whether there is not a set of cognitive values different from both the set identified as traditional and that identified as alternative which would constitute universal norms. Perhaps the verdicts of provisionality and partiality are the consequence of looking at the wrong values. But this objection must provide examples of values that could be universally binding. The only characteristics of theories or hypotheses that might qualify are truth or empirical adequacy. But truth in the context of theory adjudication reduces to empirical adequacy—truth of the observational statements of a theory. And empirical adequacy is not sufficient to eliminate all but one of a set of contesting theories. It is because the purely epistemic is not rich enough to guide inquiry and theory appraisal that the values discussed earlier come into play. (For arguments about the insufficiency of truth simpliciter, see Anderson (1995) and Grandy (1987).) One might, alternatively, specify qualities of inquirers that count as virtues, for example, open-mindedness and sensory or logical acuity, but these are not theoretical, but personal virtues, not public standards of critical discourse but qualities required to participate constructively in such discourse. Secondly, one might resist the identification of competing sets of virtues and suggest the integration of the two sets of virtues. There are two difficulties with this suggestion. In particular contexts of inquiry virtues from the two sets recommend non-reconcilable theories. (Cf. Longino 1996) Moreover, integration can be understood in at least two ways, each involving quite different presuppositions. It might be proposed as fulfilling a commitment to unified science, but that commitment needs support. It might, on the other hand, be proposed as a way of realizing theoretical pluralism within a single community. This presupposes the value of the (particular) diversity of models that inclusion of both sets of values in a community's standards might produce. If so, what is called for is not integration of the virtues by one research community, but the tolerance of and interaction with research guided by different theoretical virtues, the construction of larger or meta-communities characterized by mutual respect for divergent points of view, i.e. by pluralism.

V

Feminist Theoretical Virtues and Feminist Epistemologies. Studying professedly feminist work in order to determine what cognitive ideals and standards serve a regulative or normative function for feminist inquiry (or at least some feminist inquiry) represents an approach to feminist epistemology that differs from some of the more iconic views in feminist theory of knowledge such as feminist standpoint theory or feminist empiricism.

Feminist standpoint theory has been one of the most visible and most discussed of feminist approaches to knowledge. Standpoint theory has been well-received among feminist thinkers, because it insists on the ineluctable situatedness of knowers. Beliefs endorsed, theories produced by individuals bear the stamp of their situations, which are what provide standpoints. Feminist standpoint theorists have emphasized the difference in the situations of and knowledge/beliefs consequently produced by men and women or by individuals occupying gendered positions, such as factory foreman, managerial bureaucrat, housewife or secretary. Some versions of standpoint theory articulate the contrast in more explicitly political terms as one between masculinist or androcentric and feminist standpoints, where androcentrism would be the default or unreflective standpoint in a male dominant society and a feminist standpoint would be the achievement of reflection. The notion that (broadly speaking) social factors might play a role in the production and acceptance of theories is not unique to standpoint theory. What distinguishes standpoint theory from other forms of contextualism is its normative dimension—its interest in identifying a better or more objective standpoint. As a Marxist standpoint theory privileges the standpoint of the proletariat over that of the bourgeoisie, so a feminist standpoint theory privileges the standpoint of women (or of feminists) over that of men (or of androcentrists or masculinists).

One repeated criticism of feminist standpoint theory is that there are many systematic differences among women (race, class, nationality, . . .) that generate different standpoints. There cannot be one women's standpoint, or even one feminist standpoint, but many. Another is that the theory ends up in something of a vicious circle, since the identification of standpoints, let alone epistemologically superior ones, requires theory which in turn requires justification, which implicates a standpoint. Sandra Harding, one of the strongest philosophical defenders of standpoint theory has turned the first objection into a virtue by urging what she calls "strong objectivity." This is achieved by systematic reflexivity and by "starting

thought" from all marginalized or socially subordinated positions, i.e. the positions of women and men in postcolonial societies, the positions of working class women and men in industrialized or in post-industrialized societies, of gay men and lesbians in industrialized societies, of the same in non-industrialized societies, etc. Maximal objectivity accrues to the body of inquiry most inclusive of heretofore marginalized standpoints. This proposal is somewhat hard to interpret (what, for instance, does "starting thought" mean?) and is still subject to charges of circularity as just sketched. But what is of more interest is the kind of theory of knowledge standpoint theory, even revised as Harding proposes, is. It has been called a form of naturalized epistemology because it proceeds from some empirical premises (Thalos 1994). But it shares with traditional epistemology a commitment to a singularly correct theory or set of theories as well as to a singularly correct methodology. Even though it locates those in particular social configurations, rather than in a set of context-free universally applicable rules (such as Bayesian inference rules), in sharing epistemic ideals with traditional normative epistemology, standpoint theory is closer to traditional epistemology than the contextualism outlined above. In the latter, (1) no single position or set of positions is granted authority it does not earn as a consequence of empirical application and critical interaction with other perspectives, (2) any epistemological orientation is seen as both provisional and partial, and (3) rather than some single theory providing a best or definitive account of reality, the availability of multiple theoretical approaches each illuminating different facets of a phenomenon constitutes the best epistemological outcome.

What might be called naive feminist empiricism shares with standpoint theory the goal of a single best account and supposes that androcentric science is a matter of failing to keep personal biases out of inquiry. Better science will be bias-free science. Naive empiricism shares with contextual empiricism the emphasis given to observational data, but supposes observational data and logic are sufficient to generate and justify theories. Contextualism, on the other hand, argues in light of underdetermination arguments for the necessity of assumptions establishing the evidential relevance of data to hypotheses and theories.

VI

Feminist Theoretical Virtues and Philosophical Epistemology. Both standpoint theory and feminist empiricism are normative theories. They prescribe conditions for producing knowledge. Study of the theoretical virtues as engaged in here is not normative but descriptive/analytic. It offers an interpretation of normative claims rather than itself prescribing. I have indicated how the virtues could be integrated into the minimally prescriptive contextual empiricism, but this integration does not privilege the feminist or any other set of theoretical virtues.

The complete set of regulative standards, inclusive of theoretical virtues, guiding a community's epistemic practices could be called its epistemology. This is the way the term "epistemology" is used outside of philosophy. Given that communities will be distinguished from each other by those non-overlapping elements of community regulative standards, such epistemologies are local epistemologies. If general epistemic norms like empirical adequacy require supplementation by the more specific and distinctive norms, then normative epistemology will be local epistemology, i.e. epistemic norms (apart from general prescriptions like "establish evidential relevance") will be only locally and provisionally binding. Feminist epistemology does turn out to be partial, but not viciously so. In one sense, it is as partial as any local epistemology, in that inquiry conducted under its auspices will not reveal a total, but an incomplete, picture of reality. In a second sense, it is partial, not in being distorted by, but in being directed to the aim of providing knowledge useful or necessary to a community identified by its political goals.

What then of the general inquiry we in philosophy call epistemology? I propose that general epistemology is not a normative, but an interpretive inquiry. General epistemology inquires into what is meant by distinctively epistemic language: what is the meaning of the distinctions between knowledge and belief, truth and falsity, objectivity and subjectivity and what is the relation between the values embedded in those distinctions and the epistemic practices of communities employing those distinctions. This inquiry is not just into what *is* meant, but what *could be* meant given both particular cognitive resources and particular cognitive aims. Philosophical epistemology, I propose, makes sense of our epistemically evaluative behaviour, but does not prescribe for it. Normative or prescriptive epistemology that can make contact with actual inquiry is the task of those communities engaged in inquiry. Philosophers who engage in normative epistemology should be understood as doing so not as members of a class having special insight into knowledge, but as members of particular communities of inquiry characterized by partiality and provisionality, contributing to what from both a human's and a God's eye view is a plurality of models and theories, rather than a single account that captures all facets of reality.

VII

Conclusion. I have argued that a set of theoretical virtues can be extracted from the normative reflections of feminists engaged in inquiry. This set constitutes an alternative and a challenge to the traditional epistemic virtues, as well as a set of virtues that could guide inquiry directed to feminist cognitive aims. To the extent that feminist epistemology is work for feminist philosophers, it is work for us as members of a feminist community of inquiry. Our task, as I see it, is not to prescribe to but to participate with other members of that community in developing the criteria that will advance our cognitive aims. General philosophical epistemology, by contrast, makes sense of our most general epistemically evaluative norms and behaviour, norms and behaviour that we share with others who share concepts such as "know" and "believe." As philosophers we may be able to achieve some critical distance that facilitates our offering interpretations of our community's practices to it, but changes in those practices must be recommended from a position that is embedded in the community, not one that stands apart from it.

XI.3 Knowledge and Propaganda: Reflections of an Old Feminist

SUSAN HAACK

A biographical sketch for Susan Haack precedes Reading V.8. Haack argues that the locution *feminist* epistemology is both confused and dangerous. It is confused because there is no special female way of knowing or justifying beliefs. There is no more a feminist epistemology than there is a "Republican epistemology." It is dangerous because it leads to a "fashionable kind of intellectual apartheid of the sexes." The goals of epistemology have to do with truth-seeking, of aiming at impartial regard for the evidence, whereas feminist epistemologists are primarily concerned with political goals. As such, they are in the propaganda business, supporters of political correctness.

The philosophy which is now in vogue . . . cherishes certain tenets . . . which tend to a deliberate and factitious despair, which . . . cuts the sinews and spur of industry . . . And all for . . . the miserable vainglory of having it believed that whatever has not yet been discovered and comprehended can never be discovered or comprehended hereafter.

—Francis Bacon[1]

I have been a feminist since the age of twelve, when I got the top grade in my first chemistry exam, and the boy who got the next highest grade protested indignantly that it wasn't *fair*, "everyone knows girls can't do chemistry." And, since I have been working in epistemology for more than a decade now, I think I qualify as an epistemologist. So I must be a feminist epistemologist, right? Wrong; on the contrary, I think there is no such connection between feminism and epistemology as the rubric "feminist epistemology" requires.

Perhaps you think that only someone of extreme right-wing political views could possibly be less than enthusiastic about feminist epistemology. If so, you are mistaken; both because the only thing extreme about my political views is my dislike of extremes, and because my reasons for thinking feminist epistemology misconceived are, in any case, not political but epistemological.

The last fifteen years or so have seen a major shift within feminist philosophy: from a modest style which stressed the common humanity of women and men, focused on justice and opportunity, and was concerned primarily with issues in social and political theory; to an ambitious, imperialist feminism which stresses the "woman's point of view," and claims revolutionary significance for all areas of philosophy, epistemology included.

So, yes, the pun in my title is intentional; my feminism is of the older-fashioned, modest stripe.[2] But I am taking issue, here, only with the imperialist ambitions of the new feminism with respect to epistemology specifically.

The rubric "feminist epistemology" is incongruous on its face, in somewhat the way of, say, "Republican epistemology." And the puzzlement this prompts is rather aggravated than mitigated by the bewildering diversity of epistemological ideas described as "feminist." Among self-styled feminist epistemologists one finds quasi-foundationalists, coherentists, contextualists; those who stress connectedness, community, the social aspects of knowledge, and those who stress emotion, presumably subjective and personal; those who stress concepts of epistemic virtue, those who want the "androcentric" norms of the epistemological tradition to be replaced by "gynocentric" norms, and those who advocate the descriptivist approach. . . . Even apparent agreement, e.g., that feminist epistemology will stress the social aspects of knowledge, masks significant *dis*agreement about what this means: that inquirers are pervasively dependent on one another; that cooperative inquiry is better

This paper originally appeared in *Reason Papers* 18 (Fall 1993) under the title "Epistemological Reflections of an Old Feminist." A slightly modified and abridged version appeared under the present title in *Partisan Review* (fall 1993). It is reprinted here by permission.

than individual inquiry; that epistemic justification is community-relative; that only a social group, not an individual, can properly be said to inquire or to know; that reality is socially constructed. . . .[3]

The puzzlement is further aggravated by the reflection that neither all, nor only, females, or feminists, favor all, or indeed any, of the ideas offered under the rubric "feminist epistemology." Charles Peirce, for example, is critical of what he calls the "vicious individualism" of Descartes's criterion of truth, and has a subtle conception of the social aspects of inquiry; yet he was neither female nor (to judge by his use of "masculine intellect" to mean "tough, powerful mind") feminist. John Stuart Mill surely qualifies as feminist if any male philosopher does; yet one finds none of the supposedly feminist themes in his epistemology—anymore than one does in Ayn Rand's.[4]

So, what *is* feminist about feminist epistemology? There seem to be two routes by which feminism and epistemology are taken to be connected, corresponding to two interpretations of the phrase "the woman's point of view": as "the way women see things," or as "serving the interests of women."[5]

Sometimes we are told that feminist epistemology represents women's "ways of knowing." This reversion to the notion of "thinking like a woman" is disquietingly reminiscent of old, sexist stereotypes.[6] Still, there *are* disquieting truths, so this hardly settles the matter. But I am not convinced that there *are* any distinctively female "ways of knowing." All *any* human being has to go on, in figuring out how things are, is his or her sensory and introspective experience, and the explanatory theorizing he or she devises to accommodate it; and differences in cognitive style, like differences in handwriting, seem more individual than gender-determined.[7]

The profusion of incompatible themes proposed as "feminist epistemology" itself speaks against the idea of a distinctively female cognitive style. But even if there were such a thing, the case for feminist epistemology would require further argument to show that female "ways of knowing" (scare quotes because the term is tendentious, since "knows" is a success-word) represent better procedures of inquiry or subtler standards of justification than the male. And, sure enough, we are told that insights into the theory of knowledge are available to women which are not available, or not easily available, to men. In all honesty, I cannot see how

the evidence to date could be thought to speak in favor of this bold claim; what my experience suggests is rather that the questions of the epistemological tradition are *hard*, very hard, for anyone, of either sex, to answer or even significantly to clarify.[8]

It is said that oppressed, disadvantaged, and marginalized people are epistemically privileged in virtue of their oppression and disadvantage.[9] If this were true, it would suggest that the *truly* epistemically privileged are not the affluent, well-educated, white, Western women who (mostly) rest their claim to special insight upon it, but the most oppressed, the most disadvantaged—some of who are men. But, aside from appeals to the authority of Karl Marx on epistemological matters,[10] is there any reason to think it *is* true? Thomas Kuhn observed that revolutionary scientific innovations are often made by persons who are at the margin of a discipline;[11] but women, as a class, are not "marginal" in *this* sense. And one of the ways in which oppressed people *are* oppressed is, surely, that their oppressors control the information that reaches them. This argues, if anything, an epistemic *dis*advantage for "oppressed, disadvantaged, marginalized" people.

So no such connection between feminism and epistemology as the rubric "feminist epistemology" requires is to be found under the first interpretation of "the woman's point of view" as "the way women see things."

Under the second interpretation, "serving the interests of women," the connection is supposed to be made, rather, by way of feminist criticisms of sexism in scientific theorizing.[12] The two routes connecting feminism and epistemology would merge on the assumption—which, of course, I do not accept—that sexism in scientific theorizing is the result of the exclusion of female "ways of knowing." A very faint trace of the first route would be detectable along the second on the assumption—which, with the caveat that it would be naive to suppose that only men subscribe to sexist stereotypes, I am inclined to grant—that women are a bit more likely than men to notice such sexism.

In the social sciences and biology, theories which are not well-supported by the evidence do seem sometimes to have come to be accepted by scientists, most often male scientists, who have taken stereotypical ideas of masculine and feminine behavior uncritically for granted.[13] Those who think that criticisms of sexism in scientific theorizing require a new, feminist epistemology insist that we are obliged, in the light of these criticisms, to acknowledge political considerations as legitimate ways to decide between theories.

But on the face of it these criticisms suggest exactly the opposite conclusion—that politics should be kept out of science.[14] I can make sense of how things get so startlingly transmuted only by looking at feminist epistemology, not just as part of a larger development in feminism, but also as part of a larger development in epistemology. Here the last thirty years or so have seen a major shift: from the old deferentialist view, which took science to deserve a kind of epistemic authority in virtue of its peculiarly objective method of inquiry; to a new cynicism, which sees science as a value-permeated social institution, stresses the importance of politics, prejudice, and propaganda, rather than the weight of the evidence, in determining what theories are accepted, and sometimes goes so far as to suggest that reality is constructed by us, and "truth" a word not to be used without the precaution of scare quotes.[15]

My diagnosis is that the new cynicism in philosophy of science has fed the ambition of the new feminism to colonize epistemology. The values with which science is permeated, it is argued, have been, up till now, androcentric, sexist, inhospitable to the interests of women. Feminist criticisms of sexism in scientific theorizing, the argument continues, cannot be seen merely as criticisms of bad science; the moral to be drawn is that we must abandon the quixotic quest for a science that is value-free, in favor of the achievable goal of a science informed by feminist values. There would be a genuinely feminist epistemology if the aspiration *to legitimate the idea that feminist values should determine what theories are accepted* could be achieved.

The arguments offered to motivate the shift from feminist criticisms of sexism in scientific theorizing to feminist epistemology are of precisely the kind this diagnosis would predict. I can consider here only the two most important lines of argument, each of which focuses on a notion dear to the hearts of the new cynics: underdetermination and value-ladenness.

The first appeals to "the underdetermination of theories by data," claiming that, since there is unavoidable slack with respect to what theories are accepted, it is proper to allow political preferences to determine theory choice.[16] Suppose, first, that

the appeal to underdetermination is intended only to point to the fact that sometimes the available evidence is not sufficient to decide between rival theories, and that in some cases (e.g., with respect to theories about the remote past, "man the hunter" and all that) additional evidence may be, in practice, unobtainable. The proper response is that, unless and until more evidence is available, scientists had better suspend judgment—and that the lay public, philosophers included, should not be too uncritically deferential to scientists' sometimes unwarrantedly confident claims about what they have discovered. Underdetermination, in this sense, has not the slightest tendency to show that we may legitimately choose to believe whatever theory suits our political purposes.

Suppose, next, that the appeal to underdetermination is intended, rather, to rest on the Quinean thesis that there can be incompatible theories with the same observational consequences—theories, therefore, between which not even all possible evidence could decide. Fortunately the issues at stake here do not depend on whether or not the thesis is proven. (Quine himself at one point suggests that what he formerly described as empirically equivalent but incompatible theories would really only be verbal variants of one theory.) For in any case, if the thesis were true, it would presumably be true only of the genuinely theoretical (in the sense of "unobservable"); it would be irrelevant, therefore, to such questions as whether men's hunting or women's gathering mainly sustained prehistoric communities. And if it *were* relevant to such questions, the feminists' appeals to it would be self-defeating, since in that case it would undermine their presumption that we can know what theories conduce to the interests of women, or what those interests are.[17]

The second line of argument urges the necessity of "rubbing out the boundary between science and values,"[18] and hence, again, the appropriateness of allowing feminist values to determine theory choice. In one version, the argument seems to be that the idea that feminist values could not constitute evidence with respect to this or that theory rests on an untenable distinction of descriptive versus normative. This argument is only as good as the reasons for thinking the required distinction untenable. What is at issue is not whether moral or political criticisms of priorities within science, or of uses of the findings of science, are ever appropriate; not whether an evolutionary account of moral values is defensible; not whether simplicity, e.g., might have a more than pragmatic role; not whether some epistemic norms may turn out to be covertly of a descriptive, means-end character; but *whether it is possible to derive an "is" from an "ought."*[19] I can find no argument in the literature that even purports to show this, and neither can I think of one. That it is false is manifest as soon as one expresses it plainly: that propositions about what states of affairs are *desirable* to *deplorable* could be evidence that things *are*, or *are not*, so.

In another version, the second line of argument seems to rest on the claim that it is impossible entirely to exclude "contextual" (i.e., external, social, and political) values from science. In this version, the argument is a non sequitur. Perhaps it is true that the scientists are never entirely without prejudice; perhaps it is impossible that they should entirely put their prejudices out of sight when judging the evidence for a theory; it doesn't follow that it is proper to allow prejudice to determine theory choice. Even if it is not possible to make science perfect, it doesn't follow that we shouldn't try to make it better.

The failure of these arguments is symptomatic of the false presupposition on which the second proposed route to connect feminism and epistemology depends: that, since the old deferentialist picture is not defensible, there is no option but the new cynicism. These are not the only options; the truth lies, as it so often does, between the extremes.[20] The old deferentialist overstresses the virtues, the new cynicism the vices, of science; the old deferentialist focuses too exclusively on the logical, the new cynicism too exclusively on the sociological, factors that an adequate philosophy of science should combine. Science is neither sacred nor a confidence trick. It has been the most successful of human cognitive endeavors, but it is thoroughly fallible and imperfect—and, in particular, like all human cognitive endeavors, it is susceptible to fad and fashion, partiality and politics.

Implicit here is a conception of the epistemological role of the sociology of science which is worth making explicit, since it challenges an assumption which, it seems, both some old deferentialists and some new cynics take for granted—that the sociology of knowledge somehow constitutes a threat to traditional epistemological concerns. It is manifest as soon as it is stated plainly that no sociological investigation or theory could be sufficient by itself to show that the idea of theories being better or worse supported by evidence is untenable. But to say this is not to deny that the sociology of knowledge has any possible relevance to epistemology. Sometimes scientists are scrupulous in seeking out and assessing relevant evidence; sometimes not. Presumably, there is always some explanation of why they behave as they do, sometimes an explanation appealing to the individual psychology of the scientists concerned, sometimes an explanation appealing to considerations of a more sociological kind (e.g., that political pressures led these scientists to ignore or gloss over the relevance of such-and-such easily available evidence; that the knowledge that their work would come under the critical scrutiny of a rival team also aspiring to the Nobel prize ensured that those scientists left no stone unturned; etc.). The value of such sociological investigations to epistemology is that they may suggest what ways of organizing science are apt to encourage, and what to discourage, scrupulous attention to the evidence.[21]

If my diagnosis is correct, then though it is not inevitable that all the themes offered under the rubric "feminist epistemology" are false, it *is* inevitable that only those themes can be true which fail in their cynical intent. It is true, e.g., that inquirers are profoundly and pervasively dependent on each other; it is true that sometimes scientists may perceive relevant evidence *as* relevant only when persuaded, perhaps by political pressure, out of previous prejudices. But such truths have no radical consequences; it does not follow, e.g., that reality is however some epistemic community determines it to be, or that what evidence *is* relevant is not an objective matter.

And the epistemological significance of feminist criticisms of sexism in scientific theorizing, though real enough, is undramatic and by no means revolutionary. One traditional project of epistemology is to give rules, or, better, guidelines, for the conduct of inquiry; another is to articulate criteria of evidence or justification.[22] One sub-task of the "conduct of inquiry" project is to figure out what environments are supportive of, and what hostile to, successful inquiry. One sub-task of this sub-task is to figure out how to minimize the effect of unquestioned and unjustifiable preconceptions in encouraging the acceptance of theories which are not well-supported by evidence. (Greater diversity within science may be one way to do this. If we cannot ensure that scientists leave all their prejudices at the laboratory door, it may nevertheless be possible to ensure that there is enough diversity within the laboratory for prejudices and counter-prejudices to cancel out.)[23] Feminist criticisms of sexist science, like studies of the disasters of Nazi or Soviet science, can be a useful resource in the sub-sub-task of the "conduct of inquiry" project. But this is a role that requires the conception of theories as better or worse supported by the evidence, and the distinction of evidential and non-evidential considerations, traditionally investigated in the "criteria of justification" project; it is not a role that allows us to abandon or requires us radically to revise the concepts of evidence or truth or reality.[24]

Still, you may ask, given that I have not denied that some themes presented under the rubric "feminist epistemology" are true, and that I grant that some feminist criticisms of sexist science seem well-founded and have a bona fide epistemological role, why do I make all this fuss about the label? Well, since the idea that there is an epistemology properly called "feminist" rests on false presuppositions, the label is at best sloppy. But there is more at stake than dislike of sloppiness; more than offense at the implication that those of us who don't think it appropriate to describe our epistemological work as "feminist" don't care about justice for women; more than unease at sweeping generalizations about women and embarrassment at the suggestion that women have special epistemological insight. What is most troubling is that the label is designed to convey the idea that *inquiry should be politicized*. And *that* is not only mistaken, but dangerously so.

It is dangerously mistaken from an epistemological point of view, because the presupposition on which it rests—that genuine, disinterested inquiry is impossible—is, in Bacon's shrewd phrase, a "factitious despair" which will, indeed, "cut the sinews and spur of industry." Serious intellectual work is hard, painful, frustrating; suggesting that it is legitimate to succumb to the temptation to cut corners can only block the way of inquiry.[25]

I would say that inquiry really is best advanced by people with a genuine desire to find out how things are, who will be more persistent, less dogmatic, and more candid than sham reasoners seeking only to make a case for some foregone conclusion; except that, since it is a tautology that inquiry aims at the truth, the sham reasoner is not really engaged in inquiry at all.[26] This should remind us that those who despair of honest inquiry cannot be in the truth-seeking business (as they should say, "the 'truth' racket"); they are in the propaganda business.[27]

And this makes it apparent why the idea that inquiry should be politicized is dangerously mistaken, also, from a political point of view, because of the potential for tyranny of calls for "politically adequate research and scholarship."[28] Think what "politically *in*adequate research" refers to: research informed by what some feminists deem "regressive" political ideas—and research not informed by political ideas at all, i.e., honest inquiry. Have we forgotten already that in *Nineteen Eighty-Four* it was *thoughtcrime* to believe that two plus two is four if the Party ruled otherwise?[29] This is no trivial verbal quibble, but a matter, epistemologically, of the integrity of inquiry and, politically, of freedom of thought. Needlessly sacrificing these ideals would not help women; it would hurt humanity.

Notes

[1] Francis Bacon, *The New Organon* (1620), Book 1, aphorism LXXXVIII.

[2] The clash of "old" and "new" feminisms is nothing new; here is British novelist and feminist Winifred Holtby, writing in 1926:

> The New Feminism emphasizes the importance of the "woman's point of view," the Old Feminism believes in the primary importance of the human being. . . . Personally I am . . . an Old Feminist, because I dislike everything that feminism implies. I desire an end to the whole business, the demands for equality. . . . But while. . . opportunity [is] denied, I shall have to be a feminist. . . . (Cited in Rosalind Delmar, "Afterword," to Vera Brittain, *Testament of Friendship* [1945; London: Virago, 1980], p. 450.)

It ought to be said that fewer opportunities are now denied, that the "end to the whole business" is, hopefully, closer than it was in 1926.

[3] For example, Lorrain Code represents herself as an "empirico-realist," acknowledging the affinity of this conception with foundationalism (*Epistemic Responsibility* [Hanover, NH: University Press of New England, 1987], p. 6); Lynn Hankinson Nelson follows Quine, whom she interprets as holding a coherentist theory of evidence (*Who*

Knows: From Quine to a Feminist Empiricism
[Philadelphia, PA: Temple University Press, 1990], pp. 25–27, 85–86, 91–94, 112–17); Jane Duran represents herself as a contextualist (*Toward a Feminist Epistemology* [Savage, MD: Rowman and Littlefield, 1991], pp. 119ff.). But matters are not really as straightforward as this suggests, since there are in each case apparent inconsistencies: after aligning herself with "empirico-realism," Code bemoans the "aridity" of the whole issue of foundationalism versus coherentism (p. 7) and hints that it is somehow misconceived; Nelson acknowledges (pp. 22ff.) that Quine's conception of evidence allows an important role for experience; Duran describes the female point of view as instinctively coherentist (p. 14). Again, Duran appears to hold that feminist epistemology should be "naturalistic" in the sense of descriptivist (pp. 204ff.); *and* that it should focus on other conceptions of justification than the epistemological (pp. 12–13); *and* that it should replace androcentric norms with gynocentric ones (pp. 73ff).

It is all very confusing. Sandra Harding tells us that it is to be expected that feminist epistemology will "contain contradictions," that it is "multiple and contradictory knowledge" out of which we are "to learn and think" (*Whose Science? Whose Knowledge?* [Ithaca, NY: Cornell University Press, 1991], pp. 180, 285, 275). This is not very reassuring.

[4]The critique of Descartes is to be found in Charles S. Peirce, *Collected Papers*, ed. Charles Hartshorne, Paul Weiss, and Arthur Burks (Cambridge, MA, and London: Harvard University Press, 1931–58), 5.213–310; Peirce's social conception of inquiry is already apparent in perhaps his best-known paper, "The Fixation of Belief," 5.358–77. See also Susan Haack, "Descartes, Peirce, and the Cognitive Community," *The Monist*, vol. 65 no. 2 (1982), pp. 156–81, and in Eugene Freeman, ed., *The Relevance of Charles Peirce* (La Salle, IL: Monist Library of Philosophy, 1983), pp. 238–63. For Peirce's use of "masculine intellect," see *Collected Papers*, 5.368, and his review of Lady Welby's *What is Meaning?*, 8.171: "Lady Victoria Welby's book . . . is a feminine work, and too masculine mind might think it painfully weak." Other themes sometimes described as "feminist" are also to be found in Peirce (e.g., a penchant for replacing dichotomies by trichotomies); and different "feminist" themes are to be found in other pragmatists (e.g., William James's Will to Believe doctrine, allowing a legitimate cognitive role to "our passional nature"). But, for obvious reasons, I think it inappropriate to attempt to trace "anticipations of feminist epistemology/metaphysics/philosophy of language/ etc." in pragmatism (as in the symposium in *Transaction of the Charles S. Peirce Society*, vol. XXVII, no. 4 [1991]).

For John Stuart Mill, see *A System of Logic* (1843; London: Longman, 1970), and *The Subjection of Women* (1869; Chicago, IL: Phoenix Books, University of Chicago Press, 1970). I say Mill counts as a feminist "if any male philosopher does" to draw attention to Harding's discussion of the male feminist—"The Monster," as she calls him (*Whose Science? Whose Knowledge?*, p. 284)—and to note that some writers, though not Harding, suspect that the monster may be mythical, an impossible beast; see Scarlet Friedman and Elizabeth Sara, eds., *On the Problem of Men* (London: Women's Press, 1982), and Alice Jardine and Paul Smith, eds., *Men in Feminism* (New York: Methuen, 1987).

For Ayn Rand, see *Introduction to Objectivist Epistemology* (New York: Mentor, 1966).

[5]Of course, some of those who describe themselves as "feminist epistemologists" do so only because they are picking up some theme described elsewhere as "feminist"; and some, perhaps, for no better reason than that, since they are female and doing epistemology, what they are doing must be feminist epistemology.

[6]Cf. this observation, from p. 1 of Nancy Holland, *Is Women's Philosophy Possible?* (Savage, MD: Rowman and Littlefield, 1990): "Women's philosophy seems to entail a healthy skepticism about universal generalizations." (My thanks to John Nuechterlein for drawing this gem to my attention.)

The tendency for feminists' generalizations to mirror old stereotypes can hardly escape attention; Andrea Nye's "feminist critique" of logic (*Words of Power* [New York and London: Routledge, 1990]), mirroring the old cliche that "women are so illogical," being a striking case in point. Ironically enough, where they are at all plausible Nye's criticisms of formal logic are familiar from the work of earlier (male) writers who stressed the inadequacy of symbolic logic to represent pragmatic aspects of reasoning. See Ferdinand C. S. Schiller, *Formal Logic: A Scientific and Social Problem* (London: MacMillan, 1912); Peter F. Strawson, *Introduction to Logical Theory* (London: Methuen, 1952); Stephen Toulmin, *The Uses of Argument* (Cambridge: Cambridge University Press, 1958). And, of course, the notion of "reading" which Nye favors derives from the work of male writers such as Paul de Man.

[7]I am skeptical of attempts to establish this by appeal to Object Relations theory, as in, e.g., the paper by Jane Flax in Sandra Harding and Merrill Hintikka, eds., *Discovering Reality: Feminist Perspectives on Epistemology, Metaphysics, Methodology, and Philosophy of Science* (Dordrecht: Reidel, 1983); Evelyn Fox Keller, *Reflections on Gender and Science* (New Haven and London: Yale University Press, 1985). Not only is the theory very speculative, it is also very vague, and its pertinence to the claim that women have different ways of knowing than men is tenuous at best.

Mary Field Belenky et al., *Women's Ways of Knowing* (New York: Basic Books, 1986) purports to offer direct, empirical evidence of "women's ways of knowing." In this, I think, it entirely fails. It reports only studies *of women*; and these studies do not replicate, with female subjects, the studies already undertaken by William Perry with male subjects (*Forms of Intellectual and Ethical Development in the College Years* [New York: Rinehart and Winston, 1970]). The authors chose to ask their subjects different questions than Perry asked his because they already believed that "there is a masculine bias at the heart of most academic disciplines, methodologies and theories" (p. 8)—

a proposition, they claim, "convincingly argued" by feminist academics, among whom they mention Fox Keller and the authors collected in Harding and Hintikka, *Discovering Reality*. The issue here is not the merits or demerits of Perry's categories, but the fact that Belenky et al. make no attempt to study *both* men *and* women under *one* set of categories—surely a minimally necessary condition of discovering whether there are or aren't male and female cognitive styles. The question was begged in the design of the study.

[8]And, I should add, that the capacity for original, creative philosophical thought is quite a rare and unusual talent. I recall, in this context, the observation attributed to Peirce by Eric Temple Bell: "There is a kink in my damned brain that prevents me from thinking as other people think" (*The Development of Mathematics* [New York and London: McGraw Hill, 1949], p. 519). It is just such individual idiosyncrasies—not the "group-think" apparently admired by some feminists—that philosophical (and scientific, artistic, etc.) innovation requires.

[9]See, e.g., Alison Jaggar, "Love and Knowledge: Emotion in a Feminist Epistemology," in Anne Garry and Marilyn Pearsall, eds., *Women, Knowledge, and Reality* (Boston: Unwin Hyman, 1989), p. 146; Harding, *Whose Science? Whose Knowledge?*, p. 271; Nelson, *Who Knows: From Quine to a Feminist Empiricism*, p. 40. Some, seeing that the "privilege of disadvantage" thesis suggests *greater* privilege for the *more* marginalized, claim special epistemological privilege for lesbians (see, e.g., Marilyn Frye's essay in *Women, Knowledge, and Reality*, p. 77).

[10]See, e.g., Nancy Hartstock's essay in Harding and Hintikka, *Discovering Reality*; Harding, *Whose Science? Whose Knowledge?*, p. 58.

[11]Thomas Kuhn, *The Structure of Scientific Revolutions* (Chicago and London: University of Chicago Press, 1962). I owe to correspondence with Mary Hesse the neat observation that Kuhn is himself such an "outsider" (with respect to the philosophy of science, that is).

[12]This labored phrase is necessary in order to make it clear that the issue concerns feminist criticisms focusing on the content of scientific theories, not feminist criticisms of the choice of problems on which scientists work, or of there being relatively few, and mostly relatively junior, women scientists. I am not saying that the latter kinds of criticism are never justified, only that they are not relevant to the line of argument under consideration here.

I should also make it clear that I am using the term "sexist" in such a way that a theory counts as sexist only if it is false. See my review of Harding and Hintikka, eds., *Discovering Reality*, in *Philosophy*, vol. 60 (1985), pp. 265–70.

[13]Ruth Bleier's criticisms, in Bleier, ed., *Feminist Approaches to Science* (New York: Pergamon Press, 1986), of some claims about hormonal determinism are among the most convincing. I have two cents' worth of my own to contribute here: the claim that male dominance is hormonally determined is confidently reiterated by critics of

feminism such as Nicholas Davidson and Michael Levin, both of whom cite Steven Goldberg as their source; Goldberg cites a medical researcher called Money. Imagine my astonishment, then, on tracking down Money's work, to find that he says specifically that questions about dominance *were not addressed* in his study of genetic females exposed before birth to high levels of male hormones! For details, see my review on Davidson and Levin, in *International Studies in Philosophy*, vol. 23, no. 1 (1991), pp. 107–9.

Other feminist criticisms of sexism in scientific theorizing are to be found in, e.g., Anne Fausto-Sterling, *Myths of Gender: Biological Theories about Women and Men* (New York: Basic Books, 1986), and Helen Longino and Ruth Doell, "Body, Bias, and Behavior: A Comparative Analysis of Reasoning in Two Areas of Science," in Jean O'Barr and Sandra Harding, eds., *Sex and Scientific Inquiry* (Chicago: University of Chicago Press, 1989).

Let me make it as clear as I can that my view is that each feminist critique of this or that bit of scientific theorizing has to be considered on its own merits; of course, in some instances it may be difficult for someone outside the field to determine what those merits are. But I should also say that I am skeptical of the idea that sexism infects theorizing not only in the social sciences and biology, but also in the physical sciences; at any rate, I have never encountered a convincing example.

[14]This seems an appropriate time for a comment about the use of the term "feminist empiricism," which is potentially confusing. In both *The Science Question in Feminism* (Ithaca, NY: Cornell University Press, 1986) and *Whose Science? Whose Knowledge?*, Sandra Harding distinguished three positions within feminist epistemology: feminist empiricism, feminist standpoint theories, and feminist postmodernism; and she characterizes "feminist empiricism" as holding that feminist criticisms of sexism in scientific theorizing are criticisms of "bad science" (her scare quotes), not requiring any change in the appraisal of "science as usual." As Helen Longino observes ("Science, Objectivity, and Feminist Values," *Feminists Studies*, vol. 14, no. 3 [1988], p. 571), *this* "feminist empiricism" seems to be characterized just so as to be a foil to the feminist standpoint theories Harding favors; as I would say, "feminist" in "feminist empiricism" seems redundant. In this sense, Stephen Jay Gould, or myself, qualify as "feminist empiricists," even though we both deny that a specifically feminist epistemology is required. (See Gould's review of Ruth Bleier, ed., *Feminist Approaches to Science*, in *New York Times Book Review*, August 12, 1984, p. 7.)

But Nelson, who entitles her book *Who Knows: From Quine to Feminist Empiricism*, is no such pallid creature; hers is a feminist empiricism which insists that feminist political considerations should determine theory choice.

[15]My description is, of course, very simplified. But I think it is true to the spirit of the shift.

[16]Helen Longino, "Can There Be a Feminist Science?" in Garry and Pearsall, eds., *Women, Knowledge, and Reality*, p. 206; Nelson, *Who Knows: From Quine to a Feminist*

Empiricism, pp. 173–74, 187–88, 248. I have the impression that Longino favors the first of the two versions of the argument distinguished below, Nelson the second.

17Willard Van Orman Quine, "Empirically Equivalent Theories of the World," *Erkenntnis*, vol. 9 (1975), pp. 313–28, and "Empirical Content," in Quine, *Theories and Things* (Cambridge, MA and London: Belknap Press of Harvard University Press, 1981), pp. 24–30. This passage from the latter (pp. 29–30) is unambiguous enough:

> Being incompatible, the two theory formulations that we are imagining must evaluate some sentence oppositely. Since they are nevertheless empirically equivalent, that sentence must contain terms that are short on observational criteria. But then we can . . . pick out one of those terms and treat it as if it were two independent words, one in one theory formulation and another in the other. We can mark this by changing the spelling of the word in one of the two theory formulations.
>
> Pressing this trivial expedient, we can resolve all conflict between the two theory formulations . . .

Theories and Things appears in Nelson's bibliography, but I have not been able to find any discussion of this passage from "Empirical Content."

What I have said here, of course, falls way short of a thorough discussion of the undetermination thesis, which would require, *inter alia*, consideration of the status of such pragmatic values as simplicity in theory choice. Two recent discussions which illustrate the complexities of the issues here are Laurens Laudan, "Demystifying Underdetermination," in *Scientific Theories*, ed. C. Wade Savage (Minneapolis, MN: University of Minnesota Press, 1990), pp. 267–97, and Brian Ellis, "What Science Aims to Do," in Paul Churchland and Christopher Hooker, eds., *Images of Science* (Chicago: University of Chicago Press, 1985), pp. 48–74.

18Nelson, *From Quine to a Feminist Empiricism*, p. 248. See also Longino, "Can There Be a Feminist Science?" Once again, my impression is that Nelson favors the in-principle version of the argument, Longino the in-practice variant. See also Harding, *Whose Science? Whose Knowledge?*, pp. 57ff.

19Or more strictly speaking, whether the statement that *p* ought [not] to be the case could be evidence that *p* is [not] the case.

20"[L]et us remember how common the folly is, of going from one faulty extreme into the opposite" (Thomas Reid, *Essays on the Intellectual Powers* [1785], in Thomas Reid, *Inquiry and Essays*, ed. R. E. Beanblossom and K. Lehrer [Indianapolis: Hackett, 1983], Essay VI, ch. 4, p. 262).

21After Peirce, Michael Polanyi seems to me to have best understood these issues. See "The Republic of Science," in Marjorie Grene, ed., *Knowing and Being* (Chicago: University of Chicago Press, 1969), p. 49–62. I think one might attribute Polanyi's insights in part to his having worked as a scientist, at different stages of his career, on both sides of the Iron Curtain, an experience which left him acutely aware of the dangers of politicizing science.

22Reliabilists, however, confuse the two projects. Cf. chapter 10 of Susan Haack, *Evidence and Inquiry: Towards Reconstruction in Epistemology* (Oxford: Blackwell, 1993) for a more careful articulation of the differences between them. Note that I there argue that the "conduct of inquiry" project is more hospitable to pluralism, and to the social aspects of epistemology, than the "criteria of justification" project.

23Implicit in this is a deflationary interpretation of the grain of truth in the "multiple standpoints" account of objectivity suggested by Harding in *Whose Science? Whose Knowledge?*

24*Contra* Harding, *Whose Science? Whose Knowledge?*, p. 38: "Issues of access for women in the practices of science turn out to have . . . radical consequences for the logic of inquiry and explanation."

25"Do not block the way of inquiry" is, according to Peirce, a proposition that "deserves to be written on every wall of the city of philosophy" (*Collected Papers*, 1.135).

26*Webster's*. "*Inquiry*: search for truth, information or knowledge."

See Susan Haack, "The First Rule of Reason," (1992), in *The Rule of Reason: The Philosophy of Charles Sanders Peirce*, eds Jacqueline Brunning and Paul Forester (Toronto: Toronto University Press, 1997), 246–61 for a detailed defense of the claims made in this paragraph. The term "sham reasoning," and its characterization, are both due to Peirce.

In this paper I also suggest a diagnosis of the organizational pressures which encourage the fashion in contemporary philosophy for exaggerated claims (that developments in neurophysiology show epistemology misconceived, that feminism requires a radically new epistemology, etc., etc.,). I agree with Longino, by the way, that to improve the condition of science would probably require changes in the way in which it is presently organized and funded—though not, of course, that more politicization, provided it was of the "right" sort, would constitute improvement.

27Some admit this unambiguously, e.g., Elizabeth Gross, who writes: "[F]eminist theory . . . is not a true discourse . . . It could be appropriately seen, rather, as a *strategy*, . . . [an] intervention with definite political . . . aims . . . intellectual guerrilla warfare" ("What is Feminist Theory?" in *Feminist Challenges*, eds. Carole Pateman and Elizabeth Gross [Sydney, London, and Boston: Allen and Unwin, 1986], p. 177; cited in David Stove, "A Farewell to Arts," *Quadrant*, May 1986, pp. 8–11).

Consider also this passage from Nelson, *Who Knows: From Quine to a Feminist Empiricism*, p. 102: " 'Nazi Science' [sic] indicates that . . . a mix of science and politics can enable cruelty and suffering . . . But while the dangers are real, . . . the 'noble lie' [that politics can and should be kept out of science] is far more dangerous."

Others are more equivocal: e.g., Harding, who, after stating boldly that "[t]he truth—whatever that is—cannot set us free" (*Whose Science, Whose Knowledge?*, p. xi), suggests that feminist theorizing could be, if not "true," "less false" (pp. 58, 185). The impression I get from *Whose*

Science? Whose Knowledge? is that Harding's view is that the notion of a theory's being true is unintelligible, but the notion of one theory's being less false than another is intelligible. This is pretty puzzling. However, in "Who Knows? Identities and Feminist Epistemology," in Joan E. Hartmen and Ellen Messer-Davidow, eds., *(En)gendering Knowledge* (Knoxville: University of Tennessee Press, 1991), pp. 100–115, Harding suggests, instead, the much less startling thesis that scientists claim only that this or that theory is better supported by the evidence, not that this or that theory is true. (My thanks to Ruth Manor for drawing this paper to my attention.) This isn't nearly so puzzling: it is, however, at odds with Harding's insistence, both in *The Science Question in Feminism* and in *Whose Science? Whose Knowledge?*, that feminist criticisms of sexism in science lead inevitably to revolutionary epistemological conclusions.

[28]Harding, *Whose Science? Whose Knowledge?*, p. 98: "The model for good science should be research programs directed by liberatory political goals." And, p. 280: "The authority to say what is theoretically and politically adequate research and scholarship must remain [*sic*] in the hands of the marginalized."

Duran, *Toward a Feminist Epistemology*, pp. 145–46: "[W]ould a model like the . . . computational model [of mind], be the result of politically incorrect theorizing that

is, apart from being grossly androcentric, also the very sort of thing feminists have labeled oppressive to minorities, Third World points of view, and, indeed, to anyone who is not white, male and well-educated?" And now consider Conor Cruise O'Brien's shrewd account of the insidiousness of political pressures within the academy:

> Young scholars in . . . sensitive fields are likely to believe that if they write with excessive candor about certain realities . . . doors will close to them: certain grants will be out of reach, participation in certain organized research programs denied, influential people alienated, the view propagated that the young man is unbalanced or unsound. These fears may be exaggerated . . . but they are not without foundation. . . . Inevitably some young men . . . will adapt to this situation with such concessions as they believe are necessary. And the scholars who adapt successfully are likely to be highly influential in the fields in the next generation.

("Politics and the Morality of Scholarship," in *Morality and Scholarship*, ed., Max Black [Ithaca, NY: Cornell University Press, 1967], p. 73.) I invite you to enjoy the irony of O'Brien's unselfconscious assumption that "young scholars" are "young men."

[29]George Orwell, *Nineteen Eighty-Four* (1949; Harmondsworth, Middlesex, UK: Penguin Books, 1954), pp. 184, 198.

XI.4 Dismantling Truth: Solidarity Versus Objectivity

RICHARD RORTY

Richard Rorty (1931–   ) is professor of comparative literature and philosophy at Stanford University and the author of several works, including *Philosophy and the Mirror of Nature* (1979), from which the first part of this selection is taken.

In Part I of this selection, "Epistemological Pragmatism," Rorty argues that truth means, not what corresponds to the facts, as is the dominant definition of truth in Western philosophy, but what it is *better* for us to believe. He describes truth as "what you can defend against all comers . . . what our peers will [all things considered] let us get away with saying." He defends the thesis that we should give up metaphysical and epistemological notions of reality and truth in favor of those built on ethnocentric solidarity.

In Part II, "Solidarity Versus Objectivity," Rorty attacks the distinction between objectivity and subjectivity as well as the correspondence theory of truth. He sides with Thomas Kuhn in arguing that we can have no theory-independent notion of reality and proposes to erase the essential difference between science, on the one hand, and the humanities and art, on the other. Embracing the title of "the new fuzzies," Rorty further develops his thesis that a notion of social solidarity replace the enlightenment notion of objective truth.

Part I

Epistemological Pragmatism

Quine asks how an anthropologist is to discriminate the sentences to which natives invariably and whole-heartedly assent into contingent empirical platitudes on the one hand and necessary conceptual truths on the other. Sellars asks how the authority of first-person reports of, for example, how things appear to us, the pains from which we suffer, and the thoughts that drift before our minds differ from the authority of expert reports on, for example, metal stress, the mating behavior of birds, or the colors of physical objects. We can lump both questions together and simply ask, "How do our peers know which of our assertions to take our word for and which to look for further confirmation of?" It would seem enough for our peers to believe there to be no better way of finding out our inner states than from our reports, without their knowing what "lies behind" our making them. It would also seem enough for us to know that our peers have this acquiescent attitude. That alone seems sufficient for that inner certainty about our inner states which the tradition has explained by "immediate presence to consciousness," "sense of evidence," and other expressions of the assumption that reflections in the Mirror of Nature are intrinsically better known than nature itself. For Sellars, the certainty of "I have a pain" is a reflection of the fact that nobody cares to question it, not conversely. Just so, for Quine, the certainty of "All men are animals," and of "There have been some black dogs." Quine thinks that the "meanings" drop out as wheels that are not part of the mechanisms, and Sellars thinks the same of "self-authenticating non-verbal episodes." More broadly, if assertions are justified by society rather than by the character of the inner representations they express, then there is no point in attempting to isolate *privileged* representation.

Explaining rationality and epistemic authority by reference to what society lets us say, rather than the latter by the former, is the essence of what I call "epistemic behaviorism," an attitude common to Dewey and Wittgenstein. This sort of behaviorism can best be seen as a species of holism—but one which requires no idealist metaphysical underpinnings. It claims that if we understand the rules of a language-game, we understand all that there is to understand about why moves in that language-game are made . . . If we are behaviorists in this sense, then it will not occur to us to invoke either of the traditional Kantian distinctions. But can we just go ahead and be behaviorists? Or, as Quine and Sellars' critics suggest, doesn't behaviorism simply beg the question? Is there any reason to think that fundamental epistemic notions *should* be explicated in behavioral terms?

The last question comes down to: Can we treat the study of "the nature of human knowledge" just as the study of certain ways in which human beings interact, or does it require an ontological foundation (involving some specific philosophical way of describing human beings)? Shall we take "S knows that p" (or "S knows noninferentially that p," or "S believes incorrigibly that p," or "S's knowledge that p is certain") as a remark about the status of S's reports among his peers, or shall we take it as a remark about the relation between subject and object, between nature and its mirror? The first alternative leads to a pragmatic view of truth and a therapeutic approach to ontology (in which philosophy can straighten out pointless quarrels between common sense and science, but not contribute any arguments of its own for the existence or [non]existence of something). Thus for Quine, a necessary truth is just a statement such that nobody has given us any interesting alternatives which would lead us to question it. For Sellars, to say that a report of a passing thought is incorrigible is to say that nobody has yet suggested a good way of predicting and controlling human behavior which does not take sincere first-person contemporary reports of thoughts at face-value. The second alternative leads to "ontological" explanations of the relations between minds and meanings, minds and immediate data of awareness, universals and particulars, thought and language, consciousness and brains, and so on. For philosophers like Chisholm and Bergmann, such explanations *must* be attempted if the realism of common sense is to be preserved. The aim of all such explanations is to make truth something more than what Dewey called "warranted assertability": more than what our peers will, *ceteris paribus,* let us get away with saying. Such explanations, when ontological, usually take the form of a redescription of the object of knowledge so as to "bridge the gap" between it and the knowing subject. To choose between these approaches is to choose between truth as "what it is good for us to believe" and truth as "contact with reality."

Part II

Solidarity Versus Objectivity

In our culture, the notions of "science," "rationality," "objectivity" and "truth" are bound up with one another. Science is thought of as offering "hard," "objective" truth—truth as correspondence to reality, the only sort of truth worthy of the name. Humanists—philosophers, theologians, historians, literary critics—have to worry about whether they are being "scientific"—whether they are entitled to think of their conclusions, no matter how carefully argued, as worthy of the term "true." We tend to identify seeking "objective truth" with "using reason," and so we think of the natural sciences as paradigms of rationality. We also think of rationality as a matter of following procedures laid down in advance, of being "methodical." So we tend to use "methodical," "rational," "scientific" and "objective" as synonyms.

Worries about "cognitive status" and "objectivity" are characteristic of a secularized culture in which the scientist replaces the priest. The scientist is now seen as the person who keeps humanity in touch with something beyond itself. As the universe was depersonalized, beauty (and, in time, even moral goodness) came to be thought of as "subjective." So truth is now thought of as the only point at which human beings are responsible to something non-human. A commitment to "rationality" and to "method" is thought to be a recognition of this responsibility. The scientist becomes a moral exemplar, one who selflessly exposes himself again and again to the hardness of facts.

One result of this way of thinking is that any academic discipline which wants a place at the trough, but is unable to offer the predictions and the technology provided by the natural sciences, must either pretend to imitate science or find some way of obtaining "cognitive status" without the necessity of discovering facts. Practitioners of these disciplines must either affiliate themselves with this quasi-priestly order by using terms like "behavioral sciences" or else find something other than "fact" to be concerned with. People in the humanities typically choose the latter strategy. They describe themselves either as concerned with "values" as opposed to facts, or as developing and inculcating habits of "critical reflection."

Neither sort of rhetoric is very satisfactory. No matter how much humanists talk about "objective values," the phrase always sounds vaguely confused. It gives with one hand what it takes back with the other. The distinction between the objective and the subjective was designed to parallel that between fact and value, so an objective value sounds vaguely mythological as a winged horse. Talk about the humanists' special skill at critical reflection fares no better. Nobody really believes that philosophers or literary critics are better at critical thinking, or at taking big broad views of things, than theoretical physicists or microbiologists. So society tends to ignore both these kinds of rhetoric. It treats humanities as on a par with the arts, and thinks of both as providing pleasure rather than truth. Both are, to be sure, thought of as providing "high" rather than "low" pleasure. But an elevated and spiritual sort of pleasure is still a long way from the grasp of a truth.

These distinctions between hard facts and soft values, truth and pleasure, and objectivity and subjectivity are awkward and clumsy instruments. They are not suited to divide up culture; they create more difficulties than they resolve. It would be best to find another vocabulary, to start afresh. But in order to do so we first have to find a new way of describing the natural sciences. It is not a question of debunking or downgrading the natural sciences, but simply of ceasing to see him on the model of the priest. We need to stop thinking of science as the place where the human mind confronts the world. We need a way of explaining why scientists are, and deserve to be, moral exemplars which does not depend on a distinction between objective fact and something softer, squishier and more dubious.

To get to such a way of thinking we can start by distinguishing two senses of the term "rationality." In one sense, the one I have already discussed, to be rational is to be methodical: that is, to have criteria for success laid down in advance. We think of poets and painters as using some other faculty than "reason" in their work because, by their own confession, they are not sure of what they want to do before they have done it. They make up new standards of achievement as they go along. By contrast, we think of judges as knowing in advance what criteria a brief will have to satisfy in order to invoke a favorable decision, and of businessmen as setting well-defined goals and being judged by their success in achieving them. Law and business are good examples of rationality, but the scientist, knowing in advance what would count as disconfirming his hypothesis and prepared to abandon that hypothesis as a result of the unfavorable outcome of a single experiment, seems a truly heroic example. Further, we seem to have a clear criterion of the success of a scientific theory—namely, its ability to predict, and thereby to enable us to control some portion of the world. If to be rational means to be able to lay down criteria in advance, then it is plausible to take natural science as the paradigm of rationality.

The trouble is that in this sense of "rational" the humanities are never going to qualify as rational activities. If the humanities are concerned with ends rather than means, then there is no way to evaluate their success in terms of antecedently specified criteria. If we already knew what criteria we wanted to satisfy, we would not worry about whether we were pursuing the right ends. If we thought we knew the goals of culture and society in advance, we would have no use for the humanities—as totalitarian societies in fact do not. It is characteristic of democracies and pluralistic societies to redefine their goals continually. But if to be rational means to satisfy criteria, then this process of redefinition will be bound to be non-rational. So if the humanities are to be viewed as rational activities, rationality will have to be thought of as something other than the satisfaction of criteria which are statable in advance.

[The second] meaning of "rational" is, in fact, available. In this sense, the word means something like "sane" or "reasonable" rather than "methodical." It names a set of moral virtues: tolerance, respect for the opinion of those around one, willingness to listen, reliance on persuasion rather than force. These are the virtues which members of a civilized society must possess if the society is to endure. In this sense of "rational," the word means something more like "civilized" than like "methodical." When so construed, the distinction between the rational and the irrational has nothing in particular to do with the difference between the arts and the sciences. On this construction, to be rational is simply to discuss any topic—religious, literary, or scientific—in a way which eschews dogmatism, defensiveness, and righteous indignation.

There is no problem about whether, in this latter, weaker sense the humanities are "rational disciplines." Usually humanists display the moral virtues in question. Sometimes they do not, but then sometimes scientists don't either. Yet these moral virtues are felt to be not enough. Both humanists and the public hanker after rationality in the first, stronger sense of the term: a sense which is associated with objective truth, correspondence to reality, method and criteria.

We should not try to satisfy this hankering, but rather try to eradicate it. No matter what one's opinion of the secularization of culture, it was a mistake to try to make the natural scientist into a new sort of priest, a link between the human and the non-human. So was the idea that some sorts of truths are "objective" whereas others are merely "subjective" or "relative"—the attempt to divide up the set of true sentences into "genuine knowledge" and "mere opinion," or into the "factual" and the "judgmental." So was the idea that the scientist has a special method which, if only the humanists would apply it to ultimate values, would give us the same kind of self-confidence about moral ends as we now have about technological means. I think that we should content ourselves with the second, "weaker" conception of rationality and avoid the first, "stronger" conception. We should avoid the idea that there is some special virtue in knowing in advance what criteria you are going to satisfy, in having standards by which to measure progress.

Is Science Rational?

One can make these issues somewhat more concrete by taking up the current controversy among philosophers about the "rationality of science." For some twenty years, ever since the publication of Thomas Kuhn's book *The Structure of Scientific Revolutions,* philosophers have been debating the question of "whether science is rational." Attacks on Kuhn for being "irrational" are now as frequent and urgent as, in the 1930s and 1940s, were attacks on the logical positivists for saying that moral judgments were "meaningless." We are constantly being warned of the danger of "relativism" which will beset us if we give up our attachment to objectivity and to the idea of rationality as obedience to criteria.

Whereas Kuhn's enemies routinely accuse him of reducing science to "mob psychology," and pride themselves on having (by a new theory of meaning or reference or verisimilitude) vindicated the "rationality of science," his pragmatic friends (such as myself) routinely congratulate him on having softened the distinction between science and non-science. . . . [H]e has said that "there is no theory-independent way to reconstruct phrases like 'really there.' " He has asked whether it really helps "to imagine that there is some one full, objective, true account of nature and that the proper measure of scientific achievement is the extent to which it brings us closer to the ultimate goal." We pragmatists quote these passages incessantly in the course of our effort to enlist Kuhn in our campaign to drop the objective-subjective distinction altogether.

What I am calling "pragmatism" might also be called "left-wing Kuhnianism." It has also been rather endearingly called (by one of its critics, Clark Glymour) "the new fuzziness," because it is an attempt to blur just those distinctions between the objective and the subjective and between fact and value which the criterial conception of rationality has developed. We fuzzies would like to substitute the idea of "unforced agreement" for that of "objectivity." We should like to put all culture on an epistemological level (or get rid of the idea of "epistemological level"). . . . On our view, "truth" is a univocal term. It applies equally to the judgments of lawyers, anthropologists, physicists, philologists and literary critics. There is point in assigning degrees of "objectivity" or "hardness" to such disciplines. For the presence of unforced agreement in all of them gives us everything in the way of "objective truth" which one could possibly want: namely, intersubjective agreement.

As soon as one says that all there is to objectivity is intersubjectivity, one is likely to be accused of being a relativist. That is the epithet traditionally applied to pragmatists. But this epithet is ambiguous. It can name any of three different views:

1. the silly and self-refuting view that every belief is as good as every other.
2. the wrong-headed view that "true" is an equivocal term, having as many meanings as there are contexts of justification.
3. the ethnocentric view that there is nothing to be said about either truth or rationality apart from descriptions of the familiar procedures of justification which a given society—*ours*—uses in one or another area of inquiry.

The pragmatist does hold this third, ethnocentric view. But he does not hold the first or the second view of relativism.

But "relativism" is not an appropriate term to describe this sort of ethnocentrism. For we pragmatists are not holding a positive theory which says that something is relative to something else. Instead, we are making the purely *negative* point that we would be better off without the traditional distinctions between knowledge and opinion, construed as the distinction between truth as correspondence to reality and truth as a commendatory term for well-justified beliefs. Our opponents call this negative claim "relativistic" because they cannot imagine that anybody would seriously deny that truth has an intrinsic nature. So when we say that there is nothing to be said about truth save that each of us will commend as true those beliefs which he or she finds good to believe, the realist is inclined to interpret this as one more positive theory about the nature of truth: a theory according to which truth is simply the contemporary opinion of a chosen individual or group. Such a theory would, of course, be self-refuting. But we pragmatists do not have a theory of truth, much less a relativistic one. As partisans of solidarity, our account of the value of cooperative human enquiry has only an ethical base, not an epistemological or metaphysical one.

To say that we must be ethnocentric may sound suspicious, but this will only happen if we identify ethnocentricism with pigheaded refusal to talk to representatives of other communities. In my sense of ethnocentricism, to be ethnocentric is simply to work by our own lights. The defense of ethnocentrism is simply that there are no other lights to work by. Beliefs suggested by another individual or another culture must be tested by trying to weave them together with beliefs which we already have. . . .

This way of thinking runs counter to the attempts, familiar since the eighteenth century, to think of political liberalism as based on a conception of the nature of man. To most thinkers of the Enlightenment, it seemed clear that the access to Nature which physical science had provided should now be followed by the establishment of social, political and economic institutions which were "in accordance with Nature." Ever since, liberal social thought has centered around social reform as made possible by objective knowledge of what human beings are like—not knowledge of what Greeks or Frenchmen or Chinese are like, but of humanity as such. This tradition dreams of a universal human community which will exhibit a non-parochial solidarity because it is the expression of an a historical human nature.

Philosophers who belong to this tradition, who wish to ground solidarity in objectivity, have to construe truth as correspondence to reality. So they must construct an epistemology which has room for a kind of justification which is not merely social but natural, springing from human nature itself, and made possible by a link between that part of nature and the rest of nature. By contrast we pragmatists, who wish to reduce objectivity to solidarity, do not require either a metaphysics or an epistemology. . . . We see the gap between truth and justification not as something to be bridged by isolating a natural and trans-cultural sort of rationality which can be used to criticize certain cultures and praise others, but simply as the gap between the actual good and the possible better. From a pragmatist point of view, to say that what is rational for us now to believe may not be *true*, is simply to say that somebody may come up with a better idea. . . .

Another reason for describing us as "relativistic" is that we pragmatists drop the idea that enquiry is destined to converge to a single point— that Truth is "out there" waiting for human beings to arrive at it. This idea seems to us an unfortunate attempt to carry a religious conception over into a secular culture. All that is worth preserving of the claim that rational inquiry will converge to a single point is the claim that we

must be able to explain why past false views were held in the past, and thus explain how we go about re-educating our benighted ancestors. To say that we think we're heading in the right direction is just to say, with Kuhn, that we can, by hindsight, tell the story of the past as a story of progress.

But the fact that we can trace such a direction and tell such a story does not mean that we have come closer to a goal which is out there waiting for us. We cannot, I think, imagine a moment at which the human race could settle back and say, "Well, now that we've finally arrived at the Truth we can relax." Paul Feyerabend is right in suggesting that we should discard the metaphor of inquiry, and human activity generally, as converging rather than proliferating, becoming more unified rather than more diverse. On the contrary, we should *relish* that thought that the sciences as well as the arts will *always* provide a spectacle of fierce competition between alternative theories, movements and schools. The end of human activity is not rest, but rather richer and better human activity. We should think of human progress as making it possible for human beings to do more interesting things and be more interesting people, not as heading toward a place which has somehow been prepared for us in advance. To drop the criterial conception of rationality in favor of the pragmatist conception would be to give up the idea of Truth as something to which we were responsible. Instead we should think of "true" as a word which applies to those beliefs upon which we are able to agree, as roughly synonymous with "justified." . . .

. . . Pragmatists would like to replace the desire for objectivity—the desire to be in touch with a reality which is more than some community with which we identify ourselves—with the desire for solidarity with that community. They think that the habits of relying on persuasion rather than force, of respect for opinions of colleagues, of curiosity and eagerness for new data and ideas, are the *only* virtues which scientists have. They do not think that there is an intellectual virtue called "rationality" over and above these moral virtues. . . .

Pragmatists interpret the goal of inquiry (in any sphere of culture) as the attainment of an appropriate mixture of unforced agreement with tolerant disagreement (where what counts as appropriate is determined, within that sphere, by trial and error). Such a reinterpretation of our sense of responsibility would, if carried through, gradually make unintelligible the subject-object model of enquiry, the child-parent model of moral obligation, and the correspondence theory of truth. A world in which those models, and that theory, no longer had any intuitive appeal would be a pragmatist's paradise.

When Dewey urged that we try to create such a paradise he was said to be irresponsible. For, it was said, he left us bereft of weapons to use against our enemies; he gave us nothing with which to "answer the Nazis." When we new fuzzies try to revise Dewey's repudiation of criteriology we are said to be "relativistic." We must, people say, believe that every coherent view is as good as every other, since we have no "outside" touchstone for choice among such views. We are said to leave the general public defenseless against the witch doctor, the defender of creationism, or anyone else who is clever and patient enough to deduce a consistent and wide-ranging set of theorems from his "alternative first principles."

Nobody is convinced when we fuzzies say that we can be just as morally indignant as the next philosopher. We are suspected of being contritely fallibilist when righteous fury is called for. Even when we actually display appropriate emotions we get nowhere, for we are told that we have no *right* to these emotions. When we suggest that one of the few things we know (or need to know) about truth is that it is what wins in a free and open encounter, we are told that we have defined "true" as "satisfies the standards of our community." But we pragmatists do not hold this relativist view. We do not infer from "There is no way to step outside communities to a neutral standpoint" to "There is no rational way to justify liberal communities over totalitarian communities." For that inference involves just the notion of "rationality" as a set of ahistorical principles which pragmatists abjure. What we in fact infer is that there is no way to beat totalitarians in argument by appealing to shared common premises, and no point in pretending that a common human nature makes the totalitarians unconsciously hold such premises.

The claim that we fuzzies have no right to be furious at moral evil, no right to commend our views as true unless we simultaneously refute ourselves by claiming that there are objects out there which *make* those views true, begs all the theoretical questions. But it gets to the practical and moral heart of the matter. This is the question of whether notions like "unforced agreement" and "free and open encounter"—descriptions of social situations—can take the place in our moral lives of notions like "the world," "the will of God," "the moral law," "what our beliefs are trying to represent accurately" and "what makes our beliefs true." All the philosophical presuppositions which make Hume's fork seem inevitable are ways of suggesting that human communities must justify their existence by striving to attain a non-human goal. To suggest that we can forget about Hume's fork [the radical separation of facts from values], forget about being responsible to what is "out there," is to suggest that human communities can justify their existence only by comparisons with other actual and possible human communities. . . .

Imagine . . . that a few years from now you open your copy of the *New York Times* and read that the philosophers, in convention assembled, have unanimously agreed that values are objective, science rational, with a matter of correspondence to reality, etc. Recent breakthroughs in semantics and meta-ethics, the report goes on, have caused the last remaining non-cognitivists in ethics to recant. Similarly breakthroughs in the philosophy of science have led Kuhn formally to abjure his claim that there is no theory-independent way to reconstruct statements about what is "really there." All the new fuzzies have repudiated all their former views. By way of making amends for the intellectual confusion which the philosophical profession has recently caused, the philosophers have adopted a short, crisp set of standards of rationality and morality. Next year the convention is expected to adopt the report of the committee charged with formulating a standard of aesthetic taste.

Surely the public reaction to this would not be "Saved!" but rather "Who on earth do these philosophers think they *are*?" It is one of the best things about the form of intellectual life we Western liberals lead that this *would* be our reaction. No matter how much we moan about the disorder and confusion of the current philosophical scene, about the treason of the clerks, we do not really want things any other way. What prevents us from relaxing and enjoying the new fuzziness is perhaps no more than cultural lag, the fact that the rhetoric of the Enlightenment praised the emerging natural sciences in a vocabulary which was left over from a less liberal and tolerant era. This rhetoric enshrined all the old philosophical opposition between mind and world, appearance and reality, subject and object, truth and pleasure. Dewey thought that it was the continued prevalence of such opposition which prevented us from seeing that modern science was a new and promising invention, a way of life which had not existed before and which ought to be encouraged and imitated, something which required a new rhetoric rather than justification by an old one.

Suppose that Dewey were right about this, and that eventually we learn to find the fuzziness which results from breaking down such opposition spiritually comforting rather than morally offensive. What would the rhetoric of the culture, and in particular of the humanities, sound like? Presumably it would be more Kuhnian, in the sense that it would mention particular concrete achievements—paradigms—more, and "method" less. There would be less talk about rigor and more about originality. The image of the great scientist would not be of somebody who got it right but of somebody who made it new. The new rhetoric would draw more on the vocabulary of Romantic poetry and socialist politics, and less on that of Greek metaphysics, religious morality or Enlightenment scientism. A scientist would rely on a sense of solidarity with the rest of her profession, rather than a picture of herself as battling through the veils of illusion, guided by the light of reason.

If all this happened, the term "science," and thus the opposition between the humanities, the arts and the sciences might gradually fade away.

Once "science" was deprived of an honorific sense, we might not need it for taxonomy. . . . The people now called "scientists" would no longer think of themselves as members of a quasi-priestly order, nor would the public think of themselves as in the care of such an order.

In this situation, the "humanities" would no longer think of themselves as such, nor would they share a common rhetoric. Each of the disciplines which now fall under that rubric would worry as little about its method, cognitive status or "philosophical foundations" as do mathematics, civil engineering or sculpture. For terms which denoted disciplines would not be thought to divide "subject matter," chunks of the world which had "interfaces" with each other. Rather, they would be thought to denote communities whose boundaries were as fluid as the interests of their members. In this heyday of the fuzzies, there would be as little reason to be self-conscious about the nature and status of one's discipline as, in the ideal democratic community, about the nature and status of one's race or sex. For one's ultimate loyalty would be to the larger community which permitted and encouraged this kind of freedom and insouciance. This community would serve no higher end than its own preservation and self-improvement, the preservation and enhancement of civilization. It would identify rationality with that effort, rather than with the desire for objectivity. So it would feel no need for a foundation more solid than reciprocal loyalty.

XI.5 A Defense of Objectivity

Margarita Rosa Levin

Margarita Rosa Levin received her Ph.D. from the University of Minnesota and teaches philosophy at Stern College. She is the author of several articles in philosophy of science and environmental ethics. In this essay, she defends the notion of objective knowledge against contemporary critics such as Richard Rorty, radical feminists, Marxists, Jacques Derrida, and others. After defining *objectivity* as "intersubjectively accessible knowledge . . . independent of anyone's biases, traditions, wishes, or other influences," she examines (1) the general philosophical arguments against the possibility of objectivity, (2) those grounded in the history and sociology of science, and (3) those specifically grounded in the social sciences. Levin argues that the anti-rationalist arguments not only fail but also presuppose objectivity even in their attempt to undermine it.

Upholding Truth: Objectivity Versus Skepticism and Nihilism

It is a paradox that the twentieth century, which has witnessed the greatest triumphs of science and technology, should also be the century in which the ideal of objectivity has been subjected to the most severe challenges. By *objectivity* I mean intersubjectively accessible knowledge, by definition truly independent of anyone's biases, traditions, wishes, or other influences. The idea that objectivity is not only possible but also regularly realized continues to underpin modern natural science. This same objectivity was a goal that initially inspired the social sciences.[1]

Just *why* the denial of objectivity is so alluring to modern thinkers is perhaps best left to future psychologists and historians. I confine myself to classifying, analyzing, and replying to the various arguments purporting to establish nihilism—the thesis that there is no fixed reality—or skepticism—the thesis that we can't know what that reality is. I claim no great originality or completeness. What follows is meant as a representative sample of current positions.

The order I have chosen sorts arguments against objectivity into four (somewhat artificial) categories that descend in degree of generality. I begin by examining *general* philosophical arguments against the possibility of objectivity in the construction of theories. Then I turn to arguments with similar conclusions but which are grounded in the *history and sociology of science*. Since the social sciences seem particularly vulnerable to charges of bias, I next focus on arguments that single them out. I conclude with arguments against objectivity based on specific claims about *the nature of society and communication*.

General Skeptical and Nihilist Arguments

One hallmark of objective theory-making is testability. A theory must be tested; if it fails its test, if its predictions turn out false, or it is somehow incompatible with the evidence, it must be rejected. But W. V. O. Quine and Pierre Duhem have separately pointed out that it is never *logically* necessary to discard a hypothesis or theory because of disconfirming evidence. Their position, generally referred to as the Quine–Duhem thesis, is that one can always consistently alter one's "auxiliary assumptions" to accommodate the new evidence. Such assumptions are inevitable: The factors mentioned in one's hypotheses always connect with other factors. There is no getting around this; you can't test everything at once. But it does mean that the seeming failure of a hypothesis to pass its test

This article was commissioned for this anthology and appeared in print in the second edition for the first time.

could, *in principle,* be attributed to an erroneous auxiliary assumption. For example, when testing whether a new medicine will lower high fevers, we must make certain assumptions about how thermometers work. If after administering the medicine we find thermometers inserted in treated patients continue to register high fevers, we *could* argue that the medicine has impaired the ability of the thermometers to record body temperature.[2] There is no logical absurdity in this. If *A* and *B* together imply *C* but *C* turns out to be false, all that follows is that *either A* or *B* (or possibly both) is false.

The relevance of this point to objectivity is that, if we can always save any theory in the face of conflicting evidence, then we can never know any theory to be true. If you *know A,* you can not believe or reasonably assert not-*A,* no matter what the evidence. Since, given the Quine–Duhem thesis, you can *always* believe or assert not-*A,* you can never know *A.* To put the point intuitively, the world never forces acceptance or rejection of theories. Within very wide limits we can believe what we want.

This argument contains two themes that will recur. The first is the implicit use of mathematical certainty as a paradigm: If the data do not *entail* some one theory, then either there is no objective "fact of the matter" or (a weaker conclusion) we can never know what that fact is. The second theme is revealed when it is asked how the theorizer, or the Quinean himself, *knows* that an experiment requires some adjustment to his theory. The situation is evidently one in which it must be assumed to be *objectively true* that evidence and theory conflict. Hence, the second theme: appeal to the concept of objective knowledge in arguments that purport to dispose of it. Even the enemies of objectivity rely on it.

This latter point might be blunted if one could strongly distinguish theory from data—perhaps we can know the *data* are true, for example that the mercury in a thermometer has reached a certain level, but we cannot know that any *theory* is true. But even if this distinction is drawn, surely the knowledge that data conflict with theory would be located on the *theoretical* side of such a line.

However that may be, and whatever the merits of the Quine–Duhem thesis as such, it cannot justify doubts about objectivity. Quine's point, it must be remembered, is a *logical* one—that it is always logically possible to preserve any theory. Another way of saying this is that the language of theories is not definable in terms of the data language. But this observation does not show that there are no objective truths beyond the data; it does not even address that question. Nor does Quine's thesis entail that we cannot *know* that one interpretation of the data is right—unless, again, it is assumed that knowledge requires mathematical certainty. Just because you can *believe* not-*A* doesn't mean you can *rationally* believe it. When you look at any concrete case, you realize how irrational it is, after a certain point, to continue to "make changes elsewhere" rather than accept the failure of a hypothesis. For example, we were not compelled to accept Copernicus's heliocentric account of planetary motion. We could have kept Ptolemy's geocentric model by assuming the other planets followed strange orbits that circled back on themselves (epicycles) and that would have accounted for the observations of their motion in the night skies. But that would have required assuming far more complexity than expected and only for the purpose of saving a particular theory, not for any independent reason. The accepted position since Copernicus has been that heliocentrism is the simplest theory that fits the data. Data need not entail a theory to compel acceptance.

As noted, skepticism based on Quine's thesis works best with a sharp line between theory and data. The next argument rests on the opposite claim: "Theory informs observation." This is the view that theory influences observation to such an extent that the two cannot be distinguished. Two observers with different theories will allegedly disagree on what is supposed to be a common database. Furthermore, on this view, it is impossible to even experience data without unconsciously interpreting them according to some theory. It is therefore impossible to achieve a neutral perspective from which to judge competing theories.

The *locus classicus* of this position is a passage from *Patterns of Discovery* in which Norwood Hanson imagines the dawn as viewed by Tycho Brahe, a Ptolemaic, and Johannes Kepler, a Copernican:

> Tycho sees the sun beginning its journey
> from horizon to horizon. He sees that from
> some celestial vantage point the sun . . .
> could be watched circling our fixed earth . . .

Kepler will see the horizon dipping, or turning away, from our local fixed star. The shift from sunrise to horizon-turn is . . . occasioned by differences between what Tycho and Kepler think they know.[3]

We are supposed to conclude that two observers with different theories *see* differently and therefore lack common ground. Fortunately, this thought experiment is one we can all perform ourselves. Modern Americans have assimilated more thoroughly than Kepler the idea that Earth goes around the Sun, yet we do not summon our children to view the data by saying "come see this beautiful Earth-turn." Sunrise looks to us just as it did to Brahe. The difference between ourselves and him is that we know that the Sun's apparent motion is deceptive.

So the argument in this particular case fails because one of its premises is false. Despite holding different theories, observers will see the same thing. Nor is the fault in the example. Consider the series of experiments in which several people around a table were asked to compare two objects that were clearly of different lengths. All but one person had been secretly instructed to insist that the objects were the same length. The test subject was therefore under social pressure to deny the evidence of his senses and quite often succumbed and agreed with the rest. This experiment makes no sense and establishes nothing about the influence of nonperceptual factors on perception unless there is an objective fact of the matter as to how the objects appeared to the participants and what their true lengths were. Furthermore, critics of objectivity can get no mileage from this example unless they claim that it actually happened. Once again the critics of objectivity must rely on it for their arguments.

A different version of nihilism is encapsulated in the phrase "we make the world." Many distinguished contemporary philosophers—Nelson Goodman, Richard Rorty, Hillary Putnam—defend some version of it. I will first discuss the fairly accessible version presented by Robert Schwartz in "Let Me Make You a Star." Schwartz argues that human beings, through the order they impose by their thinking, somehow determine what the world is. (What they impose the order *on* is not made clear.) This is reminiscent of Kant's theory of knowledge, but it differs in that the

mind's categories are not seen as fixed and a priori. Here is Schwartz:

> Whether there are stars, and what they are like, are facts that can *emerge* only in our attempts to describe and organize the world. The world is not given to us ready-made with stars . . . [T]he property of being a star would lack definitive character and boundaries until fashioned in the course of describing the heavens and accounting for its doings.[4]

To the natural objection that surely people don't *literally* make stars, he responds "Of course they don't! . . . We never compressed huge quantities of gas and set them aglow in the heavens above . . . *It,* the sun, was in the ready-made world all along. Yet, independent of our fashioning the relevant properties and kinds, questions about what *it* is really like *have neither any force nor any answers*" (pp. 437–438).

Schwartz seems to be confusing our freedom to *talk* about something—we can call the Missouri River a separate river or an arm of the Mississippi—with our inability to change the facts of what we're talking about; for example, the Missouri is wet and cold. However much we theorize about it, if we fall in it and can't swim, we will drown.

Schwartz does grant that "there are constraints on our scientific schemes of classification and organization," although these are not spelled out. They are *not* a function of an independently existing world because the idea of "[an] external ready-made version of the world—untinged by our cognitive efforts—is not a notion we can have much confidence in making sense of."[5]

Well, if someone insists that he doesn't understand an idea, you can't force him to admit he does. The most you can do is compare it to another idea that he does understand. So consider a newborn baby lying in his crib, lacking a theoretical framework to make sense of those enduring entities we know to be mother, light, walls, and so on. It hardly makes sense to speak of his knowledge of them, yet the world contains those things anyway. Everything Schwartz says about us can be said of the baby, and that is quite consistent with a definite world existing independently of our knowledge.

Schwartz's promise to "make" a star is most plausible when seen as a promise to remake classification schemes. Most would say that Jupiter is not a star because, unlike our Sun, it is not a burning globe of gas. But one could classify Jupiter as a star because it is a gas giant and just say it is nonburning. In this sense, we "make" Jupiter a star when we so classify it. But it is trivial to switch from one scheme to the other. There is no real disagreement between someone who says there are nine planets and someone who says there are eight planets and one nonburning star, just alternate ways of describing the same facts. So Schwartz's point is the triviality that the world can be described in several ways, not that there is no fixed world until we get around to describing it

Another opponent of objectivity with a preference for words over facts is Richard Rorty. In *Philosophy and the Mirror of Nature,* he rejects all metaphors about knowledge that suggest that true statements about the world accurately reflect an independent reality, that reality needs to be uncovered or illuminated. He also repudiates any sharp distinction between the sciences and the humanities, between knowledge and opinion, between fact and value.[6] Adopting the term "fuzziness" for his position, he writes:

> We fuzzies would like to substitute the idea of "unforced agreement" for that of "objectivity." We should like to put all culture on an epistemological level . . . [Truth] applies equally to the judgments of lawyers, anthropologists. physicists, philologists and literary critics. There is no point in assigning degrees of "objectivity" or "hardness" to such disciplines. For the presence of unforced agreement in all of them gives us everything in the way of "objective truth" which one could possibly want: namely, intersubjective agreement.[7]

Rorty gives no specific examples of *how* people arrive at "unforced agreement" other than by pointing to evidence. We can certainly imagine fashions in literary criticism as arising from "unforced agreement." If there are several incompatible theories about whether Hamlet's madness is real or feigned, no one will much care. But how do we handle the case of a significant fraction of our population coming to "unforced agreement" to give up the germ theory of disease and adopt the view that illness is due to negative thoughts? Suppose they act on their agreement and refuse immunizations, knowingly sell contaminated meat, and let animals foul the water supply. Does Rorty really think there's no objective truth here, that agreement is the end of the matter? Won't *reality* force them to change their minds?

He does anticipate that critics will misread him:

> [W]hen we say that there is nothing to be said about truth save that each of us will commend as true those beliefs which he or she finds good to believe, the realist is inclined to interpret this as one more positive theory about the nature of truth: a theory according to which truth is simply the contemporary opinion of a chosen individual's group. Such a theory would, of course, be self-refuting. But pragmatists do not have a theory of truth, much less a relativistic one. As partisans of solidarity, our account of the value of cooperative human enquiry has only an ethical base, not an epistemological or metaphysical one.[8]

Well, Rorty can *say* he doesn't have a theory—but if you declare that talk of *X* is meaningless. that opposing views of *X* are wrong, that *X* does not exist, then you certainly *do* have a theory of *X*.

Rorty keeps mocking the picture of human knowledge as seeking to come *closer* to the truth, of progress in reaching "a place which has somehow been prepared in advance." Michael Devitt[9] has an apt response: Belief in objective truth, realism about the world, is *not* the thesis that people *will* know everything. Realism has nothing to do with human activity. To say that there is life on planets in other solar systems is not to say that we will ever contact them, that they have ever visited here, or that some other group is responsible for seeding life both here and there. It is to say that there is life on other planets, period.

Finally, when Rorty says that "from a pragmatist point of view, to say that what is rational for us now to believe may not be *true,* is simply to say that somebody *may come up with a better* idea,"[10] one has to ask how it can be better if it isn't true or truer. How does one sort out the unpleasant truth from the delightful delusion? This is an old objection to pragmatism, and Rorty does not avoid it.

More Specific Skeptical and Nihilistic Arguments

Even if unbiased investigation is theoretically possible, it is sometimes argued, in practice, investigators are human. They have blindspots, preconceptions, and unconscious motives. You cannot expect objectivity from an investigator even if he sincerely believes he has rid himself of bias.

This is an argument that feminists stress: Because of their male gender and their socialization, men are unreliable about any area where gender plays a role. (Feminists are inconsistent—sometimes they attack objectivity *in toto;* at other times they only question the possibility of male objectivity.) At a minimum this includes research in animal and human behavior; more extreme feminists extend this claim to the physical sciences Feminists cite as an example the work of early male entomologists who erroneously assumed that the large insects that seemed to dominate hives and anthills were "kings."

Now this example clearly has no force unless one can go on to say that further research showed that the "ruling" insects were more properly labeled "queens." Speaking generally, one cannot present an example of investigator bias without also presenting the objective fact that the investigator has missed. So it is unnecessary to examine in detail any instances of bias from the history of science that are produced to support skepticism or nihilism. All such instances self-destruct in the same way.

Let us now consider a more sophisticated argument from the history and sociology of science, namely, that the concept of truth is *unnecessary* for describing what scientists do. On this view, first proposed by Thomas Kuhn in *The Structure of Scientific Revolutions* and adopted by many others, the history of science is significantly like the history of fashion. Just as hemlines go up or down, and different parts of the body are exaggerated or hidden, so too do scientific theories change through time. Experiments are performed, some problems are solved, others go unsolved, new theories are proposed—the old guard defends its views, the young rebels take over. But, just as there is no "correct" dress, there is no "true" theory. We need make no reference to external reality in explaining why scientists believe their theories.

I would make three points about this view. First, not just science but any activity whatever can be redescribed in terms (technically known as "metalinguistic") that make no apparent reference to an external reality. Consider traffic control. The Department of Transportation could be said to be concerned not with actual collisions and traffic jams but with written reports. The department is not out to reduce pedestrian deaths at intersections but to solve the pedestrian-death problem by reducing the number of pedestrian-death-at-intersection reports (the sort of "success" bureaucracies are said to pursue). The history of traffic technology, of the introduction of parking meters and traffic lights, could be told "internally" in terms of decisions taken to install such devices, of satisfaction with their effect on traffic reports, and possibly physical descriptions of the apparatus—all in language that made no commitment to the existence of actual automobiles. Such recasting into metalinguistic form hardly proves that cars are needless conceptual baggage.

It should also be stressed that Kuhn's view is not one scientists take of their own activity. Most scientists believe they are coming ever closer to the truth about how nature works. They may well be mistaken about whether they are succeeding, but it is arrogance for philosophers to claim to know better than scientists what scientists are trying to do.

The third and strongest point is that the nihilist account makes the success of science inexplicable. This is an old problem nihilists have never resolved. Even if they deny any predictive power or explanatory success to the social sciences, they must acknowledge the success of the physical sciences, especially in applications such as engineering. Yet if there is no objective truth, if scientists are merely playing games with each other, this success is a miracle.

Perhaps the most promising response to the success of science is to hark back to the Quine–Duhem thesis and argue that the success of a scientific theory does not logically entail its truth. This is correct. It is also true that many theories can be consistent with a narrow set of observations. But as a theory is tested, refined, and reconfirmed under many different circumstances, it becomes less and less likely that a wildly different theory will do a better job. It is safe to say that we know that certain diseases are caused by germs

XI.5 A Defense of Objectivity

even though the data do not *entail* this, and many questions about germs remain open. To demand that knowledge have the certainty of mathematics is to use the word *knowledge* in a nonstandard way. You *know* you are reading this article even though it is theoretically possible that you are under a hypnotically induced illusion. Indeed, the demand for absolute certainty is unsatisfiable even in mathematics, since it is always possible that we are systematically confused about some basic rule of inference.

It appears to be rhetorically effective to label the position just stated "naive" realism. One is evidently expected to retract one's views rather than admit to naiveté, but I, for one, will not back off. I won't buy the Brooklyn Bridge, but I will buy the idea that the simplest explanation is the likeliest and the simplest explanation for the success of science is that we are indeed coming nearer to understanding some external reality. Rather than calling my opponents names ("decadent"?), let me challenge them to provide a positive alternative account of the success of science, one that scientists themselves will accept.

General Arguments for Skepticism and Nihilism in the Social Sciences

The arguments in this category are variations on a single theme: You cannot be objective about what is subjective in nature. The social sciences involve people, and people attach values to their activities, so the social sciences have a normative dimension. Far from seeing it as a problem for social science, some see it as an inevitable, even welcome, aspect of dealing with human beings. Thus, William Outhwaite notes:

> The fact that we are ourselves human beings makes it possible for us to understand what it is like to be another human being, what it is (probably) like to hold the beliefs which other human beings hold, and so on. But this also means that we cannot simply record, in an objective and value-free way, the practices and beliefs of other human beings. The social scientist does not go out into the field as a *tabula rasa* and return with an account of what it is like to be a European car-worker or an African peasant; it is precisely the

encounter between the social scientist's own belief and practices and those of the people he . . . is studying which makes up whatever understanding we can have of another social reality.[11]

Indeed, as Outhwaite observes, people and their values are involved on both sides of any inquiry in social science. It is therefore convenient to divide the arguments in this section into those that focus on the values of the human *objects* of social inquiry and those that focus on the values of the inquirer himself.

So let us first ask whether values can be neutrally identified and neutrally attributed to others. It seems to me that such attribution is indeed possible. Wittgenstein's celebrated attacks on private languages apply with full force to a private language of values. If evaluating were a private act, people could not learn—as they obviously do learn—what someone means when he says that he "admires" something or "despises" it. There are public indicators of valuing; most clearly, what a culture encourages and discourages—which it is possible to determine at least in principle—is a good sign of what it values. Of course, the values an individual will publicly assent to may not be the values he secretly holds, and ferreting out his true preferences may require considerable ingenuity, but again this is not *in principle* impossible. On the whole, determining values poses no less but no more difficulty than detecting the presence of a shy nocturnal animal.

But people aren't raccoons, it will be said; detecting guilt is not like detecting leaf eaters in your garden. Two equally remorseful individuals may differ in how much of their feelings they let show and how they show them. There is surely something here inaccessible to ordinary observation. In reply, we must focus again on how we ordinarily spot, for example, guilt. Regret over some past action or inaction typically leads to reluctance to discuss it, expressions of desire that it not be generally known, and possibly the wish that it had never been committed, as well as a desire to be punished for it. These are the sorts of clues that lead me to conclude that a person is experiencing guilt.

To be sure, establishing the same fact about a subject from a different culture requires certain preliminaries, such as acquiring a working knowledge of his language. Aha, says the skeptic, a working knowledge of another language means being able to translate such terms as *guilt* in the first place, and how do we know on the basis of sheer behavior that we are correctly translating such words? Once again, it must be insisted that observable behavior is, in the end, all we *ever* have to go on. No child at his mother's knee has access to his mother's inner states. He knows only what she says and does when she corrects his speech and if this is sufficient to allow the child to learn his mother's words for emotions, it suffices for penetrating an alien language.

However—the skeptic now urges—the problem isn't as simple as just finding the alien's word for "guilt." Correctly identifying his values means, in addition, finding out the sorts of things his culture thinks *ought* to be regretted, the ways in which his culture understands personal responsibility, the culturally approved forms of public displays of emotion—a whole "system of meanings" that must be grasped before guilt can be properly understood. The Irish at a wake behave differently than Jews sitting shiva, yet both are presumably "distressed." In fact, the whole issue of judging foreign values is a special case of *verstehen*. This phrase encapsulates the view that at least some types of behavior are incomprehensible without a certain sympathetic understanding ("verstehen") from the inside of what the behavior means to the participants. Peter Winch had this requirement in mind when he wrote: "A historian or sociologist of religion must himself have some religious feeling if he is to make sense of the religious movement he is studying and understand the considerations which govern the lives of its participants."[12]

Thus, Winch might say, you cannot understand why a born-again Christian might quit his job unless you yourself have experienced a comparable spiritual rebirth. Only then will you realize how even the most pressing material concerns might come to seem unimportant.

Plausible as this may seem, it is simply not true. One need not oneself believe in a world to come to reason that someone who does believe might well lose interest in this world. One need not know what it feels like to have such a belief to make and test predictions about his actions. A great many people understand *Othello* without having endured irrational jealousy. We would do well to remember a quip by Albert Einstein, often cited in this context: It is not the job of science "to *give* the taste of the soup." It *is* the job of science to describe and account for the taste of the soup. Similarly, it is not the job of social science to give the feeling of guilt or "reproduce"[13] the feeling of someone acting within a normative tradition. Its job is to describe the mental state of the agent by the behavior it evokes and its relation to other phenomena.

What do we expect of a social science? Is it information, lawlike statements, predictions, correlations, and unification of seemingly disparate data? Or are social scientists expected to be professional empaths who feel and act like the people they study? Social science should not be conceived so narrowly that one questions whether there has ever been a successful study of human behavior.

The fact is that we *do* understand certain alien "forms of life." Consider the treaties between the various Native American tribes and European settlers. Native Americans did not have the concept of land ownership or, consequently, any idea of the significance that the signing of treaties had for the Europeans. Many of us, accustomed to talk of selling air rights, buying lots, and the distinction between public and private land, find it hard to put ourselves in the natives' frame of mind. Yet we can grasp their system of meanings enough to see how its conflict with that of the European system would have led to trouble on the frontier. You might say that it is not difficult to see the natives' point of view (many environmentalists do say this) and that is why we think we understand them. Well then, consider the focus of the ancient Egyptians on the afterlife, their custom of preserving the body through mummification, filling the tomb with actual goods (food) and representations of goods (statuettes of slaves) needed in the next world. Today's theology is not so literal-minded, and those who expect an afterlife imagine that they will take purely spiritual forms. We can nonetheless discuss and interpret ancient Egyptian finds and even make predictions about future discoveries.

Indeed, it is possible to predict and even influence the behavior of beings whose view of the world we cannot experience, namely, nonhumans. None of us, except possibly the blind, have an inkling of what it is like to navigate by echolocation as bats do. Scientists have nevertheless analyzed echolocation thoroughly enough to convince bats to try to land on a ledge that isn't there by sending the sort of signals the bat would receive from a genuine ledge.

Having considered the values of the investigated, let us consider the values of the investigator.

Neutrally describing behavior to which one is indifferent is hard enough, runs the argument; it is impossible to do justice to practices one considers inhumane, depraved, or unjust. Well, that all depends on what is meant by "doing justice." It certainly seems possible in actual practice to separate fact from values and establish the concrete facts about such institutions as slavery in the antebellum South and Nazi concentration camps. One can deplore these institutions yet ask how they were run and what beliefs sustained them. Did different kinds of plantation workers enjoy different social status? Did German farmers think they would gain anything from the elimination of the Jews?

Let us remember that facts normally *precede* judgments of value, and changes in awareness of facts can and do lead to changes in evaluations. Two recent controversies show at least an intuitive awareness of this on the part of partisans of what might seem like purely normative positions. Opponents of the death penalty, even those who say their opposition is not based on questions of deterrence, almost always deny that capital punishment deters. They thus recognize that how people assess capital punishment depends in large part on what they believe to be its empirical effects. Similarly, those who criticize Harry Truman for dropping the atomic bomb on Japan commonly argue that Japan was on the point of surrender, and they often try to produce documentary evidence for this factual claim. Revisionist historians realize that it is difficult to dispute the decision once it is admitted that it saved millions of lives.

"But," the skeptic asks, "what about the 'big picture'? What caused the Civil War? Did the New Deal hasten the end of the Depression? The facts may not be in dispute, little facts anyway—it's the interpretation of the facts that allows personal values to enter. Values may wait upon facts, but this only tempts historians to shade the facts to reinforce their own values."

The quick answer to this is, "Speak for yourself." A more careful answer begins by admitting that, indeed, we may never have enough data to definitely establish what factors caused the Civil War or even to rank several possible causes in order of importance. And since (for instance) we may never know all of Lincoln's motives for declaring war on the Confederacy, those who approve Lincoln's decision are free to believe that he was acting as he thought his oath of office

required, while his critics are free to attribute less flattering motives. The sensible response to the selectivity forced on us by the gaps in the record is not that we can't know *anything* but that there is a difference between uncovering some truths and uncovering them *all*. That we can't know the whole truth does not mean that we can't know any of it. What is more, our inability to find out about something in the past doesn't imply that nothing definite ever happened. Unavoidable ignorance does not justify nihilism, and it is worth noting that ignorance can never be known to be irremediable. A Lincoln diary might turn up tomorrow in some forgotten closet that would help us determine what Lincoln was thinking.

The skeptic is apt to retreat another step and claim that it is the choice of problems and interests that is dictated by values. While true to some extent—although it ignores the contribution of pure curiosity—this is logically irrelevant to the issue of objectivity. Why you become interested in something has no bearing on the quality or validity of your research. A study of driving habits sponsored by General Motors may have merit; a study commissioned by Kelloggs that determines that women prefer Rice Krispies while men prefer Corn Flakes can be as trustworthy as any other study of cereal preferences. To think otherwise is to commit a particularly blatant form of the genetic fallacy. Indeed, a commercially sponsored survey might be *more* reliable, since Kelloggs needs accurate data and doesn't want to be lied to.

It is an *empirical* question whether choice of a topic implies a desire for certain conclusions and, more significantly, whether that desire will blind the investigator to contrary evidence. A relevant experiment involved the submission of papers with identical protocols but different results to social work journals.[14] The version reporting social work intervention in children's environment to be ineffective was rejected significantly more often than the version reporting such intervention to be effective. Interestingly, the negative paper was criticized on methodological grounds when it was identical in that respect to the positive paper. Yet, while this experiment does show something—that social work journals are biased toward reports of the effectiveness of environmental intervention—it *cannot* show that the evaluation of research is always subject to bias. Anyone accepting that strong conclusion would have to think that he accepted it because he was biased (in favor of finding bias everywhere) and not because the conclusion was supported by the evidence. As usual, skepticism defeats itself. There *can't* be evidence that all investigation is biased.

Social scientists are quite aware of the problem of wishes and commitments swaying the critical eye. It is precisely to neutralize such factors that "double-blind" experiments are routinely deployed in experiments. This is especially true for such emotionally charged subjects as beauty and intelligence, or any placebo effect. For instance, a psychologist studying the connection between attractiveness and perceived intelligence would not rely on his own opinion of who was attractive. He—or, better, an assistant unaware of the purpose of the experiment—would show an assortment of photos to a panel of respondents to establish which were generally seen as attractive. Another panel would then be asked for estimates of intelligence based on the photos.

Because investigators, like anyone else, sometimes let their emotions or predilections cloud their judgments, science must be not done in a vacuum. This is why results must be replicable, why raw data must be published so that others may evaluate the arguments and the statistical analyses. It is why people should not be discouraged from engaging in research about those whose background is significantly different from theirs. Failure to appreciate this is *the* error in the often-heard remarks that only blacks should study blacks, only women should study women, and the like. Far from its being the case that you need to be an *X* to study *X*s, non-*X*s are needed to check and correct blindspots that *X*s may have about their own group.

The final objection in this group concerns the reality of social constructs. Personality traits, social forces and institutions, and morale have no obvious physical embodiments. Hence, they might seem more like the impositions of our minds on reality than are the constructs of physics. Proponents of such skepticism generally view the constructs of social theory as vehicles for prejudices and hidden values.

Is there really a problem here? As long as talk about social forces and institutions can be appropriately anchored in talk about observable traits of individuals, there is no *new* objectivity problem. Thus, "socioeconomic status" is epistemologically

acceptable because it can be measured in terms of individuals' income, health, and occupation. A more interesting example is the concept of general intelligence, a theoretical construct that is applied to individuals rather than groups but that has drawn criticism for allegedly being arbitrary and value-laden. "Intelligent" is sometimes said to be no more than a label for the middle-class cognitive style or for members of an economic elite that wishes to preserve itself. In fact, although neither a structure nor a process in the brain has been identified as "intelligence," a number of tests of information processing are found to correlate highly with each other, with independent indicators such as academic achievement, and with what people have in mind when they use the word *intelligent*. So talk of intelligence can be anchored in such observables as reaction speed and memorization ability. It is no more suspect than talk of magnetism.

Deconstructionist Skepticism and Nihilism

I have not yet addressed doubts concerning objective knowledge of society stemming from Marxism and its currently popular offshoot, deconstuctionism.

Classical Marxism is determinedly iconoclastic and puts great stress on "tensions" and "contradictions" in extant social institutions. Marriage, school, and the legal system supposedly serve the pursuit of power by some economic class. People are unaware of this because they are brainwashed from infancy to see social artifacts as objective and universal. Such institutions need to be "demystified" so people can see what interests they really serve. For example, Marxists claim the family is an economic unit raising future workers for those who control the means of production. The supposed absolute obligation of parents to their children is part of the "false consciousness" induced by capitalism. The way to raise people's consciousness about the function of institutions is to analyze the "contradictions." Television under capitalism, for instance, sells merchandise and keeps workers docile, but by presenting a glamorous world beyond their grasp, it also sows resentment, weakening the capitalist structure.[15]

Michel Foucault stretches this analysis to include language and concepts. Whoever controls discourse controls the categories of thought and hence has "power/knowledge." Categories of description purporting to be objectively correct are merely weapons for seizing control. Thus, psychologists get the power to define what is mentally abnormal and needs treatment, and physicians get to define physical abnormality.

It should be clear that Marxism and all its variations get into trouble when applied to themselves. If all ideas are believed simply because they serve the interests of some class, presumably a Marxist's belief in Marxism is caused by its effectiveness in helping him seize power. On the Marxist's own theory, it is impossible to attain the neutral perspective required to see that his theory is true. The same goes for Foucault, of course; why not label (and dismiss) him as someone seeking to control discourse with his own arbitrary inventions?

An even more extreme position is taken by Jacques Derrida, perhaps the most widely known deconstuctionist. His original field was literary criticism, his theme that an author has no privileged knowledge of the meaning of his own work. There is "no transcendental signified," no independent meaning; each reader brings his own interpretation to a text. But Derrida has extended his reach to encompass virtually all human activity: "any apparently coherent system of thought can be shown to have underlying, unresolvable antinomies . . . multiple and conflicting readings that must be held simultaneously."[16] Everything, even nature itself, becomes a "text" open to interpretation. If that seems too bizarre, then certainly *theories* about nature can be treated as text. Science and philosophy are just other fictional genres.

To the extent that there can be an argument for a view like Derrida's, it rests on identifying the meaning of a word with every association the word calls up in anyone's mind. If meaning is so understood, it follows immediately that no word has a stable intersubjective meaning, or a stable intrasubjective meaning across time, and that mutual understanding is impossible. The word *elephant* reminds me of Dumbo but reminds you of Republicans. If both associations partly define the word, we are asking the zookeeper different questions when we each inquire the way to the elephant house. But all this shows is the silliness of defining "meaning" so broadly. It is clearly prefer-

able to restrict the meaning of a word to a core of associations shared by all its users, so that "elephant" means "big gray mammal with floppy ears and a trunk." Our expectation that everyone means *that* by "elephant" is what makes communication possible. It is revealing that deconstructionists commonly support their view of communication by analyzing passages from literature, which of course depend for their effect on the myriad resonances of words. Their view loses all plausibility when applied to literal or technical language. What "unresolvable antinomies" is one likely to find in instructions for changing a fuse?

Conclusion

We have found that virtually all critics of objectivity say something like the following:

1. It is an objective fact that there are no objective facts.

2. It is absolutely true that everything is relative to a framework.

3. No one can divorce himself from his social milieu to examine his society with a critical eye, and that conclusion is the result of my having done so.

4. There is evidence for the position that there is no such thing as evidence.

In each case, the skeptic states a position that cannot possibly be substantiated or rationally believed. In each case he is in effect asking that you not apply his assertion to his own position, without giving any reason for exempting his words from his own general claim. His position is futile and self-refuting; it can be stated, but it cannot convince anyone who recognizes its implications.

It might be argued that, strictly speaking, these arguments are not literally contradictory. Consider "theory always influences perception; therefore, there is no objective verification of any claim." The conclusion of this argument (being about theories) does not contradict its premise (which is about observation). To defend skepticism this way, however, overlooks the point of presenting an argument. If we are supposed to accept a conclusion on the basis of a premise, then there must be a reason for accepting the premise. The skeptic must be claiming that we can verify his premise that theory influences perception if he thinks his argument proves that there is no such thing as verification. Merely observing that a premise entails a conclusion accomplishes nothing; I display valid but unsound arguments in logic class every semester. The skeptic must claim that there is some reason to accept his premise as true, in which case his argument really does lead him to contradict himself. If it is replied that the skeptic does not think that his premises are rationally compelling, but only "relatively compelling" to those who share his biases, then his argument loses any point. It can only persuade those who already accept its conclusion and cannot persuade nonskeptics.

Ironically, what the skeptic is attempting is one of the few instances in which inherent contradiction a la Derrida does make a hash out of the whole enterprise. You can't use reason to attack the very idea of reason, and you can't use arguments to convince anyone that arguments are useless. In fact, the ultimate source of Derrida's theory may lie here. Having grasped at some level that the skeptical project is doomed, undermined from within, he may have unconsciously sought to disguise the futility of his own argument by asserting that *all* argument, *all* writing, *all* thinking suffers from this instability, so skeptics are no more misguided than anyone else.

That the self-refuting character of skepticism and nihilism has long been noted makes the persistence of arguments against objectivity curious—like influenza they reappear periodically in slightly different forms and must be attacked with adjusted medications. I suspect that nihilism survives because it resembles a somewhat more benign claim—not that there are no truths or that there is no knowledge, but that we can never be certain which of our beliefs amount to knowledge. The idea that we might know things but not know which ones we know is reminiscent of a paradox about belief. Each of us will grant that, being fallible, not everything we believe is true. But of no particular belief p can we say both that p is false and that we believe p. From this it does not follow that we really are infallible, anymore than the impossibility of being aware that we are dreamlessly asleep shows that we are always awake.[17] Similarly, those of us who hold out for objective knowledge will argue that we can come to know some truths but, alas, may never be in a position to state positively of any given belief that it is one that we know.

Notes

[1] What drew my attention to this topic were recent feminist attacks against traditional science. Their particular spin is that objectivity is a male contrivance, engendered—pun intended—by the male propensity for domination and psychological distancing. Having discussed these views elsewhere, I refer to them only briefly here. See "Caring New World: Feminism and Science," *American Scholar* (winter 1988).

[2] The same maneuver occurs when someone who claims paranormal powers but can't perform in a controlled laboratory setting argues that the presence of doubters diminishes the power. Here the auxiliary assumption being challenged is that perception is independent of the opinions of witnesses.

[3] Norwood Russell Hanson, *Patterns of Discovery* (London: Cambridge University Press), 23–24.

[4] Robert Schwartz, "Let Me Make You a Star," *Midwest Studies in Philosophy 12* (1986), 435.

[5] Schwartz, 437.

[6] It has been argued that science is laden with value words, as when we speak of a "good" fit between hypothesis and data or what an experiment's outcome "should" be. This almost pre-Socratic argument would show that every activity is value-laden, from selling cars ("it gets good mileage") to folding laundry ("you should sort the socks first"). But in each case we can substitute nonnormative words that refer to some standard being met, e.g., that a hypothesis is probable given specified antecedents.

[7] Richard Rorty, Reading XI.4 in this book, p. 624.

[8] Rorty, p. 628.

[9] Michael Devitt, *Realism and Truth*, 2d ed. (Cambridge: Blackwell, 1991).

[10] Rorty, p. 629.

[11] William Outhwaite, "Gadamer," in *The Return of Grand Theory in the Human Sciences*, ed. Quentin Skinner, (London: Cambridge University Press, 1985), p 29.

[12] Peter Winch, *The Idea of a Social Science*. (London: Routledge & Kegan Paul, 1965), p. 88.

[13] Richard Rudner's phrase.

[14] D. Peters and S. Ceci, "Peer-Review Practices of Psychological Journals," *The Behavioral and Brain Sciences* (June 1982).

[15] Feminists speak of men controlling the means of reproduction and urge raising women's consciousness.

[16] David Hoy, "Michel Foucault," in Skinner, 52.

[17] The whole topic of impossible mental states is discussed in Roy Sorensen, *Blindspots* (New York: Oxford University Press, 1989).

XI.6 Epistemology without a Knowing Subject

KARL POPPER

Karl Popper (1902–1994), an Austrian-born philosopher, spent most of his career at the London School of Economics. He is the author of several works in philosophy of science, epistemology, and political philosophy.

In "Epistemology Without a Knowing Subject," Popper argues that here really are three different worlds existing in the same universe; the physical world of matter, the mental world of consciousness and mental events, and the Platonic world of propositions, theories, arguments, and problems. This third world, an idea anticipated by Frege, is objective and autonomous. Although it has been created by humans, it doesn't depend on humans for its continued existence. As long as a record (e.g., a library) survived the extinction of humanity, a new race might discover these ideas and bring them back to the public domain. Unlike Jacques Derrida and the deconstructivists, this world of ideas does not depend on human interpretation. The *text* remains objective and autonomous, even though individuals may interpret it differently (or misinterpret it).

Allow me to start with a confession. Although I am a very happy philosopher I have, after a lifetime of lecturing, no illusions about what I can convey in a lecture. For this reason I shall make no attempt in this lecture to convince you. Instead I shall make an attempt to challenge you, and, if possible, to provoke you.

I. Three Theses on Epistemology and the Third World

I might have challenged those who have heard of my adverse attitude towards Plato and Hegel by calling my lecture '*A theory of the Platonic world*', or '*A theory of the objective spirit*'.

The main topic of this lecture will be what I often call, for want of a better name, '*the third world*'. To explain this expression I will point out that, without taking the words 'world' or 'universe' too seriously, we may distinguish the following three worlds or universes: first, the world

of physical objects or of physical states; secondly, the world of states of consciousness, or of mental states, or perhaps of behavioural dispositions to act; and thirdly, the world of *objective contents of thought*, especially of scientific and poetic thoughts and of works of art.

Thus what I call 'the third world' has admittedly much in common with Plato's theory of Forms or Ideas, and therefore also with Hegel's objective spirit, though my theory differs radically, in some decisive respects, from Plato's and Hegel's. It has more in common still with Bolzano's theory of a universe of propositions in themselves and of truths in themselves, though it differs from Bolzano's also. My third world resembles most closely the universe of Frege's objective contents of thought.

It is not part of my view or of my argument that we might not enumerate our worlds in different ways, or not enumerate them at all. We might, especially, distinguish more than three worlds. My term 'the third world' is merely a matter of convenience.

In upholding an objective third world I hope to provoke those whom I call "*belief philosophers*": those who, like Descartes, Locke, Berkeley, Hume, Kant, or Russell, are interested in our subjective beliefs, and their basis or origin. Against these belief philosophers I urge that our problem is to find better and bolder theories; and that *critical preference* counts, but *not belief.*

I wish to confess, however, at the very beginning, that I am a realist: I suggest, somewhat like a naive realist, that there are physical worlds and a world of states of consciousness, and that these two interact. And I believe that there is a third world, in a sense which I shall explain more fully.

Among the inmates of my 'third world' are, more especially, *theoretical systems;* but inmates just as important are *problems* and *problem situations.* And I will argue that the most important inmates of this world are *critical arguments,* and what may be called—in analogy to a physical state or to a state of consciousness—*the state of a discussion* or the *state of a critical argument;* and, of course, the contents of journals, books, and libraries.

Most opponents of the thesis of an objective third world will of course admit that there are problems, conjectures, theories, arguments, journals, and books. But they usually say that all these entities are, essentially, symbolic or linguistic *expressions* of subjective mental states, or perhaps of behavioural dispositions to act; further, that these entities are means of *communication*—that is to say, symbolic or linguistic means to evoke in others similar mental states or behavioural dispositions to act.

Against this, I have often argued that one cannot relegate all these entities and their content to the second world.

Let me repeat one of my standard arguments[1] for the (more or less) *independent existence of the third world.*

I consider two thought experiments:

Experiment (1). All our machines and tools are destroyed, and all our subjective learning, including our subjective knowledge of machines and tools, and how to use them. But *libraries and our capacity to learn from them* survive. Clearly, after much suffering, our world may get going again.

Experiment (2). As before, machines and tools are destroyed, and our subjective learning, including our subjective knowledge of machines and tools, and how to use them. But this time, *all libraries are destroyed also*, so that our capacity to learn from books becomes useless.

If you think about these two experiments, the reality, significance, and degree of autonomy of the third world (as well as its effects on the second and

first worlds) may perhaps become a little clearer to you. For in the second case there will be no reemergence of our civilization for many millennia.

I wish to defend in this lecture three main theses, all of which concern epistemology. Epistemology I take to be the theory of *scientific knowledge.*

My first thesis is this. Traditional epistemology has studied knowledge or thought in a subjective sense—in the sense of the ordinary usage of the words 'I know' or 'I am thinking'. This, I assert, has led students of epistemology into irrelevances: while intending to study scientific knowledge, they studied in fact something which is of no relevance to scientific knowledge. For *scientific knowledge* simply is not knowledge in the sense of the ordinary usage of the words "I know." While knowledge in the sense of 'I know' belongs to what I call the 'second world', the world of *subjects*, scientific knowledge belongs to the third world, to the world of objective theories, objective problems, and objective arguments.

Thus my first thesis is that the traditional epistemology, of Locke, Berkeley, Hume, and even of Russell, is irrelevant, in a pretty strict sense of the word. It is a corollary of this thesis that a large part of contemporary epistemology is irrelevant also. This includes modern epistemic logic, if we assume that it aims at a theory of *scientific knowledge.* However, any epistemic logician can easily make himself completely immune from my criticism, simply by making clear that he does not aim at contributing to the *theory of scientific knowledge.*

My first thesis involves the existence of two different senses of knowledge or of thought: (1) *knowledge or thought in the subjective sense*, consisting of a state of mind or of consciousness or a disposition to behave or to react, and (2) *knowledge or thought in an objective sense*, consisting of problems, theories, and arguments as such. Knowledge in this objective sense is totally independent of anybody's claim to know; it is also independent of anybody's belief, or disposition to assent; or to assert, or to act. Knowledge in the objective sense is *knowledge without a knower*: it is *knowledge without a knowing subject.*

Of thought in the objective sense Frege wrote: 'I understand by a *thought* not the subjective act of thinking but its *objective content. . . .*'

The two senses of thought and their interesting interrelations can be illustrated by the following highly convincing quotation from Heyting (1962, p. 195), who says about Brouwer's act of inventing his theory of the continuum: 'If recursive functions had been invented before, he [Brouwer] would perhaps not have formed the notion of a choice sequence which, I think, would have been unlucky.'

This quotation refers on the one hand to some *subjective thought processes* of Brouwer's and says that they might not have occurred (which would have been unfortunate) had the *objective problem situation* been different. Thus Heyting mentions certain possible *influences* upon Brouwer's subjective thought processes, and he also expresses his opinion regarding the value of these subjective thought processes. Now it is interesting that influences, *qua* influences, must be subjective: only Brouwer's subjective acquaintance with recursive functions could have had that unfortunate effect of preventing him from inventing free choice sequences.

On the other hand, the quotation from Heyting points to a certain objective relationship between the *objective contents* of two thoughts or theories: Heyting does not refer to the subjective conditions or the electrochemistry of Brouwer's brain processes, but to an *objective problem situation in mathematics* and its possible influences on Brouwer's subjective acts of thought which were bent on solving these objective problems. I would describe this by saying that Heyting's remark is about the objective or third-world *situational logic* of Brouwer's invention, and that Heyting's remark implies that the third-world situation may affect the second world. Similarly, Heyting's suggestion that it would have been unfortunate if Brouwer had not invented choice sequences is a way of saying that the *objective content* of Brouwer's thought was valuable and interesting; valuable and interesting, that is, in the way it changed the objective problem situation in the third world.

To put the matter simply, if I say 'Brouwer's thought was influenced by Kant' or even 'Brouwer rejected Kant's theory of space' then I speak at least partly about acts of thought in the subjective sense: the word 'influence' indicates a context of thought processes or acts of thinking. If I say, however, 'Brouwer's thought differs vastly from Kant's', then it is pretty clear that I speak mainly about contents. And, ultimately, if I say 'Brouwer's thoughts are incompatible with Russell's', then, by using a

logical term such as '*incompatible*', I make it unambiguously clear that I am using the word 'thought' only in Frege's objective sense, and that I am speaking only about the objective content, or the logical content, of theories.

Just as ordinary language unfortunately has no separate terms for 'thought' in the sense of the second world and in the sense of the third world, so it has no separate terms for the corresponding two senses of 'I know' and of 'knowledge'.

In order to show that both senses exist, I will first mention three subjective or second-world examples:

(1) 'I *know* you are trying to provoke me, but I will not be provoked.'

(2) 'I *know* that Fermat's last theorem has not been proved, but I believe it will be proved one day.'

(3) From the entry 'Knowledge' in *The Oxford English Dictionary: knowledge* is a 'state of being aware or informed'.

Next I will mention three objective or third-world examples:

(1) From the entry 'Knowledge' in *The Oxford English Dictionary: knowledge* is a 'branch of learning; a science; an art'.

(2) 'Taking account of the present state of *metamathematical knowledge*, it seems possible that Fermat's last theorem may be undecidable.'

(3) 'I certify that this thesis is an original and significant *contribution to knowledge*.'

These very trite examples have only the function of helping to clarify what I mean when I speak of 'knowledge in the objective sense'. My quoting *The Oxford English Dictionary* should not be interpreted as either a concession to language analysis or as an attempt to appease its adherents. It is not quoted in an attempt to prove that 'ordinary usage' covers 'knowledge' in the objective sense of my third world. In fact, I was surprised to find in *The Oxford English Dictionary* examples of objective usages of 'knowledge'. (I was even more surprised to find some at least *partly* objective usages of 'know': 'to distinguish . . . to be acquainted with (a thing, a place, a person); . . . to understand'. That these usages may be partly objective will emerge from the sequel.) At any rate, my examples are not intended as arguments. They are intended solely as illustrations.

My *first thesis*, so far not argued but only illustrated, was that traditional epistemology with its concentration on the second world, or on knowledge in the subjective sense, is irrelevant to the study of scientific knowledge.

My *second thesis* is that what is relevant for epistemology is the study of scientific problems and problem situations, of scientific conjectures (which I take as merely another word for scientific hypotheses or theories), of scientific discussions, of critical arguments, and of the role played by evidence in arguments; and therefore of scientific journals and books, and of experiments and their evaluation in scientific arguments; or, in brief, that the study of a *largely autonomous* third world of objective knowledge is of decisive importance for epistemology.

An epistemological study as described in my second thesis shows that scientists very often do not claim that their conjectures are true, or that they 'know' them in the subjective sense of 'know', or that they believe in them. Although in general they do not claim to know, in developing their research programmes they act on the basis of guesses about what is and what is not fruitful, and what line of research promises further results in the third world of objective knowledge. In other words, scientists act on the basis of a guess or, if you like, of a *subjective belief* (for we may so call the subjective basis of an action) concerning what is promising of impending *growth in the third world of objective knowledge.*

This, I suggest, furnishes an argument in favour of both my *first thesis* (of the irrelevance of a subjectivist epistemology) and of my *second thesis* (of the relevance of an objectivist epistemology).

But I have a *third thesis*. It is this. An objectivist epistemology which studies the third world can help to throw an immense amount of light upon the second world of subjective consciousness, especially upon the subjective thought processes of scientists; but *the converse is not true.*

These are my three main theses.

In addition to my three main theses, I offer three supporting theses.

The first of these is that the third world is a natural product of the human animal, comparable to a spider's web.

The second supporting thesis (and an almost crucial thesis, I think) is that the third world is largely *autonomous*, even though we constantly act upon it and are acted upon by it: it is autonomous in spite of the fact that it is our product and that it has a strong feed-back effect upon us; that is to say, upon us *qua* inmates of the second and even of the first world.

The third supporting thesis is that it is through this interaction between ourselves and the third world that objective knowledge grows, and that there is a close analogy between the growth of knowledge and biological growth; that is, the evolution of plants and animals.

2. A Biological Approach to the Third World

In the present section of my talk I shall try to defend the existence of an autonomous world by a kind of biological or evolutionary argument.

A biologist may be interested in the behaviour of animals; but he may also be interested in some of the *non-living structures* which animals produce, such as spiders' webs, or nests built by wasps or ants, the burrows of badgers, dams constructed by beavers, or paths made by animals in forests.

I will distinguish between two main categories of problems arising from the study of these structures. The first category consists of problems concerned with *the methods used* by the animals, or *the ways the animals behave* when constructing these structures. This first category thus consists *of problems concerned with the acts of production*; with the behavioural dispositions of the animal; and with the relationships between the animal and the product. The second category of problems is concerned with the *structures themselves*. It is concerned with the chemistry of the materials used in the structure; with their geometrical and physical properties; with their evolutionary changes, depending upon special environmental conditions; and with their dependence upon or their adjustments to these environmental conditions. *Very* important also is the *feedback relation* from the properties of the structure to the behaviour of the animals. In dealing with this second category of problems—that is, with the structures themselves—we shall also have to look upon the structures from the point of view of their biological *functions*. Thus some problems of the first category will admittedly arise when we discuss problems of the second category; for example 'How was this nest built?' and 'What aspects of its structure are typical (and thus presumably traditional or inherited) and what aspects are variants adjusted to special conditions?'

As my last example of a problem shows, problems of the first category—that is, problems concerned with the production of the structure—will sometimes be suggested by problems of the second category. This must be so, since both categories of problems are dependent upon *the fact that such objective structures exist*, a fact which itself belongs to the second category. Thus the existence of the *structures themselves* may be said to create both categories of problems. We may say that the second category of problems—problems connected with the structures themselves—is more fundamental: all that it presupposes from the first category is the bare fact that the structures are somehow *produced by* some animals.

Now these simple considerations may of course also be applied to products of *human* activity, such as houses, or tools, and also to works of art. Especially important for us, they apply to what we call 'language', and to what we call 'science'.

The connection between these biological considerations and the topic of my present lecture can be made clear by reformulating my three main theses. My first thesis can be put by saying that in the present problem situation in philosophy, few things are as important as the awareness of the distinction between the two categories of problems—production problems on the one hand and problems connected with the produced structures themselves on the other. My second thesis is that we should realize that the second category of problems, those concerned with the products in themselves, is in almost every respect more important than the first category, the problems of production. My third thesis is that the problems of the second category are basic for understanding the production problems: contrary to first impressions, we can learn more about production behaviour by studying the products themselves than we can learn about the products by studying production behaviour. This third thesis may

be described as an anti-behaviouristic and anti-psychologistic thesis.

In their application to what may be called 'knowledge' my three theses may be formulated as follows.

(1) We should constantly be aware of the distinction between problems connected with our personal contributions to the production of scientific knowledge on the one hand, and problems connected with the structure of the various products, such as scientific theories or scientific arguments, on the other.

(2) We should realize that the study of the products is vastly more important than the study of the production, even for an understanding of the production and its methods.

(3) We can learn more about the heuristics and the methodology and even about the psychology of research by studying theories, and the arguments offered for or against them, than by any direct behaviouristic or psychological or sociological approach. In general, we may learn a great deal about behaviour and psychology from the study of the products.

In what follows I will call the approach from the side of the products—the theories and the arguments—the 'objective' approach or the 'third-world' approach. And I will call the behaviourist, the psychological, and the sociological approach to scientific knowledge the 'subjective' approach or the 'second-world' approach.

The appeal of the subjective approach is largely due to the fact that it is *causal*. For I admit that the objective structures for which I claim priority are caused by human behaviour. Being causal, the subjective approach may seem to be more scientific than the objective approach which, as it were, starts from effects rather than causes.

Though I admit that the objective structures are products of behaviour, I hold that the argument is mistaken. In all sciences, the ordinary approach is from the effects to the causes. The effect raises the problem—the problem to be explained, the explicandum—and the scientist tries to solve it by constructing an explanatory hypothesis.

My three main theses with their emphasis on the objective product are therefore neither teleological nor unscientific.

3. The Objectivity and the Autonomy of the Third World

One of the main reasons for the mistaken subjective approach to knowledge is the feeling that a book is nothing without a reader: only if it is understood does it really become a book; otherwise it is just paper with black spots on it.

This view is mistaken in many ways. A wasp's nest is a wasp's nest even after it has been deserted; even though it is never again used by wasps as a nest. A bird's nest is a bird's nest even if it was never lived in. Similarly a book remains a book—a certain type of product—even if it is never read (as may easily happen nowadays).

Moreover, a book, or even a library, need not even have been written by anybody: a series of books of logarithms, for example, may be produced and printed by a computer. It may be the best series of books of logarithms—it may contain logarithms up to, say, fifty decimal places. It may be sent out to libraries, but it may be found too cumbersome for use; at any rate, years may elapse before anybody uses it; and many figures in it (which represent mathematical theorems) may never be looked at as long as men live on earth. Yet each of these figures contains what I call 'objective knowledge'; and the question of whether or not I am entitled to call it by this name is of no interest.

The example of these books of logarithms may seem farfetched. But it is not. I should say that almost every book is like this: it contains objective knowledge, true or false, useful or useless; and whether anybody ever reads it and really grasps its contents is almost accidental. A man who reads a book with understanding is a rare creature. But even if he were more common, there would always be plenty of misunderstandings and misinterpretations; and it is not the actual and somewhat accidental avoidance of such misunderstandings which turns black spots on white paper into a book, or an instance of knowledge in the objective sense. Rather, it is something more abstract. It is its possibility or potentiality of being understood, its dispositional character of being understood or interpreted, or misunderstood or misinterpreted, which makes a thing a book. And this potentiality or disposition may exist without ever being actualized or realized.

To see this more clearly, we may imagine that after the human race has perished, some books or libraries may be found by some civilized successors of ours (no matter whether these are terrestrial animals which have become civilized, or some visitors from outer space). These books may be deciphered. They may be those logarithm tables never read before, for argument's sake. This makes it quite clear that neither its composition by thinking animals nor the fact that it has not actually been read or understood is essential for making a thing a book, and that it is sufficient that it might be deciphered.

Thus I do admit that in order to belong to the third world of objective knowledge, a book should—in principle, or virtually—be capable of being grasped (or deciphered, or understood, or 'known') by somebody. But I do not admit more.

We can thus say that there is a kind of Platonic (or Bolzanoesque) third world of books in themselves, theories in themselves, problems in themselves, problem situations in themselves, arguments in themselves, and so on. And I assert that even though this third world is a human product, there are many theories in themselves and arguments in themselves and problem situations in themselves which have never been produced or understood and may never be produced or understood by men.

The thesis of the existence of such a third world of problem situations will strike many as extremely metaphysical and dubious. But it can be defended by pointing out its biological analogue. For example, it has its full analogue in the realm of birds' nests. Some years ago I got a present for my garden—a nesting-box for birds. It was a human product, of course, not a bird's product—just as our logarithm table was a computer's product rather than a human product. But in the context of the bird's world, it was part of an objective problem situation, and an objective opportunity. For some years the birds did not even seem to notice the nesting-box. But after some years, it was carefully inspected by some blue tits who even started building in it, but gave up very soon. Obviously, here was a graspable opportunity, though not, it appears, a particularly valuable one. At any rate, here was a problem situation. And the problem may be solved in another year by other birds. If it is not, another box may prove more adequate. On the other hand, a most adequate box may be removed before it is ever used. The question of the adequacy of the box is clearly an objective one; and whether the box is ever used is partly accidental. So it is with all ecological niches. They are potentialities and may be studied as such in an objective way, up to a point independently of the question of whether these potentialities will ever be actualized by any living organism. A bacteriologist knows how to prepare such an ecological niche for the culture of certain bacteria or moulds. It may be perfectly adequate for its purpose. Whether it will ever be used and inhabited is another question.

A large part of the objective third world of actual and potential theories and books and arguments arises as an unintended by-product of the actually produced books and arguments. We may also say that it is a by-product of human language. Language itself, like a bird's nest, is an unintended by-product of actions which were directed at other aims.

How does an animal path in the jungle arise? Some animal may break through the undergrowth in order to get to a drinking-place. Other animals find it easiest to use the same track. Thus it may be widened and improved by use. It is not planned—it is an unintended consequence of the need for easy or swift movement. This is how a path is originally made—perhaps even by men— and how language and any other institutions which are useful may arise, and how they may owe their existence and development to their usefulness. They are not planned or intended, and there was perhaps no need for them before they came into existence. But they may create a new need, or a new set of aims: the aim-structure of animals or men is not 'given', but it develops, with the help of some kind of feedback mechanism, out of earlier aims, and out of results which were or were not aimed at.

In this way, a whole new universe of possibilities or potentialities may arise: a world which is to a large extent *autonomous*.

A very obvious example is a garden. Even though it may have been planned with great care, it will as a rule turn out partly in unexpected ways. But even if it turns out as planned, some unexpected interrelationships between the planned objects may give rise to a whole universe of possibilities, of possible new aims, and of new *problems*.

The world of language, of conjectures, theories, and arguments—in brief, the universe of objective knowledge—is one of the most important of these man-created, yet at the same time largely autonomous, universes. . . .

Note

[1]The argument is adapted from Popper, 1962, vol. ii; cp. p. 108.

Bibliography

Alcoff, Linda, and Elizabeth Potter, eds. *Feminist Epistemologies.* New York: Routledge, 1993.

Anderson, Elisabeth. "Feminist Epistemology: An Interpretation and a Defense." *Hypathia 10,* no. 3 (1995).

Birke, Linda. *Women, Feminism, and Biology: The Feminist Challenge.* New York: Methuen, 1986.

Bloor, David. *Knowledge and Social Imagery.* London: Routledge, 1991.

Cartwright, Nancy. "The Truth Doesn't Explain Much." In *How the Laws of Physics Lie.* New York: Oxford University Press, 1983.

Code, Lorraine. *What Can She Know?* Ithaca, N.Y.: Cornell University Press, 1991.

Code, Lorraine. *Gendered Species.* New York: Routledge, 1995.

Grandy, Richard. "Information-Based Epistemology, Ecological Epistemology and Epistomology Naturalized." *Synthese 70* (1987).

Haraway, D. *Primate Visions: Gender, Race and Nature in the World of Modern Science.* New York: Routledge, 1989.

Harding, Sandra. *The Science Question in Feminism.* Ithaca, NY: Cornell University Press, 1986.

Harding, Sandra. *Whose Science? Whose Knowledge?* Ithaca, NY: Cornell University Press, 1991.

Harding, Sandra, and Merrill Hintikka, eds. *Discovering Reality: Feminist Perspectives on Epistemology, Metaphysics, Methodology, and Philosophy of Science.* Dordrecht: Reidel, 1983.

Haslinger, Sally, ed. *Feminist Perspectives on Language, Knowledge, and Reality. Philosophical Topics 23,* no. 2 (Fall 1995).

Kitcher, Philip. "Socializing Knowledge." *Journal of Philosophy 88* (1991).

Kuhn, Thomas. "Objectivity, Values and Theory Choice." In *The Essential Tension.* Chicago: University of Chicago Press, 1971.

Latour, Bruno. *Science in Action.* Cambridge, MA: Harvard University Press, 1989.

Lloyd, Genevieve. *The Man of Reason: Male and Female in Western Philosophy.* Minneapolis: University of Minnesota Press, 1984.

Longino, Helen. *Science and Social Knowledge.* Princeton, NJ: Princeton University Press, 1990.

Longino, Helen. "In Search of a Feminist Epistemology." *The Monist 77,* no. 4 (1994).

Longino, Helen. "Cognitive and Non-Cognitive Values in Science: Rethinking the Dichotomy." In *Feminism, Science and the Philosophy of Science,* edited by L. Nelson and J. Nelson. Kluwer Academic Publishers, 1996.

Martin, Jane. "Science in a Different Style." *American Philosophical Quarterly 25* (1988).

Rooney, Phyllis. "Recent Work in Feminist Discussions of Reason." *American Philosophical Quarterly 31,* no. 1 (1994).

Rorty, Richard. *Philosophy and the Mirror of Nature.* Princeton NJ: Princeton University Press, 1979.

Rorty, Richard. *The Consequences of Pragmatism.* Minneapolis: University of Minnesota Press, 1980.

Schmitt, Fred. ed. *Socializing Epistemology.* Totowa, NJ: Rowman and Littlefield, 1994.

Seller, Anne. "Realism Versus Relativism: Towards a Politically Adequate Epistemology." In *Feminist Perspectives in Philosophy,* edited by M. Griffiths and M. Whitford. Bloomington: Indiana University Press, 1988.

Solomon, Miriam. "A More Social Epistemology." In *Socializing Epistemology,* edited by Fred Schmitt. Totowa, NJ: Rowman and Littlefield, 1994.

Stanley, Liz. ed. *Feminist Praxis.* New York: Routledge, 1990.

Thalos, Mariam. "The Common Need for Classic Epistemological Foundations: Against a Feminist Alternative." *The Monist 77,* no. 4 (1994), 531–553.

CPSIA information can be obtained
at www.ICGtesting.com
Printed in the USA
FFOW01n0455261213
2848FF